FUNDAMENTALS OF PROPERTY LAW

FUNDAMENTALS OF PROPERTY LAW

Fourth Edition

Barlow Burke
*John S. Myers and Alvina Reckman Myers Scholar
and Professor of Law
American University Washington College of Law*

Ann M. Burkhart
*Curtis Bradbury Kellar Professor of Law
University of Minnesota Law School*

Thomas P. Gallanis
*Associate Dean for Research,
N. William Hines Chair in Law and Professor of History
The University of Iowa College of Law*

R.H. Helmholz
*Ruth Wyatt Rosenson Distinguished Service Professor of Law
The University of Chicago Law School*

ISBN: 978-1-6328-0977-3
ISBN: 978-1-6328-0979-7 (eBook)
ISBN: 978-1-6328-0978-0 (looseleaf)

Library of Congress Cataloging-in-Publication Data

Burke, D. Barlow, 1941- author
  Fundamentals of property law / Barlow Burke, John S. Myers and Alvina Reckman Myers Scholar and Professor of Law, American University Washington College of Law; Ann M. Burkhart, Curtis Bradbury Kellar Professor of Law, University of Minnesota Law School; Thomas P. Gallanis, Associate Dean for Research, N. William Hines Chair in Law and Professor of History, The University of Iowa College of Law; R.H. Helmholz, Ruth Wyatt Rosenson Distinguished Service Professor of Law, The University of Chicago Law School. -- Fourth edition.
    pages cm.
  Includes index.
  ISBN 978-1-63280-977-3 (hardbound)
  1. Property--United States--Cases. I. Burkhart, Ann M., 1952- author. II. Gallanis, Thomas P. III. Helmholz, R.H. IV. Title.
  KF560.B865 2015
  346.7304--dc23
  2015006756

NOTE TO USERS
To ensure that you are using the latest materials available in this area, please be sure to periodically check the LexisNexis Law School web site for downloadable updates and supplements at www.lexisnexis.com/lawschool.

Editorial Offices
630 Central Ave., New Providence, NJ 07974 (908) 464-6800
201 Mission St., San Francisco, CA 94105-1831 (415) 908-3200
www.lexisnexis.com

MATTHEW◆BENDER

Dedication

The memory of my father,
D. Barlow Burke, Philadelphia lawyer
—B.B.

For Alex, Jessica, and Daniel Kranz,
a wonderful branch of the family tree
—A.M.B.

With gratitude to R.H. Helmholz, who taught me Property and much more
—T.P.G.

For my uncles,
Bourne Bean and Howard Burchell
—R.H.H.

Preface

Our intention as editors of this casebook is to provide students with a firm grasp of the fundamentals of the law of real and personal property and to help them enjoy the experience. We do not think the two are mutually exclusive. With these objectives in mind, we have followed four guidelines in preparing the casebook.

(1) Our case selection has emphasized rules that are widely accepted in practice. We have included opinions that adopt a minority view only when they also state the majority position clearly, so that students will not be misled about the current state of the law.

(2) Shorter cases have been preferred over longer ones, and short expositions of the rules have been preferred over treatise-like opinions. We think students should also become familiar with the treatises and law review literature on the subjects raised in the cases. Casebooks are a necessary, but not sufficient, guide to the law.

(3) Many of the cases and notes that follow deal with questions of statutory interpretation. The law of real property is less affected by statutory change than many areas of the first year curriculum, but learning to understand the role statutes play in our legal system is of vital importance for all students of the law.

(4) The nature of the law of property is illuminated by many disciplines. We have emphasized no particular discipline in selecting cases, writing notes, or defining problems, but we think that much of the material in the casebook lends itself to a broad approach to the law.

For research assistance, Barlow Burke thanks Les Anderson, Catherine Brown, Julie Richmond, Stephanie Quaranta, Erica Gaspar, Alison Fultz, Rachael Reuben, and William Weaver; Ann Burkhart thanks Travis Anderson, Emily Flynn, Michael Klemm, Thayer Thompson, and Steven Schaefer; and Thomas Gallanis thanks Michael Conroy.

B.B.
A.M.B.
T.P.G.
R.H.H.
2015

Table of Contents

Chapter 1	**PERSONAL PROPERTY**	**1**
I.	WILD ANIMALS	1
	Pierson v. Post	1
	Notes	4
	Buster v. Newkirk	6
	Notes	6
	Keeble v. Hickeringill	7
	Notes	9
	Dapson v. Daly	9
	Note	10
	Notes on Larceny	11
	Ghen v. Rich	13
	Note	15
	State of North Dakota v. Dickinson Cheese Co., Inc.	16
	Note	17
II.	ACQUIRING ABANDONED PROPERTY	17
	Eads v. Brazelton	17
	Note	19
	Haslem v. Lockwood	19
	Note	21
III.	FINDERS' RIGHTS	22
	Armory v. Delamirie	22
	Clark v. Maloney	23
	Barker v. Bates	23
	Notes	24
	South Staffordshire Water Co. v. Sharman	24
	Hannah v. Peel	26
	Notes	29
	Favorite v. Miller	31
	Notes	33
IV.	WRONGFUL TAKING OF POSSESSION	36
	Anderson v. Gouldberg	36
	Notes	37
	Russell v. Hill	38
	Note	40
	A Note on the Scope of Conversion	40
V.	BAILMENTS	42
	Adams v. The New Jersey Steamboat Co.	43

Table of Contents

Notes 45

Peet v. The Roth Hotel Co. 46

Notes 49

Allen v. Hyatt Regency-Nashville Hotel 50

Note 54

Cowen v. Pressprich 55

Notes 58

Carr v. Hoosier Photo Supplies, Inc. 59

Notes 62

A Note on Pawnbrokers 64

VI.   GIFTS 65

    Flower's Case 65

    Irons v. Smallpiece 65

    Notes 66

    Gruen v. Gruen 67

    Notes 72

VII. SALES AND BONA FIDE PURCHASERS 73

    Midway Auto Sales, Inc. v. Clarkson 74

    Note 76

    Porter v. Wertz 76

    Note 82

VIII. ACCESSION 83

    Ballard v. Wetzel 85

    Notes 87

IX.   FIXTURES 88

    First Tr. and Sav. Bank of Moville v. Guthridge 88

    Notes 92

X.   ADVERSE POSSESSION OF PERSONALTY 94

    Chapin v. Freeland 94

    Notes 96

    Solomon R. Guggenheim Foundation v. Lubell 97

    Note 102

Chapter 2   **THE LAW OF NEIGHBORS** **105**

I.   ADVERSE POSSESSION 105

  A.   The Statutory Basis 105

    Fleming v. Griswold 106

    Notes and Problems 107

  B.   The Elements of Adverse Possession 108

    Anderson v. Cold Spring Tungsten, Inc. 108

    Grace v. Koch 111

Table of Contents

Notes 114

C.   The Future of Adverse Possession 115

         Meyer v. Law 116

         Notes 119

II.   RIGHTS OF LATERAL AND SUBJACENT SUPPORT 120

  A.   Lateral Support 120

         Noone v. Price 121

         Notes 125

  B.   Modifying the Duty of Support by Statute 126

  C.   Subjacent Support 127

         Island Creek Coal Co. v. Rodgers 128

III.   NUISANCE 131

         Griffin v. Northridge 132

         Notes 135

         Boomer v. Atlantic Cement Co. 135

         Notes 140

         Robert C. Ellickson, *Alternatives to Zoning: Covenants, Nuisance*
         Rules, and Fines as Land Use Controls 142

         Notes 143

IV.   AIR AND LIGHT 146

  A.   Airspace 146

         Murphy v. Bolger 146

         Notes 147

         Allegheny Airlines, Inc. v. Village of Cedarhurst 148

         Notes 150

  B.   Rights in Air and Light 153

         Sundowner, Inc. v. King 153

         Notes 155

         Fontainebleau Hotel Corp. v. Forty-Five Twenty-Five, Inc. 156

         Notes 160

         Prah v. Maretti 161

         Notes 164

V.   WATER RIGHTS 167

  A.   Diffuse Surface Water 167

         Westland Skating Ctr., Inc. v. Gus Machado Buick, Inc. 167

         Note 172

  B.   Groundwater 172

         Maddocks v. Giles 172

         Note 175

         MacArtor v. The Graylyn Crest III Swim Club, Inc. 176

         Note 178

Table of Contents

C.   Riparian and Littoral Rights 179
         Notes 181

Chapter 3   ESTATES IN LAND **183**

I.   THE FEE SIMPLE 183
         Johnson v. Whiton 183
         Notes 185
         Epting v. Mayer 186
         Hall v. Hall 187
         Note 190
         Peters v. East Penn Township School District 190
         Notes 193
         Oldfield v. Stoeco Homes, Inc. 193
         Notes 195
         Bank of Powhattan v. Rooney 196
         Notes 198
         Estate of Elizabeth Beck 199
         Note 200
II.   THE FEE TAIL 201
         Morris v. Ulbright 203
         Notes and Problems 205
III. THE LIFE ESTATE 205
         Thompson v. Baxter 206
         Note 209
         Smith v. Smith 209
         Notes 211
         Brokaw v. Fairchild 212
         Notes 216
         New York, O. & W. R. Co. v. Livingston 216
         Notes 219
IV.   MARITAL ESTATES 219
   A.   The Common Law 219
            Melenky v. Melen 220
            Notes 222
   B.   Statutory Changes in Marital Estates 222
   C.   Community Property 224
            In Re Kessler's Estate 224
            Notes and Problems 229
   D.   Homestead Rights 229
V.   CONCURRENT ESTATES 230
   A.   Basic Characteristics 230

Table of Contents

	Problems	232
B.	Creation of Concurrent Tenancies	232
	Camp v. Camp	232
C.	Relations Among Concurrent Tenants	235
	Mosher v. Van Buskirk	237
	Notes	238
D.	The Termination of Joint Tenancies	239
	Riddle v. Harmon	239
	Notes	243
	Allison v. Powell	243
	Notes	245
VI.	REVERSIONS, POSSIBILITIES OF REVERTER, AND RIGHTS OF ENTRY	246
	Village of Peoria Heights v. Keithley	247
	Notes and Problems	248
	Trustees of Calvary Presbyterian Church v. Putnam	248
	Note	250
	Richardson v. Holman	250
VII.	REMAINDERS	253
A.	Creation and Classification of Remainders	253
	Edwards v. Hammond	256
	Notes	256
	Guilliams v. Koonsman	257
	Notes	258
	Linkous v. Candler	259
	Notes	261
	Browning v. Sacrison	261
	Notes	264
B.	Three Special Rules Regarding Remainders	264
	Popp v. Bond	264
	Notes	266
	Finley v. Finley	266
	Notes and Problems	269
	Doctor v. Hughes	270
	Notes	271
	Stewart v. Merchants Nat'l Bank of Aurora	272
VIII.	THE STATUTE OF USES AND EXECUTORY INTERESTS	275
	Blackman v. Fysh	277
	Notes	278
	Problems	279
IX.	POWERS OF APPOINTMENT	280
A.	The Nature of Powers	280

Table of Contents

		Gilman v. Bell	280
		Bank of Dallas v. Republic Nat'l Bank of Dallas	281
		Notes	283
B.		Varieties of Powers	284
		Problems	284
		Problems	285
X.		THE RULE AGAINST PERPETUITIES	285
A.		The Orthodox Rule	286
		United Virginia Bank/Citizens & Marine v. Union Oil Co.	286
		Notes	289
		Jee v. Audley	290
		Laughlin v. Elliott	291
		Note	293
		Warren v. Albrecht	293
		Problems	296
B.		Reform of the Orthodox Rule	297

Chapter 4	**LANDLORD AND TENANT**	**299**
I.	TYPES OF TENANCIES	299
	Alfano v. Donnelly	300
	Notes	301
II.	CREATION	302
	Note on Tenant's Right to Possession	302
	Hannan v. Dusch	302
	Notes	308
III.	ILLEGALITY AND FRUSTRATION OF PURPOSE	309
A.	Illegality	309
B.	Frustration	310
	Smith v. Roberts	311
	Notes	313
IV.	THE COVENANT OF QUIET ENJOYMENT	313
	Blackett v. Olanoff	313
	Notes	315
	Echo Consulting Servs., Inc. v. North Conway Bank	316
V.	THE COVENANT TO REPAIR	320
	Sparkman v. Hardy	321
	Harts v. Arnold Bros.	323
	Note	325
	Atlantic Discount Corp. v. Mangel's of North Carolina, Inc.	325
	Rose v. Freeway Aviation, Inc.	327
	Note	328

Table of Contents

Reste Realty Corp. v. Cooper 329

VI. THE IMPLIED COVENANT OF HABITABILITY 333

    Wade v. Jobe 333

    Notes 337

    Hilder v. St. Peter 339

    Notes 340

VII. A LANDLORD'S TORT LIABILITY 341

    Borders v. Roseberry 341

    Notes 346

    Feld v. Merriam 347

    Notes 352

VIII. ASSIGNMENTS AND SUBLEASES 353

    Davis v. Vidal 355

    Notes 360

  A. Assumption and Novation 362

    First American Nat'l Bank Of Nashville v. Chicken Sys.

    of America, Inc. 363

      Notes 367

  B. Transfer Restrictions 368

    Julian v. Christopher 367

      Notes 372

  C. Assignments and Real Covenants 374

    Abbott v. Bob's U-Drive 374

      Note 377

IX. TERMINATION 378

  A. Notice of Termination 378

    1. Term for Years 378

    2. Periodic Tenancy 378

      S.D.G. v. Inventory Control Company 379

      Note 380

    3. Tenancy at Will 380

    4. Tenancy at Sufferance 380

  B. Surrender and Abandonment 380

    1. The Traditional Rule 380

    2. A Corollary Rule, Accepted in a Majority of States 381

      Sagamore Corp. v. Willcutt 381

      Notes 383

      Austin Hill Country Realty, Inc. v. Palisades Plaza, Inc. 383

      Notes 389

      Schneiker v. Gordon 391

      Notes 396

Table of Contents

C. The Holdover Tenant 398

   A.H. Fetting Mfg. Jewelry Co. v. Waltz 399

   Notes 402

X. THE LANDLORD'S SELF-HELP 404

   Bass v. Boetel & Co. 404

   Question 408

XI. SUMMARY PROCEDURE 409

   Problems 410

XII. RETALIATORY EVICTION 411

   Building Monitoring Sys., Inc. v. Paxton 411

   Notes 415

XIII. SECURITY DEPOSITS 417

   Notes 419

Chapter 5   **LAND CONVEYANCING** **421**

I. INTRODUCTION 421

II. REAL ESTATE AGENTS 422

   Notes 423

   Blank v. Borden 424

   Notes 430

   Cornett v. Nathan 430

   Notes 432

III. CONTRACTS OF SALE 434

 A. The Statute of Frauds 435

   Cash v. Maddox 436

   Note 437

 B. Equitable Conversion 438

   Bryant v. Willison Real Estate Co. 439

   Notes 442

   Cannefax v. Clement 444

   Notes 448

 C. Contract Contingencies 450

 D. Disclosures about the Property 451

 E. Time for Performance of the Contract 451

 F. Express "Subject to Financing" Contract Terms 452

   Luttinger v. Rosen 453

   Bruyere v. Jade Realty Corp. 455

   Note 456

 G. Implied Contract Terms 456

   Notes 458

 H. Breaks in the Chain of Title 459

Table of Contents

		Trimboli v. Kinkel	459
I.		Express Title Standards in Contracts	461
J.		Contract Remedies	462
	1.	Damages	462
		Wolofsky v. Behrman	463
		Note	464
	2.	Specific Performance	465
		Kies v. Warrick	466
		Note	468
	3.	Rescission	468
		Gordon v. Tafe	469
	4.	Other Remedies	470
IV.		LAND TRANSFERS	470
A.		History of Common Law Conveyancing	470
B.		Modern Conveyancing	471
		Anderson v. Anderson	474
		Notes	478
C.		Statutory Short Form Deeds	478
		Notes and Problems	480
D.		Deed Covenants	484
	1.	Breach of Covenants	485
	2.	Running with the Land	486
		Deason v. Finley	486
		Proffitt v. Isley	487
		Notes	488
		St. Paul Title Insurance Corp. v. Owen	489
		Notes	493
E.		Legal Descriptions	494
	1.	Government Survey System	495
	2.	Metes and Bounds	498
	3.	Recorded Subdivision Plat	500
	4.	Conflicts and Ambiguities in Descriptions	502
F.		Intent, Delivery, and Acceptance	503
		Brtek v. Cihal	503
		Notes	509
		Turner v. Mallernee	510
		Notes	516
V.		DEEDS CHARACTERIZED AS MORTGAGES	517
		Seaman v. Seaman	517
		Notes	519
VI.		RECORDING ACTS	520

Table of Contents

A.   History of the Recording Acts 521

B.   Operation of the Recording Acts 522

         GRANT S. NELSON, DALE A. WHITMAN, ANN M. BURKHART &
         R. WILSON FREYERMUTH, REAL ESTATE TRANSFER, FINANCE,
         AND DEVELOPMENT 522

         Problems 525

C.   Indexes 527

   1.   Grantor-Grantee Index 527

   2.   Tract Index 531

D.   Bona Fide Purchasers 533

   1.   Lack of Notice 533

         In Re Barnacle 535

         Note 537

         J.C. Penney Co. v. Giant Eagle, Inc. 538

         Notes 541

         Methonen v. Stone 542

         Note 545

   2.   Payment of Consideration 545

         Geo. M. McDonald & Co. v. Johns 545

         Notes and Problems 547

E.   Recording and Indexing 549

         Notes and Problems 549

F.   Exclusions from the Recording Act 552

VII.   TORRENS REGISTRATION 553

         Notes 558

VIII.   TITLE INSURANCE 558

         Notes 566

         Swanson v. Safeco Title Insurance Co. 567

         Notes 571

IX.   CLOSINGS AND ESCROWS 572

         Ferguson v. Caspar 573

         Notes 580

         Lechner v. Halling 582

         Note 590

Chapter 6   **SERVITUDES AND EASEMENTS** **591**

I.   EASEMENTS 591

A.   Creation of Easements 592

         Estate of Thomson v. Wade 592

         Notes 593

         Baseball Publishing Co. v. Bruton 594

Table of Contents

		Bunn v. Offutt	596
		Notes	598
B.		Easements Implied by Necessity	599
		Kingsley v. Gouldsborough Land Improvement Co.	599
		Notes	600
		Chandler Flyers, Inc. v. Stellar Development Corp.	601
		Notes	602
		Hollars v. Church of God of Apostolic Faith, Inc.	603
		Notes	605
C.		Easements Implied by Past Usage	606
		Flax v. Smith	606
D.		Prescriptive Easements	608
		Reed v. Piedimonte	608
		Notes	609
		State ex rel. Haman v. Fox	610
		Notes	615
E.		Scope of the Easement	616
		Hayes v. Aquia Marina, Inc.	616
		Notes	619
		Ephrata School District v. County of Lancaster	620
		Notes	626
F.		Transferability of Easements	626
	1.	Appurtenant Easements	626
		Martin v. Music	626
	2.	Easements in Gross	629
		Miller v. Lutheran Conference & Camp Ass'n	629
		Note	634
G.		Termination of Easements	634
		Lindsey v. Clark	635
		Note	638
II.		REAL COVENANTS	638
		Rogers v. Watson	638
		Note	640
		Neponsit Property Owners Ass'n v. Emigrant Industrial Savings Bank	642
		Note	647
		Feider v. Feider	648
III.		EQUITABLE SERVITUDES	650
A.		Creation	650
		Tulk v. Moxhay	650
		Notes	652

Table of Contents

B.   Enforcement 652

         Houghton v. Rizzo 652

         Notes 656

         Citizens for Covenant Compliance v. Anderson 567

IV.   TERMINATION OF COVENANTS 666

         Grange v. Korff 666

         Note 669

Chapter 7   TAKINGS AND LAND USE CONTROLS 671

I.   TAKINGS 671

A.   Public Use 671

         Kelo v. City of New London 672

         Notes 680

B.   Taking 683

  1.   Federal Constitution 683

         Pennsylvania Coal Co. v. Mahon 683

         Notes 689

         Keystone Bituminous Coal Association v. DeBenedictis 691

         Notes 702

  2.   State Constitution 703

         Pratt v. State, Department of Natural Resources 703

         Notes 708

  3.   Categorical Takings 709

         Notes 710

         Lucas v. South Carolina Coastal Council 712

         Notes 722

  4.   Exactions and Impact Fees 724

         Dolan v. City of Tigard 724

         Notes 734

C.   Private Property 736

         City of Oakland v. Oakland Raiders 736

         Notes 741

         Walker v. State 741

         Notes 744

D.   Just Compensation 745

         First English Evangelical Lutheran Church v. County of

         Los Angeles 745

         Notes 750

II.   LAND USE CONTROLS 751

A.   Zoning Actions 751

  1.   Zoning 752

Table of Contents

Village of Euclid v. Ambler Realty Co. 752

Notes 760

2.   Nonconforming Use 761

Village of Valatie v. Smith 761

Notes 766

3.   Zoning Amendment 767

City of Pharr v. Tippitt 767

Notes 772

4.   Variance 773

Alumni Control Board v. City of Lincoln 773

Notes 776

5.   Special Exception 777

Schultz v. Pritts 778

Notes 784

B.   Modern Zoning Techniques 785

Rodgers v. Village of Tarrytown 786

Notes 791

C.   Exclusionary Zoning 791

1.   Federal Courts 791

*Village of Arlington Heights v. Metropolitan Housing
Development Corporation* 791

Notes 800

2.   State Courts 801

Britton v. Town of Chester 802

Notes 807

D.   Residency Restrictions 809

Village of Belle Terre v. Boraas 810

Notes 813

Costley v. Caromin House, Inc. 815

Notes 819

E.   Aesthetic Regulation 820

State ex rel. Stoyanoff v. Berkeley 821

Notes 827

Society for Ethical Culture v. Spatt 828

Notes 831

Chapter 8   **CREATING INTANGIBLE AND INTELLECTUAL
PROPERTY** **833**

I.   MISAPPROPRIATION OF INFORMATION 833

International News Service v. The Associated Press 833

RCA Mfg. Co. v. Whiteman 842

Table of Contents

Board of Trade of Chicago v. Dow Jones & Co. 845

Note 849

II. COPYRIGHTS 849

Rockford Map Publishers, Inc. v. Directory Serv. Co. 850

Notes 853

Random House, Inc. v. Rosetta Books LLC 857

Notes 858

III. MORAL RIGHTS OF ARTISTS 860

Martin v. City of Indianapolis 862

Notes 867

Moakley v. Eastwick 869

Notes 873

IV. THE RIGHT TO PUBLICITY 874

Haelan Laboratories, Inc. v. Topps Chewing Gum, Inc. 875

Notes 877

Martin Luther King, Jr. Center v. American Heritage Products 878

Notes 886

Stephano v. News Group Publications, Inc. 887

Notes 891

Wendt v. Host International, Inc. 891

Notes 895

V. TRADEMARKS 895

VI. PATENTS 897

35 U.S.C. § 102(a) (2014) 900

Notes 900

Ebay Inc. v. Mercexchange LLC 901

Notes 904

VII. IDEAS AS PROPERTY 905

Garrido v. Burger King Corp. 905

Notes 908

Table of Cases TC-1

Index I-1

*· Case of first impression, court looks to proced.
from philosophers, and old professors.*

*· Following, Court held that P did not have a claim
b/c there was no ACTUAL CAPTURE or even
mortal wounding.*

*· MERE PURSUIT is not enough for
possession.*

Chapter 1

PERSONAL PROPERTY

I. WILD ANIMALS

fox case   *NY Supreme court*

PIERSON v. POST

3 Cai. R. 175, 2 Am. Dec. 265 (N.Y. 1805)

This was an action of trespass on the case commenced in a justice's court, by the present defendant against the now plaintiff. The declaration stated that *Post*, being in possession of certain dogs and hounds under his command, did "upon a certain wild and uninhabited, unpossessed and waste land, called the beach, find and start one of those noxious beasts called a fox," and whilst there hunting, chasing and pursuing the same with his dogs and hounds, and when in view thereof, *Pierson*, well knowing the fox was so hunted and pursued, did, in the sight of *Post*, to prevent his catching the same, kill and carry it off. A verdict having been rendered for the plaintiff below [*Post*], the defendant there [*Pierson*] sued out a *certiorari*, and now assigned for error, that the declaration and the matters therein contained were not sufficient in law to maintain an action.

TOMPKINS, J. This cause comes before us on a return to a *certiorari* directed to one of the justices of *Queens* county. The question submitted by the counsel in this cause for our determination is, whether *Lodowick Post*, by the pursuit with his hounds in the manner alleged in his declaration, acquired such a right to, or property in, the fox as will sustain an action against *Pierson* for killing and taking him away? . . . It is admitted that a fox is an animal *ferae naturae*, and that property in such animals is acquired by occupancy only. These admissions narrow the discussion to the simple question of what acts amount to occupancy, applied to acquiring a right to wild animals.

If we have recourse to the ancient writers upon general principles of law, the judgment below is obviously erroneous. *Justinian's Institutes*, lib.2, tit.1, s.13 and *Fleta*, lib.3, c. 2, p.175, adopt the principle, that pursuit alone vests no property or right in the huntsman; and that even pursuit, accompanied with wounding, is equally ineffectual for that purpose, unless the animal be actually taken. The same principle is recognized by *Bracton*, lib.2, c.1, p.8.

Puffendorf, lib.4, c.6, s.2, and 10, defined occupancy of beasts *ferae naturae*, to be the actual corporal possession of them. . . . It is indeed with hesitation that *Puffendorf* affirms that a wild beast mortally wounded, or greatly maimed, cannot be fairly intercepted by another, whilst the pursuit of the person inflicting the wound continues. The foregoing authorities are decisive to show that mere pursuit

1

gave *Post* no legal right to the fox, but that he became the property of *Pierson*, who intercepted and killed him.

It therefore only remains to inquire whether there are any contrary principles, or authorities, . . . which ought to induce a different decision. Most of the cases which have occurred in *England*, relating to property in wild animals, have . . . arisen between the huntsman and the owner of the land upon which beasts *ferae naturae* have been apprehended; the former claiming them by title of occupancy, and the latter *ratione soli*. Little satisfactory aid can, therefore, be derived from the *English* reporters.

Barbeyrac, in his notes on *Puffendorf*, does not accede to the definition of occupancy by the latter, but, on the contrary, affirms, that actual bodily seizure is not, in all cases, necessary to constitute possession of wild animals. He does not, however, describe the acts which, according to his ideas, will amount to an appropriation of such animals to private use, so as to exclude the claims of all other persons, by title of occupancy, to the same animals; and he is far from averring that pursuit alone is sufficient for that purpose. To a certain extent, and as far as *Barbeyrac* appears to me to go, his objections to *Puffendorf*'s definition of occupancy are reasonable and correct. That is to say, that actual bodily seizure is not indispensable to acquire a right to, or possession of, wild beasts; but that, on the contrary, the mortal wounding of such beast, by one not abandoning his pursuit, may, with the utmost propriety, be deemed possession of him; since, thereby, the pursuer manifests an unequivocal intention of appropriating the animal to his individual use, has deprived him of his natural liberty, and brought him within his certain control. So also, encompassing and securing such animals with nets and toils, or otherwise intercepting them in such a manner as to deprive them of their natural liberty, and render escape impossible, may justly be deemed to give possession of them to those persons who, by their industry and labor, have used such means of apprehending them. . . . The case now under consideration is one of mere pursuit, and presents no circumstances or acts which can bring it within the definition of occupancy by *Puffendorf* . . . or the ideas of *Barbeyrac* upon that subject.

The case cited from 11 *Mod.* 74–130, I think clearly distinguishable from the present; inasmuch as there the action was for maliciously hindering and disturbing the plaintiff in the exercise and enjoyment of a private franchise; and in the report of the same case, 3 *Salk.* 9[,] *Holt*, Ch. J., states, that the ducks were in the plaintiff's decoy pond, and so in his possession, from which it is obvious the court laid much stress in their opinion upon the plaintiff's possession of the ducks, *ratione soli*.

We are the more readily inclined to confine possession or occupancy of beasts *ferae naturae*, within the limits prescribed by the learned authors above cited, for the sake of certainty, and preserving peace and order in society. If the first seeing, starting, or pursuing such animals, without having so wounded, circumvented or ensnared them so as to deprive them of their natural liberty, and subject them to the control of their pursuer, should afford the basis of actions against others for intercepting and killing them, it would prove a fertile source of quarrels and litigation.

However uncourteous or unkind the conduct of *Pierson* towards *Post*, in this instance, may have been, yet his act was productive of no injury or damage for which a legal remedy can be applied. We are of opinion the judgment below was erroneous, and ought to be reversed.

LIVINGSTON, J. My opinion differs from that of the court. . . . This [case] should have been submitted to the arbitration of sportsmen, without poring over *Justinian, Fleta, Bracton, Puffendorf, Locke, Barbeyrac,* or *Blackstone,* all of whom have been cited; they would have had no difficulty in coming to a prompt and correct conclusion. . . .

By the pleadings it is admitted that a fox is a "wild and noxious beast." . . . His depredations on farmers and on barn yards, have not been forgotten; and to put him to death wherever found, is allowed to be meritorious, and of public benefit. Hence it follows, that our decision should have in view the greatest possible encouragement to the destruction of an animal, so cunning and ruthless in his career. But who would keep a pack of hounds; or what gentlemen, at the sound of the horn, and at peep of day, would mount his steed, and for hours together, . . . pursue the windings of this wily quadruped, if just as night came on, and his stratagems and strength were nearly exhausted, a saucy intruder, who had not shared in the honors or labors of the chase, were permitted to come in at the death, and bear away in triumph the object of pursuit? Whatever *Justinian* may have thought of the matter, it must be recollected that his code was compiled many hundred years ago, and it would be very hard indeed, at the distance of so many centuries, not to have a right to establish a rule for ourselves. In his day, we read of no order of men who made it a business, in the language of the declaration in this cause, "with hounds and dogs to find, start, pursue, hunt, and chase," these animals, and that, too, without any other motive than the preservation of Roman poultry; if this diversion had been then in fashion, the lawyers who composed his institutes, would have taken care not to pass it by, without suitable encouragement. If any thing, therefore, in the digests . . . shall appear to militate against the defendant in error, who, on this occasion, was the fox hunter, we have only to say . . . if men themselves change with the times, why should not laws undergo an alteration?

I have examined [the authorities cited] and feel great difficulty in determining, whether to acquire dominion over a thing, before in common, it be sufficient that we barely see it, or know where it is, or which for it, or make a declaration of our will respecting it; or whether, in the case of wild beasts, setting a trap, or lying in wait, or starting, or pursuing, be enough; or if an actual wounding, or killing, or bodily tact and occupation be necessary. Writers in general law, who have favored us with their speculations on these points, differ on them all; but, great as is the diversity of sentiment among them, some conclusion must be adopted on the question immediately before us. After mature deliberation, I embrace that of *Barbeyrac,* as the most rational, and least liable to objection. . . .

Now . . . the pursuit here, for aught that appears on the case, being with dogs and hounds of imperial stature, we are at liberty to adopt one of the provisions just cited, which comports also with the learned conclusion of *Barbeyrac,* that property in animals *ferae naturae,* may be acquired without bodily touch or manucaption, provided the pursuer be within reach, or have a reasonable prospect (which certainly existed here) of taking, what he has thus discovered an intention of converting to his own use.

When we reflect also that the interest of our husbandmen, the most useful of men in any community, will be advanced by the destruction of a beast so pernicious and incorrigible, we cannot greatly err, in saying that a pursuit like the present, through waste and unoccupied lands, and which must inevitably and speedily have terminated in corporal possession, or bodily *seisin*, confers such a right to the object of it, as to make any one a wrongdoer, who shall interfere and shoulder the spoil. The *justice's* judgment ought therefore, in my opinion, to be affirmed.

NOTES

1. Trespass? Trespass on the case? What's the difference? What was the issue on appeal? When might it have been raised during the litigation in the trial court? The majority and the dissent in this case have different ideas of the role of social policy plays in the law. Which of these policies (if any) persuades you? If the case had involved a deer, not a fox, would your answer change? See Ray Brown, Personal Property 13–23 (Walter B. Raushenbush ed., 3d ed. 1975). See generally Andrea McDowell, *Legal Fictions in Pierson v. Post*, 105 Mich. L. Rev. 735 (2007); Bethany Rogers, *It's Not About The Fox: The Untold Story of Pierson v. Post*, 55 Duke L.J. 1089 (2006).

2. Restatement (Second) of Torts § 506(1) (1977) defines a wild animal as one "not by custom devoted to the service of mankind at the time and in the place in which it is kept." The next subsection of this Restatement defines a domestic animal as one that is "by custom devoted to the service of mankind." *Ibid.*, § 506(2). "The owner, keeper, or possessor of a wild animal is strictly liable if the animal injures another." Furthermore, "if the animal is one of a class that is not indigenous to the locality, its escape does not prevent its possessor from being liable for the harm done by the animal no matter how long after its escape; in this case the risk of liability continues until some third person takes possession of the animal." *Ibid.*, § 507, cmt. d. Many farm animals serve mankind primarily at the slaughterhouse and many zoo animals arguably serve mankind but are by custom regarded a wild. What of a wolfdog biting a child? Does its wolf-like ferocity made it wild, or does its pet-like submissiveness make it domestic? See *Tipton v. Town of Tabor*, 567 N.W.2d 351, 361–363 (S. Dak. 1997) (discussing strict liability). What if Post trapped the fox alive and was putting it into a cage when it snarled, bit him, escaped, fled with Post in pursuit, and was shot by Pierson as before? Would the court's judgment change? See *Young v. Hichens*, 115 Eng. Rep. 228 (Q.B. 1844) (an analogous fishing case). What if Post trapped the fox alive and caged it, but left the cage beside the nearest road while he went back for his pickup, and Pierson came along, took the fox from the cage and took it away? What if Pierson killed it instead?

William Blackstone, 2 Commentaries on the Laws of England 391–94 (1st ed. 1766, reprinted by U. Chi. Press 1979), wrote:

> "[A] man may be invested with a qualified, but not an absolute, property in all creatures that are *ferae naturae*. . . ." A qualified property may subsist in animals *ferae naturae, per industriam hominis*: by a man's

reclaiming and making them tame by art, industry, and education; or by so confining them within his own immediate power, that they cannot escape and use their natural liberty. . . . [O]ur law apprehends the most obvious distinction to be, between such animals as we generally see tame, and are therefore seldom, if ever, found wandering at large, which calls *domitae naturae*; and such creatures as are usually found at liberty, which are therefore supposed to be more emphatically *ferae naturae*, though it may happen that the latter shall be sometimes tamed and confined by the art and industry of man. Such as are deer in a park, hares or rabbits in an enclosed warren, doves in a dovehouse, pheasants or partridges in a mew, hawks that are fed and commanded by their owner, and fish in a private pond or in trunks. These are no longer the property of a man, than while they continue in his keeping or actual possession: but, if at any time they regain their natural liberty, his property instantly ceases; unless they have *animum revertendi*, which is only to be known by their usual custom of returning. * * * The law therefore extends this possession farther than the mere manual occupation; for my tame hawk that is pursuing his quarry in my presence, though he is at liberty to go where he pleases, is nevertheless my property; for he had *animum revertendi*. So are my pigeons, that are flying at a distance from their home (especially those of the carrier kind). . . . * * * Bees also are *ferae naturae*; but, when hived and reclaimed, a man may have a qualified property in them, by the law of nature, as well as by the civil law. And to the same purpose, not to say in the same words, with the civil law, speaks Bracton: occupation, that is, hiving or including them, gives the property in bees; for, though a swarm lights upon my tree, I have no more property in them till I have hived them, than I have in the birds which make their nests thereon; and therefore if another hives them, he shall be their proprietor: but a swarm, which flies from and out of my hive, are mine so long as I can keep them in sight, and have power to pursue them; and in these circumstances no one else is entitled to take them. But it hath been also said, that with us the only ownership in bees is *ratione soli*. . . .

In all these creatures, reclaimed from the wildness of their nature, the property is not absolute, but defeasible: a property, that may be destroyed if they resume their ancient wildness, and are found at large. For if the pheasants escape from the mew, or the fishes from the trunk, and are seen wandering at large in their proper element, they become *ferae naturae* again and are free and open to the first occupant that has ability to seise them. But while they thus continue my qualified or defeasible property, they are as much under the protection of the law, as if they were absolutely and indefeasibly mine: and an action will lie against any man that detains them from me, or unlawfully destroys them. It is also as much felony by common law to steal such of them as are fit for food, as it is to steal tame animals: but not so, if they are only kept for pleasure, curiosity, or whim, as dogs, bears, cats, apes, parrots, and singing birds; because their value is not intrinsic, but depending only on the caprice of the owner: though it is such an invasion of property as may amount to a civil injury, and be redressed by a civil action. Yet to steal a reclaimed hawk is felony both by common law and statute; which seems to be relic of the tyranny of our ancient sportsmen. * * * And thus much of qualified property in wild animals, reclaimed *per industriam.*

BUSTER v. NEWKIRK
20 Johns. 75 (N.Y. Sup. Ct. 1822)

IN ERROR, on *certiorari* to a justice's court. Newkirk brought an action of trover against Buster for a deer skin. It appeared that N. was hunting deer on the 31st of December, 1819, and had wounded one, about six miles from B.'s house, which he pursued with his dogs. He followed the track of the deer, occasionally discovering blood, until night; and on the next morning resumed the pursuit, until he came to B.'s house, where the deer had been killed the evening before. The deer had been fired at by another person, just before he was killed by B., and fell, but rose again, and ran on, the dogs being in pursuit, and the plaintiff's dog laid hold of the deer about the same time, when B. cut the deer's throat. N. demanded the venison and skin of B., who gave him the venison, but refused to let him have the skin. The jury found a verdict for the plaintiff for seventy-five cents, on which the justice gave judgment.

PER CURIAM. The principles decided in the case of *Pierson v. Post*, 3 Caines' Rep. 175, are applicable here. The authorities cited in that case establish the position that property can be acquired in animals *ferae naturae* by *occupancy* only, and that in order to constitute such an occupancy it is sufficient if the animal is deprived of his natural liberty, by wounding or otherwise, so that he is brought within the power and control of the pursuer. In the present case the deer, though wounded, ran six miles; and the defendant in error had abandoned the pursuit that day, and the deer was not deprived of his natural liberty, so as to be in the power or under the control of N. He therefore cannot be said to have had a property in the animal so as to maintain the action. The judgment must be reversed.

NOTES

1. Does this opinion accurately restate the rule of *Pierson v. Post*? See *Liesner v. Wanie*, 145 N.W. 374 (Wis. 1914) (involving the hunt for a wolf in a vigorous pursuit that cornered the animal and made actual possession "practically inevitable," putting the hunter in constructive possession of the animal; holding that a directed verdict for the plaintiff hunter was proper and ordering that the defendant intervening in the hunt and taking the wolf return it). What is the rule of *Liesner*? What is its rationale?

2. A common law action in trover redressed an interference with the plaintiff's personal property that is substantial enough to justify compelling the defendant to pay for it, as in a forced sale; that is, the measure of damages in trover becomes the value of the property at the time and place of the interference, in effect the sale price. The interference or appropriation came over time to be called a conversion (or the tort for which trover is maintainable), and emerged as both the last element of trover and a separate cause of action that rests on proving the loss of a plaintiff's immediate right to possession by the defendant. See William Prosser, *The Nature* *of Conversion*, 42 Cornell L.Q. 168 (1957). Conversion (a/k/a trover and conversion) was distinguished from trespass in *Fouldes v. Willoughby*, 151 Eng. Ret. 1153 (1841) (defendant's wrongfully refusing to carry plaintiff's horses on a ferry boat, and putting them off while plaintiff remained on board, held to be a trespass, but not a conversion of the horses because defendant did not interfere with the plaintiff's "general right of dominion" over them — even though plaintiff lost them).

3. What difference would it have made if either Buster or Newkirk — or Pierson or Post — were trespassing on the land of a third party? Would it make any difference if the land were posted with no hunting signs? See *McKee v. Gratz*, 260 U.S. 127 (1922) (Holmes, J.). See also *Bizzell v. Booker*, 16 Ark. 308, 320 (Ark. 1855). Based on statutes requiring posting to withhold the right of a landowner to exclude, a majority of states have a rule that if land is not posted, a hunter is immune from both civil and criminal trespass. Does such a "welcome hunters" rule make sense today? Would it make any difference if the hunter stalked the animal on one owner's land, but killed or captured on another's? Post starts a fox on L's land and pursues it onto O's land, where Pierson intercepts and kills it while Post is still in pursuit. Who owns the fox? What if Post killed the fox on O's land, but when Post turned away, Pierson took its body off? What if Post had placed a box on L's land to attract bees, who swarmed to the box and then swarmed again in a hollow tree on O's land, where Pierson removed the hive and carried it off? See *Rexroth v. Coon*, 23 A. 37 (R.I. 1885). What if Pierson came and cut down the tree for firewood?

KEEBLE v. HICKERINGILL
11 East 574, 103 Eng. Rep. 1127,
sub nom. Keble v. Hickringill, 11 Mod. 74, 130
sub nom., Keeble v. Heckeringhall, 3 Salk 9 (Q.B. 1707)

ACTION upon the case. Plaintiff declares that he was, 8th *November* in the second year of the queen, lawfully possessed of a close of land called *Minott's Meadow, et de quodam vivario*, vocato a decoy pond, to which divers wildfowl used to resort and come; and the plaintiff had at his own costs and charges prepared and procured divers decoy-ducks, nets, machines, and other engines for the decoying and taking of the wildfowl, and enjoyed the benefit in taking them; the defendant, knowing which, and *intending to damnify the plaintiff in his vivary, and to fright and drive away the wildfowl used to resort thither, and deprive him of his profit*, did, on the 8th of *November* resort to the head of the said pond and vivary, and did discharge the said gun several times that was then charged with the gunpowder against the said decoy pond, whereby the wildfowl was frighted away, and did forsake the said pond [for four months]. Upon not guilty pleaded a verdict was found for the plaintiff and 20 lbs. damages.

Plaintiff's Decoy Pond
(courtesy of Brian Simpson)

HOLT, C.J. I am of opinion that this action doth lie. . . . For, 1st, This using or making a decoy is lawful. 2dly, This employment of the ground to that use is profitable to the plaintiff, as is the skill and management of that employment. As to the first, Every man that hath a property may employ it for his pleasure and profit, as for alluring and procuring decoy ducks to come to his pond. To learn the trade of seducing other ducks to come here in order to be taken is not prohibited either by the law of the land or the moral law; but it is as lawful to use art to seduce them, to catch, them, and destroy them for the use of mankind, as to kill and destroy wildfowl or tame cattle. Then when a man useth his art or his skill to take them, to sell and dispose of for his profit this is his trade; and he that hinders another in his trade or livelihood is liable to an action for so hindering him. . . . [W]here a violent or malicious act is done to a man's occupation, profession, or way of getting a livelihood; there an action lies in all cases. But if a man doth him damage by using the same employment; as if Mr. Hickeringill had set up another decoy on his own ground near the plaintiff's, and that had spoiled the custom of the plaintiff, no action would lie because he had as much liberty to make and use a decoy as the plaintiff. This is like the case of 11 *H*. 4.47. One schoolmaster sets up a new school to the damage of an ancient school, and thereby the scholars are allured from the old school to come to his new. (The action there was held not to lie.) But suppose Mr. Hickeringill should lie in the way with his guns, and fright the boys from going to school, and their parents would let them go thither; sure that schoolmaster might have an action for the loss of his scholars. A man hath a market, to which he hath toll for horses sold: a man is bringing his horse to market to sell; a stranger hinders and obstructs him from going thither to the market; an action lies because it imports damage. . . . Now considering the nature of the case, it is not possible to declare of the number, that were frighted away; because the plaintiff had not possession of them, to count them. Where a man brings trespass for taking his goods, he must declare of the quantity, because he, by having had the possession, may know what he had, and therefore must know what he lost. . . . And when we do know that of long time in the kingdom these artificial contrivances of decoy ponds and decoy ducks have been used for enticing into those ponds wildfowl, in order to be taken for the profit of the owner of the pond, who is at the expense of servants, engines, and other management, whereby the markets of the nation may be furnished; there is great reason to give encouragement thereunto; that the people who are so instrumental by their skill and industry so to furnish the markets should reap the benefit and have their action. But in short, that which is the true reason, is, that this action is not brought to recover damage for the loss of the fowl, but for the disturbance. . . . So is the usual and common way of declaring.

NOTES

1.   Is the text of the *Keeble* opinion reported here consistent with the description of the case in *Pierson v. Post*? How might Post's counsel have used *Keeble* to argue his client's case? See *State of South Dakota v. Rumpca*, 652 N.W.2d 795 (S. Dak. 2002).

2.   O has a pond on her land, to which she attracts wild geese. The geese eat the crops of a farmer F whose land adjoins O's. F sues O for the value of the crops eaten. In F's suit, what result and why? See *Andrews v. Andrews*, 88 S.E.2d 88 (N.C. 1955). Suppose that a pond in a state wildlife refuge attracts wildfowl, who eat crops on F's adjoining farms. F sues the state for the value of the crops eaten. Will F win her suit? See *Sickman v. United States*, 184 F.2d 616 (7th Cir. 1950). Suppose that pesticides from F's farm sicken and kill waterfowl in a wildlife refuge adjoining F's farm. The state sues F for the damage to the wildlife. Will the state win its suit? See *State v. Dickenson Cheese Co., Inc.*, 200 N.W.2d 59 (N.D. 1972), reprinted *infra*.

DAPSON v. DALY
153 N.E. 454 (Mass. 1926)

Rugg, C.J.

This is an action of replevin to recover the carcass of a deer. There was evidence tending to show that both the plaintiff and defendant were on the same day and in the open season hunting deer, that the plaintiff and his companion fired shots at the deer in question, and that, shortly thereafter, while the deer was galloping, although it may have fallen before, the defendant also fired a shot, whereupon it immediately fell, and was dead when he reached it, and that the defendant carried it away.

The finding was that the court was not satisfied that the deer, an animal *ferae naturae*, was so wounded by the plaintiff that it was about to be deprived of its natural liberty, and that the fatal shot was fired by the defendant. There was evidence to support these findings. Hence they must stand.

In this commonwealth the title to wild animals and game is in the commonwealth in trust for the public, to be devoted to the common welfare. The Legislature has made provision for the hunting of deer during a restricted period by those duly licensed. G. L. c. 131, §§ 3, 62, 63. These regulations are valid. The right to hunt deer exists and can be exercised only in accordance therewith. *Commonwealth v. Hilton*, 174 Mass. 29, 31, 54 N.E. 362. *Geer v. Connecticut*, 161 U.S. 519.

The plaintiff in the case at bar failed to show that he was duly authorized by law to hunt. Unless so licensed, he was not entitled to the rights of a huntsman. It was an essential part of his case to show that he was a lawful huntsman before he could invoke in his own behalf the law of the chase. The plaintiff, in order to prevail, was bound to show title in himself and could not rely on the weakness of the defendant's rights. (Citation omitted.) The plaintiff never acquired physical possession of the deer. The first step toward showing title in himself was to prove that he was licensed to hunt. The nature of the plaintiff's claim was such as not to require the defendant to set up in his answer the illegal conduct of the plaintiff. The burden of proof in this as in all other essential particulars was on the plaintiff. (Citations omitted.)

The plaintiff bases his case on the ground that he was pursuing and had wounded a deer during the open season and was therefore entitled to its ownership, even if the mortal wound was given by the defendant. It is conceded that the deer in question was a wild animal not doing damage to property. The controlling principle of the common law is that the huntsman acquires no title to a wild animal by pursuit alone, even though there is wounding, unless the animal is followed up and reduced to occupation, that is, to actual possession. *Pierson v. Post*, 3 Caines, 175, where the authorities are reviewed. *Buster v. Newkirk*, 20 Johns. 75; *Young v. Hichens*, 6 Q. B. 606, 1 Bracton, (Twiss' Ed.) 67 (2nd book, c. 1, 3). On this point the finding of fact was against the plaintiff. It cannot be set aside on this record. It follows that there was no error of law. . . .

NOTE

Dapson is a case involving an action in replevin. On this cause of action, *Doughty v. Sullivan*, 661 A.2d 1112, 1118–1120 (Me. 1995), states:

> Replevin is one of the oldest legal remedies available under the common law. Historically, replevin lay to recover immediate possession of a specific chattel as compared with other common law actions for trespass or conversion which lay to recover damages for the wrongful taking of a chattel. Replevin sought only to establish the right to possession and not the right to legal title. The common law action of replevin could be commenced only by the issuance of a writ of replevin and seizure of the property which was deemed necessary for the court to obtain jurisdiction over the action.
>
> The plaintiff would apply for a writ of replevin from the court by supplying an affidavit alleging the right to immediate possession of the goods currently in the wrongful possession of a third party. If the affidavit satisfied the common law formalities, the court would issue the writ

directing the sheriff to seize the chattel and to deliver the same to the plaintiff. Before the sheriff could serve the writ and seize the property, however, he had to obtain a bond from the plaintiff for twice the value of the goods sought to be replevied. Upon receiving possession, the plaintiff would bring the action in replevin seeking a judicial determination of his right to possession and any damages incurred by the defendant's wrongful retention of the chattel. Hence, replevin was a unique common law action that entitled a plaintiff to a prejudgment seizure of the chattel, leaving the merits of the plaintiff's claim of right to be tried later.

In some states the common law replevin action was eventually subsumed by a broader statutory action, commonly called an action to recover a chattel, in which a writ of replevin is but one remedy available to the plaintiff and not essential to commencing the action. . . . Other states have also concluded that, pursuant to their statutes, a writ of replevin is merely ancillary to the statutory action to recover a chattel. * * * [In these states] a plaintiff may obtain pre-judgment possession as a provisional remedy within a larger cause of action.

Other states, interpreting their own statutes, have concluded that if the property were not seized pursuant to a writ prior to the court hearing the case, the action was transformed into an action in trover or conversion. In such actions, the plaintiff could seek only damages instead of possession. Some states interpret their statutes to have retained the common law rule that the court has no jurisdiction to hear a replevin action until the property has been replevied. (Citations omitted.)

NOTES ON LARCENY

1. In *State of Ohio v. Shaw*, 65 N.E. 875 (Ohio 1902), the defendant was convicted of the crime of larceny. Larceny consists of stealing the property of another. It is a crime with five elements: it is (1) a trespass (2) resulting in the taking or carrying away (3) of tangible personalty (4) of another (5) with the implied or express intent to take exclusive possession and permanently deprive the other of it. See *State v. Parsons*, 773 A.2d 1034 (Me. 2001). Some states add lack of consent by the owner as a sixth element. See *State v. Calonico*, 770 A.2d 454 (Conn. 2001). Grand larceny is larceny that is also a breach of the peace and often depends on the value of the thing taken. If Heckeringill had shot and killed one of Keeble's ducks, would that be larceny? No, because there is no asportation (no taking away from the scene of a defendant's taking possession). Likewise, "let me borrow this" is not larceny because there is no intent to deprive an owner of possession permanently. Likewise, abandoned property cannot be the subject of larceny. Is refusal to pay a taxi fare larceny? No. The refusal is not tangible. Is the taxi driver's picking your wallet off the seat after you leave the cab larceny? It might be. *Shaw* involved the defendant's taking 100–150 pounds of fish from two "pound nets" set by others in open water in Lake Erie. A pound net has tunnel-like entrance was about 40 feet long and 35 feet underwater, ending in an opening 3 feet in diameter leading into the net and extending 5 to 6 feet into the net; the opening of the tunnel into the holding area of the net was left open so it was possible for the fish to get out the way they got in and the holding area rose several feet above the Lake's surface.

The *Shaw* opinion's concluding paragraph states: "In the present case the fish were not at large in Lake Erie. They were confined in nets, from which it was not absolutely impossible for them to escape, yet it was practically so impossible; for it seems that under ordinary circumstances few, if any, of the fish escape. The fish that were taken had not escaped, and it does not appear that they would have escaped, or even that they probably would have escaped. They were so safely secured that the owners of the nets could have taken them out of the water at will as readily as the defendants did. The possession of the owners of the nets was so complete and certain that the defendants went to the nets and raised them with absolute assurance that they could get the fish that were in them. We think, therefore, that the owners of the nets, having captured and confined the fish, had acquired such a property in them that the taking of them was larceny." But in a criminal case like *Shaw*, wouldn't you expect the court to have a clearer rule as to what constitutes possession? Is the crime in *Shaw* against the owners' possession or their right to exclude others from using their net? Compare *Shaw* with *Sollers v. Sollers*, 26 A. 188 (Md. 1893) (holding that fish driven into and trapped in an inlet by a net laid along the length of the inlet's mouth are still subject to capture). Can *Shaw* and *Sollers* be reconciled? See also *State v. House*, 65 N.C. 315 (N.C. 1871) (larceny of an otter from a trap).

2. A fisherman is convicted of violating fishery regulations requiring that inshore nets be set at least 1000 feet apart. His defense is that his net was set first, at a time when another fisherman's net was not within 1000 feet. Is this defense a good one? See *Clucas v. State of Alaska*, 815 P.2d 384 (Alaska Ct. App. 1991). What if the other fisherman says that she might not have been the first to set her net, but was the first to haul a catch from her net? If a fisherman has his net illegally seized under this regulation, does he have a remedy against the fisherman whose catch becomes legal, but who otherwise would be in violation of the regulation? Would the problems be the same if the fisherman were fishing with a prohibited type of gear, such as a drift net? See *Haggren v. State of Alaska*, 829 P.2d 842 (Alaska Ct. App. 1992). Does a fisherman legally setting and hauling a net under the regulation have the right to exclude the public from fishing within the prohibited distance? See *CWC Fisheries, Inc. v. Bunker*, 755 P.2d 1115 (Alaska 1988).

3. Hunting licenses and regulations and criminal law are but two approaches used to regulate wildlife. The leading citation for wildlife regulation in *Daly* is *Geer v. Connecticut*, 161 U.S. 519 (1896) (concluding that the police power of the state was sufficient to prohibit the interstate transportation of birds killed during hunting season and to allow their use, purchase, or sale only within the state, without violating the interstate Commerce Clause of the U.S. Constitution). Other approaches are contained in statutes prohibiting the inhumane treatment of animals (e.g., the neglect of animals in possession) or the exploitation of designated animals (e.g., outlawing bear-baiting, cock-fighting, or greased pig contests), and those prohibiting possession of live wild animals. What if a hunter without a license were attacked by a six point rutting buck? What if an unlicensed person saved a baby squirrel after it fell out of its nest and raised it? Might she be prosecuted for not having a license to possess a wild animal? See *Commonwealth of Pennsylvania v. Gosselin*, 861 A.2d 997 (Pa. Super. Ct. 2004). Hunters' and animal rights activists' interests sometimes conflict today. See, e.g., *Seeton v. Pennsylvania Game Comm'n*, 937 A.2d 1028 (Pa. 2007) (involving a "canned hunt"). Right to hunt and hunter harassment statutes are the result in many states, and 14 states have constitutional guarantees regarding the right to hunt. And seven more guarantee the right to bear arms and hunt. See Stephen P. Halbrook, *The Constitutional Right to Hunt: New Recognition of an Old Liberty in Virginia*, 19 W. & Mary Bill of Rts. J. 197 (2010). Virginia also has a statute prohibiting the penning of foxes in preparation for a fox hunt with hounds. See Va. Code § 2.9.1–5252(2) (2014).

whale case [handwritten]

GHEN v. RICH

8 Fed. 159 (D. Mass. 1881)

NELSON, J.

Issue: did I have possession of whale b/c of the fact that he had hunted and killed it, and were his actions continued pursuit? [handwritten]

This is a libel to recover the value of a fin-back whale. The libellant lives in Provincetown and the respondent in Wellfleet. The facts, as they appeared at the hearing, are as follows:

In the early spring months the easterly part of Massachusetts bay is frequented by the species of whale known as the fin-back whale. Fishermen from Provincetown pursue them in open boats from the shore, and shoot them with bomb-lances fired from guns made expressly for the purpose. When killed they sink at once to the bottom, but in the course of from one to three days they rise and float on the surface. Some of them are picked up by vessels and towed into Provincetown. Some float ashore at high water and are left stranded on the beach as the tide recedes. Others float out to sea and are never recovered. The person who happens to find them on the beach usually sends word to Provincetown, and the owner comes to the spot and removes the blubber. The finder usually receives a small salvage for his services. Try-works are established in Provincetown for trying out the oil. The business is of considerable extent, but, since it requires skill and experience, as well as some outlay of capital, and is attended with great exposure and hardship, few persons engage in it. The average yield of oil is about 20 barrels to a whale. It swims with great swiftness, and for that reason cannot be taken by the harpoon and line. Each boat's crew engaged in the business has its peculiar mark or device on its lances, and in this way it is know by whom a whale is killed.

Court found he did in fact have possession of the whale b/c the spear he had used to kill it was tagged so people would know it was his. [handwritten]

The usage on Cape Cod, for many years, has been that the person who kills a whale in the manner and under the circumstances described, owns it, and this right has never been disputed until this case. The libellant has been engaged in the business for ten years past. On the morning of April 9, 1880, in Massachusetts bay, near the end of Cape Cod, he shot and instantly killed with a bomb-lance the whale in question. It sunk immediately, and on the morning of the 12th was found stranded on the beach in Brewster, within the ebb and flow of the tide, by one Ellis, 17 miles from the spot where it was killed. Instead of sending word to [Provincetown], as is customary, Ellis advertised the whale for sale at auction, and sold it to the respondent, who shipped off the blubber and tried out the oil. The libellant

Judge this accepts [handwritten]

It is custom of the area and industry that if you found a dead whale w/ a tag you notify the person and get a finder's fee. [handwritten]

heard of the finding of the whale on the morning of the 15th, and immediately sent one of his boat's crew to the place and claimed it. Neither the respondent nor Ellis knew the whale had been killed by the libellant, but they knew or might have known, if they had wished, that it had been shot and killed with a bomb-lance, by some person engaged in this species of business.

The libellant claims title to the whale under this usage. The respondent insists that this usage is invalid. It was decided by Judge Sprague, in *Taber v. Jenny*, 1 Sprague 315, that when a whale has been killed, and is anchored and left with marks of appropriation, it is the property of the captors; and if it is afterwards found, still anchored, by another ship, there is no usage or principle of law by which the property of the original captors is diverted, even though the whale may have drifted from its anchorage. The learned judge says: "When the whale had been killed and taken possession of by the boat of the Hillman, [the first taker,] it became the property of the owners of that ship, and all was done which was then practicable in order to secure it. They left it anchored, with unequivocal marks of appropriation."

In *Bartlett v. Budd*, 1 Low. 223, the facts were these: The first officer of the libellant's ship killed a whale in the Okhotsk sea, anchored it, attached a waif to the body, and then left it and went ashore at some distance for the night. The next morning the boats of the respondent's ship found the whale adrift, the anchor not holding, the cable coiled around the body, and no waif or irons attached to it. Judge Lowell held that, as the libellants had killed and taken actual possession of the whale, the ownership vested in them. In his opinion the learned judge says: "A whale, being *ferae naturae*, does not become property until a firm possession has been established by the taker. But when such possession has become firm and complete, the right of property is clear, and has all the characteristics of property." * * *

In *Swift v. Gifford*, 2 Low. 110, Judge Lowell decided that a custom among whalemen in the Arctic seas, that the iron holds the whale, was reasonable and valid. In that case a boat's crew from the respondent's ship pursued and struck a whale in the Arctic ocean, and the harpoon and the line attached to it remained in the whale, but did not remain fast to the boat. A boat's crew from the libellant's ship continued the pursuit and captured the whale, and the master of the respondent's ship claimed it on the spot. It was held by the learned judge that the whale belonged to the respondents. It was said by Judge Sprague, in *Bourne v. Ashley*, an unprinted case referred to by Judge Lowell in *Swift v. Gifford*, that the usage for the first iron, whether attached to the boat or not, to hold the whale was fully established; and he added that, although local usages of a particular port ought not to be allowed to set aside the general maritime law, this objection did not apply to a custom which embraced an entire business, and had been concurred in for a long time by every one engaged in the trade.

In *Swift v. Gifford*, Judge Lowell also said: "The rule of law invoked in this case is one of very limited application. The whale fishery is the only branch of industry of any importance in which it is likely to be much used, and if a usage is found to prevail generally in that business, it will not be open to the objection that it is likely to disturb the general understanding of mankind by the interposition of an arbitrary exception."

I see no reason why the usage proved in this case is not as reasonable as that sustained in the cases cited. Its application must necessarily be extremely limited, and can affect but a few persons. It has been recognized and acquiesced in for many years. It requires in the first taker the only act of appropriation that is possible in the nature of the case. Unless it is sustained, this branch of industry must necessarily cease, for no person would engage in it if the fruits of his labor could be appropriated by any chance finder. It gives reasonable salvage for securing or reporting the property. That the rule works well in practice is shown by the extent of the industry which has grown up under it, and the general acquiescence of a whole community interested to dispute it. It is by no means clear that without regard to usage the common law would not reach the same result. If the fisherman does all that it is possible to do to make the animal his own, that would seem to be sufficient. Such a rule might well be applied in the interest of trade, there being no usage or custom to the contrary. Holmes, Com. Law, 217. But be that as it may, I hold the usage to be valid, and that the property in the whale was in the libellant.

The rule of damages is the market value of the oil obtained from the whale, less the cost of trying it out and preparing it for the market, with interest on the amount so ascertained from the date of conversion. * * * Decrees for libellant for $71.05, without costs.

NOTE

"Custom is what men do, not what they think." John Chipman Gray, The Nature and Sources of the Law 285 (2d. ed. 1921). What preconditions does the *Ghen* opinion impose on the use of custom? Is custom a defense of the whaling industry, or a means of extending the reach of the common law? Does its use by a court depend on its reasonableness or its general acceptance? Other industries have well recognized customs — horse breeding and racing, for example. See *Marsh v. Gentry*, 642 S.W.2d 574 (Ky. 1982). Would the result in *Ghen* have been the same under the common law? The rule of capture taken from *Pierson* and *Ghen*, when applied to fisheries, is subject to much criticism:

> Commercial ocean fishing combines difficult and risky labor with large capital investments to make money from a resource owned by no one, the fish. Unlimited access tends to cause declining fisheries. The reason is that to get title to a fish, a fisherman has to catch it before someone else does. *Pierson v. Post*, 3 Caines 175, 2 Am. Dec. 264 (N.Y. 1805). This gives each fisherman an incentive to invest in a fast, large boat and to fish as fast as possible. As boats and crews get more efficient, fewer fish escape the fishermen and live to reproduce. "The result is lower profits for the too many fishermen investing in too much capital to catch too few fish." Terry L. Anderson and Donald R. Leal, *Free Market Environmentalism* 123 (1991).

Alliance Against IFQS v. Brown, 84 F.3d 343, 345 (9th Cir. 1996).

[handwritten: Cheese fish case.]

STATE OF NORTH DAKOTA v.
DICKINSON CHEESE CO., INC.
200 N.W.2d 59 (N.D. 1972)

[handwritten: Issue: does ND have property rights to fish while they are in the river in a free state?]

STRUTZ, J.

The State of North Dakota, by its State Game and Fish Commissioner, brought this action to recover damages for the value of fish killed as a result of pollution of the Heart River near Dickinson, in Stark County. The complaint alleges that the discharge of whey into the river by the defendant Dickinson Cheese Company caused the death of thousands of fish, totaling some 36,000 pounds, thereby damaging the environment in and around the river for a distance of some twelve miles and destroying the fish; that all fish located in any public waters in this State are the property of the State of North Dakota; and that the plaintiff is responsible for such fish for the benefit of the people of the State. The action was commenced against the defendant cheese company and John Gurtner, its manager, for monetary damages for destruction of the fish and damage to the environment and for exemplary damages. * * *

The trial court dismissed the complaint of the plaintiff as well as the complaint of the third-party plaintiff, on the ground that the complaints failed to state claims upon which relief could be granted, and the plaintiff takes this appeal. The sole question before us on this appeal is whether the State of North Dakota, as represented by the State Game and Fish Department, has such property rights in fish, while they are in the river in a free state, that the invasion of those property rights by the defendants will support an action for damages.

Fish swimming in streams of the State are *ferae naturae*. . . . Ownership of and title to fish while they are in such state of freedom is in the State for the purpose of regulating the enjoyment, use, possession, disposition, and conservation thereof for the benefit of the people. Sec. 20-01-02, N.D.C.C. The regulatory power of the State extends not only to the taking of its fish but also over the waters inhabited by the fish. . . . It has been held that although the law provides that the ownership of fish, while they are in a state of freedom, is in the State for the purposes of regulation of their taking and conservation, the interest of the State in fish running wild in the streams of the State is that of a sovereign, and not that of an owner. *Commonwealth v. Agway, Inc.*, 232 A.2d 69 (Pa. Super. 1967) (a trespass action — Eds.). As sovereign, the State has the power to determine when and under what conditions fish running wild may be taken and thus reduced to ownership, but it does not have such property interest in the fish while they are in a wild state sufficient to support a civil action for damages for the destruction of those fish which have not been reduced to possession. *Commonwealth v. Agway, Inc., supra.*

Did the law enacted by the Legislative Assembly in 1967, . . . Ch. 61-28 of the N.D.C.C., commonly referred to as the "Antipollution Act," bestow upon the State of North Dakota the power to maintain an action for monetary damages for the unlawful killing of fish in the wild state? We think not. That chapter was enacted to give to the State the power to control, prevent, and abate the pollution of surface waters in the State. It gives to the State of North Dakota . . . the authority to

[handwritten left margin: "Court says no. Fish are ferae natura and the fish, despite being state sovereign water, they are not captured, pursued or confined, so they are not the personal property of anyone.]

adopt, amend, or repeal rules, regulations, and standards of quality of the waters of the State, and it fixes penalties for the violation thereof. It does not give to the State ownership sufficient to support a civil action for damages against one who unlawfully pollutes a stream and thus causes the destruction of fish while they are running wild in such water.

For reasons stated in this opinion, the order dismissing the complaint of the plaintiff . . . is in all things affirmed.

NOTE

Why did the state bring this suit? Why didn't it base its suit on the statutes cited in the opinion, one involving game management and the other involving water pollution? Would the case have been stronger if public lands were affected in some way by the fish kill? See *In re Stewart Transp. Co.*, 495 F. Supp. 38 (E.D. Va. 1980) (holding that the public trust includes waterfowl and that both the federal government and Virginia had an action for damages caused by an oil spill killing 30,000 waterfowl lost to the trust); see also *California Trout, Inc. v. State Water Resources Control Bd.*, 255 Cal. Rptr. 184 (Cal. App. 1989). In a few states, wildlife is made a public trust resource in the state constitution. See, e.g., Alaska Const. Art VIII, § 3.

II. ACQUIRING ABANDONED PROPERTY

Shipwreck case

EADS v. BRAZELTON
22 Ark. 499, 79 Am. Dec. 88 (Ark. 1861)

Issue: Did P have possession of the wreck as a finder? Court says NO. They said a finder must take possession of the prop. they wish to find. There need to be ACTUAL CAPTURE, just marking it is not enough.

FAIRCHILD, J. . . .

The bill in this case is founded upon a right of occupancy which Brazelton, the plaintiff, insists was vested in him by his discovery of the wreck of the steam-boat America and by his intentions and acts relating thereto. Because this right was not respected by the defendants, partners and servants of a firm of wreckers doing business in the Mississippi River and its tributaries under the style of Eads and Nelson, Brazelton filed his bill on the chancery side of the Circuit Court of Mississippi County, to obtain the protection of the court, to relieve him from the interference of the defendants in his own intended labors, to recover the property in the wreck, and to obtain compensation for what they had taken therefrom.

From what is before us it may be taken as shown in the case that in November, 1827, the boat named sank in the Mississippi River within the limits of Mississippi County; that, of her cargo, shot and bundles of bar lead of an unascertained quantity and lead in pigs to about the number of three thousand remained in the river, wholly abandoned by the owners; that Brazelton, having information of the place where the boat sank, proceeded in December, 1854, to ascertain its exact locality in the bed of the river with the view of raising the sunken lead; that in January, 1855, he arrived at the vicinity of the wreck with his diving boat to carry out his intention and fastened a buoy to a weight that rested upon the wreck with the expectation of putting his boat over it the next day; but that he was detained by other business and by the difficulties and dangers of the work in the existing state of water with boats like his and by the necessity for making repairs upon his boat and apparatus for raising the cargo, till the defendants, upon the 18th of September, 1855, caused one of their boats to stop at the shore near the wreck, to search for and find it, to place their boat over it, and to commence raising the lead. . . . [The trial judge enjoined interference by the defendants and gave damages to the plaintiff.]

When Brazelton found the wreck he traced lines to it from different points on the Arkansas side of the river, so that their intersection would show the situation of the wreck, and the lines were indicated by marks upon the trees. It was upon the return of Brazelton from St. Louis with his bell boat that a float or buoy was placed by Brazelton over the wreck, and this was done with the intention of signifying the place to which the diving boat was to be dropped the next morning. It was not to be expected that such objects would remain permanent fixtures, as the wreck was in the main channel of the river, and it is evident that Brazelton considered them as guides to the situation of the wreck, as the marked trees were, as he stated to Seth Daniel, in the presence of Reese Bowen, that it would make no difference if they should be washed away, as he could find the wreck from the ranges of his lines. Brazelton does not pretend to have put his boat over the wreck, or to have had any claim to the wreck but by occupancy, which depended upon his finding it, upon his providing means for easy approaches to it by land-marks, and floats upon water, and upon his being in the neighborhood of the wreck from January to the last of September, without any other appropriation of the wreck, but with a continual assertion of his claim, and with the intention of making it good by future action. . . .

With reference to the tree marks of Brazelton it may be said that there is no satisfactory evidence that they were used on the part of the defendants in finding the wreck. . . . It is not established that the defendants knew that Brazelton was about to work upon the America, although a witness so inferred from the conversation of the Captain and others of the boat, while there is no room for suspicion that they intended to interfere with any occupancy of the boat by Brazelton, and the whole case is, that they did not do so according to their understanding of Brazelton's right.

But what that right was remains to be determined. Notwithstanding the point made by the defendants, that Brazelton had no right to the lead which the law would protect, it being the property of the original owners of the cargo, there is no room for doubt that the lead was abandoned by its owners; and even without the positive testimony of an owner of the boat and cargo in affirmation of the fact the law would so imply from the term of the loss and from the fact of its having been covered by an island formed upon it which sustained trees growing to a height of thirty to forty feet. All reasonable hope of acquiring the property must have been given up from the nature of the case; and the evidence shows that during the two years that intervened between the sinking of the boat and its being covered by the tow head and island no effort was made to save that part of the cargo. . . .

The occupation or possession of property lost, abandoned or without an owner must depend upon an actual taking of the property with the intent to reduce it to possession. . . . Brazelton's act of possession need not have been manual; he was not obliged to take the wreck or the lead between his hands; he might take such possession of them as their nature and situation permitted; but that his circumstances should give a legal character to his acts, make that to be possession which the law declares not to be possession, assumes more than a court can sanction. Marking trees that extend across the wreck and affixing temporary buoys to it were not acts of possession; they only indicated Brazelton's desire or intention to appropriate the property. Placing his boat over the wreck, with the means to raise its valuables and with persistent efforts directed to raising the lead, would have been keeping the only effectual guard over it, would have been the only warning that intruders — that is, other longing occupants — would be obliged to regard, and would have been such acts of possession as the law would notice and protect. . . . The decree . . . is reversed. . . .

NOTE

How might an intent to abandon the lead be contested? What if its owners produced the lading receipts or the bills of sale for it? An insurer of a cargo long lost has reclaimed it on the basis of paying policyholders and taking their rights. See *Columbus-America Discovery Group v. Atlantic Mut. Ins. Co.*, 974 F.2d 450 (4th Cir. 1992) (involving the insurers of a cargo of gold in the *S.S. Central America*, sinking in a storm off the coast of South Carolina in 1857), discussed in Gary Kinder, Ship of Gold in the Deep Blue Sea (1998). After the steamboat sinks, suppose that a passenger's chest is found floating in the river, empty, except for money in its lining. Is the chest abandoned? See *Hollingsworth v. Seventy Doubloons and Three Small Pieces of Gold*, 12 F. Cas. 380 (E.D. Pa. 1820). See generally Barlow Burke, *A Reprise of the Case of Eads v. Brazelton*, 44 Ark. L. Rev. 425 (1991).

HASLEM v. LOCKWOOD
37 Conn. 500 (1871)

[handwritten: (Court says it wasn't abandoned by P since had an intention of returning in a reasonable time. 'P put in the time and effort]

[handwritten: manure case]

Trover for a quantity of manure. On the trial it appeared that plaintiff, on the evening of April 6, 1869, gathered into heaps manure lying on a public highway in the borough of Stamford, intending to remove the same to his own lands the next evening. Before noon the next day defendant removed the manure so gathered. The fee of the said highway was in the borough, and neither plaintiff nor defendant had permission from the authorities to remove the manure, although its removal was beneficial to the health and appearance of the borough. The manure was worth $6.

Plaintiff claimed that the manure was abandoned personal property, and became the property of the first possessor, which he became by gathering it into heaps. The defendant claimed that the manure was a part of the realty, and belonged to the owner of the fee of the highway; and, further, that if it was personalty the plaintiff had abandoned it, by leaving it after having raked it into heaps. The court ruled that the plaintiff had not made out title or right of possession to the manure, and rendered judgment for defendant. Plaintiff moved for a new trial.

Park, J. We think the manure scattered upon the ground, under the circumstances of this case, was personal property. The cases referred to by the defendant to show that it was real estate are not in point. The principle of those cases is, that manure made in the usual course of husbandry upon a farm is so attached to and connected with the realty that, in the absence of any express stipulation to the contrary, it becomes appurtenant to it. The principle was established for the benefit of agriculture. It found its origin in the fact that it is essential to the successful cultivation of a farm that the manure, produced from the droppings of cattle and swine fed upon the products of the farm, and composted with earth and vegetable matter taken from the land, should be used to supply the drain made upon the soil in the production of crops, which otherwise would become impoverished and barren; and in the fact that manure so produced is generally regarded by farmers in this country as a part of the realty and has been so treated by landlords and tenants from time immemorial. *Daniels v. Pond*, 21 Pick., 367; 1 Washb. on Real Prop., 5, 6.

But this principle does not apply to the droppings of animals driven by travelers upon the highway. The highway is not used, and cannot be used, for the purpose of agriculture. The manure is of no benefit whatsoever to it, but on the contrary is a detriment; and in cities and large villages it becomes a nuisance, and is removed by public officers at public expense. The finding in this case is, "that the removal of the manure and scrapings was calculated to improve the appearance and health of the borough." It is therefore evident that the cases relied upon by the defendant have no application to the case.

But it is said that if the manure was personal property, it was in the possession of the owner of the fee, and the scraping it into heaps by the plaintiff did not change the possession, but it continued as before, and that therefore the plaintiff cannot recover, for he neither had the possession nor the right to the immediate possession.

The manure originally belonged to the travelers whose animals dropped it, but it being worthless to them was immediately abandoned; and whether it then became the property of the borough of Stamford which owned the fee of the land on which the manure lay, it is unnecessary to determine; for, if it did, removal of the filth would be an improvement to the borough, and no objection was made by any one to the use that the plaintiff attempted to make of it. Considering the character of such accumulations upon highways in cities and villages, and the light in which they are everywhere regarded in closely settled communities, we cannot believe that the borough in this instance would have had any objection to the act of the plaintiff in removing a nuisance that affected the public health and the appearance of the streets. At all events, we think the facts of the case show a sufficient right in the plaintiff to the immediate possession of the property as against a mere wrong doer.

The defendant appears before the court in no enviable light. He does not pretend that he had a right to the manure, even when scattered upon the highway, superior to that of the plaintiff; but after the plaintiff had changed its original condition and greatly enhanced its value by his labor, he seized and appropriated to his own use the fruits of the plaintiff's outlay, and now seeks immunity from responsibility on the ground that the plaintiff was a wrong doer as well as himself. The conduct of the defendant is in keeping with his claim, and neither commends itself to the favorable consideration of the court. The plaintiff had the peaceable and quiet possession of the property; and we deem this sufficient until the borough of Stamford shall make complaint.

It is further claimed that if the plaintiff had a right to the property by virtue of occupancy, he lost the right when he ceased to retain the actual possession of the manure after scraping it into heaps. We do not question the general doctrine, that where the right by occupancy exists, it exists no longer than the party retains the actual possession of the property, or till he appropriates it to his own use by removing it to some other place. If he leaves the property at the place where it was discovered, and does nothing whatsoever to enhance its value or change its nature, his right by occupancy is unquestionably gone. But the question is, if a party finds property comparatively worthless, as the plaintiff found the property in question, owing to its scattered condition upon the highway, and greatly increases its value by his labor and expense, does he lose his right if he leaves it a reasonable time to procure the means to take it away, when such means are necessary for its removal?

Suppose a teamster with a load of grain, while traveling the highway discovers a rent in one of his bags, and finds that his grain is scattered upon the road for a distance of a mile. He considers the labor of collecting his corn of more value than the property itself, and he therefore abandons it, and pursues his way. A afterwards finds the grain in this condition and gathers it kernel by kernel into heaps by the side of the road, and leaves it a reasonable time to procure the means necessary for its removal. While he is gone for his bag, B discovers the grain thus conveniently collected in heaps and appropriates it to his own use. Has A any remedy? If he has not, the law in this instance is open to just reproach. We think under such circumstances A would have a reasonable time to remove the property, and during such reasonable time his right to it would be protected. If this is so, then the principle applies to the case under consideration.

A reasonable time for the removal of this manure had not elapsed when the defendant seized and converted it to his own use. The statute regulating the rights of parties in the gathering of sea-weed, gives the party who heaps it upon a public beach twenty-four hours in which to remove it, and that length of time for the removal of the property we think would not be unreasonable in most cases like the present one. We therefore advise the Court of Common Pleas to grant a new trial.

NOTE

In *Goddard v. Winchell*, 52 N.W. 1124 (Iowa 1892), a 66 pound meteorite fell to earth, embedded itself in Goddard's field (leased at the time to a tenant as a pasture), was found and dug up by someone let onto the field by the tenant, and was then sold by its finder to Winchell. Goddard sued Winchell in replevin for its recovery and won. Why, in *Haslem*, protect a person who gathers manure into a pile, but not someone who brings a meteorite to public attention? Was the meteorite to be treated as part of the soil in the field, or a boulder cast there during the last Ice Age? The opinion concludes:

> It is said that the aerolite is without adaptation to the soil, and only valuable for scientific purposes. * * * That it may be of greater value for scientific or other purposes may be admitted, but that fact has little weight in

determining who should be its owner. We cannot say that the owner of the soil is not as interested in, and would not as readily contribute to, the great cause of scientific advancement, as the finder, by chance or otherwise, of these silent messengers. * * * The subject of this controversy was never lost or abandoned. Whence, it came is not known, but, under the natural law of its government, it became part of this earth, and, we think, should be treated as such. . . . Affirmed.

Ritz v. Selma United Methodist Church, 467 N.W.2d 266 (Iowa 1991), held that a person burying money in the ground and dying years later without moving it, had not abandoned it, and so his legatees had a claim on it superior to the subsequent owner of the land. Is *Ritz* distinguishable from *Goddard?*

Problem: Adam (A) and Ben (B) attend a major league baseball game in which the renowned slugger, Mac McWire, was expected to hit a home run breaking the league record for runs hit in one season. Both A and B position themselves in the area of the stands where most of McWire's home run balls have landed. In the first inning, McWire comes to bat and hits the record-breaking home run. A raises his catching arm high into the air, snaring the ball in the webbing of the softball glove he brought along; a melee instantly ensues around A who, glove and all, is sucked into a gathering mob. B, initially standing next to A, is also forced into the melee, and winds up on the bottom of it, where he sees the ball on the ground. B picks it up and pockets it, showing it seconds later to the roving cameraman from a local TV news channel. A sues B in replevin. In A's suit, what result and why? See *Popov v. Hayashi*, 2002 WL 31833731 (Cal. Super. Ct., Dec. 8, 2002).

[handwritten: A finder must perform a legally significant act of control.]

III. FINDERS' RIGHTS

[handwritten: The law of finders is comparing the finder's rights to the original owner's.]

ARMORY v. DELAMIRIE
1 Strange 505 (K.B. 1722)

[handwritten: Chimney case]

[handwritten left margin: Court says that P had possession that was not absolute, b/c if the OO came and said he wanted it back P would have to give it, but D is not the OO so P has a better claim to it.]

The plaintiff being a chimney sweeper's boy found a jewel and carried it to the defendant's shop (who was a goldsmith) to know what it was, and delivered it into the hands of the apprentice, who under the pretense of weighing it, took out the stones, and calling to the master to let him know it came to three halfpence, the master offered the boy the money, who refused to take it, and insisted to have the thing again; whereupon the apprentice delivered him back the socket without the stones. And now in trover against the master these points were ruled:

1. That the finder of a jewel, though he does not by such finding acquire an absolute property or ownership, yet he has such a property as will enable him to keep it against all but the rightful owner, and consequently may maintain trover.

2. That the action well lay against the master, who gives a credit to his apprentice, and is answerable for his neglect.

3. As to the value of the jewel several of the trade were examined to prove what a jewel of the finest water that would fit the socket would be worth; and the Chief Justice directed the jury, that unless the defendant did produce the jewel, and show it not to be of the finest water, they should presume the strongest against him, and

make the value of the best jewels the measure of the damages: which they accordingly did.

[handwritten: Issue: P has to prove the logs were his and D converted them for his own use.]

CLARK v. MALONEY
3 Harr. 68 (Del. Super. Ct. 1840)

[handwritten: tied up log case]

Action of trover to recover the value of ten white pine logs. The logs in question were found by plaintiff floating in the Delaware bay after a great freshet, were taken up and moored with ropes in the mouth of Mispillion creek. They were afterwards in the possession of defendants, who refused to give them up, alleging that they had found them adrift and floating up the creek.

[handwritten right margin: Court says P was the original finder, D was not original owner.]

BAYARD, C.J., charged the jury: The plaintiff must show first, that the logs were his property; and secondly, that they were converted by the defendants to their own use. In support of his right of property, the plaintiff relies upon the fact of his possession of the logs. They were taken up by him, adrift in the Delaware bay, and secured by a stake at the mouth of Mispillion creek. Possession is certainly prima facie evidence of property. It is called prima facie evidence because it may be rebutted by evidence of better title, but in the absence of better title it is as effective a support of title as the most conclusive evidence could be. It is for this reason, that *the finder of a chattel, though he does not acquire an absolute property in it, yet has such a property, as will enable him to keep it against all but the rightful owner.* The defense consists, not in showing that the defendants are the rightful owners, or claim under the rightful owner; but that the logs were found by them adrift in Mispillion creek, having been loosened from their fastening either by accident or design, and they insist that their title is as good as that of the plaintiff. But it is a well settled rule of law that the loss of a chattel does not change the right of property; and for the same reason that the original loss of these logs by the rightful owner, did not change his absolute property in them, but he might have maintained trover against the plaintiff upon refusal to deliver them, so the subsequent loss did not divest the special property of the plaintiff. It follows, therefore, that as the plaintiff has shown a special property in these logs, which he never abandoned, and which enabled him to keep them against all the world but the rightful owner, he is entitled to a verdict. Verdict for the plaintiff.

BARKER v. BATES
30 Mass. 255 (Mass. 1832)

SHAW, C.J.

The sole and single question in the present case is, which of these parties has the preferable claim, by mere naked possession, without other title, to a stick of timber, driven ashore under such circumstances as lead to a belief that it was thrown overboard or washed out of some vessel in distress, and never reclaimed by the owner. It does not involve any question of the right of the original owner to regain his property, in the timber, with or without salvage, or the right of the sovereign to claim title to property as wreck, or of the power and jurisdiction of the governments, either of the commonwealth or of the United States, to pass such laws and adopt such regulations on the subject of wreck, as justice and public policy may require. . . . Considering it as . . . established, that the place upon which this timber was thrown up and had lodged, was the soil and freehold of the plaintiff, that the defendants cannot justify their entry, for the purpose of taking away or marking the timber, we are of opinion that such entry was a trespass, and that as between the plaintiff and the defendants, neither of whom had or claimed any title except by mere possession, the plaintiff had, in virtue of his title to the soil, the preferable right of possession, and therefore that the plaintiff has a right to recover the agreed value of the timber, in his claim of damages.

NOTES

1. Three boys — Huey, Louie, and Dewey — are playing near a railroad track. Huey picks up a bag. They all toss it around. As Huey tosses it to Louie, the bag breaks open, but before Louie realizes what's inside it, Dewey catches it and the money falling out of it. Who found the money? See *Keron v. Cashman*, 33 A. 1055 (N.J. Ch. 1896).

2. Did the opinion in *Clark v. Maloney* correctly use the rule of the *Armory* opinion? Does *Armory* dictate the result in *Clark*? Does *Armory* also dictate the result in *Barker*? The plaintiff in *Armory v. Delamirie* sued in trover, but *Armory*'s rule of prior possession is used in real property as well as personal property disputes, where the cause of action is called ejectment. See, e.g., *Tapscott v. Cobbs*, 52 Va. 172 (1854).

3. Paragraph 3 in *Armory* makes the full value of the jewel the basis for the measure of damages given the plaintiff in trover. Is that because the defendant can't produce it for valuation? In a replevin case, when the goods are damaged when returned or the plaintiff also sues for loss of use, what would be the measure of damages? See *Dado v. Jeeninga*, 743 N.E.2d 291 (Ind. Ct. App. 2001) (involving an automobile); *Wallender v. Barnes*, 671 A.2d 962, 971–974 (Md. 1996) (involving an automobile lease). What alternative measures might a court choose? See Alan Brownstein, *What's the Use? A Doctrinal and Policy Critique of the Measurement of Loss of Use Damages*, 37 Rutgers L. Rev. 433, 436 (1985).

4. Suppose that after the goldsmith satisfied the judgment in the case, the true owner of the jewel walks into the goldsmith's shop and demands the return of the jewel, or that the goldsmith give him its value. Is the goldsmith's plea that he paid once a good defense? See *The Winkfield*, [1902] P. 42 (1901), discussed in Comment, *Bailment — The Winkfield Doctrine*, 34 Cornell L. Rev. 615 (1949).

SOUTH STAFFORDSHIRE WATER CO. v. SHARMAN
[1896] 2 Q.B. 44 (1896)

LORD RUSSELL, C.J. . . .

The action was brought in detinue to recover the possession of two gold rings from the defendant. The defendant did not deny that he had possession of the rings, but he denied the plaintiffs' title to recover them from him. Under those circumstances the burden of proof is cast upon the plaintiffs to make out that they have, as against the defendant, the right to the possession of the rings.

Now, the plaintiffs, under a conveyance from the corporation of Lichfield, are the owners in fee simple of some land on which is situate a pool known as the Minster Pool. For purposes of their own the plaintiffs employed the defendant, among others, to clean out that pool. In the course of that operation several articles of interest were found, and amongst others the two gold rings in question were found by the defendant in the mud at the bottom of the pool.

The plaintiffs are the freeholders of the locus in quo, and as such they have the right to forbid anybody coming on their land or in any way interfering with it. They had the right to say that their pool should be cleaned out in any way that they thought fit, and to direct what should be done with anything found in the pool in the course of such cleaning out. It is no doubt right, as the counsel for the defendant contended, to say that the plaintiffs must shew that they had actual control over the locus in quo and the things in it; but under the circumstances, can it be said that the Minster Pool and whatever might be in that pool were not under the control of the plaintiffs? In my opinion, they were. The case is like the case, of which several illustrations were put in the course of the argument, where an article is found on private property, although owners of that property are ignorant that it is there. The principle on which this case must be decided* . . . is to be found in a passage in Pollock and Wright's Essay on Possession in the Common Law, p. 41: "The possession of land carries with it general, by our law, possession of everything which is attached to or under that land, and, in the absence of a better title elsewhere, the right to possess it also. And it makes no difference that the possessor is not aware of the thing's existence. . . . It is free to any one who requires a specific intention as part of a de facto possession to treat this as a positive rule of law. But it seems preferable to say that the legal possession rests on a real de facto possession constituted by the occupier's general power and intent to exclude unauthorized interference."

That is the ground on which I prefer to base my judgment. There is a broad distinction between this case and those cited from Blackstone . . . in which a thing was cast into a public place or into the sea — into a place, in fact, of which it could not be said that any one had a real de facto possession, or a general power and intent to exclude unauthorized interference. . . .

[T]he general principle seems to me to be that where a person has possession of house or land, with a manifest intention to exercise control over it, and the things which may be upon or in it, then, if something is found on that land, whether by an employee of the owner or by a stranger, the presumption is that the possession of that thing is in the owner of the locus in quo. . . . Appeal allowed. Judgment for plaintiff.

---

* Here the words "and the distinction which must be drawn between this case and that of *Bridges v. Hawkesworth*, 21 L.J. Q.B. 75 (1851), . . ." have been deleted. You will find it useful to return to them later, after you read *Hannah v. Peel, infra*, in which *Bridges* is discussed and quoted. — Eds.

Issue: does P have more rights as the finder than D as the property owner?

HANNAH v. PEEL

broach case.

[1945] 1 K.B. 509 (K.B. 1945)

Action tried by BIRKETT, J.

Normally, court would say D has better rights as property owner, but the military circumstance negated that.

On December 13, 1938, the freehold of Gwernhaylod House, Overton-on-Dee, Shropshire, was conveyed to the defendant, Major Hugh Edward Ethelston Peel, who from that time to the end of 1940 never himself occupied the house and it remained unoccupied until October 5, 1939, when it was requisitioned. . . . In August, 1940, the plaintiff, Duncan Hannah, a lance-corporal, serving in a battery of the Royal Artillery, was stationed at the house and on the 21st of that month, when in a bedroom, used as a sick-bay he was adjusting the black-out curtains when his hand touched something at the top of a window frame, loose in a crevice, which he thought was a piece of dirt or plaster. The plaintiff grasped it and dropped it on the outside window ledge. On the following morning he saw that it was a brooch covered with cobwebs and dirt. Later, he took it with him when he went home on leave and his wife having told him it might be of value, at the end of October, 1940, he informed his commanding officer of his find and, on his advice, handed it over to the police, receiving a receipt for it. In August 1942, the owner not having been found the police handed the brooch to the defendant, who sold it in October, 1942, for £66, to Messrs. Spink & Son, Ltd., of London, who resold it the following month for £88. There was no evidence that the defendant had any knowledge of the existence of the brooch before it was found by the plaintiff. The defendant had offered the plaintiff a reward for the brooch, but the plaintiff refused to accept this and maintained throughout his right to the possession of the brooch as against all persons other than the owner, who was unknown. By a letter, dated October 5, 1942, the plaintiff's solicitors demanded the return of the brooch from the defendant, but it was not returned and on October 21, 1943, the plaintiff issued his writ claiming the return of the brooch, or its value, and damages for its detention. By his defense, the defendant claimed the brooch on the ground that he was the owner of Gwernhaylod House and in possession thereof.

BIRKETT, J. There is no issue of fact in this case between the parties. As to the issue in law, the rival claims of the parties can be stated in this way: The plaintiff says: "I claim the brooch as its finder and I have a good title against all the world, save only the true owner." The defendant says: "My claim is superior to yours inasmuch as I am the freeholder. The brooch was found on my property, although I was never in occupation, and my title, therefore, ousts yours and in the absence of the true owner I am entitled to the brooch or its value." . . .

Bridges v. Hawkesworth, 21 L.J. Q.B. 75, was an appeal against a decision of the county court judge at Westminster. The facts appear to have been that in the year 1847 the plaintiff, who was a commercial traveler, called on a firm named Byfield & Hawkesworth on business, as he was in the habit of doing, and as he was leaving the shop he picked up a small parcel which was lying on the floor. He immediately showed it to the shopman, and opened it in his presence, when it was found to consist of a quantity of Bank of England notes, to the amount of £65. The defendant, who was a partner in the firm of Byfield & Hawkesworth, was then called, and the plaintiff told him he had found the notes, and asked the defendant to keep them until the owner appeared to claim them. Then various advertisements were put in the papers asking for the owner, but the true owner was never found. No person having appeared to claim them, and three years have elapsed since they were found, the plaintiff applied to the defendant to have the notes returned to him, and offered to pay the expenses of the advertisements, and to give an indemnity. The defendant refused to deliver them up to the plaintiff, and an action was brought in the county court of Westminster in consequence of that refusal. The county court judge decided that the defendant, the shopkeeper, was entitled to custody of the notes as against the plaintiff, and gave judgment for the defendant. Thereupon the appeal was brought which came before the court composed of Patteson, J. and Wightman, J. Patteson, J., said: "The notes which are the subject of this action were incidentally dropped, by mere accident, in the shop of the defendant, by the owner of them. The facts do not warrant the supposition that they had been deposited there intentionally, nor has the case been put at all upon that ground. The general right of the finder to any article which has been lost, as against all the world, except the true owner, was established in the case of *Armory v. Delamirie*, 1 Str. 505, which has never been disputed. This right would clearly have accrued to the plaintiff had the notes been picked up by him outside the shop of the defendant and if he once had the right, the case finds that he did not intend, by delivering the notes to the defendant, waive the title (if any) which he had to them, but they were handed to the defendant merely for the purpose of delivering them to the owner should he appear." Then a little later: "The case, therefore, resolves itself into the single point on which it appears that the learned judge decided it, namely, whether the circumstance of the notes being found inside the defendant's shop gives him, the defendant, the right to have them as against the plaintiff, who found them. . . . If the discovery had never been communicated to the defendant, could the real owner have had any cause of action against him because they were found in his house? Certainly not. The notes never were in the custody of the defendant, nor within the protection of his house, before they were found, as they would have been had they been intentionally deposited there; and the defendant has come under no responsibility, except the communication made to him by the plaintiff, the finder, and the steps taken by way of advertisement. . . . We find, therefore, no circumstances in this case to take it out of the general rule of law, that the finder of a lost article is entitled to it as against all persons except the real owner, and we think that rule must prevail, and that the learned judge was mistaken in holding that the place in which they were found makes any legal difference. Our judgment, therefore, is that the plaintiff is entitled to these notes as against the defendant." . . .

With regard to *South Staffordshire Water Co. v. Sharman*, [1896] 2 Q.B. 44, the first two lines of the head note are: "The possessor is generally entitled, as against the finder, to chattels found on the land." I am not sure that this is accurate. The facts were that the defendant Sharman, while cleaning out, under the orders of the plaintiffs, the South Staffordshire Water Company, a pool of water on their land, found two rings embedded in the mud at the bottom of the pool. He declined to deliver them to the plaintiffs, but failed to discover the real owner. In an action brought by the company against Sharman in detinue it was held that the company were entitled to the rings. Lord Russell of Killowen, C.J., said [1896] 2 Q.B. 46: "[Quoting the opinion *supra* and the excerpt from Pollock and Wright's Essay, and then . . .] . . . It has been said that it [*South Staffordshire Water Co. v. Sharman*] establishes that if a man finds a thing as the servant or agent of another, he finds it not for himself, but for that other, and indeed that seems to afford a sufficient explanation of the case. The rings found at the bottom of the pool were not in the possession of the company, but it seems that though Sharman was the first to obtain possession of them, he obtained them for his employers and could claim no title for himself.

The only other case to which I need refer is *Elwes v. Brigg Gas Co.*, 33 Ch. D. 562, in which land had been demised to a gas company for ninety-nine years with a reservation to the lessor of all mines and minerals. A prehistoric boat embedded in the soil was discovered by the lessees when they were digging to make a gasholder. It was held that the boat, whether regarded as a mineral or as part of the soil in it which it was embedded when discovered, or as a chattel, did not pass to the lessees by the demise, but was the property of the lessor though he was ignorant of its existence at the time of granting the lease. Chitty, J., said (33 Ch. D. 568) "The first question in this case is whether the boat belonged to the plaintiff at the time of granting of the lease. I hold that it did, whether it ought to be regarded as a mineral, or as part of the soil, or as chattel. If it was a mineral or part of the soil, then it clearly belonged to the owners of the inheritance as part of the inheritance itself. But if it ought to be regarded as a chattel, I hold the property in the chattel was vested in the plaintiff. Obviously the right of the original owner could not be established. . . . The plaintiff, then, had a lawful possession, good against all the world, and therefore the property in the boat. In my opinion it makes no difference, in these circumstances, that the plaintiff was not aware of the existence of the boat."

A review of these judgments show that the authorities are in an unsatisfactory state. . . . It is fairly clear from the authorities that a man possesses everything which is attached to or under his land. Secondly, it would appear to be the law from the authorities I have cited, and particularly from *Bridges v. Hawkesworth*, that a man does not necessarily possess a thing which is lying unattached on the surface of his land even though the thing is not possessed by someone else. . . . [T]he rule which governs things an occupier possesses as against those which he does not, has never been clearly formulated. . . .

There is no doubt that in this case the brooch was lost in the ordinary meaning of that term, and I should imagine it had been lost for a very considerable time. But the moment the plaintiff discovered that the brooch might be of some value, he took the advice of his commanding officer and handed it to the police. His conduct was commendable and meritorious. The defendant was never physically in possession of these premises at any time. It is clear that the brooch was never his, in the ordinary acceptation of the term, in that he had the prior possession. He had no knowledge of it, until it was brought to his notice by the finder. A discussion of the merits does not seem to help, but it is clear on the facts that the brooch was "lost" in the ordinary meaning of that word; that it was "found" by the plaintiff in the ordinary meaning of that word, that its true owner has never been found, that the defendant was the owner of the premises and had his notice drawn to this matter by the plaintiff, who found the brooch. In those circumstances I propose to give judgment in this case for the plaintiff for £66.

NOTES

1. A customer in a barbershop found a pocketbook with money in it on a table and said "See what I found" to the barber, who asked where the customer found it, to which the customer replied, "I found it right there," showing the place on the table. The defendant barber took the pocketbook and counted the money. The customer told him to keep the pocketbook, give it to its owner if he or she showed up, and otherwise to advertise the find. The defendant promised to do this. Afterwards "the customer made three demands to have the money and the defendant [the barber] never claimed to hold the money till the last demand." The customer sued the barber in tort to recover the sum of money. The parties stipulated that the pocketbook was placed on the table and accidentally left there by another transient customer, that it was first seen and taken up by the plaintiff, and that its owner had not been found. At trial, the judge ruled that the plaintiff could not maintain his action and so a verdict was returned for the defendant. The plaintiff appealed. In *McAvoy v. Medina*, 93 Mass. 548 (1866), the court said:

> It seems to be the settled law that the finder of lost property has a valid claim to the same against all the world except the true owner, and generally that the place in which it is found creates no exception to this rule. *Bridges v. Hawkesworth*, 7 Eng. L. & Eq. R. 424.

> But this property is not, under the circumstances, to be treated as lost property in that sense in which a finder has a valid claim to hold the same until called for by the true owner. This property was voluntarily placed upon a table in the defendant's shop by a customer of his who accidentally left the same there and has never called for it. The plaintiff also came there as a customer, and first saw the same and took it up from the table. The plaintiff did not by this acquire the right to take the property from the shop, but it was rather the duty of the defendant, when the fact became thus known to him, to use reasonable care for the safekeeping of the same until the owner should call for it. In the case of *Bridges v. Hawkesworth* the property, although found in a shop, was found on the floor of the same, and had not been placed there voluntarily by the owner, and the court held that the finder was entitled to the possession of the same, except as to the owner. But the present case more resembles that of *Lawrence v. The State*, 1 Humph. (Tenn.) 228, and is indeed very similar in its facts. The court there distinguished between the case of property thus placed by the owner and neglected to be removed, and property lost. It was there held that "to place a pocket-book upon a table and to forget to take it away is not to lose it, in the sense in which the authorities referred to speak of lost property." We accept this as the better rule, and especially as one better adapted to secure the rights of the true owner.

> In view of the facts of this case, the plaintiff acquired no original right to the property, and the defendant's subsequent acts in receiving and holding the property in the manner he did does not create any. Exceptions overruled.

What if the true owner shows up and is told by other customers that the plaintiff had offered to deposit the pocketbook with the barber, but the latter refused to accept it and the plaintiff has disappeared? Would you advise the owner to sue the barber? Why didn't the opinion in *Hannah v. Peel* cite *McAvoy*? See *Terry v. Lock*, 37 S.W.3d 202 (Ark. 2001); *Franks v. Pritchett*, 197 S.W.3d 5 (Ark. Ct. App. 2004) (both mislaid property cases). Would you be in favor of a statute providing that property classified as mislaid by the courts be, after the effective date of the statute, treated as lost? See, e.g., N.Y. Pers. Prop. Law 251(3) (2009) (defining lost to include mislaid property and abolishing the distinction). What policy justifies such a statute?

2. *Sharman* has not been followed much in the United States, where employees finding things at their place of employment have prevailed over the owner of the locus in quo. See, e.g., *Erickson v. Sinykin*, 26 N.W.2d 172 (Minn. 1947); *Toledo Tr. Co. v. Simmons*, 3 N.E.2d 661 (Ohio Ct. App. 1935) (attendant in safe deposit company); *Hamaker v. Blanchard*, 90 Pa. 377 (Pa. 1879) (chambermaid in hotel).

3. Iowa Code § 556F.6–556F.12 (2014):

§ 556F.6. If any person shall find any lost goods, money, bank notes, or other things of any description whatever, of the value of five dollars and over, such person shall inform the owner thereof, if known, and make restitution thereof.

§ 556F.7. If the owner is unknown, the finder shall, within five days after finding the property, take the money, bank notes, and a description of any other property to the county sheriff of the county or the chief of police of the city in which the property was found, and provide an affidavit describing the property, the time when and place where the property was found, and attesting that no alteration has been made in the appearance of the property since the finding. The sheriff or chief of police shall send a copy of the affidavit to the county auditor who shall enter a description of the property and the value of the property, as nearly as the auditor can determine it, in the auditor's lost property book, together with the copy of the affidavit of the finder.

§ 556F.8–.10. [These sections impose requirements for advertisements by the finder of a description of the find, as well as proof of their publication.]

§ 556F.11. If no person appears to claim and prove ownership to said goods, money, bank notes, or other things within twelve months of the date when proof of said publication and posting is filed in the office of the county auditor, the right to such property shall irrevocably vest in said finder.

§ 556F.12. In any case where a claim is made to property found . . . , and the ownership of the property cannot be agreed upon by the finder and claimant, they may make a case before any district judge . . . in the county, who may hear and adjudicate it, and if either of them refuses to make such case the other may make an affidavit of the facts which have previously occurred, and the claimant shall also verify the claim by the claimant's affidavit, and the district judge . . . may take cognizance of and try the matter on the other party having one day's notice, but there shall be no appeal from the decision. This section does not bar any other remedy given by law.

How would this statute change the result in *Hannah v. Peel*?

4.   If you think that the true owner seldom turns up to claim lost property, read the opinion in *Ganter v. Kapiloff*, 516 A.2d 611 (Md. Ct. Spec. App. 1986).

FAVORITE v. MILLER
407 A.2d 974 (Conn. 1978)

BOGDANSKI, J.

On July 9, 1776, a band of patriots, hearing news of the Declaration of Independence, toppled the equestrian statue of King George III, which was located in Bowling Green Park in lower Manhattan, New York. The statue, of gilded lead, was then hacked apart and the pieces ferried over Long Island Sound and loaded onto wagons at Norwalk, Connecticut, to be hauled some fifty miles northward to Oliver Wolcott's bullet-molding foundry in Litchfield, there to be cast into bullets. On the journey to Litchfield, the wagoners halted at Wilton, Connecticut, and while the patriots were imbibing, the loyalists managed to steal back pieces of the statue. The wagonload of the pieces lifted by the Tories was scattered about in the area of the Davis swamp in Wilton and fragments of the statue have continued to turn up in that area since that time.

Although the above events have been dramatized in the intervening years, the unquestioned historical facts are: (1) the destruction of the statue; (2) cartage of the pieces to the Wolcott foundry; (3) the pause at Wilton where part of the load was scattered over the Wilton area by loyalists; and (4) repeated discoveries of fragments over the last century.

In 1972, the defendant, Louis Miller, determined that a part of the statue might be located within property owned by the plaintiffs. On October 16 he entered the area of the Davis Swamp owned by the plaintiffs although he knew it to be private property. With the aid of a metal detector, he discovered a statuary fragment fifteen inches square and weighing twenty pounds which was embedded ten inches below the soil. He dug up this fragment and removed it from the plaintiffs' property. The plaintiffs did not learn that a piece of the statue of King George III had been found on their property until they read about it in the newspaper, long after it had been removed. In due course, the piece of the statue made its way back to New York City, where the defendant agreed to sell it to the Museum of the City of New York for $5500. The museum continues to hold it pending resolution of this controversy.

In March of 1973, the plaintiffs instituted this action to have the fragment returned to them and the case was submitted to the court on a stipulation of facts. The trial court found the issues for the plaintiffs, from which judgment the defendant appealed to this court. The sole issue presented on appeal is whether the claim of the defendant, as finder, is superior to that of the plaintiffs, as owners of the land upon which the historic fragment was discovered.

Traditionally, when questions have arisen concerning the rights of the finder as against the person upon whose land the property was found, the resolution has turned upon the characterization given the property. Typically, if the property was found to be "lost" or "abandoned," the finder would prevail, whereas if the property was characterized as "mislaid," the owner or occupier of the land would prevail.

Lost property has traditionally been defined as involving an involuntary parting, i.e., where there is no intent on the part of the loser to part with the ownership of the property. Abandonment, in turn, has been defined as the voluntary relinquishment of ownership of property without reference to any particular person or purpose; i.e., a "throwing away" of the property concerned; while mislaid property is defined as that which is intentionally placed by the owner where he can obtain custody of it, but afterwards forgotten.

It should be noted that the classification of property as "lost," "abandoned," or "mislaid" requires that a court determine the intent or mental state of the unknown party who at some time in the past parted with the ownership or control of the property.

The trial court in this case applied the traditional approach and ruled in favor of the landowners on the ground that the piece of the statue found by Miller was "mislaid." The factual basis for that conclusion is set out in the finding, where the court found that "the loyalists did not wish to have the pieces [in their possession] during the turmoil surrounding the Revolutionary War and hid them in a place where they could resort to them [after the war], but forgot where they put them."

The defendant contends that the finding was made without evidence and that the court's conclusion "is legally impossible now after 200 years with no living claimants to the fragment and the secret of its burial having died with them." While we cannot agree that the court's conclusion was legally impossible, we do agree that any conclusion as to the mental state of persons engaged in events which occurred over two hundred years ago would be of a conjectural nature and as such does not furnish an adequate basis for determining rights of twentieth century claimants.

The defendant argues further that his rights in the statue are superior to those of anyone except the true owner (i.e., the British government). He presses this claim on the ground that the law has traditionally favored the finder as against all but the true owner, and that because his efforts brought the statue to light, he should be allowed to reap the benefits of his discovery. In his brief, he asserts: "As with archeologists forever probing and unearthing the past, to guide man for the betterment of those to follow, explorers like Miller deserve encouragement, and reward, in their selfless pursuit of the hidden, the unknown."

There are, however, some difficulties with the defendant's position. The first concerns the defendant's characterization of himself as a selfless seeker after knowledge. The facts in the record do not support such a conclusion. The defendant admitted that he was in the business of selling metal detectors and that he has used his success in finding the statue as advertising to boost his sales of such metal detectors, and that the advertising has been financially rewarding. Further, there is the fact that he signed a contract with the City Museum of New York for the sale of the statuary piece and that he stands to profit thereby.

Moreover, even if we assume his motive to be that of historical research alone, that fact will not justify his entering upon the property of another without permission. It is unquestioned that in today's world even archeologists must obtain permission from owners of property and the government of the country involved before they can conduct their explorations. Similarly, mountaineers must apply for permits, sometimes years in advance of their proposed expeditions. On a more familiar level, backpackers and hikers must often obtain permits before being allowed access to certain of our national parks and forests, even though that land is public and not private. Similarly, hunters and fishermen wishing to enter upon private property must first obtain the permission of the owner before they embark upon their respective pursuits.

Although few cases are to be found in this area of the law, one line of cases which have dealt with this issue has held that except where the trespass is trivial or merely technical, the fact that the finder is trespassing is sufficient to deprive him of his normal preference over the owner of the place where the property was found. *Barker v. Bates*, 30 Mass. 255 (1832). The basis for the rule is that a wrongdoer should not be allowed to profit by his wrongdoing. Another line of cases holds that property, other than treasure trove, which is found embedded in the earth is the property of the owner of the locus in quo. *Schley v. Couch*, 284 S.W.2d 333 (Tex. 1955); *South Staffordshire Water Co. v. Sharman*, 2 Q.B. 44 (1896); *Elwes v. Brigg Gas Co.*, 33 Ch. 562 (1886) (prehistoric boat). The presumption in such cases is that possession of the article found is in the owner of the land and that the finder acquires no rights to the article found.

The defendant, by his own admission, knew that he was trespassing when he entered upon the property of the plaintiffs. He admitted that he was told by Gertrude Merwyn, the librarian of the Wilton Historical Society, before he went into the Davis Swamp area, that the land was privately owned and that Mrs. Merwyn recommended that he call the owners, whom she named, and obtain permission before he began his explorations. He also admitted that when he later told Mrs. Merwyn about his discovery, she again suggested that he contact the owners of the property, but that he failed to do so.

In the stipulation of facts submitted to the court, the defendant admitted entering the Davis Swamp property "with the belief that part of the 'King George Statue' . . . might be located within said property and with the intention of removing [the] same if located." The defendant has also admitted that the piece of the statue which he found was embedded in the ground ten inches below the surface and that it was necessary for him to excavate in order to take possession of his find.

In light of those undisputed facts the defendant's trespass was neither technical nor trivial. We conclude that the fact that the property found was embedded in the earth and the fact that the defendant was a trespasser are sufficient to defeat any claim to the property which the defendant might otherwise have had as a finder. . . . There is no error.

NOTES

1.   Embedded property is property (1) other than gold or silver that is (2) buried in the ground under circumstances indicating that the owner will not return. The court "concludes" that the statuary fragment was embedded property and not treasure trove. Is this dicta? If the property was lying on the surface, and the

defendant trespassed to retrieve it, would the result be the same? Further, as to government lands or seabed, can one even "find" embedded goods?

2.   Many courts hold that the passage of time, standing alone, does not work an abandonment. Does the court mean to say that here it does? Who has the burden of proving an abandonment? Does the trespasser have the burden here?

3.   Treasure trove is personal property that is (1) not lost or mislaid, because the owner meant to put it where it is found for safekeeping, (2) money or coin, gold or silver, plate or bullion, and (3) an antiquity, having been hidden long enough ago to indicate that the owner is dead, or was prevented from reclaiming it (as when the Romans were driven out of Britain). Why was the statue's head in *Favorite* not treasure trove? A majority of cases give treasure trove to the finder in this country. In Great Britain, however, treasure trove belongs to the Crown. Who inherited the power of the Crown in this country — "WE the people"? Or maybe a state government? What is the rationale for continuing to recognize treasure trove today? The *Schley* case, cited in the opinion, rejects the rules pertaining to treasure trove for Texas.

4.   The law of salvage for shipwrecks is similar to the law of finders, but, unlike finders, salvors have a right to compensation for recovering sunken cargos. How should such an award be computed? Should this feature be added to the law of finders? Many states have codified the law of finders and many of those authorize an award to the finder. See, e.g., Iowa Code § 556F.13 (2008) (awarding a 10% fee, plus the finder's costs). For a comparison of the law of finds and the law of salvage, both of which may be applied to shipwrecks, see *Bemis v. The RMS Lusitania*, 884 F. Supp. 1042, 1049–1051 (E.D. Va. 1995) (citations omitted):

> LAW OF FINDS. The common law of finds, expresses "the ancient and honorable principle of 'finders, keepers.'" *Martha's Vineyard Scuba HQ v. Unidentified Vessel*, 833 F.2d 1059, 1065 (1st Cir. 1987). Traditionally, the law of finds was applied only to maritime property which had never been owned by anybody. Yet recent trends suggest applying the law of finds when there has been a finding that the sunken property has been abandoned by its previous owners. E.g., *Columbus-America Discovery Group v. Atlantic Mut. Ins. Co.*, 974 F.2d 450, 464 (4th Cir. 1992), *cert. denied*, 113 S. Ct. 1625 (1993); *Moyer v. Wrecked and Abandoned Vessel known as the Andrea Doria*, 836 F. Supp. 1099, 1104–05 (D.N.J. 1993) [hereinafter *Andrea Doria*]. The key to ownership is whether the owner has abandoned the property. Abandonment by the owner can be express or implied. Lapse of time and non-use by the owner may give rise to an inference of an intent to abandon. *Andrea Doria*, 836 F. Supp. at 1105. Additionally, the Fourth Circuit has stated that abandonment can be inferred in the case of a historic shipwreck when no owners come forward during the action to claim ownership rights. . . . Pursuant to the common law of finds, the ownership of abandoned property depends on the finder taking possession. "Title to abandoned property is acquired by the finder who demonstrates 'occupancy', which is defined as 'taking possession of the property and exercising dominion or control over it.'" *Andrea Doria*, 836 F. Supp. at 1106. . . . Once the finder establishes possession, he holds title to

the property which is good against all, including the original owner since abandonment forfeits all the owner's rights. . . . The early American case of *Eads v. Brazelton* suggests that if a salvor keeps a ship over the wreck and carries on a continual salvage operation, the salvor establishes possession of all the contents. *Eads v. Brazelton*, 22 Ark. 499, 511 (1861). * * *

LAW OF SALVAGE. Three elements must be established in order to assert a salvage claim. First, the property rescued must be in marine peril. Courts will usually find that underwater shipwrecks are in marine peril, because sunken vessels and their cargoes are in danger of being lost forever. See, e.g., *Treasure Salvors, Inc. v. Unidentified Wrecked and Abandoned Sailing Vessel*, 569 F.2d 330, 336–37 . . . (5th Cir. 1978). Next, the salvage service must be voluntary. Finally, the salvage must be successful, in whole or in part. The salvor can receive a salvage award only through actual recovery of the property. Although the law of salvage, like the law of finds, requires a salvor to establish possession over property before obtaining the right to exclude others, "possession" means something less in salvage law than in finds law. In the salvage context, only the right to compensation for service, not the right to title, usually results; "possession" is therefore more readily found than under the law of finds. [Hener v. United States, 525 F. Supp. 350,] . . . 357 [(S. D. N.Y. 1981).] Furthermore, the possession need not be continuous, but only as such the "nature and situation" of the salvage operations permit. *Id.* at 354 (quoting *Eads v. Brazelton*, 22 Ark. at 511). Generally, the Court will grant an exclusive right to salvage if the salvor's effort is ongoing and there is likelihood of success.

A finder cannot exclude others from their attempts to obtain first possession. See *Sea Hunters, LP v. The Unidentified, Wrecked & Abandoned Vessel*, 599 F. Supp. 2d 57 (D. Me. 2009). This leads some courts to apply the law of salvage as a general rule, reserving the law of finds for later use and deferring questions of title. Thus a salvor might in turn gain a maritime lien over goods actually salvaged and then an exclusive right to salvage once in actual or constructive possession of the wreck, but subject to a presumption that title remains with the true owner of the wreck, regardless of the passage of time. Once the true owner abandons goods in a sunken wreck, should courts apply the law of salvage? After all, the object of salvage is to return the goods to the true owner, and if he has abandoned, there is no one to whom the salvor can return the goods. See *Zych v. Unidentified, Wrecked, and Abandoned Vessel, Believed to be the SB "Seabird,"* 811 F. Supp. 1300, 1310 (N.D. Ill. 1992), *aff'd*, 19 F.3d 1136 (7th Cir. 1994). And what about the rights of the cargo's insurance underwriters? Moreover, once the salvor has possession of and a maritime lien on the goods, the title to them might not be worth much: when the salvage is expensive, that lien may be worth more than the title. See *Columbus-America Discovery Group, Inc. v. Unidentified, Wrecked and Abandoned Sailing Vessel*, 2014 U.S. Dist. LEXIS 97996 (E.D. Va. 2014) (reporting a salvor's lien of 90% of value). Finally, as to the law of finds, taking possession of a wreck strewn over a swath of seabed presents questions of facts (involving control) and law (involving constructive possession). All this means that the law of finds is "incorporated into admiralty law but only rarely applied." See *RMS Titanic, Inc. v. The Wrecked and*

Abandoned Vessel, 435 F.3d 521, 532 (4th Cir. 2006).

5.　See generally John Orth, *What's Wrong with the Law of Finders & How to Fix It*, 4 Green Bag 391 (2001); Patty Gerstenblith, *Identity and Cultural Property: The Protection of Cultural Property in the United States*, 75 B.U. L. Rev. 559, 587–95 (1995); Edward Cohen, *The Finders Cases Revisited*, 48 Tex. L. Rev. 1001 (1970); David Riesman, *Possession and the Law of Finders*, 52 Harv. L. Rev. 1105 (1939).

IV.　WRONGFUL TAKING OF POSSESSION

ANDERSON v. GOULDBERG
53 N.W. 636 (Minn. 1892)

Appeal by defendants, Hans J. Gouldberg and D.O. Anderson, from an order of the District Court of Isanti County, . . . refusing a new trial. This action was brought by the plaintiff, Sigfrid Anderson, against the defendants, partners as Gouldberg & Anderson, to recover the possession of ninety-three pine logs, marked L S X, or for the value thereof. Plaintiff claimed to have cut the logs on section 22, township 27, range 15, Isanti County, in the winter of 1889–1890, and to have hauled them to a mill on section 6, from which place defendants took them. The title to section 22 was in strangers, and plaintiff showed no authority from the owners to cut logs thereon. Defendants claimed that the logs were cut on section 26, in the adjoining township, on land belonging to the Ann River Logging Company, and that they took the logs by direction of the Logging Company, who were the owners. The court charged that even if plaintiff got possession of the logs as a trespasser, his title would be good as against any one except the real owner or some one who had authority from the owner to take them, and left the case to the jury on the question as to whether the logs were cut on the land of the Logging Company, and taken by defendants under its authority. The jury found a verdict for the plaintiff and assessed his damages at $153.45. From an order denying their motion for a new trial, defendants appeal. . . .

MITCHELL, J. It is settled by the verdict of the jury that the logs in controversy were not cut upon the land of the defendants, and consequently that they were entire strangers to the property.

For the purposes of this appeal, we must also assume the fact to be (as there was evidence from which the jury might have so found) that the plaintiffs obtained possession of the logs in the first instance by trespassing upon the land of some third party. Therefore the only question is whether bare possession of property, though wrongfully obtained, is sufficient title to enable the party enjoying it to maintain replevin against a mere stranger, who takes it from him. We had supposed that this was settled in the affirmative as long ago, at least, as the early case of *Armory v. Delamirie*, 1 Strange 505, so often cited on that point.

When it is said that to maintain replevin the plaintiff's possession must have been lawful, it means merely that it must have been lawful as against the person who deprived him of it; and possession is good title against all the world except those having a better title.

Counsel says that possession only raises a presumption of title, which, however, may be rebutted. Rightly understood, this is correct; but counsel misapplies it. One who takes property from the possession of another can only rebut this presumption by showing a superior title in himself, or in some way connecting himself with one who has. One who has acquired the possession of property, whether by finding, bailment, or by mere tort, has a right to retain that possession as against a mere wrongdoer who is a stranger to the property. Any other rule would lead to an endless series of unlawful seizures and reprisals in every case where property had once passed out of the possession of the rightful owner. Order affirmed.

NOTES

1. The same principle applies to real property. Those in possession of realty can sue trespassers who cannot show that their entry is privileged, even if the trespasser shows that the plaintiff is liable to be ousted by a third party unconnected to the defendant. See *Hall v. Schoenwetter*, 686 A.2d 980 (Conn. 1996). A trespasser may not rely on the rule of *jus tertii*. The leading English case on the *jus tertii* defense is *Jefferies v. The Great Western Railway*, 119 Eng. Rep. 680 (Q.B. 1856):

> Trover for trucks. On the trial before Pollock, C.B., . . . the plaintiff proved that he had possession of the trucks in question, which he claimed as his own property under an assignment from one Owen, and that the defendants had seized them, also claiming them as their own property under an assignment from Owen, executed after the assignment to the plaintiff, but before the plaintiff took possession, and whilst Owen was apparent owner of the goods. The defendants' counsel, in opening their case, stated that he should contend . . . that, before the plaintiff took possession of the trucks, Owen had become a bankrupt . . . and that the Court of Bankruptcy had made an order that they should be sold for the benefit of the creditors under the bankruptcy; so that, at the time of the conversion, the goods were not the plaintiff's. . . . The learned Chief Baron then stated that . . . the defendants, if wrongdoers, could not set up the *jus tertii* as a defense. The defendants' counsel, after arguing against this ruling, in submission to it abstained from tendering any evidence to that effect. . . .

> CAMPBELL, C.J. I am of opinion that the Chief Baron did right in refusing to admit evidence to impeach the title of the plaintiff. The defendants were strangers to the title which they proposed to set up; and the plaintiff had been for some time in possession, when the defendants seized the goods, claiming them as their own, but having, as we must now take it, no right to the goods; and I think that, under such circumstances, the *jus tertii* could not be set up, by the defendants averring that they themselves were mere wrongdoers at the time of the conversion, but that there were strangers who then had a right to take the goods. I am of opinion that the law is that a person possessed of goods as his property has a good title as against every stranger, and that one who takes them from him, having no title in himself, is a wrongdoer, and cannot defend himself by showing that there

was title in some third person; for against a wrongdoer possession is a title. The law is . . . essential for the interests of society, that peaceable possession should not be disturbed by wrongdoers. And I do not find that this doctrine has been impeached by any of the cases cited. It is not disputed that the *jus tertii* cannot be set up as a defense to an action of trespass for disturbing the possession. In this respect I see no difference between trespass and trover; for in truth the presumption of law is that the person who has possession has the property. Can that presumption be rebutted by evidence that the property was in a third person, when offered as a defense by one who admits that he himself had no title and was a wrongdoer when he converted the goods? I am of opinion that this cannot be done, and consequently that the Chief Baron's ruling was right. . . .

WIGHTMAN, J. Here the plaintiff was in possession of the trucks on the railway as his own. The defendants took them out of his possession and converted them; and they seek to defeat an action for that conversion by showing title, not in themselves, or in any one under whom they acted, but title in a stranger against whom they would be wrongdoers; and they ask, by doing this, to defeat the prima facie right arising from possession. . . . I find no case where the person in actual possession has been defeated in an action of trover because the defendant was permitted to set up the *jus tertii*. . . . Therefore I think that the Chief Baron was right.

2. "No court has allowed an admitted, or even a clearly proved, thief without claim of right to recover, and it seems improbable that one ever will." Dan Dobbs, et al., Torts 103 (5th ed. 1984) (also describing *Anderson* as a case in which the rule of *Armory* and *Clark* "has even been applied to permit recovery by one whose possession is wrongful, and in defiance of the owner, although in all such cases the plaintiff has been in possession under some colorable claim of right"). See generally R.H. Helmholz, *Wrongful Possession of Chattels: Hornbook Law and Case Law*, 80 Nw. U. L. Rev. 1221, 1242–44 (1986).

RUSSELL v. HILL
34 S.E. 640 (N.C. 1899)

MONTGOMERY, J.

This case was heard upon an agreed state of facts, the material parts of which are as follows: In 1887, after entry and survey, F.H. Busbee, trustee, received a grant from the state for a tract of land in Swain county. Iowa McCoy made a subsequent entry and survey, and received a grant from the state for a part of the land embraced in the grant to Busbee, trustee. Busbee, trustee, was the owner of the land by virtue of his grant, which was properly registered, and registered before the entry, survey, and grant of Mrs. McCoy. Mrs. McCoy had no knowledge of Busbee's grant, except the notice which the law implies from the fact of registration. Mrs. McCoy sold to the plaintiff certain timber standing on the land embraced in her grant, and the plaintiff cut the timber, and carried the same, in the shape of logs, to the bank of Nantahalla river, a floatable stream, for the purpose of floating them to the Asheville Furniture Company. While the logs were lying on the river bank, the defendants, without any claim of right or title to them from Busbee, trustee, or from any one else, so far as the record shows, took possession of the logs without the consent of the plaintiff, and sold and delivered them to the Asheville Lumber Company for $686.84. The lumber company is insolvent. The court, upon the facts agreed, adjudged that the plaintiff could not recover, and rendered judgment accordingly.

We are of the opinion that there was no error in the ruling and judgment of the court. Busbee, trustee, was the legal owner of the land. Mrs. McCoy was not in possession. If she had been in adverse possession, the title to the logs would have passed to the plaintiff, and he could have maintained this action; and Busbee would have been compelled to proceed against Mrs. McCoy for damages to the freehold. The present action is in the nature of the old action of trover, and, before the plaintiff could recover in an action of that nature, he had to show both title and possession, or the right of possession.

The cases in our Reports seem to be all one way on that point. In *Laspeyre v. McFarland*, 4 N.C. 620, . . . this court, in sustaining the judgment below, said: "It is one of the characteristic distinctions between this action [trover] and trespass that the latter may be maintained on possession; the former, only on property and the right of possession. Trover is to personalty what ejectment is to realty. In both, title is indispensable. It is true that, as possession is the strongest evidence of the ownership, property may be presumed from possession. And therefore the plaintiff may not in all cases be bound to show a good title by conveyances against all the world, but may recover in trover upon such presumption against the wrongdoer. Yet it is but a presumption, and cannot stand when the contrary is shown. Here it is completely rebutted by the deed, which shows the title to be in another, and not in the plaintiff."

So, in the case before us, the title to the land from which the timber was cut is shown by the agreed state of facts to have been in Busbee, trustee, and not in the plaintiff or Mrs. McCoy. The same point arose in *Barwick v. Barwick*, 33 N.C. 80. . . . The court said: "But if it appears on the trial that the plaintiff, although in possession, is not in fact the owner, the presumption of title inferred from the possession is rebutted, and it would be manifestly wrong to allow the plaintiff to recover the value of the property; for the real owner may forthwith bring trover against the defendant, and force him to pay the value a second time, and the fact that he paid it in a former suit would be no defense. . . . Consequently trover can never be maintained unless a satisfaction of the judgment will have the effect of vesting a good title in the defendant, except where the property is restored, and the conversion was temporary. Accordingly, it is well settled as the law of this state that, to maintain trover, the plaintiff must show title and the possession, or a present right of possession." In the last-mentioned case the court went on to say, in substance, that in some of the English books, and in some of the Reports of our sister states, cases might be found to the contrary, but that those cases were all founded upon a misapprehension of the principle laid down in the case of *Armory v. Delamirie*, 1 Strange, 505. There a chimney sweep found a lost jewel. He took it into his possession, as he had a right to do, and was the owner, because of having it in possession, unless the true owner should become known. That owner was not known, and it was properly decided that trover would lie in favor of the finder against the defendant, to whom he had handed it for inspection, and who refused to restore it. But the court said the case would have been very different if the owner had been known. . . . Affirmed.

NOTE

Does *Anderson* or *Russell* have the better argument? A discussion of both *Anderson* and *Russell* is found in John Orth, *Russell v. Hill (N.C. 1899): Misunderstood Lessons*, 73 N.C. L. Rev. 2031 (1995).

A NOTE ON THE SCOPE OF CONVERSION

In a common law system, judges constantly consider whether to extend causes of action into new fields and facts. For example, John Moore, a leukemia patient, consented to the surgical removal of his spleen that was then used for cultivating, over the next three years, a patented cell line from his blood cells. Moore was informed by his surgeon that his blood and bodily substances has no commercial value, when in fact the patented cell line was commercially developed by a drug company. Do these events constitute a conversion of Moore's cells? In *Moore v. The Regents of the University of California*, 793 P.2d 479 (Cal. 1990), the Supreme Court of California decided that no cause of action for conversion lay, although Moore did state a contract claim for breach of the surgeon's fiduciary duty to disclose research interests in potential conflict with Moore's medical needs (a conflict that arose at the time of the pre-operative instructions to hospital staff). Why was there no cause of action for conversion? First, because no precedent supported it. (But then, neither did precedent preclude it either.) Second, there was no warrant for it under existing laws relating to (1) specialized statutes dealing with limited use and eventual disposal of human tissue, organs, glands, blood, fetuses, and dead bodies, (2) right to publicity cases, and (3) right to privacy cases. Third, the balancing of policy considerations — particularly the protection of a patient's right to autonomous medical decisions and the encouragement of socially useful research by "innocent parties" — (a) argues against extending conversion to this situation, (b) suggests a situation better left to legislative decision and control, and (c) is unnecessary when patients are given a cause of action for breach of fiduciary duty. Medical patients like John Moore are in effect told to re-think and re-order their relationships with their doctors, insisting on both a confidentiality and a use agreement with them for their organs and cells. When is that practical? How practical is that for Moore?

Moore lost his conversion case because he could not begin to do with his cells what the researchers did, or because he did not complete the research process. We protect a person's privacy and, in the instance of famous people, their persona because that is the result of their labor and effort. We don't protect an abstract idea, but we do protect scripts, articles, or books, with a copyright. Same underlying principle? Probably. Compare *Cameco, Inc. v. Gedicke*, 690 A.2d 1051, 1058 (N.J. Super. Ct. App. Div. 1997) (stating that plaintiff "fails to cite any support for the proposition that anything other than tangible personal property or tangible evidence of title to intangible . . . property is subject to conversion so that a cause of action may lie"), with *Thrifty-Tel Inc. v. Bezenek*, 54 Cal. Rptr. 2d 468, 472 (Cal. App. 1996) (opining that: "When the value of a stock certificate is not the cost of the paper, but the intangible interests that it represents. When the certificate is stolen or placed in another's name without the owner's permission, the value of the loss is not the cost of the paper — a tangible — but the worth of the stock — an intangible."). Similarly, a person who misappropriates a computer disk is liable for the value of what's on the disk.

The traditional, bright-line rule is that intangible personal property cannot be converted. See *Northeast Coating Tech., Inc. v. Vacuum Metallurgical Co.*, 684 A.2d 1322 (Me. 1996). Examples might be unpatented ideas, undocumented trade secrets, or business goodwill. This rule is based on the conversion action's origins in trover, which requires as its subject something that may be lost and found. A tangibility requirement also avoids the difficulty of deciding what has been taken, that being a precondition to measuring damages accurately. However, some courts have held that a share of stock is merged with its certificate so that the certificate is treated as property. See *Allied Inv. Corp. v. Jasen*, 731 A.2d 957 (Md. 1999). This "merger exception" to the traditional rule has been applied to a bankbook and a computer code. Likewise, only ideas that are novel, reduced to a concrete expression such as a protocol, plan, or manual, can be protected. See Chapter 8, *infra*. How about a computerized client list? Everything stored in a computer can be reduced to print, and today a "document" often may either be read on its screen or by using the print button, reduced to paper. What about an internet domain name? See *Kremen v. Cohen*, 337 F.3d 1024, 1035 (9th Cir. 2003), noted and discussed at 42 Hous. L. Rev. 489 (2005). A phone number? Is the merger exception wise? As in the case of John Moore's spleen, will other remedies suffice? Is torching a file room any different from deleting computer data? See *Thyroff v. Nationwide Mutual Ins. Co.*, 864 N.E.2d 1272 (N.Y. 2007) (reviewing the cases and the history of conversion). What about a conversion cause of action for a wire transfer of funds? See *Quincey Cablesystems, Inc. v. Sully's Bar, Inc.*, 650 F. Supp. 838, 848 (D. Mass. 1986) (allowing a conversion action involving satellite cable signals). What about a wi-fi signal? What if someone wires his home to by-pass the electric utility's meter? Has the electricity been converted? See *Narragansett Elec. Co. v. Carbone*, 898 A.2d 87 (R.I. 2006).

Does the proprietor of an email system have an action in trespass and conversion for its unauthorized use? See *Intel Corp. v. Hamidi*, 71 P.3d 296 (Cal. 2003) (holding that the corporation had no trespass to chattels action against a former employee emailing 8,000 to 35,000 present employees at work "on six occasions over almost two years," the emails criticizing corporate employment practices when there was no physical equipment damage or functional disruption of the corporation's email system). Spamming the system, the *Hamidi* opinion said, might well produce a different result, but then it is the *quantity* of the emails, not their *contents*, that constitute the disruption to a system. Does the corporation have an interest in preventing a lot of reading and deleting in the workplace? But see *Register.com v. Verio*, 126 F. Supp. 2d 238 (S.D.N.Y. 2000) (finding, under New York law, a trespass when crawling a competitor's database).

[handwritten top margin: Rightful possession of a chattel by one who is not actually the owner, though it it not absolute ownership.]

V. BAILMENTS

*[handwritten: bailor: person giving prop.
bailee: person getting prop.]*

A bailment is the transfer of possession of personal property to a person who is not its owner and for a limited purpose. It requires the possession of the property by the bailor, its delivery to the bailee pursuant to a contract or other agreement, and its acceptance by the bailee. Your delivery of your clothes to the dry cleaners, of your coat to the restaurant checkroom, of your vacuum cleaner to the repair shop, or your automobile at the mechanic's garage for repair — all create bailments. They involve many types of businesses, including warehousemen, pawnbrokers, and hotels — the last three types being governed by special state statutes. Decisions on whether a bailment exists can involve newer types of transactions too: the deposit of reproductive materials with doctor for *in vitro* fertilization procedures and a scientist's use of biological substances in laboratories. See *York v. Jones*, 717 F. Supp. 421 (E.D. Va. 1989) (deposit of IVF materials); *Yao v. Chapman*, 705 N.W.2d 272 (Wis. App. Ct. 2005) (professor's substances deposited in university science lab). Blackstone wrote:

> Bailment, from the French *bailler*, to deliver, is a delivery of good in trust, upon a contract expressed or implied, that the trust shall be faithfully executed on the part of the bailee. As if cloth be delivered, or (in our legal dialect) bailed, to a taylor to make a suit of clothes, he has it upon an implied contract to render it again when made, and that in a workmanly manner. If money or goods be delivered to a common carrier, to convey from Oxford to London, he is under a contract in law to pay, or carry, them to the person appointed. If a horse, or other goods, be delivered to an inn-keeper or his servants, he is bound to keep them safely, and restore them when his guest leaves the house. If a man takes in a horse, or other cattle, to graze and depasture in his grounds . . . , he takes them upon an implied contract to return them safe to the owner. . . . If a friend delivers any thing to his friend to keep for him, the receiver is bound to restore it on demand: and it was formerly held that in the mean time he was answerable for any damage or loss it might sustain, whether by accident or otherwise; unless he expressly undertook to keep it only with the same care as his own goods, and then he should not be answerable for theft or other accidents. But . . . if the bailee undertakes specially to keep the goods safely and securely, he is bound to answer all perils and damages, that may befall them for want of the same care with which a prudent man would keep his own.

> In all these instances there is a special qualified property transferred from the bailor to the bailee, together with the possession. It is not an absolute property in the bailee, because of his contract for restitution; and the bailor hath nothing left in him but the right to a *chose* in action, grounded upon such contract, the possession being delivered to the bailee. And, on account of this qualified property of the bailee, he may (as well as the bailor) maintain an action against such as injure or take away these chattels. The taylor, the carrier, the innkeeper, the agisting farmer, the pawnbroker, the distreinor, and the general bailee, may all of them vindicate, in their own right, this their possessory interest, against any stranger or third person. For, as such bailee is responsible to the bailor, if

*[handwritten left margin: 2 elements:
1. delivery by bailor
2. acceptance by bailee

• Burden of proof of proving a bailment happened is on bailor.
• Burden of proof that negligence did not cause a loss is on bailee.

Test of a bailment: Was there a full transfer, either actual or constructive, of the property to the bailee?]*

[handwritten bottom margin: This means that bailee ~~has~~ has sole custody AND control.]

the goods are lost or damaged by his wilful default or gross negligence, or if he do not deliver up the chattels on lawful demand, it is therefore reasonable that he should have a right to recover either the specific goods, or else a satisfaction in damages, against all other persons, who may have purloined or injured them; that he may always be ready to answer the call of the bailor.

William Blackstone, 2 Commentaries on the Laws of England 452–54 (1st ed. 1766, reprinted by U. Chi. Press 1979). Would Blackstone classify a finder as a bailee?

ADAMS v. THE NEW JERSEY STEAMBOAT CO.
45 N.E. 369 (N.Y. 1896)

O'Brien, J.

On the night of the 17th of June, 1889, the plaintiff was a cabin passenger from New York to Albany on the defendant's steamer Drew, and for the usual and regular charge was assigned to a stateroom on the boat. The plaintiff's ultimate destination was St. Paul, in the state of Minnesota, and he had upon his person the sum of $160 in money for the purpose of defraying his expenses of the journey. The plaintiff, on retiring for the night, left this money in his clothing in the stateroom, having locked the door and fastened the windows. During the night it was stolen by some person who apparently reached it through the window of the room.

The plaintiff's relations to the defendant as a passenger, the loss without negligence on his part, and the other fact that the sum lost was reasonable and proper for him to carry upon his person to defray the expenses of the journey, have all been found by the verdict of the jury in favor of the plaintiff. The appeal presents, therefore, but a single question, and that is, whether the defendant is in law liable for this loss without any proof of negligence on its part. The learned trial judge instructed the jury that it was, and the jury, after passing upon the other questions of fact in the case, rendered a verdict in favor of the plaintiff for the amount of money so stolen. The judgment entered upon the verdict was affirmed at General Term, and that court has allowed an appeal to this court.

The defendant has, therefore, been held liable as an insurer against the loss which one of its passengers sustained under the circumstances stated. The principle upon which innkeepers are charged by the common law as insurers of the money or personal effects of their guests originated in public policy. It was deemed to be a sound and necessary rule that this class of persons should be subjected to a high degree of responsibility in cases where an extraordinary confidence is necessarily reposed in them, and where great temptation to fraud and danger of plunder exists by reason of the peculiar relations of the parties. (Story on Bailments, § 464; 2 Kent's Com. 592; *Hulett v. Swift*, 33 N.Y. 571.) The relations that exist between a steamboat company and its passengers, who have procured staterooms for their comfort during the journey, differ in no essential respect from those that exist between the innkeeper and his guests. The passenger procures and pays for his room for the same reasons that a guest at an inn does. There are the same opportunities for fraud and plunder on the part of the carrier that was originally supposed to furnish a temptation to the landlord to violate his duty to the guest. A steamer carrying passengers upon the water, and furnishing them with rooms and entertainment, is, for all practical purposes, a floating inn, and hence the duties which the proprietors owe to the passengers in their charge ought to be the same. No good reason is apparent for relaxing the rigid rule of the common law which applies as between innkeeper and guest, since the same considerations of public policy apply to both relations.

The defendant, as a common carrier, would have been liable for the personal baggage of the plaintiff unless the loss was caused by the act of God or the public enemies, and a reasonable sum of money for the payment of his expenses, if carried by the passenger in his trunk, would be included in the liability for loss of baggage. (*Merrill v. Grinnell*, 30 N.Y. 594. . . .) Since all questions of negligence on the part of the plaintiff, as well as those growing out of the claim that some notice was posted in the room regarding the carrier's liability for the money, have been disposed of by the verdict, it is difficult to give any good reason why the measure of liability should be less for the loss of the money under the circumstances than for the loss of what might be strictly called baggage. * * *

It was held in *Carpenter v. N.Y., N.H. & H. R.R. Co.* (124 N.Y. 53) that a railroad running sleeping coaches on its road was not liable for the loss of money taken from a passenger while in his berth, during the night, without some proof of negligence on its part. That case does not, we think, control the question now under consideration. Sleeping-car companies are neither innkeepers nor carriers. A berth in a sleeping car is a convenience of modern origin, and the rules of the common law in regard to carriers or innkeepers have not been extended to this new relation.

This class of conveyances are attached to the regular trains upon railroads for the purpose of furnishing extra accommodations, not to the public at large nor to all the passengers, but to that limited number who wish to pay for them. The contract for transportation and liability for loss of baggage is with the railroad, the real carrier. All the relations of passenger and carrier are established by the contract implied in the purchase of the regular railroad ticket, and the sleeping car is but an adjunct to it only for such of the passengers as wish to pay an additional charge for the comfort and luxury of a special apartment in a special car. The relations of the carrier to a passenger occupying one of these berths are quite different with respect to his personal effects from those which exist at common law between the innkeeper and his guest, or a steamboat company that has taken entire charge of the traveler by assigning to him a stateroom. While the company running sleeping cars is held to a high degree of care in such cases, it is not liable for a loss of this character without some proof of negligence. The liability as insurers which the common law imposed upon carriers and innkeepers has not been extended to these modern appliances for personal comfort, for reasons that . . . do not apply in the case at bar. (*Ulrich v. N.Y.C. & H.R. R.R. Co.*, 108 N.Y. 80. . . .)

But aside from authority, it is quite obvious that the passenger has no right to expect, and in fact does not expect, the same degree of security from thieves while in an open berth in a car on a railroad as in a stateroom of a steamboat, securely locked and otherwise guarded from intrusion. In the latter case, when he retires for the night, he ought to be able to rely upon the company for his protection with the same faith that the guest can rely upon the protection of the innkeeper, since the two relations are quite analogous. In the former the contract and the relations of the parties differ at least to such an extent as to justify some modification of the common-law rule of responsibility. The use of sleeping cars by passengers in modern times created relations between the parties to the contract that were unknown to the common law, and to which the rule of absolute responsibility could not be applied without great injustice in many cases. But in the case at bar no good reason is perceived for relaxing the ancient rule and none can be deduced from the authorities. The relations that exist between the carrier and the passenger who secures a berth in a sleeping car or in a drawing-room car upon a railroad are exceptional and peculiar. The contract which gives the passenger the right to occupy a berth or a seat does not alone secure to him the right of transportation. It simply gives him the right to enjoy special accommodations at a specified place in the train. The carrier by railroad does not undertake to insure the personal effects of the passenger which are carried upon his person against depredation by thieves. It is bound, no doubt, to use due care to protect the passenger in this respect, and it might well be held to a higher degree of care when it assigns sleeping berths to passengers for an extra compensation than in cases where they remain in the ordinary coaches in a condition to protect themselves. But it is only upon the ground of negligence that the railroad company can be held liable to the passenger for money stolen from his person during the journey. The ground of the responsibility is the same as to all the passengers, whether they use sleeping berths or not, though the degree of care required may be different. Some proof must be given that the carrier failed to perform the duty of protection to the passenger that is implied in the contract before the question of responsibility can arise, whether the passenger be in one of the sleeping berths or in a seat in the ordinary car. The principle upon which the responsibility rests . . . must be measured by the danger to which the passenger is exposed from thieves and with reference to all the circumstances of the case. The carrier of passengers by railroad, whether the passenger be assigned to the ordinary coaches or to a berth in a special car, has never been held to that high degree of responsibility that governs the relations of innkeeper and guest. . . .

But the traveler who pays for his passage, and engages a room in one of the modern floating palaces that cross the sea or navigate the interior waters of the country, establishes legal relations with the carrier that cannot well be distinguished from those that exist between the hotelkeeper and his guests. The carrier in that case undertakes to provide for all his wants, including a private room for his exclusive use, which is to be as free from all intrusion as that assigned to the guest at a hotel. The two relations, if not identical, bear such close analogy to each other that the same rule of responsibility should govern. We are of the opinion, therefore, that the defendant was properly held liable in this case for the money stolen from the plaintiff without any proof of negligence. The judgment should be affirmed.

NOTES

1. The traditional rule was that the liability of an innkeeper extended to a guest's property *infra hospitum* — within the walls of the inn. See *Waterton v. Linden Motor Co.*, 810 N.Y.S.2d 319 (N.Y. Civ. Ct., King's Cty., 2006) (reviewing the history of innkeeper liability).

2. In *Ellish v. Airport Parking Co. of America, Inc.*, 345 N.Y.S.2d 650, 653 (N.Y. App. Div. 1973), *aff'd*, 316 N.E.2d 882 (N.Y. 1974), the court said that a bailment "describes a result which in many instances does not flow from the conscious promises of the parties made in a bargaining process but from what the law regards as a fair approximation of their expectations. . . . Hence, in formulating a rule to determine the extent of the liability of the defendant, we must concern ourselves with the realities of the transaction in which the parties engaged. The nature of the circumstances themselves leads to the determination whether the transaction should be considered a bailment, in which event the defendant is liable to the plaintiff, or whether the transaction should be considered a license to occupy space, in which event the defendant is not liable to the plaintiff." See also R.H. Helmholz, *Bailment Theories and the Liability of Bailees: The Elusive Uniform Standard of Reasonable Care*, 41 Kan. L. Rev. 97 (1992).

PEET v. THE ROTH HOTEL CO.
253 N.W. 546 (Minn. 1934)

Action in the district court for Ramsey county to recover judgment against defendant for the value of a ring belonging to plaintiff, valued at $2,500, which became lost after plaintiff had left it with defendant's cashier to be delivered to a guest in its hotel. . . . Plaintiff recovered a verdict of $2,140.66. Defendant appealed from an order denying its alternative motion for judgment or a new trial. Affirmed.

STONE, J.

* * * The record is the story of a ring. Defendant operates the St. Paul Hotel in St. Paul. Mr. Ferdinand Hotz is a manufacturing jeweler. For 20 years or more he has visited St. Paul periodically on business, making his local headquarters at the St. Paul Hotel. He has long been one of its regular patrons, personally known to the management. Plaintiff's engagement ring, a platinum piece set with a large cabochon sapphire surrounded by diamonds, was made to order by Mr. Hotz. One of its small diamonds lost, plaintiff had arranged with him to have it replaced and for that purpose was to leave it for him at the St. Paul Hotel. November 17, 1931, he was a guest there on one of his seasonal visits. About four p.m. of that day plaintiff went to the cashier's desk of the hotel, wearing the ring. The cashier on duty was a Miss Edwards. At this point plaintiff may as well tell her own story, for upon it is based the jury's verdict. She thus testified:

> I had it [the ring] on my finger and took it off my finger. The cashier — I told the cashier that it was for Mr. Ferdinand Hotz. She took out an envelope and wrote "Ferdinand Hotz." I remember spelling it to her, and then I left. . . . I handed the ring to the cashier, and she wrote on the envelope. . . . The only instructions I remember are telling her that it was for Mr. Ferdinand Hotz, who was stopping at the hotel.

Plaintiff's best recollection is that Miss Edwards told her that Mr. Hotz was registered but was not in at the moment. Miss Edwards frankly admitted, as a witness, that the ring had been delivered to her. It is conceded that it was immediately lost, doubtless stolen, probably by an outsider. Miss Edwards herself is beyond suspicion. But the ring, where she placed it upon its delivery to her by plaintiff, was on her desk or counter and within easy reach of anyone standing or passing just outside her cashier's window.

The loss was not then reported either to plaintiff or Mr. Hotz. About a month later he was again in St. Paul, and then plaintiff was advised for the first time that her ring had never reached him. Upon inquiry at the hotel office, it was learned that it had been lost. The purpose of this action is to recover from defendant, as bailee of the ring, its reasonable value, fixed by the jury at $2,140.66. The reasonableness of that figure is not questioned.

1. The jury took the case under a charge that there was a bailment as a matter of law. Error is assigned upon the supposition that there was at least a question of fact whether the evidence showed the mutual assent prerequisite to the contract of bailment which is the sine qua non of plaintiff's case. The supporting argument is put upon the cases holding that where the presence or identity of the article claimed to have been bailed is concealed from the bailee he has not assented to assume that position with its attendant obligation, and so there is no bailment. *Samples v. Geary* (Mo. App.) 292 S.W. 1066 (fur piece concealed in coat checked in parcel room); *United States v. Atlantic C.L.R. Co.*, 206 F. 190 (cut diamonds in mail package with nothing to indicate nature of contents); *Riggs v. Bank of Camas Prairie*, 34 Idaho, 176, 200 P. 188 (bailee of locked box supposed to contain only "papers and other valuables" not liable for money therein of which it had no knowledge).

The claim here is . . . that plaintiff . . . failed to divulge the unusual value of her ring when she left it with Miss Edwards. The latter testified that at the moment she did not realize its value. Taking both facts and their implications as favorably as we may for defendant, the stubborn truth remains that plaintiff delivered and defendant accepted the ring with its identity and at least its outward character perfectly obvious.

The mutual assent necessary to a contract may be expressed as well by conduct as by words; or it may be manifested by both. The latter is the case here. The expression of mutual assent is found in what passed between plaintiff and Miss Edwards. The former delivered and the latter accepted the ring to be delivered to Mr. Hotz. Below that irreducible minimum the case cannot be lowered. No decision has been cited and probably none can be found where the bailee of an article of jewelry, undeceived as to its identity, was relieved of liability because of his own erroneous underestimate of its value.

If there was mistake with legal effect worthwhile to defendant, it must have been of such character as to show no mutual assent and so no contract. There was no such error here. Identity of the property and all its attributes, except only its value, were as well known to defendant as to plaintiff. The case is identical in principle with *Wood v. Boynton*, 64 Wis. 265, 215 N.W. 42. There the plaintiff had sold to defendant, for one dollar, a stone which she supposed was at best a topaz. It turned out to be an uncut diamond worth $700. Neither its true character nor value was known to either buyer or seller at the time of the sale. There being neither fraud nor mistake as to identity, the mutual mistake as to value was held no obstacle to completion of the contract. Plaintiff was denied recovery.

2. The jury was instructed also that defendant was a "nongratuitous" bailee. By that it doubtless intended to say that the bailment was "reciprocally beneficial to both parties." 1 Dunnell, Minn. Dig. (2d ed.) § 732. Clearly, that was a correct interpretation of the proof. The ring was accepted in the ordinary course of business by defendant in rendering a usual service for a guest, and so, plainly, it was for defendant's advantage, enough so, at least, to make the bailment as matter of law one for the benefit of both bailor and bailee.

3. The jury was charged also that, the bailment being for the reciprocal benefit of the parties, defendant as bailee was under duty of exercising, in respect to the subject matter, ordinary care, that is, the degree of care which an ordinarily prudent man would have exercised in the same or similar circumstances. The instruction was correct. The former distinction between bailments for the sole benefit of the bailor; those for the mutual benefit of both bailor and bailee; and those for the sole benefit of the latter, in respect to the degree of care required of the bailee in order to protect him from liability for negligence, has long since been pretty much discarded here as elsewhere. "It is evident that the so-called distinctions between slight, ordinary and gross negligence over which courts have perhaps somewhat quibbled for a hundred years, can furnish no assistance." *Elon College v. Elon B. & T. Co.*, 182 N.C. 298, 303, 109 S.E. 6.

Defendant's liability, if any, is for negligence. In that field generally the legal norm is a care commensurate to the hazard, i.e. the amount and kind of care that would be exercised by an ordinarily prudent person in the same or similar circumstances. The character and amount of risk go far, either to decrease or increase the degree of care required. The value of the property, its attractiveness to light-fingered gentry, and the ease or difficulty of its theft have much to say with triers of fact in determining whether there has been exercised a degree of care commensurate to the risk, whether the bailment be gratuitous or otherwise. However unsatisfactory it may be, until legal acumen has developed and formulated a more satisfactory criterion, that of ordinary care should be followed in every case without regard to former distinctions between slight, ordinary, and great care. Even the courts which adhere to the former distinctions will be found in most cases to be demanding no other degree of care than one commensurate to the risk and other relevant circumstances; e.g. in *Ridenour v. Woodward*, 132 Tenn. 620, 179 S.W. 148, 149, it was held that a gratuitous bailee was answerable only for his gross negligence or bad faith. But, as the court proceeded to say, the care to be taken was (132 Tenn. 632) "to be measured, however, with reference to the nature of the thing placed in his keeping." The defendant was relieved of liability because it was held as matter of law that he had (132 Tenn. 628) "acted with a fairly commensurate discretion" in handling the bailed property. . . .

4. The rule of our decision law (*Hoel v. Flour City F.&T. Co.*, 144 Minn. 280, 175 N.W. 300) puts upon the bailee the burden of proving that the loss did not result from his negligence. This burden, in the language of the late Mr. Justice Dibell (144 Minn. 281), is "not merely the burden of going forward with proofs, nor a shifting burden, but a burden of establishing before the jury that its negligence did not cause the loss." That proposition we adopted as "the practical working rule." We are not disposed to depart from it.

5. With the foregoing statement concerning the burden of proof, we go to an assignment of error questioning an instruction that "it makes no difference what care the defendant may have taken of its own property, that being its own concern, and the care it may give to its own property is of no importance in the determination of this case." That instruction was given in connection with and in explanation of the rule concerning the due or ordinary care required of defendant.

Because the care required was that of the ordinary person in the same or similar circumstances, it is but obvious that, whatever defendant's care of its own property may have been, it would not alter the standard of care applicable to plaintiff's property in its hands as bailee. It may have been too much to say that defendant's care of its own property "is of no importance." There may be cases where the care of his own property exercised by a defendant bailee would have some relevancy as evidence. But, if in that respect, the charge went a bit too far, and was pro tanto error, no prejudice could have resulted to defendant, for no issue was made as to the *quantum* of care exercised by it, concerning its own property, if any, of a kind and value comparable to those of plaintiff's "cabochon sapphire." . . . Order affirmed.

NOTES

1. Are the rules stated in paragraph number 4 in *Peet* changed by the following statutes?

Cal. Civ. Code § 1838 (2014):

If a thing is lost or injured during its deposit, and the depositary refuses to inform the depositor of the circumstances under which the loss or injury occurred, so far as he has information concerning them, or willfully misrepresents the circumstances to him, the depositary is presumed to have willfully, or by gross negligence, permitted the loss or injury to occur.

Georgia Code Ann. § 44-12-44 (2014):

In all cases of bailment, after proof of loss by the bailor, the burden of proof is on the bailee to show proper diligence.

And see the Tennessee statute cited in the *Allen* opinion, *infra*:

Tenn. Code Ann. § 24-5-111 (2014):

In all actions by a bailor against a bailee for loss or damage to personal property, proof by the bailor that the property was delivered to the bailee in good condition and that it was not returned or redelivered according to the contract, or that it was returned or redelivered in a damaged condition, shall constitute prima facie evidence that the bailee was negligent, provided the loss or damage was not due to the inherent nature of the property bailed.

2. Article 7 of the Uniform Commercial Code is applicable to bailments in a warehouse. One section of this article states:

§ 7-204(1). A warehouseman is liable for damages for loss of or injury to the goods caused by his failure to exercise such care in regard to them as a reasonably careful man would exercise under like circumstances but unless otherwise agreed he is not liable for damages which could not have been avoided by the exercise of such care.

Does this statute codify or modify the common law rule for bailments? Is it intended to be a minimum standard? See Drew Kershen, *Comparing the United States Warehouse Act and U.C.C. Article 7*, 27 Creighton L. Rev. 735, 754–57 (1994). Suppose that a warehouseman shows that a fire originated on neighboring premises and then spread to the warehouse, destroying the bailor's goods. Is the bailee liable for their loss under § 7-204(1)?

3. "The degree of diligence exacted of each of the several classes of bailees, in respect to the care of the thing bailed, has ordinarily no application to the liability of the bailee in respect to its return or delivery. A misdelivery by [the bailee] even if procured by fraud and made without negligence, would be a conversion." *Dolitsky v. Dollar Sav. Bank*, 118 N.Y.S.2d 65, 67 (N.Y., Bronx County Mun. Ct., 1952).

ALLEN v. HYATT REGENCY-NASHVILLE HOTEL
668 S.W.2d 286 (Tenn. 1984)

HARBISON, J.

In this case the Court is asked to consider the nature and extent of the liability of the operator of a commercial parking garage for theft of a vehicle during the absence of the owner. Both courts below, on the basis of prior decisions from this state, held that a bailment was created when the owner parked and locked his vehicle in a modern, indoor, multi-story garage operated by appellant in conjunction with a large hotel in downtown Nashville. We affirm.

There is almost no dispute as to the relevant facts. Appellant is the owner and operator of a modern high-rise hotel in Nashville fronting on the south side of Union Street. Immediately to the rear, or south, of the main hotel building there is a multi-story parking garage with a single entrance and a single exit to the west, on Seventh Avenue, North. As one enters the parking garage at the street level, there is a large sign reading "Welcome to Hyatt Regency-Nashville." There is another Hyatt Regency sign inside the garage at street level, together with a sign marked "Parking." The garage is available for parking by members of the general public as well as guests of the hotel, and the public are invited to utilize it.

On the morning of February 12, 1981, appellee's husband, Edwin Allen, accompanied by two passengers, drove appellee's new 1981 automobile into the parking garage. Neither Mr. Allen nor his passengers intended to register at the hotel as a guest. Mr. Allen had parked in this particular garage on several occasions, however, testifying that he felt that the vehicle would be safer in an attended garage than in an unattended outside lot on the street. The single entrance was controlled by a ticket machine. The single exit was controlled by an attendant in a booth just opposite to the entrance and in full view thereof. Appellee's husband entered the garage at the street level and took a ticket which was automatically dispensed by the machine. The machine activated a barrier gate which rose and permitted Mr. Allen to enter the garage. He drove to the fourth floor level, parked the vehicle, locked it, retained the ignition key, descended by elevator to the street level and left the garage. When he returned several hours later, the car was gone, and it has never been recovered. Mr. Allen reported the theft to the attendant at the exit booth, who stated, "Well, it didn't come out here." The attendant did not testify at the trial.

Mr. Allen then reported the theft to security personnel employed by appellant, and subsequently reported the loss to the police. Appellant regularly employed a number of security guards, who were dressed in a distinctive uniform, two of whom were on duty most of the time. These guards patrolled the hotel grounds and building as well as the garage and were instructed to make rounds through the garage, although not necessarily at specified intervals. One of the security guards told appellee's husband that earlier in the day he had received the following report: "He said, 'It's a funny thing here. On my report here a lady called me somewhere around nine-thirty or after and said that there was someone messing with a car.'" The guard told Mr. Allen that he closed his office and went up into the garage to investigate, but reported that he did not find anything unusual or out of the ordinary.

Customers such as Mr. Allen, upon entering the garage, received a ticket from the dispensing machine. On one side of this ticket are instructions to overnight guests to present the ticket to the front desk of the hotel. The other side contains instructions to the parker to keep the ticket and that the ticket must be presented to the cashier upon leaving the parking area. The ticket states that charges are made for the use of parking space only and that appellant assumes no responsibility for loss through fire, theft, collision or otherwise to the car or its contents. The ticket states that cars are parked at the risk of the owner, and parkers are instructed to lock their vehicles. The record indicates that these tickets are given solely for the purpose of measuring the time during which a vehicle is parked in order that the attendant may collect the proper charge, and that they are not given for the purpose of identifying particular vehicles. . . .

It is legally and theoretically possible, of course, for various legal relationships to be created by the parties, ranging from the traditional concepts of lessor-lessee, licensor-licensee, bailor-bailee, to that described in some jurisdictions as a "deposit." Several courts have found difficulty with the traditional criteria of bailment in analyzing park-and-lock cases. One of the leading cases is *McGlynn v. Parking Authority of City of Newark*, 432 A.2d 99 (N.J. 1981). There the Supreme Court of New Jersey reviewed numerous decisions from within its own state and from other jurisdictions, and it concluded that it was more "useful and straightforward" to consider the possession and control elements in defining the duty of care of a garage operator to its customers than to consider them in the context of bailment. That Court concluded that the "realities" of the relationship between the parties gave rise to a duty of reasonable care on the part of operators of parking garages and parking lots. It further found that a garage owner is usually better situated to protect a parked car and to distribute the cost of protection through parking fees. It also emphasized that owners usually expect to receive their vehicles back in the same condition in which they left them and that the imposition of a duty to protect parked vehicles and their contents was consistent with that expectation. The Court went further and stated that since the owner is ordinarily absent when theft or damage occurs, the obligation to come forward with affirmative evidence of negligence could impose a difficult, if not insurmountable, burden upon him. After considering various policy considerations, which it acknowledged to be the same as those recognized by courts holding that a bailment is created, the New Jersey Court indulged or authorized a presumption of negligence from proof of damage to a car parked in an enclosed garage. *Id.* at 105.

Although the New Jersey Court concluded that a more flexible and comprehensive approach could be achieved outside of traditional property concepts, Tennessee courts generally have analyzed cases such as this in terms of sufficiency of the evidence to create a bailment for hire by implication. We believe that this continues to be the majority view and the most satisfactory and realistic approach to the problem, unless the parties clearly by their conduct or by express contract create some other relationship. The subject has been discussed in numerous previous decisions in this state. One of the leading cases is *Dispeker v. New Southern Hotel Co.*, 373 S.W.2d 904 (Tenn. 1963). In that case the guest at a hotel delivered his vehicle to a bellboy who took possession of it and parked it in a lot adjoining the hotel building. The owner kept the keys, but the car apparently was capable of being started without the ignition key. The owner apparently had told the attendant how to so operate it. Later the employee took the vehicle for his own purposes and damaged it. Under these circumstances the Court held that a bailment for hire had been created and that upon proof of misdelivery of the vehicle the bailee was liable to the customer.

In the subsequent case of *Scruggs v. Dennis*, 440 S.W.2d 20 (Tenn. 1969), upon facts practically identical to those of the instant case, the Court again held that an implied bailment contract had been created between a customer who parked and locked his vehicle in a garage. Upon entry he received a ticket dispensed by a machine, drove his automobile to the underground third level of the garage and parked. He retained his ignition key, but when he returned to retrieve the automobile in the afternoon it had disappeared. It was recovered more than two weeks later and returned to the owner in a damaged condition.

In that case the operator of the garage had several attendants on duty, but the attendants did not ordinarily operate the parked vehicles, as in the instant case.

Although the Court recognized that there were some factual differences between the Scruggs case and that of *Dispeker v. New Southern Hotel Co., supra,* it concluded that a bailment had been created when the owner parked his vehicle for custody and safe keeping in the parking garage, where there was limited access and where the patron had to present a ticket to an attendant upon leaving the premises. . . . On the contrary, in the case of *Rhodes v. Pioneer Parking Lot, Inc.,* 501 S.W.2d 569 (Tenn. 1973), a bailment was found not to exist when the owner left his vehicle in an open parking lot which was wholly unattended and where he simply inserted coins into a meter, received a ticket, then parked the vehicle himself and locked it. . . .

In the instant case, appellee's vehicle was not driven into an unattended or open parking area. Rather it was driven into an enclosed, indoor, attended commercial garage which not only had an attendant controlling the exit but regular security personnel to patrol the premises for safety. Under these facts we are of the opinion that the courts below correctly concluded that a bailment for hire had been created, and that upon proof of nondelivery appellee was entitled to the statutory presumption of negligence provided in T.C.A. § 24-5-111.

We recognize that there is always a question as to whether there has been sufficient delivery of possession and control to create a bailment when the owner locks a vehicle and keeps the keys. Nevertheless, the realities of the situation are that the operator of the garage is, in circumstances like those shown in this record, expected to provide attendants and protection. In practicality the operator does assume control and custody of the vehicles parked, limiting access thereto and requiring the presentation of a ticket upon exit. As stated previously, the attendant employed by appellant did not testify, but he told appellee's husband that the vehicle did not come out of the garage through the exit which he controlled. This testimony was not amplified, but the attendant obviously must have been in error or else must have been inattentive or away from his station. The record clearly shows that there was no other exit from which the vehicle could have been driven.

Appellant made no effort to rebut the presumption created by statute in this state (which is similar to presumptions indulged by courts in some other jurisdictions not having such statutes). While the plaintiff did not prove positive acts of negligence on the part of appellant, the record does show that some improper activity of tampering with vehicles had been called to the attention of security personnel earlier in the day of the theft in question, and that appellee's new vehicle had been removed from the garage by some person or persons unknown, either driving past an inattentive attendant or one who had absented himself from his post, there being simply no other way in which the vehicle could have been driven out of the garage.

Under the facts and circumstances of this case, we are not inclined to depart from prior decisions or to place the risk of loss upon the consuming public as against the operators of commercial parking establishments such as that conducted by appellant. We recognize that park-and-lock situations arise under many and varied factual circumstances. It is difficult to lay down one rule of law which will apply to all cases. The expectations of the parties and their conduct can cause differing legal relationships to arise, with consequent different legal results. We do not find the facts of the present case, however, to be at variance with the legal requirements of the traditional concept of a bailment for hire. In our opinion it amounted to more than a mere license or hiring of a space to park a vehicle, unaccompanied by any expectation of protection or other obligation upon the operator of the establishment.

The judgment of the courts below is affirmed at the cost of appellant. The cause will be remanded to the trial court for any further proceedings which may be necessary.

DROWOTA, J., dissenting.

From its earliest origins, the most distinguishing factor identifying a bailment has been delivery. * * * Certainly Defendant cannot be said to have sole custody of Plaintiff's vehicle, for Defendant could not move it, did not know to whom it belonged, and did not know when it would be reclaimed or by whom. Anyone who manually obtained a ticket from the dispenser could drive out with any vehicle he was capable of operating. Also, a cashier was not always on duty. When on duty, so long as the parking fee was paid — by what means could the Defendant reasonably exercise control? The necessary delivery and relinquishment of control by the Plaintiff, the very basis upon which the bailment theory was developed, is missing. . . .

NOTE

Consider *Swarth v. Barney's Clothes, Inc.*, 242 N.Y.S.2d 922 (N.Y. Sup. App. Term 1963):

The plaintiff sued in the Small Claims Court for $350 for the loss of a wallet claimed to have been left in her automobile while parked in the defendant's parking lot. The defendant, Barney's Clothes, Inc., maintains the lot for the free use of its patrons. The plaintiff testified that she had $350 in cash in the wallet when she left her home, had removed the wallet from her purse only to pay a toll, and, in attempting to replace it, inadvertently left it on the seat of the car. On the request of the parking lot attendant, she left the keys with him after locking the car. It is not claimed that the plaintiff informed the attendant when she parked the car with him that she had left her wallet on the seat. Indeed, she testified that when she left the keys with him she did not even know the wallet was in the car. There is thus a complete absence of notice to the defendant of the presence of the wallet in the car, much less the value of its contents. The attendant unlocked the car and left the keys in the ignition. On the completion of her shopping in the defendant's store an hour later the plaintiff missed her wallet and immediately returned to the car. A search of the car and subsequent search by the police of the attendant failed to yield the wallet. The plaintiff charged the defendant with negligence and recovered below.

When the defendant accepted the plaintiff's automobile for parking, it unquestionably became its bailee and assumed the liability flowing from that relation. It by no means follows, however, that it thereby also undertook the bailment of the wallet, whose presence in the vehicle was neither disclosed nor reasonably to be expected. Delivery, actual or constructive, to the person sought to be held as bailee is not enough to create a bailment; acceptance, actually or constructively, by the latter is equally essential. *Cowen v. Pressprich*, 194 N.Y.S. 926 (N.Y. App. Div.), rev'd on dissenting opinion of LEHMAN, J, at Appellate Term, 192 N.Y.S. 242, 249 (N.Y. 1922). Acceptance is absent when the property is not such as is usually and customarily left with a custodian in like circumstances and no disclosure of this fact is made. In that situation, the person sought to be charged as bailee having no reason to suppose the property has been delivered to him, is liable only if on express notice, "for the bailee cannot by artifice be compelled to assume a liability greater than he intended." *Waters v. Beau Site Co.*, 186 N.Y.S. 731 (N.Y. City Ct. 1920). Self-evidently valuable and easily stolen articles are not left in parked automobiles, and the operator of a parking lot, without notice that they have been so left, is not liable as bailee in respect to them. . . . It follows that the judgment must be reversed. . . .

COWEN v. PRESSPRICH
192 N.Y.S. 242 (Sup. Ct., App. Term, 1922)

[The plaintiffs were a firm of stock brokers (hereafter Cowen). They sued the defendants, another brokerage firm (hereafter Pressprich) for conversion of a $1000 bond of the Oregon & California R.R. Co. Cowen alleged that he agreed to deliver a bond of the Oregon Short Line R.R. Co. to Pressprich, but by mistake delivered a bond of the Oregon & Calif. R.R. Co.; that Cowen is entitled to the return of the Oregon & Calif. R.R. Co. bond, has demanded the bond, but defendants have refused to deliver it.

The plaintiff's evidence showed [that] Cowen sent a runner, Goldberg, age 17, to make delivery of an Oregon Short Line bond which had been sold to Pressprich. By mistake he took an Oregon & Calif. R.R. bond. For receiving deliveries of securities Pressprich had a small room into which the delivery boys entered; in one wall of the room was a slot for depositing the securities and above it a ground-glass window, which could be opened from the inside; securities pushed through the slot fell on the desk of Pressprich's clerk whose job it was to receive deliveries. All deliveries were accompanied by slips describing the item delivered. Goldberg came into the small room and pushed through the slot the Oregon & Calif. bond and a slip describing an Oregon Short Line bond; then he left to make other deliveries. Pressprich's clerk noticed the discrepancy between the bond and slip. He opened the ground-glass window and called "Cowen." A boy who was there stepped up. (The boy was not Goldberg, nor any agent of Cowen, but Pressprich's clerk knew none of the runners.) The clerk said, "Make your statement agree with the bond," handing the boy the bond and slip. The boy took them and left. The bond was negotiable and was never recovered.

The defendants requested a ruling that the plaintiff's evidence was insufficient to sustain a cause of action. The court denied this motion and found for the plaintiffs. Defendants appealed.]

MULLAN, J.

. . . The defendants have refused to make good the plaintiffs' loss, contending that they were chargeable only with due diligence, and that, accepting the version of the plaintiffs as given by Goldberg, it appears that they exercised all the care required of them. The plaintiffs contend that there was an absolute obligation on the part of the defendants to redeliver the bond to the plaintiffs, and that no question of negligence enters into the case. They also argue that, if the negligence question does enter, there was sufficient evidence to warrant a finding that the defendants did not, in fact, exercise due care. The learned trial judge did not state the ground of his decision in plaintiffs' favor.

A person who has been put, through no act or fault of his own, in such a situation as that in which the defendants were put upon the delivery to them of the wrong bond, has come to be known as "involuntary bailee." . . .

In the field of voluntary bailments, whether they be for hire or be otherwise coupled with an interest on the part of the bailee, or whether they be merely gratuitous, no rule is better settled than that it is the duty of the bailee to deliver the bailed article to the right person and that delivery to the wrong person is not capable of being excused by any possible showing of care or good faith or innocence.

Such distinctions as have been drawn between the duties of voluntary bailees for compensation and voluntary gratuitous bailees relate solely to the degree of care the bailee should exercise in respect of the *custody* of the thing bailed. In respect of *delivery* to the proper person, no such distinction is drawn; the duty in both cases is absolute.

What, then, is the difference, if any, between the duty of a voluntary gratuitous bailee and that of a wholly involuntary bailee? . . . [A]ll that can be found upon [the question] points to the conclusion that the involuntary bailee, as long as his lack of volition continues, is not under the slightest duty to care for or guard the subject of the bailment, and cannot be held, in respect of custody, for what would even be the grossest negligence in the case of a voluntary bailment, but that, in case the involuntary bailee shall exercise any dominion over the thing so bailed, he becomes as responsible as if he were a voluntary bailee. . . .

[While] it may seem to be imposing upon the defendants an unduly severe rule of conduct to hold them to an absolute liability, the rule is no more severe than the occasion calls for. . . . The defendants could easily have protected themselves by telephoning the plaintiffs that the wrong bond had been delivered, or they could have sent the bond back to the plaintiffs by one of their own messengers. Instead, they chose to take the chance of delivering it to the wrong messenger. As the delivery window was closed when the bond was dropped through the slot, and remained close for an appreciable time, they could not have known what messenger had made the delivery. . . . Judgment affirmed.

LEHMAN, J., dissenting.

[The Appellate Division relied upon Judge Lehman's dissent on appeal, App. Div., 194 N.Y.S. 926 (1922) (reversing Mullan, J.) — Eds.] It is unnecessary now to consider whether the complaint sufficiently sets forth any cause of action; for no motion was made by the defendants to dismiss the complaint on the ground of insufficiency, and no such point is raised on this appeal. It is to be noted, however, that the complaint does not allege any negligence on the part of the defendants, and I agree with Mr. Justice MULLAN that no such issue was litigated, and that the judgment can be sustained only if, as a matter of law, the defendants' mistake in returning the bond to the wrong messenger constituted a conversion of the bond or at least a breach of an implied agreement on their part to return the bond only to the plaintiffs.

. . . The defendants had not consented to accept the bond as a deposit, they claimed no title to it, and they were not subject to any trust or obligation as bailees, for a bailment arises only through an express or implied contract. They were put in possession of the bond without any agreement on their part, express or implied, to accept the deposit of the bond; and, though persons who come into possession of the property of others without their consent are sometimes for convenience called "involuntary" or "quasi bailees," they incur no responsibility to the true owner in respect thereof. It is only where they commit some "overt act" of interference with the property that an implied contract of bailment is created.

. . . In other words, an implied contract of bailment with its consequent obligations arises only where a person in possession of the property of another does some act which is inconsistent with the view that he does not *accept* the possession which has been thrust upon him. . . . In the present case the defendants were put in possession of the bond by mistake; they discovered the mistake promptly, and thereafter they committed no "overt act" of interference with the bond except that they attempted to divest themselves of this possession by delivering the bond to a person whom they believed to be the messenger of the plaintiffs. That act was not only consistent with the continued title and right of dominion in the plaintiffs, but was an honest attempt to restore possession to the true owners. An attempt to return the bond to the true owner or to the person who delivered it cannot be considered as inconsistent with a recognition of the complete ownership and right of dominion by the true owner, and certainly shows no intent to accept the possession thrust upon the defendants by plaintiffs' mistake, and I fail to see how, in the absence of such elements, any implied contract of bailment can arise. If in making an attempt to return the goods, which was lawful and proper in itself, the defendants used means which were not reasonable and proper, and as a result thereof the goods were lost or misdelivered, then the defendants would be liable for negligence or possibly for conversion, for every man is responsible for his own acts; but, if the defendants had a right to divest themselves of possession and attempt to return the goods, then, in the absence of some obligation resting upon contract to deliver the goods only to the true owner or upon his order, I do not see how the mere fact that through innocent mistake the defendants handed the bond to the wrong messenger could constitute a conversion. . . .

Even if under these pleadings we could consider the question of negligence, I find no evidence upon this question to sustain a judgment in favor of the plaintiffs. There is no doubt that the defendants acted in good faith and in the honest belief that they were handing back the bond to the messenger who delivered it. They had assumed no obligation of any kind to the plaintiffs; any act they performed was for the plaintiffs' benefit, and it was through plaintiffs' mistake that they were called upon to act at all in the premises. Doubtless, if they had foreseen the possibility of mistake, they would not have delivered the bond to the wrong messenger; but it was not unreasonable to suppose that the messenger might be waiting or that, if he had left, no thief would be in the office who would claim to represent the plaintiffs. They probably committed an error of judgment, but for such error they cannot be held liable. Since they owed no obligation to the plaintiffs and acted in good faith under the reasonable belief that they were returning the bond to the messenger who delivered it, I see no ground for imposing upon them liability for the loss of a bond which would never have been lost but for the plaintiffs' mistake, due apparently to the plaintiffs' negligence. . . . [T]he judgment should be reversed . . . and the complaint dismissed. . . .

NOTES

1. The type of bailment created here is often called a constructive bailment. Was this the type of bailment involved in *Peet*? See also *Shamrock Hilton Hotel v. Caranas*, 488 S.W.2d 151 (Tex. Civ. App. 1972) (involving a pocketbook left on the floor by a hotel guest in the hotel's coffee-shop and delivered by a busboy to the shop's cashier, who gave it to an unknown person before its owner attempted to reclaim it), discussed in Note, *Bailment — An Innkeeper Is Liable for the Unknown Contents of Bailed Property Which He Could Reasonably Expect to Find Contained Within the Bailed Property*, 5 Tex. Tech. L. Rev. 141 (1973). Texas and many other states have statutes requiring that a hotel provide its guests with a safe in which to store their valuables and with notices posted to inform them of the availability of the safe, and further providing that the hotel's liability shall not be more than (say) $100 if it complies with the statute and unless it is negligent otherwise. Tex. Rev. Civ. Stat. Ann. art. 4592 (2003). See, e.g., N.Y. Gen. Bus. L. § 203-a (2003):

> No hotel or motel keeper shall be liable in any sum exceeding the sum of two hundred and fifty dollars for the loss of or damage to property of a guest delivered to such keeper, his agent or employee, for transport to or from the hotel or motel, unless at the time of delivering the same such value in excess of two hundred and fifty dollars shall be stated by such guest and a written receipt stating such value shall be issued by such keeper; provided, however, that where such written receipt is issued the keeper shall not be liable beyond five hundred dollars unless it shall appear that such loss or damage occurred through his fault or negligence.

Would this statute control the facts of *Peet*? Of *Caranas*?

2. Consider the impact of the following statute governing the warehousing of goods under the Uniform Commercial Code:

> § 7-404. A bailee who in good faith including observance of reasonable commercial standards has received goods and delivered or otherwise disposed of them according to the terms of the document of title or pursuant to this Article is not liable therefor. This rule applies even though the person from whom he received the goods had no authority to procure the document or to dispose of the goods and even though the person to whom he delivered the goods had no authority to receive them.

What would be the common law rule when a bailee delivers goods to a third party presenting proper documents showing ownership? Does that rule change under § 7-404? See *Turner v. Scobey Moving & Storage Co.*, 515 S.W.2d 253 (Tex. 1974).

Suppose that you check your baggage with a checkroom in a waiting room of a railroad station or airport. How do you know the terms of the agreement under which the bags are held? You typically take a receipt for the goods. What is the effect of that receipt? See Ray Brown, Personal Property 270–276 (Walter B. Raushenbush ed., 3d ed. 1975).

Issue: was the waiver of liability enough for P to be not liable? Court says Yes. P was well educated and a lawyer, so the waiver applied.

V.   BAILMENTS   59

CARR v. HOOSIER PHOTO SUPPLIES, INC.
441 N.E.2d 450 (Ind. 1982)

Givan, C.J.

Litigation in this cause began with the filing of a complaint in Marion Municipal Court by John R. Carr, Jr., seeking damages in the amount of $10,000 from defendants Hoosier Photo Supplies, Inc. and Eastman Kodak Company. Carr was the beneficiary of a judgment in the amount of $1,013.60. Both sides appealed. The Court of Appeals affirmed the trial court in its entirety. Kodak and Hoosier now petition to transfer this cause to this Court. We hereby grant that petition and vacate the opinion of the Court of Appeals. For reasons we shall set out below, we remand the cause to the trial court with instructions to enter a judgment in favor of Carr in the amount of $13.60 plus interest. Each party is to bear its own costs.

The facts were established by stipulation agreement between the parties and thus are not in dispute. In the late spring or early summer of 1970, Carr purchased some Kodak film from a retailer not a party to this action, including four rolls of Kodak Ektachrome-X 135 slide film that are the subject matter of this dispute. During the month of August, 1970, Carr and his family vacationed in Europe. Using his own camera Carr took a great many photographs of the sites they saw, using among others the four rolls of film referred to earlier. Upon their return to the United States, Carr took a total of eighteen rolls of exposed film to Hoosier to be developed. Only fourteen of the rolls were returned to Carr after processing. All efforts to find the missing rolls or the pictures developed from them were unsuccessful. Litigation commenced when the parties were unable to negotiate a settlement.

The film Carr purchased, manufactured by Kodak, is distributed in boxes on which there is printed the following legend:

> READ THIS NOTICE. This film will be replaced if defective in manufacture, labeling, or packaging, or if damaged or lost by us or any subsidiary company even though by negligence or other fault. Except for such replacement, the sale, processing, or other handling of this film for any purpose is without other warranty of liability.

In the stipulation of facts it was agreed though Carr never read this notice on the packages of film he bought, he knew there was printed on such packages "a limitation of liability similar or identical to the Eastman Kodak limitation of liability." The source of Carr's knowledge was agreed to be his years of experience as an attorney and as an amateur photographer. When Carr took all eighteen rolls of exposed film to Hoosier for processing, he was given a receipt for each roll. Each receipt contained the following language printed on the back side:

> Although film price does not include processing by Kodak, the return of any film or print to us for processing or any other purpose, will constitute an agreement by you that if any such film or print is damaged or lost by us or any subsidiary company, even though by negligence or other fault, it will be replaced with an equivalent amount of Kodak film and processing and,

except for such replacement, the handling of such film or prints by us for any purpose is without other warranty or liability.

Again, it was agreed though Carr did not read this notice he was aware Hoosier "[gave] to their customers at the time of accepting film for processing, receipts on which there are printed limitations of liability similar or identical to the limitation of liability printed on each receipt received by Carr from Hoosier Photo."

It was stipulated upon receipt of the eighteen [18] rolls of exposed film only fourteen were returned to Hoosier by Kodak after processing. Finally, it was stipulated the four rolls of film were lost by either Hoosier or Kodak.

Kodak and Hoosier petition to transfer this cause to this Court. They allege the Court of Appeals erred when it decided two new questions of law. These errors are alleged to be: (1) that Hoosier's limitation of liability as a bailee for its own negligence, as reflected on the receipts given to Carr, was ineffective; and (2) that Kodak's limitation for its own negligence, as reflected on the boxes of film sold to Carr, was ineffective. . . . At the time Carr purchased the film in question the sale contract was completed. The box in which the film was packaged contained an offer by Kodak to enter into a bailment contract to process the film. This offer of bailment was accepted by Carr when he turned the film over to Hoosier and Kodak for processing. We thus find the breach of contract occurring in the case at bar was a breach of a contract for bailment between the parties. In 8 Am. Jur.2d, Bailments, § 34, pp. 769–770 (1980), it is stated: "Where property in an unmanufactured state is delivered by one person to another, on an agreement that it shall be manufactured or converted in form, or there is a delivery of chattels under an agreement that the party receiving them shall improve them by his labor or skill, whether the transaction is a sale or a bailment depends generally on whether the product of the identical articles delivered is to be returned to the original owner, though in a new form. If it is to be so returned, it is a bailment. . . . The intention of the parties is the controlling factor. . . ."

That either Kodak or Hoosier breached the bailment contract, by negligently losing the four rolls of film, was established in the stipulated agreement of facts. Therefore, the next issue raised is whether either or both, Hoosier or Kodak, may limit their liability as reflected on the film packages and receipts.

With regard to the limitation on the back of Hoosier's receipts, we are unable to agree with the position of Carr and the Court of Appeals that there is such an ambiguity in the wording of that clause that it is impossible to determine to whom it applies. Again we call attention to the limitation of liability that appears on the back of the receipts from Hoosier. . . . The argument as to the construction of this language centers around the words "return" and "us" as they appear on the receipts. * * * The language of the receipt refers to Kodak. The word Kodak is on the front of the receipt as well as twice in the body of the receipt itself as above quoted. Even though this is a receipt which was presented by Hoosier to Carr it obviously was speaking to the interests of Kodak. Hoosier's participation was as an agent for Kodak in this regard. Therefore, as we read the receipt, the word "return" refers to the returning of film manufactured by Kodak to Kodak for processing. The word "us" refers to Kodak. We, therefore, hold the receipt issued by Hoosier primarily refers to Kodak and includes Hoosier to the extent of their participation on behalf of Kodak.

We next turn to a consideration of whether Kodak may be insulated from liability for its negligence in losing the four rolls of film by virtue of its limitation of liability printed on the film packages or on the receipt issued by Hoosier. At the time Carr purchased the film, the box contained an offer by Kodak to process the film under the stated conditions. At that time no contract existed between Carr and Kodak. When Carr submitted the film for processing, he in effect accepted the terms and conditions of Kodak's offer. We view the receipt issued by Hoosier as a reiteration of the offer by Kodak and a memorialization of the acceptance of the contract by the person submitting the film for processing. Hoosier was acting as the agent for Kodak in this regard.

* * * *Weaver v. American Oil Co.*, 276 N.E.2d 144 (Ind. App. 1971) held . . . an exculpatory clause in a lease limiting American Oil's liability to Weaver, the lessee, for damages caused by American Oil's negligent acts was unconscionable and hence void. We pointed out in that case the facts showed Weaver had only a year and a half of high school education, that he "was not one who should be expected to know the law or understand the meaning of technical terms," and "the evidence showed Weaver had never read the lease prior to signing and that the clauses in the lease were never explained to him in a manner from which he could grasp their legal significance." *Weaver, supra*, 276 N.E.2d at 146. We summarized our view in *Weaver*, 276 N.E.2d at 148, in the following language:

> When a party can show that the contract, which is sought to be enforced, was in fact an unconscionable one, due to a prodigious amount of bargaining power on behalf of the stronger party, which is used to the stronger party's advantage and unknown to the lesser party, causing a great hardship and risk on the lesser party, the contract provision, or the contract as a whole, if the provision is not separable, should not be enforceable on the grounds that the provision is contrary to public policy. The party seeking to enforce such a contract has the burden of showing that the provision was explained to the other party and came to his knowledge and there was in fact a real and voluntary meeting of the minds and not merely an objective meeting.

The language quoted above, and the facts of the *Weaver* case, show a prerequisite to finding a limitation of liability clause in a contract unconscionable and therefore void is a showing of disparity in bargaining power in favor of the party whose liability is thus limited. . . .

In the case at bar the stipulated facts foreclose a finding of disparate bargaining power between the parties or lack of knowledge or understanding of the liability clause by Carr. The facts show Carr is an experienced attorney who practices in the field of business law. He is hardly in a position comparable to that of the plaintiff in *Weaver, supra*. Moreover, it was stipulated he was aware of the limitation of liability on both the film packages and the receipts. We believe these crucial facts belie a finding of disparate bargaining power working to Carr's disadvantage.

Contrary to Carr's assertions, he was not in a "take it or leave it position" in that he had no choice but to accept the limitation of liability terms of the contract. As cross-appellants Hoosier and Kodak correctly point out, Carr and other photographers like him do have some choice in the matter of film processing. They can, for one, undertake to develop their film themselves. They can also go to independent film laboratories not a part of the Kodak Company. We do not see the availability of processing as limited to Kodak.

Nor can we agree with Carr's contention, focusing on . . . the necessity of assent to such a term. Carr contends "knowledge" or "notice" do not constitute "assent." However, where, as here, a knowledgeable party, aware that such terms are part of the proposed contract, enters into the contract without indicating any non-acquiescence to those terms, we must assume he has assented to those terms. . . .

In the case at bar, Carr's act of bringing the film to Hoosier and Kodak for processing, coupled with the awareness and understanding of the effect of the limitation of liability clause in the contracts, constitutes a manifestation of assent to those terms.

We hold the limitation of liability clauses operating in favor of Hoosier and Kodak were assented to by Carr; they were not unconscionable or void. Carr is, therefore, bound by such terms and is limited in his remedy to recovery of the cost of four boxes of unexposed Kodak Ektachrome-X 135 slide film. The Court of Appeals' opinion in this case is hereby vacated. The cause is remanded to the trial court with instructions to enter a judgment in favor of appellant, John R. Carr, Jr., in the amount of $13.60, plus interest.

NOTES

1. On a prepaid film mailer, the following statement appears: "Enclosed mailer entitles the user to processing and mounting of one 36 exposure roll of film size 135. Slides will be returned on 2x2 inch mounts." Would this statement change the result in *Carr*? See *Morgenstern v. Eastman Kodak Co.*, 569 F. Supp. 474, 476 (N.D. Ohio 1983). Would an indemnity agreement between a bailor and bailee (requiring the bailee to carry insurance for the bailed property) be subject to the same level of judicial scrutiny as the exculpatory provision in *Carr*? See *Buckey v. Indianhead Truck Line, Inc.*, 48 N.W.2d 534, 535 (Minn. 1951).

2. *Williams v. McMahan*, 2002 Wash. App. LEXIS 307 (Wash. App., Feb. 15, 2002), discusses the measure of damages in cases with facts similar to *Carr*, as follows, describing:

> three measures of damage, each alternative to the others. The first is to be used when the personal property in issue has a fair market value (in other words, when personal property of like kind is regularly bought and sold on the open market). It provides that a claimant can recover fair market value if the personal property was left without value after the tort (or, as is sometimes said, if the personal property was "completely destroyed"). It provides that a claimant can recover fair market value beforehand less fair market value afterward if the personal property was left with some value afterward (or, as is sometimes said, if the personal property was "damaged" or "partially destroyed"). The second measure is to be used if the personal property in issue lacks a fair market value but can be replaced or

restored to its former condition. It provides that a claimant can recover the cost to replace or reproduce if the personal property has been wholly lost or completely destroyed. It also provides that a claimant can recover the cost to restore or repair if the personal property has been damaged (i.e., partially but not completely destroyed). * * * The third measure is to be used when the personal property in issue has no fair market value and cannot be replaced or restored. It provides that a claimant can recover the property's value to him or her, exclusive of sentimental value.

The third measure (value to the owner) is sometimes referred to as "actual value." What are the components of such a measure? See *Cherry v. McCutchen*, 16 S.E.2d 167 (Ga. App. 1941), opinion after new trial, 23 S.E. 2d 587 (Ga. App. 1942). The second opinion in *Cherry* excluded sentimental value as a component. But see *Bond v. A.H. Belo Corp.*, 602 S.W.2d 105 (Tex. App. 1980), for a contrasting view. Which measure would apply to a pet with a fair market value? Compare *Hyland v. Borras*, 719 A.2d 662 (N.J. Super. Ct. 1998) (involving defendant's dog injuring plaintiff's dog, plaintiff incurring a $2,500 veterinary bill when his dog's fair market value was $500), with *Green v. Leckington*, 236 P.2d 335 (Or. 1951), noted at 55 Hastings L.J. 1009 (2004). Would the *Hyland* plaintiff recover $2,500? See generally *Anzalone v. Kragness*, 826 N.E.2d 472 (Ill. App. 2005).

3.   Consider the following section of the Uniform Commercial Code governing the liability of warehousemen:

§ 7-204. (2) Damages may be limited by a term in the warehouse receipt or storage agreement limiting the amount of liability in case of loss or damage, and setting forth a specific liability per article or item, or value per unit of weight, beyond which the warehouseman shall not be liable; provided however, that such liability may on written request of the bailor at the time of signing such storage agreement or within a reasonable time after receipt of the warehouse receipt be increased on part or all of the goods thereunder, in which event increased rates may be charged based on such increased valuation, but that no such increase shall be permitted contrary to a lawful limitation of liability contained in the warehouseman's tariff, if any. No such limitation is effective with respect to the warehouseman's liability for conversion to his own use.

Are warehousemen given more authority or latitude than Hoosier Photo is? For model receipts and limitations authorized by this section, see the annotations in Cal. Unif. Com. Code § 7204 (Deering 1996).

4.   A bailment requires the return to the bailor of the identical property or its byproduct. Thus, when logs are delivered to the sawmill, the fact that boards are to be returned does not prevent a bailment from arising. Similarly, when leather is to be made into shoes, grapes into wine, wheat into flour, etc., the rule is the same: When the product of the identical property is to be returned, a bailment may be found, even though the identical goods are not returned. When the purpose of the bailment is to alter or manufacture goods, and the bailee under contract for compensation is to work on the property delivered, there is a bailment *locatio operis faciendi*. Suppose the owner of a cider press agrees to deliver so many galleons of cider and after delivery has some applies left over. Does he get to keep the

leftovers? See *B.A. Ballou and Co. v. Citytrust*, 591 A.2d 126, 129–130 (Conn. 1991). In contrast to this type of bailment, under the doctrine of accession, when the labor of a person is combined with the property of another, so that either the identity of the property is destroyed, its nature is substantially altered, or its value is greatly increased, the owner loses ownership to the manufacturer, and retains only a cause of action for the value of the property lost. This doctrine is discussed in Section VII Accession, *infra*, this chapter.

Problem: C is a customer of B Bank. C rents a safe deposit box from B and stores currency and coins in the box. While B's burglary alarm was inoperative, the box's contents disappeared when most of the boxes in the bank were burglarized. C sues B for their value, and B produces the following signature card, signed by C: "In consideration of the undersigned customer's checking account, B Bank rents safety Deposit Box <u>7877</u> to <u>C</u> for one year beginning _____, the undersigned to hold bank harmless for loss of currency or coin left in the box." Is the card a defense to C's action?

A NOTE ON PAWNBROKERS

A pawn is a bailment of tangible personal property as security for the payment of a debt and in which the creditor also holds the property and has a power of sale on default. It is also known as a pledge of personalty, except that a pledge is also possible for intangible personalty — securities (stocks) and bonds, as well as commercial paper (personal and corporate notes). Pawnbroking is one of the oldest types of money-lending. The English common law (L. of England, ch. 24 1757) required that pawnbrokers record the identity of the personalty pledged, the amount loaned, the name and address of the pledgor, and a receipt for the pawn — and these requirements are reinforced by regulation in most states. Added to such regulations sometimes are others that require transaction reports to the police. *Newman v. Carson*, 280 So. 2d 426 (Fla. 1973).

How is the pawn structured? It is typically either (1) a purchase of the personalty with the pledgee promising to hold it for a specified period of time and the pledgor having the exclusive right to repurchase it within that time (the repurchase price is set at a higher amount than the original) or (2) a loan of money collateralized by a pledge of personalty, again for a specified period, with the pledgee having the right to sell it to third parties thereafter. In each of these two arrangements, the specific period of time is typically set by state regulation as a minimum period of time, say 30 or 60 days. Which of these arrangements do you think pawnbrokers prefer? A third arrangement, more controversial but used in some states, though prohibited by statute in still others, permits a title pledge or pawn of a title certificate to an automobile, or the pawn of a personal check.

[Handwritten margin notes: "• Intervivos — intent — delivery — acceptance"; "• Causa mortis — intent — delivery"; "— realistic apprehension of imminent death — personal property"; "acceptance"; "Can be revoked any time b4 death."]

VI.   GIFTS

FLOWER'S CASE
74 Eng. Rep. 1035 (K.B. 1587)

A borrowed one hundred pounds of B, and at the day brought it in a bag and cast it upon the table before B, and B said to A, being his nephew, I will not have it, take it you and carry it home again with you. And by the Court, that is a good gift by parol, being cast upon the table. For then it was in the possession of B, and A might well wage his law. By the Court, otherwise it had been, if A had only offered it to B, for then it was chose in action only, and could not be given without a writing.

IRONS v. SMALLPIECE
106 Eng. Rep. 467 (K.B. 1819)

[Handwritten: "Worst case"; "① fulfilled the requirement of the gift inter vivos b/c there was a"]

TROVER for two colts. Plea, not guilty.

The defendant was the executrix and residuary legatee of the plaintiff's father, and the plaintiff claimed the colts, under the verbal gift made to him by the testator twelve months before his death. The colts however continued to remain in possession of the father until his death. It appeared further that about six months before the father's death, the son having been to a neighboring market for the purpose of purchasing hay for the colts, and finding the price of that article very high, mentioned the circumstance to his father; and that the latter agreed to furnish the colts any hay they might want at a stipulated price, to be paid by the son. None however was furnished to them till within three or four days before the testator's death. Upon these facts, Abbott, C.J., was of opinion, that the possession of the colts never having been delivered to the plaintiff, the property therein had not vested in him by the gift; but that it continued in the testator at the time of his death, and consequently that it passed to his executrix under the will; and the plaintiff was therefore non-suited.

ABBOTT, C.J.

I am of opinion that by the law of England, in order to transfer property by gift there must either be a deed or instrument of gift, or there must be an actual delivery of the thing to the donee. Here the gift is merely verbal, and differs from a *donatio mortis causa* only in this respect, that the latter is subject to a condition, that if the donor live the thing shall be restored to him. Now it is a well established rule of law, that a *donatio mortis causa* does not transfer the property without an actual delivery. The possession must be transferred, in point of fact; and the late case of *Bunn v. Markham*, 2 Marsh. 532, where all the former authorities were considered, is a very strong authority upon that subject. There Sir G. Clifton had written upon the parcels containing the property the names of the parties for whom they were intended, and had requested his natural son to see the property delivered to the donees. It was therefore manifestly his intention that the property should pass to the donees; yet as there as no actual delivery, the Court of Common Pleas held that it was not a valid gift. I cannot distinguish that case from the present, and therefore think that this property in the colts did not pass to the son by the verbal gift; and I cannot agree that the son can be charged with the hay which was provided for these colts three or four days before the father's death; for I cannot think that that tardy supply can be referred to the contract which was made so many months before.

HOLROYD, J.

I am also of the same opinion. In order to change the property by a gift of this description, there must be a change of possession: here there has been no change of possession. If indeed it could be made out that the son was chargeable for the hay provided for the colts, then the possession of the father might be considered as the possession of the son. Here however no hay is delivered during a long interval from the time of the contract, until within a few days of the father's death; and I cannot think that the hay so delivered is to be considered as delivered in execution of that contact made so long before, and consequently the son is not chargeable of the price of it.

NOTES

1. A donee, once in possession, need not afterwards be in continuous possession. A donee might establish a bailment of the gift with the donor as a bailee. A donee's possession may also be constructive, as when the donor delivers the gift to a third party to hold for the donee. For a case similar to *Irons*, see *Whatley v. Mitchell*, 100 S.E. 229 (Ga. Ct. App. 1919) (validating a grandfather's gift of a heifer to a grandchild although the animal did not thereafter leave the grandfather's possession: delivery is essential, but actual manual delivery is not required), discussed in Harlan Fiske Stone, *Delivery in Gifts of Personal Property*, 20 Colum. L. Rev. 196 (1920). The rule of *Irons* was reaffirmed in *Cochrane v. Moore*, 25 Q.B.D. 57 (Q.B. 1890).

2. The opinion refers to a gift *causa mortis*. This is a gift of personalty with some distinctive, well-settled elements. "First, there must be an intent to make a gift. Second, the gift must be of personal property. Third, the gift must be made while the donor is under the apprehension of imminent death, upon the essential condition that the property shall belong to the donee if the donor dies as anticipated leaving the donee surviving, and the gift is not revoked in the meantime. Fourth, possession of the property given must be delivered at the time of the gift to the donee, or to someone for the donee, and the donee must accept the gift. . . ." *Woo v. Smart*, 442 S.E.2d 690 (Va. 1994) (adopting the majority rule and holding "that a donor's own check drawn on a personal checking account is not, prior to acceptance or payment by the bank" delivered because the check is neither money nor an assignment of funds on account) and *Coley v. Walker*, 680 So. 2d 352 (Ala. Civ. App. 1996) (holding that a gift made just before surgery was in "immediate apprehension of death"). The recovery of the donor from the anticipated cause in some states is an automatic revocation of the gift. In other states, revocation is not automatic: the donor may elect to revoke the gift when he recovers. A grave physical illness is the typical precondition to finding that a gift *causa mortis* has been made, but, with some older cases to the contrary, there is authority that a mental illness, resulting in suicidal feelings induced by a terminal illness, may also be a basis for such a gift.

[handwritten at top: Ownership of property can be divided by force.]

Compare *In re Estate of Smith*, 694 A.2d 1099 (Pa. Super. Ct. 1997), and *Scherer v. Hyland*, 380 A.2d 698 (N.J. 1977) (both validating gifts from a person subsequently committing suicide), with *Pikeville Nat'l Bank & Trust Co. v. Shirley*, 135 S.W.2d 426 (Ky. 1939) (invalidating such a gift). May a gift *causa mortis* be revoked by the donor's will? See *Nicholas v. Adams*, 2 Wharton 17 (Pa. 1836). If it can only be revoked during the life of the donor, the latter's death by definition ends the power to revoke, and the gift is valid just before the will is effective at the donor's death. This sequence of legal events denies the will its evidentiary value to show the donor's intent (to revoke). There is, however, a tension between the doctrine of gifts *causa mortis* and the Statute of Wills. That Statute (and the state probate codes enacted subsequently on the same subject) require a written instrument indicating a person's testamentary intent, signed by the testator and by witnesses. Finally, courts generally require that a gift *causa mortis* be shown by the donee with clear and convincing evidence.

[handwritten margin: Condition subsequent indicates present intent.]

3. "By the rules of the ancient common law, there could be no future property, to take place in expectancy, created in personal goods and chattels; because, being things transitory, and by many accidents subject to be lost, destroyed, or otherwise impaired, and the exigencies of trade requiring also a frequent circulation thereof, it would occasion perpetual suits and quarrels, and put a stop to the freedom of commerce, if such limitations in remainder were *generally* tolerated and allowed. But yet in last wills and testaments such limitations of personal goods and chattels, in remainder after a bequest for life, were permitted. . . . * * * But now . . . if a man either by deed or will limits his books or furniture to A for life, with remainder over to B, this remainder is good. But, where an estate-tail in things personal is given to the first or any subsequent possessor, it vests in him the total property, and no remainder over shall be permitted on such a limitation. For this, if allowed, would tend to a perpetuity . . . and therefore the law vests in him at once the entire dominion of the goods, being analogous to the fee-simple which a tenant in tail may acquire in a real estate." William Blackstone, 2 Commentaries on the Laws of England 398 (1st ed. 1766, reprinted by U. Chi. Press 1979).

[handwritten: Issue: did Dad intend to transfer any present interest when he sent the letter or did he mean it only after death.]

GRUEN v. GRUEN
496 N.E.2d 869 (N.Y. 1986)

SIMONS, J.

[handwritten: Dad has a present intention to transfer a future interest.]

Plaintiff commenced this action seeking a declaration that he is the rightful owner of a painting which he alleges his father, now deceased, gave to him. He concedes that he has never had possession of the painting but asserts that his father made a valid gift of the title in 1963 reserving a life estate for himself. His father retained possession of the painting until he died in 1980. Defendant, plaintiff's stepmother, has the painting now and has refused plaintiff's requests that she turn it over to him. She contends that the purported gift was testamentary in nature and invalid insofar as the formalities of a will were not met or, alternatively, that a donor may not make a valid inter vivos gift of a chattel and retain a life estate with a complete right of possession. Following a seven-day nonjury trial, Special Term found that plaintiff had failed to establish any of the elements of an inter vivos gift

[handwritten margin: Court says there was also symbolic delivery.]

and that in any event an attempt by a donor to retain a present possessory life estate in a chattel invalidated a purported gift of it. The Appellate Division held that a valid gift may be made reserving a life estate and, finding the elements of a gift established in this case, it reversed and remitted the matter for a determination of value. That determination has now been made and defendant appeals directly to this court . . . from the subsequent final judgment entered in Supreme Court awarding plaintiff $2,500,000 in damages representing the value of the painting, plus interest. We now affirm.

The subject of the dispute is a work entitled "Schloss Kammer am Attersee II" painted by a noted Austrian modernist, Gustav Klimt. It was purchased by plaintiff's father, Victor Gruen, in 1959 for $8,000. On April 1, 1963 the elder Gruen, a successful architect with offices and residences in both New York City and Los Angeles during most of the time involved in this action, wrote a letter to plaintiff, then an undergraduate student at Harvard, stating that he was giving him the Klimt painting for his birthday but that he wished to retain the possession of it for his lifetime. This letter is not in evidence, apparently because plaintiff destroyed it on instructions from his father. Two other letters were received, however, one dated May 22, 1963 and the other April 1, 1963. Both had been dictated by Victor Gruen and sent together to plaintiff on or about May 22, 1963. The letter dated May 22, 1963 reads as follows:

Dear Michael: I wrote you at the time of your birthday about the gift of the painting by Klimt. Now my lawyer tells me that because of the existing tax laws, it was wrong to mention in that letter that I want to use the painting as long as I live. Though I still want to use it, this should not appear in the letter. I am enclosing, therefore, a new letter and I ask you to send the old one back to me so that it can be destroyed.

I know this is all very silly, but the lawyer and our accountant insist that they must have in their possession copies of a letter which will serve the purpose of making it possible for you, once I die, to get this picture without having to pay inheritance taxes on it. Love, s/Victor.

Enclosed with this letter was a substitute gift letter, dated April 1, 1963, which stated:

Dear Michael: The 21st birthday, being an important event in life, should be celebrated accordingly. I therefore wish to give you as a present the oil painting by Gustav Klimt of Schloss Kammer which now hangs in the New York living room. You know that Lazette and I bought it some 5 or 6 years ago, and you always told us how much you liked it. Happy birthday again. Love, s/Victor.

Plaintiff never took possession of the painting nor did he seek to do so. Except for a brief period between 1964 and 1965 when it was on loan to art exhibits and when restoration work was performed on it, the painting remained in his father's possession, moving with him from New York City to Beverly Hills and finally to Vienna, Austria, where Victor Gruen died on February 14, 1980. Following Victor's death plaintiff requested possession of the Klimt painting and when defendant refused, he commenced this action.

[handwritten note in top margin: inter vivos: referring to the transfer of property by agreement b/w living persons and not by a gift through a will]

The issues framed for appeal are whether a valid inter vivos gift of a chattel may be made where the donor has reserved a life estate in the chattel and the donee never has had physical possession of it before the donor's death and, if it may, which factual findings on the elements of a valid inter vivos gift more nearly comport with the weight of the evidence in this case, those of Special Term or those of the Appellate Division. Resolution of the latter issue requires application of two general rules. First, to make a valid inter vivos gift there must exist the intent on the part of the donor to make a present transfer; delivery of the gift, either actual or constructive to the donee; and acceptance by the donee (*Matter of Szabo*, 10 NY2d 94, 98). Second, the proponent of a gift has the burden of proving each of these elements by clear and convincing evidence.

There is an important distinction between the intent with which an inter vivos gift is made and the intent to make a gift by will. An inter vivos gift requires that the donor intend to make an irrevocable present transfer of ownership; if the intention is to make a testamentary disposition effective only after death, the gift is invalid unless made by will.

Defendant contends that the trial court was correct in finding that Victor did not intend to transfer any present interest in the painting to plaintiff in 1963 but only expressed an intention that plaintiff was to get the painting upon his death. The evidence is all but conclusive, however, that Victor intended to transfer ownership of the painting to plaintiff in 1963 but to retain a life estate in it and that he did, therefore, effectively transfer a remainder interest in the painting to plaintiff at that time. Although the original letter was not in evidence, testimony of its contents was received along with the substitute gift letter and its covering letter dated May 22, 1963. The three letters should be considered together as a single instrument and when they are they unambiguously establish that Victor Gruen intended to make a present gift of title to the painting at that time. But there was other evidence for after 1963 Victor made several statements orally and in writing indicating that he had previously given plaintiff the painting and that plaintiff owned it. Victor Gruen retained possession of the property, insured it, allowed others to exhibit it and made necessary repairs to it but those acts are not inconsistent with his retention of a life estate. Furthermore, whatever probative value could be attached to his statement that he had bequeathed the painting to his heirs, made 16 years later when he prepared an export license application so that he could take the painting out of Austria, is negated by the overwhelming evidence that he intended a present transfer of title in 1963. Victor's failure to file a gift tax return on the transaction was partially explained by allegedly erroneous legal advice he received, and while that omission sometimes may indicate that the donor had no intention of making a present gift, it does not necessarily do so and it is not dispositive in this case.

Defendant contends that even if a present gift was intended, Victor's reservation of a lifetime interest in the painting defeated it. She relies on a statement from *Young v. Young* (80 NY 422) that "[any] gift of chattels which expressly reserves the use of the property to the donor for a certain period, or . . . as long as the donor shall live, is ineffectual" (*id.*, at 436). The statement was dictum, however, and the holding of the court was limited to a determination that an attempted gift of bonds in which the donor reserved the interest for life failed because there had been no delivery of the gift, either actual or constructive (see also *Speelman v. Pascal*, 10

NY2d 313, 319–320). The court expressly left undecided the question "whether a remainder in a chattel may be created and given by a donor by carving out a life estate for himself and transferring the remainder" (*Young v. Young, supra*, at 440). We answered part of that question in *Matter of Brandreth* (169 NY 437, 441–442, *supra*) when we held that "[in] this state a life estate and remainder can be created in a chattel or a fund the same as in real property." The case did not require us to decide whether there could be a valid gift of the remainder.

Defendant recognizes that a valid inter vivos gift of a remainder interest can be made not only of real property but also of such intangibles as stocks and bonds. Indeed, several of the cases she cites so hold. That being so, it is difficult to perceive any legal basis for the distinction she urges which would permit gifts of remainder interests in those properties but not of remainder interests in chattels such as the Klimt painting here. The only reason suggested is that the gift of a chattel must include a present right to possession. The application of Brandreth to permit a gift of the remainder in this case, however, is consistent with the distinction, well recognized in the law of gifts as well as in real property law, between ownership and possession or enjoyment (see, *Speelman v. Pascal*, 10 NY2d 313, 318). Insofar as some of our cases purport to require that the donor intend to transfer both title and possession immediately to have a valid inter vivos gift, they state the rule too broadly and confuse the effectiveness of a gift with the transfer of the possession of the subject of that gift. The correct test is " 'whether the maker intended the [gift] to have no effect until after the maker's death, or whether he intended it to transfer some present interest' " (*McCarthy v. Pieret*, 281 NY 407, 409). As long as the evidence establishes an intent to make a present and irrevocable transfer of title or the right of ownership, there is a present transfer of some interest and the gift is effective immediately (Brown, *Personal Property* § 48, at 133–136 [2d ed.]). Thus, in *Speelman v. Pascal* (*supra*), we held valid a gift of a percentage of the future royalties to the play "My Fair Lady" before the play even existed. There, as in this case, the donee received title or the right of ownership to some property immediately upon the making of the gift but possession or enjoyment of the subject of the gift was postponed to some future time.

Defendant suggests that allowing a donor to make a present gift of a remainder with the reservation of a life estate will lead courts to effectuate otherwise invalid testamentary dispositions of property. The two have entirely different characteristics, however, which make them distinguishable. Once the gift is made it is irrevocable and the donor is limited to the rights of a life tenant not an owner. Moreover, with the gift of a remainder title vests immediately in the donee and any possession is postponed until the donor's death whereas under a will neither title nor possession vests immediately. Finally, the postponement of enjoyment of the gift is produced by the express terms of the gift not by the nature of the instrument as it is with a will.

In order to have a valid inter vivos gift, there must be a delivery of the gift, either by a physical delivery of the subject of the gift or a constructive or symbolic delivery such as by an instrument of gift, sufficient to divest the donor of dominion and control over the property (see, *Matter of Szabo*, 10 NY2d 94, 98–99, *supra*; *Speelman v. Pascal*, 10 NY2d 313, 318–320, *supra*; *Matter of Cohn*, 187 App Div 392, 395). As the statement of the rule suggests, the requirement of delivery is not rigid or inflexible, but is to be applied in light of its purpose to avoid mistakes by donors and fraudulent claims by donees (see *Matter of Cohn, supra*, at 395–396). Accordingly, what is sufficient to constitute delivery "must be tailored to suit the circumstances of the case" *(Matter of Szabo, supra*, at 98). The rule requires that " '[the] delivery necessary to consummate a gift must be as perfect as the nature of the property and the circumstances and surroundings of the parties will reasonably permit' " *(id.)*.

Defendant contends that when a tangible piece of personal property such as a painting is the subject of a gift, physical delivery of the painting itself is the best form of delivery and should be required. Here, of course, we have only delivery of Victor Gruen's letters which serve as instruments of gift. Defendant's statement of the rule as applied may be generally true, but it ignores the fact that what Victor Gruen gave plaintiff was not all rights to the Klimt painting, but only title to it with no right of possession until his death. Under these circumstances, it would be illogical for the law to require the donor to part with possession of the painting when that is exactly what he intends to retain.

Nor is there any reason to require a donor making a gift of a remainder interest in a chattel to physically deliver the chattel into the donee's hands only to have the donee redeliver it to the donor. As the facts of this case demonstrate, such a requirement could impose practical burdens on the parties to the gift while serving the delivery requirement poorly. Thus, in order to accomplish this type of delivery the parties would have been required to travel to New York for the symbolic transfer and redelivery of the Klimt painting which was hanging on the wall of Victor Gruen's Manhattan apartment. Defendant suggests that such a requirement would be stronger evidence of a completed gift, but in the absence of witnesses to the event or any written confirmation of the gift it would provide less protection against fraudulent claims than have the written instruments of gift delivered in this case.

Acceptance by the donee is essential to the validity of an inter vivos gift, but when a gift is of value to the donee, as it is here, the law will presume an acceptance on his part. Plaintiff did not rely on this presumption alone but also presented clear and convincing proof of his acceptance of a remainder interest in the Klimt painting by evidence that he had made several contemporaneous statements acknowledging the gift to his friends and associates, even showing some of them his father's gift letter, and that he had retained both letters for over 17 years to verify the gift after his father died. Defendant relied exclusively on affidavits filed by plaintiff in a matrimonial action with his former wife, in which plaintiff failed to list his interest in the painting as an asset. These affidavits were made over 10 years after acceptance was complete. . . .

Accordingly, the judgment appealed from and the order of the Appellate Division brought up for review should be affirmed, with costs.

NOTES

1. To make a gift effective, there must be a present intent to transfer the chattel, delivery of the chattel, and acceptance of that delivery. Absent consideration, a promise to make a gift in the future is unenforceable. See *Lewis v. Poduska*, 481 N.W.2d 898, 904 (Neb. 1992) (holding that when the gift is absolute, the postponement of its enjoyment until the donor's death will not invalidate it); Phillip Mechem, *The Requirement of Delivery in Gifts of Chattels and of Choses in Action Evidenced by Commercial Instruments*, 21 U. Ill. L. Rev. 341 (1926); Ray Brown, Personal Property 154 (Walter Rauschenbush ed., 3d ed. 1975). If avoiding or minimizing inheritance taxes was the issue for Victor, what do you think was wrong with the first letter? See I.R.C., § 2036(a); and compare *Estate of D'Ambrosio v. C.I.R.*, 101 F.3d 309 (3d Cir. 1996), with *United States v. Allen*, 293 F.2d 916 (10th Cir. 1961). Would you have advised Victor Gruen to destroy his first letter (the one not in evidence) to Michael? See Model Rules of Professional Conduct Rule 3.04(a). What if Victor, in his second letter, had reserved the right to revoke the gift? Would it still have been effective?

2. Some deliveries involve more than a transfer to the donee, but instead involve third parties, acting either as an agent for the donor or as a trustee for the donee. Many such cases involve the gift of corporate shares. See *In the Matter of the Estate of Szabo*, 176 N.E.2d 395 (N.Y. 1961). A delivery of shares will at inception be a symbolic delivery (often an endorsement on the share certificate). Endorsement evidences intent, but even this type of delivery must reach a point where the donor cannot recall it. For shares, that point is a transfer of ownership in the corporate books. Up to that point, the donor may have a change of mind and withdraw the directive to the corporate transfer agent to put the donee's name in place of his own. Since the agent acts at the donor's directive, the donor's death normally revokes the agency. See also *Young v. Young*, 393 S.E.2d 398 (Va. 1990). If the donee's name is put on the corporate books, but the returned certificate is retained by the donor in his safe, the delivery is once again in doubt. See *Malek v. Patten*, 678 P.2d 201 (Mont. 1984). Suppose that the donee has access to the box, but never used it. Suppose the donor gave the donee the safe's combination, but when the donee open the safe, the shares were found elsewhere. See *Teague v. Abbott*, 100 N.E. 27 (Ind. App. 1912). In other situations, when the alleged donor and donee jointly establish a bank account, the issue of delivery turns on the use made of the funds on account. See *In the Matter of Bobeck*, 531 N.Y.S.2d 340 (N.Y. App. Div. 1988).

3. A father wishes to make a gift of a heavy antique cabinet to his visiting daughter. In her presence, he points to it on Christmas morning and says to her, "This is yours; we'll empty it and you can take it away when you can." Is the gift effective at this point? If months later, they empty it of its contents, and the daughter takes it away, only to discover an old, but negotiable bond taped to the bottom of a drawer, who owns that bond?

4. John gives Jane a ring as a symbol of their engagement. The ring has a market value of $10,000. John went house hunting, but when Jane refused to sign the mortgage loan documents for the house that John found, John broke the engagement and asked for the ring back. Jane refused. John sues Jane in replevin to recover its possession. What result and why? See *Fowler v. Perry*, 830 N.E.2d 97

(Ind. App. 2005); *Fierro v. Hoel*, 465 N.W.2d 669 (Iowa 1990). Should it matter who broke off the engagement? What if John died during the engagement? What if, after John broke off the engagement, Jane in a fury threw the ring off a bridge and into a river. Would she liable for its value to John in trover?

VII.   SALES AND BONA FIDE PURCHASERS

No person may sell or transfer a better title to a chattel than she has. Many courts repeat and use this rule. One implication of it is that someone who has no right to the chattel (such as a thief) may transfer none, even though the transferee pays a reasonable price and has no reason to believe that the transferor is not the chattel's owner. Beyond this implication, courts sometimes depart substantially from it, and statutes also limit its scope.

Large markets for goods and various types of documents — markets in which the transferor and transferee are not likely to have personal knowledge of each other — require that purchasers (who must also be attracted in volume) be protected against third-party claims. Drafted in the 1950s and adopted in every state except Louisiana, the Uniform Commercial Code (UCC), art. 2, is one response to the needs of many such markets. UCC § 2-403 states:

> (1) A purchaser of goods acquires all title which his transferor had or had power to transfer except that a purchaser of a limited interest acquires rights only to the extent of the interest purchased. A person with voidable title has power to transfer a good title to a good faith purchaser for value. When goods have been delivered under a transaction of purchase the purchaser has such power even though (a) the transferor was deceived as to the identity of the purchaser, or (b) the delivery was in exchange for a check which is later dishonored, or (c) it was agreed that the transaction was to be a "cash sale", or (d) the delivery was procured through fraud punishable as larcenous under the criminal law.

> (2) Any entrusting of possession of goods to a merchant who deals in goods of that kind gives him power to transfer all rights of the entruster to a buyer in ordinary course of business.

> (3) "Entrusting" includes any delivery and acquiescence in retention of possession regardless of any condition expressed between the parties to the delivery or acquiescence and regardless of whether the procurement of the entrusting or the possessor's disposition of the goods have been such as to be larcenous under the criminal law.

> (4) The rights of other purchasers of goods and of lien creditors are governed by [separate codes of rules for Secured Transactions (Article 9), Bulk Transfers (Article 6) and Documents of Title (Article 7)-ed.].

For further discussions of § 2-403, see *Kenyon v. Abel*, 36 P.3d 1161 (Wyo. 2001), and *Tempur-Pedic Internat'l v. Waste to Charity*, 2008 U.S. Dist. LEXIS 8866 (W.D. Ark., Feb. 6, 2008); for a discussion of its common law origins, see *Provident Bank v. Tri-County Southside Asphalt, Inc.*, 804 N.E.2d 161, 165 (Ind. App. 2004):

The famous case of *Phelps v. McQuade*, 115 N.E. 441 (N.Y. 1917), was the genesis of Uniform Commercial Code section 2-403. In *Phelps*, Gwynne falsely represented himself to a jewel vendor and obtained jewelry on credit from Phelps. Gwynne then sold the jewelry to McQuade. Phelps filed a claim for replevin of the jewelry, arguing that under common law title did not pass to McQuade. The *Phelps* court, however, noted that it was the "intention of the person having title to the goods and delivering them to another" that determined whether good title then passed to a purchaser for value. *Id.* at 442. Thus, the *Phelps* court held that Phelps had to bear the economic loss due to Gwynne's false representation because Phelps had dealt directly with Gwynne.

The Uniform Commercial Code drafters incorporated the sound policy behind the result in *Phelps*. The drafters noted that U.C.C. section 2-403 was "predicated on the policy that where a transferor has voluntarily delivered the goods to a purchaser, he, the transferor, ought to run the risk of the purchaser's fraud as against innocent third parties." U.C.C. § 2-403, comment 4 (2002). The policy is just inasmuch as he who deals directly with a person is in the best position to prevent a financial injury.

MIDWAY AUTO SALES, INC. v. CLARKSON
29 S.W.3d 788 (Ark. App. 2000)

Robbins, C.J.

* * * Midway argues that Clarkson [the vendor of a car sold to Midway after its purchase from Bowen, who bought it from Haddock who had purchased the car with an "open title" from a person in Oklahoma and had paid with a computer generated check on a non-existent bank account. — Eds.] breached his warranty of title because the Corvette was confiscated as a stolen vehicle by the sheriff. According to Ark. Code Ann. § 4-2-312 (1)(a), in a contract for sale, there is a warranty by the seller that the title conveyed is good and its transfer rightful. See *Smith v. Russ*, 13 S.W.3d 920 (Ark. App. 2000). Clarkson relies on Ark. Code Ann. § 4-2-403, which recognizes the legal distinction between a sale of stolen goods and a sale of goods procured through fraud. Absent exigent circumstances, one who purchases from a thief acquires no title as against the true owner. *Eureka Springs Sales Co. v. Ward*, 290 S.W.2d 434 (Ark. 1956). However, under section 4-2-403, the result is different when property obtained by fraud is conveyed to a bona fide purchaser: "(1) * * * A person with voidable title has power to transfer a good title to a good faith purchaser for value. When goods have been delivered under a transaction of purchase the purchaser has such power even though:. . . . (b) The delivery was in exchange for a check which is later dishonored; or. . . . (d) The delivery was procured through fraud punishable as larcenous under the criminal law." This section of the Uniform Commercial Code has been explained as follows:

> Under 2-403, voidable title should be distinguished from void title. A thief, for example, "gets" only void title and without more cannot pass any title to a good faith purchaser. "Voidable title" is a murky concept. The Code does not define the phrase. The comments do not even discuss it. Subsections

(1)(a)–(d) of 2-403 clarify the law as to particular transactions which were "troublesome under prior law." Beyond these, we must look to non-Code state law. In general voidable title passes to those who lie in the middle of the spectrum that runs from best faith buyer at one end to robber at the other. These are buyers who commit fraud, or are otherwise guilty of naughty acts (bounced checks), but who conform to the appearance of a voluntary transaction; they would never pull a gun or crawl in through a second story window. Presumably these fraudulent buyers get voidable title from their targets, but second story men get only void title because the targets of fraud are themselves more culpable than the targets of burglary. * * * Subsection (1)(b) of 2-403 deals with a more common occurrence: the "rubber check." Even when Bert Buyer pays Sam Seller with a check that returns to Sam marked "NSF," a good faith purchaser from Bert takes good title. * * * Subsection (1)(d) of 2-403 provides that even where delivery was procured through criminal fraud, voidable title passes. Thus if Bert acquired goods from Sam with a forged check, a good faith purchaser from Bert would obtain good title.

James White & Robert Summers, Uniform Commercial Code 187–89 (4th ed. 1995).

In his letter opinion, the circuit judge relied on *Pingleton v. Shepherd*, 242 S.W.2d 971 (Ark. 1951), decided before the Uniform Commercial Code was enacted. There, it was held that the appellee, who had purchased an automobile in good faith from an individual who had given the appellant a worthless check, had good title. In so holding, the court relied upon a provision of the Uniform Sales Act . . . , which stated: "Where the seller of goods has a voidable title thereto, but his title has not been avoided at the time of the sale, the buyer acquires a good title to the goods, provided he buys them in good faith, for value, and without notice of the seller's defect of title." The court held that a fraudulent purchase of personal property accompanied with delivery is not void, but only voidable at the election of the seller; until it is avoided by the seller, the buyer has power to make a valid sale of the goods to a bona fide purchaser who has no notice of the fraud.

Section 4-2-403 is consistent with the court's decision in *Pingleton v. Shepherd*. Therefore, it follows that: (1) Mr. Haddock obtained a voidable title from the original seller, with whom he entered into a voluntary transaction of purchase; (2) until the sale was avoided by the original seller, Mr. Haddock had the power to transfer good title to a good-faith purchaser; (3) if Mr. Bowen was a good-faith purchaser, he had good title to convey to Clarkson, who would have conveyed good title to Midway; and, (4) if the title Clarkson conveyed to Midway was good, the warranty of title was not breached. Therefore, the issue is whether Mr. Bowen and Mr. Clarkson were good-faith purchasers. "Good faith" is defined at Ark. Code Ann. § 4-1-201(19) as "honesty in fact in the conduct or transaction concerned." Generally speaking, whether a party has acted in good faith in a commercial transaction is a question of fact. *Adams v. First State Bank*, 778 S.W.2d 611 (Ark. 1989). * * * Mr. Bowen testified that, before consummating his purchase, he contacted the Oklahoma licensing agency and was informed that the Corvette's title was good. Mr. Clarkson testified that Mr. Bowen related this information to him. * * * Midway now makes much of the fact that neither . . . registered the vehicle; however, it has provided no citation to authority holding that this failure will prevent one's buyer from acquiring good faith purchaser status. We hold . . . that Mr. Clarkson and Mr. Bowen were good faith purchasers. Accordingly, Clarkson did not breach the warranty of title. Affirmed.

NOTE

For a case involving an automobile title holding that the assignee of the title was not a bona fide purchaser, see *Landshire Food Service, Inc. v. Coghill*, 709 S.W.2d 509 (Mo. Ct. App. 1986).

PORTER v. WERTZ
416 N.Y.S.2d 254 (N.Y. App. Div. 1979)

BIRNS, J.

Plaintiffs-appellants, Samuel Porter and Express Packaging, Inc. (Porter's corporation), owners of a Maurice Utrillo painting entitled "Chateau de Lion-sur-Mer," seek in this action to recover possession of the painting or the value thereof from defendants, participants in a series of transactions which resulted in the shipment of the painting out of the country. The painting is now in Venezuela.

Defendants-respondents Richard Feigen Gallery, Inc., Richard L. Feigen & Co., Inc., and Richard L. Feigen, hereinafter collectively referred to as Feigen, were in the business of buying and selling paintings, drawings and sculpture.

The amended answer to the complaint asserted, inter alia, affirmative defenses of statutory estoppel (Uniform Commercial Code, § 2-403) and equitable estoppel. The trial court, after a bench trial, found statutory estoppel inapplicable but sustained the defense of equitable estoppel and dismissed the complaint. On this appeal, we will consider whether those defenses, or either of them, bar recovery against Feigen. We hold neither prevents recovery.

Porter, the owner of a collection of art works, bought the Utrillo in 1969. During 1972 and 1973 he had a number of art transactions with one Harold Von Maker who used, among other names, that of Peter Wertz. One of the transactions was the sale by Porter to Von Maker in the spring of 1973 of a painting by Childe Hassam for $150,000, financed with a $50,000 deposit and 10 notes for $10,000 each. At about that time, Von Maker expressed an interest in the Utrillo. Porter permitted him to have it temporarily with the understanding that Von Maker would hang it in his (Von Maker's) home, pending Von Maker's decision whether to buy the painting. On a visit to Von Maker's home in Westchester in May, 1973, Porter saw the painting hanging there. In June, 1973, lacking a decision from Von Maker, Porter sought its return, but was unable to reach Von Maker.

The first note in connection with Von Maker's purchase of the Childe Hassam, due early July, 1973, was returned dishonored, as was the balance of the notes. Porter commenced an investigation and found that he had not been dealing with Peter Wertz — but with another man named Von Maker. Bishop reports, dated July 10 and July 17, 1973, disclosed that Von Maker was subject to judgments, that he had been sued many times, that he had an arrest record for possession of obscene literature, and for "false pretenses," as well as for "theft of checks," and had been convicted, among other crimes, of transmitting a forged cable in connection with a scheme to defraud the Chase Manhattan Bank and had been placed on probation for three years. Porter notified the FBI about his business transactions concerning the notes. He did not report that Von Maker had defrauded him of any painting, for, as will be shown, Porter did not know at this time that Von Maker had disposed of the Utrillo.

Porter did, however, have his attorney communicate with Von Maker's attorney. As a result, on August 13, 1973, a detailed agreement, drawn by the attorneys for Porter and Von Maker, the latter still using the name Peter Wertz, was executed. Under this agreement the obligations of Von Maker to Porter concerning several paintings delivered by Porter to Von Maker (one of which was the Utrillo) were covered. In paragraph 11, Von Maker acknowledged that he had received the Utrillo from Porter together with a certain book on Utrillo, that both "belong to [Porter]", that the painting was on consignment with a client of Von Maker's, that within 90 days Von Maker would either return the painting and book or pay $30,000 therefor, and that other than the option to purchase within said 90-day period, Von Maker had "no claim whatsoever to the Utrillo painting or Book."

Paragraph 13 provided that in the event Von Maker failed to meet the obligations under paragraph 11, i.e., return the Utrillo and book within 90 days or pay for them, Porter would immediately be entitled to obtain possession of a painting by Cranach held in escrow by Von Maker's attorney, and have the right to sell that painting, apply the proceeds to the amount owing by Von Maker under paragraph 11, and Von Maker would pay any deficiency. Paragraph 13 provided further that "[the] above is in addition to all [Porter's] other rights and remedies, which [Porter] expressly reserved to enforce the performance of [Von Maker's] obligations under this Agreement."

We note that the agreement did not state that receipt of the Cranach by Porter would be in full satisfaction of Porter's claim to the Utrillo and book. Title to the Utrillo and book remained in Porter, absent any payment by Von Maker of the agreed purchase price of $30,000. Indeed, no payment for the Utrillo was ever made by Von Maker.

At the very time that Von Maker was deceitfully assuring Porter he would return the Utrillo and book or pay $30,000, Von Maker had already disposed of this painting by using the real Peter Wertz to effect its sale for $20,000 to Feigen. Von Maker, utilizing Sloan and Lipinsky, persons in the art world, had made the availability of the Utrillo known to Feigen. When Wertz, at Von Maker's direction, appeared at the Feigen gallery with the Utrillo, he was met by Feigen's employee, Mrs. Drew-Bear. She found a buyer for the Utrillo in defendant Brenner. In effecting its transfer to him, Feigen made a commission. Through a sale by Brenner the painting is now in Venezuela.

We agree with the conclusion of the trial court that statutory estoppel does not bar recovery. The provisions of statutory estoppel are found in § 2-403 of the Uniform Commercial Code. Subdivision (2) thereof provides that "[any] entrusting of possession of goods to a merchant who deals in goods of that kind gives him power to transfer all rights of the entruster to a buyer in the ordinary course of business." Subdivision (9) of § 1-201 of the UCC defines a "buyer in the ordinary course of business" as "a person who in good faith and without knowledge that the sale to him is in violation of the ownership rights or security interest of a third party in the goods buys in ordinary course from a person in the business of selling goods of that kind."

In order to determine whether the defense of statutory estoppel is available to Feigen, we must begin by ascertaining whether Feigen fits the definition of "a buyer in the ordinary course of business". (UCC, § 1-201, subd [9].) Feigen does not fit that definition, for two reasons. First, Wertz, from whom Feigen bought the Utrillo, was not an art dealer — he was not "a person in the business of selling goods of that kind". (UCC, § 1-201, subd [9].) If anything, he was a delicatessen employee.[6] Wertz never held himself out as a dealer. Although Feigen testified at trial that before he (Feigen) purchased the Utrillo from Wertz, Sloan, who introduced Wertz to Feigen told him (Feigen) that Wertz was an art dealer, this testimony was questionable. It conflicted with Feigen's testimony at his examination before trial where he stated he did not recall whether Sloan said that to him. Second, Feigen was not "a person . . . in good faith" (UCC, § 1-201, subd [9]) in the transaction with Wertz. Section 2-103 (subd [1], par [b]) of the Code defines "good faith" in the case of a merchant as "honesty in fact and the observance of reasonable commercial standards of fair dealing in the trade." Although this definition by its terms embraces the "reasonable commercial standards of fair dealing in the trade," it should not — and cannot — be interpreted to permit, countenance or condone commercial standards of sharp trade practice or indifference as to the "provenance," i.e., history of ownership or the right to possess or sell an object d'art, such as is present in the case before us.

We note that neither Ms. Drew-Bear nor her employer Feigen made any investigation to determine the status of Wertz, i.e., whether he was an art merchant, "a person in the business of selling goods of that kind." (UCC, § 1-201, subd [9].) Had Ms. Drew-Bear done so much as call either of the telephone numbers Wertz had left, she would have learned that Wertz was employed by a delicatessen and was not an art dealer. Nor did Ms. Drew-Bear or Feigen make an effort to verify whether Wertz was the owner or authorized by the owner to sell the painting he was offering. Ms. Drew-Bear had available to her the Petrides volume on Utrillo which included "Chateau de Lion-sur-Mer" in its catalogue of the master's work.[8] Although this knowledge alone might not have been enough to put Feigen on notice that Wertz was not the true owner at the time of the transaction, it could have raised a doubt as to Wertz' right of possession, calling for further verification before the purchase by Feigen was consummated. Thus, it appears that statutory estoppel provided by subdivision (2) of § 2-403 . . . was not, as Trial Term correctly concluded, available as a defense to Feigen.

---

[6] Wertz is described as a seller of caviar and other luxury food items (because of his association with a Madison Avenue gourmet grocery) and over whom the Trial Term observed, Von Maker "cast his hypnotic spell . . . and usurped his name, his signature and his sacred honor."

[8] Page 32 of that book clearly contained a reference to the fact that that painting, at the time of publication of the book in 1969, was in the collection of Mrs. Donald D. King of New York, supposedly the party from whom Porter obtained it.

We disagree with the conclusion of the trial court that the defense of equitable estoppel (see *Zendman v. Harry Winston, Inc.*, 305 N.Y. 180) raised by Feigen bars recovery.

We pause to observe that although one may not be a buyer in the ordinary course of business as defined in the Code, he may be a good-faith purchaser for value and enjoy the protection of precode estoppel (see . . . UCC, § 1-103). We now reach the question whether the defense of equitable estoppel has been established here.

In general terms: "Equitable estoppel or estoppel in pais is the principle by which a party is absolutely precluded, both at law and in equity, from denying, or asserting the contrary of, any material fact which, by his words or conduct, affirmative or negative, intentionally or through culpable negligence, he has induced another, who was excusably ignorant of the true facts and who had a right to rely upon such words or conduct, to believe and act upon them thereby, as a consequence reasonably to be anticipated, changing his position in such a way that he would suffer injury if such denial or contrary assertion were allowed." 21 N.Y. Jur., Estoppel, § 15.

As the Court of Appeals reiterated in *Zendman* (*supra*, p. 185), an " 'owner may be estopped from setting up his own title and the lack of title in the vendor as against a bona fide purchaser for value where the owner has clothed the vendor with possession and other indicia of title, 46 Am. Jur., Sales, § 463.' " Indeed, "[the] rightful owner may be estopped by his own acts from asserting his title. If he has invested another with the usual evidence of title, or an apparent authority to dispose of it, he will not be allowed to make claim against an innocent purchaser dealing on the faith of such apparent ownership" (*Smith v. Clews*, 114 NY 190, 194).

In *Zendman*, a diamond merchant in New York City sent a ring to Brand, Inc., a corporation which conducted auctions on the boardwalk in Atlantic City, New Jersey, with a memorandum reciting that the ring was for examination only and that title was not to pass until the auctioneer had made his selection, and had notified the sender of his agreement to pay the indicated price and the sender had indicated acceptance thereof by issuing a bill of sale. The ring was placed in a public show window at the auctioneer's place of business, remaining there for more than a month, before being sold to the plaintiff at a public auction. Under circumstances where it was demonstrated that the defendant had permitted other pieces of jewelry it owned to be exhibited and sold by the auctioneer, it was held that the defendant by his conduct was estopped from recovering the ring from the plaintiff.

In the case at bar, Porter's conduct was not blameworthy. When the first promissory note was dishonored, he retained Bishop's investigative service and informed the FBI of the financial transactions concerning the series of notes. His attorney obtained a comprehensive agreement covering several paintings, within which was the assurance (now proven false) by Von Maker that he still controlled the Utrillo. Although Porter had permitted Von Maker to possess the painting, he conferred upon Von Maker no other indicia of ownership. Possession without more is insufficient to create an estoppel (*Zendman*, *supra*, pp. 186–187).

We find that the prior art transactions between Porter and Von Maker justified the conclusion of the trial court that Porter knew that Von Maker was a dealer in art. Nevertheless, the testimony remains uncontradicted, that the Utrillo was not consigned to Von Maker for business purposes, but rather for display only in Von Maker's home. In these circumstances, it cannot be said that Porter's conduct in any way contributed to the deception practiced on Feigen by Von Maker and Wertz.

Finally, we must examine again the position of Feigen to determine whether Feigen was a purchaser in good faith. In purchasing the Utrillo, Feigen did not rely on any indicia of ownership in Von Maker. Feigen dealt with Wertz, who did not have the legal right to possession of the painting. Even were we to consider Wertz as the agent of Von Maker or merge the identities of Von Maker and Wertz insofar as Feigen was concerned, Feigen was not a purchaser in good faith. As we have commented, neither Ms. Drew-Bear nor Feigen made, or attempted to make, the inquiry which the circumstances demanded.

The Feigen claim that the failure to look into Wertz' authority to sell the painting was consistent with the practice of the trade does not excuse such conduct. This claim merely confirms the observation of the trial court that "in an industry whose transactions cry out for verification of . . . title . . . it is deemed poor practice to probe." Indeed, commercial indifference to ownership or the right to sell facilitates traffic in stolen works of art. Commercial indifference diminishes the integrity and increases the culpability of the apathetic merchant. In such posture, Feigen cannot be heard to complain.

In the circumstances outlined, the complaint should not have been dismissed. Moreover, we find that plaintiffs-appellants are the true owners of the Utrillo painting and are entitled to possession thereof, that defendants-respondents wrongfully detained that painting and are obligated to return it or pay for its value at the time of trial. . . . Judgment, Supreme Court, New York County, reversed, on the law and the facts, and vacated, the complaint reinstated, judgment entered in favor of plaintiffs-appellants on liability, and the matter remanded for an assessment of damages.

Porter v. Wertz, 421 N.E.2d 500 (N.Y. 1981) (affirming the opinion below):

The judgment appealed from and order of the Appellate Division brought up for review should be affirmed, with costs. We agree with the Appellate Division's conclusion that subdivision (2) of § 2-403 of the Uniform Commercial Code does not insulate defendants from plaintiff Porter's lawful claim to the Utrillo painting. Subdivision (2) of § 2-403 . . . provides: "Any entrusting of possession of goods to a merchant who deals in goods of that kind gives him power to transfer all rights of the entruster to a buyer in ordinary course of business." The "entruster provision" of the Code is designed to enhance the reliability of commercial sales by merchants (who deal with the kind of goods sold on a regular basis) while shifting the risk of loss through fraudulent transfer to the owner of the goods, who can select the merchant to whom he entrusts his property. It protects only those who purchase from the merchant to whom the property was entrusted in the ordinary course of the merchant's business.

While the Utrillo painting was entrusted to Harold Von Maker, an art merchant, the Feigen Gallery purchased the painting not from Von Maker, but from one Peter Wertz, who turns out to have been a delicatessen employee acquainted with Von Maker. It seems that Von Maker frequented the delicatessen where Peter Wertz was employed and that at some point Von Maker began to identify himself as Peter Wertz in certain art transactions. Indeed, Von Maker identified himself as Peter Wertz in his dealings with Porter.

Defendants argued that Feigen reasonably assumed that the Peter Wertz who offered the Utrillo to him was an art merchant because Feigen had been informed by Henry Sloan that an art dealer named Peter Wertz desired to sell a Utrillo painting. Feigen therefore argues that for purposes of subdivision (2) of § 2-403 of the Code it is as though he purchased from a merchant in the ordinary course of business. Alternatively, he claims that he actually purchased the Utrillo from Von Maker, the art dealer to whom it had been entrusted, because Peter Wertz sold the painting on Von Maker's behalf. Neither argument has merit.

Even if Peter Wertz were acting on Von Maker's behalf, unless he disclosed this fact to Feigen, it could hardly be said that Feigen relied upon Von Maker's status as an art merchant. It does not appear that the actual Peter Wertz ever represented that he was acting on behalf of Von Maker in selling the painting.

As to the argument that Feigen reasonably assumed that Peter Wertz was an art merchant, it is apparent from the opinion of the Appellate Division that the court rejected the fact finding essential to this argument, namely, that Peter Wertz had been introduced to Feigen by Henry Sloan as an art merchant. The court noted that in his examination before trial Richard Feigen had testified that he could not recall whether Henry Sloan had described Peter Wertz as an art dealer and concluded that this substantially weakened the probative force of Feigen's trial testimony on this point. Indeed, Peter Wertz testified that Von Maker had not directed him to the Feigen Gallery but had simply delivered the painting to Wertz and asked him to try to find a buyer for the Utrillo. Wertz had been to several art galleries before he approached the Feigen Gallery. Thus, the Appellate Division's finding has support in the record.

Because Peter Wertz was not an art dealer and the Appellate Division has found that Feigen was not duped by Von Maker into believing that Peter Wertz was such a dealer, subdivision (2) of § 2-403 . . . is inapplicable for three distinct reasons: (1) even if Peter Wertz were an art merchant rather than a delicatessen employee, he is not the same merchant to whom Porter entrusted the Utrillo painting; (2) Wertz was not an art merchant; and (3) the sale was not in the ordinary course of Wertz' business because he did not deal in goods of that kind (Uniform Commercial Code, § 1-201, subd [9]).

Nor can the defendants-appellants rely on the doctrine of equitable estoppel. It has been observed that subdivision (1) of § 2-403 . . . incorporates the doctrines of estoppel, agency and apparent agency because it states that a purchaser acquires not only all title that his transferor had, but also all title that he had power to transfer (White & Summers, Uniform Commercial Code, § 3-11, p. 139).

An estoppel might arise if Porter had clothed Peter Wertz with ownership of or authority to sell the Utrillo painting and the Feigen Gallery had relied upon Wertz' apparent ownership or right to transfer it. But Porter never even delivered the painting to Peter Wertz, much less create apparent ownership in him; he delivered the painting to Von Maker for his own personal use. It is true, as previously noted, that Von Maker used the name Peter Wertz in his dealings with Porter, but the Appellate Division found that the Feigen Gallery purchased from the actual Peter Wertz and that there was insufficient evidence to establish the claim that Peter Wertz had been described as an art dealer by Henry Sloan. Nothing Porter did influenced the Feigen Gallery's decision to purchase from Peter Wertz a delicatessen employee. Accordingly, the Feigen Gallery cannot protect its defective title by a defense of estoppel.

The Appellate Division opined that even if Von Maker had duped Feigen into believing that Peter Wertz was an art dealer, subdivision (2) of § 2-403 . . . would still not protect his defective title because as a merchant, Feigen failed to purchase in good faith. Among merchants good faith requires not only honesty in fact but observance of reasonable commercial standards (UCC, § 2-103, subd [1], par.[b]). The Appellate Division concluded that it was a departure from reasonable commercial standards for the Feigen Gallery to fail to inquire concerning the title to the Utrillo and to fail to question Peter Wertz' credentials as an art dealer. On this appeal we have received amicus briefs from the New York State Attorney-General urging that the court hold that good faith among art merchants requires inquiry as to the ownership of an object d'art, and from the Art Dealers Association of America, Inc., arguing that the ordinary custom in the art business is not to inquire as to title and that a duty of inquiry would cripple the art business which is centered in New York. In view of our disposition we do not reach the good faith question. Judgment appealed from and order of the Appellate Division brought up for review affirmed. . . .

NOTE

This case involves two affirmative defenses. To which of the several transactions in the facts does each apply? How do these defenses differ from one another? What is the general rule of § 2-403? Is this section taken to repeal the pre-existing cases (such as *Zendman v. Harry Winston, Inc.*) involving equitable estoppel? Should any purchaser of a work of art become a bona fide purchaser without inquiring into the state of the title to the work? What if such an inquiry is not routinely made in the locale? What if it was done badly, or proved futile? As these questions suggest, the degree of diligence required of purchasers of works of art has continued to trouble courts. See *Lindholm v. Brant*, 925 A.2d 1048 (Conn. 2007).

VIII.   ACCESSION

The use of ↑ *to improve personal prop. that belongs to another.*

Bancorp Leasing & Fin. Corp. v. Stadeli Pump & Constr., Inc., 739 P.2d 548, 551–53 (Or. 1987):

Doesn't Apply)

IF THERE IS BAD FAITH!

[T]he common-law rule of accession is that "[w]hen the goods of two different owners are incorporated together, the title to the resulting product goes to the owner of the principal goods." Brown, The Law of Personal Property § 6.3, at 52 (Raushenbush ed., 3d ed 1975). . . . The common-law doctrine of accession was taken from Roman law by Bracton and was said by Blackstone to have been grounded on the right by occupancy. 2 Blackstone, Commentaries 404–05 [a citation to U. Chi. Press ed. (1979)-ed.]. Thus, the owner of a parchment acquired title to writings on the parchment, and the owner of a garment acquired title to embroidery on the garment. *Id.* at 404–07. The concept of title by occupancy precluded joint ownership of the combined substances, although in certain circumstances, for example, when a writer used the parchment of another by mistake, the person acquiring title to goods by accession would be required to compensate the former owner of the goods. See 2 Gaius, Institutes §§ 77–78; 2 Justinian, Institutes, title 1, §§ 26–34.

Accession did not occur through the mere physical attachment of goods. The incorporation of the goods had to be such that the component goods could not be recovered, as with ink and parchment in a writing, or could be recovered only at substantial economic cost, as with thread interwoven into a garment. 2 Justinian, title 1, §§ 26, 33. This principle of severability can also be seen in the related doctrines of specification and confusion. A specification is the application of labor to a thing or substance to create a new product. Because the labor is always inseparable from the new product, title to the whole of the new product is always in either the laborer or the owner of the original thing or substance, depending upon the nature of the transformation effected. 2 Blackstone, at 404–05. A confusion is the combination of similar substances or things into a uniform mass such that the identities of the original substances are lost, as when the grain of two separate owners is mixed together. Because the mass is practically infinitely divisible, there is no need to place title to the mass in a single person, absent some extraneous consideration such as the prevention of fraud. Thus, the owners of the original substances will own the mass in common in proportion to their respective shares. Accession, then, is a doctrine that is meant to vest in a single person the ownership of products that are not, as a practical matter, severable into their component parts or shares.

In the United States, the severability limitation came to be a rule that "the principle of accession does not apply when the attached articles can be separated and removed from the principal thing without damage to the latter." Brown, § 6.3, at 52. The leading case articulating this rule, *Clark v. Wells*, 45 Vt. 4, 12 Am. Rep. 187 (1872), is factually somewhat similar to the present case. In *Clark* the plaintiff made a conditional sale of wheels and axles that he used to repair a wagon. The owner of the wagon on which the wheels and axles were installed subsequently sold the wagon with wheels and axles to the defendant before payment was completed on the wheels and axles. The court rejected the defendant's contention that the wheels and axles were accessions to the wagon, stating, "[The wheels and axles] could be followed, identified, severed, without detriment to the wagon, and appropriated to other use without loss." *Clark*, 12 Am. Rep. at 188. . . . Under the rule articulated in *Clark*, the issue is not damage to the whole, but damage to the principal part. Even under a somewhat broader rule of practical severability, i.e., severability that does not result in substantial economic loss, as with the unraveling of embroidery from a garment, the focus is still on the aggregate value of the parts rather than the functional value of the whole. Because the aggregate value of the truck and engine is not substantially less than the value of the truck with the engine installed, the engine is severable.

Nevertheless, courts in certain circumstances ignore the severability principle in order to hold that a part is an accession. Brown, § 6.3, at 52–53. Accession in these instances turns less on the degree and form of attachment than on the circumstances of the attachment and the perceived equities of the case. The doctrine thus becomes a vehicle for the application of various other distinct principles of law.

One such principle is that the law creates a presumption that a debtor's improvements to property in which there is a security interest are intended to benefit the secured party. Perhaps the most commonly litigated circumstance in which this principle is operative is a security interest in a motor vehicle. Thus, where the owner of a vehicle subject to a security interest attaches the owner's own parts to the vehicle, the parts are usually deemed to be accessions to the vehicle and thereby subject to the security interest, particularly if the parts are functional necessities such as an engine or tires. Brown, § 6.3, at 53. The rationale for this result is that otherwise the secured party's interest would evaporate as parts failed and were replaced. Moreover, if the debtor is entitled to the surplus or obligated to pay the deficiency resulting from the repossession and sale of the goods, the debtor theoretically is neither harmed nor benefitted by the conclusion that the added part is an accession.

Where, however, the added part is owned by a third party . . . , or where a third party has a security interest in the part, under the common law courts ordinarily will not conclude that the part acceded to the vehicle unless it is not severable. See Brown, § 6.3, at 53. (Where the third party holds a security interest in the part, UCC § 9-314 now controls. — Eds.) The reason for this distinction is that, unlike the debtor, the third party has no obligation to maintain the secured party's security interest. Moreover, the third party has no debt to which the value of the part can be applied. . . .

A more general principle that might motivate a court to conclude that a severable part was an accession would be the protection of persons who detrimentally rely on an apparent association of parts to the whole.

Although there are no court decisions couched in these terms, the principle appears to be the source of . . . UCC § 9-314(3)(c), which gives creditors with a prior perfected security interest in the whole priority over an attached security interest in a part to the extent of advances subsequent to the attachment.

BALLARD v. WETZEL
1997 Tenn. App. LEXIS 699 (Oct. 16, 1997)

FRANKS, J.

In this action to recover a Corvette motor vehicle, the Trial Judge, after trial, ruled that the defendant was entitled to possession of the vehicle and said: "The Court finds . . . the son . . . was the person who was responsible for the disappearance of plaintiff's Corvette automobile." The vehicle was taken from the garage of the plaintiff, after being stored in the garage because the Corvette had been substantially damaged due to a previous accident. After the vehicle had been removed from the garage, restoration began. The defendant describes the vehicle at the time of beginning restoration as being a mere hull. Plaintiff claimed the vehicle was wrecked, but was whole. Plaintiff claims that she did not immediately report the vehicle stolen because her son assured her that he was having the vehicle restored for her. This Court resolves all factual issues in favor of the defendant, Johnny Wetzel. In making this ruling, the Court finds that the defendant was a "good faith purchaser for value" and the auto hull once restored became the property of the defendant by "accession." Any cause the plaintiff would have should be addressed against her son. * * *

The Trial Judge correctly determined that defendant was a good faith purchaser for value. * * * Defendant qualifies as a purchaser because he acquired the car parts by sale and paid valuable consideration. Defendant also acted in good faith. T.C.A. § 47-1-201(19) defines "good faith" as "honesty in fact in the conduct or transaction concerned." Therefore, a buyer is not a good faith purchaser if he had notice "of facts that would put a reasonably prudent person on inquiry." *Liles Bros. & Son v. Wright*, 638 S.W.2d 383 (Tenn. 1982). In this case, defendant purchased the "hull" from Lambert Auto Parts, whose regular business is selling parts. Also, defendant received a receipt from Lambert's documenting the purchase of the parts from a George Martin. Defendant took additional steps to ensure the parts were not stolen, by checking the VIN numbers through the County Clerk's Office. * * * The defendant's sales receipt from Lambert's Auto Parts shows that George Martin purchased the parts from Tyrone Ballard, the plaintiff's son, and there is nothing in the record to put defendant on notice that plaintiff's son did not have auto parts to sell.

The fact that defendant did not obtain a certificate of title at the time of purchasing the parts is not dispositive. We have held the fact that a seller presents no indicia of title is not alone sufficient to demonstrate a buyer's lack of good faith. *Jernigan v. Ham*, 691 S.W.2d 553, 557 (Tenn. App. 1984). In *Jernigan*, the Court noted that it was not customary to ask for title to a used piece of equipment, since it was usually unavailable. Similarly, George Martin testified that he usually received a title when he bought "whole" vehicles. According to his testimony, Martin purchased only a "hull." Moreover, T.C.A. § 55-3-201 states that "any owner dismantling . . . any registered vehicle shall immediately forward to the division, the certificate of title." Thus, Martin's subsequent purchasers had no apparent reason to believe that a certificate of title would be available. * * *

Defendant's status as a good faith purchaser for value, alone, does not establish good title to the vehicle. T.C.A. § 47-2-403 states that "a purchaser of goods acquires all title which his transferor had or had power to transfer. . . ." The statute also provides that "[a] person with voidable title has power to transfer a good tile to a good faith purchaser for value." Although the Trial Court correctly determined that the defendant was a good faith purchaser for value, the statute requires that the transferor have at least "voidable" title in order to confer good title. In this case, the record shows that Tyrone Ballard had no authority to sell plaintiff's vehicle. We have held that the selling of a vehicle without authority to do so constitutes theft. *Butler v. Buick Motor Co.*, 813 S.W.2d 454 (Tenn. App. 1991). If "goods are stolen or otherwise obtained against the will of the owner, only void title can result, and the thief only has void title to the goods." 77A C.J.S. Sales § 232 (1994). Tyrone Ballard and the subsequent purchasers had a void, not voidable, title. Accordingly, defendant's good faith purchase status is not itself sufficient to create good title under T.C.A. § 47-2-403. The defendant, however, as the Court held, acquired good title by accession.

Our courts have held that title may pass, however, to an innocent purchaser, where there is a great disparity in the value between the original article and the new product resulting from the purchaser's labor and/or materials. *Eusco, Inc. v. Huddleston*, 835 S.W.2d 576 (Tenn. 1992); *Capitol Chevrolet Co. v. Earheart*, 627 S.W.2d 369 (Tenn. App. 1981).

Defendant acquired title by accession because his labor significantly increased the value of the vehicle. He acquired the hull of a vehicle for $900.00 and spent approximately $5,000.00 restoring the vehicle, and invested approximately 100 hours of restoration labor. There is evidence in the record that the restoration has a market value of $7,950.00. There is ample evidence to support the Trial Court's finding that title passed by accession.

Finally, plaintiff argues that accession cannot apply because there is not adequate disparity between the value of the vehicle when owned by her, and the value of defendant's restore vehicle. The only evidence of the pre-sale value of the vehicle was plaintiff's estimate of its value. Assuming for purposes of argument that this estimate was correct, plaintiff's argument is founded upon an improper comparison. In *Earheart*, the Court did not compare the value of the original Corvette to the value of the restored Corvette. Rather, the Court compared the value of the hull purchased by Sartin to the value Sartin created. Thus, the Trial Court made the proper comparison of value in this case. We affirm the judgment of the Trial Court. . . .

NOTES

1. A thief steals three automobiles and in his chop shop, makes a fourth auto from the chassis of one, the frame of the second, and the engine from the third automobile. Which of the true owners could claim the fourth auto? This situation shows one limitation of the doctrine of accession — that is, the doctrine solves two party, but not three party disputes. See *Atlas Assurance Co. v. Gibbs*, 183 A. 690 (Conn. 1936). This limitation will also make accession useless in disputes where two automobiles were stolen, but one was financed, or contained an engine sold on the installment basis. "The general rule holds that detachable parts added to an automobile do not become accessions to the automobile sold under a lien instrument containing an after-acquired accessory clause if the seller of the parts retains title to the parts by a conditional sales agreement." What the automobile owner does not own, cannot be subject to the after-acquired accessory clause. See *Bank of America v. J.&S. Auto Repairs*, 694 P.2d 246 (Ariz. 1985) (holding that such an engine could be removed without damage and was not an accession). Would the same rule make the tires, or the transmission, accessions? See *Paccar v. Schwab*, 920 P.2d 977 (Mont. 1996).

O owns an automobile. A takes it to mechanic M who installs a new engine, but A disappears and does not pay M's bill. O brings replevin against M to recover the automobile. Should *J.&S.*'s general rule (that detachable parts are not accessions) be applied whenever a mechanic shows that he did not intend to make repairs and install parts (e.g., an engine, transmission, or tires) gratuitously? No, because that fact is significant only if the owner was unjustly enriched by the repair, and so long as the owner does not sell it, the engine adds no value. O gets a judgment entitling him to repossess the whole automobile in its repaired state, just as M left it after finishing the repair and installation.

In the case of a lien holder, replacing an engine (say) only made the auto run again, just as it did when the sale under the lien instrument occurred. To the extent that a used, repaired car is more valuable than a used, unrepaired but operative car to the lien holder — that is, to the extent that such an auto is more valuable in the used car market — the lien holder (not wanting just to operate the car) is enriched, and the mechanic can seek restitution for the uncompensated repair, not to the extent of the repair bill, but to the extent that the fair market value of the auto is increased. *AM Leasing, Ltd. v. Baker*, 786 P.2d 1045 (Ariz. App. 1989). Why this limitation on the *J.&S.* rule? Because the lien holder repossessing the auto, being in a position similar to the true owner of the auto who did not authorize the repairs, is not a party to the agreement to repair, and so cannot be bound by it. One cannot be made a debtor against one's will. See *Tom Growney Equipment, Inc. v. Ansley*, 888 P.2d 992 (N.M. App. 1994).

If O sued M in replevin, as before, but if (as many states would require) M posted a bond instead of giving the automobile to the court, M actually has a choice of forfeiting the bond or yielding possession of the automobile. Then the hearing setting the amount of the bond will be crucial to M's decision. If O brought an action for conversion against M, would the value M added to the car off-set any damages O might recovery? Yes. If O doesn't want the car back, but only wants money for it, the value M added should be accounted for. See generally Robert Casad, *The*

Mistaken Improver, 19 Hastings L.J. 1039 (1968); Earl C. Arnold, *The Law of Accession of Personal Property*, 22 Colum. L. Rev. 103 (1922). Would a trailer attached to a truck become an accession? See *Valley Chevrolet Co. v. O.S. Stapley Co.*, 72 P.2d 945 (Ariz. 1937).

2. For a discussion of the law of accession in the context of the mistaken improvement of real property, see Kelvin Dickinson, *Mistaken Improvers of Real Estate*, 64 N.C. L. Rev. 37 (1985). For a case avoiding the harshness of the common law rules on mistaken improvers of realty, see *DeAngelo v. Brazauskas*, 655 N.E.2d 165 (N.Y. 1995).

3. The doctrine of confusion applies when goods of one type, owned by different persons, are intermingled in such a way that they cannot thereafter be separated. Like accession, it applies when different owners contribute to a whole — as when grain is deposited in a grain elevator — but unlike accession, no labor is added to the whole and the whole is no different from the particular contributions in quality; only the quantity increases. When the confusion occurs unintentionally with goods of the same type, quality, and unit value, or when each owner consents to the intermingling, each contributor owns the whole in proportion to her contribution. When there is an intentional confusion, the party confusing the goods, the "confuser" has the burden of establishing the extent of proportional ownership, and every reasonable doubt is resolved against the intentional confuser. In the extreme, then, the intentional confuser forfeits all rights to the intermingled goods to the nonconsenting owner. See *Somers v. Kane*, 210 N.W. 287 (Minn. 1926), noted in 25 Mich. L. Rev. 683 (1927). Can you see that the last, extreme rule will seldom control the facts of a particular case? See Ray Brown, Personal Property 62–75 (Walter B. Raushenbush ed., 3d ed. 1975).

IX. FIXTURES

FIRST TR. & SAV. BANK OF MOVILLE v. GUTHRIDGE
445 N.W.2d 401 (Iowa App. 1989)

Sackett, J.

In this replevin action we must determine whether there is substantial evidence to support the trial court's decision feed bunks on a farm now owned by defendant-appellant Bernice Guthridge are the property of plaintiff-appellee First Trust and Savings Bank of Moville, Iowa. Bernice's son Larry Guthridge gave a security interest in the bunks to plaintiff in 1983 to secure a loan. At the time the security interest was given the bunks were located on the land. Bernice at that time had a life estate in the land and her son Larry owned the remainder interest. Larry was farming the land as Bernice's tenant and in 1985 conveyed by quit claim deed his interest in the farm to Bernice in satisfaction of two years of unpaid rents. Defendant appeals the trial court order contending the bunks were fixtures conveyed to her when her son gave her the quit claim deed. We disagree. . . .

A replevin action is an enforcement of a plaintiff's right to immediate possession of property wrongfully taken or detained. Replevin is a law action, Iowa Code

§ 643.2, and the findings of fact made by the trial court are binding on us if supported by substantial evidence.

Defendant contends the bunks were fixtures. The Iowa Uniform Commercial Code provides "goods are 'fixtures' when they become so related to particular real estate that an interest in them arises under real estate law." Iowa Code § 554.9313(1)(a) (1989). However, a fixture continues to be characterized by Iowa realty law. *Ford v. Venard*, 340 N.W.2d 270, 271 (Iowa 1983) (court applied common law rule on issue of when personal property becomes a fixture). Under common law personal property becomes a fixture when (1) it is actually annexed to the realty, or to something appurtenant thereto; (2) it is put to the same use as the realty with which it is connected; and (3) the party making the annexation intends to make a permanent accession to the freehold. *Ford*, 340 N.W.2d at 271; *Cornell College v. Crain*, 235 N.W. 731, 732 (Iowa 1931); *Speer v. Donald*, 207 N.W. 581, 582 (Iowa 1926); *Rahm v. Domayer*, 114 N.W. 546, 546 (Iowa 1908); *Teaff v. Hewitt*, 1 O. St. 511.

The intention of the party annexing the improvement is an important factor in assessing the issue. *Ford*, 340 N.W.2d at 272. The character of the attachment is important in determining the intent. *Speer*, 207 N.W. at 582. Because there was some attachment, the burden to show the bunks were not fixtures was on the bank. See *Rahm*, 114 N.W. at 546. At the time Larry gave the security interest he was a mere tenant on the land. We agree with the trial court his action in giving a security interest was evidence he intended the bunks to remain his personal property and not become attached to the property in which his mother held a life interest. We note also the fact the only attachment other than gravity was an easily removable steel cable. Additionally, we look to the fact that when the bunks were brought on the farm Larry was but a tenant which would negate against their being determined fixtures. *Speer*, 207 N.W. at 582. Also, they were intended to be used in the livestock business and the use of the bunks was limited by the requirements of the business rather than the boundaries of the farm. *Id.* There is substantial evidence to support the trial court's decision.

The plaintiff had filed a financing statement with the secretary of state covering Larry's personal property. . . . Therefore, Bernice's interest would be subject to the bank's even if the bunks were sold or transferred to her. * * * AFFIRMED.

DONIELSON, J.

I respectfully dissent. I would reverse the trial court's judgment issuing a writ of replevin in the Bank's favor for recovery of the forty fence-line feed bunks. * * * The intention of the party annexing the improvement is the "paramount factor" in determining whether the improvement is a fixture. *Ford*, 340 N.W.2d at 272. While the united application of the three factors determines whether an item is a fixture, "the character of the physical attachment, whether slight or otherwise, and the use, are mainly important in determining the intention of the party making the annexation." *Speer*, 207 N.W. at 582. "This intention is not the secret purpose of the owner, but that which should be inferred" from the application of the other two factors. *Id.*

The Supreme Court in *Rahm v. Domayer*, when considering the first factor as it relates to intention, pointed out "that physical attachment need be of no particular kind or degree, and that any annexation which, however slight it may be, indicates the intent, is sufficient to meet the demands of the rule . . . [T]he true rule is that articles not otherwise attached to the realty than by their own weight are prima facie personalty, and articles affixed to the land in fact, although only slightly, are prima facie realty, and that the burden of proof is on the one contending that the former is realty or the latter is personalty." *Rahm*, 114 N.W. at 546.

The Supreme Court in *Ford* stated "physical attachment of the structure to the soil or to an appurtenance thereto is not essential to make the structure a part of the realty." *Ford*, 340 N.W.2d at 272. * * * Iowa law does not require the attachment be so great as to cause damage upon removal of the fixture. The Supreme Court found in *Cornell College v. Crain* that a granary and a corncrib constructed on movable skids were intended to be fixtures. *Cornell College*, 235 N.W. at 732. Although these buildings were not attached to the realty, and, therefore, prima facie personalty, the court found the first factor was not controlling and the determinative factor was intent. *Id.* The *Cornell College* court emphasized the practical necessity for and the use to be made of the buildings on the premises. *Id.* The court found the buildings were essential to the proper conduct and operation of the farm and were well suited to the purposes for which they were erected. *Id.* Based on the second factor, the court found the appellee's obvious intention was to occupy and maintain the buildings upon the premises as permanent structures. *Id.* * * *

The Supreme Court ruled movable hog houses were not fixtures in *Speer v. Donald*, 207 N.W. at 583. This case is similar to *Cornell College* in that the hog houses were placed upon runners (skids), were not attached to the land except by their own weight, and were designed to be moved from place to place. * * * In *Speer*, the hog houses were used in connection with the business of raising hogs and cattle. *Id.*, at 581. However, the business was not confined to the farm in question. *Id.* The buildings had in fact been moved from farm to farm. The court found that the fact the buildings were movable and the manner of their use in connection with other farms evidenced an intent not to make them a part of the realty.

The trial court in the present case found the fence-line feed bunks consisted of concrete bunks, each weighing 2,000 pounds. The forty bunks were installed by setting them on concrete blocks on the ground. The fence was secured by wooden fence posts at each end of the line of bunks. A steel cable runs through each bunk and attaches to the wooden posts at each end. The trial court determined the feed bunks were movable by their nature and were only attached by their own weight and therefore concluded they were not fixtures. * * *

The trial court determined that under the first factor the bunks were movable and therefore not fixtures. First, the bunks, although movable, were affixed to the land by a cable and posts. Although the attachment is slight, under *Rahm*, the bunks are *prima facie* realty and the burden of proof is on the bank to show they were intended to be personalty. Second, under *Ford*, physical attachment is not essential to make the bunks a part of the realty. Therefore, the law doesn't allow the inference the bunks were personalty based merely on the fact they are movable.

In evaluating the use of the bunks, the court concluded the bunks were no more a part of the fence than a building placed in a fence line would be a fence. The court's conclusion . . . fails to take into account the fact that the bunks were specifically made and purchased for the purpose of making them a part of the fence. I find the nature of the use of the bunks evidences an intent that they become part of the real estate. The bunks were used as a fence to contain cattle and an apparatus for feeding them. The bunks were well suited for use as a fence and were used in connection with the business of raising cattle. Unlike *Speer*, the use of the bunks in this case was confined to one farm. There is no evidence in the record that the bunks in question were ever moved. The trial court seems to rely on the fact that it is not uncommon for farmers to move the bunks in finding that under the second factor the bunks were not intended to be used as fixtures. The paramount factor here is the intent of Larry, not other farmers owning such bunks.

The trial court found Larry intended the bunks to be personalty because he entered into a security agreement rather than a second mortgage to finance the bunks. No such intent may be inferred because the U.C.C. provides for the perfection of a security agreement involving fixtures. Iowa Code § 554.9313 (1987).

The majority determined the trial court's finding that the bunks were intended to be personalty was supported by substantial evidence. The majority relies on the fact Larry was "a mere tenant on the land" at the time he gave the bank a security interest in the bunks. The majority concludes, citing *Speer*, 207 N.W. at 582, that this evidences his intention the bunks remain his personal property. First, . . . the landlord-tenant relationship was but one factor in *Speer*. That court relied more heavily on the fact that the movable hog houses and feed bunks were not attached to the land, save by their own weight, and were in fact moved from farm to farm. Second, Larry was not a "mere tenant" when he gave the bank a security interest in the bunks. Larry had a remainder interest in the land upon which the bunks were placed and was renting from the life tenant, his mother. I find no intent the bunks be personalty can be inferred from the fact that Larry was a tenant at the time he placed the bunks on the land under these circumstances. Further, the majority also relies on the fact the bunks were intended to be used in the livestock business, and the bunks were limited by the requirements of the business rather than the boundaries of the farm. The court in *Speer* found such was the case "as his operations in the prosecution of that business seem not to have been confined to the farm in question." In the present case, the use of the bunks was limited to one farm. There is no evidence that even if Larry moved the bunks, they would be moved for use off the farm. I do not find any evidence that Larry's intent, based on the use of the bunks, was that the bunks be personalty.

The majority seems to be inferring that since the bunks were movable, Larry intended them to be personalty. That inference is not supported by the law. The extent of the attachment is but one factor in determining Larry's intent. *Speer*, 207 N.W. at 582. However, the mere fact that the bunks were movable does not require a finding they were intended to be personalty. Instead, the issue with regard to movable buildings and feeders is whether the owner intended they become a permanent part of the premises. *Cornell College*, 235 N.W. 731, 732. In *Cornell College*, the Supreme Court determined that although a hog house and farrowing pens could be moved about on the premises, the owner's intent was clearly that they be used only on the premises and become a permanent part of the premises. That case is analogous to the present situation. Larry used the bunks on the farm in the livestock business. Although the bunks were movable, there is no evidence he intended to use the bunks off the premises. Instead, the evidence shows that even if Larry were to move the bunks (there is no evidence they were ever moved), he would have moved them for use elsewhere on the premises. This case is not like *Speer*, where the livestock operation was not limited to one farm. Accordingly, the majority's emphasis on Speer is misplaced. I find no substantial evidence in the record . . . that Larry did not intend the bunks to be permanent fixtures. The Bank did not sustain its burden of proof and the trial court erred in holding the bunks were not fixtures.

The trial court held the Bank had properly perfected its security interest in the feed bunks by filing a financing statement with the Secretary of State. Appellant contends the trial court erred in granting the Bank a writ of replevin because the Bank did not file with the County Recorder. * * * Fixtures pass with the realty upon conveyance absent notice of a lien. Notice of a security interest in these fixtures is governed by the Iowa Uniform Commercial Code. The U.C.C. requires a "fixture filing," a filing in the office where a mortgage on the real estate would be recorded, to perfect a security interest in fixtures. Iowa Code § 554.9313(1)(b). Real estate records are filed in the office of the county recorder. The Bank did not file a fixture filing and therefore did not perfect its security interest in the feed bunks. The purpose of perfection is to give purchasers notice. When a filing is made in an improper place but the buyer nonetheless has actual notice of the security interest, the buyer takes subject to the security interest. There is no evidence in the record that Bernice knew the Bank had a security interest in the feed bunks. Therefore, under the conveyance of the real estate, she takes the feed bunks free of the Bank's security interest. I would rule the trial court erred in granting the Bank a writ of replevin.

NOTES

1. In *Cornell College v. Crain*, cited in the opinions you just read, the intention of the annexor is called "the paramount consideration" in deciding whether chattel has become a fixture. Does it lose that status in these opinions? See generally Ronald W. Polston, *The Fixtures Doctrine: Was It Ever Really the Law?*, 16 Whittier L. Rev. 455 (1995), adapted for use in 5 Thompson on Real Property, ch. 46 (David Thomas ed., 1994) and discussed in *Arizona Dept. of Highways v. Arizona Outdoor Advertisers, Inc.*, 41 P.3d 639 (Ariz. App. 2002). Is it only the intent of the annexor that matters? After attaching the object to the real property, the annexor may then engage in various types of transactions involving the property, and it is only then that an annexation is likely to be of interest to more than one person. Does it make sense to classify the law according to the type of later transaction involved? Whether an object is a fixture is an issue arising in three transactional contexts:

    (1)   when a vendor removes an object from realty after agreeing to sell it to a purchaser who expects the object to be his when the sale is complete [see, e.g., *Everitt v. Higgins*, 838 P.2d 311 (Idaho 1992) (finding a woodstove not a fixture)],

(2)   when a mortgage lender seeks foreclosure of a lender's lien on real property, including its fixtures [see, e.g., *K & L Distributors, Inc. v. Kelly Elec., Inc.*, 908 P.2d 429 (Alaska 1995)], and

(3)   when a landlord claims that an object is a fixture when a lease is terminated.

In the first instance, will a vendor be subject to temptation to strip the property after the purchaser has agreed to buy it? Similarly, will the borrower or the lessee be tempted to strip the property when a mortgage loan is in foreclosure, or when a lease's term is about to expire? Should the test be different in each instance? Should the issue of intent be settled first, before the mode and the purpose of annexation is reviewed? Often the intent of the parties will have to be inferred because there is no direct evidence of that intent.

Consider *Everitt v. Higgins, supra,* concerning a dispute between parties to a real estate contract and the ownership of a wood cook stove; the trial court found that the stove was the personal property of the vendor and the purchaser appealed, arguing: (a) that the stove was a fixture passing to him by deed with the real property and in the alternative, (b) that the stove passed to him under the terms of the contract. The court states the facts as follows:

> Paul and Shelly Higgins owned a home in Rathdrum, Idaho. Although the home was equipped with a modern, gas heating system, it also contained two antique wood cook stoves, one in the downstairs portion of the home, and one upstairs in the master bedroom. Each stove rested on, but was not attached to, a built-in brick platform, which was slightly higher than the surrounding wood flooring. However, only the downstairs wood stove was connected to the chimney flu. Its heat was incorporated into the forced-air distribution of the home's heating system. The upstairs stove was not operational but exclusively decorative: it had no stove pipe connecting it to the chimney. In fact, prior to the Higgins' occupancy of the home, the chimney flu had been blocked by a concrete plug where the stove pipe would have attached. This plug was never removed but was concealed by a decorative device.

If there is no further evidence of intent available in the record, what result?

2.   If the law of fixtures applied to the relationship between landlords and tenants, chattel adapted by a tenant to leasehold premises would risk becoming the landlord's property when the lease terminates. However, the chattel of commercial tenants has long received special treatment. This treatment is traditionally justified by its encouraging tenants to put the premises to the best use. A commercial tenant does not have an absolute right of removal. This right is extended only when an actual or implied intent to permit removal can be found, and when the law of accession does not dictate otherwise. There is sometimes a presumption that a tenant installed the fixture for his own benefit and intended to remove it from the premises if the removal occurs before the termination of the lease. See *Lehmann v. Keller*, 684 A.2d 618, 621 (Pa. Super. Ct. 1996). What if a tenant builds a structure on the premises? Suppose that the lease provides for a right of removal, but is extended without a similar provision? And if a residential tenant installs a chandelier, should an exception similar to the trade fixture exception be made? See Polston, supra, n.1, 5 Thompson on Real Property, § 46.02(f).

3. Some industries and situations have created considerable case law with unique definitions of a fixture. See, e.g, *Droney v. Droney*, 651 A.2d 415 (Md. 1995) (mobile homes and manufactured housing); *Comcast Cablevision of Sterling Heights, Inc. v. City of Sterling Heights*, 553 N.W.2d 627 (Mich. App. 1996) (cable television equipment).

X. ADVERSE POSSESSION OF PERSONALTY

Porter v. Wertz shows that a bona fide purchaser of personal property may transfer the property to another who can then defeat the rights of its true owner. In a sense, bona fide purchasers may transfer more rights than they acquire. Do you see why this is so? Another way of achieving the same result is through the law of adverse possession, which is, in most states, applied to both personal and real property. See Chapter 2, § I, *infra*. Adverse possessors, be they bona fide purchasers or thieves, obtain absolute ownership of personalty by meeting the requirements of the law of adverse possession.

Every jurisdiction has a statute limiting the amount of time after which a cause of action for the recovery of possession of property is barred. Such statutes are read like a Statute of Limitations. Such statutes provide that "[n]o action shall be brought, unless within. . . ." To these statutes, courts have often added a judicial gloss, requiring that the possessor of the property have been in actual, open, continuous, exclusive, and hostile possession for the required amount of time. Other states have statutes providing that: "Any person with a cause of action for the recovery of property from a person in adverse possession of that property, shall sue within. . . ." Should such statutes bar suits against those who have hidden property claimed by potential plaintiffs? As you read the statute in the following case, keep this question in mind as you ask yourself where, among its words, judges have gleaned the requirements of adverse possession.

CHAPIN v. FREELAND
8 N.E. 128 (Mass. 1886)

HOLMES, J.

This is an action of replevin for two counters. There was evidence that they belonged to the defendant in 1867, when one Warner built a shop, put the counters in, nailed them to the floor, and afterwards, on January 2, 1871, mortgaged the premises to one De Witt. In April, 1879, De Witt's executors foreclosed and sold the premises to the plaintiff. The defendant took the counters from the plaintiff's possession in 1881. The court found for the defendant. Considering the bill of exceptions as a whole, we do not understand this general finding to have gone on the ground either of a special finding that the counters remained chattels for all purposes, and were not covered by the mortgage, or that there was a fraudulent concealment of the cause of action within Gen. St. c. 155, § 12, but we understand the court to have ruled or assumed that although the statute would have run in favor of Warner or De Witt before the transfer to the plaintiff, that circumstances would not prevent the defendant from taking possession if she could or entitle the plaintiff to sue her for doing so if she was the original owner.

A majority of the court are of opinion that this is not the law, and that there must be a new trial. We do not forget all that has been said and decided as to the statute of limitations going only to the remedy, especially in cases of contract. We do not even find it necessary to express an opinion as to what would be the effect of a statute like ours if a chattel, after having been held adversely for six years, was taken into another jurisdiction by the originally wrongful possessor. What we do decide is that, when the statute would be a bar to a direct proceeding by the original owner, it cannot be defeated by indirection within the jurisdiction where it is law. If he cannot replevy, he cannot take with his own hand. A title which will not sustain a declaration will not sustain a plea.

It is true that the statute in terms only limits the bringing of an action. But, whatever importance may be attached to that ancient form of words, the principle we lay down seems to us a necessary consequence of the enactment. Notwithstanding the disfavor with which the statute of limitations was formerly regarded, all the decisions or dicta which we know of, directly bearing upon the point, favor or go beyond that principle. . . .

As we understand the statutory period to have run before the plaintiff acquired the counters, we do not deem it necessary to consider what would have been the law if the plaintiff had purchased or taken the counters, within six years of the original conversion, from the person who first converted them, and the defendant had taken them after the action against the first taker had been barred, but within six years of the plaintiff's acquisition. We regard the purchaser from one against whom the remedy is already barred as entitled to stand in as good a position as his vendor. Whether a second wrongful taker would stand differently, because not privy in title, we need not discuss. Exceptions sustained.

FIELD, J. (dissenting).

I am unable to assent to the opinion of the court. . . . As the plaintiff first took possession of the counters as his own in 1879, the statute of limitations would have been no defense to him if the defendant had brought trover against him. His only defense would have been title in himself, derived from his vendors, and this title rests ultimately upon the possession of Warner. . . . Our statute of limitations of real actions (Pub. St. c. 196, § 1) provides that "no person shall commence an action for the recovery of land, nor make any entry thereon, unless within twenty years after the right to bring such action, or to make such entry, first accrued, or within twenty years after he, or those by or under whom he claims, have been seized or possessed of the premises, except as hereinafter provided." Gen. St. c. 154, § 1. As writs of right and of formedon, and all writs of entry except those provided by Gen. St. c. 134, were abolished, (Gen. St. c. 134, § 48) it follows that, with certain exceptions not necessary to be noticed, after 20 years from the time when the right to bring a writ of entry, or to enter upon the land, first accrued, the former owner can neither maintain any action to recover a freehold, nor enter upon the land; and as all remedy, either by action or by taking possession, is gone, his title is held to have been lost. The effect of the statute has been to extinguish the right, as well as to bar the remedy. . . . Our statute of limitations of personal actions was taken from St. 21 Jac. I. c. 16; and this statute has been held not to extinguish the right, but only to bar the remedy. . . .

Pub. St. c. 197, § 1, is that "the following actions shall be commenced within six years after the cause of action accrues, and not afterwards: . . . Actions of replevin, and all other actions for taking, detaining, or injuring goods or chattels." There is no statute and no law prohibiting the owner of personal chattels from peaceably taking possession of them wherever he may find them. It is established in this commonwealth that a debt barred by the statute of limitations of the place of the contract is not extinguished. The statute only bars the remedy by action within the jurisdiction where the defendant has resided during the statutory period. . . . There is nothing in the statute which suggests any distinctions between actions to recover chattels and actions to recover debts, and it does not purport to be a statute relating to the acquisition of title to property, but a statute prescribing the time within which certain actions shall be brought. There is not a trace to be found in our reports of the doctrine that possession of chattels for the statutory period of limitations for personal actions creates a title, and I can find no such doctrine in the English reports, or in the reports of a majority of the courts of the states of the United States.

NOTES

1.   Holmes and Field have different ways of dealing with the statute involved in this case. How would you characterize that difference? With what type of property — real or personal — does each of them think that he is dealing? When does each classify the property in the way that he does? What difference does the classification make to the purpose(s) each sees for the law of adverse possession?

2.   In your torts course, you probably have or will soon read a case in which a statute of limitations, similar to the one quoted by Judge Field, is interpreted to mean that an action "accrues" when the plaintiff discovers the tortious injury caused by the defendant. When the cause of action involves a stolen chattel, a court might similarly hold that the statute of limitations starts to run not on the date of the theft, which might be years in the past, but when the owner discovers the identity of the person in possession of it. See *Naftzger v. American Numismatic Soc'y*, 49 Cal. Rptr. 2d 784, 792 (Cal. App. 1996) (holding just that, in a case involving stolen coins that had been "switched" by the thief substituting fakes in their place). See *Society of California Pioneers v. Baker*, 50 Cal. Rptr. 2d 865 (Cal. App. 1996). See also Cal. Code Civ. Pro. § 338(c) (enacted in 1983) stating: "The cause of action in the case of theft . . . of any art or artifact is not deemed to have accrued until the discovery of the whereabouts of the art or artifact by the aggrieved party, his or her agent, or the law enforcement agency which originally investigated the theft." As you read the next case, consider whether this statute is consistent with the rule of that case.

3.   When applied to personal property, the law of adverse possession required that stolen animals be held "openly and notoriously" in the vicinity of the theft and, if grazed there, and not kept in the barn, owners ignored the animal's presence at their peril. See, e.g., *Luter v. Hutchinson*, 70 S.W. 1013, 1014 (Tex. App. 1902) (denying the true owner of a horse its possession). For other types of personalty, such as violins and pianos, some courts required use "as openly as an ordinary owner would" and confirmed the rights of possessors, time-barring the true owners' suits. See, e.g., *Reynolds v. Bagwell*, 198 P.2d 215 (Okla. 1948) (finding residential use of a violin, carried to occasional music lessons, to be open and notorious). Other (but fewer) courts required such openness and notoriety as would give true owners reasonable opportunities to discover the property. See, e.g., *San Francisco Credit Clearing House v. Wells*, 239 P. 319, 321 (Cal. 1925) (finding the residential use of a piano "not open and notorious, but clandestine" leaving the owner "without means of knowing in whose possession it actually was").

Problem: O owns two famous oil paintings. She agrees to an indefinite loan to M museum of art. She dies ten years after the loan. Her will makes no mention of the paintings and when the will is probated, they are not listed as assets of O's estate. H is O's residual legatee. Fifty years later, H learns of the loan and promptly demands that M return them. M refuses. H sues M in replevin. In this suit, what result? See *Estate of McCagg*, 450 A.2d 414 (D.C. 1982).

SOLOMON R. GUGGENHEIM FOUNDATION v. LUBELL
569 N.E.2d 426 (N.Y. 1991)

WACHTLER C.J.

The backdrop for this replevin action is the New York City art market, where masterpieces command extraordinary prices at auction and illicit dealing in stolen merchandise is an industry all its own. The Solomon R. Guggenheim Foundation, which operates the Guggenheim Museum in New York City, is seeking to recover a Chagall gouache worth an estimated $200,000. The Guggenheim believes that the gouache was stolen from its premises by a mailroom employee sometime in the late 1960s. The appellant Rachel Lubell and her husband, now deceased, bought the painting from a well-known Madison Avenue gallery in 1967 and have displayed it in their home for more than 20 years. Mrs. Lubell claims that before the Guggenheim's demand for its return in 1986, she had no reason to believe that the painting had been stolen.

On this appeal, we must decide if the museum's failure to take certain steps to locate the gouache is relevant to the appellant's Statute of Limitations defense. In effect, the appellant argues that the museum had a duty to use reasonable diligence to recover the gouache, that it did not do so, and that its cause of action in replevin is consequently barred by the Statute of Limitations. The Appellate Division rejected the appellant's argument. We agree with the Appellate Division that the timing of the museum's demand for the gouache and the appellant's refusal to return it are the only relevant factors in assessing the merits of the Statute of Limitations defense. We see no justification for undermining the clarity and predictability of this rule by carving out an exception where the chattel to be returned is a valuable piece of art. Appellant's affirmative defense of laches remains viable, however, and her claims that the museum did not undertake a reasonably diligent search for the missing painting will enter into the trial court's evaluation of the merits of that defense. Accordingly, the order of the Appellate Division should be affirmed.

The gouache, known alternately as Menageries or Le Marchand de Bestiaux (The Cattle Dealer), was painted by Marc Chagall in 1912, in preparation for an oil painting also entitled Le Marchand de Bestiaux. It was donated to the museum in 1937 by Solomon R. Guggenheim.

The museum keeps track of its collection through the use of "accession cards," which indicate when individual pieces leave the museum on loan, when they are returned and when they are transferred between the museum and storage. The museum lent the painting to a number of other art museums over the years. The last such loan occurred in 1961–1962. The accession card for the painting indicates that it was seen in the museum on April 2, 1965. The next notation on the accession card is undated and indicates that the painting could not be located.

Precisely when the museum first learned that the gouache had been stolen is a matter of some dispute. The museum acknowledges that it discovered that the painting was not where it should be sometime in the late 1960s, but claims that it did not know that the painting had in fact been stolen until it undertook a complete inventory of the museum collection beginning in 1969 and ending in 1970. According to the museum, such an inventory was typically taken about once every 10 years. The appellant, on the other hand, argues that the museum knew as early as 1965 that the painting had been stolen. It is undisputed, however, that the Guggenheim did not inform other museums, galleries or artistic organizations of the theft, and additionally, did not notify the New York City Police, the FBI, Interpol or any other law enforcement authorities. The museum asserts that this was a tactical decision based upon its belief that to publicize the theft would succeed only in driving the gouache further underground and greatly diminishing the possibility that it would ever be recovered. In 1974, having concluded that all efforts to recover the gouache had been exhausted, the museum's Board of Trustees voted to "deaccession" the gouache, thereby removing it from the museum's records.

Mr. and Mrs. Lubell had purchased the painting from the Robert Elkon Gallery for $17,000 in May of 1967. The invoice and receipt indicated that the gouache had been in the collection of a named individual, who later turned out to be the museum mailroom employee suspected of the theft. They exhibited the painting twice, in 1967 and in 1981, both times at the Elkon Gallery. In 1985, a private art dealer brought a transparency of the painting to Sotheby's for an auction estimate. The person to whom the dealer showed the transparency had previously worked at the Guggenheim and recognized the gouache as a piece that was missing from the museum. She notified the museum, which traced the painting back to the defendant. On January 9, 1986, Thomas Messer, the museum's director, wrote a letter to the defendant demanding the return of the gouache. Mrs. Lubell refused to return the painting and the instant action for recovery of the painting, or, in the alternative, $200,000, was commenced on September 28, 1987.

In her answer, the appellant raised as affirmative defenses the Statute of Limitations, her status as a good-faith purchaser for value, adverse possession, laches, and the museum's culpable conduct. The museum moved to compel discovery and inspection of the gouache and the defendant cross-moved for summary judgment. In her summary judgment papers, the appellant argued that the replevin action to compel the return of the painting was barred by the three-year Statute of Limitations because the museum had done nothing to locate its property in the 20-year interval between the theft and the museum's fortuitous discovery that the painting was in Mrs. Lubell's possession. The trial court granted the appellant's cross motion for summary judgment, relying on *DeWeerth v. Baldinger* (836 F2d 103), an opinion from the United States Court of Appeals for the Second Circuit. The trial court cited New York cases holding that a cause of action in replevin accrues when demand is made upon the possessor and the possessor refuses to return the chattel. The court reasoned, however, that in order to avoid prejudice to a good-faith purchaser, demand cannot be unreasonably delayed and that a property owner has an obligation to use reasonable efforts to locate its missing property to ensure that demand is not so delayed. Because the museum in this case had done nothing for 20 years but search its own premises, the court found that its conduct was unreasonable as a matter of law. Consequently, the court granted Mrs. Lubell's cross motion for summary judgment on the grounds that the museum's cause of action was time barred.

The Appellate Division modified, dismissing the Statute of Limitations defense and denying the appellant's cross motion for summary judgment. The Appellate Division held that the trial court had erred in concluding that "delay alone can make a replevin action untimely." The court stated that the appellant's lack of diligence argument was more in the nature of laches than the Statute of Limitations and that as a result, the appellant needed to show that she had been prejudiced by the museum's delay in demanding return of the gouache. The court also held that summary judgment was inappropriate because several issues of fact existed, including whether the museum's response to the theft was unreasonable, when the museum first realized that the gouache was missing, when the museum should have realized that the gouache had been stolen, whether it was unreasonable for the museum not to have taken certain steps after it realized that the gouache was missing but before it realized that it had been stolen, and when the museum learned of the defendant's possession of the gouache. The Appellate Division granted leave to this Court, certifying the following question: "Was the order of this Court, which modified the order of the Supreme Court, properly made?" We answer this certified question in the affirmative.

New York case law has long protected the right of the owner whose property has been stolen to recover that property, even if it is in the possession of a good-faith purchaser for value (see, *Saltus & Saltus v. Everett*, 20 Wend 267, 282). There is a three-year Statute of Limitations for recovery of a chattel (CPLR 214 [3]). The rule in this State is that a cause of action for replevin against the good-faith purchaser of a stolen chattel accrues when the true owner makes demand for return of the chattel and the person in possession of the chattel refuses to return it (see, e.g., *Goodwin v. Wertheimer*, 99 NY 149, 153). Until demand is made and refused, possession of the stolen property by the good-faith purchaser for value is not considered wrongful (see, e.g., *Gillet v. Roberts*, 57 NY 28, 30–31). Although seemingly anomalous, a different rule applies when the stolen object is in the possession of the thief. In that situation, the Statute of Limitations runs from the time of the theft (see, *Sporn v. MCA Records*, 58 NY2d 482, 487–488), even if the property owner was unaware of the theft at the time that it occurred (see, *Varga v. Credit Suisse*, 5 AD2d 289, 292–293, affd 5 NY2d 865).

In *DeWeerth v. Baldinger (supra)*, which the trial court in this case relied upon in granting Mrs. Lubell's summary judgment motion, the Second Circuit took note of the fact that New York case law treats thieves and good-faith purchasers differently and looked to that difference as a basis for imposing a reasonable diligence requirement on the owners of stolen art. * * * We have reexamined the relevant New York case law and we conclude that the Second Circuit should not have imposed a duty of reasonable diligence on the owners of stolen art work for purposes of the Statute of Limitations.

While the demand and refusal rule is not the only possible method of measuring the accrual of replevin claims, it does appear to be the rule that affords the most protection to the true owners of stolen property. Less protective measures would include running the three-year statutory period from the time of the theft even where a good-faith purchaser is in possession of the stolen chattel, or, alternatively, calculating the statutory period from the time that the good-faith purchaser obtains possession of the chattel. Other States that have considered this issue have applied a discovery rule to these cases, with the Statute of Limitations running from the time that the owner discovered or reasonably should have discovered the whereabouts of the work of art that had been stolen (see, e.g., *O'Keeffe v. Snyder*, 83 NJ 478, 416 A2d 862; Cal Civ Proc Code § 338[c]).

New York has already considered-and rejected-adoption of a discovery rule. In 1986, both houses of the New York State Legislature passed Assembly Bill 11462-A (Senate Bill 3274-B), which would have modified the demand and refusal rule and instituted a discovery rule in actions for recovery of art objects brought against certain not-for-profit institutions. This bill provided that the three-year Statute of Limitations would run from the time these institutions gave notice, in a manner specified by the statute, that they were in possession of a particular object. Governor Cuomo vetoed the measure, however, on advice of the United States Department of State. . . . The Governor . . . had been advised by the State Department that the bill, if it went into effect, would have caused New York to become "a haven for cultural property stolen abroad since such objects [would] be immune from recovery under the limited time periods established by the bill."

The history of this bill and the concerns expressed by the Governor in vetoing it, when considered together with the abundant case law spelling out the demand and refusal rule, convince us that that rule remains the law in New York and that there is no reason to obscure its straightforward protection of true owners by creating a duty of reasonable diligence. Our case law already recognizes that the true owner, having discovered the location of its lost property, cannot unreasonably delay making demand upon the person in possession of that property (see, e.g., *Heide v. Glidden Buick Corp.*, 188 Misc 198). Here, however, where the demand and refusal is a substantive and not a procedural element of the cause of action (see, *Guggenheim Found. v. Lubell*, 153 AD2d, at 147; compare, CPLR 206 [where a demand is necessary to entitle a person to commence an action, the time to commence that action is measured from when the right to make demand is complete]), it would not be prudent to extend that case law and impose the additional duty of diligence before the true owner has reason to know where its missing chattel is to be found.

Further, the facts of this case reveal how difficult it would be to specify the type of conduct that would be required for a showing of reasonable diligence. Here, the parties hotly contest whether publicizing the theft would have turned up the gouache. According to the museum, some members of the art community believe that publicizing a theft exposes gaps in security and can lead to more thefts; the museum also argues that publicity often pushes a missing painting further underground. In light of the fact that members of the art community have apparently not reached a consensus on the best way to retrieve stolen art, it would be particularly inappropriate for this Court to spell out arbitrary rules of conduct that all true owners of stolen art work would have to follow to the letter if they wanted to preserve their right to pursue a cause of action in replevin. All owners of stolen property should not be expected to behave in the same way and should not be held to a common standard. The value of the property stolen, the manner in which it was stolen, and the type of institution from which it was stolen will all necessarily affect the manner in which a true owner will search for missing property. We conclude that it would be difficult, if not impossible, to craft a reasonable diligence requirement that could take into account all of these variables and that would not unduly burden the true owner.

Further, our decision today is in part influenced by our recognition that New York enjoys a worldwide reputation as a preeminent cultural center. To place the burden of locating stolen artwork on the true owner and to foreclose the rights of that owner to recover its property if the burden is not met would, we believe, encourage illicit trafficking in stolen art. Three years after the theft, any purchaser, good faith or not, would be able to hold onto stolen art work unless the true owner was able to establish that it had undertaken a reasonable search for the missing art. This shifting of the burden onto the wronged owner is inappropriate. In our opinion, the better rule gives the owner relatively greater protection and places the burden of investigating the provenance of a work of art on the potential purchaser.

Despite our conclusion that the imposition of a reasonable diligence requirement on the museum would be inappropriate for purposes of the Statute of Limitations, our holding today should not be seen as either sanctioning the museum's conduct or suggesting that the museum's conduct is no longer an issue in this case. We agree with the Appellate Division that the arguments raised in the appellant's summary judgment papers are directed at the conscience of the court and its ability to bring equitable considerations to bear in the ultimate disposition of the painting. As noted above, although appellant's Statute of Limitations argument fails, her contention that the museum did not exercise reasonable diligence in locating the painting will be considered by the Trial Judge in the context of her laches defense. The conduct of both the appellant and the museum will be relevant to any consideration of this defense at the trial level, and as the Appellate Division noted, prejudice will also need to be shown. On the limited record before us there is no indication that the equities favor either party. Mr. and Mrs. Lubell investigated the provenance of the gouache before the purchase by contacting the artist and his son-in-law directly. The Lubells displayed the painting in their home for more than 20 years with no reason to suspect that it was not legally theirs. These facts will doubtless have some impact on the final decision regarding appellant's laches defense. Because it is impossible to conclude from the facts of this case that the museum's conduct was unreasonable as a matter of law, however, Mrs. Lubell's cross motion for summary judgment was properly denied.

We agree with the Appellate Division that the burden of proving that the painting was not stolen properly rests with the appellant Mrs. Lubell. Accordingly, the order of the Appellate Division should be affirmed. . . .

NOTE

The traditional rule involved in this type of case, and applied by the trial court, is that the statute of limitations runs from the time of a theft. The New York rule used in *Lubell* establishes a second approach, using an "accrual" type of statute of limitations for replevin. It is that the action runs from the time the owner made a demand for the return of the chattel from its possessor, not from the time of either the theft or its discovery. A third approach is taken in the much discussed opinion in *O'Keeffe v. Snyder*, 416 A.2d 862 (N.J. 1980), followed in *DeWeerth*. The New Jersey court wrote:

> The discovery rule provides that, in an appropriate case, a cause of action will not accrue until the injured party discovers, or by exercise of reasonable diligence and intelligence should have discovered, facts which form the basis of a cause of action. The rule is essentially a principle of equity, the purpose of which is to mitigate unjust results that otherwise might flow from strict adherence to a rule of law. . . . [W]e conclude that the discovery rule applies to an action for replevin of a painting. . . .

> We are persuaded that the introduction of equitable considerations through the discovery rule provides a more satisfactory response than the doctrine of adverse possession. The discovery rule shifts the emphasis from the conduct of the possessor to the conduct of the owner. The focus of the inquiry will no longer be whether the possessor has met the tests of adverse possession, but whether the owner has acted with due diligence in pursuing his or her personal property. . . . [I]f an artist diligently seeks the recovery of a lost or stolen painting, but cannot find it or discover the identity of the possessor, the statute of limitations will not begin to run. The rule permits an artist who uses reasonable efforts to report, investigate, and recover a painting to preserve the rights of title and possession.

> Properly interpreted, the discovery rule becomes a vehicle for transporting equitable considerations into the statute of limitations for replevin. . . .

> To summarize, the operative fact that divests the original owner of title to either personal or real property is the expiration of the period of limitations. In the past, adverse possession has described the nature of the conduct that will vest title of a chattel at the end of the statutory period. Our adoption of the discovery rule does not change the conclusion that at the end of the statutory period title will vest in the possessor.

We next consider the effect of transfers of a chattel from one possessor to another during the period of limitation under the discovery rule. Under the discovery rule, the statute of limitations on an action for replevin begins to run when the owner knows or reasonably should know of his cause of action and the identity of the possessor of the chattel. Subsequent transfers of the chattel are part of the continuous dispossession of the chattel from the original owner. The important point is not that there has been a substitution of possessors, but that there has been a continuous dispossession of the former owner. . . . An owner who diligently seeks his chattel should be entitled to the benefit of the discovery rule although it may have passed through many hands. Conversely an owner who sleeps on his rights may be denied the benefit of the discovery rule although the chattel may have been possessed by only one person.

Id. at 869–75. What will be the impact of such a rule on the law of adverse possession?

Chapter 2

THE LAW OF NEIGHBORS

INTRODUCTION

This chapter considers the rights and duties of the owners of neighboring lands. As used here, neighbors include landowners whose property lies next to or near to the land in question. It also covers owners in a common watershed. We will also continue studying the legal importance of possession, this time with regard to the acquisition of title to real property.

I. ADVERSE POSSESSION

A. The Statutory Basis

Every American jurisdiction has a statute of limitations requiring that an action to recover property be brought within a certain number of years from the time when the right to bring the action arose. We expect a person with a legal claim to bring it within a reasonable period of time. Virtually all Western legal systems have similar provisions, normally described as the law of prescription. Prescription, or long usage, is a direct means of acquiring a right in property. See Reinhard Zimmermann, The Law of Obligations 767–70 (1990). Although couched in the right of owners to recover their property, American statutes also permit a wrongful possessor of land to obtain good title to it whenever the rightful owner fails to sue to recover the land within the statutory period. As in *Chapin v. Freeland*, 8 N.E. 128 (Mass. 1886), *supra*, Chapter 1, once the right of action is extinguished, so is the owner's right to the land. The law in effect creates a new title in the person who had once been a wrongful possessor.

Although earlier precedents did exist, the first effective English statute of limitations was enacted in 1623–24 (21 Jac. I, c. 16). It stated:

> For quieting of men's estates and avoiding of suits, Be it enacted that . . . writs [to recover land] at anytime hereafter to be sued or brought by occasion or means of any title or cause hereafter happening, shall be sued and taken within twenty years next after the title and cause of action first descended or fallen, and at no time after the said twenty years.

Early American statutes adopted the same basic pattern. The New York statute at issue in the following case read:

> § 1. The people of this state will not sue or implead any person for, or in respect to, any lands, tenements or hereditaments, or for the issues or

profits thereof, by reason of any right or title of the said people to the same, unless,

    1. Such right or title shall have accrued within twenty years before any suit, or proceeding, for the same shall be commenced. . . .

§ 16. If any person entitled to commence any action in this Article specified, . . . be at the time such title shall first descend or accrue, either: (1) within the age of twenty-one years; or (2) insane; or (3) imprisoned on any criminal charge or in execution upon some conviction of a criminal offence for any term less than for life; or (4) a married woman. The time during which such disability shall continue shall not be deemed any portion of the time in this Article limited for the commencement of such suit, . . . but such person may bring such action . . . within ten years after such disability [be] removed, but not after that period.

disability case

FLEMING v. GRISWOLD
3 Hill 85 (N.Y. 1842)

P claims clock stopped due to her disability.

Ejectment, tried at the Tompkins Circuit, in September, 1841, before MONELL, C.J.

The plaintiffs claimed the premises in question in right of Mrs. Fleming, one of the plaintiffs, who was heir of Peter Tallman. At the trial the following facts appeared: Tallman acquired a valid title to the premises on the 27th of January, 1795. In 1805, Edward Griswold held the premises adversely to Tallman, under a warranty deed from one Earll; and in 1811, the former, being still in possession, conveyed to Abraham Griswold, the defendant, who thereupon entered and continued to hold the premises till the commencement of this suit, in 1840. Tallman died in 1815; Mrs. Fleming, his daughter, having married the other plaintiff, J.B. Fleming, in 1807, while she was under the age of 21 years.

Disability must exist at the time the title is first adversely possessed.

The circuit judge charged the jury that, the defendant having shown in himself and the one under whom he claimed an adverse possession for more than twenty-five years, he was entitled to a verdict, notwithstanding Mrs. Fleming's disabilities by reason of infancy and coverture. The plaintiffs excepted, and a verdict having been rendered against them, they now moved for a new trial on a bill of exceptions.

S. Sherwood, for the plaintiffs, said, he found the opinion of the bar much against him on the question raised by the bill of exceptions, and some cases looked that way; but he thought the latter distinguishable from the present. He should contend, if the court deemed the case open for discussion, that inasmuch as at the time Mrs. Fleming's right of entry accrued she was under disability, the statute (2 R.S. 293,) did not run against her. (*Id.* 295, § 16.)

But the Court were clear that the opposite doctrine must prevail; and they did not think their opinion could be changed by discussion, or any reflection they might bestow on the question. They considered the rule entirely settled, that where the statute has begun to run against the ancestor or the other person under whom the plaintiff claims, it continues to run against the plaintiff, notwithstanding any disability when the right accrues to the latter. The revised statutes have not changed the law on this subject. New trial denied.

NOTES AND PROBLEMS

1. Problems regarding accrual of a cause of action and disabilities arise in a variety of contexts. Under the New York statute, how long would B have to bring suit to recover Blackacre in these situations?

a. In 1990, O grants Blackacre to B, who is under a disability. In 1991, X enters and possesses the property adversely. In 2005, B's disability is removed.

b. In 1990, O grants Blackacre to B, who is under a disability. In 1991, X enters and possesses the property adversely. In 1995, B's disability is removed.

c. In 1990, O grants Blackacre to A during A's lifetime, then to B at A's death. In 1991, X enters and possesses the property adversely. A dies in 2010.

d. In 1990, X enters Blackacre and possesses it adversely to O. In 2000, O grants the property to A during A's lifetime, then to B at A's death. A dies in 2010.

e. In 1990, O dies leaving B, who is a minor, as his heir. In 1991, X enters Blackacre and possesses it adversely. In 1995, B is convicted of a felony and imprisoned. In 2000, B reaches the age of majority. In 2005, B is released from prison.

2. In these problems, suppose that X conveyed his interest in Blackacre to Y before the statute had run. Would that change the outcome? Not necessarily. The doctrine of "tacking" allows Y to add the period of X's possession to Y's own if privity of possession between them exists. Privity of possession ordinarily requires some kind of formal connection, such as a grant, a devise, or passage of title by intestate succession. If, therefore, Y entered Blackacre adversely to X, privity between them would not exist and a new statutory period would begin, allowing O a longer period to bring suit. Problems in establishing privity have sometimes been raised where (as often happens) the deed from X to Y does not describe the land adversely possessed. See, e.g., *Senez v. Collins*, 957 A.2d 1057, 1075–76 (Md. App. 2008).

3. Once the statute of limitations has run, the adverse possessor's title is treated as though it had existed from the moment his possession began. This is the "relation back" doctrine. Among other things, it means that the holder of the record title has no claim to damages to the land during any part of the period of adverse possession, even though the statute of limitations for injury to property may not have run out on damage of recent occurrence. It would be "a contradiction in terms" to give the possessor full title and at the same time hold the possessor liable for damages "for his acts of possession done while his inchoate title was being perfected." *Counce v. Yount-Lee Oil Co.*, 87 F.2d 572, 575 (5th Cir. 1937). Suppose a creditor of the holder of record title secured a statutory lien against the property before the adverse possessor's title had ripened. Would it follow that the lien would be lost automatically once the adverse possessor's claim ripened?

B. The Elements of Adverse Possession

Although sometimes formulated in slightly different terms, a five-part test has evolved to determine whether title has been acquired by adverse possession. The theory behind the test is that the record owner does not have a true cause of action against the adverse possessor if one or more of these elements is lacking. In order to acquire title, the occupant's possession must be: (a) actual; (b) continuous for the statutory period; (c) exclusive; (d) hostile; and (e) open and notorious.

It is not difficult to see the statutory basis at work here. Unless the occupant's possession is open and notorious, for example, the record owner has no meaningful way of bringing an action of ejectment against him. The record owner cannot know of the adverse possessor's occupancy. Similarly, if the occupant makes only sporadic use of the property, the statute will not run because no real cause of action in ejectment can be brought by the record owner.

The following two cases illustrate some of the problems (and solutions) that occur in applying this five-part test.

cabin case

ANDERSON v. COLD SPRING TUNGSTEN, INC.
458 P.2d 756 (Colo. 1969)

Doctrine of Constructive AP: constructive possession of part gets you the whole — only if there's a deed.

PRINGLE, J.

Cold Spring Tungsten, Inc. (hereinafter referred to as the plaintiff) filed an action in the Boulder District Court under R.C.P. Colo. 105 in 1966 naming as defendants June B. Anderson, James A. Anderson, and William J. Doherty (all hereinafter referred to as the defendants or by name) and seeking to quiet title to certain real property located in the County of Boulder.

The defendants counterclaimed for judgment establishing title in themselves to a portion of the said property based on their alleged adverse possession for a period in excess of the statutory period. The trial judge found that the defendants were entitled to the cabin situated on the property, but not to the land upon which it was situated. He therefore denied the counterclaim and quieted the title in the plaintiff.

The facts are not in dispute. The plaintiff holds the record title to the property in question. William J. Doherty purchased a cabin located upon this property from the Boulder Rotary Club in 1930. Mr. Doherty made improvements on the cabin, and from 1930 until the time when this action was commenced, he and the members of his family including the other defendants in this action have made use of the cabin by spending weekends there during the summer months and occasionally remaining for a month or longer. The defendants have kept the cabin in repair, have posted it at one time or another to warn off trespassers, and have kept the cabin door locked and the windows shuttered during periods of nonuse. They used a portion of the land in question as follows: on one side of the cabin for toilet facilities and on the other side of the cabin for trash and garbage facilities. Mr. Doherty has paid the real estate taxes for each year since his entry on the property.

It is the contention of the defendants that (1) the trial judge committed error in finding that the original entry onto the property by Mr. Doherty in 1930 was not hostile because it was "peaceable," and (2) that the trial judge committed error in finding that the continued use and occupation of the cabin by the defendants did not amount to adverse possession of any of the property in dispute. We agree with the position of the defendants. We therefore reverse the judgment of the trial judge and remand the case to the district court for further proceedings consistent with this opinion.

The trial judge found that the entry onto the property in dispute by Mr. Doherty was "peaceable" and therefore was not adverse or hostile as required by law in order to sustain a claim of adverse possession. It is true that the record here shows no evidence of force employed by the party making the entry against either the holder of the record title or against the public. But such a showing of force or actual dispute is not necessary to constitute hostile entry so as to lay a foundation for a claim of adverse possession. The requirement that adverse possession be both hostile and adverse does not mean that there need be any violence connected with the entry onto the property or that there be any actual dispute as to ownership between the adverse possessor and the owner of the property. Such a contention was expressly rejected by this Court in *Moss v. O'Brien*, 165 Colo. 93, 437 P.2d 348, in which we stated: "Plaintiffs argue that the evidence failed to establish a 'hostile claim,' or that defendants ever claimed to own more land than their record title showed. Implicit in their argument is the assumption that a deliberate attempt to steal a neighbor's property, or an actual dispute at some previous time is necessary in order to show an intention to hold adversely. This is not the law in Colorado."

Hostility arises from the intention of the adverse possessor to claim exclusive ownership of the property occupied. No specific intent directed toward the property owner is required. This has been made amply clear in the boundary cases decided by this Court and particularly in *Vade v. Sickler*, 118 Colo. 236, 195 P.2d 390, where the court found hostile and adverse possession even though the adverse possessor had stated that he was claiming only to what he believed to be the true boundary of his land and had no intention of claiming the land of another. All that the court in *Vade* required to establish hostility was that the person claiming adverse possession occupy the property with belief that the property is his and not another's.

Whether possession is hostile or adverse is ordinarily a question of fact. *Moss v. O'Brien, supra*. Hostile intent is to be determined not only from the declarations of the parties but from reasonable deductions from the facts as well. *Vade v. Sickler, supra*. In reviewing such issues of fact, this Court has taken the position that it will not set aside the findings of the trial judge where they are sustained by competent and adequate evidence, amply appearing from the record. *Segelke v. Atkins*, 144 Colo. 558, 357 P.2d 636. But such restraint in no way limits the power of this Court to reject the findings and conclusions of the trial judge where they are not supported by any evidence in the record or where the law has not been applied correctly.

Limiting our discussion to the property actually occupied by the defendants, we find no basis in the record to support the conclusion of the trial judge that entry upon the property was not hostile and adverse. This is not a case in which the judge has been called upon to consider conflicting evidence. The uncontroverted testimony of Mr. Doherty, who is the party who made the original entry onto the property in 1930, was that he believed he had acquired ownership to and was the actual owner of some of the property upon which the cabin was situated. Testimony by the other defendants reveals that they thought that they owned the property.

There is nothing in the facts and circumstances revealed by the record that would justify a finding of non-hostile intent in the face of the specific and unrebutted testimony of the defendants to the contrary, and their actions during the years they occupied the cabin site. Nor is there any other evidence in the record from which the trial court could infer that the defendants did not claim the cabin site as their own. The trial judge stated that his finding of non-hostile intent was required because there was no evidence that the property claimed by the defendants was ever fenced or that the boundaries were ever marked, and that such failure shows a willingness to share the use and possession of the property with the public. But the failure to fence does not alone evidence non-hostile intent. The facts and circumstances in this record reveal an uncontradicted, definite intent to claim ownership to the land associated with the defendants' exclusive use of the cabin. The circumstances relied upon by the trial judge only serve to limit the claim of the defendants and do not support a finding that there was no hostile claim to any of the property described in the counterclaim.

Because it is clear that the original entry by the defendants was hostile and adverse, it is not necessary for us to consider the weight placed by the trial judge on *Lovejoy v. School District*, 129 Colo. 306, 269 P.2d 1067. In *Lovejoy* the original entry by the school district onto the property was not adverse since the property was then owned by the state. There was no evidence that at the time the patent was issued to private owners or thereafter the school district made any claim to ownership of the property upon which the school was located. On the contrary, there was evidence that at the time the school was built on the property it was the custom of landowners to encourage use of their private property in order to obtain the services of the school for their children. Since *Lovejoy* is thus limited by its facts to a situation where original entry is not adverse, it does not control or contribute to disposal of the present controversy.

The trial judge found that, because the public used part of the property in question for picnicking, there was no exclusive possession of the property for the statutory period. In order for possession to be exclusive, it is not necessary that all use of that property by the public be prevented. In *McKelvy v. Cooper*, 165 Colo. 102, 437 P.2d 346, this Court held that casual intrusion by fishermen would not defeat a claim of exclusive possession. In *McKelvy* the Michigan case of *Pulcifer v. Bishop*, 246 Mich. 579, 225 N.W. 3, was cited with approval. The Michigan court held that the defendant had established a claim by adverse possession to a portion of the beach even though the beach was commonly used by others for recreation and stated: ". . . In view of the well-known tendency of people to make rather free use of shores and beaches, we think defendant exercised all control of these premises that reasonably could be expected in view of their character. . . ." In the present case, the defendants testified that during the times they occupied the cabin they would ask picnickers to leave the property. During periods of nonuse, the cabin door was locked and shutters were placed on the windows. There is no evidence of any public use of the cabin or the land which immediately surrounds it. In light of the nature of the property claimed by the defendants and in light of the nature of their use of the property as a vacation cabin, the record reveals that the defendants acted as the average landowner would act under such circumstances to assert the exclusive nature of their possession.

There remains to be considered the question of the boundaries to be fixed on the property acquired by the defendants. The boundaries of the land which the defendants claim have not been established by fences or barriers for the period of the statute of limitations. There is no deed which describes the extent of their holding. In such a case as this the parties claiming title by adverse possession may not claim any property not actually occupied by them for the statutory period.

The extent of actual occupancy must be determined by the court when ascertaining the extent of the adverse interest. While this Court has not had the opportunity to specifically discuss the concept of actual occupancy in determining the extent of an adverse claim, other courts have considered the problem. ". . . Adverse possession without enclosure need not be characterized by a physical, constant, visible occupancy or improved by improvements of every square foot of the land. . . . Actual occupancy is not limited to structural encroachment which is common but is not the only physical characteristic of possession. Actual occupancy means the ordinary use to which the land is capable and such as an owner would make of it. Any actual visible means, which gives notice of exclusion from the property to the true owner or to the public and of the defendant's dominion over it, is sufficient." *Burkhardt v. Smith*, 17 Wis.2d 132, 138, 115 N.W.2d 540, 543–44.

This case is remanded to the district court for a determination of the boundaries of the property to which the defendants have acquired title by actual occupancy and adverse possession. In making such boundaries and quieting defendants' title thereto, the trial court is to determine the land necessarily appurtenant to the cabin, taking into consideration the location and nature of the property, and the uses to which the property lends itself, the uses made of the property by the defendants, and the evidence of visible occupation of the property by the defendants which would give notice of their exclusive and adverse claim to the owner and the public. The judgment is reversed and the cause is remanded with directions to proceed in accordance with the views outlined herein.

GRACE v. KOCH
692 N.E.2d 1009 (Ohio 1998)

In the early 1960s, Leonard L. Grace, Jr. built a house on Wuest Road in Colerain Township. The land ("parcel 44") had been given to him by his parents from a larger tract ("parcel 43") that they owned. Grace constructed a house and driveway on parcel 44, and he and his father built a split-rail fence thirty-four feet to the north of the driveway to keep livestock from straying onto parcel 44. The fence did not follow the property line, and the thirty-four-foot strip between the driveway and the fence was wholly inside parcel 43.

In 1970, Grace sold parcel 44 to Anthony H. and Elizabeth A. Koch. To facilitate the sale, Grace obtained an easement from his parents over parcel 43 so that the Kochs could use the existing driveway, which encroached on parcel 43 by five feet, and conveyed this easement to the Kochs. The Kochs knew at the time and testified subsequently that they did not own the land between the driveway and the fence ("the strip"), which was part of parcel 43. Nevertheless, the Kochs began using the strip as a sideyard and continued to use it as such through the time of the current litigation.

In 1991, after his father passed away, Grace became the owner of parcel 43. In January, 1992, he mortgaged parcel 43 to Mayflower Savings & Loan Company ("Mayflower").

At some point in 1970, Anthony Koch sought permission from Grace to mow the grass on the strip and received express permission. Grace's parents agreed. Koch testified that he had never discussed his use of the strip as a sideyard with either Grace or Grace's parents. Neighbors testified that they assumed that the Kochs owned the strip but that no one had ever told them so. Grace's parents never used the strip. The record is unclear as to whether Grace used it since obtaining title to parcel 43. It is not disputed that the Kochs used the strip, from the time they purchased parcel 44 through the time of litigation, by parking cars on it, installing a swing set, planting a tree, storing oil drums, and erecting a car port.

There is no indication in the record that there were any disputes over the ownership or use of the strip from 1970 through 1991. That changed in 1992. Grace became upset about the noise from a race car belonging to the Kochs' son. In July 1992, when Koch spread gravel over the strip, Grace objected and ordered Koch to stop trespassing. When Koch refused, Grace parked on the strip to prevent Koch from spreading more gravel. He removed the portions of the fence that separated the strip from the remainder of parcel 43.

In September 1992, Grace filed a complaint against the Kochs for trespass, seeking an injunction and damages for trespass. The Kochs filed a counterclaim to quiet title in them through adverse possession and for damages. The Kochs joined Mayflower as a party defendant. After trial, the trial court found that the Kochs owned the strip by adverse possession and awarded them $577.49 in damages.

On appeal, the court of appeals reversed, stating that the Kochs "did not prove by clear and convincing evidence, not even by a preponderance, that their use of the strip was sufficiently exclusive, hostile, or notorious for the required twenty-one years to take title to the strip by adverse possession." The court remanded to the trial court with instructions that title to the strip should be restored to Grace and that damages for the Kochs' trespass should be determined.

The cause is now before this court pursuant to the allowance of a discretionary appeal.

PFEIFER, J.

In this case, we examine the common-law doctrine of adverse possession. For the reasons that follow, we hold that adverse possession must be proven by clear and convincing evidence and affirm the court of appeals' determination that the Kochs had not established title by adverse possession.

To acquire title by adverse possession, the party claiming title must show exclusive possession and open, notorious, continuous, and adverse use for a period of twenty-one years. . . . Failure of proof as to any of the elements results in failure to acquire title by adverse possession. *Pennsylvania Rd. Co. v. Donovan*, 111 Ohio St. at 349–50, 145 N.E. at 482.

As a preliminary matter, we must clarify the quantum of proof needed to establish each element of an adverse possession claim, something this court has not done definitively apart from the cotenant context. See *Demmitt v. McMillan* (1984), 16 Ohio App. 3d 138, 140, 474 N.E.2d 1212, 1215, 16 Ohio B. Rep. 146, 148.

The court of appeals spoke at length about adverse possession being disfavored. We agree. A successful adverse possession action results in a legal titleholder forfeiting ownership to an adverse holder without compensation. Such a doctrine should be disfavored, and that is why the elements of adverse possession are stringent. See 10 Thompson on Real Property (Thomas Ed. 1994) 108, Section 87.05 ("there are no equities in favor of a person seeking to acquire property of another by adverse holding"). We believe that the burden of proof should be equally rigorous. A substantial majority of our sister states agree and already apply the clear and convincing evidentiary standard, or a variant thereof, to adverse possession claims. We hold that to acquire title by adverse possession a party must prove, by clear and convincing evidence, exclusive possession and open, notorious, continuous, and adverse use for a period of twenty-one years.

Grace first took action to assert ownership in July 1992 when Anthony Koch began spreading gravel over the strip and Grace attempted to stop him. Therefore, to establish adverse possession, the Kochs must prove by clear and convincing evidence that each element of adverse possession had been established since 1971. We find it unnecessary to address each of the elements of adverse possession because the Kochs did not establish by clear and convincing evidence that they held the strip adversely to Grace for the entire statutory period.

This court has stated that "it is the visible and adverse possession with an intent to possess that constitutes [the occupancy's] adverse character," *Humphries v. Huffman* (1878), 33 Ohio St. 395, 402, and that "the occupancy must be such as to give notice to the real owner of the extent of the adverse claim." *Id.* at 404. In *Lane v. Kennedy* (1861), 13 Ohio St. 42, this court stated that to make possession adverse, "there must have been an intention on the part of the person in possession to *claim title, so manifested* by his declarations or his acts, that a failure of the owner to prosecute within the time limited, raises a presumption of an extinguishment or a surrender of his claim," (Emphasis *sic.*) *Id.* at 47.

The Vermont Supreme Court stated the same proposition more colorfully when it declared that to establish adversity, "the tenant must unfurl his flag on the land, and keep it flying so that the owner may see, if he will, that an enemy has invaded his dominions and planted his standard of conquest." *Darling v. Ennis* (1980), 138 Vt. 311, 313, 415 A.2d 228, 230. See, also, *Philbin v. Carr* (1920), 75 Ind. App. 560, 591, 129 N.E. 19, 30.

There is no question that the Kochs used the strip. They mowed the grass, parked cars in the strip, and their children played in the strip. The Kochs also placed firewood, oil drums, and a swing set in the strip. While we consider the case a close one, we conclude that the record does not contain clear and convincing evidence that Grace or his parents were on notice that their dominions had been invaded in 1971. The Kochs asked for the Graces' permission before proceeding to mow the strip. Mr. Koch conceded that he knew that the strip belonged to Grace and that he never would have used it without permission. Absent clear and convincing evidence of the adversity of the Kochs' claim to the strip for the entire statutory period, adverse possession must fail.

Accordingly, we affirm the judgment of the court of appeals and remand the cause to the trial court for restoration of title to the strip to Grace and determination of damages for the Kochs' trespass on the strip. *Judgment affirmed.*

NOTES

1. A common addition to the five elements of adverse possession is the requirement that the adverse possessor's claim be accompanied by a "claim of right" or a "claim of title." Very often, it is stated as one aspect of the requirement of hostility. Some cases hold that it adds nothing in substance, meaning no more than that the claimant did not enter with the permission of the record owner. *Patterson v. Reigle*, 4 Pa. 201 (Pa. 1846). Other cases treat it as requiring that an adverse possessor must claim to have been the actual owner while the statute was running. *Howard v. Kunto*, 477 P.2d 210 (Wash. Ct. App. 1970). Many cases do not explain the term's exact meaning. See 3 Amer. L. Prop. § 15.4, at 774.

2. An investigative reporter discovered that three Colorado judges had successfully made claims to land adjacent to their own by making use of it for the statutory period, even though they were aware that they had no right to do so. Joey Bunch, *Land-seizure cases no rarity in Colorado*, Denv. Post, Nov. 26, 2007, at A-01. The judges who tried the resulting cases held that their fellow judges were simply taking advantage of a right the law provided and awarded title to them. The incidents caused a small outcry and also attracted the attention of the Colorado legislature, which enacted a statute requiring that an adverse possessor have "a good faith belief that [he or she was] the actual owner of the property" and that "the belief was reasonable" under the circumstances. Colo. Rev. Stat. § 38-41-101(3)(b)(II). Is this a sensible step? Some observers think it is not. Professor Lee Fennell believes it would be sensible actually to limit the doctrine to cases of "bad faith" possession. See *Efficient Trespass: The Case for "Bad Faith" Adverse Possession*, 100 Nw. U. L. Rev. 1041 (2006). See also Eduardo Moisés Peñalver & Sonia Katyal, *Property Outlaws*, 155 U. Pa. L. Rev. 1095 (2007); Thomas Merrill & Henry Smith, *Law and Morality: Property Law, the Morality of Property*, 48 Wm. & Mary L. Rev. 1850 (2007).

3. To what extent does the law of adverse possession serve legitimate economic goals? Some scholars contend that it does. They say first, that it "prevents valuable resources from being left idle for long periods of time," and second, that it "lowers the administrative costs of establishing rightful ownership claims in the event of a delayed dispute." See Robert Cooter & Thomas Ulen, Law and Economics 154–56 (1988); Thomas Miceli & C.F. Sirmans, *An Economic Theory of Adverse Possession*, 15 Int'l Rev. L. & Econ. 161 (1995). It may also be said that the doctrine puts the property into the hands of the party who values it most highly. See Stewart Sterk,

Neighbors in American Land Law, 87 Colum. L. Rev. 55 (1987). On the other hand, critics of the doctrine contend that it discourages conservation of land in its natural state and indirectly leads to degradation of the environment. See, e.g., John Sprankling, *The Antiwilderness Bias in American Property Law*, 63 U. Chi. L. Rev. 519 (1996).

4. When a person enters property with the permission of the owner, as under a lease, can he ever acquire title by adverse possession? What must that person do to start the statutory clock running? Cease paying rent? Convert the property to a use inconsistent with the rental? Give notice to the owner, actual or constructive, repudiating the lease? Actually exclude the owner from the land? See, e.g., *Dobbs v. Knoll*, 92 S.W.3d 176 (Mo. App. 2002). Establishing hostility is particularly difficult if a familial relationship exists between the parties, or if the record owner has allowed use of the land in dispute as a "neighborly accommodation." See, e.g., *Watkins v. Watkins*, 775 A.2d 841 (Pa. Super. 2001); *Gray v. Fitzhugh*, 576 P.2d 88 (Wyo. 1978).

C. The Future of Adverse Possession

Like Colorado, several American states have enacted statutes dealing specially with the requirements for establishing title by adverse possession. Most of them have added requirements to the traditional law based on the Statute of Limitations, seemingly in order to discourage easy acquisition of title by adverse possessors. The law of New York, for example, provides that "non-structural encroachments including, but not limited to, fences, hedges, shrubbery, plantings, sheds, and non-structural walls shall be deemed to be permissive and non-adverse." Similarly held to be deemed as permissive are "lawn mowing or similar maintenance across the boundary line." N.Y. RPAPL § 543 (enacted in 2008). For a decision that this statute may apply only prospectively, and not to an adverse possession claim that had already ripened into title by 2008, see *Franza v. Olin*, 897 N.Y.S.2d 804 (N.Y. App. Div. 2010).

Some states have enacted more elaborate statutory provisions to deal with the subject. Florida, for example, adopted the following measures:

> Fla. Stat. § 95.16 (1971): Whenever it appears that the occupant, or those under whom he claims, entered into possession of premises under claim of title exclusive of any other right, founding such claim upon a written instrument as being a conveyance of the premises in question, or upon a decree or judgment of a competent court, and that there has been a continued occupation and possession of the premises included in such instrument, decree, or judgment for seven years, the premises so included shall be deemed to have been held adversely, except that, where the premises so included consist of a tract divided into lots, the possession of one lot shall not be deemed a possession of any other lot of the same tract; provided, that adverse possession commencing after December 31, 1945, shall not be deemed to be adverse possession under color of title unless and until the instrument of conveyance of the premises in question upon which such claim of title is founded shall be duly recorded in the office of the clerk of the circuit court of the county in which the premises are situated.

Fla. Stat. § 95.17 (1971): For the purpose of constituting an adverse possession by any person claiming a title founded upon a written instrument, or a judgment or decree, land shall be deemed to have been possessed and occupied in any of the following cases: (1) Where it has been usually cultivated or improved; or (2) Where it has been protected by a substantial enclosure. All contiguous land protected by such substantial enclosure shall be deemed to be premises included within the written instrument, judgment, or decree, within the purview of § 95.16; or (3) Where [although not enclosed] it has been used for the supply of fuel, or of fencing timber for the purpose of husbandry, or for the ordinary use of the occupant; or (4) Where a known lot or single farm has been partly improved, the portion of such farm or lot which may have been left not cleared or not enclosed according to the usual course and custom of the adjoining county shall be deemed to have been occupied for the same length of time as the part improved or cultivated.

Fla. Stat. § 95.18 (1971): Where it shall appear that there has been an actual continued occupation for seven years of premises under a claim of title exclusive of any other right, but not founded upon a written instrument, or a judgment or decree, the premises so actually occupied, and no other, shall be deemed to have been held adversely; provided that during the period of seven years aforesaid the person so claiming adverse possession without color of title shall have within a year after entering into possession made a return of said property by proper legal description to the assessor of the county wherein situated and has subsequently, during each year paid all taxes theretofore or thereafter levied and assessed against the same and matured installments of special improvement liens theretofore or thereafter levied and assessed against the same by the state and county and by city or town, if such property be situated within any incorporated city or town, before such taxes become delinquent.

These provisions have been amended slightly since first enacted, but their character remains intact. Florida courts have been faced with the necessity of interpreting them. See, e.g., *Seton v. Swann*, 650 So. 2d 35 (Fla. 1995); *Turner v. Valentine*, 570 So. 2d 1327 (Fla. Ct. App. 1990): *Candler Holdings Ltd. I v. Watch Omega Holdings*, 947 So. 2d 1231 (Fl. Ct. App. 2007). Among their earliest and most notable responses has been:

MEYER v. LAW
287 So. 2d 37 (Fla. 1973)

BOYD, J.

This cause is before us on petition for writ of certiorari to review the decision of the District Court of Appeal, Second District, reported at 265 So.2d 737. Our jurisdiction is based on conflict between the decision sought to be reviewed and [several other Appellate District opinions — Eds.]. . . .

Petitioners owned land contiguous to the property of respondents. Relying upon an incorrect survey, respondents built and maintained a fence for twenty-five years, enclosing a portion of petitioners' land, in the belief that it was part of their own. Both petitioners and respondents had deeds of record reflecting the true boundary; both parties returned their lands for taxes according to the record titles, and paid taxes only on their respective properties as shown by such record titles. Respondents apparently thought the fence was on the true line, and petitioners took no action for legal determination to the contrary.

The District Court held that the respondents acquired valid title to the enclosed lands of petitioners under "color of title", although there was neither a decree nor a written instrument of any kind in the public records to show color of title in respondents, and although there had been no return of the encroached lands for taxes or payment thereof by respondents.

The foregoing cases, cited for conflict, clearly hold that without color of title or payment of taxes, as prescribed by Sections 95.16, 95.17, 95.18, and 95.19. Florida Statutes, and without seven years of actual, adverse, open, hostile, and continuous enclosure or cultivation, or adverse claim cannot ripen into a valid legal title. . . .

In light of these cases, we now turn to the essence of the issue upon which this Court must reverse the District Court in the instant case. Relying upon cases cited in the opinion, and other legal writings, both the Circuit Court and the District Court concluded that subsection (2) of Section 95.17 should be construed to mean that when a person claims certain specific lands under color of title, such claimant may enclose or cultivate the properties of contiguous owners for seven years, without returning or paying taxes, and without having paper title to the land upon which he has encroached, and thus perfect his claims to the property of adjoining owners, who return and pay their taxes, and who have ownership of record by deed, decree, or other written instrument. In this fashion, all owners of real property described in the statute would be subject to losing parts of their yards, farms, ranches, or other lands, to contiguous owners who happen to plant flowers, vegetables, or fences thereon. Surely, the Legislature did not intend such a result.

Reading the foregoing subsection in pari materia with the other quoted sections, we think its proper construction is that persons who claim land adversely under a paper title relating to a certain area, and who fence in or cultivate an area beyond that which is described in the paper title, but who do not pay any taxes on the additional area, can secure good title by adverse possession only to the portion of land described by the deed, decree, or other written instrument of record. We believe that, in enacting the foregoing subsection, the Legislature intended to provide that, where one has color of title to a larger area than is fenced or cultivated, and he pays no taxes on any of the land described in the title, he may acquire title by adverse possession only to that portion of land shown on the paper title which he actually fences or cultivates. It requires little imagination to realize that one who holds an uncertain or doubtful color of title, by deed, decree, or other recorded written instrument, to a large piece of property which may likely be claimed by others, might wisely fence, cultivate, or pay taxes on a portion of the same, in order to avoid controversy, for seven years, and then reach out in like manner for another piece. Obviously, in such circumstances, only the part occupied adversely could be included, regardless of the lands shown on the color of title, or the taxes paid.

In the case before us, we hold that the respondents' color of title was limited to the property shown in the public records, and no color of title extended from that ownership to the contiguous lands of the petitioners. In Florida, there are only two ways to acquire land by adverse possession. First, without color of title, the claimant must show seven years of open, continuous, actual possession, hostile to all who would challenge such possession, must both pay all taxes for the seven year period, returning said land for taxes during the first year of occupation, and enclose or cultivate said lands for the seven year period. Second, with color of title, the claimant must show he entered into possession of the premises under a claim based upon a written instrument of conveyance of the premises in question, or deed, or judgment of a competent court, and there has been a continued occupation and possession of the premises, as defined by Section 95.17, Florida Statutes, F.S.A. (and, of course, including the above criteria of openness, etc.), for a period of seven years. It should be noted that Section 95.16, Florida Statutes, F.S.A., provides that adverse possession commencing after December 31, 1945, shall not be deemed to be adverse possession under color of title unless the instrument purporting to convey the premises is recorded. One who enters into possession of realty is presumed to do so subordinately to the legal titleholder, and not adversely thereto. One who claims adversely has the burden of overcoming this presumption.

The concept of adverse possession is an ancient and, perhaps, somewhat outdated one. It stems from a time when an ever-increasing use of land was to be, and was, encouraged. Today, however, faced, as we are, with problems of unchecked over-development, depletion of precious natural resources, and pollution of our environment, the policy reasons that once supported the idea of adverse possession may well be succumbing to new priorities. A man who owns some virgin land, who refrains from despoiling that land, even to the extent of erecting a fence to mark its boundaries, and who makes no greater use of that land than an occasional rejuvenating walk in the woods, can hardly be faulted in today's increasingly "modern" world. Public policy and stability of our society, therefore, require strict compliance with the appropriate statutes by those seeking ownership through adverse possession. In this case, respondents have not demonstrated sufficient compliance with the requirements of the law to perfect their claim by adverse possession. Accordingly, the opinion of the District Court is quashed and the cause remanded for further proceedings consistent herewith. It is so ordered.

ADKINS, J., dissenting.

Respectfully, I must dissent. To reach the conclusion set forth in the majority opinion requires that one totally ignore the language of Fla.Stat. § 95.17(2), F.S.A., which provides: "All contiguous land protected by such substantial enclosure shall be deemed to be premises included within the written instrument, judgment, or decree, within the purview of § 95.16." Fla.Stat. § 95.16, F.S.A., deals with adverse possession under color of title, so that, to be given any meaning at all, the language of Fla.Stat. § 95.17(2), F.S.A., must be interpreted as an extension of the applicability of the color of title doctrine. . . .

The majority opinion seeks to enjoin the taking of land from a goodly and nature-loving man whose boundaries are unmarked by fences. Such a goal is indeed laudatory, but would require that the doctrine of adverse possession be totally abolished in this State — whether or not it was joined by the payment of taxes. Such a result would also work to the detriment of one such as the respondent in the case sub judice, a man who bought a section of land and diligently seeking to act properly, obtained a survey of his land. Relying, in good faith, on that survey, he placed a fence at what he honestly thought were the boundaries of his land. For seven long years, this man was allowed to believe that he was openly and notoriously tilling, improving, and fencing his own land. Under the rationale of the majority opinion, he was actually toiling for the benefit of his neighbor. Under the rationale of the statute, he acquired title by adverse possession.

Neither neighbor is actually in the wrong; and, the best result would be that neither had to suffer. However, this is not possible within the limitations of land, and the Legislature has determined that, under the facts of the case sub judice, the man who had, through a good faith mistake, protected, enclosed and improved the land in question for seven years without complaint of his neighbor should have the benefit of his toils. The majority opinion gives the land to the man who did not bother to check his boundaries for seven years to determine whether or not his land has been invaded.

This is not to suggest that the intentional fencing of surrounding land in an attempt to grab that which is not rightfully the property of the one so reaching would dictate a similar result. The exception to the color of title doctrine provided by Fla.Stat. § 95.17(2), F.S.A., is such that it could apply only to good faith mistakes, because, otherwise, the adverse possessor could not be claiming the land under the good title which he holds to the neighboring land. The burden of proving a good faith error would be on the adverse possessor. However, under the facts of the case sub judice, especially the reliance on a survey for the setting of a boundary, I feel that the burden has been met.

Because I feel that it is the duty of this Court to apply all of an applicable statute to the facts of a case, unless some portion of the statute violates a provision of the Constitution of Florida or of the United States, I would affirm the decision below because this is the result dictated by a simple application of the statutory language to the facts. I dissent to the majority opinion.

NOTES

1. Payment of taxes is not ordinarily a pre-requisite for establishing adverse possession and traditionally has played little role in litigation. However, as in *Meyer*, there does appear to be a legislative movement to require it. Minnesota, for example, requires payment of taxes for at least five of the 15-year period of possession. The statute provides, however, that it "shall not apply to actions relating to the boundary line of lands." Minn. Stat. § 541.02 (2002). The meaning of that exception is not free from doubt. See, e.g., *Ganje v. Schuler*, 659 N.W.2d 261 (Minn. App. 2003). In some states, an adverse possessor who pays taxes may benefit from a shorter limitations period. See, e.g., Colo. Rev. Stat. § 38-41-101 (providing for a baseline limitations period of 15 years), § 38-41-108 (shortening the limitations period to seven years for an adverse possessor who pays taxes and who claims under "color of title").

2. "Color of title" refers to an instrument that purports to pass title but does not actually do it, perhaps because the instrument is defective or because the person making the instrument does not have title in the first place. At common law and under most American statutes, an adverse possessor need not have color of title, or indeed have an instrument at all. But if the adverse possessor does have color of title, it can be helpful in some instances, for example in proving good faith in jurisdictions requiring it or — in states such as Colorado, see the previous note — shortening the limitations period.

3. Under American law, except where permitted by statute, title to land held by the federal or state governments cannot be acquired by adverse possession. See *Adverse Possession of Public Land: A Look at the Recommendations of the Public Land Law Review Commission*, 1971 Law and the Social Order 131. Is this merely a holdover of the English feudal law that a vassal could not hold adversely to his lord, or does it make sense in modern conditions? In some states, there is a narrow exception for property not being held for public purposes, such as land taken for failure to pay property taxes and meant for re-sale. *Miller v. Metropolitan Water Reclamation Dist.*, 870 N.E.2d 1040 (Ill. App. 2007); *Devins v. Borough of Bogota*, 592 A.2d 199 (N.J. 1991). Should it be extended? Should it apply to charitable institutions more generally? A few states do so. See, e.g., Mo. Ann. Stat. § 516.090, excepting from adverse possession those lands "given, granted, sequestered or appropriated to any public, pious or charitable use."

II. RIGHTS OF LATERAL AND SUBJACENT SUPPORT

A. Lateral Support

Landowners are entitled to lateral support for their soil, in its natural condition, by nearby neighbors or adjacent owners. They have a correlative duty to such owners to provide the same support for neighboring and adjacent soils; this duty is not delegatable. Both the right and the duty are incidents of land ownership and do not depend on the words of a grant or conveyance; as such, they are called natural rights and duties. See *Wilde v. Minsterly*, 2 Rolle Abr. 564 (1639), quoted in *Gilmore v. Driscoll*, 23 Am rep. 312, 314–315 (Mass. 1877):

> . . . if A. be seised in fee of copyhold land next adjoining to the land of B., and A. erects a new house upon his copyhold land, and some part of the house is erected upon the confines of his land next adjoining to the land of B., and B. afterwards digs his land so near to the foundation of A.'s house, but no part of A.'s land, that thereby the foundation of the house and the house itself fall into the pit, yet no action lies by A. against B., because it was A.'s own fault that he built his house so near the land of B., for he by his act cannot hinder B. from making the best use of his own land that he can. But it seems that a man who has land next adjoining to my land cannot dig his land so near my land that thereby my land shall go into his pit; and therefore, if the action had been brought for this, it would lie.

Crumbling wall case

NOONE v. PRICE
298 S.E.2d 218 (W. Va. 1982)

NEELY, J.   *Strictly liable for the cause of damages to house if its determined the land collapsed b/c of the land itself, not the if it was caused by added weight of the house.*

Damages: house and land or land only.

In 1960 the plaintiffs below, and appellants in this Court, Mr. and Mrs. William H. Noone, bought a house located on the side of a mountain in Glen Ferris, West Virginia. This house had been constructed in 1928 or 1929 by Union Carbide, and in 1964, four years after plaintiffs purchased the house, plaintiffs became aware that the wall under their front porch was giving way and that the living room plaster had cracked.

The defendant below, appellee in this Court, Mrs. Marion T. Price, lived directly below the plaintiffs at the foot of the hill in a house that was built in 1912. Sometime between 1912 and 1919 a wall of stone and concrete was constructed along the side of the hill, ten to twelve feet behind the defendant's house. This wall was a hundred to a hundred and twenty-five feet long, approximately four feet high, and of varying degrees of thickness. The wall lay entirely on the defendant's property, and was approximately ten to twelve feet from the property line that divided the defendant's property from the plaintiffs' property. The defendant purchased her house in 1955 and lived there until 1972, when she sold the property. Before the defendant's purchase, the wall had fallen into disrepair. When the plaintiffs discovered that their house was slipping down the hill, they complained to the defendant that their problem was the result of deterioration in the defendant's retaining wall. The defendant did nothing to repair the wall and the plaintiffs repaired the damage to their house at a cost of approximately $6,000.

The action before us now was filed in 1968 for damages of $50,000 for failure of the defendant to provide lateral support for the plaintiffs' land, and her negligent failure to provide lateral support for their house. Plaintiffs alleged that the wall was constructed to provide support to the slope upon which their house was built, and that the disrepair and collapse of the wall caused the slipping and eventual damage to their property.

The defendant denied that the wall on her property provided support to the slope, or that the condition of her wall caused the slipping and damage to the plaintiffs' property. In addition, the defendant asserted that the plaintiffs were negligent in failing to take reasonable precautions to protect their own property and were estopped from suing her because the wall on her property was erected by her predecessor in title and the plaintiffs had purchased their property with knowledge of the wall's deteriorating condition.

Defendant made a motion for summary judgment that the circuit court granted in part. The circuit court concluded that the plaintiffs had no right to recover for damage to their dwelling house and buildings, but the court left open the question of whether plaintiffs could recover for damage to their land. The circuit court stated on the record that "there is a duty of lateral support to the land but not to a structure on the land." Unfortunately, while the circuit court stated an entirely correct principle of law, his disposition of this case on summary judgment was inappropriate. While an adjacent landowner has an obligation only to support his neighbor's property in its raw or natural condition, if the support for land in its raw, natural condition is insufficient and the land slips, the adjacent landowner is liable for both the damage to the land and the damage to any buildings that might be on the land. Consequently, we reverse and remand.

This case provides an opportunity . . . to address the obligations of adjoining landowners to provide lateral support to each other's land. Support is lateral when the supported and supporting lands are divided by a vertical plane. The withdrawal of lateral support may subject the landowner withdrawing the support to strict liability or to liability for negligence. We have recognized both forms of liability in *Walker v. Strosnider*, 67 S.E. 1087 (W. Va. 1910) and this case, remarkably enough, is still in harmony with the modern weight of authority as articulated in the Restatement (Second) of Torts.

As a general rule, "[a] landowner is entitled, ex jure naturae, to lateral support in the adjacent land for his soil." Point 2, syllabus, *McCabe v. City of Parkersburg*, 79 S.E.2d 87 (W. Va. 1953). Therefore, as we said in syllabus point 2 of *Walker*, *supra*:

> An excavation, made by an adjacent owner, so as to take away the lateral support, afforded to his neighbor's ground, by the earth so removed, and cause it, of its own weight, to fall, slide or break away, makes the former liable for the injury, no matter how carefully he may have excavated. Such right of support is a property right and absolute.

An adjacent landowner is strictly liable for acts of commission and omission on his part that result in the withdrawal of lateral support to his neighbor's property. This strict liability, however, is limited to land in its natural state; there is no obligation to support the added weight of buildings or other structures that land cannot naturally support. However, the majority of American jurisdictions hold that if land in its natural state would be capable of supporting the weight of a building or other structure, and such building or other structure is damaged because of the subsidence of the land itself, then the owner of the land on which the building or structure is constructed can recover damages for both the injury to his land and the injury to his building or structure. The West Virginia cases are largely consistent with this position, although none has expressly so held.

The converse of the preceding rule is also the law: where an adjacent landowner provides sufficient support to sustain the weight of land in its natural state, but the land slips as a direct result of the additional weight of a building or other structure, then in the absence of negligence on the part of the adjoining landowner, there is no cause of action against such adjoining landowner for damage either to the land, the building, or other structure.

The issue in the case before us concerns the proper application of the strict liability rule. The circuit court improperly awarded summary judgment because the plaintiffs should have been allowed to prove that their land was sufficiently strong in its natural state to support the weight of their house, and that their house was damaged as a result of a chain reaction that began when the land in its natural state, toward the bottom of the hill, slipped as a result of the withdrawal of lateral support occasioned by the deterioration of the retaining wall, causing, in turn, successive parts of the hillside to subside until the ripple effect reached the foundation of the plaintiffs' house.

The cases recognize that lateral support sufficient to hold land in its natural state may be insufficient to support the additional weight of a building or other structure. If, therefore, as a result of the additional weight of a building or other structure, so much strain is placed upon existing natural or artificial lateral support that the support will no longer hold, then in the absence of negligence, there is no liability whatsoever on the part of an adjoining landowner. In the case before us, this means that if the weight of the plaintiff's house placed so much pressure on the soil that the house itself caused the subsidence, and the land would not have subsided without the weight of the house, then the plaintiffs cannot recover.

A theoretical problem that presents itself in all of these cases is the extent to which the obligation of support runs with the land. The weight of authority appears to be that where an actor, whether he be an owner, possessor, lessee, or third-party stranger, removes necessary support he is liable, and an owner cannot avoid this liability by transferring the land to another. Nevertheless, when an actor who removes natural lateral support substitutes artificial support to replace it, such as a retaining wall, the wall then becomes an incident to and a burden on the land upon which it is constructed, and subsequent owners and possessors have an obligation to maintain it.

In the case sub judice, the plaintiffs' land had no buildings erected on it at the time the defendant's predecessor in title built the retaining wall on his property; therefore, he needed only to erect a retaining wall sufficient to provide support for their soil. He was not required to furnish a wall sufficient to support any structure which they might erect upon their property. The defendant, as his successor, merely had the obligation to maintain the wall to support the plaintiffs' land in its natural condition. Defendant was not required to strengthen the wall to the extent that it would provide support for the weight of plaintiffs' buildings.

Since the pleadings in the case before us make reference to negligence, it is appropriate here to address the scope of a negligence theory. In general, it has been held that while an adjoining landowner has no obligation to support the buildings and other structures on his neighbor's land, nonetheless, if those structures are actually being supported, a neighbor who withdraws such support must do it in a non-negligent way. In an action predicated on strict liability for removing support for the land in its natural state, the kind of lateral support withdrawn is material, but the quality of the actor's conduct is immaterial; however, in a proceeding based upon negligence, the kind of lateral support withdrawn is immaterial, and the quality of the actor's conduct is material. Comment e, Restatement (Second) of Torts § 819 (1979) succinctly explains the nature of liability for negligence.

> The owner of land may be unreasonable in withdrawing lateral support needed by his neighbor for artificial conditions on the neighbor's land in either of two respects. First, he may make an unnecessary excavation, believing correctly that it will cause his neighbor's land to subside because of the pressure of artificial structures on the neighbor's land. If his conduct is unreasonable either in the digging or in the intentional failure to warn his neighbor of it, he is subject to liability to the neighbor for the harm caused

by it. The high regard that the law has by long tradition shown for the interest of the owner in the improvement and utilization of his land weighs heavily in his favor in determining what constitutes unreasonable conduct on his part in such a case. Normally the owner of the supporting land may withdraw lateral support that is not naturally necessary, for any purpose that he regards as useful provided that the manner in which it is done is reasonable. * * * Thus, if the actor's sole purpose in excavating his land is to harm his neighbor's structures, the excavation itself is unreasonable. Furthermore, although for the purpose of permanently leveling the land it may be reasonable to withdraw support that is not naturally necessary, it may be unreasonable to make an excavation for a building that will itself require a foundation, without providing for the safeguarding of the neighbor's structures during the progress of the work. Likewise it is normally unreasonable not to notify an adjacent landowner of excavations that certainly will harm his structures, unless the neighbor otherwise has notice.

Secondly, the owner of land may be negligent in failing to provide against the risk of harm to his neighbor's structures. * * * The owner in making the excavation is therefore required to take reasonable precautions to minimize the risk of causing subsidence of his neighbor's land. In determining whether a particular precaution is reasonably required, the extent of the burden that the taking of it will impose upon the actor is a factor of great importance. . . .

The plaintiffs contend that the defendant should be held liable for negligence in removing the support required by their dwelling, in addition to the strict liability for removing support for their soil, relying on *Walker v. Strosnider, supra*. . . . *Walker* and *Beaver* [*v. Hitchcock*, 151 W.Va. 620, 153 S.E.2d 886 (1967)] imposed liability for damages to structures caused by negligent excavation and failure to shore up an excavation; however, they involved situations where the structures were already in existence at the time of the acts that deprived them of lateral support, and the owner of the property was the actor who caused the excavation to be made. If there are no structures on the land at the time of the excavation, the excavator owes no further duty than to refrain from removing the lateral support for the soil, or to substitute artificial support for that which is removed. His duty of support cannot be enlarged by the addition of artificial structures to the land; therefore, the duty of his successor in title cannot be greater, where she has done no act to deprive the structures of their support.

It would appear that the case before us either stands or falls on a question of strict liability. It is admitted that the retaining wall on the defendant's property was constructed at least sixty years ago, before the construction of the plaintiffs' house, and that all parties to this action were aware of the condition of the wall. Furthermore, there is no allegation that the defendant did anything to cause the collapse of the wall, but rather only failed to keep it in repair. Therefore, if the plaintiffs can recover, they must do so by proving that the disrepair of the retaining wall would have led ineluctably to the subsidence of their land in its natural condition. If, on the other hand, the land would not have subsided but for the weight of the plaintiffs' house, then they can recover nothing.

Since the proper resolution of this issue will require the development of an appropriate factual record, the judgment of the Circuit Court of Fayette County is reversed and the case is remanded for further proceedings consistent with this opinion.

NOTES

1. If the defendant had an obligation to maintain the wall to support the plaintiffs' land in its natural condition, but not to provide support for the weight of the plaintiffs' buildings, what advice would you give a client about to undertake the construction of such a wall? Would the ease of its application support a rule stating that any damage to the land may be recovered under a theory of strict liability, but that negligence must be alleged and proven in order to recover for injury to an improvement, such as a house, on the land? See *Prete v. Cray*, 141 A. 609, 613 (R.I. 1928) (Rathbun, J., dissenting). Once the wall is in place, what difference does it make whether the right to support is viewed as a right to have the soil supported or a right in the supporting land? In *Klebs v. Yim*, 772 P.2d 523, 526–527 (Wash. Ct. App. 1989), the plaintiffs were upper landowners who sued lower owners when a retaining wall on the defendants' lower lot collapsed, causing injury to the plaintiffs' upper lot; the upper lot had been improved with a swimming lot and concrete apron around the pool; the court cites and quotes from *Noone* and then states:

> Although adjacent landowners each have an absolute property right to have their land laterally supported by the soil of their neighbor, this right does not include the right to have the weight of buildings or improvements placed on the land also supported. The landowner cannot, by placing an improvement upon his land, increase his neighbor's duty to support the land laterally. Accordingly, the owner of the lot with the duty to maintain the wall should only be required to reconstruct the wall under the right of lateral support if the failure of the wall was due to its inability to support the natural, unimproved land, rather than improvements on the supported lot. Otherwise the party with the duty to maintain the wall would be responsible for improving the wall to hold more than the natural land would have held. . . .

> Here, the trial court . . . found that the retaining wall collapsed due to hydrostatic pressure behind the wall that was caused by inadequate drainage, footings, and rebar. However, the trial court here made an additional finding that Klebs and Hutter "presented no evidence to show that the change in runoff resulting from the concrete deck sloping toward the wall did not cause the wall to collapse." As previously stated, these findings are not challenged and, therefore, are treated as verities on appeal.

> The concrete deck sloping toward the wall was placed upon Klebs' and Hutter's property by their predecessor in interest when he built a swimming pool on the property. To hold Yim responsible for reconstructing the wall under the right of lateral support, Klebs and Hutter must show that these improvements would have been supported by the natural land which the retaining wall replaced. Klebs and Hutter have failed to support

this burden. Therefore, it was not error to refuse to hold Yim responsible for reconstructing the retaining wall.

2. Is the right to lateral support in *Noone* affected by a subsequent transfer of the supporting property? If the right arises with the excavation, and accrues with the subsidence of the supported land, what if the ownership of the supporting land changes in the meantime? Should the present landowner of the supporting land be under a duty to furnish or restore lateral support removed by a predecessor in title? See *Frederick v. Burg*, 148 F. Supp. 673 (W.D. Pa. 1957).What would happen if the wall in *Noone* were struck by lightning? Who would have the obligation to repair it? See *Urosevic v. Hayes*, 590 S.W.2d 77 (Ark. Ct. App. 1979).

3. Defendant excavates along the boundary of the plaintiff's land, observing all reasonable precautions while doing so, including shoring up its ditch with sturdy planks, driven into place with a steam hammer. When the defendant's ditch was 10 feet wide and 40 feet deep, the defendant struck a fine quicksand, unknown to either the plaintiff or the defendant. The sand quickly seeped around the defendant's shoring, bubbling up in the ditch and causing the plaintiff's land to slide into the ditch from under the plaintiff's land and so damaging the plaintiff's house. What result in the plaintiff's suit, and why? See *Prete v. Cray*, 141 A. 609 (R.I. 1928). What if the quicksand extended under several lots, so that not just adjoining owners, but others more distant, sued as well. Would the liability extend as far as the quicksand, to nonadjacent owners as well? Annotation, *Liability of Excavators for Damages to Non-Coterminous Tract from Removal of Lateral Support*, 87 A.L.R.2d 710 (1963).

B. Modifying the Duty of Support by Statute

When reading the following statute, ask yourself what changes, both procedural and substantive, it makes in the common law regarding the right to lateral support. Does the statute change who can sue to enforce the right, the nature of the right, or the remedies available to those able to sue under it?

765 Ill. Comp. Stat. Ann. 140/1 (2014):

Sec. 1. Each adjacent owner is entitled to the continuous lateral and subjacent support which his land receives from the adjoining land, subject to the right of the owner of the adjoining land to make proper and usual excavations on the same for purposes of construction or improvements, under the following conditions:

1. Any owner or possessor of land intending to make or to permit an excavation to be made on his land shall give due and reasonable notice in writing to the owner or owners of adjoining lands and of adjoining buildings and other structures stating the depth to which the excavation is intended to be made and when the excavation will begin. If the excavation is to be of a depth of not more than the standard depth of foundations, as herein defined, and if it appears that the excavation is to be of a greater depth than the walls or foundations of any adjoining building or other structure and is to be so close as to endanger the building or other structure in any way, then the owner of the building or other structure on the adjoining land shall be allowed a reasonable time, but in no event less than thirty (30) days, in

which to take measures to protect the same from any damage or in which to extend the foundations thereof, and he must be given, for the said purpose, a license to enter on the land on which the excavation is to be or is being made.

2. Any owner or possessor of land upon which an excavation is made, who does not comply with the provisions of subparagraph 1, when so required, is liable to the owner of adjacent property for any damage to the land or to any buildings or other structure thereon arising from such excavation, and is also liable to occupants and tenants of the adjoining land or structures for any damage to their property or business, proximately resulting from injury to such land or structures, caused by the failure of such owner or possessor to so comply.

3. In making any excavation, reasonable care and precautions shall be taken to sustain the adjoining land as such, without regard to any building or other structure which may be thereon, and there is no liability for damage done to any building or other structure by reason of the excavation except as herein provided or otherwise provided or allowed by law.

4. Standard depth of foundations, as used herein, is a depth of eight (8) feet below the established grade of a street, highway or other public way upon which such land abuts, or if there is no established grade, below the surface of the adjoining land.

5. If the excavation is intended to be or is deeper than the standard depth of foundations as herein defined, then the owner of the land on which the excavation is being made, if given the necessary license to enter on adjoining land, and not otherwise, shall protect the said adjoining land and any building or other structure thereon, without cost to the owner thereof, by furnishing lateral and subjacent support to said adjoining land and all buildings and structures thereon, in such a manner as to protect the same from any damage by reason of the excavation and shall be liable to the owner of such property for any damage to the land or to any buildings or other structures thereon.

6. The owner or possessor of the land upon which the excavation is being made shall also be liable to occupants and tenants of such adjoining lands or structures thereon for any damage to their property or business, proximately resulting from injury to such land or structures, caused by the failure of such owners or possessor, making such excavation, to fulfill the duty set forth in subparagraph 5.

C. Subjacent Support

Subjacent support is the support that the surface of the land receives from underlying strata. It arises when the title to the land surface is severed from that of the underlying strata, as for example, when that strata contains minerals. All states recognize the possibility of such severances. In general, the rules that apply to lateral support apply as well to subjacent support. The traditional rule is that removal of either lateral or subjacent support results in absolute or strict liability in the excavator, miner, or other defendant. In England, the right to lateral support was one of four permissible subjects for a negative easement — the others being light, air, and the right to the flow of a non-natural watercourse.

bomb case

ISLAND CREEK COAL CO. v. RODGERS
644 S.W.2d 339 (Ky. Ct. App. 1982)

McDONALD, J. *Minority: forseeable improvement.*

damages: diff b/w fair market value before and after the incident.

This is an appeal of a blasting case. It was tried as a lead case, and many others remain to be tried. The appellants, Island Creek Coal Company and Cimarron Coal Corporation, received adverse judgments against them in the circuit court. They prosecute their appeals separately.

The jury awarded the Rodgers $50,000 in damages for injury to their home. Fifty percent of the award was assessed against Island Creek and 50 percent against Cimarron. In addition, Cimarron Coal Corporation was assessed $45,000 in punitive damages.

The appellees, Jewell and Elsie Rodgers, sued to recover damages to their home located in Sharp Subdivision, just east of Madisonville in Hopkins County. The subdivision is located above Island Creek's East Diamond Mine which is composed of 5,000 acres of underground mines, containing seams of coal 90 feet and 250 feet below the surface. The mining operations under Sharp Subdivision were begun in 1905 by the West Kentucky Coal Company, Island Creek's predecessor in title. The operations have been abandoned since 1971.

Mr. Jewell Rodgers has been employed by Bearing Service Company for over 30 years. His employment is related to the mining industry, and he personally makes business calls on mine operations. In 1966 the appellees built their home, knowing that the house was situated over underground mines and that other subdivisions in the area built over mines had trouble with subsidence. Subsidence is defined as "any movement of the soil from its natural position. This movement may be in any direction. It may be of surface or subsurface soil. A shifting, falling, slipping, seeping or oozing of the soil is a subsidence. . . ." Restatement (Second) of Torts § 817, comment h at 68 (1977).

Cimarron Coal Corporation engaged in strip mining in various areas south and east of Sharp Subdivision, within 5,600 to 23,000 feet of the subdivision. The property Cimarron was mining had been acquired from Island Creek in 1967. Cimarron used strip mining methods with explosives in order to fragmentize the rock and soil so the coal would be exposed. . . .

According to Island Creek, uncontradicted evidence showed that in 1905, when the mineral fee severance occurred, modern-day land development and subdivisions were not only unheard of but unthought of. Island Creek did not begin mining by the underground method until 1948, and they continued until 1963.

An expert for Island Creek testified as follows:

[Island Creek had] done an excellent job of designing and mining both the Number 11 and Number 9 coal seams and had left more than adequate coal to support the surface in its natural state for an indefinite time (100 years or more) and that the only known conditions which could have produced subsidence in the Sharps area were the discharge of sewage into the old mines, or blasting operations of Cimarron, or a combination of the two.

He further explained that the sewage discharge would result in a softening of the fire clay which in turn would permit the remaining pillars to "punch" down through the fire clay, increasing the load and strain upon the large sandstone layers which support the surface. He explained that the repeated blasting from Cimarron resulted in the failure or fracture of the support members which caused a subsidence.

The Rodgers testified that on April 29, 1977, at 11:40 p.m., there was a shaking and jolting of their home followed by a terrific blast. The next morning they discovered their damage.

Cimarron's blasting records established that the blast shot consisted of 16 drill holes 32 feet deep, each containing 275 pounds of anfo, a mixture of ammonium nitrate and fuel oil. The holes were shot 25 milli-seconds apart. The blast site was located about 13,200 feet from the nearest part of Sharp subdivision.

Cimarron's expert testified that the blast, if more than 5,600 feet from the house, would be too remote to cause direct damage as the Rodgers complain. Cimarron's experts concluded that the blasting did not contribute to or accelerate the subsidence. The subsidence, they felt, was caused by Island Creek's extracting coal from the seams under the subdivision; by the seams' having inadequate support in the mines; and by the use of an unacceptable mining practice of not lining up the panels or passageways of Nos. 9 and 11 seams. They theorized that when Island Creek abandoned or closed the mine and terminated its pumping operations, water accumulated in the mine and the fire clay softened, causing the support pillars to sink. Lastly, Cimarron's experts stated that Island Creek failed to leave a barrier pillar for support immediately under the Sharp subdivision.

The trial, expertly handled by the trial court, spanned 20 days and included an exhaustive list of witnesses. A review of the record shows that the array of expert testimony corroborates and then, on the other hand, contradicts each and every claim and defense made by the parties. . . . Island Creek proved that the severance of the coal from the fee occurred in 1905. It argues that the uncontradicted evidence established that when the severance occurred, the subdivision in which the Rodgers' property was located was a remote woodland and it was not possible for a modern-day subdivision to have been developed upon the property. It is argued further that in 1905 bare subsistence required at least 50 acres, and a one-half (1/2) acre subdivision lot certainly would not have been adequate for that purpose. Beyond that, running water, electricity, indoor plumbing and gas service, which are indispensable to the development and use of modern day subdivisions, were not available in rural Kentucky. Island Creek vigorously contends that there was no obligation, legal or otherwise, to support the surface in contemplation of development of a modern subdivision.

The unquestioned law of Kentucky is that an underground mine operator is obligated to support the surface and leave it in its "natural state." *West Kentucky Coal Company v. Dilback*, 294 S.W. 478, 479 (Ky. 1927), states: "As we have said, the right to mine is subservient to the right of the surface owners to have the surface maintained in its natural state free from subsidence or partings of the soil, and this right of support is absolute and not dependent upon any questions of negligence."

The question of liability of an underground mine operator for damages to structures on the surface which were built after the underground operations had been abandoned is a matter of first impression in Kentucky. What constitutes "natural state"? Island Creek advances the argument that the definition of "natural state" is the surface as it was when the coal rights were severed (in this case, 1905). The Rodgers argue to the contrary. They claim it makes no difference when the coal rights were severed because strict or absolute liability on the underground mine operator for any damage to the surface is applicable, the only exception being that if subsequent structures are put on the surface, the underground operator would not be liable for any damage attributable to the structures themselves causing or contributing to the subsidence. The Rodgerses remind us that the weight of the house had nothing to do with the cause of the subsidence, as their uncontradicted expert testimony verified.

It is easy to follow Island Creek's argument to the contrary, and it's a good one. If Island Creek's responsibility is fixed at the year 1905, the year of the fee severance, then it would be responsible for only remote and rural farmland; certainly no liability would exist for damage to a modern house in a subdivision 72 years later. Island Creek is armed with authority from foreign jurisdictions to support this position, (e.g.) *Drummond v. White Oak Fuel Co.*, 140 S.E. 57 (W. Va. 1927); and *Noonan v. Pardee*, 50 A. 255 (Pa. 1901). To the contrary, we define "natural state" as the condition of the surface, including reasonable and forseeable improvements thereon, at the time the coal is severed, not from the fee, but from the earth.

Also, our review of Kentucky law convinces us that strict liability is applicable. In *West Kentucky Coal Co. v. Dilback*, *supra*, the court dealt with damage to a well. There the coal company was operating an underground mine not a far distance from the house of the appellee. The Dilbacks' complaint stated that the coal company was negligent because it did not leave sufficient support for the overlying surface after removing the coal, which caused a cave-in, thereby destroying the Dilbacks' well. Even though the case was one concerning lateral support, as opposed to subjacent support as in our case, the court made the following statement:

> * * * As we have said, the right to mine is subservient to the right of the surface owners to have the surface maintained in its natural state free from subsidence or partings of the soil, and this right of support is absolute and not dependent upon any question of negligence. But this doctrine ought not to be extended any further than applying it to the surface above the mining operation. . . . If the operation had been carried on under the land of appellees, the appellant would have owed to them the absolute duty not to disturb the natural condition of the surface, but as the operation was not

going on under the land of appellees, the appellant is responsible only if it can be shown that the operation was conducted negligently.

III. NUISANCE   *Reasonableness test.*   *Private or public.*

What can a landowner do when a neighbor's property use creates annoying odors, noises, or sights? The owner may have an action for trespass, but trespass requires a physical intrusion. In many cases, there is no physical intrusion, but the harm to the owner can be just as great. See, e.g., *Labbe v. Steffens*, 752 P.2d 1067 (Colo. App. 1988) (trucks waiting in line at 24-hour car wash emitted noxious fumes to neighboring residential properties); *Lambert v. Matthews*, 757 So. 2d 1066 (Miss. App. 2000) (the crowing of nineteen roosters kept on neighbors' land was unreasonable interference with enjoyment of property); *Taylor v. Leardi*, 502 N.Y.S.2d 514 (App. Div. 1986) (defendant's blasting operations caused serious emotional distress and discomfort to plaintiffs). Compare *Schuman v. Greenbelt Homes Inc.*, 69 A.3d 512 (Md. Ct. Spec. App. 2013) (cigarette smoking by owner of adjoining cooperative unit is not a nuisance); *Christmas v. Exxon Mobile Corp.*, 138 So. 3d 123 (Miss. 2014) (wild alligators on neighboring property are not an actionable nuisance); *Hale v. Ward County*, 818 N.W.2d 697 (N.D. 2012) (shooting range is not a nuisance).

Nuisance law developed to fill the void left by the strict requirements of trespass. Nuisance prevents property owners from using their land in a way that causes an unreasonable and substantial interference with another's use or enjoyment of land. Obviously, this definition casts a broad net, and property owners tend to look to nuisance when no other legal rule applies to the bothersome activity. In fact, Dean Prosser has called nuisance "a legal garbage can." William L. Prosser, *Nuisance Without Fault*, 20 Tex. L. Rev. 399, 410 (1942). However, this flexibility has made nuisance a very handy tool for property owners.

Although nuisance and trespass frequently overlap, fundamental differences exist between them. The law of trespass protects a property owner's right to *exclusive possession,* and thus it requires some intrusion onto the property. Damages need not be proved, because the owner's right of exclusive possession is absolute. Conversely, the law of nuisance protects the property owner's right to *use and enjoyment* of the property, which can be infringed even without a physical intrusion. This right is not absolute, and thus the plaintiff must prove actual damages.

Two distinctions have been drawn in nuisance law. First, nuisances are either *public* or *private*. Public nuisance originated as a criminal offense and focuses on harm to society at large. For example, if homeowners block the street in front of their home, everyone in the community is affected. For a long time, only the government could bring an action for public nuisance. It is now generally accepted, however, that private citizens may bring a public nuisance suit if their injuries are different from those suffered by the general public. Therefore, if the street obstruction eliminates neighboring homeowners' access to their property, those homeowners have suffered special damages; members of the community at large can find other ways to get to their property, but the neighbors cannot.

In contrast, private nuisances affect only one person or a small group of persons. For instance, property owners might change the grade of their land in a way that causes all the surface water to drain onto their neighbor's land. The public at large is not affected by such an action. Therefore, this conduct constitutes a private, but not a public, nuisance.

The second distinction to be drawn is between *nuisance per se* and *nuisance per accidens*. A nuisance per se is an act or thing that is a nuisance wherever or whenever it occurs or that is prohibited by statute or ordinance. For instance, releasing toxic waste into the environment is a nuisance under any circumstance. On the other hand, a nuisance per accidens, or nuisance in fact, is a lawful activity that constitutes a nuisance only because of where or when it takes place. For instance, a hog farm is not a nuisance in a rural area, but it may be a nuisance in a city. Keep these distinctions in mind as you read the following cases.

bitch case (private nuisance)

GRIFFIN v. NORTHRIDGE
153 P.2d 800 (Cal. Ct. App. 1944)

MOORE, J.

The question for decision is whether the facts established justify the finding of a nuisance on adjacent premises and the consequent award of damages.

In the fall of 1940, plaintiffs purchased a lot on Oporto Drive in a hillside district. The area was restricted exclusively to residential structures with minimum building requirements of $10,000. The lot had dimensions of 109 feet frontage and a depth of 100 feet. At the time plaintiffs acquired their building site defendants had already erected their home on the adjoining lot. In February, 1941, plaintiffs commenced their structure which was completed in October, 1941. At the time of its completion plaintiffs had an unobstructed view of the neighboring hills, the territory which formerly comprised the suburban town of Hollywood and vast stretches of the metropolitan area. Both lots had a long descent at the rear, but there was no alley or other means of access from the street below. Both houses were built according to a plan which placed the kitchen and service quarters to the side. Each house was approximately the same distance from the common property line.

Immediately following plaintiffs' occupancy of their home defendants commenced a course of exhibiting malice toward plaintiffs by both words and deeds. Mrs. Northridge trespassed upon flower beds of plaintiffs, ground her heel into the flowers and removed plaintiffs' only blooming hibiscus plant from a flower pot. Defendants removed their garbage can from the place originally constructed for it on the east side of the Northridge home and placed it on the west side, against the property line and almost directly under plaintiffs' dining room window. They raised a line along the common boundary to which they tied many tin can tops which by their constant clanging caused plaintiffs to be annoyed in the daytime and to be kept awake at night. They wilfully caused paint to be cast upon the walls and windows of plaintiffs' home. To add insult to injury, at many times and on divers occasions Mrs. Northridge approached the common property line and called to Mrs. Griffin that she was a "tin-pan-alley queen," "cheap people," "dirty people," "a sloppy wench," "a sloppy huzzy," "an alley cat," and by directing to her such statements as "There you go you old sloppy wench with your trash;" "Why don't you do something about your figure?" "Why don't you spend a little of your dirty money to have your car washed?" Also, at times, while the Griffins were entertaining friends she advanced to the plaintiffs' windows, screamed that plaintiffs' guests had parked their cars in front of defendants' property and demanded their removal. Along and by the common property line defendants planted eucalyptus trees which grew to some 18 feet in height. They obstructed the eastward view from plaintiffs' home, deprived plaintiffs of light and air, and sent their roots beneath the soil of the Griffin lot and imperiled the foundations of plaintiffs' residence. During the period of plaintiffs' occupancy of their property defendants maintained a wall adjacent to the common property line with huge dirt and concrete foundations with an ugly, hideous board fence upon it, which obstructed the sun, light, ventilation and view for portions of the Griffin home and which wall so excluded sunlight from the plants on the east side of the Griffin lot as to cause them to die. And to crown their deeds with a shocking display of ill-will they exposed the fangs of their malice by dissuading a buyer from completing her acquisition of plaintiffs' home after she had deposited $1,000 on the purchase price. These acts of defendants were done with malice and with intent to harm and injure plaintiffs in the peaceful occupancy of their home. Plaintiffs declared that the alleged acts constituted a nuisance and demanded the abatement thereof with damages. But prior to the trial they sold their home and submitted only their prayer for damages which were assessed in the sum of $1,000 without comment as to what portion of the award was by way of punishment.

In their brief defendants have attempted to minimize the significance of each of their several acts with a view of demonstrating that by reason thereof no damage could have been suffered by plaintiffs. They assert that there is no sufficient evidentiary support for any one of the acts found to constitute a nuisance. . . .

We are not impressed by the claim that the evidence is insufficient to support the several findings. While it may be true that no one finding alone would justify the judgment for $1,000, yet the sum total of all of defendants' behavior abundantly warrants such decision. That the acts were done by defendants in person makes them even more culpable, more dreadful and repulsive than if robots had acted. The financial value of the trespasses committed, of plant or flowers destroyed, of walls and windows marred by paint, of peace and quiet disturbed, of cruel epithets spoken, of unsightly walls that precluded view and darkened the home, of the spreading roots of the eucalypti — the detriment caused by any one of these factors measured by its money value alone is of little importance in appraising the sum total of them all as a nuisance to those who occupy the adjoining home. The old proverb that a man's home is his castle embodies a rich heritage of truth. All things in it or about it are as fine gold to them that dwell there. It is their palace to their friends, their refuge from toil and unkind foes. There they commune with the thoughts of the wise and virtuous, thrill under the spell of music, enjoy laughter and love. He who maliciously aims and attempts to destroy the peace and recreative value of a home robs its inmates of immeasurable riches and does an inestimable damage.

But because financial recompense is an inadequate exchange for the deprivation of home comforts it is no good reason for denying pecuniary award for the damage sustained thereby. In deriving a determination of the extent of the detriment suffered in such event the court may consider the sentimental and aesthetic values of things destroyed, the owner's affection for his possessions, as well as his peace, comfort and quiet which have been scorned by his neighbor. *Judson v. Los Angeles Suburban Gas Co.*, 157 Cal. 168, 106 P. 581, 26 L.R.A., N.S., 183, 21 Ann. Cas. 1247. The owner of a residence occupied as a home is entitled to just compensation for annoyance, discomfort and inconvenience caused by a nuisance on the adjoining property. *Green v. General Petroleum Corporation*, 205 Cal. 328, 333, 337, 270 P. 952, 60 A.L.R. 475; *Dauberman v. Grant*, 198 Cal. 586, 246 P. 319, 48 A.L.R. 1244; 39 American Jurisprudence, p. 398. While the *Green* judgment was for eviction and other special damages resulting from oil and mud blown onto their home from an oil well near by, without negligence, and the *Dauberman* judgment was for the inconvenience suffered from smoke and rain waters from Grant's adjoining property, yet we see no reason why such acts as those of defendants would not be a nuisance to the occupants of a home as much as smoke, water and oil. Especially is this true where the acts complained of were activated by sheer malice. * * *

That the acts of defendants created a nuisance is established by the proof that the acts committed were of such a nature as to harass and annoy plaintiffs continuously and to interfere with their comfortable enjoyment of life and of their home. Civil Code § 3479; *Los Angeles Brick & Clay Products Co. v. City of Los Angeles*, 60 Cal. App. 2d 478, 141 P.2d 46. If the contention were established that defendants did no unlawful acts and therefore created no nuisance, the maintenance of a comfortable home in a city would be imperiled by the presence of a neighbor who would wilfully frustrate the peace and comfort of another without just cause. Where people attempt to dwell side by side in urban life, where their interests are common if not intertwined, the liberties we might unrestrictedly enjoy on a forty-acre farm must be foregone if the metropolitan areas are to succeed in the development of wholesome culture and in the extension of civilization. While we take pride in the towering structures that adorn a city, its parks, its paved boulevards and its utilities, these marks of grandeur and facilities are as naught if homes are rendered untenantable by those who on adjacent properties delight in their display of malice and hatred for a fellow man.

The judgment is not excessive. For the personal discomfort and annoyance to which a person had been subjected by a nuisance on adjoining property, the determination of the amount of his compensation is a question for the trial court. *Dauberman v. Grant, supra*, 198 Cal. page 590, 246 P. 319, 48 A.L.R. 1244 . It is not necessary that compensation for a nuisance should be denied because it is not continuous. Neither should a plaintiff be denied recovery because he is deprived of only a part of his property, comfort or life. *Judson v. Los Angeles Suburban Gas Co., supra*, 157 Cal. page 172, 106 P. 581, 26 L.R.A., N.S., 183, 21 Ann. Cas. 1247. A judgment will not be disturbed so long as it is supported by any substantial evidence. *Bellman v. San Francisco H.S. Dist.*, 11 Cal. 2d 576, 581, 82 P.2d 894. A single intentional trespass on the rights of another justifies an award of punitive damages against the wrongdoer. If the act is maliciously done the damages may be enhanced to such extent as will afford complete redress. Judgment affirmed.

NOTES

1.   Although damages are generally the preferred remedy in nuisance actions, courts routinely will grant an injunction in certain situations. For instance, if the harm is continuing in nature, a court will grant an injunction rather than require the plaintiff to return to court periodically to recover additional damages for its ongoing injuries. See *Scott v. Jordan*, 661 P.2d 59 (N.M. Ct. App. 1983) (injunction against livestock feeding operation because pollution, flies, and noxious odors could not be prevented). Additionally, if the nuisance is only prospective — that is, if the harm is threatened but has not yet occurred — an award of damages is inappropriate, and an injunction is necessary to prevent the harm from occurring. *Village of Wilsonville v. SCA Servs., Inc.*, 426 N.E.2d 824, 836 (Ill. 1981) (injunction against operation of a chemical-waste landfill based on proof that it would constitute a public nuisance in the future). Note, however, that in *Boomer v. Atlantic Cement Co.*, which is the next case, the court refused to grant an injunction even though the defendant's ongoing conduct constituted a nuisance.

2.   What about abnormally sensitive plaintiffs? Suppose, for instance, that the sound of a lawn mower, which causes no discomfort to most people, drives a hypersensitive invalid into convulsions and threatens his health. The lawn mower does not constitute a nuisance. The standard is a person of ordinary sensitivity. Restatement (Second) of Torts § 821F, cmt. d (1977). Similarly, courts will not enjoin an activity that harms a plaintiff's hypersensitive use of land. Thus, courts have refused to enjoin outdoor lighting that would be unobjectionable to most people but that seriously interferes with the operation of a drive-in movie theater. See *Belmar Drive-In Theater Co. v. Illinois State Toll Highway Comm'n*, 216 N.E.2d 788 (Ill. 1966).

BOOMER v. ATLANTIC CEMENT CO.
257 N.E.2d 870 (N.Y. 1970)

BERGAN, J.

Defendant operates a large cement plant near Albany. These are actions for injunction and damages by neighboring land owners alleging injury to property from dirt, smoke and vibration emanating from the plant. A nuisance has been found after trial, temporary damages have been allowed; but an injunction has been denied.

The public concern with air pollution arising from many sources in industry and in transportation is currently accorded ever wider recognition accompanied by a growing sense of responsibility in State and Federal Governments to control it. Cement plants are obvious sources of air pollution in the neighborhoods where they operate.

But there is now before the court private litigation in which individual property owners have sought specific relief from a single plant operation. The threshold question raised by the division of view on this appeal is whether the court should resolve the litigation between the parties now before it as equitably as seems possible; or whether, seeking promotion of the general public welfare, it should channel private litigation into broad public objectives.

A court performs its essential function when it decides the rights of parties before it. Its decision of private controversies may sometimes greatly affect public issues. Large questions of law are often resolved by the manner in which private litigation is decided. But this is normally an incident to the court's main function to settle controversy. It is a rare exercise of judicial power to use a decision in private litigation as a purposeful mechanism to achieve direct public objectives greatly beyond the rights and interests before the court.

Effective control of air pollution is a problem presently far from solution even with the full public and financial powers of government. In large measure adequate technical procedures are yet to be developed and some that appear possible may be economically impracticable.

It seems apparent that the amelioration of air pollution will depend on technical research in great depth; on a carefully balanced consideration of the economic impact of close regulation; and of the actual effect on public health. It is likely to require massive public expenditure and to demand more than any local community can accomplish and to depend on regional and interstate controls.

A court should not try to do this on its own as a by-product of private litigation and it seems manifest that the judicial establishment is neither equipped in the limited nature of any judgment it can pronounce nor prepared to lay down and implement an effective policy for the elimination of air pollution. This is an area beyond the circumference of one private lawsuit. It is a direct responsibility for government and should not thus be undertaken as an incident to solving a dispute between property owners and a single cement plant — one of many — in the Hudson River valley.

The cement making operations of defendant have been found by the court of Special Term to have damaged the nearby properties of plaintiffs in these two actions. That court, as it has been noted, accordingly found defendant maintained a nuisance and this has been affirmed at the Appellate Division. The total damage to plaintiffs' properties is, however, relatively small in comparison with the value of defendant's operation and with the consequences of the injunction which plaintiffs seek.

The ground for the denial of injunction, notwithstanding the finding both that there is a nuisance and that plaintiffs have been damaged substantially, is the large disparity in economic consequences of the nuisance and of the injunction. This theory cannot, however, be sustained without overruling a doctrine which has been consistently reaffirmed in several leading cases in this court and which has never been disavowed here, namely that where a nuisance has been found and where there has been any substantial damage shown by the party complaining an injunction will be granted.

The rule in New York has been that such a nuisance will be enjoined although marked disparity be shown in economic consequence between the effect of the injunction and the effect of the nuisance.

The problem of disparity in economic consequence was sharply in focus in

Whalen v. Union Bag & Paper Co., 208 N.Y. 1, 101 N.E. 805. A pulp mill entailing an investment of more than a million dollars polluted a stream in which plaintiff, who owned a farm, was "a lower riparian owner". The economic loss to plaintiff from this pollution was small. This court, reversing the Appellate Division, reinstated the injunction granted by the Special Term against the argument of the mill owner that in view of "the slight advantage to plaintiff and the great loss that will be inflicted on defendant" an injunction should not be granted (p. 2, 101 N.E. p. 805). "Such a balancing of injuries cannot be justified by the circumstances of this case," Judge Werner noted (p. 4, 101 N.E. p. 805). He continued: "Although the damage to the plaintiff may be slight as compared with the defendant's expense of abating the condition, that is not a good reason for refusing an injunction" (p. 5, 101 N.E. p. 806). . . .

Although the court at Special Term and the Appellate Division held that injunction should be denied, it was found that plaintiffs had been damaged in various specific amounts up to the time of the trial and damages to the respective plaintiffs were awarded for those amounts. The effect of this was, injunction having been denied, plaintiffs could maintain successive actions at law for damages thereafter as further damage was incurred.

The court at Special Term also found the amount of permanent damage attributable to each plaintiff, for the guidance of the parties in the event both sides stipulated to the payment and acceptance of such permanent damage as a settlement of all the controversies among the parties. The total of permanent damages to all plaintiffs thus found was $185,000. This basis of adjustment has not resulted in any stipulation by the parties.

This result at Special Term and at the Appellate Division is a departure from a rule that has become settled; but to follow the rule literally in these cases would be to close down the plant at once. This court is fully agreed to avoid that immediately drastic remedy; the difference in view is how best to avoid it.*

One alternative is to grant the injunction but postpone its effect to a specified future date to give opportunity for technical advances to permit defendant to eliminate the nuisance; another is to grant the injunction conditioned on the payment of permanent damages to plaintiffs which would compensate them for the total economic loss to their property present and future caused by defendant's operations. For reasons which will be developed the court chooses the latter alternative.

If the injunction were to be granted unless within a short period — e.g., 18 months — the nuisance be abated by improved methods, there would be no assurance that any significant technical improvement would occur. . . .

Moreover, techniques to eliminate dust and other annoying by-products of cement making are unlikely to be developed by any research the defendant can undertake within any short period, but will depend on the total resources of the

---

* Respondent's investment in the plant is in excess of $45,000,000. There are over 300 people employed there.

cement industry nationwide and throughout the world. The problem is universal wherever cement is made. . . .

On the other hand, to grant the injunction unless defendant pays plaintiffs such permanent damages as may be fixed by the court seems to do justice between the contending parties. All of the attributions of economic loss to the properties on which plaintiffs' complaints are based will have been redressed. . . .

It seems reasonable to think that the risk of being required to pay permanent damages to injured property owners by cement plant owners would itself be a reasonable effective spur to research for improved techniques to minimize nuisance. . . .

The damage base here suggested is consistent with the general rule in those nuisance cases where damages are allowed. "Where a nuisance is of such a permanent and unabatable character that a single recovery can be had, including the whole damage past and future resulting therefrom, there can be but one recovery" (66 C.J.S. Nuisances § 140, p. 947). It has been said that permanent damages are allowed where the loss recoverable would obviously be small as compared with the cost of removal of the nuisance (*Kentucky-Ohio Gas Co. v. Bowling*, 264 Ky. 470, 477, 95 S.W.2d 1). . . .

There is some parallel to the conditioning of an injunction on the payment of permanent damages in the noted "elevated railway cases" (*Pappenheim v. Metropolitan El. Ry. Co.*, 128 N.Y. 436, 28 N.E. 518 and others which followed). Decisions in these cases were based on the finding that the railways created a nuisance as to adjacent property owners, but in lieu of enjoining their operation, the court allowed permanent damages.

Judge Finch, reviewing these cases in *Ferguson v. Village of Hamburg*, 272 N.Y. 234, 239–240, 5 N.E.2d 801, 803, said: "The courts decided that the plaintiffs had a valuable right which was being impaired, but did not grant an absolute injunction or require the railway companies to resort to separate condemnation proceedings. Instead they held that a court of equity could ascertain the damages and grant an injunction which was not to be effective unless the defendant failed to pay the amount fixed as damages for the past and permanent injury inflicted." . . .

Thus it seems fair to both sides to grant permanent damages to plaintiffs which will terminate this private litigation. The theory of damage is the "servitude on land" of plaintiffs imposed by defendant's nuisance. (See *United States v. Causby*, 328 U.S. 256, 261, 262, 267, where the term "servitude" addressed to the land was used by Justice Douglas relating to the effect of airplane noise on property near an airport.)

The judgment, by allowance of permanent damages imposing a servitude on land, which is the basis of the actions, would preclude future recovery by plaintiffs or their grantees (see *Northern Indiana Public Service Co. v. W.J. & M.S. Vesey, supra*, p. 351, 200 N.E. 620).

The orders should be reversed, without costs, and the cases remitted to the Supreme Court, Albany County, to grant an injunction which shall be vacated upon payment by defendant of such amounts of permanent damage to the respective plaintiffs as shall for this purpose be determined by the court.

JASEN, J., dissenting.

I agree with the majority that a reversal is required here, but I do not subscribe to the newly enunciated doctrine of assessment of permanent damages, in lieu of an injunction, where substantial property rights have been impaired by the creation of a nuisance.

It has long been the rule in this State, as the majority acknowledges, that a nuisance which results in substantial continuing damage to neighbors must be enjoined. (*Whalen v. Union Bag & Paper Co.*, 208 N.Y. 1, 101 N.E. 805; *Campbell v. Seaman*, 63 N.Y. 568; *see, also, Kennedy v. Moog Servocontrols*, 21 N.Y.2d 966, 290 N.Y.S.2d 193, 237 N.E.2d 356.) To now change the rule to permit the cement company to continue polluting the air indefinitely upon the payment of permanent damages is, in my opinion, compounding the magnitude of a very serious problem in our State and Nation today. . . .

The specific problem faced here is known as particulate contamination because of the fine dust particles emanating from defendant's cement plant. The particular type of nuisance is not new, having appeared in many cases for at least the past 60 years. (See *Hulbert v. California Portland Cement Co.*, 161 Cal. 239, 118 P. 928 (1911).) It is interesting to note that cement production has recently been identified as a significant source of particulate contamination in the Hudson Valley. This type of pollution, wherein very small particles escape and stay in the atmosphere, has been denominated as the type of air pollution which produces the greatest hazard to human health. We have thus a nuisance which not only is damaging to the plaintiffs, but also is decidedly harmful to the general public.

I see grave dangers in overruling our long-established rule of granting an injunction where a nuisance results in substantial continuing damage. In permitting the injunction to become inoperative upon the payment of permanent damages, the majority is, in effect, licensing a continuing wrong. It is the same as saying to the cement company, you may continue to do harm to your neighbors so long as you pay a fee for it. Furthermore, once such permanent damages are assessed and paid, the incentive to alleviate the wrong would be eliminated, thereby continuing air pollution of an area without abatement.

It is true that some courts have sanctioned the remedy here proposed by the majority in a number of cases, but none of the authorities relied upon by the majority are analogous to the situation before us. In those cases, the courts, in denying an injunction and awarding money damages, grounded their decision on a showing that the use to which the property was intended to be put was primarily for the public benefit. Here, on the other hand, it is clearly established that the cement company is creating a continuing air pollution nuisance primarily for its own private interest with no public benefit.

This kind of inverse condemnation (*Ferguson v. Village of Hamburg*, 272 N.Y. 234, 5 N.E.2d 801) may not be invoked by a private person or corporation for private gain or advantage. Inverse condemnation should only be permitted when the public is primarily served in the taking or impairment of property. (*Matter of New York*

City Housing Auth. v. Muller, 270 N.Y. 333, 343, 1 N.E.2d 153, 156; *Pocantico Water Works Co. v. Bird*, 130 N.Y. 249, 258, 29 N.E. 246, 248.) The promotion of the interests of the polluting cement company has, in my opinion, no public use or benefit. . . .

I would enjoin the defendant cement company from continuing the discharge of dust particles upon its neighbors' properties unless, within 18 months, the cement company abated this nuisance. It is not my intention to cause the removal of the cement plant from the Albany area, but to recognize the urgency of the problem stemming from this stationary source of air pollution, and to allow the company a specified period of time to develop a means to alleviate this nuisance.

I am aware that the trial court found that the most modern dust control devices available have been installed in defendant's plant, but, I submit, this does not mean that *better* and more effective dust control devices could not be developed within the time allowed to abate the pollution.

Moreover, I believe it is incumbent upon the defendant to develop such devices, since the cement company, at the time the plant commenced production (1962), was well aware of the plaintiffs' presence in the area, as well as the probable consequences of its contemplated operation. Yet, it still chose to build and operate the plant at this site.

In a day when there is a growing concern for clean air, highly developed industry should not expect acquiescence by the courts, but should, instead, plan its operations to eliminate contamination of our air and damage to its neighbors.

* * * In each action: Order reversed, without costs, and the case remitted to Supreme Court, Albany County, for further proceedings in accordance with the opinion herein.

NOTES

1. The trial court in *Boomer* found that the defendant had installed the most modern dust control devices in its plant. If nuisance focuses on protection of use and enjoyment of property, why does it matter that the defendant is using the best available precautionary devices? A few courts refuse to consider the defendant's precautionary measures when deciding whether an activity is a nuisance. See *Bell v. Gray-Robinson Constr. Co.*, 62 N.W.2d 390, 392–93 (Wis. 1954) ("A nuisance does not rest on the degree of care used . . . but on the degree of danger existing even with the best of care."). However, the vast majority of courts follow *Boomer* in taking defendants' precautions into consideration. Is this a good rule for an industrialized nation?

2. Would the court in *Boomer* have granted an injunction if the plaintiffs had brought their nuisance action before the cement plant was built? Courts normally will not enjoin an anticipatory (or prospective) nuisance unless the plaintiff can prove that the proposed use necessarily will constitute a nuisance in its proposed location. If the plaintiff cannot prove that the proposed use essentially will be a nuisance per se, the plaintiff must wait until the use is commenced and proves to be a nuisance in fact. What difficulties does this rule create for potential plaintiffs?

One notable exception to the usual rule is a funeral home in a residential area. Although funeral homes generally are well-maintained and quiet, courts regularly have enjoined them from locating in residential neighborhoods even though the discomfort they cause arguably is irrational. See, e.g., *Travis v. Moore*, 377 So. 2d 609 (Miss. 1979); *Fraser v. Fred Parker Funeral Home*, 21 S.E.2d 577 (S.C. 1942).

3. In determining whether to grant an injunction, the court relied on an approach known as "balancing the equities." The court weighed the gravity of the harm caused by the defendant's plant operations against their utility. In assessing the gravity of the harm and the utility of the defendant's operations, what factors did the court consider? What other factors should it have considered?

4. Should a court balance the equities in deciding whether to award damages? Consider the following comment from the Restatement:

> The process of comparing the general utility of the activity with the harm suffered as a result is adequate if the suit is for an injunction prohibiting the activity. But it may sometimes be incomplete and therefore inappropriate when the suit is for compensation for the harm imposed. The action for damages does not seek to stop the activity; it seeks instead to place on the activity the cost of compensating for the harm it causes. . . . In a damage action . . . , therefore, the invasion is unreasonable not only when the gravity of the harm outweighs the utility of the conduct, but also when the utility outweighs the gravity — provided the financial burden of compensating for the harms caused by the activity would not render it unfeasible to continue conducting the activity. If imposition of this financial burden would make continuation of the activity not feasible, the weighing process for determining unreasonableness is similar to that in a suit for injunction.

Restatement (Second) of Torts § 826 cmt. f (1977). In at least one action for damages, the court refused to consider any evidence of the utility of the defendant's conduct. See *Jost v. Dairyland Power Coop.*, 172 N.W.2d 647, 653 (Wis. 1969) ("We know of no acceptable rule of jurisprudence that permits those who are engaged in important and desirable enterprises to injure with impunity those who are engaged in enterprises of lesser economic significance.").

5. As noted in the majority opinion, the effect of the court's failure to grant an injunction is to impose a servitude on the plaintiffs' lands. However, the federal and state constitutions permit the involuntary transfer of a property interest only for a public use and not for a private use. Has the court acted unconstitutionally in permitting the defendant to impose this servitude? Compare *Board of County Commissioners of County of Morgan v. Kobobel*, 176 P.3d 860 (Colo. App. 2007) (unconstitutional for county to condemn land for access road to private cemetery), with *City of Las Vegas Downtown Redevelopment Agency v. Pappas*, 76 P.3d 1 (Nev. 2003) (city agency can condemn land for privately owned parking garage).

The *Boomer* decision raises the question of the proper distribution of rights and resources. The New York court awarded the property owners damages but permitted the pollution to continue. The distribution issue has provoked a flood of commentary from the law and economics perspective, including the article from which the following excerpt is taken:

Robert C. Ellickson, *Alternatives to Zoning: Covenants, Nuisance Rules, and Fines as Land Use Controls*
40 U. Chi. L. Rev. 681, 722–24 (1973)*

In an important economic analysis of the problem of external cost,** Professor R.H. Coase showed that if administrative costs are zero, the same resource allocation will result regardless of the initial distribution of rights. Assume, for example, that there is a grocery store in the Santa Monica Mountains, the only external harm to the neighbors is added noise, and administrative costs are zero. The Coase theorem states that if the cost to the grocer of going out of business is less than his neighbors' gains from the reduction in noise resulting from the termination of his enterprise, the grocer will shut down regardless of the initial distribution of rights. If homeowners have the right to recover for injury caused by the noise, the grocer will choose to absorb the smaller loss of going out of business rather than pay for the damage he causes by staying open. If the law does not require the grocer to compensate the homeowners for noise, the homeowners will combine to pay the grocer to close. The grocer will agree if the bounty is larger than his losses from closing, and the homeowners will be willing to offer more than the amount of his loss if their total damage exceeds that amount.

On the other hand, when the cost to the grocer of closing exceeds the resulting benefit to the homeowners, the grocer will continue to operate. If the homeowners have the right to recover, the grocer will pay damages rather than absorb the larger costs of terminating his business. If the grocer need not pay damages, the homeowners will not pay him to adopt a more neighborly course of action, because the minimum payment he would insist on to shut down exceeds the value of the damage they are currently suffering. In brief, the Coase theorem states that private bargaining will tend to reduce the sum of nuisance and prevention costs over time, regardless of assignment of rights.

The Coase theorem does not imply that the policy maker need not be concerned about how rights are assigned. First, as Coase reminds us, administrative costs in bargaining situations are not zero, and consequently the assignment of rights does affect resource allocation. Second, the policy maker cannot ignore the equities of resource distribution, as Coase intentionally does, to focus solely on the efficiency of resource allocation. Any unexpected alteration of the distribution of rights among landowners is almost certain to affect their relative shares of wealth. Decisions on the distribution of rights in cases of external cost thus must accommodate the complex considerations of administrative costs and fairness.

** R.H. Coase, *The Problem of Social Cost*, 3 J.L. & Econ. 1 (1960).

NOTES

1. The Coase theorem states that, ignoring transaction costs, the parties to a nuisance conflict will reach the most efficient solution to their conflict through market and bargaining processes, regardless of any initial judicial allocation of liability. As Ellickson points out, Coase is concerned not just about bargaining, but with the assignments of rights or liabilities. Coase's theorem is narrowly focused on economic issues but also is consistent with courts producing a fair result.

Today, entitlements and rights routinely are thought to be separate from the choice of remedies. Thus, a four-rule framework has emerged in nuisance law: (1) Boomer (B) enjoins Atlantic Cement (A) from operating. This rule is one of two traditional results in nuisance cases, which Coase says is only the start of negotiations between the two parties. (2) A is required to pay damages for B's injuries. (3) A is permitted to operate status quo ante — the inverse of rule 1. (4) A ceases operations, but B pays A for its damages, such as A's relocation costs. See Saul Levmore, *Unifying Remedies: Property Rules, Liability Rules, and Startling Rules*, 106 Yale L.J. 2149, 2152–53 (1997) (using this four-rule framework), in Symposium, *Property Rules, Liability Rules, and Inalienability: A Twenty-Five Year Retrospective*, 106 Yale L.J. 2149 (1997).

2. At the same time that Coase wrote, the use of injunctions in nuisance cases was criticized as making the litigation a zero sum game that often produced unjust results. First, injunctions allowed plaintiffs to extort defendants; in Coase negotiations thereafter, the results were biased toward the plaintiffs, who, when successful, acquired the right to shut defendants down, gaining a right to share in the defendants' trade in excess of plaintiffs' injuries. Second, enforcing injunctions became inefficient when courts incorrectly estimated their value to plaintiffs. However, the same judicial mistakes can as easily be made when damages are sought. Third, damage remedies can be measured dollar for dollar, whereas injunctions are less flexible, although the strategic use of injunctions makes this difference uncertain. See Mitchell Polinsky, *Resolving Nuisance Disputes: The Simple Economics of Injunctive and Damage Remedies*, 32 Stan. L. Rev. 1075, 1110–1111 (1980) (contending that "the arguments favoring damage remedies are logically incoherent"). See also Jeff L. Lewin, *Compensated Injunctions and the Evolution of Nuisance Law*, 71 Iowa L. Rev. 775, 803–31 (1986).

Some scholars have harshly criticized the law and economics approach to nuisance remedies. One recurrent criticism is that the value of rights is defined by willingness to pay for them. Defining value by willingness to pay gives disproportionate power to the wealthy, who are obviously much more "willing" to pay for the right to cause nuisances or to be free from them. See Ronald Dworkin, *Is Wealth a Value?*, *in* A Matter of Principle 237 (1985). Professor Ward Farnsworth, in his article *Do Parties to Nuisance Cases Bargain After Judgment?: A Glimpse Inside the Cathedral*, 66 U. Chi. L. Rev. 373 (1999), makes a more fundamental criticism. Based on his examination of twenty actual nuisance cases, Professor Farnsworth concludes that Coase's theory that parties to nuisance actions will bargain after the conclusion of the litigation is incorrect. The parties' mutual animosity after the litigation and their unwillingness to sell the rights at issue apparently prevent them from negotiating.

3. For further discussions of the law and economics approach to nuisance and other remedies, see Guido Calabresi, *The Pointlessness of Pareto: Carrying Coase Further*, 100 Yale L.J. 1211 (1991); Donald Gjerdingen, *The Coase Theorem and the Psychology of Common-Law Thought*, 56 S. Cal. L. Rev. 711 (1983); Louise Halper, *Untangling the Nuisance Knot*, 26 B.C. Envt'l. Aff. L. Rev. 89 (1998); Frank Michelman, *Property, Utility, and Fairness: Comments on the Ethical Foundations of "Just Compensation" Law*, 80 Harv. L. Rev. 1165 (1967); George Smith, *Nuisance Law: The Morphogenesis of an Historical Revisionist Theory of Contemporary Economic Jurisprudence*, 74 Neb. L. Rev. 658 (1995).

4. *Spur Industries, Inc. v. Del E. Webb Development Co.*, 494 P.2d 700 (Ariz. 1972), provides an interesting example of a case in which a court enjoined a nuisance but awarded damages to the defendant for the injuries suffered as a result of the injunction. In *Spur*, the defendant, Spur Industries, operated a cattle feedlot in an agricultural area that was approximately fifteen miles outside Phoenix. The plaintiff, Del Webb, built Sun City, a large retirement community, in the immediate vicinity of the feedlot. Del Webb then brought suit to enjoin the feedlot as a nuisance because of the flies and odors associated with it. Despite Spur's good management practices for the feedlot, the court held that the feedlot constituted a public nuisance. However, as the following excerpt from the opinion demonstrates, the court did not consider Spur to be a wrongdoer and awarded it damages.

> There was no indication in the instant case at the time Spur and its predecessors located in western Maricopa County that a new city would spring up, full-blown, alongside the feeding operation and that the developer of that city would ask the court to order Spur to move because of the new city. Spur is required to move not because of any wrongdoing on the part of Spur, but because of a proper and legitimate regard of the courts for the rights and interests of the public.

> Del Webb, on the other hand, is entitled to the relief prayed for (a permanent injunction), not because Webb is blameless, but because of the damage to the people who have been encouraged to purchase homes in Sun City. It does not equitably or legally follow, however, that Webb, being entitled to the injunction, is then free of any liability to Spur if Webb has in fact been the cause of the damage Spur has sustained. It does not seem harsh to require a developer, who has taken advantage of the lesser land values in a rural area as well as the availability of large tracts of land on which to build and develop a new town or city in the area, to indemnify those who are forced to leave as a result.

> Having brought people to the nuisance to the foreseeable detriment of Spur, Webb must indemnify Spur for a reasonable amount of the cost of moving or shutting down. It should be noted that this relief to Spur is limited to a case wherein a developer has, with foreseeability, brought into a previously agricultural or industrial area the population which makes necessary the granting of an injunction against a lawful business and for which the business has no adequate relief.

Id. at 707–08.

5. In *Spur*, the court places great importance on the fact that the plaintiff "came to the nuisance" by building Sun City in a rural area. The doctrine of "coming to the nuisance" is essentially a specialized application of the general tort doctrine of assumption of risk. Should such a defense be available to nuisance defendants? How about the defense of contributory negligence? Generally, contributory negligence is unavailable as a defense if nuisance liability is based on the defendant's intentional creation of a dangerous condition but is available if liability is based on negligence. On the other hand, assumption of risk (and thus "coming to the nuisance") is a defense regardless of the basis of the action. See Morris Denton, Comment, *Nuisance: Contributory Negligence or Assumption of Risk as Defense*, 28 Tenn. L. Rev. 561, 568–69 (1961). Some commentators have criticized the doctrine as being arbitrary; it allows priority in time to determine the permissible future development of an area. See Donald Wittman, *First Come, First Served: An Economic Analysis of "Coming to the Nuisance,"* 9 J. Legal Stud. 557 (1980); Daniel Mandelker, Land Use Law § 4.04 (5th ed. 2003). Another problem with the doctrine is that it assumes that areas are definable as commercial, industrial, or residential, when in fact an area's character is often in transition. See *Storey v. Central Hide & Rendering Co.*, 226 S.W.2d 615 (Tex. 1950). Despite criticism, the doctrine still exists. *E.g., Toftoy v. Rosenwinkel*, 983 N.E.2d 463 (Ill. 2012).

Should the *Spur* remedy be used only when the plaintiff has "come to the nuisance"? See Osborne Reynolds, *Of Time and Feedlots: The Effect of* Spur Industries *on Nuisance Law*, 41 Wash. U. J. Urb. & Contemp. L. 75, 94 (1992) (yes); but see Guido Calabresi & Douglas Melamed, *Property Rules, Liability Rules, and Inalienability: One View of the Cathedral*, 85 Harv. L. Rev. 1089, 1120–23 (1972) (suggesting other situations in which such a remedy would be appropriate).

6. Continuing urban expansion into agricultural areas has increased the number of nuisance actions like *Spur Industries*, in which residential owners seek to enjoin livestock operations. To provide some protection from these suits, several states have enacted a "Right to Farm Law." These laws generally provide that a preexisting livestock operation does not become an actionable nuisance when residences subsequently are built in its vicinity. For example, the Georgia law provides:

> No agricultural facility, agricultural operation, any agricultural operation at an agricultural facility, agricultural support facility, or any operation at an agricultural support facility shall be or shall become a nuisance, either public or private, as a result of changed conditions in or around the locality of such facility or operation if the facility or operation has been in operation for one year or more. The provisions of this subsection shall not apply when a nuisance results from the negligent, improper, or illegal operation of any such facility or operation.

Ga. Code Ann. § 41-1-7(c). The stated purposes for the law are "to conserve, protect, and encourage the development and improvement of . . . agricultural and forest land and facilities for the production . . . of food and other agricultural products." *Id.* at § 41-1-7(a). See H.W. Hannah, *Farming in the Face of Progress*, September/ October 1997 Prob. & Prop. 8.

In *Bormann v. Board of Supervisors*, 584 N.W.2d 309 (Iowa 1998), the Iowa Supreme Court held that a similar Iowa statute constituted an unconstitutional taking. The court reasoned that, because the right to maintain a nuisance is an easement, the statute created an easement in the neighboring lands for the benefit of the farm owners. The court concluded that the creation of this easement without the payment of just compensation violated the Fifth Amendment of the federal Constitution and the parallel provision in the Iowa Constitution. Other courts have declined to adopt the *Bormann* court's characterization of a nuisance as an easement. *Moon v. North Idaho Farmers Ass'n*, 96 P.3d 637 (Idaho 2004); *Lindsey v. DeGroot*, 898 N.E.2d 1251 (Ind. 2009).

IV.   AIR AND LIGHT

A.   Airspace

*Cujus est solum, ejus est usque ad coelum et ad inferos.** Land can be subdivided horizontally into the surface, subsurface, and airspace. Normally, the owner of the land's surface also owns the space above and beneath it. In fact, a deed that describes only the surface is deemed to convey the subsurface and airspace as well even though the deed does not mention them. However, title to the subsurface and to the airspace can be severed from the title to the surface and can be conveyed to different owners. For example, a coal mining company might buy just the subsurface estate under a parcel of land to conduct its mining operations. Similarly, airspace can be conveyed for a billboard, skyway, or even an entire building. During the past century, the laws affecting airspace have changed dramatically as illustrated by the materials in this section.

extending roof case

MURPHY v. BOLGER
60 Vt. 723 (1888)

TYLER, J.   *uses old common law, from ground to air.*

* * * The precise question in the case at bar is whether the projection of the side of the defendants' roof over plaintiff's land and sixteen feet above it was an ouster of plaintiff's possession of his land, or a mere intrusion upon, and interference with, a right incident to his enjoyment of the land.

Blackstone, book 2, page 18, says: "Land hath also, in its legal signification, an indefinite extent upwards as well as downwards"; . . . "the word 'land' includes not only the face of the earth, but everything under it or over it."

Defendants' counsel insists that this action cannot be maintained because there was no intrusion upon the plaintiff's soil, but upon the air or space above it, while plaintiff's counsel claims the rule to be that the action will lie provided the intrusion

---

* "Whoever owns the soil owns everything up to the sky and down to the depths." Black's Law Dictionary 1824 (9th ed. 2009).

extends over the line of plaintiff's premises, no matter how slight it is nor how far above the soil.

If the defendants had constructed their barn so that the foundation wall and the building itself had been wholly or in part over the line upon plaintiff's land, there could have been no question as to the plaintiff's right to maintain ejectment. But suppose they had built their foundation wall strictly upon their own land, but close to the line, and had projected the entire side of the building itself a few inches over the line and above the plaintiff's land, could the plaintiff maintain ejectment for the intrusion? If not, it would be because the intrusion was not upon the land itself but the space above it. If he could not maintain ejectment, he would be obliged to submit to the invasion and only have his damages therefor. But the law says the land is his even to the sky, and therefore he has a right to it, and should not be compelled to part with any portion of it upon the mere payment of damages by the trespasser. . . .

It clearly is not essential that the intruding object should actually rest upon the plaintiff's soil to entitle him to the action of ejectment, for this action will lie for an upper room in a dwelling-house or other building.

As the law gives the owner of the land all above it within its boundaries, we can find no reason, resting in principle, why, for the projection by one party of a portion of his building over the land of another, as in this case, he may not be liable in ejectment. The plaintiff was disseised of his land, and the defendant was in the wrongful possession thereof by his projecting roof. . . . There is no more difficulty in describing in a declaration a projection above the soil than one upon it, nor can there be any difficulty in the sheriff delivering possession to the plaintiff. No question was raised in the court below as to the sufficiency of the declaration. The judgment of that court is affirmed.

NOTES

1.   The court states that the issue in this case is whether the intruding roof ousted plaintiff's possession of his land or merely interfered with his enjoyment of the land. The answer to that question determines the plaintiff's appropriate cause of action. If the plaintiff had been ousted, he had an action for ejectment. On the other hand, if the roof merely infringed on his enjoyment of the land, nuisance would have been the correct cause of action. Which cause of action did the court determine was appropriate in this case?

2.   If the statute of limitations had been satisfied, could the defendant have claimed a prescriptive easement in the plaintiff's airspace? The majority rule is no. See *Pierce v. Casady*, 711 P.2d 766 (Kan. App. 1985) (tree branch overhanging neighbor's property could not create prescriptive easement; "[a]n easement through the airspace generally may not be obtained by prescription."); but see *Matthys v. Swedish Baptist Church*, 112 N.E. 228 (Mass. 1916) (roof of church that extended four feet over property line held sufficiently adverse to create a prescriptive easement). See also *Slotoroff v. Nassau Assocs.*, 428 A.2d 956 (N.J. Super. Ct. 1980) (recognizing possibility of an easement by necessity or implication in airspace).

3. Would the court's reasoning apply to space beneath the plaintiff's land, such as a cave? In *Edwards v. Sims*, 24 S.W.2d 619 (Ky. Ct. App. 1929), the court had to determine whether a portion of the Great Onyx Cave in Kentucky was owned by the surface owner, who apparently did not have an entry to the cave on his land, or by the person who owned an entry to the cave and had prepared the cave for commercial exhibition. The majority applied the maxim *cujus est solum, ejus est usque ad coelum et ad inferos* and held that the surface owner owned the portion of the cave beneath his land. In a strongly worded opinion, the dissenting judge said that the cave should belong to the person who owns the entrance and that the surface owner has title only to so much of the subsurface as can "be taken from the earth and used for his profit or happiness." What is the difference in focus between the majority and dissent? Which approach is preferable? While industrialized nations generally follow the majority's approach, subsistence cultures generally follow the dissent's approach. What accounts for the difference?

4. Note that the maxim *cujus est solum, ejus est usque ad coelum et ad inferos* reflects an early and relatively uninformed view of the world. Because the earth rotates, no one can claim title to a particular cone of airspace extending into the heavens. But, pursuant to the courts' analyses in *Murphy v. Bolger* and in *Edwards v. Sims*, do landowners have a cause of action against a pilot who flies directly over their land?

ALLEGHENY AIRLINES, INC. v. VILLAGE OF CEDARHURST
132 F. Supp. 871 (E.D.N.Y. 1955), *aff'd*, 238 F.2d 812 (2d Cir. 1956)

Bruchhausen, J.

The action involves the constitutionality of an ordinance, prohibiting air flights over the Village of Cedarhurst, below 1,000 feet. . . .

The plaintiffs, comprising ten Airline Companies, The Port of New York Authority, The Air Line Pilots Association International and nine air pilots in their individual capacities, having interests in and concerning New York International Airport, known as "Idlewild," situated in Queens County, State of New York, instituted this action against the Village of Cedarhurst and various named defendants in their official and individual capacities for a decree, adjudging unconstitutional and void and enjoining enforcement of an ordinance adopted by the said Village which prohibited the operation of aircraft below an altitude of 1,000 feet above the village. The Village is situated within a mile of the Airport.

The Administrator of Civil Aeronautics and the Civil Aeronautics Board intervened as plaintiffs in the action. * * *

While property owners in Cedarhurst are not now parties to this action, and their claims for nuisance and trespass have been withdrawn, it is appropriate to consider their positions in that the defendants base some of their contentions upon the theory that the landowners possess the title to the airspace above their property up to the sky or to infinity. The theory is founded upon the ancient doctrine, termed "Cujus est solum ejus est usque ad coelum", meaning that he who owns the land owns the airspace above it. The origin of the doctrine and its application are mentioned in the cases of *Swetland v. Curtiss Airports Corporation, D.C.*, 41 F.2d 929 and *Hinman v. Pacific Air Transport*, 9 Cir., 84 F.2d 755. None of the decisions, including the case of *Butler v. Frontier Telephone Co.*, 186 N.Y. 486, 79 N.E. 716, 11 L.R.A.,N.S., 920, cited by the defendants, involved airspace at an altitude of more than 100 feet or airspace which would be normally used by an aviator. Whether the doctrine ever was the law in this jurisdiction need not be considered. There is no doubt that it is not now the law. In the case of *United States v. Causby*, 328 U.S. 256, 260, 66 S.Ct. 1062, 1065, 90 L.Ed. 1206, the Court said:

> It is ancient doctrine that at common law ownership of the land extended to the periphery of the universe. * * * But that doctrine has no place in the modern world.

In several recent cases our highest Court has reiterated that principle. Mr. Justice Jackson in a concurring opinion in the case of *Northwest Airlines v. State of Minnesota*, 322 U.S. 292, 302, said:

> Aviation has added a new dimension to travel and to our ideas. The ancient idea that landlordism and sovereignty extend from the center of the world to the periphery of the universe has been modified. Today the landowner no more possesses a vertical control of all the air above him than a shore owner possesses horizontal control of all the sea before him. The air is too precious as an open highway to permit it to be "owned" to the exclusion or embarrassment of air navigation by surface landlords who could put it to little real use. * * * Air as an element in which to navigate is even more inevitably federalized by the commerce clause than is navigable water. Local exactions and barriers to free transit in the air would neutralize its indifference to space and its conquest of time.

In the case of *Chicago & Southern Air Lines v. Waterman S.S. Corp.*, 333 U.S. 103, 107, the Court said:

> Ancient doctrines of private ownership of the air as appurtenant to land titles had to be revised to make aviation practically serviceable to our society.

In the case of *United States v. Causby*, as appears from the opinion, in the lower Court, reported in 60 F.Supp. 751, 104 Ct. Cl. 342, a landowner sued the United States, the operator of an airport near his property, for damages. It appeared that planes taking off or landing at the airport, flew over his property at an altitude of 83 feet, clearing his house and barn, by less than 65 feet, so close in fact as to blow leaves off the tallest tree on the property. The Supreme Court, on the appeal in that case, 328 U.S. 256, held that all airspace is in the public domain other than the airspace in the immediate reaches above the land. The language of the opinion, 328 U.S. at page 266, so holding, is:

> The airspace, apart from the immediate reaches above the land, is part of the public domain. We need not determine at this time what those precise limits are. Flights over private land are not a taking, unless they are so low and so frequent as to be a direct and immediate interference with the enjoyment and use of the land.

In the *Hinman* case, *supra*, 84 F.2d at page 758, the Court said:

> We own so much of the space above the ground as we can occupy or make use of, in connection with the enjoyment of our land. This right is not fixed. It varies with our varying needs and is coextensive with them. The owner of land owns as much of the space above him as he uses, but only so long as he uses it. All that lies beyond belongs to the world.

> When it is said that man owns, or may own, to the heavens, that merely means that no one can acquire a right to the space above him that will limit him in whatever use he can make of it as a part of his enjoyment of the land. To this extent his title to the air is paramount. No other person can acquire any title or exclusive right to any space above him.

> Any use of such air or space by others which is injurious to his land, or which constitutes an actual interference with his possession or his beneficial use thereof, would be a trespass for which he would have remedy. But any claim of the landowner beyond this cannot find a precedent in law, nor support in reason.

In the case at bar the evidence established that most of the flights above the Village of Cedarhurst were at altitudes exceeding 1,000 feet, that occasionally, under unusual conditions, a plane might fly over the Village at an altitude of 450 or 500 feet, but not lower than 450 feet. No claim is now made by the defendants that those flights interfered with the enjoyment of the land beneath. * * *

Accordingly, the aforesaid ordinance of the Village of Cedarhurst is declared unconstitutional and void and the defendants are permanently enjoined and restrained from enforcing it.

NOTES

1. No court continues to adhere to the ancient principle that a landowner has exclusive ownership of the airspace above the land. However, courts have been unable to agree on exactly what rights the landowner does have in the airspace. For example, courts have held that the landowner has fee title to:

(a) all the airspace above the land subject to a public aviation easement;

(b) as much of the airspace as is necessary to use the land without substantial interference from flights; or

(c) the airspace up to a fixed height above the land, which typically is the minimum safe flying altitude set by the Federal Aviation Administration (generally, 500 feet over "open water or sparsely populated areas" and 1,000 feet over the "highest obstacle" in a "congested area" 14 C.F.R. § 91.119).

Some states have attempted to address this issue statutorily. For example, Wis. Stat. § 114.03 provides: "The ownership of the space above the land and waters of this state is declared to be vested in the several owners of the surface beneath, subject to the right of flight described in s. 114.04." Section 114.04 grants the right to flight "unless at such a low altitude as to interfere with the then existing use to which the land or water, or the space over the land or water, is put by the owner, or unless so conducted as to be imminently dangerous or damaging to persons or property lawfully on the land or water beneath."

For discussions of this interesting issue, see *Brenner v. New Richmond Regional Airport Comm'n*, 816 N.W.2d 291 (Wis. 2012); Colin Cahoon, Comment, *Low Altitude Airspace: A Property Rights No-Man's Land*, 56 J. Air L. & Com. 157 (1990).

2. Municipalities have dealt with the noise and flight pattern problems caused by airports through land use or building height regulations. Courts generally have upheld these regulations against takings challenges. See *Smith v. County of Santa Barbara*, 52 Cal. Rptr. 292 (1966); *Fitzgarrald v. City of Iowa City*, 492 N.W.2d 659 (Iowa 1992); *Greenberg v. State*, 502 A.2d 522 (Md. Ct. App. 1986); but see *Sneed v. County of Riverside*, 32 Cal. Rptr. 318 (1963) (taking found when zoning regulations prohibited owner of land adjacent to airport from building higher than three inches on land closest to the runway); *McShane v. City of Faribault*, 292 N.W.2d 253 (Minn. 1980) (height restrictions caused a taking because they substantially diminished the land's fair market value).

3. Landowners successfully have sued airports in nuisance. However, to date, courts have awarded only damages in nuisance cases against airports. No court has enjoined a public airport as a nuisance. Scott Hamilton, *Allocation of Airspace as a Scarce National Resource*, 22 Transp. L.J. 251 (1994).

4. Drones (remotely operated aircraft) may present courts with their next challenge in addressing the law of airspace. Drones can be used for a wide variety of useful purposes, such as firefighting, pipeline inspections, and photography. Recognizing drones' potential utility, Congress enacted legislation in 2012 that directs the Federal Aviation Administration to expedite the promulgation of new regulations to facilitate their use. Federal Aviation Administration Modernization and Reform Act of 2012, Pub. L. No. 112-95, 126 Stat. 11. Drones may fly not only in public airspace but potentially also in airspace that is owned by people who own the land beneath it (think pizza delivery). Will incursions into private airspace constitute trespass or give rise to a nuisance action, or will courts create a common law right for drones to enter private space? Stay tuned! See Timothy T. Takahashi, *Drones in the National Airspace*, 77 J. Air L. & Com. 489 (2012).

As cities have become more congested and land available for development has become scarcer, developers increasingly maximize the use of land by severing ownership of airspace from the land surface beneath it. Severing the airspace promotes development of the spaces over highways, railroad lines, and even buildings. For example, the Marina City Apartments and the Merchandise Mart in Chicago were built over separately-owned railroad lines. Similarly, the United Nations Plaza in New York, as well as projects in Detroit, Washington, D.C., Hartford, Birmingham, Little Rock, and many other cities, have been constructed in separately owned or leased airspace. Recognizing the development potential over streets and highways, the Federal Highway Act and an increasing number of state statutes authorize governments to lease or to sell the airspace above roadways.

Unlike the common law countries, many civil law countries do not permit separate ownership of airspace. These countries base their prohibition on an absolutist construction of the maxim *cujus est solum, ejus est usque ad coelum.* However, the development potential in airspace has caused legislation to be introduced in some civil law countries to permit separate ownership. See Gerrit Pienaar, *Legal Aspects of Private Airspace Development*, 20 Comp. & Int'l L.J. of So. Africa 94 (1987).

American law concerning airspace has now evolved to permit the transfer of "air rights." As used in this context, air rights are different from airspace. Airspace is the area physically located over the land's surface. Title to it can be transferred to someone other than the surface owner, but it cannot be moved. The airspace is used where it is located.

In contrast, air rights are used to benefit other parcels of land. One type of air right benefits its owner by restricting a neighboring owner's use of his airspace. For example, a landowner concerned about preserving the view from her land can acquire an easement across neighboring property that prevents its owner from building in a way that interferes with the view.

A second type of air right is the statutorily created transferable development right (TDR). Some jurisdictions permit a person who owns adjoining parcels of land to transfer development rights from one parcel to the other. For example, assume that the zoning code would permit a ten-story building on each parcel. If the owner builds only a two-story building on one of the parcels, he then could build an eighteen-story building on the adjoining parcel. See, e.g., *Wing Ming Properties (U.S.A.) Limited v. Mott Operating Corp.*, 561 N.Y.S.2d 337 (1990).

Some jurisdictions also grant TDRs to a landowner when land use regulations prevent it from developing its property to the same extent as is permitted for neighboring properties. For example, when Grand Central Terminal was designated a landmark pursuant to New York City's Landmarks Preservation Law, the Terminal's owners were limited in their ability to build in the airspace above the Terminal. To mitigate the resulting damages to the Terminal's owners, the Landmarks Law authorized them to transfer the unused development rights over the Terminal to other land (the "transfer site"). The transfer site owner can use the TDRs to exceed the height restrictions to which the property otherwise would be subject. See *Penn Central Transportation Co. v. City of New York*, 438 U.S. 104 (1978). In addition to landmarks preservation programs, TDRs have been used in historic district and environmental and agricultural preservation programs. However, restrictions on where TDRs can be transferred and poorly developed TDR markets in most cities have prevented TDRs from becoming widely used, except in New York City. Despite these obstacles, some commentators predict that TDRs increasingly will be used in populous areas and in open areas.

B.   Rights in Air and Light

spite fence

SUNDOWNER, INC. v. KING
509 P.2d 785 (Idaho 1973)

SHEPARD, J.

If a "sign" or fence is built purely out of malicious intent, it is actionable.

This is an appeal from a judgment ordering partial abatement of a spite fence erected between two adjoining motels in Caldwell, Idaho. This action is evidently an outgrowth of a continuing dispute between the parties resulting from the 1966 sale of a motel. See: *King v. H.J. McNeel, Inc.*, 94 Idaho 444, 489 P.2d 1324 (1971).

In 1966 Robert Bushnell sold a motel to defendants-appellants King. Bushnell then built another motel, the Desert Inn, on property immediately adjoining that sold to the Kings.

The Kings thereafter brought an action against Bushnell (H.J. McNeel, Inc.) based on alleged misrepresentations by Bushnell in the 1966 sale of the motel property. . . . In 1968 the Kings built a large structure, variously described as a fence or sign, some 16 inches from the boundary line between the King and Bushnell properties. The structure is 85 ft. in length and 18 ft. in height. It is raised 2 ft. off the ground and is 2 ft. from the Desert Inn building. It parallels the entire northwest side of the Desert Inn building, obscures approximately 80% of the Desert Inn building and restricts the passage of light and air to its rooms.

Bushnell brought the instant action seeking damages and injunctive relief compelling the removal of the structure. Following trial to the court, the district court found that the structure was erected out of spite and that it was erected in violation of a municipal ordinance. The trial court ordered the structure reduced to a maximum height of 6 ft.

The Kings appeal from the judgment entered against them and claim that the trial court erred in many of its findings of fact and its applications of law. The Kings assert the trial court erred in finding that the "sign" was in fact a fence; that the structure had little or no value for advertising purposes; that the structure cuts out light and air from the rooms of the Desert Inn Motel; that the structure has caused damage by way of diminution of the value of the Desert Inn Motel property; that the erection of the structure was motivated by ill-feeling and spite; that the structure was erected to establish a dividing line; and that the trial court erred in failing to find the structure was necessary to distinguish between the two adjoining motels.

We have examined the record at length and conclude that the findings of the trial court are supported by substantial although conflicting evidence. The trial court had before it both still and moving pictures of the various buildings. The record contains testimony that the structure is the largest "sign" then existing in Oregon, Northern Nevada and Idaho. An advertising expert testified that the structure, because of its location and type, had no value for advertising and that its cost, i.e., $6,300, would not be justified for advertising purposes. Findings of fact will not be set aside on appeal unless they are clearly erroneous, and when they are supported by substantial though conflicting evidence they will not be disturbed on appeal. *Hisaw v. Bishop*, 95 Idaho 145, 504 P.2d 818 (1972); I.R.C.P. 52(a).

* * * The pivotal and dispositive issue in this matter is whether the trial court erred in requiring partial abatement of the structure on the ground that it was a spite fence. Under the so-called English rule, followed by most 19th century American courts, the erection and maintenance of a spite fence was not an actionable wrong. These older cases were founded on the premise that a property owner has an absolute right to use his property in any manner he desires. See: 5 Powell on Real Property, 696, p. 276 (1949 ed. rev'd 1968); *Letts v. Kessler*, 54 Ohio St. 73, 42 N.E. 765 (1896).

Under the modern American rule, however, one may not erect a structure for the sole purpose of annoying his neighbor. Many courts hold that a spite fence which serves no useful purpose may give rise to an action for both injunctive relief and damages. See: 5 Powell, *supra*, 696, p. 277; IA Thompson on Real Property, § 239 (1964 ed.). Many courts following the above rule further characterize a spite fence as a nuisance. See: *Hornsby v. Smith*, 191 Ga. 491, 13 S.E.2d 20 (1941); *Barger v. Barringer*, 151 N.C. 433, 66 S.E. 439 (1909); Annotation 133 A.L.R. 691.

One of the first cases rejecting the older English view and announcing the new American rule on spite fences is *Burke v. Smith*, 69 Mich. 380, 37 N.W. 838 (1888). Subsequently, many American jurisdictions have adopted and followed *Burke* so that it is clearly the prevailing modern view. . . .

In *Burke* a property owner built two 11 ft. fences blocking the light and air to his neighbors' windows. The fences served no useful purpose to their owner and were erected solely because of his malice toward his neighbor. Justice Morse applied the maxim *sic utere tuo ut alienum non laedas*, and concluded:

> "But it must be remembered that no man has a legal right to make a malicious use of his property, not for any benefit or advantage to himself, but for the avowed purpose of damaging his neighbor. To hold otherwise would make the law a convenient engine, in cases like the present, to injure and destroy the peace and comfort, and to damage the property, of one's neighbor for no other than a wicked purpose, which in itself is, or ought to be, unlawful. The right to do this cannot, in an enlightened country, exist, either in the use of property, or in any way or manner. There is no doubt in my mind that these uncouth screens or 'obscurers' as they are named in the record, are a nuisance, and were erected without right, and for a malicious purpose. What right has the defendant, in the light of the just and beneficent principles of equity, to shut out God's free air and sunlight from the windows of his neighbor, not for any benefit or advantage to himself, or profit to his land, but simply to gratify his own wicked malice against his neighbor? None whatever. The wanton infliction of damage can never be a right. It is a wrong, and a violation of right, and is not without remedy. The right to breathe the air, and to enjoy the sunshine, is a natural one, and no man can pollute the atmosphere, or shut out the light of heaven, for no better reason than that the situation of his property is such that he is given the opportunity of so doing, and wishes to gratify his spite and malice towards his neighbor." 37 N.W. at 842.

We agree both with the philosophy expressed in the *Burke* opinion and with that of other jurisdictions following what we feel is the better-reasoned approach. We hold that no property owner has the right to erect and maintain an otherwise useless structure for the sole purpose of injuring his neighbor. The trial court found on the basis of substantial evidence that the structure served no useful purpose to its owners and was erected because of the Kings' ill will and enmity toward their neighboring competitor. We therefore hold that the trial court did not err in partially abating and enjoining the "sign" structure as a spite fence.

Our decision today is not entirely in harmony with *White v. Bernhart*, 41 Idaho 665, 241 P. 367 (1925). *White* held that an owner could not be enjoined from maintaining a dilapidated house as a nuisance, even though the house diminished the value of neighboring property. *White* is clearly distinguishable from the case at bar. Rather than a fence, it involved a dwelling house which was not maliciously erected. The rule announced herein is applicable only to structures which serve no useful purpose and are erected for the sole purpose of injuring adjoining property owners. There is dictum in *White* which suggests that a structure may only be enjoined when it is a nuisance per se. Such language is inconsistent with our decision today and it is hereby disapproved.

Appellants King assign error to findings and conclusions of the trial court relating to the applicability and interpretation of Caldwell Zoning Ordinance No. 1085. Our disposition of this appeal makes it unnecessary to consider those issues. The judgment of the trial court is affirmed. Costs to respondent.

NOTES

1.　Although the court appears to apply nuisance law to determine whether the fence should be removed, the court did not balance the gravity of the harm to the plaintiffs against the utility of the defendant's conduct, as normally would be done in a nuisance action. Why not? When a person acts maliciously — with the sole purpose to harm another — the conduct is presumed to have no utility. Therefore, balancing harm against utility is unnecessary. See Powell on Real Property § 62.05 (Michael Allan Wolf ed., 2009); Restatement (Second) of Torts § 829, cmt. c. Not every court has adopted this view. See, e.g., *44 Plaza, Inc. v. Gray-Pac Land Co.*, 845 S.W.2d 576 (Mo. Ct. App. 1992) ("[I]f the conduct is lawful, it may not be prohibited, even if it is done for motives of pure malice, because to prohibit lawful, but malicious, acts would be controlling moral conduct, not protecting a legal right."); *Cohen v. Perrino*, 50 A.2d 348 (Pa. 1947) ("[T]he motive for doing a lawful act will not be inquired into by the court").

Mixed motives traditionally have been insufficient to enjoin a spite fence; the motive must be purely malicious. *Roper v. Durham*, 353 S.E.2d 476 (Ga. Ct. App. 1987); but see *Schork v. Epperson*, 287 P.2d 467, 470 (Wyo. 1955).

2.　Spite fences are common enough that many states have statutes prohibiting them and providing remedies. For example, a Rhode Island statute provides:

> A fence or other structure in the nature of a fence which unnecessarily exceeds six feet (6') in height and is maliciously erected or maintained for the purpose of annoying the owners or occupants of adjoining property,

shall be deemed a private nuisance, and any owner or occupant who is injured, either in the comfort or enjoyment of his or her estate thereby, may have an action to recover damages for the injury.

R.I. Gen. Laws § 34-10-20.

Does this statute provide adequate relief? See also Cal. Civ. Code § 841.4; Conn. Gen. Stat. §§ 52-480 & 52-570; Me. Rev. Stat. tit. 17, § 2801; Mass. Ann. Laws ch. 49 § 21; Minn. Stat. §§ 561.02–.03; N.Y. Real Prop. Acts § 843; 53 Pa. Cons. Stat. § 15171; Wash. Rev. Code § 7.40.030; Wis. Stat. § 844.10. Some courts interpreting these statutes have held that malice need not be the sole motive for the fence to be actionable. See Powell on Real Property § 62.05 (Michael Allan Wolf ed., 2009).

3. Under the English doctrine of ancient lights, a landowner could acquire a prescriptive easement for light and air over neighboring lands. The easement arose if the landowner had unobstructed and uninterrupted access to light and air across the neighboring land for twenty years. Based on the easement, the neighboring landowner could be enjoined from significantly interfering with the passage of light and air. The doctrine has been universally rejected in this country because negative easements generally cannot be acquired by prescription in the United States.

4. What type of legal right, if any, does a property owner have to air and light? How does the court in *Sundowner* characterize the property owner's right? Cf. *Hornsby v. Smith*, 13 S.E.2d 20, 25 (Ga. 1941) ("The air and light no matter from which direction they come are God-given, and are essential to the life, comfort, and happiness of every one."); *Burke v. Smith*, 37 N.W. 838, 842 (Mich. 1888) ("The right to breathe the air, and to enjoy the sunshine, is a natural one."); *Barger v. Barringer*, 66 S.E. 439, 440 (N.C. 1909) ("Light and air are as much a necessity as water, and all are the common heritage of mankind."). In the following two cases, focus on the court's characterization of the legal right, if any, to air and light.

blocked pool case

FONTAINEBLEAU HOTEL CORP. v. FORTY-FIVE TWENTY-FIVE, INC.

114 So. 2d 357 (Fla. Dist. Ct. App. 1959)

No malicious intent, so you can do what you want with your property.

PER CURIAM.

This is an interlocutory appeal from an order temporarily enjoining the appellants from continuing with the construction of a fourteen-story addition to the Fontainebleau Hotel, owned and operated by the appellants. Appellee, plaintiff below, owns the Eden Roc Hotel, which was constructed in 1955, about a year after the Fontainebleau, and adjoins the Fontainebleau on the north. Both are luxury hotels, facing the Atlantic Ocean. The proposed addition to the Fontainebleau is being constructed twenty feet from its north property line, 130 feet from the mean high water mark of the Atlantic Ocean, and 76 feet 8 inches from the ocean bulkhead line. The 14-story tower will extend 160 feet above grade in height and is 416 feet long from east to west. During the winter months, from around two o'clock in the afternoon for the remainder of the day, the shadow of the addition will extend over the cabana, swimming pool, and sunbathing areas of the Eden Roc, which are located in the southern portion of its property.

In this action, plaintiff-appellee sought to enjoin the defendants-appellants from proceeding with the construction of the addition to the Fontainebleau (it appears to have been roughly eight stories high at the time suit was filed), alleging that the construction would interfere with the light and air on the beach in front of the Eden Roc and cast a shadow of such size as to render the beach wholly unfitted for the use and enjoyment of its guests, to the irreparable injury of the plaintiff; further, that the construction of such addition on the north side of defendants' property, rather than the south side, was actuated by malice and ill will on the part of the defendants' president toward the plaintiff's president; and that the construction was in violation of a building ordinance requiring a 100-foot setback from the ocean. It was also alleged that the construction would interfere with the easements of light and air enjoyed by plaintiff and its predecessors in title for more than twenty years and "impliedly granted by virtue of the acts of the plaintiff's predecessors in title, as well as under the common law and the express recognition of such rights by virtue of Chapter 9837, Laws of Florida 1923. . . ." Some attempt was also made to allege an easement by implication in favor of the plaintiff's property, as the dominant, and against the defendants' property, as the servient, tenement.

The defendants' answer denied the material allegations of the complaint, pleaded laches and estoppel by judgment.

The chancellor heard considerable testimony on the issues made by the complaint and the answer and, as noted, entered a temporary injunction restraining the defendants from continuing with the construction of the addition. His reason for so doing was stated by him, in a memorandum opinion, as follows:

> "In granting the temporary injunction in this case the Court wishes to make several things very clear. The ruling is not based on any alleged presumptive title nor prescriptive right of the plaintiff to light and air nor is it based on any deed restrictions nor recorded plats in the title of the plaintiff nor of the defendant nor of any plat of record. It is not based on any zoning ordinance nor on any provision of the building code of the City of Miami Beach nor on the decision of any court, nisi prius or appellate. It is based solely on the proposition that no one has a right to use his property to the injury of another. In this case it is clear from the evidence that the proposed use by the Fontainebleau will materially damage the Eden Roc. There is evidence indicating that the construction of the proposed annex by the Fontainebleau is malicious or deliberate for the purpose of injuring the Eden Roc, but it is scarcely sufficient, standing alone, to afford a basis for equitable relief."

This is indeed a novel application of the maxim *sic utere tuo ut alienum non laedas.*[*] This maxim does not mean that one must never use his own property in such a way as to do any injury to his neighbor. *Beckman v. Marshall*, Fla. 1956, 85 So.2d 552. It means only that one must use his property so as not to injure the lawful *rights* of another. *Cason v. Florida Power Co.*, 74 Fla. 1, 76 So. 535, L.R.A. 1918A, 1034. In *Reaver v. Martin Theatres*, Fla. 1951, 52 So.2d 682, 683, 25 A.L.R.2d 1451, under this maxim, it was stated that "it is well settled that a property owner

---

[*] "So use your own as not to injure another's property." Black's Law Dictionary 1872 (9th ed. 2009).

may put his own property to any reasonable and lawful use, so long as he does not thereby deprive the adjoining landowner of any right of enjoyment of his property *which is recognized and protected by law, and so long as his use is not such a one as the law will pronounce a nuisance.*"

No American decision has been cited, and independent research has revealed none, in which it has been held that — in the absence of some contractual or statutory obligation — a landowner has a legal right to the free flow of light and air across the adjoining land of his neighbor. Even at common law, the landowner had no legal right, in the absence of an easement or uninterrupted use and enjoyment for a period of 20 years, to unobstructed light and air from the adjoining land. *Blumberg v. Weiss*, 1941, 129 N.J.Eq. 34, 17 A.2d 823; 1 Am. Jur., *Adjoining Landowners*, § 51. And the English doctrine of "ancient lights" has been unanimously repudiated in this country. 1 Am. Jur., *Adjoining Landowners*, § 49, p. 533; *Lynch v. Hill*, 1939, 24 Del.Ch. 86, 6 A.2d 614, *overruling Clawson v. Primrose*, 4 Del. Ch. 643.

There being, then, no legal right to the free flow of light and air from the adjoining land, it is universally held that where a structure serves a useful and beneficial purpose, it does not give rise to a cause of action, either for damages or for an injunction under the maxim *sic utere tuo ut alienum non laedas*, even though it causes injury to another by cutting off the light and air and interfering with the view that would otherwise be available over adjoining land in its natural state, regardless of the fact that the structure may have been erected partly for spite. . . .

We see no reason for departing from this universal rule. If, as contended on behalf of plaintiff, public policy demands that a landowner in the Miami Beach area refrain from constructing buildings on his premises that will cast a shadow on the adjoining premises, an amendment of its comprehensive planning and zoning ordinance, applicable to the public as a whole, is the means by which such purpose should be achieved. (No opinion is expressed here as to the validity of such an ordinance, if one should be enacted pursuant to the requirements of law. Cf. *City of Miami Beach v. State ex rel. Fontainebleau Hotel Corp.*, Fla. App. 1959, 108 So.2d 614, 619; *certiorari denied*, Fla. 1959, 111 So.2d 437.) But to change the universal rule — and the custom followed in this state since its inception — that adjoining landowners have an equal right under the law to build to the line of their respective tracts and to such a height as is desired by them (in the absence, of course, of building restrictions or regulations) amounts, in our opinion, to judicial legislation. As stated in *Musumeci v. Leonardo, supra* [77 R.I. 255, 75 A.2d 177], "So use your own as not to injure another's property is, indeed, a sound and salutary principle for the promotion of justice, but it may not and should not be applied so as gratuitously to confer upon an adjacent property owner incorporeal rights incidental to his ownership of land which the law does not sanction."

We have also considered whether the order here reviewed may be sustained upon any other reasoning, conformable to and consistent with the pleadings, regardless of the erroneous reasoning upon which the order was actually based. See *McGregor v. Provident Trust Co. of Philadelphia*, 119 Fla. 718, 162 So. 323. We have concluded that it cannot.

The record affirmatively shows that no statutory basis for the right sought to be enforced by plaintiff exists. The so-called Shadow Ordinance enacted by the City of Miami Beach at plaintiff's behest was held invalid in *City of Miami Beach v. State ex rel. Fontainebleau Hotel Corp., supra.* It also affirmatively appears that there is no possible basis for holding that plaintiff has an easement for light and air, either express or implied, across defendants' property, nor any prescriptive right thereto — even if it be assumed, arguendo, that the common-law right of prescription as to "ancient lights" is in effect in this state. And from what we have said heretofore in this opinion, it is perhaps superfluous to add that we have no desire to dissent from the unanimous holding in this country repudiating the English doctrine of ancient lights.

The only other possible basis — and, in fact, the only one insisted upon by plaintiff in its brief filed here, other than its reliance upon the law of private nuisance as expressed in the maxim *sic utere tuo ut alienum non laedas* — for the order here reviewed is the alleged violation by defendants of the setback line prescribed by ordinance. The plaintiff argues that the ordinance applicable to the Use District in which plaintiff's and defendants' properties are located, prescribing "a front yard having a depth of not less than one hundred (100) feet, measured from the ocean, . . . ," should be and has been interpreted by the City's zoning inspector as requiring a setback of 100 feet from an established ocean bulkhead line. As noted above, the addition to the Fontainebleau is set back only 76 feet 8 inches from the ocean bulkhead line, although it is 130 feet from the ocean measured from the mean high water mark.

While the chancellor did not decide the question of whether the setback ordinance had been violated, it is our view that, even if there was such a violation, the plaintiff would have no cause of action against the defendants based on such violation. The application of simple mathematics to the sun studies filed in evidence by plaintiff in support of its claim demonstrates conclusively that to move the existing structure back some 23 feet from the ocean would make no appreciable difference in the problem which is the subject of this controversy. Cf. *Taliaferro v. Salyer,* 162 Cal. App. 2d 685, 328 P.2d 799 (1958)], *supra.* The construction of the 14-story addition is proceeding under a permit issued by the city pursuant to the mandate of this court in *City of Miami Beach v. State ex rel. Fontainebleau Hotel Corp., supra,* which permit authorizes completion of the 14-story addition according to a plan showing a 76-foot setback from the ocean bulkhead line. Moreover, the plaintiff's objection to the distance of the structure from the ocean appears to have been made for the first time in the instant suit, which was filed almost a year after the beginning of the construction of the addition, at a time when it was roughly eight stories in height, representing the expenditure by defendants of several million dollars. In these circumstances, it is our view that the plaintiff has stated no cause of action for equitable relief based on the violation of the ordinance — assuming, arguendo, that there has been a violation.

Since it affirmatively appears that the plaintiff has not established a cause of action against the defendants by reason of the structure here in question, the order granting a temporary injunction should be and it is hereby reversed with directions to dismiss the complaint. Reversed with directions.

NOTES

1. What could the Eden Roc Hotel's owner have done to protect the flow of sunlight to its property? A protected right to light, air, and view across another's land can be created by express easement or by restrictive covenant. See, e.g., *Pacifica Homeowners' Association v. Wesley Palms Retirement Community*, 224 Cal. Rptr. 380 (1986); *Pierce v. Northeast Lake Washington Sewer and Water Dist.*, 870 P.2d 305 (Wash. 1994); POWELL ON REAL PROPERTY § 34.11[5] (Michael Allan Wolf ed., 2009). Such easements also may be implied but only in cases of real and obvious necessity and only if the intent to create the easement is clear. See *Nomar v. Ballard*, 60 S.E.2d 710 (W. Va. 1950); *Rohde v. Beztak of Arizona, Inc.*, 793 P.2d 140 (Ariz. Ct. App. 1990); *Highway 7 Embers, Inc. v. Northwestern Nat'l Bank*, 256 N.W.2d 271, 276 (Minn. 1977); but see *Miller v. Hoeschler*, 105 N.W. 790 (Wis. 1905). For example, in *Ramsey v. Lewis*, 874 S.W.2d 320 (Tex. Civ. Ct. App. 1994), the court refused to recognize an implied easement for view when the defendant, a land developer, represented in his promotional sales materials that the property featured a "magnificent view of [the] city skyline." The court held that the statement did not adequately demonstrate a promise not to obstruct the view.

2. The City of Miami Beach attempted to protect the Eden Roc Hotel when the Fontainebleau building plans became public by adopting the Shadow Ordinance referred to in the decision. The ordinance provided:

> [O]n lots fronting on the ocean no building shall be erected to a height in excess of thirty (30) feet, except that for each foot of the total number of feet that the building sets back from the ocean and/or sets back from the northerly property line, one-half (1/2) foot may be added to the height limit specified, not exceeding, however, the maximum height herein specified.

The City's stated purpose for the ordinance was to provide for more orderly development along the ocean by "taking due consideration to the necessities for light, air and reflection of sunshine and the general appearance of the hotels and apartments along the Ocean front. . . ." The Florida appellate court invalidated the ordinance because the City did not provide the legally required notice and public hearing. The court expressly reserved the issue of the validity of the ordinance's substance. *City of Miami Beach v. State ex rel. Fontainebleau Hotel Corp.*, 108 So. 2d 614 (Fla. Dist. Ct. App. 1959).

3. Several states have enacted statutes expressly providing for easements and other restrictions to ensure access to sunlight. See, e.g., Ill. Stat. Ch. 30, § 725/1.2; Ky. Rev. Stat. Ann. § 381.200(2); 33 Me. Rev. Stat. §§ 1401–02; N.M. Stat. Ann. 1978, §§ 47-3-1 *et seq.*; Wyo. Stat. Ann. §§ 34-22-101 *et seq.*

4. How would you draft an easement for access to sunlight? See Colleen McKann Kettles, *A Comprehensive Review of Solar Access Law in the United States*, Solar America Board for Codes and Standards (Oct. 2008), available at www.solarabcs.org/solaraccess.

5. Courts universally hold that obstructing a view does not constitute a nuisance. See *Venuto v. Owens-Corning Fiberglass Corp.*, 99 Cal. Rptr. 350 (Cal. 1971); *Mohr v. Midas Realty Corp.*, 431 N.W.2d 380 (Iowa 1988); *44 Plaza, Inc. v. Gray-Pac Land Co.*, 845 S.W.2d 576 (Mo. App. 1992); *Collinson v. John L. Scott,*

Inc., 778 P.2d 534 (Wash. Ct. App. 1989); but see *Heston v. Ousler*, 398 A.2d 536 (N.H. 1979); *O'Neil v. Atwell*, 598 N.E.2d 110 (Ohio Ct. App. 1991). The court in *Mohr* articulated the two reasons that courts routinely reject a nuisance claim for obstructing a view: (1) holding that the obstruction constituted a nuisance would essentially grant a prescriptive easement; and (2) because nearly every new building obstructs someone's view, a flood of litigation would result from finding a nuisance. *Mohr*, 431 N.W.2d at 382.

PRAH v. MARETTI
321 N.W.2d 182 (Wis. 1982)

ABRAHAMSON, J.

This appeal from a judgment of the circuit court for Waukesha County, Max Raskin, circuit judge, was certified to this court by the court of appeals, sec. (Rule) 809.61, Stats. 1979–80, as presenting an issue of first impression, namely, whether an owner of a solar-heated residence states a claim upon which relief can be granted when he asserts that his neighbor's proposed construction of a residence (which conforms to existing deed restrictions and local ordinances) interferes with his access to an unobstructed path for sunlight across the neighbor's property. This case thus involves a conflict between one landowner (Glenn Prah, the plaintiff) interested in unobstructed access to sunlight across adjoining property as a natural source of energy and an adjoining landowner (Richard D. Maretti, the defendant) interested in the development of his land.

The circuit court concluded that the plaintiff presented no claim upon which relief could be granted and granted summary judgment for the defendant. We reverse the judgment of the circuit court and remand the cause to the circuit court for further proceedings.

According to the complaint, the plaintiff is the owner of a residence which was constructed during the years 1978–1979. The complaint alleges that the residence has a solar system which includes collectors on the roof to supply energy for heat and hot water and that after the plaintiff built his solar-heated house, the defendant purchased the lot adjacent to and immediately to the south of the plaintiff's lot and commenced planning construction of a home. The complaint further states that when the plaintiff learned of defendant's plans to build the house he advised the defendant that if the house were built at the proposed location, defendant's house would substantially and adversely affect the integrity of plaintiff's solar system and could cause plaintiff other damage. Nevertheless, the defendant began construction. The complaint further alleges that the plaintiff is entitled to "unrestricted use of the sun and its solar power" and demands judgment for injunctive relief and damages.

After filing his complaint, the plaintiff moved for a temporary injunction to restrain and enjoin construction by the defendant. In ruling on that motion the circuit court heard testimony, received affidavits and viewed the site.

The record made on the motion reveals the following additional facts: Plaintiff's home was the first residence built in the subdivision, and although plaintiff did not build his house in the center of the lot it was built in accordance with applicable restrictions. Plaintiff advised defendant that if the defendant's home were built at the proposed site it would cause a shadowing effect on the solar collectors which would reduce the efficiency of the system and possibly damage the system. To avoid these adverse effects, plaintiff requested defendant to locate his home an additional several feet away from the plaintiff's lot line, the exact number being disputed. Plaintiff and defendant failed to reach an agreement on the location of defendant's home before defendant started construction. The Architectural Control Committee and the Planning Commission of the City of Muskego approved the defendant's plans for his home, including its location on the lot. After such approval, the defendant apparently changed the grade of the property without prior notice to the Architectural Control Committee. The problem with defendant's proposed construction, as far as the plaintiff's interests are concerned, arises from a combination of the grade and the distance of defendant's home from the defendant's lot line.

The circuit court denied plaintiff's motion for injunctive relief, declared it would entertain a motion for summary judgment and thereafter entered judgment in favor of the defendant.

* * * We consider first whether the complaint states a claim for relief based on common law private nuisance. This state has long recognized that an owner of land does not have an absolute or unlimited right to use the land in a way which injures the rights of others. The rights of neighboring landowners are relative; the uses by one must not unreasonably impair the uses or enjoyment of the other. VI-A American Law of Property sec. 28.22, pp. 64–65 (1954). When one landowner's use of his or her property unreasonably interferes with another's enjoyment of his or her property, that use is said to be a private nuisance. *Hoene v. Milwaukee*, 17 Wis.2d 209, 214, 116 N.W.2d 112 (1962); *Metzger v. Hochrein*, 107 Wis. 267, 269, 83 N.W. 308 (1900). See also Prosser, Law of Torts sec. 89, p. 591 (2d ed. 1971).

The private nuisance doctrine has traditionally been employed in this state to balance the rights of landowners, and this court has recently adopted the analysis of private nuisance set forth in the Restatement (Second) of Torts. . . .

Although the defendant's obstruction of the plaintiff's access to sunlight appears to fall within the Restatement's broad concept of a private nuisance as a nontrespassory invasion of another's interest in the private use and enjoyment of land, the defendant asserts that he has a right to develop his property in compliance with statutes, ordinances and private covenants without regard to the effect of such development upon the plaintiff's access to sunlight. In essence, the defendant is asking this court to hold that the private nuisance doctrine is not applicable in the instant case and that his right to develop his land is a right which is per se superior to his neighbor's interest in access to sunlight. This position is expressed in the maxim *"cujus est solum, ejus est usque ad coelum et ad inferos,"* that is, the owner of land owns up to the sky and down to the center of the earth. The rights of the surface owner are, however, not unlimited. *United States v. Causby*, 328 U.S. 256, 260–1 (1946). See also 114.03, Stats. 1979–80. . . .

Many jurisdictions in this country have protected a landowner from malicious obstruction of access to light (the spite fence cases) under the common law private nuisance doctrine. If an activity is motivated by malice it lacks utility and the harm it causes others outweighs any social values. VI-A Law of Property sec. 28.28, p. 79

(1954). This court was reluctant to protect a landowner's interest in sunlight even against a spite fence, only to be overruled by the legislature. Shortly after this court upheld a landowner's right to erect a useless and unsightly sixteen-foot spite fence four feet from his neighbor's windows, *Metzger v. Hochrein*, 107 Wis. 267, 83 N.W. 308 (1900), the legislature enacted a law specifically defining a spite fence as an actionable private nuisance. Thus a landowner's interest in sunlight has been protected in this country by common law private nuisance law at least in the narrow context of the modern American rule invalidating spite fences. See, e.g., *Sundowner, Inc. v. King*, 95 Idaho 367, 509 P.2d 785 (1973); Restatement (Second) of Torts, sec. 829 (1977).

This court's reluctance in the nineteenth and early part of the twentieth century to provide broader protection for a landowner's access to sunlight was premised on three policy considerations. First, the right of landowners to use their property as they wished, as long as they did not cause physical damage to a neighbor, was jealously guarded. *Metzger v. Hochrein*, 107 Wis. 267, 272, 83 N.W. 308 (1900).

Second, sunlight was valued only for aesthetic enjoyment or as illumination. Since artificial light could be used for illumination, loss of sunlight was at most a personal annoyance which was given little, if any, weight by society.

Third, society had a significant interest in not restricting or impeding land development. *Dillman v. Hoffman*, 38 Wis. 559, 574 (1875). This court repeatedly emphasized that in the growth period of the nineteenth and early twentieth centuries change is to be expected and is essential to property and that recognition of a right to sunlight would hinder property development. The court expressed this concept as follows:

> "As the city grows, large grounds appurtenant to residences must be cut up to supply more residences. . . . The cistern, the outhouse, the cesspool, and the private drain must disappear in deference to the public waterworks and sewer; the terrace and the garden, to the need for more complete occupancy. . . . Strict limitation [on the recognition of easements of light and air over adjacent premises is] in accord with the popular conception upon which real estate has been and is daily being conveyed in Wisconsin and to be essential to easy and rapid development at least of our municipalities." . . .

Considering these three policies, this court concluded that in the absence of an express agreement granting access to sunlight, a landowner's obstruction of another's access to sunlight was not actionable. . . . These three policies are no longer fully accepted or applicable. They reflect factual circumstances and social priorities that are now obsolete.

First, society has increasingly regulated the use of land by the landowner for the general welfare. *Euclid v. Ambler Realty Co.*, 272 U.S. 365 (1926); *Just v. Marinette*, 56 Wis. 2d 7, 201 N.W.2d 761 (1972).

Second, access to sunlight has taken on a new significance in recent years. In this case the plaintiff seeks to protect access to sunlight, not for aesthetic reasons or as a source of illumination but as a source of energy. Access to sunlight as an energy source is of significance both to the landowner who invests in solar collectors and to a society which has an interest in developing alternative sources of energy.

Third, the policy of favoring unhindered private development in an expanding economy is no longer in harmony with the realities of our society. *State v. Deetz*, 66 Wis. 2d 1, 224 N.W.2d 407 (1974). The need for easy and rapid development is not as great today as it once was, while our perception of the value of sunlight as a source of energy has increased significantly.

Courts should not implement obsolete policies that have lost their vigor over the course of the years. The law of private nuisance is better suited to resolve landowners' disputes about property development in the 1980s than is a rigid rule which does not recognize a landowner's interest in access to sunlight. As we said in *Ballstadt v. Pagel*, 202 Wis. 484, 489, 232 N.W. 862 (1930), "What is regarded in law as constituting a nuisance in modern times would no doubt have been tolerated without question in former times." We read *State v. Deetz*, 66 Wis. 2d 1, 224 N.W.2d 407 (1974), as an endorsement of the application of common law nuisance to situations involving the conflicting interests of landowners and as rejecting per se exclusions to the nuisance law reasonable use doctrine. . . .

Private nuisance law, the law traditionally used to adjudicate conflicts between private landowners, has the flexibility to protect both a landowner's right of access to sunlight and another landowner's right to develop land. Private nuisance law is better suited to regulate access to sunlight in modern society and is more in harmony with legislative policy and the prior decisions of this court than is an inflexible doctrine of non-recognition of any interest in access to sunlight across adjoining land.

We therefore hold that private nuisance law, that is, the reasonable use doctrine as set forth in the Restatement, is applicable to the instant case. Recognition of a nuisance claim for unreasonable obstruction of access to sunlight will not prevent land development or unduly hinder the use of adjoining land. It will promote the reasonable use and enjoyment of land in a manner suitable to the 1980s. That obstruction of access to light might be found to constitute a nuisance in certain circumstances does not mean that it will be or must be found to constitute a nuisance under all circumstances. The result in each case depends on whether the conduct complained of is unreasonable.

Accordingly we hold that the plaintiff in this case has stated a claim under which relief can be granted. Nonetheless we do not determine whether the plaintiff in this case is entitled to relief. In order to be entitled to relief the plaintiff must prove the elements required to establish actionable nuisance, and the conduct of the defendant herein must be judged by the reasonable use doctrine. . . . The judgment of the circuit court is reversed and the cause remanded for proceedings not inconsistent with this opinion.

NOTES

1. Should the court's analysis in *Prah* have been different if:

    a. The plaintiff had a backup electrical system that he could use if the solar system failed or became less efficient;

  b. The plaintiff could have avoided the problem by building his home in a different location on his lot; or

  c. State legislation authorized local governments to issue solar access permits to prevent interference with solar collectors but only after giving notice and an opportunity to be heard to the owner of the land to be restricted?

All three additional facts were part of the record in *Prah*.

  2. In a vigorously worded dissent, Justice Calloway disagreed with the *Prah* holding on a number of grounds, including:

  a. The plaintiff could have avoided this problem by locating his home on a different part of his lot or by acquiring the lot that the defendant later purchased;

  b. The defendant's building plans complied with all applicable laws;

  c. Solar collectors are used on few properties because of their cost and "limited efficiency";

  d. The majority's decision is legislative, rather than judicial;

  e. The plaintiff's solar collectors constitute an unusually sensitive use; and

  f. The defendant had no notice when he bought his lot that he might be subject to a limitation on its use.

  3. The New Hampshire Supreme Court has followed *Prah*. In *Tenn v. 889 Assocs., Ltd.*, 500 A.2d 366, 370 (N.H. 1985), Justice Souter cited *Prah* and stated that "there is no reason in principle why the law of nuisance should not be applied to claims for the protection of a property owner's interests in light and air, and . . . we believe that considerations of policy support just such an application of nuisance concepts." However, two other courts considering the question of rights to sunlight have rejected the *Prah* approach. In *Sher v. Leiderman*, 226 Cal. Rptr. 698 (Cal. Ct. App. 1986), a California appellate court stated that the concerns raised by the court in *Prah* are better handled through legislative action. The court noted: "Though the Solar Age may indeed be upon us, it is not so easily conceded that individual property rights are no longer important policy considerations." See also *Residences at Riverbend Condo. Ass'n v. City of Chicago*, 2013 U.S. Dist. LEXIS 164526 (N.D. Ill. Nov. 19, 2013).

  4. Consider the following statement by the court in *Prah*:

  We do not find the reasoning of *Fontainebleau* persuasive. The court leaped from rejecting an easement by prescription (the doctrine of ancient lights) and an easement by implication to the conclusion that there is no right to protection from obstruction of access to sunlight. The court's statement that a landowner has no right to light should be the conclusion, not its initial premise. The court did not explain why an owner's interest in unobstructed light should not be protected or in what manner an owner's interest in unobstructed sunlight differs from an owner's interest in being free from obtrusive noises or smells or differs from an owner's interest in unobstructed use of water. The recognition of a per se exception to private nuisance law may invite unreasonable behavior.

321 N.W.2d at 190 n.13. Which court's approach is more consistent with modern American property law and expectations?

5. *Prah* has generated a great deal of academic comment, nearly all positive. See, e.g., Sara C. Bronin, *Solar* Rights, 89 B.U. L. Rev. 1217 (2009); Steven Cherin, *Casting a Shadow on a Solar Collector — A Cause of Action Recognized, An Alternative Resolution Framework Suggested*: Prah v. Maretti, 68 Cornell L. Rev. 941 (1983); Troy A. Rule, *Shadows on the Cathedral: Solar Access Laws in a Different Light*, 2010 U. Ill. L. Rev. 851. However, at least one scholar has criticized *Prah*. Denis Brion, *Rhetoric and the Law of Enterprise*, 42 Syracuse L. Rev. 117, 125–27 (1991). Brion argues that the *Prah* decision does not make economic sense because it ignored the initial distribution of rights to the airspace over the defendant's land. The parties simply could have bargained for ownership of those rights. More importantly, he argues, the decision does not satisfy distributive justice because the court allowed Prah to expropriate value from Maretti's land without compensating Maretti for the loss. "If the public is the beneficiary of the subsidy to the solar cell owner, then it, and not the expropriated landowner, ought to bear the cost of the subsidy."

6. Another form of alternative energy, wind power, has generated nuisance cases in which the court considered wind power's public benefit in the balancing of harms. *Sowers v. Forest Hills Subdivision*, 294 P.3d 427 (Nev. 2013) ("evidence concerning the noise, diminution in property value, shadow flicker, and aesthetics far outweighs any potential utility of the proposed wind turbine within the Forest Hills Subdivision"). See also *Burch v. Ned Power Mount Storm, LLC*, 647 S.E.2d 879 (W. Va. 2007) (noise and unsightliness can cause wind turbine to be a nuisance); *Rassier v. Houim*, 488 N.W.2d 635 (N.D. 1992) (wind turbine does not constitute a nuisance); *Rankin v. FPL Energy, LLC*, 266 S.W.3d 506 (Tex. App. 2008) (neighbors' emotional response to loss of view caused by wind turbines does not constitute a nuisance); *Rose v. Chaikin*, 453 A.2d 1378 (N.J. Super. Ct. 1982) (defendants erected a 60-foot wind turbine in a residential area to conserve energy and to reduce their electric bills; court weighed the turbine's social utility against the harms it was causing). Jennifer R. Andriano, *The Power of Wind: Current Legal Issues in Siting for Wind Power*, 61 Plan. & Envtl. L. 3 (May 2009); Robert S. Guzek, Comment, *Addressing the Impacts of Large Wind Turbine Projects to Encourage Utilization of Wind Energy Resources*, 27 Temp. J. Sci., Tech. & Envtl. L. 123 (2008); Ernest Smith, *Wind Energy: Siting Controversies and Rights in Wind*, 1 Envtl. & Energy L. & Pol'y J. 281 (2007).

7. Does a property owner have any right to the clouds over the property or to the rain in those clouds? Compare *Southwest Weather Research, Inc. v. Rounsaville*, 320 S.W.2d 211, 216 (Tex. Civ. App. 1958) (court enjoined defendant's cloud seeding over plaintiff's ranch, which caused the clouds to dissipate, because "the landowner is entitled to such precipitation as Nature deigns to bestow"), with *Slutsky v. City of New York*, 97 N.Y.S.2d 238, 239 (1950) (resort owners cannot prevent New York City from attempting to induce rain artificially because plaintiffs "clearly have no vested property rights in the clouds or the moisture therein").

V. WATER RIGHTS

A. Diffuse Surface Water

flooded state park

WESTLAND SKATING CTR., INC. v.
GUS MACHADO BUICK, INC.
542 So. 2d 959 (Fla. 1989)

GRIMES, J.

* * * This case involves a dispute among occupiers of adjacent parcels of land that used to be part of the Everglades and later became pastureland, but which now comprise commercially developed property in Dade County. Petitioner, Westland Skating Center, Inc., operated a skating rink on property leased from petitioner, Hialeah Skating Center, Ltd. An auto dealership, now operated by respondent, Gus Machado Buick, Inc., occupied abutting property. There has been some alteration of all the land involved, but the parties agree that the natural drainage flow was generally and gradually toward the southwest, that is from the skating rink property onto and toward the rear of the auto dealership property.[3] When the auto dealership was built in 1970, a miniature-golf course occupied the skating rink property, and apparently neither landowner had unusual problems in dealing with rainwater.

Trouble began in April 1980, however, after the construction of the skating rink. The building's roof was 200 by 120 feet. A 200-by-60-foot section sloped toward the auto dealership; it ended about 10 feet from the property line. Water drained off the roof through five downspouts. During a rainstorm the auto dealership, then Seipp Buick, experienced flooding extensive enough to damage several cars. This sort of flooding had occurred only once before, and then during much heavier rain. Seipp blamed the new skating rink, with its sloping roof and downspouts, for increasing the flow of water onto his property.

Talks between Seipp and Revitz to alleviate the problem were unavailing, and in 1980 Seipp decided to take action. He built a wall, 8 feet high and 2 feet deep between the two tracts along the 900-foot length of his property. This project took several months to complete; the skating center did not object to the presence of the wall during that time.

August of 1981 brought a heavy rain and profoundly different results than the 1980 downpour. This time, water ran off the roof and down toward Seipp's wall, which acted as a dam. The water then backed up under the skating rink's floor, inflicting heavy damage. The floor was replaced, but another heavy rain a month or so later resulted in more flooding, which the skating rink's employees alleviated by

---

[3] The only evidence at trial of this "natural" flow was from a surveyor, who based his conclusions on a 1961 survey which was done before the area was commercially developed. Apparently, there was no survey of the land while it was actually the Everglades. The surveyor said the average slope was about 1 inch every 30 feet, and that some of the land sloped to the south, rather than the southwest.

sledgehammering holes in Seipp's wall. More repairs to the rink ensued, but eventually it closed.

Westland and Hialeah sued Seipp for damages and sought a mandatory injunction to remove the wall. Seipp counterclaimed for damages and to enjoin Westland from damaging the wall. During the litigation, Machado bought the Seipp land and the dealership and was substituted as a party.[4]

Before trial, Westland and Hialeah obtained a partial summary judgment to the effect that as long as the skating rink was constructed in accordance with the South Florida Building Code, Machado's lower-elevation lot remained the servient tenement for all surface water flowing from the skating center.

The case proceeded to trial where the jury, after receiving an instruction that tracked the language of the partial summary judgment, found in favor of Westland and Hialeah in excess of one million dollars in damages.

The Third District Court of Appeal reversed the judgment against Machado in a six-to-three split decision. The court held that the trial judge had applied an incorrect rule of law in granting the summary judgment and that the jury instruction based on the summary judgment also was error.

Originally, disputes involving the interference of surface waters were resolved by one of two doctrines: the common enemy rule or the civil law rule. See generally F. Maloney, S. Plager, R. Ausness, B. Canter, Florida Water Law 589 (1980), [hereinafter Maloney & Plager]; Annot., *Modern Status of Rules Governing Interference With Drainage of Surface Waters*, 93 A.L.R.3d 1216 (1979). The common enemy rule held that landowners had an unlimited privilege to deal with the surface water on their land as they pleased without regard to the harm which may be caused to others. The civil law rule recognized that higher elevation tracts had an easement or servitude over lower tracts for all surface water that naturally flowed downhill. However, anyone who increased or interfered with the natural flow of surface waters so as to cause invasion of another's interests was subject to liability to the other.

Neither of these doctrines, in its pure form, was perfect, especially as the population increased. While the common enemy rule permitted the free improvement of property, it also carried with it the potential of self-help engineering contests in which the winner was the person who most effectively turned the excess water upon his neighbor's land. On the other hand, the civil law rule acted as an impediment to the improvement of land since almost any development by an upper landowner was likely to increase the flow of surface water upon the land below and most efforts by the lower owner to dam the natural flow had the effect of throwing the water back onto the land of the upper owner. As a consequence, some jurisdictions adopted a third rule, known as the reasonable use rule. Under this rule, a possessor of land is not unqualifiedly entitled to deal with surface waters as he pleases nor is he absolutely prohibited from increasing or interfering with the

---

[4] The counterclaim was dismissed in return for Westland and Hialeah agreeing not to seek punitive damages. The record is silent as to the fate of the injunction, but apparently improvements to both lots eliminated the flooding and mooted the issue.

natural flow of surface waters to the detriment of others. Each possessor is legally privileged to make reasonable use of his land even though the flow of surface waters is altered thereby and causes some harm to others. He incurs liability only when his harmful interference with the flow of surface waters is unreasonable.

Because of the inequities which would result from a strict application of either the common enemy or the civil law rule, most of the states which had adopted either of these rules began to apply modifications in given cases. Often, these hybrid rules produced the same result as would have occurred through the application of the reasonable use rule. The reasonable use rule has been adopted by Restatement (Second) of Torts § 833 (1979), which recommends that claims of interference with the flow of surface waters should be decided under principles of nuisance. See *Pendergrast v. Aiken*, 236 S.E.2d 787 (N.C. 1977) (if the interference is intentional, the conduct of the offending party is measured in terms of reasonableness; if unintentional, the test is negligence).

The Florida position with respect to the interference with surface waters is not entirely clear. After explaining the common enemy and the civil law rules in *Brumley v. Dorner*, 83 So. 912 (Fla. 1919), this Court noted that both of these rules had been modified considerably by the courts to the extent that each case must stand upon its own facts. The Court, 83 So. at 914, then stated:

> The almost universal rule, as gathered from the decisions, is that no person has the right to gather surface waters that would naturally flow in one direction by drainage, ditches, dams, or otherwise, and divert them from their natural course and cast them upon the lands of the lower owner to his injury.

Later in the opinion, *id.*, 83 So. at 914–15, the Court observed:

> The law as to surface waters and other waters accumulated and thrown upon the lands of adjoining property, that would not naturally flow across it, is stronger than the rule against accumulating water in quantities and casting it upon the lower proprietor, which would under natural conditions receive the water from the upper proprietor, as it naturally flows upon the lower proprietor. . . .

There are several subsequent cases in which the First District Court of Appeal announced principles which appear consistent with the strict civil law rule. *Koger Properties, Inc. v. Allen*, 314 So.2d 792 (Fla. 1st DCA 1975), *cert. denied*, 328 So.2d 842 (Fla. 1976) (further citations omitted.) On the other hand, in *Seminole County v. Mertz*, [415 So. 2d 1286, 1289 (Fla. 5th DCA), *rev. denied*, 424 S. 2d 763 (Fla. 1982) — Eds.] the court said:

> Courts of Florida have applied, in an almost unbroken line of decisions, practically all the elements of the modified civil law rule of surface water. (Citation omitted.) The general rule today is that the upper owner may improve and enhance the natural drainage of his land as long as he acts reasonably and does not divert the flow, and that the lower owner is subject to an easement for such flow as the upper owner is allowed to cast upon him.

The majority opinion of the Third District Court of Appeal below adopted the strict civil law rule. The court reasoned that whether Westland's use of the property was reasonable was irrelevant. The court held that if Westland's improvement of the property caused an increase in the amount or a diversion of the surface water flowing onto Machado's property, Machado could not be liable to Westland for erecting the wall to protect its property. This holding directly conflicted with the foregoing statement from *Mertz*.

Upon analysis, we have elected to adopt the reasonable use rule in cases involving the interference with surface waters.[6] In so doing, we join approximately twenty-one other states, (citation omitted), many of which have taken this position in recent years. E.g., . . . *Hall v. Wood*, 443 So.2d 834 (Miss. 1983); *McGlashan v. Spade Rockledge Terrace Condo. Dev. Corp.*, 402 N.E.2d 1196 (Ohio 1980). . . .

The rule we announce appears much like the modified civil law rule; however, we believe it desirable to state our position through the adoption of the separate rule of reasonable use. As noted by Maloney and Plager, *supra*, at 596:

> Although the courts have treated the doctrine of reasonable use as a separate rule on equal footing with the civil law and common enemy rules, it is in reality merely the general tort principle which would decide such cases in the absence of the application of either of the two "property" rules. The relationship between adjoining landowners, in the absence of specific property rights, has always been governed by the maxim "*Sic utere tuo ut alienum non laedas*" ("Use your property in such a manner as not to injure that of another"). Much confusion and strained reasoning could be avoided if the courts would limit the application of the traditional rules to the narrowest possible situation or discard them altogether.

The principle that an upper landowner enjoys an easement across the lower tract for all naturally occurring surface water continues to apply to land in its natural state. However, when any party improves his land, thereby causing surface waters to damage his neighbor's property, the reasonable use rule shall be applied in order to settle the controversy. The rule applies not only in cases involving the conduct of the upper owner but also to improvements by the lower owner, such as the construction of dams designed to protect against the natural flow of surface waters across the lower land. Regardless of whether a counterclaim has been filed when both parties have made improvements, the reasonableness of the conduct of each will be in issue and may be compared in order to arrive at a fair determination.

We recognize that the application of the reasonable use rule may make the outcome of certain controversies less predictable. Yet, if the rigidity of the traditional doctrines made cases predictable, it also led to such arbitrary results that the courts began to modify those rules. Predictability should not be achieved at the expense of justice. We believe that the rule of reasonable use employs the proper balance and will best enable surface water controversies to be fairly decided. As stated in *McGlashan v. Spade Rockledge Terrace Condominium Development Corp.*:

---

[6] This Court has previously recognized that subject to legislative regulation, the reasonable use rule is applicable to subsurface waters. *Village of Tequesta v. Jupiter Inlet Corp.*, 371 So.2d 663 (Fla. 1979).

The basic issue in these controversies is normally whether liability for the damage resulting from an interference with surface water flow should be borne by the person causing it. In this regard, an analysis centering on the reasonableness of a defendant's conduct, in view of all the circumstances, is more likely to produce an equitable result than one based on arbitrary property concepts. It is true that the law should not inhibit reasonable land development, but neither should it allow a landowner to expel surface water without regard to the consequences. As eloquently stated by Justice Brennan in *Armstrong v. Francis Corp.* (1956), 20 N.J. 320, 330, 120 A.2d 4, 10, "no reason suggests itself why, in justice, the economic costs incident to the expulsion of surface waters in the transformation of the rural or semi-rural areas of our State into urban or suburban communities should be borne in every case by adjoining landowners rather than by those who engage in such projects for profit. Social progress and the common well-being are in actuality better served by a just and right balancing of the competing interests according to the general principles of fairness and common sense which attend the application of the rule of reason."

402 N.E.2d at 1199–1200.

While it is evident that we do not accept the application of the strict civil law rule by the district court of appeal, we do not disagree with its analysis of the disputed jury instruction. The jury instruction read as follows:

Higher elevation land imposes a servitude on the owner of neighboring lower elevation land to accept the runoff of water naturally flowing from the higher elevation to the lower. The owner of higher elevation land has a right to use and improve his land by constructing a building on his property in accordance with applicable building code requirements. Where the higher elevation owner complies with the applicable building code, and rainwater then falls onto the building constructed on the higher elevation land, and from that building onto the lower elevation land, a servitude on the lower elevation landowner is still imposed as it is for naturally flowing water. The owner of lower elevation land may not lawfully construct a barrier between its land and the adjoining higher elevation land for the purpose, in whole or in part, of preventing water from flowing from the higher elevation land to the lower elevation land unless: (a) The owner of the higher elevation land grants permission for the barrier constructed by the lower elevation landowner; or (b) The building on the higher elevation was not constructed in accordance with applicable building code requirements which deviates from code cause the natural water flow to be increased or made more burdensome; or (c) The barrier built by the lower landowner provides adequate drainage to protect the higher elevation landowner from flood.

This instruction had the practical effect of requiring the jury to determine the reasonableness of Westland's conduct based upon whether or not it complied with the South Florida Building Code. As noted by the court below, while one's compliance with a statute or an ordinance may amount to evidence of reasonableness, such compliance is not tantamount to reasonableness as a matter of law. Thus, evidence of Westland's compliance with the code could be properly considered as evidence of the reasonableness of its conduct, but not to the exclusion of other relevant evidence on that issue. Moreover, this case involved an evaluation and comparison of the reasonableness of the conduct of both parties. Therefore, the entry of the partial summary judgment and the resultant giving of the disputed jury instruction constituted reversible error. Accordingly, while we have expressed differing views with respect to the law applicable to the interference with surface waters, we approve the decision of the district court of appeal reversing the judgment and directing a new trial. It is so ordered.

NOTE

May diffused surface water be discharged into a watercourse? See *City of Columbus v. Barngrover*, 552 S.E.2d 536 (Ga. App. Ct. 2001). Are flood and overflow waters from a watercourse diffused surface water? How about irrigation runoff? Does a landowner have the right to impound such water? More generally, can a landowner acquire use rights in this type of water? See *Hendrickson v. Wagners*, 598 N.W.2d 507 (S.D. 1999). If both common enemy and civil law jurisdictions have modified their law for this type of water, then what differences remain between the two types of jurisdictions? What are the advantages and disadvantages of using rules of reasonable use for diffused surface water, percolating water, and water in watercourses? See *Heins Implement Co. v. State Highway Comm'n*, 859 S.W.2d 681, 690–691 (Mo. 1993). Does the word natural in the civil law rule for surface water have the same meaning that it has in the law of subjacent and lateral support?

B. Groundwater

MADDOCKS v. GILES
728 A.2d 150 (Me. 1999)

CALKINS, J.

Sewall and Janice Maddocks appeal from the entry of judgment in the Superior Court (Lincoln County) after a jury verdict finding that Elbridge Giles' excavation activities on his land did not interfere with the flow of an underground watercourse benefitting the Maddockses' land. The Maddockses argue that the trial court erred by instructing the jury on the absolute dominion rule, and they urge us to adopt a new rule governing groundwater usage. We decline to adopt a new rule, and we affirm the judgment.

The Maddockses own property adjacent to a gravel pit owned by Giles. The Maddockses do not live on this property; in fact, there is no house on the property. An underground spring that produced large quantities of water has historically flowed beneath the Maddockses' property. In 1994 the Maddockses filed a complaint alleging that Giles' excavation activities at the gravel pit caused the spring to run dry. Giles moved to dismiss on the ground that there is no cause of action for the diminution or exhaustion of a neighbor's spring by the lawful excavation of land through which underground water percolates. The motion was granted, but we vacated the dismissal in *Maddocks v. Giles*, 686 A.2d 1069 (Me. 1996) [*Maddocks I*]. We recognized the general rule that a person may use his land as he pleases for lawful purposes, but we noted that a landowner may not disrupt a watercourse to the injury of neighboring landowners. *Id.* at 1071. Because we concluded that the complaint sufficiently alleged that Giles' excavation activities disrupted a watercourse running beneath Giles' property to the Maddockses' spring, we remanded for further proceedings.

At trial, the Maddockses testified that Giles' excavation activities, including dewatering the gravel pit to allow ever-deeper digging, caused the spring to become exhausted. Their expert hydrogeologist conceded that the water underneath Giles' land flowing into the spring is presumed to be percolating,[1] but added that percolating water can constitute a watercourse because there is a general flow and predictable course. Giles' expert hydrogeologist testified that the water feeding the spring was percolating water and that it could not constitute a watercourse because it has no sides or bed, as a surface watercourse does. He further testified that underground watercourses do not exist in Maine, as these appear primarily in areas of limestone deposits.

The absolute dominion rule, which has been the law in this jurisdiction for a over a century, is reflected in the instructions given to the jury in this case.[2] The court gave the jury a verdict form that required it to make a preliminary determination of whether the water feeding the spring was a watercourse. The judge instructed the jury to go no further if it found the aquifer on Giles' land was not a watercourse. The jury returned a unanimous verdict that the source aquifer for the spring was not a watercourse, and judgment was granted to Giles.

The sole issue presented on appeal is whether we should depart from the common law absolute dominion rule and adopt the groundwater use rules set forth in Restatement (Second) of Torts § 858 (1979). The absolute dominion rule is based on the premise that groundwater is the absolute property of the owner of the land, just like the rocks and soil that compose it. *See* Roger A. Cunningham, et al., The Law of Property § 7.5 (1984). In *Chase v. Silverstone*, 62 Me. 175, 183–84 (1873), we held that a landowner who digs a well on his own property, thereby causing percolating water to a neighbor's spring to dry up, is not liable for damages. The rule was affirmed in *Chesley v. King*, 74 Me. 164, 170 (1882):

---

[1] Most underground water gradually percolates through the various strata and is not flowing in a watercourse. *See* 3 Waters and Water Rights § 20.07(a)(4) (Robert Beck ed., 1991). This has led to a judicial presumption that underground water is percolating, and therefore the party asserting the existence of an underground stream has the burden of proof. *Id.* § 20.07(a)(2).

[2] The trial court instructed the jury that a property owner may use his land as he pleases for all lawful purposes but the owner may not interrupt or interfere with a watercourse benefitting another's land, whether that watercourse is above ground or below ground. The court further instructed the jury that a property owner could dig a well or make other excavations and not be subject to a claim for damages even though the effect of the excavation was to cut off and divert water which percolates through the ground or hidden veins to feed the neighbor's well or spring. The court defined a watercourse as a course of water flowing in a particular direction by a regular channel having a bed with banks and sides and usually discharging itself into some other body or stream of water. The court added that although it must have a well-defined and substantial existence, a watercourse need not flow continuously or never be dry.

One may, for the convenience of himself or the improvement of his property, dig a well or make other excavations within his own bounds, and will be subject to no claim for damages although the effect may be to cut off and divert the water which finds its way through hidden veins which feed the well or spring of his neighbor.

As we noted in *Maddocks I*, there is a limit to this rule of unfettered capture: a landowner cannot stop or divert the flow of a watercourse to the injury of his neighbor. *See Morrison v. Bucksport & Bangor R.R. Co.*, 67 Me. 353, 356 (1877). The scope of this exception, however, is limited by the narrow definition of a watercourse: "To constitute a water course, it must appear that the water usually flows in a particular direction; and by a regular channel, having a bed with banks and sides; and (usually) discharging itself into some other body or stream of water. It may sometimes be dry. It need not flow continuously; but it must have a well defined and substantial existence." *Id.* . . .

The absolute dominion rule is now the minority rule in the United States. A few states in addition to Maine continue to recognize the rule. *See Wiggins v. Brazil Coal & Clay Corp.*, 452 N.E.2d 958, 964 (Ind. 1983) (further citations omitted).

Most jurisdictions have adopted the reasonable use, or American, rule or some variation of it.[5] See Cunningham at § 7.5. A representative sample of these jurisdictions includes [Ala., N.H., Pa., and Tenn. — Eds.]. The reasonable use rule requires that all uses of the water on the land from which it is extracted must be reasonable. See 6 Thompson on Real Property § 50.1 1(a) and (d) (David A. Thomas ed., 1994). The usual interpretation of reasonable simply prevents the landowner from wasting the water or from transporting it off of the land for use elsewhere. *See* Cunningham at § 7.5.

The Restatement approach abandons the common law distinction between underground watercourses and percolating water. *See* Restatement (Second) of Torts § 845. It provides that a landowner who withdraws groundwater, whether in a watercourse or percolating, and "uses it for a beneficial purpose is not subject to liability for interference with the use of water by another." *Id.* § 858(1). If the withdrawal, however, unreasonably causes harm to a neighbor by lowering the water table, exceeds the owner's reasonable share, or has a direct effect on a watercourse and unreasonably causes harm to one entitled to that water, then the owner may be liable. *Id.* The Restatement rule is derived from principles of reasonable use, but it differs from its predecessors. The reasonable use rule, of which there are variations, usually only requires that water not be wasted, but the "Restatement balances the equities and hardships between competing users." Linda Malone, *The Necessary Interrelationship Between Land Use and Preservation of Groundwater Resources*, 9 UCLA J. Envtl. L. & Pol'y 1, 11 (1990). Three states have adopted the Restatement approach. *See Cline v. American Aggregates Corp.*, 474 N.E.2d 324, 328 (Ohio 1984). . . .

The Maddockses argue that we should abandon the absolute dominion rule because it is based upon faulty science. It is generally accepted that the absolute

---

[5] A few jurisdictions, notably California, have adopted a rule of correlative rights as a variant on reasonable use principles. *See City of Pasadena v. City of Alhambra*, 207 P.2d 17, 28–29 (Cal. 1949). . . .

dominion rule was established because courts did not understand how water flows underground. Instead, courts looked to established principles of property law that would allow them to resolve disputes without having to probe beneath the surface. *See* 1 Waters and Water Rights § 4.05(c) (Beck ed., 1991). In rejecting the absolute dominion rule, several courts have given modern science as a basis for abandoning the old rule. *See, e.g., Cline,* 474 N.E.2d at 328.

We decline to abandon the absolute dominion rule. First, we are not convinced that the absolute dominion rule is the wrong rule for Maine. We recognize that we are not bound by the doctrine of *stare decisis* when the underpinnings of the previous decisions are disproved and when the conditions of society have changed so that the prior law no longer fulfills a need and is counterproductive. *See Myrick v. James,* 444 A.2d 987, 998 (Me. 1982). Although modern science has enlightened our knowledge of groundwater, this does not mean that the rule itself has interfered with water use or has caused the development of unwise water policy. The Maddockses did not present evidence or point to any studies showing that the absolute dominion rule has not functioned well in Maine. Furthermore, for over a century landowners in Maine have relied on the absolute dominion rule. (Citation omitted.) In the absence of reliable information that the absolute dominion rule is counterproductive and a hindrance to achieving justice, we will not depart from our prior decisions.

Second, we are not persuaded that we, as opposed to the Legislature, should be weighing the heavy policy considerations involved in this issue, not the least of which is the reliance of land owners on the present property laws. The Legislature can study the ramifications of a change in policy; it can call upon experts to give their opinions as to the best water policy for Maine; and it can survey Maine's water needs. We conclude that at this time the question of whether to depart from our common law on groundwater issues is best left to the Legislature.

Finally, we are further constrained in making the requested change because the Legislature has taken action in this area by creating the Water Resources Management Board to do a comprehensive study of water law in Maine. The Board reported to the Legislature and suggested that it adopt reasonable use principles. The Legislature chose to leave the common law as it currently stands. * * * Judgment affirmed.

NOTE

Outside of the bounds of an underground watercourse, a rule of capture does not apply when there is a malicious injury to a neighboring landowner, a willful waste of water, or (sometimes) subsidence of a neighbor's land because of the withdrawal. How useful are these exceptions? Many reasonable use rules involve courts in balancing the social values of competing uses. Is a court equipped for that task? Hydrological data requires trained professionals to evaluate; that evaluation can baffle unassisted judicial analysis and the professionals otherwise providing it can be expensive. See *Spear T Ranch, Inc. v. Knaub,* 691 N.W.2d 116 (Neb. 2005) (permitting suit by surface water user against a hydrologically connected groundwater user); *Sipriano v. Great Springs Water of America, Inc.,* 1 S.W.3d 75 (Tex. 1999) (reaffirming the state's rule of capture for groundwater).

[handwritten margin note top: Minority: absolute dominion rule, ground water is absolutely prop. of land owner.]

[handwritten margin note: for percolating water (undefined channels)]

MacARTOR v. THE GRAYLYN CREST III SWIM CLUB, INC.
187 A.2d 417 (Del. Ch. 1963)

[handwritten note above title: Pool drains well case.]

SEITZ, J. *[handwritten: Majority: reasonable use]*

[handwritten margin note: Restatement combines percolating and water course and uses reasonable use rule.]

This is the decision after final hearing on plaintiffs' application to enjoin defendant Swim Club from further use of its well, . . . and for damages in the sum of $73.49. This case raises in capsule form very important problems of allocation of rights in percolating water. It is not susceptible of an easy solution, because the controlling test is "objective" reasonableness.

Plaintiffs live on the east side of Marsh Road in Brandywine Hundred and have for their water supply what I will call a bricked well 4 feet 7 inches long, 2 feet 11 inches wide, and just over 4 feet deep. The "normal" water depth is of course much less than the height of the well. The defendant leased land directly across Marsh Road but back about 150 feet from the road and constructed thereon a swimming pool with accompanying facilities. The parties' wells are about 200 feet apart. Defendant proceeded to sink a well of approximately 200 feet, which passed through almost solid rock below the 42 foot level, at an expense of about $2,500. The first 42 feet of the well are encased in steel.

[handwritten margin note: Reasonable use is: — amount of water — when water is being used — what for water.]

Defendant began pumping operations from its well on the afternoon of July 7, 1960 for the purpose of filling its pool. The plaintiffs' water fell below the intake pipe at least by the next morning. There followed a series of disagreements resulting in the filing of this action. At the motion stage this court rejected the so-called English rule of absolute ownership of percolating water. The court stated that it preferred to adopt an appropriate legal principle in the light of the fully developed facts.

The trial resulted in one important change in the record from that presented at the motion stage. At the motion stage, it was contended on affidavit by plaintiffs' expert, and denied by defendant's expert, that there was a hydrological connection between the two wells. At the trial defendant's expert stated that he then agreed with plaintiff's expert that such a connection did exist. Thus, as strange as it may seem, in view of their relative depths and the other factors mentioned, both wells are drawing from a common pool or reservoir of water.

The defendant's swimming pool requires about 240,000 gallons to fill. It appears that defendant's pump must run constantly for about three weeks to fill the pool. I find that this results in plaintiffs' well being unusable for at least the same period. It also would appear that the amount drawn out by defendant intermittently for miscellaneous pool use during the swimming "season" continues to render plaintiffs' well unusable. Are plaintiffs entitled to relief under the circumstances?

The answer to the question posed first requires the court to determine the applicable legal principle. The doctrine of "reasonable user" commends itself here. This rule permits the court to consider and evaluate the various factors on both sides and arrive at an "accommodation" of the conflicting rights, if that is feasible. It also permits the court to consider the intentions of the offending party and his actions subsequent to the discovery of the consequences of his use of the water.

Before examining the factors relevant to the application of this announced legal principle, certain important preliminary observations are in order. First of all, plaintiffs are not entitled to have the defendant restrained from using its well merely because it can purchase the water commercially at a reasonable rate. I say this because a land owner is entitled to make "reasonable" use of the percolating water under his land. This is one of his "bundle of sticks". Indeed, defendant attempts to bring the same argument to bear against plaintiffs and the court merely reiterates its position. Nor do I think that a prior use by one party automatically preempts the water for such party merely because of such priority.

Nor does the fact that plaintiffs' well may be objectively marginal necessarily deprive them of relief. They are entitled to protection if their use is impaired by an unreasonable use of the water by plaintiff. The marginal nature of the well is however pertinent evidence in evaluating the reasonableness of the comparative uses both for the purpose of determining liability and for the purpose of affording relief.

Finally, defendant says the construction of a school and of sanitary and storm sewers next to plaintiffs' property have lowered the level of the water in the well. This is no answer to plaintiffs' claim. I say this because it appears that plaintiffs have a water supply which, even after such work they deem sufficient except when the defendant's well is being pumped.

What are the facts pertinent to the reasonable user issue? It seems clear that defendant believed and was reasonably entitled to believe that the well it sank would not interfere with wells such as plaintiffs. Moreover, plaintiffs' well is objectively marginal with a weak recovery rate. In contrast, it appears that defendant's use is recreational. While such use is not to be condemned, it is not entitled to quite the same consideration as a household use. I recognize however that the comparative number of users may also be a relevant factor. So far as appears only a few property owners are apparently affected, and only the plaintiffs complain legally. Next, the defendant is withdrawing water from the land area it occupies in amounts which far exceed what would be the "normal" residential water need for such area, assuming its building density would be about the same as that which surrounds the area. Finally the defendant takes a very large volume of water in concentrated periods.

The foregoing factors, when considered with the balance of the record, lead me to conclude that defendant's initial use of its well was made without an awareness of its consequences on plaintiffs' well. However, after it became aware of such effect defendant's use at least during the period when it pumped to fill the pool was not unqualifiedly reasonable. * * *

What relief is here warranted? Certainly there are "equities" on both sides. As noted, I do not believe this case justifies a permanent injunction against the use of defendant's well. One immediately asks whether defendant could not pump in amounts and over a time period that would not result in plaintiffs' well going dry. On the record before me there seems to be substantial doubt that the schedule could be sufficiently drawn out to accomplish its purpose without being impractical at least time wise. At least this is so with respect to the filling operation.

The next suggestion that comes to mind is to consider whether plaintiffs' well could be deepened with the hope of obviating the problem. There is of course no assurance that the deepening of plaintiffs' type of well to a reasonable extent would solve the problem created by defendant's pumping. But there is testimony that a nearby similar type well of some 14 feet is adequate despite the pumping. I think the first approach to a balancing of the conflicting interests for purpose of affording relief is to deepen plaintiffs' well a reasonable distance and see what happens. This can be accomplished by an order made subject to appropriate later change.

I therefore conclude that plaintiffs' request to enjoin defendant from pumping from its well will be granted until further order of the court on the condition that plaintiffs deepen or agree to permit defendant to cause their well to be deepened to a reasonable depth with the cost to be equally divided. Plaintiffs must run the risk of permanent loss of water inherent in deepening the well. Defendant must also arrange for a substitute water supply for plaintiffs in the interim.

As an alternative remedy, if not objectionable to third parties involved, plaintiffs may elect to run at their own expense a permanent connection to the defendant's supply of water from the Suburban Water Company which they may thereafter use so long as they bear their proportion of the costs attributable to such use. If the parties accept one of the alternative remedies and the conditions applicable to it, the order will fix a time schedule and provide for a report on the results of the work. If plaintiffs reject both alternatives or the applicable conditions, no injunction will be granted against the use of the defendant's well. If defendant rejects the conditions applicable to the remedy selected by plaintiffs, a permanent injunction against the use of its well will be granted. * * *

Finally, I consider plaintiffs' claim for damages. Defendant does not challenge the amount or reasonableness of the expenses. Its defense is that it offered plaintiffs a substitute water supply which was rejected. I accept defendant's defense and decline to assess damages. Unless defendant desires to be heard court costs will be assessed against it.

NOTE

In *State v. Michels Pipeline Constr., Inc.*, 217 N.W.2d 339, 344–345 (Wis. 1974), the court stated:

> The basis for this rule of absolute ownership of percolating ground water was a feeling that the ways of underground water were too mysterious and unpredictable to allow the establishment of adequate and fair rules for regulation of competing rights to such water. So the English courts adopted the position that everyone was permitted to take and use all of which they could get possession. . . . And the early American case of *Roath v. Driscoll* [20 Conn. 533, 541 (1850)] said with regard to percolating water: "The laws of its existence and progress . . . cannot be known or regulated. It rises to great heights, and moves collaterally, by influences beyond our apprehension. These influences are so secret, changeable and uncontrollable, we cannot subject them to the regulations of law, nor build upon them a system of rules, as has been done, with streams upon the surface."

And again in *Haldeman v. Bruckhart* [45 Pa. 514, 519 (1863)] the Pennsylvania court said: "A surface stream cannot be diverted without knowledge that the diversion will affect a lower proprietor. Not so with an unknown subterranean percolation or stream. One can hardly have rights upon another's land which are imperceptible, of which neither himself or that other can have any knowledge."

Even in 1903 when the [leading Wisconsin opinion] was written, the awe of mysterious, unknowable forces beneath the earth was fast becoming an outmoded basis for a rule of law. The court . . . discussed the subject of artesian water with a certain degree of sophistication. However, artesian water may have been better understood than other types of percolating ground water. However, today scientific knowledge in the field of hydrology has certainly advanced to the point where a cause and effect relationship can be established between a tapping of underground water and the level of the water table in the area so that liability can be fairly adjudicated consonant with due process. Our scientific knowledge also establishes the interdependence of all water systems. "The hydrologic cycle traces all existing water from the oceans to the atmosphere, to the land and ultimately back to the oceans. In nature, there is an inseparable relationship between all water, whether in the atmosphere, on the earth's surface, or under the earth's surface." J.H. Beuscher, *Wisconsin's Law of Water Use*, 31 Wis. Bar Bull. (Oct. 1958), p. 30.

It makes very little sense to make an arbitrary distinction between the rules to be applied to water on the basis of where it happens to be found. There is little justification for property rights in ground water to be considered absolute while rights in surface streams are subject to a doctrine of reasonable use.

What reasons might justify different rules for groundwater as opposed to watercourses (creeks, streams, rivers, etc.)? How is the reasonable use rule modified in *MacArtor* for situations that involve drawing percolating water from a well? Under a reasonable use rule, may the Swim Club recover against a polluter of the groundwater it pumped into its pool? See *Artesian Water Co. v. New Castle Cty.*, 659 F. Supp. 1269 (D. Del. 1987). What if withdrawing groundwater caused surface subsidence? Is a rule of reasonable use an effective anti-pollution device? See also *Martin v. City of Linden*, 667 So. 2d 732 (Ala. 1995) (reviewing another state's cases dealing with *MacArtor* issues).

C. Riparian and Littoral Rights

The basic doctrines governing the rights of owners of land abutting lakes and watercourses (rivers, streams, creeks) are set out in *Harris v. Brooks*, 283 S.W.2d 129, 132–133 (Ark. 1955), as follows:

Generally speaking two separate and distinct theories or doctrines regarding the right to use water are recognized. One is commonly called the "Appropriation Doctrine" and the other is the "Riparian Doctrine."

Appropriation Doctrine. * * * Generally speaking, under this doctrine, some governmental agency, acting under constitutional or legislative authority, apportions water to contesting claimants. It has . . . been in about 17 western states. This doctrine is inconsistent with the common law relative to water rights in force in this and many other states. One principal distinction between this doctrine and the riparian doctrine is that under the former the use is not limited to riparian landowners.

Riparian Doctrine. This doctrine, long in force in this and many other states, is based on the old common law which gave to the owners of land bordering on streams the right to use the water therefrom for certain purposes, and this right was considered an incident to the ownership of land. Originally it apparently accorded the landowners the right to have the water maintained at its normal level, subject to use for strictly domestic purposes. Later it became evident that this strict limitation placed on the use of water was unreasonable and unutilitarian. Consequently it was not long before the demand for a greater use of water caused a relaxation of the strict limitations placed on its use and this doctrine came to be divided into (a) the natural flow theory and (b) the reasonable use theory.

(a) Natural Flow Theory. Generally speaking again, under the natural flow theory, a riparian owner can take water for domestic purposes only, such as water for the family, livestock, and gardening, and he is entitled to have the water in the stream or lake upon which he borders kept at the normal level. There are some expressions in the opinions of this court indicating that we have recognized this theory, at least to a certain extent.

[(b)] Reasonable Use Theory. This theory appears to be based on the necessity and desirability of deriving greater benefits from the use of our abundant supply of water. It recognizes that there is no sound reason for maintaining our lakes and streams at a normal level when the water can be beneficially used without causing unreasonable damage to other riparian owners. The progress of civilization, particularly in regard to manufacturing, irrigation, and recreation, has forced the realization that a strict adherence to the uninterrupted flow doctrine placed an unwarranted limitation on the use of water, and consequently the courts developed what we now call the reasonable use theory. This theory is of course subject to different interpretations and limitations. In 56 Am. Jur., p. 728, it is stated that "The rights of riparian proprietors on both navigable and unnavigable streams are to a great extent mutual, common, or correlative. The use of the stream or water by each proprietor is therefore limited to what is reasonable, having due regard for the rights of others above, below, or on the opposite shore. In general, the special rights of a riparian owner are such as are necessary for the use and enjoyment of his abutting property and the business lawfully conducted thereon, qualified only by the correlative rights of other riparian owners, and by certain rights of the public, and they are to be so exercised as not to injure others in the enjoyment of their rights." It has been stated that each riparian owner has an equal right to make a reasonable use of waters subject to the equal rights of other owners to make the reasonable use. . . . The purpose of the law is to secure to each riparian owner equality in the use of water as near as may be by requiring each to exercise his right reasonably and with due regard to the rights of others similarly situated.

NOTE

Some jurisdictions have held that riparian water may neither be taken nor used by riparian owners outside the watershed and that extra-watershed uses are unreasonable per se. Does this prohibition makes sense in both natural flow and reasonable use jurisdictions? See, e.g., *Roberts v. Martin*, 77 S.E. 535 (W. Va. 1913) (recognizing this prohibition); *Stratton v. Mt. Hermon Boys' Sch.*, 103 N.E. 87 (Mass. 1913) (discussing this prohibition, but not finding it dispositive, requiring instead proof of actual damages before giving the plaintiff damages even nominal in amount). Should the application of such a prohibition depend on the remedy (injunction or damages) a plaintiff seeks? The watershed limitation has been one of the most criticized restrictions on the riparian right. Some states, such as Kentucky and Florida, authorize trans-basin diversions of water by statute. See Ky. Rev. Stat. § 151.200(2) (1987). In Florida water is diverted, with statutory authority, from the northern part of the state to the south. Fla. Stat. Ann. § 373.223 (1987). A watershed limitation may at least hold intrastate political problems in check. See generally 1 Waters and Water Rights § 7.02 (Robert Beck ed., 1991).

The doctrine of prior appropriation, mentioned in *Harris*, allocates rights to water in the western United States. The needs of miners and ranchers in the nineteenth century had much to do with the development of this doctrine. Where it is used, it is everywhere codified and is written into seven state constitutions. Eighteen western states rely solely on prior appropriation as the method for water rights acquisition and allocation. The allocation of prior appropriation rights is based on a "first in time, first in right" rule. 2 Waters and Water Rights § 12.02 (Robert Beck ed., 1991). Each state, however, has a slightly different version of and different interpretations of the doctrine. Eight states — Arizona, Colorado, Idaho, Montana, Nevada, New Mexico, Utah, and Wyoming — have the purest appropriation systems. Other states — Alaska, California, Kansas, North Dakota, Oklahoma, Oregon, South Dakota, Texas, and Washington — use a hybrid system — a mixture of riparian and appropriation doctrines; of these, however, only a few make it possible to acquire new riparian rights.

Although specific statutory provisions serve to define the elements of each state's doctrine, an appropriation generally has five elements. First, a qualified "person" must acquire the right. A "person" is not confined to natural persons, but extends to different types of legal entities, such as corporations.

Second, the person must establish that he or she is the first to appropriate the water. The priority of a particular right is usually determined by reference to filing and pursuing an appropriation permit with due diligence, plus an actual appropriation with an intent to appropriate. The rationale underlying the first in time analysis is a policy favoring the encouragement and protection of investment based on an actual use of the water. Traditionally, the action manifesting appropriation was equated to a diversion of the water from the watercourse. This requirement has been subject to attack and it is argued that, in the absence of an express statutory mandate, there is nothing to require an actual diversion of the water flow. See generally 2 Waters and Water Rights § 12.03(c)(1) (Robert Beck ed., 1991). Thus in-stream uses, as well as diversions, may be subject to appropriation.

The third element involves the water appropriated: the appropriation statutes and cases define the quantity of water allocated to the user and further define what waters and water courses are subject to the prior appropriation doctrine. Almost all statutes place some water sources beyond the reach of potential appropriators. The modern trend is towards excluding bodies of water such as wild or scenic rivers and wetlands.

The fourth element involves the use of the water: it requires that the water appropriated be put to an actual and beneficial use. Thus, to satisfy the element of appropriation, there must be an intent to appropriate, accompanied by an overt act manifesting the intent, with the appropriation intended for a "beneficial use." Requiring such use means that a water allocation is not just a quantity-based right. All states require that an appropriation be for a beneficial use. Moreover, some states recently added a "reasonable use" requirement, similar in nature to the reasonable use doctrine of riparian rights. The policy rationale underlying the beneficial use requirement examines the actual use of the water, recognizing a concern for environmental and societal effects as opposed to a purely economic determination of the benefit of the use.

Fifth and finally, the water right created is a property right, although more limited than other such rights. Restrictions on the alienability of water rights are common and, more importantly, the right is subject to discontinuance by a prior water right drawn from the same water source. Thus the last appropriated right is the first to be terminated in the event of a water shortage. 2 Waters and Water Rights § 12.03(e) (Robert Beck ed., 1991). Additionally, there is a growing trend toward attempting to accommodate all uses through a rotation process.

The doctrine of prior appropriation originated to meet the needs for water in the arid western states. It provides for the use of water far beyond riparian parcels. Later conveyances of these water rights has given rise, in the western states, to a unique system for transferring and recording water rights, title searches, and deeds — everything needed for a law practice in this special branch of conveyancing. However, the ability to use or transfer the right to benefit another location is limited. Among common state restrictions are those which require that the water be utilized only in the area for which an initial permit is issued; those that forbid the transfer of water out of state; and restrictions on changes in senior uses that might adversely affect junior uses.

Chapter 3

ESTATES IN LAND

I. THE FEE SIMPLE

At common law, estates in land were divided into two classes: freehold estates and leasehold estates. Only the former signified a lifelong bond between a free man and his feudal lord. Freehold estates were of three types: the fee simple, the fee tail, and the life estate. All were (and are) present possessory interests. The fee simple remains the basic unit of ownership of land in American law. The fee simple can either be *absolute* if it is unlimited in duration or *defeasible* if it is subject to termination upon the happening of an event specified in the grant. A fee simple absolute is the greatest interest holders of land can possess, and it is what we think of when we describe someone as owner of a parcel of land. Holding a fee simple allows owners to convey it inter vivos and to devise it by will. It allows them to use it in the ways they desire, free from the claims of their children or their ancestors. In the United States, it allows them to extract the minerals found under the land.

Possession of a fee simple, even a fee simple absolute, does not mean that holders enjoy unfettered dominion over the land. Think of zoning laws, for example, and the restrictions they impose on the permissible uses of land. Or think of the possibility that interests in the same property may be held by others, easements to walk across the land, for example, or the very real interest held by a bank to which the land is mortgaged. Such interests are not thought incompatible with the existence of a fee simple in the land, although they do restrict the powers of the holder of the fee. Despite the existence of such restrictions, the fee simple nevertheless gives the holder extensive powers over the land, and it will almost always be in the interest of persons holding land to claim a title in fee simple absolute.

"heirs on fathers side case"

JOHNSON v. WHITON

34 N.E. 542 (Mass. 1893)

Numerus Clausus: you can't make up your own fees.

Contract, to recover a deposit paid under an agreement to purchase land, which provided that in case the title was defective the vendor should refund the deposit. The case was submitted to the Superior Court, and, after judgment for the defendant, to this court, on appeal, on agreed facts, the material portions of which appear in the opinion.

HOLMES, J.

This is an action to recover a deposit paid under an agreement to purchase land. The land in question passed under the seventh clause of the will of Royal Whiton to his five grandchildren, and a deed executed by them was tendered to the plaintiff, but was refused on the ground that one of the grandchildren, Sarah A. Whiton, could not convey a fee simple absolute, and this action is brought to try the question. The clause of the will referred to is as follows: "After the decease of all my children, I give, devise, and bequeath to my granddaughter, Sarah A. Whiton, and her heirs on her father's side, one third part of all my estate, both real and personal, and to my other grandchildren and their heirs respectively the remainder, to be divided in equal parts between them."

We see no room for doubt that the legal title passed by the foregoing clause. We think it equally plain that the words "and her heirs on her father's side" are words of limitation, and not words of purchase. The only serious question is whether the effect of them was to give Sarah A. Whiton merely a qualified fee, and whether by reason of the qualification she is unable to convey a fee simple. We do not think that it would be profitable to follow the discussions to be found in 1 Prest. Est. 449 et seq., and Challis, Real Prop. 215 et seq. By the old English law, to take land by descent a man must be of the blood of the first purchaser; Co. Lit. 12a; 2 Bl. Com. 220; and by the St. 3 & 4 Will. IV. c. 106, sec. 2, descent is traced from the purchaser. For instance, if the land had been acquired in fee simple by Sarah A. Whiton's father, it could have descended from her only to her heirs on her father's side. The English rule means that inherited property does not pass from one line to the other, and is like the rule of the French customary law. Propres ne remontent pas. P. Viollet, Hist. du Droit Civil Franc. (2d Ed.) 845. In this state of the law of descent it was no great stretch to allow a limitation in the first instance to Sarah of a fee with the same descendible quality that it would have had in the case supposed. Challis, Real Prop. 216, 222, 224. Co. Lit. 220b. *Blake v. Hynes*, 11 L.R. Ir. 284. 1 Prest. Est. 474. See 22 & 23 Vict. c. 35, sec. 19. Especially is this true if, as Mr. Challis argues, the grantee under such a limitation could convey a fee simple, just as he or she could have done if the estate actually had descended from the father. But our statute of descent looks no further than the person himself who died seised of or entitled to the estate. In other words, inherited property may pass from one line to the other in Massachusetts. Pub. Sts. c. 125. The analogy on which is founded the argument for the possibility of limitations like that under discussion is wanting. A man cannot create a new kind of inheritance. Co. Lit. 27. Com. Dig. Estates by Grant (A6). These and other authorities show, too, that except in the case of a grant by the King, if the words "on her father's side" do not effect the purpose intended, they are to be rejected, leaving the estate a fee simple, which was Mr. Washburn's opinion. 1 Washb. Real Prop. (5th ed.) 61. Certainly it would seem that in this Commonwealth an estate descending only to heirs on the father's side was a new kind of inheritance.

What we have to consider, however, is not the question of descent, but that of alienability; and that question brings a further consideration into view. It would be most unfortunate and unexpected if it should be discovered at this late day that it was possible to impose such a qualification upon a fee, and to put it out of the power of the owners to give a clear title for generations. In the more familiar case of an estate tail, the Legislature has acted and the statute has been carried to the farthest verge by construction. Pub. Sts. c. 120, sec. 15. *Coombs v. Anderson*, 138 Mass. 376. It is not too much to say that it would be plainly contrary to the policy of the law of Massachusetts to deny the power of Sarah A. Whiton to convey an unqualified fee. Judgment for defendant.

NOTES

1. It is by no means clear that in its early days English law allowed those who held a fee simple to alienate the property freely. Where a feudal lord (or the king himself) granted a fee (*feudum* in Latin) to a tenant, the lord might wish to make sure that he retained any new tenant's loyalty and feudal services. This required retention of a right to prevent alienation without his consent. When the tenant died, the lord might want to ensure that the successor adequately filled the tenant's role. Some Continental laws also placed considerable restrictions on the alienability of estates in land. See S.E. Thorne, *English Feudalism and Estates in Land*, in idem, Essays in Legal History 13 (1985). Contrast J.G.H. Hudson, Land, Law, and Lordship in Anglo-Norman England (1994). In England, the question was settled, however, by the statute *Quia emptores*, 18 Edw. I (1290). Its enacting clause read:

> [H]enceforth every freeman shall be permitted to sell his land or tenement, or a part of it, at pleasure: yet so that the feoffee shall hold that land or tenement of the same principal lord [of whom the feoffor held] and by the same services and customs by which the feoffor earlier held.

2. At common law, an appropriate form of the phrase "to B and his (or her) heirs" was necessary in all inter vivos conveyances if an estate in fee simple was to be created in B. The words of inheritance were required to create a fee simple estate. A grant merely "to B" conveyed an estate that lasted only during B's lifetime. It was even held that a grant "for as long as the waters of the Delaware flow" created only a life estate in the grantee because of the absence of the words "and his heirs." See 2 Thompson on Real Property § 17.06(a). This was never the rule, however, for wills, and today (either by statute or judicial decision) the rule has been abrogated throughout the United States. In most jurisdictions, the presumption is in favor of construing grants as conveying a fee simple. However, the phrase "and his heirs" continues to be in wide use in deeds, usually coupled with the words "and assigns and successors." Perhaps it is out of lawyerly inertia. Perhaps it is used to leave no room for ambiguity.

3. Limiting the kinds of interests in real property permitted under the law is a feature of many legal systems. A basic Italian manual on private law, for example, explains a similar phenomenon: "In the general interest of production, the juridical order does not consider it appropriate to permit individual citizens the power to burden property by limitations differing from those provided for by the law, since the latter correspond to socially relevant interests: thus real interests are a *numerus clausus*. The will of an individual citizen is not free to create forms of real interests not provided by the law." Andrea Torrente & Piero Schlesinger, Manuale di diritto privato § 131, at 252 (19th ed. 2009). Why should this be so? It is not true, for example, in the law of contracts. For suggestions, see Thomas Merrill & Henry Smith, *Optimal Standardization in the Law of Property: The Numerus Clausus Principle*, 110 Yale. L.J. 1 (2000); Henry Hansmann & Reinier Kraakman, *Property, Contract, and Verification: The Numerus Clausus Problem and the Divisibility of Rights*, 31 J. Legal Studies 373 (2002).

EPTING v. MAYER
323 S.E.2d 797 (S.C. Ct. App. 1984)

SHAW, J.

This appeal involves the construction of devise in a will. The question we review is: what estate is devised to respondent Chloe Epting by Item V of Mahalie Cummings Epting's will? Item V states:

> I will, devise and bequeath unto my two daughters, Eula Epting and Chloe Epting, all real estate of which I may die seized and possessed, to have and to hold in fee simple absolute and in case of the death of either of my said two daughters, then to the survivor of the two, and in the event my said two daughters should die without issue, either before or after my death, then and in that event the said property shall go to my two sons, J. Cornelius Epting and Quincy A. Epting, share and share alike, and in case either or both of my said sons should die before my said two daughters, then and in that event, the child or children of either or both of them shall take the portion their parent or parents would have taken if they had been alive at the said time.

Mahalie Cummings died in 1939 leaving four children, Chloe, Eula, J. Cornelius, and Quincy A. Chloe is the only living child. Eula died unmarried and without children. J. Cornelius was survived by three children and Quincy A. was survived by five. Chloe brought this action naming her eight nieces and nephews as defendants alleging she had received an offer to buy the timber on the land devised in Item V and further alleging the timber was infested with insects and would soon lose its value. Chloe asked the court to define "the extent and nature" of her title under Item V. Quincy A.'s children answered denying title in Chloe and seeking either an injunction against removal of the timber or protection of the proceeds. The trial court found Mahalie Cummings gave Chloe a fee simple estate and further found the language of defeasance in the same sentence repugnant to the conveyance. Quincy A.'s children appeal. We affirm.

On this appeal our jurisdiction is limited to the correction of errors of law. The guiding principles for this task were well summarized by our Supreme Court in Rogers v. Rogers, 211 S.C. 360, 70 S.E. (2d) 637, 641 (1952):

> There is no doubt of the soundness of the rule to the effect that a bequest or devise in terms sufficient to unequivocally give the property absolutely or in fee will not be deemed cut down by subsequent language which is less clear and distinct than that of the original gift. . . . It is equally well settled that an estate devised in fee cannot by subsequent limitation be stripped of its legal incidents, and where it appears that the controlling intention is to give an absolute estate, subsequent language inconsistent therewith must be held ineffective. "But before this doctrine may be invoked, it must appear clearly, from a reading of the whole will, that testator's intention was to vest in the first taker an estate of absolute ownership. The use of words of restriction after language which in itself

would be sufficient to create an absolute estate may of course be evidence — to be considered with other provisions in the will — of an intent to create a less estate."

In re Byrne's Estate, 320 Pa. 513, 181 A. 500, 502. The court there summed up the applicable principles as follows:

> If the intention of the testator is to be given effect, as it must be, courts must be permitted, considering each case separately, to hold ineffective words of restriction and to enforce an absolute estate, where such an estate was intended, or, conversely, to disregard words of absolute gift and to declare the estate created to be a limited estate where a clear intention to that effect appears.

Applying the *Rogers* test, we hold the will gave Chloe a fee simple absolute. First of all, the will clearly manifests an intention on the part of the testatrix to vest an absolute estate in the surviving daughter as evidenced by the testatrix's overall scheme to provide for her two daughters and the survivor of them. Secondly, language expressly bestowing at the outset a fee simple estate has been generally treated as controlling.

. . . . For the reasons stated, Chloe possesses a fee simple title to the subject property.

Affirmed.

HALL v. HALL
604 S.W.2d 851 (Tenn. 1980)

BROWN, J.

This case involves the interpretation and legal effect of a deed wherein the grantor gave the grantee an estate in land with an apparent unlimited power of disposition and conversely placed a condition upon her right of ownership.

On December 20, 1920, T.A. Hall conveyed three tracts of land by warranty deed to his wife, Ms. Betty Hall, the plaintiff. In the granting clause of this deed, the grantor stated:

> I do this day Give and bequeath my Entire Rite (sic) and title to the following described tracks (sic) of land to wit (property described).

Later in the habendum clause, he states:

> [the] condition of this deed is as follows: In case I, T.A. Hall, should die before my wife and leave her a widow then she shall have full control and full power to handle or do just as she should see fit with the above described property just so long as she lives my widow but if she should every (sic) mary (sic) any other man then this deed becomes void to her and the above described property shall fall to my children.

T.A. Hall died in 1957 and on August 16, 1978, the plaintiff, still a widow, and numerous family members including children, daughters-in-law and grandchildren, conveyed the land by deed to Ronnie and Randall Dixon, also plaintiffs in the present action. The validity of this conveyance was questioned by the defendant, Opal Hall, one of the plaintiff's daughters-in-law, and several grandchildren. Thereafter, the plaintiffs brought this suit in chancery court to determine the nature and extent of their estate, alleging that Ms. Hall held a fee simple absolute estate and that the Dixons derivatively held a similar estate. The defendants answered alleging that Ms. Hall held the land in a fee simple subject to a conditional limitation or executory interest and not in fee simple absolute. They contend that the Dixons' ownership of the property is subject to the condition that Ms. Hall not remarry. In a memorandum opinion, the Chancellor held that the defendants failed to overcome the presumption that T.A. Hall had given Ms. Hall a fee simple absolute, created in T.C.A. § 64-501, which provides:

> Every grant or devise of real estate, or any interest therein, shall pass all the estate or interest of the granter or devisor, unless the intent to pass a less estate or interest shall appear by express terms, or be necessarily implied in the terms of the instrument.

. . . .

In a split decision, the Court of Appeals affirmed the Chancellor, but on slightly different grounds. The majority correctly stated that the intent of the grantor controls a deed interpretation. Without addressing the aforementioned statute they concluded, however, that where the conveyance is accompanied by an unlimited power of disposition in the grantee, the future interest created in or limitation over to a third party, i.e., the children in the present case, was void, citing *Erwin National Bank v. Riddle*, 18 Tenn. App. 561, 79 S.W.2d 1032 (1934) as controlling. In his dissent, Judge Todd stated that it was the unequivocal intent of the deed that Ms. Hall have absolute ownership and control of the subject property unless and until she should remarry, in which event the Dixons' title, derived through Ms. Hall, would cease and the title would revert to the heirs of T.A. Hall.

The overriding purpose of any deed interpretation is the determination of the grantors' intent of the conveyance. *Collins v. Smithson*, 585 S.W.2d 598 (Tenn. 1979). In this case, as in many cases where the grantor is not trained in the law and the deed is handwritten, it is difficult to determine the subjective intent of the grantor. This task is made more difficult by the presence of repugnant or conflicting clauses. The product of this interpretative process can therefore only be the judicially ascertained intent of the grantor. This intent is normally derived by examining "the language employed in [the] conveyance, read as an entirety and in the light of circumstances of its formulation" and assuming that these evidence the grantor's subjective intent. 3 Restatement of Property § 242 (1940). For reasons stated hereinafter we are of the opinion that the Chancellor and the Court of Appeals erred in their interpretation of the present deed.

Before addressing the issues in dispute, we believe it necessary to address two secondary matters briefly. First, although not raised as an issue, Tennessee courts have long recognized that a limitation upon remarriage in derogation of an estate in land is valid. See *Overton v. Lea*, 108 Tenn. 505, 547, 68 S.W. 250, (Tenn. 1902); *Hinton v. Bowen*, 190 Tenn. 463, 230 S.W.2d 965 (Tenn. 1950). Secondly, the Dixons, as purchasers are:

[chargeable] with notice, by implication, of every fact affecting the title which would be discovered by an examination of the deed or other muniments of title of his vendor, and of every fact as to which the purchaser, with reasonable prudence or diligence, ought to become acquainted. If there is sufficient contained in any deed or record, which a prudent person ought to examine, to produce an inquiry in the mind of an intelligent person, he is chargeable with knowledge or notice of the fact so contained.

Teague v. Sowder, 121 Tenn. (13 Cates) 132, 151, 114 S.W. 484 (1908) citing 2 Devlin on Deeds § 100. In the present case, the limitation is clearly evident on the face of the deed. The Dixons hold their title derivatively and hold no greater title than Ms. Hall held and hold it subject to the same limitations as Ms. Hall.

The construction of the deed sub judice involves the consideration of two possible estates, one, a fee with an apparent unlimited power of disposition and the other a fee simple subject to an executory interest or conditional limitation. The latter is an estate which upon the happening of a stated condition or event, other than its natural termination, will automatically divest the fee holder and vest in the holder of the executory interest, who must not be the original grantor. *Yarbrough v. Yarbrough*, 151 Tenn. 221, 269 S.W.2d 36, 38 (Tenn. 1924); 4 Thompson on Real Property § 1872 (1979 Replacement). The fee holder possesses all the powers and rights of a fee simple absolute, i.e., it may be sold, rented, mortgaged, devised and descend to heirs, so long as the event which terminates does not occur.

At common law and in some Tennessee decisions the rule was generally stated that where a second clause in a deed, usually the habendum, conflicted with and reduced a greater estate given in an earlier clause, the granting clause would usually govern. See *Bennett v. Langham*, 214 Tenn. 674, 383 S.W.2d 16 (Tenn. 1964); *Roberts v. Hale*, 216 Tenn. 578, 393 S.W.2d 155 (Tenn. 1965).

Although not totally abandoning this rule of construction, we recently noted:

> It has long been the preferred rule in this state, however, that all of the provisions of an instrument be considered together and that the intent of the grantor of a deed be ascertained from the entire document, not from the separate parts thereof, if at all possible.

Collins, supra, at 603.

. . . .

While it is true that the courts have a general attitude of disfavor toward restrictions on the fee and are slow to imply a construction from ambiguous language, such restrictions or conditions are valid and, where legal, will be enforced. Since the condition is an "express term" the statute states that the presumption does not arise. See *Magevney v. Karsch*, 167 Tenn. 32, 65 S.W.2d 562 (1933).

The grantor's intent in the present case is clear and unequivocal. The estate is subject to a condition, the happening of which will forfeit the holder's estate.

Under the interpretation given the deed by the Chancellor and the Court of Appeals, the clause containing the conditional limitation of forfeiture upon remarriage is merely precatory and idle verbiage. Under the interpretation of *Overton v. Lea*, and Judge Todd, the clause "she shall have full power to handle or do just as she shall see fit" would also be verbiage. This interpretation, however, would not distort the grantor's intent because even with its omission, the grantee would still possess all the powers and rights of ownership the clause allegedly conveys. We are, therefore, of the opinion that Ms. Hall acquired the estate of fee simple subject to a conditional limitation or executory interest in the deed from her husband. When she sold the real property to the Dixons, she could convey no more of an estate than she possessed. The Dixons, therefore, acquired the property subject to their forfeiture upon the remarriage of Ms. Hall.

The decision of the Court of Appeals is reversed.

NOTE

The Restatement of Property (1936) § 16 explains that an "estate in fee simple defeasible is an estate in fee simple which is subject to a special limitation (defined in § 23), a condition subsequent (defined in § 24), an executory limitation (defined in § 25) or a combination of such restrictions."

A word is appropriate here about the third of these. An estate in fee simple subject to an executory limitation "exists when any limitation, in an otherwise effective conveyance of land [in fee simple], . . . provides that the estate subject thereto, upon the occurrence of a stated event is to be divested, before the normal expiration thereof, in favor of another interest in a person other than the conveyor, or his successor in interest." *Id.*, § 46.

School case

PETERS v. EAST PENN TOWNSHIP SCHOOL DISTRICT
126 A.2d 802 (Pa. Super. Ct. 1956)

RHODES, J.

recognized language for creating a ~~statutory~~ fee simple determinable

Habendum: clause in a deed or lease that defines the type of interest and rights to be enjoyed by the grantee or lessee.

This is an action of ejectment brought by Earl C. Peters against the East Penn Township School District, Carbon County, to establish that its title to forty square rods (1/4 acre) of ground was a determinable fee which terminated when the use of the land for school purposes was discontinued. On a case stated the court below filed an opinion and entered a special verdict in favor of the school district. Earl C. Peters appealed to this Court.

The controversy arises from certain language in a deed of November 9, 1893, by which James F. Peters, of whom Earl C. Peters is an heir, conveyed the property in question to the East Penn Township School District. The habendum clause of the deed provides: "To have and to hold the said piece of ground, and appurtenances, to the School District aforesaid, and its assigns as long as it is used for public school purposes." The warranty clause provides that the grantor will warrant and defend the premises to the school district "as long as it is used for public school purposes." The property is no longer used for school purposes, and the school district has instituted separate proceedings for the purpose of selling the property to a prospective buyer to whom it desires to give a fee simple title. It could not do so, however, according to the case stated, while the present action of ejectment remains as a cloud on the title.

The contention of appellant is that the words "as long as it is used for public school purposes" created "a base fee determinable," and that, since the property is no longer used for the stated purpose, the land has reverted. On the other hand, the school district contends that these words express only a purpose for which the conveyance was made, and that they are not a limitation on the title. The effect of a deed and the extent of the estate conveyed are controlled by the intention of the grantor as expressed therein. In view of the public policy favoring the free alienability of land, a deed which would convey an estate in fee simple except for certain words, or for a phrase or clause must be interpreted strictly against any such limitation unless the grantor's intention to so limit the fee is clearly expressed or necessarily implied. *Sapper v. Mathers*, 286 Pa. 364, 367, 133 A. 565, 47 A.L.R. 1172; *Abel v. Girard Trust Company*, 365 Pa. 34, 38, 73 A.2d 682. Words which merely express the purpose for which the conveyance is made are not considered words of limitation on the title; such words are viewed as superfluous to the grant. *T.W. Phillips Gas & Oil Co. v. Lingenfelter*, 262 Pa. 500, 502, 105 A. 888, 5 A.L.R. 1495.

The court below, after discussing a number of cases in which purported limiting expressions were held to be statements of purpose, concluded that the words in the instant deed were similar thereto, that they were expressive merely of a purpose, and that they did not import a limitation. The court thereupon held that an absolute fee passed to the school district.

We find various expressions used in those cases in which it has been held that only a purpose had been expressed. Examples of such expressions are: "for the use of the inhabitants," *Pearson v. Nelley*, 331 Pa. 376, 378, 200 A. 654, 655; "for school purposes only," *T.W. Phillips Gas & Oil Co. v. Lingenfelter, supra*, 262 Pa. 500, 501, 105 A. 888, 889; "for the use and benefit of the inhabitants . . . and to and for no other use of purpose whatsoever." *Abel v. Girard Trust Company, supra*, 365 Pa. 34, 36, 73 A.2d 682, 683; "for no other purpose whatsoever than a cemetery or burial ground," *Sapper v. Mathers, supra*, 286 Pa. 364, 365, 133 A. 565. It is to be noted that in not one of the cases were the words "as long as" used.

We have cases in which there was not only an expression of a purpose or use, but in which there was a specific reverter clause as well: "to be used for the establishment and maintenance of the common schools . . . and for no other purpose . . . said lot to revert to the grantors, their heirs and assigns, as soon as said parties . . . cease to use it for said purpose," *Calhoun v. Hays*, 155 Pa. Super. 519, 521, 39 A.2d 307, 308; "so long as they use it for that purpose and no longer, and then to return back to the original owner," *Henderson v. Hunter*, 59 Pa. 335, 340; "for school purposes so long as it shall be used for school purposes, . . . after which this shall be null and void," *Beaver Township School District v. Burdick*, 51 Pa. Super. 496, 497.

In the instant case there is no specific reverter clause. The absence of such clause, however, is not determinative of the effect of the words if the intent to limit the fee is otherwise clear. In such instances there is an implied reverter to the grantor. (citations omitted)

The issue before us in the instant case is limited to whether the use of the words "as long as" clearly indicates an intention on the part of the grantor to create at most an estate in fee simple determinable.

Our courts have frequently said that the words "so long as" and "as long as" are technical words which limit a fee. In *Pearson v. Nelley, supra,* 331 Pa. 376, 379, 200 A. 654, one of the cases in which a clause was held to be a mere expression of purpose and not a limitation, the absence of such apt words is fully discussed. Mr. Justice Linn, quoting from *Stuart v. City of Easton,* 170 U.S. 383, 397, 18 S.Ct. 650, 655, 42 L.Ed. 1078, 1083, said (at pages 379, 380 of 331 Pa., at page 655 of 200 A.): "There are no apt, technical words, such as 'so that,' 'provided,' 'if it shall happen,' etc. . . . . contained in the grant, nor is the declaration of the use coupled with any clause of re-entry or a provision that the estate conveyed should cease or be void on any contingency. . . . So, also, we fail to find in the patent the usual and apt words to create a limitation, such as 'while,' 'so long as,' 'until,' 'during,' . . . , or words of similar import." For the same quotation, see *Abel v. Girard Trust Company, supra,* 365 Pa. 34, 38, 73 A.2d 682, 684.

As used in the deed in the instant case, the words "as long as" have a greater significance than the introduction of a statement of purpose; they impose a limitation which is directly connected with the declared purpose of the grant. Of course it is the rule that the mere expression of purpose will not of and by itself debase the fee. *T.W. Phillips Gas & Oil Co. v. Lingenfelter, supra,* 262 Pa. 500, 503, 105 A. 888; *Abel v. Girard Trust Company, supra,* 365 Pa. 34, 38, 73 A.2d 682. However, we point out that the grantor here said more than that the conveyance was "for public school purposes"; he significantly added that the school district was "to have and to hold the said piece of ground . . . as long as" it was so used. We think the necessary implication is that the estate was to expire upon the occurrence of the stated event. See Restatement, Property, § 44, p. 121.

There are other cases where, under similar circumstances, the words "as long as" or "so long as" have been given the above interpretation and effect. For example, a devise of real estate to a wife "so long as she remains my widow" has been held to be a defeasible fee without any expression of a gift over (citations omitted). See, also, *In re Burpee's Estate,* 367 Pa. 329, 336, 80 A.2d 721. If it is clear that the intention of one who devises property to his wife "so long as she remains my widow" creates an estate which is defeasible upon her remarriage, then it would seem to be equally apparent that the intention of one who conveys land to a school district "as long as it is used for public school purposes" creates a fee which is determinable when the land is no longer used for the stated purpose. Although a reverter clause could have been added, its absence is not material as the words used were appropriate technical words which definitely indicated the extent of the interest which the grantor intended to create and were not limited to a purpose in making the conveyance. The words can have no other reasonable interpretation and effect. See Restatement, Property, § 44, p. 121.

The judgment is reversed, and now entered on the case stated for plaintiff.

NOTES

1. As mentioned in the note following *Hall v. Hall*, the Restatement of Property (1936) § 16 explains that an "estate in fee simple defeasible is an estate in fee simple which is subject to a special limitation (defined in § 23), a condition subsequent (defined in § 24), an executory limitation (defined in § 25) or a combination of such restrictions." A word is appropriate here about the first of these. An estate in fee simple determinable "is created by any limitation which, in an otherwise effective conveyance of land [in fee simple] . . . , provides that the estate shall automatically expire upon the occurrence of a stated event." *Id.*, § 44. Standard language to create such a limitation includes "as long as," "so long as," "during," "until," and "while."

2. Several American states have enacted statutes restricting the time period during which a fee simple may be made defeasible by special limitation. For example, Fla. Stat. § 689.18 declares that "No reverter or forfeiture provision contained in any deed conveying real estate or any interest therein in the state, executed on and after July 1, 1951, shall be valid and binding more than 21 years from the date of such deed, and upon the expiration of such period of 21 years, the reverter or forfeiture provision shall become null, void, and unenforceable." The statute also limited such provisions created prior to its enactment, and it was declared unconstitutional to the extent that it invalidated them. *Biltmore Village v. Royal*, 71 So. 2d 727 (Fla. 1954); *J.C. Vereen & Sons, Inc. v. City of Miami*, 397 So. 2d 979 (Fla. Dist. Ct. App. 1981). The statute excepts from invalidity all provisions made to governmental, educational, and charitable institutions.

OLDFIELD v. STOECO HOMES, INC.
139 A.2d 291 (N.J. 1958)

BURLING, J.

This is a proceeding in lieu of prerogative writ. Suit was instituted by plaintiffs, residents and taxpayers of the City of Ocean City, with the object of having several resolutions of the City of Ocean City extending the time for performance of certain conditions in a deed declared invalid, and for the further relief of having lands owned by the defendants forfeited and returned to the city. . . .

In 1951 Ocean City held title to a large number of lots of undeveloped land in a low lying area of the city. The locale of the lots is roughly divisible into two large segments, with Bay Avenue forming a dividing line between east and west. . . . It is the lots in the eastern segment which are the subject matter of this litigation. . . .

While the deed from Ocean City to Stoeco contained various conditions and restrictions, the core provisions around which this dispute centers are:

(a) Within (1) year from the date of this Deed, the party of the second part shall fill all of the listed lots of land now owned by the party of the first part and which are not being conveyed.

(Here follows a list of lots by lot number and block number.) . . .

(b) Within one (1) year following the date of this Deed, the party of the second part shall fill all of the lots of land sold to said party of the second part as a result of this sale. . . .

(d) All such land shall be filled to at least the now established and existing grades of the City of Ocean City, New Jersey for the areas and lots to be filled.

The City of Ocean City reserves the right to change or modify any restriction, condition or other requirements hereby imposed in a manner agreeable to or as permitted by law.

A failure to comply with the covenants and conditions of paragraphs (a), (b) and (d) hereof will automatically cause title to all lands to revert to the City of Ocean City . . . .

By June 29, 1952, one year after obtaining the deed, Stoeco had still not completed the substantial portion of filling and grading, nor had it done so by February of 1953. Ocean City, more interested in redevelopment than declaring a default, passed a resolution on February 20, 1953, to change and modify the terms and conditions of the sale of land. . . .

The general import of the resolution was that Stoeco was to be given until December 31, 1954, to complete the filling and grading . . . .

. . . On December 30, 1954, Ocean City passed the second of the disputed resolutions, . . . [extending] the time for performance of the original conditions [as to some lots] . . . until January 1, 1958, and . . . [as to other lots] until January 1, 1960. . . .

Plaintiffs were present at the commissioners' meeting of December 30, 1954, when the second resolution was adopted, and voiced their objections. Sometime later, on October 3, 1955, plaintiffs instituted the instant proceeding attacking the two resolutions and seeking a forfeiture of all the lands to Ocean City for failure to comply with the original one year time limitation. . . .

The court below held that the nature of the defeasible estate created was one in fee simple, subject to a condition subsequent . . . and that the proceeding was barred on all the grounds advanced. The issues raised below are again urged on appeal.

First, we consider the issue relating to the nature of the estate granted. It is said that a fee simple determinable differs from a fee simple subject to a condition subsequent in that, in the former, upon the happening of the stated event the estate "*ipso facto*" or "automatically" reverts to the grantor or his heirs, while in the latter the grantor must take some affirmative action to divest the grantee of his estate. The interest remaining in the grantee in a fee simple determinable has been denominated a possibility of reverter. *Restatement, Property*, §§ 44, 154, while the interest remaining in the grantee of a fee simple subject to a condition subsequent, i.e., the right to re-enter upon the happening of a prescribed contingency, has been denominated a power of termination. *Restatement, Property*, §§ 45, 155.

It is further alleged that a fee simple determinable estate is more onerous than an estate in fee simple subject to a condition subsequent . . . .

While language is the primary guide for the ascertainment of whether a given deed attempts to condition or limit an estate, still it is the instrument as a whole, and not a particular phrase aborted from the context which provides the basis for the attainment of our ultimate task which is to effectuate the intention of the parties. The particular words, upon which are predicated the right, or lack of it, to a forfeiture are often emphasized. Thus, it has been said that words such as "so long as," "until" or "during," followed by words of reverter, are appropriate to create a fee simple determinable, whereas such words as "upon condition that" or "provided that" are usual indicators of an estate upon condition subsequent. But that particular forms of expression standing alone and without resort to the purpose of the instrument in question are not determinative is at once apparent to a discerning surveyor of the case authorities. . . .

To hold that the condition as to time was so essential to the scheme of the parties that to violate it by a day would result in an immediate and automatic forfeiture of the estate is to distort beyond recognition what the parties intended. There is no indication that time was of the essence of the agreement. . . . A certain amount of flexibility is inherent among such large scale undertakings as the one under consideration. . . .

It is our conclusion that the parties contemplated that the estate created was not to expire automatically at the end of a year and that therefore it is one subject to a condition subsequent.

The remaining questions asserted need not long detain us. . . .

The judgment appealed from is affirmed.

NOTES

1.   As mentioned in the note following *Hall v. Hall*, the Restatement of Property (1936) § 16 explains that an "estate in fee simple defeasible is an estate in fee simple which is subject to a special limitation (defined in § 23), a condition subsequent (defined in § 24), an executory limitation (defined in § 25) or a combination of such restrictions." A word is appropriate here about the second of these. An estate in fee simple subject to a condition subsequent "is created by any limitation which, in an otherwise effective conveyance of land [in fee simple] . . . , provides that upon the occurrence of a stated event the conveyor or his successor in interest shall have the power to terminate the estate so created." *Id.*, § 45.

2.   In *Wood v. Board of County Comm'rs*, 759 P.2d 1250 (Wyo. 1988), the grantors had conveyed land to the county in a 1948 deed containing this language in its granting clause: "Said tract is conveyed to Fremont County for the purpose of constructing and maintaining thereon a County Hospital in memorial to the gallant men of the Armed Forces of the United States of America from Fremont County, Wyoming." A hospital occupied the site until November 1983, when the land was put up for sale. The grantors brought suit to enforce their rights under the deed. On the defendant's motion for summary judgment, it was held that the

language created neither a determinable fee nor a fee simple upon condition subsequent, but a fee simple absolute.

3. A grant of land "to be used for an irrigation canal," which stated that the grantee "shall build and maintain one wagon bridge across said canal" and that "a flume will be constructed and maintained on the north side of the land across said canal for the purposes of B.T. Biggs [the grantor] conveying water for the irrigation of lands lying on the west side of said Rocky Ford Canal" was held to create an easement in favor of the land retained by Biggs, and not a defeasible fee. *Beckham v. Ward County Irrigation Dist. No. 1*, 278 S.W. 316 (Tex. Civ. App. 1925). Grants of land for railroad rights of way have been particularly difficult to interpret, most significantly when the railroad pulls up its track and ceases to use the land. See, e.g., *Hash v. United States*, 454 F. Supp. 2d 1066 (D. Idaho 2006).

4. A grant of land "unto the second party, his heirs and assigns, forever, upon the express condition that the second party shall lay out and set aside and dedicate [the property described] for a park and recreation center, and to be forever maintained as such" was held to create a covenant, not a condition. This distinction meant that the grantor could maintain an action for damages where the land ceased to be used as indicated, but he could not assert a right of forfeiture. *Gordon v. Whittle*, 57 S.E.2d 169 (Ga. 1950).

5. A grant of land made "[i]n consideration that the [grantee] erect a building and maintain a county high school therein or revert to the owner" was held to leave no interest in the grantors where a high school had been built on the land and maintained for 11 years. *Board of Comm'rs of Trego Cty v. Hays*, 145 P. 847 (Kan. 1915). A 1885 deed containing a clause stating that the land "is to revert to [grantor] when it shall fail to be used for school purposes" was held to allow the grantor's successor to retake the land after abandonment of the school in 1959. *Thompson v. Godfrey*, 379 P.2d 269 (Kan. 1963).

BANK OF POWHATTAN v. ROONEY
72 P.2d 993 (Kan. 1937)

SMITH, J.

This was an action on a note. Judgment was for defendant. Plaintiff appeals.

The facts are simple. L. E. Laflin is the assignee of a judgment rendered in the district court of Brown county on March 30, 1922, in favor of the Bank of Powhattan against D. P. Rooney for approximately $2,500. The judgment has been kept alive by executions, and on May 20, 1936, was a valid judgment and unsatisfied.

In the early part of 1936 Hugh Rooney, the father of defendant, D. P. Rooney, died testate in Nemaha county. He made a cash bequest to his son, Hugh F. Rooney, and various devises of real estate to his children, Charles J. Rooney, John E. Rooney, Mark Rooney, Eliza Ann Rooney, Eva C. Studer, and Sarah Isabelle Studer.

He devised to D. Pat Rooney a life estate in 40 acres of land in Brown county, with the provision that, after the death of D. Pat Rooney, his interest should descend to and become the property of his heirs. By another provision he devised the residue of his estate share and share alike to his children, naming them. The ninth paragraph of the will was as follows: "Ninth: It is my will that any of the beneficiaries under this will shall have the privilege of selling their interest in lands bequeathed to them to any other beneficiary at any time, but shall not sell to an outsider until three (3) years after my death."

On the 20th day of May, 1936, Laflin caused an execution to be issued from the district court of Brown county in the case in which he had his judgment directed to the sheriff of Brown county, Kan., and also caused an execution to be issued from the same court directed to the sheriff of Nemaha county, Kan. On May 22, 1936, the sheriff of Brown county, finding no personal property of the defendant upon which to levy, levied execution upon the right, title, and life estate of D. Pat Rooney in the land in which he had been given a life estate by his father's will. On the same day the sheriff of Nemaha county, Kan., finding no personal property of the defendant upon which to levy, levied the execution which had been issued to him upon the interest of D. Pat Rooney in certain real estate in Nemaha county in which D.P. Rooney had an undivided one-eighth interest under the residuary clause in his father's will. The real estate was fully advertised for sale. Prior to the date of the sale one of the executors of the estate of Hugh Rooney filed a motion in the district court of Brown county, Kan., for an order staying the sale of both the Brown county and the Nemaha county real estate.

. . . .

The motion was heard by the court and the sales were enjoined. In the journal entry the trial court stated that the sales were enjoined because the real estate in question was not subject to sale on execution for a period of three years from the date of the death of Hugh Rooney on account of the provision in the will we have already noted. It was provided in the journal entry that the enjoining of these sales should not affect the judgment lien which Laflin had on the interest of D.P. Rooney in the real estate. The assignee of the judgment has appealed from the order enjoining these sales.

The question we have before us is whether the ninth clause in the will prevented this real estate from being sold to anybody but one of the beneficiaries thereof until three years had elapsed from the date of the death of the testator. In other words, Was the restriction on alienation contained in the will a valid one? It will be noted that there is no provision for a trustee having active duties to discharge during the restrictive period by a provision for re-entry or alternative grant or devise over on breach of conditions prescribed in the instrument itself. The provision in the will amounts to no more than an admonitory gesture.

This question has been settled contrary to the contention of appellees by the holding of this court in *Guarantee Title & Trust Co. v. Siedhoff*, 144 Kan. 13, 58 P.(2d) 66. In that case there was a will with a clause about as appears in this will.

It will be noted that the restriction on alienability in this will was somewhat limited, that is, the restraint was made effective by the terms of the will for three years only and the will provided that any one of the devisees might sell to any of the other devisees during that time. There are some authorities holding that a restraint on the power to alienate for a limited time is valid. The great weight of authority, however, is to the effect that a restraint, even though limited as to time, is void. In *Wright v. Jenks*, 124 Kan. 604, 261 P. 840, this court recognized that a reasonable restraint on alienation to prevent or hinder a testator's estate being dissipated by grandchildren or for some similar purpose might be valid, but held that, in order to make it valid, there must have been some practical bar to a breach of the restriction. There is no such bar in this case. To the same effect is 21 R.C.L. 330–333. (citations omitted)

We now pass to the question of whether the fact that the restriction on alienation is limited so that the land in question might have been sold to the other devisees renders it valid. We have concluded that the weight of authority is to the effect that a provision in a will that property may not be alienated except to a particular class or group of persons is void. (citations omitted).

It is well established that the rule as to restrictions on the right to alienate applies to life estates as well as to estates in fee simple. See 21 R.C.L. 333, also *Wool v. Fleetwood*, 136 N.C. 460, 48 S.E. 785, 67 L.R.A. 444; also *Guarantee Title & Trust Co. v. Siedhoff, supra*.

We have concluded that the ninth clause of the will of Hugh Rooney was ineffective to prevent the interest of D. Pat Rooney from being sold on execution. The court below based the decision upon the ground to which reference has already been made. However, appellee in this court argues that the sales should have been enjoined upon the ground that they had been prematurely had. Upon this question we have concluded that the interest of D. Pat Rooney in the estate vested in him at once upon the death of the testator. A life estate in land or an undivided interest in land may be sold on execution to pay a judgment. See G.S. 1935, 60-3403; also *Poole v. French*, 71 Kan. 391, 80 P. 997, and *McCartney v. Robbins*, 114 Kan. 141, 217 P. 311.

It is true that sufficient time had not elapsed since the death of testator for the estate to be wound up. However, should the sales be made as appellant seeks to have them made, the land will be sold subject to the right of the executor to sell the real estate to pay debts if the personalty of the estate is insufficient. It is clear that nothing more than the interest of D. Pat Rooney in the real estate may be sold.

The judgment of the trial court is reversed, with directions to set aside the order enjoining the sale of the real estate in question.

ALLEN, J., concurring.

I agree that the attempted restraint on alienation is void.

NOTES

1. Chancellor Kent, the great commentator on American law, gave these reasons for the invalidity of restraints on alienation: "Conditions are not sustained when they are repugnant to the nature of the estate granted, or infringe upon the essential enjoyment and independent rights of property, and tend manifestly to public inconvenience." 4 James Kent, Commentaries on American Law 131 (2d ed.

1832). Most recent commentators have concentrated on practical and economic factors, arguing that by taking land out of the flow of commerce, restraints cause harm to the economy. Many reasons have also been advanced for invalidating restraints: they are said to discourage improvement of property; to hamper effective use of property where a buyer could put it to better use than the seller; to allow individuals to appear to be more prosperous than they are; and to perpetuate dead hand control at the expense of the living. See Herbert Bernhard, *The Minority Doctrine Concerning Direct Restraints on Alienation*, 57 Mich. L. Rev. 1173, 1177 (1959).

2.   A number of "indirect" restraints upon alienation have been the subject of litigation in recent years. Examples are: rights of first refusal where a property owner desires to sell; "due on sale" clauses in mortgage agreements; and condominium agreements forbidding alienation without the consent of a management board. The results have not been wholly harmonious, but recent cases have shown a greater willingness to evaluate restraints according to their perceived reasonability. See, e.g., *Abbott v. Forward Design Development, Inc.*, 957 So. 2d 23 (Fla. Ct. App. 2007); *Melton v. Melton*, 221 S.W.3d 391 (Ky. Ct. App. 2007). What about a restriction that prevents a grantee from alienating to buyers below the age of fifty? Would that be invalid in states that permit some indirect or reasonable restraints on alienation?

3.   This is not a new subject in Western law. Hugo Grotius (1583–1645), the great Dutch jurist, wrote, "After the introduction of ownership, men who are masters of their own goods have by the law of nature the power of transferring all or any part of their property to other persons, for this is the very nature of ownership." De iure belli ac pacis (1625), Lib. II, ch. 6, sec. 1. On the other hand, European law has also admitted a variety of forms of restrictions of what Grotius called a right guaranteed by the law of nature, and freedom of alienation of freehold land in England was fully established only by statute. In fact, various means of fettering alienability have long been thought consistent with the underlying principle.

ESTATE OF ELIZABETH BECK
19 A. 302 (Pa. 1890)

Paxson, C.J.

Elizabeth Beck, the testator, in and by her last will and testament gave to her step-daughter, also named Elizabeth Beck, a one fourth interest in her estate, upon the following condition: "And whereas, the said Elizabeth Beck was unfortunate in business transactions, whereby she became indebted, part of which still remains unpaid, and having no means to pay the same, now it is my will that the above equal share in my estate, as well as the specific bequest given to her, are given to her expressly upon condition that they shall not be liable to be attached or seized for the debts or moneys which said Elizabeth Beck may owe at the time of my decease, but that the whole amount of her share shall be paid directly to said Elizabeth Beck by my executor, without diminution for the payment of her said indebtedness."

The share aforesaid has not yet been paid to the said legatee, for the reason that the appellant, who held a judgment against her, attached the fund in the hands of the executor. The learned court below held that the attachment would not bind the fund in the hands of the executor, and awarded it to the legatee. From this decree the attaching creditor has appealed.

No one doubts that it was competent for the testator to have placed this fund forever beyond the reach of the creditors of her legatee, by creating a trust for that purpose. This she has not done, and the question which arises is, whether she has protected the fund in its transit from the executor to the legatee. That she had a right to do this must be conceded. Has she done so? We may dismiss from the case the learning about vested and contingent legacies. This was not, as was assumed by the learned counsel for appellant, an absolute gift of the property. It was a gift upon the express condition that, in the hands of her executor, it should not be liable to the debts of the legatee, but should "be paid directly to the said Elizabeth Beck by my executor, without diminution for the payment of her said indebtedness." The executor was thus clothed with an express trust in regard to this share.

It is true, the trust would end the moment the money was paid to the legatee, but during the transit, while the money remained in his hands, it was as much protected from creditors as if a separate trust had been created for that purpose. It was the right of the testatrix to say that her estate should not go to pay her step-daughter's creditors. She has said so as emphatically as language can express it, for the time that the money remains in the hands of her executor. Does the fact that she did not protect it further, by raising up another trustee of the fund, after it left the executor's hands, destroy the trust she did create, and nullify the positive directions of the will that it should not be attached in transit? Why shall the will of the testator be defeated in this respect? She had a right to do what she willed with her own. The creditors of her legatee had no claim upon her estate, and when she directed that the share should be paid to her step-daughter, and not to the creditors of the latter, who shall gainsay her? The creditor is not injured, and has no right to complain.

I have not discussed the authorities, because we have no case which precisely covers this; but, upon reason, and analogy to the decisions we have, this case must be affirmed.

The decree is affirmed, and the appeal dismissed, at the costs of the appellant.

NOTE

Tall oaks grow from tiny acorns. This case, and others like it from Pennsylvania and Massachusetts, at length permitted the creation of the "spendthrift trust" that permits the creation of interests in real and personal property that are not alienable or reachable by the creditors of the person holding the beneficial interests. Of cases like *Beck*, John Chipman Gray had this to say, "[I]t would be absurd to say that the learned judges who have aided in the introduction of spendthrift trusts have been secret socialists, but it is none the less true, I believe, that they have been influenced . . . by that spirit, in short, of paternalism, which is the fundamental essence alike of spendthrift trusts and of socialism." Restraints on the Alienation of Property, p. ix (2d ed. 1895). A modern view of the old problem is provided in Adam J. Hirsch, *Spendthrift Trusts and Public Policy: Economic and*

Cognitive Perspectives, 73 Wash. U. L.Q. 1 (1995).

II. THE FEE TAIL

In English history, the most common, or at least the most celebrated, kind of defeasible fee was undoubtedly the fee tail, often called an entail for short. It was created by a grant "to B and the heirs of B's body." By virtue of the statute, *De donis conditionalibus*, 13 Edw. I, c. 1 (1285), such a grant had the effect of controlling the devolution of the property from one generation to another. As the words imply, the land passed from the ancestor (B) to B's children, grandchildren, great-grandchildren etc. (the heirs of the body). Collateral heirs were excluded, this being considered to have been the intent of the grantor. Takers in tail thus held a kind of fee simple, because the estate was of potentially infinite duration, but they did not have the power to alienate it for a period beyond their own lives or to devise it, because it passed by operation of law to the heirs of their body at their death. If there were no heirs of the body, then the land reverted automatically either to the grantor (or his heirs) or passed to a remainderman if the grantor had limited an estate in remainder to follow the fee tail. *De donis* made available a writ called formedon to enforce these rights.

About some of the possible variants of the fee tail, William Blackstone, 2 Commentaries on the Laws of England *113, wrote:

> Next, as to the several species of estates-tail, and how they are respectively created. Estates-tail are either general or special. Tail-general is where lands and tenements are given to one, and the heirs of his body begotten; which is called tail-general, because, how often soever such donee in tail be married, his issue in general by all and every such marriage is, in successive order, capable of inheriting the estate-tail, per formam doni. Tenant in tail special is where the gift is restrained to certain heirs of the donee's body, and does not go to all of them in general. And this may happen several ways. I shall instance in only one; as where lands and tenements are given to a man and the heirs of his body, on Mary his now wife to be begotten; here no issue can inherit but such special issue as is engendered between them two; not such as the husband may have by another wife; and therefore it is called special tail. And here we may observe, that the words of inheritance (to him and his heirs) give him an estate in fee; but they being heirs to be by him begotten, this makes it a fee-tail; and the person being also limited, on whom such heirs shall be begotten (viz., Mary, his present wife), this makes it a fee-tail special. Estates, in general and special tail, are further diversified by the distinction of sexes in such entails; for both of them may either be in tail male or tail female. As if lands be given to a man, and his heirs male of his body begotten, this is an estate in tail male, general; but if to a man and the heirs female of his body on his present wife begotten, this is an estate tail female special. And in case of an entail male, the heirs female shall never inherit, nor any derived from them; nor, e converso, the heirs male, in case of a gift in tail female. Thus, if the donee in tail male hath a daughter, who dies leaving a son, such grandson in this case cannot inherit the estate-tail; for

he cannot deduce his descent wholly by heirs male. And as the heir male must convey his descent wholly by males, so must the heir female wholly by females. And therefore if a man hath two estates tail, the one in tail male, the other in tail female; and he hath issue a daughter, which daughter hath issue a son; this grandson can succeed to neither of the estates; for he cannot convey his descent wholly either in the male or female line.

As the word heirs is necessary to create a fee, so in farther limitation of the strictness of the feodal donation, the word body, or some other words of procreation, are necessary to make it a fee-tail, and ascertain to what heirs in particular the fee is limited. If, therefore, either the words of inheritance, or words of procreation be omitted, albeit the others are inserted in the grant, this will not make an estate-tail. As, if the grant be to a man and his issue of his body, to a man and his seed, to a man and his children, or offspring; all these are only estates for life, there wanting the words of inheritance, his heirs. So, on the other hand, a gift to a man, and his heirs male or female, is an estate in fee-simple, and not in fee-tail: for there are not words to ascertain the body out of which they shall issue. Indeed, in last wills and testaments, wherein greater indulgence is allowed, an estate-tail may be created by a devise to a man and his seed, or to a man and his heirs male; or by other irregular modes of expression.

. . . .

Thus much for the nature of estates tail; the establishment of which family law (as it is properly styled by Pigott) occasioned infinite difficulties and disputes. Children grew disobedient when they knew they could not be set aside: farmers were ousted of their leases made by tenants in tail; for, if such leases had been valid, then under color of long leases the issue might have been virtually disinherited; creditors were defrauded of their debts; for, if a tenant in tail could have charged his estate with their payment, he might also have defeated his issue, by mortgaging it for as much as it was worth: innumerable latent entails were produced to deprive purchasers of the lands they had fairly bought; of suits in consequence of which our ancient books are full; and treasons were encouraged, as estates tail were not liable to forfeiture longer than for the tenant's life. So that they were justly branded as the source of new contentions, and mischiefs unknown to the common law; and almost universally considered as the common grievance of the realm.

Blackstone's description does not tell the full story. By the fifteenth century, it had become possible to convert a fee tail into a fee simple by means of a collusive action at law called a common recovery. An action at law to recover the land to be disentailed was brought against a tenant in tail that had the effect of barring the rights held by reversioners or remaindermen under the original fee tail. This was commonly called "barring" or "docking" the entail. It was a complicated and costly process. See Joseph Biancalana, The Fee Tail and the Common Recovery in Medieval England (2001). Blackstone himself (2 Commentaries **358–61) inveighed against "such subtle refinements and such strange reasoning" by which barring an entail was accomplished. In 1833, an adult tenant in tail in possession was permitted by statute to bar the entail by enrollment of a deed in the Court of Chancery, and the process was simplified further in 1925.

Other legal systems have known institutions similar to the fee tail. The Spanish *mayorazgo* is an example. See B. Clavero, Mayorazgo: propiedad feudal en Castilla, 1369–1836 (2d ed. 1989). However, modern times have brought their demise, and in the United States, where the dynastic principle upon which the fee tail rested has never been strong, statutes have largely eliminated the possibility of creating a fee tail in its classic form. See Gregory Alexander, *Time and Property in the American Republican Legal Culture*, 66 N.Y.U. L. Rev. 273, 295–302 (1991). In Texas, the State Constitution of 1876 (art. 1 § 26) itself mandates this result:

> Perpetuities and monopolies are contrary to the genius of a free government, and shall never be allowed, nor shall the law of primogeniture or entailments ever be in force in this State.

Such enactments, however mandatory in language, cannot prevent the attempt, or at least the use of words in wills or conveyances which would have created a fee tail at common law. When this happens, statutory modifications fall into one of four groups:

> (a) Converts the fee tail into a fee simple absolute in the first taker. This is the most common solution;

> (b) Converts the fee tail into a life estate in the first taker, with a remainder in fee simple in the first taker's lineal descendants;

> (c) Preserves the fee tail in the hands of the first taker, but converts it into a fee simple absolute in the hands of the lineal descendants;

> (d) Preserves the fee tail but allows any taker to convert it into a fee simple by making an inter vivos conveyance of the property.

In consequence, American courts have continued to wrestle with establishing workable rules about the fee tail. One example is found in the following case.

MORRIS v. ULBRIGHT
558 S.W.2d 660 (Mo. 1977)

DONNELLY, J.

This is an action to quiet title to land. On March 8, 1947, Lina A. Ulbright and Frank O. Ulbright, her husband, executed a deed which conveyed the property in question to Logan Mitchell Ulbright "and his bodily heirs." The natural son, and only child, of Logan Mitchell Ulbright was Logan M. Ulbright, Jr. On October 4, 1950, Marion V. Morris and Ruby N. Morris adopted Logan M. Ulbright, Jr. and his name was changed to Logan Marion Morris. Lina A. Ulbright and Frank O. Ulbright are deceased. On February 9, 1964, the heirs of Lina A. Ulbright conveyed to T.B. Alspaugh and Sara Jane Alspaugh. On February 12, 1972, Logan Mitchell Ulbright died. On January 24, 1973, the Alspaughs conveyed to Dorothy A. Ulbright and Ralph C. Ulbright. Logan Marion Morris is plaintiff and claims title under the deed executed March 8, 1947. Dorothy A. Ulbright and Ralph C. Ulbright are defendants and claim title under the deed executed January 24, 1973. The trial court entered summary judgment in favor of defendants. Plaintiff appealed to the Kansas City District of the Court of Appeals where the judgment of the trial court was reversed. The case was then transferred to this Court, by order of this Court, and will be decided here "the same as on original appeal." Mo. Const.Art. V, 10. The parties agree that the deed of March 8, 1947, created an estate tail; that under the deed and Section 442.470, RSMo 1969, the first taker (Logan Mitchell Ulbright) took a life estate; and that the heir of the body (Logan M. Ulbright, Jr. — Logan Marion Morris) took a contingent remainder in the fee. *Davidson v. Davidson*, 350 Mo. 639, 167 S.W.2d 641 (1943). It is not seriously disputed that had Logan M. Ulbright, Jr., not been adopted on October 4, 1950, he would have taken in fee simple absolute upon the death of Logan Mitchell Ulbright on February 12, 1972. Defendants contend, however, that because of the provisions of Section 453.090, RSMo 1969, the adoption of plaintiff on October 4, 1950, "acted to remove the Plaintiff from the bloodstream of his natural father Logan Mitchell Ulbright and with no exception ceased and determined all rights and duties between Plaintiff and his natural father." Section 453.090, RSMo 1969, provides that when a child is adopted in accordance with the provisions of Chapter 453, "all legal relationships and all rights and duties between such child and his natural parents * * * shall cease and determine." The essential question in this case then becomes: Does plaintiff's interest, if any, in the land derive from Lina A. Ulbright and Frank O. Ulbright (grantors in the deed of March 8, 1947) or is plaintiff's interest, if any, one of inheritance from his natural father Logan Mitchell Ulbright (life tenant under the deed of March 8, 1947)? If the latter, plaintiff's interest was cut off by the adoption. If the former, it was not. In 1 H. Tiffany, The Law of Real Property 48 at 70 (3rd ed. 1939), we find the following:

> On the death of a tenant in tail, the land passes to the next heir of the body of the original donee; but such heir, though he takes because he is the heir of the body, takes not by descent, but as a substituted purchaser from the original donor, per formam doni, as it is expressed * * *.

This proposition finds express support in *Pollock v. Speidel*, 17 Ohio St. 439, 49 Am.Dec. 467 (1867) and implied support in *Davidson v. Davidson, supra*, and *Byrd v. Allen*, 351 Mo. 99, 171 S.W.2d 691 (1942). See also 31 C.J.S. Estates 21, at 47 (1964). In addition, Section 442.490, RSMo 1969, provides that when a remainder shall be limited to the heirs of the body of a person to whom a life estate is given, the remaindermen who qualify as heirs of the body "shall be entitled to take as *purchasers* in fee simple, by virtue of the remainder so limited in them." (Emphasis ours). Accordingly, we are of the opinion that plaintiff derived his title as purchaser under the deed from Lina A. Ulbright and Frank O. Ulbright and not by inheritance from his natural father. *Grimes v. Rush*, 355 Mo. 573, 197 S.W.2d 310 (1946). We hold that his interest in the land was not extinguished by the adoption and provisions of 453.090, *supra*, because his interest in the land does not derive from his natural father. The judgment is reversed and the cause remanded.

[Dissenting opinion of Finch, J. omitted. — Eds.]

NOTES AND PROBLEMS

1. Adoption was a common feature of Roman law but unknown except as an informal arrangement at common law. In the United States, it has been universally accepted but remains a creature of statute law. It has not always fit well within established private law. A later decision that faced a variant of the same problem raised by the case is *Unsel v. Meier*, 972 S.W.2d 466 (Mo. 1998).

2. What is the result of a grant "from A to B, but if B dies without issue, to C"? At common law, this created a fee tail (at least if words of inheritance were included or if it were by devise), since the law favored an indefinite failure of issue construction, i.e. "die without issue" meant "if the takers (B and his heirs) should *ever* die without issue." Most courts now favor a definite failure of issue construction, under which the time of determination is the death of the first taker, B in this example. Where this is so, the first taker would normally take a fee simple, subject to defeasance upon his death without issue. See Joseph Warren, *Gifts over on Death without Issue*, 39 Yale L.J. 332 (1930). An illustrative case is *Friedman v. Marshall*, 876 S.W.2d 745 (Mo. App. 1994).

3. Under each of the statutes changing the effect of words that would otherwise create a fee tail, what interests would be created by the following conveyance: "O to A and the heirs of A's body, remainder to B and B's heirs"?

III. THE LIFE ESTATE

An estate in land measured by the duration of the life or lives of one or more persons is called a life estate. Normally the measuring life is that of the person who holds the estate, but it is also possible to use the life of another to fix the duration of the estate, in which case it is called a life estate *pur autre vie*. If the holder of a life estate *pur autre vie* dies, the estate passes to the person's heirs in case of intestacy, but what the heirs obtain lasts only as long as the measuring life. The life estate *pur autre vie* may also be devised, but of course the same restriction applies; the estate lasts no longer than the measuring life.

A standard life estate — in which the person holding the estate is also the measuring life — is not an estate of inheritance, as the fee simple is, since it cannot be devised and will not pass upon intestacy to the persons' heirs. At common law, the life estate was treated as a freehold estate. This was perhaps a vestige of the early feudal era when the life estate was the basic unit of land holding. The life tenant was regarded as being seized of the estate in the technical sense, something which was not true of the tenant for a term of years. The life estate can be alienated inter vivos, although there is not much of a market in life estates because of the uncertainty of duration that attends them. A mortgage lender, for example, is likely to require some extra security for making a loan secured by a life estate, perhaps a life insurance policy on the tenant's life, payable to the lender for any loan amount not repaid at the death of the tenant.

The life tenant ordinarily has a duty to maintain the property in a reasonable state of repair as necessary to preserve the property's value for the holders of subsequent future interests. A failure to repair is treated as permissive waste, and the holders of future interests in the land have a cause of action in waste against the life tenant. The rents and profits from the land must be, however, sufficient to allow the tenant to make repairs.

In order to make reasonable repairs and to provide fuel and fencing, the life tenant traditionally has had the right to cut timber sufficient for such purposes. This is the right to take estovers. The tenant also is entitled to keep existing mines open and conduct existing timber operations without liability for waste. These rights do not extend, however, to opening new mines, leasing drilling rights for oil and gas, or clearing all the standing timber on the property. The life tenant may not do so without first obtaining the consent of future interest holders.

There is no duty on the life tenant to make extraordinary repairs. Improvements destroyed by earthquake or fire, through no fault of the life tenant, also need not be rebuilt. Neither can future interest holders be held liable for the costs of rebuilding in such situations, if the tenant does choose voluntarily to undertake the rebuilding. Whether the life tenant has a duty to insure buildings on the premises for the benefit of the remaindermen is the subject of doubt. See 2 Thompson on Real Property § 19.11.

THOMPSON v. BAXTER
119 N.W. 797 (Minn. 1909)

BROWN, J.

Proceedings in forcible entry and unlawful detainer, instituted in justice court, where defendant had judgment. Plaintiff appealed to the district court, where a like result followed. From the judgment of that court she appealed to this court.

The action involves the right to the possession of certain residence property in the city of Albert Lea, and was submitted to the court below upon the pleadings and a stipulation of facts. It appears that plaintiff is the owner of the premises; that she acquired title thereto by purchase from a former owner, who had theretofore entered into a contract by which he leased and demised the premises to defendant at an agreed monthly rent of twenty two dollars; and plaintiff's title is subject to all rights that became vested in defendant thereby. The lease, after reciting the rental of the premises and other usual conditions, contained upon the subject of the term of the tenancy, the following stipulation: "To have and to hold the above-rented premises unto the said party of the second part [the tenant] his heirs, executors, administrators, and assigns, for and during the full term of while he shall wish to live in Albert Lea, from and after the first day of December, 1904." The only question involved under the stipulation is the construction of this provision of the lease. Defendant has at all times paid the rent as it became due; but, if plaintiff has the right to terminate the tenancy and eject him, proper notice for that purpose has been given. Appellant contends that the lease created either a tenancy at will, at sufferance, or from month to month, and that plaintiff could terminate the same at any time by proper notice. The trial court held, in harmony with defendant's contention, that the contract created a life estate in defendant, terminable only at his death or removal from Albert Lea. Appellant assigns this conclusion as error.

A determination of the question presented involves a construction of the lease and a brief examination of some of the principles of law applicable to tenancies at will, at sufferance, from month to month, and life estates. Deeds, leases, or other instruments affecting the title to real property are construed, guided by the law applicable to the particular subject, precisely as other contracts are construed, and effect given the intention of the parties. (citations omitted). The contract before us, though somewhat peculiar and unusual as to the term of the tenancy intended to be created, is nevertheless clear and free from ambiguity. It granted the demised premises to defendant "while he shall wish to live in Albert Lea." The legal effect of this language is, therefore, the only question in the case.

Tenancies at will may be created by express words, or they may arise by implication of law. Where created by express contract, the writing necessarily so indicates, and reserves the right of termination to either party, as where the lease provides that the tenant shall occupy the premises so long as agreeable to both parties. *Richardson v. Langridge*, 4 Taunt. 128; *Say v. Stoddard*, 27 Oh. St. 478. Such tenancies arise by implication of law where no definite time is stated in the contract, or where the tenant enters into possession under an agreement to execute a contract for a specific term and he subsequently refuses to do so, or one who enters under a void lease, or where he holds over pending negotiations for a new lease. The chief characteristics of this form of tenancy are (1) uncertainty respecting the term, and (2) the right of either party to terminate it by proper notice; and these features must exist, whether the tenancy be created by the express language of the contract or by implication of law. An accurate definition is given in 1 Wood, Landlord & Tenant, 43, in the following language: "A tenant at will is one who enters into the possession of the lands or tenements of another, lawfully, but for no definite term or purpose, but whose possession is subject to termination by the landlord at any time he sees fit to put an end to it. He is called a tenant at will 'because he hath no certain or sure estate, for the lessor may put him out at what time it pleaseth him.'"

A tenancy at sufferance arises where the tenant wrongfully holds over after the expiration of his term, differing from the tenancy at will, where the possession is by the permission of the landlord. 4 Kent, Com. 117; *Edwards v. Hale*, 9 Allen (Mass.) 462. He has a naked possession without right, and, independent of statute, is not entitled to notice to quit. 1 Wood, Landlord & Tenant § 8. It also arises where a mortgagor holds over after the expiration of the period of redemption on foreclosure. *Stedman v. Gassett*, 18 Vt. 346. In fact, this relation exists in all cases where a person who enters lawfully into the possession wrongfully holds possession after his estate or right has ended. (citations omitted).

A tenancy from month to month or year to year arises where no definite time is agreed upon and the rent is fixed at so much per year or month, as the case may be, and is terminable at the expiration of any period for which rent has been paid. *Finch v. Moore*, 50 Minn. 116, 52 N.W. 384. This form of tenancy can never exist where the lease or contract prescribes a fixed time. The mere fact that rent is payable monthly does not alone determine the character of the tenancy. The monthly or yearly payments and an intention to limit the term to a month or year must in all cases concur to create this species of tenancy.

From these general principles of the law of tenancy it is quite clear that the lease under consideration does not come within either class mentioned. Its language does not expressly define it as a tenancy at will, and no such relation arises by implication, for the reason that the term is not indefinite, within the meaning of the law on this subject, nor is the right to terminate the lease reserved to the lessor. Indefiniteness or uncertainty as to the term of the lease is illustrated by instances where one occupies land by the naked permission of the owner (*Hull v. Wood*, 14 Mees. & W. 681; *Williams v. Deriar*, 31 Mo. 13; *Larned v. Hudson*, 60 N.Y. 102), or a person who holds under a void deed (*Stamper v. Griffin*, 20 Ga. 312, 65 Am. Dec. 628; *Executors v. Houston*, 16 Ala. 111), or where he enters under an agreement for a lease not yet executed (*Emmons v. Scudder*, 115 Mass. 367), or under a lease until the premises are sold (*Lea v. Hernandez*, 10 Tex. 137; *Ela v. Bankes*, 37 Wis. 89), and under various circumstances where no time is specifically agreed upon. In the lease under consideration the tenancy is limited by the time defendant shall continue to dwell in Albert Lea, and this limitation takes the case out of the class of tenancies at will. It is equally clear that a tenancy at sufferance was not created by the contract. There has been no wrongful or unlawful holding over after the expiration of the term. Nor does the rule of tenancy from month to month apply for the reasons already pointed out.

We therefore turn to the question, the turning point in the court below, whether the instrument created a life estate in defendant within the principles of law applicable to that branch of land titles. It is thoroughly settled that a life estate may be created by a deed, lease, or devise, either with or without a stipulation for the payment of rent. This class of tenancies differs in many essential respects from tenancies at will, or from year to year, or at sufferance; the principal distinction being that the former confers a freehold upon the tenant, and the latter a mere chattel interest. The lease under consideration embodies all the essentials of a life tenancy. It contains the usual words of inheritance, necessary at common law, running to defendant, "his heirs, executors, administrators, and assigns," and grants the right of occupancy for the term stated therein.

Life estates or life tenancies are clearly defined in the books, and the lease here involved brings it within this class of estates. 1 Taylor, Landlord & Tenant, §§ 52, 53, states the rule as follows: "An estate for life may be created either by express limitation or by a grant in general terms. If made to a man for the term of his own life, or for that of another person, he is called a tenant for life. But the estate may also be created by a general grant, without defining any specific interest, as where a grant is made to a man, or to a man and his assigns without any limitation in point of time, it will be considered as an estate for life, and for the life of the grantee only. . . . Where a grant is made, subject to be defeated by a particular event, and there is no limitation in point of time, it will be ab initio a grant of an estate for life, as much as if no such event had been contemplated. Thus, if a grant be made to a man so long as he shall inhabit a certain place, or to a woman during her widowhood, as there is no certainty that the estate will be terminated by the change of habitation or by the marriage, respectively, of the lessees, the estate is as much an estate for life, until the prescribed event takes place, as if it had been so granted in express terms."

The author's statement of the law is sustained by the other writers on the subject

(4 Kent, Com. 27; 2 Blackstone, 121), and by the adjudicated cases. In *Warner v. Tanner*, 38 Oh. St. 118, a life estate was held to be created by a lease for a yearly rent extending during the time the lessee should continue to occupy the premises for a particular purpose. In *Mickie v. Lawrence*, 5 Rand. (Va.) 571, 574, the grant was to continue so long as the tenant should pay the stipulated rent. It was held a life estate. A grant "so long as the waters of the Delaware shall run" was held in *Foster v. Joice*, 3 Wash. C.C. 498, Fed. Cas. No. 4,974, to create a life estate. In *Hurd v. Cushing*, 24 Mass. 169, the premises were leased at a fixed yearly rent for the term "so long as the salt works" to be located thereon should continue in operation. It was held a life estate. In *Thomas v. Thomas*, 17 N.J. Eq. 356, it was held that a right given by a will to occupy at a specified annual rent certain premises so long as the devisee "may desire to occupy the same as a drug store" amounted to an estate for life. (citations omitted)

The lease in the case at bar comes within the rule of these authorities, and the trial court properly held that it vested in defendant a life estate, terminable only at his death or his removal from Albert Lea.

Judgment affirmed.

NOTE

A more recent New York case, *Garner v. Gerrish*, 473 N.E.2d 223 (1984), reached the same result, with a lease that provided it should continue "for and during the term of quiet enjoyment from the first day of May, 1977 which term will end — [lessee] has the privilege of termination [sic] this agreement at a date of his own choice." The opinion noted that, "[a]t early common law according to Lord Coke, 'when the lease is made to have and to hold at the will of the lessee, this must be also at the will of the lessor' (1 Co Litt 55a). This rule was generally adopted in the United States during the 19th century and at one time was said to represent the majority view. . . . [However, it] has been widely criticized, particularly in this century, as an antiquated notion which violates the terms of the agreement and frustrates the intent of the parties (citations omitted). It has been noted that the rule has its origins in the doctrine of livery of seisin (Tiffany, Real Property § 159; *Effinger v. Lewis*, 32 Penn. 367 (1859)), which required physical transfer of a clod of earth, twig, key or other symbol on the premises in the presence of witnesses, to effect a conveyance of land (2 Blackstone's Comm, 315, 316; Black's Law Dictionary, 4th ed., p. 1084)."

SMITH v. SMITH
241 S.W.2d 113 (Ark. 1951)

SMITH, J.

This is a complaint in equity filed by the appellant against his sister, the appellee. The complaint alleges that under the will of Dollie Smith, the mother of these litigants, the appellee received a life estate in a certain house and lot in Blytheville. (An alternative allegation is that the devise is void for uncertainty, but we consider this contention to be without merit.) It is further alleged that Dollie Smith died intestate as to the remainder, which passed to these parties as the only heirs of their mother. The complaint charges that as life tenant the appellee is committing waste. The prayer is that the court declare a forfeiture of the life tenancy, appoint a receiver to make repairs, and grant a partition in kind or by sale. The chancellor sustained a demurrer to this complaint and dismissed the suit when the plaintiff refused to plead further.

This is the disputed paragraph in Dollie Smith's will: "I give my home in Blytheville . . . to my daughter, Lorene (Smith) Smith to be used by her as a home as long as she wishes, and in case she should not use it as such and wish to sell it, then the proceeds to be divided between my son, Floyd Smith, and my daughter, Lorene (Smith) Smith in equal shares." Floyd contends that this language created a life estate in Lorene, while she contends that the fee was devised to her.

We agree that only a life estate was created. This will does not expressly describe the estate intended, which distinguishes this case from *Bernstein v. Bramble*, 81 Ark. 480, 99 S.W. 682, 8 L.R.A., N.S., 1028, and other cases in which a fee was definitely defined. If Dollie Smith had intended to devise the fee there would have been no need for her to mention the use of the property as a home or to provide that in the event of a sale the proceeds should be divided. Hence these clauses tend to rebut the suggestion of a fee simple. As we said in *Jackson v. Robinson*, 195 Ark. 431, 112 S.W.2d 417, 419: "If the property were given to her in fee simple, there would be no reason to say anything about her power to sell." See also Rest. Prop. § 112, Illustration 2.

The appellee relies also upon the presumption against partial intestacy to support her contention that she owns the fee. But this is merely a presumption, and it certainly does not operate to convert a life estate into a fee in every case in which the life estate might have been more accurately described. Here the presumption is materially weakened by the existence of other instances of partial intestacy in the same will. In devising her other two parcels of land Dollie Smith made no provision for their devolution in the event that both her children died without issue, and hence the testatrix died partly intestate as to these tracts. In this situation we are more readily inclined to accept the existence of partial intestacy as to the land now in controversy.

A second question is whether the complaint sufficiently alleges facts constituting waste. Construed liberally on demurrer, the complaint charges that the house on the property is old and rapidly deteriorating, that it has rotten flooring and a leaking roof, that Lorene and her husband refuse to make repairs, and that a receiver should be appointed to restore the property to the condition it was in when Lorene received it. It is permissive waste for the life tenant to fail to make such ordinary repairs as are necessary to protect the building from the effects of wind and rain, if the structure was in good condition when the life tenancy began. Tiffany, Real Property (3d Ed.) § 641. We may reasonably infer from the appellant's complaint that failure to repair the roof has caused the floors to rot, and hence waste is adequately alleged.

A cause of action being stated, the prayer for relief is relatively unimportant. *Grytbak v. Grytbak*, 216 Ark. 674, 227 S.W.2d 633. The remainderman is entitled to various remedies for waste, Simes, Future Interests, § 616; so in this case the trial court may grant whatever relief the proof justifies, regardless of the plaintiff's prayer. Nevertheless it may be helpful to the chancellor and to the litigants for us to discuss briefly the forms of relief that are prayed in this complaint.

Floyd first asks that Lorene's life estate be forfeited, but he is not entitled to this drastic action. Forfeiture of the life tenancy for the commission of waste is enforced only when specifically authorized by statute, and in Arkansas we have no such statute. It is true that forfeiture and triple damages were allowed by the Statute of Gloucester, enacted in 1278, 6 Edw. I, c. 5. But this statute soon became obsolete in England and was finally repealed in 1879. The strict English law of waste has never been appropriate to a new country like ours, in which timber must be cut to permit the nation to expand through the cultivation of wooded areas. Tiffany, *supra*, § 630. Hence it is uniformly held in America that the Statute of Gloucester did not become a part of our common law merely by the enactment of laws similar to Ark. Stats. 1947 § 1-101, which adopted English statutes of a general nature that were passed prior to 1607. Rest. Property § 198. Since our legislature has not re-enacted the English statute, the remedy of forfeiture is not available in this State. *Ibid.* § 199.

Floyd's complaint also asks for a receivership and for partition. The former is one of the remainderman's remedies for waste and may be granted by the chancellor if the proof justifies it. And even without a forfeiture of the life estate the plaintiff may demand partition if he likes, since our statute permits a partition subject to an outstanding life estate. § 34-1801. It follows that the complaint is not demurrable.

Reversed, with direction that the demurrer be overruled.

NOTES

1. Suppose A writes a letter to B incorporating this language: "I want to give you my house and lot for your residence. Please don't sell it. Let your sister have the rest of my property." What estate, if any, is transferred by these words? Is the sister entitled to any interest in the lot? See, e.g., *Trobaugh v. Trobaugh*, 397 N.W.2d 401 (Minn. Ct. App. 1987).

2. A one-sentence will read in its entirety: "I, C.E. Spurlock, leave all my property and holdings to Blanche Spurlock so long as she remains my widow." This was held to create a life estate only in Blanche Spurlock. *Cain v. Finnie*, 785 N.E.2d 1039 (Ill. Ct. App. 2003). Can this decision be reconciled with *Hall v. Hall*, *supra*?

3. A tenant for life or for a term of years "without impeachment of waste" is "entitled to cut down all the ordinary timber, as well as other trees upon the estate; but it has long been established that equity will restrain him from committing what is called 'equitable waste,' as by felling timber planted or left standing for the shelter or ornament of the mansion house or grounds. . . ." Broom's Legal Maxims, 264 (10th ed. 1939).

BROKAW v. FAIRCHILD
237 N.Y.S. 6 (1929)

HAMMER, J.

This is an action under section 473 of the Civil Practice Act and Rules of Civil Practice 210 to 212, in which plaintiff asks that it be declared and adjudged that the plaintiff, upon giving such security as the court may direct, has the right and is authorized to remove the present structures and improvements on or affecting the real property No. 1 East Seventy-Ninth street, or any part thereof, except the party wall, and to erect new structures and improvements thereon in accordance with certain proposed plans and specifications.

. . . .

In the year 1886 the late Isaac V. Brokaw bought for $199,000 a plot of ground in the borough of Manhattan, city of New York, opposite Central Park, having a frontage of 102 feet 2 inches on the easterly side of Fifth avenue and a depth of 150 feet on the northerly side of Seventy-Ninth street. Opposite there is an entrance to the park and Seventy-Ninth street is a wide crosstown street running through the park. Upon the corner portion, a plot of ground 51 feet 2 inches on Fifth avenue and a depth of 110 feet on Seventy-Ninth street, Mr. Brokaw erected in the year 1887, for his own occupancy, a residence known as No. 1 East Seventy-Ninth street, at a cost of over $300,000. That residence and corner plot is the subject-matter of this action. The residence, a three-story, mansard and basement granite front building, occupies the entire width of the lot. The mansard roof is of tile. On the first floor are two large drawing rooms on the Fifth avenue side, and there are also a large hallway running through from south to north, a reception room, dining room, and pantry. The dining room is paneled with carved wood. The hallway is in Italian marble and mosaic. There are murals and ceiling panels. There is a small elevator to the upper portion of the house. On the second floor are a large library, a large bedroom with bath on the Fifth avenue side, and there are also four other bedrooms and baths. The third floor has bedrooms and baths. The fourth floor has servants' quarters, bath, and storage rooms. The building has steam heat installed by the plaintiff, electric light and current, hardwood floors, and all usual conveniences. It is an exceedingly fine house, in construction and general condition as fine as anything in New York. It is contended by plaintiff that the decorations are heavy, not of a type now required by similar residences, and did not appeal to the people to whom it was endeavored to rent the building. (See Stenographer's minutes pp. 79, 130, 131, 132, and 133.) (Stenographer's minutes p. 33): It is "a masonry house of the old-fashioned type with very thick walls and heavy reveals in the windows, very high ceilings, monumental staircase and large rooms." (S.M. p. 53): "Such as has not been built for probably twenty-five years." (S.M. p. 54): "Utterly impractical to remodel for occupancy by more than one family." It "was offered to a great many people for rental at $25,000 with the statement that a lower figure might be considered and no offer of rental was obtained (S.M. p. 27). Mr. Brokaw (the plaintiff) directed that the asking rental be $30,000 to start and finally reduced to $20,000. There is no demand for rental of private houses. There is a sporadic demand for purchase and sale on Fifth avenue for use as private homes. Once in a while somebody will want a private house." The taxes are $16,881, upkeep for repairs $750, and watchman $300. The taxes for 1913 were $8,950.77 (S.M. p. 92).

Since 1913, the year of the death of Isaac V. Brokaw and the commencement of the life estate of plaintiff, there has been a change of circumstances and conditions in connection with Fifth avenue properties. Apartments were erected with great rapidity and the building of private residences has practically ceased. Forty-four apartments and only 2 private residences have been erected on Fifth avenue from Fifty-Ninth street to 110th street. There are to-day but 8 of these 51 blocks devoted exclusively to private residences (Exhibits 11 and 12). Plaintiff's expert testified: "It is not possible to get an adequate return on the value of that land by any type of improvement other than an apartment house. The structure proposed in the plans of plaintiff is proper and suitable for the site and show 172 rooms which would rent for $1,000 per room. There is an excellent demand for such apartments. . . . There is no corner in the City of New York as fine for an apartment house as that particular corner."

The plaintiff testified also that his expenses in operating the residence which is unproductive would be at least $70,542 greater than if he resided in an apartment. He claims such difference constitutes a loss and contends that the erected apartment house would change this loss into an income or profit of $30,000. Plaintiff claims that under the facts and changed conditions shown the demolition of the building and erection of the proposed apartment is for the best interests of himself as life tenant, the inheritance, and the remaindermen. The defendants deny these contentions and assert certain affirmative defenses: (1) That the proposed demolition of the residence is waste, which against the objection of the adult defendant remaindermen plaintiff cannot be permitted to accomplish.

. . . .

Coming, therefore, to plaintiff's claimed right to demolish the present residence and to erect in its place the proposed apartment, I am of the opinion that such demolition would result in such an injury to the inheritance as under the authorities would constitute waste. The life estate given to plaintiff under the terms of the will and codicil is not merely in the corner plot of ground with improvements thereon, but, without question, in the residence of the testator. Four times in the devising clause the testator used the words "my residence." This emphasis makes misunderstanding impossible. The identical building which was erected and occupied by the testator in his lifetime and the plot of ground upon which it was built constitute that residence. By no stretch of the imagination could "my residence" be in existence at the end of the life tenancy were the present building demolished and any other structure, even the proposed 13-story apartment, erected on the site.

It has been generally recognized that any act of the life tenant which does permanent injury to the inheritance is waste. The law intends that the life tenant shall enjoy his estate in such a reasonable manner that the land shall pass to the reversioner or remainderman as nearly as practicable unimpaired in its nature, character, and improvements. The general rule in this country is that the life tenant may do whatever is required for the general use and enjoyment of his estate as he received it. The use of the estate he received is contemplated, and not the exercise of an act of dominion or ownership. What the life tenant may do in the future in the way of improving or adding value to the estate is not the test of what constitutes waste. The act of the tenant in changing the estate, and whether or not such act is lawful or unlawful, i.e., whether the estate is so changed as to be an injury to the inheritance, is the sole question involved. The tenant has no right to exercise an act of ownership. In the instant case the inheritance was the residence of the testator — "my residence" — consisting of the present building on a plot of ground 51 feet 2 inches on Fifth avenue by 110 feet on Seventy-Ninth street. "My residence," such is what the plaintiff under the testator's will has the use of for life. He is entitled to use the building and plot reasonably for his own convenience or profit. To demolish that building and erect upon the land another building, even one such as the contemplated 13-story apartment house, would be the exercise of an act of ownership and dominion. It would change the inheritance or thing, the use of which was given to the plaintiff as tenant for life, so that the inheritance or thing could not be delivered to the remaindermen or reversioners at the end of the life estate. The receipt by them at the end of the life estate of a 13-story $900,000 apartment house might be more beneficial to them. Financially, the objecting adults may be unwise in not consenting to the proposed change. They may be selfish and unmindful that in the normal course of time and events they probably will not receive the fee. With motives and purposes the court is not concerned. In *Matter of Brokaw's Will*, 219 App. Div. 337, 219 N.Y.S. 734; *id.*, 245 N.Y. 614, 157 N.E. 880, their right to object to a proposed building loan and mortgage for the erection of the proposed apartment was established by decision. They have the same right of objection in this action. To tear down and demolish the present building, which cost at least $300,000 to erect and would cost at least as much to replace, under the facts in this case, is clearly and beyond question an act of waste.

. . . .

The cases given by plaintiff are either cases where a prohibitory injunction against future waste has been sought and the parties have been refused the injunction and relegated to an action for damages for waste, or where, in condemnation proceedings or actions in equity, it appears that the equities between the parties are such that the technical waste committed has been ameliorated. The three cases upon which the plaintiff principally relies are *Melms v. Pabst Brewing Co.*, 104 Wis. 7, 79 N.W. 738, 46 L.R.A. 478, and *New York, O. & W. R. Co. v. Livingston*, 238 N.Y. 300, 144 N.E. 589, 34 A.L.R. 1078, and *Doherty v. Allman*, 3 L.R. App. Cas. 709, 717, 721. These are readily distinguishable from the case at bar. In *Melms v. Pabst Brewing Co., supra*, there was a large expensive brick dwelling house built by one Melms in the year 1864. He also owned the adjoining real estate and a brewery upon part of the premises. He died in 1869. The brewery and dwelling were sold and conveyed to Pabst Brewing Company. The Pabst Company used the brewery part of the premises. About the year 1890 the neighborhood about the dwelling house had so changed in character that it was situated on an isolated lot standing from 20 to 30 feet above the level of the street, the balance of the property having been graded down to fit it for business purposes. It was surrounded by business property, factories, and railroad tracks with no other dwellings in the neighborhood. Pabst Brewing Company, in good faith regarding itself as the owner, tore down the building and graded down the ground for business purposes. Thereafter it was held, in the action of *Melms v. Pabst Brewing Co.*, 93 Wis. 140, 66

N.W. 244, that the brewing company had only acquired a life estate in the homestead, although in another action between the same parties (93 Wis. 153, 66 N.W. 518, 57 Am. St. Rep. 899) it was held that as to the other property the brewing company had acquired full title in fee. The action for waste in which the decision of 104 Wis. was delivered was brought and decided after the decisions in the other actions. We find it there said at page 9 (79 N.W. 738): "The action was tried before the court without a jury, and the court found, in addition to the facts above stated, that the removal of the building and the grading down of the earth was done by the defendant in 1891 and 1892, believing itself to be the owner in fee simple of the property, and that by the said acts the estate of the plaintiffs in the property was substantially increased, and that the plaintiffs have been in no way injured thereby."

Again, it was stated at page 13 of 104 Wis., 79 N.W. 740, 46 L.R.A. 478: "There are no contract relations in the present case. The defendants are the grantees of a life estate, and their rights may continue for a number of years. The evidence shows that the property became valueless for the purpose of residence property as the result of the growth and development of a great city. Business and manufacturing interests advanced and surrounded the once elegant mansion, until it stood isolated and alone, standing upon just enough ground to support it, and surrounded by factories and railroad tracks, absolutely undesirable as a residence, and incapable of any use as business property. Here was a complete change of conditions, not produced by the tenant, but resulting from causes which none could control. Can it be reasonably or logically said that this entire change of condition is to be completely ignored, and the ironclad rule applied that the tenant can make no change in the uses of the property because he will destroy its identity? Must the tenant stand by, and preserve the useless dwelling house, so that he may at some future time turn it over to the reversioner, equally useless?"

The facts in the above case are clearly not analogous to the facts here. Especially is this recognized from the fact that the plaintiff's dwelling house is far from being "isolated and alone, standing upon just enough ground to support it, surrounded by factories and railroad tracks, absolutely undesirable as a residence." It is located on the northeast corner of Fifth avenue and Seventy-Ninth street. Across the avenue to the west is Central Park. To the south across Seventy-Ninth street the block Seventy-Eighth to Seventy-Ninth streets is restricted to private dwellings. The residence itself is surrounded by the three other palatial Brokaw dwellings, forming a magnificent residential layout of the four plots (Exhibit B). It may, of course, be that the situation will change in the future. The decision here is concerned only with the present.

. . . .

From the foregoing I am of the opinion, and it will accordingly be adjudged and declared, that upon the present facts, circumstances, and conditions as they exist and are shown in this case, regardless of the proposed security and the expressed purpose of erecting the proposed 13-story apartment, or any other structure, the plaintiff has no right and is not authorized to remove the present structures on or affecting the real estate in question.

NOTES

1. That the Brokaw mansion was an "exceedingly fine house" was an opinion not shared by at least one of its occupants — Mrs. Brokaw. She later became a public celebrity as Clare Boothe Luce. About the house she wrote, "Its interior was morbidly grandiose. Dreary yellow marble and peeling gold-leaf ceilings blighted the entrance hall. Opaque La Farge stained glass windows on the staircase kept out light. Heavy French and Italian Renaissance furniture, faded tapestries, and soiled Japanese screens oppressed the formal rooms. Littered throughout were drab shawls, antimacassars, and hand-painted calendars pinned to damask walls. Innumerable clocks ticked and chimed." See Sylvia Jukes Morris, Rage for Fame: The Ascent of Clare Boothe Luce 129 (1997). George Brokaw died in 1935; the mansion was razed in the 1960s in order to erect an apartment house. New York Times, Sept. 17, 1964, at 1, col. 2.

2. Should the age of the life tenant at the time of the litigation make any difference to the outcome of cases like *Brokaw*? What about the tenant under a long-term lease? If the lease is silent about the rights of the lessee, should the tenant be free to make changes that would be classified as waste under the ordinary test? The New York legislature subsequently enacted legislation giving life tenants and tenants for years greater power to alter or replace existing structures in ways that would not "reduce the market value" of the land. One of its requirements was that the life expectancy of the life tenant or the duration of the lease be more than five years. See N.Y. RPAPL § 803.

NEW YORK, O. & W. R. CO. v. LIVINGSTON
144 N.E. 589 (N.Y. 1924)

CARDOZO, J.

Edward Livingston, who died in 1864, devised to his nephew, Charles Octavius Livingston, a farm of 200 acres at Livingston Manor, Sullivan county, New York, "said farm and its appurtenances to be used and enjoyed by my said nephew during the term of his natural life, and at his decease to descend to the eldest son of my said nephew who shall then be living; and if my said nephew shall die leaving no son, then the said farm shall descend to the daughters of my said nephew, who shall then be living, and the issue of such daughters as may before that time have died," with a gift over to others in other contingencies. He enjoined upon his "nephews and such of their children who may at any time become possessed of the said farm under this will that they do not sell or in any manner part with the same," it being his "desire that the said farm with the appurtenances shall remain in the possession of" his "family, and that the same should not be sold or pass into the possession of strangers."

In 1871 the nephew, Charles Octavius Livingston, who by this will was at least a life tenant, and who claimed the fee, conveyed the farm to one Morss, and his heirs and assigns forever, covenanting that "the children and descendants of the party of the first part, each and every of them, shall be forever estopped and barred from claiming any title, estate or interest in the said lands or any portion thereof." In

1872 the New York & Oswego Midland Railroad Company constructed its railroad upon and over the farm under an agreement with Morss for the conveyance of a right of way. In 1880 Morss, pursuant to this agreement, executed a conveyance in fee, with covenant of warranty, to the appellant, the New York, Ontario & Western Railroad Company, the successor in interest of the New York & Oswego Midland Railroad Company. Other portions of the farm were purchased later. Upon the land so acquired the railroad company built a passenger station, a freight house, and other structures as well as tracks and sidings.

The life tenant, Charles Octavius Livingston, died in 1914, survived by the respondent, Charles Victor Livingston, his eldest son. The latter made claim against the railroad company to the ownership of the land, and in 1917 began an action of ejectment to recover the possession. The railroad company answered that it was the owner of the fee, but judgment went against it after a trial of the issues and an appeal (193 App. Div. 523, 184 N.Y. Supp. 665). This proceeding was then begun, in April, 1921, under section 17 of the Railroad Law (Cons. Laws, c. 49), to acquire title to the land as necessary for a public use in the exercise of the power of eminent domain. The commissioners' report, which was confirmed by the court, fixed the value of the land without the improvements at $15,000, and the value of the improvements at $49,000, a total of $64,000. This total the appellant has been required to pay as the price of condemnation. The question is whether there was error in including the value of improvements.

We think a railroad company, or other public agency, which enters lawfully upon land and improves it in good faith, may exclude the value of the improvements in proceedings brought thereafter to condemn a hostile right. *Searl v. School District No. 2 in Lake County*, 133 U.S. 553, 561, 562, 10 Sup. Ct. 374, 33 L. Ed. 740; . . . 2 Lewis on Eminent Domain, § 507. Some courts go farther and concede a like privilege though the entry in its inception was unlawful, if only the trespasser acted innocently, under a mistaken claim of title. (citations omitted). How we should rule in such circumstances we need not now determine. Other courts go even farther, and concede a like privilege even to the willful wrongdoer. *Justice v. Nesquehoning Valley R. R. Co.*, 87 Pa. 28; *Jones v. New Orleans & S. R. R. Co.*, 70 Ala. 227; *Lewis on Eminent Domain, supra*. By our decision in *Village of St. Johnsville v. Smith*, 184 N.Y. 341, 77 N.E. 617, 5 L.R.A. (N. S.) 922, 6 Ann. Cas. 379, we refused to place upon lawlessness a premium so tempting. There a village without color of right, and in advance of the initiation of any proceeding to condemn, had made an entry upon land in defiance of the express command and remonstrance of the owner. 184 N.Y. at page 344 (77 N.E. 617). We held that the price was not subject to abatement, but we did not fail to observe that equities exacting a different conclusion might flow from an entry that was lawful in its origin. 184 N.Y. at page 349 (77 N.E. 617). As authorities supporting the rule applicable to wrongdoers, we cited *Matter of New York, West Shore & Buffalo Ry. Co.*, 37 Hun, 317, and *Matter of Long Island R. Co.*, 6 Thomp. & C. 298, where a naked or willful trespass was again the decisive feature. On the other hand, in this state as elsewhere, the rigor of the rule enforced against the willful wrongdoer has been tempered to relieve the occupant who has entered innocently and lawfully. (citations omitted) In such circumstances, "just compensation" does not exact the addition of the value of the improvements to the value of the land. The maxim, quicquid plantatur solo, solo cedit, "has always had exceptions, and they increase with the ever-varying necessities and exigencies of society." *St. Johnsbury & L. C. R. Co. v. Willard, supra,* at page 138 (17 Atl. 39); *Consol. Turnpike Co. v. Norfolk & O. V. Ry. Co.,* 228 U.S. 596, 602, 57 L. Ed. 982. Commissioners in these proceedings are to ascertain and determine the compensation which ought "justly" to be made by the public or its delegate to the owners of the property. Condemnation Law (Consol. Laws, c. 73), § 14. Cf. N.Y. Constitution, art. 1, § 6. "It is the duty of the state, in the conduct of the inquest by which the compensation is ascertained, to see that it is just, not merely to the individual whose property is taken, but to the public which is to pay for it." *Searl v. School District No. 2 in Lake County,* 133 U.S. at pages 553, 562, 10 Sup. Ct. 374, 377 (33 L. Ed. 740). No formula will be adequate unless its breadth of view and flexibility of adaptation are fitted and proportioned to the scheme and purpose of the inquest. The problem is one of justice between the individual proprietor on the one hand and on the other hand the sovereign, or the representative of sovereign power.

When the test of these principles is applied to the case before us, the conclusion is hardly doubtful. The railroad company was not a willful trespasser when it entered upon this farm and placed improvements thereon. It was not a trespasser at all. It was the owner of an estate for the life of Livingston, the grantor, and it held a deed which gave support to a reasonable, though mistaken, belief that it was the owner of the fee. The life tenant had covenanted that his children and descendants were barred and estopped from assailing the validity of the grant, and the assumption was not a strained one that he knew whereof he spoke. In such circumstances, we cannot doubt that the value of the improvements would have been excluded if the railroad company had brought proceedings during the life estate to acquire the remainder. We think it is not a sufficient reason for applying a harsher rule that the proceedings were not begun till the particular estate had ended. The owner of the remainder has been compensated for the delay by the award of mesne profits during the period of detention. Civ. Prac. Act, § 1011. We find no basis for a holding that he is entitled to something more. The improvements had been completed while the life tenant was yet in being, and the failure to yield possession at once upon his death would be penalized overmuch if the increment of value were held to be forfeit altogether. The position of this railroad company as an actual tenant for life and a supposed owner in fee is very similar to that of the railroad company in a case in Illinois, where there was entry under the deed of a tenant for life, and allowance in condemnation proceedings for improvements placed upon the land. *Chicago, Peoria & St. Louis R. R. Co. v. Vaughn,* 206 Ill. 234, 247, 69 N.E. 113. The circumstances of this entry dictate a like conclusion.

We do not overlook the argument that a life tenant who turns a farm into a railroad yard commits an act of waste. The effect of the so-called waste in this instance was to add $49,000 to the value. The act, if waste at all (citations omitted), was at the utmost meliorating waste, improving instead of injuring the remainderman's inheritance (*Doherty v. Allman,* 3 App. Cas. 709). We think a wrong so technical does not destroy the equities that would otherwise be available for the protection of the occupant, at all events in a case where to the ownership of a life estate there is added color of lawful claim to the ownership of the fee.

Nothing inconsistent with our present ruling was held in *Philadelphia, R. & N. E. R. R. Co. v. Bowman,* 23 App. Div. 170, 48 N.Y. Supp. 901; *id.,* 163 N.Y. 572, 57

N.E. 1122. There the improvements were made upon land subject to a mortgage, and title had passed to a stranger who bought at the foreclosure sale in the belief that the improvements were covered by the deed. Just compensation is determined by "equitable principles" (*United States v. Rogers*, 257 Fed. 397, 400, 168 C.C.A. 437, 440), and its measure varies with the facts.

The order of the Appellate Division and that of the Special Term should be modified by deducting the sum of $49,000 from the payment of $64,000 therein directed to be made, and as modified affirmed, without costs to either party. Condemnation Law, § 20.

NOTES

1. Suppose the railroad had commenced condemnation proceedings during the lifetime of Charles Octavius Livingston. Should he, as life tenant, be entitled to an absolute share of the award? If so, should he receive the value his life estate would have brought on the open market, or would some other way of calculating its value be more appropriate? See *Matter of Estate of Fisher*, 645 N.Y.S.2d 1020 (N.Y. Surr. Ct. 1996). On the more general problem, see Alison Dunham, *Valuing Life Estates and Remainders*, 107 Tr. & Est. 12 (1968), and Victor Goldberg, Thomas Merrill & Daniel Unumb, *Bargaining in the Shadow of Eminent Domain: Valuing and Apportioning Condemnation Awards between Landlord and Tenant*, 34 UCLA L. Rev. 1083 (1987).

2. If the life tenant takes out a policy of insurance on the premises and the buildings on the property are destroyed by fire or lightning, would the remainderman be entitled to share in the proceeds of the policy under the court's reasoning in *Livingston*? See Restatement of Property § 123 (1936); *Morris v. Morris*, 544 P.2d 1034 (Ore. 1976).

3. Under ordinary circumstances, the life tenant is responsible for the payment of property taxes, unless the intent of the grantor requires a different result. However, if the land ceases to be productive during the life estate, the tenant will be entitled to reimbursement for the taxes paid on the unproductive land. *In re Frenz's Will*, 108 N.Y.S.2d 446 (N.Y. Surr. Ct. 1951). However, assessments for permanent improvements to the land, such as establishing a drainage system, are normally apportioned between the life tenant and the remainderman. See *Chambers v. Chambers*, 39 A. 243 (R.I. 1898).

IV. MARITAL ESTATES

A. The Common Law

In most American jurisdictions, unless they choose otherwise, spouses hold title individually to property they acquire during the marriage. Each spouse may take title in his or her own name, just as they hold property they brought to the marriage. They may of course choose to take title as joint tenants or tenants in common; but if they do not, their income and the property purchased with their income belong to them individually.

Historically, exceptions to this regime of separate property existed at common law. The idea that marriage created a unity between husband and wife was strong. One consequence was that, during a wife's lifetime, her husband had the right to control property to which she held legal title. This was known as his right *iure uxoris*, and it permitted him to alienate the property during the marriage, even without her consent. The wife was entitled to support from the husband during the marriage, and she would retake full ownership of her individual property at his death.

At the death of a spouse, the early common law gave the surviving spouse, whether husband or wife, a right in the land of the other. Neither was considered the heir to the other spouse, but under ordinary circumstances, both husband and wife took a life estate in the real property the other had held during the marriage. A widow was entitled to a one-third share of lands in which the husband had been seised of an estate of inheritance at any time during their marriage. A widower was entitled to a life estate in any lands the wife held in fee simple or fee tail during the marriage, provided a child had been born alive to them during their marriage. The former was called dower; the latter curtesy. Thus, as long as the technical requirements were met, if the husband alienated land that belonged to his wife without her consent, she was entitled to a life estate in one-third of it even though it was in the hands of the purchaser. A modern example, from a jurisdiction where dower is still in force, is *Webber v. Webber*, 962 S.W.2d 345 (Ark. 1998).

MELENKY v. MELEN
134 N.E. 822 (N.Y. 1922)

CARDOZO, J.

The case is here on a demurrer to the complaint. In December, 1913, Reuben Melenky conveyed land in the city of Rochester to his son Asher P. Melenky, now Asher P. Melen. The deed was made that the son might manage the property in the absence of the father, and was coupled with an oral promise to reconvey upon demand. In August, 1914, the father married again; and the plaintiff is his wife. Before the marriage, he told her that he was the owner of valuable real estate in Rochester. She relied upon his statement in consenting to the marriage. Four years later, the son, when asked to reconvey, made a deed of an estate for life, but refused to reconvey the fee. The father, under pressure of age, infirmity, and want, accepted the deed as tendered. The purpose of the son in retaining the fee was to deprive the plaintiff of her dower. She prays that an inchoate right of dower be established and a reconveyance adjudged. Father and son are joined as defendants. The demurrer is by the son.

> A widow shall be endowed with a third part of all the lands whereof her husband was seized of an estate of inheritance, at any time during the marriage. Real Property Law § 190 (Consol. Laws, c. 50).

The plaintiff's husband is not seized of such an estate, nor has he been since the conveyance. A different question would be here if the trust had been declared in writing. There would be no need, in such circumstances, of the judgment of a court.

The beneficial owner (there being none of the four express trusts) would have the legal estate by force of the mandate of the statute. Real Prop. Law, §§ 92, 93; *Wright v. Douglass*, 7 N.Y. 564; *Murray v. Miller*, 178 N.Y. 316, 322, 70 N.E. 870; *Monypeny v. Monypeny*, 202 N.Y. 90, 93, 95 N.E. 1. This trust, however, was oral. The statute, far from executing it automatically, pronounced it unenforceable in its creation. Real Prop. Law § 242. True, a court of equity, finding an abuse of confidence, might give relief upon the ground of fraud (citations omitted). Even then, its jurisdiction would be exerted to undo rather than to enforce, or to enforce only as a substitute for undoing, since justice might fail if remedies were rigid. Until the entry of a decree, the defrauded grantor is not the owner of an estate. He is the owner of an obligation, a chose in action (*Wheeler v. Reynolds*, 66 N.Y. 227, 236; Ames, Lectures on Legal History, 425, 429, *supra*; Hohfeld, Fundamental Legal Conceptions, 24, 106, 108; Pound, 33 Harvard L. R. 420; cf. Real Prop. Law, § 100; *Schenck v. Barnes*, 156 N.Y. 316, 321, 50 N.E. 967, 41 L.R.A. 395). The right which is his during his life may pass upon his death to his heirs or devisees (*Williams v. Haddock*, 145 N.Y. 144, 39 N.E. 825), but it is still "a remedial expedient" (Pound, *supra*). Seizin there is none either "in deed" or "in law" (2 Pollock & Maitland, History of English Law, p. 60; Co. Litt. 31a). Reconveyance does not evidence a seizin continuously retained. It reinstates a seizin that would otherwise be lost.

This grantor has not attempted to enforce his chose in action. He has not asked a court of equity to undo the conveyance and re-establish the divested title. He is willing to let the transaction stand, or unwilling, at all events, to take active measures to annul it. We are now asked to say that the wife may reclaim what the husband would abandon. This means, of course, that the chose in action is not solely his, but is hers also, to the extent of the benefit that would come to her if he had chosen to enforce it. We find no adequate basis for such a conclusion either in principle or in precedent. Decisions, hardly to be distinguished, announce a different ruling. (citations omitted). Dower attaches, not to choses in action, but to estates. *Seaman v. Harmon*, 192 Mass. 5, 78 N.E. 301. The law will not create the estate in order to subject it to the incident. This is not a case where the grantee has abused a confidence reposed in him by the wife. She was not a party to the conveyance, which was made before the marriage. This is not a case where the grantor has attempted by a clandestine transfer of the title to modify the incidents of a marriage about to be contracted. *Youngs v. Carter*, 10 Hun, 194; *Bookout v. Bookout*, 150 Ind. 63, 49 N.E. 824, 65 Am. St. Rep. 350. The transfer was made to promote his business convenience, when no marriage was in view. He is not subject to the reproach of plotting a fraud upon his wife. *Walker v. Walker*, 66 N.H. 390, 31 Atl. 14, 49 Am. St. Rep. 616, 27 L.R.A. 799; *Brownell v. Briggs*, 173 Mass. 529, 54 N.E. 251. No such charge, indeed, was made. The most that can be said is that he is unwilling to assume the burden of seeking redress for a fraud which another has practiced upon him. In this, we find no breach of duty. The right of election is his, either to submit or to contend. His wife may not elect for him, nor overrule his choice. One might as well say that while he was yet alive, she could compel the specific performance, of a contract of purchase which he was willing to forego. *Hawley v. James*, 5 Paige, 318, 452, 453, 454. The wrong to the husband may be the misfortune of the wife. We think it is nothing more.

The order of the Appellate Division should be reversed, and the interlocutory judgment of the Special Term affirmed, with costs in the Appellate Division and in this court, and the question certified answered in the negative.

NOTES

1. In *Couch v. Eastham*, 73 S.E. 314 (W. Va. 1912), the will of Samuel Couch contained the following provision:

> I give and devise unto my son Peter S. Couch the farm on which I reside in Mason County, West Virginia, . . . but in [the] event the said Peter S. Couch shall die leaving no lawful children surviving him, but leaving his wife Mary Catherine Couch surviving him, it is my will and desire that the title to all my real estate aforesaid shall pass to and be vested in my daughter Sarah Frances Eastham or her children.

Peter died without surviving issue but was survived both by his wife Mary and his sister Sarah. Mary's claim to dower in the farm was upheld.

2. During the marriage, the wife's interest is called inchoate dower; it becomes consummate at the husband's death. Although it is not a possessory estate, it is a present interest and can be extinguished only by a voluntary act of the wife. Sir Francis Bacon (d. 1626) wrote that the common law held in special favor three things: "Life Liberty and Dower." Reading on the Statute of Uses 31-2 (1642 ed.).

3. A New Jersey statute abolished "the estates and interests of dower, and right of dower and curtesy" but went on to provide that "nothing in this act shall affect any of such estates or interests which may have become vested heretofore." In *Class v. Strack*, 96 A. 405 (N.J. Chan. 1915), the court upheld the rights to dower of a woman married at the time of the passage of the statute but whose husband died afterwards. However, in *Randall v. Kreiger*, 90 U.S. (23 Wall.) 137, 148 (1874), the U.S. Supreme Court held that legislation could diminish the wife's dower upon the husband's death, since "[d]uring the life of the husband, the right is a mere expectancy or possibility."

B. Statutory Changes in Marital Estates

Dower and curtesy continue to exist to the extent that the common law relating to them has not been changed. However, in fact, they have both been amended, or indeed replaced, in many American jurisdictions. See generally Ralph Brashier, *Disinheritance and the Modern Family*, 45 Case W. Res. L. Rev. 84 (1994). Among the most common changes in the common law's regime are the following:

(a) making the surviving spouse an heir upon intestacy;

(b) widening coverage to include both personal and real property;

(c) equalizing the rights of husband and wife;

(d) restricting the property subject to them to that held at death;

(e) changing the estate taken from a life estate to a fee simple interest in a percentage of the decedent's estate; and

(f) giving the surviving spouse an election either to take under the will of the first to die, or to take a statutory share as the decedent's heir.

The Ohio statute on dower (Ohio Rev. Code § 2103.02) reads in part:

A spouse who has not relinquished or been barred from it shall be endowed of an estate for life in one third of the real property of which the consort was seized as an estate of inheritance at any time during the marriage. Such dower interest shall terminate upon the death of the consort except:

(a) To the extent that any such real property was conveyed by the deceased consort during the marriage, the surviving spouse not having relinquished or been barred from dower therein;

(b) To the extent that any such real property during the marriage was encumbered by the deceased consort by mortgage, judgment, lien except tax lien, or otherwise, or aliened by involuntary sale, the surviving spouse not having relinquished or been barred from dower therein. If such real property was encumbered or aliened prior to decease, the dower interest of the surviving spouse therein shall be computed on the basis of the amount of the encumbrance at the time of the death of such consort or at the time of such alienation, but not upon an amount exceeding the sale price of such property.

The Connecticut statute (Conn. Gen. Stat. § 45a-436) reads in part:

(a) On the death of a spouse, the surviving spouse may elect, as provided in subsection (c) of this section, to take a statutory share of the real and personal property passing under the will of the deceased spouse. The "statutory share" means a life estate of one-third in value of all the property passing under the will, real and personal, legally or equitably owned by the deceased spouse at the time of his or her death, after the payment of all debts and charges against the estate. The right to such third shall not be defeated by any disposition of the property by will to other parties.

(b) If the deceased spouse has by will devised or bequeathed a portion of his or her property to his or her surviving spouse, such provision shall be taken to be in lieu of the statutory share unless the contrary is expressly stated in the will or clearly appears therein; but, in any such case, the surviving spouse may elect to take the statutory share in lieu of the provision of the will.

The Uniform Probate Code has brought a thorough-going revision of the law on this subject. It abolishes estates of dower and curtesy, and it expands the forced share available to the surviving spouse. This "augmented estate" concept gives the surviving spouse the right to elect to take a sliding scale percentage (from 3% to 50% depending on the length of the marriage) not only of the property held at death by the first spouse to die, but also assets subject to certain inter vivos transactions that are functionally equivalent to probate transfers. Property held in a revocable trust, for example, is included in the augmented estate. So is property held in joint tenancy, to be examined in the next section.

The calculations necessary to figure the elective share are complex. They are the subject of courses in trusts and estates. The drafters of the UPC felt that the complexity was necessary if an adequate "safety-net" was to be provided for surviving spouses. Without taking lifetime transfers into account, it becomes too easy to defeat the law's purpose by illusory transactions, in which one spouse retains effective control over property but nevertheless prevents it from becoming a part of his or her probate estate. Remember, however, that the process is elective and that the surviving spouse cannot ordinarily take this elective share *and* also what is allotted under the decedent's will. As this is commonly put, the elective share is a right to take *against* the will.

C. Community Property

The regime of community property goes beyond the system of spousal protection found in the common law. It rests on the principle that property that is earned by either spouse during the marriage belongs to a marital community of which each spouse is half owner. Property owned prior to the marriage, however, and property acquired by inheritance, devise, or gift during the marriage remain the separate property of each spouse. Some states treat the income from separate property — interest and rent for example — as part of the community. In others it retains the same status as its source.

Community property regimes prevail in some form in nine American states (Arizona, California, Idaho, Louisiana, Nevada, New Mexico, Texas, Washington, and Wisconsin). Alaska now permits it if the couple enters into an explicit agreement. Alaska Stat. § 34.77.090. In most of the others, however, couples are free to take property as separate property by agreement and also to convert property from one regime to the other. However, the default rule presumes that what the spouses acquire during their marriage is part of the community. Upon the death of either, that spouse may dispose of half of the community property by will, but the other half belongs to the survivor. For this reason, there is no need for a forced share system.

According to the accepted rule, property acquired under a community property regime retains that character even if the couple moves to a common-law state (and vice versa). This may lead to a number of different problems, of which the following case provides an example.

IN RE KESSLER'S ESTATE
203 N.E.2d 221 (Ohio 1964)

HOVER, J. . . .

From 1947 until 1957, the decedent and his wife lived in the state of California. While there the husband acquired and had issued in his name certain shares of stock which, although slightly changed as to form and number of certificates, remained in his possession until his death in Ohio in 1961. Decedent and his wife, from 1957 until the date of death on January 20, 1961, lived in the state of Ohio. Decedent died testate. His executor, and appellee herein, both for inventory and tax purposes, determined that one-half of 28,700 shares of stock acquired while the couple was domiciled in California became, upon the husband's death, the outright property of the widow under the law of the state of California relating to community property. The courts below upheld this contention and determined that no tax was due as to her half of the above shares.

The concept of community property is a basic law of property in eight states. These states have in common an early inheritance of French or Spanish civil law as distinguished from the common law generally prevalent in the remainder of the states. Although the community-property states differ one from the other in various respects, the basic concept is the same, to wit, that property acquired during coverture, other than by gift or descent, is the joint property of husband and wife and is properly designated as "community property." On the other hand, property held both in use and title for the exclusive benefit of either husband or wife is "separate property." It is particularly in the state of California, the community-property state with which we are here concerned, that various community-property principles have been reduced to statute, apparently for the sake of clarity and certainty. There is no doubt that the property involved here became community property when it was acquired by Louis R. Kessler during the period of the family's residence in California. The California Civil Code provides in regard to such property that "[t]he respective interests of the husband and wife in community property during continuance of the marriage relation are present, existing and equal interests under the management and control of the husband." Section 161a, California Civil Code.

It is generally recognized that the character of community property, even though it is personalty, does not change as to the nature of the holding, where the married couple remove themselves from a community-property state to a common-law state. The converse is also true, that is, the character of property acquired in a common-law state is not altered merely by the removal of the couple to a community-property state. 15 American Jurisprudence (2d), 832, Community Property, Sections 15, 16 and 17; annotation, 171 A.L.R. 1343. See, also, *Succession of Popp*, 83 So. 765, 146 La. 464, citing *Succession of Packwood*, 9 Rob. 438, 41 Am.Dec. 341, the latter case apparently being the first of its kind since it arose shortly after the first of the community-property states, Louisiana, was admitted to the Union. *People ex rel. Dunbar v. Bejarano* (1961), 145 Colo. 304, 358 P.2d 866; *In re Will of Clark* (1955), 59 N.M. 433, 285 P.2d 795. An attempt of the state of California by legislation to alter this general rule by creating a species of holding known as "quasi community property" was declared to be unconstitutional by the Supreme Court of California in *In re Estate of Thornton*, 1 Cal. 2d 1, 33 P.2d 1, 92 A.L.R. 1343.

Therefore, one-half of the shares involved here remained the community property of the wife upon the removal of the couple from California to Ohio in 1957. In other words, her interest in the community property "vested" as of the date and place of acquisition and, as stated by the California statute, her interest in such property was present, existing and equal.

It is necessary, however, to consider the real nature of the interest acquired by the wife in order to determine its status in respect to the succession tax. . . . Although it has been said, as pointed out in the arguments of counsel, that the wife's interest in the community property is more than a mere expectancy, it is equally certain that the interest accorded her by the community-property law generally, and more specifically by the California statute, is certainly not in the nature of outright ownership until the dissolution of the marriage, as upon the death of the husband. The nature of the wife's interest in community property is summarized in *Willcox v. Penn. Mutual Life Ins. Co.* (1947), 357 Pa. 581, 55 A.2d 521, 174 A.L.R. 220, wherein the Supreme Court of Pennsylvania found legislation attempting to establish the principle of community property in that state to be unconstitutional. The court observes:

> . . . it is obvious that an alleged interest in property over which another person has the right of control, management and disposal, which the creditors of such other person can take in satisfaction of his debts, and as to which there is no practical means of protection, is not a genuine right of property no matter what name or alleged title of ownership may have been given it.

It thus appears that, although one-half of the shares here in question became the outright property of the wife upon the death of the husband, the transition from community property to property of which the wife is the sole owner is a matter of real and substantial value which may become the basis for a succession tax.

In *Fernandez, Collr., Internal Revenue v. Wiener* (1945), 326 U.S. 340, 66 S.Ct. 178, the Supreme Court discusses at length the ultimate and complete vesting of community property in one spouse upon death of the other. . . . The court states on page 355, 366, S.Ct. on page 186:

> With these general principles in mind we turn to their application to federal death taxes laid with respect to the interests in community property. As we have seen, the death of the husband of the Louisiana marital community not only operates to transfer his rights in his share of the community to his heirs or those taking under his will. It terminates his expansive and sometimes profitable control over the wife's share, and for the first time brings her half of the property into her full and exclusive possession, control and enjoyment. The cessation of these extensive powers of the husband, even though they were powers over property which he never "owned", and the establishment in the wife of new powers of control over her share, though it was always hers, furnish appropriate occasions for the imposition of an excise tax. . . .

It therefore becomes necessary to examine whether this specific succession is one upon which a tax is levied by the Ohio statute. . . . Such a tax, if any, is levied by Section 5731.02, Revised Code, wherein it is provided that a tax is levied upon the succession to any property passing to or for the use of a person in certain categories, and it should be observed, of necessity, in those categories only. Among such categories is subsection (E) of the section cited, which provides:

> Whenever property is held by two or more persons jointly, so that upon the death of one of them the survivor has a right to the immediate ownership or possession and enjoyment of the whole property, the accrual of such

right by the death of one of them shall be deemed a succession taxable under this section, in the same manner as if the enhanced value of the whole property belonged absolutely to the deceased person, and he had bequeathed the same to the survivor by will, provided when the persons holding said property jointly are a husband and wife, the survivor shall be deemed to have a succession taxable to the extent of one-half the total value of the property without regard to enhancement.

The problem arises whether a party to a community-property relationship has a right to the immediate ownership or possession and enjoyment of the "whole property" upon the death of the other party to the joint ownership. If, in regard to community property, the "whole property" is the entirety of the community holding, obviously, subsection (E) does not apply because the survivor does not succeed to the entirety of the community property but to only one-half thereof. However, under the concept of community property each spouse has, during the life of the community, a qualified and restricted ownership in the whole which, upon the death of one of the parties, becomes an outright and total ownership of one-half; but, whether accrued or not, the one-half interest of the survivor in community property exists in one form or another at all times and, upon the death of one, vests the "right to the immediate ownership or possession and enjoyment of the whole property" in the survivor. It is by virtue of the death that the previously commingled and inseparable ownership of either of the parties in the whole property becomes complete and ascertainable as to one-half, so that when community property exists the survivor, upon death, does become entitled to the immediate ownership and possession and enjoyment of the whole of his share of the community property.

Subsection (E), with which we are here concerned, provides that, when the joint owners of such property as described above are husband and wife, the survivor shall be deemed to have a taxable succession to the extent of one-half of the total value of the property without regard to enhancement.

The total value of the property here is the number of shares standing in the husband's name upon death, multiplied by the then market value thereof. The taxable succession to the wife as the survivor of the community ownership is one-half of such total value.

In this case, by virtue of the death of Louis R. Kessler, his wife acquired the full and complete enjoyment of one-half of the shares of stock acquired as community property in California totally divested of the many restrictions and contingencies which had theretofore diluted her vested interest in that property. It is, accordingly, held that the acquisition by the widow, through the operation of the community-property law, of one-half of the 28,700 shares of stock in the name of her husband at his death constitutes a taxable succession under the succession tax law of Ohio.

Accordingly, the judgment of the Court of Appeals is, hereby, reversed, and the cause is remanded to the Probate Court for further proceedings in accordance with this opinion. Judgment reversed.

GIBSON, J., dissenting.

. . . The litigants disagree only as to the nature of Mrs. Kessler's interest in this community property. On the one hand, the Tax Commissioner contends that even in California the wife had only a mere expectancy in the community property until the termination of the marriage relation in California by divorce or death. On the other hand, the appellees contend that Mrs. Kessler acquired a vested ownership interest in one-half of the community property while domiciled in California, and that this identifiable one-half interest continues to be hers, even though she and the decedent were domiciled in Ohio at the time of his death. Section 161a, California Civil Code, enacted in 1927, provides as follows: "The respective interests of the husband and wife in community property during continuance of the marriage relation are present, existing and equal interests under the management and control of the husband as is provided in sections 172 and 172a of the Civil Code. This section shall be construed as defining the respective interests and rights of husband and wife in community property." The plain meaning of this provision is that the wife's ownership interest is equal to the husband's. If he has a vested interest, as he obviously does, then she also has a vested interest, otherwise the word, "equal," means nothing. If she has no vested interest then he can have none, which would be absurd. The words "present" and "existing," reinforce the conclusion that both husband and wife have equal vested interests in community property in California. The California courts have defined the wife's ownership interest in community property as a vested interest during the continuance of the marriage relation. . . .

Although it is easy to confuse management rights with ownership rights, it is clear that the management rights conferred upon the husband by Section 172, California Civil Code, do not detract from the wife's vested ownership rights in community property acquired during the marriage relation. To say that the husband's powers of management and control over the wife's equal interest in the community property are property rights owned by the husband would be to deny that the wife has the equal interest in the community property which Section 161a confers. In fact, it is well settled in California that the husband, in exercising his right of management, acts as a fiduciary with respect to the one-half interest in the community property owned by the wife. . . . Defuniak, Commonwealth v. Terjen: *Common Law Mutilates Community Property*, 43 Va. L. Rev. 49 (1957). . . .

Although the General Assembly apparently could lawfully impose a tax upon the cessation of an exercise of powers of management and control of a vested community property interest, even if we assume there was such a cessation at the death of the decedent in the instant case, the General Assembly has not done so.

In my opinion, one-half interest in the 28,700 shares of stock acquired by Mr. Kessler while the Kesslers were domiciled in California belonged to Mrs. Kessler at the time of the death of her husband in Ohio, and thus were not subject to the Ohio succession tax.

NOTES AND PROBLEMS

1.   At the time this case was decided, California law gave management powers over the community to the husband. Later, California amended its law to provide that, "either spouse has the management and control of the community property, . . . but both spouses, either personally or by a duly authorized agent, must join in executing any instrument [alienating the property for longer than one year]." Had this statute been in effect at the time, would the result of the case have been the same?

2.   Suppose a couple acquires property in Ohio, then moves to California. Since the property retains the character it had in Ohio, and since California law does not provide for the surviving spouse to "elect against the will," this would appear to leave a gap. California law attempts to fill it with the concept of "quasi-community property," which is referred to briefly in the case. It allows the surviving spouse to take half of property acquired by a decedent "while domiciled elsewhere which would have been community property if the spouse who acquired the property had been domiciled in this state at the time of its acquisition." Cal. Fam. Code § 125. See generally Comment, *Community Property and the Problem of Migration*, 66 Wash. U. L.Q. 773 (1988); Annot., 14 A.L.R.3d 404 (1967).

3.   Are the contents of the laws and statutes of a foreign jurisdiction a question of fact or of law? The traditional rule is the former, requiring proof and submission to the finder of fact. See 9 J.H. Wigmore, Treatise on the Anglo-American System of Evidence § 2558 (3d ed. 1940). The Uniform Judicial Notice of Foreign Law Act promulgated in 1936 by the National Conference of Commissioners on Uniform State Laws, by contrast, treated it as a question of law, reserving its interpretation for determination by the judge alone. A form of the Act was adopted by many American states, but NCCUSL withdrew its recommendation of the Act in 1966; consequently the Act does not appear in Uniform Laws Annotated. At the federal level, the Act has been substantially replaced by Fed. R. Civ. P. 44.1.

D.   Homestead Rights

Still another form of marital interest, established by statute or even by the state constitution in many jurisdictions, is the right to a homestead exemption from the claims of creditors of either spouse. It is a property interest that cannot be defeated by the conveyance by one spouse without the other's consent. The homestead exemption generally applies to a married couple's principal residence.

The residence is normally defined as a dwelling and the land on which it is located, the extent sometimes being limited to a certain area or value, or both. In some states, a homestead right is not self-executing; there must be a recorded declaration of homestead, defining its extent.

As a shield against the claims of creditors, the homestead is sometimes of limited effectiveness. This is because the homestead is typically limited to a stated value. That value, adequate when enacted into law, can become outmoded.

Still, the objective of homestead is to protect the eligible property from the claims of creditors and from alienation by one of the spouses without the other's consent, and thus to insure a home during the marriage and for the life of the surviving spouse, and in some jurisdictions, for the minority of surviving children.

Like the elective share, a right of homestead may not be defeated by the will of the deceased spouse. In some states, the survivor must elect against the will, however.

Claims for money that had made purchase or improvement of homestead property possible are not defeated by this right. Thus, a claimant for repayment of a down payment for the otherwise eligible property, the lender of loan proceeds secured by a purchase money mortgage, or a mechanic's lienor who has improved or otherwise added value to the property, is not subject to homestead rights.

Other creditors can reach homestead property (that is, subject it to levy and sale) to the extent that its value or acreage exceeds the permitted exemption.

V. CONCURRENT ESTATES

A. Basic Characteristics

Concurrent estates permit co-ownership of land by two or more persons. A feature basic to them all is the right of each tenant to possess the whole. This should be familiar from considering parcels of land owned by a family unit. It may violate a family understanding for one member to enter another's room, for example, but no legally cognizable wrong arises therefrom. It is a right held by all tenants. Co-owners may agree among themselves to give exclusive possession to one of their number, however, and they can agree to share the burdens of property ownership in any fashion they wish. If any of them wishes to end the co-ownership, that tenant also has the right to partition the property, causing it to be divided into its several parts or else sold where such a division in kind is impracticable. Partition may be sought by judicial order or by agreement among the tenants.

The common law recognized four principal types of concurrent estates from an early date: joint tenancy, tenancy in common, tenancy by the entirety, and coparcenary. Coparcenary existed where lands passed to two or more female descendants by operation of law, normally where no male descendant survived. It became obsolete with the end of the system of primogeniture. The other three, although subject to statutory change in many jurisdictions, are more or less intact. They may exist in both real and personal property, and are often used, among other things, for the ownership of bank accounts and automobiles. Other than tenancy by the entirety, which exists only between spouses, the concurrent estates may exist in two persons or in more than two persons.

Joint tenancy. Joint tenants were regarded as holding *per my et per tout* at common law (by the half and by the whole). This meant that each owned an undivided interest in the whole, and that upon the death of one tenant, the property passed automatically to the survivor(s). This feature, the element which distinguishes it from tenancy in common, is also called the *ius accrescendi*, signaling the right of the surviving tenant to succeed to the estate without the formalities of inheritance. It is what allows the joint tenancy to be used as an "estate planning device" by which property passes outside of probate. *right of survivorship*

At common law, four unities were required for the creation of a joint tenancy: interest, time, title and possession. If there were two tenants, the estate became a tenancy in common if any of the unities was severed. A conveyance by one tenant severed the unities of time and title, thus automatically ending the joint tenancy and rendering the grantee a tenant in common with the original tenant. If there were three or more original joint tenants, and one tenant acted so as to destroy the unities, the tenancy continued between the others, but a tenancy in common was created between the grantee and the other tenants. These unities meant:

> Title: All joint tenants must acquire title by the same instrument or by joint *(How?)* adverse possession;

> Time: The interest of all joint tenants must be acquired at the same time;

> Interest: The shares of all joint tenants must be equal, undivided, and *(what?)* identical in duration;

> Possession: All joint tenants have equal rights to possess the whole, in the absence of express agreement to the contrary.

A very common way of creating a joint tenancy is to convey property "to A and B as joint tenants, and not as tenants in common." This is done to make the grantor's intention safe against the argument that a tenancy in common also involves a form of "joint" ownership and that the term was used in a general sense. Blackstone referred to this as adding "express words of exclusion as well as description." 2 Bl. Comm. *180. Sometimes, drafters also add express mention that the right of survivorship between the tenants is intended. In creating a joint tenancy, you will be well advised to consult the precedents in your jurisdiction for the best form to use.

no right of survivorship

Tenancy in common. Only the unity of possession is necessary to create or perpetuate a tenancy in common. Tenants in common have an undivided interest in the property, but there is no survivorship right. Thus, upon the death of each tenant in common, the undivided share passes to the takers under that tenant's will or by intestacy. In earlier days, the presumption was that a grant to named individuals created a joint tenancy. Today, by statute or judicial decision, the opposite presumption prevails. A conveyance "to A and B" creates a tenancy in common. However, it remains very common for draftsmen to insert specific mention that A and B are to take as tenants in common in order to avoid possibilities for argument.

Tenancy by the entirety. A tenancy by the entirety (or by the entireties) can exist only between spouses. They hold as one person, and (unlike estates held in dower and curtesy) the surviving spouse takes the whole upon the death of the other. Although spouses acting together can sever the tenancy by the entirety, neither acting alone can do so. Nor does either spouse have the individual right to partition. Divorce does terminate a tenancy by the entirety, however, because it also terminates the marriage that is the essential feature. Only thirteen American states now recognize tenancies by the entirety; in them, the estates are normally created by conveying "to A and B, husband and wife, as tenants by the entirety." In *United States v. Craft*, 535 U.S. 274 (2002), the U.S. Supreme Court held that a federal tax lien attached to a husband's interest in land held with his wife as tenants by the entirety. The Supreme Court's decision made an evident inroad on the basis of this tenancy; it remains to be seen how far its utility (and continued viability) has been undermined.

PROBLEMS

Suppose O conveys land "to A, B, and C as joint tenants and not as tenants in common." What is the state of the title to the land in the following cases:

a. A dies, devising her interest in the land to X.

b. B conveys his interest to Y.

c. B conveys his interest to A.

d. C leases her interest to Z for five years.

e. A dies, survived by H in a jurisdiction where the right to curtesy exists.

f. B marries C.

g. A, B, and C agree to hold as tenants in common.

B. Creation of Concurrent Tenancies

Despite the apparent clarity of the different categories of concurrent tenancies and the existence of legal presumptions that resolve many apparently uncertain cases, difficulties have not been altogether eliminated in the creation of concurrent tenancies.

CAMP v. CAMP
260 S.E.2d 243 (Va. 1979)

COMPTON, J.

In this appeal, we must construe a deed to determine the title acquired by a mother and son to real property conveyed to them "as tenants in common with the right of survivorship as at common law." . . . .

The issue arose in the following manner, as revealed by the pleadings and a summary statement of the facts prepared by the trial judge. In 1955, Robert Camp, Jr., unmarried, and appellee Tincy Camp, his mother, agreed to purchase a house and lot located in the City of Richmond. Tincy Camp consulted a Richmond attorney who, at her request, drew the deed in question, which was duly executed and admitted to record.

The deed contained the usual formal parts. The premise included the names of the three grantors as "parties of the first part" and the son and mother as "parties of the second part." The next paragraph contained the consideration, the recital of payment of purchase money, and the granting clause (there was no habendum), as follows:

> That for and in consideration of the sum of Ten ($10.00) Dollars, receipt whereof is hereby acknowledged, and other good and valuable consideration, the said parties of the first part do grant and convey with general warranty of title unto the said parties of the second part, as tenants in common with the right of survivorship as at common law, the following described real estate, to-wit:

Next came the description followed by a paragraph making the conveyance subject to recorded restrictions affecting the property. Then the deed provided for assumption by the grantees of the obligations of two prior deeds of trust on the property. These provisions were followed by a paragraph containing the English covenants of title and by the conclusion executed by all five parties.

Robert Camp, Jr., married appellant Hilda Camp in 1956. He died in 1966 survived by his widow, six children (who are also appellants), and by his mother. Thereafter, a dispute arose between the mother and the widow as to the ownership of the property in question.

Subsequently, the widow, in her own name and on behalf of her children, filed the instant petition for declaratory judgment in equity against the mother asserting that the property was conveyed to mother and son as tenants in common and seeking a declaration that the widow and children had "a one-half legal interest in said property." In response, the mother maintained she was a joint tenant under the deed and, because she survived her son, had a fee simple interest in the property.

The chancellor received the ore tenus testimony of the attorney who drew the deed and, after considering argument of counsel for the parties, decided in favor of the mother. The trial court, in the August 1977 order appealed from, found that when the deed was drafted, the intention of the mother and son was to have the real estate conveyed to them as joint tenants with the right of survivorship as at common law. The court also found that the attorney "was in error . . . as to the correct terminology to be used to create survivorship between the parties," that "tenants in common" was intended to be "joint tenants," and "that it manifestly appear[ed] to the court from the tenor of the deed and from the evidence in the case, that it was intended that the part of the first to die should then belong to the other." Consequently, the court below ruled that the real estate passed by operation of law to the mother, Tincy Camp, in fee simple. We think the trial court erred.

Initially, several fundamental rules for the construction of deeds should be reviewed. The prime consideration, as with any writing, is to determine the intention of the parties executing the instrument. The intention, including a finding as to the estate conveyed, should be ascertained from the language used in the deed, if possible. *Phipps v. Leftwich*, 216 Va. 706, 710, 222 S.E.2d 536, 539 (1976). If the language is explicit and the intention is thereby free from doubt, such intention is controlling, if not contrary to law or to public policy, and auxiliary rules of construction should not be used. 4 H. Tiffany, The Law of Real Property § 977 (3d ed. 1975). If, on the other hand, the instrument is uncertain and ambiguous, oral evidence may be received to show all the attendant circumstances existing at the time the deed was executed, including the situation of the parties and their relationship. But "[p]arol contemporaneous evidence is, in general, inadmissible to contradict or vary the terms of a valid written instrument [because] . . . [t]he writing is the only outward and visible expression of the meaning of the parties, and to allow it to be varied or contradicted by verbal testimony of what passed at or before its making, would be to postpone the more certain and reliable mode of proof, to the more precarious and less trustworthy; to prefer the less good to the best evidence." 2 J. Minor, Institutes of Common and Statute Law 1059 (4th ed. 1892). Finally, where two clauses are irreconcilably repugnant in a deed, the first prevails. *Mills v. Embrey*, 166 Va. 383, 387, 186 S.E. 47, 49 (1936). The foregoing rule is to be applied, however, only in the case of "rigorous necessity" and when the two clauses are absolutely incapable of reconciliation. 2 J. Minor, *supra*.

Against this background, we now turn to the facts of this case. The attorney who drew the deed, testifying 22 years after the event, stated that he recalled talking to Tincy Camp about preparing the deed. She told counsel, he said, that her son was to buy the property for her and that the son wanted her to live there for the remainder of her life. The attorney stated the mother said the "longer liver" of the mother and son was "to get all of the property." Counsel testified he had never before drawn a deed between "tenants by the entireties" except when a husband and wife were involved and, because of this, he consulted other attorneys about the problem. They told him, he testified, that he should use the phrase "tenants in common" instead of "tenants by the entireties" when the deed did not involve husband and wife. The attorney further testified that the grantees intended to receive the property "with the right of survivorship between them."

It is manifest from the trial court's ruling that the chancellor considered all of the foregoing evidence dehors the deed in reaching his decision. Yet, as we have noted, the terms of a valid deed may not be varied or contradicted by testimonial evidence of that which passed at or before its making. Consequently, the trial court should not have relied on the attorney's statements dealing with the intention of the parties. Thus, we shall cast aside that evidence and examine the deed, uncertain in meaning, in the light of the circumstances under which it was written.

The remaining evidence merely shows that residential urban property was to be purchased by a mother and her unmarried son, and that the mother consulted counsel with reference to the purchase. No definitive conclusion can be drawn from those meager facts as to the parties' intention with reference to the nature of the title to be acquired. Turning to the provisions of the instrument as contained within its four corners, we likewise obtain little, if any, guidance as to the parties' intention, except as revealed by the disputed provision. We do know from the deed that the mother and son became obligated to pay the unpaid balances on prior encumbrances affecting the property. But that fact may not be the basis for a positive judgment as to the parties' intention. Such an obligation would just as likely be incurred by tenants in common as by joint tenants. . . . .

Consequently, we are left with the disputed provision of the deed as the sole means to ascertain the parties' intention about the title to be acquired. The language "as tenants in common" is totally repugnant to the words "with the right of survivorship as at common law." The two portions are absolutely incapable of being reconciled. Accordingly, we are left with no alternative but to hold, applying the foregoing rule of repugnant clauses to this situation, that the portion first appearing in the deed controls, and that the mother and son were conveyed the property as tenants in common, not as joint tenants. The effect of this holding is, of course, to treat the latter portion of the disputed provision as surplusage. This is a case of "rigorous necessity" in which the harsh common-law rule must be applied if the deed is to have some effect rather than being a nullity.

. . . .

For these reasons, the order appealed from will be reversed and final judgment will be entered here decreeing that Robert Camp. Jr. and Tincy Camp took the property as tenants in common under the 1955 deed. Reversed and final judgment.

POFF, J., dissenting. I respectfully dissent. The majority's conclusion results from a mechanistic application of an arbitrary rule devised for other cases and offends the spirit, if not the letter, of statutes enacted by the General Assembly.

Under Code § 55-20, the interest of a "joint tenant" passes at death "as if he had been a tenant in common." Yet, the legislature has not abolished the estate of joint tenancy; § 55-21 states that: "The preceding section (§ 55-20) shall not apply to . . . an estate conveyed or devised to persons in their own right when it manifestly appears from the tenor of the instrument that it was intended the part of the one dying should then belong to the others." Thus, the fundamental issue in this case is whether "it manifestly appears from the tenor of the instrument that it was intended the part of the one dying should then belong to the others." I believe such an intent so appears from the face of this deed.

While it is true that a tenant in common has no right of survivorship, it is also true that a survivorship interest is the interest distinguishing a joint tenancy from a tenancy in common. The use of the phrase "as tenants in common with the right of survivorship as at common law" was obviously an attempt, albeit inartful, to create a joint tenancy by appending a right of survivorship to a tenancy in common. Why would the words "with the right of survivorship as at common law" be used except to create a right of survivorship? In my view, the language the majority considers "surplusage" is the very language that manifests the intent that "the part of the one dying should then belong to the [survivor]."

Since the two parts of the phrase in dispute are reconcilable, the rule of *Mills v. Embrey*, 166 Va. 383, 186 S.E. 47 (1936), designed for cases involving two irreconcilably repugnant clauses, does not apply. Adhering to the rule prescribed by the legislature, I would affirm the chancellor's construction of the deed.

C.   Relations Among Concurrent Tenants

The holders of any concurrent estate enjoy the unity of possession. This gives each cotenant the right to possess and enjoy the whole. Accordingly, a cotenant in exclusive possession does not owe rent to the other cotenants.

Conversely, no cotenant has the right to exclude the other cotenants. Such exclusion would be an ouster, enabling the ousted cotenant to regain possession (and a share of any profits). Indeed, if the ousted cotenant did not bring an action, he or she could eventually lose title by adverse possession.

It frequently happens that not all cotenants are in possession at any given time. It is worth repeating that this is not, by itself, an ouster (and would not lead to title by adverse possession) because each cotenant has the right to possess the whole. Still, when not all cotenants are in possession, questions arise about the rights and obligations of the cotenants who are in possession with respect to those who are not.

The rule at common law was that cotenants in possession may treat the property as their own. There were (and are) two important limitations on this rule, however. First, the Statute of Anne in 1704 (4 Anne c. 16 § 27), as strictly interpreted by the English judges, required cotenants in possession to account to the other cotenants for any rents received from a third person. Most American jurisdictions follow this English statute, either by legislation or by declaring it to be part of their common law. Indeed, some American jurisdictions extend the statute to other forms of income and profits generated by the cotenant in possession himself or herself, rather than being limited to income and profits from a third party. For example, suppose G transferred land "to A and B" as cotenants. A occupied the land; B lived elsewhere. A removed and sold minerals from the land, earning a net profit. In some U.S. jurisdictions, the duty to account (rather than the duty to avoid waste, see the next paragraph) would apply to these facts, meaning that B would be entitled to a pro rata share of the profits. If A refuses to pay, B may bring an action of account to force the payment. See, e.g., *White v. Smyth*, 214 S.W.2d 967 (Tex. 1948).

The second limitation to the rule at common law (that cotenants in possession may treat the property as their own) is that a cotenant in possession may not permit or cause the property to suffer permanent damage, known as "waste." An action for waste has been available to cotenants out of possession since the Statute of Westminster II in 1285 (13 Edw. I c. 22). What constitutes waste varies widely from one U.S. jurisdiction to another, and even when damage such as cutting timber or removing minerals is labeled waste, a typical remedy is simply the same as we have already observed for rents and profits: an accounting to the other cotenants for the net profits received. Rarely is the traditional English penalty for waste — treble damages — imposed against cotenants by American courts. But it does happen. See, e.g., *Watts v. Krebs*, 962 P.2d 387 (Idaho 1998). See also Iowa Code § 658.1A ("If a guardian, tenant for life or years, joint tenant, or tenant in common of real property commit waste thereon, that person is liable to pay three times the damages which have resulted from such waste, to the person who is entitled to sue therefor.").

If the cotenants in possession spend money on the property without the consent (express or implied) of the cotenants not in possession, the extent to which the former may require contribution from the latter depends on whether the expenditures were for necessary repairs or for improvements. If for improvements, the widespread rule is that no contribution is required. (At least, this is true while the cotenancy exists. In an action for partition (to end the cotenancy), the cotenants in possession can obtain contribution as a part of the final accounting if the improvements increased the value of the land.) If the expenditures were for necessary repairs, American jurisdictions are split. Some permit contribution if consent was requested but denied, on the theory that the withholding of consent was unreasonable; other jurisdictions do not permit contribution because no consent from the other cotenants was obtained. If a cotenant pays more than his or her share of an obligation imposed by law or by agreement — e.g., a tax or a mortgage — he or she of course is entitled to contribution from the other cotenants.

American authorities are divided on whether cotenants are fiduciaries to each other. Compare William Stoebuck & Dale Whitman, The Law of Property (3d ed. 2000) at 210 ("it seems clear that a fiduciary relationship exists among most groups of cotenants"), with Jesse Dukeminier et al., Property (7th ed. 2010) at 350 ("Generally, cotenants are not fiduciaries with respect to each other. Each cotenant is expected to look after his or her interest."). Perhaps the best that can be said is that, in some circumstances, courts have treated cotenants as if they have fiduciary obligations. If the cotenants are family members, for example, then sometimes the family relationship is held to imply a fiduciary relationship.

What if one cotenant purchases title to the property at a tax sale or foreclosure of a mortgage? Does the purchasing cotenant acquire the title for his or her sole benefit, or also for the benefit of the cotenants? It would seem that the former answer is logically compelled because title is acquired on the termination of the concurrent estate. With the concurrent estate at an end, so too should be any notion of a fiduciary relationship. But consider the following case.

MOSHER v. VAN BUSKIRK
144 A. 446 (N.J. Ch. 1929)

BACKES, V.C.

The title to the land involved was in the adult children and two infant grandchildren of William H. Mosher, his heirs-at-law. An adult heir filed a bill for partition. At the partition sale Elizabeth Van Buskirk, one of the heirs, was the purchaser at $5,000, under an arrangement among the adult heirs that she should bid in the land and hold it in trust for them for an advantageous price at private sale, and they authorized her to sell for not less than $14,000. It was the design to exclude the infant grandchildren. Mrs. Van Buskirk later entered into a contract to sell two of the three tracts, forty-eight acres, in Livingston, Essex County, to the Herbert Investment Company for $15,000. Thereupon the complainant, one of the heirs, apparently apprehensive, filed this bill to have the trust declared in favor of all the heirs, including the grandchildren, and the Herbert Investment Company, being let into the suit as a party defendant, filed a counter-claim to enforce the contract of sale.

Mrs. Van Buskirk's agreement to hold the land in trust for the adult heirs only is abortive. It was her and their duty as tenants in common in possession to protect the common title and consequently they could not defeat the common right of the infant grandchildren by collusively procuring a judicial sale to one of them for an inadequate price. In the circumstances the law raises a trust in favor of the infants.
. . .

Mrs. Van Buskirk's contract to sell the land, including the infants' estate, is unenforceable unless the contract be sanctioned by this court, and the court's consent will not be given unless the contract be of advantage to the infants. That is not shown. The burden is on the purchaser to show the consideration to be reasonably fair. *Bettcher v. Knapp*, 94 N.J. Eq. 433, 120 A. 39. The price is inadequate. The land is desirable for subdivision and it is in demand. There is dependable evidence that the tracts were worth $650 per acre at the time of the contract and that they are now worth $1,000. There is testimony that the price of $15,000 was fair, but [the] most convincing proof that it was not is the fact that the purchaser immediately sold his contract for $20,000. The court would fail in its duty if it ratified the sale of the infants' estate in the face of this proof.

The Herbert Investment Company's equitable defense of bona fide purchaser for value is not sustained. It had paid but $500 of the purchase price when it learned of the trust and the infants' beneficial interest. It is settled law that the defense of bona fide purchaser can be maintained only if the entire consideration price has been paid before notice of prior equities. Where part of the consideration has been paid before notice and he thus becomes a bona fide purchaser *pro tanto* the measure of his relief against the prior equity is the return of his money. *Haughwout v. Murphy*, 22 N.J. Eq. 531.

The trust will be declared, the Herbert Investment Company will be decreed its down money.

NOTES

1. Where one of several cotenants purchases title to the property at a tax sale or foreclosure of a mortgage, it is generally held that the title acquired by the purchasing cotenant inures to the benefit of the other cotenants. It is said that "there exists between cotenants a peculiar relationship of mutual trust and confidence in respect of the common estate" that requires that result. See, e.g., *Johnson v. Johnson*, 465 S.W.2d 309, 310 (Ark. 1971). The purchasing cotenant usually has a right of contribution from the others, however, so that they bear their fair share of the cost of removing the encumbrance.

2. Suppose one cotenant purposefully damages property held in joint tenancy. Can he or she be convicted under a statute that makes it a crime to "recklessly deface or damage the property of another person"? See *State v. Superior Court*, 936 P.2d 558 (Ariz. Ct. App. 1997). What should occur when one cotenant makes use of property held in cotenancy in such a way that a statute authorizes the forfeiture of property? See *Bennis v. Michigan*, 516 U.S. 442 (1996).

3. Do the rules regulating the rights of cotenants make sense from the point of view of equity or economic efficiency? And what about the difference between the law's treatment of repairs to the premises and improvements that enhance the property's value? See Lawrence Berger, *An Analysis of the Economic Relations Between Cotenants*, 21 Ariz. L. Rev. 1015 (1979).

D.   The Termination of Joint Tenancies

Under traditional law, each joint tenant has the right to sever the tenancy and destroy the survivorship feature, even without the agreement of the others. The conveyance itself will destroy the four unities. The necessity of making that conveyance today is a matter of some uncertainty.

[handwritten: lady breaking joint tenancy.]

RIDDLE v. HARMON

102 Cal. App. 3d 524 (Cal. Ct. App. 1980)

POCHE, J.   *[handwritten: Court said any joint tenant can sever tenancy and destroy right of survivorship w/o agreement.]*

We must decide whether Frances Riddle, now deceased, unilaterally terminated a joint tenancy by conveying her interest from herself as joint tenant to herself as tenant in common. The trial court determined, via summary judgment quieting title to her widower, that she did not. The facts follow.

Mr. and Mrs. Riddle purchased a parcel of real estate, taking title as joint tenants. Several months before her death, Mrs. Riddle retained an attorney to plan her estate. After reviewing pertinent documents, he advised her that the property was held in joint tenancy and that, upon her death, the property would pass to her husband. Distressed upon learning this, she requested that the joint tenancy be terminated so that she could dispose of her interest by will. As a result, the attorney prepared a grant deed whereby Mrs. Riddle granted to herself an undivided one-half interest in the subject property. The document also provided that "The purpose of this Grant Deed is to terminate those joint tenancies formerly existing between the Grantor, FRANCES P. RIDDLE, and JACK C. RIDDLE, her husband. . . ." He also prepared a will disposing of Mrs. Riddle's interest in the property. Both the grant deed and will were executed on December 8, 1975. Mrs. Riddle died 20 days later.

The court below refused to sanction her plan to sever the joint tenancy and quieted title to the property in her husband. The executrix of the will of Frances Riddle appeals from that judgment.

The basic concept of a joint tenancy is that it is one estate which is taken jointly. Under the common law, four unities were essential to the creation and existence of an estate in joint tenancy: interest, time, title and possession. (*Tenhet v. Boswell* (1976) 18 Cal. 3d 150, 155, 133 Cal. Rptr. 10, 554 P.2d 330.) If one of the unities was destroyed, a tenancy in common remained. (*Id.*) Severance of the joint tenancy extinguishes the principal feature of that estate, the Jus accrescendi or right of survivorship. This "right" is a mere expectancy that arises "only upon success in the ultimate gamble — survival — and then only if the unity of the estate has not theretofore been destroyed by voluntary conveyance . . . , by partition proceedings . . . , by involuntary alienation under an execution . . . , or by any other action which operates to sever the joint tenancy." (*Id.*, at pp. 155–156, 133 Cal. Rptr. at p. 14, 554 P.2d at p. 334, citations omitted.)

An indisputable right of each joint tenant is the power to convey his or her separate estate by way of gift or otherwise without the knowledge or consent of the other joint tenant and to thereby terminate the joint tenancy. (*Delanoy v. Delanoy* (1932) 216 Cal. 23, 26, 13 P.2d 513; *Estate of Harris* (1937) 9 Cal. 2d 649, 658, 72 P.2d 873; *Wilk v. Vencill* (1947) 30 Cal. 2d 104, 108–109, 180 P.2d 351.) If a joint tenant conveys to a stranger and that person reconveys to the same tenant, then no revival of the joint tenancy occurs because the unities are destroyed. (*Hammond v. McArthur* (1947) 30 Cal. 2d 512, 183 P.2d 1; Comment, *Severance of Joint Tenancy in California* (1957) 8 Hastings L.J. 290, 291.) The former joint tenants become tenants in common.

At common law, one could not create a joint tenancy in himself and another by a direct conveyance. It was necessary for joint tenants to acquire their interests at the same time (unity of time) and by the same conveyancing instrument (unity of title). So, in order to create a valid joint tenancy where one of the proposed joint tenants already owned an interest in the property, it was first necessary to convey the property to a disinterested third person, a "strawman," who then conveyed the title to the ultimate grantees as joint tenants. This remains the prevailing practice in some jurisdictions. Other states, including California, have disregarded this application of the unities requirement "as one of the obsolete 'subtle and arbitrary distinctions and niceties of the feudal common law,' (and allow the creation of a valid joint tenancy without the use of a strawman)." (4 A. Powell on Real Property (1979) p. 616, p. 670, citation omitted.)

By amendment to its Civil Code, California became a pioneer in allowing the creation of a joint tenancy by direct transfer. Under authority of Civil Code section 683, a joint tenancy conveyance may be made from a "sole owner to himself and others," or from joint owners to themselves and others as specified in the code. (See Bowman, Real Estate Law in California (4th ed. 1975) p. 105.) The purpose of the amendment was to "avoid the necessity of making a conveyance through a dummy" in the statutorily enumerated situations. (Appendix to Journal of the Senate, California, Reg. Sess. 1955, Vol. 2, Third Progress Report to the Legislature, March 1955, p. 54.) Accordingly, in California, it is no longer necessary to use a strawman to create a joint tenancy. (*Donovan v. Donovan* (1963) 223 Cal. App. 2d 691, 697, 36 Cal. Rptr. 225.) This court is now asked to reexamine whether a strawman is required to terminate a joint tenancy.

Twelve years ago, in *Clark v. Carter* (1968) 265 Cal. App. 2d 291, 295, 70 Cal. Rptr. 923, the Court of Appeal considered the same question and found the strawman to be indispensable. As in the instant case, the joint tenants in *Clark* were husband and wife. The day before Mrs. Clark died, she executed two documents without her husband's knowledge or consent: (1) a quitclaim deed conveying her undivided half interest in certain real property from herself as joint tenant to herself as tenant in common, and (2) an assignment of her undivided half interest in a deed of trust from herself as joint tenant to herself as tenant in common. These documents were held insufficient to sever the joint tenancy.

After summarizing joint tenancy principles, the court reasoned that:

> [U]nder California law, a transfer of property presupposes participation by at least two parties, namely a grantor and a grantee. Both are essential to the efficacy of a deed, and they cannot be the same person. A transfer of property requires that title be conveyed by one living person to another

(Civ. Code § 1039). Foreign authority also exists to the effect that a person cannot convey to himself alone, and if he does so, he still holds under the original title. Similarly, it was the common law rule that in every property conveyance there be a grantor, a grantee, and a thing granted. Moreover, the grantor could not make himself the grantee by conveying an estate to himself. (*Clark, supra*, at pp. 295–96, citations omitted.)

That "two-to-transfer" notion stems from the English common law feoffment ceremony with livery of seisin. (Swenson and Degnon, *Severance of Joint Tenancies* (1954) 33 Minn.L.Rev. 466, 467.) If the ceremony took place upon the land being conveyed, the grantor (feoffor) would hand a symbol of the land, such as a lump of earth or a twig, to the grantee (feoffee). (Burby, Real Property (3d ed. 1966) p. 281.) In order to complete the investiture of seisin it was necessary that the feoffor completely relinquish possession of the land to the feoffee. (Moynihan, Preliminary Survey of the Law of Real Property (1940) p. 86.) It is apparent from the requirement of livery of seisin that one could not enfeoff oneself — that is, one could not be both grantor and grantee in a single transaction. Handing oneself a dirt clod is ungainly. Just as livery of seisin has become obsolete, so should ancient vestiges of that ceremony give way to modern conveyancing realities.

"We are given to justifying our tolerance for anachronistic precedents by rationalizing that they have engendered so much reliance as to preclude their liquidation. Sometimes, however, we assume reliance when in fact it has been dissipated by the patent weakness of the precedent. Those who plead reliance do not necessarily practice it." (Traynor, *No Magic Words Could Do It Justice* (1961) 49 Cal. L. Rev. 615, 622–623.) Thus, undaunted by the *Clark* case, resourceful attorneys have worked out an inventory of methods to evade the rule that one cannot be both grantor and grantee simultaneously.

The most familiar technique for unilateral termination is use of an intermediary "strawman" blessed in the case of *Burke v. Stevens* (1968) 264 Cal. App. 2d 30, 70 Cal. Rptr. 87. There, Mrs. Burke carried out a secret plan to terminate a joint tenancy that existed between her husband and herself in certain real property. The steps to accomplish this objective involved: (1) a letter written from Mrs. Burke to her attorney directing him to prepare a power of attorney naming him as her attorney in fact for the purpose of terminating the joint tenancy; (2) her execution and delivery of the power of attorney; (3) her attorney's execution and delivery of a quitclaim deed conveying Mrs. Burke's interest in the property to a third party, who was an office associate of the attorney in fact; (4) the third party's execution and delivery of a quitclaim deed reconveying that interest to Mrs. Burke on the following day. The *Burke* court sanctioned this method of terminating the joint tenancy, noting at one point: "While the actions of the wife, from the standpoint of a theoretically perfect marriage, are subject to ethical criticism, and her stealthy approach to the solution of the problems facing her is not to be acclaimed, the question before this court is not what should have been done ideally in a perfect marriage, but whether the decedent and her attorneys acted in a legally permissible manner." (*Burke, supra*, at p. 34, 70 Cal. Rptr. at p. 91.)

Another creative method of terminating a joint tenancy appears in *Reiss v. Reiss* (1941) 45 Cal. App. 2d 740, 114 P.2d 718. There a trust was used. For the purpose of destroying the incident of survivorship, Mrs. Reiss transferred bare legal title to her son, as trustee of a trust for her use and benefit. The son promised to reconvey the property to his mother or to whomever she selected at any time upon her demand. (*Id.*, at 746, 114 P.2d 718.) The court upheld this arrangement, stating, "[w]e are of the opinion that the clearly expressed desire of Rosa Reiss to terminate the joint tenancy arrangement was effectively accomplished by the transfer of the legal title to her son for her expressed specific purpose of having the control and the right of disposition of her half of the property." (*Id.*, at 747, 114 P.2d at 722.)

In view of the rituals that are available to unilaterally terminate a joint tenancy, there is little virtue in steadfastly adhering to cumbersome feudal law requirements. "It is revolting to have no better reason for a rule of law than that so it was laid down in the time of Henry IV. It is still more revolting if the grounds upon which it was laid down have vanished long since, and the rule simply persists from blind imitation of the past." (Justice Oliver Wendell Holmes, Collected Legal Papers (1920) 187.) Common sense as well as legal efficiency dictate that a joint tenant should be able to accomplish directly what he or she could otherwise achieve indirectly by use of elaborate legal fictions.

Moreover, this will not be the first time that a court has allowed a joint tenant to unilaterally sever a joint tenancy without the use of an intermediary. In *Hendrickson v. Minneapolis Federal Sav. & L. Ass'n* (Minn. 1968) 281 Minn. 462, 161 N.W.2d 688, decided one month after *Clark*, the Minnesota Supreme Court held that a tenancy in common resulted from one joint tenant's execution of a "[D]eclaration of election to sever survivorship of joint tenancy." No fictional transfer by conveyance and reconveyance through a strawman was required.

Our decision does not create new powers for a joint tenant. A universal right of each joint tenant is the power to effect a severance and destroy the right of survivorship by conveyance of his or her joint tenancy interest to another "person." (Swenson and Degnon, *supra*, at 469.) "If an indestructible right of survivorship is desired — that is, one which may not be destroyed by one tenant — that may be accomplished by creating a joint life estate with a contingent remainder in fee to the survivor; a tenancy in common in simple fee with an executory interest in the survivor; or a fee simple to take effect in possession in the future." (Swenson and Degnon, *supra*, at 469, fn. omitted.)

We discard the archaic rule that one cannot enfeoff oneself which, if applied, would defeat the clear intention of the grantor. There is no question but that the decedent here could have accomplished her objective termination of the joint tenancy by one of a variety of circuitous processes. We reject the rationale of the *Clark* case because it rests on a common law notion whose reason for existence vanished about the time that grant deeds and title companies replaced colorful dirt clod ceremonies as the way to transfer title to real property. One joint tenant may unilaterally sever the joint tenancy without the use of an intermediary device.

The judgment is reversed.

NOTES

1.   Does the decision in *Riddle* increase the likelihood of opportunistic behavior by joint tenants? Professor Samuel Fetters argues that it does — permitting an effective "secret severance" allows one joint tenant a tempting choice: either taking all the property if he survives (by suppressing the deed of severance) or by passing half to his heirs if he dies first (by having someone produce the deed of severance after his death). See Samuel M. Fetters, *An Invitation to Commit Fraud: Secret Destruction of Joint Tenant Survivorship Rights*, 55 Fordham L. Rev. 173 (1986). Is that what happened in *Riddle*?

2.   One Minnesota judge, asked to reject the four unities requirement, refused to do so in all cases, saying that it was "premature to do away with the 'unities' doctrine as its usefulness may better be determined on a case-by-case basis." *Cornell v. Heirs of Walik*, 235 N.W.2d 828, 829 n.1 (Minn. 1975). Is such a case-by-case determination actually possible? Is it desirable? The State of Minnesota now has a statute which provides: "The common law requirement for unity of time, title, interest, and possession in the creation of a joint tenancy is abolished." Minn. Stat. § 500.19, subd. 3.

ALLISON v. POWELL
481 A.2d 1215 (Pa. Super. Ct. 1984)

WIEAND, J.

Does a pending action to partition real estate owned by joint tenants with right of survivorship survive the death of the joint tenant at whose instance the action was commenced? The trial court held that the action did not survive and entered judgment on the pleadings in favor of the surviving joint tenant and against the executrix of the deceased joint tenant. We affirm.

Harold N. Allison and Robert O. and Mary Jane Powell, husband and wife, owned title to real estate in Chester County as joint tenants with right of survivorship. On July 31, 1981, Harold Allison filed a complaint in equity seeking to obtain partition of the real estate. The complaint was not served on Mr. and Mrs. Powell until March 9, 1982. Meanwhile, on January 10, 1982, Harold Allison had died. Powells' answer to the complaint contained an averment that Allison had died and that title had passed to the Powells by right of survivorship. Allison's executrix was substituted as a party plaintiff for the decedent and filed a Reply containing New Matter in which she alleged an agreement "that the defendants would pay Twenty Thousand ($20,000.00) Dollars in cash to the plaintiff" for Allison's interest in the real estate. As evidence thereof, she attached a copy of a letter sent by Allison's attorney to Powells' attorney as follows:

November 4, 1981
Frank L. White, Jr., Esquire
Duane, Morris and Heckscher
45 Darby Road, Paoli, Pa., 19301

Re: Mr. and Mrs. Robert O. Powell

Dear Mr. White:

My client will accept the $20,000.00 cash to sign off the property. This would mean that all costs of transfer would have to be borne by your client. He is pressing me to bring the matter to a rapid conclusion and I would appreciate hearing from you as soon as possible what the time frame the Powells would need to get the money.

Sincerely, William R. Keen, Jr.

The trial court sustained a motion for judgment on the pleadings and dismissed the complaint. On appeal, Allison's executrix argues that the commencement of the action for partition, together with the decedent's alleged agreement to sell his interest, manifested an irrevocable determination by the parties to sever the joint tenancy.

A joint tenancy in real estate with right of survivorship is created by the co-existence of the four unities of interest, title, time and possession. *Sheridan v. Lucey*, 395 Pa. 306, 307, 149 A.2d 444, 445 (1959); *Yannopoulos v. Sophos*, 243 Pa.Super. 454, 459, 365 A.2d 1312, 1314 (1976). A joint tenancy in real estate with right of survivorship is severable by the act, voluntary or involuntary, of either of the parties. *Angier v. Worrell*, 346 Pa. 450, 452, 31 A.2d 87, 88 (1943). When this occurs, the tenancy becomes one in common. *Yannopoulos v. Sophos, supra*, 243 Pa.Super. at 459, 365 A.2d at 1314. Although the joint tenancy may be severed by a joint tenant's act which destroys one of the four unities, "that act must be of sufficient manifestation that the actor is unable to retreat from the position of creating a severance of the joint tenancy." *Sheridan v. Lucey, supra*, 395 Pa. at 309, 149 A.2d at 446. Accord: *Yannopoulos v. Sophos, supra*, 243 Pa.Super. at 461, 365 A.2d at 1315. The commencement of a partition action is alone insufficient to sever a joint tenancy, because the plaintiff-joint tenant can always retreat from his demand for partition so long as a final judgment has not been entered. *Sheridan v. Lucey, supra*. It follows that in the event a joint tenant dies during the pendency of the action to partition, title to the jointly owned real estate passes by right of survivorship to the surviving joint tenant. *Id.*

In *Yannopoulos v. Sophos, supra*, this Court held that a valid and enforceable agreement to sell the real estate by both joint tenants was sufficient to sever the joint tenancy. In such case, the Court said, the agreement was effective to pass equitable title to the real estate to the purchaser. Because the parties had placed themselves in a position from which they could not retreat, the Court said, the joint tenancy was severed upon execution of the sales agreement. *Id.* at 461, 365 A.2d at 1315.

In the case sub judice, it is readily apparent that no enforceable agreement of sale existed between Allison and the Powells. Counsel's letter of November 4, 1981 evidenced not an agreement but only continuing negotiations between the attorneys for the parties. Moreover, even if we were somehow to conclude that terms and conditions of sale had been agreed upon, it is patently clear that failure to comply with the statute of frauds rendered the agreement unenforceable. Not only were the terms of the sale not defined, but neither the real estate to be sold nor the grantor was identified in counsel's letter. See: *American Leasing v. Morrison Co.*, 308 Pa.Super. 318, 322, 454 A.2d 555, 557 (1982); *Williams v. Stewart*, 194 Pa.Super. 601, 607, 168 A.2d 769, 771 (1961). The purported agreement was not signed by the grantor-seller, and there is no suggestion that the seller's attorney was duly authorized in writing to execute a written agreement on his client's behalf. See: *Charles v. Henry*, 460 Pa. 673, 677, 334 A.2d 289, 291 (1975). The trial court properly concluded, therefore, that the parties had not executed an enforceable agreement. *Polka v. May*, 383 Pa. 80, 118 A.2d 154 (1955); *Weir v. Rahon*, 279 Pa.Super. 508, 512, 421 A.2d 315, 317 (1980). Without an enforceable agreement, the parties had not placed themselves in a position from which they could not retreat. Equitable title had not passed from Allison during his lifetime; and the four unities of the joint tenancy remained undisturbed. See: *Gerlock v. Gabel*, 380 Pa. 471, 476, 112 A.2d 78, 81 (1955). See also: 1 Ladner on Conveyancing in Pennsylvania § 2:08 (rev. 4th ed. 1979). It is apparent from the pleadings, therefore, that Allison had not divested himself of his interest in the real estate prior to his death.

Because appellant's decedent had not divested himself of his interest in the real estate prior to death, his interest passed upon death by right of survivorship to the surviving joint tenant. The joint tenancy had not been severed, and the right of survivorship was not defeated by the pendency of the action in partition.

The order entering judgment on the pleadings is affirmed.

NOTES

1.   The prevalence of divorce has created an increasing number of problems relating to title of land the couple owned as joint tenants. A divorce decree severs a tenancy by the entirety automatically, but not a joint tenancy. Unless there is a property settlement incident to the divorce, the question of whether there has been a severance invites courts to scrutinize the parties' behavior in search of an agreement to sever the joint tenancy. A few states have enacted statutes terminating the right of survivorship and creating a tenancy in common in its place. E.g., Ohio Rev. Code § 5302.20(C)(5).

2.   Suppose one joint tenant kills the other. Is the joint tenancy severed? None of the four unities is destroyed thereby, but allowing the survivor to take the whole has seemed wrong to observers and judges. Uniform Probate Code § 2-803 creates a severance by operation of law if one joint tenant "feloniously and intentionally kills another."

3.   What does the future hold for concurrent tenancies? Professor Orth suggests that the tenancy in common seems destined to flourish; it is "ideally suited to the modern ethos of individualism" because of its "freedom of alienation and devise, its inheritable shares, and its right of partition." He goes on to suggest that the real question "is whether any form of concurrent ownership other than tenancies in common will continue to exist." 4 Thompson on Real Property § 32.09.

VI. REVERSIONS, POSSIBILITIES OF REVERTER, AND RIGHTS OF ENTRY

When owners of property convey or devise less than their entire ownership interest, they necessarily retain an interest in the property. The name given to the retained interest depends on (1) the estate held by the owner before the transfer and (2) the estate transferred. Here are the most common examples. If the owner of an estate in fee simple transfers a present estate less than fee simple — for example, a life estate or a lease — the interest retained by the owner is called a *reversion*. If the owner of an estate in fee simple absolute transfers a fee simple determinable, the interest retained by the owner is called a *possibility of reverter*. If the owner of an estate in fee simple absolute transfers a fee simple subject to a condition subsequent, the interest retained by the owner is called a *right of entry for condition broken*, often called simply a *right of entry*. The reversion, the possibility of reverter, and the right of entry are future interests. They are interests in which the right to possession of the property is postponed, and depending on the terms of the future interest, possession might or might not occur eventually. The reversion, the possibility of reverter, and the right of entry are known as *reversionary* future interests because they are retained by or created in the grantor. They are contrasted with the two nonreversionary future interests — the remainder and the executory interest — which the grantor creates in a grantee. The nonreversionary future interests are discussed in later sections.

The reversionary future interests can arise by implication of law even if they are not stated expressly, e.g. in a deed or will. This means that a grant from O "to A for life" leaves a reversion in O, even if the reversion is not expressly mentioned in the grant. Similarly a grant from O "to A for life, remainder to B if B survives A" leaves a reversion in O, since B may not survive A. Still, it is common practice and good drafting to state these interests expressly. Doing so leaves no doubt about the grantor's intention to retain the interest.

Reversions have long been held to be fully transferable, both inter vivos and at death. Thus, in the examples in the preceding paragraph, O can transfer O's reversion to a third party during O's lifetime. If O dies with the reversion, the reversion passes under O's will to O's devisees or, if O does not have an effective will, to O's heirs in intestacy.

The rules governing the transferability of possibilities of reverter and rights of entry are more complex. In most American jurisdictions, these interests are descendible (capable of passing by intestacy) and devisable (capable of passing by will). With respect to transfer inter vivos, American jurisdictions are divided. Some permit the inter vivos transfer of one or both of the possibility of reverter and right of entry. Others do not.

All three of the reversionary future interests are exempt from the Rule Against Perpetuities; hence in the absence of legislation restricting their duration, they continue to exist indefinitely. Some states have passed laws limiting the period during which these future interests may exist. These statutes extinguish the future interests if they are too remote, turning (for example) what was a defeasible fee simple estate into a fee simple absolute.

VILLAGE OF PEORIA HEIGHTS v. KEITHLEY
132 N.E. 532 (Ill. 1921)

THOMPSON, J.

Prior to January 4, 1904, G.W.H. Gilbert was the owner of the major part of Seiberling's addition to the village of Peoria Heights. On that date he conveyed by warranty deed to the village, lots 28 and 29 in block 6 of said addition, the expressed consideration being "the sum of $600 in hand paid and the observance of the provisions hereinafter named." The deed contained the following conditions:

> The consideration for this deed is that the village shall use the said lots for the purpose of a town hall and the location of the village water works and other village buildings of a public nature, provided, however, that the said village shall by ordinance provide that no saloon license for the sale of any intoxicating, malt, vinous, mixed or fermented liquors, and no license for the keeping of dram-shops or saloons, shall ever be granted to operate within said Seiberling's addition to Peoria Heights, and if there is a breach of such conditions, which form the consideration of his deed, such breach shall work a forfeiture of the said lots and the title to same shall revert to the grantors, their heirs and assigns, together with all the improvements thereon.

No cash was paid by the village. February 1, 1904, the village passed an ordinance prohibiting the sale of intoxicating liquors in the addition. In 1907 the village purchased a lot outside of the addition and built thereon a village hall. The village has erected no buildings on the lots in question. It has occasionally piled drain tile on the lots, and about the time this litigation was begun it set a few posts around the lots and stretched a single wire on these posts. Since the conveyance to the village the lots have been listed as public property and have been exempted from general taxation, and special assessments against said lots have been paid by the village. December 20, 1910, Gilbert and wife by an unconditional form of Warranty deed conveyed said property to appellant, Arthur Keithley. There is no evidence that appellant paid anything for these lots nor that he has ever had possession of them. March 1, 1920, Gilbert by quit-claim deed conveyed to the village all his present and future interests in said lots, including all interest that he then had or could or might acquire through forfeiture or otherwise. December 30, 1920, appellee filed its bill in the circuit court of Peoria county, praying that the deed to appellant be canceled and removed as a cloud upon appellee's title to said lots and for other relief. Appellant answered the bill, admitting most of the averments of fact but denying that appellee has any right, title or interest in the lots. Appellant filed his cross-bill asking that the title be quieted in him. The cross-bill was dismissed on demurrer. The court found that appellee was in possession of the lots in question, and that at the time Gilbert executed his deed to appellant he had no interest in the premises capable of being assigned or conveyed and that appellant obtained no interest and that his deed was void. A decree was entered canceling appellant's deed and declaring that he had no interest in the premises. From that decree this appeal was prosecuted.

By his deed of January 4, 1904, Gilbert conveyed to appellee the lots in question on certain conditions, and provided that if these conditions were not fulfilled the village would forfeit the lots and the title to them would revert to him. This conveyance clearly created in appellee an estate on condition subsequent. (1 Tiffany on Real Property, 2d ed. sec. 78; Kales on Estates and Future Interests, 2d ed. sec. 219; 8 R.C.L. 1109.) This being true, a breach of the condition can be taken advantage of only by the grantor or his heirs. His grantee, whether before or after the breach, acquires no right to enforce a forfeiture. (*O'Donnell v. Robson*, 239 Ill. 634; *Golconda Northern Railway v. Gulf Lines Railroad*, 265 *id.* 194.) Appellant acquired no title to or right or interest in the lots by the conveyance of December 20, 1910, and the court properly canceled the deed and removed it as a cloud upon appellee's title.

The decree of the circuit court is affirmed.

NOTES AND PROBLEMS

1. If the Village had broken the conditions of the 1904 deed between 1910 and 1920, could Gilbert or his heirs have enforced the right of entry, or is it destroyed by the attempt to alienate it to Keithley? Compare Restatement of Property § 140 (1940) (no forfeiture) with *United Methodist Church v. Dobbins*, 369 N.Y.S.2d 817 (N.Y. App. Div. 1975) (forfeiture).

2. O conveys Blackacre "to A for life, but if A ceases to use the property for residential purposes, O shall have the right to re-enter and retake the property." Ten years later, O conveys all his interest in Blackacre to B. Then A ceases to use the premises for residential purposes. Has B any right to Blackacre? Compare *Rice v. Boston & Worcester R.R.*, 94 Mass. (12 Allen) 141 (1866), with *Jones v. Oklahoma City*, 145 P.2d 971 (1943). See also Am. L. Prop. §§ 4.68–69 (A.J. Casner ed., 1952).

3. Suppose O conveys Blackacre to A and his heirs for so long as the premises are used for residential purposes, expressly reserving a possibility of reverter in himself and his heirs. Years later, the property ceases to be so used, but none of O's heirs appear to claim the property. Does the property escheat to the state as unowned, or does it remain in the successors to A? Would it make a difference if it were a fee simple subject to a condition subsequent?

TRUSTEES OF CALVARY PRESBYTERIAN
CHURCH v. PUTNAM
162 N.E. 601 (N.Y. 1928)

Appeal, by permission, from a judgment of the Appellate Division of the Supreme Court in the fourth judicial department, entered November 9, 1927, unanimously affirming a judgment in favor of plaintiff entered upon a decision of the court on trial at Special Term.

O'BRIEN, J.

Sixty-six years ago George Palmer and Harriet his wife conveyed to plaintiff a parcel of realty on Delaware avenue in Buffalo. In their deed several conditions were attached, one of which prescribes that the premises shall be perpetually maintained for religious purposes, and a covenant provides that upon the breach of any of the conditions the grantor or his heirs may re-enter and take possession, and thereupon plaintiff's estate shall cease and determine. Mr. Palmer died two years after the execution of that deed and thirty-five years ago all his living heirs and next of kin, for a consideration, gave a quitclaim deed and covenanted with plaintiff that they would not at any time or in any manner enter upon or interfere with the enjoyment of the premises by plaintiff or its successors or assigns nor in any manner seek to enforce the covenants and conditions of the deed of 1862. In 1926 plaintiff brought this action against all the heirs then living. The complaint alleges that, in the event of a breach of the conditions of the deed, defendants claim a right of reverter and re-entry and it prays for a judgment declaring, among other things, whether any possibility of reverter exists as to defendants and whether they or any other Palmer heirs who may hereafter be born would have any interest in or claim upon the premises in the nature of a right of re-entry or otherwise. It seeks a general declaration respecting the validity of its own title and the rights of the Palmer heirs.

The conditions imposed by the deed clearly are subsequent rather than precedent. No one can doubt this proposition. Indeed, all the parties assume or concede it. Conditions subsequent are not favored. They are strictly construed because they tend to destroy estates. Public interest dictates that real property shall be readily transferable and that titles shall be reasonably marketable. *Nicoll v. New York & Erie R.R. Co.*, 12 N.Y. 121, 131; *Seneca Nation v. Appleby*, 196 N.Y. 318, 323; *St. Stephen's Church v. Church of Transfiguration*, 201 N.Y. 1, 10. The grantor himself certainly was authorized to release the grantee from its obligation to perform conditions and, even prior to a breach, to waive his possible right of reverter. He could have taken any course agreeable to him by which this possible right might have been divested. No one disputes the proposition that, as long as the conditions existed unbroken, all interest in the estate remained out of the grantor and his heirs. Until the contingency happens the whole title is in the grantee. *Vail v. L.I.R.R. Co.*, 106 N.Y. 283, 287. Neither the grantor nor his heirs possessed anything except a right to take advantage of a breach. This is not an estate. *Fowler v. Coates*, 201 N.Y. 257. This possibility of reverter, this possible right of re-entry, passes to the heirs not by descent but by force of representation. *Upington v. Corrigan*, 151 N.Y. 143.

After condition broken, the heirs could unquestionably waive their rights of re-entry. The case is, therefore, reduced to this issue; the grantor, in behalf of himself and his heirs, born and unborn, having power, prior to a breach, to waive all possible right of reverter and the heirs having the same power, after condition broken, can the living heirs, prior to a breach, waive their own possible rights and foreclose those of unborn heirs? In respect to remote contingent rights in an estate, the policy of the law encourages their release to parties already possessed of some substantial estate. All rights, titles and actions may be released to the terre-tenant for securing his repose and quiet and for avoiding contentions and suits. *Miller v. Emans*, 19 N.Y. 384, 390, 391. No rule of law is invoked which would tend to prevent the living heirs, prior to a breach, from waiving a right or a possible right of which they could thereafter divest themselves. No reason presents itself for the creation of such a rule. If, prior to the release by the heirs in 1893, plaintiff had violated the conditions, they, in their representative capacity, had also been vested with power either to stand passive or approve actively of the violation. They could have exercised or have refrained from exercising any power which would have existed in the grantor had he been alive. They represented him and his possible rights. The rights of unborn heirs are surely no more extensive than those of the grantor which were represented by the living heirs. The judgment should be affirmed, with costs.

NOTE

Suppose the grantor or the heirs of the grantor give, on one occasion, permission to a grantee, allowing the use of the property contrary to the terms of the grant. Alternatively, they allow use of a portion of the premises for a purpose that would otherwise trigger the right of entry. There is authority for the proposition that they would not later be able to assert the right of entry as to either a subsequent violation or a violation as to the portion of the premises not covered by the initial permission. This is the so-called "Rule in Dumpor's Case." It is discussed in Simes & Smith, The Law of Future Interests § 260 (3d ed. 2003).

RICHARDSON v. HOLMAN
33 So. 2d 641 (Fla. 1948)

On June 24, 1910, Eugene Holtsinger, by warranty deed, conveyed to Tampa and Sulphur Springs Traction Company a certain described parcel of land, with the following reservation:

> Provided however, and this conveyance is made subject to and upon the express condition that should the party of the second part cease to use the foregoing land for railroad purposes, then and in that event the title to said property shall *revert to and vest in the said Eugene Holtsinger and his heirs and assigns*.

On December 26, 1910, Eugene Holtsinger and his wife, by warranty deed, conveyed to G. A. Henderson and Monroe C. Gaither, all of Government Lots 1-25-28. The description in this deed included the lands conveyed by Holtsinger to Tampa and Sulphur Springs Traction Company and contained the following reservation: "This deed is made subject to a certain deed from the parties of the first part to the Tampa and Sulphur Springs Traction Company, a corporation, dated the 24th day of June, A.D. 1910, and recorded in Deed Book 128 on page 35 of the land records of Hillsborough County, State of Florida."

Some time in 1945 or 1946, the Tampa and Sulphur Springs Traction Company, hereinafter referred to as the Traction Company, ceased to operate street cars and abandoned the property in question. The appellants have by mesne conveyance become successors in title to Henderson and Gaither, instituted suit in ejectment to recover title and possession of the premises. The appellee, as defendant, demurred to the declaration, his demurrer was sustained, the suit was dismissed and plaintiffs prosecuted this appeal.

As frequently occurs, the parties are not in accord as to what questions are brought up for determination. Appellants urge two questions and appellee urges three, but in our view, they all turn on that of whether or not the reservation in the deed by Holtsinger to the Traction Company left any right of reverter in the grantor that he could assign and if so, did he assign it to Henderson and Gaither by the deed he executed to them.

Appellants contend that the reservation in the deed to the Traction Company created an estate in fee simple determinable, while appellee asserts that it created an estate upon condition subsequent. It seems to be admitted that if it creates an estate upon condition subsequent, the power reserved to terminate under the common law, was personal to the grantor and his heirs and was not assignable, while if it created a fee simple determinable, then there was the possibility of reverter which might or might not be assignable under the common law.

Appellee contends that whether or not a fee simple determinable or an estate upon condition subsequent is created, depends upon the words employed by the grantor in the conveying instrument. The words employed are of course a very important determining factor, at the same time words or phrases in isolation will not be permitted to defeat the purpose of the grantor when that may be unmistakably gleaned from the four corners of the instrument.

We do not think it essential to the disposition of the question here, to participate in a discourse in semantics on the difference between a fee simple determinable and estate on condition subsequent, when a possibility of reverter is or is not alienable, or when a fee is qualified, what constitutes a naked possibility, a conditional limitation, or any other uncertain interest in lands. These old common law concepts had much to do with conveyance in their day, but even in States like Florida, where the common law is in effect except as repealed or substituted by statute, many of them have become obsolete or have been set aside.

Some of the text books say, that the distinction between a fee simple determinable and an estate on condition subsequent, is that as to the former, the words creating it limit the continuation of the estate to the time preceding the happening of the contingency, while in the latter, the words creating the condition do not originally limit the term, but merely permit its termination upon the happening of the contingency. The main difference is whether the estate automatically expires upon the occurrence of a stated event, whether the conveyor has the power to terminate it upon the happening of the event if he desires to do so.

Appellee reviews a great many cases from different jurisdictions to show that the reservation in the deed from Holtsinger to the Traction Company created an estate on condition subsequent which properly construed, left no assignable interest in the grantor, and being so, he contends that no right of reverter passed to appellants by virtue of having acquired their title through Henderson and Gaither.

A review of the cases cited in both briefs discloses that even under the common law, some of them hold that a possibility of reverter attached to a fee simple determinable and may be alienated, while others interpret the same rule to the contrary. Some of these cases hold that the rule in the United States is different because the reasons that actuated the common law rule have vanished. In our view, the sounder rule supported by Blackstone, Kent and a wealth of decisions is that the operation and effect of a deed depends less on artificial rules than it does on the application of common sense and sound equity to the object and purpose of the contract under review.

We do not think there is any escape from the conclusion that the reservation in the deed from Holsinger to the Traction Company withheld the possibility of reverter which materialized when the traction company ceased to use the lands for street railroad purposes. The words of reverter "The title to said property shall revert to and vest in the said Eugene Holtsinger and his heirs," could hardly be more conclusive as to his purpose. The record discloses that this deed conveyed a strip of land 222 feet long by 65 feet wide, and that six months later the second deed by the same grantor to Henderson and Gaither conveyed the same with other lands, subject to the reservation in the deed to the Traction Company.

Subject to the reservation in the deed to the traction company, the deed to Henderson and Gaither carried the usual covenants of warranty, seisin and possession, and we think vested in the grantees all of Holtsinger's title, including his right to reverter, preserved in the deed to the Traction Company. The language used in both deeds is not materially different from that used under similar circumstances, in conveying to Churches, schools, lodges and other institutions for benevolent or public purposes, and when not used for the purpose of the grant, the lands so conveyed have been held to revert.

As heretofore pointed out, the final test to determine whether the language in a deed creates an estate upon condition subsequent, or an estate in fee simple determinable, is whether the language used provides for automatic reverter when the determining event takes place, or whether under the terms used, the grantor or his heirs were clothed with the right immediately to step in and declare a reverter. The language employed in the reservation in the deed to the traction company is consistent with, and we think sufficient to accomplish an automatic reverter.

In the latter holding we do not overlook appellee's contention supported by numerous authorities to the contrary, but we think that both the statutes and the philosophy of conveyancing in Florida, rule the point against him. We think the reservation in the deed to the traction company contained a possibility of reverter to Holtsinger and that it materialized when the traction company ceased to use the lands for street railway purposes. It is also our view that Holtsinger parted with his right of reverter, including all other interest he had in the lands, when he executed the deed to Henderson and Gaither.

We are not unmindful of the fact that the case law is in hopeless conflict on the point of whether or not a possibility of reverter may be assigned. Some of this confusion arises from a muddled view as to what constitutes an estate upon conditions subsequent and what constitutes a fee simple determinable. Some of it arises on account of statutes affecting these concepts, some of it arises from confusing it with other common law rules, and concepts. Notwithstanding the confusion, there is a line of well reasoned cases that supports the assignment of this and other uncertain interest in land. *Hamilton v. City of Jackson*, 157 Miss. 284. 127 So. 302; *Caruthers v. Leonard*, (Tex.) 254 S.W. 779; *Juif v. Dillman*, 287 Mich. 35. 282 N.W. 892; *Battistone v. Banulski*, 110 Conn. 267, 147 Atl. 820; American Law

Institute, Restatement of the law of property.

The statutes of Florida abrogate many of these old feudal concepts and contemplates that any interest in land may be the subject of conveyance. Section 689.01, Florida Statutes 1941, provides that "No estate or interest of freehold, or for a term of more than one year, or an uncertain interest of, in, or out of any messuages, lands, tenements or hereditaments, shall be created, made, granted, transferred or released in any other manner than by instrument in writing, signed in the presence of two subscribing witnesses by the parties creating, making, granting, conveying, transferring or releasing such estates, interest for a term more than one year." Section 731.05, Florida Statutes 1941, and other statutes with reference to passing by will is of similar import, so it appears that in Florida all restraints on alienation have been removed. A possibility of reverter is an uncertain interest in land that may under our law be conveyed or devised, regardless of what the common law rule was.

The foregoing and other statutes are the product of a growing liberal philosophy in the matter of land conveyancing coupled with a purpose to shake off the old restrictions of the common law, such as livery of seisin and sale of pretended titles sometimes spoken of as maintenance. The latter has never had a place in the law of this country and our system of recording deeds rendered the former obsolete. Under the feudal system possession was an indispensable prerequisite to alienation, but at present the tendency is to permit one to alienate any interest in lands he may claim. It will be noted that our statute, among other things, permits the alienation of "hereditaments" which under the common law of England included lands and tenements, whether corporeal or incorporeal, real, personal or mixed.

In fine, the right of contract so rigidly canalized by the common law, has, by the constitution and statutes, been liberalized till at the present any citizen who is sui juris may enter into any contract that is not illegal, fraudulent, immoral or contrary to public policy. Under the common law a right of action, choses in action, future or contingent interests, possible and existing estates or interests, were not assignable, but all of these are now assignable by statute or in equity. In view of the law as thus reflected in this state, we see no escape from this conclusion.

It is accordingly our view that Holtsinger's deed to the traction company reserved a reversionary interest in the lands in question which he conveyed to Henderson and Gaither and they in turn assigned it to their successors in title. It follows that the order sustaining the demurrer to the declaration was erroneous.

Reversed.

VII.   REMAINDERS

A.   Creation and Classification of Remainders

Sir Edward Coke defined a remainder as "a remnant of an estate in lands or tenements, expectant upon a particular estate created with the same at one time." Co. Lit. 143a. The American Law Institute has formulated this definition: "any future interest limited in favor of a transferee in such manner that it can become a present interest upon the expiration of all prior interests simultaneously created, and cannot divest any interest except an interest left in the transferor." Restatement of Property § 156 (1936).

Perhaps the most obvious difference between the two definitions is the exclusion of interests in personal property from Coke's definition. It is now settled, however, that future interests, including remainders, can be created in personalty. Indeed, most trusts today consist primarily of personalty rather than land.

Taken together, Coke's definition and the definition from the Restatement of Property point to five essential characteristics of a remainder:

(1)   a remainder is created simultaneously with and in the same document as the prior possessory interest, and is what "remains" after that prior interest;

(2)   the prior possessory interest must be a "particular estate," a term of art referring to an estate less than fee simple, such as a life estate or a lease;

(3)   the prior possessory interest must be immediately prior to the remainder and there must be no gap in seisin between them; if there is, the future interest is not a remainder but instead an executory interest (a future interest discussed in the next section);

(4)   the prior estate must end naturally, meaning that it cannot be cut short by a divesting event (in which case, the future interest can take effect only as an executory interest); and,

(5)   the remainder must be created in a "transferee," meaning someone other than the grantor.

Here is a standard example. Suppose O conveys Blackacre "to A for life, and at A's death to B and her heirs." This grant creates a life estate in A and a remainder in B. The future interest in B satisfies all five of the requirements above. (1) B's remainder is created at the same time and in the same document as A's life estate and is what remains after A's life estate expires. (2) The prior estate, held by A, is a particular estate. (3) A's life estate is immediately prior to the remainder, and there is no gap in seisin in between. (4) A's life estate will end naturally, on the natural termination of A's life, rather than being cut short by a divesting event. (5) B is a transferee.

A remainder can be a remainder in fee or for life or for a term of years. A remainder need not be limited to a named individual. In practice, remainders are often created in a class, such as "A's descendants," or in a charity.

Remainders are classified into four main categories. A remainder is *indefeasibly vested* if it is not subject to any conditions or limitations. In other words, the remainder is certain to become a possessory fee simple absolute at some time in the future. A remainder is *vested subject to open* if it is subject to no conditions precedent and is in favor of a class (such as "A's descendants") that contains at least one living member and is still "open," i.e., where it is possible for additional individuals to become class members, typically through birth or adoption. A remainder is *vested subject to divestment* if it is subject to one or more conditions subsequent ("to B and his heirs, but if"). A remainder is *contingent* if it is subject to one or more conditions precedent ("to B and his heirs if").

Here are some illustrations. Suppose that O conveys "to A for life," and then follows A's life estate with one of the following:

(1) ". . . then to B and B's heirs." This is an indefeasibly vested remainder. Under traditional rules, there is no implied condition that B survive A. If B dies before A, B's remainder passes to B's heirs or devisees.

(2) ". . . then to B's children" and B is childless at the time of the conveyance. This is a contingent remainder and will remain so until B has a child, either by birth or adoption. When B has a child, then that child will be said to have a vested remainder subject to open (upon the birth of each sibling, the first child's share will be reduced pro rata). As a point of good drafting, it is better to use the word "descendants" rather than "children" in this conveyance. This change in wording will permit B's grandchildren to share the remainder; otherwise the parent's share, predeceasing A, may pass by will or descent to others.

(3) ". . . but when A dies, to B and B's heirs." This is an indefeasibly vested remainder. The words "but when A dies" are words of limitation for A's life estate and really do no more than define it, indicating when A's life estate will naturally terminate. These words are not a condition on the remainder.

(4) ". . . then, if B survives A, to B and B's heirs." B has a contingent remainder. The express condition of survivorship is a condition precedent. Once the remainder is classified as contingent, O has not given away all O has; B's contingent remainder is followed by a reversion in O, subject to divestment upon B's surviving A.

When the words "but if B does not survive A, to C and C's heirs" are added to this conveyance, B and C's remainders are both contingent; they are called alternative contingent remainders, meaning that the condition precedent attached to one interest is the opposite of the condition attached to the other. At the time of the termination of the life estate, one of the two conditions will be satisfied and one of the two remainders will vest in possession. While the remainders are both contingent, O technically retains a reversion.

(5) ". . . then to B for life, then to C and C's heirs." B's remainder for life is vested. In technical parlance, it is *vested subject to limitational defeasance*, meaning that it will end naturally when B dies. The point to notice for present purposes is that it is *not* contingent. The fact that B must survive A is taken as inherent in the remainder for life, and is not viewed as a "condition" on it. C's remainder is indefeasibly vested.

(6) ". . . to B and B's heirs, but if B does not survive A, to C and C's heirs." B's remainder is vested subject to divestment. The condition of survivorship is phrased as a condition subsequent. The future interest is C is not a remainder because it will take effect, if at all, by divesting the interest in B. Recall that a remainder takes effect only on the natural termination of the prior estate, not by divesting it. C's interest is called an executory interest, discussed in the next section.

Does it matter whether a remainder is classified as vested or contingent? At common law, remainders and executory interests were descendible and devisable whether they were vested or contingent, but only vested remainders were alienable inter vivos. Contingent remainders and executory interests were not. Today, most U.S. jurisdictions consider all contingent future interests alienable inter vivos. For some other consequences of the classification of remainders, consider the following materials.

EDWARDS v. HAMMOND
3 Lev. 132, 83 Eng. Rep. 614 (C.P. 1683)

Ejectment upon not guilty, and special verdict, the case was. A copyholder of land, burrough English, surrendered to the use of himself for life, and after to the use of his eldest son and his heirs, if he live to the age of 21 years: provided, and upon condition, that if he die before 21, that then it shall remain to the surrenderer and his heirs. The surrenderer died, the youngest son entered; and the eldest son being 17 brought an ejectment; and the sole question was, whether the devise to the eldest son be upon condition precedent, or if the condition be subsequent? *scil.* that the estate in fee shall vest immediately upon the death of the father, to be divested if he die before 21. For the defendant it was argued, that the condition was precedent, and that the estate should descend to the youngest son in the mean time, or at least shall be in contingency and in abeyance 'till the first son shall attain to one and twenty; and so the eldest son has no title now, being no more than 17. On the other side it was argued, and so agreed by the Court; that though by the first words this may seem to be a condition precedent, yet, taking all the words together, this was not a condition *precedent*, but a present devise to the eldest son, subject to and defeasible by this condition subsequent, *scil.* his not attaining the age of 21. . . .

NOTES

1. Copyholders were free men holding land by unfree tenure. The freehold and seisin of the copyholder's estate resided in his lord. The copyholder's evidence of title was his copy of the roll of the court of the manor; the court's roll served as a form of land registry. The rules governing the landholding of a copyholder were not uniform, but were to be found in the custom of the manor concerned. Borough English was a custom whereby the youngest son, not the eldest son, inherited lands subject to the custom. See A.W.B. Simpson, A History of Land Law 14 (2d ed. 1986). The surrenderer in *Edwards* was trying to reverse this rule of inheritance by transferring (surrendering) his copyhold to his lord who would, upon the surrenderer's death, admit the grantee. The surrender would have been registered on the court rolls by the steward of the manor. The surrender did not completely cut out the surrenderer's youngest son, for by virtue of the custom of borough English, the surrenderer's youngest son was his heir and, as such, was scheduled to take the land if the eldest son failed to reach 21. Apparently, however, when the surrenderer died, the youngest son was admitted immediately; at least, he entered. This precipitated the action of ejectment, which was brought by the surrenderer's 17-year-old eldest son.

2. In *Edwards*, what was the result of holding that the remainder was vested subject to divestment? What would have happened if the court had held the remainder to be contingent?

life estate or fee simple?

GUILLIAMS v. KOONSMAN
279 S.W.2d 579 (Tex. 1955)

CALVERT, J.

If a condition precedent is used, it creates contingent remainder.

Our main problem involves the construction of the fourth paragraph of the will of J. J. Koonsman, deceased, which reads as follows:

> I give and devise to my son, Alvin Koonsman, all of my undivided interest in all of the remainder of my real property situated in Scurry County, Texas, which I may own at the time of my death, and to his child or children if any survive him, and in the event of Alvin's death without issue surviving him, then to my son and daughter, Jesse J. Koonsman and Mrs. Cora Guilliams, share and share alike, and to their heirs and assigns forever. . . .

The only evidence in the record before us, other than the will itself and the probate proceedings in connection therewith, is the testimony of Alvin Koonsman that J. J. Koonsman, the testator, died March 6, 1942, and that he (Alvin) has only one child, John Billy Koonsman, born October 15, 1942. From this testimony it appears that John Billy was in esse for the purpose of taking under the will on the date it became effective, that is, the date of J. J. Koonsman's death.

What is the meaning of the words "and to his child or children if any survive him" following the devise to Alvin? We have been cited to and have found no case squarely in point. If the words "if any survive him" had been omitted and we were to follow the weight of authority, heretofore noted, we would be compelled to hold that Alvin and his son, John Billy, took the first estate created as cotenants. But those words were not omitted, and we ascribe to them a two-fold effect: first, they limited the interest of Alvin Koonsman to a life estate, and secondly, they operated to make the remainder to be taken by the child or children of Alvin contingent rather than vested.

The words "if any survive him," qualifying the devise to the children of Alvin, clearly indicate that his children were not to take as cotenants with Alvin but were to take in succession to him, with the result that the devise to Alvin is limited to a life estate. No particular form of words is necessary to the creation of a life estate.

> It has been said that where the construction of a will devising property to one and his children is doubtful, the courts lean toward giving the parent a life estate, and that even a slight indication of an intention that the children shall not take jointly with the parent will give a life estate to the parent with a remainder to the children. 33 Am. Jur. 474.

The conclusion that the remainder in the child or children is contingent rather than vested is also impelled by the words "if any survive him." Survival is made a condition precedent to the vesting of the remainder rather than a condition of defeasance. While it has been said that "The law favors the vesting of estates at the earliest possible period, and will not construe a remainder as contingent where it can reasonably be taken as vested," *Caples v. Ward*, 107 Tex. 341, 179 S.W. 856, 858, nevertheless, when the will makes survival a condition precedent to the vesting of the remainder, it must be held to be contingent. . . . The rule for determining whether a remainder is vested or contingent is thus stated by Gray in his work on The Rule Against Perpetuities:

> If the conditional element is incorporated into the description of, or into the gift to the remainder-man, then the remainder is contingent; but if, after words giving a vested interest, a clause is added divesting it, the remainder is vested.

3d Ed., § 108(3), page 85. The rule as thus stated has been approved and adopted by the courts of this state. Here the condition of survival is incorporated into the gift to Alvin Koonsman's child or children.

There remains to be determined the nature of the estate devised to Jesse J. Koonsman and Mrs. Cora Guilliams by the fourth paragraph of the will. They are to take the fee "in the event of Alvin's death without issue surviving him." Their estate must be held to be a contingent remainder also. It is to take effect upon Alvin's death, but only if he dies "without issue surviving him." It is an alternative contingent remainder. . . .

The judgments of the trial court and Court of Civil Appeals are reformed to . . . decree that the true meaning and effect of the fourth paragraph of the will is that the plaintiff, Alvin Koonsman, is therein and thereby given an estate for life in the property therein described, with a remainder in fee to the child or children of Alvin Koonsman, conditioned upon their surviving him, and an alternative remainder in fee to Jesse J. Koonsman and Mrs. Cora Guilliams, or their heirs and assigns, conditioned on the death of Alvin Koonsman without a child or children surviving him, and as so reformed the judgments of those courts are affirmed.

NOTES

1.   A disposition to a named individual and his or her "children" or "issue" is ambiguous. Wild's Case, 6 Coke 16b (K.B. 1599), promulgated what has come to be known as the Rule in Wild's Case. The rule applied only to a devise of land and provided that, if the parent had no children at the date of the devise, the parent would take a fee tail estate; but, if the parent then had children, the parent and the children would take concurrently as joint tenants. The rule is repudiated in the Restatement Third of Property: Wills and Other Donative Transfers § 14.2, Comment f (2011). Under the Restatement Third, the presumptive meaning of a disposition to a named individual and his or her "children" or "issue," or a similar class-gift term, is that it creates successive rather than concurrent interests.

2.   Can you reconcile *Edwards* and *Guilliams*? *Guilliams* is supported by the Restatement of Property § 278 (1940), but a few courts have held that a disposition such as that in *Guilliams* creates a vested remainder subject to divestment. See, e.g., *Safe Deposit & Trust Co. of Baltimore v. Bouse*, 29 A.2d 906 (Md. 1943). Do you think the grantor, or the grantor's lawyer, intends different consequences by framing a condition as precedent or subsequent?

LINKOUS v. CANDLER
508 S.E.2d 657 (Ga. 1998)

Thompson, J.

Does the language of the trust agreement in this case indicate an intent to prohibit acceleration of the trust? Because such an intent need not be express, but can be implied from the four corners of the agreement, *Wetherbee v. First State Bank & Trust Co.*, 266 Ga. 364, 365, 466 S.E.2d 835 (1996), we hold that the trust agreement does indeed prohibit acceleration, and that the superior court erred in ruling otherwise.

On June 3, 1961, while in the midst of a pending divorce, C. Howard Candler, Jr. and Ruth O. Candler created an irrevocable trust in full settlement of Howard Candler's support obligations to Ruth Candler. Trust Company of Georgia (now SunTrust Bank) was named as trustee. The trust provided that Ruth Candler was to have a life estate in the net income of the trust assets and that, upon Ruth Candler's death, the net income of the trust was to be distributed among the then living children of Howard and Ruth Candler. The trust also provided for a per stirpes distribution to the issue of any child of Howard and Ruth Candler who pre-deceased Ruth Candler. Upon the death of the "last survivor" of Howard and Ruth Candler's children, the trust was to be divided equally among the "then living" grandchildren of Howard and Ruth Candler with the issue of any then deceased grandchild taking per stirpes its deceased parent's share.

At the time the trust was created, Howard and Ruth Candler had four living children: C.H. Candler III; Samuel O. Candler; Ruth C. Lovett; and Flora G. Candler Fuller. Howard Candler died in 1988, and Ruth Candler died on September 2, 1996. Ruth Candler was survived by three of her children: C.H. Candler III; Samuel O. Candler; and Flora G. Candler Fuller. (Ruth C. Lovett died before either one of her parents in 1964, leaving three children.)

On March 4, 1997 the surviving children of Howard and Ruth Candler filed a petition requesting the superior court to construe the 1961 trust agreement and give direction to the trustee with regard to its obligations under the agreement. The petition named the trustee, all 13 of the grandchildren of Howard and Ruth Candler, and "all otherwise unrepresented descendants, born and unborn" as respondents. The court appointed William J. Linkous, Jr., as guardian ad litem, to protect the interests of the unrepresented descendants of Howard and Ruth Candler. Thereafter, petitioners filed a written instrument, pursuant to OCGA § 53-2-115 seeking renunciation, release, and termination in full of their interests in the trust.

In a final order entered on September 17, 1997, the court ordered the trustee to distribute the trust to Howard and Ruth Candler's 13 grandchildren. The court reached that decision after concluding (1) that there was no language in the trust agreement which indicated an intent to prohibit acceleration; and (2) that petitioners' renunciation of their interests in the trust produced the same result as if they had predeceased Ruth Candler.

The guardian ad litem appeals. Relying upon *Wetherbee v. First State Bank & Trust Co.*, supra, he asserts that the trust agreement indicates an intent on the part of Howard and Ruth Candler to prohibit acceleration of the trust. We agree. . . .

In *Wetherbee*, Mr. Wetherbee created a trust for the maintenance and support of his wife for life. Upon his wife's death, a specified percentage of the trust was to be placed into a trust for each of his then living sons for their support for life. Upon the termination of the trust created for each son, the remainder was to go to his surviving wife and descendants. After Mr. Wetherbee died, his sons renounced their interests in the trust. When Mrs. Wetherbee died, the remaindermen sought to accelerate their interests. The Court observed that "the principle of acceleration of remainders is limited to those cases wherein the testator has not 'otherwise indicated' a contrary intent." *Wetherbee*, supra. The Court then found a contrary intent because the testator had provided that the holder of the future interest must survive the holder of the renounced interest. In so doing, the court stated that the indication of the testator's contrary intent need not be express, but may be implied from the provisions and language of the trust.

Wetherbee controls the outcome of this case. Just as the instrument in *Wetherbee* provided that the holder of the remainder (the wife and descendants) must survive the holder of the renounced life interest (the sons), so too the instrument in this case provides that the grandchildren must survive their parents in order to take their interests in the trust. Accordingly, just as the instrument in *Wetherbee* indicated an intent to prohibit acceleration, so too the instrument in this case must be viewed as indicating an intent to prohibit acceleration.

Although other jurisdictions might take an approach which differs from *Wetherbee*, see generally Anno., 7 A.L.R.4th 1084 (1981), it cannot be said that Georgia lies outside the mainstream in this regard. Many jurisdictions hold, as does Georgia, that a substitutionary gift in a will indicates a contrary intent on the part of the testator with respect to acceleration of the remainder interests. See, e.g., *Trenton Banking Co. v. Hawley*, 7 N.J. Super. 301, 70 A.2d 896 (1950) (the gift of the remainder was made to a class that would have to stay open until the death of the life beneficiary); *Bass v. Moore*, 229 N.C. 211, 49 S.E.2d 391 (1948) (the remaindermen's right of enjoyment was contingent upon whether they survived the life beneficiary); *Compton v. Rixey's Ex'rs.*, 124 Va. 548, 98 S.E. 651 (1919) (acceleration of remainder would be contrary to intent of testator); and *Cool v. Cool*, 54 Ind. 225 (1876) (no acceleration of the remainder when widow holder of life estate elected to take against the will). This rationale is logical, for if a class of remaindermen cannot be ascertained until the death of the life beneficiary, then acceleration must not have been contemplated by the testator.

The class of remaindermen in the Candler trust is subject to open by the birth of more grandchildren. In addition, it is subject to change by the death of a grandchild, entitling that grandchild's issue to take its share. This contingency does not expire until the death of the last of Howard and Ruth Candler's children. Therefore, the remaindermen cannot be ascertained until the last child of Howard and Ruth Candler has died. To hold otherwise would be contrary to the intent of the Candlers and would deprive potential class members of their share of the trust.

Judgment reversed.

NOTES

1. The Restatement of Property § 233 (1936) provides: "When an attempted prior interest fails because it is renounced by the person to whom it is limited, a succeeding interest is not accelerated so long as a condition precedent to such succeeding interest continues unfulfilled."

2. The Uniform Disclaimer of Property Interests Act § 6(b)(4) provides that "[U]pon the disclaimer of a preceding interest, a future interest held by a person other than the disclaimant takes effect as if the disclaimant had died or ceased to exist immediately before the time of distribution, but a future interest held by the disclaimant is not accelerated in possession or enjoyment." For discussion, see William LaPiana, *Uniform Disclaimer of Property Interests*, 14 Probate and Property 57 (2000).

BROWNING v. SACRISON
518 P.2d 656 (Or. 1974)

O'CONNELL, C.J.

This is a suit in which plaintiff seeks to have a provision in the will of Kate Webb construed. The question presented is whether the remainder devised to plaintiff's husband, Franklin Browning, now deceased, and his brother, Robert Sacrison, the defendant, was vested or contingent at the time of Mrs. Webb's death. The trial court found the remainder to be contingent. Plaintiff appeals.

Kate Webb was the maternal grandmother of Franklin Browning and Robert Sacrison. Her will, executed in 1943 when Franklin was 20 and Robert 13, contained the following provision (paragraph III):

> I give and devise to my daughter, Ada W. Sacrison, a life estate for the term of her natural life in and to all real property belonging to me at the time of my death, excepting only the residence property at Pilot Rock described in paragraph II of this will, with remainder over at the death of the said Ada W. Sacrison, share and share alike, to my grandsons, Francis Marion Browning[1] and Robert Stanley Browning,[2] or, if either of them be dead, then all to the other, subject to a like condition as to the use of the same or any portion of the proceeds thereof for Clyde Browning, as mentioned in paragraph II of this my last will.

Kate Webb died in 1954. She was survived by her daughter, Ada, and grandchildren, Franklin and Robert. At the time of her death, Mrs. Webb owned 960 acres of farmland in Umatilla County. This is the land devised by paragraph III of the will. Franklin died in 1972 without issue. He did not survive the life tenant Ada, who is still alive.

Plaintiff takes the position that the language in paragraph III of the will,

---

[1] Francis Marion Browning is the same person as Franklin M. Browning.

[2] Robert Stanley Browning is the same person as Robert Stanley Sacrison.

creating an interest in the two grandsons "or, if either of them be dead, then all to the other" refers to the death of the testatrix not the death of their mother Ada, the life tenant. Thus, she argues the estate vested at the time of Mrs. Webb's death.

Conversely, defendant contends that the grandsons each took a remainder contingent upon surviving the life tenant.

Plaintiff relies upon the constructional preference favoring the early vesting of estates. It cannot be denied that there is considerable case support, including our own cases, for the view that the law favors the early vesting of estates. And it is clear that at an earlier day the rule was widely, if not universally accepted. The policy reason for this preference is that it "quickens commerce in the ownership of property by facilitating alienability to a considerable degree." But with the passage of time the rule was eroded by exceptions and by a closer analysis of the rationale for the early vesting preference, until today that constructional preference probably no longer represents the prevailing view. The most severe criticism of the constructional preference for vesting is found in 5 American Law of Property, § 21.3 at 130 (Casner ed. 1952), where it is said:

> The preference for vested interests undoubtedly originated in connection with conveyances of interests in land and at a time in feudal England when contingent interests in land had not attained a dignified statute. Under such conditions, it may be reasonable to attribute to a transferor the intention to give the transferee an estate of recognized quality. Today, however, unfortunate tax consequences may follow a determination that an interest is vested and most transferors who consider all the consequences which attach to a vested interest are inclined to postpone vesting until the time set for enjoyment of the interest in possession. Thus continued adherence to this preference in modern times is at least of doubtful validity in many situations.

The foregoing critique has in turn been criticized for being a "harsh, unbalanced assessment of the rule, . . . as unfortunate as the more common tendency to accept the rule uncritically." Thus a middle position has evolved which urges that "what is needed is a more discriminating evaluation rather than outright rejection of the rule."

We adopt this latter approach. It is true that the reasons which prompted the creation of the rule favoring early vesting no longer obtain. Nevertheless, early vesting still may be desirable for other reasons which have application today.

On the other hand, the factors supporting early vesting must compete against other factors favoring the postponement of vesting. All of the factors "must be given their respective weights in the ultimate determination of the judicially ascertained intent of the conveyor." 3 Restatement, Property § 243 at 1209 (1940).

In the present case, competing with the constructional preference for early vesting is the preference for that construction which conforms more closely to the intent commonly prevalent among conveyors similarly situated than does any other possible construction. In modern law it is felt that when a devise is made to a life tenant with a remainder conditioned upon an ambiguous form of survivorship, the intent "commonly prevalent among conveyors similarly situated" is deemed to require that the remainderman survive the life tenant rather than the testator. Cf. 3 Restatement, Property § 264 (1940). The application of this constructional preference would make Franklin's interest subject to the condition that he survive his mother Ada, as the trial court held.

The trial court based its decision in part upon a comparison of the language in other parts of the will with the language in paragraph III. For example, paragraph II provided as follows:

> I give and devise to my grandsons, Francis Marion Browning and Robert Stanley Browning, share and share alike, the real property owned by me in the Town of Pilot Rock, in Umatilla County, Oregon, subject to the condition that no portion of said property or the proceeds thereof shall ever go to or be used for the benefit of their father, Clyde Browning, and if either of said grandchildren be not living at the time of my death, then the other shall take all of such property, subject to said condition.

In this paragraph the testatrix expressly designates that the time for vesting of the Pilot Rock property in the survivor shall be "at the time of my death." The trial court reasoned that "it must be assumed that when these specific words were not used [in paragraph III] after the estate of Ada Sacrison, but the words, 'or, if either of them be dead, then to the other,' the testatrix intended that the interest became vested at the time of the death of the life tenant, and not at the date of her death."

The principle employed by the trial court is well recognized as one of the canons of construction. However, it loses some of its force here because the disposition in paragraph II, being directly to the devisees or the survivor without the intervention of a life estate, would necessarily have to vest, if it were going to vest at all, upon the death of the testatrix and therefore the survivorship provision could not relate to any other person's death insofar as it affected the vesting of the estate. This factor, standing alone, therefore would not justify the trial court's decision.

The trial court did, however, point to another factor which we think is more significant in ascertaining the testatrix's intent. The trial court noted that "all provisions of the will specifically excluded Clyde Browning from sharing in any interest in the estate." The court then concluded that "[i]f the construction propounded by the plaintiff were to be followed, the grandsons of Kate Webb would have had a vested transferable interest at the death of Kate Webb, and had they died intestate without issue prior to the death of the life tenant, their father, Claude (sic) Browning would have shared in his interest to the estate of Kate Webb as an heir of his child, contrary to the testatrix's specific wishes."

To strengthen this conclusion, the trial court could have pointed out that at the time the will was executed in 1943 Robert was only 13, Franklin was 20, and neither of them was married. (Indeed, neither had married by 1954 when the testatrix died.) There was, then, at least in the case of Robert, a rather long period of time during which a beneficiary might die intestate and before marriage and/or the birth of issue could divert the estate from vesting in whole or in part in Clyde Browning. It must be noted, of course, that even if the estate is regarded as vesting only upon the death of Ada, the life tenant, the survivor who out-lived Ada might not have married or had issue, in which case Clyde would share in the estate upon his son's death.

Moreover, if a grandson did have issue and predeceased the life tenant, treating the vesting event as the death of Ada would result in the disinheritance of the grandson's issue. However, we can only indulge in assumptions as to her possible objectives. We think that the assumption made by the trial court, supported by the preference for the construction which more closely conforms to the intent commonly prevalent among testators similarly situated, is the most reasonable.

The decree of the trial court is affirmed.

NOTES

1. The desire to minimize tax consequences inspires an understandable desire to construe remainders as contingent. About the temptation to "reinterpret" the intention of the grantor, a Pennsylvania judge wrote: "It is incontestable that almost every settlor and testator desires to minimize his estate burden to the greatest extent possible. However, courts cannot be placed in the position of estate planners, charged with the task of reinterpreting deeds of trust and testamentary dispositions so as to generate the most favorable possible tax consequences for the estate. Rather, courts are obliged to construe the settlor's or testator's intent as evidenced by the language of the instrument itself, the overall scheme of distribution, and the surrounding circumstances." *In re Estate of Benson*, 285 A.2d 101, 106 (Pa. 1971).

2. The drafters of the Uniform Probate Code have adopted a rule that reverses the traditional preference for vested estates. UPC § 2-707(b) provides: "A future interest under the terms of a trust is contingent on the beneficiary's surviving the distribution date." Thus a grant "to T in trust for A for life, remainder to B and his heirs" would require B to survive A in order to take the remainder. If B does not survive A, the UPC creates a substitute gift in B's then-surviving descendants. The provision is criticized by Jesse Dukeminier, *The Uniform Probate Code Upends the Law of Remainders*, 94 Mich. L. Rev. 148 (1995), and defended by Lawrence Waggoner, *The Uniform Probate Code Extends Antilapse-Type Protection to Poorly Drafted Trusts*, 94 Mich. L. Rev. 2309 (1996).

3. What preference about vesting should courts adopt where general and potentially ambiguous language is used? Suppose, for example, a testator sets up a trust to last for twenty years, the proceeds "then to be distributed to my heirs at law"? Is heirship to be determined as of the date of the testator's death, or at the expiration of the twenty years? See Uniform Probate Code § 2-711.

B. Three Special Rules Regarding Remainders

unborn kids case

POPP v. BOND
28 So. 2d 259 (Fla. 1946)

TERRELL, J. *under destructibility, kids contingent remainder is extinguished.*

John B. Franke died testate, leaving his wife, Amelia A. Franke, and a daughter, Lucile Margarite Louise Franke, surviving. The widow has since deceased and the daughter was married and has two minor children, H. Leslie Popp, Jr., and John F. Popp. The father, H. L. Popp, has been duly appointed guardian of the minor children. Paragraph VIII of the John B. Franke will in so far as pertinent is as follows:

> Item VIII. I will and bequeath all the remainder of my property . . . to . . . my daughter, Lucile Margarite Louise Franke . . . to have and to hold for and during (her) natural life . . . and at death . . . , one-half of the remainder and fee thereof to the child or children of my daughter, Lucile Margarite Louise Franke, if any, and one-half thereof to the Theological Seminary of the Evangelical Lutheran Church at Chicago, Illinois . . . if my said daughter shall die without children surviving, then the entire remainder thereof shall go to the said Seminary.

The estate of John B. Franke has been closed and the interest of the Theological Seminary of the Evangelical Lutheran Church, at Chicago, has been acquired by the life tenant, who with her husband, H. L. Popp, individually and as guardian of the minor children, have agreed to sell the real estate devised under Paragraph VIII to the appellee, but he declined to pay for and accept the deed without a court decree holding the title to be merchantable. This cause was instituted on the part of appellants to coerce specific performance. Appellee answered the bill and the case was heard on an agreed statement of facts. The Chancellor found the title to be not merchantable, and this appeal is from [his] decree.

The question for determination is whether or not under the facts detailed the life tenant, Mrs. H. L. Popp, joined by her husband individually and as guardian of the minor children, can convey a fee simple title to the real estate devised under Paragraph VIII of the will to appellee, free and clear of all claims of future born children of the life tenant.

In our judgment this question is answered in the affirmative by *Blocker v. Blocker*, 103 Fla. 285, 137 So. 249. . . .

This holding was predicated on the rule of the common law which is in effect in this State and provides in substance that contingent remainders may be defeated by destroying or determining the particular estate upon which they depend, before the contingency happens whereby they became vested. The contingency involved here was the adverse claim of prospective children of the life tenant. Under the rule as above stated such a contingent remainder was extinguished when the title of the infant remaindermen in being was merged with that of the life tenant in appellee.

An examination of the final decree discloses that the Chancellor held the title not merchantable on authority of *Deem v. Miller et al.*, 303 Ill. 240, 135 N.E. 396, 25 A.L.R. 766, Annotation 770. It is quite true that the Illinois court there held that when a will, as in this case, creates a life estate with remainder to the children of the life tenant, the life tenant and the living children, by making a conveyance, do not destroy the interest of after born children, because the remainder is vested in quality, although contingent in quantity. This holding is in direct conflict with the holding in *Blocker v. Blocker* and other Florida cases cited, but we are not convinced that we should reverse these cases. In addition to being supported by the rule of the common law they are supported by good logic. It is of course competent for the

Legislature to prescribe a different rule, which is doubtless the case in Illinois.

It follows that the judgment appealed from must be and is hereby reversed. . . .

NOTES

1. The rule of the destructibility of contingent remainders, which dates from the late sixteenth century, provides that a legal contingent remainder — meaning a contingent remainder created directly in land rather than in a trust — is destroyed if it does not vest by the time the preceding freehold estate terminates. The rule does not apply to: vested remainders, even if the remainder is vested subject to divestment; executory interests; contingent remainders in personal property; contingent remainders in a trust, even if land is a trust asset; or contingent remainders if the preceding estate is nonfreehold, such as a lease. Did the court in *Popp* correctly apply the rule?

2. The rule typically is triggered in one of two scenarios. One involves a gap in time between the termination of the freehold estate and the vesting of the remainder. For an example, suppose a grant of land "to A for life, remainder to B if B lives to age 21" where B is under 21 at A's death. B's remainder is contingent at the termination of the preceding freehold estate (A's life estate), so B's remainder is destroyed. The second scenario involves the doctrine of merger. The doctrine of merger provides that if, after creation, a life estate and a successive vested future interest in fee come into the hands of the same person, the life estate terminates by merging into the other interest. For an illustration of the interplay between the destructibility rule and the doctrine of merger, suppose a grant of land "to A for life, remainder to B if B survives A" (notice that the grantor has retained a reversion) followed by a grant of the reversion to A. Once A holds both the life estate and the successive vested future interest in fee (the reversion), those two interests merge to form a fee simple absolute in A, and B's contingent remainder is destroyed.

3. Most American jurisdictions have abolished the rule by statute or abrogated it by judicial decision. In the remaining minority of states, the question is largely open, although the Restatement of Property § 240 (1936) takes the position that the rule is not part of American law. Accord, Restatement (Third) of Property: Wills and Other Donative Transfers § 25.5 (2011). However, at least in Florida, one can find decisions endorsing the rule. See, e.g., *In re Estate of Rentz*, 152 So. 2d 480 (Fla. Dist. Ct. App. 1963).

FINLEY v. FINLEY
318 S.W.2d 478 (Tex. Civ. App. 1958)

COLLINGS, J.

This suit was brought by Norman L. Finley against Eugene Lee Finley, Ross Alvord Finley and Kathy Elizabeth Finley, his children, individually and as representatives of the unborn and unknown legal heirs of Norman L. Finley. Plaintiff sought a construction of the will of his father and mother, E. L. Finley and Ella S. Finley, and an adjudication of the rights of the devisees under the wills . . . .

It was urged by plaintiff, Norman L. Finley, that under the Rule in Shelley's Case, fee title to all of the real estate owned by E. L. Finley and Ella S. Finley at the time of their deaths vested in him.

Judgment was entered holding that the Rule in Shelley's Case was not applicable to the will of E. L. Finley and that plaintiff Norman L. Finley took only a life estate in the lands owned by E.L. Finley at the time of his death . . . .

It was further decreed that the Rule in Shelley's Case was applicable to the will of Ella S. Finley and that Norman L. Finley took fee simple title to all of the real estate owned by Ella S. Finley at the time of her death. . . .

It was stipulated that E. L. Finley died February 26, 1943, and that his will was duly probated in the County Court of Taylor County on March 15, 1943; that Ella S. Finley died on July 12, 1950, and that her will was duly probated in the County Court of Taylor County on July 31, 1950; that E. L. Finley and Ella S. Finley were husband and wife and that neither had ever entered into any other marriage; that Norman L. Finley was the only child of E. L. Finley and Ella S. Finley; that Norman L. Finley has been married twice, first on July 28, 1920, to which marriage two children were born, to wit, Eugene Lee Finley and Ross Alvord Finley; that Norman L. Finley's first marriage was terminated by a divorce in 1940; that he married again in September, 1942, and of the latter marriage one child, Kathy Elizabeth Finley was born.

Certified copies of the wills were introduced in evidence. The pertinent part of the will of Ella S. Finley is as follows:

> As to my real estate, I give, devise and bequeath all of my real estate to my son, Norman L. Finley, during his natural life to be used and enjoyed by him so long as he shall live. But upon the death of my son, Norman L. Finley, I give, devise and bequeath said lands to the legal heirs of the said Norman L. Finley. This will, however, shall not be construed to give to Norman L. Finley a fee simple title, but only a life estate in said lands. However, during the life of my said son, Norman L. Finley, he shall have the right to lease any lands owned by me at my death for oil or gas or other minerals upon such terms and conditions as to him may seem best. He shall have the right to use all the bonus and rental monies and royalties under any lease or leases which he may make, and same shall be his property the same as if he owned the property in fee simple.

Established law in this state requires us to hold that the will of Ella S. Finley comes within the Rule in Shelley's Case and that Norman L. Finley took fee simple title to the land owned by Ella S. Finley at the time of her death. . . .

In the instant case there was no explanatory language in the will of Ella S. Finley which would authorize us to say that the words "legal heirs" should not be read in their technical sense. There was no language which would reasonably permit the words "legal heirs" to be construed to mean "children." *Robinson v. Glenn*, 150 Tex. 169, 238 S.W.2d 169; *Lacey v. Floyd*, 99 Tex. 112, 87 S.W. 665, 667. There was no language qualifying the words "legal heirs" . . . such as a provision that the "legal heirs" should "share and share alike" or share "equally" in a partition and division of the land. *Wallace v. First National Bank of Paris*, 120 Tex. 92, 93, 35 S.W.2d 1036;

Calvery v. Calvery, 122 Tex. 204, 55 S.W.2d 527; *Gardner v. Dillard*, Tex. Civ. App., 258 S.W.2d 93, Writ Ref.; *Hancock v. Butler*, 21 Tex. 804.

The provision that "This will, however, shall not be construed to give Norman S. Finley a fee simple title, but only a life estate in said lands" is likewise not controlling. This language does clearly show an intention to limit the interest of Norman L. Finley in the lands to a life estate only. It does not, however, qualify or limit the meaning of the words "legal heirs," which is required to avoid the application of the rule. In this connection it is stated in *Crist v. Morgan*, Tex. Com. App., adopted by Supreme Court, 245 S.W. 659, 660, that: "The uniform conclusion is reached that no matter how clear and unequivocal the language by which a life estate only is sought to be given to the ancestor, this purpose and intention is overturned by granting in the same instrument a remainder to his heirs."

We overrule the contention of appellants that the court erred in holding the Rule in Shelley's Case applicable to the will of Ella S. Finley and in holding that fee simple title to all the lands owned by Ella S. Finley at the time of her death vested in fee simple in Norman L. Finley.

The pertinent part of the will of E. L. Finley is as follows:

> And I give to my said wife for her sole use and benefit for so long as she shall live, all of the real estate situated in Callahan County, Texas, that I may own or have an interest in at the time of my death. And I direct that upon the death of my said wife, all of said real estate situated in Callahan County, Texas, shall pass to my son, Norman L. Finley, to be used and enjoyed by him so long as he shall live, and I direct that upon the death of my said son all of said Callahan County real estate shall pass to and vest in fee simple in the legal heirs then living of my said son, according to the statutes of descent and distribution now in force in Texas.
>
> And I further direct that my said wife, during the time that she may have the use of said real estate, and my said son, during the time that he may have the use of said real estate under the terms of this will, shall have full power and authority to lease any or all of said real estate for oil, gas and mineral development to such person or persons, and on such terms as the one having the use of said land hereunder may see fit, and all such oil, gas and mineral leases by the one having the use of said real estate by the terms of this will shall be valid and binding, although the term of any such lease extend beyond the life of the one then having authority to lease.

Cross-appellant Norman L. Finley has appealed from that portion of the judgment holding that the Rule in Shelley's Case was not applicable to the will of E. L. Finley, and that under the will Norman L. Finley took only a life estate in the lands owned by E. L. Finley at the time of his death. Norman L. Finley particularly urges that the court erred "in overruling the legal presumption that the words 'legal heirs' were used in their technical sense, in that, there is no language in any part of the will of E. L. Finley to show that such words were used other than in their technical sense."

In our opinion the words "legal heirs" as used in the will of E. L. Finley did not refer to or contemplate the legal heirs of Norman L. Finley in the technical sense

. . . . The will provided that the estate should vest "in fee simple in the *legal heirs then living*" at the time of Norman L. Finley's death (emphasis ours). It is obvious that the words "legal heirs" as used in the will did not contemplate legal heirs in the technical sense, but that the words were modified so as to designate certain specific heirs and a particular class of persons. The persons designated were the heirs of Norman L. Finley living at the time of his death. . . .

The court correctly held that the Rule in Shelley's Case did not apply to the will of E. L. Finley and that Norman L. Finley took only a life estate thereunder with certain other additional rights in the land.

The judgment of the trial court is in all things affirmed.

NOTES AND PROBLEMS

1.   The Rule in Shelley's Case derives its name from *Wolfe v. Shelley*, 1 Co. Rep. 93b (1581). The rule itself, however, was recognized at least two centuries earlier. The rule provides that a remainder interest in land in favor of the life tenant's heirs is held by the life tenant. For purposes of the Rule in Shelley's Case, most American jurisdictions interpret the word "heirs" in its standard sense: the persons who succeed to property at the owner's death if the owner dies intestate. A few American jurisdictions adopt a contrary view, holding that the rule applies only when heirs is understood in a different sense: an indefinite line including not just the takers in intestacy (heirs in the standard sense) but also their heirs, their heirs' heirs, and so on forever.

The rule applies equally to inter vivos and testamentary transfers of land. It does not apply to personalty.

The rule applies only if the life estate and remainder are "of the same quality," meaning both legal or both equitable (e.g., in trust). If one is legal and the other equitable, the rule does not apply. Nor does the rule apply if the prior estate is nonfreehold, such as a lease. Accordingly, one device for avoiding the rule is to grant a lease longer than the typical life expectancy and determinable on the tenant's death: "to A for 150 years or until A's death, then to A's heirs."

For the rule to apply, the life estate and remainder must be transferred in the same instrument. But the rule need not be triggered at the moment of transfer. The rule can be triggered after the transfer if the rule's requirements are subsequently satisfied. For an example, suppose a transfer of land "to A for life, remainder to B, but if B fails to survive A, to A's heirs" where B later died, survived by A. The rule does not apply at the time of the transfer because the future interest in A's heirs is, at that time, an executory interest, not a remainder. At B's subsequent death, however, the interest becomes a remainder, at which point the rule does apply, converting the remainder intended for A's heirs into a remainder in A. On these facts, there is a further step in the analysis: the doctrine of merger (recall the second note following *Popp v. Bond*) then operates to give A a fee simple absolute.

2.   In which of the following cases does the Rule in Shelley's Case apply?

     a.   O grants Blackacre "to A for life, then to those persons who, according to applicable law, would take A's real property if A should die intestate."

b. O grants Blackacre "to A for life, then to B and his heirs if B survives A, but to A's heirs if B does not survive A."

c. O grants Blackacre "to A and B as tenants in common for their respective lives, then to the heirs of A."

d. O grants Blackacre "to A for life, then to the heirs of A if they attend A's funeral."

e. O grants Blackacre "to T in trust to manage the property for A during A's life, and at A's death to convey to A's heirs."

3. The Rule in Shelley's Case has been abolished in most, but not all, U.S. jurisdictions. See John Orth, *Requiem for the Rule in Shelley's Case*, 67 N.C. L. Rev. 681 (1989).

A rule of the common law, often linked with the Rule in Shelley's Case, is the Doctrine of Worthier Title. It operates to convert a remainder in the heirs of the grantor into a reversionary interest in the grantor. See 3 Thompson on Real Property § 30.23. At common law, the doctrine applied irrespective of the grantor's intention. In some American jurisdictions, the doctrine has been re-framed as a rule of construction used in interpreting the grantor's probable intention. Is this wise? Consider the following materials.

daughter trust case

DOCTOR v. HUGHES
122 N.E. 221 (N.Y. 1919)

CARDOZO, J.

The action is brought by judgment creditors to subject what is alleged to be an interest in real property to the lien of a judgment.

In January, 1899, James J. Hanigan conveyed to a trustee a house and lot in the city of New York. The conveyance was in trust to pay from the rents and profits to the use of the grantor the yearly sum of $1,500. The payments might, however, exceed that sum in the discretion of the trustee. Direction was also made for the payment of some debts, and for the payment of two mortgages, then liens upon the property. The trustee was empowered to mortgage, in order to pay existing liens, or to carry into effect the other provisions of the deed. He was also empowered to sell. Upon the death of the grantor, he was to "convey the said premises (if not sold) to the heirs at law of the party of the first part." In case of a sale, he was to pay to the heirs at law "the balance of the avails of sale remaining unexpended." He was authorized at any time, if he so desired, to reconvey the premises to the grantor, and thus terminate the trust.

At the trial of this action, the grantor was still alive. His sole descendants were two daughters. By deed executed in June, 1902, one of the daughters, Mrs. Hughes, conveyed to her husband all her interest in this real estate. Judgment against Mr. and Mrs. Hughes for upwards of $4,000 was afterwards recovered by the plaintiffs. The question to be determined is whether either judgment debtor has any interest in the land. The Special Term held that there passed to Mr. Hughes under the conveyance from his wife an estate in remainder which was subject to the claims of creditors. The Appellate Division held that the creator of the trust did not intend to give a remainder to any one; that his heirs at law, if they receive anything on his death, will take by descent, and not by purchase; and hence that there is nothing that creditors can seize.

We reach the same conclusion. The direction to the trustee is the superfluous expression of a duty imposed by law. "Where an express trust is created, every legal estate and interest not embraced in the trust, and not otherwise disposed of, shall remain in or revert to, the person creating the trust or his heirs." Real Prop. Law § 102. (Consol. Laws, c. 50). What is left is not a remainder, but a reversion. To such a situation neither the rule in Shelley's Case nor the statute abrogating the rule applies. The heirs mentioned in this deed are not "the heirs of a person to whom a life estate in the same premises is given." The life estate belongs to the trustee. The heirs are the heirs of the grantor. . . . The question is whether there is any remainder at all. In the solution of that problem, the distinction is vital between gifts to the heirs of the holder of a particular estate, and gifts or attempted gifts to the heirs of the grantor. "A man cannot, either by conveyance at the common law, by limitation of uses, or devise, make his right heir a purchaser." *Pilus v. Milford*, 1674, 1 Vent. 372; *Bingham's Case*, 2 Co. Rep. 91a., 91b. To the same effect are all the commentators. . . .

At common law, therefore, and under common-law conveyances, this direction to transfer the estate to the heirs of the grantor would indubitably have been equivalent to the reservation of a reversion. In England, the rule has been changed by statute. . . . But in the absence of modifying statute, the rule persists to-day, at least as a rule of construction, if not as one of property. . . . We do not say that the ancient rule survives as an absolute prohibition limiting the power of a grantor. . . . There may be times when a reference to the heirs of the grantor will be regarded as the gift of a remainder, and will vest title in the heirs presumptive as upon a gift to the heirs of others. But at least the ancient rule survives to this extent: That, to transform into a remainder what would ordinarily be a reversion, the intention to work the transformation must be clearly expressed. Here there is no clear expression of such a purpose. . . .

NOTES

1. As a rule of law, the Doctrine of Worthier Title applied to remainders in land created inter vivos or by will. Today, the testamentary branch of the doctrine is virtually extinct in the United States. What survives is the inter vivos branch. Transformed and expanded from a rule of law into a rule of construction, that branch of the doctrine applies to remainders and executory interests, whether legal or equitable, whether in land or in personalty.

2. In the case of *In re Burchell's Estate*, 87 N.E.2d 293 (N.Y. 1949), the court stated:

It is clear from the cases in this State since *Doctor v. Hughes* . . . that, despite the language in that opinion that a reversion exists unless there is clear evidence to the contrary, the rule has been less limited in application. Where a clear intent exists, there is no problem in construing the instrument, since the doctrine no longer exists as a rule of property. But where the grantor's intent is not expressed in unmistakable language, the rule comes into play. Then we look to the instrument for those indicia deemed significant in arriving at the intent of the grantor. . . .

While we have not yet adopted a rule, either by statute or judicial construction, under which language limiting an interest to heirs is unequivocally given its full effect, the presumption which exists from the use of the common-law doctrine as a rule of construction has lost much of its force since *Doctor v. Hughes*. Evidence of intent need not be overwhelming in order to allow the remainder to stand. Whether the rule should be abrogated completely is a matter for the Legislature.

In contrast, a court in the District of Columbia refused to perpetuate the doctrine. The opinion stated: "We see no reason to plunge the District of Columbia into the ranks of those jurisdictions bogged in the morass of exploring, under the modern doctrine of worthier title, 'the almost ephemeral qualities which go to prove the necessary intent.' The alleged benefit of effectuating intent must be balanced against the resulting volume of litigation and the diversity and difficulty of decision." *Hatch v. Riggs Nat'l Bank*, 361 F.2d 559 (D.C. Cir. 1966).

3. The doctrine persists and can be a trap for the unwary. The American Law Institute and the Uniform Law Commission advocate its abolition. Uniform Probate Code § 2-710 provides: "The doctrine of worthier title is abolished as a rule of law and as a rule of construction. Language [that would call for application of the doctrine] does not create or presumptively create a reversionary interest in the transferor." Accord Restatement Third of Property: Wills and Other Donative Transfers § 16.3 (2011). Would UPC § 2-710 require the opposite result in the following case?

STEWART v. MERCHANTS NAT'L BANK OF AURORA
278 N.E.2d 10 (Ill. Ct. App. 1972)

GUILD, J.

This appeal arose out of a petition by the appellant to revoke a special ten year trust after only three years had elapsed from the date of its execution in 1967. The primary purposes of the trust were twofold: to provide for the rehabilitation of appellant from personal injuries suffered by him, and for regular payment of mortgage indebtedness on a new home in substitution for the home he owned at the time the trust was executed. The trust was spendthrift in nature. The trial court held that appellant could not revoke the trust because interests of minors and unborn heirs were involved, and this appeal was taken.

The trust in question was suggested to the appellant by his attorney following the settlement of a personal injury action wherein he represented the appellant. Appellant had been struck by an automobile while riding his motorcycle to work. Serious damage to one eye occurred as well as other injuries. In the trust instrument, appellant's attorney designated himself as the settlor and appellant as the beneficiary.

[The court held that the trust was not void as a matter of law because the attorney had acted formally as the settlor and found that the appellant was effectively the settlor.]

The more significant controversy in this appeal is whether appellant was the sole beneficiary of the trust. Thus the chief question on this appeal is whether the instant trust created such an interest in the appellant's heirs that their consent was necessary for revocation. At this point we quote the pertinent trust provision: "On May 25, 1977, upon the beneficiary's death, or upon the exhaustion of the principal and income by disbursements as herein provided, whichever first occurs, the Trust shall terminate. Upon the beneficiary's death, if there be any principal or accumulated income remaining in the Trust Estate, the Trustee shall pay the beneficiary's funeral expenses, the claims against the estate and the administration expenses of his estate, the taxes due by reason of his death, and distribute the remainder as the Last Will and Testament of the beneficiary may provide, or to the beneficiary's heirs-at-law in equal shares if beneficiary leaves no valid will." The trial court held that contingent interests were created in the appellant's heirs at-law so that their consent would be required to revoke the trust, and since such heirs would include minors and possible heirs, their consent was impossible. The trial court's statement of the applicable law was entirely correct if, in fact, the trust did create legal interests in the heirs requiring their consent for revocation. In *Pernod v. American National Bank and Trust Company*, 8 Ill.2d 16, 132 N.E.2d 540 (1956) cited by both appellants and appellees, it was held that a trust may not be revoked by consent unless "all the parties in interest are ascertained, are under no incapacity, and consent to the revocation." On the other hand, within these limits, according to *Vlahos v. Andrews*, 362 Ill. 593, 1 N.E.2d 59 (1936), "The sole beneficiaries of a trust, created by themselves as settlors, may revoke the trust without the consent of the trustee, although they do not reserve a power of revocation." As we have held that appellant was the settlor of this trust, that requirement under *Vlahos*, at least, is satisfied in our case.

One difference between this trust and that involved in *Vlahos* is that in the instant trust, the trust was expressly irrevocable. However, the Restatement (2nd) of Trusts, Sec. 339, and *Illinois Central Railroad Co. v. United States*, D.C., 263 F. Supp. 421 (1967) (construing an Illinois trust) as well as authorities cited in *Illinois Central* from other jurisdictions suggest that the insertion of such a clause does not affect the rule in *Vlahos*. In *May v. Marx*, 300 Ill. App. 144, 20 N.E.2d 821 (1939) an attempt was made to modify a trust by the execution of a supplemental trust instrument. The settlor of that trust was also the sole beneficiary thereof with regard to income, and she sought, by means of the supplemental instrument, to change the income provision from a lump sum $3000 quarterly payment out of income to a payment of all accumulated income. The trustee petitioned the trial court to construe the two instruments, and the trial court held the modification to be valid. On appeal, the same argument which we have in this appeal was raised, namely, that the trust created interests in minors or unborn heirs whose consent was necessary for modification. The argument was based on the following provision of the trust:

"This Trust shall continue for twenty five years from this 27th day of April, 1921, if I shall so long live. Upon my death the trust shall be dissolved and the property descend to my heirs, as the law provides."

The court held that this language did not create an interest in the heirs such as to require their consent for modification or revocation, as follows:

"Our opinion is that the words in the trust instrument of April 27, 1921, directing that in the event of her death prior to the termination of the trust, the 'property shall descend to my heirs, as the law provides', as words of limitation and not of purchase, and that they created no remainder interests, contingent or otherwise, in any of the defendants, and that therefore, she was the sole beneficiary of the trust and as such had the power at any time to revoke or modify without the consent of any other person."

Appellee has objected strenuously to authorities such as the *May* case herein on the ground that they are merely applications of the now obsolete "Doctrine of Worthier Title" which has been done away with by statute in Chap. 30, Sec. 188, Ill. Rev. Stat. (1955). We are aware that this statute provides that:

"Where a deed, will or other instrument purports to create any present or future interest in real or personal property in the heirs of the maker of the instrument, the heirs shall take, by purchase and not by descent."

Imperative as that language may seem, we refuse to believe that it would require a trust to be construed in such a way as to override the expressed intent of the maker of such an instrument. It is important to note that in the *May* case, *supra*, the court stated: "The determination in each case depends on the intent of the settlor as disclosed in the language used in the instrument." And in our view, that court's determination of the settlor's intent was a correct interpretation thereof. In New York, the doctrine that a remainder to "heirs" amounts to a mere reversion in the grantor has also been rejected as a rule of law, yet as recently as *Richardson v. Richardson*, 298 N.Y. 35, 81 N.E.2d 54 (1948), the Court of Appeals of New York stated that this rule remains as "at least a rule of construction," albeit "no more than a prima facie precept of construction which may serve to point the intent of the author." In our view, that is precisely how the court in *May* approached the facts in the case. See also *Berlenbach v. Chemical Bank & Trust Co.*, 260 N.Y. 539, 184 N.E. 83 (1932) a case similar to the present one and cited with approval in *Richardson*.

Having concluded that the *May* case is valid law, we next determine whether the trust in our case discloses an intent to dispose of the trust property similar to the disposition in *May*. The present trust differs from *May* concerning the relevant language regarding "heirs" only in that it provides the property shall pass to such heirs "in equal shares."

In *McKeown v. Pridmore*, 310 Ill. App. 634, 35 N.E.2d 376 (1941) an extremely complicated case, some clarity was cast on this issue by way of a statement from Griswold on Spendthrift Trusts, appearing at page 653, 35 N.E.2d at page 384 of *McKeown*: "The chief justification of spendthrift trusts should be found in the protection they furnish to the beneficiary. He cannot be protected if he has died, and the restraint should accordingly be allowed only during his lifetime. After his lifetime his property should be held liable for debts." This statement is applicable to the instant case. Since according to the trust instrument, appellant intended, if he died without a will, to pass his property to his heirs, this constituted, in our view, a general intention to keep the remaining corpus within his estate upon this contingency. This, we believe, means that he intended the trust to remain "his property" to quote the language of Griswold above, a conclusion buttressed by the fact that considerable expenditures were contemplated under the trust for payment of expenses in the event of his death, and further under the trust he could designate such legatees he might desire. In our view, it would be unjust, merely by virtue of the fact that the heirs took equal shares rather than shares in accordance with the rules of intestacy, for that property not to "be liable for his debts." We therefore hold that the consent of the heirs would not be required to revoke this trust as the appellant did not intend to vest such an interest in them.

Beyond this, the appellees have also attempted to defend the decision of the trial court on a second and independent ground, namely, that the rehabilitative purposes of the trust have not been fulfilled. In our view, that is not the law as applicable here. In *Pernod, supra*, the rule was stated, in negative form, that revocation by consent is permissible so long as all the beneficiaries are ascertained and under no incapacity. It seems inconceivable that the rule in *Pernod* would contemplate only those few cases where revocation is sought after all trust purposes have been accomplished. Specifically in this case, according to the Restatement (2nd) of Trusts, Sec. 339, p. 171: "If the settlor is the sole beneficiary of a trust, he can compel the termination of the trust, although the purposes of the trust have not been accomplished." We thus hold that appellant could revoke the trust and remand for proceedings consistent with this opinion.

Reversed and remanded.

VIII.   THE STATUTE OF USES AND EXECUTORY INTERESTS

Executory interests are nonreversionary future interests that came to be enforceable at law in consequence of the Statute of Uses in 1535. Understanding how they came to be treated as a separate kind of future interest requires examination of the Statute itself. Its operative language is:

> [W]here any person or persons stand or be seised, or at any time hereafter shall happen to be seised of and in any lands . . . to the use, confidence or trust of any other person or persons . . . by reason of any bargain, sale, feoffment . . . that in every such case, all and every such person and persons . . . that have or hereafter shall have any such use, confidence or trust . . . shall from henceforth stand and be seised . . . of and in the same . . . lands . . . of and in such like estates as they had or shall have in use, confidence or trust of or in the same, and that the estate title, right and possession that was in such person or persons that were, or hereafter shall be seised of any lands . . . to the use, confidence or trust of any such persons . . . be from henceforth clearly deemed or adjudged to be in him

or them that have, or hereafter shall have, such use, confidence or trust. . . .

From at least the fourteenth century, the practice of conveying lands to feoffees to uses for the benefit of the grantor — or other persons specified by the grantor, then or later — had become increasingly common in England. The feoffment to uses separated legal title (in the feoffees to uses) from beneficial enjoyment of the land (in the cestui que use or beneficiary). It permitted grantors to avoid some forms of feudal taxation because they applied only to legal interests, and most importantly, it permitted landowners to devise land. Prior to the Statute of Wills in 1540, 32 Hen. 8, c. 1, English law did not permit the devise of most forms of freehold land. However, where the land had been conveyed inter vivos to feoffees to uses, title remained in the feoffees at the donor's death, and it was held that no violation of the rule occurred when the will of the grantor simply designated the taker of the beneficial interest after the death of the grantor. This permitted devises of land in fact even though in theory they were impossible.

Passage of the Statute of Uses changed this regime. The Statute provided that where one person stood seised to the use of another person, that other person should be deemed seised of the legal estate he had previously held only in use. This meant that what had been an equitable right, enforceable only in the court of Chancery, became a legal estate. In effect, the feoffee to uses dropped out. Thus, if O conveyed to T to the use of A for life, remainder to B and his heirs, after the Statute of Uses, A held a legal life estate, and B held a legal remainder. T took nothing.

This was a dramatic change, and it created consternation. Sir Francis Bacon described the inheritances of the realm as being "tossed like a ship upon the sea." Reading on the Statute of Uses 1 (1642 ed.). Important consequences also occurred in conveyancing as a result of the Statute. First, prior to its enactment, actual livery of seisin was normally required to convey a legal estate. Afterward, it was possible to convey land by means of a paper transaction. One means of accomplishing this result was the bargain and sale. It had long been held that a valid bargain and sale of land raised a use in the bargainee. Thus, if O and A made an agreement by which O bargained and sold Blackacre to A and his heirs, A might have a remedy in Chancery even though he held no legal title. Passage of the Statute of Uses brought change, since the Statute itself would execute the use raised in A. A thereby gained legal title without livery of seisin. Thus it became possible to convey title to land more easily.

Second, it also became possible to create future interests that previously would not have been valid at common law. Understanding this requires knowing some of the rules of property in the medieval common law. Four are important here:

1) No freehold could be limited to commence in futuro. In other words, a so-called "springing interest" would be invalid. Thus, for example, O could not convey "to A and A's heirs to commence a year from the date of conveyance."

2) No contingent interest could be created to follow a term of years. A gap in seisin would have existed, because the termor was not seised, and this

could not be admitted at common law. Thus, O could not convey "to A for twenty years, then to the heirs of B" if B were a living person.

3) No abeyance in seisin could exist between successive freehold estates. Thus, O could not convey "to A for life, remainder to B and B's heirs if B attends A's funeral." There would inevitably be a gap between A's death and his funeral.

4) No future interest could cut short an existing freehold estate. This was a shifting interest, and at law it was invalid. The future interest had to take effect in possession on the natural termination of the prior estate. Thus, O could not convey "to A for life, but to B and B's heirs if A marries C."

The Statute of Uses permitted the creation of these future estates as valid legal interests. The old law was not abolished, however, and if the proper forms were not used, the common law rules still obtained. This required legal expertise. If O used a bargain and sale in these cases, or if O created an express use (O "to T to the use of A and A's heirs to commence a year from today"), then the future interest was valid. The Statute did not require the person for whom the property was to be held in use actually to be seised of a freehold estate, only that the feoffee be seised. In this case, T was seised by virtue of the bargain and sale. Hence, in all these cases, the Statute would execute the use raised by the conveyance, and the intended future grantees would take a valid legal future interest. Thus came into existence a new type of future interest, not subject to all the rules that regulated remainders, as the following case indicates.

BLACKMAN v. FYSH
3 Ch. 200 (Ch. App. 1892)

LINDLEY, L.J.

This case, when fully understood, appears to me to present no real difficulty. The construction put by Mr. Justice Kekewich on this will has the merit of giving effect to the testator's intention. Mr. Renshaw argued that owing to certain rules of law we could not give effect to that intention; but in my opinion there are in the present case grounds which not only enable us, but require us to give effect to it. The testator devises certain lands to his son for life, and from and after his decease he devises them "unto, between, and amongst all and every the children of my said son, whether now or hereafter to be born, who shall live to attain the age of twenty-one years, or who, being a daughter, shall marry under that age, to hold the same to such child or children, if more than one, in equal undivided shares as tenants in common, and to his, her, or their several and respective heirs and assigns." Stopping there, the limitations to the children were clearly contingent remainders, and if the son had died, those of his children only who had before his death attained twenty-one, or being daughters had married under that age, would take. Then we should have been obliged to give effect to the rules of law as to contingent remainders, and to defeat the intention of the testator that those who afterwards attained twenty-one should participate. I now pass to the clause under which the property actually went over. "I hereby expressly declare and direct that neither of them, my said son and daughters, shall have any power to sell, dispose of, mortgage or charge, or otherwise anticipate his or her life estate and interest in the estates hereby devised and given to such son or daughters respectively, or the rents or income arising from the same. And in case my said son or daughters, or any or either of them, shall attempt to sell, dispose of, mortgage, charge, or anticipate the same, or in case such son or daughters shall become bankrupt or insolvent, or the estates hereby given or devised to such son or daughters shall be taken in execution by any process of law for the benefit of any creditors or creditor, then I hereby declare that the gift and devise thereof to such son or daughter shall immediately become absolutely void and cease, as if such son or daughters were then actually dead, and that the estates so given and devised to such son or daughter shall thenceforth vest in and belong to the person or persons who under the devises and limitations hereinbefore contained would be next entitled thereto." It is impossible to treat the gift made by that clause to the children of the son as a remainder, since it is not to take effect on the determination of the life estate, but in defeasance of it. The rules as to contingent remainders, therefore, are not applicable to the case. Mr. Neville's point would deserve consideration if it were necessary to resort to it; but as we hold that the limitation is not a remainder at all, we need not deal with it. There is no doubt here that the intention of the testator was that every child of his son who should attain twenty-one should take. We are not dealing with personal estate, and there is no reason for cutting down the class of takers by excluding children born after a child had attained twenty-one.

The appeal will be dismissed.

LOPES, L.J.

Till I heard Mr. Methold's argument, I did not fully consider the effect of the forfeiture clause. If the first part of the disposition had stood alone, the limitations to the children of the son would have been contingent remainders. But the forfeiture defeats the life estate before its natural determination, and the limitations to take effect on that premature determination are not contingent remainders, but executory devises. Then, as to the persons who are to take, I think, having regard to the early part of the will, that all the children of the son whenever born who attain twenty-one are objects of the gift.

A.L. SMITH, L.J.

I am of the same opinion, and am glad that we are not compelled by cases or any rules of law to defeat the obvious intention of the testator.

NOTES

1. The rule in *Purefoy v. Rogers*, 2 Wms. Saund. 380, 85 Eng. Rep. 1181 (1670), is that if, when created, an interest can take effect as either a contingent remainder or as an executory interest, it will be treated as a contingent remainder for all purposes. Thus a remainder will not be saved from destructibility by being treated as an executory interest. If the interest does not vest at the termination of the prior estate, it falls to the ground under the doctrine of destructibility of contingent remainders. Thus, if O conveys "to A for life, remainder to B and her heirs if she reaches the age of 18," the remainder to B will not be treated as an executory interest if it turns out that B is still a minor at A's death. Because she could have reached the age of 18 at that time, her interest will be a remainder for all purposes. The most famous work on the subject, Charles Fearne, An Essay on the Learning of Contingent Remainders and Executory Devises *299 (1st ed. 1772), gives this example:

> [W]here a testator devised to his wife for life, and to her son after the death of his mother, if she should have a son, and if he should die within age, then to the right heirs of the devisor; the testator died without issue, his wife married again, then the heir of the devisor by fine conveyed the reversion to the husband and wife, who had afterwards a son born; it was adjudged that the estate limited to that son should not enure by way of executory devise; because that is never allowed where a contingent estate is limited to depend on a freehold capable of supporting it; here the mother had a preceding freehold in herself, therefore it was adjudged a contingent remainder in her son; and the heir at law, having a reversion in fee in him by descent, it was held, that the remainder was destroyed by his conveying the reversion to the particular estate of the mother before the son was born.

2. In jurisdictions where the destructibility rule has been abolished, critics maintain that the distinction between contingent remainders and executory interests should also be abolished. See J.J. Dukeminier, *Contingent Remainders and Executory Interests: A Requiem for the Distinction*, 43 Minn. L. Rev. 13 (1958); T.P. Gallanis, *The Future of Future Interests*, 60 Wash. & Lee L. Rev. 513 (2003).

3. American states have either taken over the Statute of Uses as part of the common law or enacted similar statutes themselves. They have also followed and expanded upon English precedents in holding that the Statute does not execute active uses or uses upon a use. If O conveys to T "to the use of A" and T is given active duties of management, the use is not executed. This has given rise to the "Illinois Land Trust" in which the trustee has only nominal duties, but in which it is nevertheless held that the Statute does not operate. The beneficiary's interest is in fact treated as personalty rather than an equitable interest in the land. Several advantages attending these land trusts have led to their widespread use and something like competition to see how few duties the trustee can be given and still avoid execution under the Statute. See Anthony Haswell & Barbara Levine, *The Illinois Land Trust: A Fictional Best Seller*, 33 De Paul L. Rev. 277 (1984).

PROBLEMS

Assuming that the deed involved satisfies the requirements of the Statute of Uses, what interests are created by the following inter vivos conveyances?

    a. O to A for life, then to B and B's heirs, but if B is convicted of a felony during A's lifetime, to C and C's heirs.

    b. O to A for life, then to B and B's heirs if B reaches the age of 30, but if he does not reach that age to C and C's heirs.

c. O to A for life, then to B and B's heirs for twenty years, then to C and C's heirs.

d. O to A for life, then to B and B's heirs for twenty years, then to C and C's heirs, subject to a power to revoke in A at any time during those twenty years.

e. O to A for life, then to A's children and their heirs, but if A has no children, then to B and B's heirs.

f. O to A for life, then to his wife B and B's heirs if she survives A and so long as she does not remarry thereafter.

g. O to A for twenty years, then to his wife B and B's heirs if she survives A, whether or not she remarries thereafter.

h. O to A for twenty years, then to his wife B and B's heirs so long as she does not remarry thereafter.

Donor: creates power
Donee: holds power (powerholder)
appointee.

IX. POWERS OF APPOINTMENT

W. Barton Leach once wrote these words about the subject of this section: "The power of appointment is the most efficient dispositive device that the ingenuity of Anglo-American lawyers has ever worked out." See *Powers of Appointment*, 24 A.B.A. J. 807 (1938). Others have been more critical, noting that its primary use over the centuries has been to allow evasion of settled rules of law. See Simes & Smith, The Law of Future Interests § 914 (3d ed. 2003).

A. The Nature of Powers

A power of appointment is generally defined as the authority to designate recipients of beneficial interests in, or powers of appointment over, property. It is a power given by the owner of the property (the donor) to another person (the powerholder) to appoint the takers of the property (the appointees). Unless the powerholder is a fiduciary (e.g., a trustee), exercise of the power is not mandatory. However, the terms under which the power may be exercised may be circumscribed in various ways. Under the traditional rule of "relation back," the appointees take the property by virtue of the original grant from the donor, although they of course become known only after the power has been exercised.

forced appointment.
but statutes
Chs reverse it.

GILMAN v. BELL
99 Ill. 144 (1881)

Good @ common law

[Solomon Bell's will devised an estate in property in Chicago to Ellen Bell, wife of his son, Robert, for and during Robert's life, and at Robert's death to his heirs in fee, all subject to a power in Robert to appoint to himself or any other person during his lifetime. Gilman, a judgment creditor of Robert's, failed to secure payment by other means and sought to reach the real property in Robert's hands. The court first held that Robert Bell did not take a life estate or fee simple in the property, but held only a power of appointment. — Eds.]

WALKER, J.

[I]t is insisted, that, conceding it to be a mere naked power of appointment in favor of himself, in favor of creditors he should be compelled by a court of equity to appoint, or be treated as the owner, and the property subjected to the payment of his debts. The doctrine has been long established in the English courts, that the courts of equity will not aid creditors in case there is a non-execution of the power. But where there has been a defective execution, the court will supply the defective execution of the power in favor of a purchaser, creditor, wife or child. Sugden on Powers, 392; 4 Kent, 399; 1 Story's Eq. sec. 169; *Holmes v. Coghill*, 12 Ves. 306. And it has been held that where the power has been executed in favor of a volunteer, the court will seize the fund and apply it to the satisfaction of the debts of the donee of the power. *Bainton v. Ward*, 2 Atkins 172, and numerous other cases. The doctrine that a court of equity will not aid in case of the non-execution of the power, was so firmly established in England that it could only be changed by act of 1 and 2 Vict. ch. 111, sec. 113. And our statute, chap. 22, sec. 1, in conferring chancery jurisdiction on the courts, provides that they shall proceed as therein prescribed; and where no provision is made by that chapter, then according to the general usage and practice of courts of equity. Hence the courts have regarded English precedents as authority. We therefore feel constrained to conform to the unbroken chain of English decisions.

. . . Nor are the distinctions entirely without reason. No title or interest in the thing vests in the [powerholder] until he exercises the power. It is virtually an offer to him of the estate or fund, that he may receive or reject at will, and like any other offer to donate property to a person, no title can vest until he accepts the offer, nor can a court of equity compel him to accept the property or fund against his will, even for the benefit of creditors. If it should, it would be to convert the property of the person offering to make the donation to the payment of the debts of another person. Until accepted, the person to whom the offer is made has not, nor can he have, the slightest interest or title to the property. So the [powerholder] only receives the naked power to make the property or fund his own. And when he exercises the power, he thereby consents to receive it, and the title thereby vests in him, although it may pass out of him eo instanti, to the appointee. And when the appointee is a volunteer, the court holds that he, by the appointment, endeavors to misapply his property to defraud his creditors — that he must be just before he is generous. This seems to be the reason upon which the cases proceed.

We are of opinion that appellee has no interest in this property, and that no relief can be granted, and the demurrer was properly sustained to the bill, and the decree of the court below must be affirmed.

BANK OF DALLAS v. REPUBLIC NAT'L BANK OF DALLAS

540 S.W.2d 499 (Tex. Civ. App. 1976)

McDONALD, J.

The issues to be decided are: 1) can the income, and/or 2) the corpus, of an irrevocable spendthrift trust, created by the settlor for the settlor and her children's benefit, be reached by garnishment for a debt of the settlor.

Patricia Murray Fewell as Settlor, on January 28, 1971, transferred certain properties to the trustee for the "use and benefit of herself and of her children", and thereafter amended such Trust.

The Trust as amended provides in Article 1(a):

> *Distributions*. The trustee shall pay to the Settlor for her uncontrolled use and benefit, all of the net income of the trust during her lifetime. Whenever the trustee determines that the income of the Settlor from all sources known to the trustee is not sufficient for her reasonable support, comfort, and health and for the reasonable support and education of Settlor's descendants, the trustee may in its discretion pay to, or use for the benefit of, Settlor or one or more of Settlor's descendants so much of the principal as the trustee determines to be required for those purposes.

Article 11(b) provides that upon the death of the settlor the trustee shall distribute or hold the then remaining principal and undistributed income as the settlor may have appointed by will. If the settlor has not exercised her power to appoint by will, then upon her death any property remaining in the trust shall be apportioned into separate, equal trust, "one for each then living child of Settlor and one for the then living issue collectively, of each deceased child of Settlor."

Article II Sec. 2.3 provides in part that if upon death of the Settlor she has no living descendants, any undisposed portion of the trust shall be distributed to her brother and sister.

Article III Sec. 3.2 contains a spendthrift provision containing customary spendthrift language and "nor shall such income or corpus or any portion of same be subject to execution, garnishment . . . or other legal proceeding of any character . . . to the payment of such beneficiary's debts. . . ."

Appellants contend:

> The trial court erred in holding that no part of the corpus, transferred by Patricia Murray Fewell as Settlor to the Patricia Murray Trust, under which she receives all of the income from all corpus for her lifetime, and under which she holds a general power of appointment exercisable at her death by will, is garnishable.

Appellees contend:

> 1) The trial court correctly held that the corpus of the trust was not subject to garnishment; and by cross-point contend:

> 2) The trial court erred in holding that the income was subject to garnishment.

The courts of Texas recognize the validity of spendthrift trusts created by a Settlor for others, and no part of the spendthrift trust estate can be taken on execution or garnishment by creditors of the beneficiary. (citations omitted).

But the rule is otherwise in cases where the settlor creates a spendthrift trust, and makes himself the beneficiary thereof. And where a settlor creates a trust for his own benefit, and inserts a spendthrift clause, it is void as far as then existing or future creditors are concerned, and they can reach his interest under the trust by garnishment. (citations omitted).

. . . .

As to the corpus the issue is more complex, as Mrs. Fewell is not the sole beneficiary. The trust provides that the trustee may exercise its discretion to invade principal under certain circumstances "for the benefit of Settlor" or "one or more of Settlor's descendants."

Also the settlor's children have a remainder, though the settlor can defeat such interest by exercising her general powers of appointment under Article II(b).

Section 156c Restatement, Trusts & Trustees 2d, p. 326 states: "Reservation of general power to appoint principal. If the settlor reserves for his own benefit not only a life interest, but also a general power to appoint the remainder by deed or will, his creditors can reach the principal of the trust as well as the income;" and section 156d, at page 327 states: "Trust for settlor's support. Where the settlor creates a trust for his own support, . . . it can be reached by his creditors. They can compel the trustee to pay to them the maximum amount which he could pay to the settlor-beneficiary or apply for his benefit."

And Section 156e states: "Discretionary trust for the settlor. Where by the terms of the trust a trustee is to pay the settlor or apply for his benefit as much of the income or principal as the trustee may in his discretion determine, creditors can reach the maximum amount which the trustee could pay to him or apply for his benefit."

Applying the foregoing rules of law to the facts, we hold the interest of Mrs. Fewell in the trust is such that the corpus may be reached by her creditors.

. . . Affirmed in part; Reversed and remanded in part.

NOTES

1.   In some circumstances, bankruptcy law treats a power of appointment as an asset of the bankrupt even if it is not exercised. However, the law specifically excepts "any power that the debtor may exercise solely for the benefit of an entity other than the debtor." See 11 U.S.C. § 541(b)(1). State statutes may also augment the rights of creditors to reach assets subject to a power of appointment. See 3 Powell on Real Property § 33.06.

2.   Should a surviving spouse be able to claim the right of dower or curtesy, or (under modern legislation) the right to take an elective share in the estate of the spouse who is also the holder of a power of appointment? See Uniform Probate Code § 2-205(1)(A); Margaret Mahoney, *Elective Share Statutes: The Right to Elect Against Property Subject to a General Power of Appointment*, 55 Notre Dame L. Rev. 99 (1979).

3.   Suppose a person is given a power of appointment that can be exercised only by her will, and she makes an effective appointment. Her executors, who are entitled to a percentage share of the decedent's estate under state statute, seek to

have the value of the property passing under the power of appointment included in the estate. In such a case, it was held that they were not entitled to do so. *In re Estate of Wylie*, 342 So. 2d 996 (Fla. Ct. App. 1977).

4. Should a garden-variety residuary clause in a will (e.g., "I give all of my property, not otherwise disposed of, to X") be presumed to exercise a power of appointment held by the testator? The Uniform Powers of Appointment Act § 302 answers the question in the affirmative, but only if: (1) the terms of the instrument containing the residuary clause do not manifest a contrary intent; (2) the power is exercisable in favor of the powerholder's estate; (3) there is no gift-in-default clause or it is ineffective; and (4) the powerholder did not release the power. Accord, Restatement (Third) of Property: Wills and Other Donative Transfers § 19.4 (2011).

B. Varieties of Powers

Powers of appointment are differentiated in many ways. Three of the most important distinctions are (1) between presently exercisable and testamentary powers, (2) between general and nongeneral powers, and (3) between exclusionary and nonexclusionary powers. All of these distinctions relate to the scope of the powerholder's authority. An extremely important, overarching principle — followed in almost all states — is that the scope of the powerholder's authority is presumptively unlimited. The powerholder's authority as to appointees and the time and manner of appointment is limited only to the extent the donor effectively manifests an intent to impose limits. See Uniform Powers of Appointment Act § 203; Restatement (Third) of Property: Wills and Other Donative Transfers, Introductory Note to Ch. 17, Part B (2011).

If the terms of a power provide that the power can be exercised only in the powerholder's will, the power is *testamentary*. If the powerholder can exercise the power inter vivos at the time in question, the power is *presently exercisable*. In the typical case, a presently exercisable power can also be exercised in the powerholder's will, though in rare cases a presently exercisable power may be limited to inter vivos exercise. A *general* power is exercisable in favor of the powerholder, the powerholder's estate, or the creditors of either. A *nongeneral* power excludes the powerholder, the powerholder's estate, and the creditors of either as permissible appointees. An *exclusionary* power of appointment is exercisable in favor of any one or more of the permissible appointees to the exclusion of the other permissible appointees. In contrast, a *nonexclusionary* power is one in which the powerholder cannot make an appointment that excludes any permissible appointee, or one or more designated permissible appointees, from a share of the property.

PROBLEMS

Classify the powers of appointment created in the following transfers:

a. G transfers land to A for life, remainder to such persons as A may appoint or, in default of appointment, remainder to B and his heirs.

b. G transfers land to A for life, remainder to such of A's descendants as A may by will appoint or, in default of appointment, remainder to B and his heirs.

    c.   G transfers land to A for life, remainder to all of A's descendants in such shares as A may appoint or, in default of appointment, to B and his heirs.

———————

Another way that powers of appointment are differentiated is on the basis of the powerholder's property interest, if any, in the appointive property. There are three categories: collateral powers, powers in gross, and powers appendant. A power is *collateral* if the powerholder has no property interest in the appointive property. A power is a *power in gross* if the powerholder has a property interest in the appointive property but it cannot be affected by the exercise of the power. A *power appendant* exists to the extent that the powerholder has a property interest in the appointive property that can be affected by the exercise of the power. In other words, the power of appointment purports to authorize the powerholder to divest the powerholder's own property interest and confer it on someone else. A purported exercise of a power appendant is actually a transfer of the powerholder's property interest.

PROBLEMS

Classify the powers of appointment created in the following transfers:

    a.   G transfers land to A for life, remainder to such persons as P may appoint or, in default of appointment, remainder to B and his heirs.

    b.   G transfers land to A for life, remainder to B, with the proviso that A may by will appoint the land in fee simple absolute to C and his heirs. *non-general*

    c.   G transfers land to A for life, remainder to B, with the proviso that A may at any time appoint the land in fee simple absolute to C and his heirs. *non-general*

X.   THE RULE AGAINST PERPETUITIES

The purpose of the Rule Against Perpetuities is to promote the alienability of land. It is also justified as an effective check on undue concentration of property in the hands of the few, and as a way of striking a reasonable balance between generations. See Gregory Alexander, *Dead Hand and the Law of Trusts in the Nineteenth Century*, 37 Stan. L. Rev. 1189 (1985); Note, *Dynasty Trusts and the Rule Against Perpetuities*, 116 Harv. L. Rev. 2588 (2003). Like the constructional preference in favor of the fee simple absolute or the rule invalidating restraints on alienation, the Rule Against Perpetuities grows from a desire to render title to land marketable. The Rule operates when there is an otherwise valid contingent interest outstanding, but in which the takers of that interest cannot be ascertained until too remote a period. If it were possible to create future interests that remained contingent far into the future, then as a practical matter the land would be inalienable. Until one can identify the future taker with certainty, no one can give clear title to the land. Hence the Rule.

A.   The Orthodox Rule

The classic formulation of the Rule is that of John Chipman Gray: "No interest is good unless it must vest, if at all, not later than twenty-one years after some life in being at the creation of the interest." The Rule has long been subject to criticism. See, e.g., Charles Sweet, *The Monstrous Regiment of the Rule Against Perpetuities*, 18 Jurid. Rev. 132 (1906) (attacking the classic Rule as "one of the most curious examples of judicial legislation to be found in English law"). However, it remains the starting point for scholarly analysis. A fair question is how well it explains the following case.

UNITED VIRGINIA BANK/CITIZENS & MARINE v.
UNION OIL CO.
197 S.E.2d 174 (Va. 1973)

CARRICO, J.

The question for decision in this appeal is whether the provisions of a land option agreement violate the rule against perpetuities. For reasons to be later discussed, we hold that the rule is violated.

The question arose in a declaratory judgment proceeding brought by United Virginia Bank/Citizens & Marine (hereafter, the Bank), executor and trustee under the last will and testament of William Jonathan Abbitt, deceased, against Union Oil Company of California and Sanford & Charles, Inc. (hereafter, Sanford). The Bank sought a declaration that an option agreement entered into by Abbitt during his lifetime was void and unenforceable on the ground it was in violation of the rule against perpetuities. The trial court held that the agreement was valid and enforceable, and the Bank appeals.

The agreement in question was entered into on April 7, 1966, between Abbitt and Union Oil Company of California. It was later assigned by Union Oil to Sanford, the active appellee here. It granted the optionee the right and option to purchase a parcel of land 200 feet by 200 feet at the northwest corner of an intersection to be formed by two highways, "Boxley Boulevard Extension and new U.S. 60," proposed to be constructed in the city of Newport News. The option was granted for a period of 120 days. However, the agreement provided as follows:

> It is expressly understood that the 120 days option period shall begin at the time the City of Newport News, Virginia acquires the right of way of Boxley Boulevard Extension and new U.S. 60.

It is this provision which is the focal point of the controversy between the parties, the Bank contending that it results in a violation of the rule against perpetuities and Sanford insisting that it does not. Resolution of the controversy requires an examination of the status of "Boxley Boulevard Extension and new U.S. 60" at the time the option agreement was executed.

. . . .

The Bank contends that the provisions of the agreement in question, making exercise of the option contingent upon acquisition by the city of the rights-of-way of the proposed highways, violates the rule against perpetuities. The Bank says that on April 7, 1966, the date the agreement was executed, "it was not known when, if ever, the City would acquire the rights-of-way for either of [the] proposed thoroughfares." Therefore, the Bank argues, there was "every possibility" that the option might not expire within the period prescribed by the rule against perpetuities.

Sanford contends, on the other hand, that since the proposed highways were shown on the major thoroughfare plan and were contemplated to be completed at the latest by January, 1987, or within 21 years from April 7, 1966, the date of the option agreement, the limitation created by the agreement did not violate the rule against perpetuities. Alternatively, Sanford contends that if the agreement "poses a technical violation of the rule," we should hold the rule inapplicable to option contracts.

We dispose first of Sanford's alternative contention that the rule against perpetuities should be held inapplicable to option contracts. To so hold, we would have to overrule our decision in *Skeen v. Clinchfield Coal Corp.*, 137 Va. 397, 119 S.E. 89 (1923). While the reasoning of *Skeen* has been the subject of some criticism, the case clearly establishes, and we think properly so, the proposition that option contracts are unenforceable if they do not necessarily expire within the period fixed by the rule against perpetuities. In addition, it is generally recognized that the rule against perpetuities is properly applicable to option contracts. 4 Rest. Property § 393, comment a, at 2316 (1944). So we decline to depart from our holding in *Skeen*.

A preliminary matter requires attention. We must determine what period is to be employed in testing the validity of the limitation created by the option agreement under consideration. Ordinarily, the rule against perpetuities is expressed in terms of the necessity of an interest vesting within a period measured by a life or lives in being plus 21 years and 10 months. But here, the optionee is a corporate, not a human, entity, and the parties have not contracted with reference to a life or lives in being, but rather with reference to an event contemplated to occur sometime in the future. In such circumstances, a gross term of 21 years is the determinative period. *Barton v. Thaw*, 246 Pa. 348, 355, 92 A. 312, 314 (1914).

As applied to an option agreement, the rule against perpetuities requires that the option must be exercised, if at all, within the period fixed by the rule. If there exists at the time the agreement is entered into a possibility that exercise of the option might be postponed beyond the prescribed period, the agreement is invalid because it is in violation of the rule.

The question becomes, therefore, whether there existed at the time the option agreement was entered into in this case a possibility that exercise of the option might be postponed beyond a period of 21 years from the date of the agreement.

Turning to the option agreement itself, it is clear that the parties intended that the optionee would exercise the option, if at all, only upon occurrence of the specific contingency set up in the agreement, that is, the acquisition by the city of the rights-of-way of the proposed highways. It is equally as clear, from the agreement and the surrounding circumstances, that on the date the agreement was executed there existed the distinct possibility that the specified contingency might not occur until after expiration of a period of 21 years from the date of the agreement.

Sanford argues, however, that it was "the dominant intent" of the parties to the option agreement that the city would acquire the rights-of-way in question, if at all, within a reasonable time and that such time "under the circumstances of this case is less than 21 years." This being true, Sanford asserts, we should exercise the cy pres power of the judiciary and imply into the terms of the option agreement a provision that the contingency of the city's acquisition of the rights-of-way would occur within a reasonable time not more than 21 years from the date of the agreement. This, Sanford concludes, would effectuate the intention of the parties and avoid a construction of the agreement which would violate the rule against perpetuities.

The answer to this argument is three-fold. In the first place, "the dominant intent" Sanford refers to does not appear from the option agreement itself or from any other source. Secondly, the asserted intent relates to acts which parties other than those privy to the agreement must perform to bring about occurrence of the agreed contingency. So whatever may have been the intent of the contracting parties, it is of little moment. Lastly, assuming, without deciding, that the power of cy pres is otherwise available in a case such as this, it may not be employed in Virginia as a vehicle to alter an agreement so as to evade the rule against perpetuities. *Shenandoah Valley Nat'l Bk. v. Taylor*, 192 Va. 135, 149, 63 S.E.2d 786, 795 (1951).

Sanford relies upon the case of *Isen v. Giant Food, Inc.*, 295 F.2d 136, 111 U.S. App. D.C. 149 (D.C. Cir. 1961), a decision interpreting Virginia law, as authority for the argument that we should imply a reasonable time provision into the option agreement under consideration. *Isen* is, however, factually and legally different from the case at bar, and so it is not persuasive here.

Sanford next urges us to adopt the "wait and see" doctrine which has been legislatively enacted into the law of several states and judicially applied in others. Under this doctrine, the rule against perpetuities is determined to have been violated or not by taking into consideration events which occur after the period fixed by the rule has commenced. If, upon a later look, the event upon which an interest was made contingent is found to have occurred and the interest has vested or has become certain to vest within the period fixed by the rule, the rule is held not to have been violated.

Sanford does not tell us what effect adoption of the "wait and see" doctrine would have upon this case. Presumably, Sanford would say that because "new U.S. 60" is now completed or is nearing completion, we can look at this late development and see that the contingency set up in the option agreement has been or soon will be satisfied at a time within the period fixed by the rule against perpetuities. If that be Sanford's position, it overlooks the fact that the record shows nothing to have yet occurred concerning "Boxley Boulevard Extension" bordering the optioned property, an integral part of the contingency.

But aside from that, the established rule in Virginia, to which we adhere, is that a perpetuities problem may not be solved by resort to what occurs after commencement of the period fixed by the rule. In *Claiborne v. Wilson*, 168 Va. 469, 474, 192 S.E. 585, 586 (1937), we said, speaking of perpetuities cases:

> Nor is it material in such cases how the fact actually turns out. The possibility that the event may, in point of time, exceed the limits allowed, vitiates the limitation ab initio.

Finally, Sanford contends that if we should decide, as we do, that the option agreement violates the rule against perpetuities, it is nevertheless entitled to recover damages for breach of contract, and it asks us to remand the case for a hearing on damages. However, an agreement in violation of the rule against perpetuities is void ab initio. To allow recovery of damages for the failure of an optionor to comply with such an agreement would have the effect of compelling performance of an invalid contract and would, at the same time, act as a restraint upon alienation. We conclude, therefore, that damages are not allowable in such a case. 1 R. Minor, The Law of Real Property, § 823, at 1064 (2d ed. 1928); 4 Restatement of Property § 393, comment h, at 2320 (1944).

For the reasons assigned, we hold the option agreement of April 7, 1966, in violation of the rule against perpetuities and, therefore, invalid and unenforceable. Accordingly, the judgment of the trial court will be reversed and final judgment will be entered here declaring the agreement void.

NOTES

1. Under the principles of the case, would an option to renew held by the lessee to a long-term lease also violate the Rule against Perpetuities? See, e.g., *Nichols v. Day*, 91 So. 451 (Miss. 1922). What about an agreement between potential buyers of land that one of them should pay the purchase price, but the other should have the right to purchase a one-half interest for a sum equal to fifty percent in all monies invested in the premises by the other? See, e.g., *Reynolds v. Gagen*, 732 N.Y.S.2d 4 (N.Y. Sup. Ct. 2001), *rev'd*, 739 N.Y.S.2d 704 (App. Div. 2002).

2. Would a lease to begin "upon completion of a building" that is currently under construction be invalid because it violates the Rule? Would it matter if the lease covered commercial property to be constructed in a planned shopping center? See *Haggerty v. City of Oakland*, 326 P.2d 957, 66 A.L.R.2d 718 (Cal. Ct. App. 1958). Compare *Wong v. Di Grazia*, 386 P.2d 817 (Cal. 1963).

3. The Rule does not apply to all contingent future interests. For example, a contingent future interest held by a charity is not subject to the Rule if the preceding interest is valid and also held by a charity. Moreover, all reversionary future interests — reversions, possibilities of reverter, and rights of entry — are exempt from the Rule. In *Baker v. Latham Sparrowbush Assoc.*, 808 F. Supp. 992 (S.D.N.Y. 1992), for example, the court held that an option retained by a lessor to terminate a lease with 60 days' notice was a reversionary interest rather than an executory interest and hence not subject to the Rule.

JEE v. AUDLEY
1 Cox, Eq. Cas. 324 (Ch. 1787)

Edward Audley, by his will, bequeathed as follows, "Also my will is that £1000 shall be placed out at interest during the life of my wife, which interest I give her during her life, and at her death I give the said £1000 unto my niece Mary Hall and the issue of her body lawfully begotten, and to be begotten, and in default of such issue I give the said £1000 to be equally divided between the daughters then living of my kinsman John Jee and his wife Elizabeth Jee."

It appeared that John Jee and Elizabeth Jee were living at the time of the death of the testator, had four daughters and no son, and were of a very advanced age. Mary Hall was unmarried and of the age of about 40; the wife was dead. The present bill was filed by the four daughters of John and Elizabeth Jee to have the £1000 secured for their benefit upon the event of the said Mary Hall dying without leaving children. And the question was, whether the limitation to the daughters of John and Elizabeth Jee was not void as being too remote; and to prove it so, it was said that this was to take effect on a general failure of issue of Mary Hall; and though it was to the daughters of John and Elizabeth Jee, yet it was not confined to the daughters living at the death of the testator, and consequently it might extend to after-born daughters, in which case it would not be within the limit of a life or lives in being and 21 years afterwards, beyond which time an executory devise is void.

On the other side it was said, that though the late cases had decided that on a gift to children generally, such children as should be living at the time of the distribution of the fund should be let in, yet it would be very hard to adhere to such a rule of construction so rigidly, as to defeat the evident intention of the testator in this case, especially as there was no real possibility of John and Elizabeth Jee having children after the testator's death, they being then 70 years old; that if there were two ways of construing words, that should be adopted which would give effect to the disposition made by the testator; that the cases, which had decided that after-born children should take, proceeded on the implied intention of the testator, and never meant to give an effect to words which would totally defeat such intention. . . .

THE MASTER OF THE ROLLS. Several cases determined by Lord Northington, Lord Camden, and the present Chancellor, have settled that children born after the death of the testator shall take a share in these cases; the difference is, where there is an immediate devise, and where there is an interest in remainder: in the former case the children living at the testator's death only shall take: in the latter those who are living at the time the interest vests in possession; and this being now a settled principle, I shall not strain to serve an intention at the expense of removing the landmarks of the law; it is of infinite importance to abide by decided cases, and perhaps more so on this subject than any other. The general principles which apply to this case are not disputed: the limitations of personal estate are void, unless they necessarily vest, if at all, within a life or lives in being and 21 years or 9 or 10 months afterwards. This has been sanctioned by the opinion of judges of all times, from the time of the Duke of Norfolk's case to the present: it is grown reverend by age, and is not now to be broken in upon; I am desired to do in this case something which I do not feel myself at liberty to do, namely, to suppose it impossible for persons in so advanced an age as John and Elizabeth Jee to have children; but if this can be done in one case it may in another, and it is a very dangerous experiment, and introductive to the greatest inconvenience to give a latitude to such sort of conjecture. Another thing pressed upon me, is to decide on the events which have happened; but I cannot do this without overturning very many cases. The single question before me is, not whether the limitation is good in the events which have happened, but whether it was good in its creation; and if it were not, I cannot make it so. Then must this limitation, if at all, necessarily take place within the limits prescribed at law? The words are "in default of such issue I give the said £1000 to be equally divided between the daughters then living of John Jee and Elizabeth his wife." If it had been to "daughters now living," or "who should be living at the time of my death," it would have been very good; but as it stands, this limitation may take in after-born daughters; this point is clearly settled by *Ellison v. Airy*, and the effect of law on such limitation cannot make any difference in construing such intention. If then this will extended to after-born daughters, is it within the rules of law? Most certainly not, because John and Elizabeth Jee might have children born ten years after the testator's death, and then Mary Hall might die without issue 50 years afterwards; in which case it would evidently transgress the rules prescribed. I am of opinion therefore, though the testator might possibly mean to restrain the limitation to the children who should be living at the time of the death, I cannot, consistently with decided cases, construe it in such restrained sense, but must intend it to take in after-born children. This therefore not being within the rules of law, and as I cannot judge upon subsequent events, I think the limitation void. Therefore dismiss the bill, but without costs.

LAUGHLIN v. ELLIOTT
259 S.W. 1031 (Ky. 1924)

THOMAS, J.

On December 5, 1884, Anna E. Baker and her then husband, J.H. Baker, who was her second one, executed a deed to Nannie W. Neeley, a daughter of Mrs. Baker by a former husband by the name of Laughlin, conveying to the daughter a parcel of real estate in Lexington, Kentucky. The parties named in the caption of the deed are Mrs. Baker and her husband "party of the first part, and Nannie W. Neeley, wife of James E. Neeley, of the county of Simpson, state of Kentucky, party of the second part;" and in the conveying clause, after reciting the consideration of one dollar and love and affection, it is said: "The party of the first part do hereby sell and convey unto the party of the second part, and assigns, the following described real and personal property, to-wit." The habendum clause says: "To have and to hold said property unto the party of the second part, her assigns forever," which is immediately followed by a limiting condition saying: "This conveyance is made subject to the life estate of first party, Anna E. Baker. Upon her death said property shall pass to Nannie W. Neeley, second party, for, and during her natural life, to be *owned* and held by her for her sole and separate estate, free from the debts or control of her husband, and at the death of said Nannie W. Neeley, said property shall pass and belong to the grandchildren of Anne E. Baker, in equal portions."

. . . [Actions at law were brought to determine ownership of the property passing under this deed. The court first discussed the nature of the estate granted to Nannie W. Neeley — Eds.]

But, waiving that question, and coming to the one which, no doubt, influenced the court in sustaining the exceptions, we will treat that deed as conveying only a life estate to Mrs. Neeley and after her death and that of her mother then the fee to the latter's grandchildren, which perhaps is the true construction. From that view-point there can be no doubt but that the limitation in all the deeds to the grandchildren of Mrs. Baker violates the provisions of the section of the statute [section 2360, commonly known as Kentucky's statute against perpetuities], *supra*, and is inhibited thereby. As we have seen, Mrs. Baker left surviving her, and who are yet living, three sons. They were living at the time of the execution of all the deeds referred to, and it was possible that they might have children who would be born more than twenty-one years and ten months after the expiration of the lives of both Mrs. Baker and Mrs. Neeley, and if that should happen the limitations in all of the deeds would be for a longer period than during the continuance of their lives and twenty-one years and ten months thereafter, which would be in contravention of the express terms of the statute. Sustaining the construction above expressed is the text in the work of Dr. Gray on "The Rule Against Perpetuities," sections 205a, 370, 372 and 374; 30 Cyc. 1486, and the cases from this court of *Tyler v. Fidelity and Columbia Trust Co.*, 158 Ky. 280, 164 S.W. 939; *U.S. Fidelity and Guaranty Co. v. Douglas' Trustee*, 134 Ky. 374; *Beall v. Wilson*, 146 Ky. 646, 143 S.W. 55; *Brown v. Columbia Finance Co.*, 123 Ky. 775, 97 S.W. 421, and numerous others, some of which are referred to in those opinions, and from which we will not insert excerpts. Indeed it is conceded by counsel for appellants that such effect of the limitations to the grandchildren is the proper one, unless from the language employed it was the intention of the grantors to confine the estate to the grandchildren who were *in esse* at the time of the termination of the life estates created by the deeds, which, it is insisted, is the true construction of them. But, in the *Douglas*, *Beal* and *Tyler* cases, and in some of the others referred to, almost the exact language was before the court for interpretation, and it was held that the grandchildren composing the class to which the remainder interest was limited included unborn grandchildren, and that under such language the title would open up so as to let them in when they should be born. It, however, was recognized in those cases that it was competent to limit the future interest to only those members of the class who were in existence at the vesting period, and where that is done the vesting of the interest could not possibly be postponed beyond the inhibited period of the statute against perpetuities, and, of course, would be valid; but, where it was not done, either expressly or by necessary implication, the limitation to the entire class would be void. There is nothing in any of the deeds here involved, even remotely indicating the intention of the grantors to limit the general class included in the term "grandchildren," to only those living at the expiration of the life estates and under the cases referred to it must be held that the class would include all future born grandchildren, regardless of what may have been the actual though unexpressed intention of the grantors. Other cases in which it was held that the term "grandchildren" would include future born ones, in the absence of clear words of qualification or limitation, are *Caywood v. Jones*, 108 S.W. 888, 32 Ky. L. Rep. 1302; *Barker v. Barker*, 143 Ky. 66, 135 S.W. 396; *Lynn v. Hall*, 101 Ky. 738, 43 S.W. 402, and a number of others referred to in those opinions.

We are, therefore, clearly of the opinion that the court properly held that the parties to this litigation did not acquire any title to the property involved under any of the deeds referred to.

. . . .

We are also asked to determine where the title to the property is if it was not possessed by plaintiffs and defendants in this case? A number of objections may be interposed to our determining the question at this time, one of which is that "Sufficient unto the day is the evil thereof." The question is not presented nor are those who would be affected by its determination parties to this litigation, and any views which we might express thereon would be *dictum* and not binding on them. The only question presented by this appeal is, whether as between the parties to this litigation the deeds referred to vested them with title to the property. We have held that they did not, and the court properly sustained the exceptions, and the judgment is affirmed.

NOTE

In *Tuttle v. Steele*, 135 S.W.2d 436 (Ky. Ct. App. 1940), a testator devised a life estate to his wife, adding "at her death it is to go to my great-nieces and nephews including any that may be born." The court held that the Rule Against Perpetuities was not violated "as it appears that it was probably the intention of testator to limit the devise to children of his nieces and nephews living at the time of his death." At the testator's death, he had one nephew and one niece living.

WARREN v. ALBRECHT
571 N.E.2d 1179 (Ill. Ct. App. 1991)

HOWERTON, J. delivered the opinion of the court:

This appeal from an action to quiet title to land in Madison County involves the common law rule against perpetuities. James W. McGaughey devised land as follows:

> "I give, devise and bequeath to John T. McGaughey, as Trustee, in Trust for John Warren, my grand-son, the following described real estate to wit: The south Thirty-eight (38) rods of the northeast quarter (NE1/4) of the southeast quarter (SE1/4) of section ten (10), containing 19 acres more or less, and north half (N1/2) of the southwest quarter (SW1/4) of section eleven (11), containing eighty (80) acres, more or less, also the north three-fourths (N3/4) of the southwest quarter (SW1/4) of the southwest quarter (SW1/4) of section eleven (11), all of said lands in Township numbered Six (6) North, Range numbered Seven (7) West of the Third Principal Meridian, and situated in Madison County, Illinois.

> "The said John T. McGaughey, as such Trustee to have the control of said land above described, until the said John Warren becomes of the age of thirty (30) years of age ***. The above described real estate is given, devised and bequeathed too [sic] the said John Warren, and subject to said

Trust named above for and during his natural life, and at his death, and at his death [sic] to his then living child or children, or survivors thereof, and in the event there be no descendants of said child or children, then to his sisters, viz: Emma B. Warren and Goldy Maude Warren, for the sole use and benefit forever, share and share alike, subject to the following conditions, viz: That in the event of the death of either of said sisters and leaving no child or children, or descendants of said child or children, then to the survivor, and if neither of said sister are [sic] living, then to my legal heirs at law, as per the laws of descent, share and share alike and for their sole use and benefit forever."

James W. McGaughey died in 1943. John Warren, his two sons, Donald and Ronald Warren, and his two sisters, Emma B. Warren (Oliver) and Goldy Maude Warren (Albrecht), are living.

In 1987, John Warren's sons, Donald and Ronald Warren, quitclaimed their interest in the land to their father.

In 1988, John Warren, plaintiff, brought an action to quiet title claiming that James W. McGaughey's devise violated the common law rule against perpetuities. Both plaintiff and defendants filed motions for summary judgment. The circuit court granted defendants summary judgment. John Warren appealed.

The rule against perpetuities is a common law rule directed toward the remoteness of vesting. Its ultimate purpose is to prevent the "clogging of titles beyond reasonable limits in time by contingent interests, and to keep land freely alienable in the market places." (R. Boyer, Survey of the Law of Property 158 (3d ed. 1981).) The rule provides:

> "No interest is good unless it must vest, if at all, not later than twenty-one years after some life in being at the creation of the interest." Gray, The Rule Against Perpetuities § 201, at 191 (4th ed. 1942). See also Schuknecht v. Shultz (1904), 212 Ill. 43, 72 N.E. 37; Martin v. Prairie Rod & Gun Club (1976), 39 Ill. App. 3d 33, 348 N.E.2d 306; Ill. Rev. Stat. 1989, ch. 30, par. 191.

If, by any possibility, an interest cannot vest or fail within the 21-year limit, then the devise is void for remoteness. Thomas v. Pullman Trust & Savings Bank (1939), 371 Ill. 577, 21 N.E.2d 897; McKibben v. Pioneer Trust & Savings Bank (1937), 365 Ill. 369, 6 N.E.2d 619; Johnston v. Cosby (1940), 374 Ill. 407, 29 N.E.2d 608.

Interests subject to the rule are contingent remainders, executory interests (or devises), options to purchase land not incident to a lease for years, and powers of appointment. Interests not subject to the rule are present interests in possession, reversions, vested remainders, possibilities of reverter, powers of termination, charitable trusts, and resulting trusts. R. Boyer, Survey of the Law of Property 159 (3d ed. 1981).

Determining into which of these interests this case falls involves a three-step process. First, the language of the devise is explained. Secondly, the status of title is identified. Thirdly, the rule is applied.

In examining the language of the devise, the primary objective is to give effect to the testator's intent by giving the testator's words their plain and ordinary meaning. (Harris Trust & Savings Bank v. Beach (1987), 118 Ill. 2d 1, 513 N.E.2d 833.) Here, the language is plain. John Warren was to enjoy the property as beneficiary of a testamentary trust until he was 30 years old, after which the property became his for his life. At John Warren's death, his children were to take the property, and if any of those children predeceased him, the surviving children were to take the property; if no children or descendants survived John Warren, the estate was to go to John Warren's sisters, Emma and Goldy. If either Emma or Goldy died prior to taking, the survivor was to take; if both died prior to taking, the property would go to the testator's heirs at law.

In identifying the status of title, we note that title is "[t]he right to or ownership in land." (Black's Law Dictionary 1331 (5th ed. 1979).) Determining the status of title is the process of identifying present and future interests transferred by a deed or a will. Only by this process can one determine if a particular future interest in the property violates the rule.

Here, John Warren was given a life estate. His child or children were given a contingent remainder in fee simple. The descendants of his children were given an alternative contingent remainder in fee simple. Emma and Goldy were also given an alternative contingent remainder in fee simple. James W. McGaughey's heirs at law were not determined until his death, but after his death in 1943, they also possessed an alternative contingent remainder in fee simple.

Lastly, we apply the rule. In his complaint, John Warren claimed that the language — "and in the event there be no descendants of said child or children, then to his sisters" — violated the rule because John Warren's children could be divested longer than 21 years after his death if his children were to die leaving no descendants. To determine if his analysis is correct, we first ask what interest is involved. Here, the children have an alternative contingent remainder in fee simple. A contingent remainder exists if there is a condition precedent to vesting. (R. Boyer, Survey of the Law of Property 37 (3d ed. 1981).) Here, the condition is that the children survive their father. Applying the rule, we note that once John Warren dies, the interest must necessarily vest or fail. John Warren will either have children survive him, or he won't. Therefore, the devise to his children does not violate the rule. Warren argues that after the estate vests in his child or children, it can be divested if his child or children died without descendants. We disagree.

We believe that a plain reading of the devise indicates that the estate vests at the time of John Warren's death. The language in the fifth paragraph of decedent's will, in our opinion, clearly expresses his purpose. If John Warren's children survive, the estate vests in them. If the children are not alive at John's death, the estate vests in their survivors. If at the time of John's death there are no children or descendants, the estate vests in John's sisters. If the sisters or their children do not survive John's death, then John's heirs at law take the estate. The decedent provided for various alternatives, but, in any event, the estate vests at the life tenant's death. The rule against perpetuities does not apply to vested interests. Chicago Title & Trust Co. v. Shellaberger (1948), 399 Ill. 320, 334, 77 N.E.2d 675, 683; Deiss v. Deiss (1989), 180 Ill. App. 3d 600, 536 N.E.2d 120; see also McKibben v. Pioneer Trust & Savings Bank (1937), 365 Ill. 369, 6 N.E. 619.

The appellant argues only that the wording in the devise that states "in the event there be no descendants of said child or children, then to his sisters" divests the interests of John Warren's children. We do not ascribe to his argument. The ownership is vested at John's death in someone or some class. Therefore, the rule does not apply. The law, of course, favors the vesting of estates at the earliest possible moment. Fay v. Fay (1929), 336 Ill. 299, 168 N.E. 359.

The trial court was correct in its granting of defendant's motion for summary judgment, holding the devise did not violate the rule against perpetuities.

The circuit court of Madison County is affirmed.

PROBLEMS

In which of the following limitations does a future interest violate the Rule against Perpetuities? (Persons represented by letters are living when the limitation is made. Assume that none of the persons described by such words as "children" is in existence unless so stated.)

a. O devises Blackacre "upon the death of all my children and of all my grandchildren born or conceived at my death, to my eldest male descendant then living and his heirs." O leaves children and grandchildren born and in gestation at his death.

b. O devises Blackacre "twenty-one years after the death of all my children and all my grandchildren living at my death, to my issue then living per stirpes in fee." O leaves children and grandchildren at his death.

c. O devises Blackacre "thirty years after my death to my eldest descendant then living and his or her heirs." O leaves children surviving him.

d. O devises Blackacre "to the first of my grandchildren who reaches twenty-one." O leaves children at his death.

e. O devises Blackacre "to A and A's heirs, but if B or B's heirs ever pay A or A's heirs $1,000, to B and B's heirs."

f. O devises Blackacre "to my eldest child for life, remainder to its first child in fee, but if my eldest child have no child, or having such it die under twenty-one to B in fee." O leaves a child at his death.

g. O by settlement made at the time of O's marriage conveys Blackacre "to T on trust to pay the net income to O for life, on O's death to pay the net income to O's eldest child for life, and on the death of such child to convey Blackacre to its first child in fee."

h. O makes the same settlement as in (g) but reserves the power to revoke all interests created by the settlement and to dispose of Blackacre for O's own benefit. O dies without exercising the power.

i. O devises Blackacre "to A for life, remainder to any widow he may leave for life, remainder to A's children who survive the widow in fee simple."

j. O, having a term of twenty-one years, devises it "to A, but if all A's descendants ever cease to bear the name of Owen, the term shall pass to B."

    k. O devises Blackacre "to A and A's heirs, but if A leaves no child who shall attain twenty-five, to B for life."

    l. O devises Blackacre "to A in fee but if all A's children die under twenty-five, and B survives them, to B in fee simple."

    m. O devises Blackacre "to A for life, the fee simple to the first of his children who reaches twenty-five." Suppose (a) a jurisdiction where a contingent *[destructibility]* remainder fails for lack of a freehold to support it; (b) a jurisdiction where it does not fail.

    n. O bequeaths a picture "to A, but if at any time A and all her descendants are dead, the picture shall go to the children of B then living."

    o. O bequeaths a picture "to A, but if at any time A and all her descendants are dead, the picture shall go to the children of B who are living at my death and who survive A and her descendants." B has children living when O dies.

B. Reform of the Orthodox Rule

Attempts to avoid application of the Rule Against Perpetuities have taken several forms in modern American law. The most common in practice is addition of a "saving clause" to a will or other instrument in which future interests are created. Here is one example:

> In the event that any of the reservations or restrictions contained herein should result in a violation of the rule against perpetuities if enforced, then such reservation or restriction shall be deemed and construed only to extend and apply to those persons or classes who may be lawfully restricted in the selling or gifting of all or a portion of the herein-described real property without violating the aforesaid rule.

In *Smith v. Smith ex rel. Clarke*, 747 A.2d 85 (Del. Ch. 1999), it was held that this clause saved a perpetual option to purchase land from a challenge of invalidity. The clause limited the time during which the option could be exercised so that no violation of the Rule could occur.

Many proposals to "de-claw" the Rule by means of legislation have also been made. One is the adoption of a "wait and see" approach. Although "wait and see" comes in a variety of forms, most begin with the common law but look to events as they actually unfold, rather than to all the possibilities. The reasoning is that contingent future interests should not be invalidated simply because of a remote possibility of failure to vest. It is difficult, however, to determine the measuring lives under this approach. The traditional Rule has fewer problems in this, because it supposes that all persons may die at any time, which avoids the need to pick specific lives in being. "Wait and see" must face that necessity.

A second statutory approach to reforming the Rule applies a doctrine akin to *cy pres* to provisions that violate the Rule, judicially reforming those provisions to conform to the closest possible alternative that is lawful under the Rule. Under this approach, for example, a future interest stated to vest thirty years from the death of the last measuring life might be reformed to make it vest twenty-one years from that date. The argument against this alternative is that judges have no way of knowing what alternative a testator would have wished and may in fact use this doctrine to "deform" the testator's intent. Precedents from the law of charitable gifts, from which the "*cy pres*" proposal is drawn, are not entirely reassuring on this score.

A more radical statutory approach to reform legislates the Rule out of existence. A Delaware statute, for example, provides that "[n]o interest created in real property held in trust shall be void by reason of the common-law rule against perpetuities . . . and no interest created in personal property held in trust shall be void by reason of any rule . . . ." 25 Del. Code § 503(a). The same statute, however, requires that a private trust of real property must terminate no later than 110 years from the date on which the trust became irrevocable. *Id.* § 503(b). An advertisement for a bank promotes the establishment of what it calls "Dynasty Trusts" sited in Delaware. Such trusts of personal property, the advertisement states, "could potentially last forever."

So far, the most widely adopted reform has been by legislation. The Uniform Statutory Rule Against Perpetuities provides in part:

A nonvested property interest is invalid unless,

when the interest is created, it is certain to vest or terminate no later than 21 years after the death of an individual then alive;

or, the interest either vests or terminates within 90 years after its creation.

The Uniform Rule also provides that it does not apply to most nondonative transfers. USRAP § 4(1). The Uniform Rule is criticized in Jesse Dukeminier, *The Uniform Statutory Rule Against Perpetuities: Ninety Years in Limbo*, 34 UCLA L. Rev. 1023 (1987), and defended in Mary Louise Fellows, *Testing Perpetuity Reforms: A Study of Perpetuity Cases*, 25 Real Prop. Prob. & Tr. J. 597 (1991).

Another proposal that has been approved by the American Law Institute would reformulate the Rule from a rule against remote vesting to a direct time-of-termination rule. Under the Restatement (Third) of Property: Wills and Other Donative Transfers § 27.1 (2011), a trust or other donative disposition of property is subject to judicial reformation if it does not terminate on or before the end of measuring lives two generations younger than the transferor. Thus, in the typical case, a transferor can keep property in trust only through the lives of his or her grandchildren. By reformulating the Rule, the American Law Institute hopes to reinvigorate it. The ALI's official view is that the legislative movement to allow dynasty trusts is "ill advised." *Id.*, Ch. 27, Introductory Note.

Chapter 4

LANDLORD AND TENANT

I. TYPES OF TENANCIES

All leases involve a transfer by a property owner of some or all of the transferor's (lessor's or landlord's) property. This transfer is of a nonfreehold estate known as a leasehold. It entitles the transferee (lessee or tenant) to exclusive possession of the property. The lessor retains a reversion in the property, which becomes possessory at the end of the tenancy. The most common form of leasehold is a *term for years*. Of a term for years, William Blackstone, 2 Commentaries on the Laws of England 143–44 (1st ed. 1766) (reprinted by U. Chi. Press 1979), wrote:

> Every estate which must expire at a period certain and prefixed, by whatever words created, is an estate for years. And therefore this estate is frequently called a term, *terminus*, because its duration or continuance is bounded, limited, and determined: for every such estate must have a certain beginning, a certain end. But *id certum est, quod certum reddi potest*: therefore if a man make a lease to another, for so many years as J.S. shall name, it is a good lease for years; for though it is at present uncertain, yet when J.S. hath named the years, it is then reduced to a certainty. If no day of commencement is named in the creation of this estate, it begins from the making, or delivery, of the lease. A lease for so many years as J.S. shall live, is void from the beginning; for it is neither certain, nor can ever be reduced to a certainty, during the continuance of the lease. And the same doctrine holds, if a parson make a lease of his glebe for so many years as he shall continue parson of Dale; for this is still more uncertain. But a lease for twenty or more years, if J.S. shall so long live, or if he shall so long continue parson, is good: for there is a certain period fixed, beyond which it cannot last; though it may determine sooner, on the death of J.S. or his ceasing to be parson there.

> We have before remarked . . . the inferiority in which the law places an estate for years, when compared with an estate for life, or an inheritance: observing, that an estate for life, even it be *pur autre vie*, is a freehold; but that an estate for a thousand years is only a chattel, and reckoned part of the personal estate. Hence it follows, that a lease for years may be made to commence *in futuro*, though a lease for life cannot. As, if I grant lands to Titius to hold from Michaelmas next for twenty years, this is good; but to hold from Michaelmas next for the term of his natural life, is void. For no estate of freehold can commence *in futuro*; because it cannot be created at common law without livery of seisin, or corporal possession of the land: and corporal possession cannot be given of an estate now, which is not to

commence now, but hereafter. And because no livery of seisin is necessary to a lease for years, such lessee is not said to be *seised*, or to have true legal seisin, of the lands. Nor indeed does the bare lease vest any estate in the lessee; but only gives him a right of entry on the tenement, which right is called his *interest in the term*, or *interesse termini*: but when he has actually so entered, and thereby accepted the grant, the estate is then and not before vested in him, and he is *possessed*, not properly of the land, but of the term of years: the possession or seisin of the *land* remaining still in him who hath the freehold. Thus the word, *term*, does not merely signify the time specified in the lease, but the estate also and interest that passes by the lease: and therefore the *term* may expire, during the continuance of the *time*; as by surrender, forfeiture, and the like. For which reason, if I grant a lease to A for the term of three years, and after the expiration of the said *term* to B for six years, and A surrenders or forfeits his lease at the end of *one* year, B's interest shall immediately take effect: but if the remainder had been to B from and after the expiration of the said *three years*, or from and after the expiration of the said *time*, in this case B's interest will not commence till the time is fully elapsed, whatever may become of A's term.

[These commentaries were required reading for many generations of American attorneys, and Blackstone's work was annotated many times, but this passage was seldom corrected. *See, e.g.*, George Sharswood, Sharswood's Blackstone Commentaries, Book II, ch. 9, at 142–143 (1860).]

A leasehold without a definite term is either a periodic tenancy or a tenancy at will. A *periodic tenancy* is a leasehold that automatically renews from year to year, month to month, or week to week until the landlord or tenant terminates it by notice to the other. A *tenancy at will* is terminable at the option of either one or both parties. See *Napier v. Napier*, 564 S.E.2d 418 (W. Va. 2002) (person possessing property of another without being required to make periodic rent payments is a tenant at will).

A fourth type of tenancy is a tenancy in name only. A *tenancy at sufferance* arises when a tenant remains in possession after the tenancy terminates without the landlord's permission. The tenant at sufferance is characterized as a tenant, rather than as a trespasser, to avoid starting the statute of limitations for an adverse possession claim. Generally, the landlord can either evict the tenant or hold her to an additional lease term.

ALFANO v. DONNELLY
189 N.E. 610 (Mass. 1934)

Lummus, J.

The writ in this action of contract . . . is upon a written instrument by which the plaintiff "doth hereby Demise and Lease" to the defendant "the roof of the building numbered 1–3 on Chelsea Street in East Boston for the term of Five years" beginning January 1, 1931, at a rental payable in semi-annual payments of $75 each, beginning January 2, 1931. The evident intention was that the defendant should use the roof for advertising purposes. Since the signing of the instrument the defendant has removed structures which she had on the roof under an earlier use or occupancy, and has not again used the roof. But there was no evidence of surrender, or eviction, or repudiation of the contract on either side. Nothing has been paid by the defendant under the instrument. This action was begun on April 4, 1932, to recover three semi-annual payments of $75 each, with interest. The trial judge found for the plaintiff for the amount claimed in the declaration, denying several requests for rulings presented by the defendant. The appellate division dismissed a report, and the defendant appealed to this court.

The instrument bore no seal, but declared that the parties "have hereunto set their hands and seals," and consequently was in form a sealed instrument . . . . Except possibly with respect to the measure of damages, it is of no importance whether the written instrument in this case is a lease or a license. * * * But it is clear that the written instrument is a lease, and that we ought to give effect to the provision in it that "This instrument shall be construed as a lease and not merely as a license." Even if the trial judge thought otherwise, any facts that he could possibly have found from the evidence leading to a finding for the plaintiff on the theory of a license would equally have required a finding for the plaintiff on the correct theory of a lease. Therefore his failure, though requested, to state which of these theories he adopted, did not harm the defendant. Under the correct theory, at any rate, his assessment of damages in the full amount claimed in the declaration was right . . . . No error appears. Order dismissing report affirmed.

NOTES

1. If a tenant is entitled to but does not take possession of the premises, would the court treat the agreement as a lease? See 1 Am. L. Prop. 220 (James Casner ed., 1952). Would the agreement in this case be classified as a lease if the sign were to be placed on the wall of the building? See *Baseball Publishing Co. v. Bruton*, 18 N.E.2d 362 (1938), reprinted *infra*, Chapter 6. What is the difference in result as to the measure of damages that the court notes in the opinion?

2. Is a lease created when an occupancy agreement gives a person the right to occupy her parents' home and to purchase the home at a fixed price in six years, in exchange for the occupant's agreement to assume the outstanding mortgage debt, utilities, and taxes and to forfeit all such payments if she doesn't exercise her right to purchase? *Lake v. Sullivan*, 766 A.2d 708 (N.H. 2001) (agreement is a lease with an option to buy, rather than a contract for sale of the house).

3. Is an agreement to permit A to overflow B's lands likely to be classified as a lease? See *Smith v. Simons*, 1 Root 318, 1 Am. Dec. 48 (Conn. 1791). How about an agreement "in payment for a sand bar, with the exclusive right to remove its sand and gravel, and excluding others from it"? See *Haywood v. Fulmer*, 32 N.E. 574 (Ind. 1892). How about a purchaser's right to occupy the vendor's land, contained in a contract of purchase and sale, when no particular time for occupancy is given? *Druse v. Wheeler*, 22 Mich. 439 (Mich. 1871).

II. CREATION

Leaseholds generally are created in a written document labeled a lease. In most states, those with a term longer than a year are subject to the state's Statute of Frauds and so must be in writing to be enforceable. Some of these statutes permit oral leases with a shorter term, but some are silent on this matter. See 2 Am. L. Prop. 215 (James Casner ed., 1952). A tenant in possession under a lease that is void because it does not comply with the Statute of Frauds is a tenant at will, *Mauala v. Milford Management Co.*, 559 F. Supp. 1000, 1004 (S.D.N.Y. 1983), though it may be converted to a periodic tenancy by the regular payment of rent. Written leases with a term longer than one, two, or three years (depending on the state's Recording Act) can be recorded on the public records.

NOTE ON TENANT'S RIGHT TO POSSESSION

In a written lease, the use of the words "demise" or "grant" is sometimes held to imply that the landlord covenants that the latter has the power to lease. In some states, the same covenant is implied regardless of the technical words of transfer used in the lease. Whether specific technical words are required to imply such a covenant, suing for its breach is not the same as imposing on the landlord the duty to deliver possession of the premises to the tenant. The latter duty is the subject of the following case.

HANNAN v. DUSCH
153 S.E. 824 (Va. 1930)

PRENTIS, C.J.

The declaration filed by the plaintiff, Hannan, against the defendant, Dusch, alleges that Dusch had on August 31, 1927, leased to the plaintiff certain real estate in the city of Norfolk, Virginia, therein described, for fifteen years, the term to begin January 1, 1928, at a specified rental; that it thereupon became and was the duty of the defendant to see to it that the premises leased by the defendant to the plaintiff should be open for entry by him on January 1, 1928, the beginning of the term, and to put said petitioner in possession of the premises on that date; that the petitioner was willing and ready to enter upon and take possession of the leased property, and so informed the defendant; yet the defendant failed and refused to put the plaintiff in possession or to keep the property open for him at that time or on any subsequent date; and that the defendant suffered to remain on said property a certain tenant or tenants who occupied a portion or portions thereof, and refused to take legal or other action to oust said tenants or to compel their removal from the property so occupied. Plaintiff alleged damages which he had suffered by reason of this alleged breach of the contract and deed, and sought to recover such damages in the action. There is no express covenant as to the delivery of the premises nor for the quiet possession of the premises by the lessee.

The defendant demurred to the declaration on several grounds, one of which was "that under the lease set out in said declaration the right of possession was vested in said plaintiff and there was no duty as upon the defendant, as alleged in said declaration, to see that the premises were open for entry by said plaintiff."

The single question of law therefore presented in this case is whether a landlord, who without any express covenant as to delivery of possession leases property to a tenant, is required under the law to oust trespassers and wrongdoers so as to have it open for entry by the tenant at the beginning of the term — that is, whether without an express covenant there is nevertheless an implied covenant to deliver possession . . . .

It seems to be perfectly well settled that there is an implied covenant in such cases on the part of the landlord to assure to the tenant the legal right of possession — that is, that at the beginning of the term there shall be no legal obstacle to the tenant's right of possession. This is not the question presented. Nor need we discuss in this case the rights of the parties in case a tenant rightfully in possession under the title of his landlord is thereafter disturbed by some wrongdoer. In such case the tenant must protect himself from trespassers, and there is no obligation on the landlord to assure his quiet enjoyment of his term as against wrongdoers or intruders.

Of course, the landlord assures to the tenant quiet possession as against all who rightfully claim through or under the landlord.

The discussion then is limited to the precise legal duty of the landlord in the absence of an express covenant, in case a former tenant, who wrongfully holds over, illegally refuses to surrender possession to the new tenant. This is a question about which there is a hopeless conflict of the authorities. It is generally claimed that the weight of the authority favors the particular view contended for. There are, however, no scales upon which we can weigh the authorities. In numbers and respectability they may be quite equally balanced . . . .

It is conceded by all that the two rules, one called the English rule, which implies a covenant requiring the lessor to put the lessee in possession, and that called the American rule, which recognizes the lessee's legal right to possession, but implies no such duty upon the lessor as against wrongdoers, are irreconcilable.

The English rule is that in the absence of stipulations to the contrary, there is in every lease an implied covenant on the part of the landlord that the premises shall be open to entry by the tenant at the time fixed by the lease for the beginning of his term. [There are many] cases [that] appear to support that rule . . . .

It must be borne in mind, however, that the courts which hold that there is such an implied covenant do not extend the period beyond the day when the lessee's term begins. If after that day a stranger trespasses upon the property and wrongfully obtains or withholds possession of it from the lessee, his remedy is against the stranger and not against the lessor.

It is not necessary for either party to involve himself in uncertainty, for by appropriate covenants each may protect himself against any doubt either as against a tenant then in possession who may wrongfully hold over by refusing to deliver the possession at the expiration of his own term, or against any other trespasser. * * *

King v. Reynolds, 42 Am. Rep. 107 (Ala. 1880), has been said to be the leading case in this country affirming the English rule. In that case, after citing some of the cases which affirm the American rule, this is said:

> * * * The principle applicable to the case of the lessee's eviction by the lessor himself, or by a title paramount to that of the lessor, certainly rests on impregnable grounds. Such eviction is a breach of the implied covenant in every lease in general terms for quiet enjoyment, and at once bars the lessor's right to recover rent, and confers on the lessee a right of action for the lessor's breach of covenant. * * * And so, when there is no impediment to the possession at the time fixed by the terms of the lease for the lessee to take possession, it is no breach of the covenant of quiet enjoyment if a trespasser without title subsequently enter and evict the lessee in whole or in part. The lessee must meet such intrusions as that. But how about the implications at the time — the very moment — fixed by the terms of the lease for the lessee to take possession? Who is responsible if there is a trespasser, or tenant holding over, then in possession? Must the lessor clear the possession, or is this duty cast on the lessee? . . . The authorities being in conflict, how does this question stand on principle? [O]ne who accepts a lease expects to enjoy the property, not a mere chance of a lawsuit. A lease for a year, or term of years, is not a freehold. It is a chattel interest. The prime motive of the contract is, that the lessee shall have possession; as much so as if a chattel were the subject of the purchase. Delivery is one of the elements of every executed contract. When a chattel is sold, the thing itself is delivered. Formerly parties went upon the land, and there symbolical delivery was perfected. Now the delivery of the deed takes the place of this symbolical delivery. Still, it implies that the purchaser shall have possession; and without it, it would seem the covenant for quiet enjoyment is broken. Up to the time the lessee is entitled to possession under the lease, the lessor is the owner of the larger estate, out of which the leasehold is carved, and ownership draws to it the possession, unless someone else is in actual possession. The moment the lessor's right of possession ceases by virtue of the lease, that moment the lessee's right of possession begins. There is no appreciable interval between them, and hence there can be no interregnum or neutral ground between the two attaching rights of possession, for a trespasser to step in and occupy. If there be actual, tortuous occupancy, when the transition moment comes, then it is a trespass or wrong done to the lessor's possession. If the trespass or intrusion have its beginning after this, then it is a trespass or wrong done to the lessee's possession; for the right and title to the property being then in the lessee for a term, it draws to it the possession, unless there is another in the actual possession . . . . 3 Washburn on Real Property, 117, 118.

As to the suggestion in that opinion that such a lease is a chattel, we think that it should be also observed that it is not a mere chattel which passes by delivery, but a chattel real. The lease here involved is for a fifteen year term, which cannot be created in this State except by deed, and therefore the title of the lessee, Hannan, and his right of possession became perfect without more when the deed was delivered. The suggestion in the opinion that there is no appreciable interval between the expiration of the term of the former tenant and the beginning of the term of the new tenant does not seem to be significant, because just as soon as the first tenant's term ended the new tenant's term began, and there is no instant of time when the lessor had any right of possession because his tenants always had that right, and so the trespass or wrong done by the first tenant is to the lessee directly rather than to the lessor.

Another case which supports the English rule is *Herpolsheimer v. Christopher*, 107 N.W. 382, [followed] 111 N.W. 359 (Neb. 1906). In that case the court gave these as its reasons for following the English rule:

> We deem it unnecessary to enter into an extended discussion, since the reasons pro and con are fully given in the opinions of the several courts cited. We think, however, that the English rule is most in consonance with good conscience, sound principle, and fair dealing. Can it be supposed that the plaintiff in this case would have entered into the lease if he had known at the time that he could not obtain possession on the 1st of March, but that he would be compelled to begin a lawsuit, await the law's delays, and follow the case through its devious turnings to an end before he could hope to obtain possession of the land he had leased? Most assuredly not. It is unreasonable to suppose that a man would knowingly contract for a lawsuit, or take the chance of one. Whether or not a tenant in possession intends to hold over or assert a right to future term may nearly always be known to the landlord, and is certainly much more apt to be within his knowledge than within that of the prospective tenant. Moreover, since in an action to recover possession against a tenant holding over, the lessee would be compelled largely to rely upon the lessor's testimony in regard to the facts of the claim to hold over by the wrongdoer, it is more reasonable and proper to place the burden upon the person within whose knowledge the facts are most apt to lie. We are convinced, therefore, that the better reason lies with the courts following the English doctrine, and we therefore adopt it, and hold that, ordinarily, the lessor impliedly covenants with the lessee that the premises leased shall be open to entry by him at the time fixed in the lease as the beginning of the term.

In commenting on this line of cases, Mr. Freeman says this:

> The above rule practically prohibits the landlord from leasing the premises while in the possession of a tenant whose term is about to expire, because notwithstanding the assurance on the part of the tenant that he will vacate on the expiration of his term, he may change his mind and wrongfully hold over. It is true that the landlord may provide for such a contingency by suitable provisions in the lease to the prospective tenant, but it is equally true that the prospective tenant has the privilege of insisting that his prospective landlord expressly agree to put him in possession of the premises if he imagines there may be a chance for a lawsuit by the tenant in possession holding over. It seems to us that to raise by implication a covenant on the part of the landlord to put the tenant into possession is to make a contract for the parties in regard to a matter which is equally within the knowledge of both the landlord and tenant.

* * *

Referring then to the American rule: Under that rule, in such cases, "the landlord is not bound to put the tenant into actual possession, but is bound only to put him in legal possession, so that no obstacle in the form of superior right of possession will be interposed to prevent the tenant from obtaining actual possession of the demised premises. If the landlord gives the tenant a right of possession he has done all that he is required to do by the terms of an ordinary lease, and the tenant assumes the burden of enforcing such right of possession as against all persons wrongfully in possession, whether they be trespassers or former tenants wrongfully holding over." This quoted language is Mr. Freeman's, and he cites . . . [numerous] cases in support thereof.

So that, under the American rule, where the new tenant fails to obtain possession of the premises only because a former tenant wrongfully holds over, his remedy is against such wrongdoer and not against the landlord — this because the landlord has not covenanted against the wrongful acts of another and should not be held responsible for such a tort unless he has expressly so contracted. This accords with the general rule as to other wrongdoers, whereas the English rule appears to create a specific exception against lessors. It does not occur to us now that there is any other instance in which one clearly without fault is held responsible for the independent tort of another in which he has neither participated nor concurred and whose misdoings he cannot control.

In the Pennsylvania case of *Cozens v. Stevenson*, 5 Serg. & R. 421, which enforces the American rule, this is said:

> We are all clearly of opinion that the law implies no promise to deliver possession from the words of this lease. It is a bare demise for two years, without mention of the lessor's undertaking to deliver possession, although it is expressly said that at the date of the lease the house and wharf were occupied by Hugg. If a lease be made by the words "grant or demise," it amounts to a covenant by the lessor that he will make satisfaction to the lessee if he is lawfully evicted: 5 Coke 17. So covenant lies on the word "demise," if the lessor had no power to demise, although the lessee neither entered nor was evicted: Hob. 12. * * *

The case of *Gardner v. Keteltas*, 3 Hill 330, 38 Am. Dec. 637, seems to be the first case in the United States in which the question was considered. The lease there contained the ordinary covenants of title and quiet enjoyment, and this is said: "All that either of the covenants mentioned exact of the lessor is that he shall have such a title to the premises, at the time, as shall enable him to give a free, unencumbered lease for the term demised. There is no warranty, express or implied, against the acts of strangers; hence, if the lessee be ousted by one who has no title, the law leaves him to his remedy against the wrongdoer, and will not judge that the lessor covenanted against the wrongful acts of strangers unless the covenant be full and express to the purpose: *Noke's Case*, 4 Rep. 80. * * * . . . [U]pon the well-settled construction of the covenants of title and quiet enjoyment it is not the duty of the landlord, when the demised premises are wrongfully held by a third person, to take the necessary steps to put his lessee into possession. The latter being clothed with the title by virtue of the lease, it belongs to him to pursue such legal remedies as the law has provided . . . ." * * *

For the reasons which have been so well stated by those who have enforced the American rule, our judgment is that there is no error in the judgment complained of. * * *

We are confirmed in our view by the Virginia statute, providing a summary remedy for unlawful entry or detainer, Code, § 5445, et seq. The adequate, simple and summary remedy for the correction of such a wrong provided by the statute was clearly available to this plaintiff. It specifically provides that it shall lie for one entitled to possession "in any case in which a tenant shall detain the possession of land after his right has expired without the consent of him who is entitled to possession."

Certainly there should be co-operation between the lessor and the lessee to impose the resulting loss upon such a trespasser, but whatever other equities may have arisen, when the plaintiff found that the premises which he had leased were occupied by a wrongdoer who unlawfully refused to surrender possession, it is manifest that he, the lessee, Hannan, had the right to oust the wrongdoer under this statute. His failure to pursue that remedy is not explained . . . . The amount to be recovered must be proportionate to the extent of the injury, and when the injured party has failed or refused to lessen his injury by such prudent action and reasonable exertion as were in his power, recovery will be denied to him to the extent of his failure of duty . . . . *Adair v. Bogle*, 20 Iowa 238 (1866), the opinion in which was written by Judge Dillon, and is quoted with approval by this court in *Robrecht v. Marling*, 2 S.E. 827 (W. Va. 1887), cited. This eminent jurist said: "Two principles should, in cases like the present, be impressed upon juries: 1. The plaintiff should recover only such damages as have directly and necessarily been occasioned by the defendant's wrongful act or default; and, 2. That if the plaintiff by reasonable exertions or care on his part could have prevented such damages, he is bound to do so; and so far as he could have thus prevented them, he cannot recover therefor. The injured party is entitled to recover only such sums as will make him whole. This he is entitled to recover, so far as his injury has been the direct or natural cause of the wrongful act of the other party." * * *

The plaintiff alleges in his declaration as one of the grounds for his action that the defendant suffered the wrongdoer to remain in possession, but the allegations show that he it was who declined to assert his remedy against the wrongdoer, and so he it was who permitted the wrongdoer to retain the possession. Just why he valued his legal right to the possession so lightly as not to assert it in the effective way open to him does not appear. Whatever ethical duty in good conscience may possibly have rested upon the defendant, the duty to oust the wrongdoer by the summary remedy provided by the unlawful detainer statute clearly rested upon the plaintiff. The law helps those who help themselves, generally aids the vigilant, but rarely the sleeping, and never the acquiescent. Affirmed.

NOTES

1.   In a jurisdiction adopting the American rule in which you represent a tenant, what provisions would you propose inserting in an apartment lease with a term of one year? In a jurisdiction adopting the English rule, what provisions might a landlord seek? What if the jurisdiction in which you are practicing has not clearly adopted one rule or the other, what would you propose inserting in a lease to control the issue of this case?

2.   Does the Virginia statute cited in the case really "confirm" the holding of the case? Consider two further attempts at statutory reform in this area, and consider the extent to which the following state statutes would affect the outcome of the *Hannan* case:

Va. Code § 55–248.22 (2014):

If the landlord willfully fails to deliver possession of the dwelling unit to the tenant, rent abates until possession is delivered and the tenant may: terminate the rental agreement upon at least five days' written notice to the landlord and upon termination, the landlord shall return all prepaid rent and security deposits; or demand performance of the rental agreement by the landlord. If the tenant elects, he may file an action for possession of the dwelling unit against the landlord or any person wrongfully in possession and recover the damages sustained by him. If a person's failure to deliver possession is willful and not in good faith, an aggrieved person may recover from that person the actual damages sustained by him and reasonable attorney's fees.

Md. Real Prop. Code § 8-204 (2014):

(a) *Applicability of section.* — This section is applicable only to single or multi-family dwelling units.

(b) *Covenant to quiet enjoyment required.* — A landlord shall assure his tenant that the tenant, peaceably and quietly, may enter on the leased premises at the beginning of the term of any lease.

(c) *Abatement of rent for failure to deliver.* — If the landlord fails to provide the tenant with possession of the dwelling unit at the beginning of the term of any lease, the rent payable under the lease shall abate until possession is delivered. The tenant, on written notice to the landlord before possession is delivered, may terminate, cancel, and rescind the lease.

(d) *Liability of landlord.* — On termination of the lease under this section, the landlord is liable to the tenant for all money or property given as prepaid rent, deposit, or security.

(e) *Consequential damages.* — If the landlord fails to provide the tenant with possession of the dwelling unit at the beginning of the term of any lease, whether or not the lease is terminated under this section, the landlord is liable to the tenant for consequential damages actually suffered by him subsequent to the tenant's giving notice to the landlord of his inability to enter on the leased premises.

Once the tenant gains possession of the premises, damages for breach of the covenant of a power to demise are usually nominal in amount, unless there is a subsequent eviction. In the latter instance, however, a breach of the covenant of quiet enjoyment also has occurred.

3. Subject to an exception concerning the habitability of residential premises discussed later in this chapter, the tenant's covenant to pay rent is independent of many of the landlord's other duties in the lease. Nevertheless, the traditional rule on the independence or dependency of lease covenants has long been put in general, contractual terms: "[C]ovenants in leases are independent or dependent according to the nature of the obligations, their relation to each other, the intention of the parties as shown by the provisions of the governing lease, and the factual situation of each particular case . . . ." *Medico-Dental Bldg. Co. of Los Angeles v. Horton & Converse*, 132 P.2d 457, 464 (Cal. 1942). And: "Where a covenant goes only to part of the consideration on both sides, and a breach of such covenant may be paid for in damages, it is an independent covenant, and an action may be maintained for a breach of the covenant without averring performance [of other covenants in the lease — Eds.]." *Nelson v. Oren*, 41 Ill. 18, 23 (1866).

III.   ILLEGALITY AND FRUSTRATION OF PURPOSE

A.   Illegality

A lease may be illegal at its inception — void *ab initio*, as lawyers say — because it contravenes public policy or violates a statute. A contract that violates a statutory prohibition designed for police or regulatory purposes is void. It confers no right upon the wrongdoer, typically the landlord seeking to collect the rent. With a residential lease, particularly one for a low-income tenancy, the doctrine of illegality typically might involve substantial violations of a housing code. In a leading opinion, the court held that "where such conditions exist on a leasehold prior to an agreement to lease, the letting of such premises constitutes a violation of . . . the Housing Regulations, and . . . these Sections do indeed 'imply a prohibition' so as 'to render the prohibited act void.' " *Brown v. Southall Realty Co.*, 237 A.2d 834, 837 (D.C. 1968) (involving code violations known to the landlord).

A statutory penalty may imply a prohibition, unless the legislative intent is otherwise. Thus, the court in *Brown* investigated the provisions of the Housing Regulations and implied the prohibition from the following two sections of the D.C. housing code: (1) "No persons shall rent or offer to rent any habitation, or the furnishings thereof, unless such habitation and its furnishings are in a clean, safe and sanitary condition, in repair, and free from rodents or vermin;" and (2) "Every premises accommodating one or more habitations shall be maintained and kept in repair so as to provide decent living accommodations for the occupants. This part of the Code contemplates more than mere basic repairs and maintenance to keep out the elements; its purpose is to include repairs and maintenance designed to make a premises or neighborhood healthy and safe."

Older cases in many jurisdictions involve the illegal leasing of premises for the sale of intoxicating liquors, gambling, prostitution, or in violation of the antitrust laws. See 1 Am. L. Prop. 262–66 (James Casner ed., 1952); Restatement (Second) of Property, Landlord-Tenant, § 8.1, and Statutory Note ff (1977).

B. Frustration

Many decisions have involved the applicability of the contract doctrine of frustration of purpose to leases. 1 Am. L. Prop. 400 (James Casner ed., 1952). The doctrine applies only in instances of extreme hardship for the tenant:

> The general principle underlying commercial frustration is that where the purpose of a contract is completely frustrated and rendered impossible of performance by a supervening event or circumstance, the contract will be discharged. The courts in determining whether frustration will apply usually look to three factors. The first and probably most important is whether the intervening act was *reasonably foreseeable* so that the parties could and should have protected themselves by the terms of their contract. The courts then must consider the questions of whether the act was an exercise of sovereign power or *vis major*, and whether the parties were instrumental in bringing about the intervening event. The courts have generally held that if the supervening event was reasonably foreseeable the parties may not set up the defense of frustration as an excuse for non-performance. The majority of the courts stress this principle in deciding cases on frustration, and hold that if the parties could have reasonably anticipated the event, they are obliged to make provisions in their contract protecting themselves against it.

Montauk Corp. v. Seeds, 138 A.2d 907, 911 (Md. 1958). In *Lloyd v. Murphy*, 153 P.2d 47, 49–51 (Cal. 1944) (Traynor, J.), the court explained the doctrine as follows:

> [M]odern cases have recognized that the defense may be available in a proper case, even in a lease. As the author declares in 6 Williston, Contracts (1938), § 1955, pp. 5485–87,
>
>> The fact that [a] lease is a conveyance and not simply a continuing contract and the numerous authorities enforcing liability to pay rent in spite of destruction of leased premises, however, have made it difficult to give relief. That the tenant has been relieved, nevertheless, in several cases indicates the gravitation of the law toward a recognition of the principle that fortuitous destruction of the value of performance wholly outside the contemplation of the parties may excuse a promisor even in a lease . . . . Even more clearly with respect to leases than in regard to ordinary contracts the applicability of the doctrine of frustration depends on the total or nearly total destruction of the purpose for which, in the contemplation of both parties, the transaction was entered into.
>
> * * *
>
> Although the doctrine of frustration is akin to the doctrine of impossibility of performance since both have developed from the commercial necessity of excusing performance in cases of extreme hardship, frustration

is not a form of impossibility . . . , which includes not only cases of physical impossibility but also cases of extreme impracticability of performance. Performance remains possible but the expected value of performance to the party seeking to be excused has been destroyed by a fortuitous event, which supervenes to cause an actual but not literal failure of consideration.

The question in cases involving frustration is whether the equities of the case . . . require placing the risk of a disruption or complete destruction of the contract equilibrium on defendant or plaintiff under the circumstances of a given case, and the answer depends on whether an unanticipated circumstance, the risk of which should not be fairly thrown on the promisor, has made performance vitally different from what was reasonably to be expected. The . . . contract . . . must be examined to determine whether it can be fairly inferred that the risk of the event that has supervened to cause the alleged frustration was not reasonably foreseeable. If it was foreseeable there should have been provision for it in the contract, and the absence of such a provision gives rise to the inference that the risk was assumed.

The doctrine of frustration has been limited to cases of extreme hardship so that businessmen, who must make their arrangements in advance, can rely with certainty on their contracts. The courts have required a promisor seeking to excuse himself from performance of his obligations to prove that the risk of the frustrating event was not reasonably foreseeable and that the value of counterperformance is totally or nearly totally destroyed . . . . Thus laws or other governmental acts that make performance unprofitable or more difficult or expensive do not excuse the duty to perform a contractual obligation.

SMITH v. ROBERTS
370 N.E.2d 271 (Ill. App. Ct. 1977)

MILLS, J.

We have here a lease.

And with it we have the doctrine of commercial frustration.

The trial judge held that the doctrine applied and that the lease was terminated thereby.

He was right. We affirm.

The Smiths and Roberts Brothers entered into a lease agreement for the rental of the first floor and basement of property located in Springfield at 111–113 North Sixth Street. Roberts Brothers was already operating a men's clothing store next to the leased premises and intended to make an opening through their east wall and Smith's west wall in order to establish a department which would be called the Gas Light Room. Thereafter, the main store building of Roberts Brothers was completely destroyed by fire. Questions concerning the rights and liabilities of the parties under the lease were raised as a result of that conflagration and those questions then ripened into litigation.

After Roberts Brothers failed to reoccupy the leased premises — which suffered only smoke damage — the Smiths filed suit for breach of the lease. Roberts Brothers then counterclaimed for damages against the Smiths alleging that the Smiths had caused delay in the reconstruction of Roberts Brothers' premises and asked for a determination that the lease was terminated. The trial court found that the lease had been terminated because the destruction of Roberts Brothers' main store excused performance on its part . . . . We concur with the trial judge and affirm.

In their complaint, the Smiths alleged that the clothing store had violated its obligations under the lease and that the leased premises had been restored and repaired according to provisions of the lease. Roberts Brothers' defense to the complaint was . . . : the lease had been terminated because of the "doctrine of commercial frustration" . . . . ***

> "The doctrine of frustration is an extension of this exception to cases where the cessation or nonexistence of some particular condition or state of things has rendered performance impossible and the object of the contract frustrated. It rests on the view that where from the nature of the contract and the surrounding circumstances the parties when entering into the contract must have known that it could not be performed unless some particular condition or state of things would continue to exist, the parties must be deemed, when entering into the contract, to have made their bargain on the footing that such particular condition or state of things would continue to exist, and the contract therefore must be construed as subject to an implied condition that the parties shall be excused in case performance becomes impossible from such condition or state of things ceasing to exist." *Leonard v. Autocar Sales & Service Co.* (1945), 392 Ill. 182, 187–88, 64 N.E.2d 477, 479–80, *cert. denied* (1946), 327 U.S. 804.

The doctrine of commercial frustration is not to be applied liberally. However, the defense of commercial frustration is a viable doctrine in Illinois and will be applied when the defendant has satisfied two rigorous tests: (1) the frustrating event was not reasonably foreseeable; and (2) the value of counterperformance by the lessee had been totally or near totally destroyed by the frustrating cause.

The factual circumstances here satisfy these stringent tests. First, although it might be foreseeable that the main Roberts Brothers' store would be destroyed and the leased premises would remain intact, it is a remote contingency to provide for in a lease. The parties were, in fact, diligent enough to put a catastrophe clause in the lease concerning destruction of the leased premises. We find that their failure to include such a clause as to Roberts Brothers' main store was not due to a lack of diligence since such a contingency was not reasonably foreseeable.

The second horn of the two-prong test is also satisfied — the value of the Smith counterperformance was totally — or nearly totally — destroyed. Although it would be physically possible to operate the leased premises as a separate entity, testimony revealed that operations would have to be changed drastically in order to make the premises self-sufficient. Furthermore, the record clearly demonstrates that the leased premises were never intended to be autonomous. Therefore, the trial court's finding that the existence of the main store was an implied condition of the contract between the parties and that its destruction frustrated the lease is an accurate interpretation of the lease. The court's finding results in the fairest disposition of the parties' respective interests . . . . Affirmed.

NOTES

1.   Is the holding in *Smith v. Roberts* consistent with the preceding quotations from *Montauk Corp. v. Seeds* and from *Lloyd v. Murphy*? What additional facts would influence your analysis of this question?

2.   When the government takes a leasehold by using its eminent domain powers, is the tenant, once in receipt of a condemnation award, still obligated to pay rent to the landlord? See *Leonard v. Autocar Sales & Serv. Co.*, 64 N.E.2d 477, 482 (Ill. 1945), stating:

> [T]he rule seems to be well settled that in order for a tenant to be excused from the payment of rent because of the condemnation of the demised premises, it is essential that the estate of the landlord be extinguished by the condemnation proceedings. * * * We regard this rule and the reasoning upon which it is based as sound; therefore, it necessarily follows, that the taking . . . of the temporary use, only, of the premises in question does not affect the liability of appellant for the payment of rent.

IV.   THE COVENANT OF QUIET ENJOYMENT

Courts in virtually every state have held that a covenant of quiet enjoyment is implied by operation of law into every lease of real property. The covenant sometimes is implied from the words "demise" or "grant" in the operative clause of a lease, but more often, it is implied from the legal relationship between a landlord and tenant. See, e.g., *Cohen v. Hayden*, 163 N.W. 238, 239 (Iowa 1917). The latter implication permits recognition of the covenant even in an oral lease. Courts have implied the phrase "quiet enjoyment" so often and have found it written in so many leases that many have come to believe that it is not only a traditional reference to the landlord's duty to deliver a right to possession of the premises, but also to the type of possession due the tenant — in short, to the tenant's right to quiet, peaceful, enjoyable use of the premises, absent some agreement to the contrary. The following two cases show part of the law's progression in this regard. Not all states would go so far.

BLACKETT v. OLANOFF
358 N.E.2d 817 (Mass. 1977)

WILKINS, J.

The defendant in each of these consolidated actions for rent successfully raised constructive eviction as a defense against the landlords' claim. The judge found that the tenants were "very substantially deprived" of quiet enjoyment of their leased premises "for a substantial time." He ruled that the tenants' implied warranty of quiet enjoyment was violated by late evening and early morning music and disturbances coming from nearby premises which the landlords leased to others for use as a bar or cocktail lounge (lounge). The judge further found that, although the landlords did not intend to create the conditions, the landlords "had it within their control to correct the conditions which . . . amounted to a constructive eviction of each [tenant]." He also found that the landlords promised each tenant to correct the situation, that the landlords made some attempt to remedy the problem, but they were unsuccessful, and that each tenant vacated his apartment within a reasonable time. Judgment was entered for each tenant; the landlords appealed; and we transferred the appeals here. We affirm the judgments.

The landlords argue that they did not violate the tenants' implied covenant of quiet enjoyment because they are not chargeable with the noise from the lounge. The landlords do not challenge the judge's conclusion that the noise emanating from the lounge was sufficient to constitute a constructive eviction, if that noise could be attributed to the landlords. Nor do the landlords seriously argue that a constructive eviction could not be found as matter of law because the lounge was not on the same premises as the tenants' apartments. See 1 American Law of Property § 3.51, at 281 (Casner ed. 1952). The landlords' principal contention, based on the denial of certain requests for rulings, is that they are not responsible for the conduct of the proprietors, employees, and patrons of the lounge.

Our opinions concerning a constructive eviction by an alleged breach of an implied covenant of quiet enjoyment sometimes have stated that the landlord must perform some act with the intent of depriving the tenant of the enjoyment and occupation of the whole or part of the leased premises. There are occasions, however, where a landlord has not intended to violate a tenant's rights, but there was nevertheless a breach of the landlord's covenant of quiet enjoyment which flowed as the natural and probable consequence of what the landlord did, what he failed to do, or what he permitted to be done. *Charles E. Burt, Inc. v. Seven Grand Corp.*, 340 Mass. 124, 127 (1959) (failure to supply light, heat, power, and elevator services). *Westland Housing Corp. v. Scott*, 312 Mass. 375, 381 (1942) (intrusions of smoke and soot over a substantial period of time due to a defective boiler). *Shindler v. Milden*, 282 Mass. 32, 33–34 (1933) (failure to install necessary heating system, as agreed). *Case v. Minot*, 158 Mass. 577, 587 (1893) (landlord authorizing another lessee to obstruct the tenant's light and air, necessary for the beneficial enjoyment of the demised premises). *Skally v. Shute*, 132 Mass. 367, 370–371 (1882) (undermining of a leased building rendering it unfit for occupancy). Although some of our opinions have spoken of particular action or inaction by a landlord as showing a presumed intention to evict, the landlord's conduct, and not his intentions, is controlling.

The judge was warranted in ruling that the landlords had it within their control to correct the condition which caused the tenants to vacate their apartments. The landlords introduced a commercial activity into an area where they leased premises for residential purposes. The lease for the lounge expressly provided that entertainment in the lounge had to be conducted so that it could not be heard outside the building and would not disturb the residents of the leased apartments. The potential threat to the occupants of the nearby apartments was apparent in the circumstances. The landlords complained to the tenants of the lounge after receiving numerous objections from residential tenants. From time to time, the pervading noise would abate in response to the landlord's complaints. We conclude that, as matter of law, the landlords had a right to control the objectionable noise coming from the lounge and that the judge was warranted in finding as a fact that the landlords could control the objectionable conditions.

This situation is different from the usual annoyance of one residential tenant by another, where traditionally the landlord has not been chargeable with the annoyance. See *Katz v. Duffy*, 261 Mass. 149 (1927) (illegal sale of alcoholic beverages); *DeWitt v. Pierson*, 112 Mass. 8 (1873) (prostitution). Here we have a case more like *Case v. Minot*, 158 Mass. 577 (1893), where the landlord entered into a lease with one tenant which the landlord knew permitted that tenant to engage in activity which would interfere with the rights of another tenant. There, to be sure, the clash of tenants' rights was inevitable, if each pressed those rights. Here, although the clash of tenants' interests was only a known potentiality initially, experience demonstrated that a decibel level for the entertainment at the lounge, acoustically acceptable to its patrons and hence commercially desirable to its proprietors, was intolerable for the residential tenants.

Because the disturbing condition was the natural and probable consequence of the landlords' permitting the lounge to operate where it did and because the landlords could control the actions at the lounge, they should not be entitled to collect rent for residential premises which were not reasonably habitable. Tenants such as these should not be left only with a claim against the proprietors of the noisome lounge. To the extent that our opinions suggest a distinction between nonfeasance by the landlord, which has been said to create no liability, and malfeasance by the landlord, we decline to perpetuate that distinction where the landlord creates a situation and has the right to control the objectionable conditions. Judgments affirmed.

NOTES

1.   Would a court recognize a residential tenant's action for damages on a covenant for quiet enjoyment without the tenant's vacating the premises? See *Legg v. Castruccio*, 642 A.2d 906 (Md. Ct. Spec. App. 1994) (yes); *Bocchini v. Gorn Management Co.*, 515 A.2d 1179, 1184 (Md. Ct. Spec. App. 1986) (yes, involving noisy upstairs neighbors and an assertion of damages for emotional distress).

2.   If the tenants' apartments were uninhabitable, why does it matter whether the landlord had the legal ability to control the neighboring tenant's conduct? If the landlord did not have the ability to control the noise, what, if anything, could a residential tenant do?

ECHO CONSULTING SERVS., INC. v.
NORTH CONWAY BANK
669 A.2d 227 (N.H. 1995)

Brock, C.J.

The plaintiff, Echo Consulting Services, Inc., sued its landlord, North Conway Bank, claiming constructive eviction, partial actual eviction, breach of an implied covenant of quiet enjoyment, and breach of the lease. Echo appeals the decision of the Superior Court denying all of Echo's claims after a bench trial. We affirm in part, reverse in part, and remand.

Pursuant to a written lease dated March 15, 1986, Echo leased premises on the downstairs floor of a building in Conway, together with "common right of access" thereto. When the bank purchased the building from Echo's prior landlord, it assumed the lease and became Echo's landlord.

The bank undertook a series of renovations to make the building suitable for a branch banking business on the main, street-level floor. These renovations, occurring on and off through 1987, created noise, dirt, and occasional interruptions of electric service. The construction work also made the rear parking lot inaccessible. During most of 1987, therefore, many of Echo's employees used the street-level parking lot in front of the building; they gained access to Echo's downstairs office by first using the main, street-level access to the building and then walking downstairs. On October 13, the bank changed the locks on the main floor access door for security reasons, and Echo's employees were no longer able to get in or out of the building through that door after regular business hours. At that point, Echo's only means of access after hours was through the rear door, and Echo presented testimony that even that access was obstructed and difficult at times. The parties disagree as to the extent of these interferences, and as to the damage that they caused to Echo's permissible uses of its leasehold.

On appeal, Echo argues that the trial court erred by: (1) confusing the legal standards for constructive eviction and partial actual eviction; (2) finding that locking the street-level access doors did not constitute a partial actual eviction; (3) ruling that there was no constructive eviction; and (4) applying the wrong legal standard to determine the quiet enjoyment issue.

This case involves a commercial, as distinguished from a residential, lease. Since we have not addressed in the commercial context all of the issues raised here, we will draw some insight from residential lease cases, even though the applicable law may be more protective in the residential context. Compare *Golub v. Colby*, 419 A.2d 397, 398 (N.H. 1980) with *Kline v. Burns*, 276 A.2d 248, 251 (N.H. 1971).

In any lease, along with the tenant's possessory interest, the law implies a covenant of quiet enjoyment, which obligates the landlord to refrain from interferences with the tenant's possession during the tenancy. See generally 2 R. Powell, Powell on Real Property ¶¶ 231[2], 232[1] (1994). There are several ways in which a landlord might breach that covenant, each giving rise to a different claim by the tenant. The landlord's actual physical dispossession of the tenant from the leased premises constitutes an actual eviction, either total or partial, as well as a breach of the covenant. *Id.* ¶ 231[2]. "Interferences by the landlord that fall short of a physical exclusion but that nevertheless substantially interfere with the tenant's enjoyment of the premises, causing the tenant to vacate, are actionable by the tenant as 'constructive' evictions." *Id.* The landlord's general breach of the covenant of quiet enjoyment, even if not "substantial" enough to constitute a constructive eviction, nevertheless entitles the tenant to damages. We turn now to addressing each of Echo's claims separately.

I. *Partial Actual Eviction.*

A partial actual eviction occurs when the landlord deprives the tenant of physical possession of some portion of the leased property, including denial of access to the leased premises. See *Barash v. Pennsylvania Terminal Real Estate Corp.*, 256 N.E.2d 707, 709 (N.Y. 1970); Restatement (Second) of Property § 6.1 Reporter's n. 2, at 236 (1976). A landlord cannot apportion a tenant's rights under a lease. *Smith v. McEnany*, 48 N.E. 781 (Mass. 1897). Thus, the bank cannot apportion Echo's rights to choose which door to enter if the lease gives Echo a right to two different doors for access.

Echo, however, was not physically deprived of any portion of the property leased to it, nor of any appurtenant rights given to it under the lease. For its claim of partial actual eviction, Echo relies on the following language in the lease: "approximately 1,890 square feet of floor area, together with common right of access thereto, a common use of the parking lot." Echo argues that this language gives it a right of access through the main, street-level door, since that door is the only door that was actually used in common by both the bank and Echo. We disagree.

A lease is a form of contract that is construed in accordance with the standard rules of contract interpretation. When construing disputed provisions in a lease, we must analyze the entire document to determine the meaning intended by the parties. Language used by the parties to the agreement should be given its standard meaning as understood by reasonable people. In the absence of ambiguity, the intent of the parties to a lease is to be determined from the plain meaning of the language used. "The meaning of a contract is ultimately a matter of law for this court to decide, including the determination whether a contract term is ambiguous." *Walsh v. Young*, 660 A.2d 1139, 1141 (N.H. 1995).

The word "common" in Echo's lease modifies the phrase "right of access." Thus it plainly means only that the tenant's right to access is not an exclusive right; it is in "common" with the landlord's. The lease is not ambiguous; it cannot reasonably be construed to afford Echo the right in "common" to use the street-level door simply because that is the door which the bank chose actually to use. We interpret the trial court's finding that "Echo employees had access to their offices through at least one door at all times" to be a determination that such access was reasonable. That is all that is required under the language of this lease.

The trial court apparently applied the standard for constructive eviction in ruling on the actual eviction claim. Even though this was error, we affirm its decision on this issue because it reached the correct result and there are valid alternative grounds to reach that result. Since Echo was not physically deprived of any portion of the premises to which it had a right under the lease, the partial actual eviction claim was properly denied.

II. *Constructive Eviction.*

A constructive eviction is similar to a partial actual eviction except that no actual physical deprivation takes place. A constructive eviction occurs when the landlord so deprives the tenant of the beneficial use or enjoyment of the property that the action is tantamount to depriving the tenant of physical possession. *Barash*, 256 N.E.2d at 710.

The bank argues that a constructive eviction claim will not lie unless the landlord intends that its actions (1) render the premises unfit for occupancy or (2) permanently interfere with the tenant's beneficial use or enjoyment of the premises. We disagree.

It is well established that "the landlord's conduct, and not his intentions, is controlling." *Blackett v. Olanoff*, 358 N.E.2d 817, 819 (Mass. 1977); cf. Restatement (Second) of Property § 6.1 (1976 & Supp. 1995) (not mentioning any requirement that the landlord intend to evict the tenant). The bank mistakenly relies on one prior case to support its view that intent is required for a constructive eviction. See *Thompson v. Poirier*, 420 A.2d 297 (N.H. 1980). Although *Thompson* contains allegations of intentional conduct on the landlord's part, intent was not a necessary element of our decision, and the prevailing view is to the contrary. For example, even though no intent was or could have been found, courts have found a constructive eviction where a nuisance outside the leased premises — such as excessive noise from neighboring tenants — was attributable to, though not affirmatively undertaken by, the landlord. See, e.g., *Blackett*, 358 N.E.2d at 819.

The focus of the inquiry in a constructive eviction case is not on intent but on the extent of the interference, i.e., whether, in the factual circumstances of the case, the interference is substantial enough that it is tantamount to depriving the tenant of physical possession. See, e.g., *Reste Realty Corp. v. Cooper*, 251 A.2d 268, 274–75 (N.J. 1969); see also 2 Powell, *supra* ¶ 232[1], at 16B-27; Restatement (Second) of Property, *supra*. The law regarding this substantiality requirement has moved over the years "in the direction of an increase in the landlord's responsibilities." 2 Powell, *supra* ¶ 232[1], at 16B-27. Even without any affirmative activity on the landlord's part, courts have found a constructive eviction where the landlord fails to perform a lease covenant, fails to perform statutory obligations, or fails to perform a duty that is implied from the circumstances. *Sierad v. Lilly*, 22 Cal. Rptr. 580, 583 (Cal. App. 1962) (deprivation of use of parking space impliedly included in the lease); *Cherberg v. Peoples Nat'l Bank of Washington*, 564 P.2d 1137, 1142 (Wash. 1977) (landlord's failure to repair outside wall rendering it unsafe).

As we held in connection with the partial actual eviction claim, the lease here did not grant Echo a right to use the particular door of its choosing. The lease provision was satisfied since, as the trial court found, Echo employees had access to their offices through at least one door at all times. Likewise, the trial court found "the interruptions and noise [from construction activities] were intermittent and temporary and did not substantially interfere or deprive Echo of the use of the premises."

There was conflicting testimony on these points, but the credibility of witnesses and the weight to be given to testimony are questions of fact for the trial court to resolve. We will not disturb the trial court's findings of fact on the constructive eviction issue since the evidence in the record was sufficient to support its conclusion.

III. *The Covenant of Quiet Enjoyment.*

A breach of the covenant of quiet enjoyment occurs when the landlord substantially interferes with the tenant's beneficial use or enjoyment of the premises. 2 Powell, *supra* ¶ 232[1], at 16B-27. Even if not substantial enough to rise to the level of a constructive eviction, see *Reste*, 251 A.2d at 274–75, such interference may constitute a breach of the covenant of quiet enjoyment entitling the tenant to damages. See Restatement (Second) of Property § 5 (changes in the physical condition of the premises which make them unsuitable for the use contemplated by the parties), § 6 (conduct by the landlord, or by a third party under the landlord's control, which interferes with the tenant's permissible use of the premises).

The trial court concluded that quiet enjoyment only protects a tenant's possession against repossession by the landlord or one claiming title superior to the landlord. Although our prior cases have not addressed any other basis for a claim that the covenant of quiet enjoyment has been breached, they have not rejected such a claim either. We do not believe such a view of the covenant of quiet enjoyment constitutes good law today; many other courts have extended the covenant beyond mere denial of actual possession. *Pollock v. Morelli*, 369 A.2d 458, 461 n.1 (Pa. Super. 1976); see Restatement (Second) of Property §§ 5–6.

When reasons of public policy dictate, "courts have a duty to reappraise old doctrines in the light of the facts and values of contemporary life — particularly old common law doctrines which the courts themselves created and developed." *Kline v. Burns*, 276 A.2d 248, 251 (N.H. 1971). Our society has evolved considerably since the tenurial system of property law was created by the courts. The complexities, interconnectedness, and sheer density of modern society create many more ways in which a landlord or his agents may potentially interfere with a tenant's use and enjoyment of leased premises. Even without rising to the level of a constructive eviction and requiring the tenant to vacate the premises, such interferences may deprive the tenant of expectations under the lease and reduce the value of the lease, requiring in fairness an award of compensatory damages. Moreover, under modern business conditions, there is "no reason why a lessee, after establishing itself on the leased premises, should be forced to await eviction by the lessor or surrender the premises, often at great loss, before claiming a breach of the covenant for interference with the use and possession of the premises" that is not substantial enough to rise to the level of a total eviction. *Tenn-Tex Props. v. Brownell-Electro, Inc.*, 778 S.W.2d 423, 428 (Tenn. 1989). Likewise, the landlord's greater level of knowledge of and control over the leased premises and the surrounding property militates in favor of a more modern view of the covenant of quiet enjoyment than the trial court adopted. See *Kline*, 276 A.2d at 251.

Since the trial court understandably, but erroneously, believed the implied covenant of quiet enjoyment protected only Echo's possession of the property, the court did not consider Echo's claim that the bank's construction activities breached the covenant by depriving Echo of the beneficial use of the premises. There was conflicting testimony as to whether such a breach occurred, and, if so, the damages caused thereby. These are questions of fact for the trial court to determine in the first instance. Accordingly, we reverse the trial court's conclusion on this issue and remand the quiet enjoyment claim for further proceedings consistent with this opinion.

We note, however, that our holding as to the definition of a covenant of quiet enjoyment effects a change in the common law in New Hampshire, and that others might have relied on the view of the covenant that our older cases had set forth. We decline, therefore, to make this change retroactive. Instead, for anyone who is not a party to the instant action, we will only apply this new interpretation prospectively. Affirmed in part; reversed in part; remanded.

V. THE COVENANT TO REPAIR

The traditional rule is that, absent a covenant or statute imposing a duty on the landlord to repair the premises, a landlord is under no duty to repair them. See *Thomas v. Stewart*, 60 S.W.3d 415, 418 (Ark. 2001). An exception exists for the common areas of multi-unit premises; they remain the landlord's responsibility, unless a lease covenant provides otherwise. As to the tenant, the traditional rule is that when a tenant covenants unconditionally to repair or to surrender the premises in good repair and a building on the premises is destroyed and not rebuilt, he is liable for its destruction, even though the destruction occurs through fire or some other accident. See *Paradine v. Jane*, 82 Eng. Rep. 897 (K.B. 1647). A tenant also has a duty to make those repairs that are necessary to prevent waste of the premises — repairing broken windows or a leak in the roof. Thus a tenant may covenant to return the premises "in good repair" at the end of the lease. See *Perry v. J.L. Mott Iron Works Co.*, 93 N.E. 798 (Mass 1911) (holding that "repair" "means "a mending of the waste or decay incident to a removal rather than a restoration" of the premises, not the equivalent of "in good condition"). Thus, the law of waste is often held to be the basis for the tenant's duty to repair, but this is not the view everywhere: "The implied duty of the tenant is not to repair generally, but so to use the premises as to make repairs unnecessary as far as possible, and it is an implied covenant against voluntary waste only." *Earle v. Arbogast*, 36 A. 923, 924 (Pa. 1897). So lease forms often require that the tenant "maintain and repair the premises" or keep them "in good condition."

The New York legislature early on provided some relief for tenants even when the lease did not expressly exempt them from liability for accidental loss. See N.Y. Real Prop. § 227 (McKinney 2009). It provides:

> Where any building, which is leased or occupied, is destroyed or so injured by the elements, or any other cause as to be untenantable, and unfit for occupancy, and no express agreement to the contrary has been made in writing, the lessee or occupant may, if the destruction or injury occurred without his or her fault or neglect, quit and surrender possession of the

leasehold premises, and of the land so leased or occupied; and he or she is not liable to pay to the lessor or owner, rent for the time subsequent to the surrender. Any rent paid in advance or which may have accrued by the terms of a lease or any other hiring shall be adjusted to the date of such surrender.

Suppose the roof of a leased premises "became gradually out of repair so as to leak badly." Would the tenant be absolved from liability by this statute? See *Suydam v. Jackson*, 54 N.Y. 450 (1873) (holding the tenant was not absolved). Rather, this statute was intended to ameliorate the harsh legal consequences of the holding in *Paradine v. Jane, supra*. The statute which held a tenant liable for even accidental destruction of the leased premises is patterned on 6 Anne, ch. 31 (1707), as amended by 14 Geo. III, ch. 78, § 86 (1774), just in time to be received into the American common law. See 4 Kent's Commentaries, *81–82 (reprinted in its 12th and 14th editions in 1896 by Little Brown and Co., Boston). The N.Y. statute was intended to resolve any doubts about the reception of the English law on this subject. See, e.g., *Rountree v. Thompson*, 39 S.E.2d 523, 523–24 (N.C. 1946).

SPARKMAN v. HARDY
78 So. 2d 584 (Miss. 1955)

LEE, J.

This cause originated by the bill of complaint of Mrs. Edd Metts Hardy to compel the acceptance by Mrs. L. B. Sparkman of monthly advance rent in the sum of $120.00 for the first floor and the rear four rooms on the second floor, including the rear half of the hall on the second floor, of the Sparkman building in the City of Cleveland, Mississippi. The complainant alleged that she is the assignee of an original lease from Mrs. Sparkman to Marion J. Hardy, dated March 29, 1945, which was to run for a period of ten years, with the right of renewal, under certain conditions, for an additional fifteen years. It was charged that Mrs. Sparkman refused to accept the January 1952 rent; and such amount, together with the amount to accrue until the disposition of the cause, was paid into the registry of the court. * * *

The answer of Mrs. Sparkman admitted the receipt of rent from December 1945 to December 1951; that she refused acceptance of the January 1952 rent because complainant and her husband, Marion J. Hardy, made material changes and alterations in the building without her permission; and that they declined to restore the building to its former state, after she protested. She made her answer also a cross bill, in which it was charged . . . that a partition was placed in the building, . . . leaving the store proper only twenty feet instead of thirty feet wide; that a part of the glass front, installed at great expense, was removed; that the acts of the Hardys converted the building into a different kind of structure, with consequent damage to its value; that such material changes constituted waste; and that the restoration of the building to its previous state will be expensive. She therefore prayed for the cancellation of the lease and the assignment, and for recovery of damages on account of the changes.

The answer of the cross defendant, Mrs. Hardy, admitted that certain changes were made, but denied that they were material ones. * * * The court, at the conclusion of the hearing, validated the assignment to, and the title of, Mrs. Hardy in the lease, denied damages to Mrs. Sparkman on account of the changes, and directed the payment of rent . . . to Mrs. Sparkman . . . . From the final judgment, Mrs. Sparkman appealed.

When the lease was originally executed, Marion J. Hardy purposed to use the space for an electrical appliance shop, though there was no provision in the contract, which, in any case, limited the use. Neither was there a prohibition against its assignment or changes in the rental property. The changes, which are complained about, were made in August and September 1950. The partition cut the building into two parts for approximately sixty-five feet, with ten feet on the south side, which was converted into offices, and twenty feet on the north side, which was sublet for a jewelry shop. There was also a change in the front entrance. Mrs. Sparkman knew nothing about these changes until after they were made. She did not authorize them. She protested when she ascertained that they had been made, and demanded that the building be restored to its former condition. Her witnesses testified that it would cost a minimum of $840.90 and perhaps $1,000.00, or slightly more, to put the building in its former condition.

The evidence for the Hardys was to the effect that the changes were temporary in nature; that the building could be restored to its previous condition at small cost; that instead of damage to the building, the changes in fact increased its value; and that A.B. Sparkman knew about the changes at the time, he did not protest against them, but in fact expressed his approval. * * * The case turns on whether or not the changes were material, and therefore amounted to waste.

In *Moss Point Lbr. Co. v. Harrison County*, 42 So. 290, 300, 873 (Miss.), this Court said that: "Waste is defined to be any substantial injury done to the inheritance, by one having a limited estate, during the continuance of his estate." It was also there said that: "It is a universal rule in this country that, unless exempted by the terms of the lease from responsibility for waste, a tenant is responsible for voluntary waste, whenever committed." Undoubtedly material changes in a building, even though they may enhance the value, amount to waste. A good statement of the rule is given in § 1615, 4 Thompson on Real Property, p. 118, as follows: "A tenant, whether rightfully in possession or not, cannot, without the consent of the landlord, make material changes or alterations in a building to suit his taste or convenience, and, if he does, it is waste. The law is undoubtedly so settled. Any material change in the nature or character of the buildings made by the tenant is waste, although the value of the property should be enhanced by the alteration."

In the absence of a provision to the contrary, the tenant had the right to make such temporary changes as were consistent and proper for the utilization of the leased premises. (Citation omitted.) The changes did not affect the four walls, the foundation, or the roof. The reasonable value of the building was not shown; however, it appeared that it was insured for $15,000.00, and this affords a gauge by which it may be reasonably concluded that the building was worth at least that amount, and perhaps more. The parties to a ten-year lease, with a potential of fifteen additional years by renewal, in the absence of a prohibition to the contrary, must have contemplated that changes or rearrangements of the leased space could and would be made. All of the evidence showed that the former status can be restored at a cost ranging from several hundred to one thousand dollars — a small per cent of the actual value of the building. * * * Under the evidence in this case, the learned chancellor was fully warranted in finding that the changes are temporary and are not so material as to amount to waste. Affirmed.

HARTS v. ARNOLD BROS.
149 N.E. 420 (Ill. 1925)

STONE, J.

The defendant in error filed her bill in the superior court of Cook county against the plaintiff in error, a corporation, seeking an accounting for waste and an injunction. On hearing, the court granted an injunction and referred the cause to the master in chancery for an accounting of the nature, number and amount of the several acts of waste, and of the damages to the landlord, if any, on account of payment by her of increased insurance premiums. The master found that the buildings of the complainant had been damaged to the amount of $1328.28. The measure of damages applied by him was the cost of restoring the premises to the condition in which they were at the time the lease was made. Objections having been filed by the tenant, plaintiff in error here, the same, on hearing as exceptions before the chancellor, were sustained and a decree was entered, in which the chancellor held the proper measure of damages for waste to be the decrease in the market value of the buildings by reason of each of the several acts of waste. The chancellor also finds in his decree that the complainant had offered no evidence as to decrease in the market value of the buildings, and the decree entered awards the complainant, defendant in error here, nominal damages in the sum of $5. The landlord appealed to the Appellate Court. That court . . . reversed the holding of the superior court as to the measure of damages and held such to be the cost of restoring the premises to their former condition.

The premises in question consist of two old buildings, one of which had been at one time used for a mill and the other as a stable. The plaintiff in error had been in possession of both buildings under separate leases, but on May 1, 1920, a new lease was executed for a period of five years covering both buildings. The leases contained no restrictive clauses as to the use of the buildings, and during the period of the first lease the plaintiff in error made certain alterations in the buildings. It is alleged in the bill and shown on the hearing that certain other changes were subsequently made, and one building was so changed as to render it convenient for use as a soap factory. It is for these changes that this action has been brought. The bill was filed during the term of the lease.

The lease contained the following language: "The lessee having made alterations in said premises during its present tenure thereof, agrees to restore the said premises at the termination of this lease to their original condition as required, less reasonable wear and tear." The lease contained also the usual covenants regarding the care of the buildings and the condition in which they should be surrendered at the termination of the tenancy.

It is admitted that the landlord had been to no expense in repairing the buildings. The principal question to which the briefs of counsel are addressed is that of the measure of damages. Courts of this country are not in accord on the rule as to what constitutes a proper measure of damages where suit has been brought for waste during the term of the tenancy. The matter has not been squarely presented to this court. The view we take in this case, however, of the language of the lease herein quoted, does not make it necessary to go into the question as to what rule should be applied. That language, which appears not to have been presented to the Appellate Court in the briefs, if it be given meaning at all, must be construed as an understanding between the landlord and tenant that any alterations made by the tenant shall be corrected at the termination of the lease, if the landlord elects to have them so corrected, by restoring the premises to their original condition. True, such language does not consent to a depreciation of the landlord's reversion in the premises by such alterations, but, so far as the alterations are concerned, the language must be construed as an agreement that they shall be corrected at the close of the term if the landlord so elects. While it is not a matter of justification for acts of waste that the tenant agree to at some future time put the premises in such condition as they were when the lease was made, as the landlord has a right to continuation of the state of things as they existed when the injury was done, (*Klie v. Broock, 56 N.J.Eq. 18*,) yet where, as here, the parties by the terms of the lease recognize the right of the tenant to make changes on condition that he restore the premises at the close of the tenancy, such agreement must be held to prevent the application of the rule as to measure of damages. In such a situation the landlord is not entitled to recover, during the term of the tenancy, for any damage except that resulting to the reversion. Such damage, if any, is the difference between the market value before and after the changes were made. (*Watrous v. Cambridge Bank, 130 Mass. 343; Bodkin v. Arnold*, 48 W. Va. 114.) No evidence appears to have been offered of injury to the reversion by reason of the alterations complained of, and the superior court was therefore right in allowing nominal damages.

Defendant in error has cited numerous cases holding that the proper measure of damages is the cost of restoring the premises to the condition in which they were before the waste was committed. These cases, however, have been those either where the landlord has made repairs and sued for reimbursement, or where the tenant has, when called upon, refused to restore the property to its former state, or cases arising under breaches of covenants to repair the buildings and keep them in repair. Theses cases are therefore not in point here, where, as we have seen, there is language in the lease which is, in effect, a permission to the tenant to make alterations on condition that he, at the close of the term of the tenancy, shall, if ordered to do so by the landlord, restore the premises to their original condition. The lease had yet years to run, and the tenant was bound, at the close of the term, to make the necessary repairs, if ordered to do so. We are of the opinion, therefore, that it was error on the part of the Appellate Court to hold that the correct measure of damages to be applied in this case was the cost of restoration. * * * For the reasons herein given, the judgment of the Appellate Court is reversed and the decree of the superior court is affirmed.

NOTE

When a tenant covenants to "repair and maintain (not including major structural alterations to)" the premises, is he responsible for installing plumbing vents and traps, and a larger gas line because of requirements in a housing code? See *Friedman v. Le Noir*, 241 P.2d 779 (Ariz. 1952) (holding that the installation was not a repair, but an alteration; not a major, but was a minor structural alteration, stating: "The lessees were not only to 'repair' the premises but they were, in addition thereto, required to 'maintain' the entire premises except as to 'major structural alterations.' It certainly included minor structural alterations and it included all repairs. The lease agreement was executed by the parties at a time when the ordinance under which the plumbing inspector acted was in full force and effect and the ordinance therefore became a part of the lease agreement, as much so as if written therein. Both lessors and lessees are presumed to have known of the existence of such ordinance at the time the lease was executed. It follows that in the absence of an express covenant in the lease imposing the duty upon the lessors to make the repairs or alterations made by the lessees under governmental compulsion, the general covenant that the lessees should 'maintain and keep in good repair' the premises involved includes repairs made compulsory by municipal ordinance.").

ATLANTIC DISCOUNT CORP. v. MANGEL'S OF NORTH CAROLINA, INC.
163 S.E.2d 295 (N.C. App. 1968)

On 25 September 1953, plaintiff was the owner of The Carolina Building, located on the north side of East Main Street in Elizabeth City. The Carolina Building extended from McMorrine Street on the east to Martin Street on the west, having a frontage of approximately 200 feet on East Main Street, and extended northward between McMorrine and Martin Streets for a depth of approximately 100 feet. The ground level of the building had eight retail store sections of approximately 23 feet each fronting on East Main Street, and a center corridor (or arcade) 16 feet in width. The second, third, and fourth floor levels were devoted primarily to office space for rent to various tenants. By instrument dated 25 September 1953, plaintiff leased to the defendant, for a term beginning 1 October 1953 and expiring 30 September 1973, two of the retail store sections on the ground level, plus an area for storage space on the second floor. The defendant occupied the two retail store sections and made improvements therein. On 1 March 1967 The Carolina Building was wholly destroyed by fire. Plaintiff claims the lease was terminated by the complete destruction of the building which contained the leased premises. Defendant claims the lease was not terminated, and that plaintiff is under duty to restore the leased premises for defendant's use during the remaining term of the lease. This action was instituted by plaintiff under the Uniform Declaratory Judgment Act for a determination of the rights of the parties under their lease agreement. Judge Cowper heard the cause upon the pleadings and concluded that: "(1) The lease agreement between the parties dated September 25, 1953, . . . was terminated by the fire . . . which completely destroyed the building of which the leased premises was a part. (2) The land upon which the leased premises was situated is free and clear of any claim by the defendant, the plaintiff being under no duty to restore or rebuild the leased premises, the improvements therein, nor any part thereof." From entry of the judgment, defendant appealed.

BROCK, J. Those sections of the lease which are pertinent to the controversy between the parties are as follows: "* * * (9) The Landlord shall promptly make all repairs and replacements (other than those herein required to be made by the Tenant) which may be necessary to maintain the demised premises in a safe, dry and tenantable condition and in good order and repair." The defendant urges that Section 9 of the lease constitutes a general covenant to repair, and that this covenant imposes upon the landlord the duty to rebuild the building.

"The rule has become well settled that the duty created by a lessor's general covenant to repair the leased premises shall, in the absence of other controlling language in the lease or competent proof of circumstances compelling an opposite conclusion, be construed to extend to the restoration or rebuilding of structures on the premises if they are destroyed by fire." Annot., *38 A.L.R. 2d 682, at 703 (1954)*; see also, 32 Am. Jur., Landlord and Tenant, § 709, p. 586. However, it is also well settled that "the use of language which can be construed only to limit or make specific the duty of a lessor to repair structures on the leased premises may prevent an extension of the duties so as to embrace an obligation to restore or rebuild in case of substantial or total destruction by fire." Annot., 38 A.L.R. 2d 682, at 705 (1954). Also, "the view is taken that if the lease covers only a part of the building, an agreement therein to repair the building or keep it in repair will not be interpreted as imposing a duty upon the landlord to rebuild in case the whole building is destroyed by fire; such situation is said to call for an application of the principle under which the performance of a contract is excused where through no fault of the parties the subject matter without which the contract cannot be executed has ceased to exist." 32 Am. Jur., Landlord and Tenant, § 709, p. 586. * * *

Our research discloses no North Carolina case defining the duty of the lessor under a general covenant to repair in a lease of only a portion of a building, where the entire building is destroyed by fire. In *Saylor v. Brooks*, 114 Kan. 493, 220 P. 193, the Court held that an agreement by the landlord in a lease of the first floor and basement of a two-story concrete building that the premises should be "kept in good repair" does not obligate him to restore it where without his fault the building is entirely destroyed by fire. The opinion states: "We do not think the fact that a lease covering a part of a building contains the statement that the landlord agrees to keep it in repair has any fair tendency to indicate that the parties actually contemplated an obligation on his part to rebuild in case the whole house should be destroyed, and we see no sufficient grounds to interpret the language as imposing that duty upon him. The situation impresses us as one for the application of the principle under which the performance of a contract is excused, where, through no fault of the parties, its subject matter, without which it cannot be executed has ceased to exist."

A construction of the terms of a lease which would be unreasonable or unequal should be avoided, if it can be done consistently with the tenor of the agreement; and a construction which is most obviously just is to be favored as being most in accordance with the presumed intention of the parties. 32 Am. Jur., Landlord and Tenant, § 127, p. 130. The defendant lessee in this case prepared the lease which covers a little over seventeen pages . . . . It seems to be detailed as to the rights and obligations of the parties. If the parties had intended to obligate the lessor to rebuild in case of destruction of this entire building by fire, it would have been a simple matter to so provide. Instead he now seeks to impose such an obligation by asserting the provisions of Section 9 of the lease. We hold that this lease covering only a portion of a building and containing a provision that the landlord agrees to "make all repairs and replacements which may be necessary to maintain the demised premises in a safe, dry and tenantable condition and in good order and repair" does not fairly indicate, without more specific language, that the parties contemplated an obligation on the lessor to rebuild in case the entire building should be destroyed. * * * It would be harsh and unreasonable to require the lessor to restore and rebuild the *improvements* as they were in the demised premises, when the demised premises was only a portion of a building which has been entirely destroyed by fire. A construction of a contract leading to an absurd, harsh or unreasonable result should be avoided if possible. 51C C.J.S., Landlord and Tenant, § 232(4), p. 594. The judgment . . . is affirmed, and this cause is remanded . . . .

ROSE v. FREEWAY AVIATION, INC.
585 P.2d 907 (Ariz. App. 1978)

RICHMOND, J.

This is an appeal from a partial summary judgment on liability in favor of the plaintiff, Richard Rose, as tenant under a lease with Freeway Aviation, Inc. The determinative question is whether Freeway was obligated to rebuild a building after it had been destroyed by a windstorm. On March 1, 1970, the parties entered into a five-year lease of the building, which was to be used by Rose for airplane repair work. The lease provided in part: "[Freeway] shall be responsible . . . maintaining the leased premises in at least a good condition as they are presently."

The facts are not in dispute. In the latter part of 1973 the doors and frame were extensively damaged when a gasoline truck operated by a Freeway employee struck the building. Despite repeated requests to Freeway by Rose, the building was never repaired. In September, 1974, it was demolished by the storm. Thereafter, Rose tendered a check for the October rent and asked Freeway to rebuild it. Freeway refused on the ground that the lease had been terminated by the destruction of the building, and returned the check.

Rose then commenced this action for breach of the lease. In various counts, the complaint also alleged negligence, recklessness and gross negligence on the part of Freeway in refusing to repair and replace the building . . . . Although the judgment purports to determine all liability issues raised by the complaint in favor of Rose, the issue presented . . . is whether Freeway was obligated to rebuild by its covenant to maintain the leased premises in as "good condition as they are presently," or whether destruction of the building terminated all obligations under the lease.

Freeway's argument that the lease and any obligations thereunder were terminated by destruction of the building is based on the rule of supervening impossibility of performance, where a specific thing necessary for the performance of a contract is accidentally destroyed. That rule has no application, however, where the promisor has assumed by his contract the risk of the thing's continued existence. *Eggen v. Wetterborg, 237 P.2d 970 (Or. 1951)*, citing 6 Williston, Contracts (rev. ed.) 5451, § 1946. * * *

The rule is well settled that the duty created by a lessor's general covenant to repair the leased premises shall, in the absence of other controlling language in the lease or competent proof of circumstances compelling an opposite conclusion, be construed to extend to the restoration or rebuilding of structures on the premises if they are destroyed. *Atlantic Discount Corp. v. Mangel's of N.C., Inc.*, 163 S.E.2d 295, 298 (N.C. App.1968), citing Annot., 38 A.L.R.2d 682, at 703 (1954). See also 49 Am.Jur.2d, Landlord and Tenant, § 833, p. 801; but see, contra, *Heart of America Lumber Co. v. Belove*, 111 F.2d 535 (8th Cir. 1940). The same is true of a tenant's general covenant to repair. *See Anderson v. Ferguson*, 135 P.2d 302 (Wash. 1943).

"Maintain" is a broader term than "repair." *Wroblewski v. Grand Trunk Western Railway Co.*, 276 N.E.2d 567 (Ind. App. 1971). Black's Law Dictionary (revised 4th ed. 1968) at p. 1105 defines "maintain" as "keep in repair; keep up; preserve; preserve from lapse, decline, failure or cessation; provide for; *rebuild*; repair; replace." A covenant to maintain includes a covenant to rebuild. *Ponsler v. Union Traction Co.*, 132 N.E. 708 (Ind. App. 1921). Agreements which are clear and unambiguous will be enforced according to their terms and the words used will be given their normal ordinary meaning. "Maintain" is defined in Webster's Third New International Dictionary (1971) as "to keep in a state of repair, efficiency, or validity: preserve from failure or decline." Freeway did not see fit to restrict its general covenant to maintain, and the case does not present any circumstances compelling a conclusion contrary to the general rule. * * * Its covenant to maintain having obligated it to rebuild, the lease was not terminated by destruction of the building, and summary judgment as to its liability for failure to repair and rebuild was properly granted. * * * Affirmed . . . .

NOTE

Absent a covenant or statute on the issue, a tenant is typically liable for either permissive or voluntary, sometimes called commissive, waste. See *Stoup v. Robinson*, 933 S.W.2d 935 (Mo. Ct. App. 1996) ("for an action for waste by a lessee to prevail, the plaintiff must prove that the defendant either actively caused direct injury to the property or failed to exercise ordinary care in using the leased premises . . . . A tenant is liable for damages which he or she — either through negligence or willful misconduct — caused to the leased premises." Waste gives rise then to a cause of action in tort and must be pleaded as such. See *Watner v. P & C Food Mkts., Inc.*, 526 N.Y.S.2d 292 (N.Y. App. Div. 1988). There are actually three types of waste.

Permissive waste is injury that results from the tenant's neglect or omission, such as allowing a structure to deteriorate for lack of repair, failing to maintain a structure in wind and watertight condition, or permitting a third party to injure the property. Consistent with the idea that waste sounds in tort, a tenant's liability for permissive waste turns on the tenant's duty to repair and a substantial injury caused by the breach of that duty. Failing to establish the duty is grounds for dismissal of a landlord's complaint. See *Brizendine v. Conrad*, 71 S.W.3d 587 (Mo. 2002) (lease provision authorizing return of premises with "wear and tear excepted" does not authorize tenant to commit permissive waste, and a liquidated damages clause in the lease does not waive a landlord's cause of action for waste).

Voluntary waste involves a tenant's direct, deliberate, or willful injury of the premises, such as demolishing a structure, timbering the premises, or opening a mine. Voluntary waste involves a misuse or mismanagement of the premises, but a tenant is not prevented by it from making improvements. As the prior cases show, the tenant may make temporary, nonmaterial changes to the premises without incurring liability for waste. The traditional rule is that any material change constitutes waste even if the change increases the property's value. However, and as we have seen in Chapter 3, some courts may characterize this type of waste as non-compensable, *meliorating waste*. See *J.H. Bellows Co. v. Covell*, 162 N.E. 621 (Ohio Ct. App. 1927). If a tenant wishes to make material changes, the landlord may insist on a lease provision that the tenant will restore the premises to the condition in which they were received, less wear and tear. If the tenant provides this covenant, is the tenant liable for waste during the lease term? See *Harts v. Arnold Bros.*, 149 N.E. 420 (Ill. 1925). A tenant also commits waste by removing fixtures at the termination of the leasehold. Their removal, unsanctioned by a lease covenant, is waste. However, a tenant's reserving the right to remove fixtures does not imply any covenant to restore the premises. See *Leslie Pontiac, Inc. v. Novak*, 202 N.W.2d 114, 116 (Iowa 1972).

Innocent waste is an injury through accident or acts of a third party when it cannot be said that there is any act or negligence on the part of the tenant. It is seldom actionable. Cf. *Kennedy v. Kidd*, 557 P.2d 467, 470–71 (Okla. 1976) (a periodic tenant's death on the premises, undiscovered for a week and causing the premises to need fumigation and refurbishing, did not make the tenant's estate liable for waste).

A tenant at will traditionally is not liable for permissive waste. See 5 Am. L. Prop. 102 (James Casner ed., 1952).

RESTE REALTY CORP. v. COOPER
251 A.2d. 268 (N.J. 1969)

FRANCIS, J.

* * * On May 13, 1958 defendant Joy M. Cooper, leased from plaintiff's predecessor in title a portion of the ground or basement floor of a commercial (office) building at 207 Union Street, Hackensack, N.J. The term was five years . . . . The leased premises were to be used as "commercial offices" and "not for any other purpose without the prior written consent of the Landlord." More particularly, the lessee utilized the offices for meetings and training of sales personnel in connection with the business of a jewelry firm of which Mrs. Cooper was branch manager at the time. No merchandise was sold there.

A driveway ran along the north side of the building from front to rear. Its inside edge was at the exterior foundation wall of the ground floor. The driveway was not part of Mrs. Cooper's leasehold. Apparently it was provided for use of all tenants. Whenever it rained during the first year of defendant's occupancy, water ran off the driveway and into the offices and meeting rooms either through or under the exterior or foundation wall. At this time Arthur A. Donigian, a member of the bar of this State, had his office in the building. In addition, he was an officer and resident manager of the then corporate-owner. Whenever water came into the leased floor, defendant would notify him and he would take steps immediately to remove it . . . . Donigian promised to remedy the water problem by resurfacing the driveway . . . . The work was done as promised and although the record is not entirely clear, apparently the seepage was somewhat improved for a time. Subsequently it worsened, but Donigian responded immediately to each complaint and removed the water from the floor.

Donigian died on March 30, 1961. Whenever it rained thereafter and water flooded into the leased floor, no one paid any attention to defendant's complaints, so she and her employees did their best to remove it. During this time sales personnel and trainees came to defendant's premises at frequent intervals for meetings and classes. Sometimes as many as 50 persons were in attendance in the morning and an equal number in the afternoon. The flooding greatly inconvenienced the conduct of these meetings. At times after heavy rainstorms there was as much as two inches of water in various places and "every cabinet, desk and chair had to be raised above the floor." On one occasion jewelry kits that had been sitting on the floor, as well as the contents of file cabinets, became "soaked." Mrs. Cooper testified that once when she was conducting a sales training class and it began to rain, water came into the room making it necessary to move all the chairs and "gear" into another room on the south side of the building. On some occasions the meetings had to be taken to other quarters for which rent had to be paid; on others the meetings were adjourned to a later date. Complaints to the lessor were ignored. What was described as the "crowning blow" occurred on December 20, 1961. A meeting of sales representatives from four states had been arranged. A rainstorm intervened and the resulting flooding placed five inches of water in the rooms. According to Mrs. Cooper it was impossible to hold the meeting in any place on the ground floor; they took it to a nearby inn. That evening she saw an attorney who advised her to send a notice of vacation. On December 21 she asked that the place be cleaned up. This was not done, and after notifying the lessor of her intention she left the premises on December 30, 1961.

Plaintiff acquired the building and an assignment of defendant's lease January 19, 1962. On November 9, 1964 it instituted this action to recover rent for the unexpired term of defendant's lease, i.e., until March 31, 1964. * * *

The trial judge found that the "testimony is just undisputed and overwhelming that after every rainstorm water flowed into the leased premises of the defendant" and nothing was done to remedy the condition despite repeated complaints to the lessor. He declared also that the condition was intolerable and so substantially deprived the lessee of the use of the premises as to constitute a constructive eviction and therefore legal justification for vacating them.

On this appeal the plaintiff-landlord claims that under the long-settled law, delivery of the leased premises to defendant-tenant was not accompanied by any implied warranty or covenant of fitness for use for commercial offices or for any other purpose. He asserts also that by express provision . . . the tenant acknowledged having examined the "demised premises," having agreed to accept them in their "present condition," and having agreed to keep them in good repair, which acknowledgment, as a matter of law, has the effect of excluding any such implied warranty or covenant. * * *

[E]valuation of the landlord's contentions will be facilitated by first considering the lease and the factual setting attending its execution. . . . This course brings us immediately to the landlord's reliance upon the provisions of the lease that the tenant inspected the "demised premises," accepted them in their "present condition" and agreed to keep them in good condition. The word "premises," construed most favorably to the tenant, means so much of the ground floor as was leased to Mrs. Cooper for commercial offices. The driveway or its surfacing or the exterior wall or foundation under it cannot be considered included as part of the "premises." In any event there is nothing to show that the inspection by Mrs. Cooper of the driveway or the ground floor exterior wall and foundation under it prior to the execution of the lease would have given or did give her notice that they were so defective as to permit rainwater to flood into the leased portion of the interior. The condition should have been and probably was known to the lessor. If known, there was a duty to disclose it to the prospective tenant. Certainly as to Mrs. Cooper, it was a latent defect, and it would be a wholly inequitable application of *caveat emptor* to charge her with knowledge of it. The attempted reliance upon the agreement of the tenant in both leases to keep the "demised premises" in repair furnishes no support for the landlord's position. The driveway, exterior ground floor wall and foundation are not part of the demised premises. Latent defects in this context, *i.e.*, those the existence and significance of which are not reasonably apparent to the ordinary prospective tenant, certainly were not assumed by Mrs. Cooper. In fact in our judgment present day demands of fair treatment for tenants with respect to latent defects remediable by the landlord, either within the demised premises or outside the demised premises, require imposition on him of an implied warranty against such defects. * * *

This brings us to the crucial question whether the landlord was guilty of a breach of a covenant which justified the tenant's removal from the premises on December 30, 1961. We are satisfied there was such a breach.

The great weight of authority throughout the country is to the effect that ordinarily a covenant of quiet enjoyment is implied in a lease . . . . The early New Jersey cases laid down the strict rule that such a covenant would not be implied simply from the relationship of landlord and tenant. An express agreement to that effect or the use of words from which it could be implied was required. We need not deal here with problems of current serviceability of that rule because the lease in question contains an express covenant of quiet enjoyment for the term fixed. * * *

As noted above, the trial court found sufficient interference with the use and enjoyment of the leased premises to justify the tenant's departure and to relieve her from the obligation to pay further rent. In our view the evidence was sufficient to warrant that conclusion, and the Appellate Division erred in reversing it . . . .

Plaintiff claims further that *Stewart v. Childs Co.*, 86 N.J.L. 648, 92 A. 392 (E. &

A. 1914), strongly supports its right to recovery. Under the lease in that case the landlord covenanted that at all times he would keep the cellar waterproof. The cellar was known to be necessary to the conduct of the tenant's business. After the business opened, water flooded into the cellar, at times to a depth of two and three feet. There was no doubt the flooding resulted from failure of the landlord to make the place waterproof. But when the tenant moved out, a suit for rent for the unexpired term was instituted and the landlord was allowed to recover. It was held that the agreement to pay rent and the agreement to waterproof the cellar were independent covenants and breach of the covenant to waterproof was not a defense to the action for rent. We regard this holding as basically contrary to that in *Higgins v. Whiting*, 102 N.J.L. 279, 131 A. 879 (Sup. Ct. 1926), where the agreement by the landlord to heat the leased premises and the tenant's agreement to pay rent during the term were declared to be mutually dependent covenants. Thus failure to heat constituted a failure of consideration and justified vacation by the tenant without liability for further rent. We reject the rule of *Stewart v. Childs Co.* and espouse *Higgins v. Whiting* as propounding the sounder doctrine.

[W]hether the landlord's default in the present case is treated as a substantial breach of the express covenant of quiet enjoyment resulting in a constructive eviction of the tenant or as a material failure of consideration, (*i.e.*, such failure as amounts to a substantial interference with the beneficial enjoyment of the premises) the tenant's vacation was legal. Thus it is apparent from our discussion that a tenant's right to vacate leased premises is the same from a doctrinal standpoint whether treated as stemming from breach of a covenant of quiet enjoyment or from breach of any other dependent covenant. Both breaches constitute failure of consideration. The inference to be drawn from the cases is that the remedy of constructive eviction probably evolved from a desire by the courts to relieve the tenant from the harsh burden imposed by common law rules which applied principles of *caveat emptor* to the letting, rejected an implied warranty of habitability, and ordinarily treated undertakings of the landlord in a lease as independent covenants. To alleviate the tenant's burden, the courts broadened the scope of the long-recognized implied covenant of quiet enjoyment (apparently designed originally to protect the tenant against ouster by a title superior to that of his lessor) to include the right of the tenant to have the beneficial enjoyment and use of the premises for the agreed term. It was but a short step then to the rule that when the landlord or someone acting for him or by virtue of a right acquired through him causes a substantial interference with that enjoyment and use, the tenant may claim a constructive eviction. In our view, therefore, at the present time whenever a tenant's right to vacate leased premises comes into existence because he is deprived of their beneficial enjoyment and use on account of acts chargeable to the landlord, it is immaterial whether the right is expressed in terms of breach of a covenant of quiet enjoyment, or material failure of consideration, or material breach of an implied warranty against latent defects. * * * [T]he judgment of the Appellate Division is reversed and that of the trial court is reinstated.

VI. THE IMPLIED COVENANT OF HABITABILITY

At common law, no implied covenant existed that premises were fit for the purposes for which they were leased, except in leases of a furnished house. As to the exception, see *Ingalls v. Hobbs*, 156 Mass. 348 (1892), and *Smith v. Marrable*, 152 Eng. Rep. 693 (Ex. 1843) (both cases involving a short term and immediate occupancy). Additionally, as we have seen, a tenant's covenant to pay rent and the landlord's covenant to repair the premises traditionally have been regarded as being independent covenants. See *Reaume v. Brennan*, 300 N.W. 97 (Mich. 1941). Not so in the following case.

WADE v. JOBE
818 P.2d 1006 (Utah 1991)

DURHAM, J.

In June 1988, defendant Lynda Jobe rented a house in Ogden, Utah, from plaintiff Clyde Wade. Jobe had three young children. Shortly after she took occupancy, the tenant discovered numerous defects in the dwelling, and within a few days, she had no hot water. Investigation revealed that the flame of the water heater had been extinguished by accumulated sewage and water in the basement which also produced a foul odor throughout the house. The tenant notified the landlord, who came to the premises a number of times, each time pumping the sewage and water from the basement onto the sidewalk and relighting the water heater. These and other problems persisted from July through October 1988.

In November 1988, the tenant notified the landlord that she would withhold rent until the sewage problem was solved permanently. The situation did not improve, and an inspection by the Ogden City Inspection Division (the division) in December 1988 revealed that the premises were unsafe for human occupancy due to the lack of a sewer connection and other problems. Within a few weeks, the division made another inspection, finding numerous code violations which were a substantial hazard to the health and safety of the occupants. The division issued a notice that the property would be condemned if the violations were not remedied.

After the tenant moved out of the house, the landlord brought suit in the second circuit court to recover the unpaid rent. At trial, the landlord was awarded judgment of unpaid rent of $770, the full rent due under the parties' original agreement . . . . This appeal followed . . . .

At common law, the leasing of real property was viewed primarily as a conveyance of land for a term, and the law of property was applied to landlord/tenant transactions. At a time when the typical lease was for agricultural purposes, it was assumed that the land, rather than any improvements, was the most important part of the leasehold. See generally *Javins v. First Nat'l Realty Corp.*, 138 App. D.C. 369, 428 F.2d 1071, 1077 (D.C. Cir.), *cert. denied*, 400 U.S. 925 (1970). Under the rule of caveat emptor, a tenant had a duty to inspect the premises to determine their safety and suitability for the purposes for which they were leased before entering a lease. Moreover, absent deceit or fraud on the part of the landlord or an express warranty to the contrary, the landlord had no duty to make repairs during the course of the tenancy. Under the law of waste, it was the tenant's implied duty to make most repairs.

Unlike tenants in feudal England, most modern tenants bargain for the use of structures on the land rather than the land itself. Modern tenants generally lack the necessary skills or means to inspect the property effectively or to make repairs. Moreover, the rule of caveat emptor assumes an equal bargaining position between landlord and tenant. Modern tenants, like consumers of goods, however, frequently have no choice but to rely on the landlord to provide a habitable dwelling. Where they exist, housing shortages, standardized leases, and racial and class discrimination place today's tenants, as consumers of housing, in a poor position to bargain effectively for express warranties and covenants requiring landlords to lease and maintain safe and sanitary housing. *Javins*, 428 F.2d at 1079; *Green v. Superior Court*, 517 P.2d 1168, 1173 (Cal. 1974).

In consumer law, implied warranties are designed to protect ordinary consumers who do not have the knowledge, capacity, or opportunity to ensure that goods which they are buying are in safe condition. See *Henningsen v. Bloomfield Motors, Inc.*, 161 A.2d 69, 78 (N.J. 1960); Utah Code Ann. §§ 70A-2-314 to -316 (implied warranties contained in Uniform Commercial Code). The implied warranty of habitability has been adopted in other jurisdictions to protect the tenant as the party in the less advantageous bargaining position.

The concept of a warranty of habitability is in harmony with the widespread enactment of housing and building codes which reflect a legislative desire to ensure decent housing. It is based on the theory that the residential landlord warrants that the leased premises are habitable at the outset of the lease term and will remain so during the course of the tenancy. The warranty applies to written and oral leases, and to single-family as well as to multiple-unit dwellings. The warranty of habitability has been adopted, either legislatively or judicially, in over forty states and the District of Columbia. See 2 R. Powell, The Law of Real Property para. 233[2], at 16B-50 to -51 n.42 (cases), para. 233[3], at 16B-64 (statutes) (1991).

In recent years, this court has conformed the common law in this state to contemporary conditions by rejecting the strict application of traditional property law to residential leases, recognizing that it is often more appropriate to apply contract law. See *Stephenson v. Warner*, 581 P.2d 567 (Utah 1978) (landlord must use ordinary care to ensure leased premises are reasonably safe). Consistent with prevailing trends in consumer law, products liability law, and the law of torts, we reject the rule of caveat emptor and recognize the common law implied warranty of habitability in residential leases.

The determination of whether a dwelling is habitable depends on the individual facts of each case. To guide the trial court in determining whether there is a breach of the warranty of habitability, we describe some general standards that the landlord is required to satisfy. We note initially that the warranty of habitability does not require the landlord to maintain the premises in perfect condition at all times, nor does it preclude minor housing code violations or other defects. Moreover, the landlord will not be liable for defects caused by the tenant. Further, the landlord must have a reasonable time to repair material defects before a breach can be established.

As a general rule, the warranty of habitability requires that the landlord maintain "bare living requirements," see *Academy Spires, Inc. v. Brown*, 111 N.J. Super. 477, 268 A.2d 556, 559 (N.J. Dist. Ct. 1970), and that the premises are fit for human occupation. *Mease v. Fox*, 200 N.W.2d 791 (Iowa 1972); *Hilder v. St. Peter*, 478 A.2d 202, 208 (Vt. 1984). Failure to supply heat or hot water, for example, breaches the warranty. A breach is not shown, however, by evidence of minor deficiencies such as the malfunction of venetian blinds, minor water leaks or wall cracks, or a need for paint.

Substantial compliance with building and housing code standards will generally serve as evidence of the fulfillment of a landlord's duty to provide habitable premises. Evidence of violations involving health or safety, by contrast, will often sustain a tenant's claim for relief. At the same time, just because the housing code provides a basis for implication of the warranty, a code violation is not necessary to establish a breach so long as the claimed defect has an impact on the health or safety of the tenant.

In the instant case, in support of her claim that the premises were not in habitable condition, the tenant presented two city housing inspection reports detailing numerous code violations which were, in the words of the trial judge, "a substantial hazard to the health and safety of the occupants." Those violations included the presence of raw sewage on the sidewalks and stagnant water in the basement, creating a foul odor. At trial, the tenant testified that she had informed the landlord repeatedly of the problem with the sewer connection and the resulting lack of hot water, but the landlord never did any more than temporarily alleviate the problem. The landlord did not controvert the evidence of substantial problems. At trial, the court granted judgment for the landlord, concluding that Utah law did not recognize an implied warranty of habitability for residential rental premises. As discussed above, we have now recognized the warranty. We therefore remand this case to the trial court to determine whether the landlord has breached the implied warranty of habitability as defined in this opinion. If the trial court finds a breach of the warranty of habitability, it must then determine damages.

A. *Remedies.*

Under traditional property law, a lessee's covenant to pay rent was viewed as independent of any covenants on the part of the landlord. Even when a lessor expressly covenanted to make repairs, the lessor's breach did not justify the lessee's withholding rent. Under the prevailing contemporary view of the residential lease as a contractual transaction, however, the tenant's obligation to pay rent is conditioned upon the landlord's fulfilling his part of the bargain. The payment of rent by the tenant and the landlord's duty to provide habitable premises are, as a result, dependent covenants.

Once the landlord has breached his duty to provide habitable conditions, there are at least two ways the tenant can treat the duty to pay rent. The tenant may continue to pay rent to the landlord or withhold the rent.[3] If the tenant continues

---

[3] In addition, some jurisdictions recognize rent application, also known as "repair and deduct,"

to pay full rent to the landlord during the period of uninhabitability, the tenant can bring an affirmative action to establish the breach and receive a reimbursement for excess rents paid. Rent withholding, on the other hand, deprives the landlord of the rent due during the default, thereby motivating the landlord to repair the premises.[4] * * *

B. *Damages.*

In general, courts have applied contract remedies when a breach of the warranty of habitability has been shown. One available remedy, therefore, is damages. Special damages may be recovered when, as a foreseeable result of the landlord's breach, the tenant suffers personal injury, property damage, relocation expenses, or other similar injuries. See *Mease v. Fox*, 200 N.W.2d at 797; Restatement (Second) of Property, Landlord & Tenant § 10.2 (1977). General damages recoverable in the form of rent abatement or reimbursement to the tenant are more difficult to calculate.

Several different measures for determining the amount of rent abatement to which a tenant is entitled have been used by the courts. The first of these is the fair rental value of the premises as warranted less their fair rental value in the unrepaired condition. Under this approach, the contract rent may be considered as evidence of the value of the premises as warranted. Another measure is the contract rent less the fair rental value of the premises in the unrepaired condition. Methodological difficulties inherent in both of these measures, combined with the practical difficulties of producing evidence on fair market value, however, limit the efficacy of those measures for dealing with residential leases. For this reason, a number of courts have adopted what is called the "percentage diminution" (or percentage reduction in use) approach which places more discretion with the trier of fact.

Under the percentage diminution approach, the tenant's recovery reflects the percentage by which the tenant's use and enjoyment of the premises has been reduced by the uninhabitable conditions. In applying this approach, the trial court must carefully review the materiality of the particular defects and the length of time such defects have existed. It is true that the percentage diminution approach requires the trier of fact to exercise broad discretion and some subjective judgment to determine the degree to which the defective conditions have diminished the habitability of the premises. It should be noted, however, that despite their theoretical appeal the other approaches are not objectively precise either. Furthermore, they involve the use of an expert witness's subjective opinion of the "worth" of habitable and uninhabitable premises . . . . None of the approaches described above is inherently illegitimate, but we think that the percentage diminution approach has a practical advantage in that it will generally obviate the need for

---

allowing the tenant to use the rent money to repair the premises. Because this remedy has not been . . . sought in the instant case, we do not at this time make a ruling on its availability . . . .

[4] The majority of jurisdictions that permit rent withholding allow the tenant to retain the funds subject to the discretionary power of the court to order the deposit of the rent into escrow. Like the court in *Javins*, we think this type of escrow account would provide a useful protective measure in the right circumstances.

expert testimony and reduce the cost and complexity of enforcing the warranty of habitability. We acknowledge the limitation of the method but conclude that it is as sound in its result as any other and more workable in practice. We will have to depend on development of the rule in specific cases to determine whether it will be universally applicable . . . .

CONCLUSION

The decision of the trial court . . . regarding the implied warranty of habitability . . . is reversed. We remand this case to the trial court to determine whether the landlord breached the implied warranty of habitability as defined in this opinion. If the trial court determines that he was not in breach, the landlord will be entitled to payment for all the past due rent. If the trial court determines that his breach of the warranty of habitability totally excused the tenant's rent obligation (i.e., rendered the premises virtually uninhabitable), the landlord's action to recover rent due will fail. If the trial court determines that the landlord's breach partially excused the tenant's rent obligation, the tenant will be entitled to a percentage rent abatement for the period during which the house was uninhabitable.

NOTES

1.   Could the tenant successfully have claimed that she had been constructively evicted? Shouldn't the two doctrines work in tandem? See *Poyck v.Bryant*, 820 N.Y.S.2d 774 (Civ. Ct., N.Y. Cty. 2006) (a successful use of both by vacating tenants after complaining to building superintendents claiming exposure to second hand smoke in the premises).

2.   More than forty states accept the rule that a covenant or warranty of habitability is implied in residential leases. Although this acceptance largely has been the result of judicial decisions, see, e.g., *Hilder v. St. Peter*, 478 A.2d 202 (Vt. 1984), many state legislatures have enacted statutes also creating such warranties. See, e.g., Uniform Residential Landlord Tenant Act (URLTA), § 2.104 (1974) (adopted in 15 states), discussed in Samuel Jan Brakel & Donald M. McIntyre, *The Uniform Residential Landlord and Tenant Act (URLTA) in Operation: Two Reports*, 1980 Am. B. Found. Res. J. 555 (1980). The tenant's use of the warranty is contingent on affording the landlord notice of the defects on the premises and a reasonable time to repair them. See Robert Schoshinski, The American Law of Landlord and Tenant 127–28 (1980). With few exceptions, courts have refused to enforce waiver of the warranty by the tenant. See generally Edward Chase & Hunter Taylor, *Landlord and Tenant: A Study in Property and Contract*, 30 Vill. L. Rev. 571 (1985). URLTA also prohibits waiver. URLTA § 1.403(a)(1).

3.   Most courts that have considered the issue have refused to extend the warranty to commercial leases. See, e.g., *Pinzon v. A & G Properties*, 874 A.2d 347 (D.C. App. 2005); *Wesson v. Leone Enterprises, Inc.*, 774 N.E.2d 611, 620 (Mass. 2002). However, some courts have extended the implied warranty to commercial tenants or have reached a similar result by holding that the tenant's obligation to pay rent is dependent on the landlord's obligation to maintain the premises, as described by the court in *Barton Enters. v. Tsern*, 928 P.2d 368, 376–79 (Utah 1996):

We find that the principles announced in *Wade* in the context of residential leases are equally applicable to the commercial context. In addition, several other states have held that under certain circumstances, commercial lessees may withhold rent. One group of states, which includes Texas and New Jersey, holds that covenants in commercial leases are mutually dependent. Texas offers the most expansive protection for commercial leases; it extends to commercial lessees all protections available to residential lessees, including an implied warranty of suitability that the leased premises are suitable "for their intended commercial purpose." *Davidow v. Inwood North Professional Group*, 747 S.W.2d 373, 377 (Tex. 1988). The court in *Davidow* reasoned that a commercial lessee should have the same protections as those accorded a residential lessee and that contract principles rather than medieval property principles should apply. Although it stopped short of providing the same broad protections as Texas, the New Jersey Supreme Court held that "fair treatment for tenants with respect to latent defects remediable by the landlord . . . requires imposition on [the landlord] of an implied warranty against such defects." *Reste Realty Corp. v. Cooper*, 251 A.2d 268, 273 (N.J. 1969). A New Jersey appellate court thereafter noted that the state supreme court's decision heralded "the demise of the doctrine of independent covenants." *Ringwood Assocs. v. Jack's of Route 23, Inc.*, 398 A.2d 1315, 1319 (N.J. Super. Ct. App. Div. 1979).

A second group of states does not recognize implied warranties in commercial leases but nevertheless holds that covenants in commercial leases may be mutually dependent. Massachusetts and Indiana hold that the covenant to pay rent and the covenant to repair may be mutually dependent. *Erhard v. F.W. Woolworth Co.*, 372 N.E.2d 1277 (Mass. 1978). See *Welborn v. Society for Propagation of Faith*, 411 N.E.2d 1267, 1269 n.4 (Ind. App. 1980), where the court treated the covenants in a commercial lease as mutually dependent. The Supreme Court of Pennsylvania has held that a covenant to pay rent is dependent on all covenants that were significant inducements to the making of the lease. *Teodori v. Werner*, 415 A.2d 31 (Pa. 1980).

Both groups of cases recognize that the covenant to pay rent under a commercial lease is dependent on the lessor's compliance with those covenants necessary to provide the lessee with the benefits that were the essence of the bargain as reflected in the lease. This approach relieves a lessee of the obligation to abandon the premises, as is necessary under the fiction of a constructive eviction. By making the lessee's covenant to pay rent dependent on the lessor's performance of essential covenants, the legal analysis can focus, as it should, on the essential elements and purposes of the bargain between the lessor and the lessee. By employing contract principles, a court's analysis of a dispute between a lessor and a lessee should provide a more fair, realistic, and forthright analysis of whether a lessee may abate rent. The result reached on such an analysis should better comport with modern leasing practices and expectations than the result under an analysis based on the principle of independent covenants as modified by the doctrine of constructive eviction . . . .

A more complete discussion of the contract remedies in *Wade v. Jobe* is provided in the following opinion.

HILDER v. ST. PETER
478 A.2d 202 (Vt. 1984)

BILLINGS, C.J.

* * * Because we hold that the lease of a residential dwelling creates a contractual relationship between the landlord and tenant, the standard contract remedies of rescission, reformation and damages are available to the tenant when suing for breach of the implied warranty of habitability. The measure of damages shall be the difference between the value of the dwelling as warranted and the value of the dwelling as it exists in its defective condition. In determining the fair rental value of the dwelling as warranted, the court may look to the agreed upon rent as evidence on this issue. "[In] residential lease disputes involving a breach of the implied warranty of habitability, public policy militates against requiring expert testimony" concerning the value of the defect. *Birkenhead v. Coombs*, 465 A.2d 244, 247 (Vt. 1983). The tenant will be liable only for "the reasonable rental value [if any] of the property in its imperfect condition during his period of occupancy." *Berzito v. Gambino*, 308 A.2d 17, 22 (N.J. 1973).

We also find persuasive the reasoning of some commentators that damages should be allowed for a tenant's discomfort and annoyance arising from the landlord's breach of the implied warranty of habitability. See Moskovitz, *The Implied Warranty of Habitability: A New Doctrine Raising New Issues*, 62 Cal. L. Rev. 1444, 1470–73 (1974). Damages for annoyance and discomfort are reasonable in light of the fact that "the residential tenant who has suffered a breach of the warranty . . . cannot bathe as frequently as he would like or at all if there is inadequate hot water; he must worry about rodents harassing his children or spreading disease if the premises are infested; or he must avoid certain rooms or worry about catching a cold if there is inadequate weather protection or heat. Thus, discomfort and annoyance are the common injuries caused by each breach . . . ." Moskovitz, *A New Doctrine, supra*, at 1470–71. Damages for discomfort and annoyance may be difficult to compute; however, "[the] trier [of fact] is not to be deterred from this duty by the fact that the damages are not susceptible of reduction to an exact money standard." *Vermont Electric Supply Co. v. Andrus*, 315 A.2d 456, 459 (Vt. 1974).

Another remedy available to the tenant when there has been a breach of the implied warranty of habitability is to withhold the payment of future rent.[3] *King v. Moorehead*, 495 S.W.2d 65, 77 (Mo. App. 1973). The burden and expense of bringing suit will then be on the landlord who can better afford to bring the action. In an

---

[3] Because we hold that the tenant's obligation to pay rent is contingent on the landlord's duty to provide and maintain a habitable dwelling, it is no longer necessary for the tenant to first abandon the premises; thus, the doctrine of constructive eviction is no longer a viable or needed defense in an action by the landlord for unpaid rent.

action for ejectment for nonpayment of rent, 12 V.S.A. § 4773, "[the] trier of fact, upon evaluating the seriousness of the breach and the ramification of the defect upon the health and safety of the tenant, will abate the rent at the landlord's expense in accordance with its findings." [Note, *The Implied Warranty of Habitability: A Dream Deferred*, 48 UMKC L. Rev. 237, 248 (1980).] The tenant must show that: (1) the landlord had notice of the previously unknown defect and failed, within a reasonable time, to repair it; and (2) the defect, affecting habitability, existed during the time for which rent was withheld. Whether a portion, all or none of the rent will be awarded to the landlord will depend on the findings relative to the extent and duration of the breach. Of course, once the landlord corrects the defects, the tenant's obligation to pay rent becomes due again.

Additionally, we hold that when the landlord is notified of the defect but fails to repair it within a reasonable amount of time, and the tenant subsequently repairs the defect, the tenant may deduct the expense of the repair from future rent.

In addition to general damages, we hold that punitive damages may be available to a tenant in the appropriate case. Although punitive damages are generally not recoverable in actions for breach of contract, there are cases in which the breach is of such a willful and wanton or fraudulent nature as to make appropriate the award of exemplary damages. A willful and wanton or fraudulent breach may be shown "by conduct manifesting personal ill will, or carried out under circumstances of insult or oppression, or even by conduct manifesting . . . a reckless or wanton disregard of [one's] rights . . . ." *Sparrow v. Vermont Savings Bank*, 112 A. 205, 207 (Vt. 1921). When a landlord, after receiving notice of a defect, fails to repair the facility that is essential to the health and safety of his or her tenant, an award of punitive damages is proper.

> The purpose of punitive damages . . . is to punish conduct which is morally culpable . . . . Such an award serves to deter a wrongdoer . . . from repetitions of the same or similar actions. And it tends to encourage prosecution of a claim by a victim who might not otherwise incur the expense or inconvenience of private action . . . . The public benefit and a display of ethical indignation are among the ends of the policy to grant punitive damages.

Davis v. Williams, 402 N.Y.S. 2d 92, 94 (N.Y. Civ. Ct. 1977) . . . . Because of our holding in this case, the doctrine of constructive eviction, wherein the tenant must abandon in order to escape liability for rent, is no longer viable. When, as in the instant case, the tenant seeks, not to escape rent liability, but to receive compensatory damages in the amount of rent already paid, abandonment is similarly unnecessary . . . .

NOTES

1. How do the measures of damages in *Wade* and *Hilder* differ?

2. The court in *George Washington Univ. v. Weintraub*, 458 A.2d 43, 46 (D.C. 1983), held that "the implied warranty of habitability may be used as a sword (to collect damages) as well as a shield (to contest the obligation to pay rent)." See generally James Smith, *Tenant Remedies for Breach of Habitability: Tort Dimen-*

sions of a Contract Concept, 35 U. Kan. L. Rev. 505, 547–55 (1987). Whether used as a sword or a shield, the landlord is typically given a protective order giving him a right to collect rent subject to abatement or set-off for the breach of warranty; thus during the litigation the tenant pays some or all of the rent to the court for disbursal after the litigation. See *Pinzon v. A & G Properties*, 874 A.2d 347 (D.C. App. 2005). However, many jurisdictions that recognize the implied warranty do not allow shield-like remedies, such as rent withholding (rent abatement) and repair-and-deduct. See Stephen Lawrence, *George Washington University v. Weintraub: Implied Warranty of Habitability as a (Ceremonial?) Sword*, 33 Cath. U. L. Rev. 1137 (1984). What problems do these remedies create?

VII.   A LANDLORD'S TORT LIABILITY

The common law rule is that the landlord is not liable for personal injury or injury to a tenant's personal property that results from dangerous conditions on the premises, except for those conditions known to the landlord and not observable by the tenant on a reasonable inspection of the premises. *Caveat emptor* (or lessee) embodies this rule. However, the landlord's breach of an express covenant to repair or of an implied warranty or covenant to repair uninhabitable conditions may give rise to liability for consequential damages, including damages for personal injuries resulting from dangerous and uninhabitable conditions. In addition, today the rule of caveat lessee, where personal injury is concerned, is subject to many exceptions, as the following case illustrates.

BORDERS v. ROSEBERRY
532 P.2d 1366 (Kan. 1975)

PRAGER, J.

This case involves the liability of a landlord for personal injuries suffered by the social guest of the tenant as the result of a slip and fall on the leased premises. The facts in this case are undisputed and are as follows: The defendant-appellee, Agnes Roseberry, is the owner of a single-family, one-story residence located at 827 Brown Avenue, Osawatomie, Kansas. Several months prior to January 9, 1971, the defendant leased the property on a month to month basis to a tenant, Rienecker. Just prior to the time the tenant took occupancy of the house the defendant landlord had work performed on the house. The remodeling of the house included a new roof. In repairing the house the repairmen removed the roof guttering from the front of the house but failed to reinstall it. The landlord knew the guttering had been removed by the workmen, intended to have it reinstalled, and knew that it had not been reinstalled. The roof line on the house was such that without the guttering the rain drained off the entire north side of the house onto the front porch steps. In freezing weather water from the roof would accumulate and freeze on the steps. The landlord as well as the tenant knew that the guttering had not been reinstalled and knew that without the guttering, water from the roof would drain onto the front porch steps and in freezing weather would accumulate and freeze. The tenant had complained to the landlord about the absence of guttering and the resulting icy steps.

On January 9, 1971, there was ice and snow on the street and ice on the front steps. During the afternoon the tenant worked on the front steps, removing the ice accumulation with a hammer. The plaintiff-appellant, Gary D. Borders, arrived on the premises at approximately 4:00 p. m. in response to an invitation of the tenant for dinner. It is agreed that plaintiff's status was that of a social guest of the tenant. There was ice on the street and snow on the front steps when plaintiff arrived. At 9:00 p. m. as plaintiff Borders was leaving the house he slipped and fell on an accumulation of ice on the steps and received personal injuries. There is no contention that the plaintiff Borders was negligent in a way which contributed to cause his injuries. After a pretrial conference the case was tried to the court without a jury. Following submission of the case the trial court entered judgment for the defendant, making findings of fact which are essentially those set forth above. The trial court based its judgment upon a conclusion of law which stated that a landlord of a single-family house is under no obligation or duty to a social guest, a licensee of his tenant, to repair or remedy a known condition whereby water dripped onto the front steps of a house fronting north froze and caused plaintiff to slip and fall. The plaintiff has appealed to this court . . . .

At the outset it should be emphasized that we do not have involved here an action brought by a social guest to recover damages for personal injuries from his host, a possessor of real property. The issue raised involves the liability of a lessor who has leased his property to a tenant for a period of time. Furthermore, it should be pointed out that the plaintiff, a social guest of the tenant, has based his claim of liability against the landlord upon the existence of a defective condition which existed on the leased property at the time the tenant took possession.

Traditionally the law in this country has placed upon the lessee as the person in possession of the land the burden of maintaining the premises in a reasonably safe condition to protect persons who come upon the land. It is the tenant as possessor who, at least initially, has the burden of maintaining the premises in good repair. The relationship of landlord and tenant is not in itself sufficient to make the landlord liable for the tortious acts of the tenant. When land is leased to a tenant, the law of property regards the lease as equivalent to a sale of the premises for the term. The lessee acquires an estate in the land, and becomes for the time being the owner and occupier, subject to all of the responsibilities of one in possession, both to those who enter onto the land and to those outside of its boundaries. Professor William L. Prosser in his Law of Torts, 4th ed. § 63, points out that in the absence of agreement to the contrary, the lessor surrenders both possession and control of the land to the lessee, retaining only a reversionary interest; and he has no right even to enter without the permission of the lessee. There is therefore, as a general rule, no liability upon the landlord, either to the tenant or to others entering the land, for defective conditions existing at the time of the lease.

The general rule of non-liability has been modified, however, by a number of exceptions which have been created as a matter of social policy. Modern case law on the subject today usually limits the liability of a landlord for injuries arising from a defective condition existing at the time of the lease to six recognized exceptions. These exceptions are as follows:

1. Undisclosed dangerous conditions known to lessor and unknown to the lessee.

This exception is stated in Restatement, Second, Torts § 358 as follows:

(1) A lessor of land who conceals or fails to disclose to his lessee any condition, whether natural or artificial, which involves unreasonable risk of physical harm to persons on the land, is subject to liability to the lessee and others upon the land with the consent of the lessee or his sublessee for physical harm caused by the condition after the lessee has taken possession, if (a) the lessee does not know or have reason to know of the condition or the risk involved, and (b) the lessor knows or has reason to know of the condition, and realizes or should realize the risk involved, and has reason to expect that the lessee will not discover the condition or realize the risk.

(2) If the lessor actively conceals the condition, the liability stated [in] Subsection (1) continues until the lessee discovers it and has reasonable opportunity to take effective precautions against it. Otherwise the liability continues only until the vendee has had reasonable opportunity to discover the condition and to take such precautions.

In Kansas we have recognized and applied this exception . . . . It should be pointed out that this exception applies only to latent conditions and not to conditions which are patent or reasonably discernible to the tenant.

2. Conditions dangerous to persons outside of the premises. This exception is stated in Restatement, Second, Torts § 379 as follows:

A lessor of land who transfers its possession in a condition which he realizes or should realize will involve unreasonable risk of physical harm to others outside of the land, is subject to the same liability for physical harm subsequently caused to them by the condition as though he had remained in possession.

The theory of liability under such circumstances is that where a nuisance dangerous to persons outside the leased premises (such as the traveling public or persons on adjoining property) exists on the premises at the time of the lease, the lessor should not be permitted to escape liability by leasing the premises to another. The liability of the landlord for structural defects on leased property which causes injuries to persons outside of the premises was recognized and made the basis of a judgment against the landlord in *Mitchell v. Foran*, 143 Kan. 191, 53 P. 2d 490. *Mitchell* involved an awning hook which was fastened to the leased building and projected onto the public sidewalk and caused injury to a nine-year-old pedestrian.

3. Premises leased for admission of the public. The third exception arises where land is leased for a purpose involving the admission of the public. The cases usually agree that in that situation the lessor is under an affirmative duty to exercise reasonable care to inspect and repair the premises before possession is transferred, to prevent any unreasonable risk or harm to the public who may enter. This exception is stated in § 359 of Restatement, Second, Torts as follows:

A lessor who leases land for a purpose which involves the admission of the public is subject to liability for physical harm caused to persons who enter the land for that purpose by a condition of the land existing when the lessee takes possession, if the lessor (a) knows or by the exercise of reasonable care could discover that the condition involves an unreasonable risk of harm to such persons, and (b) has reason to expect that the lessee will admit them before the land is put in safe condition for their reception, and (c) fails to exercise reasonable care to discover or to remedy the condition, or otherwise to protect such persons against it.

This exception has been recognized in Kansas . . . . [Annot.,] 17 A.L.R. 3rd 873.

4. Parts of land retained in lessor's control which lessee is entitled to use. When different parts of a building, such as an office building or an apartment house, are leased to several tenants, the approaches and common passageways normally do not pass to the tenant, but remain in the possession and control of the landlord. Hence the lessor is under an affirmative obligation to exercise reasonable care to inspect and repair those parts of the premises for the protection of the lessee, members of his family, his employees, invitees, guests, and others on the land in the right of the tenant. This exception is covered in Restatement, Second, Torts §§ 360 and 361.

5. Where lessor contracts to repair. At one time the law in most jurisdictions and in Kansas was that if a landlord breached his contract to keep the premises in good repair, the only remedy of the tenant was an action in contract in which damages were limited to the cost of repair or loss of rental value of the property. Neither the tenant nor members of his family nor his guests were permitted to recover for personal injuries suffered as a result of the breach of the agreement. In most jurisdictions this rule has been modified and a cause of action given in tort to the injured person to enable him recovery for his personal injuries. This exception is found in Restatement, Second, Torts § 357 which states as follows:

> A lessor of land is subject to liability for physical harm caused to his lessee and others upon the land with the consent of the lessee or his sublessee by a condition of disrepair existing before or arising after the lessee has taken possession if (a) the lessor, as such, has contracted by a covenant in the lease or otherwise to keep the land in repair, and (b) the disrepair creates an unreasonable risk to persons upon the land which the performance of the lessor's agreement would have prevented, and (c) the lessor fails to exercise reasonable care to perform his contract.

In Kansas this exception has been followed . . . . In *Vieyra v. Engineering Investment Co., Inc.*, 205 Kan. 775, 473 P.2d 44, we held that although the landlord has a duty to keep the premises in repair by virtue of a covenant to repair in the lease, if the lease does not require the lessor to inspect the premises, the lessor is not liable until the lessee has given him notice of the need for repairs and the lessor thereafter fails to exercise reasonable care and diligence in making the repairs. In *Steele v. Latimer*, 214 Kan. 329, 521 P.2d 304, we held that the provisions of a municipal housing code prescribing minimum housing standards are deemed by implication to become a part of a lease of urban residential property, giving rise to an implied warranty on the part of the lessor that the premises are habitable and safe for human occupancy in compliance with the pertinent code provisions and will remain so for the duration of the tenancy. Such an implied warranty creates a contractual obligation on the lessor to repair the premises to keep them in compliance with the municipal housing standards as set forth in a municipal housing code.

6. Negligence by lessor in making repairs. When the lessor does in fact attempt to make repairs, whether he is bound by a covenant to do so or not, and fails to exercise reasonable care, he is held liable for injuries to the tenant or others on the premises in his right, if the tenant neither knows nor should know that the repairs have been negligently made. This exception is stated in Restatement, Second, Torts § 362:

> A lessor of land who, by purporting to make repairs on the land while it is in the possession of his lessee, or by the negligent manner in which he makes such repairs has, as the lessee neither knows nor should know, made the land more dangerous for use or given it a deceptive appearance of safety, is subject to liability for physical harm caused by the condition to the lessee or to others upon the land with the consent of the lessee or sublessee.

Section d of § 362 declares that the lessor is subject to liability if, but only if, the lessee neither knows nor should know that the purported repairs have not been made or have been negligently made and so, relying upon the deceptive appearance of safety, subjects himself to the dangers or invites or permits his licensees to encounter them. Conversely it would follow that if the lessee knows or should know that the purported repairs have not been made or have been negligently made, then the lessor is not liable under this exception. This exception has been recognized in Kansas . . . .

With the general rule and its exceptions in mind we shall now examine the undisputed facts in this case to determine whether or not the landlord can be held liable to the plaintiff here. It is clear that the exceptions pertaining to undisclosed dangerous conditions known to the lessor (exception 1), conditions dangerous to persons outside of the premises (exception 2), premises leased for admission of the public (exception 3), and parts of land retained in the lessor's control (exception 4) have no application in this case. Nor do we believe that exception 5, which comes into play when the lessor has contracted to repair, has been established by the court's findings of fact. It does not appear that the plaintiff takes the position that the lessor contracted to keep the premises in repair; nor has any consideration for such an agreement been shown. As to exception 6, although it is obvious that the repairs to the roof were not completed by installation of the guttering and although the landlord expressed his intention to replace the guttering, we do not believe that the factual circumstances bring the plaintiff within the application of exception 6 where the lessor has been negligent in making repairs. [T]hat exception comes into play only when the lessee lacks knowledge that the purported repairs have not been made or have been negligently made. Here it is undisputed that the tenant had full knowledge of the icy condition on the steps created by the absence of guttering. It seems to us that the landlord could reasonably assume that the tenant would inform his guest about the icy condition on the front steps. We have concluded that the factual circumstances do not establish liability on the landlord on the basis of negligent repairs made by him.

In his brief counsel for the plaintiff vigorously argues that the law should be changed to make the landlord liable for injuries resulting from a defective condition on the leased premises where the landlord has knowledge of that condition . . . . We do not believe that the facts and circumstances of this case justify a departure from the established rules of law discussed above. The judgment of the district court is affirmed.

NOTES

1. Landlords owe no greater duty to the tenant's guests than they owe to the tenant. See *Shump v. First Continental-Robinwood Assocs.*, 644 N.E.2d 291 (Ohio 1994); *Ortega v. Flaim*, 902 P.2d 199 (Wyo. 1995). See also *Pate v. Riverbend Mobile Home Village*, 955 P.2d 1342, 1344–45 (Kan. Ct. App. 1998) (reaffirming and summarizing *Borders*). A landlord's liability is based not on title, but on possession and control. See *Jones v. Levin*, 940 A.2d 451, 454–455 (Pa. Super. Ct. 2007). In *Borders*, the tenant may have been liable for the plaintiff's injuries. Why didn't plaintiff sue the tenant? What is the tenant's duty to a guest? If the tenant possessed a dangerous or wild animal, a tenant's liability would follow from its possession, so long as "possession" implies control of the animal. See *Frobig v. Gordon*, 881 P.2d 226, 228 (Wash. 1994). Likewise, courts are reluctant to impose strict liability on landlords. See *Dwyer v. Skyline Apartments, Inc.*, 301 A.2d 463 (N.J. Super. Ct. App. Div.), *aff'd*, 311 A.2d 1 (N.J. 1973) (mem.). California's Supreme Court held a landlord strictly liable for a latent defect but overruled the holding a decade later. See *Becker v. IRM Corp.*, 698 P.2d 116 (Cal. 1985), overruled in *Peterson v. Superior Court*, 899 P.2d 905 (Cal. 1995). Overall, though, landlords' tort liability has been the subject of much litigation during the past several decades. See, e.g., *Alcaraz v. Vece*, 929 P.2d 1239, 1245–47 (Cal. 1997). See generally Owen Browder, *The Taming of a Duty — The Tort Liability of Landlords*, 81 Mich. L. Rev. 99 (1982). In view of this large amount of litigation, would you advise a landlord, even in Kansas, to include a lease provision that exculpates the landlord from liability for negligence in repairs? What should such a provision say? Would a guest of the tenant be bound by this provision though not a party to the lease?

2. In recognition of the severe health hazards created by lead, particularly for children, the Consumer Products Safety Commission banned the residential use of lead-based paint after 1978. However, the Environmental Protection Agency estimates that more than half the homes in the United States still have lead-based paint in them. Largely as a result of exposure to lead-based paint, approximately 1,700,000 children in this country currently suffer from lead poisoning. If a residential landlord of property built before 1978 fails to inspect the premises for lead-based paint, should a tenant be able to recover damages for lead poisoning? Although older cases held that landlords did not have a duty to inspect, some modern courts are imposing that duty because the hazards of lead-based paint are now generally known. Compare *Chapman v. Silber*, 760 N.E.2d 329, 335–36 (N.Y. 2001) ("We decline to impose a new duty on landlords to test for the existence of lead in leased properties based solely upon the 'general knowledge' of the dangers of lead-based paints in older homes."), with *Antwaun A. ex rel. Muwonge v. Heritage Mutual Insurance Co.*, 596 N.W.2d 456, 463–64 (Wis. 1999) ("[W]e are persuaded that awareness of the dangers of lead paint . . . is on a different plane than the awareness of such dangers ten, twenty, or thirty years earlier. . . . [W]e conclude that a duty to test for lead paint arises whenever the landlord of a residential property constructed before 1978 either knows or in the use of ordinary care should know that there is peeling or chipping paint on the rental property.").

FELD v. MERRIAM
485 A.2d 742 (Pa. 1984)

McDermott, J.

Peggy and Samuel Feld were tenants in the large Cedarbrook Apartment complex, consisting of 150 acres and 1,000 apartments housed in three high rise buildings. For an extra rental fee the apartments are serviced by parking garages adjacent to the apartment buildings. On the evening of June 27, 1975, about 9:00 P.M., the Felds, returning from a social engagement, drove as usual to their allotted space in the parking garage. Then began the events that brings before us the question of a landlord's liability for the criminal acts of unknown third persons. We are not unaware of the social, economic and philosophic dimensions of the questions posed.

While the Felds were parking their car, they were set upon by three armed felons. At gun point, accompanied by two of the felons, they were forced to the back seat of their car. Followed by the third felon in an "old, blue broken down car," they were driven past the guard on duty at the gate, out into the night, to the ferine disposal of three criminals. To clear the car for their main criminal purpose, the felons started to force Mr. Feld into the trunk of the car. Mrs. Feld pled her husband's illness and to save him, offered herself for her husband's life. Thereupon the felons released Mr. Feld on a deserted street corner and drove Mrs. Feld to the lonely precincts of a country club. There is no need to recite the horrors that brave and loving woman suffered. Suffice it to say they extorted a terrible penalty from her defenseless innocence.

The Felds brought suit against the appellees, owners of the complex, alleging a duty of protection owed by the landlord, the breach of the duty, and injuries resulting therefrom. Named as defendants were John Merriam, Thomas Wynne, Inc., the Cedarbrook Joint Venture, and Globe Security Systems, Inc. Following an eight-day trial, the jury returned a plaintiff's verdict and a judgment totaling six million dollars against Merriam, Thomas Wynne, Inc., and the Cedarbrook Joint Venture. The jury absolved Globe Security of any liability. Common Pleas, per the Honorable Jacob Kalish, denied motions for a new trial, judgment N.O.V. and remittitur.

On appeal the Superior Court affirmed the lower court, with the exception that the award of punitive damages to Samuel Feld was reduced by one half. Both Cedarbrook and Mr. Feld filed petitions for allowance of appeal, which were granted. We now reverse.

The threshold question is whether a landlord has any duty to protect tenants from the foreseeable criminal acts of third persons, and if so, under what circumstances. Well settled law holds landlords to a duty to protect tenants from injury rising out of their negligent failure to maintain their premises in a safe condition. That rule of law is addressed to their failure of reasonable care, a failure of care caused by their own negligence, a condition, the cause of which was either known or knowable by reasonable precaution. The criminal acts of a third person belong to a different category and can bear no analogy to the unfixed radiator, unlighted steps, falling ceiling, or the other myriad possibilities of one's personal negligence. To render one liable for the deliberate criminal acts of unknown third persons can only be a judicial rule for given limited circumstances.

The closest analogy is the duty of owners of land who hold their property open to the public for business purposes. They are subject to liability for the accidental, negligent or intentionally harmful acts of third persons, as are common carriers, innkeepers and other owners of places of public resort. The reason is clear; places to which the general public are invited might indeed anticipate, either from common experience or known fact, that places of general public resort are also places where what men can do, they might. One who invites all may reasonably expect that all might not behave, and bears responsibility for injury that follows the absence of reasonable precaution against that common expectation. The common areas of an apartment complex are not open to the public, nor are the general public expected or invited to gather there for other purposes than to visit tenants.

Tenants in a huge apartment complex, or a tenant on the second floor of a house converted to an apartment, do not live where the world is invited to come. Absent agreement, the landlord cannot be expected to protect them against the wiles of felonry any more than the society can always protect them upon the common streets and highways leading to their residence or indeed in their home itself.

An apartment building is not a place of public resort where one who profits from the very public it invites must bear what losses that public may create. It is of its nature private and only for those specifically invited. The criminal can be expected anywhere, any time, and has been a risk of life for a long time. He can be expected in the village, monastery and the castle keep.

In the present case the Superior Court departed from the traditional rule that a person cannot be liable for the criminal acts of third parties when it held "that in all areas of the leasehold, particularly in the area under his control, the landlord is under a duty to provide adequate security to protect his tenants from the foreseeable criminal actions of third persons."

The Superior Court viewed the imposition of this new duty as merely an extension of the landlord's existing duty to maintain the common areas to be free from the risk of harm caused by physical defects. However, in so holding that court failed to recognize the crucial distinction between the risk of injury from a physical defect in the property, and the risk from the criminal act of a third person. In the former situation the landlord has effectively perpetuated the risk of injury by refusing to correct a known and verifiable defect. On the other hand, the risk of injury from the criminal acts of third persons arises not from the conduct of the landlord but from the conduct of an unpredictable independent agent. To impose a general duty in the latter case would effectively require landlords to be insurers of their tenants' safety: a burden which could never be completely met given the unfortunate realities of modern society.

Our analysis however does not stop here, for although there is a general rule against holding a person liable for the criminal conduct of another absent a preexisting duty, there is also an exception to that rule, i.e., where a party assumes a duty, whether gratuitously or for consideration, and so negligently performs that duty that another suffers damage.

This exception has been capsulized in Section 323 of the Restatement (Second) of Torts, which provides:

> One who undertakes, gratuitously or for consideration, to render services to another which he should recognize as necessary for the protection of the other's person or things, is subject to liability to the other for physical harm resulting from his failure to exercise reasonable care to perform his undertaking, if (a) his failure to exercise such care increases the risk of such harm, or (b) the harm is suffered because of the other's reliance upon the undertaking.

Previously we adopted this section as an accurate statement of the law in this Commonwealth . . . . Expounding on the proper application of Section 323 the drafters indicated that

> [T]his Section applies to any undertaking to render services to another which the defendant should recognize as necessary for the protection of the other's person or things. It applies whether the harm to the other or his things results from the defendant's negligent conduct in the manner of his performance of the undertaking, or from his failure to exercise reasonable care to complete it or to protect the other when he discontinues it.

Comment (a) § 323 Restatement (Second) of Torts. These comments are particularly relevant in a situation such as the present where a landlord undertakes to secure the areas within his control and possibly fosters a reliance by his tenants on his efforts.

Absent therefore an agreement wherein the landlord offers or voluntarily proffers a program, we find no general duty of a landlord to protect tenants against criminal intrusion. However, a landlord may, as indicated, incur a duty voluntarily or by specific agreement if to attract or keep tenants he provides a program of security. A program of security is not the usual and normal precautions that a reasonable home owner would employ to protect his property. It is, as in the case before us, an extra precaution, such as personnel specifically charged to patrol and protect the premises. Personnel charged with such protection may be expected to perform their duties with the usual reasonable care required under standard tort law for ordinary negligence. When a landlord by agreement or voluntarily offers a program to protect the premises, he must perform the task in a reasonable manner and where a harm follows a reasonable expectation of that harm, he is liable. The duty is one of reasonable care under the circumstances. It is not the duty of an insurer and a landlord is not liable unless his failure is the proximate cause of the harm.

A tenant may rely upon a program of protection only within the reasonable expectations of the program. He cannot expect that a landlord will defeat all the designs of felonry. He can expect, however, that the program will be reasonably pursued and not fail due to its negligent exercise. If a landlord offers protection during certain periods of the day or night a tenant can only expect reasonable protection during the periods offered. If, however, during the periods offered, the protection fails by a lack of reasonable care, and that lack is the proximate cause of the injury, the landlord can be held liable. A tenant may not expect more than is offered. If, for instance, one guard is offered, he cannot expect the same quality and type of protection that two guards would have provided, nor may he expect the benefits that a different program might have provided. He can only expect the benefits reasonably expected of the program as offered and that that program will be conducted with reasonable care.

In the present case the trial judge, when instructing the jury, was placed in the unenviable position of predicting how we would resolve this difficult question. Although we commend him on his endeavor, we are constrained to reverse the verdict, since the jury instructions which were given imposed upon the landlord a duty greater than that which we today hold to have existed.

ZAPPALA, J., concurring.

We are called upon to decide an issue of first impression-under what circumstances may a landlord be held liable to his tenant for injuries sustained as a result of criminal activity occurring on portions of the leased premises within the landlord's exclusive control. I join in the Opinion of the Court . . . . * * *

The Appellees urge this Court to hold, as did the Superior Court, that a landlord owes a duty — to provide security to protect against criminal acts of third persons — based upon the implied warranty of habitability in residential leases. This approach was adopted in the seminal case of *Kline v. 1500 Massachusetts Avenue Apartment Corp.*, 439 F.2d 477 (D.C.Cir. 1970). The United States Court of Appeals for the District of Columbia Circuit recognized that, as a general rule, a private individual does not have a duty to protect another from a criminal attack by a third person. Nevertheless, it concluded that the general rule was inapplicable to the landlord-tenant relationship in multiple dwelling houses. In arriving at its conclusion, the court emphasized the development of the modern view of the lease as a contract, and the movement away from the traditional analysis of a lease as a conveyance of a property interest. The court stated, ". . . there is implied in the contract between landlord and tenant an obligation on the landlord to provide those protective measures which are within his reasonable capacity."[1] 439 F.2d at 485.

The landmark Pennsylvania case which reflects the trend towards treating the residential lease as a contract, rather than a conveyance of land for a term, is *Pugh v. Holmes*, 486 Pa. 272, 405 A.2d 897 (1979). There this Court recognized an implied warranty of habitability in residential leases. I would expressly reject the notion advanced by the *Kline* court that a landlord is required in the first instance to provide any form of "security service" or protective measures to meet the "warranty of habitability" implied in the lease contract. The central premise of

---

[1] In *Kline*, the level of security services which had been provided by the landlord at the inception of the lease had deteriorated. The application of contract principles was, therefore, peculiarly appropriate because of this decline in the protective measures which had been in existence at the time the parties had entered into the lease. The expansive language of the opinion made it apparent, however, that the court would not be inclined to limit liability to those instances in which the level of existing measures had been relaxed.

Pugh v. Holmes was that the contemporary leasing of residences involves "a well known package of goods and services" and that, therefore, it is proper to give legal protection to the tenant's assumption that a lease guarantees him at least these well known goods and services in exchange for payment of rent. Thus, when we recognized that this package " 'includes not merely walls and ceilings, but also adequate heat, light and ventilation, serviceable plumbing facilities, secure windows and doors, proper sanitation, and proper maintenance,' " 486 Pa. at 282, 405 A.2d at 902, we focused on those qualities which by common understanding constitute the *sine qua non* of "residence." . . . It would be a gross distortion of the reasoning in *Pugh v. Holmes* to give it any part in the analysis of situations such as that presented by the case at bar. Secure doors and windows, that is, devices which serve the purpose for which they were designed and which are not merely holes in walls, are fundamental elements in distinguishing an uninhabitable structure from a residence. "Security services" are not. Only the most fainthearted and seclusive could accept the proposition that lack of such services would render a residence uninhabitable.[2]

Proceeding with the contract analysis, the *Kline* court determined that a duty was owed by a landlord to his tenants simply because the risk of harm existed. The court stated, "we place the duty of taking protective measures guarding the entire premises and the area peculiarly under the landlord's control against the perpetration of criminal acts upon the landlord, the party to the lease contract who had the effective capacity to perform these necessary acts." 439 F.2d at 482. It is an inaccurate statement of tort law, however, to say that what may be done, must be done. Duty should not be defined by ability, but by responsibility.

The Appellees suggest that a duty to protect tenants from the risk of criminal conduct is nothing more than a continuation of the landlord's existing duty to maintain the common areas of the leased premises; and that we need not impose a new duty, but merely delineate the scope of an existing obligation. This existing obligation which the Appellees perceive as the basis for their contention is a landlord's duty to maintain the common areas in a reasonably safe condition for the use of tenants and their invitees.

The term "reasonably safe" has traditionally been interpreted to include physical deficiencies, health hazards, and structural defects. Liability may be imposed upon a landlord where he had actual notice of a defective condition within the common areas or where a reasonable inspection would have disclosed the condition. The Appellees would expand "defective condition" to include not only a physical defect, but also a risk of physical harm to tenants from criminal conduct. The duty of a landlord would be two-fold — i.e., a duty to alleviate an existing condition which creates a risk of harm from criminal conduct and a duty to conduct a reasonable investigation to discover such a condition.[3] Liability would then be imposed upon a

---

[2] The implied warranty/contract analysis must also be rejected for the further reason that the remedies available thereunder are inconsistent with the remedies sought in a tort action such as this . . . . I cannot countenance the erosion of fundamental distinctions in the law which necessarily results from molding tort remedies to contract analysis.

[3] The structural soundness of the premises is readily subject to inspection and correction, even in the absence of knowledge of a particular defect. Without actual notice of criminal activity, however, the

landlord for a breach of either duty. This is neither a natural nor a logical extension.

The traditional duty which has been imposed upon a landlord who retains control over the common areas is an exception to the general rule that, absent an agreement to the contrary, a landlord who surrenders possession of the leasehold does not have an obligation to maintain the premises in repair. The exception recognizes that a landlord has exclusive authority to maintain or repair the common areas. I join in the Court's refusal to extend this duty to maintain the common areas to include security services. * * *

Where, as here, the conduct of the parties is regulated neither by statute, ordinance, or regulation, nor by the lease-contract itself, the courts have struggled with the issue of whether liability may be imposed upon a landlord for criminal acts. The conflicting resolutions of this issue result from the courts' attempts to respond to what is essentially a social problem, rather than a landlord-tenant problem. The risk of harm from criminal conduct is not peculiar to the landlord-tenant relationship. It is a risk that one encounters in society at large. Any attempt by a landlord to insulate tenants from this risk must necessarily fail. Therefore, the mere fact that a tenant may be exposed to that risk cannot be the basis for imposing liability . . . .

NOTES

1. In *Walls v. Oxford Management Co.* 633 A.2d 103, 105–107 (N.H. 1993), the court held that "while landlords have no general duty to protect tenants from criminal attack, such a duty may arise when a landlord has created, or is responsible for, a known defective condition on a premises that foreseeably enhanced the risk of criminal attack. Moreover, a landlord who undertakes, either gratuitously or by contract, to provide security will thereafter have a duty to act with reasonable care. Where, however, a landlord has made no affirmative attempt to provide security, and is not responsible for a physical defect that enhances the risk of crime, we will not find such a duty. We reject liability based solely on the landlord-tenant relationship or on a doctrine of overriding foreseeability." See also *Ward v. Inishmaan Assoc. Ltd. Partnership*, 931 A.2d 1235 (N.H. 2007); *Lacy v. Flake & Kelley Mgmt. Inc.*, 235 S.W.3d 894, 897 (Ark. 2006); *Miller v. Whitworth*, 455 S.E.2d 821, 825–26 (W. Va. 1995) (stating that a landlord does not have a duty to protect tenants from third-party criminal acts, except when (a) there is a special relationship not arising out of the landlord-tenant relationship or (b) the landlord's affirmative actions give rise to a duty to protect). Crimes committed by a landlord's employee present a further issue of landlord control. See *Rockwell v. Sun Harbor Budget Suites*, 925 P.2d 1175 (Nev. 1996) (landlord liable for tenant's murder by an employee security guard). But see *Saelzler v. Advanced Group 400*, 23 P.3d 1143 (Cal. 2001) (a delivery person who was assaulted while attempting to deliver a package to tenant did not adequately establish that the landlord's negligence proximately caused his injuries); *Yuzefovsky v. St. John's Wood Apartments*, 540 S.E.2d 134 (Va. 2001) (despite landlord's fraud, tenant was unable to establish proximate cause). Holding a landlord liable for criminal action seems most

---

protective integrity of the premises, its soundness against the risk of harm from the intentional misconduct of unknown third parties, is not similarly susceptible to meaningful examination . . . .

acceptable when the liability serves as a preventive technique to further reduce the opportunity for crime; however, when prevention is not possible, landlord liability amounts to little more than a compensation mechanism. For example, should a landlord be liable if a terrorist commits a crime on the landlord's property?

2. If the landlord can control the premises or the tenant through eviction but fails to evict a tenant with a dog, known to be vicious, is the landlord liable if the dog injures another tenant or a guest? See *Feister v. Bosack*, 497 N.W.2d 522, 523 (Mich. Ct. App. 1993) (landlord not liable when the attack occurred off-site and the tenant acquired the dog after the lease term began). That leaves bites on the premises or on common areas surrounding the leasehold as a fertile field for litigation when the tenant has the dog when the lease is signed. What if a tenant's lease had a "no pets" covenant? This issue is complicated by the widespread enactment of so-called "dog bite statutes." See, e.g., Conn. Gen. Stat. Ann. § 22–357 (1997) (making the "keeper" of a dog liable for its bites). Under such a statute, a landlord who provides an area for dogs to run might be liable when the bite occurs there. On the other hand, a keeper has a degree of control over the dog that a landlord arguably does not. See *Robison v. Stokes*, 882 P.2d 1105, 1105–06 (Okla. Ct. App. 1994).

VIII.   ASSIGNMENTS AND SUBLEASES

As discussed earlier in this chapter, a lease is both a contract between landlord and tenant and a conveyance of an estate from the landlord to the tenant. The conveyance gives the tenant the right to possess land for a period of time without interference from the landlord and imposes on the tenant certain duties including the duties to pay rent, make repairs, and not commit waste. The rights and obligations of the landlord and tenant growing out of the conveyance are based on *privity of estate*, because both have an interest in the land; the tenant has the possessory interest, and the landlord has a reversion. Leases also create a contract in which both parties make express covenants. The tenant, for example, may agree to make specified rental payments by the first day of each month, and the landlord may agree to maintain the premises. The landlord's and tenant's rights and obligations arising out of the express lease covenants are based on *privity of contract.*

The rights and obligations based on privity of contract and those based on privity of estate in the lease are often the same. That is, the rights and obligations based on privity of estate normally are included in the executed lease. Based on privity of estate, the landlord and tenant each can enforce the *real covenants*, those covenants that directly affect the land or the estate. Because they are so intimately connected to the leasehold estate in the land, they are said to "run with the land" and can be enforced by the tenant's assignee, as well as by the tenant. Conversely, the landlord can enforce real covenants against the tenant's assignee because the landlord and the assignee are in privity of estate. Promises to pay rent, make repairs, maintain common areas, refrain from waste, and to make certain uses of the premises are a few examples of covenants that run with the land.

Privity of contract enables the landlord and tenant to enforce not only the lease's real covenants, but also its *personal covenants*. Personal covenants are promises that do not affect the land or the estate. For that reason, leases normally do not include personal covenants.

A tenant can transfer all or part of her leasehold estate by means of either a sublease or an assignment. "All or part" refers to time — all or part of the time remaining in the lease. A *subletting* is a transfer of less than all of the time remaining in the lease, even one day less. It creates a new and distinct leasehold estate between the original tenant (sublessor) and the subtenant (sublessee). As a result, the original tenant (who is now a landlord) and the subtenant are in privity of estate and privity of contract, and the parties can agree to different, though not inconsistent, provisions than those in the lease. For example, the sublessor can bargain for the sublessee to pay more rent than is due under the original lease. This new landlord-tenant relationship does not affect the relationship between the original landlord and tenant. They are still in privity of estate and privity of contract. For example, if a student leases an apartment for twelve months commencing in January, subleases her interest in the apartment to a friend in June for the summer, and returns to her apartment in September to resume her studies, she remains in privity of estate and privity of contract with her landlord during the summer months and is responsible for making rental payments even if her friend does not pay her. However, because she is her friend's landlord, she has a cause of action based on her own privity of estate and privity of contract with the subtenant.

An *assignment,* on the other hand, transfers the original tenant's entire leasehold estate to the assignee who becomes the new owner of the leasehold. Because the original tenant no longer owns any interest in the land, privity of estate between the original landlord and tenant is destroyed. However, the contract created with the lease execution is still in force. Therefore, the original landlord and tenant remain in privity of contract for the remainder of the contract term. For example, if a student leases an apartment for twelve months commencing in January, but drops out of school in June to travel around the world and assigns her interest in the apartment to her friend who promises he will make rental payments, the landlord can recover from either the original tenant or the assignee if the assignee does not pay. The original tenant is liable to the landlord based on privity of contract.

The landlord also can sue the assignee for rent that has become past due since the assignment. Because the assignee now owns the original tenant's interest in the land, the assignee and the landlord are in privity of estate. They can enforce the lease's real covenants against each other. Just as the landlord can sue the assignee for rent that has come due since the assignment, the assignee can sue the landlord for breach of the covenant of quiet enjoyment. Note, however, that privity of estate exists between the landlord and assignee only for so long as the assignee has an interest in the land. If the assignee assigns his interest to a second assignee, the first assignee's liability to the landlord terminates.

How does one determine whether a transfer from a tenant to another is a sublease or an assignment? *The traditional test is whether the original tenant retains any interest in the leasehold estate.* If she does, the transfer is a sublease; if she does not, the transfer is an assignment. See *Stewart v. Long Island R. Co.*, 8 N.E. 200, 201 (N.Y. 1886) (a leading case). If, in our original example, the student transfers her apartment for only three months of the remaining lease term, the transfer is a sublease. If she transfers only part of the apartment, such as one of two bedrooms, for the remainder of the original lease term, the transfer is a sublease, though an argument can be made that it is a partial assignment. Similarly, if she transfers all of her apartment for the remainder of the original lease term but retains the right to recover possession if the transferee unduly disturbs the neighbors, the original tenant has kept a reversionary interest in the leasehold estate, and courts often will characterize the transfer as a sublease. (Reversions and similar future interests are discussed in Chapter 3, *supra*.) On the other hand, if she transfers all of her apartment for the remainder of the original lease term and keeps no reversionary interest, the transfer is an assignment under the traditional test. In a sublease, then, the tenant retains a reversion — no matter how short. How about retaining a possibility of reverter? Or right of reentry for condition broken?

DAVIS v. VIDAL
151 S.W. 290 (Tex. 1912)

DIBRELL, J.

This is a suit by Antoinette W. Davis . . . against Lewis Vidal, to recover the sum of $1,200.00 alleged to be due her by Vidal for the use of certain premises situated in the City of El Paso, of which Vidal was in possession as the assignee of the Dallas Brewery. The sole question of law involved in the case is whether a certain instrument of writing executed by the Dallas Brewery to the defendant, Vidal, on October 1, 1907, was an assignment of its lease from the plaintiff, Antoinette W. Davis, of date April 26, 1907, or a sub-letting of the premises in question. If the instrument referred to was an assignment of the lease then plaintiff was authorized to recover of the defendant the rent due on her contract of lease with the Dallas Brewery, by virtue of the privity of estate . . . that subsists between them; but if on the other hand the instrument was a sub-letting of the premises to Vidal by the original lessee the plaintiff could not recover against defendant as a sub-tenant, since in such case there is neither privity of estate nor of contract between the original lessor and the under-tenant. (Citations omitted.)

The instrument in question was construed by the trial court and the Court of Civil Appeals to be a sub-letting of the premises by the Dallas Brewery to the defendant Vidal, and in accordance with that holding judgment was rendered for the defendant. Upon appeal of the case to the Court of Civil Appeals the judgment of the lower court was affirmed. That the question involved and decided may be fully understood we embody the instrument executed by the Dallas Brewery to Vidal:

> Know All Men by These Presents, That, whereas, on the 26th day of April, 1907, Mrs. Antoinette W. Davis, acting by her agents, A.P. Coles & Brother, did lease to the Dallas Brewery the following parcel of land with the tenements thereon in the City of El Paso, County of El Paso, State of Texas, to-wit: Being the one-story and adobe composition roof building [legal description and address of premises follows — Eds.], same being leased from the 1st day of May, 1907, for three years, to be ended and completed on the 30th of April, 1910, and in consideration of same lease the

said Dallas Brewery yielding and paying therefore during said term the sum of $100.00 per month, payable in advance on the first day of each and every month; and,

Whereas, said lease provides that said premises or any part thereof may be sublet by said Dallas Brewery without the consent of said Mrs. Davis; and,

Whereas, it is desired to transfer, assign and sublet all of said above premises so leased by the said Mrs. Davis to said Dallas Brewery to Lou Vidal;

Now, therefore, in consideration of the premises and the sum of $300.00 to it in hand paid, the receipt whereof is hereby acknowledged, said, the Dallas Brewery, does hereby sublet, assign and transfer the said above premises and does assign and transfer the above said lease, to the said Lou Vidal, and in consideration therefor the said Vidal does well and truly agree and promise to pay the rents in said lease agreed to be paid, to-wit: the sum of one hundred ($100.00) dollars per month, each and every month hereafter ensuing, beginning on the first day of November, 1907, in advance, on the first day of each month so hereinafter ensuing.

And the said Vidal does agree and bind himself and obligates himself to in all respects indemnify, save and hold harmless said Dallas Brewery by reason of any of the terms or conditions in said lease contained, including the payment of rent therein provided to be paid . . . ; or if the said Vidal neglects or fails to pay said rent promptly, as in said lease provided to be paid, then and in such event the Dallas Brewery can and may at its option declare this transfer null and void, and thereupon oust the said Vidal, and assume possession thereof, and this without notice of any character or kind to the said Vidal; and the failure to pay any rent as in said lease provided to be paid, at the election of the said Dallas Brewery, can and may authorize it without notice to re-enter and repossess said premises.

In construing the effect of the foregoing instrument it is not conclusive as to its form, since it may be in form an assignment and yet be in effect a sub-lease. The question is one of law to be determined from the estate granted by the instrument. As a general proposition if the instrument executed by the lessee conveys the entire term and thereby parts with all of the reversionary estate in the property the instrument will be construed to be an assignment, but if there remains a reversionary interest in the estate conveyed the instrument is a sub-lease. The relation of landlord and tenant is created alone by the existence of a reversionary interest in the landlord. Out of this fact arises the distinction made between assignments and sub-tenancies. To state the test slightly different from that already stated, if the instrument is of such character by its terms and conditions that a reversionary interest by construction remains in the grantor of the property, he becomes the landlord and the grantee the tenant. The tenant who parts with the entire term embraced in his lease becomes an assignor of the lease and the instrument is an assignment, but where the tenant by the terms, conditions or limitations in the instrument does not part with the entire term granted him by his landlord so that there remains in him a reversionary interest, the transaction is a subletting and not an assignment. . . . Wood on Landlord & Tenant, 2 ed., sec. 65.

It will be observed that in stating the general rule as to what constitutes an assignment of a lease as distinguished from a sub-lease, the requirement is that the instrument must convey the whole *term*, leaving no interest or reversionary interest in the grantor. By the word, "term," as used in the statement of this principle of law is meant something more than the mere *time* for which the lease is given, and the instrument must convey not only the entire time for which the lease runs, but the entire estate or interest conveyed by the lease. Mr. Blackstone in his commentaries, book 2, page 144, in commenting on the significance of the word, "term," when used in leases, says: "Thus the word *term* does not merely signify the time specified in the lease, but the estate also and interest that passes by the lease; and therefore the *term* may expire, during the continuance of the *time*; as by surrender, forfeiture and the like." The meaning of the word *term* as defined by Blackstone above was adopted by the Supreme Court of Massachusetts in the case of *Dunlop v. Bullard*, 131 Mass., 162, and by a number of text writers on the subject of assignments and sub-leases.

Mr. Blackstone in his commentaries, book 2, page 327, defines an assignment to be and draws the distinction between an assignment and a lease of property as follows: "An *assignment* is properly a transfer, or making over to another, of the right one has in any estate, but it is usually applied to an estate for life or years. And it differs from lease only in this: that by a lease one grants an interest less than his own, reserving to himself a reversion; in an assignment he parts with the whole property, and the assignee stands to all intents and purposes in the place of the assignor." If we may accept this definition from so eminent authority upon the common law, which definition and distinction so concisely stated and drawn seems to have met the approval of this court in other cases, and apply it to the facts of the case at bar the conclusion must be reached that the instrument executed by the Dallas Brewery to Vidal was a sub-lease and not an assignment. The instrument speaks for itself. By its terms the whole estate granted to the Dallas Brewery by its lease from Mrs. David is not conveyed, for the reason there is reserved to the Dallas Brewery a contingent reversionary interest in the estate, to be resumed summarily upon the failure of Vidal to pay rent. More than this, and of equal significance, by the terms of the instrument the Dallas Brewery reserved the right to pay the rent to the original lessor, and thereby the right was reserved to forestall Mrs. Davis, upon the failure of Vidal to pay the rent, from exercising the right to re-enter and possess the premises. That right was reserved to the Dallas Brewery and gave it the power to control the estate in the premises upon failure by Vidal to pay it the rent.

If the instrument was an assignment of the lease the Dallas Brewery must of necessity have parted with all its estate and interest in said premises, and could therefore exercise no right in or control over the premises. If the instrument was an assignment of the lease the legal effect was to substitute Vidal in lieu of the Dallas Brewery. But this was not the case. By the terms of the instrument the Dallas Brewery retained the control of the possession of the leased premises, thereby denying the legal effect of an assignment, which would have given Mrs. Davis the right of re-entry and possession of the property upon Vidal's failure to pay the rent.

We are aware that there is great conflict of authority upon this subject, and that it would be futile to attempt to reconcile such conflict. Many of the authors of the text books on the subject of the assignment of leases and sub-letting under leases, and the decisions of a great many of the States in this Union hold that the fact that the right of re-entry is reserved in the assignment to the assignor upon failure of the assignee to pay rent does not change the instrument of assignment from such to a sub-lease. The holding of such authors and decisions is based upon the theory that the right of re-entry is not an estate or interest in land, nor the reservation of a reversion. They hold that the reservation of the right of re-entry upon failure to pay rent is neither an estate nor interest in land, but a mere chose in action, and when exercised the grantor comes into possession of the premises through the breach of the condition and not by reverter.

Those authorities which hold the contrary doctrine base their ruling upon the idea that the reservation in the instrument of the right of re-entry is a contingent reversionary interest in the premises, resulting from the conveyance of an estate upon a condition subsequent where there has been an infraction of such condition. This view of the law is strongly presented in the opinion in the case of *Dunlap v. Bullard*, 131 Mass., 163, as follows:

> Where an estate is conveyed to be held by the grantee upon a condition subsequent, there is left in the grantor a contingent reversionary interest. It was said in *Austin v. Cambridgeport Parish*, 21 Pick., 215, 223, that the grantor's contingent interest in such case was an estate which was transmissible by devise and passed under a residuary devise in the will of the grantor. It was declared to be a contingent possible estate, which, united with that of the tenants, "composed only the entire fee-simple estate, as much so as the ordinary case of an estate for life to A, remainder to B." In *Brattle Square Church v. Grant*, 3 Gray, 142, 147, it was said, that when such an estate is created "the entire interest does not pass out of the grantor by the same instrument of conveyance. All that remains, after the gift or grant takes effect, continues in the grantor, and goes to his heirs. This is the right of entry, which, from the nature of the grant, is reserved to the grantor and his heirs only, and which gives them the right to enter as of their old estate, upon the breach of the condition." These considerations are equally applicable whether the estate subject to the condition subsequent is an estate in fee, or an estate for life or years. They apply where, by the terms of an instrument which purports to be an underlease, there is left in the lessor a contingent reversionary interest, to be availed of by an entry for breach of condition which restores the sub-lessor to his former interest in the premises. The sub-lessee under such an instrument takes an inferior and different estate from that which he would acquire by an assignment of the remainder of the original term, that is to say, an interest which may be terminated by forfeiture on new and independent grounds long before the expiration of the original term. If the smallest reversionary interest is retained, the tenant takes as sub-lessee, and not as assignee.

We are not able to discern why there may not be a contingent reversionary estate or interest in land, as well as any other contingent estate or interest. It certainly cannot be contended upon sound principle that because the right of re-entry and resumption of possession of land is contingent that it is thereby any the less an estate or interest in land. The very definition of a contingent estate as distinguished from a *vested* estate is that "*the right to its* enjoyment is to accrue on an event which is dubious and uncertain." 1 Washburn on Real Property, 38. * * *

We think it deducible from respectable authority that where the tenant reserves in the instrument giving possession to his transferree the right of re-entry to the premises demised, upon failure to pay rent, he necessarily retains a part of or an interest in the demised estate which may come back to him upon the happening of a contingency.

The instrument under consideration does not convey the entire estate received by the Dallas Brewery by its lease from Mrs. Davis, but retains by the right of possible re-entry a contingent reversionary interest in the premises. That the interest retained is a contingent reversionary interest does not, it seems to us, change the rule by which an assignment may be distinguished from a sub-lease. If by any limitation or condition in the conveyance the entire term, which embraces the estate conveyed in the contract of lease as well as the length of time for which the tenancy is created, may by construction be said not to have passed from the original tenant, but that a contingent reversionary estate is retained in the premises the subject of the reversion, the instrument must be said to constitute a sub-letting and not an assignment.

The following test may be applied to determine whether the instrument in question is an assignment of the original lease, or a sub-letting of the premises. If it is an assignment its legal effect must be a transfer of the right of possession of the property conveyed to Vidal and the creation of a privity of estate . . . between Mrs. Davis, the original lessor, and Vidal, to whom the possession was granted by the Dallas Brewery. This would be essential to constitute the instrument an assignment, and if it was an assignment Vidal obligated himself to pay the rent to Mrs. Davis and the Dallas Brewery had no further connection with or interest in the transaction. But such a result can by no fair or reasonable construction of the language and provisions of the instrument be deduced therefrom. On the contrary the Dallas Brewery reserved the privilege of paying the rent to its lessor, and upon non-payment of rent by Vidal it reserved the right to declare the instrument forfeited and to repossess the premises without notice to or the consent of Vidal. There can be but one theory upon which the Dallas Brewery considered itself interested in seeing that the rent was promptly paid by Vidal, and that is that it desired to control the property in question and therefore intended and by the language and reservation in the instrument made it a sub-lease.

We do not think the proposition tenable that by the express terms of the agreement between the Dallas Brewery and Vidal, or by implication, Vidal obligated himself to pay the rent to Mrs. Davis. The provision of the contract relied upon to establish the fact that Vidal obligated himself to pay the rent to the lessor in the original lease is the following, "and in consideration therefor the said Vidal does well and truly agree and promise to pay the rents in said lease agreed to be paid, to-wit: the sum of one hundred dollars per month." Under the uniform rule of construction the latter part of the above sentence explains and qualifies the preceding part. The obligation of Vidal was to pay the rents in said lease agreed to be paid, that is, the sum of one hundred dollars per month, payable on the first day of each month in advance. There is nothing in the agreement from which it may be inferred that Vidal obligated himself to pay the rents directly to Mrs. Davis.

Having reached the conclusion that the instrument executed by the Dallas Brewery to Vidal conveying the premises in question was a sub-lease and not an assignment, by reason of the provision reserving to the Dallas Brewery the right of re-entry, which had the effect to withhold a part of the term granted by the original lease, or which retained an interest in said estate; and because by the other terms of the instrument reserving to the Dallas Brewery the discretion to pay the rents upon its own responsibility and upon the failure of Vidal to pay the same to it, the right to declare the instrument forfeited and to re-enter and take possession of the premises indicate the intention and purpose of the parties to enter into a sub-letting of the premises and not to assign the original lease, we conclude there exists no privity of estate or contract between the plaintiff, Mrs. Davis, and the defendant, Lewis Vidal, and that Mrs. Davis has no cause of action authorizing her to recover judgment against Vidal. * * * The court is of the opinion the judgments of the Court of Civil Appeals and of the trial court should be affirmed, and it is accordingly so ordered. *Affirmed.*

NOTES

1. Another test that some courts apply to determine whether a transfer is an assignment or a sublease is the parties' intention as evidenced by the totality of the factors and circumstances *surrounding the transfer*. These circumstances include the duration of the transfer, the title and form of the document of transfer, and the existence of new or different covenants in the transfer. See *Jaber v. Miller*, 239 S.W.2d 760 (Ark. 1951). In that case, the original lease between the landlord and tenant, Jaber, provided for termination of the lease if the building on the leased property was destroyed by fire. Jaber transferred his interest to Norber in exchange for Norber's agreement to pay the rent specified in the lease to the landlord and the execution of five promissory notes in favor of Jaber. Jaber retained the right to retake possession if the transferee failed to pay the rent to the landlord or the notes held by Jaber. Norber later transferred its interest to Miller in exchange for Miller's promise to pay the rent and the promissory notes. After the building was destroyed by fire, Miller claimed that the transfer from Jaber was a sublease and that the notes represented rent. Because the original lease terminated with the fire, the sublease also terminated, and Miller no longer was liable on the notes. Jaber argued that his transfer was an assignment and that the notes constituted deferred payments for the assignment. As payment for the assignment, the notes were enforceable even after the building was destroyed. That is, the fire terminated the leasehold and any rental obligation to the landlord but not the assignment and the deferred payments for the assignment.

The *Jaber* court first discussed the historical reasons for the majority rule that a transfer for less than the entire term is a sublease regardless of the parties' intention.

> The English courts therefore held that the transferee of the entire term held of the original lessor, that such a transferee was bound by the covenants in the original lease, and that he was entitled to enforce whatever duties that lease imposed upon the landlord. [The court is referring to

leasehold covenants that are deemed to "run with the land." — Eds.] The intention of the parties had nothing to do with the matter; the sole question was whether the first lessee retained a reversion that enabled him to hold his place in the chain of ownership. [Jaber retained the right to retake possession if the transferee failed to pay the rent to the landlord or the notes held by Jaber. — Eds.]

The court then rejected it as outmoded and unduly harsh. Why? Because the transferee who thinks that she is a subtenant but is really an assignee, runs the risk of paying rent twice, first to the tenant and then once an assignment is found, to the landlord. Likewise, a tenant intending to create a profitable sublease, but failing to retain a reversion for a day, will find that once an assignment is found, the tenant has no estate and thus no right to collect rent. This is a distinction that attorneys will take into account, but laymen will not: so the traditional test is a trap for the unwary. The court continued:

> For these reasons we adopt as the rule in this State the principle that the intention of the parties is to govern in determining whether an instrument is an assignment or a sublease. If, for example, a tenant has leased an apartment for a year and is compelled to move to another city, we know of no reason why he should not be able to sublease it for a higher rent without needlessly retaining a reversion for the last day of the term. The duration of the primary term, as compared to the length of the sublease, may in some instances be a factor in arriving at the parties' intention, but we do not think it should be the sole consideration.

The court then applies the intent test and concludes the Jaber-Norber transfer was an assignment and the notes represented consideration for the assignment. Miller, therefore, is still liable for the note payments:

> In the case at bar it cannot be doubted that the parties intended an assignment and not a sublease. The document is so entitled. All its language is that of an assignment rather than that of a sublease. The consideration is stated to be in payment for the lease and not in satisfaction of a tenant's debt to his landlord. The deferred payments are evidenced by promissory notes, which are not ordinarily given by one making a lease. From [Miller's] point of view it is unfortunate that the assignment makes no provision for the contingency of a fire, but [Jaber's] position is certainly not without equity. Jaber sold his merchandise at public auction, and doubtless at reduced prices, in order to vacate the premises for his assignees. Whether he would have taken the same course had the contract provided for a cancellation of the deferred payments in case of a fire we have no way of knowing. A decision either way works a hardship on the losing party. In this situation we do not feel called upon to supply a provision in the assignment which might have been, but was not, demanded by the assignees.

2. A few other courts have clearly adopted the intent test. See, e.g., *Penelko, Inc. v. John Price Assoc. Inc.*, 642 P.2d 1229, 1237 (Utah 1982). In Tennessee, the courts appear to use both the traditional and the intent test. See *Ernst v. Conditt*, 390 S.W.2d 703, 708–09 (Tenn. Ct. App. 1964). A majority of jurisdictions continue to apply the traditional "bright line" test, unless a transfer by a tenant is a sham transaction; then it is ignored for purposes of determining the transferring tenant's legal position. See *O'Donnell v. Weintraub*, 67 Cal. Rptr. 274, 278 (Cal. Ct. App. 1968). Some have recited the majority rule, interpreting it to involve an intent test. See *Hobbs v. Cawley*, 299 P.1073 (N.M. 1931).

A. Assumption and Novation

As described above, a lease assignment from a tenant to an assignee creates privity of estate between the landlord and the assignee. Based on privity of estate, the assignee is liable only for the real covenants in the lease. The assignee is not otherwise bound by the lease terms *unless* the assignee *assumes* the tenant's lease obligations to the landlord. To the extent the assignee assumes any or all of the tenant's contractual obligations, the landlord can enforce the personal covenants, as well as the real covenants, against the assignee.

For an assumption to occur, the assignee must agree to be personally liable for the lease terms. What constitutes an express assumption is the subject of many cases. "It is not every reference to, or mention of, the covenants of a lease, by an assignee, that amounts to an assumption by him. Even where he covenants that his assignment is to be 'subject' to the terms of the lease, that language, without more definite words of promise, does not make him liable as by privity of contract." See *Hart v. Socony-Vacuum Oil Co.*, 50 N.E.2d 285, 286–87 (N.Y. 1943), cited and discussed in the upcoming case. The sentence, "the assignability of such lease will be subject to its terms," is a reference to the uncertainty of the assignor's authority to assign the lease and not an express assumption by the assignee of all the lease terms. See *Kelly v. Tri-Cities Broadcasting, Inc.*, 195 Cal. Rptr. 303, 308 (Cal. Ct. App. 1983). The lease provision, "Lessee hereby warrants and represents that in the event said assignment shall ever take place, the assignee therein shall assume all of the liabilities and obligations assumed by the Lessee in the Lease Agreement," merely imposes a duty on the tenant to secure an assumption by the assignee and creates no privity of contract between the landlord and assignee. Similarly, the phrase, "[t]he assigns and/or heirs of both parties shall carry out the terms of this Lease Agreement," imposes a contractual obligation on the original landlord and tenant to obtain such assumption agreements as are necessary to perform the lease terms. It creates no privity of contract with an assignee. *Id.*

Language that does constitute an express assumption includes the following: "[I]t being understood that the said Assignee, . . . is to accept, assume, and agree to perform all of the terms, conditions, and limitations in said lease . . . ." See *Bank of America Nat. Trust & Savings Ass'n v. Moore*, 64 P.2d 460, 461–62 (Cal. 1937). In *Timm v. Brown*, 178 P.2d 10 (Cal. 1947), the court found an assumption when the assignee acknowledged in a written letter that he was holding the property as the "sole lessee" and orally promised the tenant-assignors that "he was going to live up to the terms of the lease, that he was going to continue with the payments." *Id.* at 13.

Even after an assumption by the assignee, the tenant and landlord remain in privity of contract. When the landlord is a party to the assumption agreement, the landlord also is in privity of contract with the assignee and can sue either or both parties in contract to enforce the lease provisions. When the landlord is not a party, he may be an intended third party beneficiary of the agreement and can enforce it. Once the tenant has paid the landlord, the tenant can recover from the assignee based on the agreement.

If, however, the landlord expressly releases the tenant from her contractual obligations under the lease and substitutes the assuming assignee in the tenant's place, there is a *novation* that extinguishes the privity of contract between the landlord and tenant. As a result of the assumption by the assignee and the novation by the landlord, the assignee completely takes the place of the original tenant and is exclusively in privity of estate and contract with the landlord.

FIRST AMERICAN NAT'L BANK OF NASHVILLE v. CHICKEN SYS. OF AMERICA, INC.
616 S.W.2d 156 (Tenn. Ct. App. 1980)

LEWIS, J.

This case arose out of a lease entered into on May 28, 1968, between plaintiff First American National Bank, Trustee, (First American) and defendant Chicken System of America, Inc. (Chicken System). The lease contained a provision which expressly prohibited any assignment or subletting without the written consent of First American. The lease was for a term of 180 months from May 28, 1968, at a rental of $1049.08 per month, and in addition Chicken System was required to pay premiums on all insurance and to pay all real estate taxes. [Covenants to pay rent, insurance premiums, and real estate taxes "run with the land." — Eds.] Chicken System entered and took possession of the premises under the lease and paid all obligations to and including the month of April, 1969. On April 30, 1969, the President of defendant Performance Systems, Inc. (PSI) wrote to C.H. Wright of Wriking Foods/Beverage Systems, Inc., the parent company of Chicken System. We set out the pertinent parts of that letter:

> This will confirm our mutual agreement for the purchase by us at March 30, 1969, of the Minnie Pearl's Chicken retail outlets owned by your subsidiaries at Murfreesboro Road and Nolensville Road, Nashville, Tennessee, for the sum of $137,329, plus $24,895.00. We will assume the contract payable to the Third National Bank, Nashville, Tennessee for the Nolensville Road Store, together with the rent deposit note to us on Murfreesboro Road per schedule attached. At the time of closing you will discharge your equipment note to Nashco Equipment and Supply Company in the amount of $24,895.00. For the price mentioned above and the assumption of these liabilities, we will acquire from you all inventories, store equipment, rent deposits and your franchise to operate these outlets.
>
> You understand and agree that other liabilities relating to the operation of these stores incurred by you are for your account, except that the real estate and sign leases are our responsibility after April 30, 1969.

On May 5, 1969, First American was advised by Gale Smith & Company of insurance cancellations on the leased property and was informed of Gale Smith's understanding that the business had been purchased by PSI. Prior to that time

First American had no knowledge of any agreement or possible agreement between Chicken System and PSI . . . .

Following PSI's default in the payment of rent in November, 1970, First American, along with PSI, made efforts to find another tenant for the premises and received some ten proposals. PSI wrote First American and granted approval for First American to enter the premises in the interest of subleasing the land and permanent improvements. On June 1, 1971, PSI wrote First American again and stated: "It is important that we place a tenant in the property at the earliest possible time." First American, without consulting PSI or requesting PSI's consent, entered into a lease with Rodney E. and Melanie Fortner, d/b/a Sir Pizza of Madison, for a term of 60 months beginning the first day of September, 1972, at a rental of $600 per month. The Sir Pizza lease was renewed effective September 1, 1977, for a rental of $1000 per month.

First American has brought this suit for the deficiency in the rent and other obligations occurring after September 1, 1972, the date of the Sir Pizza lease. This case was presented to the Trial Court on stipulated facts, and the Chancellor found that First American was entitled to recover $47,384.27 from PSI. PSI has appealed. While both PSI and First American have set forth issues, we are of the opinion that answering only the following question is necessary to resolve this case. Is PSI liable to First American under either privity of estate or privity of contract?

PRIVITY OF ESTATE

Three legal factors arise to create a liability running from the assignee of a leasehold to the lessor (a) privity of estate, (b) covenants in the lease running with the land, and (c) actual assumption of the covenants of the lease by the assignee. An assignee of a lease is bound by privity of estate to perform the express covenants which run with the land, but, in the absence of express agreement on his part, he is liable only on such covenants as run with the land and only during such time as he holds the term.

3A Thompson on Real Property § 1216 (1959).

An assignee, unless he has personally assumed the obligation of the lease, may absolve himself from further liability by an act which terminates his privity of estate. [The lessee's assignee] has the benefit and the burden of all covenants running with the land as long as he holds the estate. Liability of the assignee to the lessor, being based solely on privity of estate, does not continue after he transfers his interest to another. The assignee may thus put an end to his liability by making a further assignment, and this . . . although the second assignee is financially irresponsible.

1 Am. L. Property (A. Casner ed. 1952) § 3.61. In accord with this rule is *McLean v. Caldwell*, 64 S.W. 16, 16–17 (Tenn. 1901), in which the Court stated:

As a general rule, the assignee of a lease is only liable for rents while in possession, provided he reassigns the lease to the lessor or any other person; and it does not matter that such assignment is made to a beggar, a minor, a married woman, a prisoner, or an insolvent, or to one hired to take the assignment, or made expressly to rid himself of liability . . . . The reason is that such reassignment and surrender of possession terminate the privity of estate existing between him and the landlord.

A.D. Juilliard & Co. v. American Woolen Co., 32 A.2d 800 (R.I. 1943), is closely akin in facts to the case at bar. There the landlord leased premises to a lessee which, in turn, assigned the lease to the defendant. Thereafter, the defendant reassigned to a third party. The defendant assignee there, as here, had not expressly assumed the lease. The lessor there, as First American here, contended "that the assignee of a lease of real property . . . is liable for the payment of the stipulated rent for the entire unexpired term, notwithstanding that the assignee did not agree to assume such obligation and assigned the lease before the expiration of the term." *Id.*, 32 A.2d at 801. The Court, in *Juilliard*, stated:

> This contention is contrary to the overwhelming weight of authority both in England and this country . . . . [T]he courts in this country have consistently held that, in the absence of the assumption by the assignee of the obligations of the lease, the liability of such assignee to the lessor rests in privity of estate which is terminated by a new assignment of the lease made by the assignee.

Id. With this rule, First American says it "has no quarrel." It insists, however, that the rule has no relevance to the case at bar since there was not a reassignment by PSI but a reletting of the premises by First American for the benefit of PSI. This contention is a distinction without difference. While mere abandonment by PSI without reassignment of the lease would not have terminated privity of estate, there was a reletting of the premises on September 1, 1972, by First American. When First American relet the premises to Sir Pizza, PSI's possessory rights to the premises terminated just as if PSI had reassigned the lease. Privity of estate terminated, and PSI had no further leasehold interest in the premises.

First American's contention that PSI is charged with knowledge of the covenants of the lease is correct only so long as the basis of liability exists, i.e., during privity of estate. When privity of estate ended between First American and PSI, PSI was no longer charged with knowledge of the covenants of the lease. An assignee who has not assumed the lease "stands in the shoes" of the original lessee only for covenants that run with the land and then only during privity of estate. If this were not so, then the "dumping" of an unfavorable lease would not be possible. Tennessee clearly recognizes that an assignee who has not assumed the lease may "dump it."

PRIVITY OF CONTRACT

First American contends that the following stipulated facts "demonstrate that PSI assumed the obligations of the Chicken System lease thereby placing it in privity of contract with First American":

> 1. An agreement was entered into between Chicken System of America, Inc. and Performance Systems, Inc., which is reflected in a letter dated April 30, 1969, from Edward G. Nelson, President of Performance Systems, Inc., to C.H. Wright of Wriking Food/Beverage Systems, Inc., the parent

company of Chicken System of America, Inc.

2. The letter, as it related to PSI's purchase of the Nolensville Road store, provided in relevant part that "You understand and agree that other liabilities relating to the operation of these stores incurred by you are for your account except that the real estate and sign leases are our responsibility (PSI) after April 30, 1969.

3. After April 30, 1969, neither Chicken System of America, nor its parent corporation paid any rent on the property. Rent on the property was paid by PSI from May 1, 1969 through October, 1970, and PSI was in possession of the premises during that time.

First American cites *Sander v. Piggly Wiggly Stores, Inc.*, 95 S.W.2d 1266 (Tenn. App. 1936), and says that the facts there "strikingly resemble" the facts in the case at bar. We disagree . . . . In *Sander* the assignee acknowledged that it had assumed the lease contract, and the Court found that the assignee had agreed to perform the covenants of the lease. In the case at bar, we find no such acknowledgment.

In *Hart v. Socony-Vacuum Oil Co.*, 50 N.E.2d 285 (N.Y. 1943), several years after an oral assignment of the lease the assignee signed a modification agreement in regard to the insurance requirements of the lease. The modification agreement contained the following provision: "It is further mutually understood and agreed that except as herein expressly modified, all other provisions and covenants contained in said lease shall remain in full force and effect." *Id.*, 50 N.E.2d at 286. In rejecting the lessor's argument that this agreement was a personal assumption of the covenants of the lease on the part of the assignee, the Court stated:

> There is strong authority which says that to hold liable an assignee under a lease, after he has given up the lease and vacated the premises, there must be produced an express promise by him to perform the covenants of the lease . . . . [S]uch an express covenant is never assumed to have been made it must always be proven . . . . It is not every reference to, or mention of, the covenants of a lease, by an assignee, that amounts to an assumption by him. Even where he covenants that his assignment is to be "subject" to the terms of the lease, that language, without more definite words of promise, does not make him liable as by privity of contract.

Id., 50 N.E.2d at 286–87 . . . . Before there is privity of contract between the assignee and the lessor, there must be an actual assumption of the lease. In the case at bar there was not an actual assumption, only a mere acceptance of an assignment . . . . "The mere acceptance of an assignment is not an assumption. Every assignment requires acceptance, . . . yet an assignee . . . who does not assume the performance of the covenants of the lease holds the lease merely under a privity of estate. . . .'" *Packard-Bamberger & Co. v. Maloof*, 214 A.2d 45, 46–47 (N.J. Super. 1965) (internal quotation marks omitted).

While no contention is made that there was a written contract between PSI and First American, First American argues, nevertheless, that certain statements made by PSI to other parties after the assignment by Chicken System to PSI created privity of contract between First American and PSI. First American cites *Crow v.*

Kaupp, 50 S.W.2d 995, 996–97 (Mo. 1932), in support of this contention. *Crow* is readily distinguishable from the case at bar . . . . The assignee, in *Crow*, made a complete and detailed assumption of the lease. In the case at bar, the assignment to PSI by Chicken System was oral, and PSI made no promise at any time to be bound to First American.

We are of the opinion that privity of estate between First American and PSI terminated upon PSI's abandonment of the premises and the reletting of the premises to Sir Pizza by First American. We further hold that there was no privity of contract between PSI and First American . . . . The judgment of the Chancellor as to Performance Systems, Inc. is reversed and dismissed with costs to First American. The case is remanded to the Chancery Court for collection of costs and any other necessary proceedings . . . .

NOTES

1. The court did not address Chicken System's liability. Is Chicken System liable to First American for the rent deficiency? Under what theory (privity of estate, privity of contract, or both)? Is there anything Chicken System could have done when assigning its leasehold to PSI to avoid any further liability to First American? What theory would be involved in your answer? See generally Robert Kelley, *Any Reports of the Death of the Property Paradigm for Leases Have Been Greatly Exaggerated*, 41 Wayne L. Rev. 1563, 1587–1588 (1995) (providing a summary and critique of this area of landlord tenant law).

2. First American never consented to the assignment to PSI. Could PSI successfully have argued that the assignment was invalid as a result and that, therefore, it never was in privity of estate with First American? Consider the following excerpt from the *Chicken System* opinion, 616 S.W.2d 157–58, deleted from the opinion above:

> On May 8, 1969, First American's counsel wrote PSI in regard to the insurance coverage and also informed PSI that the premises could only be subleased with the written consent of First American. On June 6, 1969, First American's counsel wrote to all concerned parties. Pertinent portions of that letter are as follows:

>> Under Section 24 of the lease agreement there may be no assignment or sub-letting without the written consent of the lessor. I wish to make it plain that as of this time no such consent has been given, nor will any such consent be given unless there is a formal request in writing, requesting same. Upon our receipt of such a written request, we will submit the proposal to those three individuals who have guaranteed performance of the lease by Chicken System of America, Inc., and if they have no objection to the assignment or sub-letting and will continue bound on their guaranty agreement, the Bank will probably have no objection to consenting to a sub-lease or assignment.

> The guarantors did not at any time agree to remain bound on their guaranty agreement if the premises were sublet or assigned to PSI. The

guarantors were originally defendants in this suit, but prior to trial a nonsuit as to them was taken by First American. There were several letters written by plaintiff's counsel and PSI's counsel regarding subletting or assignment, but at no time did First American ever consent to an assignment of the lease from Chicken System to PSI.

PSI entered the premises and took possession and from May 1, 1969, through October, 1970, paid rent to First American. On November 1, 1970, PSI defaulted in payment of the rent and vacated the premises. Thereafter, First American filed suit in the Chancery Court for Davidson County against Chicken System and PSI and sought rent, insurance, taxes, and maintenance under the terms of the lease agreement due and owing until September 1, 1972. PSI's primary defense was that First American had withheld consent, that absent consent by First American the "assignment" from Chicken System to PSI was invalid and PSI was merely a tenant at sufferance, and that when PSI vacated the premises in November, 1970, its obligations and rights under the lease were suspended. The Chancellor held that the lack of consent could be waived by First American and could not be raised by PSI as a defense, that PSI's surrender of the premises in November, 1970, did not terminate privity of estate between it and First American, and that PSI was liable to First American for obligations of the lease running with the land, including the obligation to pay rent. PSI appealed, and the Supreme Court affirmed the Chancellor. *First American National Bank v. Chicken System of America, Inc.*, 510 S.W.2d 906 (Tenn. 1974) . . . . The Court stated: "[T]here is privity of estate between an original lessor and a subsequent assignee that makes the assignee fully responsible to the lessor for the lease provisions." *Id.* at 908. The Court remanded to the Chancery Court for the purpose of ascertaining damages. The damages were stipulated, but the Chancellor allowed interest on the recovery. PSI again appealed to the Supreme Court which again affirmed the Chancellor. *Performance Systems, Inc. v. First American National Bank*, 554 S.W.2d 616 (Tenn. 1977).

Did First American Bank act reasonably when it withheld its consent to Chicken System's assignment? How does the court address Performance System's argument that Chicken System's assignment to Performance System was void because it was made without First American's consent and therefore Performance System was a tenant at sufferance whose obligations terminated when Performance System vacated the premises?

B.   Transfer Restrictions

The lease in the *Chicken System* case contained a provision prohibiting the tenant from transferring its leasehold interest by sublease or assignment without the landlord's consent. Such a restraint on alienation is valid:

> The interests of the landlord and of the tenant in the leased property are freely transferable, unless: (1) a tenancy at will or sufferance is involved; (2) the lease requires significant personal services from either party and a

transfer of the party's interest would substantially impair the other party's chances of obtaining those services; or (3) the parties to the lease validly agree otherwise.

Restatement (Second) of Property § 15.1 (1977 & Supp. 1996).

JULIAN v. CHRISTOPHER
575 A.2d 735 (Md. 1990)

CHASANOW, J.

In 1961, the Court decided the case of *Jacobs v. Klawans*, 225 Md. 147, 169 A.2d 677 (1961) and held that when a lease contained a "silent consent" clause prohibiting a tenant from subletting or assigning without the consent of the landlord, landlords had a right to withhold their consent to a subletting or assignment even though the withholding of consent was arbitrary and unreasonable . . . . We now have before us the issue of whether the common law rule applied in *Klawans* should be changed. In the instant case, the tenants, Douglas Julian and William J. Gilleland purchased a tavern and restaurant business, as well as rented the business premises from landlord, Guy D. Christopher. The lease stated in clause ten that the premises, consisting of both the tavern and an upstairs apartment, could not be assigned or sublet "without the prior written consent of the landlord." Sometime after taking occupancy, the tenants requested the landlord's written permission to sublease the upstairs apartment. The landlord made no inquiry about the proposed sublessee, but wrote to the tenants that he would not agree to a sublease unless the tenants paid additional rent in the amount of $150.00 per month. When the tenants permitted the sublessee to move in, the landlord filed an action in the District Court of Maryland in Baltimore City requesting repossession of the building because the tenants had sublet the premises without his permission. At the district court trial, the tenants testified that they specifically inquired about clause ten, and were told by the landlord that the clause was merely included to prevent them from subletting or assigning to "someone who would tear the apartment up." The district court judge refused to consider this testimony. He stated in his oral opinion that he would "remain within the four corners of the lease, and construe the document strictly," at least as it pertained to clause ten. Both the District Court and, on appeal, the Circuit Court for Baltimore City found in favor of the landlord. The circuit judge noted: "If you don't have the words that consent will not be unreasonably withheld, then the landlord can withhold his consent for a good reason, a bad reason, or no reason at all in the context of a commercial lease, which is what we're dealing with." We granted certiorari to determine whether the *Klawans* holding should be modified in light of the changes that have occurred since that decision.

While we are concerned with the need for stability in the interpretation of leases, we recognize that since the *Klawans* case was decided in 1961, the foundations for that holding have been substantially eroded. The *Klawans* opinion cited *Restatement of Property* § 410 as authority for its holding. The current *Restatement (Second) of Property* § 15.2 rejects the *Klawans* doctrine and now takes the position that: "A restraint on alienation without the consent of the landlord of the tenant's interest in the leased property is valid, but the landlord's consent to an alienation by the tenant cannot be withheld unreasonably, unless a freely negotiated provision in the lease gives the landlord an absolute right to withhold consent."

Another authority cited in *Klawans* in support of its holding was 2 R. Powell, Powell on Real Property. The most recent edition of that text now states:

> Thus, if a lease clause prohibited the tenant from transferring his or her interest without the landlord's consent, the landlord could withhold consent arbitrarily. This result was allowed because it was believed that the objectives served by allowing the restraints outweighed the social evils implicit in them, inasmuch as the restraints gave the landlord control over choosing the person who was to be entrusted with the landlord's property and was obligated to perform the lease covenants.

> It is doubtful that this reasoning retains full validity today. Relationships between landlord and tenant have become more impersonal and housing space (and in many areas, commercial space as well) has become scarce. These changes have had an impact on courts and legislatures in varying degrees. Modern courts almost universally adopt the view that restrictions on the tenant's right to transfer are to be strictly construed.

2 R. Powell, Real Property § 248[1] (1988).

Finally, in support of its decision in *Klawans*, this Court noted that, "although it, apparently, has not been passed upon in a great number of jurisdictions, the decisions of the courts that have determined the question are in very substantial accord." *Klawans*, 225 Md. at 151, 169 A.2d at 679. This is no longer true. Since *Klawans*, the trend has been in the opposite direction. "The modern trend is to impose a standard of reasonableness on the landlord in withholding consent to a sublease unless the lease expressly states otherwise." *Campbell v. Westdahl*, 715 P.2d 288, 292 (Ariz. App. 1985). * * *

Traditional property rules favor the free and unrestricted right to alienate interests in property. Therefore, absent some specific restriction in the lease, a lessee has the right to freely alienate the leasehold interest by assignment or sublease without obtaining the permission of the lessor.

Contractual restrictions on the alienability of leasehold interests are permitted. Consequently, landlords often insert clauses that restrict the lessee's common law right to freely assign or sublease. Probably the most often used clause is a "silent consent" clause similar to the provision in the instant case, which provides that the premises may not be assigned or sublet without the written consent of the lessor. In a "silent consent" clause requiring a landlord's consent to assign or sublease, there is no standard governing the landlord's decision. Courts must insert a standard. The choice is usually between 1) requiring the landlord to act reasonably when withholding consent, or 2) permitting the landlord to act arbitrarily and capriciously in withholding consent. Public policy requires that when a lease gives the landlord the right to withhold consent to a sublease or assignment, the landlord should act reasonably, and the courts ought not to imply a right to act arbitrarily or capriciously. If a landlord is allowed to arbitrarily refuse consent to an assignment or sublease, for what in effect is no reason at all, that would virtually nullify any right to assign or sublease.

Because most people act reasonably most of the time, tenants might expect that a landlord's consent to a sublease or assignment would be governed by standards of reasonableness. Most tenants probably would not understand that a clause stating "this lease may not be assigned or sublet without the landlord's written consent" means the same as a clause stating "the tenant shall have no right to assign or sublease." Some landlords may have chosen the former wording rather than the latter because it vaguely implies, but does not grant to the tenant, the right to assign or sublet.

There are two public policy reasons why the law enunciated in *Klawans* should now be changed. The first is the public policy against restraints on alienation. The second is the public policy which implies a covenant of good faith and fair dealing in every contract.

Because there is a public policy against restraints on alienation, if a lease is silent on the subject, a tenant may freely sublease or assign. Restraints on alienation are permitted in leases, but are looked upon with disfavor and are strictly construed. If a clause in a lease is susceptible of two interpretations, public policy favors the interpretation least restrictive of the right to alienate freely. Interpreting a "silent consent" clause so that it only prohibits subleases or assignments when a landlord's refusal to consent is reasonable, would be the interpretation imposing the least restraint on alienation and most in accord with public policy.

Since the *Klawans* decision, this Court has recognized that in a lease, as well as in other contracts, "there exists an implied covenant that each of the parties thereto will act in good faith and deal fairly with the others." *Food Fair v. Blumberg*, 200 A.2d 166, 174 (Md. 1964). When the lease gives the landlord the right to exercise discretion, the discretion should be exercised in good faith, and in accordance with fair dealing; if the lease does not spell out any standard for withholding consent, then the implied covenant of good faith and fair dealing should imply a reasonableness standard.

We are cognizant of the value of the doctrine of *stare decisis*, and of the need for stability and certainty in the law. However, as we noted in *Harrison v. Montgomery Co. Bd. of Educ.*, 456 A.2d 894, 903 (Md. 1983), a common law rule may be modified "where we find, in light of changed conditions or increased knowledge, that the rule has become unsound in the circumstances of modern life, a vestige of the past, no longer suitable to our people." The *Klawans* common law interpretation of the "silent consent" clause represents such a "vestige of the past," and should now be changed.

In the instant case, we need not expound at length on what constitutes a reasonable refusal to consent to an assignment or sublease. We should, however, point out that obvious examples of reasonable objections could include the financial irresponsibility or instability of the transferee, or the unsuitability or incompatibility of the intended use of the property by the transferee. We also need not expound at length on what would constitute an unreasonable refusal to consent to an assignment or sublease. If the reasons for withholding consent have nothing to do with the intended transferee or the transferee's use of the property, the motivation may be suspect. Where, as alleged in this case, the refusal to consent was solely for the purpose of securing a rent increase, such refusal would be unreasonable unless the new subtenant would necessitate additional expenditures by, or increased economic risk to, the landlord.

The tenants ask us to retroactively overrule *Klawans*, and hold that in all leases with "silent consent" clauses, no matter when executed, consent to assign or sublease may not be unreasonably withheld by a landlord. We decline to do so. In the absence of evidence to the contrary, we should assume that parties executing leases when *Klawans* governed the interpretation of "silent consent" clauses were aware of *Klawans* and the implications drawn from the words they used. We should not, and do not, rewrite these contracts . . . .

For leases entered into after the mandate in this case, if the lease contains a "silent consent" clause providing that the tenant must obtain the landlord's consent in order to assign or sublease, such consent may not be unreasonably withheld. If the parties intend to preclude any transfer by assignment or sublease, they may do so by a freely negotiated provision in the lease. If the parties intend to limit the right to assign or sublease by giving the landlord the arbitrary right to refuse to consent, they may do so by a freely negotiated provision of the lease clearly spelling out this intent. For example, the clause might provide, "consent may be withheld in the sole and absolute subjective discretion of the lessor." * * *

The tenants in the instant case should get the benefit of the interpretation of the "silent consent" clause that they so persuasively argued for, unless this interpretation would be unfair to the landlord. We note that the tenants testified they were told that the clause was only to prevent subleasing to "someone who would tear the apartment up." Therefore, we will reverse the judgment of the Circuit Court with instructions to vacate the judgment of the District Court and remand for a new trial. At that trial, the landlord will have the burden of establishing that it would be unfair to interpret the "silent consent" clause in accordance with our decision that a landlord must act reasonably in withholding consent. He may establish that it would be unfair to do so by establishing that when executing the lease he was aware of and relied on the *Klawans* interpretation of the "silent consent" clause. We recognize that we may be giving the tenants a benefit that other tenants with leases entered into before our mandate will not receive . . . .

Judgment of the Circuit Court . . . reversed, and case remanded . . . with directions to vacate the judgment of the District Court and to remand the case . . . for further proceedings not inconsistent with this opinion.

NOTES

1. The majority rule remains that when a lease prohibits assignments or subleases, the landlord may withhold consent arbitrarily, for any reason or for no reason at all. However, twenty states have adopted the rule in *Julian* that a landlord cannot unreasonably withhold consent unless the lease expressly provides otherwise, leaving it still a minority rule. See Joshua Stein, *Assignment and Subletting Restrictions and What They Mean in the Real World*, 44 Real Prop. Prob. & Tr. J. 1, 17, n. 60 (2009). As the court in *Julian* noted, its holding is consistent with the position taken by the Restatement (Second) of Property. The Restatement states that, to be reasonable, a reason for withholding consent "must be objectively sensible and of some significance and not be based on mere caprice or whim or personal prejudice." § 15.2. Factors used to determine what is a reasonable withholding of consent include "the proposed assignee or subtenant's financial responsibility, the suitability of the proposed use, the need for alteration of the premises, and the nature of the occupancy." *Economy Rentals, Inc. v. Garcia*, 819 P.2d 1306, 1317 (N.M. 1991). Generally speaking, a landlord may withhold consent to protect itself from economic disadvantage relating to the ownership and operation of the leased property, such as when a proposed transfer would reduce the benefits the landlord bargained for in the original lease. On the other hand, a landlord may not withhold consent to improve his economic position, such as by sharing in the sublease rent or by securing a benefit the landlord did not bargain for in the original lease. Refusing to specify reasons for withholding consent and failing to act on a request for consent within a reasonable time constitute unreasonable withholdings of consent. When faced with an unreasonable withholding of consent, a tenant may transfer her leasehold interest without consent, but she has the burden of proving the unreasonableness of the withholding. See Restatement (Second) of Property § 15.2.

If the tenant wrongfully transfers without the landlord's required consent, the transfer is valid, and the landlord usually is limited to an action for damages. Although some authority exists that a landlord has an implied power to terminate a lease if a tenant breaches a clause forbidding a transfer, e.g., *Reynolds v. McCullough*, 739 S.W.2d 424 (Tex. App. 1987), a landlord may want to couple a consent provision with a clause that gives him the power to terminate the leasehold and recapture possession of the premises if the tenant or her transferee attempts a transfer without his consent. In *Carma Developers, Inc. v. Marathon Dev., Inc.*, 826 P.2d 710, 718 (Cal. 1992), the court held that a termination and recapture clause in a negotiated lease was not an unreasonable restraint on alienation.

A few states have codified the minority rule. See, e.g., Alaska Stat. § 34.03.060 (2014).

2. Another limitation on the effectiveness of a consent clause is the rule in *Dumpor's Case*, 4 Coke 1196, 76 Eng. Rep. 110 (1603). Pursuant to that rule, a lease clause prohibiting an assignment without the landlord's consent is extinguished if the landlord consents to one assignment. An assignee, therefore, may freely reassign without the landlord's consent. While *Dumpor's Case* has been criticized in this country as "venerable error" and has been repudiated in England by statute, it remains the law in many American jurisdictions. However, some courts limit the application of the rule. For example, it does not apply to (a) prohibitions against subleasing, (b) lease provisions that do expressly bind assigns, or (c) cases in which the landlord expressly conditions his consent to an assignment on the need to obtain his consent again for any further assignment. R. Schoshinski, American Law of Landlord and Tenant 553, 590–591 (1980 & Supp. 1996). Is the following lease provision sufficient to avoid the rule in *Dumpor's Case*? "Without the prior, express, and written consent of lessor, lessee shall not assign this lease, or sublet the premises or any part of the premises. A consent by lessor to one assignment or subletting shall not be deemed to be a consent to any subsequent assignment or subletting." 11B Am. Jur. Legal Forms 2d, *Leases of Real Property* § 161:692 (2003).

C. Assignments and Real Covenants

ABBOTT v. BOB'S U-DRIVE
352 P.2d 598 (Or. 1960)

O'CONNELL, J.

This is an appeal from a judgment based upon an arbitration award in favor of the plaintiff and against the defendants, jointly and severally . . . . In April, 1952, plaintiff leased certain premises to Robert E. Thompson under the terms of which the lessee agreed to operate an automobile "U-Drive" business and an automobile leasing business. The lease contained a provision requiring the parties to submit to arbitration any controversy arising out of the lease. In February, 1953, Thompson caused to be incorporated the defendant Bob's U-Drive, and in October, 1953, he caused to be incorporated the defendant Continental Leasing Company. Bob's U-Drive engaged in the business of making short-term rentals of automobiles, and Continental Leasing Company leased automobiles for twelve months or longer. Thompson was president and manager of both corporations and owned fifty percent of the stock of each corporation. The automobile rental and leasing business which Thompson conducted on the leasehold premises as an individual was continued by the defendant corporations after their formation. In August, 1954, Thompson assigned all of his interest in the lease to the defendant Bob's U-Drive. The assignment was in writing. No assignment was made to defendant Continental Leasing Company, although it continued to carry on its business from the leasehold premises as before.

The operations of the two corporations were not strictly segregated. All the business was conducted from one office. There was some evidence that in the operation of the business the records did not always clearly reflect which corporation was acting in the particular instance. However, each corporation kept separate business records, separate bank accounts, separate telephones and separate stationery.

A controversy arose between the parties as to the performance of the terms of the lease by the defendants and on April 22, 1957, plaintiff . . . filed a petition for the purpose of securing an order directing the defendants to proceed to arbitration. An amended petition was filed in July, 1957. The defendant Continental Leasing Company filed its answer. The defendant Bob's U-Drive prepared an answer which was never filed. At the hearing in the circuit court for Multnomah county on the petition to order arbitration the attorney for defendant Bob's U-Drive, who was also the attorney for Continental Leasing Company, indicated that Bob's U-Drive was willing to arbitrate, whereupon Bob's U-Drive ceased to participate in the proceedings and the hearing continued as to defendant Continental Leasing Company alone.

The defendant Continental Leasing Company prayed for a dismissal of the petition on the ground that there was no assignment of the lease to it and no written arbitration agreement . . . . An order was entered by the circuit court for Multnomah county requiring the defendant Continental Leasing Company to proceed forthwith to arbitrate the controversy. No order was entered directing the defendant Bob's U-Drive to arbitrate. A hearing was then held before a board of arbitrators, which culminated in an award of $2,938.88 for the plaintiff. Both defendants filed objections to the judgment setting forth various grounds. An order was entered overruling the objections and finally on July 8, 1958, a joint and several judgment was entered against the defendants in accordance with the award.

. . . [W]e are of the opinion that Bob's U-Drive, by its participation in the subsequent proceedings, submitted itself to the jurisdiction of the board of arbitrators and to the circuit court. Bob's U-Drive expressed its willingness to arbitrate and it took part in the proceedings before the board of arbitrators. . . . Bob's U-Drive made a general appearance before the board and thereafter made a general appearance before the circuit court by filing objections to the entry of the judgment and otherwise participating in the proceedings subsequent to the judgment . . . .

. . . It is urged that the defendant Continental Leasing Company could not be required to submit to arbitration . . . because it had not been a party to a written contract containing an agreement to submit to arbitration which is required by ORS 33.220.

It is conceded that no written assignment of the lease was ever made to Continental Leasing Company. The assignment ran to Bob's U-Drive only. There is no satisfactory explanation given for limiting the assignment to the one corporation. At the time of the assignment both corporations were occupying portions of the leasehold premises and had been paying rent. Until the assignment was made Thompson continued to be the lessee but he managed both corporations and apparently treated each corporation as having an equal right to the occupancy of the leasehold premises. Although the long-term leasing business of Continental Leasing Company was not developed until after the short-term rental business had been in operation by Bob's U-Drive for some time, there is no evidence that Continental Leasing Company was a sublessee under Bob's U-Drive. Both corporations had an equal status as tenants of Thompson. The looseness of the arrangement was satisfactory as long as Thompson was the common manager. It was only after Thompson decided to sell his interest in the businesses that an assignment of the lease assumed importance.

The plaintiff maintains that Continental became a party to the written lease by virtue of ratifying an act of its promoter, by adoption of a contract of its officers and by accepting the benefits under the lease.

We are of the opinion that Continental became a co-assignee of the lease together with Bob's U-Drive prior to the written assignment of lease. When a person other than the lessee is in possession of leased premises paying rent to the lessor, there is a presumption that the lease has been assigned to the person in possession.

In a majority of the modern cases applying this rule the implied assignment arising out of possession is regarded as effective to form the basis for the running of covenants in the lease so as to burden or benefit the assignee. It is said in *Leadbetter v. Pewtherer*, 121 P. 799 (Or. 1912) that "This cannot amount to or be shown to establish a formal assignment, for the purpose of binding defendant by the covenants of the lease; but it is an oral assignment, and when he enters and is recognized thereunder by the lessor he becomes liable for the rental specified therein." The court, in the *Leadbetter* case, held that the possessor was liable for the rent covenanted to be paid in the written lease. Apparently the recovery was deemed to be for use and occupation rather than for the breach of a covenant running with the land. We believe, however, that the cases holding that the implied assignment carries with it liability on the covenants which run with the land state the better rule and we adopt it. If the possessor's interest is regarded as arising out of an implied assignment, it seems only consistent to treat him as standing in the same position as an assignee who occupies the premises under a written assignment. The occupation of the premises and the payment of rent should be sufficient to take the case out of the statute of frauds. This is sometimes expressed in terms of estoppel . . . . If the policy of the statute of frauds is satisfied and if it is assumed that the privilege of occupancy arises out of an assignment of the term, there would be no reason for limiting the operative effect of the assignment as suggested in . . . *Leadbetter, supra*. In the instant case the opportunity for fraud was minimal. The gap in written proof to establish liability under the lease was in the transaction between Thompson as lessee and Thompson as manager of Continental. Under these circumstances there is little danger that the policy of the statute of frauds would be violated by recognizing the oral transaction as an assignment of the lease.

We have assumed that the covenant to submit to arbitration controversies arising out of the lease is such that it will be binding upon the assignees of the leasehold. It may be noted that the defendant Bob's U-Drive admitted that the covenant to arbitrate was binding on it. If the covenant is binding on an assignee it should make no difference whether the assignment is express or implied. We are of the opinion that the covenant to submit to arbitration ran with the assignment of the lease.

To bind the assignee of a leasehold the covenant must "touch and concern" the leasehold estate. There is considerable confusion and uncertainty as to the meaning of this requirement, not only in the adjudicated cases but among the scholars as well. The various tests and the cases on the subject of "touching and concerning" are thoroughly examined in Clark on Covenants. Probably the most definitive test is that suggested in Bigelow, *The Content of Covenants in Leases*, 12 Mich. L. Rev. 639 (1914). The Bigelow test is summarized by Judge Clark in his book Covenants and Interests Running with Land 97–98 (2d ed), as follows:

> The method he states is to ascertain the exact effect of the covenant upon the legal relations of the parties. In effect it is a measuring of the legal relations of the parties with and without the covenant. If the promisor's legal relations in respect to the land in question are lessened — his legal interest as owner rendered less valuable by the promise — the burden of the covenant touches or concerns that land; if the promisee's legal relations in respect to that land are increased — his legal interest as owner rendered more valuable by the promise — the benefit of the covenant touches or concerns that land. It is necessary that this effect should be had upon the legal relations of the parties as owners of the land in question, and not merely as members of the community in general, such as taxpayers, or owners of other land, in order that the covenant may run.

Although this analysis is frequently helpful in testing covenants for their character as "real" or "personal" covenants, it still leaves open to judicial inquiry in each case the question of whether the interests of the parties affected by the covenant are those which they have "as owners of the land in question" or separate and apart from such ownership . . . . In the case at bar the covenant to arbitrate is invoked to require the lessee to submit to arbitration a matter relating to rental payments under the lease. A covenant to pay rent clearly "touches and concerns" the land. It would seem to follow that a covenant to arbitrate a question with respect to rental payments should also be regarded as relating to the property interests of the original covenanting parties as lessor and lessee. As stated in Clark, op. cit., p. 99, "there would seem to be no reason for applying the rule of touching and concerning in an overtechnical manner, which is unreal from the standpoint of the parties themselves."

In applying this test we believe that it is important not only to consider how the original parties as laymen would naturally regard the covenant, but how one taking a lease as assignee would regard it. Assuming this to be a test to be judicially applied, we believe that the average person accepting the assignment of a lease containing a covenant to arbitrate questions relating to the terms of the lease would normally assume that he was bound by the covenant. In this connection it may be noted again that Bob's U-Drive (represented by legal counsel, to be sure) assumed that it was bound by the covenant to arbitrate. The case law on the specific question before us is sparse. *Young v. Wrightson*, 11 Ohio Dec. 104 (1890) supports the view we take. In that case the lease contained a covenant that at the end of stated periods the leasehold would be reappraised and the rent computed on the new appraised value. The court held that "It is too plain to admit of argument that the covenant in question is one which is capable of running with the land." * * *

We hold, therefore, that the possession of Continental and Bob's U-Drive made them co-assignees of the lease and that the implied assignment to Continental was sufficient to carry with it the covenant to arbitrate contained in the written lease. Were we to hold that Continental's possession was not under the lease we would, in effect, endorse a practice by which a lessee, through the formation of a corporation, could enjoy the benefits of the lease and at the same time insulate himself from liability on the covenants contained in it.

The opportunity for fraud through such a device is illustrated in the present case. The lease called for the payment of a minimum rent of $75.00 per month and an additional rental of $10.00 per month for each car over eight "owned by Thompson's U-Drive Company." Plaintiff testified that most of the cars were registered in the name of Continental Leasing Company and that a part of the cars so registered were used in the short-term rental business carried on by Bob's U-Drive. When plaintiff's accountant asked to examine the books of both companies he was denied access to Continental's books . . . . The judgment of the lower court is affirmed.

NOTE

The court in *In re Arden and Howe Assoc., Ltd.*, 152 Bankr. 971 (E.D. Cal. 1993), states: "[A] restrictive use covenant burdening contiguous land 'runs with the land' and binds the landlord's successors if three requirements are met. The contiguous real property must be particularly described in the lease; the lease must provide that successors are bound for the benefit of the demised real property; and the lease must be recorded. Cal. Civ. Code § 1470." Does this statement square with the requirements for real covenants in *Bob's U-Drive*? Why didn't the plaintiff in *Bob's U-Drive* protect itself with a covenant prohibiting or limiting an assignment or sublease or with a covenant expressly binding assignees and sublessees to all obligations of the lease? A covenant containing an option to purchase the premises is typically said to be a real covenant, the benefit of which runs to an assignee of the lease. Might the option be exercised if it were assigned separately from the lease?

IX. TERMINATION

A. Notice of Termination

1. Term for Years

Absent a statute on the subject, including statutes concerning public or federally-assisted rental housing, an estate or term for years ends without further notice at the time agreed in the lease. In some states, a further notice is required, not to end the lease, but to use summary procedures to recover possession if the lessee holds over.

Problem: L and T execute a lease that is an estate for years. With the termination date approaching, L gives T a 30-day notice to quit before the term ends. T retains possession after the end of the term. Does L have to provide another 30-day notice? See *M.L. Sigmon Forest Prod., Inc. v. Scroggins*, 446 S.W.2d 198 (Ark. 1969).

2. Periodic Tenancy

Notice is required to terminate a periodic tenancy. Absent a statute on the subject, a six-month notice is required to end a year-to-year tenancy. For periods of less than a year, notice equal to the base period is necessary. Many states have statutes on this type of notice. A 30-day minimum notice period is typical. Those statutes often provide for written notice as well. A lease for a term for years, to which the Statute of Frauds applies, becomes a periodic tenancy (or less often, a tenancy at will) when it does not conform to the Statute.

Problem: L and T have a month-to-month tenancy. L gives T written notice on June 1 that the tenancy will terminate on the last day of the period, June 30. Why is this notice ineffective? What happens when "the month" does not include a whole rental period?

Problem: L and T execute a five-year lease. The lease violates the Statute of Frauds. T takes possession of the premises. What notice requirements apply? See R. Schoshinski, American Law of Landlord and Tenant §§ 2.25–2.26, at 82 (1980). Does it matter that (a) the tenant takes possession and improves the premises, or (b) the landlord brings an eviction action nine months into the lease's term, or two years into it?

S.D.G. v. INVENTORY CONTROL COMPANY
429 A.2d 394 (N.J. Super. 1981)

PRESSLER, J.

This dispute, arising out of a commercial month-to-month tenancy, raises a novel issue in this jurisdiction regarding the consequences of a tenant's late notice to quit. Both parties agree that the applicable common-law rule requires the tenant to give at least one month's notice to the landlord of his intention to quit. The controversy here is as to the effect of a notice given during a monthly period of an intention to quit at the end of that period. The question is whether such a notice is totally ineffective or, rather, will constitute a valid notice referable to the end of the next monthly period. The trial judge held that such a late notice is totally void, obligating the tenant, after his removal, to continue paying rent for the premises until their reletting. We disagree and hold that in these circumstances the tenant's obligation continues only until the end of the monthly period following the one in which the late notice was given.

Defendant Inventory Control Company, the tenant, had leased an office in plaintiff's building for a term of five years expiring on October 31, 1976. Negotiations between the parties for a two-year extension of the lease proved to be unsuccessful, and on November 16, 1976 the tenant advised the landlord in writing that it would vacate the premises on November 30, 1976. There is some unresolved dispute as to exactly when the tenant did vacate, but there is no question that it did vacate no later than the end of the first week of December 1976. The landlord attempted to relet the premises but was unable to do so until April 1977. Accordingly, it brought this action seeking recovery of the monthly rent for December 1976 and January through March 1977. The tenant concedes its liability for the December rent. It claims, however, that its mid-November notice was effective as of December 31, 1976, shielding it from any liability for rent thereafter. The trial judge awarded plaintiff rent for all four months. We reverse . . . .

It is clear that after the termination of the lease on October 31, 1976 the tenant's status became that of a month-to-month tenant on the same terms as set forth in the lease. N.J.S.A. 46:8–10. There is no statute prescribing the requirements of a tenant's notice to the landlord of its intention to terminate a month-to-month tenancy. Thus, the common-law rule requiring at least one month's notice to quit is applicable. (Citations omitted). And although our courts have not apparently been called upon to address the question, a recognized corollary of the common-law rule is the proposition that if the notice is given during the same month in which the quit is to take place, it will be effective as of the end of the month following the month in which the short notice was given. See 3A Thompson, Real Property, § 1355 at 673–674 (1981).

We are, furthermore, satisfied that the common-law rule which refers the effective date of the late notice of vacation to the end of the next ensuing monthly period is eminently sound as a matter of public policy, common sense and customary practice. We do not believe that any legitimate interest would be served by penalizing a month-to-month tenant for his late notice by subjecting him to indefinite liability for rent in the event of the landlord's inability to relet. Certainly, such a penalty is beyond the legitimate expectations of the landlord who must be assumed to know that his month-to-month tenant can leave at any time without liability, provided one full month's notice is given. Clearly, the requirement of a month's notice is intended to afford the landlord a reasonable opportunity to secure another tenant. We are persuaded that that purpose is fully satisfied by the rule of the deferred efficacy of the notice since the landlord thereby is afforded not only a full month in which to find another tenant but, in addition thereto, that portion of the prior month remaining after the date of the notice. Consequently, we hold that when the tenant gave notice to quit on November 16, 1976, it was obligated to pay rent in the absence of an interim reletting only through December 31, 1976. The judgment below must be accordingly modified to reflect the tenant's rent obligation as encompassing one month only.

NOTE

On the issue in this case, compare *Arbenz v. Exley, Watkins & Co.*, 50 S.E. 813 (W. Va. 1905) (holding that a second notice by tenant is necessary), with *Worthington v. Moreland Motor Truck Co.*, 250 P. 30 (Wash. 1926), and *T.W.I.W., Inc. v. Rhudy*, 630 P.2d 753 (N.M. 1981) (both holding that no second notice is necessary).

3. Tenancy at Will

As a matter of common law, a tenancy at will may be ended by either party without advance notice. However, most states statutorily require advance notice. A tenancy at will also terminates by operation of law when either party dies or the landlord's or the tenant's title or interest is assigned. The tenant's interest ends if the tenant commits waste.

Problem: May a tenancy at will be, under the express provisions of the lease, terminable by the landlord alone? By the tenant alone?

4. Tenancy at Sufferance

Because this is not a formal landlord-tenant relationship, there is no tenancy to end, and the common law does not require advance notice be given the holdover tenant. However, several states have enacted statutes requiring some notice, usually 30 days.

B. Surrender and Abandonment

1. The Traditional Rule

When a tenant surrenders possession of the premises or otherwise abandons possession during the lease term, the landlord in a majority of states may take any one of three actions: (1) treat the lease as terminated and retake possession, thereby ending the tenant's liability, (2) retake possession as the tenant's agent, holding the tenant liable for the difference between the agreed rent and what the landlord is able to recover in good faith from a new tenant, or (3) do nothing, holding the tenant liable for the rent as it falls due. See *Holy Properties Ltd. v. Kenneth Cole Prod.*, 661 N.E.2d 694 (N.Y. 1995).

2. A Corollary Rule, Accepted in a Majority of States

Upon a tenant's abandonment or surrender of the premises during the term, the landlord has a duty to mitigate the tenant's damages by making a diligent and good faith effort to re-let the premises, on substantially the same terms and conditions, for the remaining portion of the term. See generally 1 Am. L. of Prop., § 3.99 (James Casner ed., 1952); H. Tiffany, 4 Law of Real Property § 963 (3d ed. 1975).

With these two rules in mind, read the following opinions.

SAGAMORE CORP. v. WILLCUTT
180 A. 464 (Conn. 1935)

BANKS, J.

The complaint alleged that on October 1, 1934, the plaintiff leased to the defendant for the term of one year from that date certain premises for the annual rental of $480 payable at the rate of $40 a month on the first day of each month in advance, that the defendant occupied the premises until February 1, 1935, on which day he moved out and thereafter notified the plaintiff that he would no longer comply with the terms of the lease and would pay no further rent, and that as a result of the defendant's breach of the lease the plaintiff has suffered as damages the difference between the rental specified in the lease and the reasonable rental value of the premises for the remainder of the term. The defendant's demurrer to the complaint, stated in four paragraphs, makes a single claim; that the breach of a covenant to pay rent creates no debt until the time stipulated for payment arrives, that the defendant owes the plaintiff no duty except to pay the rent on the first of each month during the remainder of the term, and consequently the plaintiff is not entitled, in an action brought before the expiration of the term of the lease, to recover damages for the defendant's anticipatory breach of his covenant to pay rent.

The lessee has abandoned the leased premises and refused to pay any further rent. The lessor in such a situation has two courses of action open to him. He may accept the surrender of the premises, thereby terminating the lease and effecting a rescission of the contract, or he may refuse to accept the surrender. In the latter case he may let the property lie idle and collect the balance of the rent due under the lease, or he may take possession of the property and lease it to others, in which case he may recover from the original lessee the balance of the rent due under his lease less the rent received from the new lessee. Whether the taking possession of the premises constitutes a rescission of the contract depends upon his intent . . . . The action in that case is one to recover the rent which the lessee has covenanted to pay, and of course cannot be maintained until such rent becomes due and payable under the terms of the lease. By bringing this action for damages for breach of contract, the plaintiff has manifested its intention to accept the surrender of the premises, and has acquiesced in the termination of the lease and the rescission of the contract. Its action is one for damages for the breach by the defendant of his covenant to pay rent.

The arguments and briefs of counsel appear to have proceeded largely upon the assumption that the breach arose out of the repudiation by the defendant of his obligation to pay rent which would accrue in the future and therefore constituted an anticipatory breach, or, more accurately, a breach by anticipatory repudiation of his contract. A positive statement to the promisee that the promisor will not perform his contract constitutes an anticipatory repudiation which is a total breach of contract, except in cases of a contract originally unilateral and not conditional on some future performance by the promisee and of a contract originally bilateral that has become unilateral and similarly unconditional by full performance by one party. Restatement, Contracts, v. 1, § 318. Where the contract was originally unilateral or has become so by the performance of one party, no breach can arise before the time fixed in the contract for some performance. There must be some dependency of performance in order to make anticipatory breach possible. Restatement, op. cit., Comment e. A lease is primarily a conveyance of an interest in land and its execution by the lessor may be said to constitute performance on his part, making the instrument, when considered as a contract, a unilateral agreement with no dependency of performance, which would make an anticipatory breach possible. This, we take it, is the basis for the distinction which the defendant claims to exist between a covenant to pay rent in a lease of real estate and an ordinary executory contract.

But the plaintiff is not obliged to rely solely upon the rules controlling a right to recover for an anticipatory breach arising out of the defendant's repudiation of his obligation to pay rent to accrue in the future. The complaint alleges that the rent was payable on the first day of each month in advance, that the defendant moved out on the first day of February, 1935, and thereafter notified the plaintiff that he would pay no further rent. This can only be construed as an allegation of a refusal to pay the rent which had fallen due on that date as well as that to accrue in the future. This constituted a present breach of his covenant to pay rent when due. Granting the defendant's contention that a covenant to pay rent creates no debt until the time stipulated for payment arrives, the time had arrived, so far as the rent due February 1st was concerned, and his failure to pay that rent constituted a breach of the covenants of his lease. The question remains whether this was a total or only a partial breach. If the former, the plaintiff would be entitled to maintain this action to recover the damages alleged in this complaint; if the latter, it would be limited to those resulting from the refusal to pay the rent due on February 1st. Considering a lease as a unilateral contract, or a bilateral contract that has been wholly performed by the lessor, the covenant to pay rent at certain fixed periods is a contract for the payment of money in installments, and the failure to pay any installment of rent as it falls due would constitute a partial breach of the lessee's contract. Restatement, Contracts, v. 1, § 316. But when such a partial breach is accompanied or followed by a repudiation of the entire contract, the promisee may treat it as a total breach. Restatement, Contracts, vol. 1, § 317, Comment b, Connecticut Annotations, p. 214; 3 Williston, Contracts § 131. Defendant's failure to pay the rent due on February 1st, considered alone, constituted a breach only of his agreement to pay that particular installment of rent. His subsequent statement to the plaintiff that he would no longer comply with the terms of the lease and would pay no further rent was a repudiation of his entire contract. The breach thereupon became a total one justifying an immediate action by the plaintiff to recover the damages which would naturally follow from such a breach . . . . There is no error.

NOTES

1. What are the landlord's damages, and how will the court calculate them? After the tenant's breach, can the landlord withhold further performance? What assumptions does the court make about the landlord's response to the tenant's abandonment?

2. Anticipating the landlord's problem in this case, landlords typically insert a lease provision — called an acceleration covenant — declaring that upon a specified default or any default in the payment of rent, the entire rent for the remainder of the term is immediately due and payable. After all, if the parties could agree that the whole rent is to be paid in advance, why not permit them to agree to accelerated rent? Is the landlord entitled to accelerated rent in addition to the right to sue for repossession of the premises?

3. This court assumes, but only a minority of states hold, that a landlord has no duty to mitigate damages when a tenant abandons the premises. See, e.g., *Gruman v. Investors Diversified Serv., Inc.*, 78 N.W.2d 377, 380 (Minn. 1956), stating that:

> The reasons expressed in support of this rule are that, . . . the lessor has exercised a personal choice in the selection of a tenant for a definite term . . . , that a lease is a conveyance of an interest in real property and, when a lessor has delivered the premises to his lessee, the latter is bound to him by privity of estate as well as privity of contract . . . [and] that a lessor's right to reenter the premises upon the lessee's default or abandonment thereof is at the lessor's option and not the lessee's . . . [and] that a lessee's unilateral action in abandoning leased premises, unless accepted by his lessor, does not terminate the lease or forfeit the estate conveyed thereby, nor the lessee's right to use and possess the leased premises and, by the same token, his obligation to pay the rent . . . .

Why not add that the abandoning lessee should not profit by her wrongful act, or that, by abandoning, the tenant should not be able to make the landlord seek new tenants?

AUSTIN HILL COUNTRY REALTY, INC. v. PALISADES PLAZA, INC.
948 S.W.2d 293 (Tex. 1997)

SPECTOR, J., delivered the opinion for a unanimous Court.

. . . The issue in this case is whether a landlord has a duty to make reasonable efforts to mitigate damages when a tenant defaults on a lease. The court of appeals held that no such duty exists at common law. We hold today that a landlord has a duty to make reasonable efforts to mitigate damages. Accordingly, we reverse the judgment of the court of appeals and remand for a new trial.

I.

Palisades Plaza, Inc., owned and operated an office complex consisting of four office buildings in Austin. Barbara Hill, Annette Smith, and David Jones sold real estate in Austin as a Re/Max real estate brokerage franchise operating through Austin Hill Country Realty, Inc. On September 15, 1992, the Palisades and Hill Country executed a five-year commercial office lease for a suite in the Palisades' office complex. An addendum executed in connection with the lease set the monthly base rent at $3,128 for the first year, $3,519 for the second and third years, and $3,910 for the fourth and fifth years. The parties also signed an improvements agreement that called for the Palisades to convert the shell office space into working offices for Hill Country. The lease was to begin on the "commencement date," which was defined in the lease and the improvements agreement as either (1) the date that Hill Country occupied the suite, or (2) the date that the Palisades substantially completed the improvements or would have done so but for "tenant delay." All parties anticipated that the lease would begin on November 15, 1992.

By the middle of October 1992, the Palisades had nearly completed the improvements. Construction came to a halt on October 21, 1992, when the Palisades received conflicting instructions about the completion of the suite from Hill on one hand and Smith and Jones on the other. By two letters, the Palisades informed Hill Country, Hill, Smith, and Jones that it had received conflicting directives and would not continue with the construction until Hill, Smith, and Jones collectively designated a single representative empowered to make decisions for the trio. Hill, Smith, and Jones did not reply to these letters.

In a letter dated November 19, 1992, the Palisades informed Hill Country, Hill, Smith, and Jones that their failure to designate a representative was an anticipatory breach of contract. The parties tried unsuccessfully to resolve their differences in a meeting. The Palisades then sued Hill Country, Hill, Smith, and Jones (collectively, "Hill Country") for anticipatory breach of the lease.

At trial, Hill Country attempted to prove that the Palisades failed to mitigate the damages resulting from Hill Country's alleged breach. In particular, Hill Country introduced evidence that the Palisades rejected an offer from Smith and Jones to lease the premises without Hill, as well as an offer from Hill and another person to lease the premises without Smith and Jones. Hill Country also tried to prove that, while the Palisades advertised for tenants continuously in a local newspaper, it did not advertise in the commercial-property publication "The Flick Report" as it had in the past. Hill Country requested an instruction asking the jury to reduce the Palisades' damage award by "any amount that you find the [Palisades] could have avoided by the exercise of reasonable care." The trial judge rejected this instruction, stating, "Last time I checked the law, it was that a landlord doesn't have any obligation to try to fill the space." The jury returned a verdict for the Palisades for $29,716 in damages and $16,500 in attorney's fees. The court of appeals affirmed that judgment.

II.

In its only point of error, Hill Country asks this Court to recognize a landlord's duty to make reasonable efforts to mitigate damages when a tenant breaches a lease . . . . Because there is no statute addressing this issue, we look to the common law.

The traditional common law rule regarding mitigation dictates that landlords have no duty to mitigate damages. This rule stems from the historical concept that the tenant is owner of the property during the lease term; as long as the tenant has a right to possess the land, the tenant is liable for rent. See *Reid v. Mutual of Omaha Ins. Co.*, 776 P.2d 896, 902, 905 (Utah 1989). Under this rule, a landlord is not obligated to undertake any action following a tenant's abandonment of the premises but may recover rents periodically for the remainder of the term . . . .

Texas courts have consistently followed this no-mitigation rule in cases involving a landlord's suit for past due rent. (Citations omitted.) Some Texas courts have, however, required a landlord to mitigate damages when the landlord seeks a remedy that is contractual in nature, such as anticipatory breach of contract, rather than a real property cause of action. See *Employment Advisors, Inc. v. Sparks*, 364 S.W.2d 478, 480 (Tex. Civ. App.), writ ref'd n.r.e. per curiam, 368 S.W.2d 199, 200 (Tex. 1963). * * * Other Texas courts have required a landlord to mitigate damages when the landlord reenters or resumes control of the premises. (Citations omitted.) Thus, a landlord currently may be subject to a mitigation requirement depending upon the landlord's actions following breach and the type of lawsuit the landlord pursues.

III.

In discerning the policy implications of a rule requiring landlords to mitigate damages, we are informed by the rules of other jurisdictions. Forty-two states and the District of Columbia have recognized that a landlord has a duty to mitigate damages in at least some situations: when there is a breach of a residential lease, a commercial lease, or both. Only six states have explicitly held that a landlord has no duty to mitigate in any situation. In South Dakota, the law is unclear.

Those jurisdictions recognizing a duty to mitigate have emphasized the change in the nature of landlord-tenant law since its inception in medieval times. At English common law, the tenant had only contractual rights against the landlord and therefore could not assert common-law real property causes of action to protect the leasehold. Over time, the courts recognized a tenant's right to bring real property causes of action, and tenants were considered to possess an estate in land. 2 R. POWELL, LAW OF REAL PROPERTY § 221[1], at 16–18 (1969). The landlord had to give the tenant possession of the land, and the tenant was required to pay rent in return. As covenants in leases have become more complex and the structures on the land have become more important to the parties than the land itself, courts have begun to recognize that a lease possesses elements of both a contract and a conveyance. See, e.g., *Schneiker v. Gordon*, 732 P.2d 603, 607–09 (Colo. 1987); *Reid*, 776 P.2d 896, 902, 904 (Utah 1989). Under contract principles, the lease is not a complete conveyance to the tenant for a specified term such that the landlord's duties are fulfilled upon deliverance of the property to the tenant. Rather, a promise to pay in a lease is essentially the same as a promise to pay in any other contract, and a breach of that promise does not necessarily end the landlord's ongoing duties. *Schneiker*, 732 P.2d at 610; *Wright v. Baumann*, 398 P.2d 119, 121 (Or. 1965). Because of the contractual elements of the modern lease agreement, these courts have imposed upon the landlord the contractual duty to mitigate damages upon the tenant's breach.

Public policy offers further justification for the duty to mitigate. First, requiring mitigation in the landlord-tenant context discourages economic waste and encourages productive use of the property . . . . A mitigation requirement returns the property to productive use rather than allowing it to remain idle. Public policy requires that the law "discourage even persons against whom wrongs have been committed from passively suffering economic loss which could be averted by reasonable efforts." *Wright*, 398 P.2d at 121 . . . .

Second, a mitigation rule helps prevent intentional or unintentional destruction of or damage to the leased property. If the landlord is encouraged to let the property remain unoccupied, it is more likely that waste, an accident, or vandalism will occur.

Third, the mitigation rule is consistent with the trend disfavoring contract penalties. *Reid*, 776 P.2d at 905–06. Courts have held that a liquidated damages clause in a contract must represent a reasonable estimate of anticipated damages upon breach. See *Warner v. Rasmussen*, 704 P.2d 559, 561, 563 (Utah 1985). "Similarly, allowing a landlord to leave property idle when it could be profitably leased and forcing an absent tenant to pay rent for that idled property permits the landlord to recover more damages than it may reasonably require to be compensated for the tenant's breach. This is analogous to imposing a disfavored penalty upon the tenant." *Reid*, 776 P.2d at 905–06.

Finally, the traditional justifications for the common law rule have proven unsound in practice. Proponents of the no-mitigation rule suggest that the landlord-tenant relationship is personal in nature, and that the landlord therefore should not be forced to lease to an unwanted tenant. Modern lease arrangements, however, are rarely personal in nature and are usually business arrangements between strangers. Further, the landlord's duty to make reasonable efforts to mitigate does not require that the landlord accept replacement tenants who are financial risks or whose business was precluded by the original lease.

The overwhelming trend among jurisdictions in the United States has thus been toward requiring a landlord to mitigate damages when a tenant abandons the property in breach of the lease agreement. Those courts adopting a mitigation requirement have emphasized the contractual elements of a lease agreement, the public policy favoring productive use of property, and the practicalities of the modern landlord-tenant arrangement as supporting such a duty.

IV.

We are persuaded by the reasoning of those courts that recognize that landlords must mitigate damages upon a tenant's abandonment and failure to pay rent. This Court has recognized the dual nature of a lease as both a conveyance and a contract.

See *Davidow v. Inwood North Professional Group-Phase I*, 747 S.W.2d 373, 375–76 (Tex. 1988) . . . . Under a contract view, a landlord should be treated no differently than any other aggrieved party to a contract. Further, the public policy of the state of Texas calls for productive use of property as opposed to avoidable economic waste. As Professor McCormick wrote over seventy years ago, the law "which permits the landlord to stand idly by the vacant, abandoned premises and treat them as the property of the tenant and recover full rent, [should] yield to the more realistic notions of social advantage which in other fields of the law have forbidden a recovery for damages which the plaintiff by reasonable efforts could have avoided." Charles McCormick, *The Rights of the Landlord Upon Abandonment of the Premises by the Tenant*, 23 Mich. L. Rev. 211, 221–22 (1925). Finally, we have recognized that contract penalties are disfavored in Texas. A landlord should not be allowed to collect rent from an abandoning tenant when the landlord can, by reasonable efforts, relet the premises and avoid incurring some damages. We therefore recognize that a landlord has a duty to make reasonable efforts to mitigate damages when the tenant breaches the lease and abandons the property, unless the commercial landlord and tenant contract otherwise.

V.

To ensure the uniform application of this duty by the courts of this state, and to guide future landlords and tenants in conforming their conduct to the law, we now consider several practical considerations that will undoubtedly arise. We first consider the level of conduct by a landlord that will satisfy the duty to mitigate. The landlord's mitigation duty has been variously stated in other jurisdictions. See *Reid*, 776 P.2d at 906 ("objective commercial reasonableness"); *Schneiker*, 732 P.2d at 611 ("reasonable efforts"); Cal. Civ. Code § 1951.2(c)(2) ("reasonably and in a good-faith effort") . . . . We hold that the landlord's duty to mitigate requires the landlord to use objectively reasonable efforts to fill the premises when the tenant vacates in breach of the lease.

We stress that this is not an absolute duty. The landlord is not required to simply fill the premises with any willing tenant; the replacement tenant must be suitable under the circumstances. Nor does the landlord's failure to mitigate give rise to a cause of action by the tenant. Rather, the landlord's failure to use reasonable efforts to mitigate damages bars the landlord's recovery against the breaching tenant only to the extent that damages reasonably could have been avoided. Similarly, the amount of damages that the landlord actually avoided by releasing the premises will reduce the landlord's recovery.

Further, we believe that the tenant properly bears the burden of proof to demonstrate that the landlord has mitigated or failed to mitigate damages and the amount by which the landlord reduced or could have reduced its damages. The traditional rule in other contexts is that the breaching party must show that the nonbreaching party could have reduced its damages. See generally ALLEN FARNSWORTH, CONTRACTS § 12.12 (2d ed. 1990). In the landlord-tenant context, although there is some split of authority, many other jurisdictions have placed the burden of proving mitigation or failure to mitigate upon the breaching tenant. See Dawn

Barker, *Commercial Landlords' Duty Upon Tenants' Abandonment*, 20 J. Corp. L. 627, 639 n.86.

When the tenant contends that the landlord has actually mitigated damages, the breaching tenant need not plead the landlord's actual mitigation as an affirmative defense. Rather, the tenant's evidence of the landlord's mitigation tends to rebut the measure of damages under the landlord's claim of breach and may be admitted under a general denial. The tenant's contention that the landlord failed to mitigate damages, in contrast, is similar to an avoidance defense; evidence of failure to mitigate is admissible only if the tenant pleads the failure to mitigate as an affirmative defense.

The final issue to resolve regarding the duty to mitigate is to which types of actions by the landlord the duty will apply. Traditionally, Texas courts have regarded the landlord as having four causes of action against a tenant for breach of the lease and abandonment. First, the landlord can maintain the lease, suing for rent as it becomes due. Second, the landlord can treat the breach as an anticipatory repudiation, repossess, and sue for the present value of future rentals reduced by the reasonable cash market value of the property for the remainder of the lease term. Third, the landlord can treat the breach as anticipatory, repossess, re-lease the property, and sue the tenant for the difference between the contractual rent and the amount received from the new tenant. Fourth, the landlord can declare the lease forfeited (if the lease so provides) and relieve the tenant of liability for future rent.

The landlord must have a duty to mitigate when suing for anticipatory repudiation. Because the cause of action is contractual in nature, the contractual duty to mitigate should apply. The landlord's option to maintain the lease and sue for rent as it becomes due, however, is more troubling. To require the landlord to mitigate in that instance would force the landlord to reenter the premises and thereby risk terminating the lease or accepting the tenant's surrender. We thus hold that, when exercising the option to maintain the lease in effect and sue for rent as it becomes due following the tenant's breach and abandonment, the landlord has a duty to mitigate only if (1) the landlord actually reenters, or (2) the lease allows the landlord to reenter the premises without accepting surrender, forfeiting the lease, or being construed as evicting the tenant. A suit for anticipatory repudiation, an actual reentry, or a contractual right of reentry subject to the above conditions will therefore give rise to the landlord's duty to mitigate damages upon the tenant's breach and abandonment.

VI.

In their first amended answer, Hill Country and Barbara Hill specifically contended that the Palisades failed to mitigate its damages. Because the court of appeals upheld the trial court's refusal to submit their mitigation instruction, we reverse the judgment of the court of appeals and remand for a new trial.

NOTES

1.   This case is discussed in Ian Davis, *Better Late than Never: Texas Landlords Owe a Duty to Mitigate Damages when a Tenant Abandons Leased Property*, 28 Tex. Tech. L. Rev. 1281, 1292–1307 (1997). If the holding of the case leaves the landlord with the now more tempting option of not entering the premises and then suing for the accrued rent, isn't that an exception to the required mitigation effort that will grow in use over time? Is this exception consistent with the rationales offered for the mitigation effort requirement? *Sommer v. Kridel*, 378 A.2d 767 (N.J. 1977), "presents a classic example of the unfairness which occurs when a landlord has no responsibility to minimize damages. Sommer [the landlord — Eds.] waited 15 months and allowed $4658.50 in damages to accrue before attempting to re-let the apartment. Despite the availability of a tenant who was ready, willing and able to rent the apartment, the landlord needlessly increased the damages by turning her away. While a tenant will not necessarily be excused from his obligations under a lease simply by finding another person who is willing to rent the vacated premises [citing cases in which the new tenant wants different lease terms and is insolvent — Eds.], here there has been no showing that the new tenant would not have been suitable. We therefore find that plaintiff could have avoided the damages which eventually accrued, and that the defendant was relieved of his duty to continue paying rent. Ordinarily we would require the tenant to bear the cost of any reasonable expenses incurred by a landlord in attempting to re-let the premises, but no such expenses were incurred in this case." *Id.* at 773.

2.   Who should bear the burden of proof on the issue of whether the landlord has fulfilled the duty to mitigate? *Sommer* placed this burden on the landlord, but *Palisades* put it on the tenant. If the tenant has the burden of proof to show that the landlord has made "objectively reasonable efforts" to re-let, how would you advise the tenant to go about meeting that burden? See generally Glen Weissenberger, *The Landlord's Duty to Mitigate Damages on the Tenant's Abandonment*, 53 Temp. L. Rev. 1, 10–11 (1980). So the cases on this issue are split. If the landlord shows that he or his agent offered or showed the premises to prospective tenants, the tenant might counter with evidence that he proffered suitable tenants who were rejected, but there is no standard formula for measuring and arranging such evidence. Each case must stand on its own facts. What if, while the landlord is trying to re-rent the premises, vandals damage it. Is the tenant responsible? What if a fire damages it? What if a flood sweeps away the improvements on the premises? See generally John Humbach, *The Common Law Conception of Leasing: Mitigation, Habitability, and Dependence of Covenants*, 60 Wash. U. L.Q. 1213 (1983).

3.   Consider whether the following statute achieves the same result that *Palisades* does:

> If the tenant wrongfully quits the dwelling unit and unequivocally indicates by words or deeds his intention not to resume tenancy, he shall be liable for the lesser of the following for such abandonment: (a) the entire rent due for the remainder of the term; or (b) all rent accrued during the period reasonably necessary to re-rent the premises at a fair rental, plus the difference between such fair rental and the rent agreed to in the prior rental agreement, plus a reasonable commission for the renting of the

premises. This subsection shall apply, if less than (a), notwithstanding that the landlord did not re-rent the premises.

Am. B. Found., Model Residential Landlord and Tenant Act, § 2-308(4) (1969). Compare the Uniform Landlord and Tenant Act, § 4-203 (1972), and consider the following provision of a lease promulgated by the Florida Bar Association:

> If Landlord retakes possession of the Premises for Tenant's account, Landlord must make a good faith effort to re-lease the Premises. Any rent received by Landlord as a result of the new lease shall be deducted from the rent due from Tenant. For purposes of this section, "good faith" in trying to re-lease the Premises means that Landlord shall use at least the same efforts to re-lease Premises as were used in the initial rental or at least the same efforts as Landlord uses in attempting to lease other similar property. It does not require Landlord to give a preference in leasing the Premises over other vacant properties that Landlord owns or has the responsibility to rent.

Florida Bar Re: Advisory Opinion — NonLawyer Preparation of Residential Leases up to One Year in Duration, 602 So. 2d 914, 930 (Fla. 1992) (recommending this provision for the rental of both a single family house and an apartment in a multi-unit building). How would you modify this provision if you represented a residential tenant? Does a tenant have a duty to cooperate with the landlord's re-rental efforts? What if they are strenuous, but unsuccessful? What if strenuous efforts are made but for a rent substantially higher than the tenant paid? Does it matter if the rent is higher because the landlord reasonably believes that the offering is at the current fair market rental? What if the landlord's efforts are nonexistent or consist of only a for rent sign on the outside of the premises or an advertisement in the newspaper? What impact does the duty to mitigate have on the landlord's other remedies? Upon a liquidated damages clause in the lease? What if you represented a landlord who wanted you to insert an acceleration clause into the lease, providing that upon a default by the tenant in the lease's provisions, all rent otherwise payable under the lease will become due and payable?

   4.   For a case refusing to impose a mitigation effort on a commercial landlord, see *Holy Properties Ltd. v. Kenneth Cole Productions*, 661 N.E.2d 694, 696 (N.Y. 1995). The court states:

> The law imposes upon a party subjected to injury from breach of contract, the duty of making reasonable exertions to minimize the injury. Leases are not subject to this general rule, however, for, unlike executory contracts, leases have been historically recognized as a present transfer of an estate in real property. Once the lease is executed, the lessee's obligation to pay rent is fixed according to its terms and a landlord is under no obligation or duty to the tenant to relet, or attempt to relet abandoned premises in order to minimize damages . . . .

> Defendant urges us to reject this settled law and adopt the contract rationale recognized by some courts in this State and elsewhere. We decline to do so. Parties who engage in transactions based on prevailing law must be able to rely on the stability of such precedents. In business transactions,

particularly, the certainty of settled rules is often more important than whether the established rule is better than another or even whether it is the "correct" rule. This is perhaps true in real property more than any other area of the law, where established precedents are not lightly to be set aside.

Defendant contends that even if it is liable for rent after abandoning the premises, plaintiff terminated the landlord-tenant relationship shortly thereafter by instituting summary proceedings. After the eviction, it maintains, its only liability was for contract damages, not rent, and under contract law the landlord had a duty to mitigate. Although an eviction terminates the landlord-tenant relationship, the parties to a lease are not foreclosed from contracting as they please. If the lease provides that the tenant shall be liable for rent after eviction, the provision is enforceable.

In this case, the lease expressly provided that plaintiff was under no duty to mitigate damages and that upon defendant's abandonment of the premises or eviction, it would remain liable for all monetary obligations arising under the lease (lease para. 18) . . . . Order affirmed . . . .

Is the holding of this case dependent on the express provision in the lease, or is the court adhering to the traditional no-mitigation rule? If state law imposes a duty to act reasonably in reviewing a tenant's assignee (as in *Julian v. Christopher, supra*), isn't the landlord also bound to act reasonably in responding to any prospective tenant presented by an abandoning tenant? If a landlord refuses to re-let to a reasonably acceptable substitute presented by a tenant, isn't the landlord's unreasonable action a bar on a recovery of damages for future unpaid rent from the abandoning tenant? See Robert Parella, *Real Property*, 47 Syracuse L. Rev. 681, 683–84, n. 21 (1997). See also *Stonehedge Square Ltd. Partnership v. Movie Merchants, Inc.*, 685 A.2d 1019, 1025–26 (Pa. Super. Ct. 1996) (also rejecting the mitigation rule and admonishing the trial judge who adopted it by quoting Judge Learned Hand to the effect that it is not "desirable for a lower court to embrace the exhilarating opportunity of anticipating a doctrine which may be in the womb of time but whose birth is distant.").

SCHNEIKER v. GORDON
732 P.2d 603 (Colo. 1987)

Lohr, J.

This case requires us to consider the interrelation of the law of contracts and the law of property in determining the obligations of a sublessee for payment of rent after termination of a sublease by abandonment and surrender. We granted certiorari to review the decision of the Colorado Court of Appeals that the termination of a sublease ended the sublessee's obligation to pay future rent. *Gordon v. Schneiker*, 699 P.2d 3 (Colo. App. 1984). We disagree with that decision and conclude that the rights and obligations of the parties to the sublease with respect to the covenant to pay rent survived the termination of the sublease and that the sublessee is liable for contract damages caused by breach of that covenant. We therefore reverse.

I.

Sometime before July of 1979, the defendant in this action, Jakob Schneiker (lessee-sublessor), entered into a lease (the primary lease) with the owner of certain property for use of the leased premises as a car wash. The property included a structure and attached equipment. Rent under the primary lease was payable at the rate of $600 per month, and the term of the primary lease was to extend through May of 1983.

On April 1, 1980, the lessee-sublessor entered into a sublease with the plaintiffs, Darrell W. Gordon and Gary F. Peterson (sublessees). The sublease provided for a monthly rent of $1,900 and was for a term ending at the same time as that of the primary lease. The sublease specified that the premises were to be operated as a car wash. In addition to containing a provision that the sublessees would keep the premises and equipment in good repair, the sublease also contained a "Repossession" clause which provided:

> The parties agree that in case said premises are left vacant and any part of the rent herein reserved be unpaid, then the Lessor may, without in anyway being obliged to do so, and without terminating this lease, retake possession of said premises, and rent the same for such rent and upon such conditions as the Lessor may think best, making such changes and repairs as may be required, giving credit for the amount of rent so received less all expenses of such changes and repairs, and said Lessee shall be liable for the balance of the rent herein reserved until the expiration of this lease.

After July of 1981, the sublessees ceased making rental payments, and they abandoned the premises in August of 1981. Prior to mid-November of that same year, the sublessees mailed the keys for the car wash to the lessee-sublessor. In November the lessee-sublessor reentered the premises. The equipment was in such a state of disrepair that the property could not be operated as a car wash. The trial court found that the sublessees had breached their obligation to maintain and repair the equipment, that the reasonable cost of repairs was more than $6,000, and that the reasonable rental value of the property was less than $600 per month. Being unable to afford to make the necessary repairs, the lessee-sublessor negotiated a surrender of the primary lease with the owner as of February 1982.

The sublessees brought suit against the lessee-sublessor, claiming misrepresentation on the part of the lessee-sublessor concerning the profitability of the car wash business, and requesting compensatory and punitive damages. The lessee-sublessor counterclaimed for damages caused by the sublessees' breach of the sublease and requested the full rent of $1900 per month from the time the sublessees ceased making rental payments, August of 1981, through the expiration of the lease, May of 1983. The case was tried to the court. After presentation of the sublessees' evidence, the trial court dismissed their claim. At the conclusion of the trial, the court awarded the lessee-sublessor partial relief on his counterclaim. The court found that the lessee-sublessor had acted to mitigate his damages by negotiating a surrender of the primary lease and that the lessee-sublessor had intended to hold the sublessees liable for the entire rent payable through the expiration of the sublease. However, the trial court held that the cancellation of the primary lease acted as a surrender and termination of the sublease as a matter of law, and that the lessee-sublessor was therefore entitled only to rent payable up until February 1, 1982, the date the primary lease was terminated by surrender.[1]

The lessee-sublessor appealed the denial of damages for the profits he would have received during the remainder of the original term of the sublease, from February of 1982 through May of 1983. The court of appeals affirmed the judgment of the trial court, holding that the surrender of the primary lease operated as a surrender and termination of the sublease as a matter of law, and that the sublessees' obligation to pay future rent ended when the sublease was terminated since there was no express agreement between the parties that the obligation to pay rent would survive termination of the sublease. The lessee-sublessor then filed a petition for certiorari with this court, and we granted that petition.

II.

A.

* * * Under the common law view of a lease as a conveyance, a tenant's obligation to pay rent was based upon the ownership of the leasehold estate. The rent was said to issue from the land. Therefore, so long as the tenant owned the leasehold estate the rental obligation continued, but when the leasehold was extinguished, for whatever reason, the obligation ceased . . . . Before courts began to recognize that contractual principles are relevant to the determination of a landlord's rights on abandonment by a tenant, a landlord could not rely on the contract doctrine of anticipatory repudiation to recover installments of rent that would have accrued but for the abandonment and surrender. Nor could a tenant successfully maintain that a landlord's right to collect rent accruing after abandonment, in the absence of an acceptance of the tenant's surrender, should be subject to a duty to mitigate damages by using reasonable efforts to secure a substitute tenant. 1 American Law of Property, *supra*, § 3.11, at 203 . . . .

. . . [W]e have held that if a lease expressly permits, the landlord may relet the premises abandoned by the tenant on the tenant's account and hold the tenant liable for the difference between the rent required by the original lease and the rent paid by the substitute tenant. *Ruston v. Centennial Real Estate*, 445 P.2d 64 (1968). * * * Then, in *Shanahan v. Collins*, 539 P.2d 1261 (1975), we noted that at common law the real estate lease developed in the field of real property rather than contract law but that rigid adherence to the law of property to determine the duties and obligations of the parties, implied as well as expressed, was no longer the proper approach in resolving all landlord-tenant disputes. 539 P.2d at 1262. In that case we held, contrary to traditional property law analysis, that a tenant's obligation to pay rent is not independent of a landlord's covenant to make improvements or repairs. 539 P.2d at 1263. As a result, the tenant was entitled to set off against the rent payments the cost of repairs that the landlord had refused to make although

---

[1] The trial court also awarded the lessee-sublessor $6,118.78 as damages to the equipment, less the prepaid last month's rent of $1,900 and the security deposit of $4,000. Prior to the determination of allowable attorneys' fees, the sublessees declared bankruptcy. The trial court nevertheless determined that the lessee-sublessor was entitled to $13,350 as reasonable attorneys' fees.

required to do so by a covenant in the lease. *Id.* * * *

B.

The case now before us requires us to consider once more the dual nature of a lease as contract and conveyance and to determine the implications of that dual nature for the liability of a subtenant for rent after abandonment. The sublease, in the "Repossession" clause previously referred to, specifically authorized, but did not obligate, the lessee-sublessor to retake possession, make changes and repairs, and rerent, without terminating the lease, after the sublessee departed leaving the premises vacant. The amount of the new rent less the cost of changes and repairs would be credited against the continuing obligation of the sublessee to pay the rent specified in the sublease. Upon examination of the premises after the sublessee's departure, however, it became apparent that the sublessee had left the premises in such a state that the lessee-sublessor would not be able to relet the premises without making substantial repairs. Due to a lack of funds and an inability to borrow, the lessee-sublessor could not afford to make these repairs. The ability of the lessee-sublessor to relet the premises was also adversely affected by the relatively short period of time remaining between the sublessees' departure in August 1981 and the end of the primary term in May 1983. Therefore, the trial court found that the reasonable rental value of the unrepaired premises was less than the $600 monthly rent payable by the lessee-sublessor to the owner-lessor over the remainder of the term of the primary lease.

Had the premises been in a condition permitting rerental on an economic basis, the lessee-sublessor could have elected to pursue his remedy under the "Repossession" clause. See *Ruston v. Centennial Real Estate*, 445 P.2d 64, 66 (1968). However, the terms of the "Repossession" clause implicitly apply only to circumstances in which repair and rerental is physically and economically feasible. Therefore, the actions of the sublessee rendered this remedy unavailable to the lessee-sublessor.

Being unable to make the necessary repairs or to relet the premises at an economically prudent rate, the lessee-sublessor was faced with a difficult choice. Under our early case law, he could have elected to refuse to accept the sublessees' surrender. He then could have continued to pay the $600 per month rent under the primary lease and could have held the sublessees liable for the $1900 per month rent reserved in the sublease as it became due. Rather than pursuing that uneconomic course of action, the lessee-sublessor negotiated a surrender of the primary lease, thereby eliminating the obligation to pay rent on that lease and mitigating the loss resulting from the failure of the sublessees to pay rent to $1300 per month.

* * * Traditionally, surrender and acceptance not only caused the leasehold estate to be absorbed into the lessor's reversion but also terminated the obligation of the lessee for rent that would have accrued subsequent to the surrender. As we said in *Shanahan v. Collins*, 539 P. 2d 1261 (1975), however, when faced with an appeal to apply traditional property law principles with respect to the independence of leasehold covenants, "we do not consider this to be the proper approach to the problem presented here." 539 P.2d at 1262.

We believe that it is necessary to recognize the dual nature of the lease as contract and conveyance and to analyze the lessee-sublessor's remedy for the sublessees' breach under contract principles in order to achieve a just result consonant with the intent of the parties to this modern commercial lease. A commercial lease, like other contracts, is predominantly an exchange of promises. *Wright v. Baumann*, 398 P.2d 119, 120 (Or. 1965). The covenant to pay rent represents one such promise, and the fairness of requiring fulfillment of that covenant often depends upon the landlord's performance of other covenants contained in the lease. *Shanahan*, 539 P.2d 1261, 1262–63 (Colo. 1975). We can perceive no reason why the covenant to pay rent should be treated differently than a covenant to pay contained in any other contract. See 1 American Law of Property, *supra*, § 3.11 (stating that the covenant to pay rent in a lease is a contractual provision). The parties to a commercial lease are generally sophisticated and aware of the nature of contractual obligations.

Public policy also favors the application of contract principles to these circumstances. Under traditional property law principles a landlord could allow the property to remain unoccupied while still holding the abandoning tenant liable for rent. This encourages both economic and physical waste. In no other context of which we are aware is an injured party permitted to sit by idly and suffer avoidable economic loss and thereafter to visit the full adverse economic consequences upon the party whose breach initiated the chain of events causing the loss. Furthermore, it is generally in the interests of society that property be put to practical use so far as is economically feasible. Usually, no economic value is obtained from property if a landlord allows it to remain idle. At the same time, the possibility of physical damage to the property through accident or vandalism is increased. The rules for awarding damages in the context of abandonment and breach by the tenant should discourage, rather than encourage, economic and physical waste. We believe that the contract principle of "avoidable consequences" or "duty to mitigate" should be applied in this context to prevent a landlord from passively suffering preventable economic loss, to encourage the productive use of land, and to decrease the likelihood of physical damage to property. Likewise, a landlord should be permitted to maintain an action for contract damages caused by a tenant's wrongful abandonment so that the landlord is able to receive the benefit of his bargain.

The facts of the present case readily lend themselves to analysis under familiar principles of contract law. The lessee-sublessor and the owner-lessor expressly agreed to a surrender of the primary lease on mutually satisfactory terms. At the time, the sublessees had abandoned the premises, so the intent and effect of the surrender of the primary lease was to accomplish a surrender of the sublease as well. This terminated the privity of estate between lessor and lessee-sublessor and between lessee-sublessor and sublessees. However, the lessee-sublessor intended to hold the sublessees liable for rent as parties to a contract, and privity of contract between the parties to the sublease with respect to the covenant to pay rent was not terminated. The sublessees remained under a personal obligation to carry out the terms of the covenant to pay rent contained in the lease.

Prior to surrender of the primary lease, the sublessees not only had abandoned the premises but also had returned the keys and had failed to pay installments of rent that had come due. Viewed in terms of contract law, this was in the nature of an anticipatory repudiation amounting to a total breach of the sublease. 4 A. Corbin, Corbin on Contracts §§ 959, 986 (1951). We see no reason that the surrender should operate to leave the lessee-sublessor without remedy against the sublessees, for the very purpose of the surrender upon which the sublessees rely was to mitigate damages by eliminating the lessee-sublessor's obligations under the primary lease to pay a higher rental than it could obtain by reletting the premises. Ordinarily, a landlord would be required to exercise reasonable efforts to procure a substitute tenant in order to fulfill his duty to mitigate. This course of action was not available to the lessee-sublessor in this case because of the actions of the sublessee. The necessity of the surrender was in essence forced upon the lessee-sublessor in order to minimize the economic loss, and the lessee-sublessor therefore fulfilled his duty to mitigate damages.

We must now determine the proper measure of damages in this case. This requires nothing more than application of established principles of contract law. The measure of damages is the amount it takes to place the landlord in the position he would have occupied had the breach not occurred, taking into account the landlord's duty to mitigate. Usually this will be the difference between the rent reserved in the lease and the reasonable rental value of the premises for the duration of the term of the lease, plus any other consequential damages caused by the breach . . . . However, if the landlord is unable to secure a substitute tenant after making reasonable efforts to do so or if the premises have been rendered unmarketable, the landlord is entitled to an amount equal to the full amount of rent reserved in the lease, plus any other consequential damages. If the landlord has avoided any cost by not having to perform, that cost should be deducted from his recovery in order to place him in the position he would have occupied had the tenant performed.

Under the circumstances of the present case, we conclude that the sublessees are obligated to the lessee-sublessor in the amount of $1900 per month for the entire term remaining on the sublease after the last rental payment made by the sublessees, less the $600 per month rental under the primary lease subsequent to surrender of that lease, as the damages actually suffered by the lessee-sublessor for the sublessees' breach of the covenant to pay rent in the sublease by anticipatory repudiation.

We remand this case to the court of appeals for return to the trial court for entry of judgment consistent with the views expressed in this opinion.

NOTES

1. Should the holding in this case be applied to residential leases or applied retroactively? If a sublease contains a "Repossession" covenant but no express or implied provision that it is intended to be the exclusive remedy available to the lessee-sublessor upon abandonment of the premises by the sublessee, should a court find it to be such nonetheless? Probably not, particularly when the "Repossession" clause expressly states that the lessee-sublessor is under no obligation to proceed under its terms.

2. Other courts using contract law rules to analyze the rights and obligations of a landlord and a tenant upon abandonment of premises by a tenant are *Danpar*

Assocs. v. Somersville Mills Sales Room, Inc., 438 A.2d 708 (Conn. 1980); *Wichita Properties v. Lanterman*, 633 P.2d 1154 (Kan. Ct. App. 1981); *Bernstein v. Seglin*, 171 N.W.2d 247 (Neb. 1969); *Wright v. Baumann*, 398 P.2d 119 (Or. 1965) (involving an executory contract to lease). In these cases, acceptance of surrender terminates privity of estate between the parties, while leaving privity of contract unaffected. See generally Annotation, *Landlord's Duty, on Tenant's Failure to Occupy, or Abandonment of, Premises, to Mitigate Damages by Accepting or Procuring Another Tenant*, 21 A.L.R.3d 534 (1968). As stated by the court in *Signal Management Corp. v. Lamb*, 541 N.W.2d 449 (N. Dak. 1995):

> Surrender and acceptance is a recognized method of extinguishing the leasehold. Under that doctrine, if the landlord elected to accept the surrender of the premises upon abandonment by the lessee, the lease was terminated and there was no continuing obligation for rent. But the landlord could also decline to accept the offer of a surrender that was implicit in abandonment and could continue to hold the tenant liable for rent as it became due. A surrender may be either "express" or "by operation of law." We have recognized that a surrender by operation of law results "from acts of the parties to the lease which imply mutual consent to the termination." *Sanden v. Hanson*, 201 N.W.2d 404, 409 (N.D. 1972) . . . .

> [T]his court rejected the pure common law approach and joined the modern trend, holding [that the landlord has a duty to mitigate the damages which arise out of his tenant's default — Eds.] *MAR-SON, Inc. v. Terwaho Enterprises, Inc.*, 259 N.W.2d 289, 291 (N.D. 1977). See also N.D.C.C. § 47-16-13.5 (imposing duty to mitigate damages in residential lease situations) . . . . There is an obvious tension between the common law doctrine of surrender by operation of law and the lessor's obligation to mitigate damages. One court has explained: "Common law courts have sometimes found a surrender by operation of law in certain situations where a lessor responds to the lessee's abandonment of the property, for example, by reletting or selling the property to a third party. The courts concluded that such a relet or sale was inconsistent with the original lessee's estate in the property and, therefore, based on an implied agreement or estoppel theory, constituted a binding recognition by the lessor that the estate no longer existed. The recognition of the end of the estate was crucial because under early common law, with the end of the estate necessarily came the end of the lessee's obligation with respect to future rents under the lease . . . . Reletting and selling property are two of the most direct ways for a lessor to mitigate damages. Hence, whatever may be the proper inference to draw from a relet or a sale in the absence of a duty to mitigate, if a duty to mitigate exists, it clearly cannot be presumed that the lessor's relet or sale of the leased property demonstrates an intent to accept a surrender. It is at least as likely to be merely an attempt to mitigate damages." *Sun Cal, Inc. v. United States*, 25 Cl. Ct. 426, 432–33. A tenant's burden of proving a landlord's intent to accept surrender is an onerous one when the landlord is also under an obligation to mitigate damages.

C. The Holdover Tenant

Edward Coke, in his First Part of the Institutes of the Laws of England or A Commentary on Littleton, § 72 (1st Am. ed. 1812), states that one type of "a tenant at sufferance is he that first came in by lawful demise, and after his estate ended, continueth in possession and wrongfully holdeth over." Absent some agreement to the contrary, the tenant remains in this position until the landlord makes an election, either to eject the tenant as a trespasser or accept him for an additional, although not necessarily identical, term. Once the landlord makes his election, the new tenancy arises by operation of law and irrespective of the intent, consent, or objections of the tenant. When the landlord chooses the former option, he also may recover damages caused by the holding over. An election made is irrevocable, and when the landlord does nothing, a court may hold that the tenancy has been constructively accepted for an additional term. Typically, a constructive acceptance is evidenced by the landlord's acceptance of rent when it would next be due. See generally R. Schoshinski, American Law of Landlord and Tenant § 2.23 (1980); 1 Am. L. Property § 3.35 (James Casner ed., 1952).

D.C. Code § 42-3204 (2014):

> A tenancy by sufferance may be terminated at any time by a notice in writing from the landlord to the tenant to quit the premises leased, or by such notice from the tenant to the landlord of his intention to quit on the 30th day after the day of the service of the notice. If such notice expires before any periodic installment of rent falls due, according to the terms of the tenancy, the landlord shall be entitled to a proportionate part of such installment to the date fixed for quitting the premises.

Va. Code § 55-248.37 (2014):

> (A) The landlord or the tenant may terminate a week-to-week tenancy by serving a written notice on the other at least seven days prior to the next rent due date. The landlord or the tenant may terminate a month-to-month tenancy by serving a written notice on the other at least 30 days prior to the next rent due date.

> (B) If the tenant remains in possession without the landlord's consent after expiration of the term of the rental agreement or its termination, the landlord may bring an action for possession and may also recover actual damages, reasonable attorneys' fees, and court costs, unless the tenant proves by a preponderance of the evidence that the failure of the tenant to vacate the dwelling unit as of the termination date was reasonable. The landlord may include in the rental agreement a reasonable liquidated damage penalty, not to exceed an amount equal to 150 percent of the per diem of the monthly rent, for each day the tenant remains in the dwelling unit after the termination date specified in the landlord's notice. * * *

Va. Code § 55-223 (2014):

> A tenant from year to year, month to month, or other definite term, shall not, by his mere failure to vacate the premises upon the expiration of the lease, be held as tenant for another term when such failure is not due to his

wilfulness, negligence or other avoidable cause, but such tenant shall be liable to the lessor for use and occupation of the premises and also for any loss or damage sustained by the lessor because of such failure to surrender possession at the time stipulated.

This statute is Virginia's version of the Uniform Residential Landlord and Tenant Act. It adopts part of the common law rule that when a tenant held under a lease for a term shorter than one year, that term, of whatever duration, will serve as the term for the holdover tenancy. This statute adopts that part of the common law rule applicable to terms of either a week or a month. When the tenant leases for a one-year term, is the additional term also a year? Do these statutes provide the length of the holdover term in instances when the landlord elects to hold the tenant to one?

A.H. FETTING MFG. JEWELRY CO. v. WALTZ
152 A. 434 (Md. 1930)

PARKE, J.

The plaintiffs, Ada R. Waltz, Zora A. Klare and Bertha F. Kuhnert, are the owners of an improved lot on Liberty Street, in Baltimore City, which they demised to the A.H. Fetting Manufacturing Jewelry Company, the defendant, by a lease under seal, dated October 10th, 1922, for a term of five years that would end on November 4th, 1927. The rent reserved for the first three years of the lease increased to $7,000 during the succeeding two years, and was payable in equal instalments at the beginning of every month. There are numerous covenants in the lease, whose statement is unnecessary, because the covenants of the lessee to vacate the premises at the end of the term, and to become liable to the lessors for all loss or damage which the lessors might suffer through a loss of sale or of lease or otherwise by reason of its failure to leave as agreed, are the only covenants whose effect is in controversy.

There is no material conflict in the testimony. It tended to establish that, some months before the expiration of the term, the lessee discussed with its lessors the execution of a new demise for a further period of five and ten years, but that the parties could not agree, and that the tenant wrote on August 23rd, 1927, that it was preparing to move but that it, if its plans miscarried so that it would be unable to open its new place of business before the expiration of the lease, the tenant would consider it a great favor if the lessors would extend the lease for a month or two, as might be necessary; and that it would meet the lessors for the purpose of making arrangements which would be fair to all parties. The lessors replied four days later by letters directing the tenant to confer with their agent, who was engaged in the real estate business in Baltimore, and who had the matter involved in his charge; and concluding with the statement that they felt sure a satisfactory arrangement could be made. This agent and the tenant met the first week of October, and their negotiations were fruitless, because the agent, who had full authority from his principals, would not agree to prolong the period of the lease for less than six months. After this futile meeting, nothing more was done during the term, and the original demise continued to fix the duration of the renting and the rights and liabilities of the parties.

Upon the expiration of the term the lessee did not surrender the premises as it had covenanted, but remained in actual possession until November 26th, 1927, and on December 1st, 1927, forwarded by mail to the lessors checks which aggregated $583.33, which was a sum equivalent to the monthly installment of the yearly rent reserved under the original lease. The lessors declined to receive the checks except as a payment of the monthly instalment of rent which had accrued due by the lessee as a tenant holding over for an additional year; and the lessee insisted that a payment of rent to December 4th, 1927, was a full discharge of its liability. In the assertion of those conflicting positions, the checks and keys were repeatedly sent and returned between the disputants. Ultimately the checks for $583.33 were accepted by the lessors upon an understanding that the acceptance was without prejudice to the rights of either side, and the keys were retained by the lessors under circumstances having a similar effect. Notwithstanding the effort of the owners to secure a tenant for the benefit of the lessee, the property remained unoccupied from the time the lessee left until after the owners began an action, on January 2nd, 1929, against their former lessee for the recovery of the rents issuing from the premises for the period of one year. The judgment recovered by the plaintiffs was for $6,416.67, which sum was the yearly rental under the first demise, less the payment of $585.33, which had been accepted by the plaintiffs without prejudice to the rights of any party.

The defendant's contention . . . is that the defendant was not a tenant holding over under a new renting, and that the failure of the tenant to surrender the premises at the expiration of the original period of the renting did not cause the plaintiffs any loss within the contemplation of the inclusive covenants of the lease.

The defendant was a tenant for years, and did not surrender the premises to the landlords at the expiration of the period of its tenancy, but remained for almost a month, when the tenant abandoned the premises, and then offered in full the amount of the monthly instalment of the rent which had been reserved under the original lease. Under these circumstances the defendant became a trespasser in the sense of being wrongfully in possession, or a tenant from year to year at the election of the landlords. The defendant, however, had no such election. In the language of an eminent authority: "His mere continuance in possession fixes him as tenant for another year if the landlord thinks proper to insist upon it. And the right of the landlord to continue the tenancy will not be affected by the fact, that the tenant refused to renew the lease and gave notice that he had hired other premises." *Taylor on Landlord and Tenant* (9th Ed.), § 22. In a later work of equal authority the prevailing rule is similarly stated in this language: "By the decided weight of authority in this country, one holding over may be held liable as a tenant for a further period, without reference to his actual wishes on the subject. As is frequently expressed, the landlord has the option to treat him as a tenant for a further term or a trespasser." *Tiffany's Landlord and Tenant*, §§ 209, 211, 212.

This rule does not seem to have been expressly adopted in this jurisdiction. * * * The rule is sometimes stated to be based on the theory that the tenant holding over presumably intends to prolong the duration of his tenancy by another term, and that he cannot overcome this presumption by setting up, to the disadvantage of the landlord, that he is holding as a wrongdoer. See 2 *Tiffany on Landlord and Tenant* 1472. Mr. Williston finds the rule to be an illustration of the "general principle that when an act may rightfully be done with certain consequences or effect, the actor cannot assert for his own advantage to avoid that effect, that the act was done wrongfully." 3 *Williston on Contracts.* § 1856, at 3179–3180.

It is difficult to ascribe the liability to contract, when this liability exists notwithstanding any statement, however explicit, of a contrary intention by the tenant. Mr. Tiffany prefers, and it seems the better view, to regard the liability of the tenant wrongfully holding over as one imposed by law on the tenant, without his express or implied consent, and enforceable in an action at law as a quasi-contractual obligation in order that justice may be done between the parties. 2 *Tiffany on Landlord and Tenant* 1472; 1 *Williston on Contracts*, § 3; § 21, n. 20, at 24; *Corbin's Anson on Contracts* 571 and notes . . . .

The rule imposes a penalty upon the individual tenant wrongfully holding over, but ultimately operates for the benefit of tenants as a class by its tendency to secure the agreed surrender of terms to incoming tenants who have severally yielded possession of other premises in anticipation of promptly entering into the possession of the new. This makes for confidence in leasehold transactions. Again, the terms of the leases of property which is rented for business, commercial, residential, and agricultural uses tend to begin and end at a customary date or during a particular season of the year, as determined by the nature of the use of the specific property, and as the value of any piece of property is largely dependent upon its actual or potential continuing yield in periodic rent, the social and economic importance of the landlord being able certainly to deliver, and the prospective tenant so to obtain possession on the stipulated day, is obvious. These considerations afford a sound and rational basis for the adoption of a rule which is supported by the great weight of authority in this country . . . . * * *

The testimony is clear that, when the defendant failed to surrender the premises at the end of the original period of letting, without any basis in law or fact for such action, the landlords forthwith exercised their option and elected to treat the defendant as their tenant from year to year. This new tenancy was subject to the provisions of the original lease with reference to the rent and to the other obligations so far as they are applicable, as though the new tenancy had been created by the consent of the parties. The defendant was, therefore, bound to pay $7,000 as the stipulated rent for the year next ensuing the end of period of the first lease.

The defendant further contends that, even if there were a new tenancy from year to year, the following clause of the original lease limits the loss and damage recoverable by the plaintiffs, and that there was no legally sufficient proof that the plaintiffs had sustained any injury within the contemplation of this clause:

> The tenant agrees that it will vacate the premises on the expiration date as originally fixed herein, or upon the earlier termination of said term, in the event of a sale or contract of sale as above provided or upon any other termination of said lease in accordance with the terms hereof. In the event of a failure of the tenant to so vacate, then the tenant shall be liable to the

landlords for all loss or damage which the landlords may suffer through a loss[] of sale or loss of lease or otherwise by reason for said failure to vacate and said liability and the rights of the landlords shall be in addition to all the rights which said landlords might be entitled under any present or future law for speedy ejectment or recovery of possession of said premises.

The election by the landlords to continue the defendant as their tenant for another year created a tenancy from year to year, that began with the termination of the original period of renting and made the defendant's possession rightful from this beginning of his new tenancy. So, by this election, the landlords waived all claim against the defendant with respect to its failure to surrender possession at the close of the first period, and the terms of the tenancy from year to year will determine the rights and liabilities of the parties. If the quoted provisions be assumed to be consistent with the tenancy from year to year, and, therefore, become provisions of this tenancy, they do not affect the right of the landlord to recover the unpaid instalments of the yearly rent of the new tenancy. These quoted provisions do not relate to rent, but to damages which the landlord may sustain by a failure of the tenant to surrender possession as agreed. This is made clear by the subsequent and express provision of the original lease that, if the rent be and remain in arrear for a prescribed time, the landlords may re-enter, and determine the lease, and demise the premises; and, at the option of the landlords, the tenant shall remain liable during the unexpired portion of the term for the deficit between any rent received by the landlords and the rent stipulated to be paid. Furthermore, the covenants in the lease to pay rent and to be liable for damages for a failure to surrender the premises as agreed create obligations with reference to two different undertakings.

In the instant case, the tenant did not refuse to vacate the premises during the new tenancy. On the contrary, after paying one monthly instalment of the yearly rent, the tenant repudiated the tenancy, abandoned the premises, and refused to pay the rent. The testimony shows that the landlords did not resume possession to the exclusion of the tenant, but notified the tenant that it would be held for the rent unpaid. The fact that the plaintiffs made diligent effort to procure a tenant for the unexpired term did not relieve the defendant of its liability for rent, but, by the implied terms of the tenancy, would have inured to the benefit of the defendant, if a tenant had been procured at any time before the expiration of the year of the defendant's tenancy.

For the reasons stated . . . the judgment will be affirmed.

NOTES

1.   The initial term of the tenant was five years, but there is no discussion of making the tenant pay for more than an additional year. Why not? In part, because the parties could not create such a long-term lease without a writing sufficient to satisfy the Statute of Frauds. The Statute requires that the transfer of an interest in real property, including a lease with a term of more than one year, be in writing. See *Bateman v. Maddox*, 26 S.W. 51, 54 (Tex. 1894). You may think that the Statute should not apply when the lease is implied by the law or is imposed as the result of litigation conducted under all the procedural safeguards that a court provides. However, in this area, courts follow the law as received in the Statute. This result

prevents a hardship on the very short-term holdover tenant who would be forced to accept an additional, multi-year lease.

Maryland's highest court amplified its holding in the *Fetting* opinion in *Donnelly Adver. Corp. v. Flaccomio*, 140 A.2d 165, 171–72 (Md. 1958) (reviewing a series of letters between a landlord who refused to come to an agreement in negotiations up to the end of the original term and tenant who negotiated and then held over), as follows:

> By operation of law, the tenant holding over became a trespasser, in the sense of being wrongfully in possession, or a tenant from year to year at the election of the landlord, regardless of the wishes of the tenant. *Fetting Co. v. Waltz, supra*. But in this State it is doubtful that a landlord is required to make a prompt election. The substance of the rule as expressed in Tiffany, Real Property, Sec. 175, p. 281 (3d ed. 1939), and other authorities, is to the effect that the landlord has the option to treat the tenant as wrongfully retaining possession or as rightly doing so. * * * The fact that the tenant sent a check for one month's rent after the crucial date, proposing that it be accepted as a tenant from month-to-month does not alter the situation. The landlord never agreed to the proposal, so there was no substitution of a new lease for the implied lease which arose by operation of law, nor was there any alteration in the terms and conditions of the then existing implied lease. While it is true that the landlord, in accepting the check, did not at that time expressly elect to treat the tenant as a tenant holding over, it is clear that she definitely declined the tenant's proposal. For this reason we think the acceptance of the check, which was in the exact amount the landlord was entitled to receive for a month's rent under the old lease and from a tenant holding over under the implied lease for another year, did not bar her recovery of subsequent installments . . . . We think the landlord was not barred from subsequently making the election to hold the tenant under the implied lease after her previous demand and ultimatum had been declined and ignored, and the tenant continued to remain in the premises . . . . Even if it is assumed that the acceptance by the landlord of a month's rent constituted tacit consent that the tenant could remain on the premises pending negotiations for a new written lease or a further extension of the old one, it is clear that such negotiations finally ceased on April 16, 1956 [one and a half months after the expiration of the lease — Eds.], yet the tenant continued to remain on the premises until it saw fit to vacate.

Suppose a tenant wishes to continue the lease for an additional term if the landlord makes some repairs to the premises, and at the expiration of the term, the landlord is repairing the premises as agreed, but the repairs are not yet complete. Is this tenant free to vacate after holding over?

2.   At least one court has held that a fraction of a day does not constitute a holding over; in other words, the law on this issue is subject to a *de minimis* rule. All courts and, as you see from the statutes reprinted *supra*, many statutes recognize one exception — an involuntary holding over, such as a tenant whose illness is so serious in nature that he cannot be moved or that renders his renewal

for an additional term impossible. See *In re Weinberg's Estate*, 31 N.Y.S.2d 445, 447 (N.Y. Surr. Ct. 1941); *Herter v. Mullen*, 53 N.E. 700, 701–02 (N.Y. 1899) (involving tenants who removed their personal property but did not move their ill mother on a physician's advice, thus holding over for 15 days). The Restatement (Second) of Property § 14.4 cmt. i (1977) arguably has extended the scope of this exception, stating that when the tenant intends to vacate but is prevented from doing so by circumstances beyond her control, the tenant is excused. See, e.g., *Commonwealth Bldg. Corp. v. Hirschfield*, 30 N.E.2d 790 (Ill. App. Ct. 1940) (inability of vacating tenant to obtain use of the service elevator to move out of premises in a high rise apartment building). Suppose a tenant reserves the right to remove some fixtures installed on the premises at the end of the term or covenants to restore the premises to the condition in which they were received, is the tenant a holdover if the removal or restoration takes place after the end of the term?

3. The usual measure of damages for the landlord is the reasonable rental value of the premises for the duration of the holdover. The English Landlord Tenant Act of 1730, 4 Geo. 2, ch. 28, § 1, provides that a tenant who willfully holds over after a landlord makes a written demand for possession, shall pay the landlord double rent. Florida has enacted a similar statute. See Fla. Stat. § 83.06 (1989); and see Uniform Residential Landlord and Tenant Act, § 4.301(c) (1977) (permitting treble damages).

When the premises are held by cotenants, but only one of the cotenants holds over, may the landlord sue the non-holdovers for damages as well? If the landlord sues the holdover tenant for damages, may the incoming tenant also sue the holdover? Although possibly having a basis for a suit against the landlord, has the incoming tenant acquired an interest sufficient to sue the tenant? What if the landlord, during the course of negotiations, informs the tenant of a rent increase if the tenant holds over? When the tenant disputes the amount of the increase during the term but holds over, is the tenant liable for the increase? Compare *Fields v. Conforti*, 868 N.E.2d 507 (Ind. App. 2007) (holding that the tenant is liable for the increase), with *Arnold Realty Co. v. Wm. K. Toole Co.*, 125 A. 363, 365 (R.I. 1924) (holding not liable). Many leases contain a provision dealing with the tenant's holding over. What should such a covenant provide? If it provides for a holdover rent, should that prevent the landlord from ejecting the holdover? Will that rent liquidate the landlord's damages upon ejectment?

X. THE LANDLORD'S SELF-HELP

BASS v. BOETEL & CO.
217 N.W.2d. 804 (Neb. 1974)

SPENCER, J.

Plaintiffs, dispossessed tenants of business premises at Rockbrook Center in Omaha, Nebraska, sued their landlord and the latter's agent to recover damages. Admitting default in payment of rents, they alleged that defendants, by the use of self-help, removed and detained certain personal property belonging to plaintiffs. A jury returned a verdict of $12,000 for plaintiffs, and defendants appeal.

On September 24, 1968, plaintiffs entered into a written lease of the premises with defendants' predecessor in interest. Rent was payable monthly at the rate of $400 for a period of 3 years. On April 20, 1971, the Rockbrook Center area was acquired by defendants. The transaction included an assignment of one-third of the April rent.

Carl Bass, one of the plaintiffs, operated a billiard parlor on the premises. His business was seasonal, greater in the winter than in the summer. In 1970, he was unable to pay rent to defendants' predecessor for a period of 3 months, but was permitted to make up the payments during the following 3 months. At the time of the transfer of the premises to defendants, Bass had not paid the April rent. He paid no rent to defendants. As of June 1, 1971, he was indebted to them for the rent from April 21, 1971. This is the subject of a counterclaim. Defendants were awarded a judgment of $600 against the plaintiffs. No cross-appeal was taken so this judgment is not in controversy.

When Bass attempted to open for business on June 1, 1971, he found defendants had changed the outside locks on the billiard parlor. He went to their office to discuss the matter but was refused a key. He subsequently hired a locksmith, had the locks changed, and went in to resume business. When the locksmith opened the door, the alarm went off and the security patrol showed up and asked for his identification. Shortly thereafter representatives of defendants appeared and told Bass he could no longer occupy the premises. He stayed in the premises a short while and then sought legal advice. When he left he removed his books, money from the cash register, some standing ashtrays, and a case for pool cues from the premises. When he returned to the premises the locks had again been changed, and he could not reenter. Subsequently he learned that the remainder of his equipment, with the exception of the carpeting, had been removed from the premises.

Bass was never given a written notice to quit as required by statute, nor served with legal process. Defendants removed the personal property claimed by Bass from the billiard parlor. They subsequently gave his attorney an inventory list. The property was placed in defendants' warehouse for storage pending the outcome of this litigation. The premises were relet to another tenant.

The pool and snooker tables were subject to a mortgage in favor of the seller, a corporation represented by Al Karschner. A balance of approximately $3,000 remained unpaid on this mortgage. After the lockout defendants permitted Karschner to remove the tables. Bass assented to their sale, in consideration of the discharge of the debt. The mortgagee sold the tables for $5,665, but Bass received nothing from the proceeds of the sale.

Defendants assert they possessed the right to use self-help as a matter of law; the evidence was insufficient to sustain a finding on the facts or amount of damages; erroneous exclusion of the issue of abandonment; and instructional error relating to damages.

The lease asserted ownership of the landlord, defendants' predecessor, in the tenant's fixtures, except movable office fixtures and trade fixtures. In the event of default in payment of rent, the lease provided as follows: "the Lessor may without demand or notice at once declare this lease terminated, and the Lessor may re-enter said premises without any formal notice or demand and hold and enjoy the same thenceforth as if these presents had not been made."

The lease also provided: "If the Lessee shall not promptly remove all his property whenever the Lessor shall become entitled to possession as herein agreed, the Lessor may, without notice, remove the same in any manner, or if the Lessee shall at any time vacate or abandon said premises, and leave any chattels for a period of ten days after such vacation or abandonment, or after the termination of this lease in any manner then the Lessor shall have the right to sell said chattels without notice to the Lessee, or any notice of sale, all notices required by statute or otherwise being hereby expressly waived. [A]ll chattels, fixtures and other personal property belonging to Lessee, which are, or may be put into the said leased premises during said term, whether exempt or not from sale under execution or attachment, shall at all times be bound with a first lien in favor of Lessor, and shall be chargeable for all rent which lien may be enforced in like manner as a chattel mortgage, or in any other manner afforded by law."

The lease also provided that personal property was at the risk of plaintiffs only that "the Lessor shall not be liable for any damage caused in any manner whatsoever."

Plaintiffs' second amended petition pleaded two causes of action. The first alleged breach of quiet enjoyment and loss of financial and business standing as well as public ridicule and ignominy as a result of being locked out of the business premises. The second cause of action alleged the wrongful taking and detention of plaintiffs' personal property.

Defendants argue that wrongful eviction and abandonment were issues of law and that by the terms of the lease they were given the right to take possession of the premises and the personal property. The law on forcible entry and detainer has long been otherwise. In *Myers v. Koenig*, 5 Neb. 419 (1877), this court stated: "One great object of the forcible entry act is to prevent even rightful owners from taking the law into their own hands and attempting to recover by violence, what remedial powers of a court would give them in a peaceful mode." In *Watkins v. Dodson*, 68 N.W.2d 508 (Neb. 1955), after quoting the above language, this court said: "It was the purpose of the statute relating to forcible entry and detainer to prevent parties to a litigable controversy like the present from taking the law into their own hands. The issue was not ownership or title but 'lawful and peaceable entry' . . . ."

To accept defendants' argument would scuttle our forcible entry and detainer statute. Self-help, relating to the repossession of real estate, has long been contrary to the public policy of Nebraska and is not to be condoned. The lockout herein was unlawful. The right of a landlord legally entitled to possession to dispossess a tenant without legal process is the subject of an annotation in 6 A.L.R.3d 177, 186: "An increasing number of jurisdictions uphold what seems to be the modern doctrine that a landlord otherwise entitled to possession must, on the refusal of the tenant to surrender the leased premises, resort to the remedy given by law to secure it; otherwise he would be liable in damages for using force or deception to regain possession."

Plaintiffs were in lawful possession of the premises even though they had failed to make rental payments as specified by the lease. The fact that they were in default gave defendants the right to declare a forfeiture and to recover the leased premises by legal means. Instead, they resorted to self-help and are liable for the consequences . . . .

The only issue submitted to the jury was the wrongful taking and detention of plaintiffs' personal property as the result of their being unlawfully and forcibly dispossessed of the leased premises. Defendants' unlawful seizure of the property of plaintiffs could not be justified on the ground that rent was due and owing, as defendants might have proceeded legally to enforce whatever legal or equitable claims they might have had. Instead, defendants saw fit to wrongfully and unlawfully seize and detain plaintiffs' property. The trial court properly instructed the jury that a person having a lien upon the property of another must enforce that lien by proper legal action rather than by force.

No specific damage instruction was submitted by the court. The jury was merely advised to determine the nature, extent, and amount of the damages sustained by plaintiffs as a result of the forcible taking and detention of their personal property by defendants . . . . It is always the duty of the court to instruct the jury as to the proper basis upon which damages are to be estimated. The jury should be fully and fairly informed as to the various items or elements of damage which it should take into consideration in arriving at its verdict. Otherwise, the jury may be confused and misled . . . . For the reasons given, the judgment is reversed and the cause remanded to the District Court for a new trial in conformity with this opinion. Reversed and remanded.

BOSLAUGH, J., concurring.

With respect to the matter of self-help relating to the repossession of real estate, the following statement from the opinion of Mr. Justice Marshall in *Pernell v. Southall Realty*, decided April 24, 1974 (42 Law Week 4595), seems appropriate: "Some delay, of course, is inherent in any fair-minded system of justice. A landlord-tenant dispute, like any other lawsuit, cannot be resolved with due process of law unless both parties have had a fair opportunity to present their cases. Our courts were never intended to serve as rubber stamps for landlords seeking to evict their tenants, but rather to see that justice be done before a man is evicted from his home."

CLINTON, J., dissenting.

I dissent. The case should be not only reversed, but also dismissed. The plaintiffs failed to adduce evidence from which the jury could determine the value of the converted property without indulging in speculation and conjecture. Therefore the defendants' motion for a directed verdict should have been granted. The effect of the majority opinion is to allow a new trial to the plaintiffs so that they may remedy their own deficiencies of proof. This constitutes a departure from well-established procedural rules, the substance of which is that a party who fails to obtain a verdict (or against whom a verdict should have been directed) because of failure of proof of some element of his cause of action, including the element of damages, is not entitled to a new trial so that he may have another shot at it. * * * Failure to prove damages by competent evidence should be treated the same as any other failure of proof. It seems clear to me there was no proof of the market value of the property, or its actual value, or the value of its use, and that the verdict could only be the result of conjecture or acceptance of evidence not competent for the purpose. * * *

NEWTON, J., dissenting.

I respectfully dissent. Under existing Nebraska law, a landlord cannot evict a tenant by force or artifice even though the landlord is entitled to possession. See, *Anderson v. Carlson*, 86 Neb. 126, 125 N.W. 157 . . . ; *Barnes v. Davitt*, 160 Neb. 595, 71 N.W.2d 107. These are all cases in forcible entry and detainer where the only issue was the right of possession. In such cases damages were not an issue. Furthermore, in none of these cases was a lease involved which contained a provision for reentry on breach. These cases represent an exercise in futility. In each instance the tenant, who wrongfully held possession in the first place, was returned to possession. This simply meant that the landlord would have to bring a second action in forcible entry and detainer to obtain possession from a defaulting tenant or trespasser. I believe it inadvisable to extend our rule to cases where the lease contract authorizes reentry on breach or termination of the lease . . . .

The right of a landlord to reenter for default in payment of rent or a wrongful holding over should be permitted where the lease provides for reentry and it can be accomplished without violence. This is similar to the right of a conditional sale vendor to take possession of the security on default by peaceful means. See U.C.C. § 9-503.

How can a rule such as is advocated in the majority opinion be justified? It is said that it prevents violence and therefore is required by public policy. This is untrue as the rule I have proposed, like that dealing with the repossession of a conditional sales contract security interest, authorizes only peaceful repossession. Contractual rights should not be nullified without good reason.

On the question of whether a party not entitled to possession of realty who is ejected by force or artifice may recover damages, there is a split in the authorities. There is not a single Nebraska case permitting such recovery. * * * In the absence of a willful destruction of the evicted party's property or a physical assault, I would deny recovery. This is particularly true in cases where the lease provides that the landlord shall have a lien on the tenant's property on the demised premises to secure accrued rentals. In 49 Am. Jur. 2d, Landlord and Tenant, § 677, p. 642, it is stated: "It is competent for the parties to a lease to stipulate that the landlord shall have a lien on the crops or the personal property of the tenant which may be brought upon the leased premises, which, even if invalid at common law, will be given effect in equity."

QUESTION

The common law authorized evictions through self-help, even evictions by force when force was reasonably necessary. What is the argument for continuing this traditional rule? It begins with the idea that if force is necessary, it is because the tenant forcibly resisted. How far does this idea take you? If summary procedures turn out not to be summary, is self-help available? If lockouts are authorized by statute, as in a few states, does the landlord have to give the tenant notice and a key so that he can reclaim his personal property? See Randy Gerchick, *No Easy Way Out: Making the Summary Eviction Process a Fairer and More Efficient Alternative to Landlord Self-Help*, 41 UCLA L. Rev. 759 (1994).

XI.   SUMMARY PROCEDURE

Most states have enacted statutes providing a summary eviction procedure for a landlord to recover possession of the premises. Often these statutes make summary procedure available to any "person wrongfully deprived of possession," making it available against trespassers too. By using this action, landlords do not waive their other remedies but must pursue them in separate causes of action. To recover possession through summary process, the landlord files a complaint in a jurisdiction's lowest civil trial court. The only remedy the landlord can request in this complaint is the recovery of possession. The court clerk then orders the sheriff or other official to serve a summons on the defendant, ordering her (1) to cure the breach, often within 3 days, (2) to appear for trial within 5–15 days of the summon's issue date and (3) to respond in writing to the complaint by a date set, in advance of trial, or otherwise orally at trial. The summons must be served 2–3 days before the date set for trial. If the defendant appears then, the matter is tried; if a continuance is requested and granted, it is generally for a limited period of time. To obtain a continuance, the requesting party must post a bond or pay the rent into a judicial escrow. If the defendant does not appear, the court may either adjourn the proceeding for 5–10 days or, after an inquiry into the truth of the complaint, enter judgment for the landlord. If the defendant does not appear at any adjourned proceedings, after an appropriate inquiry, the court enters judgment for the landlord. Even though such procedures limit the tenant's defenses to a denial of the plaintiff's right to possession, the U.S. Supreme Court upheld the constitutionality of such statutes under the federal Due Process and Equal Protection Clauses in *Lindsey v. Normet*, 405 U.S. 56 (1972), applying the rational basis standard of review under the Due Process Clause. The Court stated in part:

> At common law, one with the right to possession could bring an action for ejectment, a "relatively slow, fairly complex, and substantially expensive procedure." But, as Oregon cases have recognized, the common law also permitted the landlord to "enter and expel the tenant by force, without being liable to an action of tort for damages, either for his entry upon the premises, or for an assault in expelling the tenant, provided he uses no more force than is necessary, and do[es] no wanton damage." *Smith v. Reeder*, 21 Or. 541, 546, 28 P. 890, 891 (1892). The landlord-tenant relationship was one of the few areas where the right to self-help was recognized by the common law of most States, and the implementation of this right has been fraught with "violence and quarrels and bloodshed." *Entelman v. Hagood*, 95 Ga. 390, 392, 22 S.E. 545 (1895). An alternative legal remedy to prevent such breaches of the peace has appeared to be an overriding necessity to many legislators and judges. * * *

There are unique factual and legal characteristics of the landlord-tenant relationship that justify special statutory treatment inapplicable to other litigants. The tenant is, by definition, in possession of the property of the landlord; unless a judicially supervised mechanism is provided for what would otherwise be swift repossession by the landlord himself, the tenant would be able to deny the landlord the rights of income incident to ownership by refusing to pay rent and by preventing sale or rental to someone else. Many expenses of the landlord continue to accrue whether a tenant pays his rent or not. Speedy adjudication is desirable to prevent subjecting the landlord to undeserved economic loss and the tenant to unmerited harassment and dispossession when his lease or rental agreement gives him the right to peaceful and undisturbed possession of the property. Holding over by the tenant beyond the term of his agreement or holding without payment of rent has proved a virulent source of friction and dispute. We think Oregon was well within its constitutional powers in providing for rapid and peaceful settlement of these disputes.

PROBLEMS

1.   May a tenant who is sued for summary possession assert a counterclaim for the landlord's breach of the implied covenant of habitability? See *P.H. Inv. v. Oliver*, 818 P.2d 1018, 1020 (Utah 1991). May a landlord accept rent during the pendency of a summary possession case, or has he thereby waived his right to the action? See *Colonial Village, Inc. v. Pelkey*, 945 A.2d 22, 22–25 (N.H. 2008).

2.   During the term of a lease, tenant (T) improves the premises in anticipation of exercising an option provided in the lease to purchase the leased property. Rent in the lease is defined as a set, base amount, plus real property taxes, which T agrees to pay. When the taxes are levied, but tax payments are not yet due, landlord (L) raises the rent. L and T then dispute the amount of rent due. When T tenders a rent check without including the tax payment amount, L sues T in summary procedure, which is statutorily available when a tenant fails to pay rent when due. The court holds for T by using its equitable powers. L appeals. In this appeal, what result and why? See *Foundation Dev. Corp. v. Loehmann's*, 788 P.2d 1189, 1194–95 (Ariz. 1990); *Cumberland Farms, Inc. v. Dairy Mart, Inc.*, 627 A.2d 386, 390–91 (Conn. 1993).

3.   T is the lessee of premises for a supermarket in a small shopping center. The monthly rent consists of a base amount, plus a percentage of the gross income generated by the market. The base amount is now set at an amount that is currently one-third of the premise's fair rental value. The lease does not require that T continuously operate the market or that T pay anything more than the base rent. T closes the market, continues to pay the base rental amount, and opens a larger store nearby. L sues T to enjoin T from occupying the premises. T says that a suit for an injunction is improper because an action for summary process is available and moves to dismiss L's suit. How would you rule on T's motion? See *Fodor v. First Nat'l Supermarkets, Inc.*, 589 N.E.2d 17, 19–20 (Ohio 1992) (an injunction is available only if an adequate remedy at law does not exist; an action in summary procedure is an adequate legal remedy).

XII. RETALIATORY EVICTION

BUILDING MONITORING SYS., INC. v. PAXTON
905 P.2d 1215 (Utah 1995)

HOWE, J.

In December 1991, defendants Michael Paxton and Amy Lowder rented an apartment in West Jordan, Utah, from plaintiff Building Monitoring Systems, Inc., under a month-to-month rental agreement. Shortly after moving in, they notified plaintiff's resident manager that the plumbing and wiring in their apartment needed to be repaired. Although the manager attempted to make some minor repairs, the overall condition of the apartment remained unacceptable to defendants. On August 9, 1993, they complained to the Salt Lake City and County Health Department of an inoperable refrigerator, leaking sinks, decaying bathroom walls, and deteriorated carpeting. The Health Department determined that these conditions violated health department regulations and sent plaintiff a letter ordering it to make necessary repairs by September 7. On September 1, plaintiff served Paxton and Lowder with an eviction notice, effective September 30. However, the tenancy was reinstated when the manager accepted rent from them for the month of October.

On or about October 12, defendants made another complaint to the Health Department, and they also gave plaintiff a written list of needed repairs. One day after plaintiff received notice of the complaint, it served defendants with another eviction notice, demanding that they vacate by October 31. When they did not do so, plaintiff brought this unlawful detainer action against them to compel them to yield possession of the premises and to pay its costs and attorney fees pursuant to Utah Code Ann. § 78-36-3(1)(b)(i). They countered that the court should enjoin plaintiff from carrying out the eviction because it was issued in retaliation for their complaints to the Health Department. The court agreed that the eviction was retaliatory but declined to recognize the defense because of the lack of statutory or case law defining it in Utah. Defendants appeal.

At issue is whether retaliatory eviction by a landlord is an affirmative defense to an unlawful detainer action in Utah. Although at least thirty-one states statutorily prohibit retaliatory conduct by a landlord, 5 Thompson on Real Property 398 (David A. Thomas ed. 1994), the Utah legislature has not adopted such a statute. However, in many jurisdictions, courts have recognized that the promulgation of housing regulations provides support for the establishment of the retaliatory eviction defense. See, e.g., *Robinson v. Diamond Housing Corp.*, 463 F.2d 853, 862 (D.C. Cir. 1972); *Schweiger v. Superior Court*, 476 P.2d 97, 103 (Cal. 1970); *Markese v. Cooper*, 333 N.Y.S.2d 63, 69 (Monroe Cty. Ct. 1972); *Dickhut v. Norton*, 173 N.W.2d 297, 301 (Wis. 1970).

The leading case in this area is *Edwards v. Habib*, 397 F.2d 687, 700–01 (D.C. Cir. 1968), *cert. denied*, 393 U.S. 1016 (1969). In *Edwards*, the District of Columbia Circuit Court fashioned the defense of retaliatory eviction on the basis of its finding that the vital public policy of maintaining effective enforcement of the local housing code would be thwarted if landlords were permitted to evict tenants who reported housing code violations to authorities. The court did not find any explicit legislative endorsement of this public policy but concluded that endorsement was implied by the act of promulgating the code. The court explained:

> We have the responsibility to consider the social context in which our decisions will have operational effect. In light of the appalling condition and shortage of housing in Washington, the expense of moving, the inequality of bargaining power between tenant and landlord, and the social and economic importance of assuring at least minimum standards in housing conditions, we do not hesitate to declare that retaliatory eviction cannot be tolerated. There can be no doubt that the slum dweller, even though his home be marred by housing code violations, will pause long before he complains of them if he fears eviction as a consequence.

397 F.2d at 701.

Like the court in *Edwards*, we begin our analysis by determining whether the state legislature has expressed an intent to improve housing conditions by imposing specific health and safety standards for rental housing. In Utah, renters are protected by health and safety standards from two sources. First, the legislature has authorized local boards of health to promulgate housing regulations. Utah Code Ann. §§ 26A-1-114, -121. Second, the legislature has articulated certain health and safety standards for housing in the Utah Fit Premises Act (the Act). Utah Code Ann. §§ 57-22-1 to -6. The Act's § 3(1) provides in part: "Each owner and his agent renting or leasing a residential rental unit shall maintain that unit in a condition fit for human habitation and in accordance with local ordinances and the rules of the board of health having jurisdiction in the area in which the residential rental unit is located." Both of these legislative acts manifest an intent to improve housing conditions. If we were to permit retaliatory evictions, this intent might well be frustrated because tenants would be reluctant to report violations of health department regulations or to assert their rights under the Act. Cases from other jurisdictions correctly point out that private initiative in reporting violations of housing and health codes is vital to the enforcement of statutes similar to our Act. See *Edwards*, 397 F.2d at 700–01 . . . ; *Dickhut*, 173 N.W.2d at 301. Fear of reprisal by landlords must be eliminated, or tenants may be deterred from exercising this initiative . . . . Further, we . . . recognize that because of unequal bargaining power, low-income tenants must often accept substandard housing, and we will not help perpetuate this condition by allowing retaliatory eviction by a landlord.

In addition, if retaliatory evictions were tolerated, the recourse provided in the Act for renters of substandard housing would be meaningless. Section 57-22-4 imposes specific duties on the owner:

> (1) To protect the physical health and safety of the ordinary renter, each owner shall: (a) not rent the premises unless they are safe, sanitary, and fit for human occupancy; (b) maintain common areas of the residential rental unit in a sanitary and safe condition; (c) maintain electrical systems, plumbing, heating, and hot and cold water; [and] (d) maintain other appliances and facilities as specifically contracted in the lease agreement . . . .

Subsection 57-22-4(2) states that if the renter believes the residential unit does not comply with these health and safety standards, the renter may give written notice of noncompliance to the owner, who must commence corrective action within a reasonable time. Alternatively, the owner "may refuse to correct the condition . . . and terminate the rental agreement if the unit is unfit for occupancy." Utah Code Ann. § 57-22-4(4). Finally, section 57-22-6(2) provides that if a reasonable time has elapsed after the renter has served notice on the owner to correct or remedy any condition and the owner has not complied, the renter may serve a second notice on the owner to commence corrective action within three days. If the owner fails to do so, the renter may bring an action to recover damages and injunctive relief as determined by the court. Utah Code Ann. § 57-22-6(3).

It is obvious that if the owner were allowed to evict the renter upon receiving the first notice to correct or remedy a condition, the renter could not remain in possession long enough to exercise the rights afforded him or her in section 57-22-6. The scheme of the Act would be frustrated and defeated by the short circuiting of the renter's rights.

In reaching this conclusion prohibiting retaliatory eviction, we emphasize that we have not substantially altered the landlord's right to evict. We simply hold, as the court in *Edwards* (397 F.2d at 699) did, that "while the landlord may evict for any legal reason or for no reason at all, he is not . . . free to evict in retaliation for his tenant's report of housing code violations to the authorities. As a matter of statutory construction and for reasons of public policy, such an eviction cannot be permitted."

Having determined that retaliatory eviction cannot be tolerated in this state, we must define the defense and apply it to the facts of this case. The Second Restatement of Property states:

> [A] landlord has taken retaliatory action against a tenant with respect to residential property whenever [the landlord] undertakes to terminate a tenancy that is terminable by an appropriate notice, or refuses to renew a tenancy for a specified term when that term ends, if: (1) there is a protective housing statute embodying a public purpose to insure proper conditions of housing, especially multi-unit housing designated for rental to tenants of low or moderate income; (2) the landlord is in the business of renting residential property; (3) the tenant is not materially in default in the performance of his obligations under the lease at the time the landlord acts; (4) the landlord is primarily motivated in so acting because the tenant, either alone or through his participation in a lawful organization of tenants, has complained about a violation by the landlord of a protective housing statute; and (5) the tenant's complaint was made in good faith and with reasonable cause.

Restatement (Second) of Property § 14.8, and see *id.*, cmts. d-g (1977). We accept this definition because it withstands some common criticisms of the retaliatory eviction defense. For example, under this definition a homeowner who rents his home during occasional absences cannot be rendered homeless by a renter who complains of housing code violations merely to retain possession of the home because the defense applies only to landlords who are in the business of renting property. In addition, a tenant of any rental property may not secure a continued tenancy by making insincere complaints because the defense is not available unless the tenant complains in good faith and with reasonable cause. Finally, the defense does not jeopardize the landlord's right to evict for any legal reason or for no reason because the tenant must prove that the landlord's primary motivation in issuing an eviction notice was retaliatory.

The facts of this case meet all five elements of the Restatement. The first element, which requires this court to base the defense on a protective housing statute, is met by the Act, which embodies an intent to insure safe and healthy living conditions for renters. Utah Code Ann. §§ 57-22-1 to -6. The second element, which requires the landlord to be in the business of renting residential property, is clearly met because plaintiff is the owner of a large multi-unit apartment building. The third element is met because defendants were not in breach of the rental agreement when plaintiff served them a notice of eviction. The fourth element is met because the trial court found that the tenants met their burden of proving that plaintiff's primary motivation in serving both eviction notices was to retaliate against them for complaining to the Health Department. Finally, we conclude that the fifth element is met because the tenants complained to the Health Department in good faith and with reasonable cause. They complained only after making reasonable efforts to bring the defects to plaintiff's attention, and the defects they complained of were bona fide violations of health department regulations. See Restatement (Second) of Property § 14.8 cmt. g (explaining that good faith element is met if tenant complains of bona fide violations and complains only after making reasonable efforts to bring defects to landlord's attention). Also, they furnished a written list of needed repairs to plaintiff as required by the Act. Utah Code Ann. § 57-22-4(2). Thus, we conclude that the facts of this case meet the Restatement's definition of retaliatory eviction and provide a defense against the unlawful detainer action.

Next, we must examine what course is open to a landlord who has engaged in retaliatory action. Clearly, we cannot saddle the landlord with a perpetual tenant, but "at a minimum, the tenant should be permitted to remain until the landlord has made the repairs required by law." *Markese*, 333 N.Y.S.2d at 75. In determining how long a tenant may remain after the landlord has made the repairs, courts have arrived at different conclusions. One popular approach has been to allow the tenant to remain until the landlord can show that his actions are not the result of retaliatory motives. *Robinson*, 463 F.2d at 865; *Schweiger*, 476 P.2d at 103; *Dickhut*, 173 N.W.2d at 302. However, this may be a difficult burden for the landlord to carry once a retaliatory motive has been found in the initial eviction action.

An alternative approach has been explored by New York courts. These courts have recognized that a tenant may be evicted anytime after repairs have been made but that courts "should be generous in allowing the tenant sufficient time, without the pressure normally exerted in a holdover eviction proceeding, to find other suitable housing." *Markese*, 333 N.Y.S.2d at 75. We agree. Once repairs have been made, a landlord may serve the tenant with an eviction notice and bring an unlawful detainer action without proffering evidence of his intent. However, because the unlawful detainer action may still be tainted with an unlawful motive, the burden is on the landlord to show that he has given the tenant a reasonable opportunity to procure other housing. Thus, the landlord is not deprived of his right to evict a complaining tenant, but the exercise of that right is deferred until he has remedied the housing or health code violation and the tenant has had a reasonable opportunity to find other housing. Reversed.

NOTES

1. *Edwards v. Habib*, 397 F.2d 687 (U.S. App. D.C. 1968), still the leading case on retaliatory eviction, involved a summary procedure statute providing that "whenever any tenancy shall be terminated by [statutory] notice, and the tenant shall fail or refuse to surrender possession of the leased premises, the landlord may bring an action to recover possession." The statute further provided: "When a person detains possession of real property . . . after his right to possession has ceased, the [court] may issue a summons to the party complained of to appear and show cause why judgment should not be given against him for restitution of possession." The court held that these provisions did not control the case because they "are simply procedural." *Id.* at 699. One response to this statement might be that the legislature intended the tenant to have only one choice in a summary procedure — to affirm or to deny the landlord's allegation, but not to assert a retaliatory eviction defense.

2. The retaliatory eviction defense is available in summary procedure actions in a majority of states because either the courts or, more often, the legislature has recognized it. See, e.g., *Wright v. Brady*, 889 P.2d 105 (Idaho Ct. App. 1995) (recognizing the defense); and see, e.g., Ariz. Rev. Stat. Ann. § 33-1381 (2014); Minn. Stat. Ann. § 504B.285 (2014); Wash. Rev. Code § 59.18.240 (2014). When the legislature enacts a statute on this subject, all retaliatory actions, including raising the rent and lowering the level of services are prohibited, not just retaliatory evictions. See, e.g., Uniform Residential Landlord and Tenant Act § 5.101(a) (1974), 73B U.L.A. 503 (1994). Under such a statutory aegis, tenants against whom the landlord retaliates have a cause of action for damages, as well as a defense in a summary procedure or ejectment action. See *Morford v. Lensey Corp.*, 442 N.E.2d 933, 937–938 (Ill. Ct. App. 1982). Even without a statute concerning retaliatory actions, some courts have authorized damages actions. See, e.g., *Murphy v. Smallridge*, 468 S.E.2d 167, 172 (W. Va. 1996) ("A residential tenant may state an affirmative cause of action for retaliatory eviction if the landlord's conduct is in retaliation for the tenant's exercise of a right incidental to the tenancy."). The *Murphy* court explains:

> [T]o permit only a defense of retaliatory eviction would benefit a landlord whose "unknowing tenant vacates, after notice, unaware of his rights to a defense of retaliatory eviction." Without an affirmative right to state a cause of action, the landlord — as the wrongdoer in a valid case of a retaliatory eviction — escapes impunity when a tenant complies with a landlord's demands and vacates the premises after given notice. It, therefore, would serve to punish the agreeable tenant and often would frustrate the goal of ensuring habitable housing. We can find no persuasive reason to create such an inequitable dichotomy between a tenant who vacates the premises and one who chooses to remain.

Id. at 172. Would forcing the tenant to continue living on leased premises to preserve the retaliatory action defense or cause of action benefit housing code enforcement?

3.   A division of judicial authority exists as to whether a tenant's allegation of retaliation may relate only to housing code requirements or to any lease covenant. See *Goodman v. Resident Services, Inc.*, 191 Wis. 2d 362 (Wisc. App. 1995) (non-renewal of a sloppy tenant's lease is not retaliatory though the landlord did not allege breach of a lease covenant in its summary procedure action). More broadly, must the retaliation relate to a lease covenant, or may it relate to any improper motive of the landlord? Courts have split on this issue, too. What if the landlord's motive is not related directly to the lease, such as when the tenant organizes a tenant's union or testifies in favor of a local ordinance that the landlord regards as adverse to her interests? Is the landlord's motive retaliatory? In jurisdictions recognizing an implied covenant of good faith and fair dealing between contracting parties, won't the answer to the prior question usually be yes? What if the landlord retaliates after hearing that the tenant has retained counsel to represent her interests in an ongoing dispute but before counsel calls the landlord? What if the landlord retaliates by filing an eviction action after repairing the premises to code standards? See *Houle v. Quenneville*, 787 A.2d 1258 (Vt. 2001) (retaliatory eviction defense unavailable).

4.   Consider Minn. Stat. Ann. § 504B.285 (2014):

1. The person entitled to the premises may recover possession by eviction when:

(1) any person holds over real property (i) after a sale of the property on an execution or judgment; (ii) on foreclosure of a mortgage and expiration of the time for redemption; or (iii) after termination of contract to convey the property . . . ;

(2) any person holds over real property after termination of the time for which it is demised or leased to that person or to the persons under whom that person holds possession, contrary to the conditions or covenants of the lease or agreement under which that person holds, or after any rent becomes due according to the terms of such lease or agreement; or

(3) any tenant at will holds over after the termination of the tenancy by notice to quit.

2. It is a defense to an action for recovery of premises following the alleged termination of a tenancy by notice to quit for the defendant to prove by a fair preponderance of the evidence that: (1) the alleged termination was intended in whole or part as a penalty for the defendant's good faith attempt to secure or enforce rights under a lease or contract, oral or written, under the laws of the state or any of its governmental subdivisions, or of the United States; or (2) the alleged termination was intended in whole or part as a penalty for the defendant's good faith report to a governmental authority of the plaintiff's violation of a health, safety, housing, or building code or ordinance.

If the notice to quit was served within 90 days of the date of an act of the tenant coming within the terms of clause (1) or (2) the burden of proving that the notice to quit was not served in whole or part for a retaliatory purpose shall rest with the plaintiff.

3. In any proceeding for the recovery of premises upon the ground of nonpayment of rent, it is a defense if the tenant establishes by a preponderance of the evidence that the plaintiff increased the tenant's rent or decreased the services as a penalty in whole or part for any lawful act of the tenant as described in subdivision 2, providing that the tenant tender to the court or to the plaintiff the amount of rent due and payable under the tenant's original obligation.

4. Nothing contained in subdivisions 2 and 3 limits the right of the landlord pursuant to the provisions of subdivision 1 to terminate a tenancy for a violation by the tenant of a lawful, material provision of a lease or contract, whether written or oral, or to hold the tenant liable for damage to the premises caused by the tenant or a person acting under the tenant's direction or control.

Compare this statute with the rights conferred in the *Building Monitoring Sys., Inc.*

XIII.　SECURITY DEPOSITS

At least 37 states statutorily regulate the return of security deposits. See Billie Snyder, *Refunding Residential Tenant Security Deposits: A Legislative Proposal for West Virginia*, 96 W. Va. L. Rev. 549, 550, n. 7 (1993-94) (includes statutory citations). These statutes are interpreted strictly; thus a landlord's contention that his claim on a former tenant for damages exceeded the deposit is no reason not to comply with their provisions. See, e.g., *Moonlight v. Boyce*, 372 N.W.2d 479, 483 (Wis. Ct. App. 1985). The following statute is typical.

Colo. Rev. Stat. §§ 38-12-102 to -103 (2013):

§ 102. Definitions. As used in this part 1, unless the context otherwise requires: . . .

(2) "Security Deposit" means any advance or deposit of money, regardless of its denomination, the primary function of which is to secure the performance of a rental agreement for residential premises or any part thereof.

§ 103. Return of security deposit.

(1) A landlord shall, within one month after the termination of a lease or surrender and acceptance of the premises, whichever occurs last, return to the tenant the full security deposit deposited with the landlord by the tenant, unless the lease agreement specifies a longer period of time, but not to exceed sixty days. No security deposit shall be retained to cover normal wear and tear. In the event that actual cause exists for retaining any portion of the security deposit, the landlord shall provide the tenant with a

written statement listing the exact reasons for the retention of any portion of the security deposit. When the statement is delivered it shall be accompanied by payment of the difference between any sum deposited and the amount retained. The landlord is deemed to have complied with this section by mailing said statement and any payment required to the last known address of the tenant. Nothing in this section shall preclude the landlord from retaining the security deposit for nonpayment of rent, abandonment of the premises, or nonpayment of utility charges, repair work, or cleaning contracted for by the tenant.

(2) The failure of a landlord to provide a written statement within the required time specified in subsection (1) of this section shall work a forfeiture of all his rights to withhold any portion of the security deposit under this section.

(3) (a) The willful retention of a security deposit in violation of this section shall render a landlord liable for treble the amount of that portion of the security deposit wrongfully withheld from the tenant, together with reasonable attorneys' fees and court costs; except that the tenant has the obligation to give notice to the landlord of his intention to file legal proceedings a minimum of seven days prior to filing said action. (b) In any court action brought by a tenant under this section, the landlord shall bear the burden of proving that his withholding of the security deposit or any portion of it was not wrongful.

(4) Upon cessation of his interest in the dwelling unit, whether by sale, assignment, death, appointment of a receiver, or otherwise, the person in possession of the security deposit, including but not limited to the landlord, his agent, or his executor, shall, within a reasonable time: (a) Transfer the funds, or any remainder after lawful deductions under subsection (1) of this section, to the landlord's successor in interest and notify the tenant by mail of such transfer and of the transferee's name and address; or (b) Return the funds, or any remainder after lawful deductions under subsection (1) of this section, to the tenant.

(5) Upon compliance with subsection (4) of this section, the person in possession of the security deposit shall be relieved of further liability.

(6) Upon receipt of transferred funds under subsection (4)(a) of this section, the transferee, in relation to such funds, shall be deemed to have all of the rights and obligations of a landlord holding the funds as a security deposit.

(7) Any provision, whether oral or written, in or pertaining to a rental agreement whereby any provision of this section for the benefit of a tenant or members of his household is waived shall be deemed to be against public policy and shall be void.

NOTES

1. This statute is both remedial and penal. See generally Lucy Marsh Yee, *The Colorado Security Deposit Act*, 50 U. Colo. L. Rev. 29 (1978). Despite the Colorado statute's definition of "security deposit," characterization of a particular payment by a tenant can be troublesome, as demonstrated in *Mountain Queen Condominium Ass'n. v. Haan*, 753 P.2d 1234 (Colo. 1988) (holding that a reservation fee for a ski condo is not a security deposit). The American rule on attorneys' fees is that each party to a lawsuit pays its own fees and costs; the Colorado statute reverses this rule. Why? See *Martin v. Allen*, 566 P.2d 1075, 1076 (Colo. 1977) (interpreting the Colorado statute to require a landlord who wrongfully withholds a tenant's security deposit to pay the tenant's trial and appellate attorney fees). The Colorado statute does not limit the amount of money that a landlord may demand as security. Other statutes provide that the maximum amount of a security deposit is one month's rent. See, e.g., Kan. Stat. Ann. § 58-2550(a) (2009); and see Uniform Residential Landlord and Tenant Act, § 2.101(a) & comment (1974). The Colorado statute has a treble damages provision; an Ohio court interpreting an ambiguous penal, double damages provision held that only the amount wrongfully withheld should be doubled. See *Vardeman v. Llewellyn*, 476 N.E.2d 1038, 1042 (Ohio 1985). Is that holding consistent with the statutory intent? See *Sherwin v. Cabana Club Apts.*, 70 Ohio App. 2d 11, 18 (Ohio Ct. App. 1980); see also *Mau v. E.P.H. Corp.*, 638 P.2d 777, 779 (Colo. 1981); *Meyers v. Langley*, 638 N.E.2d 875 (Ind. Ct. App. 1994). In some states, statutes provide that a landlord must deposit money held as a security deposit in an interest bearing account for the tenant's benefit. See, e.g., Ohio Rev. Code § 5321.16(A) (2009); Restatement (Second) of Property § 12.1, stat. n. 6 (1977). Will this requirement make a security deposit statute more difficult to administer?

2. Disputes concerning security deposits also produce litigation concerning the landlord's commission of a deceptive trade practice. Unfair or Deceptive Trade Practice Acts are widespread, generally include landlords, and provide redress to "any person suffering an actual loss of money or property" caused by an "unfair or deceptive act in the conduct of any trade or commerce." See *Wright v. Emory*, 41 So. 3d 290 (Fla. Dist. Ct. App. 2010).

3. A tenant who anticipates a dispute about a security deposit sometimes withholds the last month's rent. A Kansas statute provides that the tenant forfeits the security deposit by doing so. See *Clark v. Walker*, 590 P.2d 1043, 1049–50 (Kan. 1979) (upholding the statute against an equal protection challenge when the forfeiture provision is included in the lease). Conversely, a landlord who anticipates a dispute about the deposit may tender to the tenant a refund check that includes language that the tenant's endorsement of the check constitutes full settlement of any dispute and evidence of the landlord's satisfaction of all statutory and contractual obligations. What problems arise in this situation? See *Anderson v. Rosebrook*, 737 P.2d 417 (Colo. 1987).

Chapter 5

LAND CONVEYANCING

I. INTRODUCTION

Land sales usually progress through four steps. First, the landowner may retain the services of a real estate agent. The owner does not have to hire an agent, but an agent can facilitate the sale by marketing the property, negotiating the sale agreement, arranging for a title examination, and providing other services related to the sale. The frequency with which sellers retain a real estate agent is evidenced by the substantially greater number of real estate agency "For Sale" signs than "For Sale by Owner" signs posted on properties.

When a buyer is found, the seller and buyer enter into a contract of sale, which is the second step in the typical real estate sale. In the contract, the seller agrees to sell the property to the buyer, and the buyer agrees to buy it. The contract normally provides that the sale will occur on a date that is one to three months in the future. The buyer needs this time, known as the executory period, to arrange for a loan, to examine the seller's title to the property, and to inspect the property's physical condition. The buyer does not want to spend the time and money for these activities unless the seller and buyer have been able to agree on a purchase price and other terms of the sale. Additionally, buyers purchasing a home may need time to sell their current home. In a well drafted contract, successful completion of each of these activities is a precondition to the buyer's obligation to purchase the property.

When the conditions in the contract of sale have been satisfied, the sale is "closed." This is the third step in the sale transaction. In some jurisdictions, it is called "settlement." At the closing, the seller conveys title to the property to the buyer by a deed, and the buyer gives the seller the consideration for the deed. In most jurisdictions, the seller and buyer are present at the same time and place for the closing. In some jurisdictions, however, the seller and buyer customarily do not meet for a closing but instead separately deliver the deed and the consideration to a third party called an "escrow agent." The escrow agent then arranges to deliver the deed to the buyer and the consideration to the seller.

Finally, in the fourth step of the transaction, the deed is recorded in the property records of the jurisdiction where the land is located. These records are maintained by the government and are open to the public. As will be described later, buyers have substantial incentives to record their deeds. But we will begin at the beginning and focus first on real estate agents. See generally Quintin Johnstone, *Land Transfers: Process and Processors*, 22 Val. U. L. Rev. 493 (1988).

II. REAL ESTATE AGENTS

A real estate agent markets another's real estate for sale or lease with an expectation of receiving compensation. This compensation is traditionally a commission computed as a percentage (often 6%) of the sale price or rent. The agent's primary services involve bringing buyers and sellers together, educating and advising them about property and the process of buying and selling it, all in order to execute a contract of sale. There is considerable reliance on agents in residential markets, where they are involved in most transactions. Agents' ancillary activities may include property appraisals, management, the sale of property and casualty insurance, and closing transactions. Before acting in this role, a person must hold a state license. Agents must be licensed for the same reasons as lawyers. Real estate sales and leasing can be complex and are important transactions for the seller and the buyer. Educational requirements are thus designed to ensure an adequate level of competence. Additionally, agents often handle money and other valuable assets belonging to other people. Therefore, the licensing process is intended to eliminate applicants who are either incompetent or untrustworthy.

States license two different classes of real estate agent — salespersons and brokers. A salesperson must complete a specified educational program and must pass an examination. A salesperson can work only under a broker's supervision and only a broker can sue for recovery of a commission. To obtain a broker's license, a person must satisfy additional educational and experience requirements. Because the definition of a real estate agent is so broad, persons such as lawyers, auctioneers, and apartment managers might be liable for unauthorized activities as a real estate agent. Therefore, many state statutes exempt people acting in these and similar capacities from the licensing requirements.

Bar associations often have accused brokers of the unauthorized practice of law. Litigation in state courts between brokerage and bar associations often center on the issue of which types of property transfer documents brokers may prepare. Often this litigation is settled by a consent decree. Under such decrees, brokers may generally fill in the blanks on standard form sales contracts. Using these forms is incidental to a broker's business. Less frequently, brokers may also prepare post-contract documents, such as mortgages, agreements that cure title defects, and deeds, but most brokers are justifiably wary of such preparing these types of documents.

A brokerage commission is set in the agency agreement employing the broker (the "listing agreement"). Three types of listing agreements are in common use. (1) In an *exclusive right to sell listing*, the employed broker is entitled to the commission even if another broker or owner finds the buyer for the listed property. (2) In an *exclusive agency listing*, the employed broker receives the commission if another broker finds the buyer, but not if the listing owner does. (3) In an *open listing*, the broker receives a commission if she finds the buyer, but not if the owner or another broker does. Thus, listings vary according to the exclusiveness of the broker's right to sell. Brokerage firms obviously prefer exclusive listings. The commission is divided between the firm obtaining the listing and the firm that finds the buyer. Within each firm, the commission is further split between participating salespersons and brokers. Some firms specialize in commercial or industrial properties.

The marketing of listed residences is enhanced by a form of cooperative enterprise among many brokers and their firms, a so-called multiple listing service (MLS). An MLS is a pooled marketing arrangement, to which participating brokers submit their listings to all other participants. Prospective buyers contacting participants thus have access to all properties listed with all participants. Listings increasingly are posted online.

The uniformity of commission rates and MLS limitations on access to listings have often attracted the attention of antitrust regulators. The ensuing litigation in both federal and state courts frequently allege conspiracies to fix commission rates, illegal price fixing, and boycotts of non-MLS brokers. Whether by agreement or tradition, uniform rates are common.

The following listing agreement is patterned on one at issue in *Stortroen v. Beneficial Finance Co.*, 736 P.2d 391 (Colo. 1987). Which type of listing agreement is it? In case of ambiguity, the agreement is construed against the agent based on the general rule of construction that a document is construed against its drafter.

> LISTING AGREEMENT: In consideration of the services of the herein-
> after named real estate broker, I hereby list with said broker, from
> _____date_____ to _____date_____ inclusive, the property described below *[handwritten: exclusive right to sell]*
> and grant said broker the exclusive and irrevocable right to (a) sell the
> same within said time at the price and on the terms herein stated, or at such
> other price and terms which may be accepted by me, (b) accept deposits
> thereon and retain same until the closing of, or termination of the
> transaction. I also authorize said broker to list the property with any
> multiple listing service in which he participates, at the broker's expense,
> and to accept the assistance and cooperation of other brokers. I hereby
> agree to pay said broker ___commission___ % of the selling price for his
> services (1) in case of any sale or exchange of same within said listing
> period by the undersigned owner, the said broker, or by any person, or (2)
> upon the said broker finding a purchaser who is ready, willing, and able to
> complete the purchase as proposed by me, or (3) in case of any such sale or
> exchange of said property within _____ days after the expiration
> of this agreement to any party with whom the said broker negotiated and
> whose name was disclosed to me by the broker during the listing period.

NOTES

1.   a. Many states require by statute or regulation that listing agreements be written. To satisfy this requirement, the agreement only has to include a description of the property, its selling price, and the seller's and agent's signatures. All other terms are measured by a reasonableness standard, including the commission rate. Of course, a well-drafted agreement will include many more terms. What else would you include?

b.   The above listing agreement authorizes the broker to list the property with a multiple listing service (MLS) and "to accept the assistance and cooperation of other brokers." Primary functions of the MLS are for brokers to pool their listings and agree to split the commission that the seller is obligated to pay. For this reason, the agent who finds the buyer (the "selling agent") usually is characterized as a subagent of the listing agent and, therefore, of the seller. As such, the selling agent owes the seller fiduciary duties of loyalty, integrity, and good faith. Do you find this characterization of the selling agent unexpected? Why do you think it is typical? Many states require agents to disclose which party they represent. Because selling agents frequently are the seller's subagent, buyers increasingly have enlisted the services of a buyer's broker, often entering into a written agency agreement that may require the buyer to pay a retainer, a commission based on a percentage of the purchase price, or an hourly rate. Frequently, however, the agency agreement provides that the buyer's broker will be compensated by sharing the listing agent's commission. See Barlow Burke, Law of Real Estate Brokers, § 2.03 (3d ed. 2007 and 2013 Supp.).

    c. The above listing agreement's last clause states that the broker is entitled to a commission if the property is sold within a specified number of days after expiration of the agreement. What is the purpose for this clause? How would you re-draft it to achieve that purpose while more carefully protecting the owner's legitimate interests?

    2. Real estate agents traditionally have been held to the same fiduciary standards as other types of agents — a duty of absolute fidelity to their principal. Is this an appropriate standard for a real estate agent? Some states authorize agents to serve as an "agent for the transaction" or as an independent contractor, rather than as an agent for the seller or the buyer. In this independent status, the agent's primary duty is to facilitate the sale. However, the agent is obligated to act in good faith with respect to the buyer and the seller and may be prohibited from revealing information that the seller or buyer wishes to keep confidential, such as the actual price at which they would be willing to contract. See, e.g., Colo. Rev. Stat. Ann. § 12-61-807 (2008). What are the advantages and disadvantages to the buyer and seller of retaining the services of an independent contractor?

BLANK v. BORDEN
524 P.2d 127 (Cal. 1974)

SULLIVAN, J.

    In the instant case we confront the question whether the familiar withdrawal-from-sale provision in an exclusive-right-to-sell contract between an owner of real property and a real estate broker exacts an unlawful penalty. . . . We conclude that it does not. * * *

    On April 26, 1970, defendant Erica Borden and plaintiff Ben Blank, a real estate broker, entered into a written agreement for the purpose of securing a purchaser for defendant's weekend home in Palm Springs. The agreement, a printed form contract drafted by the California Real Estate Association, was entitled "Exclusive Authorization and Right to Sell" and by its terms granted Blank the exclusive and irrevocable right to sell the property for the seven-month period extending from the date of the agreement to November 25, 1970. It further provided that if the property were sold during the said period the agent would receive 6 percent of the selling price, and that "if said property is withdrawn from sale, transferred, conveyed, leased without the consent of Agent, or made unmarketable by [the owner's] voluntary act during the term hereof or any extension thereof," the agent would receive 6 percent of the "price for the property" stated elsewhere in the agreement. Relevant portions of the agreement are

Exclusive Authorization and Right to Sell

California Real Estate Association Standard Form

(1) Right to Sell. I hereby employ and grant Ben Blank Company, hereinafter called 'Agent,' the exclusive and irrevocable right to sell or exchange [the described real property]. . . .

(2) Term. Agent's right to sell shall commence on April 26, 1970 and expire at midnight on November 25, 1970.

(3) Terms of Sale. (a) The price for the property shall be the sum of $85,000.00. . . .

(4) Compensation to Agent. I hereby agree to compensate Agent as follows: (a) Six% of the selling price if the property, is sold during the term hereof, or any extension thereof, by Agent, on the terms herein set forth or any other price and terms I may accept, or through any other person, or by me, or six% of the price shown in 3(a), if said property is withdrawn from sale, transferred, conveyed, leased without the consent of Agent, or made unmarketable by my voluntary act during the term hereof or any extension thereof. * * *

(5) If action be instituted on this agreement to collect compensation or commissions, I agree to pay such sum as the Court may fix as reasonable attorney's fees. * * *

Dated: April 26, 1970.

[signature] "Erica Borden," Owner, Palm Springs, California.

In consideration of the execution of the foregoing, the undersigned Agent agrees to be diligent in endeavoring to obtain a purchaser. BEN BLANK CO., Agent, By [signature] "Ben Blank"

The findings of the trial court describe subsequent events in the following terms: "Plaintiff at once began a diligent effort to obtain a purchaser for said property, including but not limited to the expenditures of monies for advertisements in the newspaper, but on or about June 26, 1970, while said exclusive sales contract was still in effect and while plaintiff was making a diligent effort to obtain a purchaser, defendant, without reason or justification, orally notified plaintiff that the property was no longer for sale and that he had no further right to make efforts to sell same or collect a commission, all in direct violation of said exclusive sales contract."

Determining that the foregoing constituted a withdrawal from sale within the terms of the agreement, the trial court concluded that plaintiff Blank was entitled to compensation according to the agreement's provisions. Accordingly it rendered judgment in favor of plaintiff Blank in the amount of $5,100 (6 percent of $85,000) plus interest. Defendant has appealed.

At the outset we quickly dispose of two contentions relating to the substantiality of the evidence in support of the findings of the trial court which we have quoted above. First, it is contended that there was no support for the finding that plaintiff was making a diligent effort to find a purchaser for the property when it was withdrawn from the market; this, it is urged, resulted in a failure of consideration. Suffice it to say that although the record contains evidence which might support a contrary finding, it also contains substantial evidence in support of the finding made by the trial court concerning plaintiff's diligence. There is evidence in the record that plaintiff contacted several parties — members of the country club on whose golf course the property fronted as well as other persons — with respect to the property, and that he ran newspaper advertisements concerning the property during the two months which preceded defendant's withdrawal of the property. The fact that plaintiff had produced no offers prior to the withdrawal of the property from the market of course does not in itself compel a finding that he was not making diligent efforts to find a purchaser.

Second, it is contended that the finding concerning defendant's withdrawal of the property from the market lacks substantial support. Again, however, our examination of the record discloses ample evidence to support the finding. The withdrawal occurred in the course of an argument which took place at the property between plaintiff and defendant's then fiancee, Dr. Archer Michael. Defendant was also present at the time. When Dr. Michael, after making statements which might reasonably be construed as threats of physical violence, told plaintiff to take his sign off the property and leave because his services were no longer wanted, plaintiff asked defendant whether she concurred. She replied that she did, and plaintiff departed. It was only after receiving a letter from plaintiff's attorney demanding payment pursuant to the contract that she attempted to soften her position and requested that plaintiff continue his efforts to sell the property. It was wholly within the province of the trial court, as finder of fact, to determine that the withdrawal was complete and unequivocal when made and that defendant's subsequent efforts through counsel to recant were ineffective and irrelevant.

* * * It has long been the law of this state that any right to compensation asserted by a real estate broker must be found within the four corners of his employment contract. (*Crane v. McCormick*, 92 Cal. 176, 182, 28 P. 222 (1891) (further citations omitted). By the same token, however, "[the] parties to a broker's contract for the sale of real property are at liberty to make the compensation depend upon any lawful conditions they see fit to place therein." (*Leonard v. Fallas*, 51 Cal. 2d 649, 652, 335 P.2d 665 (1959).) In short it is the contract which governs the agent's compensation, and that contract is strictly enforced according to its lawful terms. It is equally well settled in this state that a withdrawal-from-sale clause in an exclusive-right-to-sell contract is lawful and enforceable, a claim for compensation under such a clause being not a claim for damages for breach of that contract but a claim of indebtedness under its specific terms. (*Maze v. Gordon*, 96 Cal. 61, 66–67, 30 P. 962 (1892) (further citations omitted).

Defendant contends, however . . . that such clauses should be denied enforcement as an unlawful penalty under the terms of Civil Code sections 1670 and 1671. The same argument was urged upon the court in *Baumgartner v. Meek*, 126 Cal. App. 2d 505, 30 P. 962 (1954), and was rejected in the following language: "We think this contention cannot be sustained in view of the contrary holdings in the cases referred to [i.e., *Kimmell v. Skelly*, 62 P. 1067 (1900)] (further citations omitted). The distinction between an action for breach of the promise by the owner not to revoke or deal through others or sell himself during the stipulated term, wherein damages are sought for such breach, and a contractual provision whereby, in consideration of the services of the broker to be and being rendered, the owner directly promises that if he sells through others or by himself or revokes he will pay a sum certain, is made clear in the cited cases, particularly in the quotations we have taken from the opinion in *Kimmell v. Skelly*. The action is for money owed, an action in debt, and the only breach involved is the failure to pay the promised sum." (126 Cal. App. 2d at 512.)

We agree with the *Baumgartner* court that the withdrawal-from-sale clause in an exclusive-right-to-sell contract does not constitute a void penalty provision. In reaching this conclusion we are not unmindful of the teaching of our recent decision in *Garrett v. Coast & Southern Fed. Sav. & Loan Ass'n*, 9 Cal. 3d 735, 11 P.2d 1197 (1973), wherein we emphasized that we look to substance rather than form in determining the "true function and character" of arrangements which are challenged on this ground. (*Id.* at 735–737.) As we there stated, "when it is manifest that a contract expressed to be performed in the alternative is in fact a contract contemplating but a single, definite performance with an additional charge contingent on the breach of that performance, the provision cannot escape examination in light of pertinent rules relative to the liquidation of damages." (*Id.* at 738.) Here, however, we do not find that the contract before us is of the indicated character. Its terms in no sense contemplate a "default" or "breach" of an obligation by the owner upon whose occurrence payment is to be made. On the contrary, the clause in question presents the owner with a true option or alternative: if, during the term of an exclusive-right-to-sell contract, the owner changes his mind and decides that he does not wish to sell the subject property after all, he retains the power to terminate the agent's otherwise exclusive right through the payment of a sum certain set forth in the contract.

We do not see in this arrangement the invidious qualities characteristic of a penalty or forfeiture. As indicated above, what distinguishes the instant case from other situations in which a form of alternative performance is used to mask what is in reality a penalty or forfeiture is the element of rational choice. For an example by way of contrast we need look no further than the *Garrett* case itself. There the contract, a promissory note secured by a deed of trust on real property, provided for the assessment of certain "late charges" for failure to make timely installment payments on the note — such charges to be a percentage of the unpaid principal balance for the period during which payment was in default. We held that these charges, which did not qualify as proper liquidated damages pursuant to Civil Code section 1671, constituted illegal penalties. In characterizing the subject provision we observed that its "only reasonable interpretation . . . is that the parties agreed upon the rate which should govern the contract and then, realizing that the borrowers might fail to make timely payment, they further agreed that such borrowers were to pay an additional sum as damages for their breach[,] which sum was determined by applying the increased rate to the entire unpaid principal balance." (*Id.* at 738.) Clearly this arrangement, viewed from the time of making the contract, realistically contemplates no element of free rational choice on the part of the obligor insofar as his performance is concerned; rather the agreement is founded upon the assumption that the obligor will make the lower payment. In these circumstances, as an eminent commentator has observed, "the only purpose and effect of the formal alternative is to hold over [the obligor] the larger liability as a threat to induce prompt payment of the lesser sum." (McCormick, *Damages* § 154, p. 618 (1935).)

In the instant case, on the other hand, the contract clearly reserves to the owner the power to make a realistic and rational choice in the future with respect to the subject matter of the contract. Rather than allowing the broker to proceed with his efforts to sell the property, the owner, in the event that at any time during the term of the contract he changes his mind and decides not to sell after all, may withdraw the property from the market upon payment of a sum certain. In these circumstances the contract is truly one which contemplates alternative performance, not one in which the formal alternative conceals a penalty for failure to perform the main promise.[7]

Further considerations support our determination that the contractual provision here at issue should be enforced according to its terms. First, it is important to recognize that we are not here concerned with a situation wherein the party who seeks to enforce the clause enjoyed a vastly superior bargaining position at the time the contract was entered into. On the contrary, the contract before us was one which was freely negotiated by parties dealing at arm's length. While contracts having characteristics of adhesion must be carefully scrutinized in order to insure that provisions therein which speak in terms of alternative performance but in fact exact a penalty are not enforced . . . , we believe that in circumstances such as those before us interference with party autonomy is less justified. . . .

Moreover, it must be emphasized that the basic contract before us shares with other purely "commission" contracts the quality of being essentially result-oriented. Regardless of the amount of effort expended by the broker under such a contract,

---

[7] The distinction we make here is discussed by McCormick in the following terms: "[In] . . . an alternative contract the promise to pay may be a penalty, and void as such. If a contract provides that A will either convey land then worth about $10,000 within six months at a price of $10,000 or will pay $250, it is quite clear that a reasonable man might look forward to either choice as a reasonable possibility, and there is no reason for hesitating to enforce the promise to pay if the land is not conveyed. If, on the other hand, A's promise provides that he shall either pay $100 on January 1st or $200 on demand thereafter, a different situation is presented. No reasonable man would, when the contract was made, consider that there was any rational choice involved (conceding the ability to pay either sum) in determining which course to pursue. If he can do so, he will pay the lesser sum, and the agreement necessarily is founded on this assumption, and the only purpose and effect of the formal alternative is to hold over him the larger liability as a threat to induce prompt payment of the lesser sum. Consequently, while an alternative promise to pay money when it presents a conceivable choice is valid, yet, if a contract is made by which a party engages himself either to do a certain act or to pay some amount which at the time of the contract no one would have considered an eligible alternative, the alternative promise to pay is unenforceable as a penalty." (McCormick, *Damages, supra,* § 154, pp. 617–618.)

he is entitled to no compensation at all unless a sale occurs. By the same token, when a sale is effected, the compensation received is a percentage of the sale price-and this is paid regardless of the amount of effort which has been expended by the broker. If in this context we view the owner's exercise of a withdrawal-from-sale clause as an anticipatory "breach" of the main contract, the "damage" sustained by the broker would not be measured in the amount of effort expended by him prior to the "breach" but rather would be measured in terms of the value of the lost opportunity to effect a sale and thereby receive compensation. (Citations omitted.) The determination of this value would clearly degenerate into an examination of fictional probabilities — e.g., whether the broker, if allowed to continue his efforts for the full term of the contract, would have been successful in locating a buyer and effecting a sale. This consideration further strengthens our conviction that in these circumstances the contract of the parties, entered into in a context of negotiation and at arm's length, should govern their rights and duties.

For the foregoing reasons we hold that the withdrawal-from-sale clause in an exclusive-right-to-sell real estate contract, long a part of real estate marketing practice in this state and long held to be valid and enforceable according to its terms, does not exact an unlawful penalty in violation of sections 1670–1671 of the Civil Code. The judgment below, which enforced the clause before us upon a showing that the explicitly stated conditions for its enforcement were present, was fully supported by the evidence and correct in all respects. The judgment is affirmed.

BURKE, J. I dissent.

The majority never reach the question whether the commission-on-withdrawal clause in the instant case was an invalid penalty clause or an enforceable liquidated damages clause. (See Civ. Code, §§ 1670, 1671.) Instead, the majority neatly sidestep this issue by labeling the brokerage contract as one contemplating an "alternative performance" by the owner in the event he exercises his "true option" to withdraw the property from sale. To the contrary, the issue in this case cannot be avoided by the facile use of labels — otherwise any illegal penalty could be disguised as a "true option" by the promisor to pay a substantial sum for the privilege of breaking his contract. When we examine the essential nature of the exclusive brokerage contract, it becomes patently obvious that defendant promised to afford plaintiff broker the exclusive and irrevocable right to sell the property during a specified period, that defendant breached that promise by withdrawing the property from sale, that the contract itself specifies the damages for that breach, and that accordingly we must determine whether or not the damage provision was a penalty or liquidated damages provision. * * *

Nowhere in the contract is any mention made of any "option" given to defendant to withdraw the property from sale. Instead, the language of the contract makes it apparent that a withdrawal of the property without the broker's consent would constitute a breach of the owner's promise to grant an irrevocable right to sell the property during the specified period. Indeed, it seems wholly naive to assume, as the majority do, that a property owner would have bargained for the "option" of withdrawing the property from sale, given the consequences of exercising that option, namely, the payment of the full commission which would have been payable to the broker had he sold the property for the original $85,000 asking price. * * * The specified damages could, of course, approximate actual damages in a situation in which the broker had negotiated a sale of the property at the original asking price, for in that situation the broker's actual loss would be the commission he otherwise would have earned. But the commission-upon-withdrawal clause purports to require payment of the full commission whether or not a sale had been arranged. In that regard, the clause seemingly could not represent a reasonable effort to estimate the fair average compensation. . . . * * *At trial . . . plaintiff described the nature of his services, but he made no attempt to prove by expert testimony or otherwise, the reasonable value thereof, and the trial court made no finding on that issue. I would reverse the judgment.

NOTES

1.   Why do brokers insert withdrawal from sale clauses in exclusive right to sell listings? If there were no such clause in the listing and the listing owner withdraws, how should the broker be compensated?

2.   In most states, absent an agreement to the contrary, a broker is entitled to receive a commission when a buyer who is ready, willing, and able to purchase the listed property on the seller's terms is found. See Barlow Burke, Law of Real Estate Brokers § 5.02 (3d ed. 2007 and 2013 Supp.). Under the majority rule, the broker is entitled to a commission when the seller and buyer execute a contract of sale. The rule applies even if the sale does not close. In some states, as in the following case, the rule is otherwise.

CORNETT v. NATHAN
242 N.W.2d 855 (Neb. 1976)

WHITE, J.

This is an action for the collection of a real estate commission allegedly due the plaintiff, a real estate broker, from the defendants. The District Court granted summary judgment to the defendants. We affirm the judgment of the District Court.

The plaintiff, a licensed real estate broker, entered into a listing agreement with the defendants, who desired to sell certain realty. The defendants promised to pay the plaintiff a 7 percent commission for his services, and the defendants listed their property for $349,700. The plaintiff presented the defendants with a potential buyer who offered the defendants $251,680 for the property. The defendants accepted the offer and entered into a purchase agreement which, among other things, provided that in the event the buyer failed to complete the sale, the $5,000 in earnest money was to be considered liquidated damages. The purchase agreement also provided that the plaintiff would get a commission of $17,617.60. After the signing of the purchase agreement, but before the sale was consummated, the buyer refused to honor the purchase agreement because he was financially unable to do so. The defendants' property was not sold, but the plaintiff still demanded his $17,617.60

commission. This placed the defendants in the position where they were entitled to only $5,000 in damages from the buyer, but owed the plaintiff over $17,000 in commission. Thus, the defendants would lose over $12,000 and still be in the same position as they were before the plaintiff presented the buyer.

Both the plaintiff and the defendants moved for summary judgment, and the District Court granted the defendants' motion. The District Court held that it was not the intent of the defendants when they signed the listing agreement and the purchase agreement to be bound to pay a commission if the sale was never consummated.

The thrust of the plaintiff's contention is that a real estate broker is entitled to his commission under the purchase agreement, such as is present in this case, at the moment that the seller and the buyer, procured by the broker, enter into a purchase agreement, regardless of whether the sale is ever consummated.

This court has consistently held that a broker has not earned his commission unless he produces a buyer who is ready, able, and willing to buy on terms satisfactory to the seller. In *Wisnieski v. Coufal*, 195 N.W.2d 750 (Neb. 1972), we said: "A broker earns his commission and becomes entitled thereto when he produces a purchaser who is ready, able, and willing to purchase at a price and upon terms specified by the principal or satisfactory to him." In *Huston Co. v. Mooney*, 207 N.W.2d 525 (Neb. 1973), this court said: "Ordinarily a real estate broker, who for a commission undertakes to sell land on certain terms and within a specified period, is not entitled to compensation for his services unless he produces a purchaser within the time limited who is ready, able, and willing to buy upon the terms prescribed."

The precise question in the case is whether a purchaser who signs a purchase agreement and later backs out because of financial inability to consummate the purchase can be said to be a purchaser who is ready, able, and willing to buy. In this case, it is undisputed that the buyer was financially unable to consummate the sale. We fail to see how it can be argued that the broker produced a buyer who was "ready" and "able" to buy when he was financially unable to pay or consummate the sale at the agreed performance date of the contract to purchase. Although our holdings are clear in *Wisnieski* and *Huston Co.*, *supra*, we reexamine briefly the considerations behind those holdings. Looking to the intent of the parties in a common listing agreement, such as this is, it is clear that sellers of real estate expect to pay a commission only if the sale is completed. The very essence of the intent of the parties and the reason for the payment of substantial commission fees is the difficult task of the real estate broker producing not just a person who will sign a contract on hopes and expectation, but one who is able to pay, ready to pay, and willing to pay. Almost without exception, the only source capable of paying the commission is the proceeds from the sale of the property. A holding which would require sellers of real estate to be liable for a commission when the broker's purchaser is unable to perform would not only be contrary to the intent of the parties, as we have held, but would throw agreements for commissions on sales of real property open to confusion and possible abuse.

The position advocated by the plaintiff broker would place an almost impossible burden on the seller. The broker is employed because of his peculiar expertise. The rule advocated by the plaintiff would not only place the difficult task of determining the financial ability of the buyer on the seller, but would require that such an investigation be made prior to the time that he entered into the purchase agreement. It would require the seller to perform a function which is probably the most important reason for obligating himself to pay the broker a substantial commission fee. We point out further that many real estate transactions, as was the transaction in this case, are made between distant parties who never actually meet face-to-face. To require a seller to check the financial status of a potential buyer who might live thousands of miles away would be totally unrealistic. In a jurisprudential sense, the only realistic answer is to place this burden and the risk involved on the broker who is hired for this specific purpose. . . .

No previous Nebraska cases deal with the precise fact situation in the case at hand. However, in cases which are directly on point, courts in other jurisdictions have come to the same conclusion as we have. In *Ellsworth Dobbs, Inc. v. Johnson*, 236 A.2d 843 (N.J. 1967), the New Jersey Supreme Court held that when a prospective buyer is financially unable to complete a purchase agreement, the broker is not entitled to his commission. "When a broker is engaged by an owner of property to find a purchaser for it, the broker earns his commission when (a) he produces a purchaser ready, willing and able to buy on the terms fixed by the owner, (b) the purchaser enters into a binding contract with the owner to do so, and (c) the purchaser completes the transaction by closing the title in accordance with the provisions of the contract. If the contract is not consummated because of lack of financial ability of the buyer to perform, there is no right to commission against the seller." The New Jersey Supreme Court even went so far as to say that a provision in a listing agreement to the contrary would be "so contrary to common fairness, as to require a court to condemn it as unconscionable." * * *

The judgment of the District Court is correct and is affirmed.

NOTES

1. The *Cornett* court's quotation of the no closing/no commission rule from *Ellsworth Dobbs, Inc. v. Johnson*, 236 A.2d 843, 855 (N.J. 1967), continued: "On the other hand, if the failure of completion of the contract results from the wrongful act or interference of the seller, the broker's claim is valid and must be paid." The *Ellsworth Dobbs* rule has been adopted in about a dozen states. See, e.g., *Margaret H. Wayne Trust v. Lipsky*, 846 P.2d 904 (Idaho 1993). Why do brokers prefer the majority rule that an agent's commission right vests when the seller and buyer enter into a binding purchase agreement? If you represented a seller in a jurisdiction that follows the majority rule, what precautions would you advise the seller to take when entering into a listing agreement and when entering into a contract of sale with a buyer?

2. Can a buyer be liable to a broker for compensation even if the broker is the seller's agent? The court in *Ellsworth Dobbs, Inc. v. Johnson*, 236 A.2d 843, 859–60 (N.J. 1967) stated: "[T]here is substantial authority elsewhere to the effect that a real estate broker may sue a purchaser who refuses to carry out his contract with the vendor, even though the broker has agreed to look to the vendor for his commission." The court also quoted 12 C.J.S. Brokers § 82 (1938): "[W]here a broker is employed by the owner of property to sell the same, the purchaser is not liable for the broker's commissions, unless he has agreed to pay them or is liable therefor by way of damages for failing or refusing to carry out his contract, or for some other wrongful act or omission which interferes with the broker's right to recover commissions from his principal."

3.   States not only license real estate agents, but also regulate their conduct after they are licensed. Some regulations are open-ended, providing for suspension or revocation of the licenses of agents who have "demonstrated unworthiness or incompetency." Other requirements are more specific. For example, state law may detail how an agent must handle and account for funds being held in connection with a property sale. An agent who violates the regulatory requirements faces a variety of potential sanctions, ranging from a fine or reprimand to license revocation. Real estate agents also can be liable for violations of the federal Fair Housing Act, 42 U.S.C. §§ 3601–3619. Section 3604 of the Fair Housing Act makes it illegal:

(a) To refuse to sell or rent after the making of a bona fide offer, or to refuse to negotiate for the sale or rental of, or otherwise make unavailable or deny, a dwelling to any person because of race, color, religion, sex, familial status, or national origin.

(b) To discriminate against any person in the terms, conditions, or privileges of sale or rental of a dwelling, or in the provision of services or facilities in connection therewith, because of race, color, religion, sex, familial status, or national origin.

(c) To make, print, or publish, or cause to be made, printed, or published any notice, statement, or advertisement, with respect to the sale or rental of a dwelling that indicates any preference, limitation, or discrimination based on race, color, religion, sex, handicap, familial status, or national origin, or an intention to make any such preference, limitation, or discrimination.

(d) To represent to any person because of race, color, religion, sex, handicap, familial status, or national origin that any dwelling is not available for inspection, sale, or rental when such dwelling is in fact so available.

(e) For profit, to induce or attempt to induce any person to sell or rent any dwelling by representations regarding the entry or prospective entry into the neighborhood of a person or persons of a particular race, color, religion, sex, handicap, familial status, or national origin.

(f)(1) To discriminate in the sale or rental, or to otherwise make unavailable or deny, a dwelling to any buyer or renter because of a handicap of —

(A) that buyer or renter;

(B) a person residing in or intending to reside in that dwelling after it is so sold, rented, or made available; or

(C) any person associated with that buyer or renter.

(2) To discriminate against any person in the terms, conditions, or privileges of sale or rental of a dwelling, or in the provision of services or facilities in connection such dwelling, because of a handicap . . . .

These provisions of § 3604 apply to all participants in the real estate market, including real estate agents, lenders, and title insurers. The Act also includes provisions that focus directly on real estate agents. It prohibits agents from discriminating against members of protected classes when providing selling or brokering services, § 3605(a), and when granting access to or participation in an MLS, real estate broker's organization, or other service relating to real estate sales. § 3606. Two activities by agents clearly violate the Act: (1) "steering" (an agent's efforts to direct potential buyers toward or away from certain neighborhoods based on an impermissible criterion, such as race) violates § 3604(a) and (2) "blockbusting" (an agent's attempts to induce home owners to sell by representing that members of a protected class either have or may move into the neighborhood) violates § 3604(e).

The Fair Housing Act contains a few exceptions. For example, § 3604 does not apply to an owner-occupied dwelling with separate living quarters for up to three additional families living independently of each other. § 3603(b)(2). Housing that is restricted to older persons also is permitted despite the Act's ban on discrimination based on "familial status" (discrimination against children under the age of eighteen). § 3607(b). Religious organizations and private clubs also may limit housing they operate to members of that organization or club. § 3607(a).

A number of state and local governments have enacted legislation to supplement the Fair Housing Act. Many of these laws expand the number of statutorily protected classes of people. For example, Minnesota prohibits discrimination based on marital status, status with regard to public assistance, and sexual orientation may be included, as well as discrimination based on the criteria in the federal Act. See, e.g., Minn. Stat. Ann. § 363A.09, subd. 1. Other state and local laws eliminate exceptions contained in the federal Act.

III. CONTRACTS OF SALE

The execution of a contract of sale for the purchase and sale of real property starts what is typically called the executory period; that is, the time before the "closing" or "settlement" of the transaction when the seller conveys the property to the buyer, and the buyer gives the seller the purchase price. During the executory period, the buyer prepares for the sale by arranging for the necessary financing. The buyer also investigates the property during the executory period. For example, the buyer will investigate matters such as the seller's title to the property (the "title search"), the property's physical condition, and the applicable zoning. The buyer does not want to invest the time and money to perform these investigations without knowing whether an agreement can be reached with the seller on the purchase price and other terms of the sale. In the contract of sale, the buyer will condition the obligation to purchase on a satisfactory outcome to these investigations.

To obtain financing for the purchase, the buyer normally files a loan application with a bank or other lender. As part of the lender's process for reviewing the application, it will obtain an appraisal of the property's value and a credit report on the buyer. The lender often will require the buyer to pay a loan origination fee, discount points, interest for the period before the first loan payment, and a premium for mortgage insurance to assure the lender repayment of the first 10–20% of the mortgage loan. Additionally, the lender may require the buyer to escrow money with the lender for property tax payments and hazard insurance premiums.

A. The Statute of Frauds

The Statute of Frauds* in every state requires that contracts of sale for real property be in writing. Under the usual state statute, no action can be brought to enforce a contract of sale unless the contract or some memorandum of it is in writing and is signed by the party to be charged or by that party's agent. A second provision of the Statute of Frauds also may apply to a contract of sale: a contract that will not be closed within one year also must be in writing and signed to be enforceable.

The writing requirement can be satisfied in one of two ways. The writing either must (1) specify the parties to the transaction, the legal description of the property, and the consideration (known collectively as the "essential terms" of the transaction) or (2) include all the material terms of the transaction. It does not matter whether the parties execute a more formal contract later or that the writing does not include all the material terms. Although requiring the inclusion of all material terms might be preferable as a means of encouraging parties to memorialize and provide evidence of their agreements, limiting the Statute's reach to a few essential terms makes it easier to enforce and avoids tempting one of the parties to assert later that a term was material but was not included.

The rationale for the Statute of Frauds has been variously stated. The rationale is sometimes described as the prevention of fraud. Others describe the rationale as preventing a person from fabricating a contract when none exists. If the former is the purpose, then the Statute itself cannot be used to effect a fraud, even though all essential or material terms are included in the writing. Therefore, a person who acts fraudulently may be estopped from enforcing the contract. On the other hand, when the latter rationale is used, the Statute is treated as an evidentiary device that establishes the standard for determining the admissibility of a contract into evidence.

In jurisdictions that require all the material terms to be in writing, an interesting and complicated relationship exists between the Statute of Frauds and the Parol Evidence Rule. Under the Rule, oral terms and conditions made before execution of the written contract that contradict its express terms and conditions are inadmissible. On the other hand, if the contract is silent on a matter, it can be reformed using the Parol Evidence Rule in order to fulfill the requirements of the

---

* The original English Statute of Frauds § 4 (1677), which is the model for modern American state statutes, provided: "No action shall be brought upon any contract for the sale of lands or any interest in them . . . unless the agreement upon which such action is brought . . . shall be in writing and signed by the party to be charged. . . ."

Statute of Frauds. However, contract reformation is limited to those instances in which fraud or mutual mistake was involved in the drafting and execution of the contract.

One exception to the Statute of Frauds is the doctrine of part performance. When a buyer pays consideration for the land and takes possession of it or improves it, those actions constitute an adequate substitute for a writing. Although all courts require that the buyer have paid at least some consideration, payment alone is never sufficient to satisfy the doctrine of part performance. Instead, most courts also require possession. Some go further and require that the buyer improve the land, as well as take possession of it. Thus, the majority of courts require that the buyer pay all or part of the consideration and take possession of the property before permitting the doctrine of part performance to eliminate the necessity for a writing.

A less used, second exception is based on promissory or equitable estoppel and requires reliance and a change of position, resulting in a financial detriment. A buyer may rely on a seller's promise to sell and make costly plans to improve the land, or a seller may rely on a promise to buy and reject other offers. In any event, estoppel is used sparingly — only for those cases in which it would be unjust not to use it. See *Baililes v. Cities Service Co.*, 578 S.W.2d 621 (Tenn. 1979).

In a few states, a third exception exists for admissions of a contract in pleadings, testimony, or other court proceedings where judicial supervision eliminates the uncertainty and possibility of fraud. See *Smith v. Boyd*, 553 A.2d 131 (R.I. 1989).

check case.

CASH v. MADDOX
220 S.E.2d 121 (S.C. 1975)

Need definite location!

NESS, J.

John and Sue Maddox allegedly contracted to sell Morris and Betty Cash 15 acres of land. The trial court held there was a binding contract and ordered specific performance. The Maddoxes, appellants, contend the memorandum of the alleged contract of sale is too vague and indefinite to satisfy the Statute of Frauds. We agree and reverse the lower court.

Appellants and respondents are husband and wife respectively. The Cashes lived in Florida. They telephoned the Maddoxes who lived in Georgia, and discussed the purchase of 15 acres of land owned by the Maddoxes. The only written evidence of the contract is a check mailed by the Cashes for Two Hundred ($200.00) Dollars as part payment. Written on the check was "15 acres in Pickens, S.C., land binder, 30 days from date of check to June 3, 1970." John Maddox endorsed and cashed the check. Subsequently, the Maddoxes advised the Cashes they did not wish to sell as it would cause trouble in the family and returned the Two Hundred ($200.00) Dollars which the Cashes refused. There was testimony the Maddoxes owned a 76 acre tract of land in Pickens County, of which 15.6 acres was south of the Pickens-Greenville highway, outside of the city limits of the town of Pickens.

The Statute of Frauds does not require any particular form of writing. It may be satisfied entirely by a written correspondence. *Speed v. Speed*, 49 S.E.2d 588 (S.C. 1948). However, the writings must establish the essential terms of the contract without resort to parol evidence. . . . One of the essential terms of a contract of sale of land is the identification of the land. A decree for specific performance operates as a deed. . . . Hence, the land must be described so as to indicate with reasonable certainty what is to be conveyed. . . . Parol evidence cannot be relied upon to supplement a vague and uncertain description. . . .

The burden of proof was upon the respondents to establish the contract " 'by competent and satisfactory proof, such as is clear, definite, and certain.' . . . 'The degree of certainty required is reasonable certainty, having regard to the subject-matter of the contract.' " *Aust v. Beard*, 96 S.E.2d 558, 561 (S.C. 1957).

For a contract to meet the requirements of the Statute of Frauds, S.C. Code § 11-101, every essential element of the sale must be expressed therein.

The alleged contract gives no definite location or shape of the 15 acres. The writing does not indicate whether the subject matter of the contract was north or south of the road, or in another area of the county. The fact 15.6 acres of the entire tract may be south of the road is not legally sufficient to satisfy the Statute of Frauds. Parol evidence may be used to explain terms appearing in the description, but the description itself must clearly identify the particular parcel of land.

In the absence of equities removing the case from the operation of the Statute of Frauds, which do not here exist, we hold before a court will decree specific performance of a contract for a sale of land, the writing must contain the essential terms of the contract. They must be expressed with such definiteness, certainty and clarity that it may be understood without recourse to parol evidence to show the intention of the parties. The terms of the contract must be such that neither party can reasonably misunderstand them. It would be inequitable to carry a contract into effect where the court is left to ascertain the intention of the parties by mere guess and conjecture.

The respondents' reliance upon *Speed v. Speed* is misplaced. The case specifically states, "the writings relied upon must *in and of themselves* furnish the evidence that the minds of the parties met as to the particular property which the one proposed to sell and the other agreed to buy; and, when such evidence is not found in the writings, it cannot be supplied by parol." 49 S.E.2d at 592.

There was not a contract between these parties as would satisfy the Statute of Frauds. The land proposed to be sold was not described or designated as would enable a court to render a decree for its conveyance. The words in the check afford no means to adequately identify the property. The parties should be restored to their original status. Reversed.

NOTE

While the contract is executory on both sides, who is the "party to be charged" under the Statute of Frauds? After a vendor conveys the title but before the purchaser has paid part of the purchase price, may the purchaser use the Statute's requirement that the contract state the essential agreement's terms to defend against the vendor's suit for the unpaid price? When can those essential terms be supplied by a document other than the contract, such as the listing agreement executed by a vendor? Does an agreement to extend the time for performance have to satisfy the Statute? See *Empire Properties, Inc. v. Equireal, Inc.*, 674 A.2d 297 (Pa. Super. Ct. 1996) (permitting a purchaser bringing a suit for damages to prove the existence of an oral extension agreement).

B. Equitable Conversion

In approximately thirty-two states, the common law doctrine of equitable conversion applies as soon as the seller and buyer execute a contract of sale. Unless the contract expressly provides otherwise, the doctrine creates an equitable interest in the property in the buyer. In contrast, the seller is treated as merely holding legal title to the land in trust for the buyer. The buyer's interest in the land is characterized as a real property, and the seller's interest is characterized as personal property. In essence, the buyer becomes the property's equitable owner, and the seller holds title simply as security for the payment of the purchase price. The doctrine becomes fully effective when all the contingencies in the contract are removed or are satisfied in some way. In the case of a contract requirement that the seller furnish a marketable title, the requirement is satisfied for purposes of the doctrine of equitable conversion when the seller in fact has that title.

This doctrine has at least two primary functions. First, it settles probate and intestate disputes when one of the parties to the contract dies during the executory period. See *Paine v. Meller*, 31 Eng. Rep. 1088 (Ch. 1801).

For example, if the buyer dies during the executory period, the devisee of his real property takes his interest in the contract, free of any personal debts, absent evidence that the buyer intended some other result. When the contract is performed, the devisee will have full ownership rights in the property. On the other hand, if the seller dies, the legatee of his personalty is entitled to the sale proceeds absent evidence of a contrary intent by the seller. If a similar dispute involves intestate property, the results would be the same by operation of law. In this case, the decedent's intent is irrelevant; the property distribution is governed solely by the terms of the intestate succession statutes.

In a majority of states, the second function of the doctrine of equitable conversion is to transfer the risk of loss to the property to the buyer. If the property is damaged by fire or other casualty, the risk of loss falls on the buyer unless the vendor caused the damage, and the buyer is legally obligated to complete the contract at the specified contract price. Similarly, if the land is adversely affected by a change of the zoning or by an exercise of eminent domain, the loss falls on the buyer.

In a minority of states, the risk of loss stays with the vendor, and the contract is annulled when the loss is material. See *Skelly Oil Co. v. Ashmore*, 365 S.W.2d 582 (Mo. 1963); *Libman v. Levenson*, 128 N.E. 13 (Mass. 1920). The theory in these states is that the contract is invalidated because performance is impossible due to the destruction of its subject matter or because the contract is subject to an implied condition that the property will be transferred in substantially the same condition as when the contract was executed. Additionally, 12 states have enacted the Uniform Vendor and Purchaser Risk Act, which generally allocates the risk of loss to the party who has the legal title or is in possession of the property. The Act is reprinted in this chapter after the next case.

The majority rule on the risk of loss may surprise many buyers. They do not realize that they should obtain hazard insurance on the property as soon as the contract is signed. To avoid this unexpected result, a well-drafted contract of sale includes provisions concerning the parties' rights and liabilities in case of a casualty loss, change in zoning, exercise of eminent domain, or other injury to the property during the contract's executory period.

water damage case

BRYANT v. WILLISON REAL ESTATE CO.
350 S.E.2d 748 (W. Va. 1986)

Contract explicitly said risk would remain on seller, which trumps equitable conversion.

MILLER, C.J.

James L. Bryant and James E. Bland, the plaintiffs who were purchasers under a real estate sales contract, appeal from a judgment of the Circuit Court of Harrison County denying their claim for rescission of the contract and permitting the defendants/vendors to retain their down payment. The trial court also awarded damages against the purchasers for property loss suffered by third parties as a result of water flowing from a broken water line into two adjacent businesses.

This case was heard by the trial court judge without a jury by agreement of the parties. The facts are that on January 4, 1980, the plaintiffs entered into a contract to purchase the O.J. Morrison Building in Clarksburg for $175,000. As required by the sales contract, they paid $10,000 to Willison Real Estate Company, the agent for the vendors, at the time the contract was signed. The balance was to be paid upon delivery of the deed, at which time the purchasers would take possession of the property. No date was set for the closing.

On February 18, 1980, before the delivery of the deed, a water line broke in the sprinkler system, permitting water to run throughout the building and into two adjoining businesses. The purchasers had planned to extensively renovate the building for use as a medical office building. The purchasers were informed by an architect and an engineer who inspected the damage that the remodeling of the Morrison Building could be delayed by as much as four to six weeks because the building had to be properly dried out. The purchasers asked the vendors to correct the water damage or to permit the contract to be rescinded. The vendors declined to repair the damage and sold the building to another purchaser in July of 1980 for $140,000. The purchasers then instituted this action for rescission of the contract and return of their down payment. The trial court ruled that the purchasers must bear the risk of loss both to the Morrison Building and for the water damage to the adjoining property owned by third parties.

The purchasers contend that the trial court placed undue reliance on the doctrine of equitable conversion and rejected language in the sales contract placing the risk of loss on the vendors. Our law on the doctrine of equitable conversion with regard to real estate sales contracts is rather minimal. The doctrine of equitable conversion provides that where an executory contract for the sale of real property does not contain a provision allocating the risk of loss and the property is damaged by fire or some other casualty not due to the fault or neglect of the vendor,[2] the risk of loss is on the purchaser. This assumes the vendor has good title.

Our main case is *Maudru v. Humphreys*, 98 S.E. 259 (W. Va. 1919), where the purchaser was in possession of the property under an executory contract of sale. A fire destroyed a building on the property and this Court found the purchaser to have borne the risk of loss, stating in its single Syllabus: "Where a vendor, having good title and capacity to perform, makes a valid enforceable contract for the sale of land and, thereafter and before a deed is executed passing the legal title, a fire destroys a building thereon, without his fault or neglect, the loss is sustained by the purchaser. In such case there is no implied warranty that the condition of the property at the time of sale shall continue until after deed is made."

The Court in *Maudru* did not make an extensive analysis of the doctrine of equitable conversion, but did state that "there is no warranty or condition in the contract between Mynes and Maudru that the property should be in the same condition when the transaction is completed as it was when the contract was made." 98 S.E. at 261. This appears to be an implied recognition that the parties may allocate the risk of loss in a sales contract and thereby alter the doctrine of equitable conversion.

It is rather universally recognized that the parties to a contract of sale for real property may allocate the risk of loss for fire or other casualty occurring before the actual transfer of the legal title. If the contract allocates the risk to the vendor, then the doctrine of equitable conversion, which places the risk of loss on the purchaser, is no longer applicable. . . .

The trial court was of the view that the contract language stating that "the owner is responsible for said property until the Deed has been delivered to said purchaser" was not sufficient to cast the responsibility on the vendors. This conclusion was based, in part, on testimony of the sales agent for the vendor that this language pertained only to vandalism.

We disagree with this conclusion. The contract was on a printed form and the language is free from ambiguity. Cases in other jurisdictions have held language of similar import to place the burden of risk of loss on the vendor. . . . To permit this language to be restricted to acts of vandalism cuts across the plain meaning of its wording and would be contrary to the general rule that forecloses oral modification of contract language which is free from ambiguity. . . .

Apparently, the trial court also relied on language in the sales contract which provided: "Purchaser to carry enough fire insurance to protect Self." We do not believe that this provision can be read to place the risk of loss on the purchasers. This provision is nothing more than an acknowledgment of the general rule that

---

[2] It would appear that where the risk of loss is on the purchaser and the damage to the property is caused by the negligence of the vendor, the vendor must bear the risk of loss. E.g., . . . *DuBois v. Nye*, 584 P.2d 823 (Utah 1978). . . .

both parties to an executory contract for the sale of real property have an insurable interest. . . .

The trial court also referred to the sentence in the contract that "[t]his contract is also subject to 'As Is' condition" as indicating an intention not to deliver the building in a specific condition. We agree with this conclusion insofar as it would dispel any claim by the purchasers to require the vendors to make any improvements to the building from the condition it was in at the time the contract was signed. There was apparently no dispute that the building had been unoccupied for some period of time and was somewhat deteriorated.

However, we do not agree that this language can be read to remove the risk of loss from the vendors. The purpose of this type of provision is not to shift the risk of loss in the event the building is damaged without fault on the part of either party. Rather the use of an "as is" provision in a real estate sales contract is generally intended to negate the existence of any warranty as to the particular fitness or condition of the property. This type of clause simply means that the purchaser must take the premises covered in the real estate sales contract in its present condition as of the date of the contract. . . . M. Friedman, Contracts & Conveyances of Real Property § 1.2(n) at 69 (4th ed. 1984).

Having determined that the vendors bore the risk of loss under the contract, we believe the purchasers had the right to obtain the return of the initial down payment once the vendors refused to consider an abatement in the sale price as a result of the water damage and then sold the property to a third party.[3]

The particular remedies that may be available where there has been partial destruction or damage to buildings to be sold are not easily categorized as they depend upon particular facts and circumstances. It may be generally stated that where the risk of loss is on the vendor and the casualty damage to the property is not substantial, the purchaser is entitled to sue for specific performance, and the purchase price is abated to the extent the property was damaged. On the other hand where the risk of loss is on the vendor and there is substantial damage to the property, the appropriate remedy ordinarily is to terminate the contract and return the down payment to the purchaser. See *Dixon v. Salvation Army*, 191 Cal. Rptr. 111 (Cal. App. 1983) . . . ; 3A A. Corbin, Contracts § 668 (1960); M. Friedman, *supra* at § 4.11. See generally Annot., 11 A.L.R.2d at 430 (1950).

We have recognized that a purchaser may have specific performance of his contract to purchase real estate with an abatement in the purchase price where the vendor cannot fully perform his agreement.[4] However, it appears that we have not had occasion to speak to the remedy where the risk of loss is on the vendor and damage has been done to the building.

The purchasers, as we have seen, sued only to recover their down payment. The

---

[3] It appears that shortly after the water damage occurred, the purchasers, through their attorney, wrote to the vendors' agent on February 26, 1980, asking that the vendors either correct the water damage or permit the contract to be rescinded. This proposal was rejected by a letter of February 27, 1980, from the vendors' agent.

[4] This is the general rule elsewhere. E.g., *Miller v. Dyer*, 127 P.2d 901 (Cal. 1942); . . . M. Friedman, *supra*, at § 4.11.

vendors counterclaimed for the difference in the sales price on the original contract and what they obtained from the subsequent sale of the Morrison Building. The trial court rejected the vendors' counterclaim for reasons that are not entirely clear. However, in view of the risk of loss being placed on the vendors, the trial court's ruling with regard to the vendors' counterclaim would be correct for two reasons.

First, the vendors having the risk of loss for the water damage could not require the purchasers to pay the full purchase price. Consequently, the vendors were wrong in concluding that the purchasers had breached the sales contract when they refused to pay the full purchase price. As a result of this erroneous conclusion, the vendors breached the contract when they sold the property to the third party. If the water damage had not been substantial, the vendors could have sued the purchasers for specific performance while offering an abatement in the purchase price.

As a second alternative, if the vendors had concluded that the damages were substantial, they could have terminated the sales contract and returned the purchasers' down payment. However, with the risk of loss being on the vendors, they would bear the cost of repairing damage to the building.

Under the particular facts of this case, we conclude that where a contract places the risk of loss on the vendor and insubstantial damage to the property occurs without the fault of either party, the purchaser may recover his down payment where the vendor refuses to repair the damage or to give an abatement in the purchase price.

Finally, we note that with the risk of loss being placed on the vendors, the vendors were not entitled to recover from the purchasers the sums that they had paid to third parties whose adjacent premises were damaged by the water flowing from the vendors' building. The trial court awarded these damages on the basis that the purchasers bore the risk of loss under the doctrine of equitable conversion, which we have found inapplicable because of the terms of the contract.

In conclusion, we observe that we were somewhat handicapped on this appeal because the parties did not supply a transcript of the testimony, but submitted the findings of fact and conclusions of law made by the trial court which were most thorough. It would appear that the purchasers would be entitled to a judgment for the amount of their down payment and interest, but in view of the lack of a complete record, we are reluctant to enter such judgment here. We, therefore, reverse the judgment of the Circuit Court of Harrison County and remand the case for further proceedings not inconsistent with this opinion.

NOTES

1. The contract in the principal case provided: "This property is sold 'as is.' " Courts generally interpret an "as is" provision as negating the existence of a warranty of habitability or fitness of the property for a particular use, but the cases are split on this issue. The "as is" language normally means that the buyer must take the property at closing if it is in the same condition as when the parties executed the contract of sale. The court in the principal case considers two other contractual provisions to determine how they affect the parties' allocation of the risk of loss. Do the provisions considered, taken together, indicate anything more than

each provision would when separately considered?

2.   A seller and buyer execute a contract of sale for Blackacre, providing in part that the buyer "agrees that she has inspected the property and agrees to accept it in its present condition, except as otherwise provided" and "has the right to walk through and inspect the property forty-eight hours before closing." Will these provisions affect the allocation of the risk of loss? See *Brooks v. Bankson*, 445 S.E.2d 473, 476 (Va. 1994).

3.   As previously discussed, common law rules control the allocation of risk in the majority of states, but in the 1930s, the contracts law scholar Samuel Williston drafted the following statute, known as the Uniform Vendor and Purchaser Risk Act (1935). See, e.g., N.Y. Gen. Oblig. Law § 5-1311 (2009), which provides:

only adopted in 12 states

> 1. Any contract for the purchase and sale or exchange of realty shall be interpreted, unless the contract expressly provides otherwise, as including an agreement that the parties shall have the following rights and duties:
>
> *seller keep the rtk of loss*
>
> a. When neither the legal title nor the possession of the subject matter of the contract has been transferred to the purchaser: (1) if all or a material part thereof is destroyed without fault of the purchaser or is taken by eminent domain, the vendor cannot enforce the contract, and the purchaser is entitled to recover any portion of the price that he has paid; but nothing herein contained shall be deemed to deprive the vendor of any right to recover damages against the purchaser for any breach of contract by the purchaser prior to the destruction or taking; (2) if an immaterial part thereof is destroyed without fault of the purchaser or is taken by eminent domain, neither the vendor nor the purchaser is thereby deprived of the right to enforce the contract; but there shall be, to the extent of the destruction or taking, an abatement of the purchase price.
>
> b. When either the legal title or the possession of the subject matter of the contract has been transferred to the purchaser, if all or any part thereof is destroyed without fault of the vendor or is taken by eminent domain, the purchaser is not thereby relieved from a duty to pay the price, nor is he thereby entitled to recover any portion thereof that he has paid; but nothing herein contained shall be deemed to deprive the purchaser of any right to recover damages against the vendor for any breach of contract by the vendor prior to the destruction or taking.
>
> 2. This section shall be so interpreted and construed as to effectuate its general purpose to make uniform the law of those states which enact it.

Under this statute, if 40% of Blackacre is destroyed by fire while subject to an executory contract of sale, who bears the risk of loss? Would it make a difference if, when the property becomes subject to the contract, it is (a) under lease to a third party and (b) the contract provides that the purchaser is to receive the rents during the executory period? What if a contract provides that the buyer is to have possession of the property during the executory period and the seller leaves the property, but the property is destroyed by fire before the buyer takes possession? Would your answers to the foregoing questions change if (a) the contract was to be closed using an escrow or (b) the property was not destroyed by fire but was lost to the parties through eminent domain?

CANNEFAX v. CLEMENT
818 P.2d 546 (Utah 1991)

STEWART, J.

This case is here on certiorari from a decision of the Utah Court of Appeals which reversed a summary judgment entered by the trial court in favor of Donald and Ruth Clement. Donald and Ruth Clement are judgment creditors of George and Lila Barker, vendors of land under a uniform real estate contract. The issue before the Court is one of first impression: whether a vendor's interest in real property sold by a land sale contract is transformed by the doctrine of equitable conversion into personal property and therefore not subject to a judgment lien pursuant to Utah Code Ann. § 78-22-1 (1987). We hold that a judgment against the vendor of land under a land sale contract does not create a lien against a vendor's interest for purposes of § 78-22-1.

On August 28, 1981, pursuant to a uniform real estate contract, George and Lila Barker contracted to sell certain real property which they owned in fee simple to Diane Hodge. Ms. Hodge recorded notice of that contract on August 31, 1981. The defendants, Donald W. Clement and Ruth L. Clement, obtained and docketed a judgment against the Barkers in August 1985. On September 25, 1985, Ms. Hodge paid the amount remaining on the contract, and the Barkers executed a deed to the property to her. On the same date, Hodge gave a warranty deed to the property to the plaintiffs, Raymond and Debra Cannefax. Both transactions took place at a single real estate closing. The Cannefaxes recorded their deed the next day. Following the closing but before the Cannefaxes recorded their deed, the settlement agent, Surety Title Agency, conducted a title search which disclosed the Clements' judgment against the Barkers. Two years later, the Clements sought to enforce the judgment lien against the property through an execution sale scheduled for September 22, 1987. The Cannefaxes brought this action to quiet title. The trial court granted summary judgment in favor of the Clements, holding that the judgment created a lien on the property in the amount of $54,464.94, the unpaid amount on the contract on September 25, 1985, the closing date, less the amount of prior encumbrances. The court of appeals reversed and ordered the trial court to enter summary judgment in favor of the Cannefaxes, quieting title to their property. * * * We affirm.

The issue presented to this Court is whether a vendor's interest in an executory land sale contract is "real property" under Utah Code Ann. § 78-22-1 (1987), so that a judgment docketed against the vendor after the contract is entered into creates a lien against the vendor's interest in the property. Utah Code Ann. § 78-22-1 provides: "From the time the judgment of the district court . . . is docketed and filed . . . it becomes a lien upon all the real property of the judgment debtor, not exempt from execution, in the county in which the judgment is entered, owned by him at the time or by him thereafter acquired during the existence of said lien. . . . The lien shall continue for eight years unless the judgment is previously satisfied . . . in which case the lien of the judgment ceases."

The court of appeals held that under the doctrine of equitable conversion, a vendor's interest in an executory land sale contract is not real property for purposes of § 78-22-1. In *Butler v. Wilkinson*, 740 P.2d 1244, 1253–54 (Utah 1987), we reiterated the proposition that under the doctrine of equitable conversion, a vendee's equitable interest in an installment land sale contract constitutes real property for purposes of § 78-22-1; however, this Court has not previously decided the nature of the vendor's interest for purposes of the lien statute. We now hold that a vendor's interest in an executory land sale contract is not "real property" as that term is used in § 78-22-1.

Although we have not previously considered the nature of a vendor's interest in an installment land contract, a number of other jurisdictions have. The cases are almost evenly divided, with a slight majority allowing the judgment lien to attach to the vendor's interest. R. Cunningham, W. Stoebuck, & D. Whitman, The Law of Property § 10.13, at 701 (1984). Compare *Mooring v. Brown*, 763 F.2d 386 (10th Cir. 1985) (applying Colorado law) . . . and *Heath v. Dodson*, 110 P.2d 845, 847 (Wash. 1941) (holding that a judgment lien attaches to a vendor's interest in an executory land contract) with *Bank of Hawaii v. Horwoth*, 787 P.2d 674, 679 (Haw. 1990) . . . and *Mueller v. Novelty Dye Works*, 78 N.W.2d 881, 884 (Wis. 1956) (holding that a judgment lien does not attach to a vendor's interest in an executory land contract). See also Annot., *Right of Vendee Under Unrecorded Executory Land Contract as Against Subsequent Deed or Mortgage Executed by, or Judgment Rendered Against Vendor*, 87 A.L.R. 1505 (1933).

In other cases, this Court has previously held that the doctrine of equitable conversion applies to transform a vendor's interest in a land sale contract from a real property interest into a personal property interest. For example, in *Allred v. Allred*, 393 P.2d 791, 792 (Utah 1964), the Court stated, "As a general rule an enforceable executory contract of sale has the effect of converting the interest of the vendor of real property to personalty." Also, in *In re Estate of Willson*, 499 P.2d 1298, 1300 (Utah 1972), the Court held that a widow could not, for purposes of limiting inheritance taxes, claim an exclusion based upon a dower interest in real property subject to an executory contract of sale. The Court stated that the vendor's interest was "no longer real estate . . . but personal estate . . . and if he dies before payment, it goes to his administrators, and not to his heirs.'" *Id.* (internal quotes omitted). *Jelco, Inc. v. Third Judicial District Court*, 511 P.2d 739, 741 (Utah 1973), was a condemnation case which held that the vendee was the equitable owner of property under an executory land contract and therefore entitled to the appreciation in the value of the land occurring after the contract was executed. Although the Court declined to apply equitable conversion in *Reynolds v. Van Wagoner*, 592 P.2d 593, 594 (Utah 1979), it was the vendor who sought application of the doctrine rather than the vendee. As the Court noted, the vendor's attempt to alter the contract by relying on equitable conversion was clearly impermissible. Finally, in *Butler v. Wilkinson*, 740 P.2d 1244, 1253–54 (Utah 1987), the Court held that a vendee's equitable interest in an installment land sale contract is real property for purposes of § 78-22-1.

The Cannefaxes argue that because this Court held that a vendee's interest in a real estate contract is a real property interest, it must necessarily rule that the vendor's interest is not real property. The court of appeals relied on the above cases and the language in *Butler* which stated that if a vendee has an interest in real estate, by a "parity of reasoning" the vendor is deemed to have converted his real property interest to a monetary or legal interest. However, that language from *Butler* was intended only as a general description of the doctrine of equitable conversion. The question of the nature of the vendor's interest was not before the Court in *Butler*. In fact, we also observed in *Butler* that "the characterization of the vendee as 'owner' of the land and of the vendor as having no interest in the land is not wholly accurate. The vendor's retention of the legal title is usually coupled with a contract right to forfeit the vendee's interest and to take back the vendee's interests if the vendee defaults." 740 P.2d at 1255. We also noted that this characterization of the vendor's interest as a lien is not completely accurate: "The term 'vendor's lien' seems to have stuck even though it is inaccurately used before the vendor parts with the title. Until then, it is not, in fact, a lien at all, but rather a retained interest in the land that is derived from the vendor's retention of the fee title." 740 P.2d at 1256 n.6. In other words, the mere fact that the vendee is treated as having a real property interest does not necessarily preclude the vendor from also having such an interest.

. . . [A] judgment lien which has already attached to real property will not be destroyed by a subsequent conveyance of the property. In other words, the property passes subject to the lien. . . . [T]he fact that the contract may have "contemplate[d] a transfer of ownership by deed after all installments have been paid" is irrelevant to construing the judgment lien statute. The true issue is whether the vendor retained a sufficient interest in the property to qualify as "owning real property" for purposes of § 78-22-1.

Section 78-22-1 provides that a judgment becomes a lien upon the real property owned by the judgment debtor at the time of docketing. The position taken by the Clements and the trial court is that the judgment lien attaches to real property to the extent that the contract remains unpaid. This argument is inconsistent with the assertion that the vendor's retained title causes his interest to be real property. If the vendor's retention of legal title were sufficient to constitute real property under § 78-22-1, it follows that the judgment lien should attach to the entire property, subject to prior encumbrances. As this Court recognized in *Belnap v. Blain*, 575 P.2d 696, 699 (Utah 1978), the fact that a judgment debtor has no equity in real property because encumbrances on the property exceed its fair market value does not prevent a judgment lien from attaching to the property, subject to prior encumbrances. The Clements' position, that the lien attaches only to the extent the contract is unpaid, is actually the first step toward applying the doctrine of equitable conversion. That position recognizes that the vendor's true interest is in receiving the unpaid amount on the contract, an interest more akin to personalty than to realty.

The principle underlying *Butler*, *Allred*, *Willson*, and *Jelco* is that the vendee of an executory land sale contract holds equitable ownership of the property but not legal title. As stated in *Butler*, the vendor retains the naked legal title, which serves as the basis for forfeiting the vendee's interest and retaking possession if the vendee defaults. 740 P.2d at 1255. In *Belnap*, the Court recognized that a judgment lien does not attach to "bare legal title" to property held by a "trustee of an express, constructive, or resulting trust or [by] an agent or mere conduit for the transfer of title to the true owner." 575 P.2d at 699. Admittedly, the vendor's interest in this case constitutes more than "bare legal title." However, for purposes of § 78-22-1, that interest is more closely analogous to the examples mentioned in *Belnap* than it is to true "ownership of real property" as required by the statute. Although the vendor may forfeit the vendee's interest, he may do so only if the vendee first defaults, an event which is completely out of the hands of the vendor. Furthermore, a vendor who breaches a land sale contract in an attempt to retain the property will be subject to either damages or a decree for specific performance. See *Willson*, 499 P.2d at 1300. Even though the vendor may retain title to the property, that title is effectively held for the benefit of the vendee, to whom it will pass if the contract is carried out. As stated in *Willson*, "the transfer of legal title and record title [is] dependent only upon the acts and conduct of the buyer." *Id.* In short, the mere retention of title of land subject to a land sale contract does not amount to ownership of real property for purposes of § 78-22-1.

Policy concerns also dictate this result. If a judgment lien could attach to the vendor's interest in an executory land contract, the vendee would be forced to make payments at his or her peril, risking the chance that a subsequent judgment has been docketed after execution of the contract. For example, a vendee who has paid the entire purchase price could still be subject to an execution sale on the purchased property if a judgment was docketed after the contract had been entered into but before all the payments had been made. Because a judgment which has not yet been docketed cannot be uncovered by a title search, such a search can provide no protection to the vendee at the time the contract is entered into. Instead, the vendee would be forced to do a title search before each payment. Even if a judgment lien were discovered in this way, the vendee would be forced to choose whether to pay the vendor or the judgment creditor, thereby risking the possibility of having to pay twice. Therefore, the position which the Clements urge this Court to adopt would make real estate contracts impracticable as an alternative to conventional financing, harming those who are poor credit risks and who are unable to obtain other financing.

However, the Clements also argue that if this Court does not rule that a judgment lien attaches to the debtor's interest in the land contract at the time the judgment is docketed, the Court should at least rule that the lien attaches at the time the vendee has notice of the lien. The Clements assert that the Cannefaxes had notice of the lien at the time they purchased the property from Hodge and that the property is therefore subject to the lien. This contention would require us to rewrite § 78-22-1, which provides that the lien will attach to the property from the time the judgment is docketed. Nothing in the statute supports this construction. Furthermore, the stipulated facts would not support the Clements' argument. The settlement agent did not discover the judgment until after the closing. The judgment debtors then transfered title to Hodge before the discovery of the judgment. Therefore, there was nothing to which the lien could attach. Hodge's transfer of title to the Cannefaxes was therefore also free of the lien.

* * * The need to enforce judgments is not so great that a lien must attach to property in the process of being transferred and to which the vendor's rights are

contractually limited. * * * This holding does not prevent the judgment creditor from reaching the vendor's interest in the property, either by garnishing payments as they are made or perhaps by executing on the vendor's interest in the contract.

For the above reasons, we hold that the vendor's interest in property subject to an executory real estate contract is not real property for purposes of § 78-22-1 and, therefore, that the judgment creditor's lien did not attach to the vendor's interest. The decision of the court of appeals is affirmed.

NOTES

1. *Cannefax* highlights the difference between an executory contract of sale and an installment land contract (called a contract for deed in some states). Unlike a contract of sale, an installment land contract usually has a long executory period. It may be as short as a year or two or as long as ten or twenty years before the seller closes the contract by transferring title to the purchaser. In contrast, the executory period for a contract of sale is typically sixty or ninety days. Installment land contracts usually are used as a method of vendor financing for the sale of land. Rather than require a buyer to borrow money from a bank or other third-party lender so that the buyer can pay the full purchase price at the closing, the purchase price is paid in installments over time with interest, using a payment plan set out in the contract. Installment land contracts are often used when the interest rates charged by institutional lenders are high. The seller then agrees to finance the purchase at a below-market interest rate. This makes the deal more affordable for the buyer. More generally, they are used when the buyer cannot qualify for a loan from an institutional lender, as with a buyer with too small a down payment, too little income to meet the lender's underwriting standards, or a poor credit history. Buyers of second homes and farm families transferring land between generations also use them. A buyer avoids the closing and mortgage lending fees charged by institutional lenders. In exchange, the seller may be able to sell the property more quickly and for more money than if he insisted on being paid in full at closing. Further, the seller's gain on the sale will not be taxed in one tax year as it would be if she were paid in full. Instead, subject to the provisions of the Internal Revenue Code, the gain will be taxed only as the buyer makes payments under the contract. See I.R.C. § 453.

Unlike the executory contract of sale, the buyer under an installment land contract normally gets possession as soon as the contract is signed. By possessing the land, the buyer can farm it, rent it, or otherwise realize rents and profits in the amount necessary to make payments to the seller. This is another reason why such a contract is attractive to a lower-income buyer. In most jurisdictions, the buyer's possession provides notice to persons dealing subsequently with the seller's title (creditors and subsequent purchasers), even if the contract is unrecorded. However, the buyer takes possession long before the seller has to show that the title is marketable. The traditional common law rule for executory contracts is applied to installment contracts as well: unless the contract provides otherwise, the seller need not have marketable title until the closing. See *Luette v. Bank of Italy Nat'l Tr. & Savings Ass'n*, 42 F.2d 9 (9th Cir. 1930). Thus, the buyer cannot place the seller in default by tendering the full price prematurely or rescind the contract because of a defect in the title during the executory period. Over the course of a long executory period, applying the rule of *Luette* means that the buyer is subjected to the risk of paying the installments to keep the contract alive with no guarantee that the title will be marketable when the last installment is paid. The seller might mortgage or even sell the property during the executory period, die and tie up the property in probate proceedings, or go bankrupt and subject the property to bankruptcy proceedings. What should a buyer do to avoid these problems?

2. Who bears the risk of loss to the property during the executory period of an installment land contract? The rule applied to contracts of sale also generally applies to installment land contracts. Under the majority rule, the risk is on the buyer. That rule makes more sense in the context of an installment land contract, because the buyer is in possession of the property. Remember, though, that a minority rule does exist. Rather than rely on the common law rule, installment land contracts normally provide expressly that the buyer must maintain and insure the property and pay taxes on it. See *Wiley v. Lininger*, 204 P.2d 1083 (Colo. 1949). As with executory contracts of sale, those jurisdictions that follow the doctrine of equitable conversion normally characterize the seller's retained interest in the property as personalty and the buyer's interest as realty. As *Cannefax* indicates, both parties' interests in the property can be transferred, used as security for a debt, and, in most jurisdictions, attached by creditors. See *Capital Assets Financial Services v. Maxwell*, 994 P.2d 201 (Utah 2000) (further reviewing Utah cases on the issue of whether a buyer may convey an interest sufficient to support an institutional mortgage lien to secure a loan sought by a buyer's grantee).

3. Perhaps the most distinctive feature of the installment land contract is the remedy it provides for the buyer's default. The following provision is typical: "Should the Buyer default in the payment of said purchase price or any of the covenants and/or conditions herein provided, and if such default shall continue for 30 days, then all moneys and payments previously paid shall, at the option of the Seller without notice or demand, be and become forfeited and be taken and retained by the Seller as liquidated damages and, thereupon, this contract shall terminate and be of no further force or effect and the Seller shall be released from all obligations in law or equity to convey said property and any occupancy of said property thereafter by Buyer shall be a tenancy at sufferance and Buyer shall never acquire and expressly waives any and all rights or claims of title because of such possession." Despite the potentially draconian features of this remedy, courts traditionally have enforced these forfeiture provisions according to their terms. Why do you think this is? The effect is to deprive the purchasers of the rights they would have enjoyed if they had financed the purchase by giving a mortgage on the land, rather than by entering into an installment land contract. These rights include (1) the common law and statutory rights of redemption, which enable a borrower to prevent a forfeiture of the property by tendering the unpaid debt or the foreclosure sale price, and (2) the statutory right in some jurisdictions to prevent forfeiture by tendering just the amount in default.

Despite the benefits of the installment land contract, state courts and legislatures increasingly are questioning the fairness of forfeiture provisions. After all, rather than using an installment land contract, the seller could have financed the purchase by conveying title to the buyer immediately and taking back a mortgage on the property. Initially, courts that did not want to enforce the forfeiture clause relied on traditional contract doctrines. For example, if the seller had a pattern of accepting late payments, the court might hold that he had waived the right to enforce the forfeiture clause.

Other courts have dealt more directly with the potential harm from literal enforcement of forfeiture provisions. They allow a buyer who has forfeited the property to use the traditional contract remedy of restitution to recover payments made in excess of the land's fair rental value or the value of the buyer's equity in the property. In still other jurisdictions, the buyer may enjoy some of the protections afforded a defaulting mortgagor, such as an equitable right to redeem. See *Lewis v. Premium Investment Corp.*, 568 S.E.2d 361 (S.C. 2002) (outlining factors to consider before granting redemption). Redemption enables the purchaser to prevent the forfeiture by obtaining financing from another source and paying the balance of the contract price to the vendor. Other jurisdictions require the seller to foreclose the purchaser's interest by selling the property at public auction and keeping only so much of the sale proceeds as are necessary to pay off the contract. See *Skendzel v. Marshall*, 301 N.E.2d 641 (Ind. 1973) (the typical forfeiture clause above is from the contract in *Skendzel*).

Other courts and state legislatures have taken the next step and have characterized installment land contracts as the functional equivalent of a mortgage, particularly when the buyer took possession of the property immediately upon contract execution and thereafter paid a substantial portion of the purchase price, thereby building equity in the property. In *Skendzel*, for example, the buyer had paid seventy-one percent of the purchase price — sometimes late, but sometimes early. Cf. *Goff v. Graham*, 306 N.E.2d 758 (Ind. Ct. App. 1974) (forfeiture permitted when buyer had paid only $2,500 of a $6,200 contract price while collecting $6,300 in rent from the property). *Skendzel* held that the contract was "in the nature of a secured transaction, the provisions of which are subject to all proper and just remedies at law and in equity." See also *Sebastian v. Floyd*, 585 S.W.2d 381 (Ky. 1979), noted in 72 Ky. L.J. 917 (1984). When a contract is recharacterized as mortgage, is it a lien or a title mortgage, and what are its terms? Where the law enables such a recharacterization, it need not be automatic and does not mean that forfeiture provisions cannot be drafted fairly and enforced as written. Provisions that require the seller to provide the buyer with notice of an impending forfeiture and time to cure the default or that permit the seller to retain only so much of the payments as represent the fair rental value of the property would make forfeiture more palatable to the courts.

C.   Contract Contingencies

A contract of sale for land is rarely completely performed at the moment of its execution. Instead, it usually is replete with contingency clauses that require the parties to perform a variety of additional actions. For example, the buyer's promise to buy the property may be subject to the conditions that he is able to obtain proper financing, secure necessary zoning permissions, sell his current residence, and obtain satisfactory environmental test results for the property. In some jurisdictions, unsatisfied conditions delay the applicability of the doctrine of equitable conversion.

D. Disclosures about the Property

If the seller and her real estate agent know about a material defect in the property, they have a common law duty to disclose the defect to the buyer if it is not known by him and is not reasonably discoverable. A failure to disclose such defects constitutes the tort of "fraudulent concealment" or "fraud by omission." It is an open question whether the seller and her agent have an affirmative duty to inspect the property for material defects, which they then would be required to disclose. In determining the scope of these duties, courts hold agents to a higher standard of care than the seller. The agent must act as a reasonably prudent real estate licensee. That standard is measured by the education and experience of such a licensee. The agent's duty extends to information disclosed in the listing process. However, it normally does not extend to inaccessible areas of the property, such as the electric wiring and plumbing.

Many federal and state statutes and local ordinances require the seller and her agent to disclose a variety of other conditions or to have the property inspected for the purpose of discovering particular defects. For example, they often must tell the buyer if the property contains lead-based paint, radon, or other toxic or hazardous substances or if the property is located in a flood plain or an earthquake zone. Normally, a failure to make these disclosures does not invalidate the sale; instead, the non-disclosing person is liable in damages for the condition. Although these statutes vary from state to state, they are often quite comprehensive and require a written disclosure on a legally-mandated form. See Eric H. Franklin, *Mandating Precontractual Disclosure*, 67 U. Miami L. Rev. 553 (2013); Thomas J. Miceli, Katherine A. Pancak & C.F. Sirmans, *Evolving Property Condition Disclosure Duties: Caveat Procurator?*, 39 Real Est. L.J. 464 (2011) (discussing the law and economics of expanding sellers' and real estate agents' duty to disclose material facts to buyer); R.M. Washburn, *Residential Real Estate Condition Disclosure Legislation*, 44 DePaul L. Rev. 381 (1995).

E. Time for Performance of the Contract

Time is money, particularly for real estate sales and development. Therefore, even though the contract need not specify a closing date — the date on which title will be transferred to the buyer — it usually does. Similarly, prudent parties — particularly sellers who want to avoid prolonging the executory period with a buyer who may be unable to satisfy the contract conditions — normally also specify time limits for performing the conditions. For example, the buyer might be required to file a loan application within ten days of contract execution and to obtain a loan commitment within sixty days. If the contract is silent concerning the closing date or the time to satisfy a condition, the law implies a reasonable time.

However, most courts recognize that delays are common in real estate transactions. Therefore, unless the delay is unreasonably long or is the result of bad faith, both parties still can enforce the contract in equity with an action for specific performance. Even though the person who defaulted on the time requirement can enforce the contract, he still may be liable for damages. Thus, the seller can recover taxes she paid during the time the buyer delayed the closing, or the buyer can recover rents and profits that the property would have generated if the seller had not delayed the closing. In fact, this obligation to account may diminish or eliminate the amount of recoverable damages. When the seller seeks damages for property taxes and other expenses incurred during the period of delay, the buyer may counterclaim for rents that the seller collected during that period. The result may be that little more than nominal damages are left to recover.

An action for damages may be an inadequate remedy if timely performance is particularly important to the seller or buyer. In that case, they may specify in the contract that time is of the essence. For example, the contract may provide: "Time shall be of the essence of this contract" or "This contract shall be null and void if not performed by [date]." When the contract makes time of the essence for the closing or for the performance of a condition, timely performance becomes a condition, rather than a mere covenant. In that case, a delay permits the aggrieved party to treat the breach as total and to repudiate the contract without further liability.

F. Express "Subject to Financing" Contract Terms

Perhaps the most litigated provision of a contract of sale is the "subject to financing" clause, by which the buyer conditions his obligation to purchase on his ability to obtain a loan. See *Woodland Realty, Inc. v. Winzenried*, 262 N.W.2d 106, 108 (Wis. 1978) ("Subject to financing clauses are common and have frequently been construed by this court as constituting a condition precedent to the buyer's performance. *Gerruth Realty Co. v. Pire*, 17 Wis. 2d 89, 91, 115 N.W.2d 557 (1962). . . . As such, the condition operates to delay 'the enforceability of the contract until the condition precedent has taken place.' *Locke v. Bort*, 10 Wis. 2d 585, 588, 103 N.W.2d 555 (1960); Restatement of Contracts, § 250(a) (1932).").

If the contract contained no more detail than that the buyer's obligation was "subject to financing," many courts would use the reasonableness standard to determine the scope of the buyer's duties under this clause. Reasonableness would be measured by the customary terms and practices of the mortgage market. Within a reasonable time, particularly taking into account the closing date, the buyer would be required to make a reasonable, good faith effort to procure financing to be secured by a first priority mortgage or deed of trust from a reasonable number of conventional (nonsubsidized) mortgage lenders. "When details as to specific types or methods of financing are omitted, the clause must be interpreted as requiring that the terms of any offered mortgage be reasonable. Otherwise the buyer is not required to accept it." *Smith v. Vernon*, 286 N.E.2d 99, 101–02 (Ill. App. Ct. 1972) (stating also that "reasonableness is to be determined and interpreted by the court according to business practice and custom in the place where the contract is to be performed"). Reasonableness incorporates an objective, rather than a subjective, standard into the contract.

However, some courts have been unwilling to use the reasonableness standard to define the scope of the buyer's duty. For example, in *Neiss v. Franze*, 422 N.Y.S.2d 345 (N.Y. Sup. Ct. 1979), the contract provided: "This agreement is contingent upon purchaser obtaining approval of a conventional mortgage loan of $29,000." The court held that the reference to a "conventional mortgage" was so ambiguous as to be unenforceable because it demonstrated that the buyer and seller never had a meeting of the minds on that provision. The court held that, for the financing provision to be enforceable, it also would have to specify the interest rate and the term of the loan (the period of time over which the loan is repaid). Courts in Maryland, New York, and Wisconsin have been the strictest in interpreting financing conditions as being indefinite. See, e.g., *Perkins v. Gosewehr*, 295 N.W.2d 789 (Wis. 1981); *Imas Gruner & Assoc. Ltd. v. Stringer*, 427 A.2d 1038 (Md. App. 1981). Other state courts are less demanding. A contract "contingent on the purchaser's obtaining a loan" might survive judicial scrutiny when the purchaser files one or more applications for a loan with conventional rates and terms.

Even in less demanding states, prudent practice by buyers and their attorneys requires that, at a minimum, the contract specify the loan term, the interest rate, and the loan amount. The contract should specify the maximum term and interest rate that the buyer would have to accept and the minimum loan amount. In this way, the buyer will not be obligated to bear more debt expense than he can afford and will not be in default under the contract unless adequate loan funds can be obtained. Stating a maximum monthly mortgage payment and a maximum amount of loan closing costs also is a good idea but may require more information than the average buyer is likely to have when executing the contract. The buyer may wish to specify the type of lender (institutional or not), the type of loan (subsidized or conventional, fixed or adjustable rate, and amortized or not), the number of loan applications that must be made, and the time given the buyer to make the applications and obtain a loan commitment. The buyer may also want the lender to have the property carefully appraised in the course of evaluating the buyer's application. Appraisals may be conducted by lenders or by an independent appraiser, and they take time. Appraisers may be liable when they misstate a property's value. See *Fisher v. Comer Plantation, Inc.*, 772 So. 2d 455, 462 (Ala. 2000) ("real estate appraisers are subject to liability for negligent or wanton misrepresentation" of value); *West v. Inter-Financial, Inc.*, 139 P.3d 1059 (Utah App. Ct. 2006) (applying the economic loss rule to a professional negligence action against an appraiser); *Decatur Ventures LLC v. Daniel*, 485 F.3d 387, 390 (7th Cir. 2007) (applying Indiana law).

LUTTINGER v. ROSEN
316 A.2d 757 (Conn. 1972)

LOISELLE, J.

The plaintiffs contracted to purchase for $85,000 premises in Stamford owned by the defendants and paid a deposit of $8,500. The contract was "subject to and conditional upon the buyers obtaining first mortgage financing on said premises from a bank or other lending institution in an amount of $45,000 for a term of not less than twenty (20) years and at an interest rate which does not exceed 8½ per cent per annum." The plaintiffs agreed to use due diligence in attempting to obtain such financing. The parties further agreed that if the plaintiffs were unsuccessful in obtaining financing as provided in the contract, and notified the seller within a specific time, all sums paid on the contract would be refunded and the contract terminated without further obligation of either party.

In applying for a mortgage which would satisfy the contingency clause in the contract, the plaintiffs relied on their attorney who applied at a New Haven lending institution for a $45,000 loan at 8-1/4 percent per annum interest over a period of twenty-five years. The plaintiffs' attorney knew that this lending institution was the only one which at that time would lend as much as $45,000 on a mortgage for a single-family dwelling. A mortgage commitment was obtained for $45,000 with "interest at the prevailing rate at the time of closing but not less than 8-3/4%." Since this commitment failed to meet the contract requirement, timely notice was given to the defendants and demand was made for the return of the down payment. The defendants' counsel thereafter offered to make up the difference between the interest rate offered by the bank and the 8½ percent rate provided in the contract for the entire twenty-five years by a funding arrangement, the exact terms of which were not defined. The plaintiffs did not accept this offer and on the defendants' refusal to return the deposit an action was brought. From a judgment rendered in favor of the plaintiffs the defendants have appealed.

The defendants claim that the plaintiffs did not use due diligence in seeking a mortgage within the terms specified in the contract. The unattacked findings by the court establish that the plaintiffs' attorney was fully informed as to the conditions and terms of mortgages being granted by various banks and lending institutions in and out of the area and that the application was made to the only bank which might satisfy the mortgage conditions of the contingency clause at that time. These findings adequately support the court's conclusion that due diligence was used in seeking mortgage financing in accordance with the contract provisions. The defendants assert that notwithstanding the plaintiffs' reliance on their counsel's knowledge of lending practices, applications should have been made to other lending institutions. This claim is not well taken. The law does not require the performance of a futile act.

The remaining assignment of error briefed by the defendants is that the court erred in concluding that the mortgage contingency clause of the contract, a condition precedent, was not met and, therefore, the plaintiffs were entitled to recover their deposit. "A condition precedent is a fact or event which the parties intend must exist or take place before there is a right to performance." *Lach v. Cahill*, 85 A.2d 481, 482 (Conn. 1951). If the condition precedent is not fulfilled the contract is not enforceable. In this case the language of the contract is unambiguous and clearly indicates that the parties intended that the purchase of the defendants' premises be conditioned on the obtaining by the plaintiffs of a mortgage as specified in the contract. From the subordinate facts found the court could reasonably conclude that since the plaintiffs were unable to obtain a $45,000 mortgage at no more than 8½ percent per annum interest "from a bank or other lending institution" the condition precedent to performance of the contract was not met and the plaintiffs were entitled to the refund of their deposit. Any additional offer by the defendants to fund the difference in interest payments could be rejected by the plaintiffs. There was no error in the court's exclusion of testimony relating to the additional offer since the offer was obviously irrelevant. There is no error.

divorced loan case

BRUYERE v. JADE REALTY CORP.

375 A.2d 600 (N.H. 1977)

• Buyer voluntarily did something which changed their ability to get a loan, so they don't get deposit back.

Courts are split about this.

PER CURIAM.

The issue herein is whether the plaintiffs are entitled to recover their deposit upon a piece of real estate, where the obligations under the purchase and sale agreement were made subject to the buyers' obtaining of bank financing and such financing was first granted but then subsequently revoked due to the plaintiffs' decision to file for divorce. For the reasons which follow below, we hold that the plaintiffs are not entitled to the return of their deposit.

The plaintiffs deposited $1,000 with the defendant in accordance with a purchase and sale agreement between the parties for a piece of residential real estate, dated May 16, 1975, which provided that the contract was "subject to financing at 7 3/4 % for thirty (30) years." The closing date was set for August 1, 1975. The plaintiffs applied for financing approval from the Nashua Federal Savings and Loan Association, which was granted on June 17, 1975. Marital problems between the plaintiffs at this time led them to decide to separate and file for divorce. The lender was informed of this development on June 30, 1975, by Mrs. Bruyere, who proposed that she alone purchase the home and assume the financing terms outlined in the bank's previous letter of commitment. The bank declined, stating that one income would not suffice to carry the mortgage in question, and withdrew its financing commitment. Alternative financing could not be arranged, and the deal fell through. The plaintiffs sought the return of their deposit. They argued that they had not breached their agreement, for their obligation was expressly conditioned on the obtaining of financing, and such financing was not available to them as of August 1, 1975, the date of closing. The District Court agreed, and granted a verdict for the plaintiffs. The defendant's exceptions thereto were reserved and transferred.

We cannot adopt the plaintiffs' position. It is true, as they allege, that the grant of bank financing was a condition precedent to the obligations under the contract. See *Rogers v. Cardinal Realty Inc.*, 339 A.2d 23 (N.H. 1975). The purpose of this frequently utilized provision, however, is merely to protect prospective purchasers from committing a technical breach of contract due to their inability, based on the facts and circumstances present at the time of the signing of the purchase and sale agreement, or due to some fortuitous intervening event, to secure the funds necessary to complete the purchase. The defendant herein contracted with a married couple. The conditional financing provision was inserted under the understanding that the mortgage would be sought by two wage earners. The seller was able to weigh the plaintiffs' likelihood of success under these conditions, and accepted the studied risk of taking its property off the market despite the possibility that the transaction might fail. We do not believe the intent of the financing clause was to place upon the seller the hazard that the plaintiffs would alter their circumstances, and therefore their borrowing potential, through a voluntary act of their own.

We hold that the intent of the financing clause is to protect the buyer from involuntary breach. Where, however, the condition precedent of financing is first satisfied, but then fails because of some action voluntarily undertaken by the buyer, we find that the risk of the failure of the transaction is properly imposed upon the party who so acts, and not upon the innocent seller. Exceptions sustained.

NOTE

Assume that sellers' contract with their buyer stated that the closing was "subject to the buyer obtaining a $100,000 mortgage loan at 7½% for 30 years from the Whitewater Savings Bank." The Whitewater Savings Bank denies their loan application. May they avoid the contract on this ground? Compare *Kovarik v. Vesely*, 89 N.W.2d 279 (Wis. 1958) (holding that they could not), with *Gardner v. Padro*, 517 N.E.2d 1131 (Ill. App. Ct. 1987) (holding they could). Naming a lender in the condition does not limit a buyer to applying and obtaining a loan from that lender. *Peterson v. Wirum*, 625 P.2d 866 (Alaska 1981). What if, after a buyer files a reasonable number of mortgage applications and is denied, the seller offers to finance the purchase on terms satisfying the "subject to financing" clause? Must the buyer accept? The *Kovarik* court also held that he must, but *Luttinger* is authority to the contrary. What factors will affect a court's holding on this issue? What if a buyer experiences a reversal of fortunes in the stock market, which causes his combined net worth to decline so far that the application for a mortgage loan on the specified terms are denied? Should the contract be terminated on these facts? Will the buyer then recover his down payment? Does it matter that the buyer did or did not disclose the source of his funds to the seller?

G.　Implied Contract Terms

Contracts of sale often include two implied terms. First, in over forty states, every contract for the sale of new housing includes an implied warranty of habitability. Even if the warranty is not expressly included in the contract, state statutory law or case law implies it. The implied warranty has been extended to used housing as well, but only in ten states. However, in every state, tort actions for fraud and negligent misrepresentation also help ensure that the seller does not misstate the physical condition of the premises.

The implied warranty extends to the land as well as to the improvements on it, because unstable soil can affect the improvements as well as the lot. The warranty applies to all matters affecting the habitability of the premises. The leading cases concerning the implied warranty have involved the structural components and infrastructure of housing. For example, the warranty requires that the boiler, the plumbing, and the heating and air conditioning units must be adequate.

The second term implied into a contract of sale as a matter of law is the implied covenant of marketable title (or merchantable title). In this context, the word "marketable" is not used in the layperson's sense; it does not mean that the title is saleable. It also is not a reference to the title's fair market value. A title can be marketable, yet be valueless in monetary terms. And a finding of marketability is not proof against declines or fluctuations in market value.

has to
do w/ ability
to sell

Rather, as a legal term of art, a marketable title means a title that is reasonably free of encumbrances and other title defects and free of the risk of litigation. *Voorheesville Rod & Gun Club v. Tompkins Co.*, 626 N.E.2d 917 (N.Y. 1993). The notion is that a buyer should not "be compelled to purchase a lawsuit" along with the land. Therefore, if any significant question exists concerning the seller's title to the land, the marketable title provision is violated and the buyer cannot be compelled to purchase.

The definition of "marketable title" is flexible and has been fleshed out by the courts on a case-by-case basis. All the definitions used by courts involve the probability that a claim will be made or litigation initiated against the owner. For example, a former owner's heirs may claim the title, but they are unlikely to assert their claim successfully once the decedent's estate has been probated and and the title established in someone else by the probate decree. Similarly, although long lost heirs might in fact own part of the title in tenancy in common, their claim may be old and unlikely to be asserted. The marketable title standard does not permit buyers to refuse a title that is subject to such minor defects, but it does permit refusal when the encumbrance affects the title that the purchaser thought she was acquiring at the time of the contract.

Titles become unmarketable in three ways. First, a title is unmarketable if the seller had title but lost it in an action or proceeding. For example, the seller may have lost title to all or part of the property in a partition action, an ejectment action after a third party adversely possessed the land, or a condemnation proceeding in eminent domain.

Second, a title can be unmarketable if the vendor never acquired title because of a flaw in the chain of title. For example, a deed in the chain might be forged, undelivered, fraudulently procured, or executed by a person without legal authority, such as a corporate officer who did not have authority to convey the land. Similarly, a chain of title that depends on a judicial proceeding for which the court did not have jurisdiction or for which the statutory requirements were not followed also renders the title unmarketable.

Finally, an encumbrance on the title can cause it to be unmarketable. An "encumbrance" is a lien or other nonpossessory interest or a nonfreehold possessory interest. For example, an encumbrance can be a mortgage, mechanic's lien, or judgment lien, all of which relate to a monetary claim. An easement, restrictive covenant, irrevocable license, lease, party wall agreement, and the rights of cotenants also constitute encumbrances; all affect the use or possession of the land. The list of possible encumbrances is very long. See Powell on Real Property § 81.03[6][d][iii] (Michael Allan Wolf ed., 2009).

An encumbrance often is described as a private agreement affecting title, but this statement is overly broad. Although a private restrictive covenant is an encumbrance that can render title unmarketable, a public zoning ordinance restricting the property in the same way is not an encumbrance. The difference is not just that the covenant is a private agreement and the zoning ordinance is a public regulation. Rather, the critical distinction is that title examiners typically search the property records for private restrictive covenants but do not search the zoning laws. In part, this is because the cost of searching for private agreements in the better organized property records is less than the cost of searching the often poorly organized zoning records.

However, circumstances exist in which zoning can cause a property title to be unmarketable. For example, when a zoning ordinance violation results in a lien or judgment affecting the property, the title becomes unmarketable if the next sale of the property is materially affected. Thus, a zoning ordinance enforcement order materially affects the title. In contrast, the enforcement of a housing or building code might not, because they are so full of technical provisions that practically every structure violates one or more of their provisions. Similarly, although a tax assessment itself does not render the title unmarketable, a lien for unpaid taxes does.

A contract of sale can provide that the title need not be marketable. The contract also can provide that the buyer agrees to take subject to certain encumbrances or other matters that otherwise would render the title unmarketable. In fact, to avoid breaching the marketable title covenant, the seller must specify in the contract of sale any title encumbrances that will remain on the title after the buyer acquires it. For example, if the buyer has agreed to acquire title subject to a mortgage, the mortgage should be listed in the contract as an exception to the marketable title covenant.

Although the marketable title covenant is contained in the contract of sale, the seller need not have marketable title until the closing. One of the purposes for the executory period between the contract's execution and the closing is to give the seller time to correct any title defects. Typically, during the executory period, the seller presents evidence of his title to the buyer. The buyer then can object to any matter not listed in the contract as an exception to the marketable title covenant. The seller has until the closing to clear the title of any such title objections. Therefore, the closing is when the title must be marketable and not before.

NOTES

1. Unless otherwise provided in the contract, a buyer's obligation to pay the deposit during the executory period is independent of the marketable title covenant. A seller's title does not have to be marketable before the closing. However, if the buyer discovers that the seller knew that his title was unmarketable when the buyer executed the contract, some recent cases have permitted immediate rescission on the basis that the seller made a tortious misrepresentation. See *Seligman v. First Nat'l Inv., Inc.*, 540 N.E.2d 1057 (Ill. App. Ct. 1989).

2. Although cases to the contrary exist, the majority rule is that the buyer's agreement to accept a quitclaim deed does not waive the marketable title covenant. See, e.g., *Boekelheide v. Snyder*, 26 N.W.2d 74 (S.D. 1947). A contract provision for a quitclaim deed is arguably consistent with the implied covenant of marketable title. The quitclaim conveys whatever title the seller has; the buyer is entitled to insist that, whatever the title is, it must be marketable. Moreover, the use of deed warranties does not affect the title the seller must present; warranties merely provide the buyer with a remedy if the title is defective.

H. Breaks in the Chain of Title

In most jurisdictions, the marketable title standard does not require that the title be provable based solely on the public property records. For example, by the weight of authority, a title that can be shown to satisfy the elements of adverse possession generally is considered to be marketable, even though it has not been proven in a quiet title action. See, e.g., *Conklin v. Davi*, 388 A.2d 598 (N.J. 1978). However, because of the inherent uncertainties in a title based on adverse possession, a good argument can be made that a gap in the chain of title caused by adverse possession should be deemed to render title unmarketable. After all, a judge may not agree with the seller's interpretation of the facts. But if the buyer elects to proceed with the sale, he should obtain affidavits that document the facts on which the seller bases its claim of adverse possession and should keep track of the seller's whereabouts!

TRIMBOLI v. KINKEL
123 N.E. 205 (N.Y. 1919)

Cardozo, J.

This is an action by client against attorney. In 1906 the plaintiffs retained the defendant to search the title to land in Brooklyn which the plaintiffs were about to buy. The defendant reported that the title was good and marketable. He made up an abstract which he delivered to his clients. This abstract shows that in 1861 title was in Aaron Clark and Harriet A. Anderson as tenants in common. Mr. Clark left a will by which his real estate passed to devisees in fee. Power to sell the land and divide the proceeds was given to the executor. The executor in 1863 conveyed his testator's undivided interest to the co-tenant, Harriet A. Anderson. The grantee in return conveyed to the executor an interest in another parcel. The transaction was not a sale for money, but an exchange. Its nature is disclosed by the deed, which is described in the abstract. Harriet A. Anderson conveyed the land in 1868 to one Frederick W. Grimme, whose title passed thereafter, by mesne conveyances, to the plaintiffs' vendors. The law is settled that a power to sell and distribute the proceeds is not a power to exchange (*Woerz v. Rademacher*, 120 N.Y. 62, 68 [further citations omitted]). There was, therefore, a flaw in the record title. The defendant made no mention of it to his clients. He made no investigation of the occupation of the land. He supplied no evidence of adverse possession. He let his clients complete the purchase on the assumption that the record title was perfect. In 1910 the plaintiffs made a contract of resale. The purchaser rejected title because of the flaw in the record. The defendant represented the plaintiffs at the closing. Even then he supplied no evidence of adverse possession. He made no claim that title could be sustained upon that ground. His position still was that the record title was sufficient. The purchaser sued for the deposit and the expenses of searching title. The sellers defended. They were then represented by new counsel. The purchaser prevailed, and the title was adjudged unmarketable. This action was then brought to compel the attorney to respond for the damages resulting from his negligence. In defense he has attempted to prove that the defect in the record title has been cured by adverse possession for more than fifty years. The trial judge held that, with this evidence available, there was a marketable title, and that the defendant had not been negligent. The complaint was dismissed upon the merits. The Appellate Division ruled that "the defendant was negligent in passing the title upon the view that the executor's deed was valid." It, therefore, reversed the judgment and ordered a new trial.

We agree with the Appellate Division that negligence was proved. The executor's deed was plainly invalid. It is negligence to fail to apply the settled rules of law that should be known to all conveyancers (. . . *Watson v. Muirhead*, 57 Penn. St. 161). The defendant knew the facts, for his search went back to the executor's deed and farther. Knowing the facts, he was chargeable with knowledge of their significance. In the absence of clear and cogent evidence of adverse possession, the title was unmarketable (*Freedman v. Oppenheim*, 187 N.Y. 101). That evidence, if it existed, should have been gathered by the defendant, and preserved in fitting form, before title was accepted (*Crocker Point Association v. Gouraud*, 224 N.Y. 343, 350). Nothing of the kind was done. Mere lapse of time was insufficient without proof of a hostile holding (*Simis v. McElroy*, 160 N.Y. 156). The defendant does not acquit himself of negligence by showing that evidence could have been collected. He must show that it was collected. Until that duty had been fulfilled, the title was unmarketable.

The question remains whether there is any evidence of damage. The defendant has proved that for more than fifty years the plaintiffs and their grantors have been in hostile and unchallenged occupation of the land. The trial judge has held that they have title. We do not need to determine whether their ownership is unclouded by any reasonable doubt. At least, they cannot be said to have made good their allegation that they are not the owners (*Woolley v. Newcombe*, 87 N.Y. 605). Their title to an undivided half is independent of the power of sale, and is undoubted. Their title to the other half, if not undoubted, has been supported by evidence which would make out a prima facie case in any contest with an adverse claimant (*Koch v. Ellwood*, 138 App. Div. 584 [many out of state citations omitted]). In such circumstances, there can be no recovery either of the whole purchase price or of half of it, even if we assume this to be the proper measure of damage where title to the whole or the half has altogether failed. The cloud, if there is any, is shadowy and vague and distant. There has been no attempt to prove the extent to which the presence of such a cloud depreciates the value (*Lawall v. Groman*, 180 Penn. St. 532, 540).

The defendant argues that the damages are, therefore, nominal. But we think this does not follow. The plaintiffs relied on the defendant's assurance that they had a marketable record title. Relying upon that assurance, they made a fruitless contract of resale. They have lost the commissions paid their brokers. They have been forced to reimburse the purchaser for the cost of an examination of the title. If the defendant had been diligent, these expenses would have been saved. The consequences were to be foreseen. A marketable title is one that may be freely made the subject of resale. Resale involves certain expenses as common, if not necessary, incidents. A lawyer takes the risk that those expenses will be lost if he fails to gather in due season the evidences of title. It is a loss within the range of probable contemplation (*U.S. Trust Co. of N.Y. v. O'Brien*, 143 N.Y. 284 [further citations omitted]). A different situation would be presented if the plaintiffs had themselves been negligent in failing to supply proof of adverse possession, and had thereby thrown away the opportunity of preserving their contract and minimizing the damage. They are not chargeable with negligence, for the defendant was still their lawyer, and when title was rejected, he made no claim, and supplied no evidence, of title through possession. The fault was still his own. It is true that the plaintiffs have claimed more than they should get. They are not entitled to recover the profits of the resale (*Hadley v. Baxendale*, 9 Exch. 341 [further citations omitted]). They are still the occupants, and, it may be, the owners of the land, which, for all that the evidence shows, is equally valuable to-day. They are not entitled to recover the costs of their lawsuit with the purchaser. It was foolish as well as futile to litigate the validity of the exercise of the power of sale. Costs of litigation are not chargeable as damages unless reasonably incurred (*Gallo v. Brooklyn Savings Bank*, 129 App. Div. 698, 700 [further citations omitted]). Payments made in the reasonable endeavor to discover evidence of adverse possession may stand upon another basis (*Den Norske Am. Actiesselskabet v. Sun Printing & Pub. Ass'n*, 226 N.Y. 1). But we have said enough to show that there is some evidence of damage. Beyond that we need not go. The extent of the recovery is not important at this time. If the plaintiffs made out a right to anything, the Appellate Division did not err in granting a new trial. Upon the inquest that will follow, the defendant's stipulation for judgment absolute may charge him with heavier damages than he would otherwise have to bear. That risk, however, was assumed when the stipulation was given.

The order should be affirmed, and judgment absolute directed in favor of the plaintiffs upon the stipulation, with costs in all courts.

I.   Express Title Standards in Contracts

To avoid the problem described in the last section, a buyer should not rely on the implied covenant of marketable title. Instead, he should provide in the contract that the seller must present a marketable title "of record." See 3 Am. L. Prop. 126, § 11.47 (James Casner ed., 1952). This provision is satisfied only by a title for which each successive owner recorded the deed or other document by which it acquired its interest in the property. In real estate jargon, each link in the chain of title must be documented in the public records. Including the words "of record" in the contract of sale is particularly important if the buyer intends to obtain a mortgage loan to acquire or to develop the property.

As an alternative to the marketable title standard, many standard form contracts of sale provide that the seller must tender "insurable" title to the buyer. By the weight of authority, an insurable title is generally equivalent to a marketable title. However, a title insurance company often is willing to insure over an encumbrance for an extra premium, thereby making the title "insurable." Therefore, the insurable title standard can be dangerous for the buyer. It effectively takes the decision whether to accept the title out of the buyer's hands and puts it into the title insurance company's hands. Unsurprisingly, title insurance companies often are the source of the form contracts with the insurable title provision. If the buyer does agree to accept an insurable title, he should insist that the contract stipulate which title company must agree to insure the title and on what terms. That way, if the title turns out to be defective, he will avoid having to look to Ed's Title Insurance Company for recourse based on a "Brand X" title insurance policy.

Suppose that parties execute a contract of sale for Blackacre providing "seller shall furnish marketable and insurable title free from encumbrances, subject to those matters described herein" and the local electric utility owns an easement, described in the contract, across one corner of Blackacre. The title is unmarketable on this account, although the issue is one of contract interpretation. Does the "subject to . . ." language modify the marketable title standard so that the seller can furnish something less, or does it merely provide an exemption from the marketable title standard, meaning that the standard is unaffected? See *Laba v. Carey*, 277 N.E.2d 641, 644 (N.Y. 1971). The strong public policy of incorporating the marketable title standard into contracts of sale dictates that the latter interpretation be preferred. The buyer could have avoided this ambiguity by providing in the contract that seller "shall furnish a marketable title, but may, at buyer's option, convey the property free of encumbrances other than those named and waived by buyer herein."

J. Contract Remedies

Although contracts for the sale of land have unique features, the remedies they provide are the same as for other types of contracts — damages, specific performance, and rescission.

1. Damages

The traditional measure of damages for breach of a contract of sale for real property is nominal damages, measured on the day of the breach. This remedy is a type of restitution. It is measured by the nondefaulting party's reasonable, out-of-pocket costs incurred in the transaction up to the date of the breach. In the case of the seller, this amount is reduced by any amount recoupable when the property is resold. For example, if the seller paid for a title search that later was used in a resale, its value is not recoverable from the original defaulting buyer.

"Nominal damages" usually refers only to the nondefaulting party's expenses for the sale contemplated by the defaulted contract. Thus a buyer's greater expenditure in another transaction would not be recoverable under this measure of damages. *Floreau v. Thornhill*, 2 W. Bl. 1078, 96 Eng. Rep. 635 (1776); *Crenshaw v. Williams*, 231 S.W. 45, 48 A.L.R. 5 (Ky. 1921). The underlying premise is to avoid unduly punishing a seller who may not know the exact extent of her ownership. That determination can be made only after the title has been examined. But when the seller intentionally misrepresents the fact of ownership because in fact she owns nothing, an exception to this general rule exists.

WOLOFSKY v. BEHRMAN
454 So. 2d 614 (Fla. App. 1984)

Downey, J.

In a suit for breach of a contract to sell a condominium apartment, the trial court awarded appellant-purchaser as damages only a return of the purchaser's deposit money plus interest. Contending that he was entitled to damages for loss of his bargain, the purchaser has perfected this appeal. In developing a condominium complex, appellant, Wolofsky, sold one of the apartments to appellees, Harold and Elaine Behrman. The Behrmans intended to move into the apartment when they were successful in selling their single family residence. When the residence did not sell the Behrmans decided to sell the condominium instead. After some futile efforts to sell the apartment, Behrman accepted Wolofsky's offer to buy it for $73,000 and a memorandum contract was signed. Although Wolofsky was not interested in the furnishings therein, his sales agent agreed to try to sell them for the Behrmans for $4,000. Behrman delivered the keys to the apartment to the agent, who was able to obtain an offer of only $3,000, which Behrman refused. A few weeks before the closing was due, Behrman visited the apartment and found evidence that someone had been staying there without his permission. The electricity was on; he found a T.V. and radio, bedclothes on the bed, food in the kitchen, and a few clothes in a closet. Behrman testified he was very upset; he was outraged; he felt violated. As a consequence, he advised Wolofsky that there could be no further relationship between them and he returned the deposit and refused to close. Apparently, Wolofsky had obtained a purchaser for the apartment for $100,000 and the sales agent had allowed that purchaser to stay briefly in the apartment.

Wolofsky sued the Behrmans for specific performance and damages. The former claim was abandoned and the case went to trial on the claim for damages and Behrmans' counterclaim for trespass. The final judgment states that the Behrmans admit they breached the contract and admit they are liable therefor. However, they denied they acted in bad faith. The trial court accepted Behrmans' contention and found no showing of bad faith.

Before discussing the applicable legal principles, we think it advisable to point out that a) the Behrmans never lived in this apartment, nor did they ever intend to after contracting with Wolofsky, b) while Wolofsky did not have permission to allow anyone to occupy the apartment, the contract between the parties was silent as to possession, c) Wolofsky offered to compensate the Behrmans for the use of the apartment, d) under the doctrine of equitable conversion the equitable title was in Wolofsky and any loss or destruction to the property would fall upon him, and e) the closing was only a few weeks away.

There are numerous Florida cases involving the measure of damages for breach of a contract to sell realty. Florida has long since aligned itself with the English rule announced in *Flureau v. Thornhill*, 2 W.Bl. 1078, 96 Eng. Rep. 635, to the effect that, except where a vendor has acted in bad faith, his liability for breach of a land sale contract is limited to the amount of the deposit paid by the purchaser, with interest and reimbursement for expenses in investigating title to the property.

However, absent good faith, he is liable for full compensatory damages, including the loss of his bargain, which is the difference between the value of the property and the contract price.

In *Key v. Alexander*, 108 So. 883 (Fla. 1926), the Supreme Court of Florida quoted from Sutherland on Damages as follows: "If the person selling is in default — if he knew or should have known that he could not comply with his undertaking; if he, being an agent, contracted in his own name, depending on his principal to fulfill his contract merely because he had power to negotiate a sale; if he has only a contract of the owner to convey, or a bond for a deed; if his contract to sell requires the signature of his wife to bar an inchoate right of dower, or the consent of a third person to render his deed effectual; if he makes his contract without title in the expectation of subsequently being able to acquire it and is unable to fulfill by reason of cause so known the want of concurrence of other persons; or if he has title and refused to convey, or disables himself from doing so by conveyance to another person — in all such cases he is beyond the reach of the principle of *Flureau v. Thornhill*, 2 W. Black (Eng.) 1078, and is liable to full compensatory damages including those for the loss of the bargain." 108 So. at 885. In analyzing the good faith-bad faith dichotomy, which pertains to this rule, Professor McCormick suggests that the present refinements of the rule seem to lean heavily on the requirement that the vendor must "do his best" by reasonable efforts or expenditures to complete the conveyance. McCormick on Damages, § 179, p. 189.

The Behrmans had legal title to the property in question but refused to convey. Thus it is clear to us that the Behrmans did not "do their best" to complete the conveyance. While they may be justified in not acceding to someone's living in the apartment until closing, that is an inadequate reason for refusing to close. The trial court was correct in finding that refusing to close for the reason given constituted a breach of the contract; he erred in finding that it did not demonstrate a failure to exercise the good faith required to preclude full compensatory damages. The inability of a vendor to close for reasons beyond his control does not necessarily mean the vendee should recover the loss of his bargain. In each of the cited cases the vendor wanted to close but was precluded by factors beyond his control. Here, there were no factors beyond the Behrmans' control except their excessive pique over the unauthorized brief use of their apartment without their consent. Thus, they not only did not do their best, they did nothing to effectuate the completion of the contract. This constitutes lack of good faith. Thus, under the applicable rules, they were liable for full compensatory damages. Accordingly, the judgment appealed from is reversed and the cause is remanded for further proceedings consistent with this opinion.

NOTE

In a jurisdiction awarding "nominal damages," when will a seller's bad faith provide a basis for a damage award measured by the lost "benefit of the bargain"? See *Beard v. S/E Joint Venture*, 581 A.2d 1275 (Md. 1990). In about half the states, "benefit of the bargain," "difference money," or consequential damages are routinely awarded, measured by the difference between the contract price and the fair market value of the property. See *Browder v. Williams*, 765 So. 2d 1281 (Miss.

2000). When the current market value is higher than the contract price, this remedy provides nothing to the seller because a resale recoups the loss; conversely, the buyer recovers no damages if the contract price exceeds the current market value, because he is well out of a bad deal.

When the buyer defaults, regardless of the jurisdiction's measure of damages, the vendor is entitled in a majority of states to retain the purchaser's down payment, contract deposit, earnest money, or binder, so long as it is no more than a customary amount. In the absence of a contrary contract provision, the buyer has the burden of litigation to sue for its return. However, in a minority of states, absent a contrary contract provision, a defaulting buyer is not barred from recovering the down payment, contract deposit, earnest money, or binder to the extent that it exceeds the seller's actual damages. See *Kutzin v. Pirnie*, 591 A.2d 932 (N.J. 1991).

In response to litigation and requests from buyers for the return of down payments, standard form contracts of sale now often provide that the seller may retain the down payment as liquidated damages when the buyer defaults. Another common contract form provides that, on the buyer's default, the seller and her broker will split the down payment. This type of provision raises the issue of whether retention of the down payment constitutes an illegal penalty, rather than an enforceable liquidated damages provision. For the provision to be valid, the parties must have bargained freely for it, actual damages must be difficult or impossible to calculate, and the liquidated damages amount must represent a fair estimate of the seller's actual damages. When a standard, pre-printed form is used, these can be difficult issues for the seller to prove! However, absent a contrary contract provision, the seller is not prevented from electing either to keep the liquidated damages or to sue for actual damages, so the seller's right to actual damages is normally preserved.

States have adopted one of three different dates in determining the seller's damages when land values are falling. In a majority of states, the seller's damages are measured on the date of the buyer's breach. In a few states, they are measured from the date of the contract. In the remaining minority of states, they are measured on the date the seller resells the property if she diligently pursues a resale. What justifications can you provide for each of these rules?

2. Specific Performance

Because each parcel of real property is unique, a presumption exists that the damage remedy is inadequate. Therefore, courts traditionally grant specific performance as a remedy for purchasers. However, courts are less inclined to grant specific performance to a seller because she simply can resell the property. Courts have been particularly unsympathetic to her prayer for specific performance when the property's characteristics are less unique, such as a unit in a condominium building. Contrast *Centex Homes Corp. v. Boag*, 320 A.2d 194 (N.J. Super. 1974) (denying specific performance to a condominium vendor), with *Giannini v. First National Bank of Des Plaines*, 483 N.E.2d 924 (Ill. App. 1985) (granting specific performance to a condominium buyer), criticized in *Gordon v. Bauer*, 532 N.E.2d 855, 864 (Ill. App. 1988).

To obtain a decree for specific performance, the petitioner first must tender performance under the contract. The tender cannot impose a new contract condition or contingency not already required of the defendant. Additionally, a court will grant specific performance only if the contract of sale is legally binding. To be legally binding, the contract must have definitive terms and must be supported by adequate, as opposed to fair, consideration. The consideration is deemed to be adequate when it was fairly bargained for or is the defendant's asking price. *Surman v. Blansett*, 539 S.E.2d 890 (Ga. App. Ct. 2000). The contract must be mutually binding on the parties, and damages must be an inadequate remedy.

A contract does not lack a definitive term merely because it does not specify the closing date. The law will imply a requirement that the closing occur within a reasonable time. Likewise, when the legal description is a material term under the state's Statute of Frauds, an ambiguous description can be made definite based on extrinsic evidence concerning the parties' intent. Therefore, a party who wishes to specifically enforce a contract that is not completely definitive in its terms first can attempt to reform the contract to provide the necessary definiteness. *DeLeon v. Zaino*, 608 A.2d 829, 832 (Md. 1992).

Because specific performance is an equitable remedy, a court has discretion whether to grant or deny it. *Kessler v. Tortoise Dev., Inc.*, 1 P.3d 292 (Idaho 2000). For example, if the seller's money is tied up in land so that he needs cash, a court is more likely to grant specific performance if the buyer defaults. If the buyer drove too hard a bargain so that the purchase price is too low, a court may deny him specific performance. In this case, allowing the seller to pay damages may be the more equitable remedy.

An action for specific performance often also includes a request for additional remedies, such as: (1) a *lis pendens*, to give notice that the property title is the subject of litigation and that persons acquiring an interest in the property may lose it to satisfy the decree; (2) a temporary restraining order to prevent the seller from taking action inconsistent with the contract; (3) a petition for the court to appoint a receiver to manage the property and prevent waste; and (4) an abatement in the purchase price, particularly if improvements on the property have been destroyed by fire, flood, or other natural causes during the executory period.

KIES v. WARRICK
182 N.W. 998 (Minn. 1921)

HALLAM, J.

On October 25, 1917, defendant, Cordelia Warrick, and her husband, Isaac Warrick, contracted to sell to plaintiff an irregular tract of land in Nobles County. This action was brought to compel specific performance of the agreement. From a judgment for plaintiff, defendants appeal. There is evidence that, prior to the making of the contract sued on, the Warricks placed the land in the hands of John Mitchell, a land man of Worthington, for sale, and told him the tract contained 209 acres. Mitchell went to plaintiff and negotiated a sale at $140 an acre, and told him the farm contained 209 acres, and drew a written contract of sale stipulating for a sale at $140 an acre or $29,260. Mitchell and plaintiff went together to procure the signatures of the Warricks to this contract, but the Warricks wanted more money. They demanded $29,800. Plaintiff testified that he sat down with them and figured the price per acre on a basis of 209 acres at $142.58 per acre, and then told them he would accept the offer. He then prepared a contract of sale which described the property according to government subdivisions and as "containing in all, two hundred and nine (209) acres." The price named in the contract was $29,800, the sum of $1,000 to be paid on execution of the contract, $8,800 March 1, 1918, $20,000 on or before March 1, 1928, with interest at 5½ per cent per annum.

Thereafter, two matters of controversy arose. Plaintiff had the land surveyed and claimed the acreage was only 203.17. There were mortgages upon the land aggregating above $8,000 to one Patterson, due March 1, 1921, and the mortgagee would not accept the money and release the mortgages.

Plaintiff in his complaint asked that the court require defendants to give a deed of the premises described, that deduction be made from the price to be paid by plaintiff because of the shortage in the acreage and that the amount of the encumbrances upon the land be deducted from the purchase price. The court made its decree in accordance with these demands in the complaint. The court found "that the price of the said land was computed upon the basis of 209 acres and that the price per acre so computed was $142.58." Defendants challenge the part of this finding that the farm was sold "on an acreage basis, or for any particular price per acre." They contend that this finding is "absolutely without foundation in the evidence" and that "this being so, the whole fabric of plaintiff's case falls." There may be some question whether this contract can be considered technically a sale at the price of $142.58 per acre, but in our opinion this is by no means decisive of the case. The contract does in express terms stipulate that the tract sold is described as "containing in all two hundred and nine (209) acres," and the tract in fact falls short by 5.83 acres.

We understand the rule to be that, where the tract sold is described as of a given quantity, that quantity is a material term of the contract, and, if it is in fact deficient in quantity, the court may, at the option of the purchaser, decree a conveyance, and allow the purchaser pecuniary compensation or abatement of price proportioned to the amount of the deficiency. Pomeroy, Contracts, Specific Performance, § 434–435, 438; Warvelle, Vendors, § 749; *Tobin v. Larkin*, 67 N.E. 340 (Mass. 1903). This appeals to us as a just rule and we adopt it and hold that it is applicable, whether the land is sold by the acre or for a lump sum.

Defendants contend there is no competent evidence as to the acreage of the farm. A surveyor, H.W. Jones, gave evidence that he surveyed the farm and made notes and records of the survey at the time, and later from such original notes and records made a plat of the farm. This plat, he said, correctly showed the number of acres in the farm. The plat was received in evidence and the witness was permitted to testify, without introduction of his notes in evidence, that he found in his survey that the farm contained 203.17 acres. There was no error. Where a surveyor testifies to the accuracy of a plat made by him, it is not ordinarily error to receive the plat in evidence, even though it was made from notes which are not in evidence. The sufficiency of the verification is a question addressed to the discretion of the trial judge. *Strasser v. Stabeck*, 127 N.W. 384 (Minn. 1910). A witness who has made a survey of land for the purpose of determining its acreage and who has computed the acreage from measurements taken by him, may also testify as to the acreage found by him without introduction of the notes in evidence.

There is ample evidence that plaintiff was at all times ready, able and willing to carry out his contract. Plaintiff was not required to make tender of performance, *Lewis v. Prendergast*, 39 N.W. 802 (Minn. 1888), and was never in default because defendants were never able to fully perform.

The contract, through mistake of parties, omitted to provide that the deferred payment shall be secured by a purchase money mortgage upon the land sold. Plaintiff conceded that this provision should have been in the contract, and the decree provides that the mortgage shall be given. Defendants have no ground for complaint. That a provision, favorable to the defendant, has been omitted by mistake, is not a defense, if the plaintiff is ready, able and willing to perform the whole agreement including the omitted term. *Anderson v. Kennedy*, 16 N.W. 816 (Mich. 1883). Judgment affirmed.

NOTE

Suppose that buyers sue for specific performance of a contract for a new house and lot. In the same suit, can they also receive damages for the delay in moving in? The traditional answer is yes; delay damages are permissible. Suppose further that the construction of the house is defective? May they sue for these damages as well? Here the answer is less certain. See *Billy Williams Builders and Developers, Inc. v. Hillerich*, 446 S.W.2d 280, 282 (Ky. 1969) (noting a split in the authorities). As the *Kies* opinion indicates, once equitable jurisdiction attaches, a court will attempt to resolve all disputes between the parties in its decree.

3. Rescission

Rescission is the cancellation of the contract. The cancellation can be by mutual agreement of the parties or by court decree. The grounds for rescission include mutual mistake of fact, failure of consideration, fraud, intentional misrepresentation, undue influence, and duress. See *Halvorson v. Birkland*, 171 N.W.2d 77 (S.D. 1969), noted in 15 S.D. L. Rev. 435 (1970). Although rescission is sometimes regarded as an equitable remedy, the authority on this issue is divided. When characterized as equitable, the party seeking rescission must not be in breach because of the equitable "clean hands" doctrine. Moreover, even though grounds exist for rescission, the remedy is not automatic. For example, when the parties make a mutual mistake about the acreage, rescission may not be granted if the acreage actually conveyed can be used by its purchaser and the latter can be compensated for the deficiency with an abatement in the price. See *Harris v. Axline*, 36 N.W.2d 154 (Mich. 1949). In other jurisdictions, rescission may be unavailable when the acreage is 10–15% more or less than contracted for, even when a mutual mistake is made, but a 20% difference, regardless of the remaining use, may be grounds for rescission. See *Bigham v. Madison*, 52 S.W. 1074, 1075 (Tenn. 1899) (suggesting this). A mutual mistake about the acreage to be conveyed is a mistake of fact. However, a mutual mistake about the acreage available for building or development because of zoning restrictions, is a mistake of law, which is not a basis for rescission. See *Burggraff v. Baum*, 720 A.2d 1167 (Me. 1998).

Intentional misrepresentation is a frequent basis for rescission. In this context, a misrepresentation may be intentional even though it was innocent and not made with the intent to deceive. See *Lesher v. Strid*, 996 P.2d 988 (Or. App. Ct. 2000).

In every jurisdiction, a person seeking rescission must restore or offer to restore all that he received under the contract. This "tender back" requirement is a precondition of any decree granting rescission. Indeed, a person often goes to court to seek rescission, rather than unilaterally declaring the contract to be at an end, in order to get a decree that the other parties must return what they have received under the contract. The court proceedings also give the plaintiff time to "tender back" when an immediate tender would be difficult or impossible.

GORDON v. TAFE
428 A.2d 892 (N.H. 1981)

Per Curiam.

In June 1978, the parties entered into a contract for the purchase and sale of the defendants' house. Two months later, the plaintiffs moved in, and shortly after that they discovered that the building was infested by termites. Subsequently, the plaintiffs filed a bill in equity, seeking rescission of the contract and damages. In support of the bill, they maintained that the defendants were aware of the termite problem prior to the sale and had misrepresented the condition of the house to the plaintiffs at the time of the conveyance. After a trial which included a view, the Superior Court (Souter, J.) found that the conveyance was based on a mutual mistake of material fact and granted the relief requested by the plaintiffs. The defendants appeal. They do not challenge the trial court's finding of mutual mistake but argue that rescission was an inappropriate remedy.

Rescission is an equitable remedy, which is discretionary with the court depending upon the facts of each case. *Barber v. Somers*, 150 A.2d 408, 411 (N.H. 1959); 8A G. Thompson, Modern Law of Real Property § 4465 at 365, § 4471 at 397 (1963). It is also held as a general proposition of law that before rescinding a contract, the court must determine that the parties can be returned to the status quo and that there will be no undue hardship to the defendant. *Barber*, 150 A.2d at 411.

The defendants first argue that the parties could not be returned to status quo because they had bought a new house. If we were to accept defendants' argument, then a court could almost never grant rescission in a case like the present, for it is not unusual for sellers to buy a new home in a similar situation. Furthermore, this court has recognized that the general principle that the parties must be put in the same situation in which they stood at the time of the contract was entered into cannot be taken in a strict literal sense. Otherwise "no contract could be rescinded after there has been a change of possession, because the parties could not be put in the same situation in which they were before the contract." *Concord Bank v. Gregg*,

14 N.H. 331, 338 (1842). As a practical matter, absolute and literal restoration is not required if all that is reasonably possible and demanded by the equities is done. 17A C.J.S. Contracts § 438 (1963); *Manchester Dairy System, Inc. v. Hayward*, 132 A. 12, 18 (N.H. 1926).

It is well settled law that a determination that the parties can be restored to the status quo depends upon the facts of each case. *National Shawmut Bank v. Cutter*, 196 A.2d 706, 709 (N.H. 1963). The trial court found that the plaintiffs returned the defendants' home to them in the same condition in which they had received it. The court was not compelled to find on evidence before it that the defendants would be unable to sell their new home and move back to their former residence. Accordingly, we hold that the trial court acted well within its discretion in finding that the parties could be restored substantially to the status quo.

Next the defendants assert that the court mistakenly found that an order of rescission would not cause them undue hardship. The main basis of the defendants' argument is financial; they assert that they cannot afford to pay two mortgages. "Undue" hardship is that which is excessive. See Oxford Universal Dictionary 2296 (3d ed. rev. 1955). Although financial difficulties are a hardship, they are not necessarily "undue." (Citation omitted.) A finding of undue hardship must be made upon the facts of each case. In its order, the trial court noted that rescission would cause the defendants "serious hardship," but, in view of the plaintiffs' need for relief and the defendants' conduct, the court found that the hardship was not undue in this case. *Manchester Dairy System*, 132 A. at 18.

The trial court apparently was aware of the consequences of its ruling, because it reached its decision after several post-trial conferences at which the defendants allegedly explained the probable consequences of the court's decision to them. Because we do not have a record of those conferences, our review of the propriety of the court's judgment is restricted. See *McCrady v. Mahon*, 400 A.2d 1173, 1174 (N.H. 1979). * * * After reviewing the court's order, we conclude that it gave careful consideration to all the circumstances before granting rescission. Accordingly, we find no abuse of discretion . . . and hold on the record that the trial court properly found, ruled, and decreed as it did. Affirmed.

4. Other Remedies

Every real property seller has an equitable lien on the property that is the subject of the contract of sale. This lien is for any portion of the purchase price that is unpaid at the closing. For example, the lien protects the seller if the buyer's check for the purchase price bounces. Similarly, the buyer has an equitable lien for any portion of the purchase price paid before the vendor defaults or otherwise refuses to close the transaction.

IV. LAND TRANSFERS

A. History of Common Law Conveyancing

The earliest, and at first the only, evidence of title was possession. Thus, a transfer of title was evidenced by livery of seisin in deed or in law. No writing was necessary. Instead, livery in deed required the grantor ("feoffor") and the grantee ("feoffee") to go to the land, where the feoffor would hand the feoffee a clod of dirt, a stick, or some other object that symbolized a transfer of ownership. The feoffor and feoffee did not have to enter the land for a livery in law. Instead, they stood where they could see the land, and the feoffor directed the feoffe to take possession of it.

The Statute of Uses (1535) brought into common use written methods of conveyance that did not require livery of seisin. These included a covenant to stand seised, a contract of bargain and sale, and a deed of lease and release. In addition, when the transfer included nonpossessory interests, such as easements, a written deed was necessary because livery of seisin was impossible for them. Written deeds became customary, though optional, until the enactment of the Statute of Frauds in 1677. See Joyce Palomar, 1 Patton and Palomar on Land Titles 4-7 (3d ed. 2003). Once deeds were required, they had to be delivered and accepted. In the United States, the Statue of Uses was often relied on "to give effect to an instrument which might otherwise be ineffective to operate as a conveyance." *Id.* at 8. In addition, many states enacted statutes that prescribe short forms of deeds that are effective as a conveyance without livery of seisin. These deeds often resemble the "grant deeds" used earlier for nonpossessory interests and typically include warranties prescribed by the same statute. *Id.*

B. Modern Conveyancing

Today, a deed is normally used to convey title to real property, and a bill of sale is used to convey title to personal property. A deed can be used to convey any interest in land, whether the fee simple absolute title or a more limited interest. Each time an interest in land is conveyed, a new deed is prepared and delivered to the grantee. The most commonly used deed forms are the general warranty deed, the special warranty deed (also known as a limited warranty deed or as a bargain and sale deed), and the quitclaim deed. However, some variations exist among the states. For example, the most commonly used deed forms in California are the quitclaim deed and the grant deed, which is the equivalent of a special warranty deed.

A common law deed is divided into four parts. The first part is the "premises." It contains the names of the parties, the granting clause, and the consideration if any and generally ends with the legal description of the property. The second part is the habendum clause, which begins with the words "to have and to hold" and describes the interest that is being conveyed. The third part is the deed warranties, and the fourth and final part is the testimonium clause ("witnessed by my hand" or "Given this day" are the key introductory phrases for this clause).

Different types of deeds are characterized by the amount of protection they provide a grantee against title defects. The general warranty deed provides the most protection. It includes title covenants for any defect in the title, whether created before or during the grantor's period of ownership.

A second type of deed is the special warranty deed. Despite its name, a special warranty deed is not better for grantees than a general warranty deed. This type of deed is more aptly described by its other name, the limited warranty deed. Any limitation on the warranties in a general warranty deed causes the deed to become a limited warranty deed. For example, if the deed includes fewer than all the common law covenants, it is a limited warranty deed. More commonly, however, a limited warranty deed has all the covenants but is limited in time to the grantor's period of ownership. Therefore, the grantor would be liable on the deed covenants for an easement that attached to the title during her period of ownership, but not for an easement that already existed when she acquired title to the land.

The third type of deed, the quitclaim deed, is the least desirable for a grantee because it includes no title covenants. The quitclaim deed transfers whatever interest, if any, the grantor has in the property. The grantee does not have recourse against the grantor even if he had no interest in the property. Similarly, the grantee has no recourse if the title is encumbered by easements, mortgages, judgment liens, or any other property interests. Understandably, buyers normally are unwilling to settle for a quitclaim deed. This type of deed usually is used for more limited purposes, such as releasing a mortgage, transferring property intra-family, or settling a boundary line dispute.

Whichever type of deed the parties use, it must be in writing to satisfy the Statute of Frauds. The original English Statute of Frauds provided that any transfer of an interest in land must be in writing, and every state in this country has enacted a similar statute. Most state statutes include exceptions to the writing requirement, such as for short-term leases. But when a writing is required, it must include at least the grantor's and grantee's names, a legal description of the land, words reflecting the grantor's intent to convey the property, and the grantor's signature.

The grantor's name must appear in the body of the deed and must identify the grantor with sufficient certainty. The requirement can be satisfied by pronouns in the deed that are sufficiently linked to the grantor's signature on the deed. Although the grantor's name in the body of the instrument should be identical to the signature, courts usually will not invalidate a deed for this type of technical defect.

The requirements for the grantee's name are similar to those for the grantor. The grantee must be described with sufficient certainty, but courts generally hold that misdescriptions, misspellings, and other technical defects will not invalidate a deed. The most difficult issue concerning the grantee's identity involves the situation in which a grantor signs a deed with the grantee's name left blank and authorizes a third party to fill in the blank. Courts often uphold the deed's validity, but the cases are not uniform.

The legal description of the land must be sufficiently detailed that the land can be distinguished from every other parcel. As will be described later in this chapter, three primary types of legal descriptions are widely used in this country: (1) metes and bounds, (2) government survey system, and (3) subdivision plat. If the legal description is vague, courts sometimes admit extrinsic evidence to clarify it, rather than invalidate the deed.

The common law does not require that the deed include any particular words of conveyance. The only requirement is that the words used must demonstrate the grantor's present intent to convey. Therefore, words such as "grant," "convey," "give," and "sell" are all sufficient. However, courts have held that the grantor's promise to "warrant and defend" the title to the grantee is inadequate to satisfy this requirement. Conveyancers in an earlier era fell into the unfortunate habit of using strings of words of conveyance, such as "enfeoff, grant, bargain, sell, convey, surrender, remise, release, and confirm."

The grantor's signature generally is required for a deed to be enforceable, because the grantor is the "party to be charged" under the Statute of Frauds. The signature need only be a mark that sufficiently identifies the person who is signing the document. Therefore, a stamp or other mark adopted by an illiterate grantor can be sufficient. The grantor also may ratify the signature of another as his own, resulting in a valid deed. What if the property is owned by more than one person, but all the owners do not sign the deed? The deed is effective to convey the interests of the signing owners, unless the parties intended that it be valid only if signed by all the owners.

The grantee's signature is not needed for a valid deed even if it includes covenants that restrict the grantee's use of the land or impose affirmative obligations, such as an obligation to maintain a common wall. The grantee's acceptance of the deed is deemed to be adequate to demonstrate consent to its terms. Therefore, grantees do not sign the deed.

Some states require that a deed be signed by witnesses or acknowledged before a notary public or other specified official. "Acknowledgment" means that the grantor must appear before the specified official to confirm that the signature on the deed is hers. Of course, she also could sign the deed in the official's presence. Legislatures enacted the acknowledgment requirement as a substitute for the common law requirement of a seal. Because the acknowledgment requirement is in derogation of the common law, it is required only to the extent provided by applicable state law. In most states, acknowledgment is not a prerequisite to the deed's validity, but only to the deed's recordability in the public records.

Despite the widespread substitution of acknowledgment for the common law requirement of a seal, a few jurisdictions still require or permit the grantor to use a seal. The seal requirement originated at an early period in the common law when most people were illiterate and unable to sign their name. The seal was an alternative means of identification. Even if the jurisdiction does not require a seal for a deed to be effective, corporations sometimes provide in their by-laws or articles of incorporation that a deed or other document executed on behalf of the corporation is valid only if a corporate seal is affixed to the document. Similarly, the notary public or other official before whom the document is acknowledged must put his or her seal on the document.

Finally, although deeds routinely state at least a nominal consideration, such as one dollar, a deed need not be supported by consideration. Consideration is not required because the deed is a conveyance and not a contract. Moreover, people should be free to make gifts of land. However, when consideration is promised for a deed, can the deed be invalidated if the grantee does not give the consideration?

[handwritten: fraud case]

ANDERSON v. ANDERSON
620 S.W.2d 815 (Tex. App. 1981)

[handwritten: No consideration necessary for deeds, but if there is some then you have to say if you can't do it or its fraud and deed can be cancelled.]

SUMMERS, C.J.

This is an appeal from a judgment of the trial court cancelling a deed of conveyance.

Frank Bostick Anderson, plaintiff below and appellee here, brought this suit against defendants, William Wade Anderson (appellant) and Altha Miller seeking to rescind and set aside a deed executed by appellee's mother, Jewell Esther Anderson, to Altha Miller. Appellee alleged that said deed was fraudulently procured, that the stated consideration providing for "adequate care and maintenance" by grantee during grantor's lifetime had wholly failed and that the grantee, Altha Miller, never intended to perform this support obligation. The defendants' answer included a plea of not guilty, a general denial and plea that the consideration providing for support was a covenant rather than a condition subsequent. The case was tried to the court without the intervention of a jury. After hearing the evidence, the trial court rendered judgment which set aside and canceled the deed. From this adverse judgment only defendant William Wade Anderson has appealed. We affirm.

The following is a chronology of events leading to this suit:

(1) On May 5, 1970, Jewell Esther Anderson executed her will devising the property in question (being her homeplace consisting of four acres of land and improvements thereon in Sabine County, Texas) to her son, Frank Bostick Anderson, appellee herein. (2) On June 29, 1973, Jewell Esther Anderson executed a deed to Altha Miller which purported to convey the property in question[1] "for and in consideration of Altha Miller, my granddaughter, providing for the adequate care and maintenance of me during the remainder of my lifetime." (3) On July 1, 1975, Altha Miller deeded the property in question to William Wade Anderson (another son of Jewell Esther Anderson); no money or consideration was given for this conveyance. (4) On March 12, 1977, the said Jewell Esther Anderson died testate leaving the will devising the property in question to appellee. (5) On April 11, 1977, Jewell Anderson's will was admitted to probate as a muniment of title in Sabine County, Texas.

Charlie C. Anderson testified that he obtained the deed in question from his

---

[1] Grantor reserved a life estate with the right to full possession, benefit and use of premises, as well as the rents, issues and profits thereof, during her natural life.

mother, Jewell Esther Anderson, and was present when such instrument was signed; that he had heard his mother say several times that she would give the property in controversy to the "person or people who would come and take care of her the remainder of her life"; that it was his understanding that his mother meant for someone to come and take care of her at her place in Sabine County. He also testified that he had oral authority, or understood that he did at the time, from Altha Miller to represent her in dealing with his mother for legal papers to transfer the property to Altha in return for "Altha and her husband at that time, Richard, to come and take care of mother;" but on further questioning he stated that the authority he "really had" was oral approval from each of his brothers and sisters to make this contract with Altha and Richard and his mother. He further testified that he recalls having three conversations with Altha Miller about this matter, two over the telephone and one personally; that Altha's response to the proposal that she come to Sabine County and take care of his mother was at first quite in the affirmative; that he last talked to her about this matter about a month before he obtained the deed; that he thought he had authority from Altha to represent her in negotiating the deed because in their various conversations she said "yes, she wanted to do that" to "move down there and take care of mother," and that she had never rescinded that statement in his presence.

Altha Miller testified that Charlie Anderson called and stated if she could go to Sabine County and take care of her grandmother that he could get her grandmother to deed the property to her for such care; that her grandmother told her that if she would come to Sabine County, they would go to town, have the papers drawn and she would sign the same; that at first "they" were all enthusiastic about the matter and in the summer of 1972 she made a trip to see her grandmother to complete the transaction; that nothing was done on that occasion since the lawyers in Hemphill were out of town; that she had already begun to realize that she couldn't fulfill the obligations expected of her because she had four children at home and it would be necessary for her to sell her home and move to take care of her grandmother; that she later told her grandmother that she did not see how she could come at that time and take care of her because she had too many obligations at home; that in discussing this matter with Charlie she did not tell him he had the authority to act for her in negotiating the deed and she did not tell him not to do so; that she was ready to let the matter drop in 1972 because she realized she could not sell her home and take a chance on being able to make a living in Sabine County; that there was already a family controversy brewing and she wanted to drop the matter; that at Thanksgiving 1972 she told Charlie that she had reservations as to whether they would be financially able to come to Sabine County and take care of her grandmother and she did not see how they could come at that time. Mrs. Miller further testified that the deed in controversy had already been signed by her grandmother when she first learned of it in June of 1973; that she received the executed deed by mail and did not pay her grandmother any money for the deed nor fulfill any of the support obligation therein; that subsequently on July 1, 1975, she deeded the property in question to defendant William Wade Anderson (a brother of appellee) when he asked that she sign the property over to him, stating that since she had been unable to fulfill the requirements of the deed, he intended to take care of her grandmother; that she did not receive any money or other consideration from William Wade Anderson for such deed.

Appellant William Wade Anderson testified that he obtained the deed from Altha Miller; that he did not pay her any money or other consideration for it; that sometime before the deed from his mother to Altha Miller he learned of his mother's will leaving the property to appellee.

Appellee Frank Bostick Anderson testified that about 1972 he received a copy of his mother's will, that he is claiming title to the property in question as the devisee in such will which has been probated; that he is asking that the deed to Altha Miller be held to be null and void.

* * * We agree with appellant's contention that the promise of support set out as consideration in the deed from Jewell Esther Anderson to Altha Miller created a covenant rather than a condition subsequent. Conditions subsequent are not favored by the courts, and the promise or obligation of the grantee will be construed as a covenant unless an intention to create a conditional estate is clearly and unequivocally revealed by the language of the instrument. *Hearne v. Bradshaw*, 312 S.W.2d 948, 951 (Tex. 1958). Mere failure of consideration resulting from a failure of the grantee to perform as promised is not a sufficient ground for forfeiture of the estate granted in the absence of additional circumstances justifying equitable relief, such as fraud in that the person failing to perform had the intention not to perform at the time the deed was executed. However, cancellation of the deed is the proper remedy if the promise of support was fraudulently made with no intention to carry it out at the time of its execution. 13 Am. Jur. 2d, Cancellation of Instruments § 23 (1964). . . .

Appellant complains that there was factually insufficient evidence to support the trial court's finding that defendant, Altha Miller, had no intention of performing the promise set out as consideration in the deed. The intent not to perform the promise at the time it is made may be shown by circumstantial evidence including the acts and declarations of the person in securing the contract, as well as his subsequent conduct with respect to refusing to carry out the promise. . . . We have considered all the evidence in the case and conclude it is factually sufficient to support the court's finding that Altha Miller had no intention of keeping or performing the promise of support set out as consideration in the deed. *In re King's Estate*, 244 S.W.2d 660 (Tex. 1951). Furthermore, it is undisputed that Altha Miller did not fulfill the obligation of support which was the sole consideration set forth in the deed; there was therefore a total failure of consideration for the conveyance in issue as found by the trial court.

In order to decide whether a contract was procured by fraud, a court may properly consider the transaction as a whole, including the nature of the transaction, the extent of the consideration, the relationship and interests of the parties, the respective ages of the parties, the extent of defendant's efforts to perform, and all other relevant circumstances. *Pulchny v. Pulchny*, 555 S.W.2d 543, 545 (Tex. Civ. App. 1977). . . .

The support representation, set forth as consideration for the deed, obligating Altha Miller as grantee to provide and care for the grantor during the grantor's lifetime was first made by Charlie C. Anderson, purportedly in behalf of Altha Miller, at the time of the execution of the deed. When Altha Miller received the deed, the evidence discloses that she had already determined that she could not fulfill and had no intention of performing the support obligation at the time of the execution of the deed. Furthermore, even though she occupied a position of trust and confidence in her relationship with her grandmother, she took no action to disclose the misrepresentation in the deed or offer to reconvey the property to her grandmother. By remaining silent and failing to speak to correct the false misrepresentation in the deed, she in legal contemplation adopted the misrepresentation as her own. As further evidence of this fact, she retained the deed and approximately two years later conveyed the property in question to appellant William Wade Anderson. Where the particular circumstances impose on a person a duty to speak and he deliberately remains silent, his silence is equivalent to a false representation. 37 C.J.S. Fraud § 16 (1943).

In 25 Tex. Jur. 2d Fraud and Deceit § 35, it is stated:

> Fraud is deducible from artifice and concealment as well as from affirmative conduct of a character such as tends to deceive. If there is a duty to speak, fraud may be found in the concealment of a material fact. If a person sustains toward another a position of trust and confidence, his failure to disclose facts that it is his duty to disclose is as much fraud as would be actual misrepresentation of true facts. That is to say, fraud may exist where there is a concealment of a material fact that should be divulged, as well as where there is a positive misrepresentation of a material fact.

In passing on appellant's "no evidence" points we have reviewed the evidence in its most favorable light, considering only the evidence and inferences which support the court's findings, and find that there is evidence of probative force to support the court's implied findings of fraud, that Altha Miller by remaining silent and failing to speak to correct the false representation of support set forth as consideration in the deed made such representation her own, that her grandmother relied upon such representation and was damaged thereby. The fact that Jewell Esther Anderson executed the deed to her homeplace for the sole consideration of the representation for care and maintenance during her lifetime is evidence of her reliance on such representation. As a result of the representation not being performed she was damaged by loss of the support promised and title to the property in question. . . . Points one through six are overruled.

We find no merit in appellant's point of error seven wherein he complains that appellee had no standing to bring this suit. It is a fundamental principle that no person may maintain an action in court unless he shows that he has a justiciable interest in the subject matter in litigation, either in his own right or in a representative capacity. . . . * * * Appellee's petition alleges that on about March 12, 1977, Jewell Esther Anderson died, leaving a last will and testament dated May 5, 1970, in which the property in question was devised to him, and that said will was admitted to probate on April 11, 1977, as a muniment of title in the County Court of Sabine County. The record herein supports these allegations. By proof of the probate of such will and his interest as a devisee thereunder, appellee has shown a justiciable interest in the property in controversy which entitles him to maintain this suit for cancellation of the deed in question from Jewell Esther Anderson to Altha Miller. . . .

An equitable cause of action for rescission or cancellation is generally considered to survive the death of the person in whose favor or against whom the cause of action has accrued; and the right to maintain such a suit ordinarily passes to the heirs or to the devisees of the grantor. 12A C.J.S. Cancellation of Instruments § 63. After the death of a person who was a party to a conveyance and who had a cause of action for its cancellation, his devisees under a will admitted to probate disposing of the property in question would be the proper parties plaintiff in a suit for cancellation of the conveyance. . . .

The judgment of the trial court is affirmed.

NOTES

1. Why was Jewell Esther Anderson's deed to Altha Miller valid when Anderson already had executed a will devising the land to someone else? Was the deed from Altha Miller to William Wade Anderson valid when given?

2. The *Anderson* decision represents the great weight of authority that failure of consideration alone is an inadequate basis for cancelling a deed. If the court in *Anderson* had not found fraud, what remedy would have been available to the grandmother who was not receiving the care that constituted the consideration for the deed? Would specific performance be a desirable remedy in this situation? Because of the unique problems presented by cases in which land is transferred in exchange for the grantee's agreement to care for the grantor, at least one state has enacted a statute to permit cancellation of the deed without a showing of fraud. Alabama Code § 8-9-12 provides:

> Any conveyance of realty wherein a material part of the consideration is the agreement of the grantee to support the grantor during life is void at the option of the grantor, except as to bona fide purchasers for value, lienees and mortgagees without notice, if, during the life of the grantor, he takes proceedings to annul such conveyance.

See *Vaughn v. Carter*, 488 So. 2d 1348 (Ala. 1986) (applying this statute to invalidate a deed without requiring a showing of fraud or even failure of consideration).

C.   Statutory Short Form Deeds

To reduce the complexity and length of deeds, many states now provide by statute for so-called statutory short form deeds. The statutes specify the words that must be used when drafting a warranty deed or a quitclaim deed. Only a few words, or sometimes just one word, can be used in place of lengthier formulations used in common law deed forms. In the case of warranty deeds, the statute usually specifies the title covenants that are statutorily implied into the deed. Thus the title covenants do not have to be spelled out in the deed. Therefore, unlike the drafter of a common law deed, the drafter of a statutory short form deed must choose carefully among the possible words of conveyance to avoid creating a different type of deed than intended.

The Washington statutes that follow are a good example of short form deed legislation:

§ 64.04.030. *Warranty deed — Form and effect.* Warranty deeds for the conveyance of land may be substantially in the following form, without express covenants:

> The grantor (here insert the name or names and place of residence) for and in consideration of (here insert consideration) in hand paid, conveys and warrants to (here insert the grantee's name or names) the following described real estate (here insert description), situated in the county of _____, state of Washington.
> Dated this _____ day of _____, 20_____.

Every deed in substance in the above form, when otherwise duly executed, shall be deemed and held a conveyance in fee simple to the grantee, his or her heirs and assigns, with covenants on the part of the grantor: (1) That at the time of the making and delivery of such deed he or she was lawfully seized of an indefeasible estate in fee simple, in and to the premises therein described, and had good right and full power to convey the same; (2) that the same were then free from all encumbrances; and (3) that he or she warrants to the grantee, his or her heirs and assigns, the quiet and peaceable possession of such premises, and will defend the title thereto against all persons who may lawfully claim the same, and such covenants shall be obligatory upon any grantor, his or her heirs and personal representatives, as fully and with like effect as if written at full length in such deed.

§ 64.04.040. *Bargain and sale deed — Form and effect.* Bargain and sale deeds for the conveyance of land may be substantially in the following form, without express covenants:

> The grantor (here insert name or names and place of residence), for and in consideration of (here insert consideration) in hand paid, bargains, sells and conveys to (here insert the grantee's name or names) the following described real estate (here insert description) situated in the county of _____, state of Washington.
> Dated this _____ day of _____, 20_____.

Every deed in substance in the above form when otherwise duly executed shall convey to the grantee, his or her heirs or assigns, an estate of inheritance in fee simple, and shall be adjudged an express covenant to the grantee, his or her heirs or assigns, to wit: That the grantor was seized of an indefeasible estate in fee simple, free from encumbrances, done or suffered from the grantor, except the rents and services that may be reserved, and also for quiet enjoyment against the grantor, his or her heirs and assigns, unless limited by express words contained in such deed; and the grantee, his or her heirs, executors, administrators and assigns may recover in any action for breaches as if such covenants were expressly inserted.

§ 64.04.050. *Quitclaim deed — Form and effect.* Quitclaim deeds may be in substance in the following form:

The grantor (here insert the name or names and place of residence), for and in consideration of (here insert consideration) conveys and quitclaims to (here insert grantee's name or names) all interest in the following described real estate (here insert description) situated in the county of _____, state of Washington.

Dated this _____ day of _____, 20_____.

Every deed in substance in the above form, when otherwise duly executed, shall be deemed and held a good and sufficient conveyance, release and quitclaim to the grantee, his or her heirs and assigns in fee of all the then existing legal and equitable rights of the grantor in the premises therein described, but shall not extend to the after acquired title unless words are added expressing such intention.

NOTES AND PROBLEMS

1. Of the following three deed forms, identify the general warranty deed, the limited warranty deed, and the quitclaim deed. What is the identifying feature of each?

Individual (s) to Individual (s)

No delinquent taxes and transfer entered; Certificate
of Real Estate Value (   ) filed (   ) not required
Certificate of Real Estate Value No._____ __
_____, 19 _____

_____
                                    County Auditor

by_____
                                    Deputy

STATE DEED TAX DUE HEREON: $ _____

Date: _____January 1,_____, 19 __81__

(reserved for recording data)

FOR VALUABLE CONSIDERATION, _____James J. Dircks and Linda L. Dircks,_____
_____husband and wife_____, Grantor (s),
                                    (marital status)

hereby convey (s) and warrant (s) to _____Christopher T. Kalgren_____
_____, Grantee (s),

real property in _____Hennepin_____ County, Minnesota, described as follows:

Lot 1, Block 4, Freeway View Addition, according to the plat thereof
on file and of record in the office of the County Recorder in and for
said county,

(If more space is needed, continue on back)
together with all hereditaments and appurtenances belonging thereto, subject to the following exceptions:

Affix Deed Tax Stamp Here

James J. Dircks
_____

Linda L. Dircks
_____

_____

_____

STATE OF MINNESOTA
                              } ss.
COUNTY OF ____Hennepin____

The foregoing instrument was acknowledged before me this ____1st day of____January_____, 19 81,
by _____James J. Dircks and Linda L. Dircks, husband and wife_____
_____, Grantor (s).

NOTARIAL STAMP OR SEAL (OR OTHER TITLE OR RANK)

SIGNATURE OF PERSON TAKING ACKNOWLEDGMENT

Tax Statements for the real property described in this instrument should
be sent to (include name and address of Grantee):
        Christopher T. Kalgren
        317 North Barry Avenue
        Wayzata, Minnesota 55391

THIS INSTRUMENT WAS DRAFTED BY (NAME AND ADDRESS)

   Larson Law Firm
   326 South Broadway
   Wayzata, MN 55391

Individual (s) to individual (s)

No delinquent taxes and transfer entered; Certificate
of Real Estate Value (   ) filed (   ) not required
Certificate of Real Estate Value No._____
_____, 19_____

_____
County Auditor

by_____
Deputy

(reserved for recording data)

STATE DEED TAX DUE HEREON: $ _____

Date:____August 1_____, 19 81

FOR VALUABLE CONSIDERATION, ____James J. Dircks and Linda L. Dircks,____
husband and wife _____, Grantor (s),
(marital status)

h reby convey (s) and quitclaim (s) to _____Christopher T. Kalgren_____
, Grantee (s),

real property in _____Hennepin_____County, Minnesota, described as follows:

Lot 1, Block 4, Freeway View Addition, according to the plat thereof
on file and of record in the office of the County Recorder in and for
said county,

(If more space is needed, continue on back)
together with all hereditaments and appurtenances belonging thereto.

Affix Deed Tax Stamp Here

James J. Dircks
_____
Linda L. Dircks
_____
_____

STATE OF MINNESOTA   }
                          } ss.
COUNTY OF__Hennepin_____

The foregoing instrument was acknowledged before me this__1st__day of__August_____, 19 81,
by _____James J. Dircks and Linda L. Dircks, husband and wife,_____
, Grantor (s).

NOTARIAL STAMP OR SEAL (OR OTHER TITLE OR RANK)

SIGNATURE OF PERSON TAKING ACKNOWLEDGMENT

Tax Statements for the real property described in this instrument should
be sent to (include name and address of Grantee):

Christopher T. Kalgren
317 North Barry Avenue
Wayzata, MN 55391

THIS INSTRUMENT WAS DRAFTED BY (NAME AND ADDRESS):
Larson Law Firm
326 South Broadway
Wayzata, Minnesota 55391

This Indenture, *Made this* ____ 1st ____ *day of* September ____ , 19 83 .
between ____ ____ LLF Investments, a general partnership

of the County of ____ Hennepin ____ *and State of* ____ Minnesota
part Y *of the first part, and* ____ Christopher T. Kalgren

of the County of ____ Hennepin ____ *and State of* ____ Minnesota
part Y *of the second part.*

Witnesseth. *That the said part* Y *of the first part, in consideration of the sum of* One dollar and other good and valuable consideration ($1.00) --- *DOLLARS.* *to* ____ it ____ *in hand paid by the said part* Y *of the second part, the receipt whereof is hereby acknowledged, do* es *hereby Grant, Bargain, Sell, and Convey unto the said part* Y *of the second part,* ____ his ____ *heirs and assigns, Forever, all the tract or parcel of land lying and being in the County of* Hennepin ____ *and State of Minnesota, described as follows, to-wit:*

Lot 1, Block 4, Freeway View Addition, according to the plat thereof on file and of record in the office of the County Recorder in and for said county,

To Have and to Hold the Same, *Together with all the hereditaments and appurtenances thereunto belonging or in anywise appertaining, to the said part* y *of the second part,* his ____ *heirs and assigns, Forever. And the said* ____ LLF Investments, a general partnership,

part y *of the first part, for* itself, / its successors and assigns, *do* es *covenant with the said part* y *of the second part,* ____ his ____ *heirs and assigns, that* he *it has not made, done, executed, or suffered any act or thing whatsoever whereby the above described premises or any part thereof, now, or at any time hereafter, shall or may be imperiled, charged or incumbered in any manner whatsoever,*

____ *and the title to the above granted premises against all persons lawfully claiming the same from, through, or under* it *except items, if any, hereinbefore mentioned, the said part* y *of the first part will Warrant and Defend.*

In Testimony Whereof, *The said part* y *of the first part ha* s *hereunto set* its *hand the day and year first above written.*

LLF Investments, a general partnership

By: Jeffrey W. Lambert, a partner

2. Note that the first two deed forms are statutory short form deeds; the third form has been prepared in accordance with the common law requirements for a deed. A key difference between the statutory and common law deed forms is that the common law form includes a habendum clause. The clause's name comes from the Latin phrase "habendum et tendendum," which means "to have and to hold." The habendum clause was designed to serve two purposes. First, it includes the words of inheritance necessary in the early common law to convey fee simple absolute title, or, if less than fee simple absolute title was being conveyed, it limited the estate. Second, it specifies which title covenants the deed includes.

Modern law largely has obviated the need for the habendum clause. In all but a very few states, a deed is presumed to convey fee simple absolute title unless it expressly provides otherwise. Therefore, words of inheritance no longer need to be included in a deed. Moreover, short form deed statutes eliminate the need to describe the title covenants in the deed.

However, the habendum clause is worse than merely unnecessary. As you can see on the third deed form, the granting clause (the clause with the words of conveyance, "grant, bargain, sell, and convey") also specifies the estate being conveyed. Through the centuries, lawyers and others preparing deeds have not always been as careful as they should be. As a result, a substantial body of case law deals with the problem of granting and habendum clauses that, by their terms, convey different estates to the grantee. Thus today, habendum clauses have substantially diminished utility and desirability. However, they still are used, particularly in states without statutory short form deeds.

3. Why do the statutory deed forms reproduced above request information about the grantor's marital status? Why does the second deed form leave space to fill in "exceptions" after the legal description, but the first deed form does not?

D. Deed Covenants

[handwritten: present covenants are breached when deed becomes effective, don't run with land.]

Although there are some differences among the states, the title covenants in a general warranty deed normally are the covenants of:

[handwritten: present]

1. *Seisin.* The covenant of seisin warrants that the grantor owns the title that the deed purports to convey. For example, if the deed states that the grantor is transferring fee simple absolute title, the covenant of seisin is breached if the grantor only had a life estate. However, the covenant is not breached by property interests that are not estates in land, such as mortgages and easements. In some jurisdictions, the covenant of seisin is satisfied if the grantor merely has possession of the property and not title.

[handwritten: present]

2. *Right to Convey.* This covenant is virtually coextensive with the covenant of seisin. It warrants that the grantor has the right to convey the property interest described in the deed. If the grantor actually has a lesser interest in the land or no interest, both the covenants of seisin and of the right to convey are violated. However, the covenants differ in two ways. First, in those jurisdictions in which the covenant of seisin is not breached if a person possesses property even without owning it, the lack of title would breach the covenant of the right to convey; although the grantor has possession of the property, she has no right to convey

title. Second, a person executing a deed pursuant to a power of attorney has the right to convey the property but does not have seisin. See *Maxwell v. Redd*, 496 P.2d 1320 (Kan. 1972).

3. *Against Encumbrances.* This covenant warrants that the title is not subject to those lesser property interests that do not breach the covenant of seisin. It warrants against the existence of incorporeal interests, such as easements and real covenants, and of monetary charges against the land, such as mortgages, judgment liens, and mechanic's liens. In some jurisdictions, an outstanding life estate or tenancy is deemed to breach the covenant against encumbrances, rather than the covenant of seisin. See *Aczas v. Stuart Heights, Inc.*, 221 A.2d 589 (Conn. 1966).

present

4 & 5. *Warranty and Quiet Enjoyment.* Although these two covenants technically are separate, they are so similar as to be virtually identical, and they are almost always considered together. They protect against the same types of title defects as the covenants of seisin and against encumbrances. Any outstanding interest in the land, whether it is an estate in land, such as a life estate, or a lesser interest, such as a lien, can violate the covenants of warranty and quiet enjoyment. However, one additional element is required for a breach of these covenants. The adverse interest holder actually must assert its rights in the land. As discussed more fully later in this section, this assertion of rights must rise to the level of an actual or constructive eviction. See *Brown v. Lober*, 389 N.E.2d 1188, 1191–92 (Ill. 1979).

future

6. *Further Assurances.* This covenant is quite limited in scope and is qualitatively different than the other covenants. The other covenants provide a cause of action for damages based on a third party's interest in the property. The covenant of further assurances, on the other hand, is enforced by an action for specific performance based on the grantor's failure to convey title properly. The covenant requires the grantor to execute any additional document or take such other action as is necessary to perfect the grantee's interest. For example, if a deed was defectively executed, the grantee can use the covenant of further assurances to require the grantor to execute a new deed.

future

These six common law deed covenants are classified as being either present or future covenants. The covenants of seisin, right to convey, and against encumbrances are present covenants. The covenants of warranty, quiet enjoyment, and further assurances are future covenants. This distinction has two significant implications. It dictates when a breach of the covenant occurs, thereby triggering the statute of limitations. It also determines whether the covenant can be enforced only by the grantee of the deed that includes the covenant or also by later purchasers of the land. Using the appropriate term of art, it prescribes whether the covenant "runs with the land."

Future covenants are breached when breach occurs, do run w/ land.

1.   Breach of Covenants

Present covenants are breached, if ever, at the moment the deed becomes effective, and the statute of limitations begins to run immediately even if the grantee is unaware of the breach. In fact, the statute may cut off the cause of action before the grantee discovers the breach. In contrast, a future covenant is not breached until an "eviction" has occurred. After the statute of limitations has run on a grantee's present covenants, but before an eviction has occurred, no deed covenant protects him against encumbrances, defects, or even a failure of title. See *Brown v. Lober,* 389 N.E.2d 1188 (Ill. 1979). This means that a future covenant is an agreement to indemnify the grantee but not a guarantee of the title conveyed. "[T]he mere existence of paramount title in one other than the covenantee is not sufficient to constitute a breach of the covenant of warranty or quiet enjoyment." *Id.* at 1191–92.

Either an actual or constructive eviction breaches a future covenant. An actual eviction occurs when a paramount interest holder uses self-help or judicial action to disturb the grantee's possession. Actual eviction also occurs when the paramount interest holder already has possession of the property when the deed is delivered to the grantee. On the other hand, a constructive eviction does not require actual interference with the grantee's possession. However, it does require that the paramount interest holder has asserted its right. For example, a grantee whose deed purported to convey the entire fee simple absolute title is constructively evicted if he buys the interest of a cotenant who is threatening to or has commenced a partition action. Similarly, a grantee is constructively evicted if he pays a judgment lienor to prevent the threatened execution of the lien against the property. What purpose is served by making eviction a prerequisite to enforcing a future covenant but not a present covenant? Would the covenantee/grantee's inability to resell the property because she discovers that she does not own the title her deed purported to convey be a constructive eviction? (*Brown v. Lober* indicates not.) Because the statute of limitations begins to run only from an eviction, a grantor of a warranty deed can be liable for a breach many years after delivering the deed.

2. Running with the Land

DEASON v. FINLEY
40 So. 220 (Ala. 1906)

Anderson, J.

The complainant relies on a breach of covenant of warranty or quiet enjoyment, and not a covenant of seisin. Covenant of quiet enjoyment and of warranty runs with the land into the hands of the assignee and heirs, and may be sued upon by the heir or assignee who is in possession when the breach occurs. "But, in order that a covenant may run with the land to assignees, the grantee must by the conveyance acquire the actual or constructive seisin." Tiedman on Real Property, §§ 855, 860. It is not sufficient that the covenant is concerning land, but to make it run with the land there must be a privity of estate between the covenanting parties, and the covenant must have relation to an interest created or conveyed, in order that the covenant may pass to the grantee. 8 Am. & Eng. Ency. Law 147. In order to entitle one to recover on a covenant of warranty of a remote vendor, the plaintiff must show that he holds title by privity with the immediate covenantor of such remote vendor. *Mygatt v. Coe,* 26 N.E. 611 (N.Y. 1891). . . .

The complainant in the case at bar has shown no privity of estate with Wm.

Robertson, the covenantee of the grantor or warrantor, Murchison Findley. There is nothing to connect her with Elbert Robertson, the second grantee; she claiming under John C. Moore, who received no conveyance from any one holding under Wm. Robertson, the original covenantee of Murchison Findley. The complainant's contention that the possession of herself and those claiming under John C. Moore has been of such duration that the law presumes a conveyance from Elbert Robertson to said Moore, if correct, cannot enable her to recover for a breach as against Findley. In the case of *Beardsley v. Knight*, 4 Vt. 471, the Vermont court said: "The argument that the plaintiff was in possession, and therefore might avail himself of the covenant as running with the land, is wholly destitute of foundation. His possession, as against [the covenantee] Hotch, may have been adverse, so that he was acquiring a title by the statute of limitations as against him; but, if so, it would be at least singular if he could acquire a title against Hotch by a trespass, and at the same time, by the same trespass, acquire a right to Hotch's claim against the defendant on the covenants in his deed. Although a deed from Hotch to the plaintiff might under some circumstances be presumed, yet, as presumptions are made to quiet men in possession, I do not know that it has ever been contended before that it would create a right of action on the deed presumed. A deed might be presumed to give a legal origin to possession; but an instrument not under seal cannot be presumed to be a deed for the purpose of giving one an action of covenant thereon, or an action of covenant on a deed further back in the chain of title." The decree of the chancellor is affirmed.

breach cov

PROFFITT v. ISLEY
683 S.W.2d 243 (Ark. Ct. App. 1985)

MAYFIELD, J.   *no constructive eviction*

In 1974 Bobby and Mary Proffitt sold one and one-half acres of real estate to Truman and Earline Atkinson, who sold it to Shirley Carter in 1978, who sold it to Arthur and Bonnie Isley in 1980. About two months after the Isleys bought it they discovered that the land had been mortgaged by the Proffitts and that the mortgage was still outstanding. The Isleys sued Carter, the Atkinsons, and the Proffitts for damages based on the general warranties in the warranty deeds. The jury held for the Atkinsons and Carter, but held the Proffitts liable to the Isleys for $4,390.78 representing the unpaid balance on the mortgage plus interest and costs. The Proffitts appeal. We reverse.

The usual covenants of title in a general warranty deed are the covenants of seisin, good right to convey, against encumbrances, for quiet enjoyment and general warranty. An encumbrance is any right to an interest in land which may subsist in third persons, to the diminution of the value of the land, not inconsistent with the passing of title. Examples of encumbrances are an outstanding lease, a timber deed, dower, an easement, and a mortgage. P. Jones, The Arkansas Law of Title to Real Property, §§ 383, 386 (1935). In *Logan v. Moulder*, 1 Ark. 313, 320 (1839), the court said:

> The covenants of seizin, and of right to convey, and against incumbrances are personal covenants, not running with the land, nor passing to the

assignee, but are declared to be mere *choses in action*, not assignable at common law. The covenants of warranty, and of quiet enjoyment, are in the nature of a real covenant, and run with the land, and descend to the heirs, and are made transferable to the assignee.

In 7 G. Thompson, Thompson on Real Property § 3185 at 303 (Repl. 1962), the *Logan* case is cited in support of the general rule that a covenant against encumbrances is not assignable and does not pass to a grantee. Since the covenant against encumbrances is personal between the grantor and the grantee, the remedy for a remote grantee, when the encumbrance has not been removed from the property, is against his immediate grantor, whose recourse is against his grantor and so forth back up the chain of title to the original grantor whose conveyance breached the warranty against encumbrances. However, the covenant of general warranty may be breached where steps are taken to enforce an encumbrance. See also *Brawley v. Copelin*, 153 S.W. 101 (Ark. 1913) and *Thompson v. Dildy*, 300 S.W.2d 270 (Ark. 1957).

With some exceptions, not applicable here, unless the covenantee is evicted or has satisfied the outstanding encumbrance, he may only recover nominal damages. See *Van Bibber v. Hardy*, 219 S.W.2d 435 (Ark. 1949). In *Smith v. Thomas*, 278 S.W. 39 (Ark. 1925) the court stated:

> The measure of damages for the breach of a covenant against incumbrance is the amount necessary to remove the incumbrance, not exceeding the consideration expressed in the deed containing the covenants of warranty, and ordinarily the covenantee cannot recover on the mere existence of the incumbrance, but must first discharge it by payment, unless he has actually lost the estate in consequence of the incumbrance. In 7 R.C.L. p. 1104, the rule is stated as follows: "In a number of jurisdictions it has been held that, although a covenant against incumbrances, like a covenant of seisin, is broken if at all as soon as made, yet the covenantee can found no right to actual damages on the mere existence of incumbrances, but will be limited to a nominal recovery, unless he has paid off the incumbrance or actually lost the estate in consequence of it."

In the present case the appellees had incurred no expense because of the outstanding mortgage on the property, and the mortgagee had made no effort to either evict appellees or foreclose on the property. Therefore, appellees' only cause of action was a technical breach of the covenant against encumbrances which could be brought against their grantor, Carter, with the recovery of only nominal damages. Therefore, the judgment against the Proffitts is reversed and dismissed.

NOTES

1. The court in *Proffitt* adhered to the old common law rule that the cause of action arising from the breach of a present covenant is unassignable. Many states have changed that rule by statute or by judicial decision. In some states, present and future covenants are deemed to run with the land. See, e.g., Colo. Rev. Stat. Ann. § 38-30-121; Ga. Code Ann. § 44-5-60; W. Va. Code § 36-4-16. In other jurisdictions, a deed is treated as conveying the cause of action for breach of the present covenant, as well as title to the land. However, in other jurisdictions, the cause of action is not transferred by operation of law. Instead, it must be conveyed expressly to the property buyer. In this type of jurisdiction, a well-represented buyer will specify in the contract of sale that the seller is obligated to give him not only a deed, but also a bill of sale that conveys any causes of action relating to the property, such as causes of action for breach of a deed covenant. Why is a bill of sale, rather than a deed, used in this situation?

2.   The issue of damages for breach of a present covenant can be problematic. As in *Proffitt*, most courts will award only nominal damages if the adverse interest holder is not asserting it. To award full damages in this situation could result in a windfall to the deed grantee. If the adverse interest holder never asserts its rights or loses them by adverse possession, the grantee will not have suffered anything more than a technical breach of the present covenant. However, limiting recovery to nominal damages can create substantial problems for the grantee. If the grantee waits to enforce the present covenant until actual damages have accrued, the statute of limitations on the breach of the present covenant may have expired. Additionally, a prior recovery of nominal damages may bar a subsequent action when the adverse interest holder asserts its rights. In light of these problems, some courts have awarded full damages even when the adverse interest has not been asserted.

breach case 2

ST. PAUL TITLE INSURANCE CORP. v. OWEN
452 So. 2d 482 (Ala. 1984)

MADDOX, J.

limited warranty deeds only cover acts done by seller, not there previous sellers.

The question here is what liability do grantors have to remote grantees or their assigns under a warranty deed and a statutory warranty deed where certain covenants of title contained in the deeds are found to run with the land?

On February 18, 1976, Albert M. Owen, an unmarried man, executed a warranty deed purporting to convey certain real property in Baldwin County to his brother and sister-in-law, James R. Owen, Jr., and Cheryl C. Owen. The deed, which was recorded on March 8, 1976, in Baldwin County, contained the following covenants of title:

> The party of the first part [Albert Owen] for himself, his heirs, executors and administrators, hereby covenants and warrants to and with the said parties of the second part [James and Cheryl Owen], their heirs and assigns, that he is seized of an indefeasible estate in and to the said property; that he has a good right to convey the same as herein contained; that he will guarantee the peaceable possession thereof; that the said property is free from all liens and encumbrances, and that he will, and his heirs, executors and administrators will forever warrant and defend the same unto the said parties of the second part, their heirs and assigns, against the lawful claims of all persons.

The warranty deed form was obtained from the law office of James R. Owen, Sr., the father of Albert and James Owen.

Subsequently, James and Cheryl Owen conveyed the Baldwin County property, purportedly conveyed to them, by statutory warranty deed to Dennis C. Carlisle Jr., the brother of Cheryl Owen. The property was conveyed June 6, 1976, and the deed recorded in Baldwin County on July 14, 1976.

On June 10, 1976, Dennis Carlisle mortgaged the property to United Companies Mortgage and Investment of Mobile #2, Inc., for $17,159.52. This mortgage was recorded on July 14, 1976, in both Mobile and Baldwin counties.

Dennis Carlisle mortgaged the property to GECC Financial Services (GECC) for $17,671.29, on November 8, 1977, apparently substituting mortgages and paying off the original mortgage. The mortgage to GECC was recorded in Baldwin County and a policy of title insurance naming GECC as the insured was issued shortly thereafter by Eastern Shore Title Insurance Corp., of Daphne, the agent for St. Paul Title Insurance Corp. (St. Paul Title). The title insurance was issued at the request of Dennis Carlisle.

When Dennis Carlisle subsequently defaulted on his mortgage payments, GECC attempted to foreclose on the property. The Circuit Court of Baldwin County found, however, that because Dennis Carlisle held no right, title, or interest in or to any of the property on the day the mortgage was executed, GECC was not entitled to foreclose on the property. GECC then brought suit against St. Paul Title, to collect its debt, and in addition the costs of litigation involved, all as provided for under the terms of the title insurance policy.

St. Paul Title, as subrogee of GECC, then filed a complaint against Albert Owen, James R. Owen, Jr., and Cheryl Owen, wherein St. Paul alleged that they had breached the covenants of title contained in the deeds executed and delivered by them. The trial court, after a non-jury trial, entered a judgment on behalf of the defendants. St. Paul appeals.

I. The Liability of Albert Owen under the express covenants
of title contained in his warranty deed.

The deed executed by Albert Owen, an unmarried man, purporting to convey property to James and Cheryl Owen, contained the following express covenants of title: a covenant of seizin; a covenant of right to convey; a covenant for quiet enjoyment; a covenant against encumbrances; and a covenant of warranty. . . . Of these covenants, however, only the covenants of quiet enjoyment and warranty are said to operate *in futuro* for the benefit of the ultimate grantee. *Musgrove v. Cordova Coal, Land & Improvement Co.*, 67 So. 582, 583 (Ala. 1914). Until broken, these two covenants run with the land to the heirs of the grantee, or if the land is conveyed or assigned, to the assignee, so that when they are broken, the heir or assignee injured by the breach can maintain an action against the covenantor. . . . Thus, it is generally recognized and held that when a covenant of title runs with the land, all grantors, back to and including the original grantor-covenantor, become liable upon a breach of the covenant to the assignee or grantee in possession or entitled to the possession at the time, and the latter may sue the original or remote grantor, regardless of whether he has taken from the immediate grantor with a warranty. 21 Am. Jur. 2d, Covenants, Conditions, Etc. § 119 (1965).

Because the covenants of quiet enjoyment and of warranty are virtually identical in operation, whatever constitutes a breach of one covenant is a breach of the other. . . . Neither covenant is breached until there is an eviction under paramount title. The eviction may be either actual or constructive.

It has been said that an outstanding title that could be asserted in a judicial proceeding against the party in possession is equivalent to an eviction. *Musgrove v. Cordova Coal, Land & Improvement Co.*, 67 So. at 583. Likewise, a final judgment or decree adverse to the covenantee's title or right to possession constitutes a sufficient constructive eviction to entitle the covenantee to sue for breach of the covenant of warranty. 20 Am. Jur. 2d, Covenants, Conditions, Etc., § 62 (1965).

Here, the breach occurred when the trial court ruled in the foreclosure proceedings that Dennis Carlisle possessed no interest in the property which had been mortgaged, thereby frustrating GECC's attempt to foreclose on the property purportedly conveyed to Carlisle in fee simple.

We hold that the covenant of quiet enjoyment and warranty provided by the terms of the warranty deed executed by Albert Owen ran with the land purportedly conveyed by that instrument. We further hold that because someone other than the original grantor-covenantor in fact possessed paramount title, appellant is entitled to assert a claim for the breach of the covenants of title, as its subrogor was the ultimate grantee or assignee who was in possession at the time the covenants were broken.

II. The liability of James and Cheryl Owen under the covenants of title contained in their statutory warranty deed. *short hand for limited warranty deed*

The deed executed by James and Cheryl Owen contained no express covenants of title, but it did use the words, "grant, bargain, sell and convey." In all conveyances of estates in fee where the words "grant, bargain, and sell" appear, the deed is construed by statute as containing the following covenants of title: a covenant of seizin; a covenant against encumbrances; and a covenant of quiet enjoyment. Code 1975, § 35-4-271.

Appellant asserts that James and Cheryl Owen are liable for a breach of the implied covenant of quiet enjoyment contained in the statutory warranty deed, and that such a covenant runs with the land so as to benefit a remote grantee or assign. Unlike the express covenants of title found in a general warranty deed, however, the implied covenants of title contained in a statutory warranty deed are more limited in effect.

In the early case of *Heflin v. Phillips*, 96 Ala. 561, 11 So. 729 (1892), the Court noted: "In construing this statute [predecessor of § 35-4-271] this Court declared that the words 'grant, bargain, sell' do not import an absolute general covenant of seizin against incumbrances and for quiet enjoyment, but that they amount to a covenant *only against acts done or suffered by the grantor and his heirs.*" 96 Ala. at 562, 11 So. 730. (Emphasis added.) More than twenty years after *Heflin*, the Court remarked: "All authorities hold that the covenants implied by statute are limited to the acts of the grantor and those claiming under him, and do not extend to defects of title anterior to the conveyance to him." *Mackintosh v. Stewart*, 61 So. 956, 958 (Ala. 1913).

In *Mackintosh*, the immediate grantee (Stewart) prevailed in enforcing the implied warranty of seizin contained in a statutory warranty deed against the grantor (Mackintosh). The grantor had allowed part of the subject property to be adversely possessed during his period of ownership. Although the grantee succeeded in showing that adverse possession took place at least partially during the period in which the grantor held title to the property, the Court suggested the outcome of the case could have been different had the grantor pleaded and proved that adverse possession had ripened into title prior to the grantor's laying claim to the subject property. 61 So. at 959. This result would have ensued in that instance, because the defect in the title would have been anterior to the conveyance to Mackintosh by his grantor. Although Mackintosh would have been without good title to convey to Stewart, Mackintosh would not have been liable to Stewart under the statutory warranty deed's implied covenants of title because Mackintosh would not have suffered or caused any of the title problems.

James and Cheryl Owen conveyed their complete, albeit non-existent interest, in the subject property to Dennis Carlisle by statutory warranty deed. By so doing, they merely warranted that they had not conveyed title to anyone else; that they had not allowed the property to become encumbered while they held purported title; and that they had not caused or suffered anyone to do anything that would interfere with the property's quiet enjoyment by the grantee, the grantee's heirs or assigns. Because the record indicates that James and Cheryl did nothing to affect the purported title they conveyed, they did not breach any of the covenants of title contained in the statutory warranty deed delivered to Dennis Carlisle and are therefore not liable to the appellant, as subrogee of GECC.

III. Damages for breach of covenants of title.

Appellant asserts that it is entitled to recover, as damages, the amount of mortgage proceeds paid to Dennis Carlisle by its subrogor, plus litigation costs and interest. Appellant further contends its recovery should neither be barred nor be limited to merely nominal damages, even though appellees received no consideration for their conveyances.

In situations where there has been a complete failure of title and a grantee has sought recovery from his immediate grantor, the maximum recovery allowed has been the purchase price paid. *Allinder v. Bessemer C.I. & L. Co.*, 51 So. 234, 235 (Ala. 1909). With respect to an action against a remote grantor, however, there appears to be a difference of opinion as to whether damages are to be determined by the consideration paid by the grantee bringing the suit to his immediate grantor or by the consideration paid to the original grantor or covenantor, not exceeding in either case, however, the consideration paid for the conveyance by the defendant in the action. 20 Am. Jur. 2d Covenants, Conditions, Etc., § 163 (1965). Here, however, the facts indicate that no consideration was ever paid to or received by any of the appellees, Albert Moore Owen, James R. Owen, Jr., or Cheryl C. Owen. Consequently, since there was no evidence that the remote grantors received any consideration for their conveyances purportedly conveying title to the subject property, appellant, as subrogee of GECC, is entitled to an award of nominal damages only, for the breach of the covenant of quiet enjoyment contained in Albert Owen's deed, and not the amount of the mortgage made by GECC. *Id.* Furthermore, appellant is not entitled to recover an award of legal fees under the covenant of warranty by Albert Owen to defend the title of the grantee and his successor against all lawful claims. In *Chicago, Mobile Development Co. v. G.C. Coggin Co.*, 66 So. 2d 151 (Ala. 1953), the Court held:

> The duty to warrant and defend the title conveyed to the [grantees] against the lawful claims of all persons does not justify a charge for attorneys' fees whenever that title is brought into question in a court proceeding. As we have shown, it is no more than a warranty for quiet enjoyment. There is no authority which holds, so far as we can find, that under that warranty a duty arises to pay the expenses of litigation whenever that title is involved, but only in a suit with the claimant of an outstanding superior right, usually seeking to obtain possession in order to profit by that right. But even on the theory insisted on by the [grantees], this suit did not seek to call into question their warranty to complainant. Complainant neither sought nor obtained a decree against the [grantees] nor a decision as to any right against them on their warranty. But if it had done so, the warranty of appellant to defend them did not cover such a situation so far as we are able to discover in the law. No such authority has come to our attention. On the other hand, there is authority opposed to that theory. 21 C.J.S., Covenants, § 150, p. 1030, note 84. The cases noted are directly in point.

The facts of this case reveal that the legal actions here were not an attack on title by a third party possessing paramount title, but instead, were instigated by appellant or its subrogor, GECC. Thus, attorneys' fees in this instance are precluded under *Chicago, Mobile Development Co. v. G.C. Coggin Co., supra.* The judgment of the trial court is hereby reversed and the cause remanded to that court for a determination of the amount of nominal damages appellant is entitled to recover as consistent with the holding of this opinion.

NOTES

1. Was it appropriate for the court to hold that James and Cheryl Owen were not liable for breach of the covenants in the statutory warranty deed they gave to Dennis Carlisle? Does that holding essentially transform the warranty deed into a quitclaim deed?

2. In determining the appropriate measure of damages for breach of a covenant, courts must choose between compensating the injured party for his entire loss or simply making the liable party return the consideration that she received when she gave the covenant. The difference between these measures of damages can be dramatic. For example, suppose that seller (S) sold buyer (B) undeveloped land for $50,000 and that B subsequently constructed an apartment building on the land, which increased its value to $1,000,000. If S never had title to the land, should she be liable to B for $50,000 or for $1,000,000? The traditional rule, which the great majority of courts follow, is $50,000. If the loss is less than complete, courts award a proportionate part of the purchase price. Therefore, if S owned half the land, B could recover $25,000. The theory for limiting damages to the purchase price is that a contrary rule would make the seller liable for potentially large and unforeseeable damages. Does B have any method of recouping the money he invested in constructing the apartment building? During the early days of the common law, he did not because he was viewed as being essentially a trespasser. Today, however, this result often is changed by judicial decision or by legislation. The statutes, known as "occupying claimant acts" or "betterment acts," vary in their terms. However, they often provide that the innocent builder has a lien on the land for the value of the improvements unless the actual owner of the land sells it to the builder at a reasonable price. See Restatement of the Law (Third): Restitution and Unjust Enrichment § 52 (2011).

3. Attorneys' fees generally are recoverable for a breach of deed covenants. However, in *Owen*, the court applied an exception to that rule — fees are recoverable only if incurred while defending the title. Note also that fees cannot be recovered if the grantee of the deed successfully defends the title. If the grantee proves that the adverse claimant in fact has no interest in the property, the deed covenants have not been breached and, therefore, no damages are due. In this way, a deed covenant provides less protection to a land buyer than the marketable title standard in the contract of sale. The marketable title standard is violated not just by actual defects in the title, but also by apparent defects even if they later are proven to have no effect on the title. Unfortunately for the buyer, once she accepts a deed to the property, the doctrine of merger makes the title representations in the contract unenforceable. The underlying theory is that, by consummating the contract, the buyer has demonstrated her satisfaction with the title even if it did not meet the standard specified in the contract. Therefore, when representing a buyer, either do not close the sale until all questions about the title have been resolved or provide in the closing documents that the seller's contract representations concerning title will not be extinguished by the doctrine of merger.

4. What would happen if Albert Owen later acquired title to the land that he purported to convey by general warranty deed to James and Cheryl Owen? Under the doctrine of after-acquired title (also known as estoppel by deed), title automatically would pass to James and Cheryl. The doctrine then also would operate to transfer title automatically to Dennis Carlisle based on the statutory warranty deed he received from James and Cheryl Owen. The doctrine is based on the notion that a grantor who gives a deed warranting the title is estopped from later denying that title passed to the grantee. Because the doctrine depends on the grantor's title representations, it normally does not apply when the grantor gives a quitclaim deed. However, if the grantor makes express representations that the quitclaim deed in fact is conveying title, the doctrine will apply.

E. Legal Descriptions

The legal description identifies the parcel of land being conveyed by the deed. The description must be sufficiently detailed to distinguish the parcel from every other parcel of land. The description normally is prepared from a survey of the land or from past conveyances of it. A premium is placed on using the same legal description for each conveyance of the land to avoid creating questions concerning the scope of the conveyance; when different descriptions are used, uncertainty can be created as to whether the descriptions are coextensive. A premium also is placed on accuracy. Transposed numbers, missing information, or other errors can make the legal description meaningless and render the title unmarketable.

No particular method of legal description is required as long as the land is accurately described. To avoid rendering the title unmarketable, the legal description must be ascertainable from the public records. The deed itself need not include the complete description. It can incorporate other documents by reference to complete the description. For example, when a subdivision plat is recorded in the public records, a deed conveying a lot in the subdivision can describe the lot by reference to the recorded plat.

Deed drafters sometimes use rather informal methods of describing the land. For example, the deed may state that a property boundary extends from a certain point on a road "to the old oak tree." This type of description, although commonly used at an earlier time in this country's history, presents obvious difficulties. For example, what if the tree dies or is destroyed? What if more than one old oak tree is in the immediate vicinity? A more modern version of a commonly used but ambiguous legal description is a street address. Although street addresses routinely are used as a legal description in listing agreements and contracts of sale, courts normally hold that street addresses do not provide enough detail to be legally sufficient.

To satisfy the legal requirements for a land description, three main methods are commonly used: (1) the government survey system, (2) metes and bounds, and (3) the recorded subdivision plat. Primarily because of historic accident and development trends, one method or another will be the predominant method in any given geographic area. Legal descriptions frequently include elements of more than one method. Thus an understanding of each is essential.

1. Government Survey System

The government survey system (also known as the Jeffersonian or rectangular survey system) is used primarily in the midwestern and western states. The federal government adopted this system in 1785 as a means of surveying and describing the vast expanses of land that the government was acquiring, such as the land acquired in the Louisiana Purchase. The federal government has continued to incorporate newly-acquired land expanses, such as Alaska, into the system.

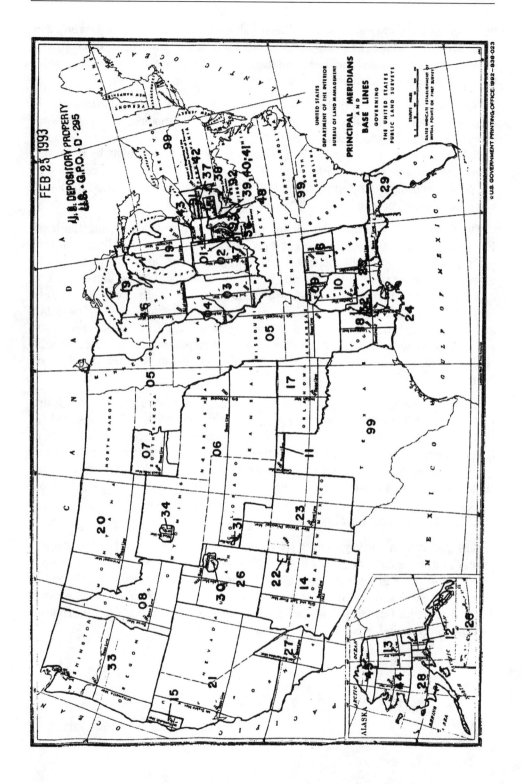

The system divides, subdivides, and then further subdivides land with a series of north-south and east-west lines. As shown on the preceding map, lands included in the government system first are divided by a paired "principal meridian," which runs north-south, and "base line," which runs east-west. For example, the Sixth Principal Meridian and Base Line intersect on the Kansas/Nebraska border.

These areas then are subdivided by lines running parallel to the principal meridians and base lines at six-mile intervals. The north-south lines, which run parallel to the principal meridians, separate land into "ranges." The east-west lines, which run parallel to the base lines, separate land into "townships."

Unfortunately, the word "township" has a second meaning in this context. It also refers to the parcels of land formed by the intersections of the range and township lines. In this second sense, a township is six miles long on each side and includes thirty-six square miles of land. As shown on the following map, each township is identified by its distance from its principal meridian and base line or, in other words, by its township and range. The second township north of the base line is Township 2 North, which is abbreviated as T2N. The third range east of the principal meridian is Range 3 East, which is abbreviated as R3E. The thirty-six square mile township formed at their intersection is described as Township 2 North, Range 3 East.

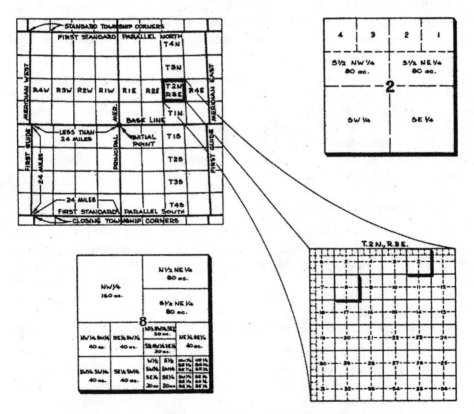

Reprinted from Jay Andriot, Township Atlas of the United States viii (1991).

Note that the range lines north of the base line do not exactly meet the range lines to the south. This discrepancy reflects the distortion caused by the earth's curvature. Because the earth is roughly spherical, each township cannot be exactly thirty-six square miles. As the range lines approach the North Pole, they converge. Therefore, the range lines are adjusted at regular intervals in an attempt to keep the townships approximately equal in size and shape.

Each thirty-six square mile township is further subdivided into thirty-six "sections." A section is one mile long on each side and includes 640 acres of land. As shown on the map of Township 2 North, Range 3 East, the sections are numbered beginning in the northeast corner of the township, continue to the northwest corner, and then wind east to west and back until reaching Section 36 in the township's southeast corner.

Because sections of 640 acres are still too large to describe most individually owned parcels of land, sections can be subdivided further. However, rather than comprehensively superimposing another set of north-south and east-west lines, further subdivisions are tailored to facilitate the description of a particular parcel. Sections can be halved or quartered and then halved or quartered again as needed.

Assume that the township illustrations on the preceding page are for the Sixth Principal Meridian and Base Line. The complete legal description for the parcel in the northeast corner of Section 8 would be "the North half of the Northeast quarter of Section 8, Township 2 North, Range 3 East, Sixth Principal Meridian and Base Line." Assuming the same Principal Meridian and Base Line, what is the legal description for the parcel numbered 4 on the map of Section 2?

The government survey system works well for describing many farms and ranches, but it is not well-suited to describing irregularly-shaped or small lots, such as lots in a residential subdivision. However, in these situations, the government survey system still can serve a valuable function because it provides a fixed and public point of reference for land. It can be used in conjunction with a metes and bounds or subdivision plat description to describe one or more boundaries or the point at which the legal description begins.

2. Metes and Bounds

The metes and bounds method of legal description has been used in this country since the colonial period. This method successively describes each boundary line of the property by a series of "calls," which consist of the distance and the direction of travel (the "bearing") of each boundary. Because each boundary is described separately, metes and bounds descriptions are lengthier and more complex than other types of descriptions and present more opportunity for mistakes. Therefore, drafters normally prefer to use one of the other methods of legal description when possible.

A metes and bounds description starts by identifying a "point of beginning" at one corner of the property being described. The point of beginning should be established by reference to a relatively permanent and identifiable source. In earlier times, natural monuments, such as a tree or large rock, often were used. Today, points of beginning are identified by reference to publicly available information, such as section lines in the government survey system or the intersection of the rights-of-way of two streets.

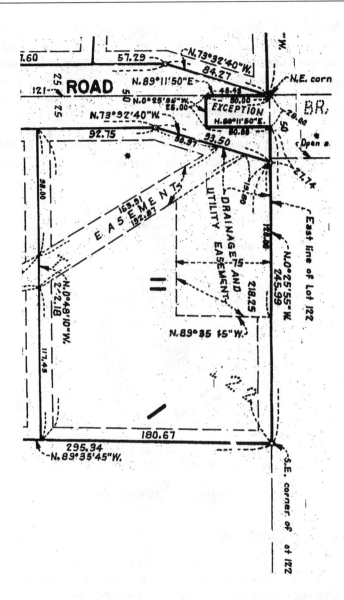

After identifying the point of beginning, a metes and bounds description gives the call for a boundary line that begins at that point. The description continues with the call for each successive boundary until the last call closes the legal description back at the point of beginning. The bearing and distance sometimes are stated rather informally, such as "travel east along the river bank to the old Hess homestead." However, the problems with this type of description are obvious, particularly with the passage of time. River banks, owners, and the dimensions of land parcels all change.

For these reasons, metes and bounds descriptions are best prepared from a survey of the property that describes the length of each boundary line and its bearing in relation to the points of a compass. For example, look at Lot 11 on the portion of the plat reproduced on the preceding page. The call for the easterly boundary is N 0°25'55"W 245.99'. This notation means that the boundary line is 245.99 feet long and is located at an angle 0 degrees, 25 minutes, 55 seconds west from magnetic north. Looking at the compass reproduced here, you can see that the bearing for this boundary also could be described as S 0°25'55"E if the legal description proceeded clockwise around the parcel, rather than counterclockwise. Prepare metes and bounds descriptions for Lot 11, first moving clockwise around the parcel and then counterclockwise. What additional information would you need to prepare a complete legal description — one that distinguishes this parcel from all others?

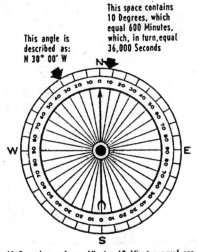

3. Recorded Subdivision Plat

In many jurisdictions, a landowner that wants to subdivide a parcel of land into two or more separate parcels must comply with the jurisdiction's subdivision regulations. The regulations typically specify minimum lot sizes, widths of any streets to be built in the subdivision, and similar matters affecting the public health, safety, and welfare. To prove compliance with the regulations, the landowner must submit a plat map of the property that shows the proposed boundary lines of the new parcels, the proposed location of any new streets and utility easements, and any other matters specified in the subdivision regulations. Before the land can be subdivided, the plat must be approved by the local zoning department, department of streets and transportation, and any other relevant local agencies.

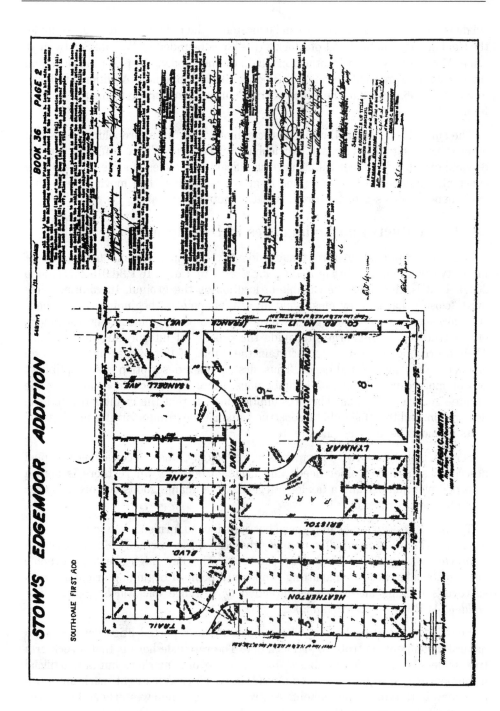

Once the plat has received the necessary approvals, it can provide the basis for the third method of legal description. If the subdivider records the plat in the public property records, subsequent conveyances of parcels in the subdivision simply can identify the subdivision and the block and lot number of the parcel being conveyed. A well-drafted legal description also will include the recording information for the subdivision plat, so that it readily can be located in the public records. For example, the legal description for Lot 1 of Block 3 (the block bounded by W. 70th St., Lynmar Lane, Mavelle Drive, and Heatherton Blvd.) on the subdivision plat reproduced on the preceding page would be: Lot 1, Block 3, Stow's Edgemoor Addition, as shown in Plat Book 36, page 2 in the Office of the County Recorder for Hennepin County, Minnesota.

The subdivision plat method is most commonly used in metropolitan areas and other areas of significant growth, particularly for housing. Where sufficient housing demand exists, a developer can achieve significant economies of scale by building a substantial number of homes on one large parcel, rather than moving crews and equipment to sites scattered throughout the metropolitan area.

4. Conflicts and Ambiguities in Descriptions

Legal descriptions must reasonably identify the quantity and boundaries of property conveyed. See *City of Kellogg v. Silver Mtn. Corp.*, 16 P.3d 915, 920 (Idaho 2000). That is, they must be capable of location on the ground. In addition, they must "close"; that is, they must wind up at their point of beginning. While these rules are simply stated, the case law involving them is voluminous. Several canons of construction have emerged to guide the process of interpreting descriptions. Their overriding purpose is to ascertain the intent of the parties and to sustain erroneous descriptions and deeds. Thus, first, when a description is susceptible of two or more constructions, or is ambiguous, the construction most favoring the grantee generally prevails. The presumption here is that the grantor drafted the description, and that it should be construed against the grantor/drafter and in favor of its intended beneficiary, the grantee.

Second, if there are two descriptions in a deed (say, where a conveyancer copied descriptions from two older deeds and included both, or where there is both a recorded plat number and a tax lot reference), the unambiguous one prevails over its ambiguous companion.

Third, if a description is ambiguous but sufficient to furnish a key to a boundary, extrinsic evidence is admissible to apply the description correctly. See *Ketchum v. Whitfield County*, 508 S.E.2d 639 (Ga. 1998). The key might be a geographic direction, a reference to an abutting property, a point of beginning or ending, or a surveyor's running an erroneous direction or distance backwards. See *Ault v. Holden*, 44 P.3d 781, 790 (Utah 2002).

Fourth (and starting here is where much of the reported litigation occurs), a natural monument controls an artificial one. The rationale here is that a rock or a tree is less susceptible of abuse than a surveyor's marker, but an artificial monument may also be a fence or a road, in which case it might mark an entire boundary. Both types of monuments control a course ("then westerly at 30 degrees off north"). *Rocamora v. Heaney*, 74 A.3d 457 (Conn. App. Ct. 2013). A course in turn controls a distance ("thence 90 feet"). See *Via v. Beckett*, 617 S.E.2d 895 (W. Va. 2005). The overall rationale is that a monument is easily located and that what is located on the ground should be more reliable than the plat or survey that preceded it. This canon often has the advantage of containing a surveyor's error within one boundary of a property, instead of permitting it to taint other boundaries as well.

Fifth, when the original monuments of a surveyor are not found but are ascertainable, they control even when they deviate from a course or distance in a metes and bounds description or on a plat. See *Scarberry v. Carr*, 571 P.2d 458, 462 (Okla. 1977). They also control later monuments and surveys. See *Steinherz v. Wilson*, 705 A.2d 710, 712, n.5 (Me. 1998). If, however, the original monuments are unascertainable, a surveyor's notes control the description or the plat. The latter are the picture, but the former become the substance, of the matter. In lieu of either monuments or notes, the boundaries of adjacent properties may be used. See *Wacker v. Price*, 216 P.2d 707, 710 (Ariz. 1950).

Sixth, when a natural monument has width, as with a boulder or a tree, the boundary line is presumed to run through its center. See *Crocker v. Cotting*, 44 N.E. 214, 215 (Mass. 1896) (Holmes, J., reviewing prior history of this canon). This canon also applies to artificial monuments like roads, as in "continuing along Mill Road," because if the roadway is ever vacated or abandoned, abutting owners should not have to quiet title to its bed.

Seventh, a particular description controls a general one. See *Ault v. Holden*, 44 P.3d 781, 791 (Utah 2002). For example, a recorded plat will likely contain more precise description terms than a tax map, and so controls. Likewise, a monument, a course, a distance — all control a statement of the acreage or area of a property.

Eighth, an inadequate description may be made good by incorporating an adequate one by reference, so long as the latter has been recorded. Do you see why the latter requirement is required? See generally John Cribbet & Corwin Johnson, Principles of the Law of Property 209–212 (3d ed. 1989) (reviewing these and other canons and discussing their overlapping and contradictory effects).

F.   Intent, Delivery, and Acceptance

A deed is effective only if (1) the grantor had a present intent to convey a property interest to the grantee, (2) the grantor delivered the deed to the grantee, and (3) the grantee accepted the conveyance.

BRTEK v. CIHAL
515 N.W.2d 628 (Neb. 1994)

HASTINGS, C.J.

This is an action by Jaroslav Brtek, also known as Jerry Brtek, and Lillian L. Brtek against Jerry's sister and her husband, Martha and Lad Cihal. By their fourth amended petition, the Brteks sought to impose a constructive or a resulting trust upon two farms, the Urbanek place and the Pedersen place, to which the Cihals held the record title. Additionally, they asked that a certain deed, which was dated April 30, 1960, conveying the Urbanek place from Joe Brtek, a deceased brother, to Joe himself and Martha Cihal, be canceled. The Cihals, in their answer, denied the Brteks' claims and counterclaimed, asking that a deed conveying certain other property not involved in this appeal from Agnes Brtek, the mother of Jerry and Martha, to Jerry be set aside because of an alleged failure of Jerry to comply with certain conditions therein.

Following a bench trial, the court entered judgment, finding that the Brteks had failed to establish a resulting or constructive trust by clear and convincing evidence and had failed to prove their allegations as to the requested deed cancellation, and that the Cihals had failed to prove the allegations of their counterclaim. Although it is difficult to trace the titles from the language of the decree because it refers to descriptions in the pleadings which do not match, it appears that titles to the Urbanek and Pedersen places were confirmed in the Cihals, and title to the home place in the Brteks. The Brteks have appealed, but the Cihals have not appealed the dismissal of their counterclaim. The Brteks assign eight errors, which may be summarized to allege that the decree of the trial court was contrary to law and was not sustained by the evidence, and that their case was wrongfully dismissed. . . .

This is an unfortunate situation in which the domineering matriarch of this family, Agnes, who was born in Czechoslovakia and barely spoke, wrote or read the English language, attempted to control the affairs of her three adult children by requiring them to convey, cross-convey, and reconvey certain real estate which was a part of a family operation. As a result, she turned sister against brother and successfully upset the titles to two parcels of real estate in Saunders County.

It must be understood at the outset that all of the business of this family unit was carried on in the Czech or Bohemian language, and much was lost or distorted in the parties' translation of those activities into English.

Upon the death of Vaclav Brtek in 1949, sons Jerry and Joe, daughter Martha, and wife Agnes inherited from Vaclav a farm known as the home place. On May 18, 1950, the children conveyed their interests in the farm to their mother, Agnes. On June 8, 1950, Agnes conveyed the home place to Jerry. Jerry and Joe continued to farm the land. Some of their earnings went into the family "pool," although Jerry and Joe put money earned from custom farming into separate bank accounts. Martha testified that she did not share in the income from the farming operation, but got "what was from the ducks and geese and chickens." From 1949 until 1961, Agnes filed one income tax return for the whole family, claiming Jerry, Joe, and Martha, her adult children, as dependents. From then on, because of the intervention of the Internal Revenue Service, the mother and the two boys, at least, started filing separate returns. On January 10, 1961, Martha married Lad Cihal and left the family home.

However, before that marriage occurred, the Urbanek place was purchased in 1952, with the various family members contributing to the purchase price of $13,200. The ledger kept by Martha at Agnes' direction revealed the source of those funds. Joe paid $3,955.92, Agnes $2,400, Jerry $4,450, and Martha $708. A note for $1,200 was also given, and that note and interest were paid from the sale of some steers and corn. The balance of approximately $486 was paid from the assets of the estate of Vaclav Brtek. Record title was taken in the name of Joe Brtek at the direction of Agnes.

Later on, at the direction of Agnes, Joe deeded the Urbanek place to himself and Martha as joint tenants. However, the deed was not given to Martha, but instead was placed by Agnes in her dresser drawer in which the family's papers were kept. Access to this dresser was available to Agnes, Joe, and Jerry, but the record does not reveal whether Martha enjoyed that privilege. Physical possession of that deed was not given to Martha before Joe's death on June 8, 1974.

Shortly after Joe's death, either Agnes brought the deed conveying the Urbanek place to Martha at the latter's home and declared that "the farm is yours" or Martha came to the home place, where Agnes gave her the deed. That deed was filed for record on July 1, 1974.

The petition for the determination of inheritance tax due and owing by reason of Joe's death was executed by both Jerry and Martha. The petition recited that the deed to the Urbanek place was executed by Joe "with instruction that said deed would be filed . . . on the death of the said Joseph Brtek." On August 23, 1974, Martha paid the inheritance tax of $370 on the property. Jerry stated that after the inheritance tax was paid, he and Martha had a conversation at attorney Clyde Worrall's office in which they discussed putting his name on the title to the Urbanek place. However, instead of doing that, Martha executed a deed on April 11, 1975, conveying the Urbanek place to herself and her husband, Lad, as joint tenants, which deed was filed for record on April 14, 1975.

Before Joe's death, he and Jerry farmed the Urbanek place and divided the income, giving one-third each to themselves and one-third to Agnes. After Joe died, Jerry continued to farm the Urbanek place, and Agnes received one-third of the income from this farm and Jerry received two-thirds. During the time that the farm was in the Agricultural Stabilization and Conservation Service program, Jerry received 60 percent of the payments and Martha received 40 percent.

Jerry stated that he did not pay any rent on the Urbanek place, but paid property taxes. Martha stated that her mother told her not to charge Jerry rent, but a few years before her mother passed away in 1982, Martha started charging rent because she needed the money and could not pay the taxes without getting any crops off the land. Martha charged Jerry $1,600 a year and stated that she did not know how she arrived at that figure but that "he paid me for the taxes and I paid it to the treasurer's." In 1985, Martha demanded that Jerry vacate the premises. . . .

THE URBANEK PLACE

In regard to the Urbanek place, the plaintiffs argue that the deed was clearly never delivered by Joe to Martha and, further, that there is clear and convincing evidence that Martha holds the Urbanek place as trustee of a resulting trust.

DELIVERY OF DEED

It seems apparent from the record that the deed from Joe to Joe and Martha was never delivered during Joe's lifetime. It is essential to the validity of a deed that there be a delivery, and the burden of proof rests upon the party asserting delivery to establish it by a preponderance of the evidence. To constitute a valid delivery of a deed, there must be an intent on the part of the grantor that the deed shall operate as a muniment of title to take effect presently. *Moseley v. Zieg*, 146 N.W.2d 72 (Neb. 1966); *Lewis v. Marker*, 18 N.W.2d 210 (Neb. 1945). One of the problems in this litigation is that the only intent supported by evidence in the record is that of Agnes, not of the grantor.

However, the essential fact to render delivery effective always is that the deed itself has left the control of the grantor, who has reserved no right to recall it, and it has passed to the grantee. No particular acts or words are necessary to constitute delivery of a deed; anything done by the grantor from which it is apparent that a delivery was intended, either by words or acts, or both combined, is sufficient. Whether a deed or other instrument conveying an interests in property has been delivered is largely a question of intent to be determined by facts and circumstances of the particular case. * * * Recordation of a deed generally presumes delivery. *Kresser v. Peterson*, 675 P.2d 1193 (Utah 1984).

In *Kresser*, the testatrix's two stepsons asserted a one-half interest in a home under the terms of a will. The testatrix, Della, had executed a will which devised the home to her two sons and two stepsons. Seven years later, she executed a warranty deed in which she named herself and her two sons as grantees, with right of survivorship. The deed was recorded and placed in a bank safe deposit box under a lease agreement which provided "exclusive access" to the box to the joint tenants. Although the agreement permitted the sons access to the box, they did not know the deed was in the box and did not have a key to the box. The Utah court stated the general rules: "An effective deed requires delivery, actual or constructive, without exclusive control or recall. Recording generally presumes delivery. Delivery to one cotenant or reservation of an estate connotes delivery to all cotenants, where the grantor is also the grantee." *Id.* at 1194. The court did not rely upon this last rule, however, noting instead that "* * * Delivery was reflected by recordation of the deed and deposit by Della in the safety deposit box with written authority that any of the grantees, who also were tenants under the box rental agreement, had exclusive right of access to the box." *Id.*

The primary issue in *Meadows v. Brich*, 606 S.W.2d 258, 260 (Mo. App. 1980), was whether the trial court was correct in finding that a deed had been delivered. In making that determination, the court stated the following governing principles, with which we agree:

> Whether or not a deed has been delivered is a mixed question of law and fact. The element which controls the resolution of that question is the intention of the parties, especially the intention of the grantor. The vital inquiry is whether the grantor intended a complete transfer — whether the grantor *parted with dominion over the instrument* with the intention of relinquishing all dominion over it and of making it presently operative as a conveyance of the title to the land.

> It is not necessary, to effectuate delivery, that the deed actually be handed over to the grantee or to another person for the grantee. There may be a delivery notwithstanding the deed remains in the custody of the grantor. If a valid delivery takes place, it is not rendered ineffectual by the act of the grantee in giving the deed into the custody of the grantor for safekeeping. It is all a question of the intention of the parties, which may be manifested by words or acts or both. If the deed, although acknowledged, is not recorded and is in the grantor's possession at the time of his

death, those circumstance, unless explained, are deemed conclusive that the parties did not intend a complete transfer. If there is an unequivocal showing that the grantee was given possession of the deed, a presumption of delivery arises. Such a presumption, however, does not arise where the evidence shows that the grantor handed the deed to one of two grantees momentarily, for the purpose of reading it, and at the grantor's direction it is immediately taken back into grantor's possession, to be kept by him until his death.

There is a presumption of *non-delivery* if the evidence shows that the deed was in grantor's possession at the time of his death and was not then recorded. Such a showing places upon grantees the burden of going forward with the evidence, "more accurately, the burden of persuasion," to rebut the presumption of non-delivery.

The parties seem to agree that it was Agnes who decided that the Urbanek farm would be put in Joe's name originally, and it was Agnes who decided that Joe should add Martha's name to the deed. Thus, it is difficult to ascertain the *grantor*'s intent. However, as noted in *Moseley v. Zieg*, 146 N.W.2d 72 (Neb. 1966), the burden of proof rests upon the party asserting delivery to establish it by a preponderance of the evidence, and to constitute a valid delivery of a deed there must be an intent on the part of the grantor that the deed shall operate as evidence of title to take effect presently. Therefore, Martha had the burden of proof to show that Joe had the intention to relinquish dominion over the deed and to make it *presently* operative as a conveyance of the title to the land.

In deposition testimony, Martha stated:

Q: After Joe died, did you get a deed to the Urbanek place?

A: Yes.

Q: How?

A: It was written in Joe's name. When he passed away, it was deeded to me.

Q: Well, but how did you get the deed?

A: It was made at the Schuyler Bank with Mr. Joe Beck when — well, the farm was Joe's, and after something happened to him, then it would be mine. . . .

Q: Did you record the deed?

A: No.

Q: Do you know what it means to record a deed?

A: Yes. . . .

Q: But you didn't record it?

A: No.

Q: Who did?

A: Nobody. Joe had it at home. He had it.

Q: In what?

A: In the dresser drawer, and it was there until —

Q: Until he died?

A: Until he died.

Martha further testified:

> Well, then that Urbanek's, it was an estate. So we decided to buy it because it was just a mile and a half from the home place where I come from.

Q: Did anybody make any decisions about how it was going to be paid for?

A: We all pitched in.

Q: Joe and Jerry and Mom and you, right?

A: Yes.

Q: And the title was put in Joe's name?

A: Yes.

Q: How did you get your name on that title?

A: I don't know which year now, but then Mother decided — Well, it was with Dad's estate. The farm was put in just Dad's name and not in Mother's, and so we had it made that Urbanek's place, which Joe had in his name, *so it would be willed to me*, something should happen to him.

Q: Why was that?

A: Mother decided it that way. . . .

Q: After your mother died, did Jerry rent this farm from you for awhile?

A: *I did not have no right to the farm until after Joe passed away.* (Emphasis supplied.)

This testimony clearly evidences the testamentary intent of the deed as to Martha. * * *

It is essential to the validity of a deed that there must be delivery, and the burden of proof rests upon the party asserting delivery to establish it by a preponderance of the evidence. *Moseley v. Zieg*, 146 N.W.2d 72 (Neb. 1966). It is true that *Moseley* states that when the deed is found in the grantee's possession during the lifetime of the grantor, this is prima facie evidence of delivery, and the burden of proof is upon the one who disputes this presumption. However, here, the deed was never in Martha's possession during Joe's lifetime.

We find that there is insufficient evidence to support a conclusion that the deed from Joe to Joe and Martha was delivered to Martha during Joe's lifetime. Accordingly, there is no valid title in the Cihals upon which a trust may be impressed. To that extent, the judgment of the district court finding that the Brteks have failed to prove the establishment of a trust as to the Urbanek place is affirmed.

By the same token, we reverse the judgment of the trial court which confirmed title to the Urbanek place in the Cihals.

Rather, we find that at Joe's death without a will, title vested immediately in his heirs or heir. * * * There is no question that Joe died in 1974, leaving no spouse or issue surviving him, so title descended to his mother, Agnes. Effective at that time was Neb. Rev. Stat. § 30-102, which provided in substance that upon the death of one leaving no spouse or heir surviving, his or her property descended to parents if living. Accordingly, title descended to Agnes. Upon Agnes' death in 1982, in effect at that time was Neb. Rev. Stat. § 30-2303(1), which provided that upon the death of a person leaving no spouse surviving, the estate passes to "the issue of the decedent. . . ." This, of course, would mean Jerry and Martha. Although this is not the lawsuit that was tried, nevertheless, the evidence supports such a conclusion. "[W]here a court of equity has obtained jurisdiction of a cause for any purpose, it will retain it for all, and will proceed to a final determination of the case, adjudicating all matters in issue, thus avoiding unnecessary litigation." *Whitehead Oil Co. v. City of Lincoln*, 515 N.W.2d 401, 405 (Neb. 1994). Therefore, title is confirmed in Jerry and Martha as tenants in common, and the deeds to the Urbanek place purporting to vest title in Martha and then Martha and Lad are ordered canceled of record. There is no problem with the statutes of limitations, because the deed to Martha was not valid and she had no title to convey to herself and Lad. The judgment of the district court confirming title to the Urbanek place in Martha and Lad Cihal is reversed. . . .

NOTES

1. The delivery requirement is rooted in the early English common law. As described at the beginning of this chapter, the earliest common law method of conveying title was by livery of seisin, which required the grantor to hand a clod of dirt or some other part or symbol of the land to the grantee. In the absence of written records, this ceremony was designed to serve as an outward manifestation of the grantor's intent to transfer ownership. Today, grantors can manifest their intent by executing a deed. As the *Brtek* opinion demonstrates, however, many courts still require a physical delivery of the deed for an effective conveyance.

Courts increasingly are recognizing that physical delivery of the deed is just one method for a grantor to manifest the requisite intent for a title transfer. If the grantor clearly has manifested intent in another way, the law should effectuate that intent, rather than defeating it based on a requirement that originated in a very different time. Unfortunately, a large body of rather confusing case law has been created by courts that are attempting to effectuate intent but that are unwilling to dispense with the requirement for a physical delivery of the deed.

2. The delivery requirement can create problems for future buyers of the property, as well as for the parties to the deed. Even if the deed is recorded in the public property records, it is completely ineffective to transfer title if it has not been delivered. *Gheen v. State ex rel. Dept. of Health, Div. of Healthcare Fin./ Equalitycare*, 326 P.3d 918 (Wyo. 2014). For example, if the grantee named in the deed takes the deed from the grantor without his permission and records it, a buyer from the grantee will not acquire title even though the buyer relied on the appearance of ownership provided by the property records. No matter how carefully the buyer inspected the recorded deed, she would be unable to determine that the deed had not been delivered.

weird brother case

TURNER v. MALLERNEE
640 S.W.2d 517 (Mo. Ct. App. 1982)

FLANIGAN, J. *Absolute unconditional delivery from lawyer to Mildred, and Arthur couldn't get to it.*

This is an action to quiet title to a 160-acre farm located in Douglas County. Plaintiffs are Harold Turner and Mildred Turner, his wife, and defendants are Roy Mallernee and Thelma Mallernee, his wife. Mildred and Roy are the children of Arthur Mallernee, who died on November 6, 1978. The parties base their respective claims of title on two competing deeds to the land, each signed and acknowledged by Arthur as grantor. In November 1975 Arthur signed a deed which named plaintiffs as grantees. The 1975 deed was never recorded. On October 3, 1978, Arthur signed a deed which named defendants as grantees. That deed was promptly recorded.

The petition was in three counts. Count I sought to establish title in plaintiffs based on the 1975 deed. Count II sought a decree invalidating the 1978 deed on the grounds that Arthur was incompetent at the time it was executed and that defendant Roy had exercised undue influence on Arthur with respect to its execution. Count III sought an order "impressing a constructive trust upon defendants" and "compelling defendants to convey the land to plaintiffs."

Sitting without a jury, the trial court found in favor of defendants on Counts I and III and in favor of plaintiffs on Count II. The trial court found that the 1975 deed was ineffective for lack of delivery. The trial court also found that the 1978 deed was ineffective because of undue influence exerted by Roy and lack of the grantor's competence. Both sides have appealed.

Although defendants have challenged the ruling on Count II, the evidence of both sides with respect to that count, including testimony from defendant Roy himself, overwhelmingly demonstrated that undue influence was exercised by Roy and that Arthur was incompetent to execute the 1978 deed. It would serve no precedential purpose to recount the evidence pertinent to Count II. The appeal by defendants has no merit.

The dispositive issue is whether the 1975 deed was delivered. The parties agree that Arthur owned the farm prior to the execution of the 1975 deed, that Arthur was competent when the 1975 deed was executed, and that the 1975 deed was not tainted by undue influence. . . .

There is little, if any, dispute with regard to the facts on which hinges the issue of delivery or non-delivery of the 1975 deed. Several years prior to November 1975 Arthur had conveyed another 160-acre farm, adjacent to the one here in dispute, to Roy. Arthur had stated on several previous occasions that he intended for the disputed farm "to be Mildred's."

In November 1975 plaintiffs Harold and Mildred drove to the farm where Arthur was then living alone. There they met Arthur and Roy, who lived on the adjacent farm, and the four people went to the office of attorney Daniel Wade in Ava, Missouri. During the "15 to 30 minutes" they were at Wade's office, Wade prepared a deed to the land, using a description the four laymen had first obtained at the recorder's office. In the presence of attorney Wade and his three companions, Arthur signed and acknowledged the deed which contained a description of the farm and named the plaintiffs as grantees. After Wade had "notarized" the deed, Wade placed it in an envelope and gave it to grantee Mildred in the presence of the other people, including Arthur. It is a reasonable, if not inescapable, inference from the evidence that Wade's act of handing the deed to Mildred was done with the knowledge and consent of Arthur.

Although Harold, Mildred and Roy all testified at the trial, there was no testimony concerning any specific statement made by Arthur during the conference in the attorney's office or indeed on that day.

After Mildred was in physical possession of the deed, Roy suggested to Mildred that the deed be left with Roy to be put by him in a safety deposit box. Mildred agreed and handed the deed to Roy. Mildred and Roy decided that the deed would not be recorded. Mildred testified that Roy "was supposed to keep the deed in a lock box and the deed was supposed to be returned" to her at Arthur's death.

Neither of the grantees, Harold and Mildred, saw the deed again. Roy testified that he placed the deed in his, Roy's, safety deposit box, to which Arthur had no access. Indeed it was Roy's testimony that Arthur did not know where the deed was. In 1978 Roy burned the 1975 deed shortly before Arthur's death and after the execution of the defective 1978 deed. Mildred did not learn of the destruction of the 1975 deed nor the existence of the 1978 deed until three weeks after Arthur's funeral.

On cross-examination by defense counsel, Harold testified that attorney Wade made the statement "that if [Arthur] trusted [Mildred] that she could always reconvey the property." There was conversation between Mildred and Roy that Arthur "might need the property — not that he would need it — if he got badly sick, that he would need to borrow against it."

Mildred testified that "the purpose in Roy having the deed was in case Dad did have some kind of sickness or had a need of borrowing money against the place" but "that was never necessary." Mildred also testified that attorney Wade told her "if Arthur ever really needed it, you could convey it back." Mildred admitted that on her deposition she had given an affirmative answer to the question, "So you realized your father still had control of the property?" Explaining her foregoing answer the witness said, "I realized he could borrow money on the property if he needed to before his death. But it was also understood I was to receive the deed at my father's death. It was to be recorded."

Roy testified that the decision not to record the deed was made by Mildred and Roy and that decision had been made "without talking to Dad." Roy said, "My intentions at that time [were] to bring the deed back at Dad's passing away." Asked whether Arthur had instructed the witness on what to do with the deed, Roy replied, "I don't know as he really said."

In November 1975, when the events in the attorney's office occurred, plaintiffs Harold and Mildred were in the process of moving to Arkansas where Harold was employed. Arthur continued to live alone on the farm for a few months, but his health failed and thereafter he made his home with Roy except for the last summer of his life which he spent with the plaintiffs in Arkansas. The plaintiffs did not occupy the farm or make improvements on it between November 1975 and the date of Arthur's death three years later. Although plaintiffs admitted they did not pay taxes on the farm, the record does not show who paid the taxes during that period or even if they were paid at all.

Significantly, after the conference in the attorney's office Arthur did not incur substantial medical expenses. No need arose for the farm to be mortgaged to obtain funds for Arthur's expenses, medical or otherwise, and it was not mortgaged.

In their attack upon the ruling of the trial court that the 1975 deed was not delivered, Harold and Mildred argue that delivery was accomplished when the deed, signed and acknowledged by Arthur, was handed by attorney Wade to Mildred in the presence of Arthur with the latter's knowledge and consent. Their brief states: "There was absolutely no evidence that the grantor, Arthur, participated in any of the discussions between Mildred and Roy concerning the handling of the deed which had been given to her by Arthur. Arthur, after executing the deed, allowed it to be handed to Mildred and at no time made any request that it be redelivered to either himself or any other person. The decision not to record the deed was reached between Mildred and Roy. These discussions were all had after the execution and delivery of the deed to Mildred. The deed was then placed in a safety deposit box to which Arthur did not have access, except through Roy. Thus, it is clear that from the time Arthur executed the deed which conveyed the property in question to Harold and Mildred, he had no further control or dominion over the deed." The foregoing argument may not be totally lacking in its appeal but its soundness need not be determined because, for reasons to be stated, this court holds, as Harold and Mildred alternatively contend, that there was a valid conditional delivery of the 1975 deed which, upon satisfaction of the condition, ripened into an absolute delivery.

Seeking to uphold the ruling of the trial court that the 1975 deed was not delivered, Roy argues that the circumstances demonstrate that Arthur "intended to retain control" of the deed and "intended to be able to recall the deed if necessary." Roy points to the testimony of Harold that Harold was aware that "if Arthur wanted to mortgage the farm, he had the right to do so." He also points to the testimony of Mildred that she realized that her father "still had control of the property." Of course, if Roy's position is correct, the trip to attorney Wade's office and the proceedings which occurred there were a total waste of time.

It has long been the law in Missouri that the delivery of a deed by the grantor to a third person with *unconditional* instructions that it be held by him and delivered to the grantee upon the grantor's death is a valid delivery, if there is no reservation by the grantor of dominion over the deed. *Haer v. Christmas*, 312 S.W.2d 66, 68 (Mo. 1958). In *Haer* the court said, "[T]he requirement that there be an intention on the part of the grantor to convey to the grantee a present interest in the land does not mean that he must intend to transfer the present right of possession."

It is also true that a deed's delivery, if otherwise effective, is not impaired by a contemporaneous agreement between the grantor and the grantee that the deed not be recorded until after the death of grantor, and this is so "even if the parties entertained the erroneous idea that it would not be in force until recorded." III American Law of Property § 12.66 (A.J. Casner ed. 1952).

"Delivery" of a deed is a legal concept which is not to be equated with the mere physical handing of the document by the grantor to the grantee. That physical act, however, if it takes place, is a circumstance to be considered in determining whether the grantor intended to convey a present interest. The circumstances may be such that there is delivery without physical transfer, or there may be no delivery although a physical transfer took place. It has been said, however, "The least questionable proof [of delivery] is a manual transfer of the instrument by the grantor to the grantee, requiring strong evidence to overcome it." III American Law of Property § 12.64 (A.J. Casner ed. 1952).

The rule in the majority of jurisdictions is "that delivery to the *grantee* of a deed absolute on its face passes title though the grantor, by an oral condition, wishes to postpone its operative effect." . . . Some Missouri cases have alluded to the rule. *Commerce Trust Co. v. White*, 158 S.W. 457, 460[8] (Mo. App. Ct. 1913); *Whelan v. Tobener*, 71 Mo. App. 361, 370 (1897).

It is unnecessary to decide whether the foregoing rule would have come into operation if Roy had not been present and the Mildred-Roy conversation had taken place between Mildred and Arthur. This opinion assumes, arguendo, that Arthur, by his physical presence, was a participant in the Mildred-Roy conversation. In other words, whether or not it is necessary for this court to view the evidence as showing a conditional delivery of the deed by Arthur to *Roy*, the evidence will be so viewed. From Roy's standpoint, such is the most favorable view.

The conversation in the attorney's office indicates that it was the intention of Roy and Mildred (and, arguendo, Arthur) that Mildred (and her husband) receive title to the farm if, during the balance of his life, Arthur escaped serious illness necessitating major medical expenses. That view of the evidence may involve a condition precedent to a posthumous delivery. On the other hand the intention of the parties may be viewed as contemplating a present passage to the grantees of an interest subject to defeasance if Arthur incurred major medical expenses, a condition subsequent. The difference, however theoretical, between these views becomes academic because the fact is that the condition precedent was satisfied and the condition subsequent did not occur.

If the act of Mildred in handing the deed to Roy be deemed equivalent to the act of Arthur in handing the deed to Roy, subject to the content of the Mildred-Roy conversation, the transaction may properly be viewed as "a conditional delivery" or as a delivery "in escrow." The general topic of conditional delivery of a deed has been the subject of considerable discussion.

An excellent treatment of the subject of conditional delivery of a deed is found in Tiffany, Real Property, Third Ed., Vol. IV, § 1048–1054, p. 418, *et seq*. Certain principles stated in that source are applicable here and are set forth in the next six paragraphs.

"The delivery of a conveyance, or of any other instrument which takes effect by delivery, may be conditioned upon the performance of some act or the occurrence of some event. . . . A conditional delivery is usually referred to as to delivery 'in escrow,' or it is said that an instrument conditionally delivered is delivered as an 'escrow.' . . . [A]n instrument in the form of a deed, which is conditionally delivered, is delivered as a deed, an instrument capable of legal operation, and not as a mere piece of paper. Otherwise it could not become legally operative upon the satisfaction of the condition. In the case of a conditional delivery, a delivery in escrow, the maker of the instrument in effect says: 'I now deliver this as my act and deed, provided such a condition is satisfied,' ". . . § 1048.

"The manual transfer of the instrument, which is ordinarily assumed to be essential to a conditional delivery, must, according to a great majority of the authorities in this country, be to a person other than the grantee, it being held that if the grantor, intending to make a conditional delivery, hands the instrument to the grantee, there is necessarily an absolute delivery." § 1049.

"The question whether, when the instrument has been handed by the grantor to a third person, it is to be regarded as having been conditionally delivered, is to be determined with reference to the language used by him, construed in the light of the surrounding circumstances, as showing the grantor's intention. That is, as absolute delivery is a question of the grantor's intention, so conditional delivery is a question of his intention. Such a manual transfer of the instrument to a third person is compatible with either an absolute delivery, a conditional delivery, or no delivery whatsoever; that is, the grantor may hand the instrument to a third person with the intention that it become immediately operative, that it become operative in case a certain condition is satisfied, or with no intention as to its becoming operative. A conditional delivery differs from an absolute delivery merely in the fact that it is subject to a condition, and it is in its nature as final as an absolute delivery. For this reason it is difficult to yield our assent to occasional decisions and dicta that the grantor may, when handing the instrument to a third person by way of conditional delivery, retain a right of revocation, so-called, by an express statement that the instrument is not to become operative even on satisfaction of the condition if he, the grantor, in the meantime indicates a desire to the contrary. It is recognized that, after making a conditional delivery without expressly retaining any such right of control, the grantor cannot prevent the instrument from becoming operative upon the satisfaction of the condition, and there is no reason why he should be allowed to retain a right of control by an express statement to that effect while making delivery." . . . § 1050.[2]

---

[2] "Sometimes the contingency is not the ultimate death of the grantor but his death by a certain date, or prior to that of the grantee, or if he fails to recover from a present illness or from an operation about to be performed. A number of courts have held that under such circumstances the grantor has thus reserved a conditional right of recall in the event that he survives and that accordingly the transaction lacks the necessary intent to convey a present interest by an unconditional first delivery. Walsh makes the logical comment that the decisions in these cases confuse an allowable reservation of a right of recall

"When the conditions of the escrow have been met, the depository becomes the agent of each party under a duty to deliver, so that, if the depository fails to deliver when he should, the delivery is held to have legally occurred." § 1051.

"It has been asserted in a number of cases that there can be no delivery in escrow unless it takes place as the result of an actual contract of sale between the parties to the instrument, as, for instance, when the delivery is conditioned upon the payment by the grantee of an agreed price for the land. . . . The idea at the basis of this asserted requirement of an auxiliary contract in connection with conditional delivery appears to be that, in the absence of such a contract, the grantor can control the operation of the instrument, that, in other words, he may revoke the delivery. Such an idea is, it is conceived, absolutely erroneous, and involves an entire misapprehension of the nature of conditional delivery. After the delivery of the instrument of conveyance, whether absolutely or conditionally, the parties stand in the relation, not of vendor and purchaser under a contract but of grantor and grantee under a conveyance, and consequently the question of the existence of a valid contract of sale is immaterial. There is no more reason for regarding the conditional delivery of a conveyance as invalid in the absence of an enforceable contract of sale than for so regarding an absolute delivery. . . . [A] valid conditional delivery may occur in connection with transactions not involving a sale, in the case of a gift, for instance. There can obviously be no contract of sale in such case to support the validity of the delivery, yet if a contract of sale is necessary to support a conditional delivery in the one case, how can such a delivery be valid without a contract of sale in the other? . . . The idea that, in the absence of a contract, the grantor can recall the deed is, as before remarked, without any support in principle, and there is, it is submitted, no more necessity of a contract in regard to its custody when the delivery is conditional than when it is unconditional. . . . § 1052.

"Properly considered, conditional delivery, or delivery in escrow, is the same as any other delivery, except that it is subject to the satisfaction of a condition. After the condition has been satisfied, there is an operative conveyance which is to be regarded as having been delivered at the time of its conditional delivery, for the obvious reason that it was then, and then only, that it was delivered, though the ownership cannot be regarded as having passed until it actually did pass, that is, until the satisfaction of the condition. The grantor in effect says, at the time of handing the instrument to the intended custodian, 'I now deliver this as my deed provided such a thing is done or occurs.' " . . . § 1053.

In *Seibel v. Higham*, 216 Mo. 121, 115 S.W. 987, 990 (1908), the court said: " 'The distinctive feature of an escrow is the delivery of a deed to a third person to await

---

if a contingent event should take place with the unallowable absolute right of recall. He contends that there is no more retention of control by the grantor in these cases than in any other case of accepted delivery in escrow and that the courts have so held in decisions involving some conditional rights of recall." III American Law of Property § 12.67 (A.J. Casner ed. 1952).

the performance of some condition, whereupon the deed is to be delivered to the grantee and the title is to pass.'. . . In such case it is not a deed until the condition is performed. The depositary of an escrow is sometimes spoken of as the agent of the grantor and sometimes as the agent of both parties. . . . If he were the agent of the grantor, his agency would cease on the grantor's death, and he would have no authority to receive the purchase money from the grantee and deliver the deed. But the death of the grantor does not annul the depositary's authority to do what he was appointed to do, and it does not impair the right of the grantee to perform the condition and take down the deed."

In *Donnelly v. Robinson*, 406 S.W.2d 595, 598 (Mo. 1966), the court said: "[U]pon final delivery by a depository of a deed deposited in escrow the instrument will be treated as relating back to, and taking effect at the time of the original deposit in escrow. This shall apply even though one of the parties to the deed dies before the second delivery. This relation back doctrine has wide and general acceptance." * * *

In light of the foregoing principles this court holds that there was a conditional delivery of the 1975 deed, that the condition was satisfied, and that the 1975 deed was an operative conveyance. The trial court erred in denying plaintiffs relief on Count I and in finding that the 1975 deed was ineffective for lack of delivery. In all other respects the judgment is affirmed. The judgment is reversed and the cause is remanded for entry of judgment consistent with this opinion.

NOTES

1.   If Arthur's deed to Mildred was not to be delivered to her until his death, why isn't the deed invalid as an attempted testamentary gift? Presumably, the deed did not satisfy the requirements of the Statute of Wills.

2.   In *Turner*, the court proceeded on the assumption that Arthur had delivered the 1975 deed to Roy subject to an oral condition. What if Arthur had delivered the deed directly to Mildred subject to the same oral condition? The great majority of courts would hold that title immediately transferred to Mildred free of the condition. To enforce the condition would violate the Statute of Frauds because the condition was not in writing. Additionally, upholding the condition after Arthur delivered the deed to Mildred would violate the requirement that the grantor intend to transfer title immediately upon delivery of the deed, rather than upon the future satisfaction of a condition. Therefore, a grantor that wants to make a conditional delivery of a deed should give it to a third party with instructions to deliver it to the grantee only when the condition has been satisfied.

3.   If the grantor does make a conditional delivery to a third party, whose agent is she?

> Such decisions [that a conditional delivery to a third party constitutes a valid delivery] are sometimes explained on the theory that there is an irrevocable transfer to the agent, which puts the deed beyond the dominion, control and recall of the grantor. However, if the deed is beyond the recall of the grantor, the agent cannot be the agent of the grantor since an agent is always subject to the control of his or her principal. It would also be improper to designate the third party as the agent for the grantee, since

doing so would force the agent into an impossible dilemma — in order to comply with the grantee's direction to transfer the deed to him or her, the agent would have to violate the terms of the condition imposed by the grantor. The only realistic interpretation is that the agent is an independent agent or an escrow agent.

Powell on Real Property § 81A.04[2][a][v][D] (Michael Allan Wolf ed., 2014).

4. Courts frequently state that a deed conveys title "upon delivery." Does this mean that title automatically transfers to the grantee subject to defeasance if the grantee refuses to accept the title? What are the legal consequences if the title transfers to the grantee before he has had an opportunity to accept or reject the conveyance? Acceptance is not always a foregone conclusion. A grantee may refuse to accept a conveyance for any one of a number of reasons. For example, the property may be environmentally contaminated, thereby creating the possibility for a large liability for cleanup costs. The conveyance might be subject to covenants that would restrict the grantee's ability to use the land or that would impose affirmative obligations on the grantee, such as an obligation to pay condominium association fees. The conveyance might upset the grantee's estate plan. An owner may attempt to convey property to a taxing authority for unpaid taxes, or to a mortgagee or creditor in payment of a debt. A grantee can refuse to accept land for any reason or for no reason. "Acceptance consists of two elements: some *conduct* by or on behalf of the grantee and an *intent* to accept the grant. Anno. 74 A.L.R.2d 992, 996 ('an intention to take the legal title to the property which the deed purports to convey, and the manifestation of such intention by some act, conduct, or declaration'). . . . Under certain circumstances, the law presumes acceptance even when the grantee is unaware of the grant. Such is the case where the grant is beneficial to the grantee and not onerous; or where the grantee is an infant; or of unsound mind." *County of Worth v. Jorgenson*, 253 N.W.2d 575, 578 (Iowa 1977).

5. Suppose that O executes a deed to his farm, conveying it to his son S for life, remainder to S's children. S resents the limitations on his life estate and, in O's presence, tears up the deed and throws it in a wastebasket. O then dies, leaving the farm to his daughter D. Both S's children and D claim title to the farm. Who has the title? Compare *Underwood v. Gillespie*, 594 S.W.2d 372 (Mo. Ct. App. 1980), with *Martin v. Adams*, 62 So. 2d 328 (Miss. 1953).

V. DEEDS CHARACTERIZED AS MORTGAGES

SEAMAN v. SEAMAN
477 A.2d 734 (Me. 1984)

SCOLNIK, J.

The plaintiff, Earle Seaman, appeals from a judgment of the Superior Court, York County, ordering the defendant, Malcolm Seaman, be allowed to redeem his interest in a cottage which was the subject of an equitable mortgage held by the plaintiff. The defendant cross-appeals, assigning error to the court's calculation of the amount due to effectuate the redemption. We grant the defendant's cross-appeal, and remand for recalculation of the mortgage debt, but affirm the judgment of the Superior Court in all other respects.

The facts are not in dispute. Between 1962 and 1964 the plaintiff Earle Seaman lent his brother Malcolm Seaman $4500. On September 9, 1965, the defendant and his wife executed a promissory note for that amount plus five percent annual interest, the total to be repaid in five years. As security for the note, the defendant assigned to his brother his future interest in a cottage in Ogunquit which he had received under his grandfather's will. The defendant's interest was a vested remainder subject to divestment if the defendant predeceased the life tenant. The defendant made no payments on the note during the five year period. In 1971, the plaintiff recorded the note, the assignment, and an affidavit of default in the York County Probate Court, but did not institute foreclosure proceedings. In 1973, the parties made a new agreement, whereby the defendant promised to make monthly payments of $50.00 on the note. The plaintiff received four $100 payments in 1977 and $500 in 1979.

On March 9, 1982, the life tenant died, and the defendant's interest in the Ogunquit cottage was no longer subject to divestment. On March 25, 1982, the defendant tendered payment of $5848.55 to the plaintiff, representing the total amount he calculated to be due on the note. The plaintiff refused to accept this payment, and instead, on April 2, 1982, instituted this action for specific performance. The defendant counterclaimed, seeking, *inter alia*, an order that he be allowed to redeem the property by payment of the amount due on the note.

By order dated November 3, 1983 the Court directed that the defendant be given 90 days in which to redeem his interest in the cottage, by tendering to the plaintiff $4500, plus five percent annual interest, computed from September 9, 1965.

The Superior Court correctly characterized the interest transferred between the parties as an equitable mortgage, rather than a true assignment. It is clear the parties intended the transfer of the defendant's future interest in the cottage to secure his obligation on the promissory note. As we stated in *Smith v. Diplock*, 127 Me. 452, 457, 144 A. 383, 386 (1929). No matter what the form and phraseology of the written evidence of a conveyance, if the court is satisfied that, at its inception, the agreement of transfer was as security, such conveyance, though in form a deed absolute, is in effect an equitable mortgage. *Accord Fulton v. McBurnie*, 134 Me. 6, 180 A. 921 (1935); G. Osborne, Handbook on the Law of Mortgages § 29 (2d ed. 1970). This court has repeatedly recognized that a right of redemption is incident to a mortgage, and is an equitable right upon which the mortgagor may justifiably rely. *Portland Savings Bank v. Landry*, 372 A.2d 573 (Me. 1977). While not disputing that he held an equitable mortgage on the Ogunquit cottage, the plaintiff argues that by the terms of the "assignment," the defendant expressly waived his right of redemption. In prior decisions we have held that while a mortgagor may release or surrender his right of redemption, such an agreement must be made subsequent to the giving of the mortgage, and for valuable consideration. *Bither v. Packard*, 115 Me. 306, 98 A. 929 (1916).

In the present case there is no evidence the defendant agreed to waive his equity of redemption, and, in fact, the plaintiff's acceptance of payments on the note in 1977 and 1979 gave the defendant justifiable grounds for believing his period of redemption was open-ended. Furthermore, until he refused to accept the defendant's tendered payment in March of 1982, the plaintiff repeatedly indicated he would accept payments on the note at any time. We agree with the finding of the Superior Court: "The defendant . . . was led to believe by the words of the plaintiff and by the action of the plaintiff in accepting irregular payments that he could repay at any time. . . . The plaintiff cannot refuse the defendant's tender of final payment within their agreed redemption period nor can the plaintiff unilaterally end the open-ended redemption period without giving some reasonable period of time in which to redeem." We find no error in the Superior Court's decision that the defendant has the right to redeem his interest in the cottage.

The court's order determined the amount owed by the defendant to be $4500 plus five percent interest calculated from September 9, 1965. The defendant is certainly correct in arguing, as he does on his cross-appeal, that the $900 in payments he has already made on the note must be deducted from the total amount due. We therefore remand this case to the Superior Court for its recalculation of the amount owed by the defendant. . . . Judgment affirmed in all other respects.

NOTES

1.   A mortgage is a document that transfers a lien from grantor/mortgagor to grantee/mortgagee. Its consideration is most typically a monetary loan from the mortgagee to the mortgagor. If the mortgagor does not repay the debt, the mortgagee is entitled to declare a default and foreclose. Foreclosure is typically the subject of long and detailed procedures set out in every state's code. See Nelson, Whitman, Burkhart & Freyermuth, Real Estate Finance Law 568–675 (6th ed. 2015). These procedures now also often regulate so-called predatory lending practices, which is lending when the mortgagee knows or has reason to know that the mortgagor does not have the financial assets to repay the loan. A mortgage usually involves two documents — a note or IOU as evidence of the debt and a mortgage that creates the lien as security for the debt. 765 Ill. Comp. Stat. Ann. 5/11 (2013) provides the following illustrative short mortgage form:

> Mortgages of lands may be substantially in the following form:
>
> The Mortgagor (here insert name or names), mortgages and warrants to (here insert name or names of mortgagee or mortgagees), to secure the payment of (here recite the nature and amount of indebtedness, showing when due and the rate of interest, and whether secured by note or otherwise), the following described real estate (here insert description thereof), situated in the County of _____, in the State of Illinois.
>
> _____ Dated (insert date).
>
> _____ (signature of mortgagor or mortgagors)

2.   A court may exercise its equitable power to recharacterize a deed that is absolute on its face as a mortgage — that is, the deed's effect may be cut back, so that a document not styled as a mortgage will nonetheless function as the parties to it intended. See Restatement (Third) of Property (Mortgages), § 3.2 (1997); Nelson, Whitman, Burkhart & Freyermuth, Real Estate Finance Law § 3.1 (6th ed. 2015).

Underlying an action to recharacterize a deed as a mortgage is, as *Seaman* indicates, the idea that debts secured by real property are unlike all other types of secured transactions. No matter how desperate Malcolm was to borrow money from his brother Earle, no amount of contract language in the note Malcolm signed could, once the document is characterized as mortgage, trump his implied equity of redemption. This equity is the mortgagor's right to avoid foreclosure by repaying the outstanding debt; it prevents Earle from simply taking the secured property (the cottage) from Malcolm. See *Humble Oil & Refining Co. v. Doerr*, 303 A.2d 898 (N.J. Super. Ct., Ch. Div., 1973). A mortgagor has this right even though, as *Seaman* again indicates, it is in effect a right of late redemption. Once a document is deemed a mortgage, even the most impecunious mortgagor has this right against even the most powerful financial institution in the country.

3.   A mortgage is only enforceable when "the obligation whose performance it secures is measurable in terms of money or is reducible to a monetary value" when the foreclosure action is brought. See Restatement (Third) of Property (Mortgages) § 1.4 (1997). This requirement does not prevent the debt amount from being open ended at its inception or from being disbursed in the future in installments, as are most construction loans. See *Potwin State Bank v. J.B. Houston & Son*, 327 P.2d 1091 (Kan. 1958); *Northridge Bank v. Lakeshore Commercial Finance Corp.*, 365 N.E.2d 382 (Ill. App. Ct. 1977). The mortgagor's promise to consent to a future rezoning cannot be secured by a mortgage, but a promise to construct improvements is reducible to a monetary amount and can be secured. See *Application of Jeffery Towers, Inc.*, 297 N.Y.S.2d 450 (N.Y. App. Div. 1969), *aff'd*, 257 N.E.2d 897 (N.Y. 1970). A mortgage lien may provide the only recourse or remedy of a mortgagee. A mortgagor need not be personally liable for the obligation that the mortgage secures. See *Bedian v. Cohn*, 134 N.E.2d 532 (Ill. App. Ct. 1956) (finding a mortgage to be "non-recourse," meaning that the mortgagee has no recourse to the mortgagor's personal assets). Finally, a mortgage lien is defeasible, which means that it is incidental to the debt and is no longer enforceable when the debt is canceled or satisfied. "A mortgage lives and dies with the debt" is a maxim of the common law. See *Egbert v. Egbert*, 132 N.E.2d 910, 918 (Ind. 1956) (stating that when the debt "is discharged the mortgage become *functus officio* and legally dead."). A "*mort gage*," is a dead pledge — get it?

VI.   RECORDING ACTS

The real property recording system provides the means by which title to a parcel of land can be determined. Pursuant to the state recording act, all instruments affecting title to land can be recorded as public documents in the recorder's office for the jurisdiction where the land is located. Anyone can search these public property records to determine the state of title to any parcel of land. The recording act also establishes priorities among conflicting claims to land and promotes certainty of titles. However, a range of complex issues can arise when applying the terms of a recording act. For example, who has the right to record a document? When is the document "recorded"? Was the recording free from defects? What type of notice, if any, did the purchaser have before recording? These questions must be answered to determine the state of title.

Simply recording a document is insufficient to accomplish the purposes of the recording act. Accurate indexing of the records also is essential if the recording system is to have any practical effect. Indexing provides the organizational system for the documents in the recorder's office, and, for all practical purposes, the index provides the only way to search a property title. Two basic systems of indexing are used in the United States-the grantor-grantee index (also known as the "name index") and the tract index (also known as the "parcel index"). Not surprisingly, the indexes, particularly the grantor-grantee index, present their own set of complexities and questions. For example, is indexing an essential element of recording or is it separate and distinct? What if a document is incorrectly indexed or is not indexed at all?

The materials in this section of the book will provide an overview of the mechanics and operation of the recording system. Recording acts are indispensable to the proper functioning of the real estate market in the United States. Moreover, with increasing technological advancements in the real estate industry, the potential now exists to eliminate many of the problems in the current recording system.

A.   History of the Recording Acts

In early English common law, title to real property was transferred by enfeoffment, a public ceremony conducted on or within sight of the land. Conflicting claims to the land were resolved by application of the common law principle "first in time, first in right." Pursuant to this principle, after enfeoffment, the transferor had no remaining interest in the land and, therefore, any subsequent conveyances by him were ineffective. However, when the Statute of Frauds was enacted in 1677, land was no longer transferred by public livery of seisin. Rather, land generally could be transferred only by a written conveyance. But at this time England did not have a formal system for preserving evidence of written conveyances; no public record existed for them.

American colonists quickly saw the need for a public record. This country's mobile population meant that land titles changed hands with increasing frequency. Titles could be transferred to someone unknown to the community. This was the impetus for the establishment of a public recording system, first established in Massachusetts in 1640. Like today's recording acts, this statute resolved conflicting claims to land and made land transfers a matter of public record. This 1640 statute and similar statutes marked the modern departure from the English common-law rule of "first in time, first in right." In its place came a system pursuant to which a subsequent purchaser of land could acquire title to land free of prior unrecorded conveyances.

The court in *Phoenix Title & Trust Co. v. Old Dominion Co.*, 253 P. 435, 438–39 (Ariz. 1927), summarized the purpose of the modern recording system:

> Until the establishment of the system of recording conveyances, it was extremely difficult for any man who purchased property to ascertain whether or not he had in fact secured a good title. In many cases innocent purchasers who had made the utmost effort to determine whether there were outstanding incumbrances, and who had in all good faith and sincerity

paid a full consideration for the property, lost it on account of hidden equities of which they had neither knowledge, nor means of obtaining it. This condition, which was bad enough in the early days of the English and American law when conveyances were comparatively rare, grew intolerable as the complexity and frequency of such transactions increased, and the various recording acts were passed for the express purpose of providing a place and a method by which an intending purchaser could safely determine just what kind of a title he was in fact securing. . . . [T]here has grown up, not only in the bar, but among the general laity, the profound conviction that, if the public records show a clear title in a grantor, the prospective purchaser may safely buy the property, unless he has notice of such facts as would at least put him on inquiry. That such an interpretation of the recording acts is beneficial in the long run to all honest owners or prospective owners of real property is obvious. If the law provides a place where any man who owns an interest in real estate can give notice of it to all the world with the assurance that his rights will be protected thereby, and a prospective purchaser, on the other hand, can with equal safety investigate, and be confident that no rights not disclosed therein are valid against him in the absence of his knowledge thereof, we can hardly imagine a more beneficial institution.

B. Operation of the Recording Acts

There are different types of recording acts and indexing systems used in the United States. As you study them, consider whether the recording system has achieved the purpose articulated by the court in *Phoenix Title & Trust Co.*

NELSON, WHITMAN, BURKHART & FREYERMUTH, REAL ESTATE TRANSFER, FINANCE, AND DEVELOPMENT
204–09 (8th ed. 2009)*

Why do people who enter into real estate transactions ever take their papers to the courthouse to be recorded? It is clear in virtually every state that recording is unnecessary to the validity of a deed; as between grantor and grantee, it is effective whether filed in the public records or not. Yet the law gives certain incentives for filing, and most people respond by doing so. To understand the incentives, imagine the simple case in which Oscar (O) is the owner in fee simple of land. On day 1 he sells the land to Alice (A), giving A a deed and receiving a handsome price. On day 2, feeling greedy and a bit corrupt, O decides to sell *the same land* to Betty (B)! Obviously, this scam is likely to work only if A has not taken possession of the land yet, since A's presence would probably tip off B that O is no longer the owner. If B bites, we can diagram the transactions this way:

$$\text{Deed}$$
$$\text{Day 1: O} \;\text{—}\;\text{—}\;\text{—}\;\text{→ A}$$

Deed

Day 2: O — — — → B

Don't be disturbed by the fact that there are two deeds in the picture; remember that a deed is not a unique piece of paper, and O can make up as many of them (to the same land) as he wishes. The question, of course, is who owns the land? In a jurisdiction without a recording act (and there are none in the United States, so we must imagine one hypothetically), strict legal logic would tell us that A is the owner. B cannot prevail, since at the time O purported to deed the land to B, O had nothing. So B has nothing either.

Astounding as it may seem, recording acts can (and often do) change this result. In effect, they give O a power, under certain circumstances, to give B a valid deed notwithstanding the prior deed to A. This is a strange concept — that one with no title can still transfer good title — and it takes a little getting used to. Under what circumstances can it occur? First (and this is true under every American recording act), it can occur only if A fails to record her deed before B buys. You can immediately see that this provides a powerful incentive for A to record; the law tells her that, while she now has title, she may lose it if her grantor makes a later conveyance of the same land *unless she records*. True, she will probably have a claim against O if this occurs (particularly if she received a deed containing full covenants of title), but this is much less satisfactory to A than keeping the land she bought. So A will usually be very careful to record her deed immediately, thereby cutting off O's power to deprive A of her title.

Even if A fails to record, B will not always prevail, for the recording acts of the various states impose certain criteria upon B's status and behavior as well. There are three categories of such acts, and by oversimplifying a little we can present some basic information about them in the form of a table. The table's purpose is to answer the question, "Assuming that A has failed to record, what must B do to qualify herself under the recording act and take the title as against A?"

What must B do to prevail against A?	Type of act	Prevalence of this type of act
1. B must be a purchaser for value and without notice	"Notice" type	About half the states
2. B must record his own conveyance before A records	"Race" type	Only three states: Delaware, Louisiana, and North Carolina[4]

---

[4] A few other states have specialized race-type statutes which apply to specific types of conveyances; they include Arkansas (mortgages), Ohio (mortgages and oil and gas leases), and Pennsylvania (mortgages except for purchase money). Note that the North Carolina statute, reproduced in the text *infra*, is not quite a pure race-type statute, since the subsequent purchaser is protected only if he pays value. See IV Am. L. Prop. § 17.5 (1952).

What must B do to prevail against A?	Type of act	Prevalence of this type of act
3. B must both be a purchaser for value and without notice, and also record before A	"Notice-race" or "Race-notice" type	About half the states

These requirements which the statutes impose on B have a moralistic ring about them. The "notice" and "notice-race" states seem to say, "Why should we let B take advantage of A's failure to record if B knew about A anyway, or if B paid nothing for the land (so that she has nothing to lose)?" The "race" and "notice-race" states seem to say, "Why should we let B take advantage of A's failure to participate in the public recording process if B herself also fails to participate?" Consider whether either the bona fide purchaser ("BFP") or recording-first requirements are really essential to a rational and workable recording system. Would it be equally satisfactory (and simpler) if the statutes allowed *all* subsequent grantees to prevail against A's unrecorded deed? Or should we take the next step, and simply announce that all unrecorded conveyances are void? No American recording system goes this far.

Our example above assumed that both A and B were given deeds purporting to convey fee simple title, but the same principles apply if one or both of them transfer lesser interests. For example, if both are mortgages, the common law would say that A has the first mortgage, and that B's is junior or subordinate to it; but a notice-type recording act will reverse those priorities if A failed to record and B is a good faith "purchaser" (many of the statutes add the words "or creditor" just to take care of mortgagees) for value. Similarly, if the deed to A granted A only an easement across O's land, the question becomes whether B (whose deed conveys a fee simple) takes free of the easement or subject to it. In general, we can say that the recording acts may give B priority over an interest to which she would otherwise be subordinate.

At this point it will be helpful to examine a few recording statutes in some depth. * * * Perhaps the most common format is represented by the Washington statute, Rev. C. Wash. § 65.08.070:

> Every . . . conveyance not . . . recorded is void as against any subsequent purchaser or mortgagee in good faith and for valuable consideration from the same vendor . . . whose conveyance is first duly recorded.

The statute is of the "notice-race" type, since the subsequent purchaser, to prevail, must both be a BFP and record first. The legislature could easily amend the statute to make it a pure "notice" type by deleting the last phrase quoted, ". . . whose conveyance is first duly recorded." Many "notice" type statutes follow this form. An alternative type of wording for "notice" statutes, also very common, is represented by Iowa C. Ann. § 558.41:

> An instrument affecting real estate is of no validity against subsequent purchasers for a valuable consideration, without notice . . . , unless . . . filed and recorded in the county in which the real estate is located. . . .

* * *

Finally, examine the North Carolina statute, N.C. Gen. Stat. § 47-18: "No . . . conveyance of land . . . shall be valid to pass any property interest as against lien creditors or purchasers for a valuable consideration from the donor . . . but from the time of registration thereof."

If you compare this statute with those of Washington and Iowa, above, you will note that the word "subsequent" does not appear before "creditors or purchasers" in the North Carolina version. You might think of the North Carolina statute as working "both ways" — that is, denying unrecorded conveyances validity both as against subsequent *and prior* purchasers. Nobody is safe from anybody else until he or she records! Of course, the statute is not quite "pure" race, since to prevail against an unrecorded conveyance, one must have paid value. * * *

Incidentally, the "race" designation applied to the North Carolina statute is a bit misleading in another sense; it seems to suggest that A and B are literally racing one another to the courthouse, and the first one to arrive and record will own the land. In reality, each of them is usually entirely unaware of the other for many months or years, and there is no race going on at all. Still, the first one to arrive will win (although for B to do so he or she must have paid value.)

PROBLEMS AND NOTES

1.   Categorize the following recording acts as race, race-notice, or notice:

a. Del. Code Ann. tit. 25, § 153 (1989):

A deed concerning lands or tenements shall have priority from the time that it is recorded in the proper office without respect to the time that it was signed, sealed and delivered.

RACE

b. Tex. Prop. Code Ann. § 13.001(a) (2003):

A conveyance of real property or an interest in real property or a mortgage or deed of trust is void as to a creditor or to a subsequent purchaser for a valuable consideration without notice unless the ^(A's deed) instrument has been acknowledged, sworn to, or proved and filed for record as required by law.

NOTICE

c. Ind. Code Ann. § 32-21-4-1 (2009):

(a) The following must be recorded in the recorder's office of the county where the land is situated:

(1) A conveyance or mortgage of land or of any interest in land.

(2) A lease for more than three (3) years.

RACE-NOTICE

(b) The conveyance, mortgage, or lease is fraudulent and void as against any subsequent purchaser, lessee, or mortgagee in good faith and for a valuable consideration if the purchaser's, lessee's, or mortgagee's deed, mortgage, or lease is first recorded.

2.   For each of the following problems, what is the state of title under the common law rule of "first in time, first in right" and under each type of recording

statute? Assume that O has an estate in fee simple absolute, the same property is involved in each transfer, the facts occurred in the order given, all persons gave value unless otherwise noted, and no one has recorded or has actual knowledge of a conflicting claim unless otherwise noted:

a. O conveys to A, who does not record. O then conveys to B, who does not record. O then conveys to C, who does not record. A records.

b. O conveys to A, who does not record. O then conveys to B. A learns about the conveyance to B and then conveys to C, who is unaware of the conveyance to B.

c. O conveys to A, who does not record. O then conveys to B, who takes with notice of A's deed. B records. A records. B conveys to C, and C records. Compare *Angle v. Slayton*, 697 P.2d 940, 942 (N.M. 1985) (holding for A) ("a property owner [A] should not be divested of title by a subsequent purchaser when the owner has done all that the law requires him to do"), with *Kiser v. Clinchfield Coal Corp.*, 106 S.E.2d 601 (Va. 1959) (holding for C) ("It was not incumbent upon [C]'s attorney to search the record for adverse conveyances by [O] recorded after the recordation of [B]'s deed."). Which is the better view?

d. O conveys to A. A does not record. O dies, leaving B as his heir. B conveys to C. C records. Who prevails? It is very likely that C will prevail. As stated by the court in *Earle v. Fiske*, 103 Mass. 491, 494 (1870): "As a purchaser without notice, [C] is in a position to say that the unrecorded deed had no legal force or effect; that [O] died seised; that the property descended to [B]. Upon that assumption, [B's] deed would take precedence over the unrecorded deed of [O], in exactly the same manner as a deed from [O] in [his] lifetime would have done over any unrecorded deed from [himself]."

e. O conveys to A. O then conveys to B. O then conveys to C. B records. C records. A records.

f. O conveys to A. O then gives a mortgage to B. O then gives an easement to C. B records. A records. C records.

3.   In some older cases, courts held that purchasers could not be bona fide purchasers if they had acquired title by a quitclaim deed. These courts regarded a quitclaim as suspicious, thinking that if grantors had a title that they believed to be unimpaired by outstanding interests, they would have executed a deed with covenants. So the restrictive language of the deed was deemed equivalent to notice of outstanding interests. See, e.g., *Rich v. Downs*, 105 P. 9 (Kan. 1909). Most states have since abandoned this notion, either through statute or judicial decision. See, e.g., Minn. Stat. Ann. § 507.06; Fla. Stat. Ann. § 695.01. The most influential cases in this regard were two Supreme Court decisions permitting purchasers who took quitclaim deeds to be bona fide purchasers for value, provided they were, in all other respects, bona fide purchasers. See *Moelle v. Sherwood*, 148 U.S. 21 (1893); *United States v. California and Or. Land Co.*, 148 U.S. 31 (1893).

4.   The recording of a deed or other instrument is not essential to an effective conveyance in most jurisdictions. Thus "an unrecorded conveyance is binding on the

parties to the instrument, the parties' heirs, and all those who have knowledge of the conveyance." See *Burris v. McDougald*, 832 S.W.2d 707, 709 (Tex. App. 1992). See generally John Scheid, *Down Labyrinthine Ways: A Recording Acts Guide for First Year Law Students*, 80 U. Det. Mercy L. Rev. 91 (2002).

C. Indexes

While the recorded documents are essential to the operation of the recording system, they are not sufficient. The recording system also must include an index so that a title examiner can locate the documents. Once the records are properly indexed, a title examiner can determine the identity of each current and past owner of the property, with each period of ownership constituting a link in the "chain of title." Ideally, the property records will include all the documents necessary to connect the links in the chain from the current owner to the government's first conveyance of title to the land.

1.   Grantor-Grantee Index

The most commonly used index is the grantor-grantee index. This index actually consists of two indexes — one that is arranged alphabetically by the name of the grantee of each recorded instrument and one that is arranged alphabetically by the name of the grantor of each recorded instrument. When a document is filed with the county recorder, it is entered in both the grantor index and the grantee index. Typically, each volume of the grantor and grantee indexes includes entries for documents recorded during a specified time period.

To see how this type of index works, examine the following index pages from the Hennepin County, Minnesota Recorder's Office. Assume that you have entered into an agreement to purchase Lot 1, Block 1 of the Cedar Isles West subdivision in Maple Grove, Minnesota from Richard Dvorak. To examine the title to this land using the grantor-grantee index, you would start with the grantee index and look for the name Richard Dvorak and you will find the deed by which Dvorak acquired title to the land. If Dvorak remembers when he acquired the title, you can begin your search in the index volume that includes that year. If you are not so fortunate, you would need to begin with the volume that includes the present year and search in reverse chronological order until you find Dvorak's name in connection with this particular parcel of property. By looking at the sample grantee index page, you can see Richard Dvorak's name on the third line from the bottom, dated November 24, 1981. You will also see the grantor's name, Cedar Isles Inc. You then would continue your search in earlier volumes of the grantee index under the name Cedar Isles Inc. until you find its name and discover from whom it acquired title. You can continue this process in the grantee index until each link in the chain of ownership is located back to the original conveyance from the government. Of course, the time and expense of a search all the way back to the first conveyance normally is unnecessary because it is a rare title problem that would manifest itself so many years later.

After completing your search of the grantee index, you are ready for the second step in the title examination — search of the grantor index. You use the grantor index to discover all the property interests conveyed by each owner. For example, on the sample grantor index page, you can see that Cedar Isles Inc. conveyed an easement in the property to the City of Bloomington before conveying fee title to Dvorak. You should check the grantor index for the name of each current and former owner to discover all the other interests that they conveyed, including mortgages, leases, and restrictive covenants. You also should check the grantor index for the name of each owner of any such interest to determine whether the interest has been transferred or released. For example, the notation "S MTG" on the sample grantor index page shows that a satisfaction of mortgage has been recorded.

GRANTEE ALPHA INDEX — ABSTRACTS

INDEX	INSTRMT	TYPE	DATE TIME	FEE	GRANTEE	LEGAL DESCRIPTION	GRANTOR
2	4693577	C D	01-04-82 01:11	5.00	DVORAK PAUL G	L 4 BLK 5 EXCELSIOR ADN TO MPLS	O'ROURKE THOMAS
2	4713689	C D	04-29-82 12:24	5.00	DVORAK PAUL G	L 6 BLK 5 WOODBRIDGES 2ND ADN TO MPLS	MYREN BRUCE
2	4743792	Q C D	09-30-82 12:27	5.00	DVORAK PAUL G	L 1 F W MALMSTENS ADN TO MPLS	MAYER ROSE
2	4849641	Q C D	12-06-83 01:27	5.00	DVORAK PAUL G	L 3 BLK 26 GALES ADN TO SHERBURNE	ILLIFF STEWART
2	4849642	A C D	12-08-83 01:28	5.00	DVORAK PAUL G	DOC 4705060	ILLIFF STEWART
2	4893306	CANC C D	05-25-84 11:50	5.00	DVORAK PAUL G	L 3 BLK 28 GALES SUB OF SHERBURNE	MANSHURA GORDON
2	4951812	CANC C D	12-17-84 02:13	5.00	DVORAK PAUL G	L 4 BLK 5 EXCELSIOR ADN TO MPLS	O'ROURKE THOMAS
2	5120887	CANC C D	06-18-86 02:08	10.00	DVORAK PAUL G	L 8 BLK 5 WOODBRIDGES 2ND ADN TO MPLS	MYREN BRUCE
2	5145611	CANC C D	06-19-86 03:35	10.00	DVORAK PAUL G	L 1 F W MALMSTENS ADN	SUTTON EVELYN
2	5347783	AFT SURV	11-17-87 11:12	10.00	DVORAK RALPH B (DCD)	DOC 4201107	
2	4525111	S MTG	11-28-79 12:18	3.00	DVORAK RALPH W	BK 3309 M 145 DOC 3348097	FIRST NATL BANK
2	4660963	Q C D	06-03-81 01:07	5.00	DVORAK RAYMOND J	L 16 BLK 5 GIBBS FIRST ADN TO MPLS	DVORAK RAYMOND
2	4660964	Q C D	06-03-81 01:07	5.00	DVORAK RAYMOND J	L 18 BLK 5 GIBBS FIRST ADN TO MPLS	DVORAK RICHARD
2	4660962	DEC DIST	08-03-81 01:06	5.00	DVORAK RAYMOND ET AL	L 18 BLK 5 GIBBS FIRST ADN TO MPLS	DVORAK ALBION
2	5194940	C D	12-05-86 10:18	10.00	DVORAK REBECCA J	L 10 BLK 12 MPLS THIRD DIV	CLIFT BRADLEY
2	4656421	W D	11-24-81 12:44	5.00	DVORAK RICHARD	L 1 BLK 1 CEDAR ISLES W MAPLE GROVE	CEDAR ISLES INC.
2	4660962	DEC DIST	08-03-81 01:06	5.00	DVORAK RICHARD A	L 10 BLK 5 GIBBS FIRST ADN TO MPLS	DVORAK ALBION
2	4819476	Q C D	08-19-83 12:18	5.00	DVORAK RICHARD L	L 16 BLK 3 TINGDALE BROS LINCOLN HILLS T	DVORAK HARRY

GRANTOR ALPHA INDEX — ABSTRACTS

INDEX	INSTRMT	TYPE	DATE TIME	FEE	GRANTOR	LEGAL DESCRIPTION	GRANTEE
1	5028046	W D	06-30-85 02:21	10.50	CEDAR INVSTS	L 1 BLK 2 HOYT ADN	CEDAR INVSTS LTD PTN
1	4860697	MOD AGR	01-19-84 11:29	5.50	CEDAR INVSTS ET AL	DCC 4795616	NORTHLAND MTG CO
1	4944394	PLAT	11-19-84 08:30	15.00	CEDAR INVSTS ET AL	SEE RECORD	HOYT ADN
1	5028047	MTG ETC	08-30-85 02:21	19.00	CEDAR INVSTS LTD PTN	L 1 BLK 1 HOYT ADN	NORTH ATLANTIC LIFE
1	5028048	A LS & K	08-30-85 02:22	11.00	CEDAR INVSTS LTD PTN	L 1 BLK 1 HOYT ADN	NORTH ATLANTIC LIFE
1	4481678	W D	06-25-79 03:04	3.00	CEDAR ISLES INC	L 3 BLK 1 CEDAR ISLE W	MOUSSA EZZAT
1	4953498	ESMT	12-24-80 10:29	.00	CEDAR ISLES INC	L 1 BLK 1 CEDAR ISLE W MAPLE GROVE	BLOOMINGTON CITY
1	4675421	W D	11-24-81 12:44	5.00	CEDAR ISLES INC	L 1 BLK 1 CEDAR ISLE W MAPLE GROVE	DVORAK RICHARD
1	4954046	W D	12-27-84 11:05	5.00	CEDAR ISLES INC	OUTL A CEDAR ISLE W	DICKEY JANE
1	5056897	W D	11-27-85 11:06	10.00	CEDAR ISLES INC	L 2 BLK 1 PADDOCK TERRACE 2ND ADN	GREENWALDT CONSTR INC
1	5069679	W D	01-09-86 02:34	10.00	CEDAR ISLES INC	L 1 BLK 1 L 1-5 BLK 2 PADDOCK TERRACE	GREENWALDT CONSTR INC
1	5133865	S MTG	07-24-86 10:32	10.00	CEDAR ISLES INC	DOC 5069681	GREENWALDT CONSTR INC
1	5133866	S MTG	07-24-86 10:32	10.00	CEDAR ISLES INC	DOC 5069682	GREENWALDT CONSTR INC
1	5133867	S MTG	07-24-86 10:32	10.00	CEDAR ISLES INC	DOC 5069683	GREENWALDT CONSTR INC
1	5133868	S MTG	07-24-86 10:32	10.00	CEDAR ISLES INC	DOC 5069680	GREENWALDT CONSTR INC
1	5133869	S MTG	07-24-86 10:32	10.00	CEDAR ISLES INC	DOC 5069684	GREENWALDT CONSTR INC
1	4766614	W D	01-19-83 03:29	5.50	CEDAR LAKE CORP	L 4 BLK 6 CEDAR LAKE PARK ADN TO MPLS	JONES WINTON
8	4600938	CHG NAME	11-04-80 08:11	5.00	CEDAR LAKE FLORAL CO	SEE RECORD	CLF INC

After locating the index entry for all the documents affecting title to the land, you should get a copy of each of those documents. The instrument number on the index tells you the location of the recorded document in the record books. You must examine the documents to determine their validity, their effect on the property title, and whether they have been released properly. Only then will you have an accurate picture concerning the state of title.

However, examination of the grantor-grantee index will not provide a complete picture of the state of title. Documents kept in a number of government offices other than the recorder's office can affect title to land. For example, the title might be subject to tax assessments documented in the tax assessor's office, by pending law suits concerning title to the land, or by a will filed with the probate court. A purchaser of property acquires title subject to all matters that are included in a public record. Thus a land purchaser cannot rely simply on the grantor-grantee index and documents in the recorder's office; he or she also must examine records kept in other government offices.

2. Tract Index

The tract index is easier to use than the time consuming grantor-grantee index. Under this system, each parcel of land in the jurisdiction is assigned an index page that lists every recorded document affecting title to that parcel. As each document is submitted to the recorder, an entry is made in the tract index on the appropriate page. At a minimum, this entry includes the grantor's and grantee's names and the page and volume number of the official record book in which the document is recorded.

When conducting a search using the tract index, the title examiner must find the page in the tract index assigned to the relevant parcel of land. On this page, the searcher will find an entry for every document affecting title to the parcel, whether recorded before or during the current owner's period of ownership. For example, on the following tract index page from the Hennepin County Recorder's Office, you can see entries for all the documents that affect title to Dvorak's Cedar Isle West property, beginning with the original conveyance from the City of Maple Grove. As with a search in the grantor-grantee index, you should examine a copy of each of these documents to determine its effect on the title. Also like the grantor-grantee index, you must check other sources of government documents that may affect title to the land. Finally, you should note the statement "For Current Records Check Computer." Like many urban counties, Hennepin County has begun computerizing its land records. Documents recorded after the introduction of computerized records are no longer included in the tract index volumes, but are entered only in the computer.

Although the tract index is easier for title examiners to use, it is far less available than the grantor-grantee index. Its relative unavailability is attributable in part to the terms of the recording acts. Most recording acts provide for a grantor-grantee index as the official index. The predominance of the grantor-grantee index is also due to the greater ease with which recorder's office personnel can maintain it; when a document is recorded, the recorder's office only needs to determine the grantor's and grantee's names. In contrast, use of a tract index requires the recorder's office to determine what land is affected by the conveyance. This task is particularly difficult if the legal description on the conveyance does not match the description in the tract index.

D. Bona Fide Purchasers

The recording acts in all but a very few states protect only those subsequent purchasers who are bona fide purchasers (bfps). To qualify for bfp status, a purchaser (1) must not have had notice of the conflicting claim when it acquired its interest in the property and (2) must have given consideration for the conveyance. What language in the Washington and Iowa recording statutes, *supra*, imposes these requirements?

1. Lack of Notice

Clearly, a purchaser of land will acquire title to land subject to any property interest about which it had actual knowledge. Actual notice, however, is not the only type of notice that will destroy a purchaser's ability to qualify for bfp status. See, e.g., *In re Ryan*, 851 F.2d 502 (1st Cir. 1988) (involving a deed lacking a witness, required at the time, but no longer required, under Vermont's recording act), stating in part:

> *Why Notice Matters.* Under Vermont property law, as in most states, a real property transaction memorialized in an unrecorded deed will not hold the land from any person, *except* from persons who have notice of the transaction.[5] See, e.g., *Gilchrist v. Van Dyke*, 21 A. 1099 (Vt. 1890). The addition of the notice requirement to the land recording system was an invention of the courts of equity. The theory was that a subsequent purchaser, with notice of a prior, unrecorded deed, commits a "fraud upon the first purchaser" if he attempts to avail himself of the protection of the recording statutes. 4 American Law of Property § 17.5, at 539. Accordingly, a court of equity will give the prior purchaser priority over a subsequent purchaser who had notice of the first purchase. . . .
>
> *Types of Notice.* "Notice" is sometimes broken down into various types: constructive, actual, record, implied, imputed, inquiry, etc. The classifications of notice employed in Vermont case law and in many of the treatises are often confusing and seemingly contradictory. See 5 H. Tiffany, Law of Real Property § 1284 (B. Jones ed. 1939) (hereinafter Tiffany's Real Property) (noting that "the cases and textbooks are absolutely lacking in harmony"). A helpful formulation, however, appears in Tiffany's Real Property. Separating notice into two main types, actual and constructive, the treatise continues,

---

[5] Forty-five of the 50 states do not permit a subsequent purchaser with notice to have priority over prior purchasers who failed to record. 4 American Law of Property § 17.5, at 545 n. 63 (A. Casner ed. 1952).

> It would seem that one might properly be said to have *actual notice* when he has information in regard to a fact, or information as to circumstances an investigation of which would lead him to information of such fact, while he might be said to have *constructive notice* when he is charged with notice by a statute or rule of law, irrespective of any information which he might have, *actual notice* thus involving a mental operation on the person sought to be charged, and *constructive notice* being independent of any mental operation on his part.

5 Tiffany's Real Property § 1284, at 50 (emphasis added). Thus "constructive notice" is not really "notice," as that word is commonly used, at all. Instead, constructive notice is a positive rule of state law that permits the prior purchaser to gain priority over a latter purchaser, *regardless* of whether the latter purchaser really knows of the prior purchase.

Constructive notice is an essential element of the land recording system: if a deed is properly recorded, all future purchasers have constructive knowledge of the deed. See 4 American Law of Property § 17.17. A purchaser, therefore, can protect his interest by the act of recording his deed of purchase. To clarify, we present three examples of actual and constructive notice: (1) a subsequent purchaser has actual notice when he knows of the existence of a prior, unrecorded deed, *Gilchrist v. Van Dyke*, 21 A. 1099 (Vt. 1890); (2) he has constructive notice (whether or not he has actual knowledge) of a prior deed if that deed is properly recorded . . . ; and (3) he has both actual and constructive notice if he knows of the existence of a properly recorded deed.

A term sometimes used as a third and distinct type of notice is "inquiry notice." But we do not believe "inquiry notice" is a type of notice separate from "actual" or "constructive" notice. Rather, it is a corollary of both types. See 5 Tiffany's Real Property § 1285 (inquiry notice as a form of actual notice); 4 American Law of Property § 17.11, at 565 (inquiry notice as a form of constructive notice). Inquiry notice follows from the duty of a purchaser, when he has actual or constructive knowledge of facts which would lead a prudent person to suspect that another person might have an interest in the property, to conduct a further investigation into the facts.[6]

---

[6] The Vermont Supreme Court explained inquiry notice in *Hart v. Farmers & Mechanics Bank*, 33 Vt. 252, 264–65 (1860),

> [T]he courts of equity are vigilant . . . to see that . . . purchaser[s] shall not be allowed to take any benefit resulting from any want of care and watchfulness. If there exist any circumstance of suspicion, whereby he might be said to be fairly put upon his guard, and he neglects to follow out the inquiry, he is affected with notice of all facts, which such inquiry would have brought to his knowledge, and if he purchases with his eyes shut, he acquires only the title of his grantor impeded with its attendant equity.

[handwritten: , Minority: defective instrument does.]

IN RE BARNACLE
623 A.2d 445 (R.I. 1993)

FAY, C.J.   *[handwritten: Majority: defective instrument does not count as notice]*

* * * On December 22, 1986, Sally E. Lapides (Lapides) and her husband, Michael J. Barnacle (Barnacle), executed a promissory note in favor of Greater Providence Deposit Corporation to evidence a loan for the purchase of property located in Providence. The note was secured by a mortgage document that was intended and required to be executed jointly by Barnacle and Lapides. Through inadvertence the mortgage was not signed by Lapides. The mortgage was recorded in the Providence land evidence records. On January 9, 1992, Barnacle and Lapides filed a chapter-7 petition in bankruptcy. The trustee in bankruptcy, pursuant to 11 U.S.C. § 544(a)(3) (1989), is deemed to be a bona fide purchaser of the mortgaged property as of the filing of the bankruptcy petition. The United States Bankruptcy Court . . . certified the following question of law to this court: Whether the failure of one of two joint mortgagors to execute a mortgage document, which instrument is thereafter duly recorded in the appropriate land evidence records, gives constructive notice to a bona fide purchaser five years later? * * *

We must decide whether the mortgage, if defective, although recorded, affords constructive notice to a bona fide purchaser. The general purpose of land-recording statutes is to provide a public record of transactions affecting title to land. When dealing with priority problems, courts must decide whether the emphasis of their decisions should be placed on protecting those who warrant protection, such as a purchaser without notice, or in punishing those who fail to record. Strict adherence to either approach may result in an overly rigid and unforgiving body of applicable law.

The definition of constructive notice is not one on which all authorities agree. . . . Constructive notice has been interpreted as both "record notice" and all notice that is inferred as a matter of law. Because we are analyzing notice derived from the record, constructive notice, as applied in title-priority questions, is

> notice of all claims which are revealed by the record regardless of whether or not [the purchaser] ever looks at the record or ever sees the information contained therein. In other words, notice of all properly recorded claims is inferred, as a matter of law. Indeed, a better label for this type of notice would be "record notice" or, more specifically, "notice inferred from the record." [Such an inference] is absolutely necessary for the proper operation of the recording system. Without it a subsequent purchaser could, quite intentionally, avoid any inspection of the record and claim bona fide purchaser status because he or she had not otherwise personally received actual notice of the claim. If such a principle were allowed to exist, there would be no purpose in enacting a statute designed to give notice of land transactions to the public.

6A Powell, The Law of Real Property, ¶ 905[1] at 82-40, 41 (1991).

General Laws § 34-13-2 provides in part: "Recording as constructive notice. —

Such record or filing shall be constructive notice to all persons of the contents of such instruments. . . ." Section 34-13-2 "by its terms gives the broadest possible effect to constructive notice. . . ." *Speedy Muffler King, Inc. v. Flanders*, 480 A.2d 413, 415 n.1 (R.I. 1984). "The purpose of . . . constructive notice is to bind subsequent purchasers and all other affected parties by restrictions that are clearly set forth in prior conveyances or other instruments appropriately recorded." *Id.* at 415. In analyzing the meaning of "appropriately" or "properly" (see Powell quoted above) recorded, we must review the applicable statutes. General Laws § 34-11-1 provides that

> [e]very conveyance of lands . . . by way of mortgage . . . shall be void unless made in writing *duly signed, acknowledged as hereinafter provided,* delivered, and recorded . . . Provided, however, that the same, if delivered, as between the parties . . . or those having notice thereof, shall be valid and binding though not acknowledged or recorded. (Emphasis added.)

General Laws 1956 (1984 Reenactment) § 34-12-1 provides in part that "[a]cknowledgment of any instrument . . . shall be made by all the parties executing the instrument. . . ."

The trustee contends that because the mortgage lacks Lapides's signature and the appropriate acknowledgment of the signature, the mortgage is defective and cannot afford constructive notice to a subsequent purchaser. Because this is an issue of first impression, it is necessary to review the rulings of other jurisdictions in this area.

It appears that a clear majority of jurisdictions hold that when an instrument is defective because it lacks a signature, because it is not signed by the appropriate number of witnesses, or because it is not properly acknowledged, although recorded, the instrument does not impart constructive notice. *Connecticut National Bank v. Lorenzato*, 602 A.2d 959, 961 (Conn. 1992) (an imperfectly executed instrument "is a nullity and is, therefore, incapable of giving constructive notice[,]" *id.* at 962); see also *In re Ryan*, 851 F.2d 502 (1st Cir. 1988) (reviewing cases from thirty-four jurisdictions and concluding that as a general rule instruments not properly acknowledged do not provide constructive notice). . . .

We are well aware of the majority rule and have reviewed many cases expressing the belief that a defectively executed instrument does not impart constructive notice. A well-beaten path, although more traveled, is not necessarily the correct or best reasoned one. We are of the opinion that those courts that have rushed into a determination that an instrument not executed by all parties named therein is a nullity have created a forfeiture for no reasonable or necessary purpose. Indeed, the Supreme Court of Indiana has commented upon this rule both critically and persuasively. The thrust of the "argument is . . . that documents which were not entitled to be recorded do not constitute constructive notice. The rationale for this rule remains unexplained today. . . . Judges are often called upon to extinguish the substantial property rights of a citizen. Doing so on the basis of a rule for which there appears no basis is especially difficult." *In re Sandy Ridge Oil Co.*, 510 N.E.2d at 671.

"The rule that a recorded defective instrument does not afford constructive notice has long been questioned." *Id.* at 670. If we were to adopt the majority view, a disturbing situation could arise. If there is a valid recording, a failure to search the record does not protect the prospective bona fide purchaser. However, following the majority view, if there is a defectively executed instrument recorded in the proper chain of title, failure to search the record would result in protection whereas actual discovery of the instrument would result in a duty to inquire. Adopting the majority view would result in rewarding a failure to search the chain of title. We would thus be protecting a party that failed to protect itself, most probably resulting in an unfair and an unjust windfall. What legal maxim would be served in penalizing those who search while rewarding those who do not? We find none of any value. "The overriding consideration should be that the instrument would give the purchaser a 'definite and tangible clue, which, if diligently followed up, would ordinarily bring the truth of the matter to light.'" C. Johnson, *Purpose and Scope of Recording Statutes*, 47 Iowa L. Rev. 231, 241 n.57 (1962).

We conclude that a technical deficiency that would be subject to reformation in equity ought not to create a windfall for junior encumbrancers or those who would become bona fide purchasers. A reasonable title searcher, when confronted with this instrument along with its purported acknowledgment, would be placed upon notice to inquire further concerning the validity of the instrument. Such inquiry would establish that the mortgagee had a valid interest in law that could be further perfected in equity. To suggest that such an interest is a nullity because of the missing signature is to exalt form over substance.

The Barnacle instrument was recorded in the proper chain of title and therefore would be readily discoverable by a title search. This is not an instance wherein the instrument was misfiled and could not be discovered, nor was the instrument wholly void of a signature or acknowledgment. The instrument would most assuredly give a purchaser a definite clue about an interest in the property. Our decision is restricted to a question of notice; and if a prospective bona fide purchaser had searched this title, he or she would have discovered this instrument. This discovery would have put the purchaser on notice of a possible claim.

Limited to the particular facts of this case, we conclude that this instrument, filed in the land evidence records, would impart constructive notice to a subsequent purchaser. We find no sound reasoning in allowing a title searcher to pass by this instrument and claim no knowledge of an interest in the property. Consequently, discovered or undiscovered, this instrument would destroy a purchaser's claim that he or she is bona fide. Therefore we answer the . . . certified question in the affirmative.

NOTE

Although the rule of *In re Ryan* (cited in the principal case) currently represents the majority view concerning defective recordings and notice, recent case law reveals the emergence of a strong minority view similar to the decision in *In re Barnacle*. Many of these cases are the result of legislative reversals of decisions such as *In re Ryan*. See, e.g., *In re Nies*, 183 B.R. 866, 871 (Bankr. D. N.D. 1995) (noting the 1959 amendments to the North Dakota Recording Act that legislatively reversed *Messersmith v. Smith*, 60 N.W.2d 276 (N.D. 1953), a leading case in which the court held that an unacknowledged deed was unrecordable and that, therefore, a subsequent purchaser had no notice). See also *Leeds Building Products, Inc. v. Sears Mortgage Corp.*, 477 S.E.2d 565, 568 (Ga. 1996) ("To the extent that any former cases imply that a latently defective attestation will destroy the constructive notice of an otherwise properly recorded deed, such cases are expressly overruled and will no longer be followed."). As the *Leeds* quotation indicates, some courts distinguish between types of defects. "Many courts seem to distinguish between recording defects . . . evident on the face of the instrument (e.g., absence of any acknowledgment) and those which are latent (e.g., a false acknowledgment), and give constructive notice to the latter; see, e.g., *Hildebrandt v. Hildebrandt*, 683 P.2d 1288 (Kan. App. 1984); Annot., 59 A.L.R.2d 1299, 1316 (1958)." 4 Baxter Dunaway, Law of Distressed Real Estate, § 40.14 n.13 (2013).

J.C. PENNEY CO. v. GIANT EAGLE, INC.
85 F.3d 120 (3d Cir. 1996)

GIBSON, J.

Giant Eagle, Inc. appeals from an order of the district court enjoining it from operating a pharmacy in its Quaker Village shopping center store for the duration of J.C. Penney Company's 1978 lease, including renewals. Giant Eagle argues that Penney's exclusive right to operate a pharmacy in Quaker Village ended when Penney's 1962 lease ended, and that Penney's exclusive right is unenforceable against it because it did not have notice of Penney's exclusive right. We affirm.

In 1962 the Thrift Drug Company leased a store in the Quaker Village shopping center to operate a retail drugstore. The lease required that Thrift Drug use the premises only for operation of a retail drugstore, and gave it the right to display "such articles as are displayed and sold by it in its other retail drug stores." The lease further provided that the owner of Quaker Village, as lessor, would not permit another tenant to operate a pharmacy or fill or sell prescriptions. The lease covenanted that other tenants would be Thorofare Markets, Inc., which would operate a supermarket, and Triple "A", a national chain variety store. These tenants were allowed to sell merchandise customarily sold in drugstores, provided that they did not compound or sell prescriptions, or sell merchandise limited by state law to licensed pharmacies. The lease was for a term of fifteen years, and Thrift Drug was given the right to renew and extend the lease for three additional five-year terms. Thrift Drug recorded a memorandum of the lease which set forth a description of the premises, the term of the lease, and Thrift Drug's right to renew, but made no mention of Thrift Drug's obligation to operate only a retail drugstore, nor of the shopping center's agreement prohibiting other tenants from operating a drugstore. In 1969 Penney acquired Thrift Drug and all of its rights, including the 1962 lease.

In 1977 Giant Eagle entered into a lease at Quaker Village, which provided that it was to operate a food and grocery supermarket for items "customarily sold in the markets which it operates in the Greater Pittsburgh area." Giant Eagle's lease also gave Giant Eagle the exclusive right to operate a grocery store in Quaker Village with the exception of the existing Thorofare store.

Stanley R. Gumberg, the owner of the Quaker Village shopping center, negotiated the lease with Giant Eagle, and stated that there was no reference to a pharmacy or drugstore in the lease provision describing Giant Eagle's use of the premises. He also stated that at the time the lease was negotiated there was no thought or discussion of a pharmacy in Giant Eagle's store.

In 1975 Penney began discussing with Gumberg the possibility of relocating its drugstore within Quaker Village. Throughout these discussions, Penney insisted on keeping its exclusive right to operate a pharmacy. In 1978 Penney and Gumberg agreed that Penney would relocate its drugstore within the shopping center and continue to have the exclusive right to operate a pharmacy. The 1978 lease gave Penney the exclusive right to operate a pharmacy in Quaker Village, and provided that the 1962 lease was to terminate one day after the new lease term started, thus providing an overlap between the 1962 and 1978 leases. The 1978 lease also covenanted that Giant Eagle was to operate a supermarket in the shopping center, which was a condition for Penney operating its new drugstore.

In 1990 Giant Eagle began to make plans to expand its supermarket in Quaker Village to include a pharmacy. To accommodate Giant Eagle's plans, Gumberg asked Penney several times to waive its exclusive right to operate a pharmacy in the shopping center. Penney consistently refused to waive its exclusive right. Gumberg told Giant Eagle that Penney had the exclusive right to operate a pharmacy in Quaker Village and that Penney refused to waive that right. Despite this information, Giant Eagle began its construction of a pharmacy at its Quaker Village store. Shortly thereafter Penney told Giant Eagle and Gumberg that it intended to enforce its exclusive right. On August 13, 1992 Giant Eagle opened its pharmacy in Quaker Village, and Penney sued Giant Eagle to enjoin Giant Eagle's operation of the pharmacy.

The district court granted Penney a preliminary injunction. Giant Eagle appealed the preliminary injunction to this court, and we affirmed the injunction in an unpublished opinion. The district court later granted Penney a permanent injunction against Giant Eagle for the duration of Penney's 1978 lease, including renewals. In granting the permanent injunction, the district court stated that under Penney's 1962 and 1978 leases Penney continuously held the exclusive right to operate a pharmacy in Quaker Village. The court also stated that Penney could enforce its exclusive right against Giant Eagle because the memorandum of the 1962 lease, which was filed for record, gave Giant Eagle constructive notice of Penney's exclusive right when Giant Eagle entered into its Quaker Village lease. Giant Eagle appeals from the district court's grant of the permanent injunction. . . .

Giant Eagle argues that it did not have notice of Penney's exclusive right when it entered into its Quaker Village lease in 1977 and, therefore, Penney cannot enforce that right against it.

Thrift Drug did not file for record the entire 1962 lease. Instead, it filed a memorandum of the lease as allowed by section 405 of title 21 of the Pennsylvania statutes. Section 407 of title 21 defines the effect of recording a lease memorandum. Section 407, which is titled "Effect of recording lease, sublease, agreement or memorandum," provides: "The recording of any such *lease, sublease, agreement or memorandum* in accordance with the provisions of this act *shall constitute constructive notice* to subsequent purchasers, mortgagees and judgment creditors of the lessor of the making *and of the provisions of such lease,* sublease or agreement, including any purchase or refusal provisions set forth in the lease, sublease or agreement." Pa. Stat. Ann. tit. 21, § 407 (emphasis added).

Giant Eagle argues that under section 407 the recording of a lease memorandum results in constructive notice only to "subsequent purchasers, mortgagees and judgment creditors of the lessor." Giant Eagle contends that it is a lessee, not a subsequent purchaser, mortgagee or judgment creditor, and, therefore, it received no constructive notice from the recorded lease memorandum. Penney responds that Giant Eagle is a "purchaser" within the meaning of section 407 because a lease is really a sale of land for a term of years.

A close examination of section 407 shows that the legislature intended the recording of a lease memorandum to give constructive notice of the entire lease to subsequent lessees. Section 407 not only defines the effect of recording a lease memorandum, but also the effect of filing a lease, sublease or lease agreement. This is plainly reflected in the terms of section 407. If we were to accept Giant Eagle's interpretation of section 407, not even the recording of the entire lease would constitute constructive notice to a subsequent lessee. Under Giant Eagle's interpretation, there would be no way to give constructive notice of the terms of a lease to a subsequent lessee. A more reasonable interpretation of section 407 leads to the conclusion that the legislature intended the term "purchasers," as used in section 407, to include lessees. Indeed, the Supreme Court of Pennsylvania has so held. *Commonwealth v. Monumental Properties, Inc.,* 459 Pa. 450, 329 A.2d 812 (1974) (holding that a lease of real property is a sale . . .). Consequently, the district court did not err in holding that Giant Eagle was at least constructively, if not actually, aware of the exclusive provision in Penney's lease.

The record before us supports this conclusion. Giant Eagle's Vice President, Faccenda, stated that while he was not involved with exclusive rights in 1977, Giant Eagle had a staff of real estate and legal people who were expected to handle these functions and to ensure that everything that Giant Eagle was doing was proper and legal. He would expect them to find a recorded document which restricted the use of the premises Giant Eagle was about to lease. He was aware when Giant Eagle moved into Quaker Village in 1977 that there was a Thrift Drug store there and that it was logical for Thrift to have a lease, but he would not have paid attention to details like exclusive rights in other leases. This testimony is sufficient to raise an inference that when Giant Eagle signed the lease in 1977 it knew of Penney's exclusive right in the 1962 lease. Also, Faccenda's knowledge that exclusive rights were common in 1977, as well as the exclusive right contained in Giant Eagle's lease, support the inference that this is a subject about which Giant Eagle and its representatives would have been interested. The record makes clear that both Penney and Giant Eagle were sophisticated lessees, and indeed were involved in some three other disputes in which Giant Eagle was seeking to enforce exclusive rights to operate pharmacies in other leases. While Giant Eagle argues that a single lessee would have no right to obtain information from a landlord about other lessees, the record is to the contrary. In Penney's letter to Gumberg's attorney on January 12, 1978, Penney requested copies of the use and exclusive-right provisions from the leases of other tenants within the shopping center. There was strong evidence in the record to support the district court's finding that Giant Eagle was constructively, if not actually, aware of the exclusive-right provisions in Penney's leases.

We think it also follows that when Giant Eagle decided to open a pharmacy in 1990 it was bound by the exclusive rights granted to other tenants. Giant Eagle conceded that in 1977 it was not operating a pharmacy in any of its stores and its lease certainly did not give them a right to operate a pharmacy. In 1977 Giant Eagle knew of Penney's rights under the 1962 lease. From 1978, well before Giant Eagle operated pharmacies in its supermarkets and in 1990 when it decided to open a pharmacy, it had constructive notice of Penney's exclusive right as granted both in the 1978 and 1962 leases. Accordingly, we affirm the order of the district court granting the permanent injunction.

NOTES

1.   O executed an installment land sale contract with A. A defaulted. O began foreclosure proceedings and filed a lis pendens notice. Before the foreclosure decree became final, A conveyed to B, who held the title in trust for C. A avoided having the decree become final. O then conveyed the property to A, who deposited the deed with B. A conveyed by quitclaim to D. D recorded. B recorded the O/A deed and then the A/C deed. In D v. B, what result and why? See *Kordecki v. Rizzo*, 317 N.W.2d 479, 483 (Wis. 1982). Judgment for B: "Had [D] examined the record, which he did not, he would have found the lis pendens which would have led him to the Kenosha county circuit court file on the proceedings to foreclose the land contract and more specifically to the documents terminating the period of redemption. . . ."

2.   While the lis pendens notice provides notice of a title claim to the defendant's land during a lawsuit's pendency, a judgment lien encumbers the defendant's land after judgment is entered for the plaintiff. Judgment liens are creatures of state statute. They attach to all lands (and, in a few jurisdictions, to personal property) owned by the defendant (the "judgment debtor") in the county where the judgment is docketed. Many states also authorize the successful plaintiff (the "judgment creditor") to record the lien in other counties, which causes the lien to attach to all the defendant's property in that county too. The lien enables the judgment creditor to force a sale of the encumbered land and to use the sale proceeds to satisfy the judgment. Judgment liens are useful tools for collecting on judgments for two reasons. First, they normally attach not only to property owned by the defendant when the lien is created, but also to all property subsequently acquired by the judgment debtor in the county where the lien is effective. Second, judgment liens remain effective for several years — as many as twenty years in some states. They usually do not appear in the chain of title to any particular parcel of land owned by the judgment debtor; they may not even be recorded in the county recorder's office, but are filed in a special judicially maintained record system. However, because they are a matter of public record, a purchaser of the land is deemed to have notice of the lien and takes title subject to it. Thus, as seen in the following opinion, the property records are not the only source of notice that can destroy bfp status.

METHONEN v. STONE
941 P.2d 1248 (Alaska 1997)

Rabinowitz, J.

This appeal involves a dispute over property rights pertaining to a water well which is located on one subdivision lot and has been used as a source of water by owners of other lots in the subdivision.

Facts and Proceedings

In 1970 Howard and Daniel Hede subdivided eleven lots within Tract Five of Siefker Subdivision No. 3. The Hedes retained Lot 10, drilled a well there, constructed a well house, and installed water lines which supplied water to Lots 1 through 10. The subdivision plat which the Hedes recorded indicates the location of the well but does not disclose that it services the other lots.

When the Hedes sold Lot 10 to Fermo Albertini in October 1974, the Hedes and Albertini executed an agreement (Water Agreement) to continue the water service. In part the Water Agreement provided that "[t]he Party of the First part [the Hedes] has previously agreed to furnish water to any owner of [Lots 1 through 10]." This Water Agreement was not recorded until 1985. In November 1974, Albertini conveyed Lot 10 to Dennis Oney. In June 1975, Oney sold Lot 10 to Kathryn Ostrosky. Finally, in January 1976, Ostrosky conveyed Lot 10 to Marcus and Gwendolyn Methonen. The statutory warranty deed by which Methonen took title contained the following provision: "SUBJECT TO easements, restrictions, reservations and exceptions of record, and well site as delineated on the subdivision plat."

When Methonen purchased the property, he was aware of the pipes running from the well on his property to other lots in the subdivision. However, he asserts that the real estate agent who sold him Lot 10 "led me to understand that I did not need to worry about maintaining the water system or providing water to anyone." Shortly after taking title, Methonen learned that the owners of the other lots in the subdivision believed that he was legally obligated to provide them with water. Indeed, he "accepted money for the water system from system users when they provided it [to him]."

However, Methonen refused to acknowledge an obligation to supply water to the other lots, and in February 1985 shut off the water supply to the others. Settlement negotiations ensued and service was restored. During this period, the 1974 Hedes-Albertini Water Agreement (recognizing the original community water agreement) was recorded. Also, in February 1985 the Hedes, Albertini, and Ostrosky signed an "Acknowledgment of Water Well Agreement." This document contains the statement that Albertini, Ostrosky, and Methonen were all "aware of the [Hede-Albertini] Water Well Agreement and of the need to serve the lots in the subdivision with water."

Appellees Rick Stone and Robert Talmage purchased Lots 3 and 4 respectively in November 1985 and October 1991. Methonen continued to deny any obligation to provide water and discontinued service again in July 1994. Stone and Talmage then instituted suit against Methonen, contending they had an easement for water from the well on Methonen's property. They sought a judgment permanently enjoining Methonen from "any further interference with the water supply" as well as damages.

On cross motions for summary judgment, the superior court determined that Methonen's deed created an easement in favor of Stone and Talmage. The superior court based its ruling on the provision in Methonen's deed stating that he took subject to recorded easements and the well site delineated on the subdivision plat. The superior court also relied on the 1985 "Acknowledgment of Water Well Agreement" signed by the Hedes, Albertini, and Ostrosky. Methonen now brings this appeal.

Grants of summary judgment are reviewed to determine whether genuine issues of material fact exist, drawing all reasonable inferences in favor of the opposing party, and whether any party is entitled to judgment as a matter of law. *Newton v. Magill*, 872 P.2d 1213, 1215 (Alaska 1994).

Discussion

As an initial matter, we note that Stone and Talmage in moving for summary judgment failed to demonstrate that Methonen had either actual or constructive [record] notice of a community water agreement at the time he purchased Lot 10 from Ostrosky. In granting summary judgment in favor of Stone and Talmage, the superior court held that an easement for water was created by the "subject to" provisions of the 1976 deed from Ostrosky to Methonen and the 1985 Acknowledgment of Water Well Agreement. We conclude that the superior court erred in granting summary judgment to Stone and Talmage on these grounds.

It is well established that the intention to create a servitude must be clear on the face of an instrument; ambiguities are resolved in favor of use of land free of easements. . . . Neither the Ostrosky deed to Methonen nor the subdivision plat identifies an easement for a community water system based on the well located on Lot 10. Neither document indicates that the owner of Lot 10 is obligated to supply water to any of the remaining subdivision lots. In short, these documents did not provide either actual or constructive notice to Methonen of the existence of a community water system agreement at the time he purchased Lot 10 in 1976.

Nor can notice be inferred from the post-hoc "Acknowledgment of Water Well Agreement." This 1985 document was neither signed by Methonen nor recorded when Methonen purchased Lot 10 in 1976. As such, it cannot bind him of its own force. Nor can the unverified assertions contained in the Acknowledgment serve as evidence that Methonen was aware of the community water system agreement at the time he purchased Lot 10. The statements as to Methonen's knowledge contained in the Acknowledgment are unsworn, and thus cannot support a ruling on a motion for summary judgment. *Jennings v. State*, 566 P.2d 1304, 1309–10 (Alaska 1977). A holding that Methonen is bound to supply water to Stone and Talmage must find its rationale in some basis other than the Ostrosky deed, the plat of the subdivision, and the 1985 Acknowledgment of Water Well Agreement.

Although we conclude that the superior court erred in ruling that Stone and

Talmage were entitled to summary judgment, we further hold that on this record Methonen is not entitled to the entry of summary judgment on his cross motion for summary judgment. . . .

The basis for our conclusion that genuine issues of material fact are presented by this record resides in the fact that at the time of his purchase of Lot 10, Methonen was aware of the existence of the well on the property and the water lines running from the well to the adjoining lots in the subdivision. These facts are sufficient to place Methonen on inquiry notice as to the existence of the community water system agreement.

It is well established that a purchaser will be charged with notice of an interest adverse to his title when he is aware of facts which would lead a reasonably prudent person to a course of investigation which, properly executed, would lead to knowledge of the servitude. . . . The purchaser is considered apprised of those facts obvious from an inspection of the property. . . . [5]

Lack of diligence in the prosecution of a required inquiry creates a conclusive presumption of knowledge of those facts which reasonable inquiry would have revealed. . . . Generally, a proper investigation will include a request for information from those reasonably believed to hold an adverse interest. Should these sources mislead, the purchaser is not bound. *Kelly v. Fairmount Land Co.*, 33 S.E. 598 (Va. 1899). Reliance on the statements of the vendor, or anyone who has motive to mislead, is not sufficient. . . .

Methonen did allegedly receive misleading information from the real estate agent who sold him the property. However, reliance on this source would not satisfy his duty to investigate. Since Methonen was on notice of a possible obligation to supply water to neighboring lots, the proper object of his inquiry was the owners of those lots. Should those adjoining owners have misled Methonen, he would not be bound.

Given the record before the superior court when it ruled on the parties' cross-motions for summary judgment, we conclude that there are genuine issues of material fact as to whether Stone and Talmage can establish that Methonen was on inquiry notice as to the existence of a prior agreement to a community water system that was intended to run with the land.

Conclusion

The superior court's judgment entered in favor of Stone and Talmage is reversed and vacated. The case is remanded for further proceedings. . . . Upon remand among the issues remaining for determination are whether Stone and Talmage are entitled to a water easement. . . .

---

[5] "If a purchaser or incumbrancer, dealing concerning property of which the record title appears to be complete and perfect, has information of extraneous facts, or matters in pais, sufficient to put him on inquiry respecting some unrecorded conveyance, mortgage, or incumbrance, or respecting some outstanding interest, claim, or right which is not the subject of record, and he omits to make proper inquiry, he will be charged with constructive notice of all the facts which he might have learned by means of a due and reasonable inquiry." *Petrain v. Kiernan*, 23 Or. 455, 32 P. 158, 159 (1893) (quoting 2 John Norton Pomeroy, Pom. Eq. Jur. § 613 (2d ed. 1892)).

NOTE

A similar case, with the same result, is *Richart v. Jackson*, 758 A.2d 319 (Vt. 2000). Another inquiry notice situation arises when a person mortgages a right to land that he doesn't yet have but expects to obtain, when the mortgaged land is possessed by someone whose deed is unrecorded. See *Bank of Mississippi v. Hollingsworth*, 609 So. 2d 422 (Miss. 1992) (holding that a late recording grantee in possession trumps a first-recording mortgagee of the grantor's putative heir, based on possession and inquiry notice).

2.   Payment of Consideration

Consideration Case

GEO. M. McDONALD & CO. v. JOHNS
114 P. 175 (Wash. 1911)

DUNBAR, C.J.   *Gotta pay a new consideration.*

Incorporated in the record in this case is a very lucid and forceful opinion rendered by the trial judge, and a very succinct statement of the facts, which we will adopt; there being no question raised as to the facts found by the court. Johns and wife, whom we will hereafter refer to as Johns, were indebted to appellant in the principal sum of $2,210, evidenced by three promissory notes, all executed and delivered at times prior to May 5, 1908. On May 5, 1908, Johns executed and delivered to appellant a mortgage on certain lands specified. Johns was also at the same time indebted to Bechtol, one of the respondents, in the sum of $662.16, evidenced by a promissory note executed and delivered at a time prior to May 4, 1908. On May 4, 1908, Johns executed and delivered to Bechtol a mortgage on the same lands which had been mortgaged to appellant, and above described. Both mortgages were given to secure the payment of a pre-existing indebtedness, and no new or additional consideration or extension of time of payment was given as an inducement to the execution of either of said mortgages. The Bechtol mortgage was executed and delivered first. The McDonald mortgage was recorded first. Quoting from the opinion of the court: "Upon these facts the ultimate question is: Which of these mortgages has the prior lien on the land in said sections 25 and 30? McDonald claims to be a bona fide purchaser (incumbrancer) without notice of the Bechtol mortgage prior to the execution and delivery of his own. I will assume (without finding or deciding at this time) that he had no notice. The law upon which his claim to priority must rest is found at section 4441, Pierce's Code, and reads: 'All deeds, mortgages and assignments of mortgages shall be recorded in the office of the county auditor of the county where the land is situated, and shall be valid as against bona fide purchasers from the date of their filing for record in said office; and when so filed shall be notice to all the world.' Of course, the term 'bona fide purchaser' means bona fide mortgage or incumbrancer, as well; else the statute would have no application to mortgages at all. Hence the statutory phrase will be used in that sense herein. This statute is for the protection of those who become bona fide purchasers subsequent to a given conveyance or mortgage, and has nothing to do with those who become such prior thereto. In other words, the recording act reaches forward with its benefits, and not backward. It imposes upon any given mortgagee the duty of making a public record of his mortgage for the information, guidance and protection of those who at a subsequent time may have occasion to deal concerning the land, failing in the discharge of which duty he shall lose the priority otherwise to be accorded to him. But a mortgagee owes no such duty to those who precede him, and as against them he neither gains nor loses anything by recording his mortgage, except in those states where the statutes expressly provide otherwise." In the opinion of the learned judge there are collated and distinguished the principal cases on this subject, and the court concluded, as indicated, that the priority should be accorded to the party having received the first mortgage, and judgment was entered accordingly.

A review of the authorities convinces us that the judgment in this case should be affirmed. The doctrine of mortgages was originally, of course, purely equitable, and is yet as between the mortgagor and the mortgagee; and as between them it makes no difference whether the mortgage is recorded or not. The recording statutes were for the purpose, as is universally understood now, of giving constructive notice to innocent purchasers and incumbrancers, and the practical question in all these cases is: Who are innocent purchasers and incumbrancers? Pomeroy, in the second volume of his Equity Jurisprudence (3d Ed. § 749), says: "A conveyance of real or personal property as security for an antecedent debt does not, upon principle, render the transferee a bona fide purchaser, since the creditor parts with no value, surrenders no right, and places himself in no worse legal position than before. The rule has been settled, therefore, in very many of the states, that such a transfer is not made upon a valuable consideration, within the meaning of the doctrine of bona fide purchase" — citing cases from Alabama, Arkansas, New York, Vermont, Massachusetts, New Jersey, Pennsylvania, Kentucky, Illinois, Mississippi, Tennessee, Texas, and Indiana, to sustain the text. It is also stated by the author that the doctrine is not universal, but that the weight of authority is in accordance with the text announced. It is also said, in discussing the question, at section 747: "What constitutes a valuable consideration within the meaning of the doctrine which gives protection to a bona fide purchaser? No person who has acquired title as a mere volunteer, whether by gift, devise, inheritance, postnuptial settlement on wife or child, or otherwise, can thereby be a bona fide purchaser. 'Valuable consideration' means, and necessarily requires under every form and kind of purchase, something of actual value, capable, in estimation of the law, of pecuniary measurement; parting with money or money's worth or an actual change of the purchaser's legal position for the worse." And ordinary examples are given, as a contemporaneous advance or loan of money, or a sale, transfer, or exchange of property, made at the time of the purchase or execution of the instrument; the surrender or relinquishment of an existing legal right, or the assumption of a new legal obligation which is in its nature irrevocable. Jones on Mortgages, vol. 1 (6th Ed.) p. 433, also states that the weight of authority is to the effect that the equitable mortgage, the mortgage first given, will prevail over the subsequent mortgage recorded prior to it. In *People's Savings Bank v. Bates*, 120 U.S. 556, a case which cannot be distinguished in principle from the case at bar, it was held that the doctrine that the bona fide holder for value of negotiable paper, transferred as security for an antecedent debt merely, and without other circumstances, is unaffected by equities or defenses between prior parties of which he had no notice, does not apply to instruments conveying real or personal property as security in consideration only of pre-existing indebtedness;

the court quoting from 2 Leading Cases in Equity (3 Am. Ed.) 104, where it is said: "Whatever the rule may be in the case of negotiable instruments, it is well settled that the conveyance of lands or chattels as security for antecedent debt will not operate as a purchase for value, or defeat existing equities." "A creditor who takes a mortgage on realty merely as security for the payment of a debt or demand already due to him, and without giving any new consideration or being induced to change his condition in any manner, is not entitled to the protection accorded to a bona fide purchaser for value, as against prior liens or equities." (Citations omitted.)

Outside of general authority, this view of the law has been distinctly sustained by this court in *Hicks v. National Security Co.*, 50 Wash. 16, 96 Pac. 515. That was where a surety company took a bill of sale as security for a pre-existing debt upon a breached contractor's bond where a prior unrecorded bill of sale had been given, and it was held that the surety company was not an incumbrancer for value in good faith, and that its lien was inferior to that of a prior bill of sale valid as between the parties, although not executed so as to be valid as to creditors of the vendor or subsequent incumbrancers in good faith. The court concluded its announcement in that case by saying: "The instrument under which the appellant claims was taken as security for a pre-existing debt or a pre-existing contingent liability. Under such circumstances, does it come within the definition of an incumbrancer for value and in good faith, as that term is defined in law? Under the great weight of authority it does not." And the first case cited was *People's Savings Bank v. Bates, supra.* The judgment is affirmed.

NOTES AND PROBLEMS

1. Although most courts require payment of more than nominal consideration to qualify as a bfp, payment equal to the land's fair market value is not required. For example, in *Cheatham v. Gregory*, 313 S.E.2d 368, 370 (Va. 1984), the court stated: "[A] purchaser seeking the protection of the recording acts is not required to pay 'fair and adequate' consideration. The statute applies if he simply has paid value." Even an extension of time for payment can be sufficient consideration under a recording statute. Can a judgment creditor qualify for protection as a bfp pursuant to a state recording act that requires the payment of consideration? How about a mechanic's lienor?

2. On the other hand, donees of land cannot qualify for bfp status under most state statutes. Therefore, donees are not protected from prior unrecorded conveyances. However, a few states do include donees within the protection of their state recording act. See, e.g., *Eastwood v. Shedd*, 442 P.2d 423 (Colo. 1968) (noting that the Colorado statute broadly protects "any class of persons with any kind of rights" and, therefore, protects a donee against a prior unrecorded deed). What justification exists for failing to protect a donee?

3. For each of the following problems, what is the state of title? Assume that O has an estate in fee simple absolute, the same property is involved in each transfer, the facts occurred in the order given, all persons gave value unless otherwise noted, and no one has recorded or has actual knowledge of a conflicting claim unless otherwise noted:

a. O conveys to A, a donee who does not record. O conveys to B, who does record and is in possession. B makes a payment to O and an executory promise to provide services to O. A records. See *Alexander v. Andrews*, 64 S.E.2d 487 (W. Va. 1951); John W. Fisher, II, *The Scope of Title Examination in West Virginia: Can Reasonable Minds Differ?*, 98 W. Va. L. Rev. 449, 464–69 (1996) (discussing *Alexander*).

b. O conveys to A, a donee. A records. O then conveys to B for value. B records.

c. O contracts to convey a parcel of land to A. A does not record the contract but goes into possession of the property. O then gives a mortgage on the property to M, who records. A cancels O's pre-existing debt to A, and O conveys title to the land to A. A records. See *Waldorff Insur. & Bonding Inc. v. Eglin Nat'l Bank*, 453 So. 2d 1383 (Fla. Dist. Ct. App. 1984). Judgment for A in all states.

4. A person who acquires a bona fide purchaser's interest in property also is treated as a bona fide purchaser even if she would not otherwise qualify as one. The purpose is to give the bona fide purchaser the benefit of his bargain by enabling him to sell the same title he acquired. This is sometimes called the bona fide purchaser shelter or filter. The subsequent purchaser is sheltered by the equities of his bona fide purchaser grantor. But there is an important exception to maintain the filter's integrity. An owner who was not a bona fide purchaser cannot take advantage of the shelter by selling her interest to a bona fide purchaser and then reacquiring it See *Rogis v. Barnatowich*, 89 A. 838 (R.I. 1914). The opinion states: "The respondents claim that they as assignees succeeded to the rights to which Randall would have been entitled had he retained the mortgage. In support of this position the respondents refer to the case of *Coombs v. Aborn*, 29 R.I. 40, 68 A. 817, in which our court, quoting from Pomeroy's Equity, said, 'There are two special rules on the subject which have been settled since an early day. . . . The first is that if a second purchaser for value and without notice purchases from a first purchaser who is charged with notice, he thereby becomes a bona fide purchaser, and is entitled to protection.' To the rule thus cited by our court from Pomeroy there is the exception that a title cannot be conveyed free from prior equities back to a former owner who is charged with notice. Pomeroy's Eq. Juris. 3rd Ed., § 754. Considering the relationship between the present assignees . . . and the original mortgagors, . . . we think the exception to the rule, as before stated, applies to the present case and that the present holders of the . . . mortgage cannot be regarded as bona fide holders without notice."

In *Chergosky v. Crosstown Bell, Inc.*, 463 N.W.2d 522 (Minn. 1990), the opinion stated:

Generally, a bona fide purchaser of property which was subject to a prior outstanding unrecorded interest may pass title free of the unrecorded interest to a subsequent purchaser who otherwise would not qualify as a bona fide purchaser under the recording act. (Citation omitted.) This bona fide purchaser filter rule protects the alienability of property. Without this rule the bona fide purchaser would be deprived of the full benefit of the purchase — the right to transfer good title to a subsequent purchaser. * *

* The bona fide purchaser filter principle is subject to a well-recognized exception, which prevents the grantor or former owner of the property, who held the property subject to a prior equity, from acquiring the rights of a bona fide purchaser. *Walker v. Wilson*, 469 So.2d 580, 582 (Ala. 1985); *Clark v. McNeal*, 21 N.E. 405, 407 (N.Y. 1889). Professor Cribbet wrote that this exception "prevents a holder of the title from using the [bona fide purchaser] as a 'filter' to cleanse his defective ownership." J. Cribbet, Principles of the Law of Property 287–88 (2d ed. 1975). Pomeroy expressed the rationale for the filter principle as follows: "Were this not the rule, nothing would be easier than for a trustee to take advantage of his own wrong. It would only be necessary for him to make or permit a wrongful sale, in his individual capacity buy from the innocent purchaser, and then rely on the conveyance back as a shield with which to protect himself when sued for the very property which in the first instance, through a breach of duty, he allowed to be sold." 3 J. Pomeroy, A Treatise on Equity Jurisprudence § 754b, at 62 (5th ed. 1941).

E.   Recording and Indexing

In every state, recording is required to protect a real property interest from conflicting claims. A conveyance must be recorded to protect the purchaser from subsequent claims, and in approximately half the states, recording is necessary to protect against prior claims. Courts frequently have been called upon to determine whether a particular document has been recorded within the meaning of the recording act.

NOTES AND PROBLEMS

1.   O owns fee simple absolute title to Blackacre. O mortgages Blackacre to A. A records. O conveys to B. B does not record. B mortgages to C. C records. B conveys to D. B records. D records. D conveys to E. E records. In C v. E, judgment for E. *Far West Savings and Loan Ass'n v. McLaughlin*, 246 Cal. Rptr. 872 (Cal. Ct. App. 1988). Even though C promptly recorded, C's mortgage is not in the chain of title so E did not have constructive notice. It does not matter which type of recording act applies because chain of title rules are implied into all of them.

2.   O owns fee simple absolute title to Blackacre. O conveys Blackacre to A. O conveys to bfp B. B conveys to bfp C, who records. A records. B records. In A v. C, what result in a state with a notice type recording act? In a race-notice state? See *Bank of New Glarus v. Swartwood*, 725 N.W.2d 944 (Wis. Ct. App. 2006). Does B's recording make any difference?

3.   O owns fee simple absolute title to Blackacre. O conveys one-half of Blackacre to A expressly subject to a restrictive covenant. O dies. The remaining half of Blackacre is transferred in probate to H. H conveys to B but without a similar restrictive covenant. A conveys to A1. A1 conveys to A2. B conveys to B1 with permission to build in a manner that violates the restriction. All parties promptly recorded. B1 violates the restriction. A2 sues B1 to enjoin the violation of the restriction. What result and why? See *Witter v. Taggart*, 577 N.E.2d 338 (N.Y. 1991).

Judgment for B1, but the authority is split. Why did B1 obtain express permission to build in violation of the covenant?

4. Courts are divided on whether an unindexed or misindexed document is nonetheless properly recorded. The result normally turns on the language of the recording statute. For example, in *First Citizens Nat'l Bank v. Sherwood*, 879 A.2d 178 (Pa. 2005), the court held that a subsequent purchaser had constructive notice of a document that had been recorded but misindexed because a state statute provided that the effect of "recording . . . shall be to give constructive notice to subsequent purchasers." A contrary rule would make purchasers responsible for the recorder's mistakes, and all persons seeking the protection of the recording acts would have to return to the recorder's office after initially presenting a document for recording, check the index, and ascertain that someone subsequently searching the records can in fact locate the documents. You might ask, however, "what's wrong with that?" Subsequent title searchers, often title insurance companies, describe finding a document without the use of the grantor-grantee index to be like looking for a needle in a haystack. As one court said, "a deed might as well be buried in the earth as in a mass of records without a clue as to its whereabouts. . . ." See *Barney v. McCarty*, 83 Am Dec. 427 (Iowa 1864).

Therefore, many courts have held that an improperly indexed document does not provide notice. Some of these courts base their holding on the language of the relevant recording act, while others cite equitable reasons, even in the face of statutory language that would indicate a contrary result. See *Greenpoint Mortg. Funding v. Schlossberg*, 888 A.2d 297 (Md. 2005). See also *Federal National Mortgage Ass'n v. Levine-Rodriguez*, 579 N.Y.S.2d 975, 977, 980–81 (N.Y. App. Div. 1991) (stating that the grantee of a deed "has it in his power to examine the records and satisfy himself that his paper has been duly and accurately recorded while it is impossible for a prospective purchaser or creditor to anticipate and . . . ascertain the innumerable forms which the negligence or mistakes" made in the recorder's office can take). These courts conclude that the risk of a mistake should be allocated to the person presenting a document for recording and that, as a practical matter, a title company, insurer, or abstractor can most easily perform the additional search for that person.

5. Because grantor-grantee indices rely on names, a variation in the name of a person appearing more than once in the records can be a problem. See *Frederick Ward Assocs., Inc. v. Venture, Inc.*, 636 A.2d 496, 498 (Md. Ct. Spec. App. 1994) (holding that a judgment lien was unenforceable against a subsequent purchaser because the lien was indexed under the judgment debtor's nickname, Chris Walker, although title to the disputed parcel was in his full name, John C. Walker, and stating: "We hold that where a judgment is indexed in a nickname or misnomer that is sufficiently dissimilar to the name in which the judgment debtor's property is titled, the judgment will not be enforceable as a lien against the property with respect to a subsequent bona fide purchaser for value without notice of the judgment."). In contrast, some courts have applied the rule of *idem sonans* to hold that a document indexed under a misspelled name is valid against a bfp if the misspelling sounds the same as the correct spelling. See, e.g., *Wilson Sporting Goods Co. v. Pedersen*, 886 P.2d 203 (Wash. Ct. App. 1994) (holding that a one letter misspelling of the debtor's name — Pederson instead of Pedersen — fit into the rule of *idem sonans* and was not fatal to the otherwise valid judgment lien.

6. A public record is a document that, once recorded, provides constructive notice, and is prima facie evidence, of its contents. Not all governmental records are "public records" because to be such, they must be so designated by statute. See *Skelton v. Martin*, 673 So. 2d 877 (Fla. App. 1996) (holding that electronic property tax records are not public records and could not be relied on by a title searcher when the recorder's office contained the tax certificate missing from the computerized records, and further holding that there is no due process right to accurate governmental information). The issue in *Skelton* also arises when a county indexes its recorded documents in both a grantor-grantee index and in a tract index. Because the tract index is easier to use, title examiners prefer it to save time and expense and reduce the possibility of error. However, as in *Skelton*, title examiners may rely on the tract index only at their peril. Most state recording acts specify that the grantor-grantee index is the "official" index. Therefore, if a document is indexed in the grantor-grantee index but not in the tract index, future purchasers will have constructive notice of it even if they relied solely on the tract index to perform the title examination.

7. The majority of recorders (abstract property) and registrars (registered property) offer at least some form of computerized access to their real estate records. In the near future, computerized access likely will become universal. To the extent that a recorder's or registrar's office offers on-site access to its records via computer — as opposed to the old-fashioned logbooks of the last century — those records generally are also available through remote access. Because digital recordkeeping is relatively new, title searchers today normally must search both the computer records and the older written records to obtain a complete picture of a land title. However, all real estate records eventually will be digitized, and paper record books will become a thing of the past. Therefore, title examiners and real estate attorneys must become adept at using the computerized land records.

A myriad of software platforms exist for organizing and maintaining real estate records, but they all achieve the same basic end — creation of a searchable, computerized analog to the historic indexes that recorders have maintained since the land recording system began. Like their paper counterparts, computerized land records are searchable by name (grantor/grantee index), by legal description (tract index), and by the chronological document number that the recorder or registrar stamps on a document when it is filed for recording (reception index). Some systems offer additional indexes, such as by document type or by date range, which can help locate a specific document. Many have incorporated the historic record books into the computerized system by providing scanned images of the books themselves. However, as indicated in the preceding note, knowledge of the relevant recording act is essential. For example, if the recorder is statutorily required to maintain only a grantor/grantee index, reliance on a computerized tract index — tempting as it may be — may be insufficient. See *MidCountry Bank v. Krueger*, 782 N.W.2d 238 (Minn. 2010).

F.   Exclusions from the Recording Act

The conveyance of a record title, even to a bona fide purchaser, does not extinguish a title acquired by adverse possession. See *Crescent Harbor Water Co., Inc. v. Lyseng*, 753 P.2d 555 (Wash. Ct. App. 1988) (so holding). Another way of saying this is that, because the recordings do not repeal the law of adverse possession expressly, such repeal should not be implied. More generally, the recording acts do not include all types of property interests or methods of acquiring an interest. For example, marital property and homestead rights, implied easements, and equitable or constructive trusts, like interests acquired by adverse possession, do not require a written document and, therefore, are not subject to the applicable recording act. See *Gaona v. Gonzales*, 997 S.W.2d 784 (Tex. Ct. App. 1999) (equitable right to purchase land). Similarly, the great majority of jurisdictions do not require short-term leases to be in writing. Therefore, a purchaser of land takes subject to these types of interests even without any notice of their existence.

Some interests that are not subject to the terms of the recording act are statutorily created. For example, every state has legislation that provides a mechanic's lien for persons who provide material or labor for the improvement of land. Most of these statutes provide that the lien's priority relates back to a time that may substantially precede the recording of the lien, such as the date work began on the land. Therefore, a property purchaser who was unaware that work was performed on the property may hold title subject to a mechanic's lien recorded *after* the purchaser recorded the deed by which she acquired title to the property.

Because not all property interests are documented in the public records as described in the preceding two paragraphs, a prospective property purchaser must attempt to discover these interests in other ways. As described in *Methonen*, a purchaser should inspect the property to determine whether there are short-term tenancies, recently completed improvements, encroachments, or other evidence of potential property interests. Buyers also commonly require the seller to give a certified statement, often called an "owner's affidavit" or a "seller's affidavit," concerning the title. The affidavit includes representations by the seller about matters that may affect the property title but that are undiscoverable from the public records, such as adverse possessors. Of course, such affidavits are only as reliable as the seller, but they provide recourse against the seller if any of the representations are untrue.

Finally, the recording acts only provide constructive notice to those persons who are bound to search the records. A contractor hired to excavate land may hit a buried pipe that is the subject of a recorded easement, but wouldn't it be strange if the contractor was bound to search the records before starting work? See *Mountain States Tel. and Telegraph Co. v. Kelton*, 285 P.2d 168 (Ariz. 1955). This is not to say the excavator is not liable in negligence for shoddily performed work, but that is another matter. See also *Statler Manufacturing, Inc. v. Brown*, 691 S.W.2d 445 (Mo. Ct. App. 1985) (recorded easement for aircraft right-of-way did not impart notice to building contractor).

By now, it is obvious that any recording system has weaknesses. Indexing and transcription errors creep in. Multi-instrument indexes are confusing even if accurate. Some possessory and equitable interests trump any recorded document. Not all interests are recordable. Recitals within recorded documents may give notice of other chains of title that need to be searched. And some types of recording acts (notice and race-notice types) do not give the records their greatest possible effect. Is there a better system? Read on, and see what you think.

VII. TORRENS REGISTRATION

As described in the preceding section, the recording act system is flawed. Perhaps the most serious flaw is that the system does not cover a variety of property interests, such as implied easements and marital property interests. Another significant flaw in the system is that it can be cumbersome to use, particularly if it employs the grantor-grantee index. Finally, the recording system does not provide any guarantee that the recorded documents are legally valid. For example, a recorded deed may be void because it was not delivered or because the grantor's signature was forged. Because of these weaknesses, some states have adopted the Torrens system of title registration as an alternative.

Sir Robert Torrens first introduced the Torrens title registration system in Australia in 1858. He modeled it after the English system for registering ship titles. The Torrens system spread throughout Australia, New Zealand, Canada, and the United Kingdom. In 1895, Illinois became the first American state to enact legislation authorizing use of the Torrens system. Twenty other states enacted Torrens legislation within the next few decades. Today, however, Torrens registration is legislatively authorized in only ten states, and only three states — Hawaii, Massachusetts, and Minnesota — continue to register properties in any substantial number. The highest incidences of Torrens registration in the United States are in Hawaii and in Hennepin and Ramsey Counties, Minnesota (Minneapolis and St. Paul, respectively). Approximately 40 to 45 percent of the land in those areas are registered under the Torrens system.

The Torrens system differs from the recording system in that the title itself, rather than mere evidence of title, is registered with the government. Under the recording system, the government makes no representation concerning title to property within the system ("abstract property"). Instead, the government acts as a mere custodian of documents potentially affecting land titles. The state of title to a parcel of land must be determined by each individual title examiner based on a search of the tract or grantor-grantee indexes and on an analysis of the relevant documents. In contrast, under the Torrens system, the title record maintained by the government constitutes a government certification concerning the current state of title to property within the system ("registered property"). If a property interest is not included on the certificate of title, the interest does not exist, though a few exceptions do exist. If the government's certification of title is wrong, it is liable to the injured interest owner for damages, but the interest still is extinguished.

To bring a parcel of land into the Torrens system, the property owner files a quiet title-like action before a court or other tribunal specified in the state's Torrens legislation. Because the tribunal will make a binding determination concerning the land's title, the owner is required to exercise due diligence to identify and notify all possible claimants to the property of the registration proceeding.

After the government Examiner of Titles has searched the property title and the property has been physically inspected to discover unrecorded interests, the tribunal conducts a hearing, giving all interested parties an opportunity to be heard. Based on a determination that the petitioner in fact has title to the property, the tribunal orders the system administrator, normally called the Registrar of Titles, to issue a certificate of title to the land. The original certificate is kept in the Registrar's Office as a matter of public record, and the owner receives a duplicate certificate. Only persons not receiving adequate notice of the title action may afterwards challenge the title, and they may challenge it only to establish their interest in the property. See, e.g., *Rael v. Taylor*, 876 P.2d 1210 (Colo. 1994). Thus the certificate becomes conclusive evidence of the title, and the notations on it are the only exceptions to its holder having a full fee simple absolute. The certificate thus mirrors the state of that title and draws down the curtain on all exceptions not noted. All holders of conflicting interests are relegated to filing a claim with the system's guaranty fund, maintained with the proceeds of the fees collected from applicants for a certificate. Users of Torrens titles in other countries thus often describe the underpinnings of the system as reflecting the "Mirror Principle," the "Curtain Principle," and the "Fund Principle."

Additional hearings may be required after the initial registration proceeding. For example, a hearing may be required when the property is sold at a foreclosure sale. Also, a hearing may be required if the owner's copy of the certificate of title has been misplaced or stolen.

As described in the last section, rights acquired by adverse possession are an exception to the state recording acts. However, if there is no dispute about boundaries at the time of registration and the certificate's legal description is not ambiguous, that description is conclusive of the boundaries of a registered property. Title to Torrens property cannot be lost by adverse possession. See *In re McGinnis*, 536 N.W.2d 33 (Minn. Ct. App. 1995); *In re Building D, Inc.*, 502 N.W.2d 406, 408 (Minn. Ct. App. 1993).

Some states, including Hawaii and Minnesota, have provided statutorily for nonjudicial registration when title is uncontested. In Minnesota, a property owner can register title by submitting an application and an abstract of title to the Examiner of Titles. After notice to all persons with a property interest in the land, the Examiner can issue a directive to the Registrar of Titles to issue a Certificate of Possessory Title (CPT). After five years, the CPT is converted to a regular certificate of title. Minn. Stat. §§ 508A.01–508A.85. Torrens proponents advocate this type of administrative proceeding to reduce the time and expense of the usual judicial proceeding. Kimball Foster, *Certificates of Possessory Title: A Sensible Addition to Minnesota's Successful Torrens System*, 40 Wm. Mitchell L. Rev. 112 (2013).

Two upcoming illustrations provide an example of the front and back of a Torrens certificate of title. As you can see, the certificate identifies the owner, the land, and the owner's estate in the land. The certificate also lists the liens and other interests affecting the property title. After issuance of the original certificate of title, all subsequent transactions affecting the title will become effective only when they are "memorialized" on the registrar's title certificate. For instance, when the owner grants a mortgage, it must be listed on the certificate to become a valid lien. Conversely, when the owner satisfies a mortgage, the memorial for the mortgage should be deleted from the certificate. When the owner transfers title to the property, the owner's copy of the title certificate and the deed of conveyance must be presented to the registrar. The certificate of title is then canceled, as shown on the certificate that follows, and the transferee receives a new certificate that lists the liens and other interests that are still attached to the title.

The primary benefit of Torrens registration is that the state of title can be determined simply by looking at the registrar's certificate of title and by examining the documents memorialized on it. No time-consuming search of the tract or grantor-grantee indexes is required. Despite this advantage, the Torrens registration system has not been widely implemented in the United States for three primary reasons. First and foremost, initial registration of title is costly.

Most owners have little incentive to spend a significant amount of money today so that subsequent title transfers by future owners can be consummated more quickly and cheaply. Second, Torrens coverage is subject to a variety of exceptions. Common exceptions include short-term leases, visible easements, and mineral claims. In addition, federal government claims are not subject to Torrens registration because states cannot compel the federal government to comply with the state title laws. See, e.g., *United States v. Rasmuson*, 253 F.2d 944 (8th Cir. 1958) (Torrens property was subject to an unmemorialized federal tax lien despite a state statutory requirement that liens be memorialized). Federal government claims may include tax liens and rights in streets and highways. These exceptions defeat the primary benefit of the Torrens system — the conclusiveness of the Torrens certificate of title.

MC 1030

CERTIFICATE OF TITLE

No.   687937

DISTRICT COURT No(s)   16817

Transfer from No. 453492   Originally registered the 28th day of April

A. D. 1970   Volume 1502   Page 453492

Nº 687937

CANCELED
TRANSFERRED TO:
258755

STATE OF MINNESOTA,
COUNTY OF HENNEPIN.

REGISTRATION

This is to certify that   Norman P. Johnson and Mary I. Johnson, husband and wife, as joint tenants, 3988 Lake Curve, City of Robbinsdale,

County of Hennepin, State of Minnesota

are   now the owner(s) of an estate in fee simple of and in the following described land situated in the County of Hennepin and State of Minnesota, to wit:

Lot 10, Block 1, "Lake Shore Addition to Robbinsdale", together with accretions or relictions lying between the Easterly extensions of the Northerly and Southerly lines of said Lot 10, according to the recorded plat thereof.

Subject to the rights of the State of Minnesota in its sovereign capacity to use for navigation, and reclaim for public use in the interest of the general welfare that portion of the lands herein lying between the natural ordinary low water mark and the natural ordinary high water mark of Crystal Lake;

Subject to the encumbrances, liens and interest noted by the memorial underwritten or endorsed hereon; and subject to the following rights or encumbrances subsisting, as provided in the twenty-fourth section of "An act concerning the registration of land and the title thereto" of the General laws of the State of Minnesota for the year 1905, and the amendments thereof, namely:

1. Liens, claims or rights arising under the laws or the constitution of the United States, which the statutes of this state cannot require to appear of record.
2. The lien of any real property tax or special assessment for which the land has not been sold at the date of the certificate of title.
3. Any lease for a period not exceeding three years, when there is actual occupation of the premises under the lease.
4. All rights in public highways upon the land.
5. Such right of appeal or right to appear and contest the application as is allowed by law.
6. The rights of any person in possession under deed or contract for deed from the owner of the certificate of title.
7. Any outstanding mechanics lien rights which may exist under sections 514.01 to 514.17.

That the said Norman P. Johnson and Mary I. Johnson are each of the age of 62 years, are married to each other and are under no disability.

IN WITNESS WHEREOF, I have hereunto subscribed my name and affixed the seal of my office

this   Ninth   day of   October 1986

R. Dan Carlson

Registrar of Titles,

In and for the County of Hennepin and State of Minnesota.

By   DEPUTY

MEMORIAL

OF ESTATES, EASEMENTS OR CHARGES ON THE LAND DESCRIBED IN THE CERTIFICATE OF TITLE HERETO ATTACHED.

DOCUMENT NUMBER	KIND OF INSTRUMENT	DATE OF INSTRUMENT Month/Day/Year	DATE OF REGISTRATION Month/Day/Year	How	AMOUNT	RUNNING IN FAVOR OF	SIGNATURE OF DEPUTY REGISTRAR
1494797	Mortgage	Dec 23 1982	Dec 27 1982	9	$100000.00	Twin City Federal Savings and Loan Association, Minneapolis, Minn	
1627370	Asst of Mtge Doc No 1494797	Nov 30 1984	Feb 11 1985	9		Crossland Capital Corporation Los Angeles, CA	
1763204	Mortgage	Sep 23 1986	Oct 9 1986	11	$50000.00	TCF Mortgage Corporation (a MN corp) Minneapolis, MN	H Katz
1803326	Mortgage	Sep 23 1986	Feb 11 1987	11	$50000.00	TCF Mortgage Corporation (a MN corp) Minneapolis, MN given to correct mtge doc no 1763204.	S. Uhlik

SEE OVER

No. 687937

DOCUMENT NUMBER	KIND OF INSTRUMENT	DATE OF INSTRUMENT (Month/Day/Year)	DATE OF REGISTRATION (Month/Day/Year/Hour)	AMOUNT	RUNNING IN FAVOR OF	SIGNATURE OF DEPUTY REGISTRAR
1804638	Set of Mtge. Dec. No. 1494797	Nov. 4 1986	Feb. 13 1987 — 10		(See Mtgee. Change of Name Doc. No. 1693428) David Bryce Witkowski et al.	H. Rud
1807194	Assgt. of Mtge. Doc. No. 1463204	Oct. 24 1986	Feb. 25 1987 — 9		CPS Mortgage Corporation 2120 South 72 St. Omaha, NE	S. Uhlik
1847466	Mtge. Doc. No. 1803326 Name Trans. & Warranty	May 19 1987	Jul. 6 1987 — 10		Susan J. Lilyquist, 39 yrs., is unmarried, is under no disability	Olson
2159231	Deed Warranty	Feb. 28 1991	Mar. 7 1991 — 2		Mary L. Johnson, Trustee of the Mary L. Johnson Revocable Trust U/A/D January 11, 1989	Olson
2159232	Deed	Feb. 28 1991	Mar. 7 1991 — 2			Olson

Doc. 647937
Volume 2308

𝕮𝖊𝖗𝖙𝖎𝖋𝖎𝖈𝖆𝖙𝖊
of 𝕿𝖎𝖙𝖑𝖊

Johnson
Owner (s.)

STATE of MINNESOTA,
COUNTY of HENNEPIN.

4497

Third, the technical detail involved in registering and maintaining land titles under the Torrens system requires Registrar's Office personnel to be more skilled than their counterparts in the Recorder's Office, especially because any errors they make cut off property interests. Although persons who lose their property interests as a result of such errors are eligible to recover damages from the system's guaranty fund, state funding is sometimes insufficient, and claims can be slow to be paid. So the Torrens system is unlikely ever to be widely implemented in the United States, although it has been implemented successfully in many other countries. For more extensive discussions of the Torrens system, see Dent Bostick, *Land Title Registration: An English Solution to an American Problem*, 63 Ind. L.J. 55 (1987); Barry Goldner, Comment, *The Torrens System of Title Registration: A New Proposal for Effective Implementation*, 29 UCLA L. Rev. 661 (1982).

NOTES

1. An interesting problem arises when someone other than the owner obtains possession of the Torrens certificate of title. In *Eliason v. Wilborn*, 281 U.S. 457 (1930), the appellants entrusted their certificate of title to Napletone, who subsequently presented the certificate along with a forged conveyance to himself to the registrar. Upon receiving a new certificate of title from the registrar, Napletone conveyed the property to the Wilborns, who were good faith purchasers. The United States Supreme Court held that the Wilborns had acquired title: "As between two innocent persons, one of whom must suffer the consequence of a breach of trust, the one who made it possible by his act of confidence must bear the loss." *Id.* at 462.

2. Some state statutes (often called marketable title acts) require that for certain less-than-fee interests to survive after a thirty or forty year period, the interest must be re-recorded. Are such statutes applicable to property previously registered under the Torrens system? See *Hersh Properties, LLC v. McDonald's Corp.*, 588 N.W.2d 728 (Minn. 1999) (holding in the affirmative and stating that the Minnesota Marketable Title Act could extinguish an easement if the statutorily required notice of continuance was not memorialized).

VIII. TITLE INSURANCE

Title insurance is similar to other forms of insurance, such as car insurance and homeowner's insurance. With title insurance, the risk being insured against is that title to the property is different than the title described in the insurance policy. Depending on the policy, the insured also may be insured against additional risks, such as a lack of access to the property or unmarketability of title. Because title insurers' investigations concerning the property normally are limited to an examination of the public property records, title insurance generally insures only against title defects. It usually does not indemnify the insured for so-called "matters of survey," which are those items such as encroachments that affect the land's physical condition and that are discoverable only by an on-site inspection.

Two types of insurance policies are used in this country: the owner's policy and the loan policy. As their names imply, the owner's policy indemnifies the owner of the property against title defects, and the loan policy insures a lender that holds a mortgage, deed of trust, or similar security interest in the property. The loan policy does not provide any protection for the owner, although the lender usually requires the owner to pay the premium for the policy. Thus if the owner wants insurance protection, it must purchase an owner's policy in addition to a loan policy.

Owner's and loan policies are very similar in their coverage. Both policies indemnify against loss caused by a title defect or encumbrance that is not listed as an exception or exclusion to the policy. However, a lender is interested not just in title to the land, but also in the priority of its security interest in the land. Therefore, the loan policy also insures the validity and priority of the security interest. Also, unlike the owner's policy, a loan policy is transferable to a purchaser of the lender's security interest. In fact, the secondary mortgage market, which is the market for buying and selling mortgages and other security interests in land, has been a major impetus for the growth of the title insurance industry, because purchasers on the secondary mortgage market routinely require a loan policy as a condition of buying a loan.

Anyone who wants title insurance contacts an agent for the insurance company. A variety of insurance companies compete in the marketplace; some operate nationally, and others operate in more local markets. Like other insurance companies, title insurance companies vary in the types of coverage they offer and in the quality of service they provide. Therefore, when a purchase agreement for land requires the seller to provide title insurance or proof of title from a title insurance company, the buyer should specify *which* insurance company the seller must use. The buyer wants to make sure that the seller employs a title company with high professional standards and adequate assets to pay any claim.

Before issuing a policy, the title insurance company normally will have the title examined by a private attorney or a company employee. Although the title exam may be conducted in the public property records, many insurance companies maintain their own set of property records in their "title plant." Based on the results of the title exam, the company issues a title commitment, which is also called a title binder. The commitment is an offer to issue a title insurance policy on the terms set forth in the commitment. The commitment describes the current state of title to the land and the exceptions to coverage that will be included in the insurance policy. Some exceptions are unique to the property, such as outstanding mortgages, easements, and other title encumbrances. Other exceptions are boilerplate, such as the possibility of a subsequently recorded mechanic's lien with a statutory priority that relates back to a date before the policy's effective date. Commitments also include preconditions to the title insurance company's obligation to insure the title. Commitments routinely provide that the buyer must acquire title by a warranty deed and must pay consideration for the property.

Based on the title report contained in the commitment, the buyer can notify the seller of any objections to the state of title. If required to do so by the purchase agreement, the seller must correct any defect in the title. The seller's failure to do so constitutes a breach of the purchase agreement and authorizes the buyer to refuse to buy the land. Commonly, the sale proceeds will be used to eliminate title encumbrances, such as mortgages, judgment liens, and mechanic's liens. After the title has been transferred to the buyer and the necessary documents are recorded, the title insurance company will issue the title insurance policy.

Unlike other types of insurance, the premium for title insurance is paid only once. Title insurance companies base their premiums on two primary factors: the cost of examining title to the property (if the insurance company paid for the exam) and the risk associated with insuring the title. Under certain conditions, title insurance companies will offer a discounted premium to their customers. For a sufficiently large transaction, the title company may negotiate a rate lower than its customary charge. Additionally, when the owner's and loan policies are purchased at the same time, the cost to the title insurance company is reduced because the company now only has to conduct one title search to issue two policies. To reflect this reduction in cost, title insurance companies offer a discounted premium known as the "simultaneous issue rate." This rate provides an economic incentive for the buyer to obtain both owner's and loan policies when the property is purchased.

In addition, a title insurance company often offers a discounted "reissue rate" premium if a policy has been issued on the same property within the past several years, because the company can simply update the previous title search and thus save significant time and money. Finally, a buyer may get a discounted premium by getting a seller's affidavit, because the insurance company then may have recourse against the seller if a title defect is subsequently discovered. For examinations of the law concerning title insurance, see Barlow Burke, Law of Title Insurance (3rd ed. 2000); Joyce Palomar, Title Insurance Law (1994).

Most title insurance companies use standard policy forms drafted by the American Land Title Association (ALTA), the national trade association for title insurers. The following is the most recent owner's policy form.

OWNER'S POLICY OF TITLE INSURANCE

SUBJECT TO THE EXCLUSIONS FROM COVERAGE, THE EXCEPTIONS FROM COVERAGE CONTAINED IN SCHEDULE B, AND THE CONDITIONS, BLANK TITLE INSURANCE COMPANY, a Blank corporation (the "Company") insures, as of Date of Policy and, to the extent stated in Covered Risks 9 and 10, after Date of Policy, against loss or damage, not exceeding the Amount of Insurance, sustained or incurred by the Insured by reason of:

1. Title being vested other than as stated in Schedule A.

2. Any defect in or lien or encumbrance on the Title. This Covered Risk includes but is not limited to insurance against loss from (a) A defect in the Title caused by (i) forgery, fraud, undue influence, duress, incompetency, incapacity, or impersonation; (ii) failure of any person or Entity to have authorized a transfer or conveyance; (iii) a document affecting Title not properly created, executed, witnessed, sealed, acknowledged, notarized, or delivered; (iv) failure to perform those acts necessary to create a document by electronic means authorized by law; (v) a document executed under a falsified, expired, or otherwise invalid power of attorney; (vi) a document not properly filed, recorded, or indexed in the Public Records including failure to perform those acts by electronic means authorized by law; or (vii) a defective judicial or administrative proceeding. (b) The lien of real estate taxes or assessments imposed on the Title by a governmental authority due or payable, but unpaid. (c) Any encroachment, encumbrance, violation, variation, or adverse circumstance affecting the Title that would be disclosed by an accurate and complete land survey of the Land. The term "encroachment" includes encroachments of existing improvements located on the Land onto adjoining land, and encroachments onto the Land of existing improvements located on adjoining land.

3. Unmarketable Title

4. No right of access to and from the Land.

5. The violation or enforcement of any law, ordinance, permit, or governmental regulation (including those relating to building and zoning) restricting, regulating, prohibiting, or relating to (a) the occupancy, use, or enjoyment of the Land; (b) the character, dimensions, or location of any improvement erected on the Land; (c) the subdivision of land; or (d) environmental protection, if a notice, describing any part of the Land, is recorded in the Public Records setting forth the violation or intention to enforce, but only to the extent of the violation or enforcement referred to in that notice.

6. An enforcement action based on the exercise of a governmental police power not covered by Covered Risk 5 if a notice of the enforcement action, describing any part of the Land, is recorded in the Public Records, but only to the extent of the enforcement referred to in that notice.

7. The exercise of the rights of eminent domain if a notice of the exercise, describing any part of the Land, is recorded in the Public Records.

8. Any taking by a governmental body that has occurred and is binding on the rights of a purchaser for value without Knowledge.

9. Title being vested other than as stated in Schedule A or being defective (a) as a result of the avoidance in whole or in part, or from a court order providing an alternative remedy, of a transfer of all or any part of the title to or any interest in the Land occurring prior to the transaction vesting Title as shown in Schedule A because that prior transfer constituted a fraudulent or preferential transfer under federal bankruptcy, state insolvency, or similar creditors' rights laws; or (b) because the instrument of transfer vesting Title as shown in Schedule A constitutes a preferential transfer under federal bankruptcy, state insolvency, or similar creditors' rights laws by reason of the failure of its recording in the Public Records (i) to be timely, or (ii) to impart notice of its existence to a purchaser for value or to a judgment or lien creditor.

10. Any defect in or lien or encumbrance on the Title or other matter included in Covered Risks 1 through 9

that has been created or attached or has been filed or recorded in the Public Records subsequent to Date of Policy and prior to the recording of the deed or other instrument of transfer in the Public Records that vests Title as shown in Schedule A.

The Company will also pay the costs, attorneys' fees, and expenses incurred in defense of any matter insured against by this Policy, but only to the extent provided in the Conditions.

[signed] BLANK TITLE INSURANCE COMPANY　　　　BY: _____, PRESIDENT.

EXCLUSIONS FROM COVERAGE

The following matters are expressly excluded from the coverage of this policy, and the Company will not pay loss or damage, costs, attorneys' fees, or expenses that arise by reason of:

1. (a) Any law, ordinance, permit, or governmental regulation (including those relating to building and zoning) restricting, regulating, prohibiting, or relating to (i) the occupancy, use, or enjoyment of the Land; (ii) the character, dimensions, or location of any improvement erected on the Land; (iii) the subdivision of land; or (iv) environmental protection; or the effect of any violation of these laws, ordinances, or governmental regulations. This Exclusion 1(a) does not modify or limit the coverage provided under Covered Risk 5. (b) Any governmental police power. This Exclusion 1(b) does not modify or limit the coverage provided under Covered Risk 6.

2. Rights of eminent domain. This Exclusion does not modify or limit the coverage provided under Covered Risk 7 or 8.

3. Defects, liens, encumbrances, adverse claims, or other matters (a) created, suffered, assumed, or agreed to by the Insured Claimant; (b) not Known to the Company, not recorded in the Public Records at Date of Policy, but Known to the Insured Claimant and not disclosed in writing to the Company by the Insured Claimant prior to the date the Insured Claimant became an Insured under this policy; (c) resulting in no loss or damage to the Insured Claimant; (d) attaching or created subsequent to Date of Policy (however, this does not modify or limit the coverage provided under Covered Risk 9 and 10); or (e) resulting in loss or damage that would not have been sustained if the Insured Claimant had paid value for the Title.

4. Any claim, by reason of the operation of federal bankruptcy, state insolvency, or similar creditors' rights laws, that the transaction vesting the Title as shown in Schedule A, is (a) a fraudulent conveyance or fraudulent transfer; or (b) a preferential transfer for any reason not stated in Covered Risk 9 of this policy.

5. Any lien on the Title for real estate taxes or assessments imposed by governmental authority and created or attaching between Date of Policy and the date of recording of the deed or other instrument of transfer in the Public Records that vests Title as shown in Schedule A.

SCHEDULE A

Name and Address of Company: [File No.:　　]　　　　Policy No.:
Address Reference:
Amount of Insurance: $ [Premium: $　　]　　　　Date of Policy:　　　[at　　　a.m./p.m.]

1. Name of Insured:
2. The estate or interest in the Land that is insured by this policy is:
3. Title is vested in:
4. The Land referred to in this policy is described as follows: [insert legal description of insured title]

SCHEDULE B – EXCEPTIONS FROM COVERAGE

This policy does not insure against loss or damage, and the Company will not pay costs, attorneys' fees, or expenses that arise by reason of: [Policy may include regional exceptions if so desired by the issuing Company, as well as variable exceptions such as taxes, easements, CC&R's, etc., shown here.]

CONDITIONS

1. DEFINITION OF TERMS The following terms when used in this policy mean:

(a) "Amount of Insurance": The amount stated in Schedule A, as may be increased or decreased by endorsement to this policy, increased by Section 8(b), or decreased by Sections 10 and 11 of these Conditions.

(b) "Date of Policy": The date designated as "Date of Policy" in Schedule A.

(c) "Entity": A corporation, partnership, trust, limited liability company, or other similar legal entity.

(d) "Insured": The Insured named in Schedule A. (i) the term "Insured" also includes (A) successors to the Title of the Insured by operation of law as distinguished from purchase, including heirs, devisees, survivors, personal representatives, or next of kin; (B) successors to an Insured by dissolution, merger, consolidation, distribution, or reorganization; (C) successors to an Insured by its conversion to another kind of Entity; (D) a grantee of an Insured under a deed delivered without payment of actual valuable consideration conveying the Title (1) if the stock, shares, memberships, or other equity interests of the grantee are wholly-owned by the named Insured, (2) if the grantee wholly owns the named Insured, (3) if the grantee is wholly-owned by an affiliated Entity of the named Insured, provided the affiliated Entity and the named Insured are both wholly-owned by the same person or Entity, or (4) if the grantee is a trustee or beneficiary of a trust created by a written instrument established by the Insured named in Schedule A for estate planning purposes. (ii) with regard to (A), (B), (C), and (D) reserving, however, all rights and defenses as to any successor that the Company would have had against any predecessor Insured.

(e) "Insured Claimant": An Insured claiming loss or damage.

(f) "Knowledge" or "Known": Actual knowledge, not constructive knowledge or notice that may be imputed to an Insured by reason of the Public Records or any other records that impart constructive notice of matters affecting the Title.

(g) "Land": The land described in Schedule A, and affixed improvements that by law constitute real property. The term "Land" does not include any property beyond the lines of the area described in Schedule A, nor any right, title, interest, estate, or easement in abutting streets, roads, avenues, alleys, lanes, ways, or waterways, but this does not modify or limit the extent that a right of access to and from the Land is insured by this policy.

(h) "Mortgage": Mortgage, deed of trust, trust deed, or other security instrument, including one evidenced by electronic means authorized by law.

(i) "Public Records": Records established under state statutes at Date of Policy for the purpose of imparting constructive notice of matters relating to real property to purchasers for value and without Knowledge. With respect to Covered Risk 5(d), "Public Records" shall also include environmental protection liens filed in the records of the clerk of the United States District Court for the district where the Land is located.

(j) "Title": The estate or interest described in Schedule A.

(k) "Unmarketable Title": Title affected by an alleged or apparent matter that would permit a prospective purchaser or lessee of the Title or lender on the Title to be released from the obligation to purchase, lease, or lend if there is a contractual condition requiring the delivery of marketable title.

2. CONTINUATION OF INSURANCE The coverage of this policy shall continue in force as of Date of Policy in favor of an Insured, but only so long as the Insured retains an estate or interest in the Land, or holds an obligation secured by a purchase money Mortgage given by a purchaser from the Insured, or only so long as

the Insured shall have liability by reason of warranties in any transfer or conveyance of the Title. This policy shall not continue in force in favor of any purchaser from the Insured of either (i) an estate or interest in the Land, or (ii) an obligation secured by a purchase money Mortgage given to the Insured.

3. NOTICE OF CLAIM TO BE GIVEN BY INSURED CLAIMANT The Insured shall notify the Company promptly in writing (i) in case of any litigation as set forth in Section 5(a) of these Conditions, (ii) in case Knowledge shall come to an Insured hereunder of any claim of title or interest that is adverse to the Title, as insured, and that might cause loss or damage for which the Company may be liable by virtue of this policy, or (iii) if the Title, as insured, is rejected as Unmarketable Title. If the Company is prejudiced by the failure of the Insured Claimant to provide prompt notice, the Company's liability to the Insured Claimant under the policy shall be reduced to the extent of the prejudice.

4. PROOF OF LOSS In the event the Company is unable to determine the amount of loss or damage, the Company may, at its option, require as a condition of payment that the Insured Claimant furnish a signed proof of loss. * * *

5. DEFENSE AND PROSECUTION OF ACTIONS (a) Upon written request by the Insured, and subject to the options contained in Section 7 of these Conditions, the Company, at its own cost and without unreasonable delay, shall provide for the defense of an Insured in litigation in which any third party asserts a claim covered by this policy adverse to the Insured. This obligation is limited to only those stated causes of action alleging matters insured against by this policy. The Company shall have the right to select counsel of its choice (subject to the right of the Insured to object for reasonable cause) to represent the Insured as to those stated causes of action. It shall not be liable for and will not pay the fees of any other counsel. The Company will not pay any fees, costs, or expenses incurred by the Insured in the defense of those causes of action that allege matters not insured against by this policy. (b) The Company shall have the right, in addition to the options contained in Section 7 of these Conditions, at its own cost, to institute and prosecute any action or proceeding or to do any other act that in its opinion may be necessary or desirable to establish the Title, as insured, or to prevent or reduce loss or damage to the Insured. The Company may take any appropriate action under the terms of this policy, whether or not it shall be liable to the Insured. The exercise of these rights shall not be an admission of liability or waiver of any provision of this policy. If the Company exercises its rights under this subsection, it must do so diligently. (c) Whenever the Company brings an action or asserts a defense as required or permitted by this policy, the Company may pursue the litigation to a final determination by a court of competent jurisdiction, and it expressly reserves the right, in its sole discretion, to appeal any adverse judgment or order.

6. DUTY OF INSURED CLAIMANT TO COOPERATE (a) In all cases where this policy permits or requires the Company to prosecute or provide for the defense of any action or proceeding and any appeals, the Insured shall secure to the Company the right to so prosecute or provide defense in the action or proceeding, including the right to use, at its option, the name of the Insured for this purpose. Whenever requested by the Company, the Insured, at the Company's expense, shall give the Company all reasonable aid (i) in securing evidence, obtaining witnesses, prosecuting or defending the action or proceeding, or effecting settlement, and (ii) in any other lawful act that in the opinion of the Company may be necessary or desirable to establish the Title or any other matter as insured. If the Company is prejudiced by the failure of the Insured to furnish the required cooperation, the Company's obligations to the Insured under the policy shall terminate . . . .

(b) The Company may reasonably require the Insured Claimant to submit to examination under oath by any authorized representative of the Company and to produce for examination, inspection, and copying, at such reasonable times and places as may be designated by the authorized representative of the Company, all records, in whatever medium maintained, including books, ledgers, checks, memoranda, correspondence, reports, e-mails, disks, tapes, and videos whether bearing a date before or after Date of Policy, that reasonably pertain to the loss or damage. * * * Failure of the Insured Claimant to submit for examination under oath, produce any reasonably requested information, or grant permission to secure reasonably necessary information from third parties as required in this subsection, unless prohibited by law or governmental regulation, shall terminate any liability of the Company under this policy as to that claim.

7. OPTIONS TO PAY OR OTHERWISE SETTLE CLAIMS; TERMINATION OF LIABILITY In case of a claim

under this policy, the Company shall have the following additional options: (a) * * * To pay or tender payment of the Amount of Insurance under this policy together with any costs, attorneys' fees, and expenses incurred by the Insured Claimant that were authorized by the Company up to the time of payment or tender of payment and that the Company is obligated to pay. Upon the exercise by the Company of this option, all liability and obligations of the Company to the Insured under this policy, other than to make the payment required in this subsection, shall terminate, including any liability or obligation to defend, prosecute, or continue any litigation. (b) To Pay or Otherwise Settle With Parties Other Than the Insured or With the Insured Claimant. (i) to pay or otherwise settle with other parties for or in the name of an Insured Claimant any claim insured against under this policy. In addition, the Company will pay any costs, attorneys' fees, and expenses incurred by the Insured Claimant that were authorized by the Company up to the time of payment and that the Company is obligated to pay; or (ii) to pay or otherwise settle with the Insured Claimant the loss or damage provided for under this policy, together with any costs, attorneys' fees, and expenses incurred by the Insured Claimant that were authorized by the Company up to the time of payment and that the Company is obligated to pay. Upon the exercise by the Company of either of the options provided for in subsections (b)(i) or (ii), the Company's obligations to the Insured under this policy for the claimed loss or damage, other than the payments required to be made, shall terminate, including any liability or obligation to defend, prosecute, or continue any litigation.

8. DETERMINATION AND EXTENT OF LIABILITY This policy is a contract of indemnity against actual monetary loss or damage sustained or incurred by the Insured Claimant who has suffered loss or damage by reason of matters insured against by this policy. (a) The extent of liability of the Company for loss or damage under this policy shall not exceed the lesser of (i) the Amount of Insurance; or (ii) the difference between the value of the Title as insured and the value of the Title subject to the risk insured against by this policy. (b) If the Company pursues its rights under Section 5 of these Conditions and is unsuccessful in establishing the Title, as insured, (i) the Amount of Insurance shall be increased by 10%, and (ii) the Insured Claimant shall have the right to have the loss or damage determined either as of the date the claim was made by the Insured Claimant or as of the date it is settled and paid. (c) In addition to the extent of liability under (a) and (b), the Company will also pay those costs, attorneys' fees, and expenses incurred in accordance with Sections 5 and 7 of these Conditions.

9. LIMITATION OF LIABILITY (a) If the Company establishes the Title, or removes the alleged defect, lien, or encumbrance, or cures the lack of a right of access to or from the Land, or cures the claim of Unmarketable Title, all as insured, in a reasonably diligent manner by any method, including litigation and the completion of any appeals, it shall have fully performed its obligations with respect to that matter and shall not be liable for any loss or damage caused to the Insured. (b) In the event of any litigation, including litigation by the Company or with the Company's consent, the Company shall have no liability for loss or damage until there has been a final determination by a court of competent jurisdiction, and disposition of all appeals, adverse to the Title, as insured. (c) The Company shall not be liable for loss or damage to the Insured for liability voluntarily assumed by the Insured in settling any claim or suit without the prior written consent of the Company.

10. REDUCTION OF INSURANCE; REDUCTION OR TERMINATION OF LIABILITY All payments under this policy, except payments made for costs, attorneys' fees, and expenses, shall reduce the Amount of Insurance by the amount of the payment.

11. LIABILITY NONCUMULATIVE The Amount of Insurance shall be reduced by any amount the Company pays under any policy insuring a Mortgage to which exception is taken in Schedule B or to which the Insured has agreed, assumed, or taken subject, or which is executed by an Insured after Date of Policy and which is a charge or lien on the Title, and the amount so paid shall be deemed a payment to the Insured under this policy.

12. PAYMENT OF LOSS When liability and the extent of loss or damage have been definitely fixed in accordance with these Conditions, the payment shall be made within 30 days.

13. RIGHTS OF RECOVERY UPON PAYMENT OR SETTLEMENT (a) Whenever the Company shall have settled and paid a claim under this policy, it shall be subrogated and entitled to the rights of the Insured Claimant in the Title and all other rights and remedies in respect to the claim that the Insured Claimant has against any person or property, to the extent of the amount of any loss, costs, attorneys' fees, and expenses

paid by the Company. * * *

[Here follow Conditions 14-18 on Arbitration, Entire Contract, Severability, Choice of Law, and Notices (Where Sent).]

NOTES

1. Referring to the ALTA title insurance policy, answer the following questions:

   a. What type of protection, if any, does an owner have after transferring title to the land?

   b. Does the policy insure against deeds in the chain of title that were forged or that were not legally delivered?

   c. When an insured discovers a title defect, what must it do to avoid losing its insurance coverage?

   d. Will the insurance company indemnify the insured if the insured is able to settle a title claim quickly and economically?

   e. If the title company has to pay a claim, does it have recourse against anyone?

2. If you are buying property registered under the Torrens system, do you need title insurance? Yes: title insurance still provides coverage against a variety of risks. First, as previously described, numerous statutory exceptions to Torrens coverage exist, such as short-term leases and mineral claims. Second, a time gap exists between the final title search and the recording of the insured's deed or security interest in the land. During this time gap, new encumbrances, such as mechanic's liens, may attach to the title. Title insurance normally insures over this gap. Third, litigation may be necessary to determine the validity and scope of encumbrances memorialized on the certificate of title. In addition to indemnifying the insured for loss caused by a title defect, title insurance policies usually provide that the insurer will pay to defend the title. Finally, title insurance may indemnify the insured against losses caused by errors occurring in the registrar's office. In any event, buyers often have no choice but to buy title insurance. Particularly in anticipation of a sale to the secondary mortgage market, lenders usually require buyers to purchase at least a loan title insurance policy.

3. Title insurance policies commonly provide that when the insurer is required to defend the property title, it will select the attorney. Difficult ethical issues often arise in these cases. Generally, the insured wants the broadest possible interpretation of its protection under the insurance policy, whereas the title insurer wants to minimize the scope of its liability. Despite this potential conflict of interest, a single lawyer often represents both the insured and the insurance company. A lawyer in this situation must ensure that both clients receive adequate representation. If an actual conflict arises, Rule 1.7 of the American Bar Association Model Rules of Professional Conduct requires the attorney to inform the insured of the conflict and to get the insured's informed consent in writing. Depending on the

policy terms, the title insurer may have to pay for the separate counsel, as well as for its own counsel.

4. The Federal Trade Commission Act prohibits title insurance companies from engaging in anticompetitive conduct. However, the Supreme Court has recognized an exception to this rule. In *Federal Trade Commission v. Ticor Title Insurance Co.*, 504 U.S. 621 (1992), the FTC charged six large title insurance companies with horizontal price fixing in their fees for title searches, examinations, and closings through the state-authorized rating bureau process. The title insurance companies argued that the state regulatory review of the proposed rates provided immunity for their actions. The Court ruled that, for a state regulatory scheme to provide antitrust immunity, the state must have articulated a clear and affirmative policy to allow anticompetitive conduct and must actively supervise private parties' anticompetitive conduct.

SWANSON v. SAFECO TITLE INSURANCE CO.
925 P.2d 1354 (Ariz. Ct. App. 1995)

McGREGOR, J.

Safeco Title Insurance Company (Safeco) appeals from the trial court's grant of partial summary judgment in favor of Brent and Darlene Swanson (Swansons). Swansons cross-appealed, alleging that the trial court applied an erroneous measure of damages. Because we find that genuine issues of material fact exist, we conclude that the trial court erred in granting partial summary judgment and, therefore, reverse.

I.

In 1983, Swansons purchased real property located in Maricopa County for $180,000. Swansons partially financed the purchase with a promissory note secured by a deed of trust in favor of the seller. Prior to Swansons' purchase, John Vernon Jenkinson had been named as the beneficiary on a deed of trust involving an easement over part of the property. This deed of trust encumbering the property (the Jenkinson lien) reflected a balance due on a promissory note of $100,000. Apparently, the Jenkinson lien was satisfied before the events giving rise to this action; however, no release of the deed of trust was ever recorded.

When Swansons purchased the property, they obtained title insurance through Safeco. The policy, which insured against any loss or damages resulting from, among other things, "[a]ny defect in or lien or encumbrance on [the] title," did not list the Jenkinson lien as an exception. The policy provided that the amount recoverable by an insured was the lesser of the actual loss to the insured or the amount of the policy.

In 1987, Swansons attempted to refinance the loan on the property through Erisa Mortgage Corporation (Erisa). Erisa submitted Swansons' loan application to a lender, Union National Bank of Colorado, and recommended approval of the loan. As part of the refinancing process, Guardian Title prepared a title report, which showed that Swansons did not have clear title to the property because of the Jenkinson lien. Swansons allegedly notified Safeco of the defect in the title, which Swansons claimed placed the refinancing in jeopardy.

While the refinancing transaction was pending and Guardian Title was attempting to obtain Jenkinson's consent to remove the cloud from the title, Swansons received a notice of a trustee's sale. In December 1987, the trustee conducted a sale, and title to the property was conveyed to the original seller as the highest bidder.

Swansons brought this action for damages against Safeco, alleging that, because of the cloud on the title, they were unable to obtain refinancing and therefore lost the property through foreclosure. Swansons moved for partial summary judgment on the issue of liability. The trial court determined as a matter of law that Safeco was liable for Swansons' loss and granted the motion.

At trial on the issue of damages, the trial court determined that, because the equity measure of damages was greater than the out-of-pocket loss to Swansons, Swansons were entitled to the equity measure of damages. The trial court calculated Swansons' loss as the fair market value ($140,000) less encumbrances ($108,649.52), for a total loss of $31,350.48. Safeco filed this appeal, challenging the trial court's grant of summary judgment on the issue of liability. Swansons cross-appealed, challenging the trial court's measure of damages. * * *

II.

A.

To grant a motion for summary judgment, the trial court must find that no genuine issue of material fact exists in the record and that the moving party is entitled to judgment on the merits as a matter of law. In reviewing a trial court's ruling on a motion for summary judgment, we view the facts in a light most favorable to the party opposing the judgment. We must reverse a trial court's grant of summary judgment if our review reveals that reasonable inferences about material facts could be resolved in favor of the party opposing the judgment. *United Bank v. Allyn*, 805 P.2d 1012, 1016 (Ariz. App. 1990).

Safeco argues that the evidence before the trial court raised material issues of fact as to Safeco's liability, and thus, summary judgment was inappropriate. We agree that reasonable inferences about material facts could be resolved in Safeco's favor. [The court first found that it could not conclude, based on a dispute as to whether a notice of claim was sent to the insurer — the insured claimed it was mailed by the insurer's title agent, the insurer claimed never to have received it — stating: "Because the policy limits Safeco's liability to those situations in which it receives notice, whether Safeco had notice of the claim is a material fact. Drawing all reasonable inferences in favor of Safeco as the nonmoving party, we cannot conclude as a matter of law that Safeco received adequate notice."]

We consider next whether Swansons established, as a matter of law, that they sustained an actual loss as a result of the Jenkinson lien. The title insurance policy excludes liability if no loss existed. . . . In granting summary judgment, the trial court apparently separated the issue of liability from the issue of damages. However, the clear terms of the policy do not permit liability without damages.

Nothing in the record at the time of summary judgment indicates whether the court determined that any damages resulted from the Jenkinson lien, and the record before us reveals a material factual dispute between the parties concerning whether the Jenkinson lien caused any of the damage for which Swansons seek recovery. Material issues of fact thus preclude the conclusion that Safeco was liable as a matter of law. . . . Therefore, the trial court erred in granting partial summary judgment on the issue of Safeco's liability. * * *

B.

On cross-appeal, Swansons argue that the trial court erred in determining the measure of damages. Although we reverse the trial court's grant of summary judgment, in the interest of judicial economy, we address the measure of damages to apply in the event Swansons prevail. Swansons argue that they are entitled to the greater of the equity measure of damages or their "out-of-pocket" loss. They assert that the trial court erred in determining that the equity measure of damages was greater. Safeco argues that the evidence supported the trial court's findings and that the equity measure of damages — the fair market value less encumbrances — was proper. We do not believe that either measure correctly reflects damages, if any, as contemplated by the policy.

The title insurance policy states that Safeco's liability shall not exceed the least of "the actual loss of the insured claimant" or "the amount of insurance stated in Schedule A [$180,000]. . . ." However, nothing in the policy defines the method for calculating "actual loss."

Whether the terms of an insurance policy are ambiguous is a question of law for the court to decide. *Thomas v. Liberty Mut. Ins. Co.*, 842 P.2d 1335, 1337 (Ariz. App. 1992). Any ambiguities are subject to a construction most favorable to the insured. *Id.* at 1338. We agree that the term "actual loss" is ambiguous, and if Swansons have suffered damages for which Safeco is liable, an interpretation of the term "actual loss" most favorable to Swansons is appropriate.

We know of no cases in Arizona that have interpreted the phrase "actual loss" in a title insurance policy. However, we find opinions from other jurisdictions instructive.

The measure of an insured's loss due to a title encumbrance ordinarily is the insured's expenses incurred to remove the encumbrance. *Miebach v. Safe Title Ins. Co.*, 743 P.2d 845, 847 (Wash. App. 1987). However, this measure of damages proves unsatisfactory when the encumbrance either is not or cannot be removed. In that case, the insured's damage does not result from the cost to remove the cloud on the title; rather, any damage results from the existence of the cloud itself. *Overholtzer v. Northern Counties Title Ins. Co.*, 253 P.2d 116, 122 (Cal. Ct. App. 1953). "If that cloud impairs the market value of the land, the [insureds] are entitled to whatever damages resulted from that cloud." *Id.* Title insurance does not guarantee perfect title; instead, it pays damages, if any, caused by any defects to title that the title company should have discovered but did not. In this respect, title insurance is comparable to other types of insurance: for example, fire insurance does not guarantee that a homeowner will not have a fire, only that if a fire occurs, he can recover for damages, if any, that the fire caused.

We believe that the rule announced in *Overholtzer*, and followed by other jurisdictions, provides the proper measure of damage. In *Overholtzer*, the court held that the measure of damages was the depreciation in market value caused by the existence of the title defect. *Id.* at 124. In other words, the insured's loss, if any, is the difference between the fair market value of the property if no impairment existed and the fair market value of the property with the impairment. . . .

Here, Swansons argue that the Jenkinson lien prevented Swansons from refinancing the property and, thus, caused a loss. However, Swansons' ability to refinance their loan is not an issue in measuring damages. Rather, Swansons' loss, if any, resulted from the existence of the Jenkinson lien. If that lien diminished the fair market value of the property, then Swansons are entitled to the difference between the fair market value of the property without the lien and the fair market value with the lien.[4]

Having defined the appropriate measure of damages, the next issue we consider is the proper date for the trial court to use in determining the value of the property. Other jurisdictions are not in agreement as to the date for valuation. Some use the date of purchase, some use the date of a bona fide contract of sale by the insured, and some use the date the title defect was discovered. We believe this last option is the most appropriate.

> It seems quite apparent to us that liability should be measured by diminution in the value of the property caused by the defect in the title as of the date of the discovery of the defect, measured by the use to which the property is then devoted. When a purchaser buys property and buys title insurance, he is buying protection against defects in title to the property. He is trying to protect himself then and for the future against loss if the title is defective. The policy necessarily looks to the future. . . . The insured, when he purchases the policy, does not then know that the title is defective. But later, after he has improved the property, he discovers the defect. Obviously, up to the face amount of the policy, he should be reimbursed for the loss he suffered in reliance on the policy, and that includes the diminution in value of the property as it then exists, in this case with improvements. Any other rule would not give the insured the protection for which he bargained and for which he paid.

Overholtzer, 253 P.2d at 125; . . . *L. Smirlock Realty Corp. v. Title Guar. Co.*, 469 N.Y.S.2d 415, 427 (N.Y. App. Div. 1983) (noting majority of jurisdictions use date of

---

[4] Swansons have cited no case law to support their theory of measuring damages by "out-of-pocket" loss; neither party cites to any case other than *Miebach* to support the theory of measuring damages as the fair market value minus encumbrances, nor does either party cite any authority to support the proposition that the court should compare these two measures and award the greater amount. We decline to adopt a rule that would measure damages under title insurance differently in every case, comparing the "out-of-pocket" losses and the "loss of equity." As evidenced by the parties' arguments, these terms can be as ambiguous as the term "actual loss." Moreover, to provide a different measure of damages in every case might cause inconsistent results. Furthermore, the insured may be awarded damages that were not foreseeable to the insurer or contemplated by the parties at the time the policy was issued, such as lost profits and consequential damages.

defect discovery to measure loss). Here, Swansons discovered the defect in July 1987. Therefore, the difference in the market value of the property with and without the Jenkinson lien as of that date is the appropriate measure of damages. . . .

III.

Based on the foregoing, we reverse the trial court's grant of summary judgment. . . .

NOTES

1. If the plaintiffs prevail in the case on remand, how much will they recover? An insurance company's liability on an owner's policy is limited to the amount specified in Schedule A of the policy, which typically is the property's purchase price. Therefore, if the owner improves land after acquiring it or if the land otherwise increases in value, the policy amount may be inadequate to compensate the owner in full for a loss of title. The insured can increase the amount of coverage after the land's value has increased by paying an additional premium. How does the policy reprinted previously handle this problem?

In contrast, coverage under the loan policy normally decreases over time. The most that the insured lender can recover is the unpaid principal balance of the loan, which usually decreases over the life of the loan. As with the owners in *Swanson*, the lender can recover from the insurance company only if it can show that it has suffered an actual loss. Therefore, the lender cannot collect for a title defect if the land's value still exceeds the outstanding debt or if the borrower has not defaulted in its payments to the lender.

2. If the plaintiffs in *Swanson* cannot recover based on their title insurance policy, do they have a cause of action in tort against the insurance company? The courts in only about half the states have decided the issue of whether a title insurance company or its agent can be liable for negligence in examining a title or failing to disclose a title defect or encumbrance. Of those states, a slight majority have held that, unless the insurer has voluntarily assumed a duty to conduct a reasonable search, the insurer or its agent is not liable just because it issued plaintiff a policy. See *In re Evans*, 460 B.R. 848 (Bankr. S.D. Miss. 2011); *Greenberg v. Stewart Title Guaranty Co.*, 492 N.W.2d 147 (Wis. 1992) (both cases citing leading majority and minority rule cases). The minority rule holds a company liable in negligence, as well as contract, for failing to discover and disclose a defect: "The underlying notion [of these opinions] is that the insured has the reasonable expectation that the title company will search the title." See *Walker Rogge, Inc. v. Chelsea Title & Guar. Co.*, 562 A.2d 208, 218 (N.J. 1989).

Although an insured may expect that the insurer will conduct a title search, the insurer is not an abstractor; it presents the results of any search in the title insurance commitment or report, not as the result of a separate service, but as an offer to issue a policy reflecting the title as reported. See *Lawrence v. Chicago Title Ins. Co.*, 237 Cal. Rptr. 264 (Cal. App. 1987). The final relationship between insurer and insured is primarily a matter of contract: the insured pays a premium and receives a policy. That policy is an indemnity contract, not a guarantee or warranty of title. See *Blackhawk Prod. v. Chicago Title Ins.Co.*, 423 N.W.2d 521 (Wis. 1988). A number of state legislatures have enacted statutes requiring title insurers to examine the title before issuing an insurance policy; some of these statutes also provide that the insurer's title examination report does not constitute a representation concerning the state of title. See, e.g., Ariz. Rev. Stat. Ann. § 20-1562 ("The [preliminary title] report is not a representation as to the condition of title to real property."); Cal. Ins. Code § 12340.11 (same). However, other state statutes expressly require title insurers to disclose all known title defects and encumbrances. See, e.g., Fla. Rev. Stat. § 627.784 ("A title insurance policy or guarantee of title may not be issued without regard to the possible existence of adverse matters or defects of title."); Haw. Rev. Stat. § 431:20-113 ("[N]o title insurer shall knowingly issue any title insurance policy or commitment to insure without showing all outstanding, enforceable recorded liens or other interests against the property title to which is to be insured.").

3. In jurisdictions that impose tort liability for a negligent title examination or failure to disclose a title defect or encumbrance, title insurers attempt to avoid liability by including exculpatory clauses in their policies. However, the majority of courts view such clauses with disfavor. For instance, in *Bank of California, N.A. v. First American Title Ins. Co.*, 826 P.2d 1126 (Alaska 1992), the Alaska Supreme Court held an exculpatory clause to be invalid: "A title company is engaged in a business affected with the public interest and cannot, by an adhesory contract, exculpate itself from liability for negligence." (quoting *White v. Western Title Ins. Co.*, 710 P.2d 309, 315 (Cal. 1985)). See also *Municipality of Anchorage v. Locker*, 723 P.2d 1261 (Alaska 1986), in which the court held that exculpatory clauses are unconscionable where "circumstances indicate a vast disparity of bargaining power coupled with terms unreasonably favorable to the stronger party." Why would an insured want to bring a tort cause of action, rather than simply bring a contract action based on the insurance policy?

IX. CLOSINGS AND ESCROWS

The "closing" (or "settlement") is when the seller and buyer consummate the contract of sale. If the contract provides that the parties will enter into an installment land sale contract, the seller and buyer will execute it at the closing. If the contract of sale provides that the seller will convey title to the buyer at the closing, the seller will execute a deed, and the buyer will pay the purchase price in cash, or, more typically, by executing a note and mortgage.

The time and place for the closing usually are specified in the contract of sale. The closing may be held any place that is convenient for the various parties to the transaction, such as in the offices of the lender's lawyer, the title insurance agency, the listing broker, or a commercial closing agency. When the seller and buyer are both present at the closing, it is known as a "table" closing, because the parties sit at the same table to execute the closing documents and to take the other actions necessary to close the sale.

The person conducting the closing (the "closing agent" or "settlement agent") normally has duties to perform before, during, and after the closing. The agent's pre-closing duties include gathering information, such as the amount necessary to pay off any mortgages that must be eliminated from the title. The closing agent also may be responsible for preparing the closing documents and arranging for a variety of services, such as a title examination and title insurance. At the closing, the closing agent ensures that the parties properly execute the necessary documents and collects the purchase price from the buyer. After the closing, the closing agent usually arranges for the deed and other documents to be recorded and disburses the funds for the various expenses of the closing, such as the title insurance premium and any loan payoffs.

mike drop cox

FERGUSON v. CASPAR
359 A.2d 17 (D.C. 1974)

Perfect Tender Rule: honor contract knowing it's already breached, then sue after closing.

REILLY, J.

One of the most formal transactions known to the law is the transfer of title to real estate. In order to insure finality to such transactions, the practice in this jurisdiction is for the contracting parties, including the lienors and lienees, after they are satisfied with the report on title search, to meet with one another in the office of a title company, agree on the apportionment of outstanding taxes and other charges, and execute and deliver the conveyances (deeds) necessary to close the transaction. Such a meeting, popularly called a "closing" or a "settlement", precedes the transmission by the title company of the conveyancing instruments to the Recorder of Deeds for permanent entry into the official land records.

Although hundreds of such settlements occur every year in the District of Columbia, it is seldom indeed that the parties conduct themselves in such a way as to taint the finality of the "closing." The case before us stems from one of these uncommon situations and raises the question as to what point in a settlement proceeding finality attaches.

This is an appeal from a judgment and order of the trial court dismissing an amended complaint and granting judgment in favor of the appellees after trial by the court without a jury in an action brought by the contracting purchasers — appellants — for a declaratory judgment and for specific performance of a contract for the sale of real property in this city. To bring the issues in this controversy into perspective, a brief resume of the salient facts is in order.

Appellee Mrs. Ida Caspar was the owner of an unrestored row house in the Capitol Hill area. On November 18, 1972, she entered into a contract for the sale of the premises to the appellants for the sum of $23,000.00 payment of the purchase price to be made in cash at the time of settlement. Settlement was to be made at the office of the Lawyers Title Insurance Corporation on or before February 1, 1973. The contract of sale included a provision that the seller would convey the premises free of all notices of municipal violations existing at the date of the contract, such provision to survive the delivery of the deed.[2] On October 13, 1972, Mrs. Caspar had

---

[2] The printed clause in the contract provided: "All notices of violations of Municipal orders or requirements noted or issued by any department of the District of Columbia, or prosecutions in any of the courts of the District of Columbia on account thereof against or affecting the property at the date of this contract shall be complied with by the seller and the property conveyed free thereof. This

been personally served with a deficiency notice by a District of Columbia housing inspector informing her that there existed 126 Housing Code violations upon the premises and calling for their correction within 60 days. Subsequently, Mrs. Caspar, upon her written request, obtained an extension of time for compliance to January 25, 1973.

Early in January, 1973, the appellants became aware of the existence of the Housing Code violations but did not bring this matter to the attention of the seller. Instead, they obtained an estimate of $6,125.00 from a housing contractor as the cost of correcting the deficiencies. The notice of violations was still outstanding at the time of settlement.

By agreement, the parties met at the office of the Lawyers Title Insurance Corporation for settlement on the afternoon of February 1, 1973. Mrs. Caspar was attended by her son and daughter who assisted their mother in business matters. The appellants were present with their attorney. The settlement officer, an employee of the title company, prepared settlement statements for the respective parties which each of them signed. In addition, the parties signed the requisite District of Columbia tax recordation forms. Mrs. Caspar executed and delivered her deed to the property to the settlement officer. The purchasers delivered to the settlement officer the personal check of Mr. Ferguson in the sum of $12,924.42 payable to the order of the title company, representing the balance due as set forth in the settlement statement.[6]

After the documents had been delivered to the settlement officer and as the parties were rising to leave, the attorney for the appellants handed separate letters to the settlement officer and to Mrs. Caspar's son. The letter addressed to the title company, after referring to the clause in the contract of sale requiring Mrs. Caspar to convey the premises free of any municipal violation notices, advised the title company that as of January 26, 1973, the outstanding Housing Code violations had not been corrected and that the purchasers had obtained an estimate in the amount of $6,125.00 to bring the premises into compliance. The letter concluded by stating:

> This is to put you on notice that purchasers are paying $6,125.00 of the purchase price to you as escrow agent to hold until seller has complied with the outstanding violation notices on this property. Written notice signed by the purchaser shall be sufficient to discharge you from any further obligations with respect to this sum.

The letter directed to Mrs. Caspar informed her of the existence of the notice of the Housing Code violations and her obligation under the agreement to comply with the notice. It went on to state that the Fergusons had obtained an estimate of approximately $6,125.00 as the cost of repairing the premises and concluded as follows:

> This is to advise you that Fergusons intend to enforce the requirement that these violations be corrected. Accordingly, I have written Lawyers Title

provision shall survive the delivery of the deed hereunder."

[6] Appellants had previously deposited $1000.00 with the real estate broker and had a credit of $9,387.67 with the title company from refinancing their former residence. Tax adjustments and closing costs brought the balance due from them to $12,924.42.

requesting that they withhold the above amount from the purchase price in an escrow account until you and the Fergusons have reached a final understanding as to the cost of making these corrections.

Upon receiving the letter directed to the title company, the settlement officer advised the parties that the company could not record the deed or withhold any funds without formal authority to hold any funds in escrow. He informed the parties that he could not proceed with the settlement since the contract of sale provided for payment in cash and there was no provision for withholding any funds in escrow. Mrs. Caspar's son suggested that the parties complete the settlement, have the deed recorded, and thereafter "work out or litigate" the question of the Housing Code violations. The attorney for the appellants recommended that Mrs. Caspar seek the advice of an attorney. The parties then dispersed without the matter being resolved.

On February 13, 1973, not having received any further word or instructions from the parties, the settlement officer wrote to the Fergusons, returning the personal check which had been presented at the settlement and informing them that the deed could not be recorded in view of their attorney's letter directing the title company to withhold certain monies in escrow. Two days later, the Fergusons' attorney replied, returning the personal check to the settlement officer and insisting that the deed be recorded. This letter was received by the title company on February 16 and on the same day, the deed executed by Mrs. Caspar was returned to her son. On February 17, Mrs. Caspar signed a contract of sale for the premises to the appellees, John and Mary McAteer, and her deed to them was executed and recorded on February 23.

On February 21, 1973, appellants filed a complaint against Mrs. Caspar seeking a declaratory judgment and specific performance of the contract of sale entered into between the parties. Subsequently, the complaint was amended to include the McAteers as parties defendant. In her answer to the amended complaint, Mrs. Caspar alleged *inter alia* that the appellants had breached the contract of sale and were not entitled to specific performance. The case was tried before the court without a jury. At the close of all the evidence, the court granted appellees' motion to dismiss the complaint on the ground that the plaintiffs, by imposing conditions on their tender of payment of the purchase price, had failed to make an unconditional tender of full performance of the contract on their part and had forfeited their right to specific performance. On June 15, 1973, the trial court entered its Judgment and Order of Dismissal setting forth its Findings of Fact and Conclusions of Law.

On this appeal, appellants' principal contentions are that legal title to the property in question passed to them upon the settlement between the seller and purchasers and that the trial court erred in concluding that the appellants were not entitled to specific performance of the contract of sale by reason of their failure to tender the full purchase price for the property as required by the contract. We agree with the determination of the trial court and affirm.

The initial contention of appellants is based upon the erroneous conclusion that legal title to the property in question passed to them when the settlement statements were signed by the respective parties, the seller's deed delivered to the settlement officer, and the personal check of the purchasers for the balance due delivered to the settlement officer. In this conclusion, appellants misconstrue the nature and effect of the settlement proceedings engaged in between the various parties at the meeting. In their briefs on appeal, the appellants and appellees both infer that under the circumstances of this case the title company's position in the transaction was that of an escrow agent. Our study of the contract of sale and the proceedings which ensued at the settlement meeting confirms our understanding that, as is the usual and customary practice in real estate transactions in the District of Columbia where the parties employ a third party to accept their respective tenders of performance under the contract, a valid escrow arrangement is created and the title company serves in the capacity of an escrow agent in the transaction.

Generally, an escrow agreement is created in a formal contract between the parties, setting forth the conditions and contingencies under which the instruments deposited in escrow are to be delivered and to take effect. However, no precise form of words is necessary to create an escrow but it must appear from all the facts and circumstances surrounding the execution and delivery of the instruments that they were not to take effect until certain conditions are performed.

A valid escrow agreement is a triangular arrangement. First there must be a contract between the seller and the buyer agreeing to the conditions of a deposit, then there must be delivery of the items on deposit to the escrow agent, and he must agree to perform the function of receiving and dispersing the items. The agreement by the seller and buyer to all the terms of the escrow instructions and the acceptance by the escrow agent of the position of depository create the escrow.

In the case at bar, the seller and the purchasers agreed to make full settlement in accordance with the terms of the contract of sale at the office of Lawyers Title Insurance Corporation, the title company searching the title, and that "deposit with the Title Company . . . of the purchase money, the deed of conveyance for execution and such other papers as are required of either party by the terms of this contract shall be considered good and sufficient tender of performance of the terms hereof." Significantly, the deed executed by the seller was delivered to the settlement officer. The purchasers' personal check, which included the balance of the purchase price, was made payable to the title company and delivered to the settlement officer. The deed was deposited with the settlement officer as an escrow agent with the implied understanding that delivery to the purchasers was not to be effected until the purchasers had complied with their obligation under the contract of sale to pay the amount due the seller as purchase money. On the other hand, the settlement officer was not free to disburse any of the funds deposited by the purchasers until the title company was assured that the seller's deed conveyed title "good of record and in fact". Thus, the settlement meeting was only the initial step in the transaction and until all the conditions of the contract had been fulfilled, the settlement was not complete.[9] Where a deed is deposited as an escrow, title does not pass to the grantee

---

[9] The customary practice in settlements of this nature is for the title company to deposit the purchaser's check to assure that the check is honored. After the check clears and before recording the deed, the title company brings the title down to date by making a continuation title search from the date of its initial search to the date of recordation of the deed to assure that no liens or encumbrances have been filed against the property in the interim.

unless and until the condition of its delivery is performed. Although the purchasers tendered their personal check for the balance due from them at the settlement in ostensible payment of the purchase price, their subsequent direction to the title company to withhold from the seller a substantial portion of the purchase money to which she was entitled created a deviation from the condition upon which delivery of the deed to them could be effected. The settlement officer informed the purchasers that the settlement could not be completed and the deed could not be recorded. Since the condition precedent to the delivery of the deed had not been fulfilled, legal title to the property did not pass to the purchasers.

Appellants point to the fact that settlement statements were signed by the respective parties as indicative that settlement between the parties had been completed. Each of these statements was a separate and distinct document, one being the seller's statement establishing the "AMOUNT TO BE PAID SELLER" and the other, the purchasers' statement indicating the "BALANCE REQUIRED TO COMPLETE SETTLEMENT." The seller's statement contained an itemization of charges to be borne by the seller, including a charge for the apportionment of unpaid taxes, the brokerage fee to be paid to the real estate broker, disbursements to be paid to the broker for the costs of evicting the tenants, one-half of the recordation tax, and a charge of $50 to be held for water charges. These charges and anticipated disbursements were applied against the purchase price of the property and a balance struck, establishing the net amount which would be paid to the seller by the title company as the proceeds of the sale after the disbursements had been made and the settlement completed. The seller's signature on the statement noted her approval and acceptance of the statement as correct.

The purchasers' statement itemized the credits to their account, consisting of a credit for apportionment of unpaid taxes, the amount deposited with the broker as earnest money, and a credit to the purchasers of the sum to be received by the title company as the proceeds of the refinancing of other property owned by the purchasers. Against these credits, the purchasers were charged with the purchase price of the property and miscellaneous closing costs to be paid by them, including examination of title, title insurance, settlement fee, conveyancing fees, recording fees, and their share of the recordation tax. Off-setting the credits against the charges established a balance to be paid by the purchasers to the title company at settlement.

We do not attribute to these documents the significance which appellants attach to them. In effect, the seller's statement merely indicated what the seller would receive as the net proceeds of the sale after the settlement had been fully completed. The purchasers' statement was a statement of account of what remained to be paid by the purchasers to the title company, including the closing costs to be paid to the title company, after crediting the purchasers for the earnest money paid to the real estate broker and the sum anticipated to be received from the refinancing settlement. The incidental charges set forth on each statement were the concern solely of the party charged. Neither party bound himself to the settlement statement of the other. Neither statement constituted an acknowledgment that either the seller or the title company had received the purchase money which the purchasers were obligated to pay. The individual settlement statements were in effect an account stated separately between the title company and the seller and between the title company and the purchasers. Thus we reject the contention that the signing of the individual settlement statements by each of the parties signified that the transaction had been completed.

The appellants, contending that the settlement proceeding was completed, argue further that when the legal title to the premises passed to them the title to the purchase money vested in the seller and the subsequent demand by the purchasers that the title company withhold a portion of the sellers' money was a "legal nullity" and "obviously unenforceable." In an escrow arrangement, the escrow holder is the dual agent of both parties until the performance of the conditions of the escrow agreement, whereupon he becomes the agent of each of the parties to the transaction in respect to those things placed in escrow to which each party has thus become entitled. Thus, when the conditions specified in the escrow agreement have been fully performed, the title to the premises passes to the purchaser and title to the purchase money passes to the seller. Thereupon, the escrow holder becomes the agent of the purchaser as to the deed and of the seller as to the money. However, as we have pointed out *supra*, the settlement was not completed and since the conditions upon which the seller's deed was to be delivered to the purchasers had not been performed, legal title to the property did not pass to the purchasers and title to the purchase money deposited with the settlement officer did not vest in the seller.

Furthermore, we find it difficult to comprehend appellants' present contention that their written demand upon the title company was a "legal nullity" in view of their contrary position at the settlement meeting. Upon receipt of the written demand from appellants' attorney, the settlement officer notified the parties that under the circumstances he could not proceed with the settlement. At the same time, Mrs. Caspar's son suggested that the appellants permit the settlement to proceed and that thereafter the parties "work out" the question of the Housing Code violations. Nevertheless, the appellants persisted in their demand that a portion of the purchase money be retained in escrow by the title company. The impasse was not resolved and the meeting broke up. By making the demand upon the title company, appellants placed the company in the difficult position of having to determine the rights of the respective parties. If the company honored appellants' demand, the seller could complain that the company had breached its duty to her. If the company refused to comply with the demand, the appellants would charge the title company with having disbursed the purchase money contrary to their express direction. In either event, the title company would have risked being subject to legal action by the party aggrieved. After waiting a reasonable period for the parties to adjust their differences and not having received any further word from either of them, the title company terminated its escrow agency and returned the escrow instruments to the respective parties. This turn of events was brought about by appellants' actions in serving the demand upon the title company and in persisting in their position. They cannot escape the consequences of their action by now claiming that their demand was a "nullity."

There is no dispute that a substantial number of violations of Housing Code regulations were duly noted against the premises and were in existence at the time the contract of sale was executed. Nor is there any dispute that Mrs. Caspar, as record owner of the property, was officially notified of the violations. Prior to the time for settlement, none of these violations had been corrected. Under these circumstances, the purchasers could have refused to consummate settlement and then have brought an action at law against the seller for such damages as they may have sustained. Alternatively, the purchasers could have elected to complete the settlement, and under the survival provisions of the contract, could have sued to recover from the seller such damages as they may have sustained by reason of her failure to correct the outstanding violations. The appellants here made no effort to rescind the contract but instead gave every indication of their intention to go forward with the transaction. Thus, despite the breach of the contract by the seller, the purchasers elected to proceed with the contract and obligated themselves to continue their performance of its terms.

To sustain the right to specific performance of their contract, the purchasers must show that they have performed or have offered to perform all of the obligations required of them by the contract.

> It is the fundamental doctrine upon which the specific enforcement of contracts in equity depends, that either of the parties seeking to obtain the equitable remedy against the other must, as a condition precedent to the existence of his remedial right, show that he has done or offered to do, or is then ready and willing to do, all the essential and material acts required of him by the agreement at the time of commencing the suit, and also that he is ready and willing to do all such acts as shall be required of him in the specific execution of the contract according to its terms. [J.N. Pomeroy, Specific Performance of Contracts § 322 (3d ed. 1926)].

Thus, where the purchaser under a contract for the sale of property instructed the escrow agent to hold the purchase money deposited with it until further notice and not to pay out any money to the seller, it was held that the purchaser had failed to perform his obligation under the contract to pay the purchase price to the seller and hence was not entitled to specific performance. And where an escrow contract required the purchaser to deposit a specific sum for the account of the vendor, a deposit of such sum with conditions that it could not and would not be paid to the seller did not constitute compliance with . . . the contract. Similarly, where the purchase money was paid into escrow by the purchaser with instructions not agreed to by the seller, and which instructions went beyond reasonable requirements for securing the concurrent exchange of the deed for the purchase price, it was held that there was not a sufficient tender of performance on the part of the purchaser. A tender of performance by the purchaser which contains conditions other than those specified in the contract between the parties is ineffectual, and a tender of payment by the purchaser is ineffective where the purchaser has made arbitrary deductions therefrom for unliquidated claims against the seller.

In the case at bar, the trial court concluded that the appellants "were not ready or willing to perform in accordance with the terms of the agreement" and that their "effort to impose conditions other than those specified in the contract resulted in a breach of their contractual duty, and a forfeiture of their right to specific performance of the contract." Appellants dispute this conclusion, pointing to the delivery of their personal check in the amount found to be due in accordance with the settlement sheet signed by them as proof that they were in fact ready and willing to perform their obligations under the contract. However, the evidence of record belies their contention. Appellants appeared at the settlement meeting armed with the letter demanding that a substantial portion of the purchase money be withheld from the seller. This was not a happenstance — a subsequently-formed decision — but a preconceived plan by them to compel the seller to accept a lesser sum in payment for the property. The delivery of their check in ostensible payment of the amount due was a mere pretense since appellants never intended to have the seller receive the full amount due her upon settlement. The conclusion that appellants were not ready or willing to perform their obligation under the contract to pay the purchase price in cash is adequately supported by the record. By their own conduct, the appellants precluded their right to obtain specific performance of the contract. Affirmed.

NOTES

1. The court in *Ferguson* states the usual rule of law that title to the land passes to the buyer (i.e., the sale is closed) when the last condition of the sale is satisfied. Normally, this rule means that the buyer acquires title when the seller has delivered the deed and the buyer has paid the purchase price. See, e.g., *Sturgill v. Industrial Painting Corp.*, 410 P.2d 759 (Nev. 1966). However, when buyers and sellers have express escrow instructions, they often specify that title will transfer to the buyer when the documents are recorded. See Oscar Beasley, *Escrows and Closings*, 423 PLI/Real 27 (1997). What are the consequences of this difference? The time of closing is critical, for example, when the seller and buyer stipulated in the contract of sale that the seller bears the risk of loss until closing. The difference also is significant in determining whether liens against the seller attach to the property title. After title has transferred to the buyer, subsequent claims against the seller cannot affect the land.

2. The *Ferguson* opinion mentions many of the costs involved in the sale of land, including the fees for the real estate agent, lender, title insurer, and settlement agent. In the late 1960s and early 1970s, consumers and legislators expressed significant concerns about the excessive costs associated with real estate closings. Lack of consumer knowledge and collusive conduct by closing service providers were identified as two chief reasons for the excessiveness of costs. Thus in 1974 Congress enacted the Real Estate Settlement Procedures Act (RESPA), 12 U.S.C § 2601–2617, which is designed to protect buyers and sellers against certain misconduct in the settlement industry. However, rather than attempt to regulate the amount that service providers can charge or the services they provide, Congress' approach in RESPA is to educate consumers about the different settlement services and about consumers' ability to shop for services based on cost and quality.

RESPA attempts to assist consumers in three key ways. First, it requires lending institutions to give loan applicants an information booklet about settlement costs that was prepared by the Consumer Financial Protection Bureau (CFPB). The booklet explains the different closing costs and the borrower's possible right to choose service providers. The lender also must give loan applicants a written "good faith estimate" of the anticipated closing costs. Although Congress intended the information booklet and the good faith estimate to prompt prospective borrowers to shop around for settlement services, it is questionable whether they have had this effect. They can be rather confusing and overwhelming to buyers, and, many buyers still rely heavily on their real estate agents and other real estate professionals to tell them what to do. As a result, borrowers are often steered to service providers whose economic incentive is to avoid jeopardizing the transaction rather than to provide the borrower with the best service. In an attempt to make the loan disclosures more comprehensible to buyers, the CFPB has promulgated a new "Loan Estimate" document that lenders must give prospective borrowers, beginning on August 1, 2015, in lieu of the current good faith estimate document.

A second component of RESPA has had a more significant impact in reducing the cost of closing services. RESPA expressly prohibits kickbacks and unearned fees between service providers. Section 8 of RESPA provides:

> No person shall give and no person shall accept any fee, kickback, or thing of value pursuant to any agreement or understanding, oral or otherwise, that business incident to or a part of a real estate settlement service involving a federally related mortgage loan shall be referred to any person.

Therefore, a lender, title insurer, or lawyer cannot pay a real estate agent a referral fee for sending a buyer to him or her. Such payments were common before RESPA and obviously inflated the cost of closing services.

Finally, RESPA requires closing agents to use a standard form to set forth the seller's and buyer's closing costs for residential loan closings. The form attempts to disclose as clearly as possible how much the seller and buyer are being charged for each service. Because the seller and buyer normally do not receive the form until the closing, after most of the services already have been provided, the form's educational value is limited, though it may prevent charges from being buried in the closing statement. The CFPB has promulgated a new "Closing Disclosure" document that will replace the current form on August 1, 2015. For a comprehensive discussion of RESPA, see Sheldon E. Hochberg, *What Every Real Estate Lawyer Should Know About RESPA*, 397 PLI/Real 435 (1993).

3.   The court in *Ferguson* invoked the so-called "perfect tender rule." Pursuant to that rule, a party to a contract of sale for land does not have a cause of action for breach unless she tenders her own performance at the time and place specified for the closing. The seller's obligation to tender title to the land and the buyer's obligation to tender the purchase price are treated as concurrent conditions.

The *Ferguson* case involved a table closing, because the buyers and seller were present at the closing. In some parts of the country, particularly in the mountain west, the West Coast, and Texas, real estate sales normally are closed by an "escrow closing," rather than by a table closing. In an escrow closing, the seller and buyer do not meet at a specified time and place to close the sale. Instead, before the contractually specified closing date, they separately deliver to a neutral third party (the "escrow agent") executed documents, money, and other items needed to close the sale, such as the seller's proof of title. The seller and buyer also deliver to the escrow agent a set of escrow instructions. Most importantly, the escrow instructions specify when the escrow agent should deliver the purchase price to the seller and deliver the deed to the buyer or to the county recorder's office for recording. The escrow agent also typically performs the usual functions of a closing agent, such as disbursing funds to pay off mortgages on the property and to pay the title insurance company and other service providers. Most states require escrow agents to be licensed.

Although an escrow closing can add a significant cost to a land sale, it offers several advantages. For example, the buyer and seller do not have to be present at the closing, which is desirable when the buyer and seller live a substantial distance apart or when they otherwise do not want to meet face to face. Another advantage of an escrow closing is the "relation back" feature; the escrow agent's delivery of the deed to the grantee is deemed to relate back to the date when the grantor placed the deed in escrow. This feature is advantageous when the grantor has died or been deemed incompetent while the deed was in escrow. Finally and perhaps most importantly, an escrow closing can eliminate the risk to the buyer caused by the gap between the time of the title search and the closing. Before delivering the purchase price to the seller, the escrow agent can update the title examination to ensure than no new adverse conveyances were recorded during the gap. If an adverse conveyance has been recorded, the escrow agent will not deliver the purchase price to the seller.

As a depository for the funds and documents necessary for the sale, an escrow agent is a fiduciary for the buyer and the seller. In that capacity, the escrow agent is liable to them for negligence and for breach of instructions. If the escrow agent absconds with the funds, does the buyer or the seller bear the risk of loss? See generally Robert Flores, *A Comparison of the Rules and Rationales for Allocating Risks Arising in Realty Sales Using Executory Sales Contracts and Escrows*, 59 Mo. L. Rev. 307 (1994).

embezzlement case [handwritten]

LECHNER v. HALLING
216 P.2d 179 (Wash. 1950)

while conditions are pending, escrow agent is the agent of the buyer. After all conditions are fulfilled, they become an agent of the seller. [handwritten]

ROBINSON, J.

Prior to December, 1947, appellant, Leslie A. Lechner, was the owner of some real property at Darrington, Washington, upon which he operated a beer tavern. Desiring to sell this property, he wrote a letter to the Donahue Realty Company of Seattle, requesting its assistance in the project. The realty company (which we shall hereinafter refer to as "Donahue"), acting through Mrs. C.A. Donahue and her salesman, Mr. Sant, succeeded in finding buyers in the persons of respondents Halling. The price agreed on was $13,000. Mr. Lechner agreed to accept a certain house trailer, in which the Hallings were then living, in lieu of $2,000 of this sum, and the rest was to be paid in cash. On December 22, an earnest money receipt was executed by the parties, and, pursuant to its terms, Mrs. Halling made out a check for $2,000 to the Donahue Realty Company, which she gave to Mr. Sant, the parties agreeing, apparently in accordance with Mr. Lechner's wishes, that the money should be deposited with an escrow holder, and Donahue having been selected for this purpose. At the same time, the certificate of title and the registration certificate for the trailer were delivered by the Hallings to Donahue. The parties orally agreed, however, that the Hallings would retain possession of the trailer, and continue to live in it, until such time as the occupants of the apartment above the tavern, into which the Hallings desired to move, were able to find another place to live. On December 24, in Mr. Lechner's office, the Hallings paid the remaining $9,000 to Mr. Sant. On the same date, the following writing was executed by Donahue:

> This is to certify that Lawrence S. Halling and Dorothy A. Halling his wife has this 24th day of December, 1947 paid to the C.A. Donahue Realty, the sum of $2000.00 paid as earnest money on December 23, 1947, also a check for $9000.00 December 24, 1947, title received for trailer license No. TLF1091 valued at $2000.00, making a total of $13,000.00 as full purchase price of the Pioneer Tavern, located at Darrington, Wash. Said moneys to be held in escrow until title insurance, license, warranty deed, together with bill of sale of all equipment.

> C.A. Donahue Realty, By Dorothy Null, Bkr.

No written instructions were given by the Hallings to Donahue, and the above receipt is the only evidence of the conditions under which the latter was authorized to deliver the money to Mr. Lechner.

Prior to the end of December, the Hallings took possession of the tavern. About this time there arose a dispute over the amount of inventory on hand. The parties agreed to take an inventory, and, if the merchandise exceeded $500 in value, the Hallings were to pay the excess amount. The inventory was taken, and it was found to amount to $666.10, increasing the Hallings' obligation in the amount of $166.10.

The liquor licenses were transferred to the Hallings on January 8. On January 13, Mr. Lechner went to The Citizens State Bank of Arlington and directed it to inform Donahue of the fact that the sum of $2,901.74 was due the bank on certain mortgages held by it upon the property. The bank so advised Donahue, and on the following day Mrs. Donahue paid this sum from the funds in the Halling-Lechner account. The satisfactions of the mortgages were thereupon sent to her.

Also on January 13, Mr. Lechner executed a warranty deed to the property and a bill of sale for the equipment and inventory, and deposited them, as he testified, "in escrow," with Donahue on the same evening. No written escrow instructions were given by him to Donahue. Mr. Sant testified that he then called Mr. Halling and told him that the deed and other papers had been delivered. On January 21, Mr. Halling came down to the Donahue office. He gave Donahue a check for $166.10, the amount owing as a result of the inventory. Mrs. Donahue acknowledged a bill of sale for the trailer, which had been executed by the Hallings, and turned over to Mr. Halling the warranty deed and the bill of sale for the personal property, which had been deposited with her by Mr. Lechner, and a policy of title insurance for the sale of the real property. On this occasion, Mr. Sant dictated, and Mr. Halling signed, the following:

> January 21, 1948

> To Whom It May Concern: This is to certify that we, the undersigners, namely Lawrence S. Halling and Dorothy A. Halling have taken possession of the Pioneer Tavern, Darrington, Wash., including land, building, tavern

license, and all equipment, together with a warranty deed and Title Insurance policy for same. We, hereby, authorize the payment of any and all money now held in escrow by C.A. Donahue Realty, to the seller, Leslie A. Lechner. We will also deliver house trailer to Everett at the request of Leslie A. Lechner. (Signed) Lawrence Halling

We may note that there is some dispute over whether the delivery, alleged to have preceded the drawing up of this writing, actually took place. The trial court, however, in its extensive and well-considered oral opinion, dealt with this point at length, and took the view, which seems supported by the weight of the evidence, that such a delivery had been made. The question being purely one of fact, we shall not take issue with that conclusion.

Immediately after the delivery of the deed, title insurance policy, and bill of sale, Mrs. Donahue testified that the following took place:

"Q.   When you handed those instruments to Mr. Halling on January 21st, 1948, what was said by him and what was said by you, and how does it happen they remained in your possession?

"A.   Mr. Halling asked me what he should do with them, and I told him first he must have his warranty deed recorded. He asked me how he went about doing it, and didn't seem to know just what to do, and I suggested that I would record it for him if he would like for me to. And he asked me to do that. At that time the title insurance policy here, in Schedule 'B', it showed taxes and a mortgage that hadn't been cleared. I did, however, have the satisfaction in my possession from the bank, where the mortgage had been paid off. I had sent the money up and paid it off, but it hadn't been cleared from the title policy. And in talking with Mr. Halling, I suggested that I thought it would be better if we returned the title policy and ordered a new Schedule 'B' after the satisfactions had been filed. Which I did. I returned them.

"Q.   Did he then at that time re-deliver to you. . . .

"A.   (Interposing) He handed them back to me so I could record the deed and to pay the taxes that were due, and file the satisfactions of the mortgage, and get a new Schedule 'B' for the policy."

This testimony was, in general, corroborated by that of Mr. Halling and Mr. Sant, although it is fairly clear from the statements of both of the latter two that Mr. Halling had no very clear idea of why he was leaving the title insurance policy with Mrs. Donahue. All of this testimony, in fact, indicates complete unfamiliarity with the procedure involved in real estate sales, and throughout the transaction he appears to have acted entirely as others advised.

In any event, Mrs. Donahue paid the taxes and sent the satisfactions of the mortgages which had been outstanding against the property, together with the title insurance policy, to the Snohomish County Abstract Company in order that the mortgage satisfactions might be recorded and the title policy corrected. These things were done, and the mortgage satisfactions and corrected title insurance policy were mailed back to Mrs. Donahue on January 28.

In the meantime, Mr. Lechner called Mrs. Donahue on January 24 and asked when the transaction could be closed. The substance of the conversation was disputed, Mrs. Donahue testifying that she told Mr. Lechner of the Halling release on this occasion, and Mr. Lechner denying that she did so; but it was agreed that Mrs. Donahue told him that nothing more could be done until the corrected title policy had been returned to her. Mr. Lechner testified that, to the best of his recollection, she stated that this would be in about a week. He then told her that he would go to California and would leave the matter in the hands of his secretary, who testified that Mr. Lechner had indicated to her that he hoped the deal would be closed before his return.

Mr. Lechner went to California on the 28th or 29th. The title insurance policy and mortgage satisfactions were received by Mrs. Donahue, presumably on the 29th. She testified that, when these were returned, there was nothing else preventing her payment of the money to Mr. Lechner. Mr. Lechner's secretary talked to Mrs. Halling and to Mr. Sant during Lechner's absence about "closing the deal," but apparently nothing was discussed except the matter of delivery of the trailer. It does not appear from the testimony that Mr. Lechner had authorized her to receive any money from Donahue, or indeed that at that time he was at all concerned about that aspect of the affair. Mr. Lechner returned from California on February 5, and learned from his secretary that the transaction had not been "closed."

Had the matter proceeded as the parties had contemplated, there is no doubt that the transaction would have been completed to the satisfaction of all concerned. However, on February 6, Mrs. Donahue made an assignment of her business to her stepson, and her licenses as a realtor were picked up by the state on February 9. A receivership followed shortly thereafter. A receiver was appointed on February 17. Mrs. Donahue was subsequently convicted of embezzlement, and this particular matter was one of the items for which she was convicted. Mr. Halling delivered the trailer to Mr. Lechner, either on February 7 or February 11, and he has remained in possession of it. The title insurance policy, the bill of sale for the personal property, and the warranty deed, still unrecorded, were found in the possession of Mrs. Donahue by the receiver, as was also the bill of sale for the trailer.

This action was brought by Mr. Lechner, who alleged in his complaint that he was entitled to recover the purchase price of the property from the Hallings, less, of course, the amount paid by Mrs. Donahue on the mortgages; or, in the alternative, that he was entitled, upon reconveyance of the trailer to the Hallings, and upon payment to them of the amount paid on the mortgages, to a redelivery of the premises. The Hallings answered, alleging that they had fully performed their contract, and praying that Mr. Lechner's action be dismissed and that a decree be entered quieting title to the real property in them. The court found for the defendants Halling, and entered a decree directing the receiver to convey the warranty deed, policy of title insurance, and bill of sale to the Hallings as purchasers, and further directing him to convey the bill of sale to the trailer to Mr. Lechner. Any funds in the hands of the receiver on account of the transaction involved were directed to be paid to Mr. Lechner, as and when distribution was ordered by the court in the receivership proceeding. From this decree, Mr. Lechner has appealed, it being apparent that the one to whom it is finally held that the money belongs will never be able to recover the entire amount.

As the trial court recognized, the rule to be applied in this type of case was laid down by this court in *Lieb v. Webster*, 30 Wash. 2d 43, 190 P.2d 701. It was recently reiterated in *Angell v. Ingram*, Wash., 213 P.2d 944. In those cases, we held that, when an escrow agent absconds with money he is holding in his capacity as depositary, the loss must fall upon the person as whose agent he is holding the money at the time. Both cases turned chiefly upon the circumstance that, in each of them, the terms of the escrow instructions given by the purchasers to the depositary had not been complied with at the time the latter absconded with the funds he was holding. Applying the rule, as above stated, we held that he was still holding the money as the agent of the purchasers, and that, as between them and the sellers, they, the purchasers, must stand the loss.

Mr. Lechner urges that an analogous result must be reached in the present inquiry. He contends that the money involved in this case was received by Donahue as agent for the Hallings, that Donahue never ceased to hold it for them, and that, consequently, under the holding of the *Lieb* and *Angell* cases, the Hallings must bear the loss. In order to decide whether or not he is correct in this contention, it is first necessary to determine whether all the conditions, which respondents Halling attached to the disbursement of the funds, were fulfilled prior to delivery of the deed and other instruments to them.

Although no formal instructions were given by the Hallings to Donahue, it would appear, from the receipt executed by Donahue on the occasion of the $9,000 payment to it, that Donahue was to hold the money until a policy of title insurance, the liquor license, a warranty deed, and a bill of sale of the personal property had been delivered by Mr. Lechner. Mr. Sant testified that the following occurred after this delivery had been made: "A. Mr. Lechner brought the deed in I think a couple days after the date on there. I am not sure of the dates. Then I called Mr. Halling and told him that it was there and everything was there, and so Mr. Halling came down and signed all the releases releasing Mr. Lechner of any further obligations."

Even if the receipt executed by Donahue, not having been signed by either Mr. Halling or his wife, cannot for that reason be considered valid evidence of the conditions under which Donahue was to take possession of the money on their behalf, nevertheless, the written release, signed by Mr. Halling on January 21, fully indicates his intention to part with all right to the money. In that release, it is true that Mr. Halling stated that he "authorized" the payment of the money "now held in escrow" to Mr. Lechner, and some contention is made that this had no other effect than to constitute Donahue his agent to pay the money to Mr. Lechner in the future. But the trial court said, concerning this language: "True, he used the word 'authorized,' or he adopted it, because some other dictated the language — he 'authorized' the payment of all this money to Mr. Lechner. Now, while the word 'authorized,' as counsel for Mr. Lechner contends, is an appropriate and a proper word in the constitution of another one as an agent, I think when this instrument is read in its entirety, in the light of all the evidence in the case and of what these people have done before and since, that it was no more or less than the declaration by Lawrence Halling on his own and his wife's behalf that no further right in that money resided in them. It is the disclaimer of any right in such."

We agree with the trial court that the most logical inference from this language is that Mr. Halling intended to divest himself of all right to the money — that he intended, in other words, that Donahue should cease to hold it for him as his agent. Therefore, the situation is precisely the reverse of that presented in the *Lieb* and *Angell* cases, and, applying the principle there laid down, an opposite result is required, to the effect that all of the instructions of the purchaser having been complied with by January 21, the depositary, Donahue, thereafter held the money as the agent of the seller, Lechner. Although there is some suggestion in the evidence that, on the date of the signing of the release, Donahue's escrow obligations, as a whole, were considerably greater than the amount on deposit in her escrow account, it appears that, exclusive of the item of $166.10, for which she received a check on that day, she had sufficient money deposited to have paid the full sum owing to Mr. Lechner at the time when Mr. Halling signed the release. Therefore, on the basis of the evidence before us, we are unable to say that Donahue did not cease to hold the money as agent of Mr. Halling and take possession of it as agent for Mr. Lechner.

But there is an additional problem in this case resulting from appellant's contention that Donahue had no authority, either to deliver the deed to Mr. Lechner or to collect the money in his behalf. In view of the fact that appellant himself has most vigorously urged that this transaction amounted to a deposit in escrow, the first of these conditions is particularly difficult to understand. In the early case of *Bronx Investment Co. v. National Bank of Commerce*, 47 Wash. 566, 92 P. 380, 381, we defined an "escrow" . . . as follows: "An escrow is a written instrument, which by its terms imports a legal obligation, deposited by the grantor, promisor, or obligor, or his agent with a stranger or third person . . . *to be kept by the depositary until the performance of a condition or the happening of certain event, and then to be delivered over to take effect.*" (Italics ours.)

Once deposited in escrow, an instrument passes beyond the control of the depositor, and he may not recall it. 30 C.J.S., Escrows, § 5b, Page 1198. Upon the performance of the condition named, the depositary must deliver it to the grantee. A deposit in escrow, therefore, amounts, by its terms, to a conditional delivery (4 Tiffany, Real Property (3d Ed.), p. 226, § 1048), and if the instruments involved in this case were, as appellant contends, so deposited, it is idle for him to assert that Donahue had no authority to deliver them. However, the lack of any written escrow instructions from Mr. Lechner to Donahue, the fact that Mr. Lechner testified that he never saw the receipt which was the only evidence of any such instructions from the Hallings to Donahue, and the general vagueness and informality of the whole transaction, have resulted in some uncertainty as to the conditions upon which such delivery was to be made, and caused the trial court to question whether there had been any valid escrow agreement whatsoever. Plainly, he was justified in this doubt, for there can be no escrow unless the delivery of the instrument by the depositary to the grantee or obligee is conditioned upon the performance of some act, or the happening of some event, *McPherson v. Barbour*, 93 Or. 509, 183 P. 752; and it is essential to the constitution of an escrow, not only that the grantor and the grantee are at one as to the conditions under which the deposit is to be made, but that such conditions should be communicated to the depositary.

But that the conditions upon which an instrument is deposited in escrow may rest in, and be proved by, parol (however desirable it may be that they be expressed in writing, 7 Thompson on Real Property (Perm. Ed.) 678, § 4204, as this case amply demonstrates) is well settled in this state as elsewhere. . . . Where there is a deposit of instruments, allegedly in escrow, and conflict in the testimony as to the understanding of the parties relative to the conditions of deposit, it is proper for the court to inquire into the facts and circumstances surrounding the transaction, in order to determine first, whether the parties intended a true conditional delivery, and second, whether they were in agreement as to the nature of the conditions, performance of which would authorize the depositary to convey to the grantee. Where a written instrument, importing a legal obligation, is deposited by a grantor with a third party, to be kept by the depositary until the grantee pays a stipulated sum, and then to be delivered over to the grantee, an escrow is created. *Foulkes v. Sengstacken*, 83 Or. 124, 163 P. 311, *rev'd on rehearing* 83 Or. 118, 158 P. 952. If the evidence reveals such a situation, the transaction will be treated as a deposit in escrow, regardless of whether the parties have employed that term. *Bronx Investment Co. v. National Bank of Commerce*, 47 Wash. 566, 92 P. 380. Where they have employed it, however, as is the case here, that is a circumstance which must be taken into account, as the use of the word "escrow" by any of the parties indicates more clearly than any other their actual intention. *Foulkes v. Sengstacken, supra.*

We think the evidence, considered as a whole, reveals the existence of a valid escrow agreement, and a mutual understanding among the parties as to the conditions of deposit. Respondents' analysis of the transaction, which is supported by the evidence, indicates the nature of these conditions. It is as follows: "The evidence consists of the fact that Lechner placed in Donahue's hands a warranty deed to the property involved, a bill of sale to the personal property, a policy of title insurance, a statement of the amount of the inventory, a statement of the amount due on the real estate mortgage and chattel mortgage held at the Arlington bank. These instruments were all placed by appellant in the possession of Donahue on January 13, 1948 or prior thereto with full knowledge on the part of the appellant that Donahue then had in her possession $11,000.00 in cash and the title to the house trailer, all of which he was to receive from respondents as and when he was in a position to transfer to respondents good title to the property involved in the transaction."

As we have noted, Mr. Sant testified that, when Mr. Lechner brought in the deed, he called Mr. Halling and told him that "everything was there," and that Mr. Halling came down and signed the release. Mrs. Donahue testified that Mr. Lechner was informed of this when he telephoned her on January 24. Her testimony was as follows:

"Q.   On that occasion did you have any conversation with him concerning the fact that Hallings had signed the release?

"A.   Yes, sir, I did. I told him I was prepared to pay off; that Mr. Halling had given me the authority as soon as this came back. . . .

"Q.   Are you positive, Mrs. Donahue, that on January 24th that you advised Mr. Lechner that Hallings had released this matter to you, or had signed the release authorizing you to close the deal?

"A.   Yes, sir, I certainly am."

If this testimony is to be believed, it would seem to indicate quite clearly that it was Mr. Lechner's understanding that Mrs. Donahue was authorized to deliver the various instruments to the Hallings and to take possession of the purchase money on his behalf. However, even if Mr. Lechner's statement, that Mrs. Donahue told him nothing of the release on this or any other occasion, is accepted, his subsequent conduct indicates that this was his understanding of the matter. He went to California, knowing, as both he and Mrs. Donahue testified, that the transaction could be closed (as he put it) and the payoff made (as she put it) within a week; and, though he had authorized his secretary to "close" the transaction during his absence, he said nothing to her about taking possession of the money, but seemed only concerned with getting delivery of the trailer. The logical explanation of this, as the trial court concluded, is that: "Mr. Lechner was not concerned about the money, and its payment to him, because it was in the hands of one whom he had selected as his agent, and whom he had confidence in."

Tending, to some extent at least, to support respondents' contention that Mr. Lechner knew of the delivery of the instruments to the Hallings, and that he consequently acquiesced in Donahue's holding the purchase money for his benefit, is the fact that he signed an assignment of a fire insurance policy on the tavern, reading as follows:

> The ownership of the property described in the attached policy of the insurance company below named, . . . *having actually passed* to Lawrence Halling . . . the undersigned, for value received, hereby transfers and assigns unto said transferee all the title and interest of said undersigned in said policy, subject to all the terms and conditions thereof. . . . [Italics ours.]

Leslie A. Lechner

This assignment is not dated; however, the insurance company's consent to the assignment, which follows it on the form used, is dated February 2, 1948, indicating that the assignment was signed prior to that time.

We think the fairest inference to be drawn from the whole of the evidence is that Donahue, upon receipt, on the one hand, of all of the papers necessary to give the Hallings good title to the property, and, on the other, of all of the money making up the purchase price and the papers necessary to give good title to the trailer, was authorized to deliver the former to the Hallings and to take possession of the latter for the benefit of Mr. Lechner. This having apparently been the understanding of all of the parties, the deposit created a valid escrow, and Mrs. Donahue's delivery of January 21, being in accord with the conditions thereof, was fully effective. . . .

The case is not free from doubt, due chiefly to the numerous conflicts in the testimony on many important issues. Such conflicts are, of course, quite understandable, since, by and large, they relate to minor details of the transaction, which doubtless seemed of little importance to the parties at the time they occurred, and which only assumed significance on the occasion of Mrs. Donahue's unexpected defalcation. Nevertheless, the whole of the evidence seems to justify the conclusion that there was a valid escrow agreement between the parties and that it was completely performed on January 21, when Mrs. Donahue delivered the deed, bill of sale, and title insurance policy to the Hallings. Whether Mr. Lechner learned of this delivery on January 24, or whether he only anticipated that it would occur while he was in California, is immaterial, as a delivery would have been effective at any time after he had placed all the instruments, necessary to pass good title, in Donahue's hands. From the time of the delivery, Donahue held the purchase money as agent for Mr. Lechner, and, therefore, Mr. Lechner, rather than the Hallings, must bear the burden of the subsequent loss. The decree is affirmed.

NOTE

Courts recognize the dangers of allowing a lay person to conduct closings. See, e.g., *In re First Escrow, Inc.*, 840 S.W.2d 839 (Mo. 1992). However, in *In re Opinion No. 26 of Committee on Unauthorized Practice of Law*, 654 A.2d 1344 (N.J. 1995), the court held that real estate brokers and title insurance company officers who conduct residential real estate closings without an attorney for the seller or buyer do not engage in the unauthorized practice of law if the seller and buyer are informed of the conflicting interests of the brokers and the title company and of the general risks associated with being unrepresented by an attorney. Consistent with *Opinion No. 26*, the majority of courts hold that a lay person may complete simple, standardized closing documents but may not draft such documents or give legal advice concerning them. See *Real Estate Bar Association for Massachusetts, Inc. v. National Real Estate Information Services*, 946 N.E.2d 665 (Mass. 2011); Barlow Burke, Law of Title Insurance, § 16.01 (3d ed. 2000). At closings, when attorneys continue to be involved as agents and underwriters of title insurance policies, insurers' issue, to approved attorneys, "closing protection letters." These letters indemnify insured lenders and owners against the attorneys' embezzlement or conversion of funds involved in a closing. See Burke § 13.10, for a general discussion of these letters.

Two ways to make an express easement:
· by grant
· by reservation: in yourself

Chapter 6

SERVITUDES AND EASEMENTS

I. EASEMENTS

An easement is a nonpossessory interest in the land of another person or legal entity. Restatement of Property § 450(a-e) (1944). The land that benefits from an easement is called the dominant estate or tenement; the land subject to it is called the servient estate or tenement. The holder of the former may make such use of the latter as is appropriate to the easement in question. The right to walk across the land of one's neighbor in order to gain access to a road or to the beach is a common example of an easement. The intention of the parties and the purpose of the easement ordinarily determine the rights of each to the land subject to the easement.

Easements may be affirmative or negative; that is, they may either permit use of the land of another in specified ways or restrict a person's use of the land in specified ways. An easement of light and air is one example of the latter. It prohibits the owner of the servient tenement from blocking the light from reaching adjoining land. Easements may benefit the owners of adjacent land (the dominant tenement), in which case they are called appurtenant easements, or they may benefit persons who are not necessarily owners of adjoining property, in which case they are called easements in gross. *Only pass w/ commercial conveyances.*

Appurtenant easements are ordinarily treated as integral parts of the dominant estate. When the estate is transferred, the easement passes along with it, even without an express grant of "appurtenances." An attempt to convey the benefit of the easement to a person with no interest in the dominant estate is therefore a nullity. Gerald Korngold, Private Land Use Arrangements § 5.06 (2d ed. 2004). Where the dominant tenement is divided and transferred, ordinarily the easement continues and attaches to each part of the divided estate. By contrast, in many circumstances, an easement in gross may be transferred from one holder to another, especially if the easement in gross is commercial in nature.

Easements are classified as interests in land in considering their compliance with the Statute of Frauds and for most other purposes. Thus, the creation of an easement requires a written instrument or memorandum, typically a deed. In circumstances to be examined below, easements may also be implied or acquired by prescription, estoppel, public trust, or condemnation, but ordinarily their creation follows the formal requirements established for the creation of estates in land. It follows that when the land subject to the easement is taken by eminent domain, an appropriate share of the compensation must be paid to the holder of the easement.

A. Creation of Easements

river stranger to deed case [handwritten]

ESTATE OF THOMSON v. WADE
509 N.E.2d 309 (N.Y. 1987)

PER CURIAM.

Stranger to the deed: can't make a deed granting to a 3rd party. old rule. [handwritten]

Plaintiff, executrix of the estate of A. Graham Thomson, and defendant, Judith Wade, own adjoining parcels of land on the St. Lawrence River in the Village of Alexandria Bay. Plaintiff's property, on which a motel has been built, is known as the annex parcel and fronts on the river. Defendant owns the unimproved inland parcel, which is adjacent to plaintiff's and borders the public road. Plaintiff claims an easement over defendant's parcel to the public road. Both parcels were previously owned by Edward John Noble, who, in 1945, separately conveyed them to different parties. Although Noble had always used defendant's parcel to gain access to the public road from the annex parcel, in transferring the annex parcel to plaintiff's predecessor-in-interest, he did not convey an express easement appurtenant over defendant's parcel for the benefit of the annex parcel. When Noble subsequently conveyed defendant's parcel to defendant's predecessor-in-interest, however, he "excepted and reserved" to himself personally, and to plaintiff's predecessor-in-interest, a right-of-way across defendant's parcel. In the ensuing years, members of the public generally, and the various owners of the annex parcel, including plaintiff who purchased the parcel in 1954, used this right-of-way over defendant's land to reach the public road or the waterfront. When, in 1978, plaintiff erected a 50-room motel on the annex parcel, threatening an increase in traffic across defendant's property, defendant immediately sought to bar plaintiff's use of her property to benefit the annex parcel. Plaintiff thereafter acquired from Noble's successor-in-interest, the Noble Foundation, a quitclaim deed to the right-of-way over defendant's property that Noble had reserved to himself.

In this declaratory judgment action, plaintiff claims title to an easement over defendant's property by express grant, relying not on its own deed to the annex parcel, but on the purported intent of Noble that the annex parcel benefit from an easement over defendant's property, as evidenced by his conveyance of defendant's parcel subject to a right-of-way in himself and in plaintiff's predecessor-in-interest. Plaintiff also relies on the express conveyance of Noble's personal right-of-way in the quitclaim deed from the Noble Foundation. The Appellate Division concluded that no express easement was created here. We agree.

It is axiomatic that Noble could not create an easement benefiting land which he did not own (see, 3 Powell, Real Property, Easements by Express Conveyance, § 407). Thus, having already conveyed the annex parcel, he could not "reserve" in the deed to defendant's predecessor-in-interest an easement appurtenant to the annex parcel for the benefit of plaintiff's predecessor-in-interest. The long-accepted rule in this State holds that a deed with a reservation or exception by the grantor in favor of a third party, a so-called "stranger to the deed," does not create a valid interest in favor of that third party (see *Tuscarora Club v. Brown*, 215 NY 543; *Beardslee v. New Berlin Light & Power Co.*, 207 NY 34, 39; see generally 3 Powell, Real Property, Easements by Express Conveyance, § 407; 2 Warren's Weed, New

York Real Property, Easements § 4.02 [4th ed]). Plaintiff invites us to abandon this rule and adopt the minority view which would recognize an interest reserved or excepted in favor of a stranger to the deed, if such was the clearly discernible intent of the grantor (citations omitted).

Although application of the stranger-to-the-deed rule may, at times, frustrate a grantor's intent, any such frustration can readily be avoided by the direct conveyance of an easement of record from the grantor to the third party. The overriding considerations of the "public policy favoring certainty in title to real property, both to protect bona fide purchasers and to avoid conflicts of ownership, which may engender needless litigation" (*Matter of Violi*, 65 NY2d 392, 396), persuade us to decline to depart from our settled rule. We have previously noted that in this area of law, "where it can reasonably be assumed that settled rules are necessary and necessarily relied upon, stability and adherence to precedent are generally more important than a better or even a 'correct' rule of law" (*Matter of Eckart*, 39 NY2d 493, 500). Consequently, we hold here that any right-of-way reserved to plaintiff's predecessor-in-interest in the defendant's deed was ineffective to create an express easement in plaintiff's favor.

Additionally, inasmuch as the right-of-way reserved to Noble personally was not shown to be commercial in nature, the Appellate Division correctly determined that it could not be transferred to plaintiff in the quitclaim deed by the Noble Foundation (see *Saratoga State Waters Corp. v. Pratt*, 227 NY 429, 443). Thus, neither the reservation of an easement in gross in Noble, nor the reservation of a right-of-way in plaintiff's predecessor-in-interest, entitles plaintiff to an express easement across defendant's property.

We have examined plaintiff's remaining contentions and find them to be without merit.

Accordingly, the order of the Appellate Division should be affirmed, with costs.

NOTES

1. Some states have enacted statutes similar to the following (N.D. Cent. Code 47-09-17): "A present interest and the benefit of a condition or covenant respecting property may be taken by any natural person under a grant although not named a party thereto." Should the existence of the statute affect the outcome? See *Malloy v. Boettcher*, 334 N.W.2d 8 (N.D. 1983).

2. The Restatement of Property § 472 (1944) endorses the validity of grants of third party easements when the intent of the grantor is clear, as does the Restatement (Third) of Property: Servitudes § 2.6 (2000). One court described the traditional rule as an "inapposite feudal shackle." *Willard v. First Church of Christ Scientist*, 102 Cal. Rptr. 739, 740 (1972). See also *Uhes v. Blake*, 892 P.2d 439 (Colo. Ct. App. 1995) (collecting relevant cases and adopting the Restatement's view).

3. If toxic substances are discovered along a right of way easement, would the dominant or the servient estate holder be liable for the cleanup costs? The applicable statute (CERCLA), 42 U.S.C. § 9607(a), imposes liability on the "owner and operator" of the land. See *Grand Trunk W. R.R. Co. v. Acme Belt Recoating*,

Inc., 859 F. Supp. 1125 (W.D. Mich. 1994).

BASEBALL PUBLISHING CO. v. BRUTON
18 N.E.2d 362 (Mass. 1938)

LUMMUS, J.

The plaintiff, engaged in the business of controlling locations for billboards and signs and contracting with advertisers for the exhibition of their placards and posters, obtained from the defendant on October 9, 1934, a writing signed but not sealed by the defendant whereby the defendant "in Consideration of $25.00 . . . agrees to give" the plaintiff "the exclusive right and privilege to maintain advertising sign one 10[feet] × 25[feet] on wall of building 3003 Washington St." in Boston, owned by the defendant, "for a period of one year with the privilege of renewal from year to year for four years more at the same consideration." It was provided that "All signs placed on the premises remain the personal property of the" plaintiff. The writing was headed "Lease No. —." It was not to be effective until accepted by the plaintiff.

It was accepted in writing on November 10, 1934, when the plaintiff sent the defendant a check for $25, the agreed consideration for the first year. The defendant returned the check. The plaintiff nevertheless erected the contemplated sign, and maintained it until February 23, 1937, sending the defendant early in November of the years 1935 and 1936 checks for $25 which were returned. On February 23, 1937, the defendant caused the sign to be removed. On February 26, 1937, the plaintiff brought this bill for specific performance, contending that the writing was a lease. The judge ruled that the writing was a contract to give a license, but on November 2, 1937, entered a final decree for specific performance, with damages and costs. The defendant appealed. It is stipulated that on November 3, 1937, the plaintiff tendered $25 for the renewal of its right for another year beginning November 10, 1937, but the defendant refused the money.

The distinction between a lease and a license is plain, although at times it is hard to classify a particular instrument. A lease of land conveys an interest in land, requires a writing to comply with the statute of frauds though not always a seal (*Alfano v. Donnelly*, 285 Mass. 554, 557, 189 N.E. 610; *Mayberry v. Johnson*, 3 Green 116), and transfers possession. *Roberts v. Lynn Ice Co.*, 187 Mass. 402, 406, 73 N.E. 523. A license merely excuses acts done by one on land in possession of another that without the license would be trespasses, conveys no interest in land, and may be contracted for or given orally. (citations omitted). The writing in question, however, giving the plaintiff the "exclusive right and privilege to maintain advertising sign . . . on wall of building," but leaving the wall in the possession of the owner with the right to use it for all purposes not forbidden by the contract and with all the responsibilities of ownership and control, is not a lease. *Gaertner v. Donnelly*, 296 Mass. 260, 5 N.E.2d 419, and cases cited. *Reynolds v. Van Beuren*, 155 N.Y. 120, 49 N.E. 763. The fact that in one corner of the writing are found the words, "Lease No. —," does not convert it into a lease. Those words are merely a misdescription of the writing. (citations omitted)

Subject to the right of a licensee to be on the land of another for a reasonable time after the revocation of a license, for the purpose of removing his chattels (citations omitted) Am. Law Inst. Restatement: Torts, §§ 176, 177, it is of the essence of a license that it is revocable at the will of the possessor of the land. (citations omitted) Am. Law Inst. Restatement: Torts, §§ 167–171. The revocation of a license may constitute a breach of contract, and give rise to an action for damages. But it is none the less effective to deprive the licensee of all justification for entering or remaining upon the land. . . .

If what the plaintiff bargained for and received was a license, and nothing more, then specific performance that might compel the defendant to renew the license, leaving it revocable at will, would be futile and for that reason should not be granted. 5 Williston, Contracts (Rev. Ed.) § 1442. Am. Law Inst. Restatement: Contracts, § 377. Specific performance that might render the license irrevocable for the term of the contract would convert it into an equitable estate in land, and give the plaintiff more than the contract gave. *Cheever v. Pearson*, 16 Pick. 266, 273. (citations omitted) There can be no specific performance of a contract to give a license, at least in the absence of fraud or estoppel. (citations omitted).

The writing in the present case, however, seems to us to go beyond a mere license. It purports to give "the exclusive right and privilege to maintain" a certain sign on the defendant's wall. So far as the law permits, it should be so construed as to vest in the plaintiff the right which it purports to give. *Kaufman v. Federal National Bank of Boston*, 287 Mass. 97, 100, 101, 191 N.E. 422. That right is in the nature of an easement in gross, which, whatever may be the law elsewhere, is recognized in Massachusetts. (citations omitted) We see no objection to treating the writing as a grant for one year and a contract to grant for four more years an easement in gross thus limited to five years. Similar writings have been so treated in other jurisdictions. *Thos. Cusack Co. v. Myers*, 189 Iowa, 190, 178 N.W. 401, 10 A.L.R. 1104. (further citations omitted)

An easement, being inconsistent with seisin in the person owning it, always lay in grant and could not be created by livery of seisin. *Randall v. Chase*, 133 Mass. 210, 214. It is an interest in land within the statute of frauds and, apart from prescription, requires a writing for its creation. G.L. (Ter. Ed.) c. 183 § 3, *Cook v. Stearns*, 11 Mass. 533. Indeed, the creation of a legal freehold interest in an easement, apart from prescription, requires a deed. (citations omitted). And, differing from a lease of land for not more than seven years (*Alfano v. Donnelly*, 285 Mass. 554, 557, 189 N.E. 610), a grant of an easement for as short a term as five years apparently requires a deed in order to create a legal interest. . . . But in equity a seal is not necessary to the creation of an easement. Since equity treats an act as done where there is a duty to do it enforceable in equity, or, as more tersely phrased, equity treats that as done which ought to be done, an enforceable unsealed contract such as the writing in this case, providing for the creation of an easement, actually creates an easement in equity. (citations omitted)

There is no error in the final decree granting specific performance. The affirmance of this decree will not prevent an assessment of the damages as of the date of the final decree after rescript. *Rudnick v. Rudnick*, 281 Mass. 205, 208, 183 N.E. 348.

[handwritten: license is not an interest in land]

[handwritten: apt. swimming pool]

BUNN v. OFFUTT
222 S.E.2d 522 (Va. 1976)

HARRISON, J.   *[handwritten: Issue: is P's right a licence or an easement?]*

[handwritten: a right given by some competent authority to do an act which w/o such authority would be illegal]

[handwritten: - personal and cannot be assigned.]

Edward DeV. Bunn and Sandra M. Bunn noted this appeal from a final decree of the lower court holding that they do not have an easement to go upon property owned or controlled by the appellees, T.J. Offutt, Temco, Inc. and Dittmar Co., Inc., and to use a swimming pool located thereon.

The evidence was heard ore tenus and the following appears from the statement of facts. On July 9, 1962, Temco, Inc. conveyed to Harvey W. Wynn and Rosabelle G. Wynn property known as 900 South Wakefield Street in Arlington. Prior thereto, on January 26, 1962, the Wynns had signed a contract of purchase prepared by the seller's agent. In this contract is found the following provision: "Use of apartment swimming pool to be available to purchaser and his family." The Wynns testified that the agent, Willis L. Lawrence, told them that the use of the pool went with the ownership of the home being purchased, and that subsequent purchasers would have the right to use the pool. The pool is located in an adjoining apartment complex which was being developed by appellees at the time. The Wynns said the sales agent emphasized that use of this pool would be a desirable feature in the event they subsequently decided to sell the property. No reference was made to the pool in the deed from Temco to the Wynns.

On May 31, 1969, the Bunns contracted in writing to buy the property from the Wynns through the latter's agent, Sonnett Realty Co., Inc. While no reference to the pool was made in the contract, the Wynns and a representative of Sonnett told the Bunns that the use of the pool went with the purchase of the property. However, the deed, dated July 18, 1969, conveying the property from the Wynns to the Bunns contains no reference to the pool. After the purchase was effected, and when the Bunns requested passes from appellees showing their entitlement to the use of the pool, their request was refused.

Appellants attach significance to the close relationship which they allege existed between Offutt, Temco, Dittmar and Sonnett. The appellees all have their offices in the same room of a building situated on the property where the pool is located, and Sonnett, which in 1969 was the exclusive sales agency for the appellees, has its office in the same building. Furthermore, the Wynns had agreed to purchase another house, then under construction, from appellees provided Sonnett could sell their Wakefield home. The Bunns testified that as an inducement for them to increase by $750 their offering price for the Wynn property, Sonnett stressed the value of using the swimming pool, and represented that pool membership in a club elsewhere would cost them an initial $300 fee plus annual dues.

Representatives of Sonnett attempted to persuade the appellees to grant pool privileges to appellants, but without success. Ultimately, on November 14, 1969, Sonnett wrote Mr. Bunn a letter advising that it had been unable to secure from appellees passes for the swimming pool, and that since the situation was beyond its control, Sonnett "would be only too happy to assume your existing trust and give you the cash you have invested in the property". This offer was refused.

We agree with the trial judge that the rights of the parties depend upon the nature of the transaction in 1962 between appellees, as sellers, and Mr. and Mrs. Wynn, as purchasers.

The testimony of Offutt, owner of appellee corporations, is unequivocal that at no time did he ever intend to extend the privilege of using the swimming pool beyond the original purchasers of certain houses (including 900 South Wakefield Street) which were located adjacent to his apartment development. He said that at one time he thought he would experience difficulty in selling the houses without an added inducement, and therefore included in his sales contract a clause to the effect that the use of the apartment swimming pool would be available to the purchaser and his family. Offutt further testified he never intended the right to run with the land and inure to successors in interest and in fact had never extended pool privileges to any one beyond the first purchasers.

The dispositive issue in this case is whether the language in the contract, "Use of apartment swimming pool to be available to purchaser and his family", amounted to a grant of a mere license to the Wynns and their family; or whether the Wynns acquired thereby a private easement across the land of appellees to the swimming pool and to the use of the pool, which easement was thereafter transferred to the Bunns.

A license has been described as "a right, given by some competent authority to do an act which without such authority would be illegal, a tort, or a trespass". 12 M.J., License to Real Property, § 2, p. 148. A license is personal between the licensor and the licensee and cannot be assigned. *Hodgson v. Perkins, et al.*, 84 Va. 706, 5 S.E. 710 (1888). And a grant which creates any interest or estate in land is not a license. Such a grant creates an easement. *Buckles v. Kennedy C. Corp.*, 134 Va. 1, 114 S.E. 233 (1922).

An easement has been described as "a privilege without profit, which the owner of one tenement has a right to enjoy in respect of that tenement in or over the tenement of another person; by reason whereof the latter is obliged to suffer, or refrain from doing something on his own tenement to the advantage of the former". *Stevenson v. Wallace*, 68 Va. 396, 27 Gratt. 77, 87 (1876).

> "Easements correspond to the servitudes of the civil law, and consist (1) of privileges on the part of one person to use the land of another (the servient tract) in a particular manner and for a particular purpose, or (2) of rights to demand that the owner of the servient tract refrain from certain uses of his own land, the privileges or rights in either case not being inconsistent with a general property in the owner of the servient tract. The easement further involves the right of freedom in its exercise from interference by the owner of the servient tract or other persons. Examples of easements are rights of way, of drainage, or light and air, etc." (Footnotes omitted) 1 Minor on Real Property (2d Ed., Ribble), § 87.

Easements may be created by express grant or reservation, by implication, by estoppel or by prescription. The only rights acquired by the Wynns in the property of appellees were acquired by deed from Temco. The provisions of the contract were merged in this deed. However, the deed is silent as to the pool, and the contract made the use of the pool available only to "purchaser and his family". The trial court found this language consistent with appellees' theory that a mere license only was granted to the purchasers and their families, and not an interest in land or an estate of inheritance; that the absence of any provision regarding the swimming pool in the deed to the Wynns was sufficient to preclude any easement by grant or reservation; and that the evidence and exhibits failed to show that an easement was created by estoppel, necessity or prescription. The trial court further found that no easement had been created by implication for there was neither a showing of a preexisting use of the easement prior to the conveyance by Temco to the Wynns, nor any showing that the use of the swimming pool was essential to the beneficial enjoyment of the land conveyed. . . .

In *Hamlin v. Pandapas*, 90 S.E.2d 829, 833 (1956), the court held:

> "In the construction of language contained in a deed the grantor must generally be considered as having intended to convey all that the language he employed is capable of passing to the grantee, and where the description admits of two constructions, it will be construed most favorably to the grantee. . . ."

However, the deed from Temco to the Wynns did not purport to convey an easement to the swimming pool, and the language in the sales contract between the parties is not sufficient to create an express easement. The Wynns and their family were given a mere license to use the swimming pool. It was not an interest running with the land that could subsequently be transferred by them.

The decree of the lower court under review is affirmed.

NOTES

1.   What interest is created by a grant of a long strip of public land one hundred feet in width: "to XYZ Railroad company, its successors and assigns forever, for the purpose of constructing a railroad thereon . . . to have, hold, and enjoy the lands above conveyed with the appurtenances and privileges thereto pertaining, and the right to use the said land . . . for any and all uses and purposes connected with the construction, preservation, occupation, and enjoyment of said railroad"? Compare *Bode v. Flobert Industries, Inc.*, 249 N.W.2d 750 (Neb. 1977), with *Bethlehem Township v. Emrick*, 465 A.2d 1085 (Pa. 1983). Does it matter whether a specific area or strip is granted, as opposed to the grant of a right of way generally? See *Tazian v. Cline*, 686 N.E.2d 95 (Ind. 1997).

2.   The right of access to the land of another and to take some natural product from the land is known as a "profit a prendre" (ah prôn'druh), often called a "profit" for short. Rights to take fruit from a tree (or the tree itself) or to remove minerals are common examples of profits. Historically, some were frequent enough to acquire special names; for example, the right to cut turf for fuel was called a right of turbary. Should the right to hunt and fish on the land of another, and to take away any game caught, be treated as an easement or a profit? How should the right to lateral and subjacent support from the land of a neighbor be classified? See James Ely, Jr., & Jon Bruce, The Law of Easements and Licenses in Land §§ 1:2, 1:12. For a comparative look at an important and contentious problem involving profits, see

Michael Blumm, *Native Fishing Rights and Environmental Protection in North America and New Zealand*, 8 Wis. Int'l L.J. 1 (1989).

3. Easements in gross not linked to a profit were generally not permitted in early English law. Y.B. Mich. 5 Hen. VII, pl. 15 (1489). In the United States, the same result has sometimes been reached by holding that particular easements in gross are personal to the holders and expire with their death. In *Rose Lawn Cemetery Ass'n v. Scott*, 317 S.W.2d 265 (Ark. 1958), language in a deed reserving a 25-foot strip "as a roadway for use of the parties hereto" was held to require the easement's termination with the death of the parties to the deed because the easement had been meant to be personal to them. For the most part, however, American law has recognized easements in gross and allowed them to be alienated. This is particularly true for commercial easements. See Lewis Simes, *Assignability of Easements in Gross in American Law*, 22 Mich. L. Rev. 521 (1924); Note, *The Easement in Gross Revisited: Transferability and Divisibility Since 1945*, 39 Vand. L. Rev. 109 (1986).

B.   Easements Implied by Necessity

Conveyances of landlocked property create the obvious problem of access. If grantees cannot reach the land, they cannot make use of it. Traditionally, courts have inferred an intent to create an easement in these circumstances, reasoning that it would be inconsistent with an intent to grant property rights in the grantee if the grantor would not permit access to it. The law's goal of encouraging productive use of real property also favors implying an easement in such circumstances. Established law requires the existence of three separate elements for the creation of an easement by necessity: (1) prior common ownership of the dominant and servient estates; (2) transfer of one of the estates by the common grantor, creating the lack of access; and (3) necessity of the easement for making use of the transferred estate. Although the transfer from common ownership must create the necessity, it is not necessary that the easement be used at once. "[A] right to a way of necessity can lie dormant and be activated by a remote grantee." *Pencader Associates, Inc. v. Glasgow Trust*, 446 A.2d 1097, 1100 (Del. 1982). The meaning of the third of these requirements has been a matter of particular difficulty for many American courts (and landowners).

Surrounded by water!

KINGSLEY v. GOULDSBOROUGH LAND IMPROVEMENT CO.
29 A. 1074 (Me. 1894)

Court uses strict necessity standard — it's possible to get off property by boat.

FOSTER, J.

Notwithstanding this is an action of trespass, the real and only question involved is, whether the defendant is entitled to a way from necessity over the plaintiff's premises.

The defendant's land embraces what is popularly known as Grindstone Neck in the town of Gouldsborough, and is surrounded on three sides by the waters of Frenchman's Bay and Winter Harbor. On the north, and adjoining the defendant's land, lies at the land of the plaintiff over which the way is claimed.

Admitting that both parcels were originally owned by one William Bingham, through whom, by sundry mesne conveyances, both parties derive their respective titles, we do not think the defendants entitled to the way as one originating from necessity. Such right is founded upon the doctrine of implied grant. And implied grants of this character are looked upon with jealousy, construed with strictness, and are not favored except in cases of strict necessity, and not from mere convenience. The rule is now so well settled in the State that a reference to the decided cases where this question has been fully considered is all that is necessary. *Warren v. Blake*, 54 Maine, 276 (further citations omitted).

It has long been the established rule that if one grants a close surrounded by his own land, or to which he has no access except over his own land, he impliedly grants a right of way over his adjoining lands as incident to the occupation and enjoyment of the grant. *Nichols v. Luce*, 24 Pick. 102. And the same rule applies when there has been a severance of the property and one portion of which has been a severance of property and one portion of which has been rendered inaccessible except by passing over the other, or by trespassing on the land of stranger.

Whether the same rule shall apply in a case like the present, where the property to which the right of way is claimed is partially surrounded by the sea, presents a question somewhat different from any decided case in this State. It has, however, been before the courts in other jurisdictions, and there it was held that the rule did not apply.

. . . .

In the present case the defendant's land has navigable waters upon three sides of it. Over these waters there is a public right of travel. The defendants have the free use of these waters in going to and from their land. They have erected wharves and own a steamboat which during certain portions of the year runs several times each day between there and Bar Harbor, and as occasion requires to Winter Harbor on the east. To the latter place it is only three quarters of a mile, by the way of the road or by water. It might oftentimes be more convenient to pass over a highway, or across the plaintiff's premises, than be subjected to the inconvenience of using the waters of the sea. But this inconvenience is not such as the law requires to constitute a legal necessity for the way claimed.

Nor can the defendants prevail upon the question of license. There was no such license as would entitle the defendants to enter upon the plaintiff's premises and commit the acts which the evidence shows were done in this case.

According to the stipulation in the report, the entry must be, Judgment for the plaintiff.

NOTES

1. In *Morrell v. Rice*, 622 A.2d 1156 (Me. 1993), the plaintiffs claimed an easement by necessity over adjoining land to a county road where the only other access was from the sea "over a tidal flat that at low tide recedes approximately 1,000 yards." Finding that "to dredge the area to enable boat access at all times,

assuming that all environmental and other permits could be obtained, would cost approximately $300,000," the Maine Supreme Court upheld the claim, distinguishing *Kingsley*. For contrasting views, compare *Woelfel v. Tyng*, 158 A.2d 311, 313 (Md. 1960), with *Hancock v. Henderson*, 202 A.2d 599, 602 (Md. 1964).

2.   Does it matter whether an easement by necessity is understood as arising by operation of law because of public policy or because of the presumed intent of the grantor? Some commentators prefer the former; e.g. "These fictional implications of 'intent' are actually rooted in considerations of public policy." 4 Powell on Real Property § 34.07. Both factors are commonly mentioned in the cases. Suppose the necessity ceases to exist or that it comes into existence after the date of the grant. See 7 Thompson on Real Property § 60.03(b)(5)(iii). Or suppose that there is an alternate access, but it is much more cumbersome or costly to use. See Michael A. DiSabatino, Annotation, 10 A.L.R. 4th 447 (1981); Peter Glenn, *Implied Easements in the North Carolina Courts: An Essay on the Meaning of "Necessary,"* 58 N.C. L. Rev. 223 (1979).

3.   Can an easement by necessity come into existence when the government, either by grant or reservation, becomes the owner of a landlocked parcel? See *Leo Sheep Co. v. United States*, 440 U.S. 668, 679–81 (1978); *Moores v. Walsh*, 45 Cal. Rptr. 2d 389 (Cal. App. 1995).

airplane case

CHANDLER FLYERS, INC. v. STELLAR DEVELOPMENT CORP.
592 P.2d 387 (Ariz. Ct. App. 1979)

SCHROEDER, J.

Court uses practical standard — an easement by necessity is only applicable if you can't access public roads, wanting to fly isn't enough.

Appellant, Chandler Flyers, Inc., is the owner of a parcel of land located in a project being developed for commercial and residential purposes by the appellee, Stellar Development Corporation. The project is designed as a "fly-in" development with airport, runway and hangar facilities for residents who commute to and from their homes by means of small aircraft. Appellant wishes to operate a flight school and airplane sales center on its tract and seeks an easement of necessity over appellee's property for aircraft access to the runway and airport facilities. This is an appeal from the trial court's denial of such an easement.

Appellant's tract is zoned for commercial purposes and is adjacent to a highway providing access by motor vehicle. It is also adjacent to a small taxiway leading to the main runway of the development. By virtue of deed restrictions and covenants, however, use of that taxiway is limited to owners of abutting residential properties. In a related action appellant has been enjoined from utilizing that taxiway. No appeal has been taken from that injunction, and it has become final.

Appellant now seeks an easement over other land, owned by appellee, for the purpose of providing aircraft access from the runway to appellant's tract. Appellant seeks to bolster his position by references to certain prior usage suggesting that an easement over the taxiway was intended. However, in view of the finality of the injunction barring appellant's use of the taxiway, no such questions of contractual intent are before us. The sole question is whether the appellant is entitled to an easement implied by necessity for access to the property by airplane as well as by motor vehicle. We affirm the trial court's denial of the easement.

As both parties recognize, the standard for imposing an easement of necessity is whether such an easement is required in order to provide reasonable access to the property. See *Solana Land Co. v. Murphey*, 69 Ariz.117, 125, 210 P.2d 593, 598 (1949), construing Arizona's statutory private way of necessity provisions, A.R.S. §§ 12-1201 and 1202 n1. Absolute necessity is not required. The owner need not show that without the easement there is no access whatsoever to the property. Indeed in an age of helicopters and parachutes, virtually all property is accessible in some manner. As motor vehicles have become the predominant form of transportation, courts have recognized that an easement of necessity for overland access may be imposed even though there is other access by navigable waters. E. g., *State v. Deal*, 191 Or. 661, 233 P.2d 242 (1951); 9 A.L.R.3d 600. The standard set forth in the Restatement, Property, § 476, p. 2984, is that an easement of necessity will be implied if "without it the land cannot be effectively used."

Courts have denied easements of necessity where there was reasonable access to the property even in situations where denial of the easement caused considerable hardship. (citations omitted)

In the instant case, there is access to appellant's property by means of a public highway. Although transportation by private plane is becoming more common, we cannot say as a matter of law that a property owner is entitled to aircraft access in order to make reasonable use of his property. There is no evidence in this record that the property cannot be effectively used absent air access. At best, the record reflects that the property cannot be used for the particular purpose desired by the appellant without such access, but that showing is not sufficient to justify imposition of an easement of necessity. Accordingly, the judgment of the trial court is affirmed.

NOTES

1. Courts in many states continue to say that a very high degree of necessity is required to establish an easement by necessity. "Strict necessity" or "absolute necessity" are phrases often found in the opinions. The requirement is said to promote stability in land titles. It is also said to be required because easements by necessity derogate from the spirit of recording acts and the Statute of Frauds. However, the author of a learned article on the subject concluded that "where a way is really needed the courts always seem to allow it." James Simonton, *Ways by Necessity*, 25 Colum. L. Rev. 571, 580, n.37 (1925). He was a proponent of the view that "the easement ought to be allowed whenever it is necessary to enable the owner to have the full enjoyment of the land." *Id.*

2. Should it make any difference whether the party claiming the easement was the grantor or the grantee of the property (or the successor of either)? Restatement of Property § 476, Comment g (1944) takes the position that it does not. Some cases, however, suggest a stricter standard in the former situation; e.g., *Hewitt v. Meaney*, 226 Cal. Rptr. 349, 352 (1986): "[A]n easement by necessity may more readily be found when the grantee is landlocked than when the grantor is . . . [but] lack of express reservation of an easement does not defeat the presumption of intent to retain one."

3. As the opinion in *Chandler Flyers* mentions in passing, Arizona has a statute providing for a private way of necessity that did not figure in the outcome of the case. In effect, such statutes give landowners the right to create easements of necessity by process of private condemnation. The Arizona statute, § 12-1202(A), reads:

> An owner of or a person entitled to the beneficial use of land, mines, or mining claims and structures thereon, which is so situated with respect to the land of another that it is necessary for its proper use and enjoyment to have and maintain a private way of necessity over, across, through, and on the premises, may condemn and take lands of another, sufficient in area for the construction and maintenance of the private way of necessity.

Would *Chandler Flyers* have been decided differently had the statute's provisions been applied? Consider the following statute and decision from Missouri.

> Mo. Rev. Stat. § 228.340 (pre-1991): If any person of this state shall file a verified petition in the circuit court of the proper county, setting forth that he or she is the owner of a tract or lot of land in such county, or in an adjoining county in this state, and that no public road passes through or alongside said tract or lot of land, and asking for the establishment of a private road from his or her premises, to connect at some convenient point with some public road of the county, or with any road of the state highway system within the county, in which the proceedings are had, and shall describe the place where said road is desired, and the width desired, not exceeding forty feet and alleging that the private road sought to be established is a way of strict necessity; and if the court shall find that the allegations in said petition are true, it shall appoint three disinterested citizens who are resident householders of the county as private road commissioners to view the premises and to mark out the road, and to assess the damages to the owner or owners of the land through which it will pass. Any number of persons similarly situated may join in such petition; provided, however, that the proceedings shall always be had in the county in which the premises are situated over which said proposed road is to pass.

ravine/hollow case

HOLLARS v. CHURCH OF GOD OF APOSTOLIC FAITH, INC.
596 S.W.2d 73 (Mo. Ct. App. 1980)

Prewitt, J. *statute uses strict standard, P can access public road on part of property*

Defendant appeals from a judgment establishing a private road of necessity over its property. Defendant contends that this statute is not applicable because a public road passes alongside plaintiffs' land.

Plaintiffs own 40 acres immediately west of defendant's property. An accessible public road runs along the northern boundary of plaintiffs' property. A "gorge", "canyon", "hollow", "valley", or "ravine", as it is variously described, runs in an east-west direction dividing plaintiffs' property approximately in half. We believe, based on the testimony and the photographic exhibits, and after resort to a dictionary, that this condition in plaintiffs' land is most accurately described as a "hollow". This hollow prevents vehicles from getting from one portion of the property to the other.

Plaintiffs purchased the property in 1965. They initially ran cattle on it and now have been using it to raise tomatoes and corn. Of the approximate 20 acres south of the hollow, 16 to 17 acres are tillable. No public road provides access to the southern half of plaintiffs' property. To reach it, plaintiffs used a public road along the east side of defendant's property and then went through defendant's property. When defendant sought to prevent them from passing through its property this action was brought. There was evidence that it would cost $3,500 to construct a road across or over the hollow.

The evidence on the difficulty in entering the southern part of plaintiffs' property all related to vehicular travel. It did not show if you could walk from one-half of the property to the other. Although plaintiffs' attorney contends that the photographs do not "do justice" to the hollow, they indicate that on foot you can travel through or across it and that such a hollow is not unusual for the Ozarks. There was an indication that a road might be necessary for cattle to cross the hollow, but no evidence regarding what would be necessary to construct a path or road sufficient only for cattle, or what it would cost. Whether a lack of access by vehicles prevented the south portion from being used is not in evidence. No dimensions of the hollow were given, perhaps because it would be difficult to define what would be a part of it.

The evidence indicated that establishing a private road would be of benefit to plaintiffs, with little burden or inconvenience to defendant. The trial judge found that the hollow was "impassable" and that it would not be "reasonable nor practical" to build a roadway across it. The judgment established a roadway of necessity from the southern portion of plaintiffs' property through defendant's property to a public road.

The question, as we see it, is whether the plaintiffs are entitled under § 228.340, RSMo 1969, to a roadway of necessity because a portion of their property does not have a public road "through or alongside" it; and plaintiffs do not have, and cannot reasonably provide for, vehicular access to that portion of their property from a portion with access to a public road. While we give deference to the trial judge's decision and his ability to judge the credibility of the witnesses, there is no disputed testimony before us on the question as presented. The oral descriptions of the hollow were necessarily general, and we have the exhibits before us. The record does not show that the trial judge viewed the property; and deference, as usually given in determining the facts in a non-jury case, has no application here.

The statute should be strictly construed. *Curtman v. Piezuch*, 494 S.W.2d 668, 671 (Mo. App. 1973). A literal application of it would deny plaintiffs' claim as a "public road passes through or alongside" their land. Apparently the only reported decision under this statute which has granted a roadway when a portion of the property had a road along it is *Wiese v. Thien*, 279 Mo. 524, 214 S.W. 853, 5 A.L.R. 1552 (1919). In *Wiese*, the plaintiff and his family lived on a farm on the west side of a river. The river went through his land and 200 yards of the land was east of the river. The east land apparently had no practical use. The land on both sides of the river, as well as the portion of the riverbed between them, was within *Wiese*'s legal description as initially established by government survey. Along the land on the east side was a road at the top of a bluff. The river was impassable part of the year and the evidence showed that it would be very expensive to build a road up to the top of the bluff. The court determined that for practical purposes the portions should be considered as separate tracts and affirmed the granting of a private road of necessity. Plaintiffs contend that under the facts here they are entitled to a similar holding.

None of the other cases cited by the parties appear to cover a situation where the tract has a public road along it but the road is not accessible from all portions of the land. We think that the circumstances in *Wiese* are substantially different from the present case. The river made the property such that it would be considered as two separate tracts, one on each side of the river. That is not the present situation. It appears to us that everyone would consider plaintiffs' property to be one tract. Allowing a roadway of necessity here would, in effect, be changing the statutory language. We would be allowing a private road because a vehicle cannot travel from a portion of the same tract to a public road. It is our function to apply the statute as written. This statute authorizes the establishment of a private road only for the purpose of providing egress and ingress to land not bordering upon a public road. *Seitz Packing & Manufacturing Co. v. Quaker Oats Co.*, 343 Mo. 1059, 124 S.W.2d 1177, 1179 (1938). The wording of the statute does not permit any other interpretation. *Id.* Several decisions under similar statutes have denied relief where, because of geographic conditions or other physical objects, access to all or a part of a tract of land was severely limited or denied. See (citations omitted) Annot., 5 A.L.R. 1557, *Easement of way of necessity as affected by common ownership of parcels which are not accessible one from the other.*

Plaintiffs' 40 acres is one tract of land. There is a public road alongside the tract and thus plaintiffs are not entitled to the relief sought. As § 228.340, R.S. Mo 1969 was erroneously applied, the judgment must be reversed. . . .

NOTES

1.   The statute in *Hollars* was amended (in 1991 and again in 1993), but its character remains intact. See Mo. Rev. Stat. § 228.342 *et seq.*

2.   If a statute applies, may a landlocked landowner nevertheless take advantage of the common law of easements by necessity? Or is the statute meant to cover the whole subject matter, impliedly displacing the common law? See *Snell v. Ruppert*, 541 P.2d 1042 (Wyo. 1975).

3.   Does the statute replicate the bargaining that would otherwise occur between adjacent property owners? Or does it put too much power into the hands of the claimant? Does it encourage buyers to purchase land without paying sufficient attention to problems of access?

4.   The constitutionality of statutes such as those enacted in Arizona and Missouri has been challenged on several occasions as a deprivation of private

property without due process of law. In Missouri, the matter seems to be settled in favor of the act; indeed, the Missouri State Constitution contains an express "savings clause" for its constitutionality. Mo. Const. Art. 1 § 29. In Mississippi, *Quinn v. Holly*, 146 So.2d 357 (Miss. 1962), upheld a similar provision as a valid exercise of the power of eminent domain. Such statutes have been widely adopted in Western states. In *South Dade Farms, Inc. v. B. & L. Farms Co.*, 62 So.2d 350 (Fla. 1952), the court struck down as unconstitutional a Florida statute that contained no provision for compensation. The Florida statute was then amended to make it constitutional. See *Stein v. Darby*, 126 So.2d 313 (Fla. Dist. Ct. App. 1961).

C.　Easements Implied by Past Usage

Akin to easements implied by necessity are easements implied by past use. They come into existence when property owners make use of one part of their property for the benefit of another part. Such implied easements are often described as "quasi easements," because logically no easement can exist when property is in the same hands. The requirements for establishment of such an easement are: (1) prior common ownership of the dominant and servient estates; (2) transfer of one of the estates; (3) continuous and apparent use of the quasi easement; and (4) reasonable necessity for enjoyment of the dominant estate.

sewer line case

FLAX v. SMITH
479 N.E.2d 183 (Mass. App. Ct. 1985)

FINE, J.

Apparant means discoverable through reasonable inspection.

The parties, owners of adjoining parcels in Jamaica Plain, dispute whether the property of the defendant, Herbert Smith, trustee, is burdened by an easement for water and sewer lines in favor of the property of the plaintiff, Steven Flax. . . . Lots B and C, fronting on St. John Street, contain five dwellings. Lot A, located to the rear of Lots B and C, contains two. Lot A is connected to St. John Street by a strip of land 21 feet wide and 150 feet in length. A hard surface driveway covers most of the strip. The residences on lot A are serviced by water and sewer lines, in existence and in continuous use since 1950, which run under lot C from the main lines on St. John Street.

At all times prior to 1966, the parcels were in common ownership. In 1966, the city of Boston took lot A for nonpayment of taxes. See G. L. c. 60, § 53, as amended by St. 1970, c. 85. The taking was confirmed by the Land Court in a 1974 decree. Flax acquired title from the city on August 29, 1978, having bid on the property at public auction. See G. L. c. 60, § 43, as amended by St. 1935, c. 236. Smith's predecessor trustees obtained title to lots B and C in 1977 and promptly sought to prevent the easement.

The judge found, on the basis of the evidence, that between the residences on lot A and St. John Street there is rock ledge to a depth of three to ten feet, that sewer and water lines must be at least six feet deep to prevent freezing, and that the drilling and other work required to connect water and sewer lines from the lot A residences directly to the main lines would cost $4,800, exclusive of the cost of the pipes and the connection. He concluded that there is a reasonable necessity for the claimed easement, and he ruled that when the city first acquired an ownership interest in 1966 it was the presumed intention of the city to take the property with the benefit of the existing water and sewer service. Accordingly, the judge determined that there was in existence an easement by implication.

No claim is made by Flax that he has an express easement or one obtained by prescription. See G. L. c. 187, § 2. Thus, for Flax to prevail, he must bring his case within the authority recognizing implied easements. Such interests have been recognized when land was formerly in common ownership, when use of one part of the land was made for the benefit of another part up until the time of the severance of ownership, and when the use of one part is both reasonably ascertainable and reasonably necessary for the enjoyment of the other part. (citations omitted) As far as the respective use of the two parcels is concerned, the factual situations in the illustration to comment c of § 476 of the Restatement are remarkably similar to the factual situation in the instant case.

Unquestionably, apart from issues arising out of the particular way in which ownership passed from the grantor to the city, the plaintiff has brought himself within the class protected by the authority cited. The property was formerly in common ownership. The use of the residences on lot A required that water and sewer services be supplied through lines to the street. The services had been supplied by lines on the adjoining property since 1950. If the existence of the lines on his property was not actually known to the grantor, he could reasonably have ascertained the true facts. And, finally, reasonable necessity for continued use of the existing lines was established by the evidence.

Smith contends that Flax failed to sustain his burden of proving the requisite intent for the creation of an easement by implication. Smith reasons that the grantor, parting with the property involuntarily as the result of a tax taking, did not intend to burden his remaining property (lots B and C) with the claimed easement. Smith is undoubtedly correct that the grantor, not having willingly conveyed anything to the city, did not actually intend to convey an easement. Thus, the issue is whether the fact that title passed involuntarily, pursuant to the tax title procedures (G. L. c. 60, §§ 37-60), changes what the result would have been had title passed by an ordinary voluntary conveyance.

To support his contention that the form in which title passed to lot A precludes the creation of an implied easement, Smith relies on language in those cases which suggests the importance of the grantor's intent. See *Prentiss v. Gloucester*, 236 Mass. 36, 52 (1920); *Wellwood v. Havrah Mishna Anshi Sphard Cemetery Corp.*, 254 Mass. 350, 354 (1926). What is required, however, is not an actual subjective intent on the part of the grantor but a presumed objective intent of the grantor and grantee based upon the circumstances of the conveyance. See Restatement of Property § 476 comment g (1944). One commentator has noted that "[t]hese fictional implications of 'intent' are genuinely rooted in considerations of public policy." 3 Powell, Real Property, par. 410, at 34-60 (Rohan rev. ed. 1984), citing *Buss v. Dyer*, 125 Mass. 287, 291 (1878).

In this case there are circumstances to consider even apart from the way the respective pieces of property were being used at the time of the taking. The effectiveness of the tax title procedures as a means of producing municipal revenue would be hindered if members of the public bidding on property at tax title auctions were to receive fewer rights than ordinary grantees of the same property. Such a rule would result in generally lower bids. The policy underlying the statutory tax title procedures has been stated as follows: "The importance of collecting taxes in order that governmental functions may be discharged is universally recognized. In the collection of taxes, the public interest requires that land be taken for nonpayment of taxes and sold under such circumstances that the necessary revenue may be obtained." See *Napier v. Springfield*, 304 Mass. 174, 177 (1939). See also *Leigh v. Green*, 193 U.S. 79, 89 (1904). Further, the grantor, a delinquent taxpayer, received a benefit from the conveyance since at least a portion, if not all, of his unpaid taxes were paid out of the proceeds of the sale, which proceeds presumably amounted to fair consideration. And the judge was quite correct in determining that one of the two parties to the transaction, the city, may be presumed to have intended to receive the benefit of the easement.

The recognition that an implied easement may arise out of a taking of property for nonpayment of taxes is not a departure from established law. Other types of involuntary conveyances have been held to result in the creation of implied easements. See *Viall v. Carpenter*, 14 Gray 126 (1859) (partition); *Schmidt v. Quinn*, 136 Mass. 575 (1884) (levy of an execution); 3 Powell, *supra*, par. 410, at 34-63, 34-64; Park, [Real Estate Law § 276 (2d ed. 1981),] *supra*, at 362. It may be, however, that the degree of necessity required must be greater than in the case of a voluntary conveyance. See Restatement of Property § 474 comment b. Considering the importance of continued water and sewer services to occupants of residential property and the substantial construction work required to install new lines on lot A, even that higher degree of necessity has been shown in this case. . . .

D. Prescriptive Easements

Easements may also be acquired by prescriptive use. In general, the requirements for establishing such an easement are the same as for adverse possession, although of course the scope of the right acquired is different. Some states have statutes defining the prescriptive period; see, e.g., Conn. Gen. Stat. § 47-37 (15-year prescriptive period); other jurisdictions use the ordinary statute for recovery of land, seemingly by analogy.

Little barriers case

REED v. PIEDIMONTE
526 N.Y.S.2d 273 (App. Div. 1988)

Memorandum.

Plaintiff demonstrated by clear and convincing evidence that his employees and tenants openly and notoriously used the driveway from Geddes Street to plaintiff's warehouse from 1943 until 1970 (when defendant James Piedimonte purchased the land encompassing the driveway area) and thereafter until access was permanently blocked in 1985. Although defendants presented evidence that temporary barricades were erected by the predecessors in title and others during the 1950's and by defendants in the 1970's, there was no proof that these temporary devices ever effectively interfered with, or disturbed, plaintiff's continuous use of the driveway (see *Caswell v. Bisnett*, 50 A.D.2d 672, lv. denied 38 NY2d 709).

Once the party claiming prescriptive use of an easement demonstrates that the use was open and notorious, continuous and uninterrupted for the prescriptive period, a presumption arises that such use was adverse, and the burden is on the servient landowner to prove that the use was by permission or license (*Di Leo v. Pecksto Holding Corp.*, 304 N.Y. 505, 512; *Beutler v. Maynard*, 80 A.D.2d 982, aff'd 56 N.Y.2d 538). Defendants presented no evidence that express permission was granted during the critical period between 1943 and 1958. Defendants' claim that permission may be implied from their predecessor's neighborly accommodation lacks merit. A mere claim of neighborly accommodation is not proof of permission (see *Borruso v. Morreale*, 129 A.D.2d 604), and evidence that the predecessor erected a temporary barrier on one occasion negates an implication of permission. Lastly, the trial court correctly determined that plaintiff's use could be adverse even though he was not the exclusive user (*Borruso v. Morreale, supra; Slater v. Ward*, 92 A.D.2d 667), and the record indicates that plaintiff (including his employees and tenants) was the principal user (see *Epstein v. Rose*, 101 A.D.2d 646, 647, lv denied 64 N.Y.2d 611).

The proof demonstrated that plaintiff acquired an easement by prescription well before the date defendant purchased the property. Accordingly, plaintiff is entitled to a judgment declaring that he has an easement and restraining defendants from obstructing the driveway or otherwise interfering with plaintiff's continuous use thereof.

NOTES

1. What can a landowner do, short of a bringing an action for trespass, to prevent this sort of usage from ripening into an easement? Some states have passed statutes similar to the following from Connecticut (Conn. Gen. Stat. § 47-38):

> The owner of land over which a right-of-way or other easement is claimed or used may give notice in writing, to the person claiming or using the privilege, of his intention to dispute the right-of-way or other easement and to prevent the other party from acquiring the right; and the notice, being served and recorded as provided in sections 47-39 and 47-40, shall be deemed an interruption of the use and shall prevent the acquiring of a right thereto by the continuance of the use for any length of time thereafter.

Does this statute solve the problem, or does it fail and create unnecessary new problems? See, e.g., *South Norwalk Lodge, No. 709 v. Palco Hats, Inc.*, 100 A.2d 735 (Conn. 1953).

2. What about the problem of notice and the rights of bona fide purchasers under American recording acts? The general American rule is that to be bound by an easement "a servient purchaser must have some form of notice: record notice, actual notice, or inquiry notice." 7 Thompson on Real Property § 60.07. If the subject of an easement were underground, would it be implied against a subsequent purchaser? See, e.g., *Fossum Orchards v. Pugsley*, 892 P.2d 1095 (Wash. Ct. App. 1995).

STATE EX REL. HAMAN v. FOX
594 P.2d 1093 (Idaho 1979)

McFADDEN, J.

This is an action brought by the Prosecuting Attorney of Kootenai County on behalf of the people of the state of Idaho to establish public rights in and to privately owned water front property on Lake Coeur d'Alene. The district court determined that the public had no right or interest in the property and gave judgment to the property owners. We affirm.

Defendants-respondents C.R.W. Fox and Eileen Fox, husband and wife, and Burgess K. McDonald, personal representative of the estate of Carmelita K. McDonald, deceased, own adjoining residential properties in the City of Coeur d'Alene. The properties consist of two residential lots in the Lake Shore Addition Plat together with two water front parcels abutting the waters of Lake Coeur d'Alene. The water front property is separated from the platted lots by Lake Shore Drive, a dedicated public street. Respondents' homes and yards are in the platted lots to the north of Lake Shore Drive. The water front lots to the south of Lake Shore Drive are for the most part sandy beach. The beach lots are adjoined on both sides by other privately owned lots, which together comprise what is commonly known as Sander's Beach. The beach has no public access other than from the lake itself. But the public does have access to the lake via a deeded right-of-way to the west of respondents' property and via a ten-foot wide pathway to the east of respondents' property.

Respondents' beach property extends south from Lake Shore Drive to the ordinary mean high water mark of Lake Coeur d'Alene. Their adjoining lots have a combined lake frontage of 250 feet and a depth of from 60 to 75 feet. The property is subject to the seasonal fluctuations of high water in the spring and low water in the late summer and fall. The property is also subject to the washings and erosive forces of the lake.

For many years, at least since the 1920's, respondents and their predecessors have maintained seawalls to protect a portion of their property immediately south of Lake Shore Drive from the erosive forces of the lake. In 1971 respondents obtained the necessary building permits from the City of Coeur d'Alene and constructed a new concrete seawall. The new wall is a three-sided structure extending approximately 20 feet closer to the lake than the earlier walls and running the entire 250 feet across respondents' property. The wall does not interfere with swimming or boating on the lake, nor does it extend to the ordinary high water mark of the lake. The wall has, however, eliminated the public use of the enclosed area for sunbathing, picnicking and other related activities. It is this 20 feet by 250 feet enclosed area which is in dispute here.

This action was brought to force respondents to remove the seawall and to permanently enjoin them from further interfering with the alleged right of the public to use the enclosed areas. The complaint alleged that for over thirty years the general public had enjoyed complete freedom to use the beach for recreational purposes. It was alleged that by virtue of such public use respondents had impliedly dedicated the property to the general public or in the alternative that the public had acquired an easement thereon by prescription or by custom. It was also alleged that the wall interfered with the public trust in which the waters of the lake are held. After a trial to the court sitting without a jury, the people of the state of Idaho were adjudged to have no right or interest whatever to the property. The requested injunctive relief was denied, and judgment was entered in favor of respondents. This appeal followed.

. . . .

A. Easement by Prescription

Appellant claims a right on behalf of the general public of this state to use private property for recreational purposes. In order to establish such a right by prescription, a party must submit "reasonably clear and convincing proof of open, notorious, continuous, uninterrupted use, under a claim of right, with the knowledge of the owner of the servient tenement, for the prescriptive period." *West v. Smith*, 95 Idaho 550, 557, 511 P.2d 1326, 1333 (1973) (footnotes omitted). The prescriptive right cannot arise, however, if the use of the land is with the permission of the owner. (citations omitted)

After hearing the testimony of some seventeen witnesses on the use of respondents' property, the trial court found "that the use herein by the public was open, notorious, continuous, and uninterrupted and with the knowledge of the defendants [respondents] for more than the prescriptive period." The court further found, however, that the public use was in fact "a permissive use" and that "the evidence herein does not establish an adverse or hostile use by the plaintiff [appellant] against the interest of the defendants [respondents] nor any act on the part of any member of the public that would give notice to the defendants [respondents] that the public was claiming an interest adverse to them." The court therefore concluded that no public rights had been established by prescription.

These findings, if supported by substantial and competent evidence in the record, will not be disturbed on appeal. I.R.C.P. 52(a); *Skelton v. Spencer*, 98 Idaho 417, 565 P.2d 1374 (1977); *Idaho Water Resource Board v. Kramer*, 97 Idaho 535, 548 P.2d 35 (1976). We have carefully reviewed the record and conclude that there is substantial and competent evidence to support these findings. Even so, the court's finding that the use was by permission of respondents can only be sustained from that point in time in which respondents held title to the property. Respondents Fox acquired their property in 1948. Carmelita McDonald, now deceased, acquired hers in 1924. Appellant contends that the prescriptive rights to use the beach were acquired prior to 1948 and 1924, and that respondents took their fee interests subject to the already established public rights. We find it unnecessary to answer this contention. For the reasons stated below, this court is of the opinion that the "general public" or "the people of the state of Idaho" as distinguished from specific individuals cannot, absent specific statutory authorization, acquire prescriptive rights to private property.

As a starting point, it is important that the underlying legal rationale of a prescriptive right be discussed. Many courts have relied upon the fiction of the "lost-grant," i. e. it was presumed, from long possession under claim of right and with acquiescence of the owner, that there must have originally been a grant, from the owner to the claimant, which had become lost during the course of time. 2 G. Thompson, Thompson on Real Property § 337, 171–80 (1961); 3 R. Powell, The Law of Real Property § 413 (1977); 25 Am.Jur.2d, Easements, § 39, 452–53. Under the lost grant rationale, courts have held that the general public, considered apart from legally organized or political entities, could not acquire prescriptive rights because they could not receive a grant. (citations omitted) In *Ivons-Nispel, Inc. v. Lowe*, 347 Mass. 760, 200 N.E.2d 282 (1964), a case almost identical to the case at bar, the Supreme Judicial Court of Massachusetts stated that "We are of opinion that 'persons of the local community' and the 'general public' are too broad a group to acquire by prescription an easement to use private beaches for bathing and for recreational purposes. (citations omitted.)" 200 N.E.2d at 283.

Although Idaho long ago abandoned the fiction of the lost grant, we reach the same result as the Massachusetts court in holding that the general public cannot acquire prescriptive rights in private property. In *Last Chance Ditch Co. v. Sawyer*, an action brought by the property owner to enjoin 89 persons from permitting waste water to flow into the canal, 35 Idaho 61, 66–67, 204 P. 654, 655 (1922), the court stated:

> We are of the opinion, however, that the recognized fiction of a lost grant should not be given such controlling efficacy. While it is true that the statute of limitations does not in terms apply to the acquisition of title to an easement by prescription, it is generally held that by analogy such statutes are applicable. The use of an easement constitutes a direct invasion of the dominion of the proprietor of the land, and the statute forbids maintenance of an action to prevent such use as has been enjoyed openly, continuously, adversely, and with the acquiescence of the owner for a period of five years or more. The statute announces the policy of the law. It does not appear to be founded upon the fiction of a lost grant, but upon the proposition that it is the policy of the state to discourage litigation of matters which, through the lapse of time, should be considered as settled. We think the acquiescence of the owner of land in case of continuous and adverse user of an easement is presumed, and can be disproved only by showing acts upon his part which interrupt the continuity of the use, or by appropriate action in court to prevent its continuance. (See *Lehigh Valley R. Co. v. McFarlan*, 43 N.J.L. 605.)

The statute of limitations discussed in *Last Chance Ditch Co., supra*, upon which prescriptive rights in Idaho are based, is I.C. § 5-203. This statute in effect gives an owner five years to take the necessary and appropriate legal action to have an unauthorized use of his property stopped. If the owner of the property fails to eject the trespasser or enjoin the unauthorized use, after five years his right to do so will be barred. But as against whom would the owner be barred? Only those who had actually made open, notorious, continuous, uninterrupted use, under a claim of right, with the knowledge of the owner, for the five year period. Those persons who had not made such use could be enjoined from further interfering with the owner's superior rights.

In *West v. Smith, supra*, where an individual claimant asserted a prescriptive right to moor his houseboat in front of another person's privately owned lake front lot and to maintain a catwalk onto the owner's property, this court held that any prescriptive right there acquired was purely personal to the individual claimant. The prescriptive right belonged exclusively to the actual user, and not to guests or assignees. The private owner could therefore exclude all others from making any unapproved use of his property.

As in *West v. Smith, supra*, the rights contended for here are in the nature of an easement in gross. Being a personal right, the rule is that one individual's prescriptive use cannot inure to the benefit of anyone else. Personal prescriptive rights are confined to the actual adverse user and are limited to the use exercised during the prescriptive period. *West v. Smith, supra*; *Kirk v. Schultz*, 63 Idaho 278, 119 P.2d 266 (1941); 2 G. Thompson, Thompson on Real Property, § 346, 264–66 (1961). The fact that hundreds of individuals have made use of respondents' property for the prescriptive period does not bar respondents from enjoining all future trespass to the property. Nor does the use of respondents' property by certain neighbors or friends or even total strangers accrue or inure to the benefit of others. We therefore hold that the "people of the State of Idaho" as distinguished from specific individuals cannot acquire prescriptive rights in and to private property absent some express statutory authority. The one situation where the legislature has allowed such public prescriptive rights is in public highways. When a right-of-way has been used by the general public for a period of five years and has been maintained at public expense, the right-of-way becomes a public highway. See I.C. § 40-103 and *Meservey v. Gulliford*, 14 Idaho 133, 93 P. 780 (1908). No similar statute applies to the facts of this case. The district court's denial of the prescriptive easement is affirmed.

B. Dedication

Appellant contends that respondents have made an implied dedication of their property to the public. The district court put the burden on appellant to prove that respondents had by their acts or omissions intended to dedicate the land to public use. The court found that this burden had not been sustained. We concur.

The fundamental principles in this state regarding implied dedications are found in *Village of Hailey v. Riley*, 14 Idaho 481, 495, 95 P. 686, 691 (1908), quoted with approval in *Simmons v. Perkins*, 63 Idaho 136, 143, 118 P.2d 740, 744 (1941):

> It is no trivial thing to take another's land without compensation, and for this reason the courts will not lightly declare a dedication to public use. It is elementary law that an intention to dedicate upon the part of the owner must be plainly manifest.
>
> . . . .
>
> And while long continued user, without objection, and with the knowledge and consent of the owner is some evidence of a right in the public, still there must be joined to that user an intention upon the part of the owner to dedicate, or no dedication will be consummated; for the long-continued user by the public without objection by the owner is entirely consistent with

a license to the public to use the land, and therefore evidence of long-continued user alone will not support a finding of fact that a dedication was created. Neither will a finding of fact of mere long-continued user support a conclusion of law that a public highway was created. As previously stated, in order to constitute a dedication of a highway by evidence in pais, there must be convincing evidence that the owner intended to appropriate the land to the public use.

Appellant urges this court to adopt the reasoning of the California per curiam decisions, *Gion v. City of Santa Clara* and *Dietz v. King*, 2 Cal. 3d 29, 84 Cal. Rptr. 162, 465 P.2d 50 (1970), for the proposition that five years uninterrupted public use of private property creates a conclusive presumption of the owner's intent to dedicate. We decline the opportunity. Instead we adhere to the rule that a party claiming a right by dedication bears the burden of proof on every material issue. The intent of the owner to dedicate his land to public use must be clearly and unequivocally shown and must never be presumed. . . .

C. Custom

Another theory advanced by appellant is that the public has by customary usage acquired recreation rights to respondents' property. This theory is based upon the English common law of custom, defined as: "a usage or practice of the people, which, by common adoption and acquiescence, and by long and unvarying habit, has become compulsory, and has acquired the force of a law with respect to the place or subject-matter to which it relates." Black's Law Dictionary 461 (rev. 4th ed. 1968). By the law of custom, the general public could, after many years of unrestricted common usage, acquire rights over private property. *Post v. Pearsall*, 22 Wend. 425 (N.Y.Ct.Err. 1839); 2 W. Blackstone, Commentaries, 263; 2 G. Thompson, *supra*, § 335.

The acquisition of a right through custom in England required that the use "must have continued from time immemorial, without interruption, and as a right; it must be certain as to the place, and as to the persons; and it must be certain and reasonable as to the subject matter or rights created." 3 H. Tiffany, Law of Real Property, § 935 at 623 (3d ed. 1939). See also 1 W. Blackstone, Commentaries 75–78; 3 Powell, *supra*, § 414[9]; *Public Access to Beaches*, 22 Stanford L. Rev. 564, 582 (1970); 25 Univ. of Florida L. Rev. 586, 591 (1973). Virtually all commentators are agreed that, until recently, the law of custom was a dead letter in the United States. Aside from two New Hampshire cases decided in the 1850's no state had applied the doctrine. As recently as 1935 New York refused to accept customary usage as a means of claiming an easement in a private beach for bathing and boating. *Gillies v. Orienta Beach Club*, 159 Misc. 675, 289 N.Y.S. 733 (1935). The doctrine was exhumed, however, by the Supreme Court of Oregon in *State ex rel. Thornton v. Hay*, 254 Or. 584, 462 P.2d 671 (1969), where it was held that the public had acquired customary rights to a privately owned dry sand stretch of beach on the Oregon sea coast. Because of the tract-by-tract limitations inherent in the prescription theory, the Oregon court chose to apply custom to claimed public use of oceanfront lands.

Whether the doctrine exists in this state is a matter of first impression. I.C. §§ 73-116 provides that "[the] common law of England, so far as it is not repugnant to, or inconsistent with, the constitution or laws of the United States, in all cases not provided for in these compiled laws, is the rule of decision in all courts of this state." There being no statute which expressly or impliedly rejects the doctrine of custom, this court is of opinion that the doctrine does obtain in Idaho. See *Industrial Indem. Co. v. Columbia Basin Steel & Iron, Inc.*, 93 Idaho 719, 471 P.2d 574 (1970).

The district court applied the law of custom to the facts of this case and concluded that the requisite elements had not been established. The first element, use from time immemorial, means that the use has existed for so long that "the memory of man runneth not to the contrary." *State ex rel. Thornton v. Hay, supra*, 462 P.2d at 677. In the instant case, the district court found that usage commenced as early as 1912. We agree with the district court that this does not constitute "from time immemorial." The second requirement, that the use must be uninterrupted, is not met because of the fact that respondents had personally and with police assistance removed members of the public from their land. Without further burdening this opinion, suffice it to say that of the seven essential elements of a customary right, the trial court found adversely to appellant on six of them. We find ample evidence in the record to support the findings, and we therefore affirm the district court's denial of any customary rights in this case.

D. Public Trust

Appellant's final argument is that respondents' lake front property is imbued with a public trust under the principles of the public trust doctrine. That doctrine's leading authority, Professor Sax of the University of Michigan School of Law, articulates the following as the "central substantive thought in public trust litigation": "[when] a state holds a resource which is available for the free use of the general public, a court will look with considerable skepticism upon any governmental conduct which is calculated either to relocate that resource to more restricted uses or to subject public uses to the self-interest of private parties." J. Sax, *The Public Trust Doctrine in Natural Resource Law: Effective Judicial Intervention*, 68 Mich. L. Rev. 473, 490 (1970).

It is undisputed that the land in contention here is private property, traceable to a patent from the United States Government in 1892. It is also undisputed that the seawall constructed by respondents lies above the ordinary mean high water mark of the lake and that it in no way interferes with navigability or the public's use of the lake's waters. Since no natural resource owned by the state is involved here the public trust doctrine is inapposite. The district court judgment is affirmed in all respects. Costs to respondents.

NOTES

1. As set out in the opinion in *Thornton v. Hay*, the Oregon case mentioned in *Haman*, a valid legal custom must meet seven tests under traditional law. It must (1) have existed from a time beyond human memory; (2) have been exercised without interruption; (3) be peaceable and free from dispute; (4) be reasonable; (5) be certain; (6) be obligatory, that is not subject to the option of individual landowners; and (7) not be inconsistent with or repugnant to other laws and customs. The court in that case held that the public's long-standing use of the "dry-sand area" lying between the high tide mark and the start of vegetation "meets every one of Blackstone's requisites." 462 P.2d at 677.

2. Does the use of custom as a source of law to secure public access to the beachfront amount to an unconstitutional taking of private property for public use, or does it "take from no man anything which he has had a legitimate reason to regard as exclusively his"? 462 P.2d at 678. See David Bederman, *The Curious Resurrection of Custom: Beach Access and Judicial Takings*, 96 Colum. L. Rev. 1375 (1996).

3. Does the law of custom discussed in these cases accord with its application in *Ghen v. Rich, supra*, Chapter 1?

E. Scope of the Easement

Where grants of easements are made in unambiguous terms, courts limit the extent of the easement to what was specified in those terms or reasonably implied from them. Often, however, ambiguities exist, and of course this is particularly true where the easement is acquired in some other way than by express grant. It is hornbook law that in all such situations, the holder of the dominant estate may not unreasonably increase the burden on the servient estate. Thus in *Robertson v. Bertha Mineral Co.*, 104 S.E. 832, 835 (Va. 1920), the court held that an easement for a railway to haul coal was not an easement for general railway purposes. A change of the use of the dominant estate from agricultural use to commercial use is another textbook example in which most courts have found a similar overburden. *Bartholomew v. Staheli*, 195 P.2d 824 (Cal. Ct. App. 1948). However, exact usage is not frozen. An easement permitting access to a single family house was held not to be overburdened by its extension to tenants when the house was converted into a three-family apartment building. *Westland Nursing Home, Inc. v. Benson*, 517 P.2d 862 (Colo. Ct. App. 245). In reaching their conclusions, courts commonly weigh the interests of each landowner. See *Extending the Benefit of an Easement: A Closer Look at a Classic Rule*, 62 Wash. L. Rev. 295 (1987), which criticizes the willingness of some judges to permit expansion in the scope of easements by balancing the interests involved. See also James Backman & David Thomas, A Practical Guide to Disputes Between Adjoining Landowners — Easements § 1.03.

marina case

HAYES v. AQUIA MARINA, INC.
414 S.E.2d 820 (Va. 1992)

Generally) court says reasonable expansion of same use a foe.

STEPHENSON, J.

The principal issue in this appeal is whether an easement across the servient estates will be overburdened by the proposed expanded use of the dominant estate. Robert C. Hayes and others (collectively, Hayes) brought a chancery suit against Aquia Marina, Inc., Warren E. Gnegy, and Cynthia Gnegy (collectively, Gnegy). Hayes alleged, inter alia, that a proposed expansion of a marina located on Gnegy's land (the dominant estate or marina property) would overburden the easement across Hayes's lands (the servient estates). Hayes, therefore, sought to have the trial court enjoin the proposed expanded use of the dominant estate.

The cause was referred to a commissioner in chancery. Following an ore tenus hearing, and after taking a view of the subject properties, the commissioner filed a report containing the following findings: (1) a perpetual easement exists across the servient estates for ingress to and egress from the dominant estate; (2) the easement is not limited solely for domestic use, but may be used commercially by the marina and its customers and by boat owners and their guests; (3) the proposed expansion of the marina from 84 to 280 boat slips is a reasonable use of the dominant estate; (4) the resulting increase in traffic over the easement will not change the type, only the degree, of use and will not overburden the easement; and (5) paving the easement is reasonable and a proper means of maintenance.

By a final decree, entered March 5, 1991, the trial court overruled all of Hayes's exceptions to the commissioner's report and confirmed the report in all respects. Hayes appeals.

We must view the evidence in the light most favorable to Gnegy, the prevailing party at trial. The marina property is a 2.58-acre tract situate on Aquia Creek in Stafford County. The easement is the sole means of land access to the marina property.

The litigants' predecessors in title entered into a written agreement, executed February 3, 1951, for "the establishment of a certain roadway or right of way beginning at the Northern terminus of State Highway No. 666, and terminating at the property division line between [the servient estates], and where [the dominant estate] adjoins the same on the North side thereof" and for "the continuation of said right of way." The agreement recited that "the State Department of Highways will be requested . . . to take over into the State Highway System the present roadway beginning at the North terminus of said State Highway No. 666, and leading through [the servient estates]." The roadway that was intended to be taken into the state highway system was "approximately something less than one-half mile in length." The "newly established private roadway" was "approximately 1,120 feet in length" and "fifteen feet wide along its entire distance." The agreement provided that the parties thereto "shall have an easement of right of way over the entire length [thereof]."

The record indicates that the portion of the easement, beginning at the northern terminus of State Highway No. 666, became a part of the state highway system in 1962. The record also indicates that the "private roadway" is constructed of dirt and gravel.

By 1959, three residential buildings and a wooden pier were located on the dominant estate. The pier was approximately 30 feet long and contained about 10 boat slips. This small marina was operated commercially.

Between 1961 and 1962, the current marina was constructed. This marina has been operated commercially for the general public from 1964 until the present. The marina consists of 84 boat slips, a travel lift station, a public boat launch, and a gas dock. Boats and boat parts are sold at the marina. Boats also are repaired on the marina property.

In September 1989, the Board of Supervisors of Stafford County granted Gnegy a special use permit to expand the marina by increasing the number of boat slips to 280. After the proposed expansion, the marina will continue to provide the same services it has provided since 1964.

There has never been a "traffic problem" with the easement. An expert witness on emergency services testified that there never had been a problem with access to the marina property and none was anticipated if the proposed expansion occurred. On weekends, a time of maximum use of the marina property, Gnegy anticipates that only 20 to 30 percent of the boat owners will make use of the marina.

As a general rule, when an easement is created by grant or reservation and the instrument creating the easement does not limit the use to be made of it, the easement may be used for "any purpose to which the dominant estate may then, or in the future, reasonably be devoted." *Cushman Corporation v. Barnes*, 129 S.E.2d 633, 639 (Va. 1963). Stated differently, an easement created by a general grant or reservation, without words limiting it to any particular use of the dominant estate, is not affected by any reasonable change in the use of the dominant estate. However, no use may be made of the easement which is different from that established at the time of its creation and which imposes an additional burden upon the servient estate.

Hayes contends that, by using the phrase, "private roadway," in the easement agreement, the parties to the agreement intended to limit the use of the easement to domestic purposes, thereby prohibiting commercial uses. Gnegy contends, on the other hand, that the agreement created an easement for access without limitation. The commissioner and the trial court adopted Gnegy's contention.

When the agreement is read as a whole, it is clear that the phrase, "private roadway," was used to distinguish that portion of the easement that would not become a part of the state highway system from that portion of the easement that could be taken into the system. Thus, the phrase is descriptive, not restrictive.

Consequently, we hold that the agreement creating the easement for access contains no terms of limitation upon the easement's use. Additionally, the record supports the conclusion that the operation of a marina is a use to which the dominant estate reasonably can be, and has been, devoted.

Hayes further contends that the proposed expansion of the marina will impose an additional and unreasonable burden upon the easement. Having alleged that the proposed expansion will impose an additional burden upon the easement, Hayes has the burden of proving this allegation.

A contention similar to the one advanced by Hayes was presented in *Cushman Corporation, supra*. In *Cushman Corporation*, as in the present case, the instruments creating the easement contain no language limiting the easement's use. 129 S.E.2d at 640. When the easement was established, the dominant estate, a 126.67-acre tract, was used as a farm and contained two single-family dwellings with appurtenant servant and tenant houses. A controversy arose when the dominant owner proposed to subdivide the tract for residential and commercial uses. The trial court limited the easement to its original uses. We reversed the ruling, stating, *id.* at 640, inter alia:

> The fact that the dominant estate is divided and a portion or portions conveyed away does not, in and of itself, mean that an additional burden is imposed upon the servient estate. The result may be that the degree of burden is increased, but that is not sufficient to deny use of the right of way to an owner of a portion so conveyed.

Here, after weighing the evidence, both the commissioner and the trial court concluded that the proposed expansion would not unreasonably burden the easement. On appeal, a decree confirming a commissioner's report is presumed to be correct and will be affirmed unless plainly wrong.

In the present case, we cannot say that the trial court's conclusion is plainly wrong. Indeed, we think that it is supported by the evidence and by well-established principles of law. Here, as in *Cushman Corporation*, the proposed expansion will not, "in and of itself," impose an "additional burden" upon the easement, even though the "degree of burden" may be increased. Therefore, assuming, without deciding, that an expanded use of the dominant estate could be of such degree as to impose an additional and unreasonable burden upon an easement, such is not the situation in the present case.

Finally, Hayes contends that Gnegy does not have the right to pave the easement. Hayes acknowledges, and we agree, that the owner of a dominant estate has a duty to maintain an easement. However, Hayes reasons that, because the owner of a dominant estate has a duty to maintain an easement, it follows that the owner does not have a right to improve the easement. We agree that there is a distinction between maintenance and improvement. However, we do not agree that the owner of a dominant estate does not have the right to make reasonable improvements to an easement.

Although we previously have not addressed the "improvement" issue, courts in other jurisdictions have held that the owner of a dominant estate has the right to make reasonable improvements to an easement, so long as the improvement does not unreasonably increase the burden upon the servient estate. (Citations omitted.) Such improvement may include paving a roadway. Ordinarily, the reasonableness of the improvement is a question of fact. We adopt these principles of law.

In the present case, the commissioner and the trial court found that the proposed paving of the roadway by Gnegy, under the existing facts and circumstances, is reasonable. We will affirm this finding; it is supported by the evidence and is not plainly wrong. Accordingly, the trial court's judgment will be affirmed.

NOTES

1. One of the lessons of *Hayes v. Aquia Marina* is that an easement should be limited in the deed creating it unless the owner of the servient land wishes to run the risk of this sort of litigation. A roadway may, for example, be limited to the use of automobiles. Where this is so, how would sport utility vehicles or pickup trucks be treated? The approach used in *Hayes* centers on the rights of the dominant estate holder. Other courts have sometimes relied on rules favoring the owner of the servient estate: "In determining the scope of an easement, we have repeatedly held that the owner of the servient estate retains the right to use his land in any manner

which does not unreasonably interfere with the use granted in the easement."
Walton v. Capital Land, Inc., 477 S.E.2d 499 (Va. 1996).

2. Once located by an agreement of the parties, should a roadway easement
ever be subject to unilateral relocation by the dominant or servient tenant? The
cases are split on this issue. Compare *Dowd v. Ahr*, 583 N.E.2d 911 (N.Y. 1991)
(adhering to the traditional view that no unilateral relocation is permitted), with
Umphres v. J.R. Mayer Enterprises, Inc., 889 S.W.2d 86 (Mo. Ct. App. 1994)
(permitting unilateral relocation in some instances). The second case is discussed in
a Note, *Balancing the Equities: Is Missouri Adopting a Progressive Rule for
Relocation of Easements?*, 61 Mo. L. Rev. 1039 (1996). See also Note, *The Right of
Owners of Servient Estates to Relocate Easements*, 109 Harv. L. Rev. 1693 (1996).

3. In partial consideration for granting an appurtenant sewer easement over a
parcel, a dominant owner grants the servient owner the right to tap into the line.
May this tap-in right be transferred when the servient parcel is subdivided? See
Martin v. Music, 254 S.W.2d 701 (Ky. Ct. App. 1953).

4. The traditional rule is that unless contrary to the terms of the easement, an
appurtenant easement is transferred by the dominant owner even when it is not
mentioned in the deed. What happens when the dominant owner expressly provides
that an appurtenant easement is not included in a deed to the dominant estate?
Because the easement adheres in the land, the traditional answer is that it is
extinguished when severed from the land it served. Traditionally, easements in
gross may not be transferred, although most recent cases have held otherwise,
particularly when the easement has a commercial use. See *Miller v. Lutheran
Conference & Camp Ass'n*, 200 A. 646 (Pa. 1938). "Most courts have followed the
leading case of *Miller v. Lutheran Conference & Camp Ass'n* and have allowed the
transfer of easements in gross." James Ely, Jr. & Jon Bruce, The Law of Easements
and Licenses in Land § 9:5.

EPHRATA SCHOOL DISTRICT v. COUNTY OF LANCASTER
886 A.2d 1169 (Pa. Commw. Ct. 2005)

SIMPSON, J.

In this case of first impression, we are asked whether the holder of a prior open
space easement must consent to the grant of a subsequent right-of-way which does
not interfere with the open space easement. In particular, Ephrata Area School
District (School District) asks whether it was required to obtain the approval of
Lancaster County, which secured a prior open space easement from a private
landowner, before the private landowner may grant it a right-of-way. Because
County approval is not required unless the right-of-way interferes with the existing
open space easement, we reverse.

I.

The underlying facts of this case are largely undisputed. In 2000, the School
District purchased approximately 80 acres of land on which it proposed to construct

a public elementary school on the south side of Market Street in Ephrata Township, Lancaster County. The proposed site borders Ephrata Borough.

The School District originally proposed primary access to the elementary school through Market Street. Citing serious traffic and safety concerns, Ephrata Township and Ephrata Borough objected to the use of Market Street for primary access and instead recommended primary access through Hummer Road and secondary access through Meadow Valley Road.

The School District subsequently entered into an agreement to purchase a 50-foot strip of land totaling 2.3 acres from Nelson and Miriam Nolt and David and Erma Lauver to construct an access road from Meadow Valley Road to the school. The parties later modified the agreement to reflect acquisition of a right-of-way under and subject to the rights of the Lancaster County Agricultural Preserve Board (Board), a County agency, in an open space easement over the Lauvers' property.

The Board voted to approve removal of the 50-foot strip of land from the open space easement. In addition, it subsequently voted to recommend the grant of a right-of-way over the Lauvers' land.

Thereafter, the School District requested the County approve the relinquishment of its easement over the 50-foot strip of land or, in the alternative, approve the School District's acquisition of a right-of-way from the Lauvers. The School District alleges it initially believed County approval was required but now believes such approval is unnecessary. Nevertheless, the School District, hoping to obtain County approval, proceeded with a hearing before the Lancaster County Commissioners on its request.

The County Commissioners subsequently voted to deny the School District's request that it consent to a right-of-way over the 50-foot strip of land and denied the request to extinguish the open space easement. The School District appealed the County's decision to the Court of Common Pleas of Lancaster County (trial court).

Several months later, the School District filed a declaratory judgment action in the trial court seeking a declaration that County approval was not required for the acquisition of a right-of-way over the Lauvers' land. It also sought a declaration its proposed right-of-way did not violate the County's open space easement. The trial court stayed the School District's appeal of the County's decision pending resolution of the declaratory judgment action.

After the close of the pleadings in the declaratory judgment action, the School District filed a motion for judgment on the pleadings or, in the alternative, summary judgment. The School District argued it was entitled to judgment as a matter of law because County approval was not required to obtain a right-of-way over land owned by private landowners. The County filed a cross-motion for summary judgment asserting approval was required. Of particular import here, in its submissions to the trial court, the County conceded the proposed right-of-way would not violate its open space easement.

Ultimately, the trial court issued an opinion and order granting the County's cross-motion for summary judgment and denying the School District's motion. The trial court determined, pursuant to Section 11(a) of what is commonly known as the Open Space Lands Act (Act), the School District was required to obtain County approval for the acquisition of a right-of-way over the Lauvers' property because of the County's open space easement. The trial court further determined, because the County declined to grant approval, it was entitled to summary judgment. The School District appealed to this Court.

II.

In order to fully evaluate the claims presented, some discussion of the common law principles regarding easements is necessary. We begin by determining the appropriate classification for the County's open space easement.

A.

Generally, easements are of two types: easements appurtenant and easements in gross. An easement appurtenant is a liberty, privilege or advantage without profit which the owner of one piece of land has in the land of another. See *Morning Call, Inc. v. Bell Atlantic-Pennsylvania, Inc.*, 2000 Pa. Super 294, 761 A.2d 139 (Pa. Super. 2000). Stated otherwise, "it is a service which one estate owes to another — or a right or privilege in one man's estate for the advantage or convenience of the owner of another estate." *Perkinpine v. Hogan*, 47 Pa. Super. 22, 25 (1910). The land enjoying the privilege is referred to as the "dominant tenement," and the land subject to the privilege is known as the "servient tenement." See Ladner on Conveyancing in Pennsylvania, § 11.01 at p. 1 (Bisel, 4th ed. 1979).

An easement in gross, on the other hand, is a mere personal right in the real estate of another because it is not appurtenant to other land owned by the grantee. An easement in gross benefits a particular entity rather than a particular piece of land. See Ladner, § 11.01 at p. 2. An easement in gross is an easement with a servient estate but no dominant estate. *Kent's Run P'ship, Ltd. v. Glosser*, 323 B.R. 408 (Bankr. W.D. Pa. 2005).

The open space easement at issue here is properly classified as an easement in gross because it benefits a particular entity, i.e., the County, rather than a particular piece of land, and there is no dominant estate. See, e.g., John L. Hollingshead, *Conservation Easements: A Flexible Tool for Land Preservation*, 3 Envtl. Law. 319, 328 (1997) (characterizing conservation easement as "a negative easement in gross"). Indeed, the easement agreement at issue here expressly states (with emphasis added), "the restrictions contained herein shall apply to the land as an open space *easement in gross. . . .*" Reproduced Record (R.R.) at 12a. The agreement further states, "this grant of easement in the nature of a restriction is *intended to be an easement in gross. . . .*" *Id.* (emphasis added).

B.

Easements are also properly classified as affirmative or negative. See Restatement (Third) of Property, Servitudes § 1.2 (2000). Easements are considered "affirmative" if they convey privileges on the part of one person or owner of land to use the land of another in a particular manner or for a particular purpose. *Id.* Easements are considered "negative" if they convey rights to demand the servient owner refrain from certain otherwise permissible uses of his own land. *Id.* With regard to negative easements, the Supreme Court of Virginia recently explained:

> Negative easements, also known as servitudes, do not bestow upon the owner of the dominant tract the right to travel physically upon the servient tract, which is the feature common to all affirmative easements, but only the legal right to object to a use of the servient tract by its owner inconsistent with the terms of the easement. In this sense, negative easements have been described as consisting solely of "a veto power."

> At common law, an owner of land was not permitted at his pleasure to create easements of every novel character and annex them to the land so that the land would be burdened with the easement when the land was conveyed to subsequent grantees. Rather, the landowner was limited to the creation of easements permitted by the common law or by statute. The traditional negative easements recognized at common law were those created to protect the flow of air, light, and artificial streams of water, and to ensure the subjacent and lateral support of buildings or land.

United States v. Blackman, 270 Va. 68, 76, 613 S.E.2d 442, 446 (Va. 2005) (citations omitted).

The County's open space easement is also properly classified as a "negative easement" as it requires the Lauvers to retain their property in its agricultural and open space condition. See R.R. at 9a-12a.

C.

Easements are also classified as exclusive or non-exclusive. An "exclusive easement" deprives a servient owner of all beneficial use and enjoyment of his land. 7 Summary of Pennsylvania Jurisprudence 2d, Property, § 18:20 (2000). Under Pennsylvania law, "the fee in land may be in one person and the exclusive right to use it as a right of way may be in another, but to accomplish that result the deed creating the right of way must *specifically* so covenant." *Fedorko Props., Inc. v. C.F. Zurn & Assocs.*, 720 A.2d 147, 149 (Pa. Super. 1998) (emphasis added). Absent an express provision in a grant or reservation, an easement is not an exclusive interest in the burdened land. *Id.*

Nothing in the easement agreement here indicates the Lauvers intended to grant the County an exclusive easement. To the contrary, under the agreement, the Lauvers retain the right to use their property in any manner that does not impair its open space and agricultural values. R.R. at 10a. In addition, the agreement does not prohibit the Lauvers from granting a subsequent right-of-way over their property. Therefore, the County's open space easement is non-exclusive.

D.

Finally, the particular "negative easement" at issue here is also properly characterized as a "conservation easement." See Vivian Quinn, *Preserving Farm-*

land with Conservation Easements: Public Benefit or Burden?, 1992/1993 Ann. Surv. Am. L. 235, 238 (conservation easement is designed to preserve servient land in undeveloped or natural state). With regard to the development of conservation easements in modern law, the Restatement (Third) of Property, Servitudes, explains:

> Traditional servitudes doctrines raised potential difficulties for the creation of conservation and preservation servitudes. The primary problem was caused by the rule prohibiting equitable enforcement of restrictive-covenant benefits held in gross. Since most conservation and preservation servitudes are granted to governmental bodies, land trusts, or other charitable entities that engage in conservation or preservation activities, the benefit will usually be in gross. To avoid the rule prohibiting benefits in gross, the parties could either acquire a parcel to which the benefit could be appurtenant, or substitute a negative easement, which presumably allowed a benefit in gross. However, common-law precedents cast doubt on the validity of negative easements for previously unrecognized purposes, and on the transferability of the easement benefit.

> The uncertainty and difficulties imposed by the common law of servitudes led to the widespread enactment of statutes. The Uniform Conservation Easement Act was promulgated in 1981. In 1999, only three states lacked such a statute. These statutes validate conservation and preservation servitudes without regard to common-law rules, but limit their coverage to servitudes held by governmental bodies and charitable organizations . . . whose purposes include conservation or historic preservation. With the elimination of restrictions on creation and transferability of benefits in gross in this Restatement (§§ 2.6, 4.6), there is no longer any impediment to the creation of servitudes for conservation or preservation purposes. . . .

> [Thus,] in modern servitudes law, landowners are free to grant conservation servitudes to . . . governmental bodies and conservation organizations. . . .

Restatement (Third) of Property, Servitudes § 1.6 (2000).

E.

Having determined the appropriate classifications for the County's open space easement, we next examine the rights of a servient owner at common law. Ordinarily, when a tract of land is subject to an easement, the servient owner may make any use of the land that does not unreasonably interfere with the use and enjoyment of the easement. James W. Ely, Jr. and Jon W. Bruce, The Law of Easements and Licenses in Land, § 8:17 (2005). The servient owner's right to reasonably use the land includes the right to grant additional easements in the same land to other persons. *Id.* If the first easement is not exclusive, subsequent concurrent easements that are not unreasonably burdensome or inconsistent with the original easement are valid. *Id.*

The rule that a servient owner retains the right to grant subsequent easements that do not unreasonably interfere with the rights of prior easement holders is universally accepted. See 28A C.J.S. Easements § 53 (2005) (landowner who grants easement in land may grant subsequent easements in the same land so long as subsequent easements are neither inconsistent with, or a burden upon, the prior easement); James W. Ely, Jr. and Jon W. Bruce, The Law of Easements and Licenses in Land, §§ 8:17, 8:31 (2005) (servient owner has right to grant additional easements in same strip of land, provided such action does not impair interests of first easement holder); Herbert T. Tiffany and Basil Jones, 3 Real Property § 756 (2004) (servient owner's right to reasonably use the land includes right to grant additional easements in the same land to other persons or entities); 25 Am. Jur. 2d. Easements and Licenses in Real Property § 98 (2004) (so long as they do not unreasonably interfere with the original easement or with each other, additional easements may be created in the same land, if the original easement is non-exclusive).

The Restatement (Third) of Property, Servitudes § 4.9 (2000) is in line with these authorities. It states: "except as limited by the terms of the servitude . . . the holder of the servient estate is entitled to make any use of the servient estate that does not unreasonably interfere with enjoyment of the servitude." *Id.* See also Restatement of Property, Servitudes § 486 (1944) (possessor of land subject to easement created by conveyance is privileged to make such uses of the servient tenement as are not inconsistent with the provisions of the creating conveyance). Comment e to Section 4.9 provides, "*e. Creation of additional servitudes.* Under the rule stated in this section, the holder of the servient estate may create additional servitudes in land burdened by a servitude if the additional servitudes *do not unreasonably interfere* with the enjoyment of the prior servitude holders." Restatement (Third) of Property, Servitudes § 4.9 cmt. e (emphasis added).

Moreover, in Pennsylvania, "the owner of land, who grants a right of way over it, conveys nothing but the right of passage and reserves all incidents of ownership not granted." *Louis W. Epstein Family P'ship v. Kmart Corp.*, 13 F.3d 762, 766 (3d Cir. 1994) (quoting *Mercantile Library Co. v. Fidelity Trust Co.*, 235 Pa. 5, 15, 83 A. 592, 595 (1912)). Thus, the servient owner retains all rights in the property, subject only to the easement. *Rodier v. Twp. of Ridley*, 141 Pa. Commw. 117, 595 A.2d 220 (Pa. Cmwlth. 1991). As a result, a servient owner may grant additional easements in the same strip of land, provided such action does not impair the interests of the first easement holder. *Assocs. of Philipsburg v. Hurwitz*, 292 Pa. Super. 406, 437 A.2d 447 (Pa. Super. 1981).

These general rules also apply where the servient tenement is burdened by a conservation easement. In their treatise The Law of Easements and Licenses in Land, authors James W. Ely, Jr. and Jon W. Bruce explain, "the grantor of a conservation easement retains ownership of the servient land and may use the property for any purpose *not inconsistent with the servitude.* . . ." James W. Ely, Jr. and Jon W. Bruce, The Law of Easements and Licenses in Land, § 12:2 (2005) (emphasis added). Summarizing recent case law on this issue, the authors note:

> [A] [New York appellate] court construed easement language to permit a grant by the servient owner of access over the restricted property on grounds such de minimis use did not interfere with conservation interests.

Similarly, a Connecticut appellate court ruled that the terms of a conservation easement permitted construction of a second single-family home on the servient estate. . . . A Massachusetts appellate court has determined that the right of servient owners to "pass and repass" across a marshland subject to a conservation restriction encompassed the right to make reasonable improvements. . . .

Thus, at common law, it is unnecessary for a servient owner to obtain a prior easement holder's consent in order to grant additional easements over its property. To the contrary, the universally accepted rule is that a servient owner may grant additional easements provided those easements do not unreasonably interfere with the rights of prior easement holders.

Here, before the trial court, the County conceded the School District's proposed right-of-way would not violate its open space easement. See R.R. at 30a, 48–49a. Because the proposed right-of-way would not unreasonably interfere with the County's open space easement, grant of the right-of-way is permissible at common law without approval of the County.

[Discussion of the effect of Pennsylvania's Open Space Lands Act and Dissent omitted. — Eds.]

NOTES

1. Based on an analysis of the Open Space Lands Act, the decision in *Ephrata* was later reversed by the Pennsylvania Supreme Court. 938 A.2d 264 (Pa. 2007).

2. Conservation easements have become popular in recent years; they are used to promote environmental values and to protect scenic and wild habitats. Typically, the grantee is a unit of the government or a charitable organization. See Kornfeld, *Conserving Natural Resources and Open Spaces*, 23 Envtl. L. 185 (1993). Some of their use by governmental bodies is undoubtedly explained by their relatively modest cost compared with condemnation by eminent domain.

F.   Transferability of Easements

1.   Appurtenant Easements

MARTIN v. MUSIC
254 S.W.2d 701 (Ky. 1953)

CULLEN, Comm'nr.

This action involves the construction of the following agreement:

> This mutual agreement, made and entered into by and between Marvin Music, of Prestonsburg, Kentucky, party of the first part, and Fred Martin, of Prestonsburg, Kentucky, party of the second part.

Witnesseth: That for and in consideration of the sum of One ($1.00) Dollar, and other considerations hereinafter set out, parties of the first and second part mutually agree: Party of the first part gives and grants to second party the right to construct and maintain a sewer line under and through his property located in the Layne Heirs addition to the City of Prestonsburg, Kentucky, in the Garfield Bottom, and being lots Nos. 17 through 24 inc. of said addition.

In consideration of said right, second party agrees to lay said sewer line at sufficient depth to not interfere with first party's use and enjoyment of said property; and to place an intake connection in said line for use of said party at a point to be designated by him; and further agrees to pay to first party any damage which may result to his property by reason of the laying, maintaining, repairing and operation of said sewer line.

Given under our hands, this December 3, 1949.

At the time the agreement was executed, the eight lots owned by Music were unoccupied, except for a garage building used by Music for the vehicles operated by him in his business as a bulk distributor of oil and gasoline. Martin constructed his sewer across the lots, and thereafter Music sold six of the lots to one Moore, who in turn sold three each to the appellees Wells and Allen. Wells and Allen each commenced the construction of a dwelling house on his lots, and prepared to connect with Martin's sewer. Martin then brought this action for a declaration of rights, maintaining that the right to connect with the sewer was personal to Music alone, for the purpose of serving a dwelling house which Music had planned to build, and that the right did not accrue to Wells and Allen. The court adjudged that Music, Wells and Allen each had the right to connect with the sewer, provided that the connection was made through the one intake connection provided for in the written contract. Martin appeals.

Considerable evidence was introduced concerning the circumstances surrounding the execution of the agreement, and the situation that existed at the time the agreement was made. It appears that the lots owned by Music had a depth of 120 feet, from east to west, and a width of 25 feet each, fronting on a street on the west and an alley on the east. Across the alley to the east, Martin owned six lots on which he had his private residence and a motel. Martin's northernmost lot was opposite Music's southernmost lot. The Big Sandy River lies some 600 feet west of Martin's property, and he desired to run the sewer line from his property to the river. Martin's evidence was that he first proposed to construct his sewer down the alley between his lots and those of Music, but that Music, upon learning of this plan, offered to let the sewer cross his lots, in return for an intake connection privilege. Martin testified that the understanding was that Music was to build a home on his lots, and that the sewer connection was for that purpose.

Music's evidence was that Martin did not want to run his sewer down the alley, for fear that it then would be classified as a public sewer, to which anyone could connect; that Music offered to let the sewer go across his lots in return for a connection privilege; that there was no understanding that the intake was to be limited to one dwelling to be erected by Music, but on the contrary it was clearly understood that the intake was to be available for each of the eight lots.

Martin's sewer is a six-inch main, which the appellees' evidence tends to show is capable of handling the sewage from their buildings, in addition to that from Martin's properties, with no difficulty. On the other hand, Martin testified that the sewer line had a low grade of descent, and that in times of heavy rains, when the river was high, there would be danger of the sewer backing up into his basement. He complains particularly of the proposal of the appellees to connect their eaves and downspouts to the sewer, which he claims will create too great a flow of water for the sewer line to accommodate.

Martin maintains that the agreement provides for an easement in gross, rather than one running with the land. He relies upon *Mannin v. Adkins*, 199 Ky. 241, 250 S.W. 974, which we do not consider to be in point. In that case, the grantor of a piece of property reserved the right to 'have, use, and get coal off the lands hereby conveyed for fuel for his own purposes or home consumption as fuel'. The court held that the reservation was personal to the grantor, and did not run with the adjoining land which he occupied as his home place at the time of the conveyance. There, the reserved privilege was not related to a particular piece of property as a dominant estate, and it necessarily was personal. Here, the sewer connection privilege necessarily is limited to the parcel of land over which the sewer line runs.

If an easement is to be exercised in connection with the occupancy of particular land, then ordinarily it is classified as an easement appurtenant. We think it is clear that the right to connect to Martin's sewer line was to be exercised only in connection with the occupancy of the land through which it ran, and that Music was not granted the right to run a sewer line to the intake point from some parcel of land he might own or acquire in another block. Therefore, the easement must be considered to be an easement appurtenant.

It is the general rule that easements in gross are not favored, and that an easement will never be presumed to be a mere personal right when it can fairly be construed to be appurtenant to some other estate. This rule prevails in Kentucky.

We think the controlling question is whether the use of the sewer by Wells and Allen, as well as by Music, will unduly burden the servient tenement (in this case, the sewer line). It appears to be the general rule that the dominant estate may be divided or partitioned, and the owner of each part may claim the right to enjoy the easement, if no additional burden is placed upon the servient estate.

Here, it cannot be ascertained from the written agreement, nor can it be ascertained with certainty from the evidence of the circumstances and conditions surrounding the execution of the agreement, just what burden it was contemplated might be imposed by way of connection with the sewer line. As far as the face of the agreement is concerned, Music could have built an apartment house, a hotel, or even a factory, upon his lots, and connected them with the sewer. Either of these would have required only one intake connection. The agreement does not limit the kind of use that Music was to make of the sewer. Since, under the words of the agreement, Music could have placed a much greater burden upon Martin's sewer we do not believe that two or three dwellings will increase the burden contemplated by the parties as expressed in their agreement. If we go beyond the words of the agreement, and accept all of the evidence as to what the parties intended, then we find a conflict of evidence, upon which we could not say that the chancellor erred. The judgment is affirmed.

2.   Easements in Gross

MILLER v. LUTHERAN CONFERENCE & CAMP ASS'N
200 A. 646 (Pa. 1938)

STERN, J.

This litigation is concerned with interesting and somewhat novel legal questions regarding rights of boating, bathing and fishing in an artificial lake. Frank C. Miller, his brother Rufus W. Miller, and others, who owned lands on Tunkhannock Creek in Tobyhanna Township, Monroe County, organized a corporation known as the Pocono Spring Water Ice Company, to which, in September, 1895, they made a lease for a term of ninety-nine years of so much of their lands as would be covered by the backing up of the water as a result of the construction of a 14-foot dam which they proposed to erect across the creek. The company was to have "the exclusive use of the water and its privileges." It was chartered for the purpose of "erecting a dam . . . , for pleasure, boating, skating, fishing and the cutting, storing and selling of ice." The dam was built, forming "Lake Naomi," somewhat more than a mile long and about one-third of a mile wide.

By deed dated March 20, 1899, the Pocono Spring Water Ice Company granted to "Frank C. Miller, his heirs and assigns forever, the exclusive right to fish and boat in all the waters of the said corporation at Naomi Pines, Pa." On February 17, 1900, Frank C. Miller (his wife Katherine D. Miller not joining) granted to Rufus W. Miller, his heirs and assigns forever, "all the one-fourth interest in and to the fishing, boating, and bathing rights and privileges at, in, upon and about Lake Naomi . . . ; which said rights and privileges were granted and conveyed to me by the Pocono Spring Water Ice Company by their indenture of the 20th day of March, A.D. 1899." On the same day Frank C. Miller and Rufus W. Miller executed an agreement of business partnership, the purpose of which was the erection and operation of boat and bath houses on Naomi Lake and the purchase and maintenance of boats for use on the lake, the houses and boats to be rented for hire and the net proceeds to be divided between the parties in proportion to their respective interests in the bathing, boating and fishing privileges, namely, three-fourths to Frank C. Miller and one-fourth to Rufus W. Miller, the capital to be contributed and the losses to be borne in the same proportion. In pursuance of this agreement the brothers erected and maintained boat and bath houses at different points on the lake, purchased and rented out boats, and conducted the business generally, from the spring of 1900 until the death of Rufus W. Miller on October 11, 1925, exercising their control and use of the privileges in an exclusive, uninterrupted and open manner and without challenge on the part of anyone.

Discord began with the death of Rufus W. Miller, which terminated the partnership. Thereafter Frank C. Miller, and the executors and heirs of Rufus W. Miller, went their respective ways, each granting licenses without reference to the other. Under date of July 13, 1929, the executors of the Rufus W. Miller estate granted a license for the year 1929 to defendant, Lutheran Conference and Camp Association, which was the owner of a tract of ground abutting on the lake for a distance of about 100 feet, purporting to grant to defendant, its members, guests and campers, permission to boat, bathe and fish in the lake, a certain percentage of the receipts therefrom to be paid to the estate. Thereupon Frank C. Miller and his wife, Katherine D. Miller, filed the present bill in equity, complaining that defendant was placing diving floats on the lake and "encouraging and instigating visitors and boarders" to bathe in the lake, and was threatening to hire out boats and canoes and in general to license its guests and others to boat, bathe and fish in the lake.[1] The bill prayed for an injunction to prevent defendant from trespassing on the lands covered by the waters of the lake, from erecting or maintaining any structures or other encroachments thereon, and from granting any bathing licenses. The court issued the injunction.

It is the contention of plaintiffs that, while the privileges of boating and fishing were granted in the deed from the Pocono Spring Water Ice Company to Frank C. Miller, no bathing rights were conveyed by that instrument. In 1903 all the property of the company was sold by the sheriff under a writ of fi. fa. on a mortgage bond which the company had executed in 1898. As a result of that sale the Pocono Spring Water Ice Company was entirely extinguished, and the title to its rights and property came into the ownership of the Pocono Pines Ice Company, a corporation chartered for "the supply of ice to the public."[2]

In 1928 the title to the property of the Pocono Pines Ice Company became vested in Katherine D. Miller. Plaintiffs therefore maintain that the bathing rights, never having passed to Frank C. Miller, descended in ownership from the Pocono Spring Water Ice Company through the Pocono Pines Ice Company to plaintiff Katherine D. Miller, and that Frank C. Miller could not, and did not, give Rufus W. Miller any title to them. They further contend that even if such bathing rights ever did vest in Frank C. Miller, all of the boating, bathing and fishing privileges were easements in gross which were inalienable and indivisible, and when Frank C. Miller undertook to convey a one-fourth interest in them to Rufus W. Miller he not only failed to transfer a legal title to the rights but, in attempting to do so, extinguished the rights altogether as against Katherine D. Miller, who was the successor in title of the Pocono Spring Water Ice Company. It is defendant's contention, on the other hand, that the deed of 1899 from the Pocono Spring Water Ice Company to Frank C. Miller should be construed as transferring the bathing as well as the boating and

---

[1] In 1904 Frank C. Miller, Rufus W. Miller and others had conveyed to the Pocono Pines Assembly and Summer Schools the lot of ground which by mesne conveyances was subsequently acquired by defendant. In the deed there was reserved the right to build a road 100 feet in width along the lake front, and the parties also entered into an agreement contemplating the construction of a similar strip around the entire lake for purposes of a park road and pleasure ground. This development apparently was never carried out, but in the present bill plaintiffs alleged that defendant threatened to build bath houses and erect a diving board on this strip, and prayed injunctive relief from any violation of the restrictions in the deed and the agreement. * * *

[2] There being some question as to whether the 99-year leasehold interest passed under the sheriff's levy and sale, Frank C. Miller, Rufus W. Miller, and others, in July, 1911, confirmed the title thereto in the Pocono Pines Ice Company, and in September, 1911, the Pocono Pines Ice Company confirmed to Frank C. Miller the boating and fishing rights which had been granted to him in 1899 by the Pocono Spring Water Ice Company.

fishing privileges, but that if Frank C. Miller did not obtain them by grant he and Rufus W. Miller acquired them by prescription, and that all of these rights were alienable and divisible even if they be considered as easements in gross, although they might more properly, perhaps, be regarded as licenses which became irrevocable because of the money spent upon their development by Frank C. Miller and Rufus W. Miller.[3]

Plaintiffs have filed a motion to dismiss the present appeal on the ground that defendant's license from the estate of Rufus W. Miller was only for the year 1929, and in 1930 defendant constructed another lake on a property of its own, distant about one-half mile from Lake Naomi, and has discontinued the trespasses which are the subject of the bill; it is claimed that the questions involved have thus become moot. This motion cannot be sustained. The controversy may flare up again if defendant obtains another license from the Rufus W. Miller estate, and under such circumstances the court will entertain an appeal. Moreover, the decree of the court below would render defendant ineligible to obtain a license from the estate hereafter. Nor is the question moot merely because, since the institution of the proceedings, defendant has not persisted in the actions complained of.

Coming to the merits of the controversy, it is initially to be observed that no boating, bathing or fishing rights can be, or are, claimed by defendant as a riparian owner. Ordinarily, title to land bordering on a navigable stream extends to low water mark subject to the rights of the public to navigation and fishery between high and low water, and in the case of land abutting on creeks and non-navigable rivers to the middle of the stream, but in the case of a non-navigable lake or pond where the land under the water is owned by others, no riparian rights attach to the property bordering on the water, and an attempt to exercise any such rights by invading the water is as much a trespass as if an unauthorized entry were made upon the dry land of another. (Citations omitted.)

It is impossible to construe the deed of 1899 from the Pocono Spring Water Ice Company to Frank C. Miller as conveying to the latter any privileges of bathing. It is clear and unambiguous. It gives to Frank C. Miller the exclusive right to fish and boat. Expressio unius est exclusio alterius. No bathing rights are mentioned. This omission may have been the result of oversight or it may have been deliberate, but in either event the legal consequence is the same. It is to be noted that the mortgagee to whom the company mortgaged all its property in 1898 executed in 1902 a release of the fishing and boating rights to the company and to Frank C. Miller, thus validating the latter's title to these rights under the company's deed of 1899, but in this release also the bathing rights are omitted.

---

[3] Shortly before the present action was begun the executors of the Rufus W. Miller estate brought a bill in equity against Frank C. Miller, as surviving partner, for an accounting of the assets of the partnership, and the attempt was there made to raise the questions which are now presented to this court. That case went to the Superior Court. An account was stated covering the relations between the parties down to October 11, 1925, the date of the death of Rufus W. Miller, from which it appeared he was at that time indebted, according to the partnership accounts, to Frank C. Miller, and accordingly the plaintiffs in that action were not entitled to receive anything from the partnership assets. The Superior Court held that the boating, bathing and fishing rights had not been conveyed by the two Millers to the partnership, but remained in their common ownership, and therefore could not be adjudicated in those proceedings.

But, while Frank C. Miller acquired by grant merely boating and fishing privileges, the facts are amply sufficient to establish title to the bathing rights by prescription. True, these rights, not having been granted in connection with, or to be attached to, the ownership of any land, were not easements appurtenant but in gross. There is, however, no inexorable principle of law which forbids an adverse enjoyment of an easement in gross from ripening into a title thereto by prescription. In *Tinicum Fishing Co. v. Carter*, 61 Pa. 21, it was questioned whether a fishing right could be created by prescription, although there is an intimation (p. 40) that some easements in gross might so arise if there be evidence sufficient to establish them. Certainly the casual use of a lake during a few months each year for boating and fishing could not develop into a title to such privileges by prescription. But here the exercise of the bathing right was not carried on sporadically by Frank C. Miller and his assignee Rufus W. Miller for their personal enjoyment but systematically for commercial purposes in the pursuit of which they conducted an extensive and profitable business enterprise. The circumstances thus presented must be viewed from a realistic standpoint. Naomi Lake is situated in the Pocono Mountains district, has become a summer resort for campers and boarders, and, except for the ice it furnishes, its bathing and boating facilities are the factors which give it its prime importance and value. They were exploited from the time the lake was created, and are recited as among the purposes for which the Pocono Spring Water Ice Company was chartered. From the early part of 1900 down to at least the filing of the present bill in 1929, Frank C. Miller and Rufus W. Miller openly carried on their business of constructing and operating bath houses and licensing individuals and camp associations to use the lake for bathing. This was known to the stockholders of the Pocono Spring Water Ice Company and necessarily also to Katherine D. Miller, the wife of Frank C. Miller; no objection of any kind was made, and Frank C. Miller and Rufus W. Miller were encouraged to expend large sums of money in pursuance of the right of which they considered and asserted themselves to be the owners. Under such circumstances it would be highly unjust to hold that a title by prescription to the bathing rights did not vest in Frank C. Miller and Rufus W. Miller which is just as valid, as far as Katherine D. Miller is concerned, as that to the boating and fishing rights which Frank C. Miller obtained by express grant.

We are thus brought to a consideration of the next question, which is whether the boating, bathing and fishing privileges were assignable by Frank C. Miller to Rufus W. Miller. What is the nature of such rights? In England it has been said that easements in gross do not exist at all, although rights of that kind have been there recognized. In this country such privileges have sometimes been spoken of as licenses, or as contractual in their nature, rather than as easements in gross. These are differences of terminology rather than of substance. We may assume, therefore, that these privileges are easements in gross, and we see no reason to consider them otherwise. It has uniformly been held that a profit in gross — for example, a right of mining or fishing — may be made assignable. (Citations omitted.) In regard to easements in gross generally, there has been much controversy in the courts and by textbook writers and law students as to whether they have the attribute of assignability. There are dicta in Pennsylvania that they are non-assignable. (Citations omitted.) But there is forcible expression and even definite authority to the contrary. *Tide Water Pipe Co. v. Bell*, 280 Pa. 104 (Further citations omitted.)

There does not seem to be any reason why the law should prohibit the assignment of an easement in gross if the parties to its creation evidence their intention to make it assignable. Here, as in *Tide Water Pipe Company v. Bell, supra,* the rights of fishing and boating were conveyed to the grantee — in this case Frank C. Miller — "his heirs and assigns," thus showing that the grantor, the Pocono Spring Water Ice Company, intended to attach the attribute of assignability to the privileges granted. Moreover, as a practical matter, there is an obvious difference in this respect between easements for personal enjoyment and those designed for commercial exploitation; while there may be little justification for permitting assignments in the former case, there is every reason for upholding them in the latter.

The question of assignability of the easements in gross in the present case is not as important as that of their divisibility. It is argued by plaintiffs that even if held to be assignable such easements are not divisible, because this might involve an excessive user or "surcharge of the easement" subjecting the servient tenement to a greater burden than originally contemplated. The law does not take that extreme position. It does require, however, that, if there be a division, the easements must be used or exercised as an entirety. This rule had its earliest expression in *Mountjoy's Case,* which is reported in Co. Litt. 164b, 165a. It was there said, in regard to the grant of a right to dig for ore, that the grantee, Lord MOUNTJOY, "might assign his whole interest to one, two, or more; but then, if there be two or more, they could make no division of it, but work together with one stock." In *Caldwell v. Fulton,* 31 Pa. 475, 477, 478, and in *Funk v. Haldeman,* 53 Pa. 229, that case was followed, and it was held that the right of a grantee to mine coal or to prospect for oil might be assigned, but if to more than one they must hold, enjoy and convey the right as an entirety, and not divide it in severalty. There are cases in other jurisdictions which also approve the doctrine of *Mountjoy's* Case, and hold that a mining right in gross is essentially integral and not susceptible of apportionment; an assignment of it is valid, but it cannot be aliened in such a way that it may be utilized by grantor and grantee, or by several grantees, separately; there must be a joint user, nor can one of the tenants alone convey a share in the common right.

These authorities furnish an illuminating guide to the solution of the problem of divisibility of profits or easements in gross. They indicate that much depends upon the nature of the right and the terms of its creation, that "surcharge of the easement" is prevented if assignees exercise the right as "one stock," and that a proper method of enjoyment of the easement by two or more owners of it may usually be worked out in any given instance without insuperable difficulty.

In the present case it seems reasonably clear that in the conveyance of February 17, 1900, it was not the intention of Frank C. Miller to grant, and of Rufus W. Miller to receive, a separate right to subdivide and sublicense the boating, fishing and bathing privileges on and in Lake Naomi, but only that they should together use such rights for commercial purposes, Rufus W. Miller to be entitled to one-fourth and Frank C. Miller to three-fourths of the proceeds resulting from their combined exploitation of the privileges. They were to hold the rights, in the quaint phraseology of *Mountjoy's Case,* as "one stock." Nor do the technical rules that would be applicable to a tenancy in common of a corporeal hereditament apply to the control of these easements in gross. Defendant contends that, as a tenant in common of the privileges, Rufus W. Miller individually was entitled to their use, benefit and possession and to exercise rights of ownership in regard thereto, including the right to license third persons to use them, subject only to the limitation that he must not thereby interfere with the similar rights of his co-tenant. But the very nature of these easements prevents their being so exercised, inasmuch as it is necessary, because of the legal limitations upon their divisibility, that they should be utilized in common, and not by two owners severally, and, as stated, this was evidently the intention of the brothers.

Summarizing our conclusions, we are of opinion (1) that Frank C. Miller acquired title to the boating and fishing privileges by grant and he and Rufus W. Miller to the bathing rights by prescription; (2) that he made a valid assignment of a one-fourth interest in them to Rufus W. Miller; but (3) that they cannot be commercially used and licenses thereunder granted without the common consent and joinder of the present owners, who with regard to them must act as "one stock." It follows that the executors of the estate of Rufus W. Miller did not have the right, in and by themselves, to grant a license to defendant.

NOTE

"Most courts have followed the leading case of *Miller v. Lutheran Conference & Camp Ass'n* and have allowed the transfer of easements in gross." James Ely, Jr. & Jon Bruce, The Law of Easements and Licenses in Land § 9:5. Should non-commercial easements in gross continue to be non-transferable?

G. Termination of Easements

Easements may come to an end in many ways. The principal means are: expiration, merger, release, abandonment, forfeiture for misuse, cessation of purpose, estoppel, and adverse possession. Easements by necessity normally terminate once the necessity that caused their creation is removed.

Merger occurs when the servient and dominant estates come into the same hands. The easement does not come into existence again merely by a subsequent severance of the united estates. Restatement of Property § 497, Comment h (1944). "Such a new creation may result, [however] . . . from an express stipulation in the conveyance by which the severance is made or from the implications of the circumstances of the severance." *Id.*

A frequently litigated possibility of terminating an easement is abandonment. Unlike fee simple interests in land, an easement may be lost by abandonment. However, loss through abandonment normally requires some affirmative act showing abandonment or at least its equivalent. About it, the Supreme Court of West Virginia has written:

> Having once been granted to [the easement holder], he cannot lose it by mere non-user. . . . He may lose it by adverse possession by the owner of the servient estate for the proper length of time . . . or by abandonment, not by mere non-user, but by proofs of an intention to abandon; or of course by deed or other instrument in writing.

Moyer v. Martin, 131 S.E. 859, 861 (W. Va. 1926).

abandoned wrong spot

LINDSEY v. CLARK
69 S.E.2d 342 (Va. 1952)

• Mere non-use is not enough to show abandonment, there needs to be intent and an act.

BUCHANAN, J.

This suit was instituted by the Lindseys to enjoin the Clarks from using a driveway along the north side of the Lindsey lots and to have themselves adjudged the fee simple owners of the two lots claimed by them. The trial court held that the Clarks owned a right of way on the south side of the Lindsey lots and, in effect, put the Lindseys on terms to make it available to them or else allow the Clarks to continue using the one on the north side. There is no controversy about the controlling facts.

In 1937 the Clarks were the owners of four adjoining lots, Nos. 31, 32, 33 and 34, each fronting 25 feet on the east side of Magnolia avenue in West Waynesboro, and running back 150 feet to a 20-foot alley. The Clark residence was on Nos. 31 and 32.

By deed dated July 24, 1937, the Clarks conveyed to C. W. Six and Mabel G. Six, his wife, the latter being a daughter of the Clarks, the front two-thirds of Lots 33 and 34, being a frontage of 50 feet and extending back 100 feet. On the rear one-third of these two lots Clark erected a dwelling and garage for rental purposes. After this conveyance the Sixes built a house on their property, approximately 15 feet from the Clark line on the north and about 8 feet from their own line on the south. The Clark deed to the Sixes contained this reservation: "There is reserved, however, a right-of-way ten (10) feet in width, along the South side of the two lots herein conveyed, for the benefit of the property in the rear."

By deed of January 16, 1939, the Sixes conveyed their property to William H. McGhee and wife, with the same reservation; and by deed of March 16, 1944, the McGhees conveyed the property to the Lindseys, without any reservation.

These three deeds were all made with general warranty and both the deed to the Sixes and the deed to the McGhees were duly recorded prior to the date of the deed to the Lindseys.

Notwithstanding that the 10-foot right of way was reserved by Clark along the south side of the property conveyed to the Sixes, now owned by the Lindseys, Clark proceeded to use it along the north side of the Six property, and has so used it ever since, without objection by the Sixes, or by the McGhees, or by the Lindseys until a few months before this suit was brought. There is no explanation of this change of location. Six, a witness for the Lindseys, testified that Clark stood in the driveway on the north and said, "I am reserving this driveway to get to my back property." The time of that statement is not shown, but the words suggest it was at or before the time of the conveyance to the Sixes. When the McGhees bought the property in 1939, Six pointed out to them the driveway on the north, but the reservation in the deed he made to the McGhees was, as stated, on the south.

In 1946 the Lindseys had their attorney write to Clark, referring to the right of way in the deed to the McGhees, their grantors, and complaining, not of its location, but of its being used for parking purposes. Again, on November 7, 1949, they had their attorney write Clark, calling attention to the fact that the reservation was along the south side of their property and complaining about the use of a water line on their property which had not been reserved. The Lindseys, the letter stated, wanted to erect a line fence and suggested a discussion of the matter before this was done.

The Lindseys contend that the Clarks now have no right of way across their property because none was reserved along the north side and the one reserved on the south side has been abandoned and thereby extinguished. The trial court held it had not been abandoned and that holding was clearly right.

Abandonment is a question of intention. A person entitled to a right of way or other easement in land may abandon and extinguish such right by acts in pais; and a cessation of use coupled with acts or circumstances clearly showing an intention to abandon the right will be as effective as an express release of the right. (Citations omitted.)

But mere non-user of an easement created by deed, for a period however long, will not amount to abandonment. In addition to the non-user there must be acts or circumstances clearly manifesting an intention to abandon; or an adverse user by the owner of the servient estate, acquiesced in by the owner of the dominant estate, for a period sufficient to create a prescriptive right. (Citations omitted.) Nor is a right of way extinguished by the habitual use by its owner of another equally convenient way unless there is an intentional abandonment of the former way. (Citations omitted.)

The burden of proof to show the abandonment of an easement is upon the party claiming such abandonment, and it must be established by clear and unequivocal evidence. Clark specifically reserved a right of way over the lots now owned by the Lindseys. Very clearly he had no intention of abandoning that right of way. He was evidently mistaken as to where it was located; but his grantees, the Sixes, were likewise mistaken, as were also their grantees, the McGhees. Clark's use on the wrong location of the right of way reserved by him did not establish an intention on his part to abandon his right of way on the right location. He could not have intended to abandon his easement on the south of the Lindsey lots when he did not know that was where his easement was.

The residence built by the Sixes, and now occupied by the Lindseys, encroaches by about two feet on the 10-foot alley when located on the south side, and the Lindsey property on that side within the 10-foot space is terraced and planted with shrubbery and a tree. The Lindseys argue that the Clarks are estopped from claiming a right of way on that side because Clark knew where the Sixes were building the house. The only testimony about that is from Six, who said that Clark was away at work when the house was being built but came and went every day to and from his home on the adjoining property, saw where the house was located and made no objection; but Six also said that Clark had nothing to do with locating the house. There is no evidence that Clark knew, any more than Six knew, that the house was encroaching on the right of way. Clark did not think the right of way was on that side. Even if he had known it was there, he would not likely have known that Six was building on it. The location of the house was not influenced by anything Clark did or said. Clark knew nothing about the matter that Six did not know.

"It is essential to the application of the principles of equitable estoppel, or estoppel in pais, that the party claiming to have been influenced by the conduct or declarations of another to his injury, was not only ignorant of the true state of facts, but had no convenient and available means of acquiring such information, and where the facts are known to both parties, and both had the same means of ascertaining the truth, there can be no estoppel." *Lindsay v. James*, 51 S.E.2d 326, 332. The Lindseys had both actual and constructive knowledge of the situation. The driveway was there on the north side when they bought the property and Lindsey testified he could see where cars had been using it. They negligently failed to have their title examined but they are, of course, chargeable with the information contained in the recorded deeds. (Citations omitted.)

The suit therefore developed this situation: The Clarks were entitled to a 10-foot right of way along the south side of the Lindsey property. That right of way was partially blocked by the Lindsey house with its terraces and shrubbery. To require their removal would be very expensive to the Lindseys and damaging to their property. The Clarks were willing to let their right of way continue to be located on the north side.

The court was well warranted in resolving the matter by applying the maxim "He who seeks equity must do equity." That means that "he who seeks the aid of an equity court subjects himself to the imposition of such terms as the settled principles of equity require, and that whatever be the nature of the controversy between the parties, and whatever be the nature of the remedy demanded, the court will not confer its equitable relief on the party seeking its interposition and aid, unless he has acknowledged and conceded, or will admit and provide for, all the equitable rights, claims, and demands justly belonging to the adversary party, and growing out of, or necessarily involved in, the subject matter of the controversy." 30 C.J.S., Equity § 91, p. 461.

A court of equity may in a case in which the principles and rules of equity demand it, condition its granting of the relief sought by the complainant upon the enforcement of a claim or equity held by the defendant which the latter could not enforce in any other way. (Citations omitted.)

The decree of the trial court provided: "The Court will not require the expensive removal of the obstruction, so long as the right-of-way along the north side of the property is made available. However, it is ordered that the defendants desist from the use of the right-of-way for any purpose other than the use of the rear one-third portion of Lots 33 and 34, and only for the right of passage over and across the said right-of-way to and from the property in the rear." And, further, "Should the complainants make an election under this order, a further order will be entered fixing the rights of the respective parties."

The decree appealed from is affirmed and the cause is remanded for further decree as indicated.

NOTE

Should the rule of law that allows termination of restrictive covenants where circumstances have changed dramatically be applied to conservation easements? Should the concern for free alienability of land that underlies the Rule Against Perpetuities have any effect? As yet there has been little litigation on this question. Commentators have also disagreed, though the majority have argued that the changed circumstances doctrine should not be applied to conservation easements. See, e.g., Mahoney, *Perpetual Restrictions on Land and the Problem of the Future*, 88 Va. L. Rev. 739 (2002).

II. REAL COVENANTS

Landowners may agree to use their land in particular ways for the benefit of other landowners. One may agree, for example, to build and maintain a wall on one's own property in order to safeguard the privacy of the people living on a neighbor's land. Another may promise *not* to build a wall in order to secure a right to sunlight on the neighbor's land. Each of these agreements restricts the landowner's freedom of enjoyment, as does an easement. In some circumstances, the agreements may be enforced by and against subsequent owners. They are called real covenants, and one element in the process of binding subsequent owners is the requirement that the covenant "run with the land."

ROGERS v. WATSON
594 A.2d 409 (Vt. 1991)

DOOLEY, J.

This action began with a complaint by adjoining landowners for an injunction requiring defendants, Gerald and Kay Watson, to remove a mobile home they had placed on part of their land. The complaint alleged that the mobile home violated a restrictive covenant applicable to defendants' land. It also joined the Vermont Agency of Natural Resources, seeking to require it to enforce certain subdivision regulations that were allegedly violated by the presence of the mobile home. The Agency cross-claimed against defendants to enforce the regulations. The trial court found for the plaintiffs and the Agency and granted an injunction requiring removal of the mobile home. It also imposed a fine for violation of the regulations. Defendants appeal, and we affirm.

In 1963, defendants purchased a lot in Bennington from Olaf and Edwina Bard, the first division of a 200-acre parcel into a residential development. There are no restrictions in this deed. Thereafter, the Bards sold off other parcels, and each deed, except one to the Bards' son and daughter-in-law, contained a covenant similar to the following:

> No mobile home, trailer, or other similar structure shall be placed or maintained on said premises without the prior approval in writing of the grantor herein or his heirs, executors, administrators or assigns.

In 1977, Edwina Bard (Mr. Bard having died) sold to Charles and Hazel Wilkinson a lot adjacent to that owned by defendants. The deed contained the above restrictive covenant prohibiting the placement of a mobile home on the land. In 1981, defendants purchased part of this lot from the Wilkinsons. The deed did not mention the restrictive covenant.

Because the Wilkinsons were subdividing their land, the transfer to defendants required a permit from the Agency of Natural Resources unless deferred because defendants waived development rights. Defendants applied for and received such a deferral after agreeing that they would not construct or erect any structure, "the useful occupancy of which [would] require the installation of plumbing and sewage treatment facilities" on the lot without first obtaining a permit. The deed contained this restriction.

In October 1985, defendants decided to place a mobile home on the lot they had acquired from the Wilkinsons. Their son-in-law was afflicted with a brain tumor, making it necessary for them to house him, their daughter, and two infant grandchildren. For this purpose, they purchased the mobile home, poured a slab foundation, and began to construct the septic system when they became aware that they might need a permit from the Agency. Because of soil conditions, the Agency denied a permit for a septic system. Nevertheless, defendants completed the sewage system but did not connect it within the home. Water was available from defendants' nearby house but was not connected. The mobile home does have heat and electricity. Defendants' daughter and son-in-law use the mobile home as their home, but they go to defendants' home for all living needs requiring water or sewage.

Plaintiffs in the original action are neighboring landowners, at least some of whom purchased land from the Bards after the sale from the Bards to the Wilkinsons. Edwina Bard was also a plaintiff. She died while the action was pending and was replaced by the executor of her estate.

The trial court found that the restrictive covenant ran with the land, applied to defendants, and could be enforced by plaintiffs. It further found that defendants' actions in placing the mobile home on the land required a permit under the deferral language and the applicable Agency regulation. It found the Agency regulation to be valid.

On appeal, defendants argue that the trial court erred in granting plaintiffs an injunction because there was no showing that either the benefit or the burden of the restrictive covenant was intended to run with the land. As to the Agency, they argue that the placement of the mobile home on the land without connecting the water and sewage does not require a permit under Agency regulations. Alternatively, they argue that if the regulation is applicable, it is invalid because it is unconstitutionally vague, is beyond the Agency's statutory authority and represents an excessive delegation of legislative power.

We begin with defendants' argument that it was improper to enforce the restrictive covenant against them. In order to enforce a restrictive covenant against an owner other than the original covenantee, the covenant must run with the land. At law, a covenant will run with the land if four requirements are met:

First, the covenant must be in writing. Secondly, the parties must intend that the covenant run with the land. Thirdly, the covenant must "touch and concern" the land. Lastly, there must be privity of estate between the parties.

Albright v. Fish, 394 A.2d 1117, 1120 (1978). . . .

Defendants concede that the first, third, and fourth requirements are met but argue that there is inadequate evidence of intent to have the restriction run with the land. The intent can be implied as well as expressed. Intent can also be shown by extraneous circumstances. In some instances, the "promises are so intimately connected with the land as to require the conclusion that the necessary intention for the running of the benefit is present absent language clearly negating that intent." *Albright*, 394 A.2d at 1120.

Defendants' main argument is that there is insufficient evidence that a benefit or burden was intended to run with the land, and consequently, the restriction cannot be enforced against them. We will begin with the burden side of the equation. The restriction prohibits the placement of a particular type of structure on defendants' land. This is the sort of restriction "so intimately connected with the land" that we find the "necessary intention . . . absent language clearly negating that intent." *Id.*

Extraneous factors also point strongly to the intent to have the burden run with the land. The Bards retained adjoining or nearby land. The inclusion of the restriction in most, if not all, other deeds from the Bards shows an intent to create a common development scheme even if it was implemented imperfectly.

For the above reasons, we hold that the trial court was correct in its conclusion that the burden of the restrictions ran with the land and could be enforced against defendants. Although defendants make extensive arguments that the benefit did not run with the land, we need not reach these arguments. The covenant specifically requires "the prior approval in writing of the grantor herein or his heirs, executors, administrators or assigns." Although the grantor is now deceased, the executor has joined this action and can enforce the covenant as a named beneficiary of it. We are unpersuaded by defendants' argument that the executor has no power to enforce the covenant because the real property went directly to the heirs. It is sufficient that the executor is specifically named in the covenant. The trial court did not err in granting the injunction to enforce the restrictive covenant. [Other issues involved the trial court's conclusion that placing the mobile home on the lot required a permit from the state's natural resources agency, and are omitted. — Eds.] Affirmed.

NOTE

Real covenants are usually expressly created, but may, in one situation, be implied. When, in a residential subdivision, most deeds to the lots restrict the use of the lot to residential uses, but one deed (or more) from the common grantor or developer is silent on the matter, covenants in the silent deed(s) may arise by implication.

If the owner of two or more lots, so situated as to bear the relation to a general scheme of development, sells one with an easement of benefit to the land retained, the servitude becomes mutual, and, during the period of restraint, the owner of the lot or lots retained can do nothing forbidden to the owner of the lot sold. For want of a better descriptive term this is styled a reciprocal negative easement. It runs with the land sold by virtue of the express burden placed upon it and abides with the land retained until loosened by expiration of its period of service or by events working its destruction. It is not personal to the owner but operative upon the use of the land by any owner having actual or constructive notice thereof.

Rieger v. Wessel, 319 S.W.2d 855, 857–58 (Ky. 1958). The leading case for this implied covenant doctrine is *Sanborn v. McLean*, 206 N.W. 496 (Mich. 1925) (whose holding is, with a few clarifications, copied word-for-word by the *Rieger* court). *Sanborn* discussed the rationale for reciprocal negative easements as follows: "Reciprocal negative easements are never retroactive; the very nature of their origin forbids. They arise, if at all, out of a benefit accorded land retained, by restrictions upon neighboring land sold by a common owner. Such a scheme of restriction must start with a common owner; it cannot arise and fasten upon one lot by reason of other lot owners conforming to a general plan. If a reciprocal negative easement attached to defendants' lot, it was fastened thereto while in the hands of the common owner of it and neighboring lots by way of sale of other lots with restrictions beneficial at that time to it." *Id.* at 497 (also holding that later lot purchasers would not only be on constructive notice of the covenants recorded on the land records, but would also be on inquiry notice of the covenants after viewing residences in the subdivision). One court said of this second holding: "The general appearance and character of the tract and the nature of the improvements thereon should have indicated to them [the unrestricted lot purchasers] the presence of some character of building restrictions." *Grange v. Korff*, 79 N.W.2d 743, 749 (Iowa 1956). *Chase v. Burrell*, 474 A.2d 180, 181 (Me. 1984), restates *Sanborn's* doctrine as follows:

> Many jurisdictions have adopted the doctrine of "reciprocal negative servitudes," or "implied equitable servitudes," in which a restrictive covenant will be implied in a silent deed when certain conditions are met. . . . [G]enerally, the doctrine is applied when: (1) a common owner subdivides property into a number of lots for sale; (2) the common owner has a "general scheme of development" for the property as a whole, in which the use of the property will be restricted; (3) the vast majority of subdivided lots contain restrictive covenants which reflect the general scheme; (4) the property against which application of an implied covenant is sought is part of the general scheme of development; and (5) the purchaser of the lot in question has notice, actual or constructive, of the restriction.

NEPONSIT PROPERTY OWNERS ASS'N v. EMIGRANT INDUSTRIAL SAVINGS BANK

15 N.E.2d 793 (N.Y. 1938)

LEHMAN, J.

The plaintiff, as assignee of Neponsit Realty Company, has brought this action to foreclose a lien upon land which the defendant owns. The lien, it is alleged, arises from a covenant, condition or charge contained in a deed of conveyance of the land from Neponsit Realty Company to a predecessor in title of the defendant. The defendant purchased the land at a judicial sale. . . .

It appears that in January, 1911, Neponsit Realty Company, as owner of a tract of land in Queens county, caused to be filed in the office of the clerk of the county a map of the land. The tract was developed for a strictly residential community, and Neponsit Realty Company conveyed lots in the tract to purchasers, describing such lots by reference to the filed map and to roads and streets shown thereon. In 1917, Neponsit Realty Company conveyed the land now owned by the defendant to Robert Oldner Deyer and his wife by deed which contained the covenant upon which the plaintiff's cause of action is based.

That covenant provides:

"And the party of the second part for the party of the second part and the heirs, successors and assigns of the party of the second part further covenants that the property conveyed by this deed shall be subject to an annual charge in such an amount as will be fixed by the party of the first part, its successors and assigns, not, however exceeding in any year the sum of four ($4.00) Dollars per lot 20 × 100 feet. The assigns of the party of the first part may include a Property Owners' Association which may hereafter be organized for the purposes referred to in this paragraph, and in case such association is organized the sums in this paragraph provided for shall be payable to such association. The party of the second part for the party of the second part and the heirs, successors and assigns of the party of the second part covenants that they will pay this charge to the party of the first part, its successors and assigns on the first day of May in each and every year, and further covenants that said charge shall on said date in each year become a lien on the land and shall continue to be such lien until fully paid. Such charge shall be payable to the party of the first part or its successors or assigns, and shall be devoted to the maintenance of the roads, paths, parks, beach, sewers and such other public purposes as shall from time to time be determined by the party of the first part, its successors or assigns. And the party of the second part by the acceptance of this deed hereby expressly vests in the party of the first part, its successors and assigns, the right and power to bring all actions against the owner of the premises hereby conveyed or any part thereof for the collection of such charge and to enforce the aforesaid lien therefor.

"These covenants shall run with the land and shall be construed as real covenants running with the land until January 31st, 1940, when they shall cease and determine."

Every subsequent deed of conveyance of the property in the defendant's chain of title, including the deed from the referee to the defendant, contained, as we have said, a provision that they were made subject to covenants and restrictions of former deeds of record.

There can be no doubt that Neponsit Realty Company intended that the covenant should run with the land and should be enforceable by a property owners association against every owner of property in the residential tract which the realty company was then developing. The language of the covenant admits of no other construction. Regardless of the intention of the parties, a covenant will run with the land and will be enforceable against a subsequent purchaser of the land at the suit of one who claims the benefit of the covenant, only if the covenant complies with certain legal requirements. These requirements rest upon ancient rules and precedents. The age-old essentials of a real covenant, aside from the form of the covenant, may be summarily formulated as follows: (1) it must appear that grantor and grantee intended that the covenant should run with the land; (2) it must appear that the covenant is one "touching" or "concerning" the land with which it runs; (3) it must appear that there is "privity of estate" between the promisee or party claiming the benefit of the covenant and the right to enforce it, and the promisor or party who rests under the burden of the covenant. (Clark on Covenants and Interests Running with Land, p. 74.) Although the deeds of Neponsit Realty Company conveying lots in the tract it developed "contained a provision to the effect that the covenants ran with the land, such provision in the absence of the other legal requirements is insufficient to accomplish such a purpose." (*Morgan Lake Co. v. N.Y., N.H. & H. R.R. Co.*, 262 N.Y. 234, 238.) In his opinion in that case, Judge Crane posed but found it unnecessary to decide many of the questions which the court must consider in this case.

The covenant in this case is intended to create a charge or obligation to pay a fixed sum of money to be "devoted to the maintenance of the roads, paths, parks, beach, sewers and such other public purposes as shall from time to time be determined by the party of the first part [the grantor], its successors or assigns." It is an affirmative covenant to pay money for use in connection with, but not upon, the land which it is said is subject to the burden of the covenant. Does such a covenant "touch" or "concern" the land? These terms are not part of a statutory definition, a limitation placed by the State upon the power of the courts to enforce covenants intended to run with the land by the parties who entered into the covenants. Rather they are words used by courts in England in old cases to describe a limitation which the courts themselves created or to formulate a test which the courts have devised and which the courts voluntarily apply. (Cf. *Spencer's Case*, Coke, vol. 3, part 5, p. 16; *Mayor of Congleton v. Pattison*, 10 East, 316.) In truth the test so formulated is too vague to be of much assistance and judges and academic scholars alike have struggled, not with entire success, to formulate a test at once more satisfactory and more accurate. "It has been found impossible to state any absolute tests to determine what covenants touch and concern land and what do not. The question is one for the court to determine in the exercise of its best judgment upon the facts of each case." (Clark, [Clark on Covenants and Interests Running with Land] op. cit. p. 76.)

Even though that be true, a determination by a court in one case upon particular facts will often serve to point the way to correct decision in other cases upon analogous facts. Such guideposts may not be disregarded. It has been often said that a covenant to pay a sum of money is a personal affirmative covenant which usually does not concern or touch the land. Such statements are based upon English decisions which hold in effect that only covenants, which compel the covenanter to submit to some restriction on the use of his property, touch or concern the land, and that the burden of a covenant which requires the covenanter to do an affirmative act, even on his own land, for the benefit of the owner of a "dominant" estate, does not run with his land. (*Miller v. Clary*, 210 N.Y. 127.) In that case the court pointed out that in many jurisdictions of this country the narrow English rule has been criticized and a more liberal and flexible rule has been substituted. In this State the courts have not gone so far. We have not abandoned the historic distinction drawn by the English courts. So this court has recently said: "Subject to a few exceptions not important at this time, there is now in this State a settled rule of law that a covenant to do an affirmative act, as distinguished from a covenant merely negative in effect, does not run with the land so as to charge the burden of performance on a subsequent grantee [citing cases]. This is so though the burden of such a covenant is laid upon the very parcel which is the subject-matter of the conveyance." (*Guaranty Trust Co. v. N.Y. & Queens County Ry. Co.*, 253 N.Y. 190, 204, opinion by Cardozo, Ch. J.)

Both in that case and in the case of *Miller v. Clary (supra)* the court pointed out that there were some exceptions or limitations in the application of the general rule. Some promises to pay money have been enforced, as covenants running with the land, against subsequent holders of the land who took with notice of the covenant. (Cf. *Greenfarb v. R.S.K. Realty Corp.*, 256 N.Y. 130; *Morgan Lake Co. v. N.Y., N.H. & H. R.R. Co., supra.*) It may be difficult to classify these exceptions or to formulate a test of whether a particular covenant to pay money or to perform some other act falls within the general rule that ordinarily an affirmative covenant is a personal and not a real covenant, or falls outside the limitations placed upon the general rule. At least it must "touch" or "concern" the land in a substantial degree, and though it may be inexpedient and perhaps impossible to formulate a rigid test or definition which will be entirely satisfactory or which can be applied mechanically in all cases, we should at least be able to state the problem and find a reasonable method of approach to it. It has been suggested that a covenant which runs with the land must affect the legal relations — the advantages and the burdens — of the parties to the covenant, as owners of particular parcels of land and not merely as members of the community in general, such as taxpayers or owners of other land. (Clark, op. cit. p. 76. Cf. Professor Bigelow's article on *The Contents of Covenants in Leases*, 12 Mich. L. Rev. 639; 30 Law Quarterly Review, 319.) That method of approach has the merit of realism. The test is based on the effect of the covenant rather than on technical distinctions. Does the covenant impose, on the one hand, a burden upon an interest in land, which on the other hand increases the value of a different interest in the same or related land?

Even though we accept that approach and test, it still remains true that whether a particular covenant is sufficiently connected with the use of land to run with the land, must be in many cases a question of degree. A promise to pay for something to be done in connection with the promisor's land does not differ essentially from a promise by the promisor to do the thing himself, and both promises constitute, in a substantial sense, a restriction upon the owner's right to use the land, and a burden upon the legal interest of the owner. On the other hand, a covenant to perform or pay for the performance of an affirmative act disconnected with the use of the land cannot ordinarily touch or concern the land in any substantial degree. Thus, unless we exalt technical form over substance, the distinction between covenants which run with land and covenants which are personal, must depend upon the effect of the covenant on the legal rights which otherwise would flow from ownership of land and which are connected with the land. The problem then is: Does the covenant in purpose and effect substantially alter these rights?

The opinion in *Morgan Lake Co. v. N.Y., N.H. & H. R.R. Co.* (*supra*) foreshadowed a classification based upon substance rather than upon form. It was not the first case, however, in which this court has based its decision on the substantial effect of a covenant upon legal relations of the parties as owners of land. Perhaps the most illuminating illustration of such an approach to the problem may be drawn from the "party wall" cases in this State which are reviewed in the opinion of the court in *Sebald v. Mulholland*, 155 N.Y. 455. The court there pointed out that in cases, cited in the opinion, where by covenant between owners of adjoining parcels of land, "a designated party was authorized to build a party wall, the other agreeing to pay a portion of its value when it should be used by him," the court was constrained to hold that "the agreement was a present one, the party who was to build and the one who was to pay were expressly designated, and the covenant to pay was clearly a personal one" (p. 464). At the same time, the court also pointed out that such covenants must be distinguished from the covenants (passed upon by the court in the earlier case of *Mott v. Oppenheimer*, 135 N.Y. 312), "by which the parties conferred, each upon the other, the authority to erect such [party] wall, and dedicated to that use a portion of each of their lots, with an agreement that if either should build the other might have the right to use it by paying his share of the expense" (p. 463). In such a case, it was said by the court, "It was not and could not then be known who would build, or who was to pay when the wall was used. The agreement was wholly prospective, and its purpose was to impose upon the land of each, and not upon either personally, the burden of a future party wall, and to secure to the land and, thus, to its subsequent owners, a corresponding right to the use of the wall by paying one-half of its value. . . . In that case the character of the agreement, its obvious purpose, its prospective provisions, and the situation of the lands when the agreement was made, all concurred in showing an intent that its covenants should run with the land, and clearly justified the court in so holding" (pp. 463–4).

Looking at the problem presented in this case from the same point of view and stressing the intent and substantial effect of the covenant rather than its form, it seems clear that the covenant may properly be said to touch and concern the land of the defendant and its burden should run with the land. True, it calls for payment of a sum of money to be expended for "public purposes" upon land other than the land conveyed by Neponsit Realty Company to plaintiff's predecessor in title. By that conveyance the grantee, however, obtained not only title to particular lots, but an easement or right of common enjoyment with other property owners in roads, beaches, public parks or spaces and improvements in the same tract. For full enjoyment in common by the defendant and other property owners of these easements or rights, the roads and public places must be maintained. In order that the burden of maintaining public improvements should rest upon the land benefited by the improvements, the grantor exacted from the grantee of the land with its appurtenant easement or right of enjoyment a covenant that the burden of paying the cost should be inseparably attached to the land which enjoys the benefit. It is plain that any distinction or definition which would exclude such a covenant from the classification of covenants which "touch" or "concern" the land would be based on form and not on substance.

Another difficulty remains. Though between the grantor and the grantee there was privity of estate, the covenant provides that its benefit shall run to the assigns of the grantor who "may include a Property Owners' Association which may hereafter be organized for the purposes referred to in this paragraph." The plaintiff has been organized to receive the sums payable by the property owners and to expend them for the benefit of such owners. Various definitions have been formulated of "privity of estate" in connection with covenants that run with the land, but none of such definitions seems to cover the relationship between the plaintiff and the defendant in this case. The plaintiff has not succeeded to the ownership of any property of the grantor. It does not appear that it ever had title to the streets or public places upon which charges which are payable to it must be expended. It does not appear that it owns any other property in the residential tract to which any easement or right of enjoyment in such property is appurtenant. It is created solely to act as the assignee of the benefit of the covenant, and it has no interest of its own in the enforcement of the covenant.

The arguments that under such circumstances the plaintiff has no right of action to enforce a covenant running with the land are all based upon a distinction between the corporate property owners association and the property owners for whose benefit the association has been formed. If that distinction may be ignored, then the basis of the arguments is destroyed. How far privity of estate in technical form is necessary to enforce in equity a restrictive covenant upon the use of land, presents an interesting question. Enforcement of such covenants rests upon equitable principles (*Tulk v. Moxhay*, 2 Phillips, 774; *Trustees of Columbia College v. Lynch*, 70 N.Y. 440; *Korn v. Campbell*, 192 N.Y. 490), and at times, at least, the violation "of the restrictive covenant may be restrained at the suit of one who owns property, or for whose benefit the restriction was established, irrespective of whether there were privity either of estate or of contract between the parties, or whether an action at law were maintainable." (*Chesebro v. Moers*, 233 N.Y. 75, 80.) The covenant in this case does not fall exactly within any classification of "restrictive" covenants, which have been enforced in this State (Cf. *Korn v. Campbell*, 192 N.Y. 490), and no right to enforce even a restrictive covenant has been sustained in this State where the plaintiff did not own property which would benefit by such enforcement so that some of the elements of an equitable servitude are present. In some jurisdictions it has been held that no action may be maintained without such elements. (But cf. *Van Sant v. Rose*, 260 Ill. 401.) We do not attempt to decide now how far the rule of *Trustees of Columbia College v. Lynch* (*supra*) will be carried, or to formulate a definite rule as to when, or even whether, covenants in a deed will be enforced, upon equitable principles, against subsequent purchasers with notice, at the suit of a party without privity of contract or estate. (Cf. *Equitable Rights and Liabilities of Strangers to a Contract*, by Harlan F. Stone, 18 Columbia Law Review, 291.) There is no need to resort to such a rule if the courts may look behind the corporate form of the plaintiff.

The corporate plaintiff has been formed as a convenient instrument by which the property owners may advance their common interests. We do not ignore the corporate form when we recognize that the Neponsit Property Owners Association, Inc., is acting as the agent or representative of the Neponsit property owners. As we have said in another case: when Neponsit Property Owners Association, Inc., "was formed, the property owners were expected to, and have looked to that organization as the medium through which enjoyment of their common right might be preserved equally for all." (*Matter of City of New York [Public Beach]*, 269 N.Y. 64, 75.) Under the conditions thus presented we said: "it may be difficult, or even impossible, to classify into recognized categories the nature of the interest of the membership corporation and its members in the land. The corporate entity cannot be disregarded, nor can the separate interests of the members of the corporation" (p. 73). Only blind adherence to an ancient formula devised to meet entirely different conditions could constrain the court to hold that a corporation formed as a medium for the enjoyment of common rights of property owners owns no property which would benefit by enforcement of common rights and has no cause of action in equity to enforce the covenant upon which such common rights depend. Every reason which in other circumstances may justify the ancient formula may be urged in support of the conclusion that the formula should not be applied in this case. In substance if not in form the covenant is a restrictive covenant which touches and concerns the defendant's land, and in substance, if not in form, there is privity of estate between the plaintiff and the defendant. . . .

NOTE

Homeowners associations have proliferated and hold various powers besides administering assessments. See, e.g., *Rhue v. Cheyenne Homes, Inc.*, 449 P.2d 361 (Colo. 1969) (upholding an injunction prohibiting the defendant from moving a thirty year old Spanish style house into a new subdivision that was 80% improved and contained only modern ranch style or split level homes, when the covenant said: "No building shall be erected, placed or altered on any lot until the construction plans and specifications and a plan showing the location of the structure shall have been approved by the architectural control committee."). More recent cases dealing with similar covenants have more detailed procedures for making architectural decisions, but reach similar results, upholding the covenants. See, e.g., *Goode v. Village of Woodgreen Homeowners Ass'n*, 662 So. 2d 1064, 1074–75 (Miss. 1995). In another important line of cases, group homes have been challenged as violating single-family use covenants in residential subdivisions. Compare *Omega Corp. v. Malloy*, 319 S.E.2d 728 (Va. 1984), *cert. denied*, 469 U.S. 1192 (1985), with *Blevins v. Barry-Lawrence County Ass'n for Retarded Citizens*, 707 S.W.2d 407 (Mo. 1986). The growth of gated, covenant-controlled communities has presented the courts with increasingly detailed covenant schemes, to the point where the protection of minority and nonresidents' rights has become a concern.

See Stewart Sterk, *Minority Protection in Residential Private Governments*, 77 B.U. L. Rev. 273 (1997); David Kennedy, *Residential Associations as State Actors: Regulating the Impact of Gated Communities on NonMembers*, 105 Yale L.J. 761 (1995); and see, e.g., *Nahrstedt v. Lakeside Village Condominium Ass'n*, 878 P.2d 1275 (Cal. 1994) (upholding, in line with a majority of courts considering the issue, a condominium association's no-pets covenant as applied to indoor cats), discussed in Carl Kress, *Beyond* Nahrstedt: *Reviewing Restrictions Governing Life in a Property Owner Association*, 42 UCLA L. Rev. 837 (1995).

FEIDER v. FEIDER
699 P.2d 801 (Wash. Ct. App. 1985)

GREEN, C.J.

The question presented is whether an agreement between A and B, adjoining landowners, that if A, his heirs or assigns, elects to sell his land, he will first offer the same to B and which recites it as a covenant running with B's land, is enforceable by B's heirs. We hold it is not.

In June 1951, several brothers and sisters, who had inherited undivided interests in real property in Garfield County, stipulated to a partition of those interests. Francis A. Feider received a 110-acre parcel that adjoined land owned by his brother, Andrew Feider. Access to Andrew's land was by an easement over Francis's parcel.

On October 15, 1951, Francis and Andrew executed the following agreement which, although denominated an option, the parties agree operates as a "preemptive" right or right of first refusal:

> For and in consideration of the mutual benefits accruing to the parties hereto, Francis A. Feider, party of the first part, hereby grants to Andrew S. Feider, party of the second part, an option to purchase the following described real estate situated in Garfield County, Washington, to-wit: subject to the following terms and conditions:

> In event party of the first part, his heirs or assigns, shall elect to sell the above described lands he shall first offer the same to party of the second part and said second party may accept or reject such offer at his option. In event party of the second part shall accept such offer he shall, within a reasonable time after acceptance thereof and after approval of title, pay to party of the first part, his heirs or assigns, the agreed price therefor.

> It is further agreed that party of the second part is the owner of certain lands adjacent to the foregoing lands and is also the owner of a right of way and easement over and across the foregoing described lands, the same being described in the hereinbefore named Final Decree and that this option shall be considered a covenant running with the lands owned by party of the second part.

> In Witness Whereof the parties hereto have hereunto set their hands the 15th day of October, 1951.

Twenty-nine years later, on March 17, 1980, Francis sold the property, along with other land, to Karl and Bertha Hecht. Andrew was deceased by that time. Francis did not first offer to sell to Andrew's children.

On May 10, 1982, Andrew's children brought this action against Francis Feider and the Hechts for specific performance of or damages for breach of the 1951 agreement. They alleged it was a covenant real, enforceable by Andrew's heirs. Francis answered alleging he intended the agreement to be only a personal commitment to Andrew. He further alleged by affirmative defense the agreement is void as an unlawful restraint on alienation and violates the rule against perpetuities.

Andrew's children moved for summary judgment submitting affidavits which stated they would have purchased the property on the same terms as the Hechts. In opposition to the motion, Francis submitted an affidavit stating he did not know the meaning of the words "covenant running with the lands"; he dismissed the agreement from his mind after Andrew died; it did not appear on a title report obtained before he sold the property; and if it had, he would have taken steps to declare it of no effect or would have withdrawn the parcel from the sale. His attorney submitted an affidavit stating he searched the probate records of Andrew Feider's estate as well as the estate of Andrew's wife, who died several years later, and found no reference to the agreement. Ted Feider, one of Andrew's children, was executor of his mother's estate. He recorded the agreement, but not until June 13, 1980, 3 months after Francis sold the property to the Hechts.

In a comprehensive opinion, the trial court held the agreement did not satisfy the requirements for real covenants and was thus a personal contract. Applying *Robroy Land Co. v. Prather*, 95 Wn. 2d 66, 622 P.2d 367 (1980), the court further held the agreement was effective for a reasonable time and 29 years exceeded that time. Therefore, summary judgment was granted in favor of Francis and the action was dismissed.

In *Robroy* the court held a right of first refusal is not an interest in land and, consequently, is not a restraint on alienation. However, if it does not contain a stated duration, it is presumed intended to be effective only for a reasonable time. Here, the duration of the agreement between Francis and Andrew is not stated; therefore, it is presumed to be for a reasonable time.

Andrew's children argue a reasonable time should be longer than 29 years because farmland in Garfield County is not often sold. However, there are no facts in the record that raise this question. Instead, the record shows the contract was not inventoried as part of either Andrew's or his wife's estate and was not recorded during their lifetimes. To the contrary, the matter lay dormant for 29 years. Only after Francis sold the property was the claimed right asserted. In these circumstances, and in the absence of any evidence to the contrary, the court properly ruled on summary judgment that a reasonable time had passed as a matter of law.

We also agree with the trial court that the agreement was not a covenant running with the land. An agreement concerning real property, which is enforceable by or binds successors, referred to as a running covenant, must meet the following requirements: (1) the covenants must have been enforceable between the original parties, such enforceability being a question of contract law except insofar as the covenant must satisfy the statute of frauds; (2) the covenant must "touch and concern" both the land to be benefitted and the land to be burdened; (3) the covenanting parties must have intended to bind their successors in interest; (4) there must be vertical privity of estate, i.e., privity between the original parties to the covenant and the present disputants; and (5) there must be horizontal privity of estate, or privity between the original parties. W. Stoebuck, *Running Covenants: An Analytical Primer*, 52 Wash. L. Rev. 861 (1977). (Footnotes omitted.) *Leighton v. Leonard*, 22 Wn. App. 136, 139, 589 P.2d 279 (1978). Here, horizontal privity does not exist because the right of first refusal did not pass with an estate in land or relate to coexisting or common property interests. 1 Wash. State Bar Ass'n, Real Property Deskbook § 15.7 (1979); Stoebuck, *Running Covenants: An Analytical Primer*, 52 Wash. L. Rev. 861, 877–82 (1977); 3 H. Tiffany, Real Property § 851 (3d ed. 1939). Andrew's children argue they had common property interests with Francis because of the easement across Francis's land. However, the agreement did not accompany or relate to the easement; therefore, its existence does not satisfy this requirement. W. Burby, Real Property, ch. 9, § 40, at 99 (3d ed. 1965).

Neither do we find evidence the agreement "touches and concerns" land. To satisfy this requirement, the agreement must have rendered less valuable Francis's legal interest in his land and rendered more valuable the legal interest of Andrew in his land. See 5 R. Powell, Real Property para. 673[2][a], at 60-41 (1984). Under *Robroy*, no interest in land is created by a right of first refusal; only personal rights are affected. A preemptioner acquires no present right to affect the property but holds only a right to acquire a later interest should the property owner decide to sell. *Robroy*, at 71; *Bennett Veneer Factors, Inc. v. Brewer*, 73 Wn.2d 849, 853–54, 441 P.2d 128 (1968). There is nothing in the record to indicate the value of the land of the respective parties here was increased or decreased or even affected by the agreement. See 1 Washington State Bar Ass'n, Real Property Deskbook §§ 15.3, 15.4 (1979). Thus, the right of first refusal must fail as a covenant in any event. Affirmed.

III.　EQUITABLE SERVITUDES

A.　Creation

TULK v. MOXHAY
41 E.R. 1143 (Ch. 1848)

In 1808 the plaintiff, being then the owner in fee of a vacant piece of ground in Leicester Square, London, as well as of several of the houses forming the square, sold the piece of ground by the description of "Leicester Square Garden or Pleasure Ground, with the equestrian statue then standing in the centre thereof and the iron railing and stone work round the same," to one Elms in fee. The deed of conveyance contained a covenant by Elms, for himself, his heirs, and assigns, with the plaintiff, his heirs, executors, and administrators:

> that Elms, his heirs, and assigns should, and would from time to time, and
> at all times thereafter at his own cost and charges, keep and maintain the
> said piece of ground and square garden and the iron railing round the same

in its then form, and in sufficient and proper repair as a square garden and pleasure ground, in an open state, uncovered with any buildings, in neat and ornamental order; and that it should be lawful for the inhabitants of Leicester Square, tenants of the plaintiff, on payment of a reasonable rent for the same, to have keys at their own expense and the privilege of admission therewith at any time or times into the said square garden and pleasure ground.

The piece of land so conveyed by divers mesne conveyances into the hands of the defendant, whose purchase deed contained no similar covenant with his vendor, but he admitted that he had purchased with notice of the covenant in the deed of 1808. The defendant having manifested an intention to alter the character of the square garden, and asserted a right, if he thought fit, to build upon it, the plaintiff, who remained owner of several houses in the square, filed this bill for an injunction. An injunction was granted by the Master of the Rolls, to restrain the defendant from converting or using the piece of ground and square garden and the iron railing round the same to or for any other purpose than as a square garden and pleasure ground in an open state, and uncovered with buildings. The defendant moved to discharge that order.

Lottenham, L.C. That this court has jurisdiction to enforce a contract between the owner of the land and its neighbor purchasing a part of it that the purchaser shall either use or abstain from using the land purchasing in a particular way is what I never knew disputed. Here there is no question about the contract. The owner of certain houses in the square sells the land adjoining, with a covenant from the purchaser not to use it for any other purposes than as a square garden. It is now contended, not that the vendee could violate that contract, but that he might sell the piece of land, and that the purchaser from him may violate it without this court having any power to interfere. If that were so, it would be impossible for an owner of land to sell part of it without incurring the risk of rendering what he retains worthless. It is said that, the covenant being one which does not run with the land, this court cannot enforce it, but the question is not whether the covenant runs with the land, but whether a party shall be permitted to use the land in a manner inconsistent with the contract entered into by his vendor, with notice of which he purchased. Of course, the price would be affected by the covenant and nothing could be more inequitable than that the original purchaser should be able to sell the property the next day for a greater price in consideration of the assignee being allowed to escape from the liability which he had himself undertaken.

That the question does not depend upon whether the covenant runs with the land is evident from this, that, if there was a mere agreement and no covenant this court would enforce it against a party purchasing with notice of it, for if an equity is attached to the property by the owner, no one purchasing with notice of that equity can stand in a different situation from that of the party from whom he purchased. . . .

With respect to the observations of Lord Brougham in *Keppell v. Bailey,* he never could have meant to lay down that this court would not enforce an equity attached to land by the owner unless under such circumstances as would maintain an action at law. If that be the result of his observations, I can only say that I cannot coincide with it. I think this decision of the Master of the Rolls perfectly right, and, therefore, that this motion must be refused with costs. *Appeal dismissed.*

NOTES

1. English law held that affirmative covenants between holders of fee simple interests could not run with the land. The decision in *Tulk* can be seen as a way of avoiding the hardships caused by this rule. American courts are not bound by the rule against the running of affirmative covenants, and to some American commentators, it has seemed foolish, or at least unnecessary, to perpetuate a separate law of equitable servitudes. See Uriel Reichman, *Toward a Unified Concept of Servitudes*, 55 S. Cal. L. Rev. 1177 (1982); Susan French, *Toward a Modern Law of Servitudes: Reweaving the Ancient Strands*, 55 S. Cal. L. Rev. 1261 (1982). On the other hand, these servitudes are still considered as being enforced in equity, and this allows courts to deal with changed circumstances more readily than if enforcement were at law.

2. It is normally held that equitable servitudes must meet the same "touch and concern the land" requirement that is applied to real covenants. Does a covenant not to establish a competing business meet this requirement, or does it fail because it touches only the business, not the land itself? See *Whitinsville Plaza, Inc. v. Kotseas*, 390 N.E.2d 243 (Mass. 1979); Comment, 4 Cal. W. L. Rev. 131 (1968).

B. Enforcement

HOUGHTON v. RIZZO
281 N.E.2d 577 (Mass. 1972)

Quirico, J.

This is a bill in equity for the enforcement of restrictions allegedly applicable to land owned by the defendants. The case is before us on the defendants' appeal from a final decree enforcing compliance with the alleged restrictions. . . .

The only issue presented by this case is whether the defendants' conveyance of thirteen lots shown on a subdivision plan by deeds which contained identical restrictions operated similarly to restrict the remaining lots shown on that plan and still owned by the defendants. We review the pertinent facts bearing on that issue. All of the facts are established either by the agreement of the parties or by undisputed documentary evidence.

On April 2, 1965, the defendants caused to be recorded in the appropriate registry of deeds a subdivision plan (plan) dated June 15, 1964, and approved by the planning board of the town of Norwood on March 29, 1965. The plan showed proposed ways and thirty-seven numbered lots, all owned by the defendants. Between that date and the filing of the bill in this suit on July 10, 1969, the defendants conveyed sixteen of the lots by thirteen separate deeds, all of which were duly recorded. Eleven of the deeds contained identical restrictions which provided as follows in so far as pertinent to the issue before us: "Said premises are hereby conveyed subject to the restrictions below set forth, which are hereby imposed on said premises for the exclusive benefit of the Grantors and their successors in trust and of such of their successors in title to the benefitted land, hereinafter described (or to any portion or portions thereof), to whom the exclusive benefit of these restrictions may hereafter be expressly granted of record." There then followed among other restrictions provisions restricting the use of the lots to single family residences and requiring approval of construction plans in writing by the grantors or their successors in title. The restrictions concluded: "Any person hereafter claiming under this deed may rely upon any instrument in writing signed by the Grantors or their successors in trust or their successors in title to whom the exclusive benefit of these restrictions may hereafter have been expressly granted of record, or by any agent or agents to whom authority therefor may have been delegated by the Grantors or such successors by instruments duly recorded with Norfolk Registry of Deeds or registered with Norfolk Registry District of the Land Court, purporting to approve any plans or completed construction, or waiving these restrictions in particular respects. The benefitted land above referred to consists of all the land shown on said plan dated June 15, 1964."

The plaintiffs are the present owners of eight of the lots shown on the plan and conveyed by the defendants. Although some are the original grantees from the defendants and others are successors in title to the original grantees, nothing in this decision turns on that difference. The plaintiffs also include the original grantees of two lots which the defendants conveyed without restrictions. On the view which we take of this case, it is unnecessary to consider why the restrictions were omitted from those deeds or the effect of such omissions on the rights of the owners of those lots to obtain relief. All of the restrictions contained in the deeds by which the defendants conveyed the lots now owned by the plaintiffs are still in effect.

There is nothing in the record or in the exhibits placed before this court to indicate that the defendants ever expressly either (a) granted the benefit of any of the restrictions to their successors in title or any other persons, or (b) orally or in writing, by deeds or otherwise, restricted or agreed to restrict their remaining land in any manner, or to subject it to any of the restrictions which they placed in the deeds by which they conveyed all but two of the lots.

On June 19, 1969, the defendants obtained a building permit from the building inspector of the town of Norwood for the erection of a multi-family apartment building on one of the lots on the plan which they still own, and they started to construct the building. Those developments precipitated the filing of this bill in which the plaintiffs seek a decree ordering the removal of the partially constructed building and declaring that the defendants' lot is subject to the same restrictions as were included in the deeds by which they previously conveyed other lots on the same plan. The judge entered a final decree to that effect and the defendants seasonably appealed.

The plaintiffs do not claim that the defendants ever expressly agreed to subject all of their lots on the plan to these restrictions. They argue instead that it may be inferred from the fact that identical restrictions were imposed on thirteen lots that there was a "common scheme" as a result of which they obtained "an enforceable right to have the remaining land of the common grantor within the limits of the common scheme [viz., the remaining lots on the plan], bound by similar restrictions by way of implication." For this proposition they cite and rely almost entirely on the decision in *Snow v. Van Dam*, 291 Mass. 477. This reliance is misplaced.

In *Snow v. Van Dam, supra*, at 479, all of the lots of both the plaintiffs and the defendants were subject to restrictions originally imposed by a common grantor. It was not a case in which the owners of lots previously restricted by a grantor were attempting to enforce the same restrictions against other land still owned by that grantor. The principal question involved there was whether the land owned by the defendant grantee was within the scope of the same scheme of restrictions which the common grantor had imposed some years earlier in his conveyances to the plaintiffs or their predecessors in title. *Id.* at 481.

The case before us is governed by the rule first applied in this Commonwealth in *Sprague v. Kimball*, 213 Mass. 380, decided in 1913. There the court found that the defendant owned a tract of land which she intended to develop, that she established a general building scheme for that purpose for the entire tract and that she then sold four lots by deeds incorporating restrictions to carry out that scheme and orally represented and agreed with each buyer that she would not sell the fifth and last lot except by a deed imposing the same restrictions. On a bill in equity brought by the purchasers of the four lots to enjoin the developer from conveying the fifth lot without imposing the restrictions on it, this court held they were not entitled to relief. It said (at 382–383): "The right invoked by the plaintiffs . . . is an equitable easement or servitude passing with a conveyance of the premises to subsequent grantees. . . . It is settled by our decisions, that under . . . [the statute of frauds] an equitable as well as a legal interest in land must be evidenced by some sufficient instrument in writing or it is unenforceable." To the same effect, see *Sargent v. Leonardi*, 223 Mass. 556, 558.

In *Snow v. Van Dam*, 291 Mass. 477, 482, the court said: "Where such a scheme [of restrictions] exists, it appears to be the law of England and some American jurisdictions that a grantee subject to restrictions acquires by implication an enforceable right to have the remaining land of the vendor, within the limits of the scheme, bound by similar restrictions . . . [citations omitted]. Traces of that idea can be found in our own reports . . . [citations omitted]. But it was settled in this Commonwealth by *Sprague v. Kimball*, 213 Mass. 380, that the statute of frauds prevents the enforcement against the vendor, or any purchaser from him of a lot not expressly restricted, of any implied or oral agreement that the vendor's remaining land shall be bound by restrictions similar to those imposed upon lots conveyed. Only where . . . [citations omitted] the vendor binds his remaining land by writing, can reciprocity of restriction between the vendor and the vendee be enforced."

In the recent case of *Frank v. Visockas*, 356 Mass. 227, the defendants conveyed five lots by deeds containing substantially similar restrictions which limited the use of the lots to single family dwellings, and they agreed orally with each purchaser that all lots subsequently sold would be made subject to the same restrictions. When the defendants later decided to use their remaining land for a different purpose, this court denied relief to the purchasers of the five lots and in so doing it relied (at 228–229) on much of the same language which is quoted immediately above from the decision in *Snow v. Van Dam*, 291 Mass. 477, 482.

The denial of relief in both the *Sprague* and the *Frank* cases, *supra*, was based on the absence of any writing signed by the defendants sufficient to satisfy the requirements of the statute of frauds with respect to interests in land. Not only is there no such writing in the present case, but neither is there any express oral agreement to restrict the remaining land of the defendants such as was held unenforceable in those cases. We are compelled by those two decisions to conclude that the plaintiffs in the present case are not entitled to have the restrictions applicable to their lots enforced against the remaining land of the defendants. For a collection of similar decisions from other jurisdictions, see the annotation in 5 A.L.R. 2d 1316.

We are not required to decide, and we do not decide, whether the fact that the defendants imposed identical restrictions in the deeds conveying thirteen lots on the plan requires the conclusion that they thereby impliedly agreed to impose the same restrictions on all lots on the same plan. Even if there were a common scheme giving rise to such an implication, there would still be no writing signed by the defendants sufficient to satisfy the statute of frauds. Such a common scheme, if established, would be of significance in proceedings for enforcement of restrictions between owners of different lots claiming through a common grantor who imposed the restrictions, but not as to land which the grantor has not yet sold and which he has not in writing expressly subjected to the restrictions.

In reaching our decision we have been mindful of the existence of substantial support in judicial decisions and in the writings of legal scholars for the view that if a developer conveys enough lots on a subdivision plan by deeds including uniform restrictions which prove the existence of a uniform or common scheme for the development but without expressly agreeing to insert the same restrictions on later conveyances of other lots on the plan, an agreement to do so may nevertheless be implied and enforced in equity notwithstanding the statute of frauds. (citations omitted).

In reaching our decision we have been equally mindful of the fact that the proliferation of implied rights in or servitudes upon real estate, which cannot be readily ascertained by an examination of the records of the appropriate registry of deeds or of the Land Court, will serve only further to erode the integrity and reliability of such records and will be a subversion of the fundamental purpose for which such records are required to be made and maintained. A prospective purchaser of a lot on a plan from a developer who has not previously expressly subjected that lot to any restrictions of record should not be subjected to the nearly impossible burden and risk of deciding at his peril whether, by a series of restrictions imposed on lots previously conveyed, the developer has impliedly restricted his remaining land in the same way. "It is the policy of our law in regard to the recording of deeds, that persons desiring to buy may safely trust the record as to the ownership of land, and as to incumbrances upon it which are created by deed." *McCusker v. Goode*, 185 Mass. 607, 611. If the purchasers of lots on the defendants' plan had bargained and paid for the benefit of reciprocal restrictions on the land retained by the defendants, they "would have had the right to demand that the defendant[s] insert in the title deed a stipulation or covenant" to that effect. *Sprague v. Kimball*, 213 Mass. 380, 383. This they did not do. We elect not to add another dilemma to the many which are already faced by conveyancers in determining and evaluating title to real estate as affected by matters not of record. See Philbrick, *Limits of Record Search and Therefore of Notice: Part I*, 93 U. of Pa. L. Rev. 125, 167, 171–172; Ryckman, *Notice and the "Deeds Out" Problem*, 64 Mich. L. Rev. 421, 427–445.

The plaintiffs attempt for the first time by their brief to present to us for decision the question whether the town's zoning by-law permits the use of the defendant's land for multi-family apartment buildings. The issue was not raised by the pleadings. The facts bearing on it are not included in any stipulation nor in the judge's voluntary findings. The plaintiffs have attempted to introduce the essential facts on the issue by way of their brief which gives purported dates of amendments to the zoning by-law and includes references to a transcript. We have already noted that there is no transcript before us. This issue is not properly presented in this manner and we do not pass on it.

The final decree is reversed, and a new decree is to be entered dismissing the bill with costs of appeal. So ordered.

NOTES

1. What effect would a developer's power to abolish or modify restrictions have on the validity of a scheme of covenants? See *Wright v. Cypress Shores Dev. Co.*, 413 So.2d 1115 (Ala. 1982); *Flamingo Ranch Estates, Inc. v. Sunshine Ranches Homeowners, Inc.*, 303 So.2d 665 (Fla. Dist. Ct. App. 1974); *Hall v. Gulledge*, 145 So.2d 794 (Ala. 1962). Would it matter whether the developer ever used the power? See *Suttle v. Bailey*, 361 P.2d 325 (N.M. 1961). Should the developer's power be treated differently from a power of the homeowners association to abolish or modify restrictions by majority vote? See *Ardmore Park Subdivision Ass'n, Inc. v. Simon*, 323 N.W.2d 591 (Mich. Ct. App. 1982). What about an association's power to create exceptions to restrictions? See *Appel v. Presley Co.*, 806 P.2d 1054 (N.M. 1991).

2. Is the effect of such a decision to discourage efficiency-maximizing transactions? Orderly development of land may depend on the enforcement of these servitudes. It may be said that the gain in value to the defendants' land was more than offset by the loss to the plaintiffs' land caused by the building permitted by the decision. See generally Robert Ellickson, *Alternatives to Zoning: Covenants, Nuisance Rules, and Fines as Land Use Controls*, 40 U. Chi. L. Rev. 681 (1973).

3. What is the relation between the law of servitudes and the policy against restraints on alienation found in the law of estates? Can this decision also be explained as the product of a policy against restrictions on the use of land? Critics say that allowing more than the narrowest scope for such servitudes promotes discriminatory restrictions (e.g., against families with children, against the poor, against minorities).

llama case

CITIZENS FOR COVENANT COMPLIANCE v. ANDERSON
906 P.2d 1314 (Cal. 1995)

Most states allow developers to impose restrictions on a new development w/o putting them on each deed — all you need is sufficient evidence of a common plan.

ARABIAN, J.

The Andersons want to plant and harvest grapes, operate a winery, and keep llamas on their property in Woodside. Some neighbors object, and claim such activities are prohibited by covenants, conditions and restrictions (CC & R's) that limit the Andersons' property, and theirs, to residential use. The Andersons counter, thus far successfully, that the CC & R's are not enforceable because they are not mentioned in any deed to their property. The dispute is now before us.

Its resolution requires us to penetrate a legal thicket entangled by the ancient doctrines of covenants that run with the land and equitable servitudes. Although the relevant doctrines go back centuries, they are more vital than ever today as California becomes increasingly crowded and people live in closer proximity to one another. Planned communities have developed to regulate the relationships between neighbors so all may enjoy the reasonable use of their property. Mutual restrictions on the use of property that are binding upon, and enforceable by, all units in a development are becoming ever more common and desirable. . . .

The CC & R's of this case were recorded before any of the properties they purport to govern were sold, thus giving all buyers constructive notice of their existence. They state they are to bind and benefit each parcel of property as part of a planned community. Nevertheless, the Court of Appeals held they are not enforceable because they were not also mentioned in a deed or other document when the property was sold. We disagree, and adopt the following rule: If a declaration establishing a common plan for the ownership of property in a subdivision and containing restrictions upon the use of the property as part of the common plan, is recorded before the execution of the contract of sale, describes the property it is to govern, and states that it is to bind all purchasers and their successors, subsequent purchasers who have constructive notice of the recorded declaration are deemed to intend and agree to be bound by, and to accept the benefits of, the common plan; the restrictions, therefore, are not unenforceable merely because they are not additionally cited in a deed or other document at the time of the sale. We therefore reverse the judgment of the Court of Appeal.

I. THE FACTS

Defendants Jared A. and Anne Anderson (the Andersons), own two adjacent parcels of property in Woodside that were part of separate subdivisions developed at different times. One parcel was part of Skywood Acres, created in the 1950's when Joseph and Claire Stadler subdivided land into some 60 residential building lots. On June 5, 1958, an instrument entitled "Declarations Imposing Covenants Restrictions and Agreements Affecting . . . Skywood Acres," executed by the Stadlers, was recorded in San Mateo County. It states that the Stadlers owned the property, the map of which had previously been recorded, and expresses their "desire to establish a general plan for the improvement and development of said property and to subject said property to the following conditions, restrictions, covenants and reservations upon and subject to which all of said property shall be held, improved and conveyed. . . ."

Numerous restrictions follow, the first of which is that each lot "shall be used for residential purposes only." The instrument provides that "Dogs, cats, hares, fowls and fish may be kept as household pets provided they are not kept, bred or raised for commercial purposes or in unreasonable number," and allows keeping horses on specified lots under certain conditions. It also states, "All these conditions and restrictions shall run with the land and shall be binding upon all parties and all persons claiming under them. . . ." It further provides that, as to the Stadlers and "their grantees and successors in interest of any lot or lots" in the subdivision, the conditions are to be "covenants running with the land" enforceable by "the Subdividers, grantees or assigns, or by such owners or successors in interest."

The portion of Skywood Acres involved here was sold on October 14, 1958, and, after intermediate conveyances, was eventually acquired by the Andersons. Neither the original grant deed nor any other deed in the chain of title leading to the Andersons refers to the recorded restrictions. The Andersons' title insurance report, however, identifies the Skywood Acres CC & R's.

The second parcel was part of the Friars subdivision, comprised of four lots. On January 24, 1977, the Town of Woodside adopted a resolution approving the parcel map for the subdivision upon certain conditions, including that the developer submit to the town attorney for approval "the covenants, conditions and restrictions applicable to this land division." On May 10, 1977, a "Declaration Imposing Covenants, Restrictions, Easements and Agreements," executed by the owner, was recorded. This declaration describes the property in the subdivision and states that the owner desired and intended "to subject [the property] to certain conditions, covenants and charges between them and all subsequent purchasers. . . ." It declares that the property "shall be conveyed subject to the conditions, covenants and charges" set forth, including that the property is to be used solely for single family residences, and specifically "exclude[s] every form of business, commercial, manufacturing, or storage enterprises or activity. . . ." Keeping animals other than household pets and horses is prohibited. The restrictions "are declared to constitute mutual equitable covenants and servitudes for the protection and benefit of each property in the said subdivision," and "are to run with the land." Moreover, "Each grantee of a conveyance or purchaser under a Contract or Agreement of Sale by accepting a Deed or a Contract of Sale or Agreement of purchase, accepts the same subject to any of the covenants, restrictions, easements and agreements set forth in this Declaration and agrees to be bound by the same." The owner of any of the parcels may enforce the restrictions.

The portion of the Friars subdivision involved here was sold two days after the CC & R's were recorded, and eventually was acquired by the Andersons at a foreclosure sale. The original deed refers to the parcel map, but not to the CC & R's. No other deed in the Andersons' chain of title refers to them. The title insurance report for this lot, purchased by the original buyers, identifies the Friars CC & R's.

The parties agree that both subdivisions were "developed from a general plan of uniform development." Both sets of CC & R's contain provisions regarding possible modification and termination of the restrictions. The record does not indicate whether any other deed to property in either subdivision mentions the CC & R's.

After purchasing the two parcels of property, the Andersons entered into a limited partnership agreement with a company located in the island of Guernsey in the United Kingdom to operate a winery under the name Chaine d'Or Vineyards. They have obtained permits from the Town of Woodside to grow grapes and produce wine on their property, subject to specified conditions. In addition, the Andersons have admitted to keeping seven llamas on the property as pets.

The plaintiffs, an unincorporated association named Citizens for Covenant Compliance and individual landowners representing both subdivisions (hereafter, collectively, Citizens), filed this action against the Andersons to enforce both the Skywood Acres and the Friars CC & R's, which, they claim, prohibit the wine business and the keeping of llamas. The superior court found the CC & R's unenforceable, and judgment was eventually entered for the Andersons. Citizens appealed.

The Court of Appeal affirmed. For "several reasons," it determined that the CC & R's are not covenants running with the land. It also found they are not enforceable as equitable servitudes because no deed or other written instrument exchanged between a buyer and a seller refers to the CC & R's. For this reason, the court concluded, no parcel in either subdivision was "conveyed pursuant to an express, written, agreement that it was conveyed subject to a general plan of restrictions. Absent that, it is irrelevant that the Andersons may have had actual notice of the CC & R's." We granted Citizens' petition for review.

II. DISCUSSION

A. Background

1. Covenants and Equitable Servitudes

Modern subdivisions are often built according to a general plan containing restrictions that each owner must abide by for the benefit of all. "Ordinarily, a general plan of restriction is recorded by the subdivider grantor for the purpose of insuring the uniform and orderly development and use of the entire tract by all of the original purchasers as well as their successors in interest. The restrictions are imposed upon each parcel within the tract. These subdivision restrictions are used to limit the type of buildings that can be constructed upon the property or the type of activity permitted on the property, prohibiting such things as commercial use or development within the tract, limiting the height of buildings, imposing setback restrictions, protecting views, or imposing similar restrictions." (*Sain v. Silvestre* (1978) 78 Cal. App. 3d 461, 466, 144 Cal. Rptr. 478.)

The CC & R's of this case contain such restrictions. The Andersons contend, however, that they never took effect because they were not referenced in any deed to their property. Citizens contends they are enforceable as either (1) covenants that run with the land, or (2) equitable servitudes, two doctrines of distinct lineage. The dual nature of the argument has substantially complicated the question. A detailed review of the history and elements of these doctrines is unnecessary but, given modern confusion and, among legal scholars at least, interest regarding the degree to which the doctrines remain separate, a brief overview is appropriate.

The first doctrine to develop was that of real covenants or, as generally stated in California, covenants that run with the land, which dates back at least to *Spencer's Case* (1583 Q.B.) 77 Eng.Rep. 72. A covenant is said to run with the land if it binds not only the person who entered into it, but also later owners and assigns who did not personally enter into it. (Civ. Code, § 1460; *Scaringe v. J.C.C. Enterprises, Inc.* (1988) 205 Cal. App. 3d 1536, 1543, 253 Cal. Rptr. 344.) In California, only covenants specified by statute run with the land (§ 1461), primarily those described in sections 1462 and 1468. However, prior to the amendments of section 1468 in 1968 and 1969, these sections were written and interpreted very narrowly. Under section 1462, a covenant that benefits the property may run with the land, but not one that burdens the property. Section 1468, as originally enacted in 1905, only applied to a covenant "made by the owner of land with the owner of other land," and not to a covenant between a grantor and a grantee. Because the covenants in this case are between grantor and grantee and burden the property as well as benefit it, they would not qualify as covenants that run with the land under these provisions.

Beginning with the 1848 English decision of *Tulk v. Moxhay* (1848 Ch.) 41 Eng.Rep. 1143, courts of equity sometimes enforced covenants that, for one reason or another, did not run with the land in law, and the separate doctrine of equitable servitudes arose. California adopted this doctrine, and it accumulated its own body of rules. (E.g., *Werner v. Graham* (1919) 181 Cal. 174, 183 P. 945.) Because of the statutory limitations on covenants running with the land, at least before section 1468 was amended, California courts have "[t]raditionally" analyzed CC & R's under the doctrine of equitable servitudes.

In 1968 and again in 1969, section 1468 was amended to make covenants that run with the land analytically closer to equitable servitudes. Today, that statute applies to covenants between a grantor and grantee as well as between separate landowners. Covenants governed by the amended statute might run with the land even if they formerly would not. Thus, they would apply to the 1977 Friars subdivision but not to the earlier Skywood Acres; no matter how the current issue is decided, the CC & R's of the latter would remain enforceable, if at all, only as equitable servitudes.

2. Recording Provisions

By statute, any instrument "affecting the title to . . . real property may be recorded" by the "County Recorder of the county in which the real property affected thereby is situated." (Gov. Code, § 27280(a); Civ. Code § 1169.) "Recording consists of copying the instrument in the record book and indexing it under the names of the parties." Civil Code section 1213 provides that every "conveyance" of real property recorded as prescribed by law provides "constructive notice" of its contents to subsequent purchasers. Constructive notice "is the equivalent of actual knowledge; i.e., knowledge of its contents is conclusively presumed." (4 Witkin, Summary of Cal. Law, *supra*, § 203, p. 406, 408.)

CC & R's, which affect title to real property, have long been recorded under these provisions.

B. Analysis

Two factual circumstances, and the interplay between them, are of paramount importance. First, the CC & R's were recorded before any of the property was sold, thus giving the Andersons notice of their existence. Second, no written document executed at the time of any of the conveyances of the Andersons' properties refers to the CC & R's. Properly stated, the issue here is not whether the restrictions run with the land, and thus bind successors as well as the original grantees, but whether they ever took effect in the first place so as to bind even the original grantees. Specifically, the issue is whether a purchaser is bound by previously recorded CC & R's even though none of the written documents executed at the time of the conveyance refer to them. This involves the question whether there is sufficient expression of intent on the purchaser's part to enter into the covenants. Although notice is relevant to our resolution of the issue, it is not the issue itself.

1. California Cases

In the 1919 decision of *Werner v. Graham, supra*, 181 Cal. 174, 183 P. 945, a developer subdivided a tract and recorded a map of the tract. "This map showed no building lines or anything else to indicate any purpose of restricting in any way the manner in which the different lots might be built upon or otherwise improved or the uses to which they might be put." (*Id.* at 177.) He then sold the lots. The early deeds contained "restrictive provisions, which, while differing slightly in some instances, dependent upon the location of the particular lot . . . are yet so uniform and consistent in character as to indicate unmistakably that [the developer] had in mind a general and common plan which he was following." The developer told the purchasers "that he was exacting the same restrictive provisions from all purchasers." (*Id.* at 179.) He later quitclaimed the property eventually purchased by the plaintiff. The deed to this property contained no restrictions. The issue was whether the restrictions placed in the deeds to the other property were also binding on the plaintiff.

The developer in *Riley v. Bear Creek Planning Comm.*, 17 Cal. 3d 500, 131 Cal. Rptr. 381, 55 P.2d 1213, sold the property in dispute by a deed that contained no restrictions. "[A]t the time of the conveyance there was no document of record purporting to restrict the use of" the property. (*Id.* at 504.) Nine months after the conveyance, the developer recorded a document purporting to impose uniform restrictions on a number of lots, including the one in dispute. The issue was whether these restrictions applied to the lot sold earlier.

In both *Werner* and *Riley*, we held the property was not bound by the restrictions. It is readily apparent that both are factually distinguishable from this case. In *Werner*, there was no recorded document imposing uniform restrictions on the entire subdivision, only individual deeds imposing restrictions on specific parcels. In *Riley*, the restrictions were recorded after the conveyance at issue.

Nevertheless, the Andersons cite some of the language of these decisions as aiding their position.

In *Werner, supra*, 181 Cal. at 181–182, we noted that the restrictions in the earlier deeds did not state that the land was part of a larger tract, that the restrictions were intended to benefit other land, or that the benefit was to pass to other land. . . .

It made no difference in *Werner* that the developer "in all his deeds exacted similar restrictions and clearly had in mind a uniform plan of restrictions which he intended to impose, and actually did impose, upon all the lots in the tract as he sold them." (*Werner, supra*, 181 Cal. at 183.) We recognized that if the deeds contain "appropriate language imposing restrictions on each parcel as part of a general plan of restrictions common to all the parcels and designed for their mutual benefit, mutual equitable servitudes are thereby created in favor of each parcel as against all the others." But, we stated, the "crux of the present case" was that "here there is no language in the instruments between the parties, that is, the deeds, which refers to a common plan of restrictions or which expresses or in any way indicates any agreement between grantor and grantee that the lot conveyed is taken subject to any such plan." (*Id.* at 183–184.)

We went on to explain the significance of these facts. "The intent of the common grantor — the original owner — is clear enough. He had a general plan of restrictions in mind. But it is not his intent that governs. It is the joint intent of himself and his grantees, and as between him and each of his grantees the instrument or instruments between them, in this case the deed, constitute the final and exclusive memorial of such intent. It is also apparent that each deed must be construed as of the time it is given. . . . Nor does it make any difference that . . . [the developer] gave each grantee to understand, and each grantee did understand, that the restrictions were exacted as part of a general scheme. This whole discussion may in fact be summed up in the simple statement that if the parties desire to create mutual rights in real property of the character of those claimed here they must say so, and must say it in the only place where it can be given legal effect, namely, in the written instruments exchanged between them which constitute the final expression of their understanding." (*Werner, supra*, 181 Cal. at 184–185.)

In *Riley*, we relied on *Werner* in finding the later recorded restrictions not enforceable. We stressed the key fact distinguishing that case from this — that the restrictions of *Riley* were recorded after the conveyance — and stated that "quite apart from the rule of *Werner v. Graham*, it is manifest that acknowledgment and recordation of a declaration of restrictions by the grantor after the conveyance to plaintiffs cannot affect property in which the grantor no longer has any interest." (*Riley, supra*, 17 Cal. 3d at 507.) The rule of the *Werner* case is "supported by every consideration of sound public policy which has led to the enactment and enforcement of statutes of frauds in every English-speaking commonwealth." (*Id.* at 510, internal quotes omitted.) "As a matter of policy, the understanding of the parties should be definite and clear, and should not be left to mere conjecture." *Id.*

We also emphasized the importance of recording the restrictions. " '[T]he recording statutes operate to protect the expectations of the grantee and secure to him the full benefit of the exchange for which he bargained. Where, however, mutually enforceable equitable servitudes are sought to be created outside the recording statutes, the vindication of the expectations of the original grantee, and for that matter succeeding grantees, is hostage not only to the good faith of the grantor but, even assuming good faith, to the vagaries of proof by extrinsic evidence of actual notice on the part of grantees. . . . The uncertainty thus introduced into subdivision development would in many cases circumvent any plan for the orderly and harmonious development of such properties and result in a crazy-quilt pattern of uses frustrating the bargained-for expectations of lot owners in the tract.' " (*Riley, supra,* 17 Cal. 3d at 511–512.) . . .

In both *Werner* and *Riley*, there was no prior recorded document providing a common plan and stating that the restrictions were to apply to every parcel. The only documents in existence from which the mutual intent and agreement of the parties could be discerned were the deeds themselves, which were silent. No decision by this court invalidating restrictions involves a written plan, like that here, that was applicable to an entire tract and was recorded before conveyancing. . . .

It has not taken much to satisfy the requirement of a reference in a deed. As little as a statement that the property is "subject to" restrictions of record, or even a "reference to restrictions 'of record, if any' " have been found to suffice. But to date, the Court of Appeal decisions have required some reference in the deed, however vague, to the recorded restrictions.

2. The Current Uncertainties

The Andersons argue that the CC & R's never took effect because they were not mentioned in the deeds to their properties. Under this interpretation, if the developer of a subdivision records a uniform plan of restrictions intended to bind and benefit every parcel alike, implementation of the plan depends upon the vagaries of the actual deeds, and whether they contain at least a ritualistic reference to restrictions of record. When, as may often be the case, some deeds refer to the restrictions, and others do not, the enforceability of the restrictions can hinge upon the sequence of the conveyances, and can vary depending upon what property owner seeks to enforce them and against which property.

For example, if the deed to the first conveyance refers to the restrictions, they might be effective at least as between that property and later properties, even if the later deeds do not refer to them. Moreover, under this view, even if a deed fully and expressly incorporates the CC & R's, they would not be enforceable as to an earlier sale that did not contain such a reference. Thus, the rights and duties of a later purchaser as against earlier ones would not depend on any document executed at the time of the later sale, but solely on the language of earlier sales of separate parcels.

The results can be Byzantine. One commentator has reviewed some of the possibilities: "If the subdivider fails to insert the agreement in the first deed but remembers to insert it in the fifth deed, for example, the equitable servitude springs into existence from deed five onwards. The restrictions do not apply to the first four lots because the subdivider no longer has any interest in those lots and cannot place a restriction on them in favor of the rest of the tract. Would anyone really intend a subdivision where the order in which property is sold determines what restrictions are enforceable, where some landowners are not bound by restrictions of record and cannot enforce them against anyone, where some owners can enforce them against some property but not others and not against each other, and where some landowners are bound by the restrictions as against some owners but not against others who would be powerless to enforce them? This situation dramatically complicates title searches. Instead of simply searching for restrictions of record in order to know exactly what is being purchased, a prospective buyer must search the chain of title of all previously sold property in the tract." Note, 29 Hastings L.J. 545, 569–570 (1978). . . . This situation dramatically complicates title searches. . . . Moreover, it is not certain exactly what the law is on this subject. [The court then cited a split in California cases on the issue of whether the "first deed" rule refers to the first deed out, or to the first deed in every chain of title out, of the common subdivider. — Eds.]

3. The Solution

These uncertainties can be eliminated by adopting the rule stated at the outset. In essence, if the restrictions are recorded before the sale, the later purchaser is deemed to agree to them. The purchase of property knowing of the restrictions evinces the buyer's intent to accept their burdens and benefits. Thus, the mutual servitudes are created at the time of the conveyance even if there is no additional reference to them in the deed. This rule has many advantages. The first advantage is simplicity itself. One document, recorded for all purchasers to review, would establish the rules for all parcels, not many documents that may or may not be mutually consistent.

Having a single set of recorded restrictions that apply to the entire subdivision would also no doubt fulfill the intent, expectations, and wishes of the parties and community as a whole. A buyer need only know of the single document, not study the current labyrinthine system and try to predict how a later court would apply it to the contemplated purchase. The rule would also better enable the community to protect its interests. Here, for example, Woodside's approval of the Friars subdivision was conditioned on the town attorney's review of the CC & R's. Thus the community was able to exercise oversight as to the original recorded declaration. But it is unrealistic to expect such oversight of all subsequent individual deeds. The community should be able to expect that restrictions it requires as a condition of approving the subdivision will take effect, and not run the risk that they will fall victim to careless deed drafting. By requiring recordation before execution of the contract of sale, the rule would also be fair. All buyers could easily know exactly what they were purchasing. (See *Riley, supra,* 17 Cal. 3d at p. 512, 131 Cal. Rptr. 381, 551 P.2d 1213.) Title searches would be easier, requiring only a search of restrictions of record, not of all deeds to all properties in the subdivision. "The danger that subsequent purchasers might not be aware of restrictions in prior deeds, where the developer neglects to incorporate similar restrictions in later deeds, and where the obligation of the title searcher extends only to instruments in the direct chain of title, can be easily avoided by insistence that the developer follow a simple procedure. Where a tract index is in effect, a plan of the proposed development should be recorded against the entire tract, which would give notice to all purchasers by placing the restriction in the direct chain of title to each lot in the tract." (Newman & Losey, *Covenants Running with the Land, and Equitable Servitudes: Two Concepts, or One?, supra,* 21 Hastings L.J. at 1341.) When a developer does follow this simple procedure, it should suffice; future buyers should be deemed to agree to the restrictions.

The rule is consistent with the rationale of the prior cases, and would undermine no legal or policy concerns expressed in those cases. The theoretical underpinning of the rule requiring the restrictions to be stated in the deeds is that a developer cannot unilaterally make an agreement. It takes two parties — in this case the seller and the buyer — to agree. Merely recording the restrictions does not create mutual servitudes. Rather, they "spring into existence" only upon an actual conveyance. (*Werner, supra,* 181 Cal. at p. 183) The servitudes are not effective, that is, they do not "spring into existence," until an actual conveyance subject to them is made. The developer could modify or rescind any recorded restrictions before the first sale. Some of the prior cases, however, simply assumed that the deeds must expressly refer to the restrictions to evidence the purchaser's intent and agreement. On the contrary, it is reasonable to conclude that property conveyed after the restrictions are recorded is subject to those restrictions even without further mention in the deed. "The issue in these cases is the intent of the grantors and grantees at the time of the conveyance." (*Fig Garden Park etc. Ass'n v. Assemi Corp.,* (1991), 233 Cal. App. 3d at p. 1709.) This intent can be inferred from the recorded uniform plan. It is express on the part of the seller, implied on the part of the purchaser. The law may readily conclude that a purchaser who has constructive notice, and therefore knowledge, of the restrictions, takes the property with the understanding that it, as well as all other lots in the tract, is subject to the restrictions, and intends and agrees to accept their burdens and benefits, even if there is no additional documentation evidencing the intent at the time of the conveyance.

Even under the Andersons' interpretation, a buyer may often be subject to restrictions not referenced in the deed. If an earlier deed does reference the restrictions, they would be enforceable as between that earlier property and any property purchased later even if the later deed does not mention them. It is reasonable and logical to make them enforceable upon the actual conveyance even if no deed references them if the restrictions are recorded and apply to the entire development. The overall plan, and not individual deeds, should determine what restrictions are in effect, and between whom. For these reasons, we adopt the rule, and disapprove inconsistent language and holdings of other cases.

4. Resolution of this Case

The CC & R's of this case were recorded before any of the parcels were sold, thus providing constructive notice to subsequent purchasers; they state an intent to establish a general plan for the subdivisions binding on all purchasers and their successors; and they describe the property they are to govern. Therefore, applying the rule to this case, the fact that the individual deeds do not reference them is not fatal to their enforceability. The superior court erred in finding otherwise, and in granting summary judgment for the Andersons.

[Dissent omitted. — Eds.]

IV. TERMINATION OF COVENANTS

Covenants may be terminated in many ways — according to their terms, as when they have a definite length, or are subject to a condition subsequent; and by the same means that easements may come to an end. See Section [I][G], *supra*. The most litigated doctrine involving their termination — cessation of purpose, or as it is called in the law of covenants "changed conditions" — is illustrated in the following case.

GRANGE v. KORFF

79 N.W.2d 743 (Iowa 1956)

GARFIELD, J.

This is a suit in equity to enjoin defendants from constructing and operating an auto trailer court in a suburban residential area outside the city of Cedar Rapids as in violation of building restrictions of which defendants had notice. Following trial a decree granted plaintiffs and intervenors the relief sought. Defendants appeal.

The area consists of thirty-one numbered lots and is designated Auditor's Plat 120, Linn County, commonly referred to as Lincoln Heights. It is about five miles east of the center of the Cedar Rapids business district. Defendants Carlton J. Korff and wife purchased Lot 31 for $6000 by contract dated July 14, 1950. The deed to them was made a month later. Lot 31 is in the northwest corner of the plat, contains 8.2 acres, and has a dwelling house on it. The other lots vary in size but are much smaller than 31, although considerably larger than the average city lot. After defendants acquired their lot they did grading, built a road and otherwise improved the land as a site for an auto trailer court they planned to operate from their dwelling.

Plaintiffs are twenty-one owners of most of the other lots in the plat. Intervenors John McGowan (also a plaintiff) and wife own Lot 30 adjoining defendants' Lot 31 on the east. Plaintiff Grange started the suit in July 1952. Amended petition was filed on behalf of all plaintiffs in February 1953. Lots in the plat comprise a strictly residential area. No business is conducted there although one resident near the southeast corner raises a few dogs, apparently for sale, and has a small sign hanging from a post advertising his kennels.

In February 1920, Frank B. Lane, a real-estate broker in Cedar Rapids, acquired title to the land in question. Lane was associated in the real-estate business with H. L. Nehls with whom he officed. They owned and controlled a corporation known as Nehls-Lane Co. Nehls controlled another corporation known as H. L. Nehls Investment Co. Nehls & Lane laid out streets, built a few houses and did some other work on the land. Auditor's Plat No. 120 was filed for record September 13, 1921.

The Cedar Rapids Gazette, a daily paper, for September 23, 1921, carried an advertisement, more than a half page in size, describing claimed advantages of "Lincoln Heights, Cedar Rapids' beautiful new suburban homesites" and stating the lots would go on sale the following day. Also that "improvements must conform to the standard of desirable, attractive homes." The ad bore the name and address of Nehls-Lane Company as sponsor.

Defendants call attention to the statement in this ad that Lincoln Heights "comprises 30 tracts." From this they argue it was not intended that building restrictions, hereinafter referred to, should apply to defendants' Lot 31. We are not inclined to attach much importance to this statement. The ad contained a large reproduction of the plat showing the thirty-one numbered lots and the printed matter stated they are as large as "25 city lots each." This could refer only to Lot 31. The ad clearly implied, if it did not expressly state, the entire plat was for homesites.

October 24, 1921, Frank B. Lane and wife deeded Lot 31 to Wm. McGowan and adjoining Lot 30 to intervenor John McGowan, son of William. In purchasing Lots 30 and 31 the two McGowans dealt with H. L. Nehls who told them the deeds to all lots would be restricted to a house and outbuildings. Each deed to the McGowans contained this provision:

> "it being the intention of the owners of said lot of Plat No. 120 that said lot shall be used only for private residence purposes. This conveyance is made under the restrictions and agreements which are a part of the consideration hereof and are hereby expressly agreed to bind the grantee herein for himself, his heirs, legal representatives, assigns, and grantees as covenants running with the land as follows: That no building other than a private dwelling house which shall cost not less than $2,000.00 and the necessary barn, stable and outhouses appurtenant thereto shall ever be erected or maintained upon said lot nor shall any building be erected or maintained within twenty feet from the front line of said property. It is also agreed that the foregoing covenants are for the benefit of the present owners and each and all of the several future owners and such owner, or owners, may at any time maintain a suit, or suits, in equity for the specific performance of any or all, of the said covenants and to restrain a violation thereof."

November 12, 1921, Frank B. Lane and wife deeded Lot 14 to A.L. Peet. The deed contained substantially the same provision, quoted above, as the McGowan deeds except that the dwelling house must cost not less than $2500, instead of $2000, and the building line was fixed at 25, rather than 20, feet from the front of the lot. Lot 14 faces the southwest boundary of the plat, on a different road from that along Lot 31. Before deeding Lot 14 to Peet, Lane had contracted to sell it to Florence Risley but the contract was never performed. It contained no building restrictions.

December 19, 1921, Lane and wife conveyed Lots 26 and 27 to James E. Patterson and wife and deeded to Nehls-Lane Company all thirty-one lots except Nos. 14, 26, 27, 30 and 31 which, as stated, had been conveyed to others. The two deeds to the Pattersons and the one to Nehls-Lane contained no restrictions. Before the end of 1923 Nehls-Lane Company or its grantee, Nehls or Lane, conveyed fourteen lots by deeds containing substantially the restrictions heretofore quoted from the deeds to the McGowans of Lots 30 and 31 except that these later deeds provide: "It being the intention of the owners of said Auditor's Plat 120 that all of said Auditor's Plat shall be used only for private residence purposes."

The McGowan deeds state the lot thereby conveyed, rather than all the plat, shall be used only for private residence purposes. Two other lots were deeded by Nehls, grantee from Nehls-Lane Co., in September 1923, subject to the restrictions found in the deeds to the McGowans and Peet. Thus nineteen of the thirty-one lots were conveyed by Lane, Nehls or their corporation subject to one or the other of these two sets of restrictions.

Lot 25, like 26 and 27, was deeded without restrictions although they have been used for residence purposes. The remaining nine lots were conveyed between 1925 and 1928 "subject to reservations and building restrictions of record." Grantor in these deeds was H. L. Nehls Investment Co. which had acquired them from or through Nehls-Lane Company. All the deeds we have referred to were duly recorded.

. . . We . . . consider . . . the . . . proposition defendants argue-that drastic changes have occurred in the platted area which make it unreasonable and inequitable to enforce these building restrictions against defendants. It is claimed "many of these changes" have been caused by plaintiffs and intervenors and their predecessors in title and constitute violations of the restrictions. The argument is without merit.

The proposition is mainly based upon these facts. Several plaintiffs outlet sewage from their homes into septic tanks. There is no general sewer in the tract. Some of the tanks in turn outlet along highways and some of this filtered sewage passes along the road adjoining defendants' premises and onto the lot itself. At times an odor of sewage comes from these outlets. This condition was less prevalent at the time of trial than had formerly existed. There is a garbage dump on an abandoned electric railroad right of way about 400 feet west of defendants' premises, outside the plat in question. Some plaintiffs have dumped garbage and refuse there, but not that Mr. Korff observed for some two months before the trial. Sometime between the time of platting and defendants' purchase of their property the railroad ceased to operate over this right of way which passed along the south side of Lot 31. It is claimed this abandonment rendered the lot and surrounding ground less desirable for residence purposes. (It would seem there would also be some benefits from abandonment of the railroad.) Complaint is also made of the raising of dogs by one lot owner and his sign to which we have already referred. Also that more than one house has been built on at least one lot.

Thodos v. Shirk, 248 Iowa 172, 186, 187, 79 N.W.2d 733, 742, cites several decisions for the proposition that before a defense to such an action as this, based on changed conditions, may prevail there must be a change in the character of the neighborhood sufficient to make it impossible to secure in a substantial degree the benefits sought to be realized by the restrictions. Precedents are also referred to which hold the change must be such as to render the restriction valueless to owners of the benefitted land and oppressive or unreasonable to the owner of the burdened land. (Citations omitted.)

In *Thodos v. Shirk* the raising of dogs for sale and several other minor business activities were relied upon as showing an abandonment of building restrictions except for residences. We refer to these uses as clearly of a trivial, temporary and immaterial nature, insufficient to defeat the primary residential purpose of the restriction.

We are agreed that none of the matters of which defendants complain, nor all of them combined, has resulted in any fundamental — or substantial — change in the character of this tract sufficient to constitute a defense to the suit.

Defendants' remaining proposition is that the restrictions sought to be enforced are so unreasonable, harsh and inequitable a court of equity should not enforce them.

We find nothing unreasonable or inequitable in the restriction that Lot 31 shall be used only for private residence purposes or in the other restrictions in the deed from Lane to William McGowan except the provision that at least implies only one dwelling house shall be erected on Lot 31. While we are clear defendants are properly enjoined from constructing and operating a trailer court and from using their lot for other than private residence purposes, we are not persuaded it is an exercise of sound discretion, under all the circumstances, to enjoin the erection of more than one dwelling on this suburban lot of 8.2 acres. The trial court's decree seems to do so and in this one respect we are unable to agree with it.

It is not to be inferred from this, however, that the restriction of but one dwelling on a lot is unreasonable or unenforceable as to the other, smaller lots in the plat. As applied to Lot 31 we feel its enforcement will be of little benefit to plaintiffs and intervenors but will unnecessarily punish defendants, nor is it needed in order to effectuate the purpose of the restrictions.

Our disagreement with the trial court in this one respect is reached on what we regard as fundamental principles that govern actions of this kind. It is true mere pecuniary loss to a defendant from enforcement of such restrictions will not prevent a court of equity from enforcing them. But specific performance of them is not a matter of absolute right. It rests largely in the sound discretion of the court and if a defendant will be subject to great hardship or the consequences would be inequitable, relief will be denied. . . . *Melson v. Ormsby*, 169 Iowa 522, 529, 151 N.W. 617, 820, makes this pertinent statement: "And further, before a strict literal performance of the restriction will be exacted by a court of equity, it must affirmatively appear that this is necessary to effectuate the purpose, scheme, or intent of the parties in making the restriction."

Except as modified in the respect stated in this division the decree is affirmed. One fourth the costs in this court to be taxed to plaintiffs, the rest to defendants. Modified and affirmed.

NOTE

The doctrine of changed conditions has been used both to strike down a covenant as well as to defend against enforcement of a covenant. Most courts considering the doctrine have, like the court in *Grange v. Korff*, limited the evidence of changed conditions to the original subdivision or tract to which the covenants attached. See *El Di, Inc. v. Town of Bethany Beach*, 477 A.2d 1066 (Del. 1984) (invalidating a covenant prohibiting the sale of liquor in a summer resort originally founded by a religious group); *West Almeda Heights Homeowners Ass'n v. Board of County Comm'rs*, 458 P.2d 253, 256 (Colo. 1969). Is the doctrine a particularized restatement of the contract doctrine of frustration of purpose? See Glen Robinson, *Explaining Contingent Rights: The Puzzle of "Obsolete" Covenants*, 91 Colum. L. Rev. 546 (1991) (discussing the underpinnings of the doctrine); Timothy Shepard, *Termination of Servitudes: Expanding the Remedies for "Changed Conditions,"* 31 UCLA L. Rev. 226 (1983); 2 Am. L. Prop. § 9.39 (James Casner ed., 1952).

Chapter 7

TAKINGS AND LAND USE CONTROLS

I. TAKINGS

> "[N]or shall private property be taken
> for public use without just compensation."
> — United States Constitution Amendment V

Takings law is one of the most interesting, challenging, and controversial areas of property law. It concerns the constitutional limitations on government's ability to take property from its owner. The Fifth Amendment Takings Clause applies directly to the federal government and, by incorporation into the Fourteenth Amendment Due Process Clause, to state and local governments. Additionally, every state constitution either expressly includes a takings clause or has been judicially interpreted to include one. Many state constitutions provide greater protection than the federal Constitution for private property rights. For example, some state constitutions require compensation if an owner's property is "taken, destroyed, or damaged." See, e.g., Minn. Const. art. I, § 13.

Despite the Takings Clause's brevity, it has generated four separate areas of litigation. Currently, the most contentious issue is what type of "public use" is necessary to justify a government taking. The circumstances under which government is deemed to have "taken" property is by far the most frequently litigated issue. The definition of "private property" arises in a wide variety of contexts. For example, is a sports franchise "private property" that a city can take if the team is threatening to move? Even the seemingly straightforward requirement for "just compensation" raises a number of thorny issues.

This section of the book examines each of these elements of the Takings Clause. As you read the cases, consider how the changing composition of the U.S. Supreme Court has affected takings analysis.

A. Public Use

During the mid- to late-nineteenth century, many courts interpreted the "public use" requirement quite literally. They held that a taking of private property was unconstitutional unless the public physically would be able to use the property, such as for a road. As demonstrated by *Kelo v. City of New London*, courts now define "public use" far more broadly. However, this issue is extremely controversial.

KELO v. CITY OF NEW LONDON
545 U.S. 469 (2005)

JUSTICE STEVENS delivered the opinion of the Court.

In 2000, the city of New London approved a development plan that, in the words of the Supreme Court of Connecticut, was "projected to create in excess of 1,000 jobs, to increase tax and other revenues, and to revitalize an economically distressed city, including its downtown and waterfront areas." In assembling the land needed for this project, the city's development agent has purchased property from willing sellers and proposes to use the power of eminent domain to acquire the remainder of the property from unwilling owners in exchange for just compensation. The question presented is whether the city's proposed disposition of this property qualifies as a "public use" within the meaning of the Takings Clause of the Fifth Amendment to the Constitution.

I

The city of New London (hereinafter City) sits at the junction of the Thames River and the Long Island Sound in southeastern Connecticut. Decades of economic decline led a state agency in 1990 to designate the City a "distressed municipality." In 1996, the Federal Government closed the Naval Undersea Warfare Center, which had been located in the Fort Trumbull area of the City and had employed over 1,500 people. In 1998, the City's unemployment rate was nearly double that of the State, and its population of just under 24,000 residents was at its lowest since 1920.

These conditions prompted state and local officials to target New London, and particularly its Fort Trumbull area, for economic revitalization. To this end, respondent New London Development Corporation (NLDC), a private nonprofit entity established some years earlier to assist the City in planning economic development, was reactivated. In January 1998, the State authorized a $5.35 million bond issue to support the NLDC's planning activities and a $10 million bond issue toward the creation of a Fort Trumbull State Park. In February, the pharmaceutical company Pfizer Inc. announced that it would build a $300 million research facility on a site immediately adjacent to Fort Trumbull; local planners hoped that Pfizer would draw new business to the area, thereby serving as a catalyst to the area's rejuvenation. After receiving initial approval from the city council, the NLDC continued its planning activities and held a series of neighborhood meetings to educate the public about the process. In May, the city council authorized the NLDC to formally submit its plans to the relevant state agencies for review. Upon obtaining state-level approval, the NLDC finalized an integrated development plan focused on 90 acres of the Fort Trumbull area.

The Fort Trumbull area is situated on a peninsula that juts into the Thames River. The area comprises approximately 115 privately owned properties, as well as the 32 acres of land formerly occupied by the naval facility (Trumbull State Park now occupies 18 of those 32 acres). The development plan encompasses seven parcels. Parcel 1 is designated for a waterfront conference hotel at the center of a "small urban village" that will include restaurants and shopping. This parcel will also have marinas for both recreational and commercial uses. A pedestrian "riverwalk" will originate here and continue down the coast, connecting the waterfront areas of the development. Parcel 2 will be the site of approximately 80 new residences organized into an urban neighborhood and linked by public walkway to the remainder of the development, including the state park. This parcel also includes space reserved for a new U.S. Coast Guard Museum. Parcel 3, which is located immediately north of the Pfizer facility, will contain at least 90,000 square feet of research and development office space. Parcel 4A is a 2.4-acre site that will be used either to support the adjacent state park, by providing parking or retail services for visitors, or to support the nearby marina. Parcel 4B will include a renovated marina, as well as the final stretch of the riverwalk. Parcels 5, 6, and 7 will provide land for office and retail space, parking, and water-dependent commercial uses.

The NLDC intended the development plan to capitalize on the arrival of the Pfizer facility and the new commerce it was expected to attract. In addition to creating jobs, generating tax revenue, and helping to "build momentum for the revitalization of downtown New London," the plan was also designed to make the City more attractive and to create leisure and recreational opportunities on the waterfront and in the park.

The city council approved the plan in January 2000, and designated the NLDC as its development agent in charge of implementation. The city council also authorized the NLDC to purchase property or to acquire property by exercising eminent domain in the City's name. The NLDC successfully negotiated the purchase of most of the real estate in the 90-acre area, but its negotiations with petitioners failed. As a consequence, in November 2000, the NLDC initiated the condemnation proceedings that gave rise to this case.

II

Petitioner Susette Kelo has lived in the Fort Trumbull area since 1997. She has made extensive improvements to her house, which she prizes for its water view. Petitioner Wilhelmina Dery was born in her Fort Trumbull house in 1918 and has lived there her entire life. Her husband Charles (also a petitioner) has lived in the house since they married some 60 years ago. In all, the nine petitioners own 15 properties in Fort Trumbull — 4 in parcel 3 of the development plan and 11 in parcel 4A. Ten of the parcels are occupied by the owner or a family member; the other five are held as investment properties. There is no allegation that any of these properties is blighted or otherwise in poor condition; rather, they were condemned only because they happen to be located in the development area.

In December 2000, petitioners brought this action in the New London Superior Court. They claimed, among other things, that the taking of their properties would violate the "public use" restriction in the Fifth Amendment. After a 7-day bench trial, the Superior Court granted a permanent restraining order prohibiting the taking of the properties located in parcel 4A (park or marina support). It, however, denied petitioners relief as to the properties located in parcel 3 (office space).

After the Superior Court ruled, both sides took appeals to the Supreme Court of

Connecticut. That court held, over a dissent, that all of the City's proposed takings were valid. It began by upholding the lower court's determination that the takings were authorized by chapter 132, the State's municipal development statute. That statute expresses a legislative determination that the taking of land, even developed land, as part of an economic development project is a "public use" and in the "public interest." Next, relying on cases such as *Hawaii Housing Authority v. Midkiff*, 467 U.S. 229 (1984), and *Berman v. Parker*, 348 U.S. 26 (1954), the court held that such economic development qualified as a valid public use under both the Federal and State Constitutions. * * *

We granted certiorari to determine whether a city's decision to take property for the purpose of economic development satisfies the "public use" requirement of the Fifth Amendment.

III

Two polar propositions are perfectly clear. On the one hand, it has long been accepted that the sovereign may not take the property of A for the sole purpose of transferring it to another private party B, even though A is paid just compensation. On the other hand, it is equally clear that a State may transfer property from one private party to another if future "use by the public" is the purpose of the taking; the condemnation of land for a railroad with common-carrier duties is a familiar example. Neither of these propositions, however, determines the disposition of this case.

As for the first proposition, the City would no doubt be forbidden from taking petitioners' land for the purpose of conferring a private benefit on a particular private party. See *Midkiff*, 467 U.S., at 245 ("A purely private taking could not withstand the scrutiny of the public use requirement; it would serve no legitimate purpose of government and would thus be void"). Nor would the City be allowed to take property under the mere pretext of a public purpose, when its actual purpose was to bestow a private benefit. The takings before us, however, would be executed pursuant to a "carefully considered" development plan. The trial judge and all the members of the Supreme Court of Connecticut agreed that there was no evidence of an illegitimate purpose in this case. Therefore, as was true of the statute challenged in *Midkiff*, 467 U.S., at 245, the City's development plan was not adopted "to benefit a particular class of identifiable individuals."

On the other hand, this is not a case in which the City is planning to open the condemned land — at least not in its entirety — to use by the general public. Nor will the private lessees of the land in any sense be required to operate like common carriers, making their services available to all comers. But although such a projected use would be sufficient to satisfy the public use requirement, this "Court long ago rejected any literal requirement that condemned property be put into use for the general public." *Id.*, at 244. Indeed, while many state courts in the mid-19th century endorsed "use by the public" as the proper definition of public use, that narrow view steadily eroded over time. Not only was the "use by the public" test difficult to administer (*e.g.*, what proportion of the public need have access to the property? at what price?), but it proved to be impractical given the diverse and always evolving needs of society. Accordingly, when this Court began applying the

Fifth Amendment to the States at the close of the 19th century, it embraced the broader and more natural interpretation of public use as "public purpose." See, *e.g.*, *Fallbrook Irrigation Dist. v. Bradley*, 164 U.S. 112, 158–164 (1896). Thus, in a case upholding a mining company's use of an aerial bucket line to transport ore over property it did not own, Justice Holmes' opinion for the Court stressed "the inadequacy of use by the general public as a universal test." *Strickley v. Highland Boy Gold Mining Co.*, 200 U.S. 527, 531 (1906). We have repeatedly and consistently rejected that narrow test ever since.

The disposition of this case therefore turns on the question whether the City's development plan serves a "public purpose." Without exception, our cases have defined that concept broadly, reflecting our longstanding policy of deference to legislative judgments in this field.

In *Berman v. Parker*, 348 U.S. 26 (1954), this Court upheld a redevelopment plan targeting a blighted area of Washington, D. C., in which most of the housing for the area's 5,000 inhabitants was beyond repair. Under the plan, the area would be condemned and part of it utilized for the construction of streets, schools, and other public facilities. The remainder of the land would be leased or sold to private parties for the purpose of redevelopment, including the construction of low-cost housing.

The owner of a department store located in the area challenged the condemnation, pointing out that his store was not itself blighted and arguing that the creation of a "better balanced, more attractive community" was not a valid public use. Writing for a unanimous Court, Justice Douglas refused to evaluate this claim in isolation, deferring instead to the legislative and agency judgment that the area "must be planned as a whole" for the plan to be successful. The Court explained that "community redevelopment programs need not, by force of the Constitution, be on a piecemeal basis — lot by lot, building by building." The public use underlying the taking was unequivocally affirmed:

> "We do not sit to determine whether a particular housing project is or is not desirable. The concept of the public welfare is broad and inclusive. . . . The values it represents are spiritual as well as physical, aesthetic as well as monetary. It is within the power of the legislature to determine that the community should be beautiful as well as healthy, spacious as well as clean, well-balanced as well as carefully patrolled. In the present case, the Congress and its authorized agencies have made determinations that take into account a wide variety of values. It is not for us to reappraise them. If those who govern the District of Columbia decide that the Nation's Capital should be beautiful as well as sanitary, there is nothing in the Fifth Amendment that stands in the way."

In *Hawaii Housing Authority v. Midkiff*, 467 U.S. 229 (1984), the Court considered a Hawaii statute whereby fee title was taken from lessors and transferred to lessees (for just compensation) in order to reduce the concentration of land ownership. We unanimously upheld the statute and rejected the Ninth Circuit's view that it was "a naked attempt on the part of the state of Hawaii to take the property of A and transfer it to B solely for B's private use and benefit." Reaffirming *Berman*'s deferential approach to legislative judgments in this field, we concluded that the State's purpose of eliminating the "social and economic evils of a land oligopoly" qualified as a valid public use. Our opinion also rejected the contention that the mere fact that the State immediately transferred the properties to private individuals upon condemnation somehow diminished the public character of the taking. "[I]t is only the taking's purpose, and not its mechanics," we explained, that matters in determining public use.

In that same Term we decided another public use case that arose in a purely economic context. In *Ruckelshaus v. Monsanto Co.*, 467 U.S. 986 (1984), the Court dealt with provisions of the Federal Insecticide, Fungicide, and Rodenticide Act under which the Environmental Protection Agency could consider the data (including trade secrets) submitted by a prior pesticide applicant in evaluating a subsequent application, so long as the second applicant paid just compensation for the data. We acknowledged that the "most direct beneficiaries" of these provisions were the subsequent applicants, but we nevertheless upheld the statute under *Berman* and *Midkiff.* We found sufficient Congress' belief that sparing applicants the cost of time-consuming research eliminated a significant barrier to entry in the pesticide market and thereby enhanced competition.

Viewed as a whole, our jurisprudence has recognized that the needs of society have varied between different parts of the Nation, just as they have evolved over time in response to changed circumstances. Our earliest cases in particular embodied a strong theme of federalism, emphasizing the "great respect" that we owe to state legislatures and state courts in discerning local public needs. See *Hairston v. Danville & Western R. Co.*, 208 U.S. 598, 606–607 (1908) (noting that these needs were likely to vary depending on a State's "resources, the capacity of the soil, the relative importance of industries to the general public welfare, and the long-established methods and habits of the people"). For more than a century, our public use jurisprudence has wisely eschewed rigid formulas and intrusive scrutiny in favor of affording legislatures broad latitude in determining what public needs justify the use of the takings power.

IV

Those who govern the City were not confronted with the need to remove blight in the Fort Trumbull area, but their determination that the area was sufficiently distressed to justify a program of economic rejuvenation is entitled to our deference. The City has carefully formulated an economic development plan that it believes will provide appreciable benefits to the community, including — but by no means limited to — new jobs and increased tax revenue. As with other exercises in urban planning and development, the City is endeavoring to coordinate a variety of commercial, residential, and recreational uses of land, with the hope that they will form a whole greater than the sum of its parts. To effectuate this plan, the City has invoked a state statute that specifically authorizes the use of eminent domain to promote economic development. Given the comprehensive character of the plan, the thorough deliberation that preceded its adoption, and the limited scope of our review, it is appropriate for us, as it was in *Berman*, to resolve the challenges of the individual owners, not on a piecemeal basis, but rather in light of the entire plan. Because that plan unquestionably serves a public purpose, the takings challenged here satisfy the public use requirement of the Fifth Amendment.

To avoid this result, petitioners urge us to adopt a new bright-line rule that economic development does not qualify as a public use. Putting aside the unpersuasive suggestion that the City's plan will provide only purely economic benefits, neither precedent nor logic supports petitioners' proposal. Promoting economic development is a traditional and long-accepted function of government. There is, moreover, no principled way of distinguishing economic development from the other public purposes that we have recognized. In our cases upholding takings that facilitated agriculture and mining, for example, we emphasized the importance of those industries to the welfare of the States in question; in *Berman*, we endorsed the purpose of transforming a blighted area into a "well-balanced" community through redevelopment, 348 U.S., at 33;[13] in *Midkiff*, we upheld the interest in breaking up a land oligopoly that "created artificial deterrents to the normal functioning of the State's residential land market," and in *Monsanto*, we accepted Congress' purpose of eliminating a "significant barrier to entry in the pesticide market." It would be incongruous to hold that the City's interest in the economic benefits to be derived from the development of the Fort Trumbull area has less of a public character than any of those other interests. Clearly, there is no basis for exempting economic development from our traditionally broad understanding of public purpose.

Petitioners contend that using eminent domain for economic development impermissibly blurs the boundary between public and private takings. Again, our cases foreclose this objection. Quite simply, the government's pursuit of a public purpose will often benefit individual private parties. For example, in *Midkiff*, the forced transfer of property conferred a direct and significant benefit on those lessees who were previously unable to purchase their homes. In *Monsanto*, we recognized that the "most direct beneficiaries" of the data-sharing provisions were the subsequent pesticide applicants, but benefiting them in this way was necessary to promoting competition in the pesticide market. The owner of the department store in *Berman* objected to "taking from one businessman for the benefit of another businessman," referring to the fact that under the redevelopment plan land would be leased or sold to private developers for redevelopment. Our rejection of that contention has particular relevance to the instant case: "The public end may be as well or better served through an agency of private enterprise than through a department of government — or so the Congress might conclude. We cannot say that public ownership is the sole method of promoting the public purposes of community redevelopment projects."

It is further argued that without a bright-line rule nothing would stop a city from transferring citizen *A*'s property to citizen *B* for the sole reason that citizen *B* will

---

[13] It is a misreading of *Berman* to suggest that the only public use upheld in that case was the initial removal of blight. The public use described in *Berman* extended beyond that to encompass the purpose of *developing* that area to create conditions that would prevent a reversion to blight in the future. See 348 U.S., at 34–35 ("It was not enough, [the experts] believed, to remove existing buildings that were insanitary or unsightly. It was important to redesign the whole area so as to eliminate the conditions that cause slums. . . . The entire area needed redesigning so that a balanced, integrated plan could be developed for the region, including not only new homes, but also schools, churches, parks, streets, and shopping centers. In this way it was hoped that the cycle of decay of the area could be controlled and the birth of future slums prevented"). Had the public use in *Berman* been defined more narrowly, it would have been difficult to justify the taking of the plaintiff's nonblighted department store.

put the property to a more productive use and thus pay more taxes. Such a one-to-one transfer of property, executed outside the confines of an integrated development plan, is not presented in this case. While such an unusual exercise of government power would certainly raise a suspicion that a private purpose was afoot, the hypothetical cases posited by petitioners can be confronted if and when they arise. They do not warrant the crafting of an artificial restriction on the concept of public use.

Alternatively, petitioners maintain that for takings of this kind we should require a "reasonable certainty" that the expected public benefits will actually accrue. Such a rule, however, would represent an even greater departure from our precedent. "When the legislature's purpose is legitimate and its means are not irrational, our cases make clear that empirical debates over the wisdom of takings — no less than debates over the wisdom of other kinds of socioeconomic legislation — are not to be carried out in the federal courts." *Midkiff*, 467 U.S., at 242–243. . . . The disadvantages of a heightened form of review are especially pronounced in this type of case. Orderly implementation of a comprehensive redevelopment plan obviously requires that the legal rights of all interested parties be established before new construction can be commenced. A constitutional rule that required postponement of the judicial approval of every condemnation until the likelihood of success of the plan had been assured would unquestionably impose a significant impediment to the successful consummation of many such plans.

Just as we decline to second-guess the City's considered judgments about the efficacy of its development plan, we also decline to second-guess the City's determinations as to what lands it needs to acquire in order to effectuate the project. "It is not for the courts to oversee the choice of the boundary line nor to sit in review on the size of a particular project area. Once the question of the public purpose has been decided, the amount and character of land to be taken for the project and the need for a particular tract to complete the integrated plan rests in the discretion of the legislative branch." *Berman*, 348 U.S., at 35–36.

In affirming the City's authority to take petitioners' properties, we do not minimize the hardship that condemnations may entail, notwithstanding the payment of just compensation. We emphasize that nothing in our opinion precludes any State from placing further restrictions on its exercise of the takings power. Indeed, many States already impose "public use" requirements that are stricter than the federal baseline. Some of these requirements have been established as a matter of state constitutional law, while others are expressed in state eminent domain statutes that carefully limit the grounds upon which takings may be exercised. As the submissions of the parties and their *amici* make clear, the necessity and wisdom of using eminent domain to promote economic development are certainly matters of legitimate public debate. This Court's authority, however, extends only to determining whether the City's proposed condemnations are for a "public use" within the meaning of the Fifth Amendment to the Federal Constitution. Because over a century of our case law interpreting that provision dictates an affirmative answer to that question, we may not grant petitioners the relief that they seek.

The judgment of the Supreme Court of Connecticut is affirmed.

Justice O'Connor, with whom The Chief Justice, Justice Scalia, and Justice Thomas join, dissenting.

* * * Our cases have generally identified three categories of takings that comply with the public use requirement, though it is in the nature of things that the boundaries between these categories are not always firm. Two are relatively straightforward and uncontroversial. First, the sovereign may transfer private property to public ownership — such as for a road, a hospital, or a military base. Second, the sovereign may transfer private property to private parties, often common carriers, who make the property available for the public's use — such as with a railroad, a public utility, or a stadium. But "public ownership" and "use-by-the-public" are sometimes too constricting and impractical ways to define the scope of the Public Use Clause. Thus we have allowed that, in certain circumstances and to meet certain exigencies, takings that serve a public purpose also satisfy the Constitution even if the property is destined for subsequent private use. *See, e.g., Berman v. Parker*, 348 U.S. 26 (1954); *Hawaii Housing Authority v. Midkiff*, 467 U.S. 229 (1984). * * *

The Court's holdings in *Berman* and *Midkiff* were true to the principle underlying the Public Use Clause. In both those cases, the extraordinary, precondemnation use of the targeted property inflicted affirmative harm on society — in *Berman* through blight resulting from extreme poverty and in *Midkiff* through oligopoly resulting from extreme wealth. And in both cases, the relevant legislative body had found that eliminating the existing property use was necessary to remedy the harm. Thus a public purpose was realized when the harmful use was eliminated. Because each taking *directly* achieved a public benefit, it did not matter that the property was turned over to private use. Here, in contrast, New London does not claim that Susette Kelo's and Wilhelmina Dery's well-maintained homes are the source of any social harm. * * *

In moving away from our decisions sanctioning the condemnation of harmful property use, the Court today significantly expands the meaning of public use. It holds that the sovereign may take private property currently put to ordinary private use, and give it over for new, ordinary private use, so long as the new use is predicted to generate some secondary benefit for the public — such as increased tax revenue, more jobs, maybe even esthetic pleasure. But nearly any lawful use of real private property can be said to generate some incidental benefit to the public. Thus, if predicted (or even guaranteed) positive side effects are enough to render transfer from one private party to another constitutional, then the words "for public use" do not realistically exclude *any* takings, and thus do not exert any constraint on the eminent domain power.

There is a sense in which this troubling result follows from errant language in *Berman* and *Midkiff.* In discussing whether takings within a blighted neighborhood were for a public use, *Berman* began by observing: "We deal, in other words, with what traditionally has been known as the police power." 348 U.S., at 32. From there it declared that "[o]nce the object is within the authority of Congress, the right to realize it through the exercise of eminent domain is clear." *Id.*, at 33. Following up, we said in *Midkiff* that "[t]he 'public use' requirement is coterminous with the scope of a sovereign's police powers." 467 U.S., at 240. This language was unnecessary to the specific holdings of those decisions. *Berman* and *Midkiff* simply did not put such language to the constitutional test, because the takings in those cases were within the police power but also for "public use" for the reasons I have described. The case before us now demonstrates why, when deciding if a taking's purpose is constitutional, the police power and "public use" cannot always be equated. * * *

The specter of condemnation hangs over all property. Nothing is to prevent the State from replacing any Motel 6 with a Ritz-Carlton, any home with a shopping mall, or any farm with a factory. Cf. *Bugryn v. Bristol*, 63 Conn. App. 98, 774 A.2d 1042 (2001) (taking the homes and farm of four owners in their 70's and 80's and giving it to an "industrial park"); *99 Cents Only Stores v. Lancaster Redevelopment Agency*, 237 F.Supp.2d 1123 (C.D.Cal.2001) (attempted taking of 99 Cents store to replace with a Costco); *Poletown Neighborhood Council v. Detroit*, 410 Mich. 616, 304 N.W.2d 455 (1981) (taking a working-class, immigrant community in Detroit and giving it to a General Motors assembly plant), overruled by *County of Wayne v. Hathcock*, 471 Mich. 445, 684 N.W.2d 765 (2004). * * *

JUSTICE THOMAS dissenting.

* * * The Court has elsewhere recognized "the overriding respect for the sanctity of the home that has been embedded in our traditions since the origins of the Republic," *Payton v. New York*, 445 U.S. 573 (1980), when this issue is only whether the government may search a home. Yet today the Court tells us that we are not to "second-guess the City's considered judgments," when the issue is, instead, whether the government may take the infinitely more intrusive step of tearing down petitioners' homes. Something has gone seriously awry with this Court's interpretation of the Constitution. Though citizens are safe from the government in their homes, the homes themselves are not. Once one accepts, as the Court at least nominally does, that the Public Use Clause is a limit on the eminent domain power of the Federal Government and the States, there is no justification for the almost complete deference it grants to legislatures as to what satisfies it. * * *

The consequences of today's decision are not difficult to predict, and promise to be harmful. So-called "urban renewal" programs provide some compensation for the properties they take, but no compensation is possible for the subjective value of these lands to the individuals displaced and the indignity inflicted by uprooting them from their homes. Allowing the government to take property solely for public purposes is bad enough, but extending the concept of public purpose to encompass any economically beneficial goal guarantees that these losses will fall disproportionately on poor communities. Those communities are not only systematically less likely to put their lands to the highest and best social use, but are also the least politically powerful.

NOTES

1. Before *Hawaii Housing Authority v. Midkiff*, 467 U.S. 229 (1984), constitutional commentators questioned whether the "public use" provision in the Takings Clause restricted government's ability to take property or whether the Takings Clause's only limitation was to require compensation. In *Midkiff*, the Court seemed

to adopt the latter interpretation. Justice O'Connor, writing for the Court, stated: "The 'public use' requirement is coterminous with the scope of a sovereign's police power." *Id.* at 240. In her *Kelo* dissent, Justice O'Connor said that the statement was too broad and should be limited, whereas Justice Stevens felt bound to follow the earlier case. Speaking to a bar association group after the *Kelo* decision, Justice Stevens said that, in his personal opinion, it would have been wiser for the state and local legislatures to let the free market operate, rather than to use eminent domain, but that he had to follow precedent in deciding the case. Did Justice O'Connor persuasively distinguish *Midkiff* and *Berman* from *Kelo*?

2.   Although the *Kelo* decision was consistent with the precedent, it unleashed a tremendous backlash. In a national survey, 81% of respondents said that they disagreed with the decision. The House of Representatives passed a resolution condemning the decision, and bills were introduced in the Senate and in the House to limit the use of eminent domain for private development projects. Approximately 42 states have enacted legislation limiting the circumstances in which land can be condemned or providing additional procedural requirements, such as public notice and a public hearing. See National Conference of State Legislatures, Eminent Domain Overview, http://www.ncsl.org/default.aspx?tabid=13252; The Castle Coalition: Citizens Fighting Eminent Domain Abuse, Enacted Legislation Since *Kelo*, http://www.castlecoalition.org/index.php?option=com_content&task=view&id= 510. Many commentators argued that the land use planning community had committed a disservice by failing to get its side of the story out — that economic development is beneficial and often requires private investment.

Interestingly, many of the new laws may be ineffective. In *The Limits of Backlash: Assessing the Political Response to* Kelo, 93 Minn. L. Rev. 2100 (2009), Professor Ilya Somin states that only six or seven of the new laws significantly restrict takings for economic development. For example, many new laws prohibit takings for "economic development" but permit them for "community development" or to eliminate "blight," which is broadly defined. According to Professor Somin, all the effective new laws were enacted by citizen initiative, rather than by a legislature. He argues that the legislatively-enacted laws are largely ineffective because of "widespread political ignorance." Most voters pay little or no attention to the actual language of legislation, which enabled legislators to take a strong public stand against *Kelo* but to protect real estate developers and others that benefit from takings for economic development. In contrast, property rights activists, rather than legislators, drafted the citizen initiatives. Litigation during the next several years will determine just how effectively the new laws limit government takings.

3.   Many state courts have held that the "public use" requirement of their state constitution was violated by condemnation of land for transfer to a private developer. For example, in *County of Wayne v. Hathcock*, 684 N.W.2d 765 (Mich. 2004), the county brought a condemnation action for land for a business and technology park. As in *Kelo*, the county's purpose was to "reinvigorate the struggling economy . . . by attracting businesses to the area." Because the county was going to transfer the condemned land to private parties, the court held that the condemnation did not satisfy the Michigan Constitution's "public use" requirement. See also *Gallenthin Realty Development, Inc. v. Borough of Paulsboro*, 924 A.2d 447 (N.J. 2007); *City of Norwood v. Horney*, 853 N.E.2d 1115 (Ohio 2006); *Muskogee*

County v. Lowery, 136 P.3d 639 (2006); *Manufactured Housing Communities of Washington v. Washington*, 13 P.3d 183 (Wash. 2000); *Karesh v. City Council of Charleston*, 247 S.E.2d 342 (S.C. 1978); *Hogue v. Port of Seattle*, 341 P.2d 171 (Wash. 1959).

Hathcock expressly overruled an earlier Michigan Supreme Court decision, *Poletown Neighborhood Council v. City of Detroit*, 304 N.W.2d 455 (Mich. 1981). In that case, the Michigan Supreme Court considered the constitutionality of a condemnation of land to be conveyed to General Motors Corporation for construction of a new assembly plant. The land to be condemned included a neighborhood known as Poletown, which was "a tightly-knit residential enclave of first- and second-generation Americans . . . generally elderly, mostly retired and largely Polish-American. . . ." *Id.* at 470 (dissenting opinion). The Poletown Neighborhood Council argued that the condemnation did not satisfy the state constitution's public use requirement because GM would have uncontrolled use of the land and because GM, rather than the public, would be the primary beneficiary of the condemnation. The court held that an adequate public purpose existed because the new plant would help alleviate the city's dire fiscal situation, substantial unemployment, and need for new industrial development. The *Hathcock* court said that the "majority opinion in *Poletown* is most notable for its radical and unabashed departure from the entirety of this Court's pre-1963 eminent domain jurisprudence." *Id.* at 785.

4. Despite the popular uproar after *Kelo*'s validation of government takings for private development, little attention has been paid to *private* takings for private development. Private mining companies and other natural resource developers in the interior western states have the power of eminent domain, but none of the post-*Kelo* laws in these states imposes new limits on that power. At first blush, this legislative omission seems puzzling because these companies can take land without any government review or approval. Moreover, unlike other private entities with the eminent domain power, such as railroads, lands condemned by these companies are used solely to facilitate their private business activities.

In *The Frontier of Eminent Domain*, 79 Colo. L. Rev. 651 (2008), Professor Alexandra Klass demonstrates that these companies have had the eminent domain power since the earliest years of statehood because the interior western states' economic well-being depended on exploitation of their minerals and other natural resources. Agriculture and other forms of development are far less viable in these states than in the eastern states. She also states that these private companies' power to take land is unlikely to be curtailed now because natural resource development is still crucially important to those states' economies.

5. As a result of the long delay caused by the *Kelo* litigation and the controversy surrounding it, construction on the project has not begun. Though the state has spent $73 million for environmental cleanups and for sewer and road improvements, lenders are reluctant to be involved with such a controversial project. Therefore, the land is still vacant. The project suffered another serious blow in November 2009 when Pfizer announced that it was closing the facility that triggered the redevelopment plans for Fort Trumbull. Meanwhile, Susette Kelo's home has been moved to a site in New London where it serves as a symbol of the controversy that it engendered. See George Lefcoe, *Jeff Benedict's* Little Pink House: *The Back Story* *of the* Kelo *Case,* 42 Conn. L. Rev. 925 (2010).

B. Taking

When government needs to acquire property for a public use, such as to build a school or a road, it can exercise the power of eminent domain to condemn it. In this context, "condemn" does not mean that the government is declaring the property to be unfit for use. Rather, the term "condemn" or "condemnation" refers to the government's acquisition of title by exercising its power of eminent domain. The government has the power to acquire the fee simple absolute title or a lesser interest, such as an easement. The government will be deemed to have condemned property by acquiring it outright in an eminent domain action or by physically appropriating it, such as by flooding it, even without an eminent domain action.

Several cases in this section of the book concern a different method of taking property — regulatory takings or inverse condemnation. Before *Pennsylvania Coal Co. v. Mahon,* which is the first case, federal courts routinely held that a taking occurred only if the government physically appropriated property. Courts now recognize that land use regulations can so adversely affect an owner's ability to use land that the government essentially has taken it. However, courts have been unable to articulate a bright-line test for when a regulatory taking has occurred. Courts and scholars have proposed a variety of tests and theories, but a quest for a single theory may be quixotic. Regulatory taking cases arise in such a wide variety of situations that a certain amount of ambiguity and a great deal of flexibility in the law may be an inescapable necessity.

With the increasing amount of government regulation of land and the growth of a significant private property rights movement, a substantial number of regulatory taking cases are brought each year. They usually involve a property owner suing the government for compensation when a law has diminished the property's value. The landowner's action is for "*inverse* condemnation" because the owner is the plaintiff rather than the defendant, as it would be in a condemnation action.

1. Federal Constitution

Pennsylvania Coal case represents the beginning of modern regulatory taking law. Justice Holmes and Justice Brandeis, two of our country's most respected jurists, wrote the majority and dissenting opinions, respectively, and set forth several of the tests still used today to determine whether a taking has occurred. *Pennsylvania Coal* also is important for you to study because it is still frequently cited.

PENNSYLVANIA COAL CO. v. MAHON
260 U.S. 393 (1922)

MR. JUSTICE HOLMES delivered the opinion of the Court.

This is a bill in equity brought by the defendants in error to prevent the Pennsylvania Coal Company from mining under their property in such way as to remove the supports and cause a subsidence of the surface and of their house. The bill sets out a deed executed by the Coal Company in 1878, under which the plaintiffs claim. The deed conveys the surface but in express terms reserves the right to remove all the coal under the same and the grantee takes the premises with the risk and waives all claim for damages that may arise from mining out the coal. But the plaintiffs say that whatever may have been the Coal Company's rights, they were taken away by an Act of Pennsylvania, approved May 27, 1921, P. L. 1198, commonly known there as the Kohler Act. The Court of Common Pleas found that if not restrained the defendant would cause the damage to prevent which the bill was brought but denied an injunction, holding that the statute if applied to this case would be unconstitutional. On appeal the Supreme Court of the State agreed that the defendant had contract and property rights protected by the Constitution of the United States, but held that the statute was a legitimate exercise of the police power and directed a decree for the plaintiffs. A writ of error was granted bringing the case to this Court.

The statute forbids the mining of anthracite coal in such way as to cause the subsidence of, among other things, any structure used as a human habitation, with certain exceptions, including among them land where the surface is owned by the owner of the underlying coal and is distant more than one hundred and fifty feet from any improved property belonging to any other person. As applied to this case the statute is admitted to destroy previously existing rights of property and contract. The question is whether the police power can be stretched so far.

Government hardly could go on if to some extent values incident to property could not be diminished without paying for every such change in the general law. As long recognized some values are enjoyed under an implied limitation and must yield to the police power. But obviously the implied limitation must have its limits or the contract and due process clauses are gone. One fact for consideration in determining such limits is the extent of the diminution. When it reaches a certain magnitude, in most if not in all cases there must be an exercise of eminent domain and compensation to sustain the act. So the question depends upon the particular facts. The greatest weight is given to the judgment of the legislature, but it always is open to interested parties to contend that the legislature has gone beyond its constitutional power.

This is the case of a single private house. No doubt there is a public interest even in this, as there is in every purchase and sale and in all that happens within the commonwealth. Some existing rights may be modified even in such a case. *Rideout v. Knox*, 148 Mass. 368. But usually in ordinary private affairs the public interest does not warrant much of this kind of interference. A source of damage to such a house is not a public nuisance even if similar damage is inflicted on others in different places. The damage is not common or public. *Wesson v. Washburn Iron Co.*, 13 Allen (Mass.) 95, 103. The extent of the public interest is shown by the statute to be limited, since the statute ordinarily does not apply to land when the surface is owned by the owner of the coal. Furthermore, it is not justified as a protection of personal safety. That could be provided for by notice. Indeed the very foundation of this bill is that the defendant gave timely notice of its intent to mine under the house. On the other hand the extent of the taking is great. It purports to abolish what is recognized in Pennsylvania as an estate in land — a very valuable estate — and what is declared by the Court below to be a contract hitherto binding the plaintiffs. If we were called upon to deal with the plaintiffs' position alone, we should think it clear that the statute does not disclose a public interest sufficient to warrant so extensive a destruction of the defendant's constitutionally protected rights.

But the case has been treated as one in which the general validity of the act should be discussed. The Attorney General of the State, the City of Scranton, and the representatives of other extensive interests were allowed to take part in the argument below and have submitted their contentions here. It seems, therefore, to be our duty to go farther in the statement of our opinion, in order that it may be known at once, and that further suits should not be brought in vain.

It is our opinion that the act cannot be sustained as an exercise of the police power, so far as it affects the mining of coal under streets or cities in places where the right to mine such coal has been reserved. As said in a Pennsylvania case, "For practical purposes, the right to coal consists in the right to mine it." *Commonwealth v. Clearview Coal Co.*, 256 Pa. 328, 331. What makes the right to mine coal valuable is that it can be exercised with profit. To make it commercially impracticable to mine certain coal has very nearly the same effect for constitutional purposes as appropriating or destroying it. This we think that we are warranted in assuming that the statute does.

It is true that in *Plymouth Coal Co. v. Pennsylvania*, 232 U.S. 531, it was held competent for the legislature to require a pillar of coal to be left along the line of adjoining property, that, with the pillar on the other side of the line, would be a barrier sufficient for the safety of the employees of either mine in case the other should be abandoned and allowed to fill with water. But that was a requirement for the safety of employees invited into the mine, and secured an average reciprocity of advantage that has been recognized as a justification of various laws.

The rights of the public in a street purchased or laid out by eminent domain are those that it has paid for. If in any case its representatives have been so short sighted as to acquire only surface rights without the right of support, we see no more authority for supplying the latter without compensation than there was for taking the right of way in the first place and refusing to pay for it because the public wanted it very much. The protection of private property in the Fifth Amendment presupposes that it is wanted for public use, but provides that it shall not be taken for such use without compensation. A similar assumption is made in the decisions upon the Fourteenth Amendment. *Hairston v. Danville & Western Ry. Co.*, 208 U.S. 598, 605. When this seemingly absolute protection is found to be qualified by the police power, the natural tendency of human nature is to extend the qualification more and more until at last private property disappears. But that cannot be accomplished in this way under the Constitution of the United States.

The general rule at least is that while property may be regulated to a certain extent, if regulation goes too far it will be recognized as a taking. It may be doubted how far exceptional cases, like the blowing up of a house to stop a conflagration, go — and if they go beyond the general rule, whether they do not stand as much upon tradition as upon principle. *Bowditch v. Boston*, 101 U.S. 16. In general it is not plain that a man's misfortunes or necessities will justify his shifting the damages to his neighbor's shoulders. *Spade v. Lynn & Boston Ry. Co.*, 172 Mass. 488, 489. We are in danger of forgetting that a strong public desire to improve the public condition is not enough to warrant achieving the desire by a shorter cut than the constitutional way of paying for the change. As we already have said this is a question of degree — and therefore cannot be disposed of by general propositions. But we regard this as going beyond any of the cases decided by this Court. The late decisions upon laws dealing with the congestion of Washington and New York, caused by the war, dealt with laws intended to meet a temporary emergency and providing for compensation determined to be reasonable by an impartial board. They were to the verge of the law but fell far short of the present act. *Block & Hirsh*, 256 U.S. 135; *Marcus Brown Holding Co. v. Feldman*, 256 U.S. 170; *Levy Leasing Co. v. Siegel*, 258 U.S. 242.

We assume, of course, that the statute was passed upon the conviction that an exigency existed that would warrant it, and we assume that an exigency exists that would warrant the exercise of eminent domain. But the question at bottom is upon whom the loss of the changes desired should fall. So far as private persons or communities have seen fit to take the risk of acquiring only surface rights, we cannot see that the fact that their risk has become a danger warrants the giving to them greater rights than they bought.

Decree reversed.

Mr. Justice Brandeis, dissenting.

The Kohler Act prohibits, under certain conditions, the mining of anthracite coal within the limits of a city in such a manner or to such an extent "as to cause the . . . subsidence of any dwelling or other structure used as a human habitation, or any factory, store, or other industrial or mercantile establishment in which human labor is employed." Coal in place is land, and the right of the owner to use his land is not absolute. He may not so use it as to create a public nuisance, and uses, once harmless, may, owing to changed conditions, seriously threaten the public welfare. Whenever they do, the Legislature has power to prohibit such uses without paying compensation; and the power to prohibit extends alike to the manner, the character and the purpose of the use. Are we justified in declaring that the Legislature of Pennsylvania has, in restricting the right to mine anthracite, exercised this power so arbitrarily as to violate the Fourteenth Amendment?

Every restriction upon the use of property imposed in the exercise of the police power deprives the owner of some right theretofore enjoyed, and is, in that sense, an abridgment by the State of rights in property without making compensation. But restriction imposed to protect the public health, safety or morals from dangers threatened is not a taking. The restriction here in question is merely the prohibition of a noxious use. The property so restricted remains in the possession of its owner. The State does not appropriate it or make any use of it. The State merely prevents the owner from making a use which interferes with paramount rights of the public. Whenever the use prohibited ceases to be noxious — as it may because of further change in local or social conditions — the restriction will have to be removed and the owner will again be free to enjoy his property as heretofore.

The restriction upon the use of this property cannot, of course, be lawfully imposed, unless its purpose is to protect the public. But the purpose of a restriction does not cease to be public, because incidentally some private persons may thereby receive gratuitously valuable special benefits. Thus, owners of low buildings may obtain, through statutory restrictions upon the height of neighboring structures, benefits equivalent to an easement of light and air. . . . Furthermore, a restriction, though imposed for a public purpose, will not be lawful, unless the restriction is an appropriate means to the public end. But to keep coal in place is surely an appropriate means of preventing subsidence of the surface; and ordinarily it is the only available means. Restriction upon use does not become inappropriate as a means, merely because it deprives the owner of the only use to which the property can then be profitably put. . . . Nor is a restriction imposed through exercise of the police power inappropriate as a means, merely because the same end might be effected through exercise of the power of eminent domain, or otherwise at public expense. Every restriction upon the height of buildings might be secured through acquiring by eminent domain the right of each owner to build above the limiting height; but it is settled that the State need not resort to that power. . . . If by mining anthracite coal the owner would necessarily unloose poisonous gases, I suppose no one would doubt the power of the State to prevent the mining, without buying his coal fields. And why may not the State, likewise, without paying compensation, prohibit one from digging so deep or excavating so near the surface, as to expose the community to like dangers? In the latter case, as in the former, carrying on the business would be a public nuisance.

It is said that one fact for consideration in determining whether the limits of the police power have been exceeded is the extent of the resulting diminution in value, and that here the restriction destroys existing rights of property and contract. But values are relative. If we are to consider the value of the coal kept in place by the restriction, we should compare it with the value of all other parts of the land. That is, with the value not of the coal alone, but with the value of the whole property. The rights of an owner as against the public are not increased by dividing the interests in his property into surface and subsoil. The sum of the rights in the parts can not be greater than the rights in the whole. The estate of an owner in land is grandiloquently described as extending *ab orco usque ad coelum*. But I suppose no one would contend that by selling his interest above one hundred feet from the surface he could prevent the State from limiting, by the police power, the height of structures in a city. And why should a sale of underground rights bar the State's power? For aught that appears the value of the coal kept in place by the restriction may be negligible as compared with the value of the whole property, or even as compared with that part of it which is represented by the coal remaining in place and which may be extracted despite the statute. Ordinarily a police regulation, general in operation, will not be held void as to a particular property, although proof is offered that owing to conditions peculiar to it the restriction could not reasonably be applied. . . . But even if the particular facts are to govern, the statute should, in my opinion be upheld in this case. For the defendant has failed to adduce any evidence from which it appears that to restrict its mining operations was an unreasonable exercise of the police power. . . . Where the surface and the coal belong to the same person, self-interest would ordinarily prevent mining to such an extent as to cause a subsidence. It was, doubtless, for this reason that the

Legislature, estimating the degrees of danger, deemed statutory restriction unnecessary for the public safety under such conditions.

It is said that this is a case of a single dwelling house, that the restriction upon mining abolishes a valuable estate hitherto secured by a contract with the plaintiffs, and that the restriction upon mining cannot be justified as a protection of personal safety, since that could be provided for by notice. The propriety of deferring a good deal to tribunals on the spot has been repeatedly recognized. . . . May we say that notice would afford adequate protection of the public safety where the Legislature and the highest court of the State, with greater knowledge of local conditions, have declared, in effect, that it would not? If the public safety is imperiled, surely neither grant, nor contract, can prevail against the exercise of the police power. . . . The rule that the State's power to take appropriate measures to guard the safety of all who may be within its jurisdiction may not be bargained away was applied to compel carriers to establish grade crossings at their own expense, despite contracts to the contrary . . . and, likewise, to supersede, by an Employers' Liability Act, the provision of a charter exempting a railroad from liability for death of employees, since the civil liability was deemed a matter of public concern, and not a mere private right. . . . Nor can existing contracts between private individuals preclude exercise of the police power. "One whose rights, such as they are, are subject to State restriction cannot remove them from the power of the state by making a contract about them." . . . The fact that this suit is brought by a private person is, of course, immaterial. To protect the community through invoking the aid, as litigant, of interested private citizens is not a novelty in our law. That it may be done in Pennsylvania was decided by its Supreme Court in this case. And it is for a State to say how its public policy shall be enforced.

This case involves only mining which causes subsidence of a dwelling house. But the Kohler Act contains provisions in addition to that quoted above; and as to these, also, an opinion is expressed. These provisions deal with mining under cities to such an extent as to cause subsidence of —

(a) Any public building or any structure customarily used by the public as a place of resort, assemblage, or amusement, including, but not limited to, churches, schools, hospitals, theaters, hotels, and railroad stations.

(b) Any street, road, bridge, or other public passageway, dedicated to public use or habitually used by the public.

(c) Any track, roadbed, right of way, pipe, conduit, wire, or other facility, used in the service of the public by any municipal corporation or public service company as defined by the Public Service Company Law.

A prohibition of mining which causes subsidence of such structures and facilities is obviously enacted for a public purpose; and it seems, likewise, clear that mere notice of intention to mine would not in this connection secure the public safety. Yet it is said that these provisions of the act cannot be sustained as an exercise of the police power where the right to mine such coal has been reserved. The conclusion seems to rest upon the assumption that in order to justify such exercise of the police power there must be "an average reciprocity of advantage" as between the owner of the property restricted and the rest of the community; and that here such reciprocity is absent. Reciprocity of advantage is an important consideration, and may even be an essential, where the State's power is exercised for the purpose of conferring benefits upon the property of a neighborhood, as in drainage projects . . . or upon adjoining owners, as by party wall provisions. . . . But where the police power is exercised, not to confer benefits upon property owners but to protect the public from detriment and danger, there is in my opinion, no room for considering reciprocity of advantage. There was no reciprocal advantage to the owner prohibited from using his oil tanks in 248 U.S. 498; his brickyard, in 239 U.S. 394; his livery stable, in 237 U.S. 171; his billiard hall, in 225 U.S. 623; his oleomargarine factory, in 127 U.S. 678; his brewery, in 123 U.S. 623; unless it be the advantage of living and doing business in a civilized community. That reciprocal advantage is given by the act to the coal operators.

NOTES

1. What factors were important to the majority and to the dissent in determining whether the Kohler Act caused a taking? How do the majority and dissent differ in their analyses of similar aspects of the law, such as whether the law is designed to prevent a nuisance?

2. The focus in the majority and dissenting opinions on the existence of a public nuisance is a reflection of the land use precedent that existed at the time. Under long-established principles of nuisance law, no one has a right to use land in such an unreasonable manner that it causes substantial harm to others. Therefore, if the government enacts a law to prevent the harmful conduct, the offending property owner has not been deprived of a property interest, and the law does not constitute a taking.

This nuisance exception originated in *Mugler v. Kansas*, 123 U.S. 623 (1887). In that case, Kansas enacted a law that prohibited the manufacture and sale of liquor. A brewery owner claimed that the law forced him to close his brewery because no alternative use existed for it. The U.S. Supreme Court held that the law did not cause a taking of the brewery because the state was regulating a public harm: "[W]e cannot shut out of view the fact, within the knowledge of all, that the public health, the public morals, and the public safety, may be endangered by the general use of intoxicating drinks. . . ." The Court stated that "all property in this country is held under the implied obligation that the owner's use of it shall not be injurious to the community."

The Court employed similar reasoning in another pre-*Pennsylvania Coal* decision, *Hadacheck v. Sebastian*, 239 U.S. 394 (1915). In that case, the City of Los Angeles enacted an ordinance that prohibited operation of a brick yard in certain areas. The plaintiff owned a brick yard in one of those areas, which he had purchased before it was incorporated within the city's limits. The plaintiff alleged that the ordinance caused his property's value to decrease by 92% and would force him to go out of business. He also alleged that he could not have anticipated that the city would expand far enough to reach his property. Nonetheless, the Court held that the ordinance was constitutional because it prohibited an activity that could adversely affect the community's health and comfort.

Similarly, in *Miller v. Schoene*, 276 U.S. 272 (1928), which was decided six years after *Pennsylvania Coal*, the Supreme Court upheld a Virginia statute that authorized the government to destroy privately-owned ornamental red cedar trees without compensation because they were a host for a disease that infected neighboring apple orchards. The Court held that, because the cedars were incompatible with the apple trees, the state was forced to choose between them. "When forced to such a choice, the state does not exceed its constitutional powers by deciding upon the destruction of one class of property in order to save another which, in the judgment of the legislature, is of greater value to the public." Interestingly, both Justice Holmes and Justice Brandeis signed the *Miller* opinion.

As you read the taking decisions in this chapter, focus on the role of the nuisance exception in modern takings analysis.

3. Although many courts and scholars cite *Pennsylvania Coal* as the origin of regulatory taking law, Professor Kris W. Kobach showed in her article, *The Origins of Regulatory Takings: Setting the Record Straight*, 1996 Utah L. Rev. 1211, that state courts first recognized regulatory takings in the 1810s based on their state constitution and that the U.S. Supreme Court held that a regulatory taking occurred in a case decided in 1871. *Pumpelly v. Green Bay Co.*, 80 U.S. (13 Wall.) 166 (1871).

4. After *Pennsylvania Coal*, more than fifty years passed before the U.S. Supreme Court decided another taking case in the context of a land use regulation. That case, *Penn Central Transportation Co. v. New York City*, 438 U.S. 104 (1978), established the framework for modern regulatory takings analysis. The case is notable not only because it identifies several factors that courts should consider when determining whether a taking has occurred, but also because the Supreme Court bluntly states that these factors are indeterminate. Courts still cite the case frequently, though its reasoning is somewhat confused and its facts are rather unusual.

In *Penn Central*, a Landmarks Commission designated Grand Central Station as a landmark pursuant to New York City's Landmarks Preservation Law. Under the law, a landmark owner was required to maintain the landmark's exterior in good repair, could not alter its exterior architectural features without the Commission's permission, and could not build exterior improvements on the landmark site. Penn Central, which owned Grand Central Station, applied for permission to construct an office building on top of it. Penn Central had entered into a lease with a tenant that agreed to construct the office building and to pay Penn Central $1 million per year during construction and a minimum of $3 million per year thereafter. The Commission rejected the application on the ground that the proposed building would harm the Station's historic and aesthetic features. Penn Central then filed suit, claiming that the Landmarks Law had taken its property without just compensation.

In rejecting Penn Central's taking claim, Justice Brennan stated:

> The question of what constitutes a "taking" for purposes of the Fifth Amendment has proved to be a problem of considerable difficulty. . . . In engaging in these essentially ad hoc, factual inquiries, the Court's decisions

have identified several factors that have particular significance. The economic impact of the regulation on the claimant and, particularly, the extent to which the regulation has interfered with distinct investment-backed expectations are, of course, relevant considerations. So, too, is the character of the governmental action. A "taking" may more readily be found when the interference with property can be characterized as a physical invasion by government, than when interference arises from some public program adjusting the benefits and burdens of economic life to promote the common good.

Id. at 123–24. In addition to these factors, the Court considered the other factors identified in *Pennsylvania Coal*, such as the average reciprocity of advantage. Interestingly, in determining the law's economic impact on the property, the Court adopted Justice Brandeis' dissenting position that the value of the entire parcel must be considered and not just that portion most directly affected by the law. Balancing all these factors, the Court held that the law did not take the plaintiff's property because (1) it did not interfere with the way in which the property had been used for the previous sixty-five years, (2) the property still could be operated profitably, and (3) the plaintiff had not demonstrated that the Commission would prohibit all construction in the airspace over the station.

KEYSTONE BITUMINOUS COAL ASSOCIATION v. DeBENEDICTIS
480 U.S. 470 (1987)

Justice Stevens, delivered the opinion of the Court.

In *Pennsylvania Coal Co. v. Mahon*, 260 U.S. 393 (1922), the Court reviewed the constitutionality of a Pennsylvania statute that admittedly destroyed "previously existing rights of property and contract." *Id.*, at 413. * * * In that case the "particular facts" led the Court to hold that the Pennsylvania Legislature had gone beyond its constitutional powers when it enacted a statute prohibiting the mining of anthracite coal in a manner that would cause the subsidence of land on which certain structures were located.

Now, 65 years later, we address a different set of "particular facts," involving the Pennsylvania Legislature's 1966 conclusion that the Commonwealth's existing mine subsidence legislation had failed to protect the public interest in safety, land conservation, preservation of affected municipalities' tax bases, and land development in the Commonwealth. Based on detailed findings, the legislature enacted the Bituminous Mine Subsidence and Land Conservation Act (Subsidence Act or the Act), Pa. Stat. Ann., Tit. 52, § 1406.1 *et seq.* (Purdon Supp. 1986). Petitioners contend, relying heavily on our decision in *Pennsylvania Coal*, that §§ 4 and 6 of the Subsidence Act and certain implementing regulations violate the Takings Clause, and that § 6 of the Act violates the Contracts Clause of the Federal Constitution. The District Court and the Court of Appeals concluded that *Pennsylvania Coal* does not control for several reasons and that our subsequent cases make it clear that neither § 4 nor § 6 is unconstitutional on its face. We agree.

I.

Coal mine subsidence is the lowering of strata overlying a coal mine, including the land surface, caused by the extraction of underground coal. This lowering of the strata can have devastating effects. It often causes substantial damage to foundations, walls, other structural members, and the integrity of houses and buildings. Subsidence frequently causes sinkholes or troughs in land which make the land difficult or impossible to develop. Its effect on farming has been well documented — many subsided areas cannot be plowed or properly prepared. Subsidence can also cause the loss of groundwater and surface ponds. In short, it presents the type of environmental concern that has been the focus of so much federal, state, and local regulation in recent decades.

Despite what their name may suggest, neither of the "full extraction" mining methods currently used in western Pennsylvania enables miners to extract all subsurface coal; considerable amounts need to be left in the ground to provide access, support, and ventilation to the mines. Additionally, mining companies have long been required by various Pennsylvania laws and regulations, the legitimacy of which is not challenged here, to leave coal in certain areas for public safety reasons. Since 1966, Pennsylvania has placed an additional set of restrictions on the amount of coal that may be extracted; these restrictions are designed to diminish subsidence and subsidence damage in the vicinity of certain structures and areas.

Pennsylvania's Subsidence Act authorizes the Pennsylvania Department of Environmental Resources (DER) to implement and enforce a comprehensive program to prevent or minimize subsidence and to regulate its consequences. Section 4 of the Subsidence Act, Pa. Stat. Ann., Tit. 52, § 1406.4 (Purdon Supp. 1986), prohibits mining that causes subsidence damage to three categories of structures that were in place on April 17, 1966: public buildings and noncommercial buildings generally used by the public; dwellings used for human habitation; and cemeteries. Since 1966 the DER has applied a formula that generally requires 50% of the coal beneath structures protected by § 4 to be kept in place as a means of providing surface support. Section 6 of the Subsidence Act, Pa. Stat. Ann., Tit. 52, § 1406.6 (Purdon Supp. 1986), authorizes the DER to revoke a mining permit if the removal of coal causes damage to a structure or area protected by § 4 and the operator has not within six months either repaired the damage, satisfied any claim arising therefrom, or deposited a sum equal to the reasonable cost of repair with the DER as security.

II.

In 1982, petitioners filed a civil rights action in the United States District Court for the Western District of Pennsylvania seeking to enjoin officials of the DER from enforcing the Subsidence Act and its implementing regulations. Petitioners are an association of coal mine operators, and four corporations that are engaged, either directly or through affiliates, in underground mining of bituminous coal in western Pennsylvania. The members of the association and the corporate petitioners own, lease, or otherwise control substantial coal reserves beneath the surface of property affected by the Subsidence Act. The defendants in the action, respondents here, are the Secretary of the DER, the Chief of the DER's Division of Mine Subsidence, and the Chief of the DER's Section on Mine Subsidence Regulation.

The complaint alleges that Pennsylvania recognizes three separate estates in land: The mineral estate; the surface estate; and the "support estate." Beginning well over 100 years ago, landowners began severing title to underground coal and the right of surface support while retaining or conveying away ownership of the surface estate. It is stipulated that approximately 90% of the coal that is or will be mined by petitioners in western Pennsylvania was severed from the surface in the period between 1890 and 1920. When acquiring or retaining the mineral estate, petitioners or their predecessors typically acquired or retained certain additional rights that would enable them to extract and remove the coal. Thus, they acquired the right to deposit wastes, to provide for drainage and ventilation, and to erect facilities such as tipples, roads, or railroads, on the surface. Additionally, they typically acquired a waiver of any claims for damages that might result from the removal of the coal.

In the portions of the complaint that are relevant to us, petitioners alleged that both § 4 of the Subsidence Act, as implemented by the 50% rule, and § 6 of the Subsidence Act, constitute a taking of their private property without compensation in violation of the Fifth and Fourteenth Amendments. They also alleged that § 6 impairs their contractual agreements in violation of Article I, § 10, of the Constitution. The parties entered into a stipulation of facts pertaining to petitioners' facial challenge, and filed cross-motions for summary judgment on the facial challenge. . . .

III.

Petitioners assert that disposition of their takings claim calls for no more than a straightforward application of the Court's decision in *Pennsylvania Coal Co. v. Mahon*. Although there are some obvious similarities between the cases, we agree with the Court of Appeals and the District Court that the similarities are far less significant than the differences, and that *Pennsylvania Coal* does not control this case. . . .

The holdings and assumptions of the Court in *Pennsylvania Coal* provide obvious and necessary reasons for distinguishing *Pennsylvania Coal* from the case before us today. The two factors that the Court considered relevant, have become integral parts of our takings analysis. We have held that land use regulation can effect a taking if it "does not substantially advance legitimate state interests, . . . or denies an owner economically viable use of his land." *Agins v. Tiburon*, 447 U.S. 255, 260 (1980) (citations omitted); see also *Penn Central Transportation Co. v. New York City*, 438 U.S. 104, 124 (1978). Application of these tests to petitioners' challenge demonstrates that they have not satisfied their burden of showing that the Subsidence Act constitutes a taking. First, unlike the Kohler Act, the character of the governmental action involved here leans heavily against finding a taking; the Commonwealth of Pennsylvania has acted to arrest what it perceives to be a significant threat to the common welfare. Second, there is no record in this case to support a finding, similar to the one the Court made in *Pennsylvania Coal*, that the Subsidence Act makes it impossible for petitioners to profitably engage in their business, or that there has been undue interference with their investment-backed expectations.

The Public Purpose

Unlike the Kohler Act, which was passed upon in *Pennsylvania Coal*, the Subsidence Act does not merely involve a balancing of the private economic interests of coal companies against the private interests of the surface owners. The Pennsylvania Legislature specifically found that important public interests are served by enforcing a policy that is designed to minimize subsidence in certain areas. Section 2 of the Subsidence Act provides:

> "This act shall be deemed to be an exercise of the police powers of the Commonwealth for the protection of the health, safety and general welfare of the people of the Commonwealth, by providing for the conservation of surface land areas which may be affected in the mining of bituminous coal by methods other than 'open pit' or 'strip' mining, to aid in the protection of the safety of the public, to enhance the value of such lands for taxation, to aid in the preservation of surface water drainage and public water supplies and generally to improve the use and enjoyment of such lands and to maintain primary jurisdiction over surface coal mining in Pennsylvania."
> Pa. Stat. Ann., Tit. 52, § 1406.2 (Purdon Supp. 1986).

The District Court and the Court of Appeals were both convinced that the legislative purposes set forth in the statute were genuine, substantial, and legitimate, and we have no reason to conclude otherwise.

None of the indicia of a statute enacted solely for the benefit of private parties identified in Justice Holmes' opinion are present here. First, Justice Holmes explained that the Kohler Act was a "private benefit" statute since it "ordinarily does not apply to land when the surface is owned by the owner of the coal." 260 U.S., at 414. The Subsidence Act, by contrast, has no such exception. The current surface owner may only waive the protection of the Act if the DER consents. See 25 Pa. Code § 89.145(b) (1983). Moreover, the Court was forced to reject the Commonwealth's safety justification for the Kohler Act because it found that the Commonwealth's interest in safety could as easily have been accomplished through a notice requirement to landowners. The Subsidence Act, by contrast, is designed to accomplish a number of widely varying interests, with reference to which petitioners have not suggested alternative methods through which the Commonwealth could proceed.

Petitioners argue that at least § 6, which requires coal companies to repair subsidence damage or pay damages to those who suffer subsidence damage, is unnecessary because the Commonwealth administers an insurance program that adequately reimburses surface owners for the cost of repairing their property. But this argument rests on the mistaken premise that the statute was motivated by a desire to protect private parties. In fact, however, the public purpose that motivated the enactment of the legislation is served by preventing the damage from occurring in the first place — in the words of the statute — "by providing for the conservation of surface land areas." Pa. Stat. Ann., Tit. 52, § 1406.2 (Purdon Supp. 1986). The requirement that the mine operator assume the financial responsibility for the repair of damaged structures deters the operator from causing the damage at all — the Commonwealth's main goal — whereas an insurance program would merely reimburse the surface owner after the damage occurs.

Thus, the Subsidence Act differs from the Kohler Act in critical and dispositive respects. With regard to the Kohler Act, the Court believed that the Commonwealth had acted only to ensure against damage to some private landowners' homes. Justice Holmes stated that if the private individuals needed support for their structures, they should not have "take[n] the risk of acquiring only surface rights." 260 U.S., at 416. Here, by contrast, the Commonwealth is acting to protect the public interest in health, the environment, and the fiscal integrity of the area. That private individuals erred in taking a risk cannot estop the Commonwealth from exercising its police power to abate activity akin to a public nuisance. The Subsidence Act is a prime example that "circumstances may so change in time . . . as to clothe with such a [public] interest what at other times . . . would be a matter of purely private concern." *Block v. Hirsh*, 256 U.S. 135, 155 (1921). . . .

Many cases before and since *Pennsylvania Coal* have recognized that the nature of the State's action is critical in takings analysis.[18] In *Mugler v. Kansas*, 123 U.S. 623 (1887), for example, a Kansas distiller who had built a brewery while it was legal to do so challenged a Kansas constitutional amendment which prohibited the manufacture and sale of intoxicating liquors. Although the Court recognized that the "buildings and machinery constituting these breweries are of little value" because of the Amendment, *id.*, at 657, Justice Harlan explained that a

> "prohibition simply upon the use of property for purposes that are declared, by valid legislation, to be injurious to the health, morals, or safety of the community, cannot, in any just sense, be deemed a taking or appropriation of property. . . . The power which the States have of prohibiting such use by individuals of their property as will be prejudicial to the health, the morals, or the safety of the public, is not — and, consistently with the existence and safety of organized society cannot be — burdened with the condition that the State must compensate such individual owners for pecuniary losses they may sustain, by reason of their not being permitted, by a noxious use of their property, to inflict injury upon the community." *Id.*, at 668–669.

* * * The Court's hesitance to find a taking when the State merely restrains uses of property that are tantamount to public nuisances is consistent with the notion of "reciprocity of advantage" that Justice Holmes referred to in *Pennsylvania Coal*.[20]

---

[18] Of course, the type of taking alleged is also an often critical factor. It is well settled that a " 'taking' may more readily be found when the interference with property can be characterized as a physical invasion by government, see, e.g., *United States v. Causby*, 328 U.S. 256 (1946), than when interference arises from some public program adjusting the benefits and burdens of economic life to promote the common good." *Penn Central Transportation Co. v. New York City*, 438 U.S. 104, 124 (1978). While the Court has almost invariably found that the permanent physical occupation of property constitutes a taking, see *Loretto v. Teleprompter Manhattan CATV Corp.*, 458 U.S. 419, 435–438 (1982), the Court has repeatedly upheld regulations that destroy or adversely affect real property interests. . . .

[20] The special status of this type of state action can also be understood on the simple theory that since

Under our system of government, one of the State's primary ways of preserving the public weal is restricting the uses individuals can make of their property. While each of us is burdened somewhat by such restrictions, we, in turn, benefit greatly from the restrictions that are placed on others.[21] * * * These restrictions are "properly treated as part of the burden of common citizenship." *Kimball Laundry Co. v. United States*, 338 U.S. 1, 5 (1949). Long ago it was recognized that "all property in this country is held under the implied obligation that the owner's use of it shall not be injurious to the community," *Mugler v. Kansas*, 123 U.S., at 665; see also *Beer Co. v. Massachusetts*, 97 U.S. (7 Otto) 25, 32 (1877), and the Takings Clause did not transform that principle to one that requires compensation whenever the State asserts its power to enforce it. See *Mugler*, 123 U.S., at 664.

In *Agins v. Tiburon*, we explained that the "determination that governmental action constitutes a taking, is, in essence, a determination that the public at large, rather than a single owner, must bear the burden of an exercise of state power in the public interest," and we recognized that this question "necessarily requires a weighing of private and public interests." 447 U.S., at 260–261. As the cases discussed above demonstrate, the public interest in preventing activities similar to public nuisances is a substantial one, which in many instances has not required compensation. The Subsidence Act, unlike the Kohler Act, plainly seeks to further such an interest. Nonetheless, we need not rest our decision on this factor alone, because petitioners have also failed to make a showing of diminution of value sufficient to satisfy the test set forth in *Pennsylvania Coal* and our other regulatory takings cases.

Diminution of Value and Investment-Backed Expectations

The second factor that distinguishes this case from *Pennsylvania Coal* is the finding in that case that the Kohler Act made mining of "certain coal" commercially impracticable. In this case, by contrast, petitioners have not shown any deprivation significant enough to satisfy the heavy burden placed upon one alleging a regulatory taking. For this reason, their takings claim must fail.

---

no individual has a right to use his property so as to create a nuisance or otherwise harm others, the State has not "taken" anything when it asserts its power to enjoin the nuisance-like activity. Cf. Sax, *Takings, Private Property and Public Rights*, 81 Yale L.J. 149, 155–161 (1971); Michelman, *Property, Utility, and Fairness: Comments on the Ethical Foundations of "Just Compensation" Law*, 80 Harv. L. Rev. 1165, 1235–1237 (1967).

However, as the current Chief Justice has explained: "The nuisance exception to the taking guarantee is not coterminous with the police power itself." *Penn Central Transportation Co.*, 438 U.S., at 145 (Rehnquist, J., dissenting). This is certainly the case in light of our recent decisions holding that the "scope of the 'public use' requirement of the Takings Clause is 'coterminous with the scope of a sovereign's police powers.'" See *Ruckelshaus v. Monsanto Co.*, 467 U.S. 986, 1014 (1984) (quoting *Hawaii Housing Authority v. Midkiff*, 467 U.S. 229, 240 (1984)). See generally R. Epstein, Takings 108–112 (1985).

[21] The Takings Clause has never been read to require the States or the courts to calculate whether a specific individual has suffered burdens under this generic rule in excess of the benefits received. Not every individual gets a full dollar return in benefits for the taxes he or she pays; yet, no one suggests that an individual has a right to compensation for the difference between taxes paid and the dollar value of benefits received.

In addressing petitioners' claim we must not disregard the posture in which this case comes before us. The District Court granted summary judgment to respondents only on the facial challenge to the Subsidence Act. The court explained that "[b]ecause plaintiffs have not alleged any injury due to the enforcement of the statute, there is as yet no concrete controversy regarding the application of the specific provisions and regulations. Thus, *the only question before this court is whether the mere enactment of the statutes and regulations constitutes a taking.*" 581 F. Supp., at 513 (emphasis added). The next phase of the case was to be petitioners' presentation of evidence about the actual effects the Subsidence Act had and would have on them. Instead of proceeding in this manner, however, the parties filed a joint motion asking the court to certify the facial challenge for appeal. The parties explained that an assessment of the actual impact that the Act has on petitioners' operations "will involve complex and voluminous proofs," which neither party was currently in a position to present, App. 15–17, and stressed that if an appellate court were to reverse the District Court on the facial challenge, then all of their expenditures in adjudicating the as-applied challenge would be wasted. . . .

The posture of the case is critical because we have recognized an important distinction between a claim that the mere enactment of a statute constitutes a taking and a claim that the particular impact of government action on a specific piece of property requires the payment of just compensation. This point is illustrated by our decision in *Hodel v. Virginia Surface Mining & Reclamation Ass'n, Inc.*, 452 U.S. 264 (1981), in which we rejected a pre-enforcement challenge to the constitutionality of the Surface Mining Control and Reclamation Act of 1977. We concluded that the District Court had been mistaken in its reliance on *Pennsylvania Coal* as support for a holding that two statutory provisions were unconstitutional because they deprived coal mine operators of the use of their land. The Court explained:

> "[T]he court below ignored this Court's oft-repeated admonition that the constitutionality of statutes ought not be decided except in an actual factual setting that makes such a decision necessary. . . . Adherence to this rule is particularly important in cases raising allegations of an unconstitutional taking of private property. Just last Term, we reaffirmed:
>
> > '[T]his Court has generally "been unable to develop any 'set formula' for determining when 'justice and fairness' require that economic injuries caused by public action be compensated by the government, rather than remain disproportionately concentrated on a few persons." Rather, it has examined the "taking" question by engaging in essentially ad hoc, factual inquiries that have identified several factors — such as the economic impact of the regulation, its interference with reasonable investment backed expectations, and the character of the government action — that have particular significance.' *Kaiser Aetna v. United States*, 444 U.S. 164, 175 (1979) (citations omitted).
>
> "These 'ad hoc, factual inquiries' must be conducted with respect to specific property, and the particular estimates of economic impact and ultimate valuation relevant in the unique circumstances.

"Because appellees' taking claim arose in the context of a facial challenge, it presented no concrete controversy concerning either application of the Act to particular surface mining operations or its effect on specific parcels of land. Thus, the only issue properly before the District Court and, in turn, this Court, is whether the 'mere enactment' of the Surface Mining Act constitutes a taking. See *Agins v. Tiburon*, 447 U.S. 255, 260 (1980). The test to be applied in considering this facial challenge is fairly straightforward. A statute regulating the uses that can be made of property effects a taking if it 'denies an owner economically viable use of his land. . . .' *Agins v. Tiburon, supra*, at 260; see also *Penn Central Transp. Co. v. New York City*, 438 U.S. 104 (1978)." 452 U.S., at 295–296.

Petitioners thus face an uphill battle in making a facial attack on the Act as a taking.

The hill is made especially steep because petitioners have not claimed, at this stage, that the Act makes it commercially impracticable for them to continue mining their bituminous coal interests in western Pennsylvania. Indeed, petitioners have not even pointed to a single mine that can no longer be mined for profit. The only evidence available on the effect that the Subsidence Act has had on petitioners' mining operations comes from petitioners' answers to respondents' interrogatories. Petitioners described the effect that the Subsidence Act had from 1966–1982 on 13 mines that the various companies operate, and claimed that they have been required to leave a bit less than 27 million tons of coal in place to support § 4 areas. The total coal in those 13 mines amounts to over 1.46 billion tons. See App. 284. Thus § 4 requires them to leave less than 2% of their coal in place.[24] But, as we have indicated, nowhere near all of the underground coal is extractable even aside from the Subsidence Act. The categories of coal that must be left for § 4 purposes and other purposes are not necessarily distinct sets, and there is no information in the record as to how much coal is actually left in the ground *solely* because of § 4. We do know, however, that petitioners have never claimed that their mining operations, or even any specific mines, have been unprofitable since the Subsidence Act was passed. Nor is there evidence that mining in any specific location affected by the 50% rule has been unprofitable.

Instead, petitioners have sought to narrowly define certain segments of their property and assert that, when so defined, the Subsidence Act denies them economically viable use. They advance two alternative ways of carving their property in order to reach this conclusion. First, they focus on the specific tons of coal that they must leave in the ground under the Subsidence Act, and argue that the Commonwealth has effectively appropriated this coal since it has no other useful purpose if not mined. Second, they contend that the Commonwealth has taken their separate legal interest in property — the "support estate."

Because our test for regulatory taking requires us to compare the value that has been taken from the property with the value that remains in the property, one of the critical questions is determining how to define the unit of property "whose value is

---

[24] The percentage of the total that must be left in place under § 4 is not the same for every mine because of the wide variation in the extent of surface development in different areas. For 7 of the 13 mines identified in the record, 1% or less of the coal must remain in place; for 3 others, less than 3% must be left in place; for the other 3, the percentages are 4%, 7.8%, and 9.4%. See App. 284.

to furnish the denominator of the fraction." Michelman, *Property, Utility, and Fairness: Comments on the Ethical Foundations of "Just Compensation" Law*, 80 Harv. L. Rev. 1165, 1192 (1967). In *Penn Central* the Court explained:

> " 'Taking' jurisprudence does not divide a single parcel into discrete segments and attempt to determine whether rights in a particular segment have been entirely abrogated. In deciding whether a particular governmental action has effected a taking, this Court focuses rather both on the character of the action and on the nature of the interference with rights *in the parcel as a whole* — here the city tax block designated as the 'landmark site.' " 438 U.S., at 130–131.

Similarly, in *Andrus v. Allard*, 444 U.S. 51 (1979), we held that "where an owner possesses a full 'bundle' of property rights, the destruction of one 'strand' of the bundle is not a taking because the aggregate must be viewed in its entirety." *Id.*, at 65–66. Although these verbal formulizations do not solve all of the definitional issues that may arise in defining the relevant mass of property, they do provide sufficient guidance to compel us to reject petitioners' arguments.

The Coal in Place.

The parties have stipulated that enforcement of the DER's 50% rule will require petitioners to leave approximately 27 million tons of coal in place. Because they own that coal but cannot mine it, they contend that Pennsylvania has appropriated it for the public purposes described in the Subsidence Act.

This argument fails for the reason explained in *Penn Central* and *Andrus*. The 27 million tons of coal do not constitute a separate segment of property for takings law purposes. Many zoning ordinances place limits on the property owner's right to make profitable use of some segments of his property. A requirement that a building occupy no more than a specified percentage of the lot on which it is located could be characterized as a taking of the vacant area as readily as the requirement that coal pillars be left in place. Similarly, under petitioners' theory one could always argue that a setback ordinance requiring that no structure be built within a certain distance from the property line constitutes a taking because the footage represents a distinct segment of property for takings law purposes. Cf. *Gorieb v. Fox*, 274 U.S. 603 (1927) (upholding validity of setback ordinance) (SUTHERLAND, J.). There is no basis for treating the less than 2% of petitioners' coal as a separate parcel of property.

We do not consider Justice Holmes' statement that the Kohler Act made mining of "certain coal" commercially impracticable as requiring us to focus on the individual pillars of coal that must be left in place. That statement is best understood as referring to the Pennsylvania Coal Company's assertion that it could not undertake profitable anthracite coal mining in light of the Kohler Act. There were strong assertions in the record to support that conclusion. For example, the coal company claimed that one company was "unable to operate six large collieries in the city of Scranton, employing more than five thousand men." Motion to Advance for Argument in *Pennsylvania Coal Co. v. Mahon*, O.T. 1922, No. 549, p. 2. As Judge Adams explained:

"At first blush, this language seems to suggest that the Court would have found a taking no matter how little of the defendants' coal was rendered unmineable — that because 'certain' coal was no longer accessible, there had been a taking of that coal. However, when one reads the sentence in context, it becomes clear that the Court's concern was with whether the defendants' 'right to mine coal . . . [could] be exercised *with profit*.' 260 U.S. at 414 (emphasis added). . . . Thus, the Court's holding in *Mahon* must be assumed to have been based on its understanding that the Kohler Act rendered the business of mining coal unprofitable." 771 F.2d, at 716, n. 6.

When the coal that must remain beneath the ground is viewed in the context of any reasonable unit of petitioners' coal mining operations and financial-backed expectations, it is plain that petitioners have not come close to satisfying their burden of proving that they have been denied the economically viable use of that property. The record indicates that only about 75% of petitioners' underground coal can be profitably mined in any event, and there is no showing that petitioners' reasonable "investment-backed expectations" have been materially affected by the additional duty to retain the small percentage that must be used to support the structures protected by § 4.[27]

The Support Estate

Pennsylvania property law is apparently unique in regarding the support estate as a separate interest in land that can be conveyed apart from either the mineral estate or the surface estate. Petitioners therefore argue that even if comparable legislation in another State would not constitute a taking, the Subsidence Act has that consequence because it entirely destroys the value of their unique support estate. It is clear, however, that our takings jurisprudence forecloses reliance on such legalistic distinctions within a bundle of property rights. For example, in *Penn Central*, the Court rejected the argument that the "air rights" above the terminal constituted a separate segment of property for Takings Clause purposes. 438 U.S., at 130. Likewise, in *Andrus v. Allard*, we viewed the right to sell property as just one element of the owner's property interest. 444 U.S., at 65–66. In neither case did the result turn on whether state law allowed the separate sale of the segment of property.

The Court of Appeals, which is more familiar with Pennsylvania law than we are, concluded that as a practical matter the support estate is always owned by either the owner of the surface or the owner of the minerals. It stated:

"The support estate consists of the right to remove the strata of coal and earth that undergird the surface or to leave those layers intact to support the surface and prevent subsidence. These two uses cannot co-exist and, depending upon the purposes of the owner of the support estate, one use or

---

[27] We do not suggest that the State may physically appropriate relatively small amounts of private property for its own use without paying just compensation. The question here is whether there has been any taking at all when no coal has been physically appropriated, and the regulatory program places a burden on the use of only a small fraction of the property that is subjected to regulation. See generally n. 18, *supra*.

the other must be chosen. If the owner is a mine operator, the support estate is used to exploit the mineral estate. When the right of support is held by the surface owner, its use is to support that surface and prevent subsidence. Thus, although Pennsylvania law does recognize the support estate as a 'separate' property interest, *id.*, it cannot be used profitably by one who does not also possess either the mineral estate or the surface estate. See Montgomery, *The Development of the Right of Subjacent Support and the 'Third Estate in Pennsylvania,'* 25 Temple L.Q. 1, 21 (1951)." 771 F.2d, at 715–716.

Thus, in practical terms, the support estate has value only insofar as it protects or enhances the value of the estate with which it is associated. Its value is merely a part of the entire bundle of rights possessed by the owner of either the coal or the surface. Because petitioners retain the right to mine virtually all of the coal in their mineral estates, the burden the Act places on the support estate does not constitute a taking. Petitioners may continue to mine coal profitably even if they may not destroy or damage surface structures at will in the process.

But even if we were to accept petitioners' invitation to view the support estate as a distinct segment of property for "takings" purposes, they have not satisfied their heavy burden of sustaining a facial challenge to the Act. Petitioners have acquired or retained the support estate for a great deal of land, only part of which is protected under the Subsidence Act, which, of course, deals with subsidence in the immediate vicinity of certain structures, bodies of water, and cemeteries. The record is devoid of any evidence on what percentage of the purchased support estates, either in the aggregate or with respect to any individual estate, has been affected by the Act. Under these circumstances, petitioners' facial attack under the Takings Clause must surely fail. . . . The judgment of the Court of Appeals is affirmed.

REHNQUIST, C.J. dissenting.

More than 50 years ago, this Court determined the constitutionality of Pennsylvania's Kohler Act as it affected the property interests of coal mine operators. *Pennsylvania Coal Co. v. Mahon*, 260 U.S. 393 (1922). The Bituminous Mine Subsidence and Land Conservation Act approved today effects an interference with such interests in a strikingly similar manner. The Court finds at least two reasons why this case is different. First, we are told, "the character of the governmental action involved here leans heavily against finding a taking." Second, the Court concludes that the Subsidence Act neither "makes it impossible for petitioners to profitably engage in their business," nor involves "undue interference with [petitioners'] investment-backed expectations." Neither of these conclusions persuades me that this case is different, and I believe that the Subsidence Act works a taking of petitioners' property interests. I therefore dissent. . . .

NOTES

1. In *Keystone Bituminous*, Justice Stevens stated that a court should consider two factors when determining whether a land use regulation has caused a taking: whether the law (1) substantially advances legitimate government interests or (2) denies the owner an economically viable use of the land. As noted in the opinion, this test originated in *Agins v. City of Tiburon*, 447 U.S. 255 (1980). Courts repeatedly applied it until the Supreme Court's decision in *Lingle v. Chevron U.S.A. Inc.*, 544 U.S. 528 (2005). In *Lingle*, the Court unanimously held that the "substantially advances" test is irrelevant when determining whether a taking has occurred because it does not address "the *magnitude or character of the burden* a particular regulation imposes upon private property rights" and because an "owner of property subject to a regulation that *effectively* serves a legitimate state interest may be just as singled out and just as burdened as the owner of a property subject to an *ineffective* regulation" (emphasis in original). After *Keystone Bituminous* and *Lingle*, what factors are still relevant in a regulatory taking analysis?

2. *Keystone Bituminous* and *Pennsylvania Coal* involve remarkably similar facts. Did Justice Stevens successfully distinguish them?

3. In determining the value of the petitioners' property before and after enactment of the Subsidence Act, what property did the Court consider? Is the Court's approach consistent with *Pennsylvania Coal*, *Penn Central*, or neither?

4. Can a judicial decision constitute a taking? In *Stop the Beach Renourishment v. Florida Department of Environmental Protection*, 560 U.S. 702 (2010), four Justices said it could. In that case, a city and the county in which it is located applied for state permits to restore 6.9 miles of beach on the Florida coast that had eroded as a result of hurricanes and tropical storms. The city and county wanted to add 75' of dry sand seaward of the existing beach and planned to open this new strip of beach to the public. The owners of the affected beachfront properties challenged the project, arguing that they had property rights to beach accretions (increases to the beach caused by natural forces) and to directly adjoin the water. When the Florida Supreme Court held that the project would not deprive the plaintiffs of any property interest, they petitioned for certiorari to the U.S. Supreme Court, claiming that the Florida Supreme Court's decision took their property rights by holding that they do not exist.

The U.S. Supreme Court held that the Florida Supreme Court's decision was consistent with the state's common law of property and that the plaintiffs had not been deprived of any property interest. However, four Justices went on to address the novel issue of judicial takings and held that they could occur, because the takings clause is not expressly limited to the executive and legislative branches of government. Four Justices disagreed with this conclusion (Justice Stevens did not participate in the case). They objected that, because the Court had determined that a taking had not occurred, addressing this constitutional issue was unnecessary. They also reasoned that courts do not have the power to eliminate property rights; the policy decision to do so is an executive or legislative function. They also were concerned that states could become obligated to pay substantial judgments for judicial takings, if they can occur, particularly because courts do not have a budget for compensating landowners. These Justices also observed that, if judicial takings can occur, the federal courts would have to decide large numbers of state law cases involving an area of law that is familiar to state, but not federal, court judges.

The judicial takings concept raises a number of additional knotty issues, including:

- If courts modify the common law of property based on changed circumstances and increased knowledge, will compensation be due to affected landowners?

- What is the procedure for challenging a state court decision as a taking? To satisfy the ripeness requirement for taking challenges, would the landowner first have to exhaust state court challenges to the alleged state Supreme Court taking and then petition for certiorari to the U.S. Supreme Court?

- What is the appropriate remedy for a judicial taking? In *Stop the Beach Renourishment*, Justice Scalia said that the federal court should enjoin the state court ruling unless and until the state legislature provides compensation. But in that case, the beach restoration project had been completed before the U.S. Supreme Court granted certiorari, so an injunction would have been pointless. Besides, in *Agins v. City of Tiburon*, 447 U.S. 255 (1980), the U.S. Supreme Court held that compensation must be paid for every taking.

- If the beach restoration constituted a taking, didn't the taking occur as a result of the state law that authorized the restoration and as a result of the city's and county's restoration project? Would it be more appropriate to reverse the state Supreme Court decision that the state law and the restoration project were not an unconstitutional taking, rather than holding that the court took the plaintiffs' property?

A great deal has been written on this issue. See, e.g., John D. Echevarria, Stop the Beach Renourishment: *Why the Judiciary is Different*, 35 Vt. L. Rev. 475 (2010); Thomas W. Merrill, *Supreme Court Considers the Judicial Takings Doctrine in Beach Restoration Case*, 42 No. 1 ABA Trends 12 (Sept./Oct. 2010); David S. Wheelock, Note, *Every Grain of Sand: Would a Judicial Takings Doctrine Freeze the Common Law of Property?*, 61 Duke L.J. 433 (2011).

2.   State Constitution

PRATT v. STATE, DEPARTMENT OF NATURAL RESOURCES
309 N.W.2d 767 (Minn. 1981)

SIMONETT, J.

This is an appeal by the state from a decision of the district court finding a compensable taking of plaintiff's property by reason of a legislative change in the character of the water in three sloughs from private to public. The appeal is from an order denying the state's motion for a new trial. We remand for further proceedings.

In 1975 the state advised Sheldon Pratt he could no longer harvest the wild rice on his property by mechanical picker but had to do it by hand flailing. Since Mr. Pratt felt this would substantially reduce the profitability of his wild rice operation, he submitted a claim for damages to the Legislative Claims Commission.[1] The commission directed Mr. Pratt to seek a declaratory judgment action on whether the wild rice was being grown in public waters and deferred further action on the claim.

Mr. Pratt brought his action in the Crow Wing County District Court, asking that the bodies of water on which he harvested the rice be declared private and "not subject to any control by Minnesota Statutes 105.37 and 105.38." The state interposed an answer asking for judgment that the waters be declared public and subject to state regulation. The trial court, after hearing the evidence, found the waters to be public. But the court did more. It also found the waters had been private prior to 1973; that the 1973 amendments to Minn. Stat. §§ 105.37 and 105.38 "caused previously private waters to be reclassified as public waters, thus subjecting the rice growing thereon to regulation by the state and vesting ownership of the rice in the state"; and that, consequently, there was a compensable taking under eminent domain law "since he [the plaintiff] may no longer use a mechanical picker on the above-mentioned waters."

The main facts adduced at trial were these: For some 20 years plaintiff has owned three sloughs, called Island Lake, Rice Lake and Tamarack Lake. Island Lake averages 15 inches in depth, 5 feet at the deepest, and it covers about 60 acres. Mr. Pratt owns all the land around the lake. Rice Lake is shallower than Island and covers about 65 acres. Mr. Pratt owns all the surrounding land except for one small parcel. Tamarack Lake is the shallowest of the three lakes, about 3 feet at its deepest and covers 40 acres. Mr. Pratt owns virtually all the surrounding land.

All three lakes are unmeandered, natural waterbasins. They "freeze out" each winter. None has an outlet, except Island. The lakes are not suitable for boating, swimming or fishing, but there are ducks for hunting, muskrat and beaver, and the sloughs are good for raising wild rice. Mr. Pratt purchased the three properties for his private harvesting of wild rice. He has been able to exclude others from harvesting on the lakes. Mr. Pratt harvested all three lakes since the 1950's; he originally seeded Island Lake himself.

Since 1960, Mr. Pratt has used a mechanical picker to harvest his rice. It is more efficient, and hence more profitable, than harvesting manually. The beds are reseeded as necessary.

1. The first issue is whether the evidence supports the trial court's findings that the three lakes were private waters before 1973 and public waters since. We believe the evidence does support these findings. * * *

---

[1] The Legislative Claims Commission, more properly called the Joint Senate-House Claims Subcommittee, is an organ of the finance committees of both houses. Under its rules, it considers claims of individuals against the state for which there is no recourse to either administrative or judicial remedies, and recommends payment in appropriate cases to the full Senate Finance and House Appropriations committees.

This brings us, then, to the truly troublesome issue in this case. Was there a taking?

2. First of all, reclassifying and declaring waters to be "public" does not, by itself, constitute any taking in the constitutional sense. Ownership, in a proprietary sense, does not thereby pass to the state; rather, waters, once declared public, simply become subject to the protection and control of the state under its regulatory scheme. The state exercises this control by virtue of its police power. The state is said to hold title only in a sovereign capacity, as trustee for the public good, and not in a proprietary sense. . . .

Nor, properly speaking, does Mr. Pratt "own" these lakes. One does not, at common law, have title to water in its natural state, at least not until it has been artificially confined. Water in its natural state is not property capable of being owned. . . . Rather, one may have rights to the use and enjoyment of the water, rights exclusive of the general public, through ownership of lakeshore or lakebed.[6] These rights the law calls riparian. One does not own the water; one owns riparian rights to the use and enjoyment of the water. * * *

3. Here Mr. Pratt, by reason of his ownership of all or virtually all shoreline of the three lakes had riparian rights to grow and harvest wild rice in the waters of those lakes. The issue thus becomes whether these rights of Mr. Pratt have been taken. Since the wild rice, as of 1973, is now growing in public waters, Minn. Stat. § 97.42 (1980) comes into play:

> The ownership of wild animals, and of *all wild rice* and other aquatic vegetation *growing in the public waters* of the state, insofar as they are capable of ownership, *is in the state in its sovereign capacity for the benefit of all its people*, and no person shall acquire any property therein, or destroy the same, except as authorized by chapters 97 to 102 or sections 84.09 to 84.15 and Laws 1939, Chapter 231.

(Emphasis added.) Hence Mr. Pratt cannot harvest rice except as authorized by law and the Department of Natural Resources. We next turn to Minn. Stat. § 84.111 (1980), which provides, among other things, that:

> Subdivision 1. It shall be unlawful to use, in harvesting wild rice in any public waters in this state, any water craft other than a boat, skiff, or canoe propelled by hand. . . .

. . .

---

[6] Generally, riparian owners of land on nonnavigable lakes own the lakebed in severalty, the boundary lines being fixed by extending lines from each tract to the lake center. *State v. Adams*, 251 Minn. 521, 561 n. 18, 89 N.W.2d 661, 687 n.18 (1957), and cases cited thereunder. Owning virtually the entire lakeshore of the lakes in question, Mr. Pratt also owns the lakebeds. As Minn. Stat. § 105.37, subd. 14 (1980), makes clear, private ownership of a lakebed does not, by itself, necessarily determine the character of the water as public or private.

In addition, Mr. Pratt would have a right to exclude others from the public waters. This is not a riparian right. It is simply the right any landowner has to prevent trespass over his property.

Subd. 3. It is unlawful to use in such harvesting any machine or device for gathering the grain other than a flail not over 30 inches in length nor over one pound in weight, held and operated by hand.

Mr. Pratt claims he will sustain a financial loss if these provisions forbidding mechanical harvesting are applied to him. As yet there has been no showing of any damages, but the state admits in its answer "that the use of hand flails rather than a mechanical picker is less profitable for the harvester." Citing *Penn Central Transportation Co. v. New York City*, 438 U.S. 104 (1978), and *McShane v. City of Fairbault*, 292 N.W.2d 253 (Minn. 1980), the state argues the prohibition against harvesting rice mechanically is not a taking, but merely reasonable regulation, an exercise of its police powers, like zoning. And like a land-use regulation, the bar on mechanical harvesting is valid unless it deprives Mr. Pratt of all reasonable use of his land. While the state concedes the lakes here are of little economic use beyond ricing, it contends the regulation must be presumed reasonable in the absence of evidence as to the actual losses suffered by Mr. Pratt.

To evaluate the state's argument we must first determine whether the *McShane* decision applies. In *McShane* we discussed the distinction between governmental regulation which constitutes a taking and that which does not. We adopted the test that where the law or ordinance arbitrates between competing land uses, only noncompensable regulation is involved, but —

> We hold that where land use regulations, such as the airport zoning ordinance here, are designed to benefit a specific public or governmental enterprise, there must be compensation to landowners whose property has suffered a substantial and measurable decline in market value as a result of the regulations.

292 N.W.2d at 258–59.

In other words, where the regulation only serves an arbitration function, regulating between competing private uses for the general welfare, ordinarily no taking is involved; but where the regulation is for the benefit of a governmental enterprise, where a few individuals must bear the burden for a public use, then a taking occurs. Thus in *McShane*, where the city zoning ordinance prohibited commercial development of property near the municipal airport, we found these regulations were for the benefit of a governmental enterprise (the airport) and resulted in a substantial diminution of the value of the landowner's property; we therefore held there was a taking.

Can the bar on mechanical wild rice pickers be characterized as serving either an arbitration or governmental enterprise function? We stated in *McShane* that the line between "enterprise" and "arbitration" is not always easy to discern. That is true here.

The statutory scheme of regulation of wild rice plainly serves a public purpose. But does it also benefit a particular government enterprise? Or is it simply a plan to regulate wild rice harvesting, assuring that no one gains a competitive advantage by using a more efficient means of harvesting? The legislature has stated what it has in mind. The regulations are designed to preserve the traditional wild rice harvest for the Indians. . . . [7] As section 84.09 says, the admittedly stringent regulations were enacted "to discharge in part a moral obligation to these Indians of Minnesota." This seems to us an enterprise function.

On the other hand, the regulations also serve a conservation function by arbitrating among the competing wild rice harvesters. The regulations are "to protect against undue depletion of the crop so as to retard reseeding or restocking of such area or so as to endanger its effective use as a natural food for waterfowl." Minn. Stat. § 84.15, subd. 1 (1980). The state sets a harvesting season, much like for hunting or fishing. Minn. Stat. § 84.14, subd. 3 (1980). In other words, the state is also protecting a natural resource, wild rice, for the benefit of the public generally. This seems to us more like an arbitration function.

In other words, both the enterprise and the arbitration functions emerge from the wild rice regulatory scheme. We think it would read too much into the legislative intent to characterize the regulations as either predominantly enterprise or predominantly arbitration. Both purposes are prominent.

In *McShane* we said a taking may be found where a statute or regulation serves a governmental enterprise and a substantial diminution in market value results. That case, however, presented the situation in which the governmental enterprise function of a regulation was not just predominant but exclusive. Whether a regulation effects a taking is rarely so simple an issue. The presence of multiple purposes for a regulation, as in the instant case, is, we believe, more the rule than the exception, and to be at all useful, the principles enunciated in *McShane* for determining whether a taking has occurred must be applied with some flexibility. In *Penn Central*, the United States Supreme Court characterizes the inquiry as an essentially *ad hoc* examination of many significant factors, including the extent of economic damages inflicted, the nature of the economic interests affected, the object of the regulation, and the public policy it serves. Recently, in *San Diego Gas & Electric Co. v. San Diego*, 450 U.S. 621, 101 S. Ct. 1287, 67 L. Ed. 2d 551 (1981), the court indicated, "The determination of a 'taking' is 'a question of degree and therefore cannot be disposed of by general propositions.' " (Brennan, J., dissenting, at 1302) (Rehnquist, J., concurring, agreed with Justice Brennan but determined the case to be jurisdictionally deficient, i.e., not a final judgment or decree, at 1294). We think that here, where the governmental enterprise function is *prominent*, a

---

[7] Minn. Stat. § 84.09 (1980) provides:

From time immemorial the wild rice crop of the waters of the state of Minnesota has been a vital factor to the sustenance and the continued existence of the Indian race in Minnesota. The great present market demand for this wild rice, the recent development of careless, wasteful, and despoiling methods of harvesting, together with water conditions of the past few years, have resulted in an emergency, requiring immediate stringent methods of control and regulation of the wild rice crop. The traditional methods of the Indian in such harvesting are not destructive. On the other hand, the despoilation of the rice fields as now progressing under commercial harvesting methods will result in imminent danger of starvation and misery to large bands of these Indians. . . . It is therefore declared the purpose of sections 84.09 to 84.15, and Laws 1939, Chapter 231, to meet this emergency and to discharge in part a moral obligation to these Indians of Minnesota by strictly regulating the wild rice harvesting upon all public waters of the state and by granting to these Indians the exclusive right to harvest the wild rice crop upon all public waters within the original boundaries of the White Earth, Leech Lake, Nett Lake, Vermillion, Grand Portage, Fond du Lac, and Mille Lacs reservations.

taking may occur if the landowner's property is substantially diminished in value.

Pratt's case is unique. Usually the public has access to public waters where wild rice is growing. Here, only Pratt, owner of the riparian rights, has ready access to his lakes. He is the only harvester. Pratt acquired his property for the express purpose of having exclusive harvesting rights at a time when the property contained private waters. Pratt was then free to harvest mechanically. His situation was no different from that of a grower of "domesticated" wild rice, i.e., wild rice grown in private, artificially created paddies, where the grower is free to harvest mechanically. Only now, when the designation of the lakes as public waters has triggered application of the wild rice regulation, does Pratt find his intended use of his property circumscribed and its economic value impaired. This impairment, if substantial, would disproportionately burden an individual property owner for the benefit of the public in the furtherance, at least in part, of a governmental enterprise.

We therefore hold that the wild rice regulation here at issue, as it has both prominent arbitration and governmental enterprise functions and may unequally and disproportionately affect Pratt's property, may constitute a taking. A taking occurs if there is a substantial diminution in the market value of the property as a result of the regulation. As stated in *McShane*, more than inconvenience or some limitation in use is required. *Id.* at 259.

Unfortunately, the parties did not present evidence on diminution in market value. While the state admitted in its answer that there is some loss if hand flailing is required, we do not know if it is substantial. It is to be kept in mind that, while the property rights impaired by the regulation are the riparian rights to harvest the wild rice, the diminution in market value by reason of this impairment is measured by diminution, if any, in the market value of the tracts of land.

We remand to the district court for the taking of further evidence and a determination if there has been a substantial diminution in market value of the Pratt property by reason of the prohibition of the use of mechanical harvesters. If this standard is not met, the matter ends (except as Pratt may return to the Claims Commission). * * *

Remanded for proceedings in accordance with this opinion.

NOTES

1. Mr. Pratt's claim of a regulatory taking was based on a state constitution. Could he successfully have asserted a taking claim under the U.S. Constitution?

2. In *Arcadia Development Corp. v. City of Bloomington*, 552 N.W.2d 281 (Minn. Ct. App. 1996), the Minnesota Court of Appeals had to apply the distinction articulated in *Pratt* between a land use regulation that arbitrates between competing land uses and a regulation that benefits a government enterprise. Pursuant to state enabling legislation, the Bloomington City Council enacted an ordinance that required a mobile home park owner that closed the park to pay its tenants' relocation costs or, if a mobile home could not be moved, to purchase the home. The ordinance capped the owner's liability for these costs to twenty percent of the sale price for the park. The state and local legislation were designed to help ensure that adequate housing would be available to lower income residents and to adjust the property rights between the park owner and residents because mobile homes often are not actually "mobile." How should the case have been decided?

3. Many state courts have not adopted the arbitration/enterprise distinction employed by the court in *Pratt*. To evaluate takings claims based on a state constitution, some state courts simply apply the same tests used for a taking challenge based on the federal Constitution. Other state courts have distinguished between laws that are designed to prevent harm and those that are designed to confer a public benefit. One of the most (in)famous of these cases is *Just v. Marinette County*, 201 N.W.2d 761 (Wis. 1972). In that case, the plaintiffs acquired a parcel of land on a lake shore for the purpose of subdividing it and selling the subdivided lots. Several years after acquiring the property, the county designated it as wetlands pursuant to county shoreland regulations. The regulations prohibited wetlands owners from filling them without prior government approval. Without approval, the land could be used only for natural purposes, such as hiking, horseback riding, and fishing. The plaintiffs challenged the regulations as an unconstitutional taking after being caught illegally filling the land so that a dwelling could be built on it.

The Wisconsin Supreme Court held that, although the shoreland regulations caused the plaintiffs' land to be "severely depreciated in value," the regulations did not cause a taking. Applying the harm prevention/benefit conferring distinction, the court determined that the regulations were designed to prevent harm:

> In the instant case we have a restriction on the use of a citizens' property, not to secure a benefit for the public, but to prevent a harm from the change in the natural character of the citizens' property. We start with the premise that lakes and rivers in their natural state are unpolluted and the pollution which now exists is man made. The state of Wisconsin under the trust doctrine has a duty to eradicate the present pollution and to prevent further pollution in its navigable waters. This is not, in a legal sense, a gain or a securing of a benefit by the maintaining of the natural status quo of the environment. . . . The ordinance does not create or improve the public condition but only preserves nature from the despoilage and harm resulting from the unrestricted activities of humans.

Id. at 767–68, 771. What argument can you make that the challenged ordinance actually benefits the public, rather than simply preventing harm? Based on your argument that the ordinance actually confers a benefit, what analytic difficulties do you see in the harm prevention/benefit conferring distinction?

3. Categorical Takings

The categorical takings cases are a marked contrast to *Keystone Bituminous, Penn Central,* and the other regulatory takings cases in which courts balance a variety of factors to determine whether a taking has occurred. In categorical takings cases, a law so significantly interferes with a right of ownership that it constitutes a taking regardless of the public purpose for the law or its effect on the land's value. The categorical takings cases have been limited to the most important ownership rights.

In a system of private property ownership, one of the most protected rights is the right to exclude. The leading U.S. Supreme Court taking case involving this right is *Loretto v. Teleprompter Manhattan CATV Corp.*, 458 U.S. 419 (1982). In that case, New York enacted a law that prohibited landlords from interfering with the installation of cable television facilities on their rental property. The legislation's stated purpose was the "rapid development of and maximum penetration by a means of communication which has important educational and community aspects." Before the plaintiff in *Loretto* acquired her apartment building, a cable company installed equipment on the building's exterior. The plaintiff did not notice the equipment for some time after she purchased the building, which is unsurprising because the equipment was mounted immediately above and on the roof of the building and occupied about 1-1/2 cubic feet.

The plaintiff admitted that other apartment building owners thought the cable installation enhanced their buildings' market values. She also stated that her tenants would be "upset" if the cable connection were removed. Nonetheless, the Court held that the law constituted an unconstitutional taking.

> The historical rule that a permanent physical occupation of another's property is a taking has more than tradition to commend it. Such an appropriation is perhaps the most serious form of invasion of an owner's property interests. To borrow a metaphor, . . . the government does not simply take a single "strand" from the "bundle" of property rights; it chops through the bundle, taking a slice of every strand."

Id. at 435. Therefore, the court held that the plaintiff was entitled to compensation.

NOTES

1. In *Loretto*, the Supreme Court held that a taking occurred though the cable equipment was unobtrusive and probably enhanced the building's value. In *Penn Central*, the Supreme Court held that a taking had not occurred though the plaintiffs were prevented from constructing a building that would have generated at least $3 million per year in rent. Has the Supreme Court lost the forest for the trees?

2. Landlords are legally required to equip apartment buildings with fire extinguishers, mailboxes, and other items for the tenants' benefit. After *Loretto*, are landlords entitled to compensation for complying with these laws?

3. On remand, how much compensation should the court award Ms. Loretto?

4. In 1978, California enacted the Mobilehome Residency Law, which significantly curtailed mobile home park owners' ability to terminate tenancies. The law also prohibited park owners from disapproving purchasers of homes in the park unless the purchaser was financially unable to pay the rent. Ten years later, mobile home rent control ordinances were enacted that set mobile home park rents back to their 1986 levels and prohibited rent increases without the city council's approval. Several mobile home park owners challenged the two laws as a taking of their

property. They argued that the laws constituted a physical taking because they prevented owners from choosing their tenants and rental amounts. After *Loretto*, how should this case have been decided?

In *Yee v. Escondido*, 503 U.S. 519 (1992), the U.S. Supreme Court held that the Mobilehome Residency Law and a local rent control ordinance did not cause a taking. The Court stated that the laws did not constitute a physical invasion of the mobile home park owners' properties because the owners voluntarily rented their land to mobile home owners. The Court reasoned that the laws merely constituted land use regulations. As such, the Court indicated that the laws might be challenged as a regulatory taking. However, the park owners did not properly raise that issue on appeal, so the Court did not consider it.

In *Guggenheim v. City of Goleta*, 582 F.3d 996 (9th Cir. 2009), the Ninth Circuit Court of Appeals addressed that issue. In that case, the City of Goleta had enacted a mobile home park rent control ordinance to increase the availability of affordable housing. Affected mobile home park owners argued that the ordinance constituted a regulatory taking. In examining the ordinance's economic impact, the court found that it caused a direct and substantial wealth transfer from mobile home park owners to the tenants who lived in the parks when the ordinance became effective. The ordinance forced the park owners to rent space at 80% below the fair market rental. Correspondingly, the ordinance increased the value of the existing tenants' mobile homes by 90% because anyone who purchased their homes also would enjoy the benefit of the same below-market rent. The court also found that the ordinance impermissibly singled out mobile home park owners to bear a burden of providing affordable housing that taxpayers as a whole should share. For these reasons, the court held that the ordinance caused a regulatory taking. On rehearing en banc, the Ninth Circuit vacated that opinion and held that a regulatory taking had not occurred. The court reasoned that, because the park owners purchased the park after the ordinance was in effect, they presumably paid an amount that reflected the law's existence and, therefore, could not have had an investment-backed expectation that they could collect "illegal amounts of rent." 638 F.3d 1111, 1120 (9th Cir. 2010). Is this holding consistent with the U.S. Supreme Court precedent?

5. Is the government liable for a categorical taking, as in *Lucas*, if it *temporarily* physically occupies land? The U.S. Supreme Court addressed this issue in *Arkansas Game and Fish Comm'n v. U.S.*, 133 S. Ct. 511 (2012). In that case, the Army Corps of Engineers constructed a dam upstream from a wildlife management area. The Corps periodically released water from the dam, which temporarily flooded the management area and destroyed a substantial amount of timber growing there. The U.S. Supreme Court held that the flooding could constitute a taking but that the case should be analyzed under the multi-factor balancing approach, rather than as a categorical taking. It stated that the *Loretto* holding is limited to a *permanent* physical invasion. To determine whether the flooding constituted a taking, the Court stated that it was necessary to weigh how long the land is flooded, the degree to which the flooding was an intended or foreseeable result of the Corps' water releases, the land's character, and the owner's reasonable investment-backed expectations.

In the same year that the Supreme Court decided *Yee v. Escondido*, it decided *Lucas v. South Carolina Coastal Council*. *Lucas* attracted a great deal of attention because the dissenters in the last major taking case, *Keystone Bituminous*, were now in the Court's majority. The case also was important because it starkly presented a new type of categorical taking issue — whether a landowner is entitled to compensation if a law destroys the land's value, regardless of the police power purpose for the regulation. Numerous amicus curiae briefs were filed on both sides of the issue, and a long line of spectators crowded the Supreme Court in hopes of attending the oral arguments.

The plaintiff in *Lucas* had brought an inverse condemnation action in state court because South Carolina's newly enacted Beachfront Management Act prohibited him from building any permanent structure on his beachfront property, except a small deck or walkway. The plaintiff conceded both that the Act was properly and validly designed to preserve beaches and dunes and that preservation was a "laudable goal." Nevertheless, the trial court held that his land had been taken because the Act destroyed its value. The trial court awarded compensation in the amount of $1,232,387.50.

One month after the trial court's decision, Hurricane Hugo hit the South Carolina coast and caused twenty-nine deaths and $6 billion in property damage. Much of the damage was the result of beachfront development. On appeal, the South Carolina Supreme Court overturned the trial court's decision. The Court held that, because the Beachfront Management Act was enacted to prevent a serious public harm, it did not cause a regulatory taking. Because the Court rested its decision on the nuisance exception, it did not review the trial court's finding that the Act had destroyed the value of Lucas' property though some contrary evidence existed.

As you read the U.S. Supreme Court's opinion in *Lucas*, note the tone of the majority and dissenting opinions and the ways in which the majority opinion addresses long-standing regulatory taking issues.

LUCAS v. SOUTH CAROLINA COASTAL COUNCIL
505 U.S. 1003 (1992)

JUSTICE SCALIA delivered the opinion of the Court.

In 1986, petitioner David H. Lucas paid $975,000 for two residential lots on the Isle of Palms in Charleston County, South Carolina, on which he intended to build single-family homes. In 1988, however, the South Carolina Legislature enacted the Beachfront Management Act, S.C. Code Ann. § 48-39-250 *et seq.* (Supp. 1990), which had the direct effect of barring petitioner from erecting any permanent habitable structures on his two parcels. A state trial court found that this prohibition rendered Lucas's parcels "valueless." This case requires us to decide whether the Act's dramatic effect on the economic value of Lucas's lots accomplished a taking of private property under the Fifth and Fourteenth Amendments requiring the payment of "just compensation." U.S. Const., Amdt. 5.

I.

A.

South Carolina's expressed interest in intensively managing development activities in the so-called "coastal zone" dates from 1977 when, in the aftermath of Congress's passage of the federal Coastal Zone Management Act of 1972, 86 Stat. 1280, as amended, 16 U.S.C. § 1451 *et seq.*, the legislature enacted a Coastal Zone Management Act of its own. See S.C. Code Ann. § 48-39-10 *et seq.* (1987). In its original form, the South Carolina Act required owners of coastal zone land that qualified as a "critical area" (defined in the legislation to include beaches and immediately adjacent sand dunes, § 48-39-10(J)) to obtain a permit from the newly created South Carolina Coastal Council (Council) (respondent here) prior to committing the land to a "use other than the use the critical area was devoted to on [September 28, 1977]." § 48-39-130(A).

In the late 1970's, Lucas and others began extensive residential development of the Isle of Palms, a barrier island situated eastward of the city of Charleston. Toward the close of the development cycle for one residential subdivision known as "Beachwood East," Lucas in 1986 purchased the two lots at issue in this litigation for his own account. No portion of the lots, which were located approximately 300 feet from the beach, qualified as a "critical area" under the 1977 Act; accordingly, at the time Lucas acquired these parcels, he was not legally obliged to obtain a permit from the Council in advance of any development activity. His intention with respect to the lots was to do what the owners of the immediately adjacent parcels had already done: erect single-family residences. He commissioned architectural drawings for this purpose.

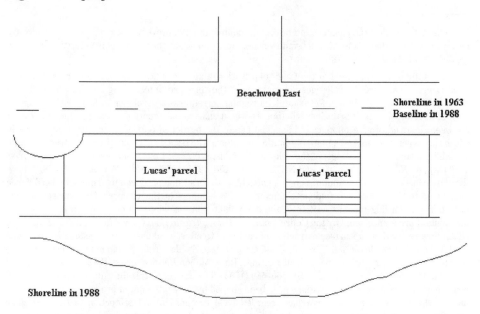

The Beachfront Management Act brought Lucas's plans to an abrupt end. Under that 1988 legislation, the Council was directed to establish a "baseline" connecting the landward-most "point[s] of erosion . . . during the past forty years" in the region of the Isle of Palms that includes Lucas's lots. S.C. Code Ann. § 48-39-280(A)(2) (Supp. 1988). In action not challenged here, the Council fixed this baseline landward of Lucas's parcels. That was significant, for under the Act construction of occupiable improvements[2] was flatly prohibited seaward of a line drawn 20 feet landward of, and parallel to, the baseline. § 48-39-290(A). The Act provided no exceptions. * * *

As we have said on numerous occasions, the Fifth Amendment is violated when land-use regulation "does not substantially advance legitimate state interests *or denies an owner economically viable use of his land." Agins, supra*, 447 U.S., at 260 (citations omitted) (emphasis added).[7]

We have never set forth the justification for this rule. Perhaps it is simply, as JUSTICE BRENNAN suggested, that total deprivation of beneficial use is, from the landowner's point of view, the equivalent of a physical appropriation. See *San Diego Gas & Electric Co. v. San Diego*, 450 U.S., at 652 (dissenting opinion). "[F]or what is the land but the profits thereof[?]" 1 E. Coke, Institutes, ch. 1, § 1 (1st Am. ed. 1812). Surely, at least, in the extraordinary circumstance when no productive or economically beneficial use of land is permitted, it is less realistic to indulge our usual assumption that the legislature is simply "adjusting the benefits and burdens of economic life," *Penn Central Transportation Co.*, 438 U.S., at 124, in a manner that secures an "average reciprocity of advantage" to everyone concerned, *Pennsylvania Coal Co. v. Mahon*, 260 U.S., at 415. And the *functional* basis for permitting the government, by regulation, to affect property values without compensation — that "Government hardly could go on if to some extent values

---

[2] The Act did allow the construction of certain nonhabitable improvements, e.g., "wooden walkways no larger in width than six feet," and "small wooden decks no larger than one hundred forty-four square feet." §§ 48-39-290(A)(1) and (2).

[7] Regrettably, the rhetorical force of our "deprivation of all economically feasible use" rule is greater than its precision, since the rule does not make clear the "property interest" against which the loss of value is to be measured. When, for example, a regulation requires a developer to leave 90% of a rural tract in its natural state, it is unclear whether we would analyze the situation as one in which the owner has been deprived of all economically beneficial use of the burdened portion of the tract, or as one in which the owner has suffered a mere diminution in value of the tract as a whole. (For an extreme — and, we think, unsupportable — view of the relevant calculus, see *Penn Central Transportation Co. v. New York City*, 42 N.Y.2d 324, 333–334, 366 N.E.2d 1271, 1276–1277 (1977), *aff'd*, 438 U.S. 104 (1978), where the state court examined the diminution in a particular parcel's value produced by a municipal ordinance in light of total value of the takings claimant's other holdings in the vicinity.) Unsurprisingly, this uncertainty regarding the composition of the denominator in our "deprivation" fraction has produced inconsistent pronouncements by the Court. Compare *Pennsylvania Coal Co. v. Mahon*, 260 U.S. 393, 414 (1922) (law restricting subsurface extraction of coal held to effect a taking), with *Keystone Bituminous Coal Ass'n v. DeBenedictis*, 480 U.S. 470, 497–502 (1987) (nearly identical law held not to effect a taking); see also *id.*, at 515–520 (REHNQUIST, C.J., dissenting); Rose, Mahon *Reconstructed: Why the Takings Issue is Still a Muddle*, 57 S. Cal. L. Rev. 561, 566–569 (1984). The answer to this difficult question may lie in how the owner's reasonable expectations have been shaped by the State's law of property — *i.e.*, whether and to what degree the State's law has accorded legal recognition and protection to the particular interest in land with respect to which the takings claimant alleges a diminution in (or elimination of) value. In any event, we avoid this difficulty in the present case, since the "interest in land" that Lucas has pleaded (a fee simple interest) is an estate with a rich tradition of protection at common law, and since the South Carolina Court of Common Pleas found that the Beachfront Management Act left each of Lucas's beachfront lots without economic value.

incident to property could not be diminished without paying for every such change in the general law," *id.*, at 413 — does not apply to the relatively rare situations where the government has deprived a landowner of all economically beneficial uses.

On the other side of the balance, affirmatively supporting a compensation requirement, is the fact that regulations that leave the owner of land without economically beneficial or productive options for its use — typically, as here, by requiring land to be left substantially in its natural state — carry with them a heightened risk that private property is being pressed into some form of public service under the guise of mitigating serious public harm. See, e.g., *Annicelli v. South Kingstown*, 463 A.2d 133, 140–141 (R.I. 1983) (prohibition on construction adjacent to beach justified on twin grounds of safety and "conservation of open space"); *Morris County Land Improvement Co. v. Parsippany-Troy Hills Township*, 40 N.J. 539, 552–553, 193 A.2d 232, 240 (1963) (prohibition on filling marshlands imposed in order to preserve region as water detention basin and create wildlife refuge). As JUSTICE BRENNAN explained: "From the government's point of view, the benefits flowing to the public from preservation of open space through regulation may be equally great as from creating a wildlife refuge through formal condemnation or increasing electricity production through a dam project that floods private property." *San Diego Gas & Elec. Co., supra*, 450 U.S., at 652 (dissenting opinion). * * *

We think, in short, that there are good reasons for our frequently expressed belief that when the owner of real property has been called upon to sacrifice *all* economically beneficial uses in the name of the common good, that is, to leave his property economically idle, he has suffered a taking.[8]

B.

The trial court found Lucas's two beachfront lots to have been rendered valueless by respondent's enforcement of the coastal-zone construction ban. Under Lucas's theory of the case, which rested upon our "no economically viable use" statements, that finding entitled him to compensation. Lucas believed it unnecessary to take issue with either the purposes behind the Beachfront Management Act, or the means chosen by the South Carolina Legislature to effectuate those purposes. The South Carolina Supreme Court, however, thought otherwise. In its view, the Beachfront Management Act was no ordinary enactment, but involved an exercise

---

[8] JUSTICE STEVENS criticizes the "deprivation of all economically beneficial use" rule as "wholly arbitrary," in that "[the] landowner whose property is diminished in value 95% recovers nothing," while the landowner who suffers a complete elimination of value "recovers the land's full value." *Post*. This analysis errs in its assumption that the landowner whose deprivation is one step short of complete is not entitled to compensation. Such an owner might not be able to claim the benefit of our categorical formulation, but, as we have acknowledged time and again, "[t]he economic impact of the regulation on the claimant and . . . the extent to which the regulation has interfered with distinct investment-backed expectations" are keenly relevant to takings analysis generally. *Penn Central Transportation Co. v. New York City*, 438 U.S. 104, 124 (1978). It is true that in at least *some* cases the landowner with 95% loss will get nothing, while the landowner with total loss will recover in full. But that occasional result is no more strange than the gross disparity between the landowner whose premises are taken for a highway (who recovers in full) and the landowner whose property is reduced to 5% of its former value by the highway (who recovers nothing). Takings law is full of these "all-or-nothing" situations.

of South Carolina's "police powers" to mitigate the harm to the public interest that petitioner's use of his land might occasion. By neglecting to dispute the findings enumerated in the Act[10] or otherwise to challenge the legislature's purposes, petitioner "concede[d] that the beach/dune area of South Carolina's shores is an extremely valuable public resource; that the erection of new construction, *inter alia*, contributes to the erosion and destruction of this public resource; and that discouraging new construction in close proximity to the beach/dune area is necessary to prevent a great public harm." In the court's view, these concessions brought petitioner's challenge within a long line of this Court's cases sustaining against Due Process and Takings Clause challenges the State's use of its "police powers" to enjoin a property owner from activities akin to public nuisances. See *Mugler v. Kansas*, 123 U.S. 623 (1887) (law prohibiting manufacture of alcoholic beverages); *Hadacheck v. Sebastian*, 239 U.S. 394 (1915) (law barring operation of

---

[10] The legislature's express findings include the following:

"The General Assembly finds that:

"(1) The beach/dune system along the coast of South Carolina is extremely important to the people of this State and serves the following functions:

"(a) protects life and property by serving as a storm barrier which dissipates wave energy and contributes to shoreline stability in an economical and effective manner;

"(b) provides the basis for a tourism industry that generates approximately two-thirds of South Carolina's annual tourism industry revenue which constitutes a significant portion of the state's economy. The tourists who come to the South Carolina coast to enjoy the ocean and dry sand beach contribute significantly to state and local tax revenues;

"(c) provides habitat for numerous species of plants and animals, several of which are threatened or endangered. Waters adjacent to the beach/dune system also provide habitat for many other marine species;

"(d) provides a natural health environment for the citizens of South Carolina to spend leisure time which serves their physical and mental well-being.

"(2) Beach/dune system vegetation is unique and extremely important to the vitality and preservation of the system.

"(3) Many miles of South Carolina's beaches have been identified as critically eroding.

"(4) . . . [D]evelopment unwisely has been sited too close to the [beach/dune] system. This type of development has jeopardized the stability of the beach/dune system, accelerated erosion, and endangered adjacent property. It is in both the public and private interests to protect the system from this unwise development.

"(5) The use of armoring in the form of hard erosion control devices such as seawalls, bulkheads, and rip-rap to protect erosion-threatened structures adjacent to the beach has not proven effective. These armoring devices have given a false sense of security to beachfront property owners. In reality, these hard structures, in many instances, have increased the vulnerability of beachfront property to damage from wind and waves while contributing to the deterioration and loss of the dry sand beach which is so important to the tourism industry.

"(6) Erosion is a natural process which becomes a significant problem for man only when structures are erected in close proximity to the beach/dune system. It is in both the public and private interests to afford the beach/dune system space to accrete and erode in its natural cycle. This space can be provided only by discouraging new construction in close proximity to the beach/dune system and encouraging those who have erected structures too close to the system to retreat from it.

. . . .

"(8) It is in the state's best interest to protect and to promote increased public access to South Carolina's beaches for out-of-state tourists and South Carolina residents alike." S.C. Code Ann. § 48-39-250 (Supp. 1991).

brick mill in residential area); *Miller v. Schoene*, 276 U.S. 272 (1928) (order to destroy diseased cedar trees to prevent infection of nearby orchards); *Goldblatt v. Hempstead*, 369 U.S. 590 (1962) (law effectively preventing continued operation of quarry in residential area).

It is correct that many of our prior opinions have suggested that "harmful or noxious uses" of property may be proscribed by government regulation without the requirement of compensation. For a number of reasons, however, we think the South Carolina Supreme Court was too quick to conclude that that principle decides the present case. The "harmful or noxious uses" principle was the Court's early attempt to describe in theoretical terms why government may, consistent with the Takings Clause, affect property values by regulation without incurring an obligation to compensate — a reality we nowadays acknowledge explicitly with respect to the full scope of the State's police power. See, e.g., *Penn Central Transportation Co.*, 438 U.S., at 125 (where State "reasonably conclude[s] that 'the health, safety, morals, or general welfare' would be promoted by prohibiting particular contemplated uses of land," compensation need not accompany prohibition); see also *Nollan v. California Coastal Comm'n*, 483 U.S., at 834–835 ("Our cases have not elaborated on the standards for determining what constitutes a 'legitimate state interest[,]' [but] [t]hey have made clear . . . that a broad range of governmental purposes and regulations satisfy these requirements"). We made this very point in *Penn Central Transportation Co.*, where, in the course of sustaining New York City's landmarks preservation program against a takings challenge, we rejected the petitioner's suggestion that *Mugler* and the cases following it were premised on, and thus limited by, some objective conception of "noxiousness":

> "[T]he uses in issue in *Hadacheck, Miller*, and *Goldblatt* were perfectly lawful in themselves. They involved no 'blameworthiness, . . . moral wrongdoing or conscious act of dangerous risk-taking which induce[d society] to shift the cost to a pa[rt]icular individual.' Sax, *Takings and the Police Power*, 74 Yale L.J. 36, 50 (1964). These cases are better understood as resting not on any supposed 'noxious' quality of the prohibited uses but rather on the ground that the restrictions were reasonably related to the implementation of a policy — not unlike historic preservation — expected to produce a widespread public benefit and applicable to all similarly situated property." 438 U.S., at 133–134, n. 30.

"Harmful or noxious use" analysis was, in other words, simply the progenitor of our more contemporary statements that "land-use regulation does not effect a taking if it 'substantially advance[s] legitimate state interests'. . ." *Nollan, supra*, 483 U.S., at 834 (quoting *Agins v. Tiburon*, 447 U.S., at 260). . . .

The transition from our early focus on control of "noxious" uses to our contemporary understanding of the broad realm within which government may regulate without compensation was an easy one, since the distinction between "harm-preventing" and "benefit-conferring" regulation is often in the eye of the beholder. It is quite possible, for example, to describe in *either* fashion the ecological, economic, and esthetic concerns that inspired the South Carolina Legislature in the present case. One could say that imposing a servitude on Lucas's land is necessary in order to prevent his use of it from "harming" South Carolina's ecological resources; or, instead, in order to achieve the "benefits" of an ecological preserve.[11] Compare, e.g., *Claridge v. New Hampshire Wetlands Board*, 125 N.H. 745, 752, 485 A.2d 287, 292 (1984) (owner may, without compensation, be barred from filling wetlands because landfilling would deprive adjacent coastal habitats and marine fisheries of ecological support), with, e.g., *Bartlett v. Zoning Comm'n of Old Lyme*, 161 Conn. 24, 30, 282 A.2d 907, 910 (1971) (owner barred from filling tidal marshland must be compensated, despite municipality's "laudable" goal of "preserv[ing] marshlands from encroachment or destruction"). Whether one or the other of the competing characterizations will come to one's lips in a particular case depends primarily upon one's evaluation of the worth of competing uses of real estate. See Restatement (Second) of Torts § 822, Comment *g*, p. 112 (1979) ("Practically all human activities unless carried on in a wilderness interfere to some extent with others or involve some risk of interference"). A given restraint will be seen as mitigating "harm" to the adjacent parcels or securing a "benefit" for them, depending upon the observer's evaluation of the relative importance of the use that the restraint favors. See Sax, *Takings and the Police Power*, 74 Yale L.J. 36, 49 (1964) ("[T]he problem [in this area] is not one of noxiousness or harm-creating activity at all; rather it is a problem of inconsistency between perfectly innocent and independently desirable uses"). Whether Lucas's construction of single-family residences on his parcels should be described as bringing "harm" to South Carolina's adjacent ecological resources thus depends principally upon whether the describer believes that the State's use interest in nurturing those resources is so important that *any* competing adjacent use must yield.[12]

When it is understood that "prevention of harmful use" was merely our early formulation of the police power justification necessary to sustain (without compensation) *any* regulatory diminution in value; and that the distinction between

---

[11] In the present case, in fact, some of the "[South Carolina] legislature's 'findings' " to which the South Carolina Supreme Court purported to defer in characterizing the purpose of the Act as "harm-preventing," 304 S.C. 376, 385, 404 S.E. 2d 895, 900 (1991), seem to us phrased in "benefit-conferring" language instead. For example, they describe the importance of a construction ban in enhancing "South Carolina's annual tourism industry revenue," S.C. Code Ann. § 48-39-250(1)(b) (Supp. 1991), in "provid[ing] habitat for numerous species of plants and animals, several of which are threatened or endangered," § 48-39-250(1)(c), and in "provid[ing] a natural healthy environment for the citizens of South Carolina to spend leisure time which serves their physical and mental well-being," § 48-39-250(1)(d). It would be pointless to make the outcome of this case hang upon this terminology since the same interests could readily be described in "harm-preventing" fashion.

JUSTICE BLACKMUN, however, apparently insists that we must make the outcome hinge (exclusively) upon the South Carolina Legislature's other, "harm-preventing" characterizations, focusing on the declaration that "prohibitions on building in front of the setback line are necessary to protect people and property from storms, high tides, and beach erosion." He says "[n]othing in the record undermines [this] assessment," apparently seeing no significance in the fact that the statute permits owners of *existing* structures to remain (and even to rebuild if their structures are not "destroyed beyond repair,") and in the fact that the 1990 amendment authorizes the Council to issue permits for new construction in violation of the uniform prohibition.

[12] In JUSTICE BLACKMUN'S view, even with respect to regulations that deprive an owner of all developmental or economically beneficial land uses, the test for required compensation is whether the legislature has recited a harm-preventing justification for its action. See *post*. Since such a justification can be formulated in practically every case, this amounts to a test of whether the legislature has a stupid staff. We think the Takings Clause requires courts to do more than insist upon artful harm-preventing characterizations.

regulation that "prevents harmful use" and that which "confers benefits" is difficult, if not impossible, to discern on an objective, value-free basis; it becomes self-evident that noxious-use logic cannot serve as a touchstone to distinguish regulatory "takings" — which require compensation — from regulatory deprivations that do not require compensation. *A fortiori* the legislature's recitation of a noxious-use justification cannot be the basis for departing from our categorical rule that total regulatory takings must be compensated. If it were, departure would virtually always be allowed. The South Carolina Supreme Court's approach would essentially nullify *Mahon*'s affirmation of limits to the noncompensable exercise of the police power. Our cases provide no support for this: None of them that employed the logic of "harmful use" prevention to sustain a regulation involved an allegation that the regulation wholly eliminated the value of the claimant's land. See *Keystone Bituminous Coal Ass'n*, 480 U.S., at 513–514 (Rehnquist, C.J., dissenting).[13]

Where the State seeks to sustain regulation that deprives land of all economically beneficial use, we think it may resist compensation only if the logically antecedent inquiry into the nature of the owner's estate shows that the proscribed use interests were not part of his title to begin with. This accords, we think, with our "takings" jurisprudence, which has traditionally been guided by the understandings of our citizens regarding the content of, and the State's power over, the "bundle of rights" that they acquire when they obtain title to property. It seems to us that the property owner necessarily expects the uses of his property to be restricted, from time to time, by various measures newly enacted by the State in legitimate exercise of its police powers; "[a]s long recognized, some values are enjoyed under an implied limitation and must yield to the police power." *Pennsylvania Coal Co. v. Mahon*, 260 U.S., at 413. And in the case of personal property, by reason of the State's traditionally high degree of control over commercial dealings, he ought to be aware of the possibility that new regulation might even render his property economically worthless (at least if the property's only economically productive use is sale or manufacture for sale). See *Andrus v. Allard*, 444 U.S. 51, 66–67 (1979) (prohibition on sale of eagle feathers). In the case of land, however, we think the notion pressed by the Council that title is somehow held subject to the "implied limitation" that the State may subsequently eliminate all economically valuable use is inconsistent with the historical compact recorded in the Takings Clause that has become part of our constitutional culture.

Where "permanent physical occupation" of land is concerned, we have refused to allow the government to decree it anew (without compensation), no matter how weighty the asserted "public interests" involved, *Loretto v. Teleprompter Manhattan CATV Corp.*, 458 U.S., at 426 — though we assuredly would permit the government to assert a permanent easement that was a pre-existing limitation upon the landowner's title. Compare *Scranton v. Wheeler*, 179 U.S. 141 (1900) (interests

---

[13] E.g., *Mugler v. Kansas*, 123 U.S. 623 (1887) (prohibition upon use of a building as a brewery; other uses permitted); *Plymouth Coal Co. v. Pennsylvania*, 232 U.S. 531 (1914) (requirement that "pillar" of coal be left in ground to safeguard mine workers; mineral rights could otherwise be exploited); *Reinman v. Little Rock*, 237 U.S. 171 (1915) (declaration that livery stable constituted a public nuisance; other uses of the property permitted); *Hadacheck v. Sebastian*, 239 U.S. 394 (1915) (prohibition of brick manufacturing in residential area; other uses permitted); *Goldblatt v. Hempstead*, 369 U.S. 590 (1962) (prohibition on excavation; other uses permitted).

of "riparian owner in the submerged lands . . . bordering on a public navigable water" held subject to Government's navigational servitude), with *Kaiser Aetna v. United States*, 444 U.S., at 178–180 (imposition of navigational servitude on marina created and rendered navigable at private expense held to constitute a taking). We believe similar treatment must be accorded confiscatory regulations, *i.e.*, regulations that prohibit all economically beneficial use of land: Any limitation so severe cannot be newly legislated or decreed (without compensation), but must inhere in the title itself, in the restrictions that background principles of the State's law of property and nuisance already place upon land ownership. A law or decree with such an effect must, in other words, do no more than duplicate the result that could have been achieved in the courts — by adjacent landowners (or other uniquely affected persons) under the State's law of private nuisance, or by the State under its complementary power to abate nuisances that affect the public generally, or otherwise.

On this analysis, the owner of a lake-bed, for example, would not be entitled to compensation when he is denied the requisite permit to engage in a landfilling operation that would have the effect of flooding others' land. Nor the corporate owner of a nuclear generating plant, when it is directed to remove all improvements from its land upon discovery that the plant sits astride an earthquake fault. Such regulatory action may well have the effect of eliminating the land's only economically productive use, but it does not proscribe a productive use that was previously permissible under relevant property and nuisance principles. The use of these properties for what are now expressly prohibited purposes was *always* unlawful, and (subject to other constitutional limitations) it was open to the State at any point to make the implication of those background principles of nuisance and property law explicit. In light of our traditional resort to "existing rules or understandings that stem from an independent source such as state law" to define the range of interests that qualify for protection as "property" under the Fifth and Fourteenth Amendments . . . this recognition that the Takings Clause does not require compensation when an owner is barred from putting land to a use that is proscribed by those "existing rules or understandings" is surely unexceptional. When, however, a regulation that declares "off-limits" all economically productive or beneficial uses of land goes beyond what the relevant background principles would dictate, compensation must be paid to sustain it.

The "total taking" inquiry we require today will ordinarily entail (as the application of state nuisance law ordinarily entails) analysis of, among other things, the degree of harm to public lands and resources, or adjacent private property, posed by the claimant's proposed activities, see, e.g., Restatement (Second) of Torts §§ 826, 827, the social value of the claimant's activities and their suitability to the locality in question, see, e.g., *id.*, §§ 828(a) and (b), 831, and the relative ease with which the alleged harm can be avoided through measures taken by the claimant and the government (or adjacent private landowners) alike, see, e.g., *id.*, §§ 827(e), 828(c), 830. The fact that a particular use has long been engaged in by similarly situated owners ordinarily imports a lack of any common-law prohibition (though changed circumstances or new knowledge may make what was previously permissible no longer so, see *id.*, § 827, Comment *g*). So also does the fact that other landowners, similarly situated, are permitted to continue the use denied to the claimant.

It seems unlikely that common-law principles would have prevented the erection of any habitable or productive improvements on petitioner's land; they rarely support prohibition of the "essential use" of land. The question, however, is one of state law to be dealt with on remand. We emphasize that to win its case South Carolina must do more than proffer the legislature's declaration that the uses Lucas desires are inconsistent with the public interest, or the conclusory assertion that they violate a common-law maxim such as *sic utere tuo ut alienum non laedas*. As we have said, a "State, by *ipse dixit*, may not transform private property into public property without compensation. . . ." *Webb's Fabulous Pharmacies, Inc. v. Beckwith*, 449 U.S. 155, 164 (1980). Instead, as it would be required to do if it sought to restrain Lucas in a common-law action for public nuisance, South Carolina must identify background principles of nuisance and property law that prohibit the uses he now intends in the circumstances in which the property is presently found. Only on this showing can the State fairly claim that, in proscribing all such beneficial uses, the Beachfront Management Act is taking nothing. . . . The judgment is reversed, and the case is remanded for proceedings not inconsistent with this opinion.

BLACKMUN, J., dissenting.

Today the Court launches a missile to kill a mouse.

The State of South Carolina prohibited petitioner Lucas from building a permanent structure on his property from 1988 to 1990. Relying on an unreviewed (and implausible) state trial court finding that this restriction left Lucas' property valueless, this Court granted review to determine whether compensation must be paid in cases where the State prohibits all economic use of real estate. According to the Court, such an occasion never has arisen in any of our prior cases, and the Court imagines that it will arise "relatively rarely" or only in "extraordinary circumstances." Almost certainly it did not happen in this case.

Nonetheless, the Court presses on to decide the issue, and as it does, it ignores its jurisdictional limits, remakes its traditional rules of review, and creates simultaneously a new categorical rule and an exception (neither of which is rooted in our prior case law, common law, or common sense). I protest not only the Court's decision, but each step taken to reach it. More fundamentally, I question the Court's wisdom in issuing sweeping new rules to decide such a narrow case. . . .

The South Carolina Supreme Court found that the Beachfront Management Act did not take petitioner's property without compensation. The decision rested on two premises that until today were unassailable — that the State has the power to prevent any use of property it finds to be harmful to its citizens, and that a state statute is entitled to a presumption of constitutionality. * * *

I [also] . . . question the Court's rationale in creating a category that obviates a "case-specific inquiry into the public interest advanced," if all economic value has been lost. If one fact about the Court's takings jurisprudence can be stated without contradiction, it is that "the particular circumstances of each case" determine whether a specific restriction will be rendered invalid by the government's failure to pay compensation. This is so because although we have articulated certain factors to be considered, including the economic impact on the property owner, the ultimate conclusion "necessarily requires a weighing of private and public interests." *Agins*, 447 U.S., at 261. When the government regulation prevents the owner from any economically valuable use of his property, the private interest is unquestionably substantial, but we have never before held that no public interest can outweigh it. Instead the Court's prior decisions "uniformly reject the proposition that diminution in property value, standing alone, can establish a 'taking.'" *Penn Central Transp. Co. v. New York City*, 438 U.S. 104, 131 (1978). . . .

The Court makes sweeping and, in my view, misguided and unsupported changes in our takings doctrine. While it limits these changes to the most narrow subset of government regulation — those that eliminate all economic value from land — these changes go far beyond what is necessary to secure petitioner Lucas' private benefit. One hopes they do not go beyond the narrow confines the Court assigns them to today. I dissent.

NOTES

1. The record in *Lucas* included evidence that: (1) Lucas' property had been under water from 1957 to 1963; (2) all or part of the property had been part of the beach or flooded twice each day by the tide during approximately half of the previous forty years; (3) the shoreline was 100–150 feet onto the property from 1963 to 1973; and (4) twelve emergency orders for sandbagging had been issued from 1981 to 1983 to protect property in the development that included the plaintiff's land. Despite these facts, the South Carolina Supreme Court held on remand that this case did not come within the nuisance exception articulated in the majority opinion and that the plaintiff was entitled to be compensated. Why didn't the plaintiff's proposed use constitute a noncompensable nuisance? What problems are created by the scope of the nuisance exception set forth in *Lucas*?

2. Are any property rights, in addition to those identified in *Loretto* and *Lucas*, so important that laws interfering with them should constitute a categorical taking? In *Hodel v. Irving*, 481 U.S. 704 (1987), the U.S. Supreme Court considered a taking challenge to a federal law that destroyed a property owner's right to transfer property at death by devise or descent. Although the Court described this right as a "valuable right" that "has been part of the Anglo-American legal system since feudal times," the Court did not treat the case as a categorical taking case. Rather, in determining whether a taking occurred, the Court applied the multi-factor balancing test. See also *Andrus v. Allard*, 444 U.S. 51 (1979) (Eagle Protection and Migratory Bird Treaty Acts' prohibitions on sale of parts of birds killed before the Acts' effective dates do not constitute a taking: "The regulations challenged here do not compel the surrender of the artifacts, and there is no physical invasion or restraint upon them. . . . In this case, it is crucial that appellees retain the right to possess and transport their property, and to donate or devise the protected birds." *Id.* at 65–66).

3. In *Penn Central Transportation Co. v. New York City*, 438 U.S. 104 (1978) (discussed in note 4 following *Pennsylvania Coal v. Mahon* in section I.B.1 of this chapter), the Supreme Court refused to consider a regulation's impact on the value of just the regulated airspace. Instead, the Court held that the regulatory taking analysis must consider "the parcel as a whole." Until *Lucas*, courts consistently applied this whole-parcel rule. See, e.g., *Concrete Pipe & Products of Cal., Inc. v. Construction Laborers Pension Trust for Southern Cal.*, 508 U.S. 602 (1993); *Keystone Bituminous Coal Association v. DeBenedictis*, 480 U.S. 470 (1987). In *Lucas*, however, the new majority on the Supreme Court opened the possibility of "conceptual severance" — examining only a portion of the property to determine whether a taking has occurred. In note 7 of the opinion, the Court states that if "a regulation requires a developer to leave 90% of a rural tract in its natural state, it is unclear whether we would analyze the situation as one in which the owner has been deprived of all economically beneficial use of the burdened portion of the tract, or as one in which the owner has suffered a mere diminution in value of the tract as a whole." Conceptual severance is particularly attractive to regulatory taking plaintiffs because, if the portion of the property that is rendered worthless by the regulation can be severed from the remainder of the parcel, *Lucas'* categorical taking rule applies.

In *Palazzolo v. Rhode Island*, 533 U.S. 606 (2001), the plaintiff tried just that. Mr. Palazzolo owned a twenty-acre undeveloped parcel of land. Eighteen acres were salt marsh. Pursuant to state law, Palazzolo could fill the salt marsh for development only if he could show that it would serve a "compelling public purpose." His application was denied because he did not satisfy that standard. Palazzolo then brought this regulatory taking action. He attempted to bring his case within the *Lucas* categorical taking analysis by arguing that the eighteen acres of salt marsh should be considered a separate parcel, rather than part of the twenty-acre parcel.

Because Palazzolo first made this argument in his brief to the U.S. Supreme Court, the Court properly declined to address it. However, rather than simply dismissing the claim, the Court used it as a platform for casting further doubt on the whole-parcel rule. The Court stated: "Some of our cases indicate that the extent of deprivation effected by a regulatory action is measured against the value of the parcel as a whole, but we have at times expressed discomfort with the logic of this rule, a sentiment echoed by some commentators."

While the conceptual severance asserted in *Palazzolo* involved severing the property, the plaintiffs in *Tahoe-Sierra Preservation Council, Inc. v. Tahoe Regional Planning Agency*, 535 U.S. 302 (2002), asserted a severance based on time. The plaintiffs were landowners in the Lake Tahoe Basin whose right to develop was substantially curtailed during a 32-month planning moratorium. The moratorium had been imposed in response to serious environmental degradation of Lake Tahoe caused by development in its basin. In an attempt to qualify as a *Lucas* categorical taking, the plaintiffs argued that their lands had been rendered totally valueless during the moratorium. In marked contrast to *Lucas* and *Palazzolo*, the Court strongly endorsed *Penn Central's* whole-parcel rule and rejected conceptual severance.

> Petitioners' "conceptual severance" argument is unavailing because it ignores *Penn Central's* admonition that in regulatory takings cases we must focus on "the parcel as a whole." * * * An interest in real property is

defined by the metes and bounds that describe its geographic dimensions and the term of years that describe the temporal aspect of the owner's interest. . . . Both dimensions must be considered if the interest is to be viewed in its entirety.

Stay tuned for further developments. This important battle undoubtedly is going to continue.

4. If you were a city attorney, what advice would you give the city council to help protect against successful takings actions based on the city's land use regulations?

4. Exactions and Impact Fees

When a developer applies for a permit to subdivide land or improve it, the government may condition the permit on the developer's contribution of land or money to build a school, park, road, or other public improvement. Alternatively, the government may require the developer to make these types of public improvements on its land. These land exactions and impact fees raise obvious takings issues, particularly when the property owner is required to deed land to the government or otherwise to allow public access to it.

This taking issue has assumed increased importance in recent years as local governments have become financially more dependent on exactions and impact fees to make needed public improvements. The following case is the U.S. Supreme Court's most important decision concerning this issue.

DOLAN v. CITY OF TIGARD
512 U.S. 374 (1994)

CHIEF JUSTICE REHNQUIST delivered the opinion of the Court.

Petitioner challenges the decision of the Oregon Supreme Court which held that the city of Tigard could condition the approval of her building permit on the dedication of a portion of her property for flood control and traffic improvements. We granted certiorari to resolve a question left open by our decision in *Nollan v. California Coastal Comm'n*, 483 U.S. 825 (1987), of what is the required degree of connection between the exactions imposed by the city and the projected impacts of the proposed development. * * *

I.

Petitioner Florence Dolan owns a plumbing and electric supply store located on Main Street in the Central Business District of the city. The store covers approximately 9,700 square feet on the eastern side of a 1.67-acre parcel, which includes a gravel parking lot. Fanno Creek flows through the southwestern corner of the lot and along its western boundary. The year-round flow of the creek renders the area within the creek's 100-year floodplain virtually unusable for commercial development. The city's comprehensive plan includes the Fanno Creek floodplain as part of the city's greenway system.

Petitioner applied to the city for a permit to redevelop the site. Her proposed plans called for nearly doubling the size of the store to 17,600 square feet and paving a 39-space parking lot. The existing store, located on the opposite side of the parcel, would be razed in sections as construction progressed on the new building. In the second phase of the project, petitioner proposed to build an additional structure on the northeast side of the site for complementary businesses and to provide more parking. The proposed expansion and intensified use are consistent with the city's zoning scheme in the Central Business District. . . .

The City Planning Commission (Commission) granted petitioner's permit application subject to conditions imposed by the city's Community Development Code (CDC) . . . . [T]he Commission required that petitioner dedicate the portion of her property lying within the 100-year floodplain for improvement of a storm drainage system along Fanno Creek and that she dedicate an additional 15-foot strip of land adjacent to the floodplain as a pedestrian/bicycle pathway. The dedication required by that condition encompasses approximately 7,000 square feet, or roughly 10% of the property. . . . The city would bear the cost of maintaining a landscaped buffer between the dedicated area and the new store.

Petitioner requested variances from the CDC standards. Variances are granted only where it can be shown that, owing to special circumstances related to a specific piece of the land, the literal interpretation of the applicable zoning provisions would cause "an undue or unnecessary hardship" unless the variance is granted. Rather than posing alternative mitigating measures to offset the expected impacts of her proposed development, as allowed under the CDC, petitioner simply argued that her proposed development would not conflict with the policies of the comprehensive plan. The Commission denied the request.

The Commission made a series of findings concerning the relationship between the dedicated conditions and the projected impacts of petitioner's project. First, the Commission noted that "[i]t is reasonable to assume that customers and employees of the future uses of this site could utilize a pedestrian/bicycle pathway adjacent to this development for their transportation and recreational needs." The Commission noted that the site plan has provided for bicycle parking in a rack in front of the proposed building and "[i]t is reasonable to expect that some of the users of the bicycle parking provided for by the site plan will use the pathway adjacent to Fanno Creek if it is constructed." In addition, the Commission found that creation of a convenient, safe pedestrian/bicycle pathway system as an alternative means of transportation "could offset some of the traffic demand on [nearby] streets and lessen the increase in traffic congestion."

The Commission went on to note that the required floodplain dedication would be reasonably related to petitioner's request to intensify the use of the site given the increase in the impervious surface. The Commission stated that the "anticipated increased storm water flow from the subject property to an already strained creek and drainage basin can only add to the public need to manage the stream channel and floodplain for drainage purposes." Based on this anticipated increased storm water flow, the Commission concluded that "the requirement of dedication of the floodplain area on the site is related to the applicant's plan to intensify development on the site." The Tigard City Council approved the Commission's final order, subject to one minor modification; the city council reassigned the responsibility for surveying and marking the floodplain area from petitioner to the city's engineering department.

Petitioner appealed to the Land Use Board of Appeals (LUBA) on the ground that the city's dedication requirements were not related to the proposed development, and, therefore, those requirements constituted an uncompensated taking of her property under the Fifth Amendment. In evaluating the federal taking claim, LUBA assumed that the city's findings about the impacts of the proposed development were supported by substantial evidence. Given the undisputed fact that the proposed larger building and paved parking area would increase the amount of impervious surfaces and the runoff into Fanno Creek, LUBA concluded that "there is a 'reasonable relationship' between the proposed development and the requirement to dedicate land along Fanno Creek for a greenway." With respect to the pedestrian/bicycle pathway, LUBA noted the Commission's finding that a significantly larger retail sales building and parking lot would attract larger numbers of customers and employees and their vehicles. It again found a "reasonable relationship" between alleviating the impacts of increased traffic from the development and facilitating the provision of a pedestrian/bicycle pathway as an alternative means of transportation.

The Oregon Court of Appeals and . . . the Oregon Supreme Court affirmed. * * *

                                    II.

The Takings Clause of the Fifth Amendment of the United States Constitution, made applicable to the States through the Fourteenth Amendment, provides: "[N]or shall private property be taken for public use, without just compensation." One of the principal purposes of the Takings Clause is "to bar Government from forcing some people alone to bear public burdens which, in all fairness and justice, should be borne by the public as a whole." Without question, had the city simply required petitioner to dedicate a strip of land along Fanno Creek for public use, rather than conditioning the grant of her permit to redevelop her property on such a dedication, a taking would have occurred. *Nollan, supra,* 483 U.S., at 831. Such public access would deprive petitioner of the right to exclude others, "one of the most essential sticks in the bundle of rights that are commonly characterized as property." *Kaiser Aetna v. United States,* 444 U.S. 164, 176 (1979).

On the other side of the ledger, the authority of state and local governments to engage in land use planning has been sustained against constitutional challenge as long ago as our decision in *Village of Euclid v. Ambler Realty Co.,* 272 U.S. 365 (1926). "Government hardly could go on if to some extent values incident to property could not be diminished without paying for every such change in the general law." *Pennsylvania Coal Co. v. Mahon,* 260 U.S. 393, 413 (1922). A land use regulation does not effect a taking if it "substantially advance[s] legitimate state interests" and does not "den[y] an owner economically viable use of his land." *Agins v. City of Tiburon,* 447 U.S. 255, 260 (1980).

The sort of land use regulations discussed in the cases just cited, however, differ in two relevant particulars from the present case. First, they involved essentially legislative determinations classifying entire areas of the city, whereas here the city made an adjudicative decision to condition petitioner's application for a building permit on an individual parcel. Second, the conditions imposed were not simply a limitation on the use petitioner might make of her own parcel, but a requirement that she deed portions of the property to the city. In *Nollan v. California Coastal Comm'n*, 483 U.S. 825 (1987), we held that governmental authority to exact such a condition was circumscribed by the Fifth and Fourteenth Amendments. Under the well-settled doctrine of "unconstitutional conditions," the government may not require a person to give up a constitutional right — here the right to receive just compensation when property is taken for a public use — in exchange for a discretionary benefit conferred by the government where the benefit sought has little or no relationship to the property. . . .

Petitioner contends that the city has forced her to choose between the building permit and her right under the Fifth Amendment to just compensation for the public easements. Petitioner does not quarrel with the city's authority to exact some forms of dedication as a condition for the grant of a building permit, but challenges the showing made by the city to justify these exactions. She argues that the city has identified "no special benefits" conferred on her, and has not identified any "special quantifiable burdens" created by her new store that would justify the particular dedications required from her which are not required from the public at large.

III.

In evaluating petitioner's claim, we must first determine whether the "essential nexus" exists between the "legitimate state interest" and the permit condition exacted by the city. *Nollan*, 483 U.S., at 837. If we find that a nexus exists, we must then decide the required degree of connection between the exactions and the projected impact of the proposed development. We were not required to reach this question in *Nollan*, because we concluded that the connection did not meet even the loosest standard. Here, however, we must decide this question.

A.

We addressed the essential nexus question in *Nollan*. The California Coastal Commission demanded a lateral public easement across the Nollans' beachfront lot in exchange for a permit to demolish an existing bungalow and replace it with a three-bedroom house. The public easement was designed to connect two public beaches that were separated by the Nollan's property. The Coastal Commission had asserted that the public easement condition was imposed to promote the legitimate state interest of diminishing the "blockage of the view of the ocean" caused by construction of the larger house.

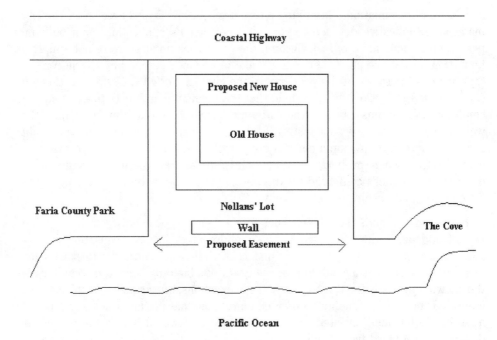

We agreed that the Coastal Commission's concern with protecting visual access to the ocean constituted a legitimate public interest. We also agreed that the permit condition would have been constitutional "even if it consisted of the requirement that the Nollans provide a viewing spot on their property for passers by with whose sighting of the ocean their new house would interfere." We resolved, however, that the Coastal Commission's regulatory authority was set completely adrift from its constitutional moorings when it claimed that a nexus existed between visual access to the ocean and a permit condition requiring lateral public access along the Nollans' beachfront lot. How enhancing the public's ability to "traverse to and along the shorefront" served the same governmental purpose of "visual access to the ocean" from the roadway was beyond our ability to countenance. The absence of a nexus left the Coastal Commission in the position of simply trying to obtain an easement through gimmickry, which converted a valid regulation of land use into " 'an out-and-out plan of extortion.' "

No such gimmicks are associated with the permit conditions imposed by the city in this case. Undoubtedly, the prevention of flooding along Fanno Creek and the reduction of traffic congestion in the Central Business District qualify as the type of legitimate public purposes we have upheld. It seems equally obvious that a nexus exists between preventing flooding along Fanno Creek and limiting development within the creek's 100-year floodplain. Petitioner proposes to double the size of her retail store and to pave her now-gravel parking lot, thereby expanding the impervious surface on the property and increasing the amount of storm water runoff into Fanno Creek.

The same may be said for the city's attempt to reduce traffic congestion by providing for alternative means of transportation. In theory, a pedestrian/bicycle pathway provides a useful alternative means of transportation for workers and shoppers: "Pedestrians and bicyclists occupying dedicated spaces for walking and/or bicycling . . . remove potential vehicles from streets, resulting in an overall improvement in total transportation system flow." A. Nelson, Public Provision of Pedestrian and Bicycle Access Ways: Public Policy Rationale and the Nature of Private Benefits 11, Center for Planning Development, Georgia Institute of Technology, Working Paper Series (Jan. 1994). See also Intermodal Surface Transportation Efficiency Act of 1991, Pub.L. 102-240, 105 Stat.1914 (recognizing pedestrian and bicycle facilities as necessary components of any strategy to reduce traffic congestion).

B.

The second part of our analysis requires us to determine whether the degree of the exactions demanded by the city's permit conditions bears the required relationship to the projected impact of petitioner's proposed development. *Nollan, supra*, 483 U.S., at 834, quoting *Penn Central Transp. Co. v. New York City*, 438 U.S. 104, 127 (1978) (" '[A] use restriction may constitute a "taking" if not reasonably necessary to the effectuation of a substantial government purpose.' "). Here the Oregon Supreme Court deferred to what it termed the "city's unchallenged factual findings" supporting the dedication conditions and found them to be reasonably related to the impact of the expansion of petitioner's business.

The city required that petitioner dedicate "to the City as Greenway all portions of the site that fall within the existing 100-year floodplain [of Fanno Creek] . . . and all property 15 feet above [the floodplain] boundary." In addition, the city demanded that the retail store be designed so as not to intrude into the greenway area. The city relies on the Commission's rather tentative findings that increased storm water flow from petitioner's property "can only add to the public need to manage the [floodplain] for drainage purposes" to support its conclusion that the "requirement of dedication of the floodplain area on the site is related to the applicant's plan to intensify development on the site."

The city made the following specific findings relevant to the pedestrian/bicycle pathway:

"In addition, the proposed expanded use of this site is anticipated to generate additional vehicular traffic thereby increasing congestion on nearby collector and arterial streets. Creation of a convenient, safe pedestrian/bicycle pathway system as an alternative means of transportation could offset some of the traffic demand on these nearby streets and lessen the increase in traffic congestion."

The question for us is whether these findings are constitutionally sufficient to justify the conditions imposed by the city on petitioner's building permit. Since state courts have been dealing with this question a good deal longer than we have, we turn to representative decisions made by them.

In some States, very generalized statements as to the necessary connection between the required dedication and the proposed development seem to suffice. We think this standard is too lax to adequately protect petitioner's right to just compensation if her property is taken for a public purpose.

Other state courts require a very exacting correspondence, described as the "specifi[c] and uniquely attributable" test. The Supreme Court of Illinois first developed this test in *Pioneer Trust & Savings Bank v. Mount Prospect*, 22 Ill. 2d 375, 380, 176 N.E.2d 799, 802 (1961).[7] Under this standard, if the local government cannot demonstrate that its exaction is directly proportional to the specifically created need, the exaction becomes "a veiled exercise of the power of eminent domain and a confiscation of private property behind the defense of police regulations." We do not think the Federal Constitution requires such exacting scrutiny, given the nature of the interests involved.

A number of state courts have taken an intermediate position, requiring the municipality to show a "reasonable relationship" between the required dedication and the impact of the proposed development. Typical is the Supreme Court of Nebraska's opinion in *Simpson v. North Platte*, 206 Neb. 240, 245, 292 N.W.2d 297, 301 (1980), where that court stated:

> "The distinction, therefore, which must be made between an appropriate exercise of the police power and an improper exercise of eminent domain is whether the requirement has some reasonable relationship or nexus to the use to which the property is being made or is merely being used as an excuse for taking property simply because at that particular moment the landowner is asking the city for some license or permit."

Thus, the court held that a city may not require a property owner to dedicate private property for some future public use as a condition of obtaining a building permit when such future use is not "occasioned by the construction sought to be permitted."

We think the "reasonable relationship" test adopted by a majority of the state courts is closer to the federal constitutional norm than either of those previously discussed. But we do not adopt it as such, partly because the term "reasonable relationship" seems confusingly similar to the term "rational basis" which describes the minimal level of scrutiny under the Equal Protection Clause of the Fourteenth Amendment. We think a term such as "rough proportionality" best encapsulates what we hold to be the requirement of the Fifth Amendment. No precise mathematical calculation is required, but the city must make some sort of individualized determination that the required dedication is related both in nature and extent to the impact of the proposed development.[8] . . .

----

[7] The "specifically and uniquely attributable" test has now been adopted by a minority of other courts. . . .

[8] JUSTICE STEVENS' dissent takes us to task for placing the burden on the city to justify the required dedication. He is correct in arguing that in evaluating most generally applicable zoning regulations, the burden properly rests on the party challenging the regulation to prove that it constitutes an arbitrary regulation of property rights. See, e.g., *Village of Euclid v. Ambler Realty Co.*, 272 U.S. 365 (1926). Here, by contrast, the city made an adjudicative decision to condition petitioner's application for a building permit on an individual parcel. In this situation, the burden properly rests on the city. See *Nollan*, 483

It is axiomatic that increasing the amount of impervious surface will increase the quantity and rate of storm water flow from petitioner's property. Therefore, keeping the floodplain open and free from development would likely confine the pressures on Fanno Creek created by petitioner's development. In fact, because petitioner's property lies within the Central Business District, the CDC already required that petitioner leave 15% of it as open space and the undeveloped floodplain would have nearly satisfied that requirement. But the city demanded more-it not only wanted petitioner not to build in the floodplain, but it also wanted petitioner's property along Fanno Creek for its greenway system. The city has never said why a public greenway, as opposed to a private one, was required in the interest of flood control.

The difference to petitioner, of course, is the loss of her ability to exclude others. As we have noted, this right to exclude others is "one of the most essential sticks in the bundle of rights that are commonly characterized as property." It is difficult to see why recreational visitors trampling along petitioner's floodplain easement are sufficiently related to the city's legitimate interest in reducing flooding problems along Fanno Creek, and the city has not attempted to make any individualized determination to support this part of its request.

The city contends that the recreational easement along the greenway is only ancillary to the city's chief purpose in controlling flood hazards. It further asserts that unlike the residential property at issue in *Nollan*, petitioner's property is commercial in character, and therefore, her right to exclude others is compromised. Brief for Respondent 41, quoting *United States v. Orito*, 413 U.S. 139, 142 (1973) (" 'The Constitution extends special safeguards to the privacy of the home.' "). The city maintains that "[t]here is nothing to suggest that preventing [petitioner] from prohibiting [the easements] will unreasonably impair the value of [her] property as a [retail store]." *PruneYard Shopping Center v. Robins*, 447 U.S. 74, 83 (1980).

Admittedly, petitioner wants to build a bigger store to attract members of the public to her property. She also wants, however, to be able to control the time and manner in which they enter. The recreational easement on the greenway is different in character from the exercise of state-protected rights of free expression and petition that we permitted in *PruneYard*. In *PruneYard*, we held that a major private shopping center that attracted more than 25,000 daily patrons had to provide access to persons exercising their state constitutional rights to distribute pamphlets and ask passers-by to sign their petitions. We based our decision, in part, on the fact that the shopping center "may restrict expressive activity by adopting time, place, and manner regulations that will minimize any interference with its commercial functions." By contrast, the city wants to impose a permanent recreational easement upon petitioner's property that borders Fanno Creek. Petitioner would lose all rights to regulate the time in which the public entered onto the greenway, regardless of any interference it might pose with her retail store. Her right to exclude would not be regulated, it would be eviscerated.

U.S., at 836. This conclusion is not, as he suggests, undermined by our decision in *Moore v. East Cleveland*, 431 U.S. 494 (1977), in which we struck down a housing ordinance that limited occupancy of a dwelling unit to members of a single family as violating the Due Process Clause of the Fourteenth Amendment. The ordinance at issue in *Moore* intruded on choices concerning family living arrangements, an area in which the usual deference to the legislature was found to be inappropriate.

If petitioner's proposed development had somehow encroached on existing greenway space in the city, it would have been reasonable to require petitioner to provide some alternative greenway space for the public either on her property or elsewhere. See *Nollan*, 483 U.S., at 836 ("Although such a requirement, constituting a permanent grant of continuous access to the property, would have to be considered a taking if it were not attached to a development permit, the Commission's assumed power to forbid construction of the house in order to protect the public's view of the beach must surely include the power to condition construction upon some concession by the owner, even a concession of property rights, that serves the same end"). But that is not the case here. We conclude that the findings upon which the city relies do not show the required reasonable relationship between the floodplain easement and the petitioner's proposed new building.

With respect to the pedestrian/bicycle pathway, we have no doubt that the city was correct in finding that the larger retail sales facility proposed by petitioner will increase traffic on the streets of the Central Business District. The city estimates that the proposed development would generate roughly 435 additional trips per day. Dedications for streets, sidewalks, and other public ways are generally reasonable exactions to avoid excessive congestion from a proposed property use. But on the record before us, the city has not met its burden of demonstrating that the additional number of vehicle and bicycle trips generated by petitioner's development reasonably relate to the city's requirement for a dedication of the pedestrian/ bicycle pathway easement. The city simply found that the creation of the pathway "could offset some of the traffic demand . . . and lessen the increase in traffic congestion."

As Justice Peterson of the Supreme Court of Oregon explained in his dissenting opinion, however, "[t]he findings of fact that the bicycle pathway system '*could* offset some of the traffic demand' is a far cry from a finding that the bicycle pathway system *will*, or is *likely to*, offset some of the traffic demand." 317 Ore., at 127, 854 P.2d, at 447 (emphasis in original). No precise mathematical calculation is required, but the city must make some effort to quantify its findings in support of the dedication for the pedestrian/bicycle pathway beyond the conclusory statement that it could offset some of the traffic demand generated.

IV.

Cities have long engaged in the commendable task of land use planning, made necessary by increasing urbanization, particularly in metropolitan areas such as Portland. The city's goals of reducing flooding hazards and traffic congestion, and providing for public greenways, are laudable, but there are outer limits to how this may be done. "A strong public desire to improve the public condition [will not] warrant achieving the desire by a shorter cut than the constitutional way of paying for the change." *Pennsylvania Coal*, 260 U.S., at 416.

The judgment of the Supreme Court of Oregon is reversed, and the case is remanded for further proceedings not inconsistent with this opinion.

Stevens, J., dissenting.

The record does not tell us the dollar value of petitioner Florence Dolan's interest in excluding the public from the greenway adjacent to her hardware business. The mountain of briefs that the case has generated nevertheless makes it obvious that the pecuniary value of her victory is far less important than the rule of law that this case has been used to establish. It is unquestionably an important case.

Certain propositions are not in dispute. The enlargement of the Tigard unit in Dolan's chain of hardware stores will have an adverse impact on the city's legitimate and substantial interests in controlling drainage in Fanno Creek and minimizing traffic congestion in Tigard's business district. That impact is sufficient to justify an outright denial of her application for approval of the expansion. The city has nevertheless agreed to grant Dolan's application if she will comply with two conditions, each of which admittedly will mitigate the adverse effects of her proposed development. The disputed question is whether the city has violated the Fourteenth Amendment to the Federal Constitution by refusing to allow Dolan's planned construction to proceed unless those conditions are met.

The Court is correct in concluding that the city may not attach arbitrary conditions to a building permit or to a variance even when it can rightfully deny the application outright. I also agree that state court decisions dealing with ordinances that govern municipal development plans provide useful guidance in a case of this kind. Yet the Court's description of the doctrinal underpinnings of its decision, the phrasing of its fledgling test of "rough proportionality," and the application of that test to this case run contrary to the traditional treatment of these cases and break considerable and unpropitious new ground. * * *

The Court . . . decides for the first time that the city has the burden of establishing the constitutionality of its conditions by making an "individualized determination" that the condition in question satisfies the proportionality requirement.

In addition, the Court ignores the state courts' willingness to consider what the property owner gains from the exchange in question. The Supreme Court of Wisconsin, for example, found it significant that the village's approval of a proposed subdivision plat "enables the subdivider to profit financially by selling the subdivision lots as home-building sites and thus realizing a greater price than could have been obtained if he had sold his property as unplatted lands." *Jordan v. Menomonee Falls*, 28 Wis. 2d, at 619–620, 137 N.W.2d, at 448. The required dedication as a condition of that approval was permissible "[i]n return for this benefit." * * *

In our changing world one thing is certain: uncertainty will characterize predictions about the impact of new urban developments on the risks of floods, earthquakes, traffic congestion, or environmental harms. When there is doubt concerning the magnitude of those impacts, the public interest in averting them must outweigh the private interest of the commercial entrepreneur. If the government can demonstrate that the conditions it has imposed in a land use permit are rational, impartial and conducive to fulfilling the aims of a valid land use plan, a strong presumption of validity should attach to those conditions. The burden of demonstrating that those conditions have unreasonably impaired the economic value of the proposed improvement belongs squarely on the shoulders of the party challenging the state action's constitutionality. That allocation of burdens has served us well in the past. The Court has stumbled badly today by reversing it. I respectfully dissent.

NOTES

1. Why do courts analyze takings cases involving exactions and impact fees differently than other types of regulatory takings cases? If the government required a landowner who was not a developer to contribute land for a public purpose, the landowner clearly would be entitled to compensation. Why is the analysis different for a developer? Consider the following explanation:

> [T]here is an elementary but vital distinction between developers and other landowners. The subdivider is a manufacturer, processer, and marketer of a product: land is but one of his raw materials. In subdivision control disputes, the developer is not defending hearth and home against the king's intrusion, but simply attempting to maximize his profits from the sale of a finished product. As applied to him, subdivision control exactions are actually business regulations.

> In a very real sense, all subdivision control exactions are grounded upon a judgment that subdivisions which do not provide adequate space for streets, utilities, parks, and other public uses are defective. Although the consumer may be able to discern the existence of such defects, his bargaining power is probably too weak to force subdividers to provide necessary improvements. From the municipality's point of view, the danger from a defective subdivision is actually greater than the threat posed by defectively manufactured automobiles, refrigerators, or other durable goods. The subdivision remains, long after the automobiles have been relegated to the junk heap, to spawn conditions of slum and blight. Further, the removal or rehabilitation of a subdivision may necessitate large expenditures of public funds. The ability of a defective environment to cripple or maim its inhabitants may not be so dramatic and obvious as that of automobiles and other inherently dangerous instrumentalities, but it is no less real.

John D. Johnston, Jr., *Constitutionality of Subdivision Control Exactions: The Quest for a Rationale*, 52 Cornell L.Q. 871, 923 (1967). Was this the rationale articulated by the Court in *Dolan*?

2. Do the holdings in *Dolan* and in *Nollan* apply only to governmentally-required land dedications or do they also apply to the imposition of impact fees? Some courts have held that *Dolan* and *Nollan* are limited to takings of an interest in land. See, e.g., *Clajon Prod. Corp. v. Petera*, 70 F.3d 1566, 1578 (10th Cir. 1995) ("Based on a close reading of *Nollan* and *Dolan*, we conclude that those cases (and the tests outlined therein) are limited to the context of development exactions where there is a physical taking or its equivalent."); *Harris v. City of Wichita*, 862 F. Supp. 287 (D. Kan. 1994); *McCarthy v. City of Leawood*, 894 P.2d 836 (Kan. 1995) ("The landowners cite no authority for the critical leap which must be made from [an

impact] fee to a taking of property." *Id.* at 845.). But see *Ehrlich v. City of Culver City*, 911 P.2d 429 (Cal. 1996); *Home Builders Association of Dayton and the Miami Valley v. City of Beavercreek*, 729 N.E.2d 349 (Ohio 2000) (in a case of first impression, the Ohio Supreme Court adopted the "dual rational nexus test" of *Dolan* to determine the constitutionality of an impact fee); *Benchmark Land Co. v. City of Battle Ground*, 14 P.3d 172 (Wash. Ct. App. 2000) (*Dolan* test applicable in cases involving impact fees). The U.S. Supreme Court settled the issue in *Koontz v. St. Johns River Water Management Dist.*, 133 S. Ct. 2586 (2013). It held that *Dolan* and *Nollan* apply to impact fees, as well as to required land dedications, because both present "the risk that the government may use its substantial power and discretion in land-use permitting to pursue governmental ends that lack an essential nexus and rough proportionality to the effects of the proposed new use of the specific property at issue, thereby diminishing without justification the value of the property."

3. In some jurisdictions, the local permitting authority does not have discretion concerning the size of the exaction or impact fee to be imposed on an individual developer. Instead, a statute or ordinance generically provides the amount of exactions or impact fees for all new development. For example, in *Collis v. City of Bloomington*, 246 N.W.2d 19 (Minn. 1976), the court considered a taking challenge to a city ordinance that required subdividers to contribute land equal in value to ten percent of the land to be subdivided or its cash equivalent. Does *Dolan* apply to this type of legislative imposition of exactions and impact fees or does it apply only to exactions and fees that are established on a case-by-case basis? Courts have limited *Dolan* to the latter situation because of the potential for administrative abuse that it presents. See, e.g., *Home Builders Ass'n v. City of Scottsdale*, 930 P.2d 993, 999 (Ariz. 1997); *Ehrlich v. City of Culver City*, 911 P.2d 429, 439 (Cal. 1996). Contra *Volusia County v. Aberdeen at Ormond Beach, L.P.*, 760 So. 2d 126 (Fla. 2000) (uniform impact fee to fund schools violates *Dolan's* dual rational nexus test when assessed against a mobile home park that is open only to people who are at least 55 years old).

4. In *City of Monterey v. Del Monte Dunes at Monterey, Ltd.*, 526 U.S. 687 (1999), the U.S. Supreme Court considered a case in which a city repeatedly denied a landowner's development plans, although the owner complied with every condition that the city requested. By the time the developer submitted its final development proposal, it had agreed to devote 17.9 acres of its 37.6 acre parcel to public open space, 7.9 acres to open, landscaped space, and 6.7 acres for public and private streets, parking, and beach access. Only 5.1 acres remained for a proposed development. Although the proposed development fully complied with the applicable land use regulations, the city again rejected the plans. The owner then claimed that a regulatory taking had occurred. In analyzing the taking claim, the Ninth Circuit Court of Appeals applied the *Dolan* test. 95 F.3d 1422 (9th Cir. 1996). The U.S. Supreme Court held that the *Dolan* standard was inapplicable because "[i]t was not designed to address, and is not readily applicable to, the much different questions arising where, as here, the landowner's challenge is based not on excessive exactions but on denial of development." How do the two situations differ? Because the *Dolan* rough proportionality standard is viewed as being more protective of landowners' rights than the multi-factor balancing test, this holding may be beneficial for local governments. See Robert H. Frielich & Jason M. Divelbiss, *Public Interest is Vindicated: City of Monterey v. Del Monte Dunes*, July 1999 Land Use Law 3. See also *Sherman v. Town of Chester*, 752 F.3d 554 (2d Cir. 2014) (based on multi-factor balancing test, town took developer's land by subjecting him to 10 years of unfair and repetitive requirements).

5. A subdivision exaction also may give rise to an equal protection challenge. In *Village of Willowbrook v. Olech*, 528 U.S. 562 (2000), the Olechs requested that the Village connect their land to the municipal water supply. The Village conditioned the connection on the Olechs' grant of a 33-foot easement to the Village, though other landowners had been required to grant only 15-foot easements. The Olechs alleged that the condition was retaliation for an earlier, unrelated suit that they won against the Village and that, therefore, the condition was irrational and arbitrary. The U.S. Supreme Court held that the Olechs had alleged adequate grounds for an equal protection claim against the Village.

C. Private Property

Two different types of issues concerning "private property" have arisen under the takings clause: (1) what types of private property interests the government can acquire by eminent domain and (2) what rights in property are compensable. *City of Oakland v. Oakland Raiders* addresses the former issue, and *Walker v. State* addresses the latter.

CITY OF OAKLAND v. OAKLAND RAIDERS
646 P.2d 835 (Cal. 1982)

RICHARDSON, J.

The City of Oakland (City) appeals from a summary judgment dismissing with prejudice its action to acquire by eminent domain the property rights associated with respondent Oakland Raiders' (the Raiders) ownership of a professional football team as a franchise member of the National Football League (NFL). We conclude that the trial court erred in granting the summary judgment and we reverse and remand the case for a full evidentiary trial of the issues on the merits.

The Raiders limited partnership is comprised of two general partners, Allen Davis and Edward W. McGah, and several limited partners, all of whom are individual respondents herein. In 1966 the Raiders and the Oakland-Alameda County Coliseum, Inc., a nonprofit corporation, entered into a five-year licensing agreement for use of the Oakland Coliseum by the Raiders. Having been given five three-year renewal options, the Raiders exercised the first three, and failed to do so for the football season commencing in 1980 when contract negotiations for renewal terminated without agreement. When the Raiders announced its intention to move the football team to Los Angeles, City commenced this action in eminent domain.

The trial court granted summary judgment for all respondents and dismissed the action. The legal confrontation between the parties is sharply defined. City insists that what it seeks to condemn is "property" which is subject to established eminent domain law. . . . In answer, respondents argue that the law of eminent domain does not permit the taking of "intangible property not connected with realty," thereby rendering impossible City's condemnation of the football franchise which respondents describe as a "network of intangible contractual rights." * * *

We have held that "The power of eminent domain is an inherent attribute of sovereignty." * * * This sovereign power has been described as "universally" recognized and "necessary to the very existence of government." (1 Nichols on Eminent Domain (3d ed. 1980) §§ 1.11, 1.14[2], pp. 1–10, 1–22.) When properly exercised, that power affords an orderly compromise between the public good and the protection and indemnification of private citizens whose property is taken to advance that good. That protection is constitutionally ordained by the Fifth Amendment to the United States Constitution, which is made applicable to the states by nature of the Fourteenth Amendment and by article I, section 19 of the California Constitution.

Because the power to condemn is an inherent attribute of general government, we have observed that "constitutional provisions merely place limitations upon its exercise." (*People v. Chevalier* [1959] 52 Cal. 2d 299, 304, 340 P.2d 598.) The two constitutional restraints are that the taking be for a "public use" and that "just compensation" be paid therefor. No constitutional restriction, federal or state, purports to limit the nature of the property that may be taken by eminent domain. In contrast to the broad powers of *general* government however, "a municipal corporation has no inherent power of eminent domain and can exercise it only when expressly authorized by law. (*City of Menlo Park v. Artino* [1957] 151 Cal. App. 2d 261, 266, 311 P.2d 135. . . .)" We examine briefly the source of City's statutory power.

In 1975, California's eminent domain statutes received extensive revision and recodification. (See Code Civ. Proc., § 1230.010 *et seq.*, all further statutory references are to this code unless otherwise indicated; see also, e.g., Gov. Code, § 37350.5.) These changes were recommended by the California Law Revision Commission after it studied our existing eminent domain law and reviewed similar laws of every jurisdiction in the United States, pursuant to legislative direction. In the words of the commission, the new law was intended "to cover, in a comprehensive manner, all aspects of condemnation law and procedure" and to produce "a modern Eminent Domain Law within the existing California statutory framework."

Certain provisions of the recodified law are particularly relevant to the issues before us. Government Code section 37350.5, as amended, provides: "A city may acquire by eminent domain *any property* necessary to carry out any of its powers or functions." (Italics added.) As newly defined, " 'Property' includes real and personal property and any interest therein." (§ 1235.170.) In implementation of the foregoing right to take, the new code also authorizes any "person" empowered to take property for a particular use to exercise certain additional power to condemn other property "necessary to carry out and make effective the principal purpose involved. . . ." Within this context, "person" includes "any public entity;" and "public entity," in turn, includes a "city." The constitutional obligation to pay compensation for property so taken also is codified.

The new law appears to impose no greater restrictions on the exercise of the condemnation power than those which are inherent in the federal and state

Constitutions. Further, the power which is statutorily extended to cities is not limited to certain types of property. In discussing the broad scope of property rights which are subject to a public taking under the new law, the Law Revision Commission comment notes that "Section 1235.170 is intended to provide the broadest possible definition of property and to include any type of right, title *or interest* in property that may be required for public use." To that end the commission eliminated the "duplicative listings of property types and interests subject to condemnation" which had appeared in the earlier eminent domain statutes.

Despite the apparent lack of any constitutional or statutory restrictions, respondents nonetheless assert that "intangible property" such as the contractual and other rights involved in the instant action has never before been taken by condemnation and that such taking should not be sanctioned now.

Initially, we note that the lack of precedent does not establish that the *legal right* to take intangibles is lacking. Further, while there is little applicable California law on the point, the Raiders, in our view, overstates its case.

Over 125 years ago, the United States Supreme Court rejected a similar claim that intangible property could not be condemned. In *The West River Bridge Company v. Dix* (1848) 47 U.S. 507, 533, 6 How. 507, the high court carefully explained: "A distinction has been attempted . . . between the power of a government to appropriate for public uses property which is corporeal . . . and the like power in the government to resume or extinguish a franchise. The distinction thus attempted we regard as a refinement which has no foundation in reason, and one that, in truth, avoids the true legal or constitutional question in these causes; namely, that of the right in private persons, in the use or enjoyment of their private property, to control and actually to prohibit the power and duty of the government to advance and protect the general good. We are aware of nothing peculiar to a franchise which can class it higher, or render it more sacred, than other property. A franchise is property, and nothing more; it is incorporeal property. . . ."

A century later, the high court reaffirmed the principle. Reasoning that "the intangible acquires a value . . . no different from the value of the business' physical property," it concluded that such intangibles as trade routes of a laundry were condemnable, upon payment of just compensation therefor, when properly taken for a public use. (*Kimball Laundry Co. v. United States* [1949] 338 U.S. 1, 10–11, 16.)

Respected treatise writers and commentators have been in full accord. Thus, "Personal property is subject to the exercise of the power of eminent domain. Intangible property, such as choses in action, patent rights, franchises, charters or any other form of contract, are within the scope of this sovereign authority as fully as land. . . ." (1 Nichols, *supra*, § 2.1[2], pp. 2-8 to 2-9.) Similarly, "Unless restricted by constitutional or statutory provisions, the right of eminent domain encompasses property of every kind and character, whether real or personal, or tangible or intangible. . . ." (26 Am. Jur. 2d, Eminent Domain, § 73, p. 733, fns. omitted.) Further, "the rule requiring compensation for property taken for or injured in connection with public use has been held to apply to personal property, such as valid contracts and contractual rights. . . ." (29A C.J.S., Eminent Domain, § 108, p. 440, fns. omitted.)

In considering the law of eminent domain within the context of inverse condemnation prior to the 1975 revision, one scholar has observed: "The constitutional provisions, both state and federal, make no verbal distinction between real property and personal property with respect to the requirement of 'just compensation.' Federal decisions under the due process clause have repeatedly applied inverse condemnation principles in cases involving both personalty and intangibles. See, e.g., *Armstrong v. United States*, 364 U.S. 40 (1960) (destruction of materialmen's liens on boats held compensable taking); *Monongahela Nav. Co. v. United States*, 148 U.S. 312 (1893) (destruction of the value of a franchise held a compensable taking). . . . [¶] The California decisions do not distinguish between real and personal property. . . . [¶] In any event, the state courts would necessarily have to yield to federal constitutional requirements in this regard, and, as noted above, takings of personalty are clearly compensable under the due process clause." (Van Alstyne, *Statutory Modification of Inverse Condemnation: The Scope of Legislative Power* (1967) 19 Stan. L. Rev. 727, 739, fn. 50.)

Citing the foregoing discussion, the appellate court in *Sutfin v. State of California* (1968) 261 Cal. App. 2d 50, 53, 67 Cal. Rptr. 665, reversed a lower court judgment in holding that under the forerunner to article I, section 19 of the California Constitution the taking or damaging of private property for public use was compensable, "whether said property be real or personal." Because condemnation and inverse condemnation, in our view, are merely different manifestations of the same governmental power, with correlative duties imposed upon public entities by the same constitutional provisions, both the *Sutfin* holding and Professor Van Alstyne's discussion are pertinent to the case before us.

Following the reasoning of *Kimball, supra*, 338 U.S. 1, numerous other decisions both federal and state have expressly acknowledged that intangible assets are subject to condemnation. (See, e.g., *Liggett & Myers v. United States* [1927] 274 U.S. 215, 220 [contract to provide tobacco products]; *Porter v. United States* [5th Cir. 1973] 473 F.2d 1329, 1333–1335 [right to exploit "collector's value" of personal effects of Lee Harvey Oswald]; *In re Fifth Avenue Coach Lines, Inc.* [1966] 18 N.Y.2d 212, 221 [273 N.Y.S.2d 52, 56, 219 N.E.2d 410] [bus system, including coach routes, operating schedules, etc. — "intangible assets are . . . equally essential to the city's" purpose]; *Milwaukee & Sub. Transp. v. Milwaukee County* [1978] 82 Wis. 2d 420, 444 [263 N.W.2d 503, 516] [intangible assets connected with a bus service].) Similar consequences occur when a private utility is taken in by eminent domain by a municipality or utility district . . . ; for the most valuable property acquired by condemnation of a utility may be intangible, namely, its franchise or right to do business. Indeed, the primary, value of any *tangible* assets, real or personal, acquired in such a taking may well be that they serve that primary *intangible* right.

For eminent domain purposes, neither the federal nor the state Constitution distinguishes between property which is real or personal, tangible or intangible. Nor did the 1975 statutory revision. Bearing in mind that the Law Revision Commission, after an extensive national study, made its legislative recommendations, including a definition of condemnable property which it characterized as "the broadest possible," we conclude that our eminent domain law authorizes the taking of intangible property. Had the trial court based its summary judgment on a contrary conclusion, it would have erred. . . .

BIRD, C.J., concurring and dissenting.

The power of eminent domain claimed by the City in this case is not only novel but virtually without limit. This is troubling because the potential for abuse of such a great power is boundless. Although I am forced by the current state of the law to agree with the result reached by the majority, I have not signed their opinion because it endorses this unprecedented application of eminent domain law without even pausing to consider the ultimate consequences of their expansive decision. It should be noted that research both by the parties and by this court has failed to disclose a single case in which the legal propositions relied on here have been combined to reach a result such as that adopted by the majority.

There are two particularly disturbing questions in this case. First, does a city have the power to condemn a viable, ongoing business and sell it to another private party merely because the original owner has announced his intention to move his business to another city? For example, if a rock concert impresario, after some years of producing concerts in a municipal stadium, decides to move his productions to another city, may the city condemn his business, including his contracts with the rock stars, in order to keep the concerts at the stadium? If a small business that rents a storefront on land originally taken by the city for a redevelopment project decides to move to another city in order to expand, may the city take the business and force it to stay at its original location? May a city condemn *any* business that decides to seek greener pastures elsewhere under the unlimited interpretation of eminent domain law that the majority appear to approve?

Second, even if a city were legally able to do so, is it proper for a municipality to drastically invade personal property rights to further the policy interests asserted here?

The rights both of the owners of the Raiders and of its employees are threatened by the City's action. Thus, one unexplored aspect of the majority's decision is the ruling that contract rights can be taken by eminent domain. The cases relied on by the majority in support of this holding chiefly concerned inverse condemnation suits. Those cases essentially held that when a state condemns a business, the government is obligated to compensate the business owner for the value of the contract rights destroyed by the taking. In this case, the City seeks to condemn employment contracts between the Raiders and dozens of its employees. Can the City acquire personal employment contracts as simply as it can acquire a tract of land? Are an employee's rights violated by this non-consensual taking of an employment contract or personal services agreement?

At what point in the varied and complex business relationships involved herein would this power to condemn end? In my view, this court should proceed most cautiously before placing a constitutional imprimatur upon this aspect of creeping statism. These difficult questions are deserving of more thorough attention than they have yet received in this litigation.

It strikes me as dangerous and heavy-handed for the government to take over a business, including all of its intangible assets, for the sole purpose of preventing its relocation. The decisional law appears to be silent as to this particular question. It appears that the courts have not yet been confronted with a situation such as that presented by this case. However, a review of the pertinent case law demonstrates that decisions as to the proper scope of the power of eminent domain generally have been considered legislative, rather than judicial, in nature. Therefore, in the absence of a legislative bar to the use of eminent domain in this manner, there appears to be no ground for judicial intervention. . . .

At this stage of the proceedings, there is no constitutional or statutory ground for barring the City's action. Despite my serious misgivings about the wisdom of the City's action and the possible future ramifications of a holding that the state has the power to take an ongoing business to prevent it from leaving a particular area, I am constrained by the law to join, albeit reluctantly, the judgment entered here.

NOTES

1. The California eminent domain law cited in the principal case provides that a city can condemn "any property *necessary* to carry out any of its powers or functions" (emphasis added). Based on this requirement of necessity, why is a challenge to a taking of personal property more likely to be successful than a challenge to a taking of real property?

2. If a company announced plans to move its operations to another state, could the state where it is currently located exercise its power of eminent domain to prevent the company from moving?

3. Although the California Supreme Court stated in the principal case that operation of a sports franchise might constitute a valid public purpose, the issue was never decided. In a subsequent decision, the California Court of Appeal held that the City's acquisition of the franchise by eminent domain would violate the Commerce Clause of the U.S. Constitution. *City of Oakland v. Oakland Raiders*, 174 Cal. App. 3d 414 (1985). The court determined that the Raiders' ability to move from Oakland affected not just the Raiders, but also the entire National Football League because every NFL member depended on the other members for income. NFL television contract proceeds and gate receipts are divided among the member teams, and thus the quality of each team's stadium was instrumental to the NFL's financial success. The court also found that the NFL had to operate at a national level because each franchise owner has an economic self-interest in the identity, financial stability, commitment, and good faith of the other owners. For these reasons, the court characterized the City's eminent domain action as "the precise brand of parochial meddling with the national economy that the commerce clause was designed to prohibit." *Id.* at 421. The court's disposition of the Commerce Clause argument made consideration of the public use issue unnecessary.

WALKER v. STATE
295 P.2d 328 (Wash. 1956)

Weaver, J.

In this action, plaintiffs pray that the state highway commission be enjoined from installing a concrete, center-line curb on that portion of primary state highway No.

2 upon which plaintiffs' property abuts until (a) the commission follows the procedures set forth in R.C.W. 47.52 (limited access facilities statute) and (b) until fair compensation shall first have been paid to plaintiffs; or, should the curb be installed during the pendency of this action, a jury be empaneled to determine plaintiffs' damages.

The trial court sustained a demurrer to plaintiffs' amended complaint. Refusing to plead further, they appeal from a judgment dismissing their action with prejudice.

Plaintiffs own various interests in certain real property. A motel is located thereon. The only access to the property is its five-hundred-foot frontage along the south side of primary state highway No. 2.

The allegations upon which plaintiffs rely to set forth a cause of action are these:

That plaintiffs' motel property abuts the south side of a four-lane highway; that tourists who travel in a westerly direction make up the bulk of plaintiffs' patronage, which requires that they make a left-hand turn across the highway, against oncoming traffic, in order to enter plaintiffs' property; that

". . . defendants State of Washington and State of Washington Highway Commission purport to install the said raised concrete bar or curb ['at the center of said highway'] pursuant to the police powers of the State of Washington and without compliance with R.C.W. Chapter 47.52";

that the state has made an administrative determination that the highway in front of plaintiffs' property is to be changed to a permanent limited-access facility, has initiated studies, prepared detailed plans, and initiated "hearings thereon pursuant to R.C.W., Chapter 47.52"; that the proposed concrete center-line curb is an integral part of, and a necessary step in, the construction of the limited-access facility as planned by the defendants;

". . . that the deprivation of egress and ingress as above described will severely damage the above described property and will seriously depress the fair market value of said property, in an amount not fully known to plaintiffs at this time. That the plaintiffs have no adequate remedy at law";

that defendants have notified plaintiffs that they will not follow the procedure of R.C.W. 47.52 for the installation of the dividing curb; and that compensation for damages allegedly arising therefrom will not be paid. . . .

The demurrer to plaintiffs' amended complaint presents a question of first impression in this jurisdiction.

Is an abutting property owner entitled to compensation under Art. I, § 16, amendment 9, of the state constitution, because an alleged diminution of the right of ingress and egress arises out of the installation, by the highway authorities, of a curb or dividing section in the center of a four-lane highway?

The owner of property abutting upon a public thoroughfare has a right to free and convenient access thereto. This right of ingress and egress attaches to the land.

It is a property right, as complete as ownership of the land itself.

On numerous occasions, this court has held that the abutting property owner is entitled to just compensation if this right is taken or damaged. *Brown v. City of Seattle*, 1892, 5 Wash. 35, 31 P. 313, 32 P. 214, 18 L.R.A. 161 (reduction of street grade in front of owner's property); *State ex rel. Smith v. Superior Court*, 1901, 26 Wash. 278, 66 P. 385 (a trestle and elevated railway built in front of relator's property); *Lund v. Idaho & Washington Northern R.*, 1908, 50 Wash. 574, 97 P. 665 (railroad tracks installed diagonally across street in front of property); *Brazell v. City of Seattle*, 1909, 55 Wash. 180, 104 P. 155 (vacation of one half of street opposite plaintiff's property); *Smith v. City of Centralia*, 1909, 55 Wash. 573, 104 P. 797 (vacation of portion of street opposite plaintiff's land); *Fry v. O'Leary*, 1927, 141 Wash. 465, 252 P. 111, 49 A.L.R. 1249 (vacation of portion of street); *State ex rel. Moline v. Driscoll*, 1936, 185 Wash. 229, 53 P.2d 622 (street grade lowered and sidewalk reduced in width).

In these cases, there was either physical injury to the owner's property or physical impairment of access. None of them involves the division of a public thoroughfare into separate roadways by division stripes or concrete curbs. Exercise of police power was not involved. Factually, they are distinguishable from the case before us.

The facts alleged in the amended complaint indicate that the real basis of plaintiffs' claim for damages is the diversion of westbound traffic from their motel business. Since there is eastbound traffic in front of plaintiffs' property, it is permissible for us to infer that westbound traffic may turn, at some point west of plaintiffs' property, and become eastbound, and thus approach plaintiffs' property.

Plaintiffs have no property right in the continuation or maintenance of the flow of traffic past their property. They still have free and unhampered ingress and egress to their property. Once on the highway, to which they have free access, they are in the same position and subject to the same police power regulations as every other member of the traveling public. Plaintiffs, and every member of the traveling public subject to traffic regulations, have the same right of free access *to* the property *from* the highway. Re-routing and diversion of traffic are police power regulations. Circuity of route, resulting from an exercise of the police power, is an incidental result of a lawful act. It is not the taking or damaging of a property right.

We have found no authority, nor has any been called to our attention, which allows, to the abutting property owner, damages allegedly arising from statutes or ordinances (a) establishing one-way streets; (b) forbidding "U" and left turns; or (c) authorizing the use of other suitable traffic-control devices deemed necessary by the proper authorities to warn, regulate, and guide traffic upon public thoroughfares.

Although an abutting property owner may be inconvenienced by one-way traffic regulation immediately in front of his property, he has no remedy if such regulation be reasonably adapted to the benefit of the traveling public. The property owner must point to illegality, fraud, or arbitrary or capricious conduct.

Plaintiffs allege that defendants propose to install the center-line curb "pursuant to the police powers of the State of Washington." They do not allege facts from which it might be concluded that this exercise of the police power is arbitrary and capricious. Statutory authority for the erection and maintenance of traffic-control devices is found in R.C.W. 43.27.100, 46.04.610, and 47.36.050.

A concrete curb erected on the center line of a four-lane highway is a physical obstruction that prevents left turns into oncoming traffic. It is a traffic-control device, within the purview of our statutes, authorized under the police power of the state.

Damages resulting from the exercise of the police power are noncompensable. . . .

The judgment is affirmed.

NOTES

1. A threshold inquiry in takings analysis is whether the alleged taking affects a legally recognized property interest. No precise formulation of the term "property" exists. Instead, courts have fleshed it out on a case-by-case basis. As the United States Supreme Court has stated: "[N]ot all economic interests are 'property rights'; only those economic advantages are 'rights' which have the law back of them, and only when they are so recognized may courts compel others to forbear from interfering with them or to compensate for their invasion." *United States v. Willow River Power Co.*, 324 U.S. 499, 502 (1945).

A variety of property interests have been asserted in takings actions with varying degrees of success. In *United States v. Willow River Power Co.*, the owner of a hydroelectric power plant claimed that the government's damming of the river on which the plant was located had taken its property interest in the river's natural flow. The Supreme Court disagreed, holding that riparian owners do not own "absolute 'property rights' in water." In a similar case, the Court held that a riparian owner had a valid property interest in water that benefited his grasslands and that the government's damming of the river that provided the water required compensation. *United States v. Gerlach Live Stock Co.*, 339 U.S. 725 (1950).

Another common takings claim occurs — albeit unsuccessfully — when the government interferes with a business' future revenues. See, e.g., *Jamesson v. Downtown Dev. Authority*, 322 So. 2d 510 (Fla. 1975) (holding that a commercial tenant's loss of profits from the condemnation of the building it occupied was not a taking because plaintiff did not have cognizable property interest in future profits); see also *United States v. General Motors Corp.*, 323 U.S. 373 (1945) (holding that loss of future profits and diminution in good will of a business caused by condemnation is not a compensable interest). In a rather unusual case, an organization of postal employees asserted that it had suffered an unlawful taking when the government prohibited the organization from operating a gun range in the post office basement. The court held that the postal employees did not have a valid property interest in the gun range or in carrying firearms and that no taking had occurred. *Minneapolis Post Office Rifle & Pistol Club v. United States*, 32 Fed. Cl. 562 (Fed. Cl. 1995).

2. When the government condemns land that is encumbered by a restrictive covenant, the government takes title free of the covenant. Clearly, the former owner of the fee title is entitled to compensation, but what about the landowners who owned the benefit of the covenant? The courts are split on this question. The issue that divides them is whether a restrictive covenant is a property interest or a mere contract right. Most courts now characterize restrictive covenants as compensable property interests. In these jurisdictions, just compensation usually is measured by the decline in fair market value of the formerly benefited land. However, a minority of jurisdictions still characterize a restrictive covenant as a contract right that does not constitute "property" for purposes of the Takings Clause. These courts sometimes are concerned about the economic burden that a contrary rule would impose on government projects or the possibility that neighbors would enter into covenants when they learn of plans to condemn land in the neighborhood solely for the purpose of obtaining compensation in the eminent domain proceedings.

D. Just Compensation

When a taking has occurred, "just compensation" normally is measured by the land's fair market value — the price that a willing buyer would pay a willing seller. If less than the full fee title or only a portion of the land is taken, the landowner is entitled to the difference between the fair market value of the property before and after the taking. However, the Takings Clause does not require compensation for anything other than the actual property that is taken. For example, the Takings Clause does not require compensation for consequential damages, such as relocation costs. For this reason, Congress and state legislatures have enacted statutes that require compensation for these types of costs. See, e.g., Uniform Relocation Assistance Act, 42 U.S.C. §§ 4601–4655; Minnesota Uniform Relocation Assistance Act, Minn. Stat. § 117.52.

Although courts uniformly have held that compensation is due when government permanently takes land, whether a landowner is entitled to compensation when his land is only temporarily taken was unclear before the U.S. Supreme Court's decision in *First English Evangelical Lutheran Church v. County of Los Angeles.*

FIRST ENGLISH EVANGELICAL LUTHERAN CHURCH v. COUNTY OF LOS ANGELES
482 U.S. 304 (1987)

CHIEF JUSTICE REHNQUIST delivered the opinion of the Court.

In this case the California Court of Appeal held that a landowner who claims that his property has been "taken" by a land-use regulation may not recover damages for the time before it is finally determined that the regulation constitutes a "taking" of his property. We disagree, and conclude that in these circumstances the Fifth and Fourteenth Amendments to the United States Constitution would require compensation for that period.

I.

In 1957, appellant First English Evangelical Lutheran Church purchased a 21-acre parcel of land in a canyon along the banks of the Middle Fork of Mill Creek in the Angeles National Forest. The Middle Fork is the natural drainage channel for a watershed area owned by the National Forest Service. Twelve of the acres owned by the church are flat land, and contained a dining hall, two bunkhouses, a caretaker's lodge, an outdoor chapel, and a footbridge across the creek. The church operated on the site a campground, known as "Lutherglen," as a retreat center and a recreational area for handicapped children.

In July 1977, a forest fire denuded the hills upstream from Lutherglen, destroying approximately 3,860 acres of the watershed area and creating a serious flood hazard. Such flooding occurred on February 9 and 10, 1978, when a storm dropped 11 inches of rain in the watershed. The runoff from the storm overflowed the banks of the Mill Creek, flooding Lutherglen and destroying its buildings.

In response to the flooding of the canyon, appellee County of Los Angeles adopted Interim Ordinance No. 11,855 in January 1979. The ordinance provided that "[a] person shall not construct, reconstruct, place or enlarge any building or structure, any portion of which is, or will be, located within the outer boundary lines of the interim flood protection area located in Mill Creek Canyon. . . ." The ordinance was effective immediately because the county determined that it was "required for the immediate preservation of the public health and safety. . . ." The interim flood protection area described by the ordinance included the flat areas on either side of Mill Creek on which Lutherglen had stood.

The church filed a complaint in the Superior Court of California a little more than a month after the ordinance was adopted. As subsequently amended, the complaint alleged two claims against the county and the Los Angeles County Flood Control District. The first alleged that the defendants were liable under Cal. Govt. Code Ann. § 835 (1980) for dangerous conditions on their upstream properties that contributed to the flooding of Lutherglen. As a part of this claim, appellant also alleged that "Ordinance No. 11,855 denies [appellant] all use of Lutherglen." The second claim sought to recover from the Flood Control District in inverse condemnation and in tort for engaging in cloud seeding during the storm that flooded Lutherglen. Appellant sought damages under each count for loss of use of Lutherglen. * * *

We reject appellee's suggestion that, regardless of the state court's treatment of the question, we must independently evaluate the adequacy of the complaint and resolve the takings claim on the merits before we can reach the remedial question. However "cryptic" — to use appellee's description — the allegations with respect to the taking were, the California courts deemed them sufficient to present the issue. We accordingly have no occasion to decide whether the ordinance at issue actually denied appellant all use of its property or whether the county might avoid the conclusion that a compensable taking had occurred by establishing that the denial of all use was insulated as a part of the State's authority to enact safety regulations. . . . These questions, of course, remain open for decision on the remand we direct today. We now turn to the question whether the Just Compensation Clause requires the government to pay for "temporary" regulatory takings.

II.

Consideration of the compensation question must begin with direct reference to the language of the Fifth Amendment, which provides in relevant part that "private property [shall not] be taken for public use, without just compensation." As its language indicates, and as the Court has frequently noted, this provision does not prohibit the taking of private property, but instead places a condition on the exercise of that power. . . . This basic understanding of the Amendment makes clear that it is designed not to limit the governmental interference with property rights *per se*, but rather to secure *compensation* in the event of otherwise proper interference amounting to a taking. Thus, government action that works a taking of property rights necessarily implicates the "constitutional obligation to pay just compensation." *Armstrong v. United States*, 364 U.S. 40, 49 (1960).

We have recognized that a landowner is entitled to bring an action in inverse condemnation as a result of " 'the self-executing character of the constitutional provision with respect to compensation. . . .' " *United States v. Clarke*, 445 U.S. 253, 257 (1980), quoting 6 P. Nichols, Eminent Domain § 25.41 (3d rev. ed. 1972). As noted in JUSTICE BRENNAN's dissent in *San Diego Gas & Electric Co.*, 450 U.S., at 654–655, it has been established at least since *Jacobs v. United States*, 290 U.S. 13 (1933), that claims for just compensation are grounded in the Constitution itself:

> "The suits were based on the right to recover just compensation for property taken by the United States for public use in the exercise of its power of eminent domain. *That right was guaranteed by the Constitution.* The fact that condemnation proceedings were not instituted and that the right was asserted in suits by the owners did not change the essential nature of the claim. The form of the remedy did not qualify the right. It rested upon the Fifth Amendment. Statutory recognition was not necessary. A promise to pay was not necessary. Such a promise was implied because of the duty to pay imposed by the Amendment. *The suits were thus founded upon the Constitution of the United States.*" *Id.*, at 16. (Emphasis added.)

Jacobs, moreover, does not stand alone, for the Court has frequently repeated the view that, in the event of a taking, the compensation remedy is required by the Constitution. . . .

The Court has recognized in more than one case that the government may elect to abandon its intrusion or discontinue regulations. See, e.g., *Kirby Forest Industries, Inc. v. United States*, [467 U.S. 1 (1984)]; *United States v. Dow*, 357 U.S. 17, 26 (1958). Similarly, a governmental body may acquiesce in a judicial declaration that one of its ordinances has effected an unconstitutional taking of property; the landowner has no right under the Just Compensation Clause to insist that a "temporary" taking be deemed a permanent taking. But we have not resolved whether abandonment by the government requires payment of compensation for the period of time during which regulations deny a landowner all use of his land.

In considering this question, we find substantial guidance in cases where the government has only temporarily exercised its right to use private property. In *United States v. Dow, supra*, at 26, though rejecting a claim that the Government may not abandon condemnation proceedings, the Court observed that abandonment "results in an alteration in the property interest taken — from [one of] full ownership to one of temporary use and occupation. . . . In such cases compensation would be measured by the principles normally governing the taking of a right to use property temporarily. . . ." Each of the cases cited by the *Dow* Court involved appropriation of private property by the United States for use during World War II. Though the takings were in fact "temporary," see *United States v. Petty Motor Co.*, 327 U.S. 372, at 375 (1946), there was no question that compensation would be required for the Government's interference with the use of the property; the Court was concerned in each case with determining the proper measure of the monetary relief to which the property holders were entitled. . . .

These cases reflect the fact that "temporary" takings which, as here, deny a landowner all use of his property, are not different in kind from permanent takings, for which the Constitution clearly requires compensation. Cf. *San Diego Gas & Electric Co.*, 450 U.S., at 657 (BRENNAN, J., dissenting) ("Nothing in the Just Compensation Clause suggests that 'takings' must be permanent and irrevocable"). It is axiomatic that the Fifth Amendment's just compensation provision is "designed to bar Government from forcing some people alone to bear public burdens which, in all fairness and justice, should be borne by the public as a whole." . . . In the present case the interim ordinance was adopted by the County of Los Angeles in January 1979, and became effective immediately. Appellant filed suit within a month after the effective date of the ordinance and yet when the California Supreme Court denied a hearing in the case on October 17, 1985, the merits of appellant's claim had yet to be determined. The United States has been required to pay compensation for leasehold interests of shorter duration than this. The value of a leasehold interest in property for a period of years may be substantial, and the burden on the property owner in extinguishing such an interest for a period of years may be great indeed. See, e.g., *United States v. General Motors, supra.* Where this burden results from governmental action that amounted to a taking, the Just Compensation Clause of the Fifth Amendment requires that the government pay the landowner for the value of the use of the land during this period. Cf. *United States v. Causby*, 328 U.S. 256, at 261 ("It is the owner's loss, not the taker's gain, which is the measure of the value of the property taken"). Invalidation of the ordinance or its successor ordinance after this period of time, though converting the taking into a "temporary" one, is not a sufficient remedy to meet the demands of the Just Compensation Clause.

Appellee argues that requiring compensation for denial of all use of land prior to invalidation is inconsistent with this Court's decisions in *Danforth v. United States*, 308 U.S. 271 (1939), and *Agins v. Tiburon*, 447 U.S. 255 (1980). In *Danforth*, the landowner contended that the "taking" of his property had occurred prior to the institution of condemnation proceedings, by reason of the enactment of the Flood Control Act itself. He claimed that the passage of that Act had diminished the value of his property because the plan embodied in the Act required condemnation of a flowage easement across his property. The Court held that in the context of condemnation proceedings a taking does not occur until compensation is determined and paid, and went on to say that "[a] reduction or increase in the value of property may occur by reason of legislation for or the beginning or completion of a project," but "[s]uch changes in value are incidents of ownership. They cannot be considered as a 'taking' in the constitutional sense." *Danforth, supra*, at 285. *Agins* likewise rejected a claim that the city's preliminary activities constituted a taking, saying that "[m]ere fluctuations in value during the process of governmental decision making, absent extraordinary delay, are 'incidents of ownership.' "

But these cases merely stand for the unexceptional proposition that the valuation of property which has been taken must be calculated as of the time of the taking, and that depreciation in value of the property by reason of preliminary activity is not chargeable to the government. Thus, in *Agins*, we concluded that the preliminary activity did not work a taking. It would require a considerable extension of these decisions to say that no compensable regulatory taking may occur until a challenged ordinance has ultimately been held invalid.

Nothing we say today is intended to abrogate the principle that the decision to exercise the power of eminent domain is a legislative function " 'for Congress and Congress alone to determine.' " *Hawaii Housing Authority v. Midkiff*, 467 U.S. 229, 240 (1984), quoting *Berman v. Parker*, 348 U.S. 26, 33 (1954). Once a court determines that a taking has occurred, the government retains the whole range of options already available — amendment of the regulation, withdrawal of the invalidated regulation, or exercise of eminent domain. Thus we do not, as the Solicitor General suggests, "permit a court, at the behest of a private person, to require the . . . Government to exercise the power of eminent domain. . . ." Brief for United States as *Amicus Curiae* 22. We merely hold that where the government's activities have already worked a taking of all use of property, no subsequent action by the government can relieve it of the duty to provide compensation for the period during which the taking was effective.

We also point out that the allegation of the complaint which we treat as true for purposes of our decision was that the ordinance in question denied appellant all use of its property. We limit our holding to the facts presented, and of course do not deal with the quite different questions that would arise in the case of normal delays in obtaining building permits, changes in zoning ordinances, variances, and the like which are not before us. We realize that even our present holding will undoubtedly lessen to some extent the freedom and flexibility of land-use planners and governing bodies of municipal corporations when enacting land-use regulations. But such consequences necessarily flow from any decision upholding a claim of constitutional right; many of the provisions of the Constitution are designed to limit the flexibility and freedom of governmental authorities, and the Just Compensation Clause of the Fifth Amendment is one of them. As Justice Holmes aptly noted more than 50 years ago, "a strong public desire to improve the public condition is not enough to warrant achieving the desire by a shorter cut than the constitutional way of paying for the change." *Pennsylvania Coal Co. v. Mahon*, 260 U.S., at 416.

Here we must assume that the Los Angeles County ordinance has denied appellant all use of its property for a considerable period of years, and we hold that invalidation of the ordinance without payment of fair value for the use of the property during this period of time would be a constitutionally insufficient remedy. The judgment of the California Court of Appeal is therefore reversed, and the case is remanded for further proceedings not inconsistent with this opinion.

Justice Stevens, dissenting.

One thing is certain. The Court's decision today will generate a great deal of litigation. Most of it, I believe, will be unproductive. But the mere duty to defend the actions that today's decision will spawn will undoubtedly have a significant adverse impact on the land-use regulatory process. The Court has reached out to address an issue not actually presented in this case, and has then answered that self-imposed question in a superficial and, I believe, dangerous way.

Four flaws in the Court's analysis merit special comment. First, the Court unnecessarily and imprudently assumes that appellant's complaint alleges an unconstitutional taking of Lutherglen. Second, the Court distorts our precedents in the area of regulatory takings when it concludes that all ordinances which would constitute takings if allowed to remain in effect permanently, necessarily also constitute takings if they are in effect for only a limited period of time. Third, the Court incorrectly assumes that the California Supreme Court has already decided that it will never allow a state court to grant monetary relief for a temporary regulatory taking, and then uses that conclusion to reverse a judgment which is correct under the Court's own theories. Finally, the Court errs in concluding that it is the Takings Clause, rather than the Due Process Clause, which is the primary constraint on the use of unfair and dilatory procedures in the land-use area. . . .

NOTES

1.   On remand, the California Court of Appeal held that the landowner had not proven a regulatory taking. The court first held that the ordinance had not denied the owner all use of its land. Although the owner could not rebuild damaged structures, it could continue to use undamaged buildings and the grounds. Second, the court held that the ordinance substantially advanced the public interest in preventing death and injury. Finally, the court determined that the ordinance was reasonable in its purpose, duration, and scope. It imposed only a moratorium for a reasonable period of time while the government assessed the situation and determined the best methods for dealing with it. *First English Evangelical Lutheran Church v. County of Los Angeles*, 258 Cal. Rptr. 893 (Cal. Ct. App. 1989), *cert. denied*, 493 U.S. 1056 (1990). See also *Woodbury Place Partners v. City of Woodbury*, 492 N.W.2d 258 (Minn. Ct. App. 1992) (two-year development moratorium during traffic flow study did not constitute a taking although it denied all economically viable use of the plaintiff's land during that period).

2.   What is the proper measure of just compensation for a temporary taking? In *First English*, the U.S. Supreme Court stated that the government must pay the owner "for the value of the use of the land" during the period of the regulatory taking. This statement, as well as the context in which it was made, indicates that the government may be liable for the land's fair rental value, at least when the owner has been deprived of all use of the land during the temporary taking. In the absence of any clearer statement concerning the proper measure of just compensation, particularly when the owner has not been deprived of all use, lower courts have devised a variety of approaches in determining compensation for a temporary taking. See, e.g., *Wheeler v. City of Pleasant Grove*, 896 F.2d 1347, 1351 (11th Cir.

1990) (city's revocation of building permit; landowner entitled to market rate return during the temporary taking on the difference between the land's fair market value with and without the permit revocation); *Nemmers v. City of Dubuque*, 764 F.2d 502 (8th Cir. 1985) (court invalidated city's rezoning of plaintiff's land from industrial to residential; plaintiff's damages equaled fifteen percent rate of return on difference between land's value when zoned industrial and when zoned residential); *Corrigan v. City of Scottsdale*, 720 P.2d 513 (Ariz. 1986) (owner's land temporarily placed in conservation district that prohibited any building; owner entitled to actual damages measured by (1) rental return, (2) option price, (3) interest on lost profit, (4) before/after valuation, or (5) benefit to the government); *Whitehead Oil Co. v. City of Lincoln*, 515 N.W.2d 401 (Neb. 1994) (city's wrongful denial of special use permit caused damages equal to the property's diminished rental value); *Kula v. Prososki*, 424 N.W.2d 117 (Neb. 1988) (crops damaged by runoff from county road before county constructed culverts; damages awarded for decrease in crop yield).

II.   LAND USE CONTROLS

A.   Zoning Actions

This section of the book examines government controls on the use of land through zoning and other forms of land use regulation. Although the common law method of land use control, nuisance law, has existed since at least the twelfth century, modern statutory land use controls did not begin until the early part of the twentieth century. As cities grew and became more crowded, nuisance law was inadequate to deal with the myriad of land use conflicts that developed. Modern land use law is designed to deal more systematically with conflicting land uses. While nuisances normally are addressed on a case-by-case basis and usually only after a conflict has developed, modern land use regulation is designed to segregate incompatible uses to provide more harmonious land use distribution, thereby preventing many problems from arising.

Land use regulation is a power that the states retained under the federal Constitution. Because it is a state power, a unit of local government, such as a city or a county, can exercise it only if the state has delegated that power and only in accordance with the terms of the delegated authority. Today, every state has delegated the power to zone to cities, and most states also have delegated the power to counties. Pursuant to this delegated authority, every major city in this country, except Houston, has enacted zoning laws.

Although modern land use regulation began with zoning, it since has expanded to include a variety of laws affecting the right to use land. For example, many environmental laws restrict land use to prevent pollution, to protect wildlife and its habitat, and to preserve scenic areas. Similarly, many jurisdictions have enacted historic preservation laws and other forms of aesthetic regulation, such as design controls on new buildings.

These types of land use restrictions are designed not just to protect the rights of private property owners from offensive uses of neighboring lands but also to preserve lands and buildings that provide a benefit to the community as a whole, such as historic buildings. However, because our history and law reflect a strong concern for the protection of private property rights, these laws often raise fundamental questions about the rights of the individual landowner versus the rights of the community. Thus, land use regulation has been a fertile area for philosophical and legal differences, particularly because society's perspectives concerning the role of property are in a state of ferment.

The Takings Clause has been central in challenges to government restrictions on land use. Equal protection and procedural due process claims also are asserted with some regularity against land use regulations. You may be surprised to learn that substantive due process also plays an important role in challenges to land use regulations. Although substantive due process has atrophied to the point of virtual extinction in most areas of law, it is alive and well in this context.

As you read the following materials, focus on the exact challenge being made to the law's legality. Concentrate on the source of the legal challenge and on whether the challenge is facial or as-applied. But also examine the philosophical underpinnings of the cases — the value placed on individual property rights versus the community good. Pay attention to the ways in which our national values have changed over time, and consider whether the change is positive or negative for our development as a society.

1. Zoning

In 1916, New York City enacted the first comprehensive zoning ordinance in this country. During the next decade, more than five hundred municipalities enacted zoning ordinances, but zoning's constitutionality was disputed until the U.S. Supreme Court's decision in *Village of Euclid v. Ambler Realty Co.*

VILLAGE OF EUCLID v. AMBLER REALTY CO.
272 U.S. 365 (1926)

Mr. Justice Sutherland delivered the opinion of the Court.

The Village of Euclid is an Ohio municipal corporation. It adjoins and practically is a suburb of the City of Cleveland. Its estimated population is between 5,000 and 10,000, and its area from twelve to fourteen square miles, the greater part of which is farm lands or unimproved acreage. It lies, roughly, in the form of a parallelogram measuring approximately three and one-half miles each way. East and west it is traversed by three principal highways: Euclid Avenue, through the southerly border, St. Clair Avenue, through the central portion, and Lake Shore Boulevard, through the northerly border, in close proximity to the shore of Lake Erie. The Nickel Plate railroad lies from 1,500 to 1,800 feet north of Euclid Avenue, and the Lake Shore railroad 1,600 feet farther to the north. The three highways and the two railroads are substantially parallel.

Appellee is the owner of a tract of land containing 68 acres, situated in the westerly end of the village, abutting on Euclid Avenue to the south and the Nickel Plate railroad to the north. Adjoining this tract, both on the east and on the west, there have been laid out restricted residential plats upon which residences have been erected.

On November 13, 1922, an ordinance was adopted by the Village Council, establishing a comprehensive zoning plan for regulating and restricting the location of trades, industries, apartment houses, two-family houses, single family houses, etc., the lot area to be built upon, the size and height of buildings, etc.

The entire area of the village is divided by the ordinance into six classes of use districts, denominated U-1 to U-6, inclusive; three classes of height districts, denominated H-1 to H-3, inclusive; and four classes of area districts, denominated A-1 to A-4, inclusive. The use districts are classified in respect of the buildings which may be erected within their respective limits, as follows: U-1 is restricted to single family dwellings, public parks, water towers and reservoirs, suburban and interurban electric railway passenger stations and rights of way, and farming, non-commercial greenhouse nurseries, and truck gardening; U-2 is extended to include two-family dwellings; U-3 is further extended to include apartment houses, hotels, churches, schools, public libraries, museums, private clubs, community center buildings, hospitals, sanitariums, public playgrounds, and recreation buildings, and a city hall and courthouse; U-4 is further extended to include banks, offices, studios, telephone exchanges, fire and police stations, restaurants, theaters and moving picture shows, retail stores and shops, sales offices, sample rooms, wholesale stores for hardware, drugs, and groceries, stations for gasoline and oil (not exceeding 1,000 gallons storage) and for ice delivery, skating rinks and dance halls, electric substations, job and newspaper printing, public garages for motor vehicles, stables and wagon sheds (not exceeding five horses, wagons or motor trucks), and distributing stations for central store and commercial enterprises; U-5 is further extended to include billboards and advertising signs (if permitted), warehouses, ice and ice cream manufacturing and cold storage plants, bottling works, milk bottling and central distribution stations, laundries, carpet cleaning, dry cleaning, and dyeing establishments, blacksmith, horseshoeing, wagon and motor vehicle repair shops, freight stations, street car barns, stables and wagon sheds (for more than five horses, wagons or motor trucks), and wholesale produce markets and salesrooms; U-6 is further extended to include plants for sewage disposal and for producing gas, garbage and refuse incineration, scrap iron, junk, scrap paper and rag storage, aviation fields, cemeteries, crematories, penal and correctional institutions, insane and feeble-minded institutions, storage of oil and gasoline (not to exceed 25,000 gallons), and manufacturing and industrial operations of any kind other than, and any public utility not included in, a class U-1, U-2, U-3, U-4, or U-5 use. There is a seventh class of uses which is prohibited altogether.

Class U-1 is the only district in which buildings are restricted to those enumerated. In the other classes the uses are cumulative-that is to say, uses in class U-2 include those enumerated in the preceding class U-1; class U-3 includes uses enumerated in the preceding classes, U-2 and U-1; and so on. In addition to the enumerated uses, the ordinance provides for accessory uses, that is, for uses customarily incident to the principal use, such as private garages. Many regulations are provided in respect of such accessory uses.

The height districts are classified as follows: In class H-1, buildings are limited to a height of two and one-half stories or thirty-five feet; in class H-2, to four stories or fifty feet; in class H-3, to eighty feet. To all of these, certain exceptions are made, as in the case of church spires, water tanks, etc.

The classification of area districts is: In A-1 districts, dwellings or apartment houses to accommodate more than one family must have at least 5,000 square feet for interior lots and at least 4,000 square feet for corner lots; in A-2 districts, the area must be at least 2,500 square feet for interior lots, and 2,000 square feet for corner lots; in A-3 districts, the limits are 1,250 and 1,000 square feet, respectively; in A-4 districts, the limits are 900 and 700 square feet, respectively. The ordinance contains, in great variety and detail, provisions in respect of width of lots, front, side, and rear yards, and other matters, including restrictions and regulations as to the use of billboards, signboards, and advertising signs.

A single family dwelling consists of a basement and not less than three rooms and a bathroom. A two-family dwelling consists of a basement and not less than four living rooms and a bathroom for each family; and is further described as a detached dwelling for the occupation of two families, one having its principal living rooms on the first floor and the other on the second floor.

Appellee's tract of land comes under U-2, U-3 and U-6. The first strip of 620 feet immediately north of Euclid Avenue falls in class U-2, the next 130 feet to the north, in U-3, and the remainder in U-6. The uses of the first 620 feet, therefore, do not include apartment houses, hotels, churches, schools, or other public and semipublic buildings, or other uses enumerated in respect of U-3 to U-6, inclusive. The uses of the next 130 feet include all of these, but exclude industries, theaters, banks, shops, and the various other uses set forth in respect of U-4 to U-6, inclusive.

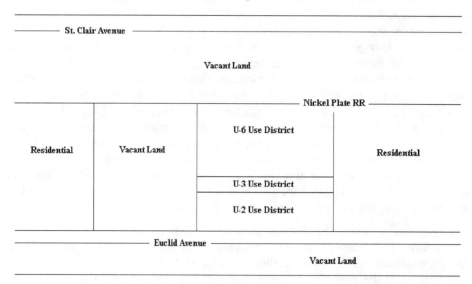

Annexed to the ordinance, and made a part of it, is a zone map, showing the location and limits of the various use, height, and area districts, from which it appears that the three classes overlap one another; that is to say, for example, both

U-5 and U-6 use districts are in A-4 area districts, but the former is in H-2 and the latter in H-3 height districts. The plan is a complicated one and can be better understood by an inspection of the map, though it does not seem necessary to reproduce it for present purposes.

The lands lying between the two railroads for the entire length of the village area and extending some distance on either side to the north and south, having an average width of about 1,600 feet, are left open, with slight exceptions, for industrial and all other uses. This includes the larger part of appellee's tract. Approximately one-sixth of the area of the entire village is included in U-5 and U-6 use districts. That part of the village lying south of Euclid Avenue is principally in U-1 districts. The lands lying north of Euclid Avenue and bordering on the long strip just described are included in U-1, U-2, U-3, and U-4 districts, principally in U-2.

The enforcement of the ordinance is entrusted to the inspector of buildings, under rules and regulations of the board of zoning appeals. Meetings of the board are public, and minutes of its proceedings are kept. It is authorized to adopt rules and regulations to carry into effect provisions of the ordinance. Decisions of the inspector of buildings may be appealed to the board by any person claiming to be adversely affected by any such decision. The board is given power in specific cases of practical difficulty or unnecessary hardship to interpret the ordinance in harmony with its general purpose and intent, so that the public health, safety and general welfare may be secure and substantial justice done. Penalties are prescribed for violations, and it is provided that the various provisions are to be regarded as independent and the holding of any provision to be unconstitutional, void or ineffective shall not affect any of the others.

The ordinance is assailed on the grounds that it is in derogation of § 1 of the Fourteenth Amendment to the Federal Constitution in that it deprives appellee of liberty and property without due process of law and denies it the equal protection of the law, and that it offends against certain provisions of the Constitution of the State of Ohio. The prayer of the bill is for an injunction restraining the enforcement of the ordinance and all attempts to impose or maintain as to appellee's property any of the restrictions, limitations or conditions. The court below held the ordinance to be unconstitutional and void, and enjoined its enforcement.

Before proceeding to a consideration of the case, it is necessary to determine the scope of the inquiry. The bill alleges that the tract of land in question is vacant and has been held for years for the purpose of selling and developing it for industrial uses, for which it is especially adapted, being immediately in the path of progressive industrial development; that for such uses it has a market value of about $10,000 per acre, but if the use be limited to residential purposes the market value is not in excess of $2,500 per acre; that the first 200 feet of the parcel back from Euclid Avenue, if unrestricted in respect of use, has a value of $150 per front foot, but if limited to residential uses, and ordinary mercantile business be excluded therefrom, its value is not in excess of $50 per front foot.

It is specifically averred that the ordinance attempts to restrict and control the lawful uses of appellee's land, so as to confiscate and destroy a great part of its value; that it is being enforced in accordance with its terms; that prospective buyers of land for industrial, commercial, and residential uses in the metropolitan district of Cleveland are deterred from buying any part of this land because of the existence of the ordinance and the necessity thereby entailed of conducting burdensome and expensive litigation in order to vindicate the right to use the land for lawful and legitimate purposes; that the ordinance constitutes a cloud upon the land, reduces and destroys its value, and has the effect of diverting the normal industrial, commercial, and residential development thereof to other and less favorable locations.

The record goes no farther than to show, as the lower court found, that the normal and reasonably to be expected use and development of that part of appellee's land adjoining Euclid Avenue is for general trade and commercial purposes, particularly retail stores and like establishments, and that the normal and reasonably to be expected use and development of the residue of the land is for industrial and trade purposes. Whatever injury is inflicted by the mere existence and threatened enforcement of the ordinance is due to restrictions in respect of these and similar uses, to which perhaps should be added — if not included in the foregoing — restrictions in respect of apartment houses. Specifically there is nothing in the record to suggest that any damage results from the presence in the ordinance of those restrictions relating to churches, schools, libraries, and other public and semipublic buildings. It is neither alleged nor proved that there is or may be a demand for any part of appellee's land for any of the last-named uses, and we cannot assume the existence of facts which would justify an injunction upon this record in respect to this class of restrictions. For present purposes the provisions of the ordinance in respect of these uses may therefore be put aside as unnecessary to be considered. It is also unnecessary to consider the effect of the restrictions in respect of U-1 districts, since none of appellee's land falls within that class.

We proceed, then, to a consideration of those provisions of the ordinance to which the case as it is made relates, first disposing of a preliminary matter.

A motion was made in the court below to dismiss the bill on the ground that, because complainant [appellee] had made no effort to obtain a building permit or apply to the zoning board of appeals for relief, as it might have done under the terms of the ordinance, the suit was premature. The motion was properly overruled, the effect of the allegations of the bill is that the ordinance of its own force operates greatly to reduce the value of appellee's lands and destroy their marketability for industrial, commercial and residential uses, and the attack is directed, not against any specific provision or provisions, but against the ordinance as an entirety. Assuming the premises, the existence and maintenance of the ordinance, in effect, constitutes a present invasion of appellee's property rights and a threat to continue it. Under these circumstances, the equitable jurisdiction is clear.

It is not necessary to set forth the provisions of the Ohio Constitution which are thought to be infringed. The question is the same under both Constitutions, namely, as stated by appellee: Is the ordinance invalid, in that it violates the constitutional protection "to the right of property in the appellee by attempted regulations under the guise of the police power, which are unreasonable and confiscatory?"

Building zone laws are of modern origin. They began in this country about twenty-five years ago. Until recent years, urban life was comparatively simple; but, with the great increase and concentration of population, problems have developed, and constantly are developing, which require, and will continue to require, additional restrictions in respect of the use and occupation of private lands in urban communities. Regulations, the wisdom, necessity, and validity of which, as applied to existing conditions, are so apparent that they are now uniformly sustained, a century ago, or even half a century ago, probably would have been rejected as arbitrary and oppressive. Such regulations are sustained, under the complex conditions of our day, for reasons analogous to those which justify traffic regulations, which, before the advent of automobiles and rapid transit street railways, would have been condemned as fatally arbitrary and unreasonable. And in this there is no inconsistency, for, while the meaning of constitutional guaranties never varies, the scope of their application must expand or contract to meet the new and different conditions which are constantly coming within the field of their operation. In a changing world it is impossible that it should be otherwise. But although a degree of elasticity is thus imparted, not to the *meaning*, but to the *application* of constitutional principles, statutes and ordinances, which, after giving due weight to the new conditions, are found clearly not to conform to the Constitution, of course, must fall.

The ordinance now under review, and all similar laws and regulations, must find their justification in some aspect of the police power, asserted for the public welfare. The line which in this field separates the legitimate from the illegitimate assumption of power is not capable of precise delimitation. It varies with circumstances and conditions. A regulatory zoning ordinance, which would be clearly valid as applied to the great cities, might be clearly invalid as applied to rural communities. In solving doubts, the maxim *sic utere tuo ut alienum non laedas*, which lies at the foundation of so much of the common law of nuisances, ordinarily will furnish a fairly helpful clew. And the law of nuisances, likewise, may be consulted, not for the purpose of controlling, but for the helpful aid of its analogies in the process of ascertaining the scope of, the power. Thus the question whether the power exists to forbid the erection of a building of a particular kind or for a particular use, like the question whether a particular thing is a nuisance, is to be determined, not by an abstract consideration of the building or of the thing considered apart, but by considering it in connection with the circumstances and the locality. *Sturgis v. Bridgeman*, L.R. 11 Ch. 852, 865. A nuisance may be merely a right thing in the wrong place, like a pig in the parlor instead of the barnyard. If the validity of the legislative classification for zoning purposes be fairly debatable, the legislative judgment must be allowed to control. *Radice v. New York*, 264 U.S. 292, 294.

There is no serious difference of opinion in respect of the validity of laws and regulations fixing the height of buildings within reasonable limits, the character of materials and methods of construction, and the adjoining area which must be left open, in order to minimize the danger of fire or collapse, the evils of overcrowding and the like, and excluding from residential sections offensive trades, industries and structures likely to create nuisances. . . .

Here, however, the exclusion is in general terms of all industrial establishments, and it may thereby happen that not only offensive or dangerous industries will be excluded, but those which are neither offensive nor dangerous will share the same fate. But this is no more than happens in respect of many practice-forbidding laws which this court has upheld, although drawn in general terms so as to include individual cases that may turn out to be innocuous in themselves. *Hebe Co. v. Shaw*, 248 U.S. 297, 303; *Pierce Oil Corp. v. City of Hope*, 248 U.S. 498, 500. The inclusion of a reasonable margin, to insure effective enforcement, will not put upon a law, otherwise valid, the stamp of invalidity. Such laws may also find their justification in the fact that, in some fields, the bad fades into the good by such insensible degrees that the two are not capable of being readily distinguished and separated in terms of legislation. In the light of these considerations, we are not prepared to say that the end in view was not sufficient to justify the general rule of the ordinance, although some industries of an innocent character might fall within the proscribed class. It cannot be said that the ordinance in this respect "passes the bounds of reason and assumes the character of a merely arbitrary fiat." *Purity Extract Co. v. Lynch*, 226 U.S. 192, 204. Moreover, the restrictive provisions of the ordinance in this particular may be sustained upon the principles applicable to the broader exclusion from residential districts of all business and trade structures, presently to be discussed.

It is said that the Village of Euclid is a mere suburb of the City of Cleveland; that the industrial development of that city has now reached and in some degree extended into the village, and in the obvious course of things will soon absorb the entire area for industrial enterprises; that the effect of the ordinance is to divert this natural development elsewhere, with the consequent loss of increased values to the owners of the lands within the village borders. But the village, though physically a suburb of Cleveland, is politically a separate municipality, with powers of its own and authority to govern itself as it sees fit, within the limits of the organic law of its creation and the State and Federal Constitutions. Its governing authorities, presumably representing a majority of its inhabitants and voicing their will, have determined, not that industrial development shall cease at its boundaries, but that the course of such development shall proceed within definitely fixed lines. If it be a proper exercise of the police power to relegate industrial establishments to localities separated from residential sections, it is not easy to find a sufficient reason for denying the power because the effect of its exercise is to divert an industrial flow from the course which it would follow, to the injury of the residential public, if left alone, to another course where such injury will be obviated. It is not meant by this, however, to exclude the possibility of cases where the general public interest would so far outweigh the interest of the municipality that the municipality would not be allowed to stand in the way.

We find no difficulty in sustaining restrictions of the kind thus far reviewed. The serious question in the case arises over the provisions of the ordinance excluding from residential districts apartment houses, business houses, retail stores and shops, and other like establishments. This question involves the validity of what is really the crux of the more recent zoning legislation, namely, the creation and maintenance of residential districts, from which business and trade of every sort, including hotels and apartment houses, are excluded. Upon that question this court has not thus far spoken. The decisions of the state courts are numerous and conflicting; but those which broadly sustain the power greatly outnumber those which deny it altogether or narrowly limit it, and it is very apparent that there is a constantly increasing tendency in the direction of the broader view. . . .

As evidence of the decided trend toward the broader view, it is significant that in some instances the state courts in later decisions have reversed their former decisions holding the other way. . . .

The decisions [following the broader view] agree that the exclusion of buildings devoted to business, trade, etc., from residential districts, bears a rational relation to the health and safety of the community. Some of the grounds for this conclusion are promotion of the health and security from injury of children and others by separating dwelling houses from territory devoted to trade and industry; suppression and prevention of disorder; facilitating the extinguishment of fires, and the enforcement of street traffic regulations and other general welfare ordinances; aiding the health and safety of the community, by excluding from residential areas the confusion and danger of fire, contagion, and disorder, which in greater or less degree attach to the location of stores, shops, and factories. Another ground is that the construction and repair of streets may be rendered easier and less expensive, by confining the greater part of the heavy traffic to the streets where business is carried on. . . .

The matter of zoning has received much attention at the hands of commissions and experts, and the results of their investigations have been set forth in comprehensive reports. These reports which bear every evidence of painstaking consideration, concur in the view that the segregation of residential, business and industrial buildings will make it easier to provide fire apparatus suitable for the character and intensity of the development in each section; that it will increase the safety and security of home life, greatly tend to prevent street accidents, especially to children, by reducing the traffic and resulting confusion in residential sections, decrease noise and other conditions which produce or intensify nervous disorders, preserve a more favorable environment in which to rear children, etc. With particular reference to apartment houses, it is pointed out that the development of detached house sections is greatly retarded by the coming of apartment houses, which has sometimes resulted in destroying the entire section for private house purposes; that in such sections very often the apartment house is a mere parasite, constructed in order to take advantage of the open spaces and attractive surroundings created by the residential character of the district. Moreover, the coming of one apartment house is followed by others, interfering by their height and bulk with the free circulation of air and monopolizing the rays of the sun which otherwise would fall upon the smaller homes, and bringing, as their necessary accompaniments, the disturbing noises incident to increased traffic and business, and the occupation, by means of moving and parked automobiles, of larger portions of the streets, thus detracting from their safety and depriving children of the privilege of quiet and open spaces for play, enjoyed by those in more favored localities — until, finally, the residential character of the neighborhood and its desirability as a place of detached residences are utterly destroyed. Under these circumstances, apartment houses, which in a different environment would be not only entirely unobjectionable but highly desirable, come very near to being nuisances.

If these reasons, thus summarized, do not demonstrate the wisdom or sound policy in all respects of those restrictions which we have indicated as pertinent to the inquiry, at least, the reasons are sufficiently cogent to preclude us from saying, as it must be said before the ordinance can be declared unconstitutional, that such provisions are clearly arbitrary and unreasonable, having no substantial relation to the public health, safety, morals, or general welfare. . . .

It is true that when, if ever, the provisions set forth in the ordinance in tedious and minute detail, come to be concretely applied to particular premises, including those of the appellee, or to particular conditions, or to be considered in connection with specific complaints, some of them, or even many of them, may be found to be clearly arbitrary and unreasonable. But where the equitable remedy of injunction is sought, as it is here, not upon the ground of a present infringement or denial of a specific right, or of a particular injury in process of actual execution, but upon the broad ground that the mere existence and threatened enforcement of the ordinance, by materially and adversely affecting values and curtailing the opportunities of the market, constitute a present and irreparable injury, the court will not scrutinize its provisions, sentence by sentence, to ascertain by a process of piecemeal dissection whether there may be, here and there, provisions of a minor character, or relating to matters of administration, or not shown to contribute to the injury complained of, which, if attacked separately, might not withstand the test of constitutionality. In respect of such provisions, of which specific complaint is not made, it cannot be said that the landowner has suffered or is threatened with an injury which entitles him to challenge their constitutionality. . . .

And this is in accordance with the traditional policy of this Court. In the realm of constitutional law, especially, this Court has perceived the embarrassment which is likely to result from an attempt to formulate rules or decide questions beyond the necessities of the immediate issue. It has preferred to follow the method of a gradual approach to the general by a systematically guarded application and extension of constitutional principles to particular cases as they arise, rather than by out of hand attempts to establish general rules to which future cases must be fitted. This process applies with peculiar force to the solution of questions arising under the due process clause of the Constitution as applied to the exercise of the flexible powers of police, with which we are here concerned.

Decree reversed.

NOTES

1.   The zoning scheme described in *Euclid* is fairly typical. The term "Euclidian zoning," which is based on this case, generally refers to the division of a municipality or county into different use districts. The different districts normally are based on a hierarchy of land uses with single-family homes at the apex. Modern zoning ordinances sometimes depart from the plan described in *Euclid* by eliminating its cumulative aspect. Rather than permitting residential uses in industrial zones, for example, modern zoning ordinances may create exclusive use districts; residences can be built only in residential zones, thereby exclusively preserving industrial and commercial zones for that type of development. The exclusion of residential uses from these zones is intended to prevent inflation in land values in nonresidential zones and to create greater efficiency in providing government services.

2.   On what legal basis did the plaintiff in *Euclid* challenge the zoning ordinance? Is this a facial challenge or an as-applied challenge?

3. Since *Euclid*, courts routinely have upheld zoning ordinances that segregate residential uses from commercial and industrial uses. Courts also usually uphold ordinances that segregate single-family residences from multifamily residences. However, many of the reasons given for separating single-family from multifamily residences apply equally to both. For example, apartment dwellers, as well as single-family residents, want safe places for their children to play, fresh air, and peace and quiet. In what ways can these goals (and the others identified in *Euclid*) be achieved without separating single-family and multifamily residences?

2.　Nonconforming Use

Although Euclidian zoning is based on the separation of different types of uses, complete separation rarely is achievable. When a city or county adopts or amends land use regulations, usually some existing uses will not conform to the regulations. For example, the owner may be operating a store in a newly-zoned residential area. An existing building may violate new height restrictions. These nonconforming uses usually are allowed to continue, though land use laws often include devices designed to hasten their demise. Note that the term "nonconforming use" applies to both nonconforming uses of property and to nonconforming structures.

VILLAGE OF VALATIE v. SMITH
632 N.E.2d 1264 (N.Y. 1994)

Simons, J.

This appeal challenges the facial validity of chapter 85 of the Village Code of the Village of Valatie, a local law that terminates the nonconforming use of a mobile home upon the transfer of ownership of either the mobile home or the land upon which it sits. Defendant argues that it is unconstitutional for the Village to use a change in ownership as the termination date for a nonconforming use. We conclude, however, that defendant has failed to carry her burden of showing that the local law is unreasonable on its face. Accordingly, we modify the order of the Appellate Division by denying defendant's cross motion for summary judgment.

In 1968, the Village enacted chapter 85 to prohibit the placement of mobile homes outside mobile home parks. Under the law, any existing mobile home located outside a park which met certain health standards was allowed to remain as a nonconforming use until either ownership of the land or ownership of the mobile home changed. According to the Village, six mobile homes, including one owned by defendant's father, fell within this exception at the time the law was passed.

In 1989, defendant inherited the mobile home from her father and the Village instituted this action to enforce the law and have the unit removed. Both the Village and defendant moved before the Supreme Court for summary judgment. The court granted defendant's motion and denied the Village's. The court characterized defendant's mobile home as a lawful nonconforming use — i.e., a use that was legally in place at the time the municipality enacted legislation prohibiting the use. Reasoning that the right to continue a nonconforming use runs with the land, the court held that the portion of the ordinance setting termination at the transfer of ownership was unconstitutional. The Appellate Division affirmed. The Court acknowledged that a municipality had the authority to phase out a nonconforming use with an "amortization period," but it concluded that this particular law was unreasonable, and therefore unconstitutional, because the period of time allowed "bears no relationship to the use of the land or the investment in that use."

Preliminarily, it is important to note that the question presented is the facial validity of the local law. The Court is not called upon to decide whether the local law *as applied* so deprived defendant of the value of her property as to constitute a governmental taking under the Fifth Amendment. Nor does defendant challenge the power of a municipality to regulate land use, including the placement of mobile homes, as a valid exercise of the police power (see, e.g., *Mobile Home Owners Protective Assoc. v. Town of Chatham*, 33 A.D.2d 78, 305 N.Y.S.2d 334; see generally 1 Anderson, New York Zoning Law and Practice, ch. 15 [3d ed.]). Finally, there is no question that municipalities may enact laws reasonably limiting the duration of nonconforming uses. . . . [1] Thus, the narrow issue is whether the Village acted unreasonably by establishing an amortization period that uses the transfer of ownership as an end point.

The policy of allowing nonconforming uses to continue originated in concerns that the application of land use regulations to uses existing prior to the regulations' enactment might be construed as confiscatory and unconstitutional (4 Rathkopf, Zoning and Planning § 51.01[2][b], at 51–6 [Ziegler 4th ed.]). While it was initially assumed that nonconforming uses would disappear with time, just the opposite proved to be true in many instances, with the nonconforming use thriving in the absence of any new lawful competition (*Matter of Harbison v. City of Buffalo*, 4 N.Y.2d 553, 560, 176 N.Y.S.2d 598, 152 N.E.2d 42). In light of the problems presented by continuing nonconforming uses, this Court has characterized the law's allowance of such uses as a "grudging tolerance," and we have recognized the right of municipalities to take reasonable measures to eliminate them (see, *Matter of Pelham Esplanade v. Board of Trustees*, 77 N.Y.2d 66, 71, 563 N.Y.S.2d 759, 565 N.E.2d 508).

Most often, elimination has been effected by establishing amortization periods, at the conclusion of which the nonconforming use must end. As commentators have noted, the term "amortization period" is somewhat misleading (see, e.g., 4 Rath-kopf, Zoning and Planning § 51B.05[1], at 51B-44, n. 3 [Ziegler 4th ed.]). "Amortization" properly refers to a liquidation, but in this context the owner is not required to take any particular financial step. "Amortization period" simply designates a period of time granted to owners of nonconforming uses during which they may phase out their operations as they see fit and make other arrangements. . . . It is, in effect, a grace period, putting owners on fair notice of the law and giving them a fair opportunity to recoup their investment. . . . Though the amortization period is typically discussed in terms of protecting the owners' financial interests, it serves more generally to protect "an individual's interest in maintaining the present use"

---

[1] Though the difference between a nonconforming use and a nonconforming structure will at times be relevant (see, *Matter of Harbison v. City of Buffalo*, 4 N.Y.2d 553, 561–562, 176 N.Y.S.2d 598, 152 N.E.2d 42), our reasoning in this case applies equally whether the mobile home is characterized as a use or a structure.

of the property (*Modjeska Sign Studios v. Berle*, 43 N.Y.2d at 479, 402 N.Y.S.2d 359, 373 N.E.2d 255).

The validity of an amortization period depends on its reasonableness (*Matter of Harbison v. City of Buffalo*, 4 N.Y.2d 553, 562–563, 176 N.Y.S.2d 598, 152 N.E.2d 42). We have avoided any fixed formula for determining what constitutes a reasonable period. Instead, we have held that an amortization period is presumed valid, and the owner must carry the heavy burden of overcoming that presumption by demonstrating that the loss suffered is so substantial that it outweighs the public benefit to be gained by the exercise of the police power. . . . Using this approach, courts have declared valid a variety of amortization periods (see, 6 Rohan, Zoning and Land Use Controls § 41.04[2], at 41-158). Indeed, in some circumstances, no amortization period at all is required. . . . In other circumstances, the amortization period may vary in duration among the affected properties. . . . We have also held that an amortization period may validly come to an end at the occurrence of an event as unpredictable as the destruction of the nonconforming use by fire (see, *Matter of Pelham Esplanade v. Board of Trustees*, 77 N.Y.2d 66, 563 N.Y.S.2d 759, 565 N.E.2d 508).

Defendant here does not challenge the local law's constitutionality under our established balancing test for amortization periods — i.e., whether the individual loss outweighs the public benefit. Instead, the challenge is a more basic due process claim: that the means of eliminating nonconforming uses is not reasonably related to the Village's legitimate interest in land use planning. More particularly, defendant makes two arguments: first, that the length of an amortization period must be related either to land use objectives or to the financial recoupment needs of the owner and, second, that the local law violates the principle that zoning is to regulate land use rather than ownership (see, *Matter of Dexter v. Town Bd.*, 36 N.Y.2d 102, 365 N.Y.S.2d 506, 324 N.E.2d 870). Neither argument withstands analysis.

We have never required that the length of the amortization period be based on a municipality's land use objectives. To the contrary, the periods are routinely calculated to protect the rights of individual owners *at the temporary expense of* public land use objectives. Typically, the period of time allowed has been measured for reasonableness by considering whether the owners had adequate time to recoup their investment in the use. . . . Patently, such protection of an individual's interest is unrelated to land use objectives. Indeed, were land use objectives the only permissible criteria for scheduling amortization, the law would require immediate elimination of nonconforming uses in all instances. Instead, the setting of the amortization period involves balancing the interests of the individual and those of the public. Thus, the real issue here is whether it was irrational for the Village, in striking that balance, to consider a nonfinancial interest of the individual owners-specifically, the individual's interest in not being displaced involuntarily.

It is significant that the six properties involved here are residential. In our previous cases dealing with amortization, we have focused almost exclusively on commercial properties, where the owner's interest is easily reduced to financial considerations. The same may not be true for the owners of residential properties, especially in instances where the property is the primary residence of the owner. Simply being able to recoup one's financial investment may be a secondary concern to staying in a neighborhood or remaining on a particular piece of land. Indeed, when mobile homes are involved, there may actually be little or no financial loss, given that the owner often will be able to relocate the structure and sell the land for legal development. Here, rather than focusing solely on financial recoupment, the Village apparently took a broader view of "an individual's interest in maintaining the present use" of the property. . . . It enacted a law that allowed owners to keep their mobile homes in place until they decided to sell, even though they may have recouped their investment long ago. By doing so, it saved the owners from a forced relocation at the end of a predetermined amortization period set by the Village. Defendant has not demonstrated why such an approach is irrational or explained why a municipality should be barred constitutionally from considering the nonfinancial interests of the owners in setting an amortization schedule. Thus, on this motion for summary judgment and the present record, defendant has failed to overcome the presumption of the law's validity and prove, as she must, unconstitutionality beyond a reasonable doubt. . . .

Equally unavailing on this facial challenge is defendant's contention that the law might prevent some owners from recouping their investment. Defendant raises the hypothetical concern that in some circumstances owners might not have adequate time to recoup — for instance, if a sale took place shortly after the law's enactment. Whatever the validity of that concern, it is not relevant to this facial challenge to the law. Defendant has not claimed that she was so injured, and her argument must fall to the general principle that a litigant cannot sustain a facial challenge to a law when that law is constitutional in its application to that litigant. . . .

Defendant's second argument is premised on the "fundamental rule that zoning deals basically with land use and not with the person who owns or occupies it." In essence, the rule is a prohibition against *ad hominem* zoning decisions. In *Dexter*, for instance, a zoning change needed to allow a supermarket was to be effective only if a certain corporation developed the site. We voided the action on the ground that the identity of the site's owner was irrelevant to its suitability for a certain type of development. Likewise, variances to accommodate the personal physical needs of the occupants have been denied on the basis that such needs are unrelated to land use (see, *Matter of Fuhst v. Foley*, 45 N.Y.2d 441, 410 N.Y.S.2d 56, 382 N.E.2d 756). In the present case, defendant claims that the Village's amortization scheme is similarly personal in that the right to the nonconforming use is enjoyed only by those who owned the property in 1968 and cannot be transferred.

Defendant misconstrues the nature of the prohibition against *ad hominem* zoning. The hallmark of cases like *Dexter* and *Fuhst* (*supra*) is that an identifiable individual is singled out for special treatment in land use regulation. No such individualized treatment is involved in the present case. All similarly situated owners are treated identically. The same is true for all prospective buyers. The only preferential treatment identified by defendant is that the owner in 1968 has rights that no future owner will enjoy. But the law has long recognized the special status of those who have a preexisting use at the time land controls are adopted. Indeed, the allowance of a nonconforming use in the first instance is based on that recognition. To the extent that defendant's argument is an attack on special treatment for the owners of nonconforming uses it flies in the face of established law.

In fact, what defendant is actually arguing is that the Village should not be allowed to infringe on an owner's ability to transfer the right to continue a nonconforming use (see, *O'Connor v. City of Moscow*, 69 Idaho 37, 202 P.2d 401). It is true that, in the absence of amortization legislation, the right to continue a nonconforming use runs with the land. . . . However, once a valid amortization scheme is enacted, the right ends at the termination of the amortization period. As a practical matter, that means the owner of record during the amortization period will enjoy a right that cannot be transferred to a subsequent owner once the period passes. In such circumstances, the law is not rendered invalid because the original owner no longer has a right to transfer or because the original owner and subsequent owners have received disparate treatment under the land use regulations.

Here, of course, the absence of the right at the time of transfer is not left to the happenstance of when the owner decides to sell but is an explicit part of the legislative plan. But that difference does not change the test for the validity of an amortization period. The test remains whether the period unreasonably inflicts a substantial loss on the owner or fails to comport to the reasonableness required by due process. Put simply, there is no independent requirement that the right to continue the nonconforming use be available for transfer at a given time. That is true whether the right to continue the nonconforming use is terminated by the passage of time, destruction of the use, abandonment or, as here, transfer of ownership. Thus, the mere fact that the right cannot be transferred or that later owners are treated disparately from the original owner is insufficient to sustain defendant's facial challenge to the ordinance.

Nor can we subscribe to the Appellate Division's theory that the amortization period here is unreasonable because it may be too long. In the Appellate Division's view, an open-ended amortization schedule does not reasonably advance land use objectives. The Appellate Division noted that if a corporation owned one of the mobile homes here, the amortization period would be limitless in theory. The Village answers by stating that all six mobile homes were owned by individuals, and thus amortization would end, at the latest, upon their deaths. Because the class of nonconforming users became closed at the law's enactment and will never contain more than those six, the concern about corporate ownership is unfounded, the Village argues. At this point in the litigation, defendant has not demonstrated that the Village is factually in error as to the ownership of the six units.

Of greater concern to us, the Appellate Division's rationale would seriously undermine the law of nonconforming uses. Amortization periods are the exceptions; in the absence of such schemes, owners of nonconforming uses are free to continue the uses indefinitely and transfer them to successor owners. Were the Appellate Division's rationale accepted, amortization periods would be *required* to avoid the problem of indefinite continuation of nonconforming uses. Amortization periods have never been mandatory as a matter of constitutional law, and consequently we must reject the Appellate Division's reasoning.

Thus, we conclude that defendant has failed to prevail on her facial challenge to the Village law. As to the remaining issues raised, further factual development is necessary.

Accordingly, the order of the Appellate Division should be modified, without costs, by denying defendant's cross motion for summary judgment and, as so modified, affirmed.

NOTES

1. Amortization is the most effective method for eliminating nonconforming uses, because the use must cease after a specified period of time. Amortization periods often vary depending on a variety of factors, including the property's value, remaining useful life, type of construction, and effect on the neighborhood. Courts usually uphold amortization laws against takings challenges because amortization enables the owner to realize a reasonable return on the property before the right to continue the nonconforming use is extinguished. If the amortization period is too brief, however, a court may invalidate it based on the Takings Clause. Other courts have held that any amortization period constitutes a taking. See, e.g., *Lamar Advertising of South Georgia, Inc. v. City of Albany*, 389 S.E.2d 216 (Ga. 1990); *Pennsylvania Northwestern Distributors, Inc. v. Zoning Hearing Board*, 584 A.2d 1372 (Pa. 1990).

2. As an alternative to amortization, many land use laws attempt to eliminate nonconforming uses by strictly limiting them. Common restrictions include:

a. *Changes or Expansion of Use.* Many ordinances prohibit any change or expansion of a nonconforming use. Although some ordinances permit limited change or expansion, the owner first may have to obtain administrative approval. Some municipalities also permit an owner to change the nonconforming use to a less intensive nonconforming use. Is this type of provision more helpful or harmful in achieving the Euclidean ideal? On one hand, the change brings the use closer to conformity with the current zoning. On the other hand, if the nonconforming use could not be changed, it might stop sooner.

b. *Repairs and Maintenance.* Some ordinances limit the extent to which a nonconforming use can be repaired or maintained. The limit often is stated as a percentage of the property's value, such as a provision that an amount not to exceed twenty percent of the land's value can be used to repair or maintain it. Although this type of restriction is designed to prevent substantial investment in continuing a nonconforming use, it can impair safety. Therefore, a court may refuse to enforce the restriction if a larger expenditure is necessary to bring the use into compliance with the building code.

c. *Reconstruction.* When more than a specified portion of a nonconforming use is destroyed, whether by fire or any other cause, its owner often is prohibited from rebuilding the nonconforming use. Ordinances commonly prohibit reconstruction if more than half the use's value is destroyed. The underlying notion is that, because the owner has to rebuild, it can rebuild in conformity with the existing law, rather than recreating a nonconforming use.

d. *Discontinuation of Use.* Some nonconforming use ordinances provide that the right to resume a nonconforming use is extinguished if the owner "abandons" the use. The problem with abandonment as a standard is that it requires not just a cessation of use, but also proof of the owner's intent not to resume that use. Because proof of intent often can be problematic, many ordinances now eliminate the right to re-establish a nonconforming use upon "discontinuation" of the use, regardless of the owner's intent. Despite the legislative goal to eliminate intent to abandon as a requirement, some courts interpret the discontinuation standard as incorporating it. Therefore, many ordinances now provide a time period after which the use may not be resumed, such as six months or a year after discontinuation.

3.   In footnote 1 of the principal case, the court refers to a difference between nonconforming structures and nonconforming uses. Which one should receive less legal protection and why?

After a parcel of land has been zoned, the zoning restrictions that apply to it may be changed in three ways: (1) a zoning amendment, (2) a variance, and (3) a special exception. In the next three sections, we will examine each one. As you read each section, consider the differences among them and how you would choose which one to use to deal with a client's land use problem.

3.   Zoning Amendment

After enacting a zoning ordinance, the local governing body has the authority to amend it. Two types of zoning amendments are available — "text amendments" and "map amendments." As indicated by its name, a text amendment changes the text of the zoning ordinance. For example, it can change the list of permitted uses or the setback requirements in an entire zoning district. In contrast, a map amendment normally affects only one parcel of land. The term "map amendment" refers to the zoning map maintained by the city. The zoning map shows the location of each zoning district. When a parcel of land is rezoned, the change is marked on the map. Which type of amendment is the subject of the following case?

CITY OF PHARR v. TIPPITT
616 S.W.2d 173 (Tex. 1981)

Pope, J.

E.A. Tippitt and fourteen other landowners filed suit against the City of Pharr, Mayfair Minerals, Inc., and Urban Housing Associates seeking a judgment declaring a zoning ordinance invalid. The district court upheld the ordinance, but the court of civil appeals nullified it. We reverse the court of civil appeals judgment and affirm that of the trial court.

Mayfair Minerals, Inc. is the owner of 10.1 acres of land which the City of Pharr rezoned from R-1, single-family residence use, to R-3, multi-family residence use. Urban Housing Associates, the developer, made the application for change of the single-family classification so that it could build fifty family units consisting of duplexes and quadruplexes. The Planning and Zoning Commission rejected its staff's recommendation that the zoning request be approved; but the City Council, by a four to one vote, enacted an ordinance which rezoned the property. After the district court upheld the validity of the zoning ordinance, Tippitt was the only person who appealed from that judgment. Tippitt's single point of error, which point was sustained by the court of civil appeals, was that the City acted arbitrarily because the amendatory ordinance was spot zoning that was not warranted by any change in conditions in the area.

The land in question is a rectangular 10.1-acre tract. It is on the west side of a larger 60-acre tract. The 60-acre tract and additional large expanses of land to the south and southeast are vacant farmlands. The lands were zoned in 1974 for single-family residences. The tract in question is about two blocks east of Highway 281, a major highway that runs from north to south toward Mexico. The land along the highway is rapidly developing as a commercial strip by reason of a proposed new bridge that will cross the Rio Grande River into Mexico. Sam Houston Street is a major traffic artery that runs from west to east. The tract in question is south of and separated from Sam Houston Street by a 2.6-acre tract of land known as the Aycock tract. Moving clockwise from the north around the 10.1-acre tract, the Aycock tract is zoned for single-family residences. Farther north of there, on the north side of Sam Houston, there are many city blocks of land that were zoned for multiple-family residences. That area, however, was built as single-family residences. The land on the east, southeast, south, and southwest are undeveloped farmlands, all zoned for single-family residences. Bordering the 10.1-acre tract on the west is Richmond Heights Subdivision, which has been developed as single-family residences on the north end, but is not yet developed toward the south. Three hundred feet to the northeast of the tract, but south of Sam Houston, there is an area that is zoned for multiple housing. Two hundred feet to the west of the 10.1-acre tract is a small area that is zoned for industrial use.

Zoning is an exercise of a municipality's legislative powers. *Thompson v. City of Palestine*, 510 S.W.2d 579 (Tex. 1974); Arts. 1011a, 1011b, 1011c, 1011d, 1011e.[1] The validity of an amendment to City of Pharr's comprehensive zoning ordinance presents a question of law, not fact. In making its determination, courts are governed by the rule stated in *Hunt v. City of San Antonio*, 462 S.W.2d 536, 539 (Tex. 1971): "If reasonable minds may differ as to whether or not a particular zoning ordinance has a substantial relationship to the public health, safety, morals or general welfare, no clear abuse of discretion is shown and the ordinance must stand as a valid exercise of the city's police power." See also *City of University Park v. Benners*, 485 S.W.2d 773 (Tex. 1972). We wrote in *City of Fort Worth v. Johnson*, 388 S.W.2d 400, 402 (Tex. 1964), that "a zoning ordinance, duly adopted pursuant to Arts. 1011a-1011k, is presumed to be valid and the burden is on the one seeking to prevent its enforcement, whether generally or as to particular property, to prove that the ordinance is arbitrary or unreasonable in that it bears no substantial relationship to the health, safety, morals or general welfare of the community." . . .

The burden on the party attacking the municipal legislative action is a heavy

---

[1] All statutory references are to Texas Revised Civil Statutes Annotated unless otherwise indicated.

one. . . . As expressed in *Weaver v. Ham*, 149 Tex. 309, 232 S.W.2d 704 (1950):

> The City had the power to enact the basic zoning ordinance, and to amend it, if a public necessity demanded it. While the presumption would be that the enactment of the amendatory ordinance was valid, that presumption disappears when the facts show and it was determined by the court that the City acted arbitrarily, unreasonably, and abused its discretion; that the ordinance is discriminatory and violates the rights of petitioners under the basic ordinance, and does not bear any substantial relation to the public health, safety, morals or general welfare; that it "constitutes unjustifiable spot zoning"; and that the ordinance is void.

These general rules for review of zoning ordinances have often been stated, but there has been little discussion of the actual legal criteria or standards against which legislative action should be tested. It has been suggested that such a statement would help to restrain arbitrary, capricious and unreasonable actions by city legislative bodies; improve the quality of the legislation; assist in eliminating *ad hoc* decisions; and focus the evidence from interested parties upon the real issues.[2] We call attention to some of the important criteria:

First: A comprehensive zoning ordinance is law that binds the municipal legislative body itself. Art. 1011c. The legislative body does not, on each rezoning hearing, redetermine as an original matter, the city's policy of comprehensive zoning. The law demands that the approved zoning plan should be respected and not altered for the special benefit of the landowner when the change will cause substantial detriment to the surrounding lands or serve no substantial public purpose. 1 R. Anderson, American Law of Zoning § 5.04 at 240 (1968). The duty to obey the existing law forbids municipal actions that disregard not only the pre-established zoning ordinance, but also long-range master plans and maps that have been adopted by ordinance. 1 R. Anderson, *supra* § 5.13 at 267.

The adoption of a comprehensive zoning ordinance does not, however, exhaust the city's powers to amend the ordinance as long as the action is not arbitrary, capricious and unreasonable. Art. 1011e. *City of University Park v. Benners, supra.*

Second: The nature and degree of an adverse impact upon neighboring lands is important. Lots that are rezoned in a way that is substantially inconsistent with the zoning of the surrounding area, whether more or less restrictive, are likely to be invalid. See *Barrington v. City of Sherman*, 155 S.W.2d 1008 (Tex. Civ. App. Dallas 1941, writ ref'd w.o.m.). For example, a rezoning from a residential use to an industrial use may have a highly deleterious effect upon the surrounding residential lands. . . .

Third: The suitability or unsuitability of the tract for use as presently zoned is a factor. Art. 1011c. The size, shape and location of a lot may render a tract unusable

---

[2] Because of the lack of standards for rezoning decisions, the exercise of pressure by . . . groups increases the likelihood that zoning bodies will be influenced by special interests rather than by the facts and circumstances bearing upon the merits of a rezoning request. Standards usually have the effect of making all of the parties concerned-the zoning body, applicant, and neighborhood opposition-concentrate more on the facts relating to the standards rather than on collateral matters. Harris, *Rezoning — Should It Be a Legislative or Judicial Function?*, 31 Baylor L. Rev. 409, 424 (1979). . . .

or even confiscatory as zoned. An example of this is found in *City of Waxahachie v. Watkins*, 154 Tex. 206, 275 S.W.2d 477 (1955), in which we approved the rezoning of a residential lot for local retail use, because the lot was surrounded by a de facto business area. See also *City of West University Place v. Ellis*, 134 Tex. 222, 134 S.W.2d 1038 (1940). This factor, like the others, must often be weighed in relation to the other standards, and instances can exist in which the use for which land is zoned may be rezoned upon proof of a real public need or substantially changed conditions in the neighborhood. See Harris, *Rezoning — Should It Be a Legislative or Judicial Function?*, 31 Baylor L. Rev. 409, 424–25 (1979).

Fourth: The amendatory ordinance must bear a substantial relationship to the public health, safety, morals or general welfare or protect and preserve historical and cultural places and areas. Arts. 1011a, 1011c. *Weaver v. Ham, supra*; 2 E. Yokley, Zoning Law and Practice § 13-6 at 243 (1978). The rezoning ordinance may be justified, however, if a substantial public need exists, and this is so even if the private owner of the tract will also benefit. . . .

Mr. Tippitt's attack upon the amendatory ordinance in this case is that it is spot zoning. The term, "spot zoning," is used in Texas and most states to connote an unacceptable amendatory ordinance that singles out a small tract for treatment that differs from that accorded similar surrounding land without proof of changes in conditions. Mr. Tippitt's present complaint of spot zoning invokes mainly inquiries about the second and third criteria stated above. Spot zoning is regarded as a preferential treatment which defeats a pre-established comprehensive plan. *Thompson v. City of Palestine*, 510 S.W.2d 579, 582 (Tex. 1974). It is piecemeal zoning, the antithesis of planned zoning. 2 E. Yokley, Zoning Law and Practice §§ 13-1 through 13-6 (1978).

Spot zoning has uniformly been denied when there is a substantial adverse impact upon the surrounding land. The size of a rezoned tract in relation to the affected neighboring lands has been said by some authorities to be the most significant consideration in rezoning. 1 R. Anderson, *supra*, § 5.07 at 252; 82 Am. Jur. 2d, Zoning and Planning, §§ 76, 77, 78 at 514–520 (1976).

Amendatory ordinances which have rezoned a single city lot when there have been no intervening changes or other saving characteristic, have almost always been voided in Texas. See *Hunt v. City of San Antonio*, 462 S.W.2d 536 (Tex. 1971), (2 city lots); *Weaver v. Ham*, 149 Tex. 309, 232 S.W.2d 704 (1950), (3 city lots); *Davis v. Nolte*, 231 S.W.2d 471 (Tex. Civ. App. Austin 1950, writ ref'd n.r.e.), (2 city block lots); *Harmon v. City of Dallas*, 229 S.W.2d 825 (Tex. Civ. App. Dallas 1950, writ ref'd n.r.e.), (1 city lot); *Barrington v. City of Sherman*, 155 S.W.2d 1008 (Tex. Civ. App. Dallas 1941, writ ref'd w.o.m.), (1 city lot). See also 1 N. Williams, American Land Planning Law § 27.03 at 563 (1974); 1 R. Anderson, *supra* § 5.08 at 2.56.

Proof that a small tract is unsuitable for use as zoned or that there have been substantial changes in the neighborhood have justified some amendatory ordinances. Here, too, the size, shape and characteristics of the tract have been determinative factors in upholding the amendments. *Waxahachie v. Watkins, supra*, (one-half acre); *Bernard v. City of Bedford*, 593 S.W.2d 809 (Tex. Civ. App. Fort Worth 1980, writ ref'd n.r.e.), (3.5 acres); *Midway Protective League v. City of Dallas*, 552 S.W.2d 170 (Tex. Civ. App. Texarkana 1977, writ ref'd n.r.e.), (7.98 acres);

McWhorter v. City of Winnsboro, 525 S.W.2d 701 (Tex. Civ. App. Tyler 1975, writ ref'd n.r.e.), (5.29-acre extension of a business zone); *Simons Land Co. v. City of Dallas*, 507 S.W.2d 828 (Tex. Civ. App. Waco 1974), *motion for reh. den.*, 510 S.W.2d 32 (1974, no writ), (90 acres out of a 100-acre tract); *Skinner v. Reed*, 265 S.W.2d 850 (Tex. Civ. App. Eastland 1954, no writ), (12 acres). On the other hand, an amendatory ordinance covering a 4.1-acre tract was invalidated in *Thompson v. City of Palestine*, *supra*. See 1 R. Anderson, *supra* § 5.07 at 253–54, for a study of size as a factor in spot zoning cases.

Amendatory zoning ordinances should be judicially tested against the same criteria that govern the action of the municipal legislative body. In this case, the 10.1-acre tract was not, as urged by the developer who made the application, an interim or automatic R-1 zoning following annexation. The tract had been previously comprehensively zoned, along with vast areas reaching south and southeast to the city limits after study, notice, and hearing. The zoning ordinance had classified lands of the city into districts known as residential, single-family (R-1); residential, two-family (R-2); residential, multi-family (R-3); residential, mobile home parks (R-MH); residential, mobile home subdivision (R-MHS); residential, townhouse subdivision (R-TH); general commercial (C); and industrial (M). See Art. 1011b.

The impact of the amendatory R-3 zoning upon the neighborhood, according to some witnesses who lived west of the rezoned tract, would depress the values of their R-1 district. According to other testimony, the new development would enhance values of the entire southeast section of Pharr, and the existing homes in Richmond Heights would be protected by the city's requirement for a conditional permit which would compel the city's prior analysis of the design before development. The new development would require the backyards of the existing residences in Richmond Heights to back upon the backyards of the buildings in the rezoned tract. Most of the traffic from the rezoned tract would be directed to the east and north away from Richmond Heights. The new housing district would have its own internal streets and off-street parking.

The number of potential structures would not be substantially increased. Zoning for single-family dwellings would permit as many as forty-four family units, whereas the rezoning for multiple-housing (R-3) would permit fifty family units. There was evidence that the impact upon the surrounding area would be slight and even beneficial.

We do not regard the ordinance as spot zoning. The ten-acre tract is located in an undeveloped farming area. Large expanses of rural lands are located to the east, south and southeast, the direction which the town must grow. To hold that the undeveloped land cannot be used for anything other than single-family residences (R-1) would mean, for all practical purposes, that there can be no more multiple housing in Pharr within its present city limits, since there is almost no presently undeveloped area which is available for R-3 housing. The size of this tract is large enough for planning as a self-contained orderly development which can in advance provide for the direction and the flow of traffic and assure a careful development of necessary public utilities. The development will not cause that measure of disharmony that occurs when there is a rezoning ordinance that permits a use that affects lands or tracts that are already developed. This is not an instance of an unplanned or piecemeal zoning of an isolated lot or small tract.

There is also evidence that rezoning would benefit and promote the general welfare of the community. The City of Pharr has a great need for multiple housing, the population has markedly increased since 1974, and there are only three small areas in Pharr that are presently zoned for multiple housing (R-3) which are not fully developed. The mayor testified that the need for multi-family housing will continue to grow. The City of Pharr, from the data included in the minutes of the zoning hearing, has 703 acres zoned for residential purposes of all kinds. Only 49 acres are actually used for multiple housing (R-3), and nine acres are actually used for duplexes (R-2). To relieve the City of Pharr's housing and utility needs, the City had agreed with the Housing and Urban Development Department to provide more space for multiple housing (R-3) construction. A block grant to the City of $3,000,000 had been made which included sums to provide needed extensions of sewer and water lines and the construction of a water reservoir. From the record it does not appear that the one complaining of the rezoning ordinance discharged his burden to prove that the City of Pharr acted arbitrarily, capriciously or unreasonably.

The judgment of the court of civil appeals is reversed and the judgment of the district court upholding the ordinance rezoning the tract in question is affirmed.

NOTES

1. What are the legal grounds for invalidating a spot zoning?

2. The rezoning in *Pharr* was initiated by a prospective developer of the land. A local legislative body and, in some jurisdictions, the voters can rezone property on their own initiative. For example, property may be rezoned to a single-family residential classification against the owner's wishes to prevent construction of a gas station or other use permitted by the existing zoning. Does the owner have a legal basis for challenging the rezoning? The owner may have purchased the land in reliance on the existing zoning or may have incurred significant expenses for architects' fees, permits, and other construction-related costs. On the other hand, valid reasons may exist for preventing the development. Local government should not be prevented from responding to newly-identified problems in the zoning code.

To deal with this problem, courts have developed a variety of doctrines. The two most widely followed doctrines are estoppel and vested rights. Although these terms often are used interchangeably in this context, they have different theoretical underpinnings. As in other situations, estoppel requires that the owner foreseeably and detrimentally relied on a governmental act or omission. In contrast, the vested rights doctrine is grounded in the constitutional protection afforded to private property rights. Despite the different theories underlying these doctrines, the method of establishing both is the same. In most jurisdictions, the owner or developer must have obtained a building permit and must have incurred significant construction costs in reliance on the permit. See *Western Land Equities, Inc. v. City of Logan*, 617 P.2d 388 (Utah 1980).

3. Because the planning process for a new development can take a long time, developers understandably are concerned about undertaking the time and expense

of planning if the local government can change the applicable land use regulations at the last minute. In response to this concern, a developer may be able to enter into a "development agreement" with the local government pursuant to which the government agrees to freeze the land use regulations for the developer's land. In *Santa Margarita Area Residents Together v. San Luis Obispo County*, 100 Cal. Rptr. 2d 740 (2000), a California Court of Appeal considered the constitutionality of development agreements. The plaintiffs argued that such agreements unconstitutionally abrogate a local government's right to exercise its police power in the future. The court rejected the challenge based on legislative findings that "lack of certainty in the approval of development projects can result in a waste of resources, escalate the cost of housing and other development to the consumer, and discourage investment in and commitment to comprehensive planning which would make efficient utilization of resources at the least economic cost to the public."

4. Variance

ALUMNI CONTROL BOARD v. CITY OF LINCOLN
137 N.W.2d 800 (Neb. 1965)

McCown, J.

This case involves an application for a building permit requiring a variance in front, rear, and side yard requirements and in off-street parking requirements of the zoning provisions of the Lincoln municipal code. The application was denied by the building inspector, by the board of zoning appeals, and by the city council, and the denial was affirmed by the district court. The plaintiff has appealed.

The property involved is a corner lot having a 50-foot frontage on one street and a 92-foot frontage on the other. The property was in single separate ownership at the time of the adoption of the Lincoln zoning code in 1953. The plaintiff purchased the property in 1955 and apparently has occupied and used the property since then as a fraternity house which, at the time of this application, housed 21 young men. The property is located in an F-restricted commercial district. Permitted uses are for single or two-family residences, multiple dwellings, fraternities, sororities, boarding and lodging houses, non-profit hospital, religious, educational, and philanthropic institutions, private clubs and lodges (where the chief activity is not a service carried on as a business), apartment hotels, and office buildings. The building proposed is a four-story building 30 by 60 feet. Under the provisions of the code, a building 28 by 48.6 feet was the maximum size permitted. The variances requested involved front, rear, and side yard reductions varying from 5 feet to 6.4 feet. The off-street parking under the zoning code was required to be on the premises or within 1,200 feet, while the off-street parking proposed was 1,280 feet from the premises.

The evidence is that a fraternity house could be built within the requirements of the city zoning code to house 48 men, but that it would not comply with the University of Nebraska housing code which became mandatory September 1, 1965. The evidence also is that a fraternity house could be built within the requirements of the city zoning code and also in compliance with the University of Nebraska housing code, but that such a fraternity house could accommodate only 36 men.

The plaintiff's position is that it is not economically desirable to construct a fraternity house for less than 48 men, and that this fact, together with the requirements of the University of Nebraska housing code, constitute "practical difficulties" sufficient to require the granting of the variances.

Use variances are customarily concerned with "hardship" while area variances are customarily concerned with "practical difficulty." A use variance is one which permits a use other than that prescribed by the zoning ordinance in a particular district. An area variance has no relationship to change of use. It is primarily a grant to erect, alter, or use a structure for a permitted use in a manner other than that prescribed by the restrictions of the zoning ordinance. Area variances are principally involved in this case.

The disposition of a case involving an area variance and "practical difficulty" under a zoning ordinance depends on the facts and circumstances of each particular case. In most instances in which courts have found that a "practical difficulty" was present in an area variance case, they have apparently relied on the fact that the case involved substandard lots as to which the practical difficulty was obvious. This case does not involve a "substandard" lot, i.e., having a smaller size or having a lesser frontage than the required minimum. 1 Rathkopf, The Law of Zoning and Planning (3d ed.), 32-1. The minimum area requirements in this zoning district are: Single family or two-family residences, 4,000 square feet; multiple family residences, 500 square feet per family; and there is no minimum area restriction for fraternities. The plaintiff's lot is 4,600 square feet and it has a 50-foot frontage which is also not substandard.

The criteria generally and properly before a board of appeals on an application for a variance from area restrictions of a zoning code are: (1) Whether compliance with the strict letter of the restrictions governing area, set backs, frontage, height, bulk, or density would unreasonably prevent the owner from using the property for a permitted purpose or would render conformity with such restrictions unnecessarily burdensome; (2) whether a grant of the variance applied for would do substantial justice to the applicant as well as to other property owners in the district, or whether a lesser relaxation than that applied for would give substantial relief to the owner of the property involved and be more consistent with justice to other property owners; and (3) whether relief can be granted in such a fashion that the spirit of the ordinance will be observed and public safety and welfare secured. 2 Rathkopf, The Law of Zoning and Planning (3d ed.), 45-28.

"The purpose of variances in the broadest sense is the rendering of justice in unique and individual cases of practical difficulties or unnecessary hardships arising from literal application of zoning ordinances; zoning statutes and ordinances commonly provide in effect that the grant of variances should be to the end of doing substantial justice." 8 McQuillin, Municipal Corporations (3d ed. Rev.), § 25.172, p. 409.

The specific provisions of the Lincoln zoning code gave the board of zoning appeals the power: ". . . to vary the strict application of the height, area, parking or density requirements to the extent necessary to permit the owner a reasonable use of his land in those specified instances where there are peculiar, exceptional and unusual circumstances in connection with a specific parcel of land, which circumstances are not generally found within the locality or neighborhood concerned." Lincoln Municipal Code, § 27.44.040.

There is no evidence that the reasons constituting the plaintiff's claim of practical difficulty are peculiar to the property involved. So far as the evidence goes, both the University of Nebraska housing code and the economic factors applying to fraternity house operations apply equally to all other fraternities in the zoning district.

Insofar as the plaintiff's basic contention that a minimum of 48 men must be accommodated to make a fraternity house operation economically feasible, the evidence is contradictory. The plaintiff's own evidence showed that for the year 1962-1963, there were 5 fraternities with less than 48 sustaining members. Four of those five, including the plaintiff, showed an income greater than expenses. Of the fraternities having 48 sustaining members or more, 6 out of 13 had expenses exceeding income. Here the evidence is clear that even within the requirements of the University of Nebraska housing code, the property could continue to be used for a fraternity house and even accommodate 60 percent more men than the plaintiff has accommodated on it for the last 10 years. The restrictions of the ordinance do not prevent the property from being used for any of the other authorized uses permitted in the district. There is essentially no difference here from any case in which an owner desires to expand, but finds himself with not enough property to do so and also meet the conditions of the ordinance. The mere fact that the plaintiff would like to have a fraternity house of larger dimensions does not establish practical difficulty in complying with the ordinance. The plaintiff's basic position is apparently that where the desire to expand a permitted use of the premises beyond the area restrictions of the zoning code is motivated by practical or economic reasons, this constitutes a "practical difficulty" and requires the granting of an area variance. We cannot agree.

Even if it be conceded that a "practical difficulty" was established, there is specific testimony that the yard requirements here are reasonable requirements, and that the granting of the variances requested would be in derogation of the spirit and intent and general plan of the zoning ordinance. The application was also opposed at the hearing by the owners of adjoining property. The fact that the plaintiff's fraternity house has now become inadequate for the plaintiff's plans for growth does not tend to show the provisions of the ordinance to be arbitrary or unreasonable. Neither does it establish that the owner is unreasonably prevented from using the property, nor that substantial justice will be done to other property owners, nor that the spirit of the ordinance will be observed and the public safety and welfare secured. The acts of the board of zoning appeals are subject to review and reversal only if they constitute an abuse of discretion and are unreasonable, arbitrary, or illegal. *Peterson v. Vasak*, 162 Neb. 498, 76 N.W.2d 420.

We have discussed above strictly area variances on the property itself. A variance of a different nature, technically involving both use and area, is involved in the off-street parking requirements.

The zoning code requires the plaintiff to provide off-street parking on the property or within 1,200 feet from the property. This is a greater distance than is permitted by any other section or provision of the zoning code. The requested variance involves off-street parking facilities 1,280 feet away from the property and in excess of the maximum distance specified. Congestion in the public streets (the basic problem giving rise to off-street parking requirements) might not be reasonably nor adequately alleviated if the required off-street private parking is so far away from the traffic generating property that it would not be reasonably or effectively used. We certainly cannot say that it is unreasonable nor arbitrary to refuse to grant a variance of an additional 80 feet where the maximum distance prescribed by the ordinance is already virtually a quarter of a mile from the location of the property. This is particularly true where there is no evidence of practical difficulty, nor unnecessary hardship, nor, in fact, of any other reason why the ordinance cannot be specifically complied with.

Under the facts in this case, we cannot say that the action of the board of zoning appeals and the city council did not permit the owner a reasonable use of the land, nor that it did not do substantial justice.

The plaintiff has directed several assignments of error to the constitutionality of the Lincoln zoning code. This court has held many times that a litigant who invokes the provisions of a statute may not challenge its validity; or seek the benefit and in the same action and at the same time question its constitutionality. *Peterson v. Vasak, supra; Shields v. City of Kearney*, 179 Neb. 49, 136 N.W.2d 174.

For the reasons set forth, the action of the board of zoning appeals and the city council in denying the requested variance was not unreasonable, arbitrary, or illegal; nor did its action violate the plaintiff's constitutional rights. The judgment of the district court was correct and is affirmed.

NOTES

1. A great deal of variation exists among the states concerning the availability of use and area variances. Some jurisdictions prohibit use variances by statute or by judicial decision but permit area variances. E.g. Cal Gov't Code § 65906; *Bradley v. Zoning Bd. of Appeals*, 334 A.2d 914 (Conn. 1973). What legally relevant distinction between the two types of variances justifies such different treatment?

In those jurisdictions that permit both types of variances, some apply the same legal standard to both. However, many jurisdictions apply different standards to each. Although a variety of standards are used, the most common are the "practical difficulties" standard for area variances and the "unnecessary hardship" standard for use variances. *Harrison v. Mayor and Board of Alderman of City of Batesville*, 73 So. 3d 1145, 1154 (Miss. 2011) ("Jurisdictions that distinguish the two terms ['practical difficulty' and 'unnecessary hardship'] do so because 'an area variance is a relaxation of one or more incidental limitations to a permitted use and does not alter the character of a district as much as a use not permitted by the ordinance.' ").

2. The court in *Otto v. Steinhilber*, 24 N.E.2d 851 (N.Y. 1939), provided a particularly cogent statement of the unnecessary hardship standard. It said that the standard requires a showing that:

(1) [T]he land in question cannot yield a reasonable return if used only for a purpose allowed in that zone; (2) that the plight of the owner is due to unique circumstances and not to the general conditions of the neighborhood which may reflect the unreasonableness of the zoning ordinance itself; and (3) that the use to be authorized by the variance will not alter the essential character of the locality.

Id. at 853. What function is served by each of the factors identified by the court? The first factor focuses on whether the landowner is entitled to relief from the existing zoning restrictions. If the owner is entitled to relief, the second factor focuses on whether a variance is the appropriate form of relief. If a variance is justified, the third factor focuses on the scope of the variance to be granted. Based on your analysis of these three factors, what is the variance's role in land use regulation? What distinguishes it from a zoning amendment?

3.   Although some jurisdictions construe the "practical difficulties" standard to have essentially the same meaning as the "unnecessary hardship" standard, e.g., *Snyder v. Waukesha County Zoning Bd. of Adjustment*, 247 N.W.2d 98 (Wis. 1976), many jurisdictions interpret the practical difficulties standard as being more lenient. E.g., *Kisil v. City of Sandusky*, 465 N.E.2d 848 (Ohio 1984). The great diversity of judicial treatment of "practical difficulties" makes further generalization difficult. However, courts normally do not require an applicant for an area variance to show that the property has no reasonable use under the existing zoning. Instead, courts consider factors such as the extent of the requested change, the effect it would have on the neighborhood, and the adverse impact of the existing zoning on the property's value. See, e.g., *Burkholder v. Twinsburg Township Bd. of Zoning Appeals*, 701 N.E.2d 766 (Ohio Ct. App. 1997).

4.   If a use variance is to be granted only when no reasonable use exists for the land as currently zoned, does a landowner who obtains a use variance automatically have a temporary taking claim for the period starting when the zoning became effective until the variance was granted? See *First English Evangelical Lutheran Church v. County of Los Angeles*, 482 U.S. 304 (1987).

5.   Special Exception

The special exception is the third type of action available to change the permitted uses of land. The special exception differs in an important respect from the zoning amendment and the variance; the zoning ordinance specifies the permissible uses for which a special exception may be granted. For example, in a single-family residential zone, the zoning ordinance may specify that single-family homes and accessory uses, such as a detached garage, are permitted as a matter of right so long as they comply with other restrictions concerning required setbacks and similar matters. The ordinance then may specify uses that are permitted in that district if a special exception is granted. In a single-family residential zone, for example, special exception uses might include churches, community centers, and schools.

The types of uses that require a special exception are generally compatible with the uses permitted as a matter of right, but they may not be appropriate at every location in the district. For example, they may serve large numbers of people, such as a church or school, and therefore create potential traffic and noise problems. Special exception uses also may be generally desirable uses that have noxious qualities, such as a gas station. Therefore, rather than permit any landowner in a zoning district to use his property for such a use, the special exception review process permits an evaluation of the proposed location and method of operation of the use before it legally can be introduced into the neighborhood.

Because permissible special exceptions are specified in the zoning ordinance, they are more aptly described by the other terms that are applied to them — special uses or conditional uses. As you read the next case, contrast the court's treatment of the special exception with the judicial treatment afforded zoning amendments and variances.

SCHULTZ v. PRITTS
432 A.2d 1319 (Md. 1981)

DAVIDSON, J.

The respondents, Robert and Ann Pritts, are contract purchasers of a 2.74 acre tract of land located in Carroll County, zoned R-20,000 (single-family residential development 20,000 square feet minimum lot size). These contract purchasers filed an application with the Board requesting a special exception use to develop a funeral establishment and a variance for reduction of the minimum front yard requirements. The Board held a hearing at which the petitioners, Roger Schultz and others (protestants), appeared in opposition. After the hearing, the Board denied the requested special exception use and held that the request for the variance was moot. . . .

The contract purchasers contend that the Board's decision denying the requested special exception use was arbitrary, capricious, and illegal. Initially, they assert that the Board did not apply the proper criteria in determining that the requested special exception use would result in dangerous traffic conditions. They claim that the Board failed to take into account the critical fact that the requested special exception use would generate less traffic than would be generated by permitted uses. In support of their position, they rely upon *Gowl v. Atlantic Richfield Co.*, 27 Md. App. 410, 417–18, 341 A.2d 832, 836 (1975).

In *Gowl*, the Court of Special Appeals reversed a Board of Appeals' decision denying a requested special exception use on the ground of traffic. There that Court stated that the proper standard by which to determine whether a requested special exception use should be denied on the ground of traffic is a comparison between the traffic problems that might arise under the requested special exception use and those that might arise under a permitted use. It held that when "the potential volume of traffic under the requested use would appear to be no greater than that which would arise from permitted uses," the requested special exception use must be granted. *Gowl*, 27 Md. App. at 417–18, 341 A.2d at 836. We do not agree.

This Court has frequently expressed the applicable standards for judicial review of the grant or denial of a special exception use. The special exception use is a part of the comprehensive zoning plan sharing the presumption that, as such, it is in the interest of the general welfare, and therefore, valid. The special exception use is a valid zoning mechanism that delegates to an administrative board a limited authority to allow enumerated uses which the legislature has determined to be permissible *absent any fact or circumstance negating the presumption*. The duties given the Board are to judge whether the *neighboring properties in the general neighborhood would be adversely affected* and whether the use in the particular case is in harmony with the general purpose and intent of the plan.

Whereas, the applicant has the burden of adducing testimony which will show that his use meets the prescribed standards and requirements, he does not have the burden of establishing affirmatively that his proposed use would be a benefit to the community. If he shows to the satisfaction of the Board that the proposed use would be conducted without real detriment to the neighborhood and would not actually adversely affect the public interest, he has met his burden. The extent of any harm or disturbance to the neighboring area and uses is, of course, material. If the evidence makes the question of harm or disturbance or the question of the disruption of the harmony of the comprehensive plan of zoning fairly debatable, the matter is one for the Board to decide. But if there is no probative evidence of harm or disturbance in light of the nature of the zone involved or of factors causing disharmony to the operation of the comprehensive plan, a denial of an application for a special exception use is arbitrary, capricious, and illegal. . . . These standards dictate that if a requested special exception use is properly determined to have an adverse effect upon neighboring properties in the general area, it must be denied.

The specific nature of the requisite adverse effect was defined in *Deen v. Baltimore Gas & Electric Co.*, 240 Md. 317, 330–31, 214 A.2d 146, 153 (1965). There the Baltimore Gas and Electric Company requested a special exception use that would permit construction of high tension transmission lines above ground. At that time, the Baltimore County Zoning Regulations stated that a special exception use could not be granted if the requested use would "be detrimental to the health, safety, or general welfare of the locality involved." The Baltimore County Board of Appeals (Board) granted the requested special exception use for that portion of the proposed transmission lines that would traverse a rural area not then serviced by public sewer or water facilities. The trial court affirmed.

On appeal, this Court affirmed stating:

> "Appellants assert that it was error for the Board to fail to consider the future effects which the high tension wires would have on the health, safety and general welfare of the locality 'which could be reasonably anticipated in the normal course of its development.' This factor was without relevance in this case, because *there was no evidence produced at the hearing which would show that the effect of high tension wires on the future health, safety and welfare of this area would be in any respect different than its effect on any other rural area. Section 502.1 implies that the effect on health, safety or general welfare must be in some sense unique or else a special exception could never be granted in such an area for the above ground location of high tension wires*. The only evidence as to future conditions was testimony revealing the possibility of future residential development of this land but

such a possibility alone does not come close to showing a future deleterious effect upon the public health, safety or general welfare." *Deen*, 240 Md. at 330–31, 214 A.2d at 153 (emphasis added).

Subsequently, a similar analysis was employed in *Anderson v. Sawyer*, 23 Md. App. at 617–18, 329 A.2d at 720. There an owner requested a special exception use that would permit construction of a funeral home in a residential zone. Protestants presented evidence to show that the requested special exception use would tend to create congestion and unsafe conditions on neighboring roads and streets and would have a depressing psychological effect that would interfere with the enjoyment of the adjoining properties, make them less saleable, and prevent them from appreciating in value as much as other homes in the area. The Board found that the grant of the requested special exception use would create traffic problems and would, in fact, "be detrimental otherwise to the general welfare of the locality involved." It denied the requested special exception use. The Circuit Court for Baltimore County reversed.

The Court of Special Appeals affirmed the order of the Circuit Court requiring the grant of the requested special exception use. The Court of Special Appeals agreed with the trial court that there was no probative evidence to show any adverse effect. More particularly, with respect to the alleged depreciation of value and enjoyment of neighboring properties, it said:

> "There can be no doubt that an undertaking business has an inherent depressing and disturbing psychological effect which may adversely affect persons residing in the immediate neighborhood in the enjoyment of their homes and which may lessen the values thereof. Indeed, it is precisely because of such inherent deleterious effects that the action of a local legislature in prohibiting such uses in a given zone or zones will be regarded as promoting the general welfare and as constitutionally sound. But in the instant case the legislature of Baltimore County has determined that as part of its comprehensive plan funeral homes are to be allowed in residential zones notwithstanding their inherent deleterious effects. By defining a funeral home as an appropriate use by way of special exception, the legislature of Baltimore County has, in essence, declared that such uses, if they satisfy the other specific requirements of the ordinance, do promote the health, safety and general welfare of the community. As part of the comprehensive zoning plan this legislative declaration shares in a presumption of validity and correctness which the courts will honor.

> "*The presumption that the general welfare is promoted by allowing funeral homes in a residential use district, notwithstanding their inherent depressing effects, cannot be overcome unless there are strong and substantial existing facts or circumstances showing that the particularized proposed use has detrimental effects above and beyond the inherent ones ordinarily associated with such uses.* Consequently, the bald allegation that a funeral home use is inherently psychologically depressing and adversely influences adjoining property values, as well as other evidence which confirms that generally accepted conclusion, is insufficient to overcome the presumption that such a use promotes the general welfare of a

local community. *Because there were neither facts nor valid reasons to support the conclusion that the grant of the requested special exception would adversely affect adjoining and surrounding properties in any way other than would result from the location of any funeral home in any residential zone, the evidence presented by the protestants was, in effect, no evidence at all.*"

Anderson, 23 Md. App. at 624–25, 329 A.2d at 724 (emphasis added) (citations omitted).

These cases establish that a special exception use has an adverse effect and must be denied when it is determined from the facts and circumstances that the grant of the requested special exception use would result in an adverse effect upon adjoining and surrounding properties unique and different from the adverse effect that would otherwise result from the development of such a special exception use located anywhere within the zone. Thus, these cases establish that the appropriate standard to be used in determining whether a requested special exception use would have an adverse effect and, therefore, should be denied is whether there are facts and circumstances that show that the particular use proposed at the particular location proposed would have any adverse effects above and beyond those inherently associated with such a special exception use irrespective of its location within the zone.

In *Gowl*, the Atlantic Richfield Company requested a special exception use that would permit construction of above ground storage for more than 10 million gallons of fuel oil and gasoline to be located on approximately 19 acres of land zoned M-2 (Manufacturing-Heavy). At a hearing before the Board of Appeals for Howard County (Board), there was much evidence presented to show that the particular use proposed at the particular location proposed would have an adverse effect on neighboring properties in the general area. There was expert and lay testimony to show, among other things, that the access roads to the property were inadequate and dangerous and that the increased traffic could not be accommodated on the existing roads. The Board found, among other things, "that the proposed use would adversely affect the surrounding and vicinal properties by creating undue traffic congestion on a presently inadequate and hazardous road network. . . ." It denied the requested special exception use.

Atlantic Richfield filed an appeal in the Circuit Court for Howard County. In a memorandum opinion filed after a hearing, the trial court said with respect to traffic:

"The finding of the Board that the use would create undue traffic congestion on a presently inadequate and hazardous road network presents a more serious question. The evidence before the Board was certainly substantial, and more than substantial, that the access roads to the property, in their present state, were inadequate to service the proposed use or, presumably, any substantial industrial use, and that the presence of any number of trailer-trucks on these roads would create a hazard."

In essence, the trial court concluded that there was sufficient evidence to support the Board's finding that the particular use proposed at the particular location proposed would have an adverse effect on traffic above and beyond the adverse effect on traffic ordinarily associated with such uses. Notwithstanding the existence of this adverse effect, the trial court concluded that the Board's denial should be reversed and that the special exception use should be granted. * * *

An analysis of the rationale underlying the statutory scheme by which certain uses are delineated as either a permitted use or a conditional or special exception use leads to the conclusion that the *Gowl* standard is logically inconsistent and in conflict with the standards established in *Turner* as explicated by *Deen* and *Anderson*. The general purpose of adequate land planning is to guide and accomplish the "coordinated, adjusted, and harmonious development of [a] juris-diction . . . which will . . . promote . . . [the] general welfare." Md. Code (1957, 1978 Repl. Vol.), Art. 66B, § 3.06. Zoning is one of the important elements of land planning that is used to further this purpose. *Board of County Comm'rs of Cecil County v. Gaster*, 285 Md. 233, 246, 401 A.2d 666, 672 (1979). The various purposes of zoning regulations, made in accordance with the plan, are:

> "[T]o control congestion in the streets; to secure the public safety; to promote health, and the general welfare; to provide adequate light and air; to promote the conservation of natural resources; to prevent environmental pollution; to avoid undue concentration of population; to facilitate the adequate provision of transportation, water, sewerage, schools, recreation, parks and other public requirements. Such regulations shall be made with reasonable consideration, among other things, to the character of the district and its suitability for particular uses, and with a view to conserving the value of buildings and encouraging the orderly development and the most appropriate use of land throughout the jurisdiction." Art. 66B, § 4.03.

Zoning provides a tool by which to establish general areas or districts devoted to selected uses. *Ellicott v. Mayor of Baltimore*, 180 Md. 176, 181, 23 A.2d 649, 651 (1942). Indeed, the very essence of zoning is the territorial division of land into use districts according to the character of the land and buildings, the suitability of land and buildings for particular uses, and uniformity of use. . . .

Generally, when a use district is established, the zoning regulations prescribe that certain uses are permitted as of right (permitted use), while other uses are permitted only under certain conditions (conditional or special exception use).[6] In determining which uses should be designated as permitted or conditional in a given use district, a legislative body considers the variety of possible uses available, examines the impact of the uses upon the various purposes of the zoning ordinance, determines which uses are compatible with each other and can share reciprocal benefits, and decides which uses will provide for coordinated, adjusted, and harmonious development of the district. P. Hagman, Urban Planning and Land Development Control Law 105 (1971). See Art. 66B, § 4.03.

Because the legislative body, in reaching its determination, is engaged in a

---

[6] Art. 66B, § 1.00 provides in pertinent part: "'Special exceptions' (conditional use) means a grant of a specific use that would not be appropriate generally or without restriction and shall be based upon a finding that certain conditions governing special exceptions as detailed in the zoning ordinance exist, that the use conforms to the plan and is compatible with the existing neighborhood."

balancing process, certain uses may be designated as permitted although they may not foster all of the purposes of the zoning regulations and, indeed, may have an adverse effect with respect to some of these purposes. Thus, when the legislative body determines that the beneficial purposes that certain uses serve outweigh their possible adverse effect, such uses are designated as permitted uses and may be developed even though a particular permitted use at the particular location proposed would have an adverse effect above and beyond that ordinarily associated with such uses. For example, churches and schools generally are designated as permitted uses. Such uses may be developed, although at the particular location proposed they may have an adverse effect on a factor such as traffic, because the moral and educational purposes served are deemed to outweigh this particular adverse effect.

When the legislative body determines that other uses are compatible with the permitted uses in a use district, but that the beneficial purposes such other uses serve do not outweigh their possible adverse effect, such uses are designated as conditional or special exception uses. . . . Such uses cannot be developed if at the particular location proposed they have an adverse effect above and beyond that ordinarily associated with such uses. For example, funeral establishments generally are designated as special exception uses. Such uses may not be developed if at the particular location proposed they have an adverse effect upon a factor such as traffic because the legislative body has determined that the beneficial purposes that such establishments serve do not necessarily outweigh their possible adverse effects.

More particularly, by definition, a permitted use may be developed even though it has an adverse effect upon traffic in the particular location proposed. By definition, a requested special exception use producing the same adverse effect at the same location must be denied. Thus, by definition, a church may be developed even if the volume of traffic that it generates causes congestion and unsafe conditions at the particular location proposed. By definition, however, a special exception use for a funeral establishment producing the same volume of traffic and, therefore, the same congestion and unsafe conditions at the particular location proposed must be denied. It is precisely because a permitted use may be developed even though it may have an adverse effect on traffic at the particular location proposed, whereas a special exception use may not, that to grant a requested special exception use on the ground that it generates traffic volume no greater than that generated by a permitted use is logically inconsistent and in conflict with previously established standards. Accordingly, the standard articulated in *Gowl* is inappropriate. We now hold that the appropriate standard to be used in determining whether a requested special exception use would have an adverse effect and, therefore, should be denied is whether there are facts and circumstances that show that the particular use proposed at the particular location proposed would have any adverse effects above and beyond those inherently associated with such a special exception use irrespective of its location within the zone. . . .

Here the purposes of the Carroll County Zoning Ordinance are "to promote the health, safety, morals, and the general welfare of the community, by regulating . . . the location and use of buildings . . . to provide for adequate light and air; to prevent congestion and undue crowding of the land; to secure safety from fire, panic, and other danger; and to conserve the value of property." Carroll County

Zoning Ordinance § 1.0. The local legislative body, the County Commissioners of Carroll County, after engaging in a balancing process, designated single-family dwellings, churches, schools, colleges, and community buildings such as libraries, cultural and civic centers as permitted uses in an R-20,000 Residence District. Carroll County Zoning Ordinance § 7.1. As a result of this designation, such uses can be developed even if they have an adverse effect on traffic. The Commissioners also designated certain other uses of land, including funeral establishments, as special exception uses in a R-20,000 Residence District. Carroll County Zoning Ordinance § 7.2. As a result of this designation, funeral establishments cannot be developed at a particular location if they have an adverse effect on traffic above and beyond that ordinarily associated with funeral establishments irrespective of location within the zone. Carroll County Zoning Ordinance § 17.6.

Here the Board determined that the grant of the requested special exception use for the proposed funeral establishment would result in dangerous traffic conditions at the proposed location and, therefore, that the special exception should be denied. However, the record here shows that the evidence primarily relied upon by the Board was based on questionable assumptions. On appeal, the trial court did not decide whether a reasoning mind could reasonably have concluded, as did the Board, that the granting of the requested special exception use would result in dangerous traffic conditions. Rather, the trial court erroneously decided only that there had been a denial of due process and reversed and remanded the matter to the Board for a new hearing. The trial court specifically refused to determine whether, on remand, the *Gowl* standard was applicable.

The Court of Special Appeals did not decide whether the question of adverse effect on traffic was fairly debatable. Rather, it erroneously decided only that the trial court's order remanding the case to the Board was not a final judgment. It dismissed the appeal, without indicating whether the *Gowl* standard was applicable.

In our view, under all of these circumstances, the purposes of justice will be advanced by permitting further proceedings in this case through the introduction of additional evidence before the Board and the application of the appropriate standard set forth in this opinion. Accordingly, we shall remand the case to the Board without affirmance or reversal for further proceedings in accordance with this opinion. Md. Rule 871.

NOTES

1. In addition to specifying the permissible uses for a special exception, zoning ordinances normally include the standards by which an application for a special exception is to be evaluated. Typical standards include compatibility with surrounding uses and the availability of adequate parking and utilities. Other ordinances include more open-ended standards, such as "furthering the general welfare." See *People's Counsel for Baltimore County v. Mangione*, 584 A.2d 1318 (Md. Ct. Spec. App. 1991). If a permit applicant can demonstrate that its proposed use satisfies the specified standards, courts often will invalidate a permit denial, but the cases are not uniform. See, e.g., *Mann v. Lower Makefield Twp.*, 634 A.2d 768 (Pa. Commw. Ct. 1993). Courts tend to be more receptive to special exceptions than to variances and zoning amendments because the legislature expressly included the permitted special exceptions in the ordinance, thereby demonstrating its determination that they are compatible with the jurisdiction's land use plan. See Daniel R. Mandelker, Land Use Law § 6.56 (5th ed. 2003).

2. To make special uses more compatible with surrounding uses, zoning ordinances normally authorize the imposition of conditions on a special use permit. For example, the permit may be conditioned on the owner's providing landscaped buffers along the property boundaries, limiting hours of operation, and limiting the location of entrances to the property. Courts routinely uphold such conditions if they are reasonable. E.g., *Leckey v. Lower Southampton Twp. Zoning Hearing Bd.*, 864 A.2d 593 (Pa. Commw. Ct. 2004).

B.   Modern Zoning Techniques

Despite its almost universal adoption in this country, Euclidean zoning presents two problems that initially may seem contradictory. First, despite the availability of variances, amendments, and special exceptions, Euclidean zoning can be too restrictive and inflexible. Particularly under zoning ordinances with exclusive use districts, each type of residential, commercial, or industrial use is segregated into a specified area. The ordinance provides little room for new forms of land use, such as mixed use developments in which people can live, work, and shop in the same area.

Euclidean zoning also can be too unrestricted. Except for residential districts, zoning districts often permit a variety of uses. For example, a retail district may include retail stores, restaurants, offices, automobile service stations, and many other uses. Therefore, the traditional zoning scheme usually does not afford methods for fine-tuning permitted uses and their methods of operation, which can be particularly problematic when the district adjoins different types of use districts or when a parcel in a district is rezoned to a different use classification.

To deal with these two types of problems, some jurisdictions now provide a variety of zoning techniques that are designed to give greater flexibility in land uses and increased control over permitted uses. The most commonly used devices are (1) the planned unit development (PUD), (2) the floating zone, and (3) contract, or conditional, zoning.

1. The *PUD*, which was first used in the 1960s, is one of the earliest zoning flexibility devices. Rather than rigidly separating different types of uses, PUDs permit a mixture. Some PUDs are exclusively residential but mix single-family with multifamily. Other PUDs also include commercial development. In fact, the seminal case upholding a PUD ordinance involved a development that included single-family residences, apartments, ski slopes, hotels, and restaurants. *Cheney v. Village 2 at New Hope, Inc.*, 241 A.2d 81 (Pa. 1968).

PUDs also may vary the usual lot size, density, and setback requirements for the district in which they are located. For example, rather than build forty single-family homes on forty identically-shaped parcels, a PUD can cluster the homes on one portion of the property. The remainder of the property could be left undeveloped as a common area for use by all the PUD residents, rather than limiting them to individually-owned yards. By permitting such variations, a developer can make the best use of the land's topography and preserve its desirable natural features, such as ponds and woods. Infrastructure costs also can be significantly less than for more traditional developments because roads and utilities do not have to be built throughout the entire development.

2. A *floating zone* is a use district that is defined in the text of the zoning ordinance but that is not given a fixed location on the zoning map. Instead, the uses allowed in a floating zone can be located anywhere that they would be appropriate and desirable, rather than being restricted to the one area designated for that use when the zoning code was enacted. Like a special exception, the landowner must apply for permission to use land for a use specified in the floating zone. However, the floating zone provides the government with greater control than does a special exception. The government more easily can refuse permission to a floating zone or impose more conditions, because special exception ordinances often specify the standards for approval and limit the types of conditions that can be imposed.

3. *Contract zoning*, which is sometimes known as *conditional zoning*, also provides the government with greater control. Under traditional Euclidean zoning, a landowner whose property is rezoned to a new use district can use the land in any way permitted in that district. In contrast, with contract zoning, the city rezones the land only if the owner legally restricts its use to just the particular use for which he is seeking the rezoning. In this way, neighboring land will not be subjected in the future to other less desirable, albeit statutorily authorized, uses of the land.

PUDs, floating zones, and contract and conditional zoning have been subjected to a variety of legal challenges. The following case, *Rodgers v. Village of Tarrytown*, is a seminal case that is representative of the judicial reaction to such challenges.

RODGERS v. VILLAGE OF TARRYTOWN
96 N.E.2d 731 (N.Y. 1951)

FULD, J.

This appeal, here by our permission, involves the validity of two amendments to the General Zoning Ordinance of the Village of Tarrytown, a suburban area in the County of Westchester, within twenty-five miles of New York City.

Some years ago, Tarrytown enacted a General Zoning Ordinance dividing the village into seven districts or zones — Residence A for single family dwellings, Residence B for two-family dwellings, Residence C for multiple dwellings and apartment houses, three business districts and an industrial zone. In 1947 and 1948, the board of trustees, the village's legislative body, passed the two amendatory ordinances here under attack.

The 1947 ordinance creates "A new district or class of zone . . . [to] be called 'Residence B-B'," in which, besides one- and two-family dwellings, buildings for multiple occupancy of fifteen or fewer families were permitted. The boundaries of the new type of district were not delineated in the ordinance but were to be "fixed by amendment of the official village building zone map, at such times in the future as such district or class of zone is applied, to properties in this village." The village planning board was empowered to approve such amendments and, in case such approval was withheld, the board of trustees was authorized to grant it by appropriate resolution. In addition, the ordinance erected exacting standards of size and physical layouts for Residence B-B zones: a minimum of ten acres of land and a maximum building height of three stories were mandated; set-back and spacing requirements for structures were carefully prescribed; and no more than 15% of the ground area of the plot was to be occupied by buildings.

A year and a half after the 1947 amendment was enacted, defendant Elizabeth Rubin sought to have her property, consisting of almost ten and a half acres in the Residence A district, placed in a Residence B-B classification. After repeated modification of her plans to meet suggestions of the village planning board, that body gave its approval, and, several months later, in December of 1948, the board of trustees, also approving, passed the second ordinance here under attack. In essence, it provides that the Residence B-B district "is hereby applied to the [Rubin] property . . . and the district or zone of said property is hereby changed to 'Residence B-B' and the official Building Zone Map of the Village of Tarrytown is hereby amended accordingly [by specification of the various parcels and plots involved]."

Plaintiff, who owns a residence on a six-acre plot about a hundred yards from Rubin's property, brought this action to have the two amendments declared invalid and to enjoin defendant Rubin from constructing multiple dwellings on her property. The courts below, adjudging the amendments valid and the action of the trustees proper, dismissed the complaint. We agree with their determination.

While stability and regularity are undoubtedly essential to the operation of zoning plans, zoning is by no means static. Changed or changing conditions call for changed plans, and persons who own property in a particular zone or use district enjoy no eternally vested right to that classification if the public interest demands otherwise. Accordingly, the power of a village to amend its basic zoning ordinance in such a way as reasonably to promote the general welfare cannot be questioned. Just as clearly, the decision as to how a community shall be zoned or rezoned, as to how various properties shall be classified or reclassified, rests with the local legislative body; its judgment and determination will be conclusive, beyond interference from the courts, unless shown to be arbitrary, and the burden of establishing such arbitrariness is imposed upon him who asserts it. In that connection, we recently said in *Shepard v. Village of Skaneateles*, 300 N.Y. 115, 118, 89 N.E.2d 619, 620: "Upon parties who attack an ordinance . . . rests the burden of showing that the regulation assailed is not justified under the police power of the state by any reasonable interpretation of the facts. 'If the validity of the legislative classification for zoning purposes be fairly debatable, the legislative judgment must be allowed to control.' *Village of Euclid v. Ambler Realty Co.*, 272 U.S. 365, 388. . . ."

By that test, the propriety of the decision here made is not even debatable. In other words, viewing the rezoning in the case before us, as it must be viewed, in the light of the area involved and the present and reasonably foreseeable needs of the community, the conclusion is inescapable that what was done not only accorded with sound zoning principles, not only complied with every requirement of law, but was accomplished in a proper, careful and reasonable manner.

The Tarrytown board of trustees was entitled to find that there was a real need for additional housing facilities; that the creation of Residence B-B districts for garden apartment developments would prevent young families, unable to find accommodations in the village, from moving elsewhere; would attract business to the community; would lighten the tax load of the small home owner, increasingly burdened by the shrinkage of tax revenues resulting from the depreciated value of large estates and the transfer of many such estates to tax-exempt institutions; and would develop otherwise unmarketable and decaying property.

The village's zoning aim being clear, the choice of methods to accomplish it lay with the board. Two such methods were at hand. It could amend the General Zoning Ordinance so as to permit garden apartments on any plot of ten acres or more in Residence A and B zones (the zones more restricted) or it could amend that Ordinance so as to invite owners of ten or more acres, who wished to build garden apartments on their properties, to apply for a Residence B-B classification. The board chose to adopt the latter procedure. That it called for separate legislative authorization for each project presents no obstacle or drawback and so we have already held. . . . Whether we would have made the same choice is not the issue; it is sufficient that the board's decision was neither arbitrary nor unreasonable.

As to the requirement that the applicant own a plot of at least ten acres, we find nothing therein unfair to plaintiff or other owners of smaller parcels. The board undoubtedly found, as it was privileged to find, that garden apartments would blend more attractively and harmoniously with the community setting, would impose less of a burden upon village facilities, if placed upon larger tracts of land rather than scattered about in smaller units. Obviously, some definite acreage had to be chosen, and, so far as the record before us reveals, the choice of ten acres as a minimum plot was well within the range of an unassailable legislative judgment. . . .

Nor did the board, by following the course which it did, divest itself or the planning board of power to regulate future zoning with regard to garden apartments. The mere circumstance that an owner possesses a ten-acre plot and submits plans conforming to the physical requirements prescribed by the 1947 amendment will not entitle him, *ipso facto*, to a Residence B-B classification. It will still be for the board to decide, in the exercise of a reasonable discretion, that the *grant* of such a classification accords with the comprehensive zoning plan and benefits the village as a whole. And — while no such question is here presented — we note that the board may not arbitrarily or unreasonably *deny* applications of other owners for permission to construct garden apartments on their properties. The action of the board must in all cases be reasonable and, whether a particular application be granted or denied, recourse may be had to the courts to correct an arbitrary or capricious determination. . . .

The charge of illegal "spot zoning" — leveled at the creation of a Residence B-B district and the reclassification of defendant's property — is without substance. Defined as the process of singling out a small parcel of land for a use classification totally different from that of the surrounding area, for the benefit of the owner of such property and to the detriment of other owners, "spot zoning" is the very antithesis of planned zoning. If, therefore, an ordinance is enacted in accordance with a comprehensive zoning plan, it is not "spot zoning," even though it (1) singles out and affects but one small plot or (2) creates in the center of a large zone small areas or districts devoted to a different use. See *Nappi v. La Guardia*, 295 N.Y. 652, 64 N.E.2d 716, *affirming* 269 App. Div. 693, 54 N.Y.S.2d 722, *affirming* 184 Misc. 775, 55 N.Y.S.2d 80 — business area in residence zone; *Marshall v. Salt Lake City*, 105 Utah 111, 126–127, 141 P.2d 704, 149 A.L.R. 282 — business district in residence zone; *Higbee v. Chicago, B. & Q.R.R. Co.*, 235 Wis. 91, 98–99, 292 N.W. 320, 128 A.L.R. 734 — railroad station in residence zone. Thus, the relevant inquiry is not whether the particular zoning under attack consists of areas fixed within larger areas of different use, but whether it was accomplished for the benefit of individual owners rather than pursuant to a comprehensive plan for the general welfare of the community. Having already noted our conclusion that the ordinances were enacted to promote a comprehensive zoning plan, it is perhaps unnecessary to add that the record negates any claim that they were designed solely for the advantage of defendant or any other particular owner. Quite apart from the circumstance that defendant did not seek the benefit of the 1947 amendment until eighteen months after its passage, the all-significant fact is that that amendment applied to the entire territory of the village and accorded each and every owner of ten or more acres identical rights and privileges.

By the same token, there is no basis for the argument that "what has been done by the board of trustees" constitutes a device for "the granting of a 'variance'," opinion of Conway, J., 302 N.Y. p. 129, 96 N.E.2d 738. As we have already shown, the village's zoning aim, the statute's purpose, was not to aid the individual owner but to permit the development of the property for the general welfare of the entire community. That being so, the board of trustees followed approved procedure by changing the General Zoning Ordinance itself. See, e.g., *Matter of Clark v. Board of Zoning Appeals*, 301 N.Y. 86, 91, 92 N.E.2d 903, 905. Accordingly, when the board was called upon to consider the reclassification of the Rubin property under the 1947 Amendment, it was concerned, not with any issue of hardship, but only with the question of whether the property constituted a desirable location for a garden apartment.

We turn finally to the contention that the 1947 ordinance is invalid because, in proclaiming a Residence B-B district, it set no boundaries for the new district and made no changes on the building zone map. The short answer is that, since the ordinance merely prescribed specifications for a new use district, there was no need for it to do either the one or the other. True, until boundaries are fixed and until zoning map changes are made, no new zone actually comes into being, and neither property nor the rights of any property owner are affected. But it was not the design of the board of trustees by that enactment to bring any additional zone into being or to affect any property or rights; the ordinance merely provided the mechanics pursuant to which property owners might in the future apply for the redistricting of their property. In sum, the 1947 amendment was merely the first step in a reasoned plan of rezoning, and specifically provided for further action on the part of the board. That action was taken by the passage of the 1948 ordinance which fixed the boundaries of the newly created zone and amended the zoning map accordingly. It is indisputable that the two amendments, read together as they must be, fully complied with the requirements of the Village Law and accomplished a rezoning of village property in an unexceptionable manner.

In point of fact, there would have been no question about the validity of what was done had the board simply amended the General Zoning Ordinance so as to permit property in Residence A and Residence B zones or, for that matter, in the other districts throughout the village to be used for garden apartments, provided that they were built on ten-acre plots and that the other carefully planned conditions and restrictions were met. It may be conceded that, under the method which the board did adopt, no one will know, from the 1947 ordinance itself, precisely where a Residence B-B district will ultimately be located. But since such a district is simply a garden apartment development, we find nothing unusual or improper in that circumstance. The same uncertainty as to the location of the various types of structures would be present if a zoning ordinance were to sanction garden apartments as well as one-family homes in a Residence A district and yet there would be no doubt as to the propriety of that procedure. . . . Consequently, to condemn the action taken by the board in effectuating a perfectly permissible zoning scheme and to strike down the ordinance designed to carry out that scheme merely because the board had employed two steps to accomplish what may be, and usually is, done in one, would be to exalt form over substance and sacrifice substance to form.

Whether it is generally desirable that garden apartments be freely mingled among private residences under all circumstances, may be arguable. In view, however, of Tarrytown's changing scene and the other substantial reasons for the board's decision, we cannot say that its action was arbitrary or illegal. While hardships may be imposed on this or that owner, "cardinal is the principle that what is best for the body politic in the long run must prevail over the interests of particular individuals." *Shepard v. Village of Skaneateles, supra*, 300 N.Y. 115, 118, 89 N.E.2d 619, 620.

The judgment of the Appellate Division should be affirmed, with costs.

CONWAY, J., dissenting.

The decision here made gives judicial sanction to a novel and unprecedented device whereby the board of trustees of a village may, in the exercise of its discretion, authorize the erection of multiple family dwellings on property, located wholly within established districts theretofore uniformly zoned for use as one- or two-family dwellings, by the simple expedient of declaring, upon the application of individuals owning a certain acreage, that henceforth such property shall constitute a new and separate zoning district. The device may have much to commend it in the way of administrative convenience, but it most assuredly is not "zoning," as that term has previously been understood. We think the action of the board of trustees of the village of Tarrytown is unauthorized by the Village Law of this State, which is the sole source of the board's power to act. Moreover, we feel that the board's action, here approved, is completely at odds with all sound zoning theory and practice, and may well prove to be the opening wedge in the destruction of effective and efficient zoning in this State. . . .

NOTES

1. Zoning flexibility devices have been the subject of a variety of legal challenges. In addition to equal protection and substantive due process, challengers have argued that the city did not have the authority to adopt them if the applicable zoning enabling legislation does not expressly authorize their use, as most do not. The flexibility devices also have been challenged as violating the statutory requirement that land use regulations be uniform, because they often permit otherwise nonconforming uses. Some litigants also have argued that flexibility devices constitute an unlawful delegation of the legislative zoning power to the administrative body that administers the zoning code. The majority of courts have rejected these challenges, just as they have rejected the spot zoning and other challenges considered in *Rodgers*. However, judicial reaction has not been uniform, and some courts have invalidated these newer zoning approaches.

2. Although courts generally uphold the legality of zoning flexibility devices, some commentators question the wisdom of their use. They argue that individually negotiated uses adversely affect the ability to achieve uniformity of use, much like other nonconforming uses. Individually negotiated zoning decisions also create enhanced possibilities for subjective and discriminatory land use decisions. Finally, a variety of land use agreements in a use district with differing conditions and permitted uses can hinder effective enforcement of the zoning code. See, e.g., Daniel Mandelker, Land Use Law § 6.62 (5th ed. 2003). Are there ways to provide flexibility in land use regulation while avoiding these potential problems?

C.   Exclusionary Zoning

By its nature, Euclidean zoning is exclusionary; property uses are excluded from every portion of the community except those that are expressly zoned for them. However, certain types of zoning restrictions also can exclude certain property *users*. For example, large lot size or minimum floor area requirements and prohibitions on multifamily residential developments and on mobile home parks can make housing in the community too expensive for low- and moderate-income families. Indirectly, these types of restrictions can cause communities to be racially segregated because members of racial minorities are disproportionately represented in the low- and moderate-income populations. The term "exclusionary zoning" refers to those types of zoning restrictions that increase the cost of housing beyond the means of all but the more affluent members of our society.

1.   Federal Courts

VILLAGE OF ARLINGTON HEIGHTS v. METROPOLITAN HOUSING DEVELOPMENT CORPORATION
429 U.S. 252 (1977)

Mr. Justice Powell delivered the opinion of the Court.

In 1971 respondent Metropolitan Housing Development Corporation (MHDC) applied to petitioner, the Village of Arlington Heights, Ill., for the rezoning of a

15-acre parcel from single-family to multiple-family classification. Using federal financial assistance, MHDC planned to build 190 clustered townhouse units for low- and moderate-income tenants. The Village denied the rezoning request. MHDC, joined by other plaintiffs who are also respondents here, brought suit in the United States District Court for the Northern District of Illinois. They alleged that the denial was racially discriminatory and that it violated, *inter alia*, the Fourteenth Amendment and the Fair Housing Act of 1968, 82 Stat. 81, 42 U.S.C. § 3601 *et seq.* Following a bench trial, the District Court entered judgment for the Village, 373 F. Supp. 208 (1974), and respondents appealed. The Court of Appeals for the Seventh Circuit reversed, finding that the "ultimate effect" of the denial was racially discriminatory, and that the refusal to rezone therefore violated the Fourteenth Amendment. 517 F.2d 409 (1975). We granted the Village's petition for certiorari, 423 U.S. 1030 (1975), and now reverse.

I.

Arlington Heights is a suburb of Chicago, located about 26 miles northwest of the downtown Loop area. Most of the land in Arlington Heights is zoned for detached single-family homes, and this is in fact the prevailing land use. The Village experienced substantial growth during the 1960's, but, like other communities in northwest Cook County, its population of racial minority groups remained quite low. According to the 1970 census, only 27 of the Village's 64,000 residents were black.

The Clerics of St. Viator, a religious order (Order), own an 80-acre parcel just east of the center of Arlington Heights. Part of the site is occupied by the Viatorian high school, and part by the Order's three-story novitiate building, which houses dormitories and a Montessori school. Much of the site, however, remains vacant. Since 1959, when the Village first adopted a zoning ordinance, all the land surrounding the Viatorian property has been zoned R-3, a single-family specification with relatively small minimum lot-size requirements. On three sides of the Viatorian land there are single-family homes just across a street; to the east the Viatorian property directly adjoins the backyards of other single-family homes.

The Order decided in 1970 to devote some of its land to low- and moderate-income housing. Investigation revealed that the most expeditious way to build such housing was to work through a nonprofit developer experienced in the use of federal housing subsidies under § 236 of the National Housing Act, 48 Stat. 1246, as added and amended, 12 U.S.C. § 1715z-1.

MHDC is such a developer. It was organized in 1968 by several prominent Chicago citizens for the purpose of building low- and moderate-income housing throughout the Chicago area. In 1970 MHDC was in the process of building one § 236 development near Arlington Heights and already had provided some federally assisted housing on a smaller scale in other parts of the Chicago area.

After some negotiation, MHDC and the Order entered into a 99-year lease and an accompanying agreement of sale covering a 15-acre site in the southeast corner of the Viatorian property. MHDC became the lessee immediately, but the sale agreement was contingent upon MHDC's securing zoning clearances from the Village and § 236 housing assistance from the Federal Government. If MHDC proved unsuccessful in securing either, both the lease and the contract of sale would lapse. The agreement established a bargain purchase price of $300,000, low enough to comply with federal limitations governing land-acquisition costs for § 236 housing.

MHDC engaged an architect and proceeded with the project, to be known as Lincoln Green. The plans called for 20 two-story buildings with a total of 190 units, each unit having its own private entrance from outside. One hundred of the units would have a single bedroom, thought likely to attract elderly citizens. The remainder would have two, three, or four bedrooms. A large portion of the site would remain open, with shrubs and trees to screen the homes abutting the property to the east.

The planned development did not conform to the Village's zoning ordinance and could not be built unless Arlington Heights rezoned the parcel to R-5, its multiple-family housing classification. Accordingly, MHDC filed with the Village Plan Commission a petition for rezoning, accompanied by supporting materials describing the development and specifying that it would be subsidized under § 236. The materials made clear that one requirement under § 236 is an affirmative marketing plan designed to assure that a subsidized development is racially integrated. MHDC also submitted studies demonstrating the need for housing of this type and analyzing the probable impact of the development. To prepare for the hearings before the Plan Commission and to assure compliance with the Village building code, fire regulations, and related requirements, MHDC consulted with the Village staff for preliminary review of the development. The parties have stipulated that every change recommended during such consultations was incorporated into the plans.

During the spring of 1971, the Plan Commission considered the proposal at a series of three public meetings, which drew large crowds. Although many of those attending were quite vocal and demonstrative in opposition to Lincoln Green, a number of individuals and representatives of community groups spoke in support of rezoning. Some of the comments, both from opponents and supporters, addressed what was referred to as the "social issue" — the desirability or undesirability of introducing at this location in Arlington Heights low- and moderate-income housing, housing that would probably be racially integrated.

Many of the opponents, however, focused on the zoning aspects of the petition, stressing two arguments. First, the area always had been zoned single-family, and the neighboring citizens had built or purchased there in reliance on that classification. Rezoning threatened to cause a measurable drop in property value for neighboring sites. Second, the Village's apartment policy, adopted by the Village Board in 1962 and amended in 1970, called for R-5 zoning primarily to serve as a buffer between single-family development and land uses thought incompatible, such as commercial or manufacturing districts. Lincoln Green did not meet this requirement, as it adjoined no commercial or manufacturing district.

At the close of the third meeting, the Plan Commission adopted a motion to recommend to the Village's Board of Trustees that it deny the request. The motion stated: "While the need for low and moderate income housing may exist in Arlington Heights or its environs, the Plan Commission would be derelict in recommending it at the proposed location." Two members voted against the motion and submitted a minority report, stressing that in their view the change to accommodate Lincoln Green represented "good zoning." The Village Board met on September 28, 1971, to consider MHDC's request and the recommendation of the Plan Commission. After a public hearing, the Board denied the rezoning by a 6-1 vote.

The following June MHDC and three Negro individuals filed this lawsuit against the Village, seeking declaratory and injunctive relief. A second nonprofit corporation and an individual of Mexican-American descent intervened as plaintiffs. The trial resulted in a judgment for petitioners. Assuming that MHDC had standing to bring the suit, the District Court held that the petitioners were not motivated by racial discrimination or intent to discriminate against low-income groups when they denied rezoning, but rather by a desire "to protect property values and the integrity of the Village's zoning plan." 373 F. Supp., at 211. The District Court concluded also that the denial would not have a racially discriminatory effect.

A divided Court of Appeals reversed. It first approved the District Court's finding that the defendants were motivated by a concern for the integrity of the zoning plan, rather than by racial discrimination. Deciding whether their refusal to rezone would have discriminatory effects was more complex. The court observed that the refusal would have a disproportionate impact on blacks. Based upon family income, blacks constituted 40% of those Chicago area residents who were eligible to become tenants of Lincoln Green, although they composed a far lower percentage of total area population. The court reasoned, however, that under our decision in *James v. Valtierra*, 402 U.S. 137 (1971), such a disparity in racial impact alone does not call for strict scrutiny of a municipality's decision that prevents the construction of the low-cost housing.[5]

There was another level to the court's analysis of allegedly discriminatory results. Invoking language from *Kennedy Park Homes Ass'n v. City of Lackawanna*, 436 F.2d 108, 112 (C.A.2 1971), *cert. denied*, 401 U.S. 1010 (1970), the Court of Appeals ruled that the denial of rezoning must be examined in light of its "historical context and ultimate effect."[6] 517 F.2d, at 413. Northwest Cook County was enjoying rapid growth in employment opportunities and population, but it continued to exhibit a high degree of residential segregation. The court held that Arlington Heights could not simply ignore this problem. Indeed, it found that the Village had been "exploiting" the situation by allowing itself to become a nearly all white community. *Id.*, at 414. The Village had no other current plans for building low- and moderate-income housing, and no other R-5 parcels in the Village were available to MHDC at an economically feasible price.

Against this background, the Court of Appeals ruled that the denial of the Lincoln Green proposal had racially discriminatory effects and could be tolerated only if it served compelling interests. Neither the buffer policy nor the desire to

---

[5] Nor is there reason to subject the Village's action to more stringent review simply because it involves respondents' interest in securing housing. *Lindsey v. Normet*, 405 U.S. 56, 73–74 (1972). See generally *San Antonio School Dist. v. Rodriguez*, 411 U.S. 1, 18–39 (1973).

[6] This language apparently derived from our decision in *Reitman v. Mulkey*, 387 U.S. 369, 373 (1967) (quoting from the opinion of the California Supreme Court in the case then under review).

protect property values met this exacting standard. The court therefore concluded that the denial violated the Equal Protection Clause of the Fourteenth Amendment.

II.

At the outset, petitioners challenge the respondents' standing to bring the suit. It is not clear that this challenge was pressed in the Court of Appeals, but since our jurisdiction to decide the case is implicated, *Jenkins v. McKeithen*, 395 U.S. 411, 421 (1969) (plurality opinion), we shall consider it.

In *Warth v. Seldin*, 422 U.S. 490 (1975), a case similar in some respects to this one, we reviewed the constitutional limitations and prudential considerations that guide a court in determining a party's standing, and we need not repeat that discussion here. The essence of the standing question, in its constitutional dimension, is "whether the plaintiff has 'alleged such a personal stake in the outcome of the controversy' [as] to warrant *his* invocation of federal-court jurisdiction and to justify exercise of the court's remedial powers on his behalf." *Id.*, at 498–499, quoting *Baker v. Carr*, 369 U.S. 186, 204 (1962). The plaintiff must show that he himself is injured by the challenged action of the defendant. The injury may be indirect, see *United States v. SCRAP*, 412 U.S. 669, 688 (1973), but the complaint must indicate that the injury is indeed fairly traceable to the defendant's acts or omissions. . . .

A.

Here there can be little doubt that MHDC meets the constitutional standing requirements. The challenged action of the petitioners stands as an absolute barrier to constructing the housing MHDC had contracted to place on the Viatorian site. If MHDC secures the injunctive relief it seeks, that barrier will be removed. An injunction would not, of course, guarantee that Lincoln Green will be built. MHDC would still have to secure financing, qualify for federal subsidies, and carry through with construction. But all housing developments are subject to some extent to similar uncertainties. When a project is as detailed and specific as Lincoln Green, a court is not required to engage in undue speculation as a predicate for finding that the plaintiff has the requisite personal stake in the controversy. MHDC has shown an injury to itself that is "likely to be redressed by a favorable decision." *Simon v. Eastern Ky. Welfare Rights Org.*, 426 U.S. 26, at 38.

Petitioners nonetheless appear to argue that MHDC lacks standing because it has suffered no economic injury. MHDC, they point out, is not the owner of the property in question. Its contract of purchase is contingent upon securing rezoning.[8] MHDC owes the owners nothing if rezoning is denied.

---

[8] Petitioners contend that MHDC lacks standing to pursue its claim here because a contract purchaser whose contract is contingent upon rezoning cannot contest a zoning decision in the Illinois courts. Under the law of Illinois, only the owner of the property has standing to pursue such an action. *Clark Oil & Refining Corp. v. City of Evanston*, 23 Ill. 2d 48, 177 N.E.2d 191 (1961); but see *Solomon v. City of Evanston*, 29 Ill. App. 3d 782, 331 N.E.2d 380 (1975).

State law of standing, however, does not govern such determinations in the federal courts. The

We cannot accept petitioners' argument. In the first place, it is inaccurate to say that MHDC suffers no economic injury from a refusal to rezone, despite the contingency provisions in its contract. MHDC has expended thousands of dollars on the plans for Lincoln Green and on the studies submitted to the Village in support of the petition for rezoning. Unless rezoning is granted, many of these plans and studies will be worthless even if MHDC finds another site at an equally attractive price.

Petitioners' argument also misconceives our standing requirements. It has long been clear that economic injury is not the only kind of injury that can support a plaintiff's standing. . . . MHDC is a nonprofit corporation. Its interest in building Lincoln Green stems not from a desire for economic gain, but rather from an interest in making suitable low-cost housing available in areas where such housing is scarce. This is not mere abstract concern about a problem of general interest. See *Sierra Club v. Morton*, 405 U.S., at 739. The specific project MHDC intends to build, whether or not it will generate profits, provides that "essential dimension of specificity" that informs judicial decision making. *Schlesinger v. Reservists to Stop the War*, 418 U.S. 208, 221 (1974).

B.

Clearly MHDC has met the constitutional requirements, and it therefore has standing to assert its own rights. Foremost among them is MHDC's right to be free of arbitrary or irrational zoning actions. . . . But the heart of this litigation has never been the claim that the Village's decision fails the generous *Euclid* test, recently reaffirmed in *Belle Terre*. Instead it has been the claim that the Village's refusal to rezone discriminates against racial minorities in violation of the Fourteenth Amendment. As a corporation, MHDC has no racial identity and cannot be the direct target of the petitioners' alleged discrimination. In the ordinary case, a party is denied standing to assert the rights of third persons. *Warth v. Seldin*, 422 U.S., at 499. But we need not decide whether the circumstances of this case would justify departure from that prudential limitation and permit MHDC to assert the constitutional rights of its prospective minority tenants. . . . For we have at least one individual plaintiff who has demonstrated standing to assert these rights as his own.[9]

Respondent Ransom, a Negro, works at the Honeywell factory in Arlington Heights and lives approximately 20 miles away in Evanston in a 5-room house with his mother and his son. The complaint alleged that he seeks and would qualify for the housing MHDC wants to build in Arlington Heights. Ransom testified at trial that if Lincoln Green were built he would probably move there, since it is closer to his job.

---

constitutional and prudential considerations canvassed at length in *Warth v. Seldin*, 422 U.S. 490 (1975), respond to concerns that are peculiarly federal in nature. Illinois may choose to close its courts to applicants for rezoning unless they have an interest more direct than MHDC's, but this choice does not necessarily disqualify MHDC from seeking relief in federal courts for an asserted injury to its federal rights.

[9] Because of the presence of this plaintiff, we need not consider whether the other individual and corporate plaintiffs have standing to maintain the suit.

The injury Ransom asserts is that his quest for housing nearer his employment has been thwarted by official action that is racially discriminatory. If a court grants the relief he seeks, there is at least a "substantial probability," *Warth v. Seldin, supra*, 422 U.S., at 504, that the Lincoln Green project will materialize, affording Ransom the housing opportunity he desires in Arlington Heights. His is not a generalized grievance. Instead, as we suggested in *Warth, supra*, at 507, 508 n. 18, it focuses on a particular project and is not dependent on speculation about the possible actions of third parties not before the court. See *id.*, at 505; *Simon v. Eastern Ky. Welfare Rights Org.*, 426 U.S., at 41–42. Unlike the individual plaintiffs in *Warth*, Ransom has adequately averred an "actionable causal relationship" between Arlington Heights' zoning practices and his asserted injury. *Warth v. Seldin, supra*, 422 U.S., at 507. We therefore proceed to the merits.

III.

Our decision last Term in *Washington v. Davis*, 426 U.S. 229 (1976), made it clear that official action will not be held unconstitutional solely because it results in a racially disproportionate impact. "Disproportionate impact is not irrelevant, but it is not the sole touchstone of an invidious racial discrimination." *Id.*, at 242. Proof of racially discriminatory intent or purpose is required to show a violation of the Equal Protection Clause. Although some contrary indications may be drawn from some of our cases, the holding in *Davis* reaffirmed a principle well established in a variety of contexts. E.g., *Keyes v. School Dist. No. 1, Denver, Colo.*, 413 U.S. 189, 208 (1973) (schools); *Wright v. Rockefeller*, 376 U.S. 52, 56–57 (1964) (election districting); *Akins v. Texas*, 325 U.S. 398, 403–404 (1945) (jury selection).

Davis does not require a plaintiff to prove that the challenged action rested solely on racially discriminatory purposes. Rarely can it be said that a legislature or administrative body operating under a broad mandate made a decision motivated solely by a single concern, or even that a particular purpose was the "dominant" or "primary" one. In fact, it is because legislators and administrators are properly concerned with balancing numerous competing considerations that courts refrain from reviewing the merits of their decisions, absent a showing of arbitrariness or irrationality. But racial discrimination is not just another competing consideration. When there is a proof that a discriminatory purpose has been a motivating factor in the decision, this judicial deference is no longer justified.

Determining whether invidious discriminatory purpose was a motivating factor demands a sensitive inquiry into such circumstantial and direct evidence of intent as may be available. The impact of the official action — whether it "bears more heavily on one race than another," *Washington v. Davis, supra*, 426 U.S., at 242 — may provide an important starting point. Sometimes a clear pattern, unexplainable on grounds other than race, emerges from the effect of the state action even when the governing legislation appears neutral on its face. *Yick Wo v. Hopkins*, 118 U.S. 356 (1886); . . . *Gomillion v. Lightfoot*, 364 U.S. 339 (1960). The evidentiary inquiry is then relatively easy. But such cases are rare. Absent a pattern as stark as that in *Gomillion* or *Yick Wo*, impact alone is not determinative,[14] and the Court must look

---

[14] This is not to say that a consistent pattern of official racial discrimination is a necessary predicate

to other evidence.

The historical background of the decision is one evidentiary source, particularly if it reveals a series of official actions taken for invidious purposes. . . . The specific sequence of events leading up to the challenged decision also may shed some light on the decision maker's purposes. . . . For example, if the property involved here always had been zoned R-5 but suddenly was changed to R-3 when the town learned of MHDC's plans to erect integrated housing,[16] we would have a far different case. Departures from the normal procedural sequence also might afford evidence that improper purposes are playing a role. Substantive departures too may be relevant, particularly if the factors usually considered important by the decision maker strongly favor a decision contrary to the one reached.[17]

The legislative or administrative history may be highly relevant, especially where there are contemporary statements by members of the decision making body, minutes of its meetings, or reports. In some extraordinary instances the members might be called to the stand at trial to testify concerning the purpose of the official action, although even then such testimony frequently will be barred by privilege. . . .[18]

The foregoing summary identifies, without purporting to be exhaustive, subjects of proper inquiry in determining whether racially discriminatory intent existed. With these in mind, we now address the case before us.

IV.

This case was tried in the District Court and reviewed in the Court of Appeals before our decision in *Washington v. Davis, supra.* The respondents proceeded on the erroneous theory that the Village's refusal to rezone carried a racially

---

to a violation of the Equal Protection Clause. A single invidiously discriminatory governmental act in the exercise of the zoning power as elsewhere would not necessarily be immunized by the absence of such discrimination in the making of other comparable decisions. See *City of Richmond v. United States,* 422 U.S. 358, 378 (1975).

[16] See, e. g., *Progress Development Corp. v. Mitchell,* 286 F.2d 222 (C.A.7 1961) (park board allegedly condemned plaintiffs' land for a park upon learning that the homes plaintiffs were erecting there would be sold under a marketing plan designed to assure integration); *Kennedy Park Homes Ass'n v. City of Lackawanna,* 436 F.2d 108 (C.A.2 1970), *cert. denied,* 401 U.S. 1010 (1971) (town declared moratorium on new subdivisions and rezoned area for parkland shortly after learning of plaintiffs' plans to build low income housing). To the extent that the decision in *Kennedy Park Homes* rested solely on a finding of discriminatory impact, we have indicated our disagreement. *Washington v. Davis, supra,* 426 U.S., at 244–245.

[17] See *Dailey v. City of Lawton,* 425 F.2d 1037 (C.A.10 1970). The plaintiffs in *Dailey* planned to build low-income housing on the site of a former school that they had purchased. The city refused to rezone the land from PF, its public facilities classification, to R-4, high-density residential. All the surrounding area was zoned R-4, and both the present and the former planning director for the city testified that there was no reason "from a zoning standpoint" why the land should not be classified R-4. Based on this and other evidence, the Court of Appeals ruled that "the record sustains the [District Court's] holding of racial motivation and of arbitrary and unreasonable action." *Id.,* at 1040.

[18] This Court has recognized, ever since *Fletcher v. Peck,* 6 Cranch 87, 130–131 (1810), that judicial inquiries into legislative or executive motivation represent a substantial intrusion into the workings of other branches of government. Placing a decision maker on the stand is therefore "usually to be avoided." *Citizens to Preserve Overton Park v. Volpe,* 401 U.S. 402, 420 (1971). . . .

discriminatory effect and was, without more, unconstitutional. But both courts below understood that at least part of their function was to examine the purpose underlying the decision. In making its findings on this issue, the District Court noted that some of the opponents of Lincoln Green who spoke at the various hearings might have been motivated by opposition to minority groups. The court held, however, that the evidence "does not warrant the conclusion that this motivated the defendants." 373 F. Supp., at 211.

On appeal the Court of Appeals focused primarily on respondents' claim that the Village's buffer policy had not been consistently applied and was being invoked with a strictness here that could only demonstrate some other underlying motive. The court concluded that the buffer policy, though not always applied with perfect consistency, had on several occasions formed the basis for the Board's decision to deny other rezoning proposals. "The evidence does not necessitate a finding that Arlington Heights administered this policy in a discriminatory manner." 517 F.2d, at 412. The Court of Appeals therefore approved the District Court's findings concerning the Village's purposes in denying rezoning to MHDC.

We also have reviewed the evidence. The impact of the Village's decision does arguably bear more heavily on racial minorities. Minorities constitute 18% of the Chicago area population, and 40% of the income groups said to be eligible for Lincoln Green. But there is little about the sequence of events leading up to the decision that would spark suspicion. The area around the Viatorian property has been zoned R-3 since 1959, the year when Arlington Heights first adopted a zoning map. Single-family homes surround the 80-acre site, and the Village is undeniably committed to single-family homes as its dominant residential land use. The rezoning request progressed according to the usual procedures. The Plan Commission even scheduled two additional hearings, at least in part to accommodate MHDC and permit it to supplement its presentation with answers to questions generated at the first hearing.

The statements by the Plan Commission and Village Board members, as reflected in the official minutes, focused almost exclusively on the zoning aspects of the MHDC petition, and the zoning factors on which they relied are not novel criteria in the Village's rezoning decisions. There is no reason to doubt that there has been reliance by some neighboring property owners on the maintenance of single-family zoning in the vicinity. The Village originally adopted its buffer policy long before MHDC entered the picture and has applied the policy too consistently for us to infer discriminatory purpose from its application in this case. Finally, MHDC called one member of the Village Board to the stand at trial. Nothing in her testimony supports an inference of invidious purpose.

In sum, the evidence does not warrant overturning the concurrent findings of both courts below. Respondents simply failed to carry their burden of proving that discriminatory purpose was a motivating factor in the Village's decision.[21] This

---

[21] Proof that the decision by the Village was motivated in part by a racially discriminatory purpose would not necessarily have required invalidation of the challenged decision. Such proof would, however, have shifted to the Village the burden of establishing that the same decision would have resulted even had the impermissible purpose not been considered. If this were established, the complaining party in a case of this kind no longer fairly could attribute the injury complained of to improper consideration of a

conclusion ends the constitutional inquiry. The Court of Appeals' further finding that the Village's decision carried a discriminatory "ultimate effect" is without independent constitutional significance.

V.

Respondents' complaint also alleged that the refusal to rezone violated the Fair Housing Act of 1968, 42 U.S.C. § 3601 *et seq.* They continue to urge here that a zoning decision made by a public body may, and that petitioners' action did, violate § 3604 or § 3617. The Court of Appeals, however, proceeding in a somewhat unorthodox fashion, did not decide the statutory question. We remand the case for further consideration of respondents' statutory claims.

Reversed and remanded.

NOTES

1.   After the *Arlington Heights* decision, who has standing in federal court to challenge a municipality's exclusionary zoning?

2.   In *Arlington Heights*, the Supreme Court stated that discriminatory intent can be inferred when "a clear pattern, unexplainable on grounds other than race, emerges from the effect of state action even when the governing legislation appears neutral on its face." 429 U.S. at 266. The Village's population of 64,000 residents included only twenty-seven African-Americans (approximately .0004%). Why was this fact inadequate to prove a pattern of racial discrimination?

3.   The Supreme Court remanded the *Arlington Heights* case to the Seventh Circuit to determine whether the failure to rezone violated the federal Fair Housing Act (FHA), 42 U.S.C. §§ 3601–3619. Section 3604(a) of the Act provided at the time of the case that "it shall be unlawful . . . [t]o make unavailable or deny . . . a dwelling to any person because of race, color, religion, or national origin." On remand, the Seventh Circuit held that exclusionary zoning could violate § 3604(a) even without proof of discriminatory intent: "Conduct that has the necessary and foreseeable consequence of perpetuating segregation can be as deleterious as purposefully discriminatory conduct in frustrating the national commitment 'to replace the ghettos "by truly integrated and balanced living patterns.' " . . . Moreover, a requirement that the plaintiff prove discriminatory intent . . . is often a burden that is impossible to satisfy." 558 F.2d 1283, 1289–90.

However, the Seventh Circuit was unwilling to hold that every zoning action that produces discriminatory effects violates the FHA. Therefore, the court created a four-part test to determine whether a zoning action violates § 3604(a): (1) magnitude of the discriminatory effect, (2) evidence of a discriminatory purpose, though it need not be sufficient to prove an equal protection violation, (3) the public purpose for the government action, and (4) the requested relief.

---

discriminatory purpose. In such circumstances, there would be no justification for judicial interference with the challenged decision. But in this case respondents failed to make the required threshold showing. See *Mt. Healthy City School Dist. Bd. of Education v. Doyle*, 429 U.S. 274.

Applying the four-part test, the Seventh Circuit held that Arlington Heights' refusal to rezone violated § 3604(a) unless it could show that other property in the Village was properly zoned and was suitable for subsidized low-cost housing. The Seventh Circuit remanded the case to the district court to make that finding, but the parties settled the action before the district court rendered a decision. Pursuant to the settlement, Arlington Heights annexed a parcel of unincorporated land on the edge of the Village and rezoned it for the proposed development. The annexed land was bounded in part by the Village of Mount Prospect. Mount Prospect intervened in the district court action to object to the settlement, but the court approved it. Does this settlement satisfy the objectives of the FHA?

The First, Second, Third, Fourth, Fifth, Sixth, Eighth, and Ninth Circuits also have held that discriminatory intent is unnecessary to establish an FHA violation. See, e.g., *Huntington Branch, NAACP v. Town of Huntington*, 844 F.2d 926 (2d Cir. 1988), *aff'd*, 488 U.S. 15 (1988) (the Supreme Court did not decide whether discriminatory effect alone is adequate); *United States v. Black Jack*, 508 F.2d 1179 (8th Cir. 1974); *Mountain Side Mobile Estates Partnership v. Secretary of Housing and Urban Development*, 56 F.3d 1243 (10th Cir. 1995). On February 8, 2013, the Department of Housing and Urban Development (HUD) promulgated a final rule that reflected its long-standing policy that "[l]iability may be established under the Fair Housing Act based on a practice's discriminatory effect . . . even if the practice was not motivated by a discriminatory intent." 24 C.F.R. § 100.500. However, the FHA does not expressly allow disparate impact claims. The U.S. Supreme Court has demonstrated significant interest in this issue. It granted certiorari in cases in 2011 and 2013 that presented this issue, but both cases were withdrawn before the oral arguments. *Mt. Holly Gardens Citizens in Action v. Township of Mount Holly*, 658 F.3d 375 (3d Cir. 2011), *cert. granted*, 133 S. Ct. 2824 (2013); *Gallagher v. Magner*, 619 F.3d 823 (8th Cir. 2010), *cert. granted*, 132 S. Ct. 548 (2011). The Court granted certiorari in yet another case in 2014 and heard oral arguments in January 2015. *The Inclusive Communities Project, Inc. v. Texas Dep't of Housing and Community Affairs*, 747 F.3d 275 (5th Cir.), *cert. granted*, 135 S. Ct. 46 (2014). See also Stacy E. Seicsnaydre, *Is Disparate Impact Having Any Impact? An Appellate Analysis of Forty Years of Disparate Impact Claims Under the Fair Housing Act*, 63 Am. U.L. Rev. 357 (2013).

2. State Courts

In some state courts, challenges to exclusionary zoning have been more successful than in the federal courts. This difference is attributable in part to the more lenient standing rules in some states. Unlike the federal Constitution, many state constitutions do not limit a court's jurisdiction to "cases or controversies." As seen in *Arlington Heights*, the federal standing requirements have substantially restricted the pool of prospective plaintiffs that can challenge exclusionary zoning.

Some state courts have interpreted their state constitution to provide broader housing rights than does the federal Constitution. The U.S. Supreme Court has held that housing is not a fundamental right under the federal Constitution. *Lindsey v. Normet*, 405 U.S. 56 (1972). Therefore, zoning devices that impede the ability to obtain housing are subject only to rational relationship review unless the plaintiff can prove racial discrimination.

Finally, as demonstrated by the next case, some state courts have been willing to grant affirmative relief from exclusionary zoning, rather than simply invalidating it.

BRITTON v. TOWN OF CHESTER
595 A.2d 492 (N.H. 1991)

BATCHELDER, J.

In this appeal, the defendant, the Town of Chester (the town), challenges a ruling by the Master (R. Peter Shapiro, Esq.), approved by the Superior Court (Gray, J.), that the Chester Zoning Ordinance is invalid and unconstitutional. In addition, the town argues that the relief granted to plaintiff Remillard, permitting him to construct multi-family housing on a parcel not currently zoned for such development, violates the separation of powers provision of the New Hampshire Constitution, N.H. Const. pt. I, art. 37, and creates an unreasonable use for this parcel. We modify the trial court's ruling that the ordinance as a whole is invalid, but we affirm the granting of specific relief to plaintiff Remillard as well as the court's ruling that the ordinance, on the facts of this case, is unlawful as applied.

The plaintiffs brought a petition in 1985, for declaratory and injunctive relief, challenging the validity of the multi-family housing provisions of the Chester Zoning Ordinance. The master's report, filed after a hearing, contains extensive factual findings which we summarize here. The town of Chester lies in the west-central portion of Rockingham County, thirteen miles east of the city of Manchester. Primary highway access is provided by New Hampshire Routes 102 and 121. The available housing stock is principally single-family homes. There is no municipal sewer or water service, and other municipal services remain modest. The town has not encouraged industrial or commercial development; it is a "bedroom community," with the majority of its labor force commuting to Manchester. Because of its close proximity to job centers and the ready availability of vacant land, the town is projected to have among the highest growth rates in New Hampshire over the next two decades.

The United States Department of Housing and Urban Development, having settled upon the median income for non-metropolitan Rockingham County as a yardstick, has determined that a low-income family in Chester is a household with annual earnings of $16,500 or less, and a moderate-income family has annual earnings of $16,501 to $25,680. Various federal and State government agencies have also determined that low- and moderate-income families should not pay in excess of 30% of their gross income for rent. Thus, a low-income family in Chester should pay less than $4,950 annually, and a moderate-income family in Chester should pay between $4,951 and $7,704 annually, for housing.

The plaintiffs in this case are a group of low- and moderate-income people who have been unsuccessful in finding affordable, adequate housing in the town, and a builder who, the master found, is committed to the construction of such housing. At trial, two plaintiffs testified as representative members of the group of low- and moderate-income people. Plaintiff George Edwards is a woodcutter who grew up in the town. He lives in Chester with his wife and three minor children in a one-bedroom, thirty-foot by eight-foot camper trailer with no running water. Their annual income is $14,040, which places them in the low-income category. Roger McFarland grew up and works in the town. He lives in Derry with his wife and three teenage children in a two-bedroom apartment which is too small to meet their needs. He and his wife both work, and their combined annual income is $24,000. Under the area standards, the McFarlands are a moderate-income family. Raymond Remillard is the plaintiff home builder. A long-time resident of the town, he owns an undeveloped twenty-three-acre parcel of land on Route 102 in the town's eastern section. Since 1979, he has attempted to obtain permission from the town to build a moderate-sized multi-family housing development on his land.

The zoning ordinance in effect at the beginning of this action in 1985 provided for a single-family home on a two-acre lot or a duplex on a three-acre lot, and it excluded multi-family housing from all five zoning districts in the town. In July, 1986, the town amended its zoning ordinance to allow multi-family housing. Article six of the amended ordinance now permits multi-family housing as part of a "planned residential development" (PRD), a form of multi-family housing required to include a variety of housing types, such as single-family homes, duplexes, and multi-family structures. * * *

We first turn to the ordinance itself, because it does, on its face, permit the type of development that the plaintiffs argue is being prohibited. The master found, however, that the ordinance placed an unreasonable barrier to the development of affordable housing for low- and moderate-income families. Under the ordinance, PRDs are allowed on tracts of not less than twenty acres in two designated "R-2" (medium-density residential) zoning districts. Due to existing home construction and environmental considerations, such as wetlands and steep slopes, only slightly more than half of all the land in the two R-2 districts could reasonably be used for multi-family development. This constitutes only 1.73% of the land in the town. This fact standing alone does not, in the confines of this case, give rise to an entitlement to a legal remedy for those who seek to provide multi-family housing. However, it does serve to point out that the two R-2 districts are, in reality, less likely to be developed than would appear from a reading of the ordinance. A reviewing court must read the entire ordinance in the light of these facts.

Article six of the ordinance also imposes several subjective requirements and restrictions on the developer of a PRD. Any project must first receive the approval of the town planning board as to "whether in its judgment the proposal meets the objectives and purposes set forth [in the ordinance] in which event the Administrator [i.e., the planning board] may grant approval to [the] proposal subject to reasonable conditions and limitations." Consequently, the ordinance allows the planning board to control various aspects of a PRD without reference to any objective criteria. One potentially onerous section permits the planning board to "retain, at the applicant's expense, a registered professional engineer, hydrologist, and any other applicable professional to represent the [planning board] and assist the [planning board] in determining compliance with [the] ordinance and other applicable regulations." The master found such subjective review for developing multi-family housing to be a substantial disincentive to the creation of such units, because it would escalate the economic risks of developing affordable housing to the point where these projects would not be realistically feasible. In addition, we question the availability of bank financing for such projects, where the developer is required to submit a "blank check" to the planning board along with his proposal, and where to do so could halt, change the character of, or even bankrupt the project.

The defendant first argues that the trial court erred in ruling that the zoning ordinance exceeds the powers delegated to the town by the zoning enabling legislation, RSA 674:16-30. In support of this argument, the town asserts that the zoning enabling act does not require it to zone for the low-income housing needs of the region beyond its boundaries. Further, the town maintains that even if it were required to consider regional housing needs when enacting its zoning ordinance, the Chester Zoning Ordinance is valid because it provides for an adequate range of housing types. These arguments fail to persuade us of any error in the master's proposed order.

RSA 674:16 authorizes the local legislative body of any city or town to adopt or amend a zoning ordinance "[f]or the purpose of promoting the health, safety, or *the general welfare of the community.*" The defendant asserts that the term "community" as used in the statute refers only to the municipality itself and not to some broader region in which the municipality is situated. We disagree.

The possibility that a municipality might be obligated to consider the needs of the region outside its boundaries was addressed early on in our land use jurisprudence by the United States Supreme Court, paving the way for the term "community" to be used in the broader sense. In *Village of Euclid v. Ambler Realty Co.*, 272 U.S. 365 (1926), the Court recognized "the possibility of cases where the general public interest would so far outweigh the interest of the municipality that the municipality would not be allowed to stand in the way." *Id.* at 390. When an ordinance will have an impact beyond the boundaries of the municipality, the welfare of the entire affected region must be considered in determining the ordinance's validity. . . .

We have previously addressed the issue of whether municipalities are required to consider regional needs when enacting zoning ordinances which control growth. In *Beck v. Town of Raymond*, 118 N.H. 793, 394 A.2d 847 (1978), we held that "[growth] controls must not be imposed simply to exclude outsiders, . . ." especially outsiders of any disadvantaged social or economic group. We reasoned that "each municipality [should] bear its fair share of the burden of increased growth." *Id.* Today, we pursue the logical extension of the reasoning in *Beck* and apply its rationale and high purpose to zoning regulations which wrongfully exclude persons of low- or moderate-income from the zoning municipality.

In *Beck*, this court sent a message to zoning bodies that "[t]owns may not refuse to confront the future by building a moat around themselves and pulling up the drawbridge." *Id.* The town of Chester appears willing to lower that bridge only for people who can afford a single-family home on a two-acre lot or a duplex on a three-acre lot. Others are realistically prohibited from crossing.

Municipalities are not isolated enclaves, far removed from the concerns of the area in which they are situated. As subdivisions of the State, they do not exist solely to serve their own residents, and their regulations should promote the general welfare, both within and without their boundaries. Therefore, we interpret the general welfare provision of the zoning enabling statute, RSA 674:16, to include the welfare of the "community," as defined in this case, in which a municipality is located and of which it forms a part.

A municipality's power to zone property to promote the health, safety, and general welfare of the community is delegated to it by the State, and the municipality must, therefore, exercise this power in conformance with the enabling legislation. . . . Because the Chester Zoning Ordinance does not provide for the lawful needs of the community, in that it flies in the face of the general welfare provision of RSA 674:16 and is, therefore, at odds with the statute upon which it is grounded, we hold that, as applied to the facts of this case, the ordinance is an invalid exercise of the power delegated to the town pursuant to RSA 674:16–30. We so hold because of the master's finding that "there are no substantial and compelling reasons that would warrant the Town of Chester, through its land use ordinances, from fulfilling its obligation to provide low[-] and moderate[-]income families within the community and a proportionate share of same within its region from a realistic opportunity to obtain affordable housing." * * *

The trial court's order declared the Chester Zoning Ordinance invalid and unconstitutional; as a result, but for this appeal, the town has been left "unzoned." To leave the town with no land use controls would be incompatible with the orderly development of the general community, and the court erred when it ruled the ordinance invalid. It is not, however, within the power of this court to act as a super zoning board. "Zoning is properly a legislative function, and courts are prevented by the doctrine of separation of powers from invasion of this field." *Godfrey v. Zoning Bd. of Adjustment*, 317 N.C. 51, 58, 344 S.E.2d 272, 276 (1986). Moreover, our decision today is limited to those sections of the zoning ordinance which hinder the construction of multi-family housing units. Accordingly, we defer to the legislative body of the town, within a reasonable time period, to bring these sections of its zoning ordinance into line with the zoning enabling legislation and with this opinion. Consequently, we will temporarily allow the zoning ordinance to remain in effect.

As to the specific relief granted to plaintiff Remillard, the town contends that the court's order effectively rezones the parcel in violation of the separation of powers provision found in part I, article 37 of the New Hampshire Constitution. It further asserts that, even if it were lawful for a court to rezone or grant specific relief, plaintiff Remillard's proposed development does not qualify for such a remedy. * * *

The trial court has the power, subject to our review for abuse of discretion, to order definitive relief for plaintiff Remillard. In *Soares v. Town of Atkinson*, 129 N.H. 313, 529 A.2d 867 (1987), we upheld the master's finding that granting a "builder's remedy," i.e., allowing the plaintiff builder to complete his project as proposed, is discretionary. *Id.* at 316, 529 A.2d at 869. Although we there upheld the decision that such relief was inappropriate, noting that the master determined that the ordered revision of the town ordinances would permit the building of the plaintiff's project, we did not reject such relief as a proper remedy in appropriate zoning cases. *Id.* In this appeal, the master found such relief to be appropriate, and the town has not carried its burden on appeal to persuade us to the contrary. A successful plaintiff is entitled to relief which rewards his or her efforts in testing the legality of the ordinance and prevents retributive action by the municipality, such as correcting the illegality but taking pains to leave the plaintiff unbenefited. . . . The Pennsylvania Supreme Court reasoned in *Casey v. Zoning Board of Warwick Township*, 459 Pa. 219, 328 A.2d 464 (1974), that "[t]o forsake a challenger's reasonable development plans after all the time, effort and capital invested in such a challenge is grossly inequitable." *Id.* 328 A.2d at 469.

The master relied on *Southern Burlington County N.A.A.C.P. v. Township of Mount Laurel*, 92 N.J. 158, 456 A.2d 390 (1983) (*Mt. Laurel II*), in determining that plaintiff Remillard was entitled to build his development as proposed. In *Mount Laurel I*, the New Jersey Supreme Court held that the municipality's zoning ordinance violated the general welfare provision of its State Constitution by not affording a realistic opportunity for the construction of its "fair share" of the present and prospective regional need for low- and moderate-income housing. *Southern Burlington Cty. N.A.A.C.P. v. Mt. Laurel Tp.*, 67 N.J. 151, 174, 336 A.2d 713, 724, *appeal dismissed*, 423 U.S. 808 (1975). *Mt. Laurel II* was a return to the New Jersey Supreme Court, eight years later, prompted by the realization that *Mt. Laurel I* had not resulted in realistic housing opportunities for low- and moderate-income people, but in "paper, process, witnesses, trials and appeals." *Mt. Laurel II, supra*, 92 N.J. at 199, 456 A.2d at 410. The court noted that the "builder's remedy," which effectively grants a building permit to a plaintiff/developer, based on the development proposal, as long as other local regulations are followed, should be made more readily available to insure that low- and moderate-income housing is actually built. *Mt. Laurel II, supra* at 279, 456 A.2d at 452.

Since 1979, plaintiff Remillard has attempted to obtain permission to build a moderate-sized multi-family housing development on his land in Chester. He is committed to setting aside a minimum of ten of the forty-eight units for low- and moderate-income tenants for twenty years. "Equity will not suffer a wrong without a remedy." 2 Pomeroy's Equity Jurisprudence § 423 (5th ed. 1941). Hence, we hold that the "builder's remedy" is appropriate in this case, both to compensate the developer who has invested substantial time and resources in pursuing this litigation, and as the most likely means of insuring that low- and moderate-income housing is actually built.

Although we determine that the "builder's remedy" is appropriate in this case, we do not adopt the *Mt. Laurel* analysis for determining whether such a remedy will be granted. Instead, we find the rule developed in *Sinclair Pipe Line Co. v. Richton Park*, 19 Ill. 2d 370, 167 N.E.2d 406 (1960), is the better rule as it eliminates the calculation of arbitrary mathematical quotas which *Mt. Laurel* requires. That rule is followed with some variation by the supreme courts of several other States, . . . and awards relief to the plaintiff builder if his development is found to be reasonable, i.e., providing a realistic opportunity for the construction of low- and moderate-income housing and consistent with sound zoning concepts and environmental concerns. Once an existing zoning ordinance is found invalid in whole or in part, whether on constitutional grounds or, as here, on grounds of statutory construction and application, the court may provide relief in the form of a declaration that the plaintiff builder's proposed use is reasonable, and the municipality may not interfere with it. The plaintiff must bear the burden of proving reasonable use by a preponderance of the evidence. Once the plaintiff's burden has been met, he will be permitted to proceed with the proposed development, provided he complies with all other applicable regulations.

The town's argument that the specific relief granted to plaintiff Remillard violates the separation of powers provision found in part I, article 37 of the New Hampshire Constitution, to the extent that the trial court exercised legislative power specifically delegated to the local zoning authority, is without merit. The rule we adopt today does not produce this result. See *Opinion of the Justices*, 121 N.H. 552, 556, 431 A.2d 783, 785–86 (1981) ("complete separation of powers would interfere with the efficient operation of government . . . consequently there must be some overlapping of the power of each branch"). This rule will permit the municipality to continue to control its own development, so long as it does so for the general welfare of the community. It will also accommodate the construction of low- and moderate-income housing that had been unlawfully excluded. * * *

The zoning ordinance evolved as an innovative means to counter the problems of uncontrolled growth. It was never conceived to be a device to facilitate the use of governmental power to prevent access to a municipality by "outsiders of any disadvantaged social or economic group." *Beck*, 118 N.H. at 801, 394 A.2d at 852. The town of Chester has adopted a zoning ordinance which is blatantly exclusionary. This court will not condone the town's conduct.

Affirmed in part and reversed in part.

NOTES

1. In *Chester*, the court granted affirmative relief in the form of a "builder's remedy." In an attempt to ensure that low- and moderate-income housing actually is built, other state courts have required municipalities to incorporate a variety of affirmative devices into their zoning codes. These "inclusionary zoning" techniques include:

    a. *Incentive Zoning.* Incentive zoning offers economic incentives to developers to build low- and moderate-income housing. For example, a developer might be allowed to build more housing units than otherwise permitted by the zoning code in exchange for the construction of a specified number of lower-income housing units.

    b. *Mandatory Set-Asides.* Whereas participation in an incentive zoning program is optional for a developer, a mandatory set-aside program requires a developer to provide lower-income housing as a condition of obtaining a building permit to construct higher-income housing. Some cities also require developers of office space to build lower-income housing or contribute money to a fund to build such housing. These programs are designed to help ameliorate the effect on the price of housing caused by an influx of new office workers. Mandatory set-aside and incentive zoning programs sometimes are combined with price controls to ensure that future owners of the homes cannot sell or rent them for prices that are unaffordable to lower-income buyers or renters.

    c. *Mandatory Zoning for Manufactured Homes.* Many municipalities ban manufactured homes (often called mobile homes) or restrict them to

very limited and potentially undesirable areas. However, because manufactured homes are a type of low cost housing, some courts have prohibited
their exclusion.

What other types of affirmative techniques can enhance the likelihood of construction of lower-income housing? What are the practical limitations of the builder's
remedy and of the other affirmative devices? What legal challenges could be made
to each of these inclusionary zoning techniques?

2.   Few state courts have been as aggressive as the *Chester* court in developing
judicial doctrines to combat exclusionary zoning, but the New Jersey Supreme
Court has been at the forefront. The most famous cases in this area are the
decisions that began with *Southern Burlington County NAACP v. Township of Mt.
Laurel*, 336 A.2d 713 (N.J. 1975). Like the court in *Chester*, the *Mt. Laurel* court
held that a municipality had to consider the housing needs of the region, rather than
only those of the municipality.

However, many other courts have reached a contrary conclusion, which has
hampered efforts to eliminate exclusionary zoning. These courts usually reason that
when a state delegates zoning authority to a city, the city is authorized to act in its
own best interests, rather than for the benefit of nonresidents. Consider, for
example, the following language from *Golden v. Ramapo Planning Board*, 285
N.E.2d 291, 299–300 (N.Y. 1972), which is a leading growth management decision:

> Experience, over the last quarter century, however, with greater tech-
> nological integration and drastic shifts in population distribution has
> pointed up serious defects and community autonomy in land use controls
> has come under increasing attack by legal commentators, and students of
> urban problems alike, because of its pronounced insularism and its
> correlative role in producing distortions in metropolitan growth patterns,
> and perhaps more importantly, in crippling efforts toward regional and
> State-wide problem solving, be it pollution, decent housing, or public
> transportation. . . .

> Recognition of communal and regional interdependence, in turn, has
> resulted in proposals for schemes of regional and State-wide planning, in
> the hope that decisions would then correspond roughly to their level of
> impact. . . . Yet, as salutary as such proposals may be, the power to zone
> under current law is vested in local municipalities, and we are constrained
> to resolve the issues accordingly.

3.   The affordable housing crisis has become acute in many popular resort areas.
New hotels and other developments create additional demands for hotel employees
and other lower income workers. However, these workers often are unable to find
housing within commuting distance of the available jobs because development
demand has driven up land prices. Telluride, Colorado attempted to address this
problem by enacting an ordinance that required developers to build affordable
housing for forty percent of the people who would be employed by the new
development. The findings for the ordinance stated: "Maintaining permanent and
long-term housing in proximity to the source of employment generation serves to
maintain the community, reduce regional traffic congestion, and minimize impacts

on adjacent communities. Housing must be affordable to the local labor force in order for the local economy to remain stable." Under the ordinance, developers could satisfy this obligation by (1) building new housing units and placing an affordable housing restrictive covenant on their titles, (2) placing an affordable housing restrictive covenant on existing housing units, (3) paying a fee, or (4) conveying land to the town in lieu of the fee. In *Telluride v. Lot Thirty-Four Venture, L.L.C.*, 3 P.3d 30 (2000), the Colorado Supreme Court invalidated the ordinance on the ground that it conflicted with a state statute prohibiting rent control. The state legislature then amended the statute to clarify that it does not apply to a voluntary agreement between a developer and a local government to provide affordable housing. Colo. Rev. Stat. § 38-12-301.

A California Court of Appeal upheld the City of Napa's requirement that ten percent of all new construction consist of affordable housing. The court held that the requirement did not violate the state constitution's taking clause or the federal Constitution Takings or Due Process Clause because lower income workers were living in crowded, substandard housing, the large homeless population was increasing, and long commutes to work were increasing traffic congestion and pollution. *Home Builders Association of Northern California v. City of Napa*, 108 Cal. Rptr. 2d 60 (2001).

4. California has implemented an alternative method to encourage the construction of affordable housing. A state statute requires local jurisdictions to permit homeowners to build "second units" on their property. Second units are independent living units attached or unattached to an existing residence. The state legislature determined that second units are a cost-effective means of creating affordable housing without public subsidies, help homeowners pay their home loans, and provide security for homeowners. To satisfy this statutory mandate, Santa Monica allowed second units but limited the occupants to the property owner and the owner's dependents or caregiver. In *Coalition Advocating Legal Housing Options v. City of Santa Monica*, 105 Cal. Rptr. 2d 802 (2001), a California Court of Appeal held that this restriction in Santa Monica's ordinance violates constitutional privacy and equal protection rights. See *Accessory Dwellings*, accessorydwellings.org.

D.   Residency Restrictions

Since the U.S. Supreme Court's decision in *Village of Euclid v. Ambler Realty Co.*, 272 U.S. 365 (1926), the constitutionality of creating a separate use district for single-family homes has not been seriously challenged. To determine specifically what types of uses are permitted in a single-family residential zone, the word "family" must be defined. Earlier zoning codes often defined "family" as a maximum number of adults who resided together and shared common cooking facilities. The legislative intent was to exclude hotels, boarding houses, and similar uses. During the 1960s, however, many jurisdictions amended their definition of "family" to restrict the number of unrelated persons who could live together. As with exclusionary zoning, the effect of the regulations was to control the users of property, rather than just the use. It was this type of restriction that prompted the U.S. Supreme Court to decide its first zoning case in almost fifty years, *Village of*

Belle Terre v. Boraas.

VILLAGE OF BELLE TERRE v. BORAAS
416 U.S. 1 (1974)

MR. JUSTICE DOUGLAS delivered the opinion of the Court.

Belle Terre is a village on Long Island's north shore of about 220 homes inhabited by 700 people. Its total land area is less than one square mile. It has restricted land use to one-family dwellings excluding lodging houses, boarding houses, fraternity houses, or multiple-dwelling houses. The word "family" as used in the ordinance means, "[o]ne or more persons related by blood, adoption, or marriage, living and cooking together as a single housekeeping unit, exclusive of household servants. A number of persons but not exceeding two (2) living and cooking together as a single housekeeping unit though not related by blood, adoption, or marriage shall be deemed to constitute a family."

Appellees, the Dickmans, are owners of a house in the village and leased it in December 1971 for a term of 18 months to Michael Truman. Later Bruce Boraas became a colessee. Then Anne Parish moved into the house along with three others. These six are students at nearby State University at Stony Brook and none is related to the other by blood, adoption, or marriage. When the village served the Dickmans with an "Order to Remedy Violations" of the ordinance, the owners plus three tenants thereupon brought this action under 42 U.S.C. § 1983 for an injunction and a judgment declaring the ordinance unconstitutional. The District Court held the ordinance constitutional, 367 F. Supp. 136, and the Court of Appeals reversed, one judge dissenting. 2 Cir., 476 F.2d 806. The case is here by appeal, 28 U.S.C. § 1254(2); and we noted probable jurisdiction, 414 U.S. 907.

This case brings to this Court a different phase of local zoning regulations from those we have previously reviewed. *Village of Euclid v. Ambler Realty Co.*, 272 U.S. 365, involved a zoning ordinance classifying land use in a given area into six categories. . . .

The main thrust of the case in the mind of the Court was in the exclusion of industries and apartments, and as respects that it commented on the desire to keep residential areas free of "disturbing noises"; "increased traffic"; the hazard of "moving and parked automobiles"; the "depriving children of the privilege of quiet and open spaces for play, enjoyed by those in more favored localities." *Id.*, at 394. The ordinance was sanctioned because the validity of the legislative classification was "fairly debatable" and therefore could not be said to be wholly arbitrary. *Id.*, at 388.

Our decision in *Berman v. Parker*, 348 U.S. 26, sustained a land use project in the District of Columbia against a landowner's claim that the taking violated the Due Process Clause and the Just Compensation Clause of the Fifth Amendment. The essence of the argument against the law was, while taking property for ridding an area of slums was permissible, taking it "merely to develop a better balanced, more attractive community" was not, *id.*, at 31. We refused to limit the concept of public welfare that may be enhanced by zoning regulations. We said:

"Miserable and disreputable housing conditions may do more than spread disease and crime and immorality. They may also suffocate the spirit by reducing the people who live there to the status of cattle. They may indeed make living an almost insufferable burden. They may also be an ugly sore, a blight on the community which robs it of charm, which makes it a place from which men turn. The misery of housing may despoil a community as an open sewer may ruin a river.

"We do not sit to determine whether a particular housing project is or is not desirable. The concept of the public welfare is broad and inclusive. . . . The values it represents are spiritual as well as physical, aesthetic as well as monetary. It is within the power of the legislature to determine that the community should be beautiful as well as healthy, spacious as well as clean, well-balanced as well as carefully patrolled." *Id.*, at 32–33.

The present ordinance is challenged on several grounds: that it interferes with a person's right to travel; that it interferes with the right to migrate to and settle within a State; that it bars people who are uncongenial to the present residents; that it expresses the social preferences of the residents for groups that will be congenial to them; that social homogeneity is not a legitimate interest of government; that the restriction of those whom the neighbors do not like trenches on the newcomers' rights of privacy; that it is of no rightful concern to villagers whether the residents are married or unmarried; that the ordinance is antithetical to the Nation's experience, ideology, and self-perception as an open, egalitarian, and integrated society.

We find none of these reasons in the record before us. It is not aimed at transients. Cf. *Shapiro v. Thompson*, 394 U.S. 618. It involves no procedural disparity inflicted on some but not on others such as was presented by *Griffin v. Illinois*, 351 U.S. 12. It involves no "fundamental" right guaranteed by the Constitution, such as voting, *Harper v. Virginia State Board*, 383 U.S. 663; the right of association, *NAACP v. Alabama*, 357 U.S. 449; the right of access to the courts, *NAACP v. Button*, 371 U.S. 415; or any rights of privacy, cf. *Griswold v. Connecticut*, 381 U.S. 479; *Eisenstadt v. Baird*, 405 U.S. 438, 453–454. We deal with economic and social legislation where legislatures have historically drawn lines which we respect against the charge of violation of the Equal Protection Clause if the law be "reasonable, not arbitrary" (quoting *Royster Guano Co. v. Virginia*, 253 U.S. 412, 415) and bears "a rational relationship to a [permissible] state objective." *Reed v. Reed*, 404 U.S. 71, 76.

It is said, however, that if two unmarried people can constitute a "family," there is no reason why three or four may not. But every line drawn by a legislature leaves some out that might well have been included. That exercise of discretion, however, is a legislative, not a judicial, function.

It is said that the Belle Terre ordinance reeks with an animosity to unmarried couples who live together. There is no evidence to support it; and the provision of the ordinance bringing within the definition of a "family" two unmarried people belies the charge.

The ordinance places no ban on other forms of association, for a "family" may, so far as the ordinance is concerned, entertain whomever it likes.

The regimes of boarding houses, fraternity houses, and the like present urban problems. More people occupy a given space; more cars rather continuously pass by; more cars are parked; noise travels with crowds.

A quiet place where yards are wide, people few, and motor vehicles restricted are legitimate guidelines in a land-use project addressed to family needs. This goal is a permissible one within *Berman v. Parker, supra.* The police power is not confined to elimination of filth, stench, and unhealthy places. It is ample to lay out zones where family values, youth values, and the blessings of quiet seclusion and clean air make the area a sanctuary for people. * * *

Reversed.

MR. JUSTICE MARSHALL, dissenting.

This case draws into question the constitutionality of a zoning ordinance of the incorporated village of Belle Terre, New York, which prohibits groups of more than two unrelated persons, as distinguished from groups consisting of any number of persons related by blood, adoption, or marriage, from occupying a residence within the confines of the township. Lessor-appellees, the two owners of a Belle Terre residence, and three unrelated student tenants challenged the ordinance on the ground that it establishes a classification between households of related and unrelated individuals, which deprives them of equal protection of the laws. In my view, the disputed classification burdens the students' fundamental rights of association and privacy guaranteed by the First and Fourteenth Amendments. Because the application of strict equal protection scrutiny is therefore required, I am at odds with my Brethren's conclusion that the ordinance may be sustained on a showing that it bears a rational relationship to the accomplishment of legitimate governmental objectives. * * *

When separate but equal was still accepted constitutional dogma, this Court struck down a racially restrictive zoning ordinance. *Buchanan v. Warley*, 245 U.S. 60 (1917). I am sure the Court would not be hesitant to invalidate that ordinance today. The lower federal courts have considered procedural aspects of zoning, and acted to insure that land-use controls are not used as means of confining minorities and the poor to the ghettos of our central cities. These are limited but necessary intrusions on the discretion of zoning authorities. By the same token, I think it clear that the First Amendment provides some limitation on zoning laws. It is inconceivable to me that we would allow the exercise of the zoning power to burden First Amendment freedoms, as by ordinances that restrict occupancy to individuals adhering to particular religious, political, or scientific beliefs. Zoning officials properly concern themselves with the uses of land — with, for example, the number and kind of dwellings to be constructed in a certain neighborhood or the number of persons who can reside in those dwellings. But zoning authorities cannot validly consider who those persons are, what they believe, or how they choose to live, whether they are Negro or white, Catholic or Jew, Republican or Democrat, married or unmarried.

My disagreement with the Court today is based upon my view that the ordinance in this case unnecessarily burdens appellees' First Amendment freedom of association and their constitutionally guaranteed right to privacy. Our decisions establish that the First and Fourteenth Amendments protect the freedom to choose one's associates. *NAACP v. Button*, 371 U.S. 415, 430 (1963). Constitutional protection is extended, not only to modes of association that are political in the usual sense, but also to those that pertain to the social and economic benefit of the members. . . . The selection of one's living companions involves similar choices as to the emotional, social, or economic benefits to be derived from alternative living arrangements.

The freedom of association is often inextricably entwined with the constitutionally guaranteed right of privacy. The right to "establish a home" is an essential part of the liberty guaranteed by the Fourteenth Amendment. *Meyer v. Nebraska*, 262 U.S. 390, 399 (1923); *Griswold v. Connecticut*, 381 U.S. 479, 495 (1965) (Goldberg, J., concurring). And the Constitution secures to an individual a freedom "to satisfy his intellectual and emotional needs in the privacy of his own home." *Stanley v. Georgia*, 394 U.S. 557, 565 (1969); see *Paris Adult Theatre I v. Slaton*, 413 U.S. 49, 66–67 (1973). Constitutionally protected privacy is, in Mr. Justice Brandeis' words, "as against the Government, the right to be let alone . . . the right most valued by civilized man." *Olmstead v. United States*, 277 U.S. 438, 478 (1928) (dissenting opinion). The choice of household companions — of whether a person's "intellectual and emotional needs" are best met by living with family, friends, professional associates, or others — involves deeply personal considerations as to the kind and quality of intimate relationships within the home. That decision surely falls within the ambit of the right to privacy protected by the Constitution. . . .

The instant ordinance discriminates on the basis of just such a personal lifestyle choice as to household companions. It permits any number of persons related by blood or marriage, be it two or twenty, to live in a single household, but it limits to two the number of unrelated persons bound by profession, love, friendship, religious or political affiliation, or mere economics who can occupy a single home. Belle Terre imposes upon those who deviate from the community norm in their choice of living companions significantly greater restrictions than are applied to residential groups who are related by blood or marriage, and compose the established order within the community. The village has, in effect, acted to fence out those individuals whose choice of lifestyle differs from that of its current residents. * * *

NOTES

1. What is the basic difference in legal theory between the majority and dissenting opinions?

2. A variety of justifications have been offered for single-family residential zones — decreased traffic and noise, the aesthetic value of compatible uses, a less transient population, better maintained properties, a greater concentration of children and parents in one area, and social homogeneity. In *Belle Terre*, the single-family ordinance prevented a group of unrelated college students from living together. But what other types of groups are excluded? By its terms, the ordinance prevents three nuns, retirees, or judges from living together. Are they more or less likely to interfere with the purposes for a single-family residential zone than a family with three teenage children?

The zoning ordinance could be re-drafted to address problems such as traffic more directly. Noise ordinances and similar laws also could be enforced to prevent other potential problems, rather than assuming that all groups of unrelated people will be detrimental to a single-family residential zone. Because alternative legal methods exist for addressing potential problems, is a valid public purpose served by reserving areas in a community for related individuals? Consider the following language from the dissenting opinion in *State v. Baker*, 405 A.2d 368, 380 (N.J. 1979):

> Appellant takes the position . . . that if a family, composed of an indefinite number of persons, may legally occupy a "single-family" residence, then an indefinite number of unrelated persons should have the same right. The majority has agreed and in so doing has deplorably denigrated one of the greatest and finest of our institutions — the family. The family should be entitled — as until now it has been — to stand on its own in a distinctly *preferred* position. There is no support in our *mores* as there should be none in our law, to justify the elevation of any group of unrelated persons to a position of parity with a family.

3. In *Moore v. City of East Cleveland*, 431 U.S. 494 (1977), the U.S. Supreme Court considered the constitutionality of a definition of "family" that limited the number of related family members who could live together. Ms. Moore was sentenced to jail for permitting her son and two grandsons, who were cousins, to live with her. By a 5-4 vote, the Supreme Court overturned the conviction. The Court distinguished *Belle Terre* on the basis that the ordinance in *Moore* infringed on the fundamental right to freedom in matters of marriage and family life, which triggered the strict scrutiny standard of review. The Court stated that, although the occupancy restriction served legitimate public purposes, it served them "marginally, at best."

4. Is a mansion a single-family home? In *Association of Friends of Sagaponack v. Southampton Zoning Board of Appeals*, 731 N.Y.S. 2d 851 (2001), a neighborhood association tried to stop the owner of a 63-acre parcel from building a home of more than 40,000 square feet by arguing that it wasn't a single-family dwelling. The house would have 29 bedrooms, 33 bathrooms, 2 bowling alleys, a 10,000 square foot playhouse, garden and beach pavilions, and a mechanical building. The New York Supreme Court upheld the Zoning Board of Appeals decision that this "large, oceanfront mansion" could be built in a single-family residential zone.

Group homes have presented a specialized set of issues with respect to single-family residential zones. The earliest zoning treatment of group homes was deplorable. For example, the zoning ordinance upheld by the U.S. Supreme Court in *Euclid* placed institutions for the "feeble minded" in the least restricted use district. The other permitted uses included "plants for sewage disposal and for producing gas, garbage and refuse incineration, scrap iron, junk, scrap paper and rag storage, aviation fields, cemeteries, crematories, penal and correctional institutions, . . . storage of oil and gasoline, . . . and manufacturing and industrial operations. . . ."

Today, it is generally accepted that a large percentage of group home occupants benefit from living in a residential setting. In response, some states have enacted statutes that require the inclusion of group homes as a permitted use in single-family residential zones. The next case considers the legality of such statutes.

COSTLEY v. CAROMIN HOUSE, INC.
313 N.W.2d 21 (Minn. 1981)

Scott, J.

This is a combined appeal from the denial of a temporary injunction sought by neighbors wishing to prohibit the construction of a home for mentally retarded adults in the City of Two Harbors, Minnesota, and the denial of a timely motion to intervene by four mentally retarded persons by the Lake County District Court. We affirm in part and reverse in part.

Respondent Caromin House, Inc. (Caromin House), a Minnesota corporation entirely owned by Garry and Gertrude Carlson, planned to operate a home for mentally retarded adults in Two Harbors, Minnesota. Land was purchased from the City of Two Harbors (City) for that purpose in December 1979. The Eighth Addition, in which the land is located, is a new subdivision platted in 1977 and 1978. Since the platting, approximately 20 single-family residences have been constructed in the Eighth Addition. Plaintiff Costley moved into the Eighth Addition in 1978. All six plaintiffs reside there. The subdivision is zoned R-2, which permits one- and two-family dwellings. In addition, the City imposed restrictive covenants on the property, limiting usage to one dwelling and one garage.

The group home planned by Caromin House would be the only facility in all of Lake County to provide a home for mentally retarded adults. Six retarded adults and their house parents would live in the home. From the exterior, the building would be indistinguishable from any other single-family dwelling in the subdivision. The interior would have five bedrooms, three baths, a living room, a dining room, a kitchen, a basement utility-furnace-storage area, and a basement recreation room. All residents would live together as a family, sharing all parts of the house except individual bedrooms. The purpose of the home is to provide a non-institutional living situation for mentally retarded adults. All of the residents, including the house parents, would share in such family functions as preparing and eating meals, planning outings, and performing household duties, all in compliance with applicable state regulations. 12 MCAR § 2.034 (1978).

Caromin House followed all necessary administrative procedures and obtained all necessary permits for construction of the home, including a Certificate of Need from the Minnesota Department of Health and approval of the location by the Minnesota Department of Public Welfare. In the course of this process, the City expressed to the Residential Licensing Supervisor its concern that the project would be a commercial enterprise or boarding house that would violate the City of Two Harbors Zoning Ordinance. The Minnesota Attorney General, in an informal written opinion, responded that Minn. Stat. §§ 462.357, subd. 7, and 245.812, subd. 3,[1] applied to the project and therefore the proposed group home would not violate the city zoning ordinance. Under these statutes, a state-licensed group home serving six or fewer mentally retarded persons shall be considered a single-family residential use for the purpose of zoning.

The Board of Zoning Appeals issued the necessary zoning permit to Caromin House on October 16, 1980, reversing the denial of the permit by the zoning administrator. While the zoning administrator had felt the project was a commercial venture, the decision of the board was "based to a large degree on the Minnesota statutes" that mandate that such a group home be considered a single-family residential use for the purpose of zoning.

On October 23, 1980, one week after the zoning permit was granted, plaintiffs obtained ex parte a temporary restraining order against construction of the group home while they sought a temporary injunction. Lori Osbakken, et al., four mentally retarded persons, through their guardians filed a timely motion to intervene. All four were potential future residents of the home and now reside there. The Lake County District Court denied both the motions for a temporary injunction and for intervention.

Plaintiffs appeal the denial of a temporary injunction on the grounds that the home is prohibited by the local zoning laws and by the applicable restrictive covenant and that Minn. Stat. §§ 462.357, subd. 7, and 245.812, subd. 3 (1980), characterizing a group home as single-family use, are unconstitutional. . . .

1. Plaintiffs contend that the group home violates the zoning ordinance because a group of persons unrelated by blood, marriage, or adoption cannot be a family. The home is located in an area zoned R-2, which permits "one and two-family dwelling groups," according to Article 6, Section 2.02. "Dwelling, single-family" is defined in Article 2, Section 1.12, as "[a] building designed for occupancy by one family."

While plaintiffs argue that the word "family" must be given "its ordinary meaning," we have stated:

> The word "family" has many different common meanings and perhaps as many legal definitions as there are fields of law in which it is used. . . . [T]he meaning necessarily depends upon the field of law in

---

[1] These statutes provide as follows:

Minn. Stat. § 462.357, subd. 7 (1980):

Permitted single family use. In order to implement the policy of this state that mentally retarded and physically handicapped persons should not be excluded by municipal zoning ordinances from the benefits of normal residential surroundings, a state licensed group home or foster home serving six or fewer mentally retarded or physically handicapped persons shall be considered a permitted single family residential use of property for the purposes of zoning.

Minn. Stat. § 245.812, subd. 3 (1980):

A licensed residential facility serving six or fewer persons or a licensed day care facility serving ten or fewer persons shall be considered a permitted single family residential use of property for the purposes of zoning.

which the word is used, the purpose intended to be accomplished by its use, and the facts and circumstances of each case."

LeRoux v. Edmundson, 276 Minn. 120, 123, 148 N.W.2d 812, 814 (1967). Here, the zoning ordinance itself defines family:

Family: One or more persons occupying a premises and living as a single housekeeping unit as distinguished from a group occupying a boarding house, lodging house or hotel as herein defined.

Two Harbors, Minn., Ordinance No. 253, Art. 2, sec. 1.16 (Oct. 15, 1979). The residents of Caromin House will constitute a family, therefore, if they live in a single housekeeping unit.

In order to qualify for state licensure, the group home must function as a single housekeeping unit. The licensing requirements of the Department of Public Welfare, 12 MCAR § 2.034 (1978), ensure that the mentally retarded residents and house parents will operate as a family.[3] The residents of Caromin House share in planning and preparation of meals, performing housekeeping duties, and planning recreational activities. The house parents provide supervision, guidance, and emotional support to the residents as would any head of household. Such a family setting differs from a boarding home, a lodging house, or a hotel which, as the zoning ordinance defines, provide limited services of food or lodging only.

Interpreting a similar ordinance in *Oliver v. Zoning Commission*, 326 A.2d 841, 31 Conn. Supp. 197 (1974), a lower Connecticut court held that a residence for eight or nine mentally retarded adults and two supervisory house parents constituted a single housekeeping unit and was a permitted single-family use. Courts have determined that almost any living arrangement that makes use of unified house-keeping facilities satisfies such an ordinance. 2 Rathkopf, The Law of Zoning and Planning § 17A.03(3)(a) (1981).

Even where local zoning ordinances have required persons to be related in order to be a family, courts have held that a group home was a single-family dwelling. . . . *City of White Plains v. Ferraioli*, 34 N.Y.2d 300, 357 N.Y.S.2d 449, 313 N.E.2d 756 (1974). . . . The word "family" is no longer limited to a traditional concept of marriage and biological ties. As the court in *Ferraioli* stated in recognizing a group home including ten foster children as a single-family unit, "So long as the group home bears the generic character of a family unit as a relatively permanent household, and is not a framework for transients or transient living, it conforms to the purpose of the ordinance." 34 N.Y.2d at 305–06, 313 N.E.2d at 758, 357 N.Y.S.2d at 453. The Caromin House group home is therefore a single-family unit within the ordinance.

Operation of the group home by a for-profit corporation does not change the

---

[3] The regulations are designed to "establish and protect the human right of mentally retarded persons to a normal living situation." 12 MCAR § 2.034 A.2 (1978). The living unit "shall be small enough to ensure the development of meaningful interpersonal relationships among residents and between residents and staff." 12 MCAR § 2.034 B.1.a. (1978). "Living-unit staff shall be responsible for the development and maintenance of a warm, family, or homelike environment that is conducive to the achievement of optimal development by the resident." 12 MCAR § 2.034 B.3.b.(1) (1978).

preceding analysis. Although Caromin House receives compensation for its services, the home does not thereby become commercial in nature. The residents interact and live as a family whether the management is by a for-profit corporation, a non-profit corporation, a religious group, or a governmental unit.

Plaintiffs' reliance on *Browndale International Ltd. v. Board of Adjustment*, 60 Wis. 2d 182, 208 N.W.2d 121 (1973), is misplaced. The court's decision in *Browndale* that therapeutic homes for emotionally disturbed children were not single-family use was influenced not only by the commercial nature but also by other factors: the house parents did not live in the house; psychiatric and medical treatment was a primary purpose of the facility; children stayed for only short terms; and six facilities were concentrated in an area that more closely resembled an institutional complex than a number of single-family dwellings. The profit nature alone would not alter the objective of providing noninstitutional living for mentally retarded persons; the home still serves a residential purpose.

The Two Harbors Zoning Ordinance prohibits in an R-2 district every use that is not specifically permitted. Article 6, Section 2. Since the group home fits within the definition of single-family dwelling that is a permitted use, it cannot be prohibited as a commercial activity. The home is therefore permitted in Two Harbors' R-2 zone.

2. Plaintiffs also contend that the group home violates the restrictive covenant applicable to the property which provides: "Only one dwelling and one garage is permitted to be constructed on each lot." "Dwelling" is undefined. Plaintiffs would interpret this limitation to permit only a "residential, single-family dwelling" and then argue that the group home violates that covenant.

Restrictive covenants are strictly construed against limitations on the use of property. *Mission Covenant Church v. Nelson*, 253 Minn. 230, 233, 91 N.W.2d 440, 442 (1958). Since the law favors the unrestricted use of property, courts will not adopt a strained construction in favor of restrictions. *Id.* According to Webster's Third New International Dictionary (1971), a dwelling is simply "a building or construction used for residence." The group home fits this description both in appearance and in use, and thus complies with the covenant.

Even if the covenant were interpreted to permit only "single-family dwellings," the group home would be a permitted use under the same reasoning as discussed above for the definition of "family" in zoning regulations. From the outside, the home looks like all the other single-family homes in the neighborhood. The residents live in a family-type setting and call the dwelling their home. Courts in other jurisdictions have found similar group homes in compliance with single-family restrictive covenants. *State ex rel. Region II Child & Family Services, Inc. v. District Court of the Eighth Judicial District*, 609 P.2d 245 (Mont. 1980) (five retarded children; one unit single-family dwelling); *Bellarmine Hills Association v. Residential Systems Co.*, 84 Mich. App. 554, 269 N.W.2d 673 (1978) (six retarded children; one single private family dwelling); *Berger v. State*, 71 N.J. 206, 364 A.2d 993 (1976) (eight to twelve multi-handicapped children under age nine; one dwelling house). Factors considered by the courts include the single housekeeping structure, the relatively permanent type of living situation, and public policy supporting such living arrangements — all factors applicable to Caromin House.

That Caromin House is compensated for its services does not change the character of the use from that of a dwelling. Deciding that a group home for four retarded adults fit within a covenant restricting use to residential purposes and one single-family dwelling, the North Carolina Supreme Court stated as follows:

> That [the group home] is paid for its efforts does not detract from the essential character of its program of non-institutional living for the retarded. Clearly, the receipt of money to support the care of more or less permanent residents is incidental to the scope of [its] efforts.

J.T. Hobby and Son, Inc. v. Family Homes of Wake County, Inc., 302 N.C. 64, 274 S.E.2d 174 (1981). The for-profit status of Caromin House is similarly irrelevant. See *Crowley v. Knapp*, 94 Wis. 2d 421, 288 N.W.2d 815 (1980) (for-profit group home for retarded adults complies with covenant restricting use to single-family dwelling used for residential purposes only). The home meets the restriction of "dwelling" whether we look at the express language or at cases involving group homes. . . .

The denial of the temporary injunction is affirmed. Since the group home is within the definition of a family as a single housekeeping unit, it is a permitted use in the R-2 zone. The group home also satisfies the restrictive covenant since it is a dwelling.

NOTES

1.   As in *Costley*, some jurisdictions have provided by legislation that group homes are a permitted use in single-family residential zones. In states without such legislation, some courts have reached a similar result by upholding the right of a group home to locate in a single-family zone, particularly if the home operates as the functional equivalent of a family. Other courts have held that excluding group homes violates substantive due process as a regulation of users, rather than of uses. However, the cases are not uniform. Some state courts follow *Belle Terre* and hold that a jurisdiction constitutionally can exclude group homes, like any other group of unrelated individuals, from single-family residential areas.

2.   Can a group home be required to obtain a special use permit as a condition of locating in a residential zone? In *City of Cleburne v. Cleburne Living Center*, 473 U.S. 432 (1985), the U.S. Supreme Court held that such a requirement violated even the rational relationship standard under the Equal Protection Clause when applied to a group home for the mentally retarded. However, the Court's decision is of rather limited precedential value. The owner of the proposed group home in *Cleburne* was denied a permit to operate the home in a district that allowed apartment houses, boarding houses, fraternities, sororities, dormitories, private clubs, and fraternal orders without a special use permit. The judicial decisions since *Cleburne* have reached conflicting results on this issue. See Daniel Mandelker, Land Use Law § 5.07 (5th ed. 2003).

3.   Three years after the *Cleburne* decision, Congress amended the Fair Housing Act, 42 U.S.C. §§ 3601–3619, to prohibit discrimination against handicapped persons. The Act defines "handicap" as "a physical or mental impairment which substantially limits one or more . . . major life activities." 42 U.S.C. § 3602(h)(1). The definition also includes a person who is "regarded as having such

an impairment" or who has "a record of having such an impairment," but it excludes current users of a controlled substance. *Id.* at § 3602(h)(2). Courts have interpreted the Fair Housing Act to prohibit the exclusion of group homes for handicapped persons from single-family residential districts. *City of Edmonds v. Oxford House, Inc.*, 514 U.S. 725 (1995); *Larkin v. State Dept. of Social Services*, 89 F.3d 285 (6th Cir. 1996). However, it does not apply to other types of group homes.

E.   Aesthetic Regulation

Before the 1930s, courts usually did not regard aesthetics as being a valid police power purpose. Rather, courts took a restrictive position concerning the permissible purposes for which government could restrict private property rights. But judicial attitudes began to shift after the U.S. Supreme Court's decision in *Berman v. Parker*, 348 U.S. 26 (1954). In that case, the Supreme Court considered the constitutionality of an urban renewal program in Washington, D.C. In upholding the program's validity, the Court stated:

> The concept of the public welfare is broad and inclusive. . . . The values it represents are spiritual as well as physical, aesthetic as well as monetary. It is within the power of the legislature to determine that the community should be beautiful as well as healthy, spacious as well as clean, well-balanced as well as carefully patrolled. . . . If those who govern the District of Columbia decide that the Nation's Capital should be beautiful as well as sanitary, there is nothing in the Fifth Amendment that stands in the way.

Id. at 33.

Since the *Berman* decision, the clear trend in the courts has been to recognize aesthetics as a valid police power purpose. In most jurisdictions, aesthetics alone can serve as an adequate purpose for a law. In some jurisdictions, however, aesthetics alone is insufficient. Some additional public purpose must support the law. These courts often rely on preservation of property values as the additional public purpose, but this factor normally is a result of aesthetic regulation, rather than a separate, independent factor.

Aesthetic regulation raises a variety of interesting issues. Perhaps the most fundamental issue is the proper definition of aesthetics. As evidenced by the design review cases, it clearly includes the quality of being visually pleasing. But, particularly because violation of a land use regulation is a misdemeanor in many jurisdictions, how can an ordinance adequately define the standards for a visually pleasing building? Who gets to decide whether the standard is satisfied? Are there any other aesthetic purposes that justify restricting private property rights? Keep these questions in mind as you read the following cases.

STATE EX REL. STOYANOFF v. BERKELEY
458 S.W.2d 305 (Mo. 1970)

PRITCHARD, COMMISSIONER.

Upon summary judgment the trial court issued a peremptory writ of mandamus to compel appellant to issue a residential building permit to respondents. The trial court's judgment is that the below-mentioned ordinances are violative of Section 10, Article I of the Constitution of Missouri, 1945, V.A.M.S., in that restrictions placed by the ordinances on the use of property deprive the owners of their property without due process of law. Relators' petition pleads that they applied to appellant Building Commissioner for a building permit to allow them to construct a single family residence in the City of Ladue, and that plans and specifications were submitted for the proposed residence, which was unusual in design, "but complied with all existing building and zoning regulations and ordinances of the City of Ladue, Missouri."

It is further pleaded that relators were refused a building permit for the construction of their proposed residence upon the ground that the permit was not approved by the Architectural Board of the City of Ladue. Ordinance 131, as amended by Ordinance 281 of that city, purports to set up an Architectural Board to approve plans and specifications for buildings and structures erected within the city and in a preamble to "conform to certain minimum architectural standards of appearance and conformity with surrounding structures, and that unsightly, grotesque and unsuitable structures, detrimental to the stability of value and the welfare of surrounding property, structures and residents, and to the general welfare and happiness of the community, be avoided, and that appropriate standards of beauty and conformity be fostered and encouraged." It is asserted in the petition that the ordinances are invalid, illegal and void, "are unconstitutional in that they are vague and provide no standard nor uniform rule by which to guide the architectural board," that the city acted in excess of statutory powers (§ 89.020, RSMo 1959, V.A.M.S.) in enacting the ordinance, which "attempt to allow respondent to impose aesthetic standards for buildings in the City of Ladue, and are in excess of the powers granted the City of Ladue by said statute."

Relators filed a motion for summary judgment and affidavits were filed in opposition thereto. Richard D. Shelton, Mayor of the City of Ladue, deponed that the facts in appellant's answer were true and correct, as here pertinent: that the City of Ladue constitutes one of the finer suburban residential areas of Metropolitan St. Louis, the homes therein are considerably more expensive than in cities of comparable size, being homes on lots from three fourths of an acre to three or more acres each; that a zoning ordinance was enacted by the city regulating the height, number of stories, size of buildings, percentage of lot occupancy, yard sizes, and the location and use of buildings and land for trade, industry, residence and other purposes; that the zoning regulations were made in accordance with a comprehensive plan "designed to promote the health and general welfare of the residents of the City of Ladue," which in furtherance of said objectives duly enacted said Ordinances numbered 131 and 281. Appellant also asserted in his answer that these ordinances were a reasonable exercise of the city's governmental, legislative and police powers, as determined by its legislative body, and as stated in the above-quoted preamble to the ordinances. It is then pleaded that relators' description of their proposed residence as " 'unusual in design' is the understatement of the year. It is in fact a monstrosity of grotesque design, which would seriously impair the value of property in the neighborhood."

The affidavit of Harold C. Simon, a developer of residential subdivisions in St. Louis County, is that he is familiar with relators' lot upon which they seek to build a house, and with the surrounding houses in the neighborhood; that the houses therein existent are virtually all two-story houses of conventional architectural design, such as Colonial, French Provincial or English; and that the house which relators propose to construct is of ultramodern design which would clash with and not be in conformity with any other house in the entire neighborhood. It is Mr. Simon's opinion that the design and appearance of relators' proposed residence would have a substantial adverse effect upon the market values of other residential property in the neighborhood, such average market value ranging from $60,000 to $85,000 each.

As a part of the affidavit of Russell H. Riley, consultant for the city planning and engineering firm of Harland Bartholomew & Associates, photographic exhibits of homes surrounding relators' lot were attached. To the south is the conventional frame residence of Mrs. T.R. Collins. To the west is the Colonial two-story frame house of the Lewis family. To the northeast is the large brick English Tudor home of Mrs. Elmer Hubbs. Immediately to the north are the large Colonial homes of Mr. Alex Cornwall and Mr. L. Peter Wetzel. In substance Mr. Riley went on to say that the City of Ladue is one of the finer residential suburbs in the St. Louis area with a minimum of commercial or industrial usage. The development of residences in the city has been primarily by private subdivisions, usually with one main lane or drive leading therein (such as Lorenzo Road Subdivision which runs north off of Ladue Road in which relators' lot is located). The homes are considerably more expensive than average homes found in a city of comparable size. The ordinance which has been adopted by the City of Ladue is typical of those which have been adopted by a number of suburban cities in St. Louis County and in similar cities throughout the United States, the need therefor being based upon the protection of existing property values by preventing the construction of houses that are in complete conflict with the general type of houses in a given area. The intrusion into this neighborhood of relators' unusual, grotesque and nonconforming structure would have a substantial adverse effect on market values of other homes in the immediate area. According to Mr. Riley the standards of Ordinance 131, as amended by Ordinance 281, are usually and customarily applied in city planning work and are: "(1) whether the proposed house meets the customary architectural requirements in appearance and design for a house of the particular type which is proposed (whether it be Colonial, Tudor English, French Provincial, or Modern), (2) whether the proposed house is in general conformity with the style and design of surrounding structures, and (3) whether the proposed house lends itself to the proper architectural development of the City; and that in applying said standards the Architectural Board and its Chairman are to determine whether the proposed house will have an adverse effect on the stability of values in the surrounding area."

Photographic exhibits of relators' proposed residence were also attached to Mr.

Riley's affidavit. They show the residence to be of a pyramid shape, with a flat top, and with triangular shaped windows or doors at one or more corners.

Although appellant has briefed the point that it is a constitutional exercise of the police power for the Legislature to authorize cities to enact zoning ordinances, it is apparent that relators do not contest that issue. Rather, relators' position is that "the creation by the City of Ladue of an architectural board for the purpose of promoting and maintaining 'general conformity with the style and design of surrounding structures' is totally unauthorized by our Enabling Statute." (§§ 89.020, 89.040, RSMo 1959, V.A.M.S.) It is further contended by relators that Ordinances 131 and 281 are invalid and unconstitutional as being an unreasonable and arbitrary exercise of the police power (as based entirely on aesthetic values); and that the same are invalid as an unlawful delegation of legislative powers (to the Architectural Board).

Section 89.020 provides: "For the purpose of promoting health, safety, morals or the general welfare of the community, the legislative body of all cities, towns, and villages is hereby empowered to regulate and restrict the height, number of stories, and size of buildings and other structures, the percentage of lot that may be occupied, the size of yards, courts, and other open spaces, the density of population, the preservation of features of historical significance, and the location and use of buildings, structures and land for trade, industry, residence or other purposes." Section 89.040 provides: "Such regulations shall be made in accordance with a comprehensive plan and designed to lessen congestion in the streets; to secure safety from fire, panic and other dangers; to promote health *and the general welfare*; to provide adequate light and air; to prevent the overcrowding of land; to avoid undue concentration of population; to preserve features of historical significance; to facilitate the adequate provision of transportation, water, sewerage, schools, parks, and other public requirements. *Such regulations shall be made with reasonable consideration, among other things, to the character of the district and its peculiar suitability for particular uses, and with a view to conserving the values of buildings and encouraging the most appropriate use of land throughout such municipality.*" (Italics added.)

Relators say that "Neither Sections 89.020 or 89.040 nor any other provision of Chapter 89 mentions or gives a city the authority to regulate architectural design and appearance. There exists no provision providing for an architectural board and no entity even remotely resembling such a board is mentioned under the enabling legislation." Relators conclude that the City of Ladue lacked any power to adopt Ordinance 131 as amended by Ordinance 281 "and its intrusion into this area is wholly unwarranted and without sanction in the law." As to this aspect of the appeal relators rely upon the 1961 decision of *State ex rel. Magidson v. Henze*, Mo. App., 342 S.W.2d 261. That case had the identical question presented. An Architectural Control Commission was set up by an ordinance of the City of University City. In its report to the Building Commissioner, the Architectural Control Commission disapproved the Magidson application for permits to build four houses. It was commented that the proposed houses did not provide for the minimum number of square feet, and "In considering the existing character of this neighborhood, the Commission is of the opinion that houses of the character proposed in these plans are not in harmony with and will not contribute to nor protect the general welfare of this neighborhood" (loc. cit. 264). The court held that § 89.020, RSMo 1949, V.A.M.S., does not grant to the city the right to impose upon the landowner aesthetic standards for the buildings he chooses to erect.

As is clear from the affidavits and attached exhibits, the City of Ladue is an area composed principally of residences of the general types of Colonial, French Provincial and English Tudor. The city has a comprehensive plan of zoning to maintain the general character of buildings therein. The *Magidson* case, *supra*, did not consider the effect of § 89.040, *supra*, and the italicized portion relating to the character of the district, its suitability for particular uses, and the conservation of the values of buildings therein. These considerations, sanctioned by statute, are directly related to the general welfare of the community. That proposition has support in a number of cases cited by appellant. *State ex rel. Carter v. Harper, Building Commissioner*, 182 Wis. 148, 196 N.W. 451, 454, quotes *Chicago B. & Q. Ry. Co. v. People of State of Illinois ex rel. Drainage Commissioners*, 200 U.S. 561, "We hold that the police power of a state embraces regulations designed to promote the public convenience or the general prosperity, as well as regulations designed to promote the public health, the public morals or the public safety." In *Marrs v. City of Oxford* (D.C.D. Kan.) 24 F.2d 541, 548, it was said, "The stabilizing of property values, and giving some assurance to the public that, if property is purchased in a residential district, its value as such will be preserved, is probably the most cogent reason back of zoning ordinances." * * * The preamble to Ordinance 131, quoted above in part, demonstrates that its purpose is to conform to the dictates of § 89.040, with reference to preserving values of property by zoning procedure and restrictions on the use of property. This is an illustration of what was referred to in *Deimeke v. State Highway Commission, Mo.*, 444 S.W.2d 480, 484, as a growing number of cases recognizing a change in the scope of the term "general welfare." In the *Deimeke* case on the same page it is said, "Property use which offends sensibilities and debases property values affects not only the adjoining property owners in that vicinity but the general public as well because when such property values are destroyed or seriously impaired, the tax base of the community is affected and the public suffers economically as a result."

Relators say further that Ordinances 131 and 281 are invalid and unconstitutional as being an unreasonable and arbitrary exercise of the police power. It is argued that a mere reading of these ordinances shows that they are based entirely on aesthetic factors in that the stated purpose of the Architectural Board is to maintain "conformity with surrounding structures" and to assure that structures "conform to certain minimum architectural standards of appearance." The argument ignores the further provisos in the ordinance: ". . . and that unsightly, grotesque and unsuitable structures, *detrimental to the stability of value and the welfare of surrounding property, structures, and residents, and to the general welfare and happiness of the community*, be avoided, and that appropriate standards of beauty and conformity be fostered and encouraged." (Italics added.) Relators' proposed residence does not descend to the "patently offensive character of vehicle graveyards in close proximity to such highways" referred to in the *Deimeke* case, *supra* (444 S.W.2d 484). Nevertheless, the aesthetic factor to be taken into account by the Architectural Board is not to be considered alone. Along with that inherent factor is the effect that the proposed residence would have upon the property values in the area. In this time of burgeoning urban areas, congested with people and structures, it is certainly in keeping with the ultimate ideal of general welfare that the Architectural Board, in its function, preserve and protect existing areas in which structures of a general conformity of architecture have been erected. The area under consideration is clearly, from the record, a fashionable one. In *State ex rel. Civello v. City of New Orleans*, 97 So. 440, 444, 154 La. 271, the court said, "If by the term 'aesthetic considerations' is meant a regard merely for outward appearances, for good taste in the matter of the beauty of the neighborhood itself, we do not observe any substantial reason for saying that such a consideration is not a matter of general welfare. The beauty of a fashionable residence neighborhood in a city is for the comfort and happiness of the residents, and it sustains in a general way the value of property in the neighborhood." See also *People v. Stover*, 12 N.Y.2d 462, 240 N.Y.S.2d 734, 191 N.E.2d 272, 274 [3]; *State ex rel. Saveland Park Holding Corp. v. Wieland*, 269 Wis. 262, 69 N.W.2d 217, 222; *Reid v. Architectural Board of Review of the City of Cleveland Heights*, 119 Ohio App. 67, 192 N.E.2d 74, 77; and *Oregon City v. Hartke*, 240 Or. 35, 400 P.2d 255, 261, for pronouncements of the principle that aesthetics is a factor to be considered in zoning matters.

In the matter of enacting zoning ordinances and the procedures for determining whether any certain proposed structure or use is in compliance with or offends the basic ordinance, it is well settled that courts will not substitute their judgments for the city's legislative body, if the result is not oppressive, arbitrary or unreasonable and does not infringe upon a valid pre-existing nonconforming use. . . . The denial by appellant of a building permit for relators' highly modernistic residence in this area where traditional Colonial, French Provincial and English Tudor styles of architecture are erected does not appear to be arbitrary and unreasonable when the basic purpose to be served is that of the general welfare of persons in the entire community.

In addition to the above-stated purpose in the preamble to Ordinance 131, it establishes an Architectural Board of three members, all of whom must be architects. Meetings of the Board are to be open to the public, and every application for a building permit, except those not affecting the outward appearance of a building, shall be submitted to the Board along with plans, elevations, detail drawings and specifications, before being approved by the Building Commissioner. The Chairman of the Board shall examine the application to determine if it conforms to proper architectural standards in appearance and design and will be in general conformity with the style and design of surrounding structures and conducive to the proper architectural development of the city. If he so finds, he approves and returns the application to the Building Commissioner. If he does not find conformity, or has doubt, a full meeting of the Board is called, with notice of the time and place thereof given to the applicant. The Board shall disapprove the application if it determines the proposed structure will constitute an unsightly, grotesque or unsuitable structure in appearance, detrimental to the welfare of surrounding property or residents. If it cannot make that decision, the application shall be returned to the Building Commissioner either with or without suggestions or recommendations, and if that is done without disapproval, the Building Commissioner may issue the permit. If the Board's disapproval is given and the applicant refuses to comply with recommendations, the Building Commissioner shall refuse the permit. Thereafter provisions are made for an appeal to the Council of the city for review of the decision of the Architectural Board. Ordinance 281 amends Ordinance 131 only with respect to the application initially being submitted to and considered by all members of the Architectural Board.

Relators claim that the above provisions of the ordinance amount to an unconstitutional delegation of power by the city to the Architectural Board. It is argued that the Board cannot be given the power to determine what is unsightly and grotesque and that the standards, "whether the proposed structure will conform to proper architectural standards in appearance and design, and will be in general conformity with the style and design of surrounding structures and conducive to the proper architectural development of the City . . ." and "the Board shall disapprove the application if it determines that the proposed structure will constitute an unsightly, grotesque or unsuitable structure in appearance, detrimental to the welfare of surrounding property or residents . . . ," are inadequate. First cited is *State ex rel. Continental Oil Company v. Waddill*, Mo., 318 S.W.2d 281, which held an ordinance provision unconstitutional which clothed the City Planning Committee with arbitrary discretion without a definite standard or rule for its guidance, following the general rule in *Lux v. Milwaukee Mechanics' Ins. Co.*, 322 Mo. 342, 15 S.W.2d 343, 345. In the *Lux* case, as well as in *State ex rel. Ludlow v. Guffey*, Mo., 306 S.W.2d 552, exceptions to the general rule were stated to be "in situations and circumstances where necessity would require the vesting of discretion in the officer charged with the enforcement of an ordinance, as where it would be either impracticable or impossible to fix a definite rule or standard, or where the discretion vested in the officer relates to the enforcement of a police regulation requiring prompt exercise of judgment" (306 S.W.2d 557). The ordinance here is similar to the ordinance in the *Guffey* case wherein it was held that general standards of the ordinance were sufficient. Although it was said that neither of the above-stated exceptions applied in the *Guffey* case, the impracticality of setting forth a completely comprehensive standard insuring uniform discretionary action by the city council was discussed. It was held that the general standards were sufficient and that the procedure for determining whether the proposed filling station would or would not promote the "health, safety, morals or general welfare of the community" or would or would not adversely affect "the character of the neighborhood, traffic conditions, public utility facilities and other matters pertaining to the general welfare" (306 S.W.2d 558) was sufficient to provide against the exercise of arbitrary and uncontrolled discretion by the city council. Here, as in the *Guffey* case, the procedures are for public hearings with notice to the applicant, not only by the Architectural Board but also by the City Council on appeal on the factual issues to be determined under the ordinance. An applicant's rights are safeguarded in this respect, and thus distinguished is the ordinance which was condemned in *State ex rel. Magidson v. Henze, supra*. Otherwise, in the respect that the *Magidson* case did not consider the purpose of § 89.040, *supra*, it should no longer be followed. Ordinances 131 and 281 are sufficient in their general standards calling for a factual determination of the suitability of any proposed structure with reference to the character of the surrounding neighborhood and to the determination of any adverse effect on the general welfare and preservation of property values of the community. Like holdings were made involving Architectural Board ordinances in *State ex rel. Saveland Park Holding Corp. v. Wieland*, 269 Wis. 262, 69 N.W.2d 217, and *Reid v.*

Architectural Board of Review of the City of Cleveland Heights, 119 Ohio App. 67, 192 N.E.2d 74, *supra.*

The judgment is reversed.

NOTES

1. What is the constitutional basis for the plaintiffs' challenge to the design review ordinance?

2. The Ladue Building Commissioner described the plaintiffs' proposed home as "a monstrosity of grotesque design." The consultant for the city planning and engineering firm also described the home as "grotesque." On the other hand, an architectural magazine commended its design. By requiring compatibility with existing uses, does a design review ordinance freeze a neighborhood into outmoded aesthetic conceptions? Did the variety of home styles already in the neighborhood waive the right to object to a new home on the grounds of compatibility?

3. The City of Ladue was a party in another important aesthetic regulation case, *City of Ladue v. Gilleo,* 512 U.S. 43 (1994). The city enacted an ordinance that banned most types of signs from residential properties. The city denied the plaintiff a variance to post a sign in her home protesting the Gulf War. She then brought suit to challenge the law's constitutionality. The U.S. Supreme Court acknowledged the validity of the aesthetic purposes for sign control, such as elimination of visual clutter, but held that the ordinance violated the First Amendment and, therefore, was invalid.

Historic preservation laws present unique issues with respect to aesthetics as a police power purpose. Although some historic sites and districts are chosen because of their appearance, many others are chosen for their historic significance or for a variety of other reasons. But these other reasons are at least as important as a visually pleasing environment. Historic preservation helps provide a sense of place and identity. Perhaps the most vivid example of the importance of these qualities is the city of Warsaw. After the city was virtually leveled during World War II, its residents chose to rebuild the Old Town area to look almost exactly as it had before the war, rather than rebuilding in more modern styles.

Historic preservation has become quite widespread in this country. The National Register of Historic Places includes more than 80,000 listings. Many state and local governments also have a variety of historic preservation programs. These programs often restrict an owner's ability to alter a building's exterior or to demolish the building. The owner also may be subjected to affirmative obligations, such as the duty to maintain or to rehabilitate the site. As with other forms of land use regulation, historic preservation programs present the issue whether these burdens should be borne by the property owner or by the community that benefits from the historic preservation.

SOCIETY FOR ETHICAL CULTURE v. SPATT
415 N.E.2d 922 (N.Y. 1980)

WACHTLER, J.

At issue in this case is the propriety of the action of New York City's Landmark Preservation Commission in designating as a landmark the Meeting House of the Society of Ethical Culture of the City of New York (Society). The Society argues that the designation, with its attendant restrictions on the use of the property, is a confiscation without due compensation and an interference with the free exercise of the Society's religious purpose. The Appellate Division held that this landmark designation was a permissible land use regulation. We affirm, 68 A.D.2d 112, 416 N.Y.S.2d 246.

The Society is a religious, educational and charitable organization founded in 1877 for the purpose of uniting interested persons to further the goal of nonsectarian moral improvement. By the early 1900s the Society had grown to the extent that a permanent home for the organization was sought. To this end, a valuable parcel of real property with an entire block frontage of 200 feet on Central Park West in the City of New York was purchased.

Two buildings eventually were constructed on the site, but only the second, known as the Meeting House, is involved in the instant controversy. That building, which comprises 40% of the lot area, was deemed worthy of landmark status due to its exemplification as the first building facade of the art nouveau style pioneered in this country by the noted architect Robert D. Kohn, who was also a president of the Society. It was the architectural distinction of the building, and the architect's personal involvement in the Society, that led the commission to conclude that the Meeting House is "a tangible symbol of the Society's permanent social contribution and a rich architectural element of the fabric of our City."

The proposal of the landmark designation was met by the Society's immediate opposition; first at the public hearing required under the Administrative Code of the City of New York (Administrative Code, § 207-2.0), and later by way of an article 78 proceeding seeking to annul the commission's designation. This proceeding was converted into an action for declaratory judgment, and after a nonjury trial the trial court agreed with the Society's contention that there was insufficient evidence that the Meeting House was of historical or architectural significance, and declared that the designation was unreasonable, confiscatory and therefore unconstitutional. The Appellate Division, in a thorough and thoughtful opinion by Mr. Justice Joseph P. Sullivan, noted that Trial Term had impermissibly substituted its subjective judgment on the landmark question for that of the Landmark Preservation Commission and unanimously reversed. The Society now appeals.

The Administrative Code of the City of New York defines a landmark as "[a]ny improvement, any part of which is thirty years old or older, which has a special character or special historical or aesthetic interest or value as part of the development, heritage or cultural characteristics of the city, state or nation" (Administrative Code, § 207-1.0, subd. n.). At the outset we note that if the only question before us were whether there is sufficient evidence in the record to support respondents' determination that the Meeting House falls within this definition, there would be no question but that the designation would be sustained. Certainly, on this record, the determination of the commission in this regard cannot be deemed irrational (see *Matter of Pell v. Board of Educ.*, 34 N.Y.2d 222, 230–231, 356 N.Y.S.2d 833, 313 N.E.2d 321). However, because the landmark designation subjects the Society to substantial restriction in its use of the property without any outright compensation, substantial questions remain concerning the constitutional application of those restrictions to the Society, a religious and charitable organization.

The Society notes, quite rightly, that the landmark designation will prevent the exploitation of the full economic value of the Central Park West property, since that development would require the demolition of the existing structures in violation of the commission's designation. Furthermore, the Society argues, the designation also effectively prevents the development of the adjacent school building portion of the tract which, although not the subject of landmark designation, is physically and functionally related to the Meeting House through common interior passageways and utility systems. This latter argument appears weaker than the first, because the record indicates that the buildings could be demolished separately, but in any event it is clear that at the present time the designation has the potential of inflicting a substantial economic impact on the Society. Inevitably the reduced development potential of the property will be reflected in its market value. The question, of course, is whether the impact on the Society and its charitable activities is so severe that the restrictions become confiscatory (*Lutheran Church in Amer. v. City of New York*, 35 N.Y.2d 121, 359 N.Y.S.2d 7, 316 N.E.2d 305).

Although the State and Federal Constitutions require that land use regulation not be so unreasonable or extreme that it amounts to an appropriation of property without due compensation, . . . it has nonetheless long been accepted that a government may reasonably restrict an owner in the use of his property for the cultural and aesthetic benefit of the community. . . . To be sure individual landmark designation involves greater problems than general zoning or historical district regulation, because unlike those types of restrictions the individual landmark designations do not involve corresponding restrictions of the surrounding parcels which operates to the benefit of the landmark owner (*Penn Cent. Transp. Co. v. City of New York*, 42 N.Y.2d 324, 330, 397 N.Y.S.2d 914, 366 N.E.2d 1271, *affd.* 438 U.S. 104). However, we have recognized that despite this particularized burden on the owner, landmark designations, if not unreasonable, are not an undue imposition under proper circumstances (*Penn Cent. Transp. Co. v. City of New York*, *supra*, 42 N.Y.2d p. 333, 397 N.Y.S.2d 914, 366 N.E.2d 1271). It must be emphasized, however, that reasonableness when related to commercial property necessarily requires that the owner not be deprived by the regulation of a reasonable return on his property. . . . However, because charitable organizations are not created for financial return in the same sense as private businesses, for them the standard is refined to permit the landmark designation restriction only so long as it does not physically or financially prevent, or seriously interfere with the carrying out of the charitable purpose. . . . With this standard now set, and the emphasis properly placed on how the restriction effects the charitable activities of the organization, it is clear that on this record the landmark designation withstands constitutional scrutiny.[*]

In *Lutheran Church* (*supra*), we found an undue interference with the church's charitable activity where the landmark structure had become so hopelessly inadequate to the church needs, that had the landmark restrictions been enforced, there was no alternative but to cause the charitable activity at that location to cease. Particularly significant in the *Lutheran Church* case was the fact that the church had tried unsuccessfully to modify the structure to suit its needs, and that no further accommodation, short of demolition and rebuilding, would have alleviated the serious space problems which had arisen. In view of these facts, the landmark restrictions were so debilitating, the impediment to the charitable use so complete, that sustaining the landmark designation without compensation was, in reality, a "naked taking" (35 N.Y.2d 121, 132, 359 N.Y.S.2d 7, 316 N.E.2d 305). The Society has shown no such compelling circumstances here.

Although the Society does argue that the physical structure of the Meeting House is ill-adapted to its present needs, by no means are we assured that the only feasible solution to this problem would entail the demolition of the now protected building facade. Instead, petitioners' arguments seem to emphasize aggrievement with respect to the prohibition against high-rise development. There is no genuine complaint that eleemosynary activities within the landmark are wrongfully disrupted, but rather the complaint is instead that the landmark stands as an effective bar against putting the property to its most lucrative use. But there simply is no constitutional requirement that a landowner always be allowed his property's most beneficial use (*Goldblatt v. Town of Hempstead*, 369 U.S. 590, 592).

It is noteworthy that the designation we are here concerned with applies only to the building facade, and it is possible that studies would reveal that without disturbing this protected portion, feasible modifications could be employed to allow the Society to continue its charitable activities in the building, as it has for over 60 years. This, of course, would be a matter for consideration at the appropriate time by the commission. In fact, the Society concedes that even minor modifications and a certain amount of normal maintenance have been held in abeyance while the questions of demolition and redevelopment were being explored. It therefore remains unclear whether both the interest of the Society and the interest of the public may yet be accommodated.

The Society also contends that the existence of the designation interferes with the free exercise of its religious activities; however, rather than argue its desire to modify the structure to accommodate these religious activities, the Society has suggested that it is improper to restrict its ability to develop the property to permit rental to nonreligious tenants. For this reason the Society's reliance on our decision *Matter of Westchester Reform Temple v. Brown*, 22 N.Y.2d 488, 293 N.Y.S.2d 297,

---

[*] Although we note that the challenge here is not to the facial validity of the statute, such a challenge would be to no avail because of the ameliorative provisions of section 207-8.0 which contains a number of alternative methods by which the commission may seek to devise a scheme so that the impediments to the owner's earning a reasonable return, created by landmark designation, may be offset by other pecuniary benefits. Failing this, the commission may recommend that the city seek to acquire an interest in the property (Administrative Code, § 207-8.0, subd. i; see *Penn Cent. Trans. Co. v. New York City*, 438 U.S. 104, 110–113, n. 13).

239 N.E.2d 891, which dealt with restrictions actually impairing religious activities, is clearly misplaced. Although the Society is concededly entitled to First Amendment protection as a religious organization, this does not entitle it to immunity from reasonable government regulation when it acts in purely secular matters (cf. *Wisconsin v. Yoder*, 406 U.S. 205, 215).

Accordingly, the order of the Appellate Division should be affirmed, with costs.

NOTES

1. The court distinguishes between the regulation of historic sites, such as the building in this case, and historic districts, such as the French Quarter in New Orleans. Which type of regulation is more susceptible to constitutional challenge and why?

2. The court states that landmark designation of a charitable institution does not constitute a taking if the designation "does not physically or financially prevent, or seriously interfere with the carrying out of the charitable purpose." Is this standard more or less stringent than the standard applied to other types of organizations?

3. As the court indicated in the *Spatt* opinion, the application of land use regulations to religious uses can raise First Amendment issues. Litigation has been brought based on both the Free Exercise Clause and the Establishment Clause. Religious groups bring free exercise cases to challenge land use regulations that restrict their use of land, such as historic preservation laws applied to places of worship and zoning regulations that prevent religious services from being conducted in a private residence. On the other hand, Establishment Clause cases challenge laws that exempt religious organizations from otherwise applicable land use requirements. The decisions involving both clauses are quite mixed.

In an attempt to provide greater protection for religious practices, Congress enacted the Religious Land Use and Institutionalized Persons Act, 42 U.S.C. §§ 2000cc-cc-5 (RLUIPA) in 2000. The Act prohibits the government from imposing or implementing a land use regulation "that imposes a substantial burden on the religious exercise of a person" unless the regulation serves a "compelling governmental interest" and is "the least restrictive means" of furthering that interest. Although this prohibition arguably violates the Establishment Clause, the courts that have considered this argument have rejected it. *Westchester Day School v. Village of Mamaroneck*, 504 F.3d 338 (2d Cir. 2007); *Midrash Sephardi, Inc. v. Town of Surfside*, 366 F.3d 1214 (11th Cir. 2004); *Lighthouse Community Church of God v. City of Southfield*, 2007 U.S. Dist. LEXIS 28 (E.D. Mich., January 3, 2007); *Murphy v. New Milford Zoning Comm'n*, 289 F. Supp. 2d 87 (D. Conn. 2003), *rev'd on other grounds*, 402 F.3d 342 (2d Cir. 2005). The U.S. Supreme Court has not addressed the issue, though it upheld RLUIPA's provision of enhanced protection for the religious rights of prisoners and other incarcerated persons. *Cutter v. Wilkinson*, 544 U.S. 709 (2005).

Chapter 8

CREATING INTANGIBLE AND INTELLECTUAL PROPERTY

I. MISAPPROPRIATION OF INFORMATION

INTERNATIONAL NEWS SERVICE v. THE ASSOCIATED PRESS
248 U.S. 215 (1918)

MR. JUSTICE PITNEY delivered the opinion of the court.

The parties are competitors in the gathering and distribution of news and its publication for profit in newspapers throughout the United States. The Associated Press, which was complainant in the District Court, is a cooperative organization, incorporated under the Membership Corporations Law of the State of New York, its members being individuals who are either proprietors or representatives of about 950 daily newspapers published in all parts of the United States. That a corporation may be organized under that act for the purpose of gathering news for the use and benefit of its members and for publication in newspapers owned or represented by them, is recognized by an amendment enacted in 1901. * * * Complainant gathers in all parts of the world, by means of various instrumentalities of its own, by exchange with its members, and by other appropriate means, news and intelligence of current and recent events of interest to newspaper readers and distributes it daily to its members for publication in their newspapers. The cost of the service, amounting approximately to $3,500,000 per annum, is assessed upon the members and becomes a part of their costs of operation, to be recouped, presumably with profit, through the publication of their several newspapers. Under complainant's by-laws each member agrees upon assuming membership that news received through complainant's service is received exclusively for publication in a particular newspaper, language, and place specified in the certificate of membership, that no other use of it shall be permitted, and that no member shall furnish or permit anyone in his employ or connected with his newspaper to furnish any of complainant's news in advance of publication to any person not a member. And each member is required to gather the local news of his district and supply it to the Associated Press and to no one else.

Defendant is a corporation organized under the laws of the State of New Jersey, whose business is the gathering and selling of news to its customers and clients, consisting of newspapers published throughout the United States, under contracts by which they pay certain amounts at stated times for defendant's service. It has wide-spread news-gathering agencies; the cost of its operations amounts, it is said, to more than $2,000,000 per annum; and it serves about 400 newspapers located in the various cities of the United States and abroad, a few of which are represented, also, in the membership of the Associated Press.

The parties are in the keenest competition between themselves in the distribution of news throughout the United States; and so, as a rule, are the newspapers that they serve, in their several districts.

Complainant in its bill, defendant in its answer, have set forth in almost identical terms the rather obvious circumstances and conditions under which their business is conducted. The value of the service, and of the news furnished, depends upon the promptness of transmission, as well as upon the accuracy and impartiality of the news; it being essential that the news be transmitted to members or subscribers as early or earlier than similar information can be furnished to competing newspapers by other news services, and that the news furnished by each agency shall not be furnished to newspapers which do not contribute to the expense of gathering it. * * *

The bill was filed to restrain the pirating of complainant's news by defendant in three ways: First, by bribing employees of newspapers published by complainant's members to furnish Associated Press news to defendant before publication, for transmission by telegraph and telephone to defendant's clients for publication by them; Second, by inducing Associated Press members to violate its by-laws and permit defendant to obtain news before publication; and Third, by copying news from bulletin boards and from early editions of complainant's newspapers and selling this, either bodily or after rewriting it, to defendant's customers.

The District Court . . . granted a preliminary injunction under the first and second heads; but refused at that stage to restrain the systematic practice admittedly pursued by defendant, of taking news bodily from the bulletin boards and early editions of complainant's newspapers and selling it as its own. The court expressed itself . . . as the legal question was one of first impression, it considered that the allowance of an injunction should await the outcome of an appeal. Both parties having appealed, the Circuit Court of Appeals [modified and — Eds.] sustained the injunction. . . .

The only matter that has been argued before us is whether defendant may lawfully be restrained from appropriating news taken from bulletins issued by complainant or any of its members, or from newspapers published by them, for the purpose of selling it to defendant's clients. Complainant asserts that defendant's admitted course of conduct in this regard both violates complainant's property right in the news and constitutes unfair competition in business. And notwithstanding the case has proceeded only to the stage of a preliminary injunction, we have deemed it proper to consider the underlying questions, since they . . . are presented upon facts that are not in dispute. As presented in argument, these questions are: 1. Whether there is any property in news; 2. Whether, if there be property in news collected for the purpose of being published, it survives the instant of its publication in the first newspaper to which it is communicated by the news-gatherer; and 3. Whether defendant's admitted course of conduct in appropriating for commercial use matter taken from bulletins or early editions of Associated Press publications constitutes unfair competition in trade.

* * * Complainant's news matter is not copyrighted. It is said that it could not, in practice, be copyrighted, because of the large number of dispatches that are sent daily; and, according to complainant's contention, news is not within the operation of the copyright act. Defendant, while apparently conceding this, nevertheless invokes the analogies of the law of literary property and copyright, insisting as its principal contention that, assuming complainant has a right of property in its news, it can be maintained (unless the copyright act be complied with) only by being kept secret and confidential, and that upon the publication with complainant's consent of uncopyrighted news by any of complainant's members in a newspaper or upon a bulletin board, the right of property is lost, and the subsequent use of the news by the public or by defendant for any purpose whatever becomes lawful. * * *

In considering the general question of property in news matter, it is necessary to recognize its dual character, distinguishing between the substance of the information and the particular form or collocation of words in which the writer has communicated it. No doubt news articles often possess a literary quality, and are the subject of literary property at the common law; nor do we question that such an article, as a literary production, is the subject of copyright by the terms of the act as it now stands. . . . But the news element-the information respecting current events contained in the literary production-is not the creation of the writer, but is a report of matters that ordinarily are publici juris; it is the history of the day. It is not to be supposed that the framers of the Constitution, when they empowered Congress "to promote the progress of science and useful arts, by securing for limited times to authors and inventors the exclusive right to their respective writings and discoveries" (Const., Art I, § 8, par. 8), intended to confer upon one who might happen to be the first to report a historic event the exclusive right for any period to spread the knowledge of it.

We need spend no time, however, upon the general question of property in news matter at common law, or the application of the copyright act, since it seems to us the case must turn upon the question of unfair competition in business. And, in our opinion, this does not depend upon any general right of property analogous to the common-law right of the proprietor of an unpublished work to prevent its publication without his consent; nor is it foreclosed by showing that the benefits of the copyright act have been waived. We are dealing here not with restrictions upon publication but with the very facilities and processes of publication. The peculiar value of news is in the spreading of it while it is fresh; and it is evident that a valuable property interest in the news, as news, cannot be maintained by keeping it secret. Besides, except for matters improperly disclosed, or published in breach of trust or confidence, or in violation of law, none of which is involved in this branch of the case, the news of current events may be regarded as common property. What we are concerned with is the business of making it known to the world, in which both parties to the present suit are engaged. That business consists in maintaining a prompt, sure, steady, and reliable service designed to place the daily events of the world at the breakfast table of the millions at a price that, while of trifling moment to each reader, is sufficient in the aggregate to afford compensation for the cost of gathering and distributing it, with the added profit so necessary as an incentive to effective action in the commercial world. The service thus performed for newspaper readers is not only innocent but extremely useful in itself, and indubitably constitutes a legitimate business. The parties are competitors in this field; and, on fundamental principles, applicable here as elsewhere, when the rights or privileges of the one are liable to conflict with those of the other, each party is under a duty so to conduct its own business as not unnecessarily or unfairly to injure that of the other.

Obviously, the question of what is unfair competition in business must be determined with particular reference to the character and circumstances of the business. The question here is not so much the rights of either party as against the public but their rights as between themselves. And although we may and do assume that neither party has any remaining property interest as against the public in uncopyrighted news matter after the moment of its first publication, it by no means follows that there is no remaining property interest in it as between themselves. For, to both of them alike, news matter, however little susceptible of ownership or dominion in the absolute sense, is stock in trade, to be gathered at the cost of enterprise, organization, skill, labor, and money, and to be distributed and sold to those who will pay money for it, as for any other merchandise. Regarding the news, therefore, as but the material out of which both parties are seeking to make profits at the same time and in the same field, we hardly can fail to recognize that for this purpose, and as between them, it must be regarded as quasi property, irrespective of the rights of either as against the public.

In order to sustain the jurisdiction of equity over the controversy, we need not affirm any general and absolute property in the news as such. The rule that a court of equity concerns itself only in the protection of property rights treats any civil right of a pecuniary nature as a property right; and the right to acquire property by honest labor or the conduct of a lawful business is as much entitled to protection as the right to guard property already acquired. It is this right that furnishes the basis of the jurisdiction in the ordinary case of unfair competition.

The question, whether one who has gathered general information or news at pains and expense for the purpose of subsequent publication through the press has such an interest in its publication as may be protected from interference, has been raised many times, although never, perhaps, in the precise form in which it is now presented. * * * Not only do the acquisition and transmission of news require elaborate organization and a large expenditure of money, skill, and effort; not only has it an exchange value to the gatherer, dependent chiefly upon its novelty and freshness, the regularity of the service, its reputed reliability and thoroughness, and its adaptability to the public needs; but also, as is evident, the news has an exchange value to one who can misappropriate it.

The peculiar features of the case arise from the fact that, while novelty and freshness form so important an element in the success of the business, the very processes of distribution and publication necessarily occupy a good deal of time. Complainant's service, as well as defendant's, is a daily service to daily newspapers; most of the foreign news reaches this country at the Atlantic seaboard, principally at the City of New York, and because of this, and of time differentials due to the earth's rotation, the distribution of news matter throughout the country is principally from east to west; and, since in speed the telegraph and telephone easily outstrip the rotation of the earth, it is a simple matter for defendant to take complainant's news from bulletins or early editions of complainant's members in the eastern cities and at the mere cost of telegraphic transmission cause it to be published in western papers issued at least as early as those served by complainant. Besides this, and irrespective of time differentials, irregularities in telegraphic transmission on different lines, and the normal consumption of time in printing and distributing the newspaper, result in permitting pirated news to be placed in the hands of defendant's readers sometimes simultaneously with the service of competing Associated Press papers, occasionally even earlier.

Defendant insists that when, with the sanction and approval of complainant, and as the result of the use of its news for the very purpose for which it is distributed, a portion of complainant's members communicate it to the general public by posting it upon bulletin boards so that all may read, or by issuing it to newspapers and distributing it indiscriminately, complainant no longer has the right to control the use to be made of it; that when it thus reaches the light of day it becomes the common possession of all to whom it is accessible; and that any purchaser of a newspaper has the right to communicate the intelligence which it contains to anybody and for any purpose, even for the purpose of selling it for profit to newspapers published for profit in competition with complainant's members.

The fault in the reasoning lies in applying as a test the right of the complainant as against the public, instead of considering the rights of complainant and defendant, competitors in business, as between themselves. The right of the purchaser of a single newspaper to spread knowledge of its contents gratuitously, for any legitimate purpose not unreasonably interfering with complainant's right to make merchandise of it, may be admitted; but to transmit that news for commercial use, in competition with complainant — which is what defendant has done and seeks to justify — is a very different matter. In doing this defendant, by its very act, admits that it is taking material that has been acquired by complainant as the result of organization and the expenditure of labor, skill, and money, and which is salable by complainant for money, and that defendant in appropriating it and selling it as its own is endeavoring to reap where it has not sown, and by disposing of it to newspapers that are competitors of complainant's members is appropriating to itself the harvest of those who have sown. Stripped of all disguises, the process amounts to an unauthorized interference with the normal operation of complainant's legitimate business precisely at the point where the profit is to be reaped, in order to divert a material portion of the profit from those who have earned it to those who have not; with special advantage to defendant in the competition because of the fact that it is not burdened with any part of the expense of gathering the news. The transaction speaks for itself, and a court of equity ought not to hesitate long in characterizing it as unfair competition in business.

* * * It is no answer to say that complainant spends its money for that which is too fugitive or evanescent to be the subject of property. That might, and for the purposes of the discussion we are assuming that it would, furnish an answer in a common-law controversy. But in a court of equity, where the question is one of unfair competition, if that which complainant has acquired fairly at substantial cost may be sold fairly at substantial profit, a competitor who is misappropriating it for

the purpose of disposing of it to his own profit and to the disadvantage of complainant cannot be heard to say that it is too fugitive or evanescent to be regarded as property. It has all the attributes of property necessary for determining that a misappropriation of it by a competitor is unfair competition because contrary to good conscience.

The contention that the news is abandoned to the public for all purposes when published in the first newspaper is untenable. Abandonment is a question of intent, and the entire organization of the Associated Press negatives such a purpose. The cost of the service would be prohibitive if the reward were to be so limited. No single newspaper, no small group of newspapers, could sustain the expenditure. Indeed, it is one of the most obvious results of defendant's theory that, by permitting indiscriminate publication by anybody and everybody for purposes of profit in competition with the news-gatherer, it would render publication profitless, or so little profitable as in effect to cut off the service by rendering the cost prohibitive in comparison with the return. The practical needs and requirements of the business are reflected in complainant's by-laws which have been referred to. Their effect is that publication by each member must be deemed not by any means an abandonment of the news to the world for any and all purposes, but a publication for limited purposes; for the benefit of the readers of the bulletin or the newspaper as such; not for the purpose of making merchandise of it as news, with the result of depriving complainant's other members of their reasonable opportunity to obtain just returns for their expenditures.

It is to be observed that the view we adopt does not result in giving to complainant the right to monopolize either the gathering or the distribution of the news, or, without complying with the copyright act, to prevent the reproduction of its news articles; but only postpones participation by complainant's competitor in the processes of distribution and reproduction of news that it has not gathered, and only to the extent necessary to prevent that competitor from reaping the fruits of complainant's efforts and expenditure, to the partial exclusion of complainant, and in violation of the principle that underlies the maxim sic utere tuo, etc.

It is said that the elements of unfair competition are lacking because there is no attempt by defendant to palm off its goods as those of the complainant, characteristic of the most familiar, if not the most typical, cases of unfair competition. But we cannot concede that the right to equitable relief is confined to that class of cases. In the present case the fraud upon complainant's rights is more direct and obvious. Regarding news matter as the mere material from which these two competing parties are endeavoring to make money, and treating it, therefore, as quasi property for the purposes of their business because they are both selling it as such, defendant's conduct differs from the ordinary case of unfair competition in trade principally in this that, instead of selling its own goods as those of complainant, it substitutes misappropriation in the place of misrepresentation, and sells complainant's goods as its own.

Besides the misappropriation, there are elements of imitation, of false pretense, in defendant's practices. The device of rewriting complainant's news articles, frequently resorted to, carries its own comment. The habitual failure to give credit to complainant for that which is taken is significant. Indeed, the entire system of appropriating complainant's news and transmitting it as a commercial product to defendant's clients and patrons amounts to a false representation to them and to their newspaper readers that the news transmitted is the result of defendant's own investigation in the field. But these elements, although accentuating the wrong, are not the essence of it. It is something more than the advantage of celebrity of which complainant is being deprived. * * * The decree of the Circuit Court of Appeals will be affirmed.

HOLMES, J., concurring.

When an uncopyrighted combination of words is published there is no general right to forbid other people repeating them — in other words there is no property in the combination or in the thoughts or facts that the words express. Property, a creation of law, does not arise from value, although exchangeable — a matter of fact. Many exchangeable values may be destroyed intentionally without compensation. Property depends upon exclusion by law from interference, and a person is not excluded from using any combination of words merely because someone has used it before, even if it took labor and genius to make it. . . .

Fresh news is got only by enterprise and expense. To produce such news as it is produced by the defendant represents by implication that it has been acquired by the defendant's enterprise and at its expense. When it comes from one of the great news-collecting agencies like the Associated Press, the source generally is indicated, plainly importing that credit; and that such a representation is implied may be inferred with some confidence from the unwillingness of the defendant to give the credit and tell the truth. If the plaintiff produces the news at the same time that the defendant does, the defendant's presentation impliedly denies to the plaintiff the credit of collecting the facts and assumes that credit to the defendant. If the plaintiff is later in western cities it naturally will be supposed to have obtained its information from the defendant. The falsehood is a little more subtle, the injury a little more indirect, than in ordinary cases of unfair trade, but I think that the principle that condemns the one condemns the other. It is a question of how strong an infusion of fraud is necessary to turn a flavor into a poison. The dose seems to me strong enough here to need a remedy from the law. But as, in my view, the only ground of complaint that can be recognized without legislation is the implied misstatement, it can be corrected by stating the truth; and a suitable acknowledgment of the source is all that the plaintiff can require. . . .

BRANDEIS, J., dissenting.

* * * News is a report of recent occurrences. The business of the news agency is to gather systematically knowledge of such occurrences of interest and to distribute reports thereof. The Associated Press contended that knowledge so acquired is property, because it costs money and labor to produce and because it has value for which those who have it not are ready to pay; that it remains property and is entitled to protection as long as it has commercial value as news; and that to protect it effectively the defendant must be enjoined from making, or causing to be made, any gainful use of it while it retains such value. An essential element of individual property is the legal right to exclude others from enjoying it. If the property is

private, the right of exclusion may be absolute; if the property is affected with a public interest, the right of exclusion is qualified. But the fact that a product of the mind has cost its producer money and labor, and has a value for which others are willing to pay, is not sufficient to ensure to it this legal attribute of property. The general rule of law is, that the noblest of human productions — knowledge, truths ascertained, conceptions, and ideas — become, after voluntary communication to others, free as the air to common use. Upon these incorporeal productions the attribute of property is continued after such communication only in certain classes of cases where public policy has seemed to demand it. These exceptions are confined to productions which, in some degree, involve creation, invention, or discovery. But by no means all such are endowed with this attribute of property. The creations which are recognized as property by the common law are literary, dramatic, musical, and other artistic creations; and these have also protection under the copyright statutes. The inventions and discoveries upon which this attribute of property is conferred only by statute, are the few comprised within the patent law. There are also many other cases in which courts interfere to prevent curtailment of plaintiff's enjoyment of incorporeal productions; and in which the right to relief is often called a property right, but is such only in a special sense. In those cases, the plaintiff has no absolute right to the protection of his production; he has merely the qualified right to be protected as against the defendant's acts, because of the special relation in which the latter stands or the wrongful method or means employed in acquiring the knowledge or the manner in which it is used. Protection of this character is afforded where the suit is based upon breach of contract or of trust or upon unfair competition.

The knowledge for which protection is sought in the case at bar is not of a kind upon which the law has heretofore conferred the attributes of property. . . . The means by which the International News Service obtains news gathered by the Associated Press is also clearly unobjectionable. It is taken from papers bought in the open market or from bulletins publicly posted. No breach of contract . . . ; or of trust . . . ; and neither fraud nor force, is involved. The manner of use is likewise unobjectionable. No reference is made by word or by act to the Associated Press. . . . Neither the International News Service nor its subscribers is gaining or seeking to gain in its business a benefit from the reputation of the Associated Press. They are merely using its product without making compensation. That, they have a legal right to do; because the product is not property. . . .

It is also suggested, that the fact that defendant does not refer to the Associated Press as the source of the news may furnish a basis for the relief. But the defendant and its subscribers, unlike members of the Associated Press, were under no contractual obligation to disclose the source of the news; and there is no rule of law requiring acknowledgment to be made where uncopyrighted matter is reproduced. The International News Service is said to mislead its subscribers into believing that the news transmitted was originally gathered by it and that they in turn mislead their readers. There is, in fact, no representation by either of any kind. . . . [N]o representation can properly be implied from omission to mention the source of information except that the International News Service is transmitting news which it believes to be credible.

Nor is the use made by the International News Service of the information taken from papers or bulletins of Associated Press members legally objectionable by reason of the purpose for which it was employed. The acts here complained of were not done for the purpose of injuring the business of the Associated Press. Their purpose was not even to divert its trade, or to put it at a disadvantage by lessening defendant's necessary expenses. The purpose was merely to supply subscribers of the International News Service promptly with all available news. * * *

The great development of agencies now furnishing country-wide distribution of news, the vastness of our territory, and improvements in the means of transmitting intelligence, have made it possible for a news agency or newspapers to obtain, without paying compensation, the fruit of another's efforts and to use news so obtained gainfully in competition with the original collector. The injustice of such action is obvious. But to give relief against it would involve more than the application of existing rules of law to new facts. It would require the making of a new rule in analogy to existing ones. The unwritten law possesses capacity for growth. . . . This process . . . should not be discontinued. Where the problem is relatively simple, as it is apt to be when private interests only are involved, it generally proves adequate. But with the increasing complexity of society, the public interest tends to become omnipresent; and the problems presented by new demands for justice cease to be simple. Then the creation or recognition by courts of a new private right may work serious injury to the general public, unless the boundaries of the right are definitely established and wisely guarded. * * *

The rule for which the plaintiff contends would effect an important extension of property rights and a corresponding curtailment of the free use of knowledge and of ideas; and the facts of this case admonish us of the danger involved in recognizing such a property right in news, without imposing upon news-gatherers corresponding obligations. A large majority of the newspapers and perhaps half the newspaper readers of the United States are dependent for their news of general interest upon agencies other than the Associated Press. The channel through which about 400 of these papers received, as the plaintiff alleges, "a large amount of news relating to the European war of the greatest importance and of intense interest to the newspaper reading public" was suddenly closed. The closing to the International News Service of these channels for foreign news (if they were closed) was due not to unwillingness on its part to pay the cost of collecting the news, but to the prohibitions imposed by foreign governments upon its securing news from their respective countries and from using cable or telegraph lines running therefrom. For aught that appears, this prohibition may have been wholly undeserved; and at all events the 400 papers and their readers may be assumed to have been innocent. For aught that appears, the International News Service may have sought then to secure temporarily by arrangement with the Associated Press the latter's foreign news service. For aught that appears, all of the 400 subscribers of the International News Service would gladly have then become members of the Associated Press, if they could have secured election thereto. It is possible, also, that a large part of the readers of these papers were so situated that they could not secure prompt access to papers served by the Associated Press. * * *

A legislature, urged to enact a law by which one news agency or newspaper may prevent appropriation of the fruits of its labors by another, would consider such facts and possibilities and others which appropriate enquiry might disclose. . . . Courts are ill-equipped to make the investigations which should precede a determination of the limitations which should be set upon any property right in news or of the circumstances under which news gathered by a private agency should be deemed affected with a public interest. Courts would be powerless to prescribe the detailed regulations essential to full enjoyment of the rights conferred or to introduce the machinery required for enforcement of such regulations. Considerations such as these should lead us to decline to establish a new rule of law in the effort to redress a newly-disclosed wrong, although the propriety of some remedy appears to be clear.

RCA MFG. CO. v. WHITEMAN
114 F.2d 86 (2d Cir. 1940)

L. HAND, J.

This case comes up upon appeals by the plaintiff, RCA Manufacturing Company, Inc., and the defendants, Paul Whiteman and W.B.O. Broadcasting Corporation. Before the action was brought Whiteman had filed a complaint against W.B.O. Broadcasting Corporation . . . , to restrain the broadcasting of phonograph records of musical performances by Whitemans's orchestra. By leave of court RCA Manufacturing Company, Inc., then filed the complaint at bar, as ancillary to Whiteman's action, asking the same relief against W.B.O. Broadcasting Corporation . . . as Whiteman had asked in his action. . . . The dispute is as to whether W.B.O. Broadcasting Corporation, as the purchaser of phonographic records prepared by RCA Manufacturing Company, Inc., of Whiteman's orchestral performances, may broadcast them by radio. Whiteman's performances took place in studios of RCA Manufacturing Company, Inc., which arranged for their reproduction upon ordinary phonographic disc records, and which, with the consent of Whiteman, sold the records to the public at large. Of the nine records here in question five were sold between November, 1932, and August 15, 1937, during which period every record bore the legend: "Not Licensed for Radio Broadcast". * * * After August 15, 1937, this notice was changed to read as follows: "Licensed by Mfr. under U.S. Pats. 1625705, 1637544 . . . (& other Pats. Pending). Only For Non-Commercial Use on Phonographs in Homes. Mfr. & Original Purchaser Have Agreed This Record Shall Not Be Resold Or Used For Any Other Purpose. See Detailed Notice on Envelope." These later records were inclosed in envelopes which even more clearly gave notice of the same limitations. W.B.O. Broadcasting Corporation every week bought from a New York company, Bruno-New York, Inc., such records as it needed; it used them thereafter to broadcast over its radio system. Bruno-New York, Inc., had bought the records in question under a contract with RCA Manufacturing Company, Inc., in which they agreed after its date (August 9, 1937) to resell "only for non-commercial use on phonographs in homes as per the notice appearing on the record labels and envelopes." It may be assumed that W.B.O. Broadcasting Corporation is charged with notice of the legends on the records, and with the contract of Bruno-New York, Inc., and that it broadcasts them on its radio system in disregard of both.

The questions raised below were whether Whiteman and/or RCA Manufacturing Company, Inc., had any musical property at common-law in the records which radio broadcasting invaded; whether Whiteman had passed any rights which he may have had to RCA Manufacturing Company, Inc., under certain agreements, not necessary to be set out; and whether, if either Whiteman or RCA Manufacturing Company, Inc., had any such common-law property, the legends and notice enabled them, or either of them, to limit the uses which the buyer might make of the records. The judge held that all of Whiteman's rights had passed to RCA Manufacturing Company, Inc., which for that reason was entitled to enjoin the broadcasting of these records; and that Whiteman was also entitled to an injunction against W.B.O Broadcasting Corporation because it was unfair competition to broadcast his performances without his consent. * * * The RCA Manufacturing Company, Inc., appealed because the judge did not recognize its common-law artistic property, arising out of the skill and art necessary to obtain good recording, and also because of the affirmative relief granted to Whiteman. Whiteman appealed because of the holding that he had lost all his rights to RCA Manufacturing Company, Inc., under its contracts with him. W.B.O. Broadcasting Corporation appealed because any relief was granted against it.

It is only in comparatively recent times that a virtuoso, conductor, actor, lecturer, or preacher could have any interest in the reproduction of his performance. Until the phonographic record made possible the preservation and reproduction of sound, all audible renditions were of necessity fugitive and transitory; once uttered they died; the nearest approach to their reproduction was mimicry. Of late, however, the power to reproduce the exact quality and sequence of sounds had become possible, and the right to do so, exceedingly valuable; people easily distinguish, or think they distinguish, the rendition of the same score or the same text by their favorites, and they will pay large sums to hear them. Hence this action. It was settled at least a century ago that the monopoly of the right to reproduce the compositions of any author — his "common-law property" in them — was not limited to words; pictures were included. *Turner v. Robinson*, 10 Ir.Ch. 121. . . . This right has at times been stated as though it extended to all productions demanding "intellectual" effort; and for the purposes of this case we shall assume that it covers the performances of an orchestra conductor, and — what is far more doubtful — the skill and art by which a phonographic record maker makes possible the proper recording of those performances upon a disc. It would follow from this that, if a conductor played over the radio, and if his performance was not an abandonment of his rights, it would be unlawful without his consent to record it as it was received from a receiving set and to use the record. Arguendo, we shall also assume that such a performance would not be an abandonment, just as performance of a play, or the delivery of a lecture is not; that is, that it does not "publish" the work and dedicate it to the public. *Ferris v. Frohman*, 223 U.S. 424, 435. . . . Nevertheless, even if Whiteman's "common-law property" in his performances survived the sale of the records on which they were inscribed, it would be very difficult to see how he, or *a fortiori* the maker of the records, could impose valid restrictions upon their resale. Concededly that could not be done (regardless of the present statutory prohibition) if the restriction went to the resale price. *Bobbs-Merrill Co. v. Straus*, 210 U.S. 339. It would also have been impossible if the restriction forbad the buyer to use the article except with other articles bought of the record maker. *Motion Picture Patents Co. v. Universal Film Co.*, 243 U.S. 502. We . . . think that the "common-law property" in these performances ended with the sale of the records and that the restriction did not save it; and that if it did, the records themselves could not be clogged with a servitude.

Copyright in any form, whether statutory or at common-law, is a monopoly; it consists only in the power to prevent others from reproducing the copyrighted work. W.B.O. Broadcasting Corporation has never invaded any such right of Whiteman; they have never copied his performances at all; they have merely used those copies which he and the RCA Manufacturing Company, Inc., made and distributed. The putatively protected performances were themselves intended for that purpose and for that alone. * * * The records at bar embodied Whiteman's "common-law property" — his contribution as a conductor — in precisely the same way that the record of such a score would embody his composition. Hence the question is no different from whether he might disseminate a musical score to the public at large, but impose a limitation upon it that buyers should not use it to broadcast for profit. * * * Restrictions upon the uses of chattels once absolutely sold are at least prima facie invalid; they must be justified for some exceptional reason, normally they are "repugnant" to the transfer of title. If "the common-law property" in the rendition be gone, then anyone may copy it who chances to hear it, and may use if as he pleases. It would be the height of "unreasonableness" to forbid any uses to the owner of the record which were open to anyone who might choose to copy the rendition from the record. To revert to the illustration of a musical score, it would be absurd to forbid the broadcast for profit of its record, if any hearer might copy it and broadcast the copy. Thus, even if Whiteman and RCA Manufacturing Company, Inc., have a "common-law property" which performance does not end, it is immaterial, unless the right to copy the rendition from the records was preserved through the notice of the restriction.

As applied to books, where the problem is precisely the same, there is not very much law as to whether such restrictions prevent complete dedication, but the judges who have passed upon the question have declared, at times with much certainty, that they are nugatory. In 1898 the Court of Appeals of New York flatly so decided in *Jewelers Mercantile Agency v. Jewelers' Weekly Publishing Co.*, 155 N.Y. 241, 49 N.E. 872, and that is the leading case. * * * In his dissenting opinion in *International News Servce v. Associated Press*, 248 U.S. 215, 256, Mr. Justice Brandeis spoke of the law as "well-settled" to that effect. * * * It is quite true that if "publication" were merely a question of intent, these decisions are wrong, for the intent is obvious not to dedicate the whole right. The problem is not so simple; in dealing with a monopoly the law imposes its own limits. Certainly when the "common-law property" is in a work which the Copyright Act, 17 U.S.C.A. § 1 et seq., covers, there can be no doubt; Congress has created the monopoly in exchange for a dedication, and when the monopoly expires the dedication must be complete. If the records were registrable under the act, the restriction would therefore certainly not limit the dedication. The fact that they are not within the act should make no difference. * * * Otherwise it would be possible, at least pro tanto, to have the advantage of dissemination of the work at large, and to retain a perpetual though partial, monopoly in it. That is contrary to the whole policy of the Copyright Act and of the Constitution. Any relief which justice demands must be found in extending statutory copyright to such works, not in recognizing perpetual monopplies, however limited their scope. * * *

Whiteman and the plaintiff also rest their case upon the theory of unfair competition, depending for that upon *International News Service v. Associated Press, supra*, 248 U.S. 215. That much discussed decision really held no more than that a western newspaper might not take advantage of the fact that it was published some hours later than papers in the east, to copy the news which the plaintiff had collected at its own expense. In spite of some general language it must be confined to that situation (*Cheney Bros. v. Doris Silk Corp.*, 2 Cir., 35 F.2d 279, 281); certainly it cannot be used as a cover to prevent competitors from ever appropriating the results of the industry, skill, and expense of others. "Property" is a historical concept; one may bestow much labor and ingenuity which inures only to the public benefit; "ideas", for instance, though upon them all civilization is built, may never be "owned". The law does not protect them at all, but only their expression; and how far that protection shall go is a question of more or less; an author has no "natural right" even so far, and is not free to make his own terms with the public. * * * If the talents of conductors of orchestras are denied that compensation which is necessary to evoke their efforts because they get too little for phonographic records, we have no means of knowing it, or any right to assume it; and it is idle to invoke the deus ex machina of a "progress" which is probably spurious, and would not be for us to realize, if it were genuine.

Finally, appeal is made to the doctrine that W.B.O. Broadcasting Corporation is guilty of a tort — or at least that it is a factor in determining its "unfair" competition — because it induces Bruno-New York, Inc., to violate its contract with RCA Manufacturing Company, Inc. * * * As between Bruno-New York, Inc., and W.B.O. Broadcasting Corporation, the contract is a nullity; RCA Manufacturing Company, Inc., had no power to impose the pretended servitude upon the records; and W.B.O. Broadcasting Corporation is free to buy and use them in entire disregard of any attempt to do so. * * * It follows that the complaint must be dismissed. . . .

BOARD OF TRADE OF CHICAGO v. DOW JONES & CO.
456 N.E.2d 84 (Ill. 1983)

GOLDENHERSH, J.

Defendant, Dow Jones & Company, Inc., appealed from the judgment of the circuit court of Cook County entered in favor of plaintiff, the Board of Trade of the city of Chicago, in its action for declaratory judgment. Plaintiff sought a declaration that its offering of a commodity futures contract utilizing the Dow Jones Industrial Average as the underlying commodity would not violate defendant's legal or proprietary rights. The appellate court reversed. . . .

* * * Defendant . . . publishes the Wall Street Journal. . . . It also maintains the Dow Jones News Service, through which it distributes financial news to subscribers. It produces . . . the Dow Jones Industrial Average . . . which [is] computed on the basis of the current prices of stocks of certain companies selected by defendant's editorial board. The financial news furnished by defendant is . . . distributed to brokerage houses, banks, financial institutions, individual investors, and others who are interested in stock market news. * * * Subscribers desiring the averages can extract them from the news service or arrange with defendant to

deliver the averages directly to them by teleprinter. * * * Plaintiff has a "Subscription Agreement" under which it pays defendant for its News Service and is allowed to compute and display the Dow Jones Averages on plaintiff's trading floor on a continuous, "real time" basis.

Plaintiff is the oldest and largest commodities exchange market in the United States. * * * Over the years plaintiff has added different types of futures contracts and now offers these contracts in a variety of fields, including agricultural products, precious metals and financial instruments. All commodities exchanges in the United States are regulated by the Commodities Futures Trading Commission (CFTC), and no exchange may trade a futures contract until the CFTC approves the futures contract and designates the exchange as a contract market for that contract.

A futures contract is a contract traded on a commodities exchange which binds the parties to a particular transaction at a specified future date. A stock index futures contract is a futures contract based upon the value of a particular stock market index. . . . [T]hese contracts have been traded since February 1982. At the time of trial they were traded on the Kansas City Board of Trade based on the Value Line Average, on the Chicago Mercantile Exchange based on the Standard & Poor's 500 Stock Index and on the New York Futures Exchange based on the New York Stock Exchange Composite Index. Unlike other futures contracts, no underlying commodity exists to be delivered at the future date, but rather the transaction is settled by the delivery of a certified promissory note in lieu of cash. . . . [T]he total risks of investing in the stock market are divided into two parts. One part is . . . "systematic risk," which is the risk associated with the broad general movements of the stock market as a whole. * * * . . . [T]here are only two ways to protect against systematic risk. The most direct way is for an investor to sell his stocks. This method is rather costly because of the transactional costs in selling and buying stocks, such as brokerage fees. Additionally, if capital gains are realized, the transaction becomes even more costly. The second method of protecting against systematic risk is to deal in stock market futures contracts. This method is more efficient, . . . since an investor holding a hypothetical $100,000 portfolio could purchase two futures contracts in the Chicago Mercantile Exchange for one-fifteenth the cost of selling his stocks. An investor who holds a diversified stock portfolio may "hedge" against systematic risk by entering into a stock index futures contract predicting that the market index would decline. * * *

Plaintiff, desiring to be designated as a contract market for stock index futures contracts, devoted more than two years to developing its own index to be used as the basis for its stock index futures contract. During the greater part of this period, the Securities and Exchange Commission and the CFTC were in a dispute concerning which agency had jurisdiction to regulate stock index futures contracts. In December 1981, the two Federal agencies agreed on the scope of their respective jurisdiction. . . . They agreed that the CFTC would regulate trading in stock market index contracts and that such trading would be permitted only if the contracts were based on widely known and well-established stock market indexes. This jurisdictional agreement effectively precluded CFTC approval of a contract based on the index developed by plaintiff.

On February 26, 1982, plaintiff submitted an application to the CFTC asking that it be designated as a contract market for Chicago Board of Trade Portfolio Futures Contracts. * * * No mention of the Dow Jones name appeared in the application, but the stocks used . . . were identical to those used in the Dow Jones. . . . The CFTC advised plaintiff that the CBT indexes . . . were identical to the Dow Jones averages and that this should be explicitly stated in its application. On May 7, 1982, plaintiff amended its application to state that the CBT indexes were identical to Dow Jones averages and that when Dow Jones changed a component stock or revised the divisor, plaintiff would make the same change so that the CBT indexes would remain identical to the Dow Jones averages. Plaintiff also added a disclaimer to the application disclaiming any association with Dow Jones. On May 13, the CFTC approved plaintiff's use of the stock market index portfolio contract. . . .

The circuit court . . . found that defendant had a "property right and valuable interest in the Dow Jones averages" but that plaintiff's use of the averages in the manner proposed did not violate those rights. The order, however, required that there be imprinted upon the CBT index contract a disclaimer disavowing any association with or sponsorship by defendant, Dow Jones. The appellate court reversed, holding that plaintiff's use of the averages constituted commercial misappropriation "of the Dow Jones index and averages." * * *

Plaintiff argues that the appellate court's holding erroneously expands the tort of misappropriation. . . . Citing . . . *International News Serv. v. Associated Press* (1918), 248 U.S. 215, plaintiff argues that competitive injury is a fundamental prerequisite essential to a finding of misappropriation. It argues that the . . . parties were not in competition with each other. It argues that it has done nothing immoral or unethical but has merely created a "new product" which is "outside the primary market which the producer of the original product originally set out to satisfy." Finally, plaintiff argues that the appellate court's decision is against public policy in that it grants what amounts to a common law patent monopoly to defendant which permits it to exclude others from using its product for any purpose "regardless of whether the producer is being injured or intends to exploit the product itself."

Defendant responds that the tort of misappropriation should be flexible so that, by carefully tailoring their misappropriation to avoid the strict rules of the tort, "enterprising pirates" cannot avoid the application of the doctrine. . . . [D]efendant argues that under the doctrine of misappropriation direct competition is not essential to tort liability. Defendant argues that plaintiff seeks to exploit defendant's reputation for accuracy and impartiality without compensating it for its good will. Finally, in response to plaintiff's argument that the appellate court's opinion is against public policy, defendant argues that the appellate court's opinion is consistent with public policy in that it maintains the incentive for the creation of intellectual property. Defendant argues that if its rights in the averages are not protected, there will be a diminished incentive for it to continue to provide the averages. Defendant points out that it does not seek to monopolize the production of stock indexes and that plaintiff is free to develop its own, but that it desires to protect its rights in the averages which it created and continues to produce. . . .

The doctrine of misappropriation as a form of unfair competition was first enunciated by the Supreme Court in *International News Serv. v. Associated Press* (1918), 248 U.S. 215. * * *

The tort of misappropriation was recognized in Illinois for the first time in *Capitol Records, Inc. v. Spies* (1970), 130 Ill. App. 2d 429. There the defendant purchased records and magnetic tapes sold by the plaintiff and recorded them on magnetic tapes. He then sold these re-recordings to his customers. A disclaimer was placed on the cassette tapes disclaiming any relationship between the defendant and plaintiff or the recorded artists. Defendant was able to sell his product at a lesser price than plaintiff since he avoided the costs of contracting with the performers, producing the master recordings, paying royalty fees, and advertising. . . . [T]he court reasoned that the manner of competition was "unfair" since the defendant was able to compete on equal terms by avoiding those costs normally associated with producing such recordings. Underlying the court's reasoning is the premise that the plaintiff's pecuniary reward for producing its intangible product would be severely reduced if other competitors could avoid production costs by merely waiting until a record became popular and then recording the work for resale.

Competing with the policy that protection should be afforded one who expends labor and money to develop products is the concept that freedom to imitate and duplicate is vital to our free market economy. Indeed, when the doctrine of misappropriation was first enunciated, Justice Brandeis recognized this competing policy: "He who follows the pioneer into a new market, or who engages in the manufacture of an article newly introduced by another, seeks profits due largely to the labor and expense of the first adventurer; but the law sanctions, indeed encourages, the pursuit." *International News Serv. v. Associated Press* (1918), 248 U.S. 215, 259 (Brandeis, J., dissenting). . . .

In balancing the factors that should determine which of the competing concepts should prevail, it appears unlikely that an adverse decision will cause defendant to cease to produce its averages or that the revenue it currently receives for the distribution of those averages will be materially affected. Defendant correctly asserts that it will lose its right to prospective licensing revenues in the event that in the future it elects to have its name associated with stock index futures contracts, but reliance upon the existence of a property right based upon the ability to license the product to prospective markets which were not originally contemplated by the creator of the product is somewhat "circular." Alternatively, holding that plaintiff's use of defendant's indexes in the manner proposed is a misappropriation may stimulate the creation of new indexes perhaps better suited to the purpose of "hedging" against the "systematic" risk present in the stock market.

Whether protection against appropriation is necessary to foster creativity depends in part upon the expectations of that sector of the business community which deals with the particular intangible. If the creator of an intangible product expects to be able to control the licensing or distribution of the intangible in order to profit from his effort, and similarly those who would purchase the product expect and are willing to pay for the use of the intangible, a better argument can be made in favor of granting protection. The record shows that the plaintiff sought to develop its own index prior to the CFTC's requirement that the contracts be based on well-known, well-established indexes. It then offered defendant 10 cents per transaction, which it estimated would be somewhere between $1 million and $2 million per year, for the use of its name and averages. * * * To hold that defendant has a proprietary interest in its indexes and averages which vests it with the exclusive right to license their use for trading in stock index futures contracts would not preclude plaintiff and others from marketing stock index futures contracts. The extent of defendant's monopoly would be limited, for as defendant points out, there are an infinite number of stock market indexes which could be devised. . . . * * *

We conclude that the possibility of any detriment to the public which might result from our holding that defendant's indexes and averages may not be used without its consent in the manner proposed by plaintiff are outweighed by the resultant encouragement to develop new indexes specifically designed for the purpose of hedging against the "systematic" risk present in the stock market. * * * The publication of the indexes involves valuable assets of defendant, its good will and its reputation for integrity and accuracy. Despite the fact that plaintiff's proposed use is not in competition with the use defendant presently makes of them, defendant is entitled to protection against their misappropriation. . . . For the reasons stated, the judgment of the appellate court is affirmed.

NOTE

Courts have struggled to define the scope of the misappropriation doctrine. It gives investors incentives to invest in the creation of intangible assets, but exclusive rights in intangibles can impede public access to valuable information and prevent the public from realizing their benefits. There is no general prohibition against copying the ideas of another or benefitting from them once they are in the public's hands; only protection of trade secrets, the commercial value of a person's identity, and contractual rights, is clear. Would you expect that a business owns the right to trade in options to buy or sell its stock? See *Golden Nugget, Inc. v. American Stock Exchange, Inc.*, 828 F.2d 586, 590 (9th Cir. 1990). See generally Restatement (Third) of Unfair Competition, § 38, Cmt. b, and the Reporter's Notes, Cmt. b (1985).

II. COPYRIGHTS

U.S. Const. art. I, § 8, cl. 8 states that "Congress shall have . . . [t]he Power to promote the Progress of Science and useful Arts, by securing for limited Times to Authors and Inventors the exclusive Right to their respective Writings and Discoveries." Congress has not regarded this clause as self-executing, so it has enacted various Copyright Acts — most recently in 1976 — defining the nature of copyrights and the procedures for obtaining and protecting them. The Copyright Act gives authors and artists some exclusive, monopolistic rights to their works: they can reproduce and distribute copies of them to the public (or perform or exhibit the work, as appropriate) as well as prepare derivative works based on them. 17 U.S.C. § 106. Anyone doing any of these things without permission is "infringing" the copyright and as such is subject to a damage or injunctive action. 17 U.S.C. § 501. See generally Robert Gorman, *An Overview of the Copyright Act of 1976*, 126

U. Pa. L. Rev. 856 (1978).

Congress has also on several occasions extended the length of time that a works might be protected by a federal copyright; it was good for 14 years after creation under the 1790 Act (renewable for another fourteen years if the author survived the initial term), for 28 years (renewable for another 14) in 1831, and for 28 (renewable for another 28) in 1909, and for 76 years after publication in 1976, and for 70 years after the author's death in 1998. Congress may "secure . . . for limited times . . . the exclusive right" to a copyrighted work. But it is up to Congress to decide how limited the right shall be. See *Eldred v. Ashcroft*, 537 U.S. 186 (2003) (regarding the 1998 Act and deferring the Congress to define the time constitutionally permitted, even though Congressional authority is "both a grant of power and a limitation" and the grant of power to enact copyright acts is "to promote the Progress of Science and the Useful Arts"). Is the fact that Congress' extension of time in each of the successive Copyright Acts applied to both existing and new works sufficient protection against a charge of not promoting the arts? Apparently so. Is the progress clause enforceable?

<h1 style="text-align:center">ROCKFORD MAP PUBLISHERS, INC. v. DIRECTORY SERV. CO.</h1>

768 F.2d 145 (7th Cir. 1985)

EASTERBROOK, J.

A plat map shows the location, size, and ownership of parcels of land. Rockford Map Publishers makes plat maps of rural counties. They are useful to local residents and to sellers of farm equipment, who can learn the identities and needs of potential customers. Doubtless they have other uses as well.

Rockford Map starts with aerial photographs distributed by the Department of Agriculture. It traces the topographical features from the photographs and draws lines showing townships and sections. Then an employee goes to places where land titles are recorded and reads the books. The employee uses the legal descriptions of the deeds to draw boundary lines indicating the location and size of each parcel. He pencils in the name of the owner. From time to time Rockford Map updates the maps as ownership of land changes. . . .

Rockford Map has repeated this process for more than 500 counties throughout the United States. The first plat of Ford County was prepared in 1948, and a new one was prepared from scratch in 1956. Rockford Map published updated versions of the Ford County plat maps in 1961, 1964, 1966, 1969, 1972, 1974, 1976, 1977, 1979, 1981, and 1983. The copyrights of several revisions, including the one in 1983, were registered. The most recent update took about 14 hours' work in the Ford County Courthouse. An employee of Rockford Map estimated that it would have taken him between 40 and 45 hours to do the research for Ford County from scratch.

Directory Service Co. also publishes plat maps. It starts with a square grid and draws in the information about ownership without regard to topographical features. When Directory Service decided to do a plat map of Ford County, it hired a local resident and gave her instructions about how to interpret information in the title records. In order to make her task easier, Directory Service enlarged Rockford Map's plat maps for Ford County. Directory Service told its agent to check the records using Rockford Map's map as a worksheet.[1] If a search of the records revealed that Rockford Map's map was correct, the agent put a green check in the space depicting the parcel of land; if the map was incorrect, the agent overwrote the map in red. The agent also recorded information about parcels Rockford Map had deemed too small to put on its plat maps. The agent estimates that she spent 75 hours on these tasks for Ford County. When she was done she sent the corrected plat maps to Directory Service, whose staff produced a new map. . . .

Rockford Map could tell by looking at Directory Service's product that its plat maps had been used as templates. Some of the names in Rockford Map's maps have bogus middle initials. These initials, if read from the top of the map to the bottom, spell out "Rockford Map Inc." Rockford Map put these trap initials in the maps of four townships in Ford County. Directory Service's maps contained 54 of the 56 trap initials.

Both Rockford Map and Directory Service sell advertising space in their books of plat maps. But Rockford Map also sells the books, while Directory Service gives the maps away as part of a directory of residents. Understandably distressed by Directory Service's methods, if not by the fact of competition, Rockford Map filed this suit, contending that Directory Service violated the copyright laws. The district court held a two-day trial and entered judgment for Rockford Map. It ordered Directory Service to turn its working materials and maps over to the court, and it enjoined further publication of infringing maps.* * *

Directory Service's principal argument on appeal is that Rockford Map's plat maps are not copyrightable. But 17 U.S.C. § 103(a) provides that "compilations" are copyrightable, subject to the limitation in § 103(b) that the copyright in a compilation "extends only to the material contributed by the author of such work, as distinguished from any preexisting material employed in such work." * * * In other words, when the contribution lies in the arrangement of facts, only the arrangement is protected by the copyright. Rockford Map could not copyright the information in the deeds on file in the county courthouse, but it could and did copyright the arrangement of that information on a plat map.

The copyright laws are designed to give people incentives to produce new works. See *Harper & Row, Publishers, Inc. v. Nation Enters.*, 471 U.S. 539 (1985). They allow people to collect the reward for their contributions. If the incremental contribution is small, so too is the reward, but a subjective assessment of the importance of the contribution has nothing to do with the existence of copyright.

Directory Service maintains that Rockford Map produced its plat maps with so little effort that the result may not be copyrighted. The court remarked in

---

[1] This is apparently a routine practice at Directory Service. An internal manual says that "the first step in the plat process is to update all of the land ownership information in the county. The best way to accomplish this is to obtain a plat map from another source that we can use as a 'base' and then have someone in the county update that information using current public records. Plat books can usually be purchased from a variety of sources, including other private publishers or the county auditor's office. . . ."

Schroeder v. William Morrow & Co., 566 F.2d 3, 5 (7th Cir. 1977), that "only 'industrious collection,' not originality in the sense of novelty, is required." The expenditure of 14 hours to update the maps of Ford County, or even 45 to start from scratch, is not very "industrious," Directory Service tells us.

The copyright laws protect the work, not the amount of effort expended. A person who produces a short new work or makes a small improvement in a few hours gets a copyright for that contribution fully as effective as that on a novel written as a life's work. Perhaps the smaller the effort the smaller the contribution; if so, the copyright simply bestows fewer rights. Others can expend the same effort to the same end. Copyright covers, after all, only the incremental contribution and not the underlying information.

The input of time is irrelevant. A photograph may be copyrighted, although it is the work of an instant and its significance may be accidental. *Burrow-Giles Lithographic Co. v. Sarony*, 111 U.S. 53 (1884). In 14 hours Mozart could write a piano concerto, J.S. Bach a cantata, or Dickens a week's installment of Bleak House. The Laffer Curve, an economic graph prominent in political debates, appeared on the back of a napkin after dinner, the work of a minute. All of these are copyrightable.[2] Dickens did not need to complete Bleak House before receiving a copyright; every chapter — indeed every sentence — could be protected standing alone. Rockford Map updates and republishes maps on more than 140 counties every year. If it put out one large book with every map, even Directory Service would concede that the book was based on a great deal of "industry." Rockford Map, like Dickens, loses none of its rights by publishing copyrightable matter in smaller units.

The contribution of a collection of facts lies in their presentation, not in the facts themselves. The collector may change the form of information and so make it more accessible, or he may change the organization and so make the data more understandable. A catalog of names and addresses is copyrightable (*Schroeder*), as is a directory of trade symbols (*Jewelers' Circular Publ'g. Co. v. Keystone Publ'g. Co.*, 274 F. 932 (S.D.N.Y. 1921) (L. Hand, J.), *aff'd*, 281 F. 83 (2d Cir.), *cert. denied*, 259 U.S. 581 (1922)) and a compilation of logarithms (*Edwards & Deutsch Lithographing Co. v. Boorman*, 15 F.2d 35 (7th Cir. 1926)). In each case the copyright depended on the fact that the compiler made a contribution — a new arrangement or presentation of facts — and not on the amount of time the work consumed.

Here Rockford Map made a contribution. Its employees dug through the records and turned the metes and bounds of the legal descriptions into a pictorial presentation. Teasing pictures from the debris left by conveyancers is a substantial change in the form of the information. The result is copyrightable, no matter how quickly Rockford Map's staff could do the work.***

All concede, as Learned Hand said in *Jewelers' Circular*, *supra*, 274 F. at 935, that "a second compiler may check back his independent work upon the original compilation." The right to "check back" does not imply a right to start with the

---

[2] * * * Only Laffer's napkin, and not the idea represented by the graph, may be copyrighted. But the principle's the thing.

copyrighted work. Everyone must do the same basic work, the same "industrious collection." "A subsequent compiler is bound to set about doing for himself what the first compiler has done." *Kelly v. Morris*, [1866] 1 Eq. 697, 701 (Wood, V.C.). The second compiler must assemble the material as if there had never been a first compilation; only then may the second compiler use the first as a check on error. Here, as in Schroeder, the second compiler started with the selection, ordering, and arrangement of the first. The district court found that Directory Service "did not make an independent production. To the contrary, it merely took the copyrighted RMP information and edited it." That Directory Service made some changes is irrelevant; the starting point itself offended. * * * AFFIRMED.

NOTES

1. See *Feist Publications, Inc. v. Rural Tel. Serv. Co.*, 499 U.S. 340 (1991), holding that copying of the listing in a residential white pages telephone directory issued by a public utility telephone company is not an infringement of copyright because the directory lacked both constitutionally- and statutorily-required originality:

> The sine qua non of copyright is originality. To qualify for copyright protection, a work must be original to the author. Original, as the term is used in copyright, means only that the work was independently created by the author (as opposed to copied from other works), and that it possesses at least some minimal degree of creativity. 1 M. Nimmer & D. Nimmer, Copyright §§ 2.01[A], [B] (1990) (hereinafter Nimmer). To be sure, the requisite level of creativity is extremely low; even a slight amount will suffice. The vast majority of works make the grade quite easily, as they possess some creative spark, "no matter how crude, humble or obvious" it might be. *Id.*, § 1.08[C][1]. Originality does not signify novelty; a work may be original even though it closely resembles other works so long as the similarity is fortuitous, not the result of copying. To illustrate, assume that two poets, each ignorant of the other, compose identical poems. Neither work is novel, yet both are original and, hence, copyrightable.

> Originality is a constitutional requirement. The source of Congress' power to enact copyright laws is Article I, § 8, cl. 8, of the Constitution, which authorizes Congress to "secure for limited Times to Authors . . . the exclusive Right to their respective Writings."

> . . . [O]riginality requires independent creation plus a modicum of creativity[.] . . . The originality requirement . . . remains the touchstone of copyright protection today. . . . It is this bedrock principle of copyright that mandates the law's seemingly disparate treatment of facts and factual compilations. "No one may claim originality as to facts." Nimmer, § 2.11[A], p. 2-157. This is because facts do not owe their origin to an act of authorship. The distinction is one between creation and discovery: The first person to find and report a particular fact has not created the fact; he or she has merely discovered its existence. "The discoverer merely finds and records." Nimmer § 2.03[E]. Census takers, for example, do not "create" the population figures that emerge from their efforts; in a sense, they copy

these figures from the world around them. Census data therefore do not trigger copyright because these data are not "original" in the constitutional sense. The same is true of all facts — scientific, historical, biographical, and news of the day. . . .

Factual compilations, on the other hand, may possess the requisite originality. The compilation author typically chooses which facts to include, in what order to place them, and how to arrange the collected data so that they may be used effectively by readers. These choices as to selection and arrangement, so long as they are made independently by the compiler and entail a minimal degree of creativity, are sufficiently original that Congress may protect such compilations through the copyright laws. Thus, even a directory that contains absolutely no protectible written expression, only facts, meets the constitutional minimum for copyright protection if it features an original selection or arrangement.

This protection is subject to an important limitation. The mere fact that a work is copyrighted does not mean that every element of the work may be protected. Originality remains the sine qua non of copyright; accordingly, copyright protection may extend only to those components of a work that are original to the author. Thus, if the compilation author clothes facts with an original collocation of words, he or she may be able to claim a copyright in this written expression. Others may copy the underlying facts from the publication, but not the precise words used to present them. In *Harper & Row* [471 U.S. 539 (1985)], for example, we explained that President Ford could not prevent others from copying bare historical facts from his autobiography, but that he could prevent others from copying his "subjective descriptions and portraits of public figures." *Id.* at 563. Where the compilation author adds no written expression but rather lets the facts speak for themselves, the expressive element is more elusive. The only conceivable expression is the manner in which the compiler has selected and arranged the facts. Thus, if the selection and arrangement are original, these elements of the work are eligible for copyright protection. No matter how original the format, however, the facts themselves do not become original through association. This inevitably means that the copyright in a factual compilation is thin. Notwithstanding a valid copyright, a subsequent compiler remains free to use the facts contained in another's publication to aid in preparing a competing work, so long as the competing work does not feature the same selection and arrangement. . . .

* * * The primary objective of copyright is not to reward the labor of authors, but "to promote the Progress of Science and useful Arts." Art. I, § 8, cl. 8. To this end, copyright assures authors the right to their original expression, but encourages others to build freely upon the ideas and information conveyed by a work. *Harper & Row, supra,* at 556–7. This principle, known as the idea/expression or fact/expression dichotomy, applies to all works of authorship. As applied to a factual compilation, assuming the absence of original written expression, only the compiler's selection and arrangement may be protected; the raw facts may be copied at will. This result is neither unfair nor unfortunate. It is the means by

which copyright advances the progress of science and art.

This Court has long recognized that the fact/expression dichotomy limits severely the scope of protection in fact-based works. . . . We reiterated this point in *Harper & Row*: "No author may copyright facts or ideas. * * * Copyright does not prevent subsequent users from copying from a prior author's work those constituent elements that are not original — for example . . . facts, or materials in the public domain — as long as such use does not unfairly appropriate the author's original contributions." 471 U.S. at 547–8." * * *

. . . Facts, whether alone or as part of a compilation, are not original and therefore may not be copyrighted. A factual compilation is eligible for copyright if it features an original selection or arrangement of facts, but the copyright is limited to the particular selection or arrangement. In no event may copyright extend to the facts themselves.

Id. at 345–51.

2. What if the compiler in *Feist* included information on the marital status, the religion, the occupation, or the educational level of telephone users? Is a book listing automobile valuations by year and model copyrightable? See *CCC Info. Servs. v. MacLean Hunter Mkt. Reports*, 44 F.3d 61 (2d Cir. 1994). Are the recipes in a cookbook copyrightable? See *Publications Int'l, Ltd. v. Meredith Corp.*, 88 F.3d 473 (7th Cir. 1996). What about a directory of cable television stations, including information on the name, address, and phone number of the station's operator, the number of subscribers, channels offered, the price of the service, and the types of equipment used — is such a directory copyrightable? Would it matter how the materials in the directory are indexed and presented as a whole? See *Warren Publ., Inc. v. Microdos Data Corp.*, 115 F.3d 1509 (11th Cir. 1997).

3. Is a title commitment or report, issued by an attorney or title insurer of real or personal property, copyright-eligible? See *Mid America Title Co. v. Kirk*, 59 F.3d 719 (7th Cir. 1995):

Mid America seeks copyright protection for the compilation of selected land title data which appears in its Title Commitment No. 125266. The Supreme Court recently clarified the standards that govern copyright protection for such fact compilations, stating that "[a] factual compilation is eligible for copyright if it features an original selection or arrangement of facts, but the copyright is limited to the particular selection or arrange-ment." See *Feist Publications, Inc. v. Rural Tel. Serv. Co.*, 499 U.S. 340, 350–51 (1991). * * *

Feist instructs that in order to establish copyright infringement, a plaintiff must prove two essential elements: "(1) ownership of a valid copyright, and (2) copying of constituent elements of the work that are original." *Id.* at 361. * * * Originality is both a statutory and constitutional requirement. See *Feist*, 499 U.S. at 347. "Original, as the term is used in copyright, means only that the work was independently created by the author . . . and that it possesses at least some minimal degree of creativity." *Id.* at 345. * * * Although the originality requirement does not impose a high threshold of creativity, the selection of facts cannot be "so mechanical or routine as to require no creativity whatsoever." *Feist*, 499 U.S. at 362. After reviewing the record in this case, we conclude that the selection process used to prepare Mid America's Title Commitment No. 125266 fails to meet this minimal level of creativity. Selecting which facts to include in this compilation of data was not a matter of discretion based on Mid America's personal judgment or taste, but instead it was a matter of convention and strict industry standards. As the affidavits introduced by Kirk suggest, all title examiners preparing a proper title commitment for the Frankfort property would have referred to the same sources of information and ultimately would have selected the same facts to include in their title commitments. . . . In essence, Mid America's selection of the facts that were allegedly copied from Title Commitment No. 125266 was too rote and mechanical a task to constitute an original element of the work. We do not mean to hold that a title commitment can never be copyrightable; rather, we hold that in this case the element of selection was not sufficiently original to merit copyright protection. * * *

In addition, we note that in preparing this title commitment for the Frankfort property, Mid America was dealing with a limited universe of available data. Since external forces dictated that Mid America was to list all facts which affect marketable title, there was no room for creativity in determining which liens or which encumbrances to include in the title commitment. The title examiner simply was not called upon to exercise his subjective judgment. * * * In short, Mid America fails to show that the selection process in this case involved some kind of creative spark. The evidence demonstrates that [the title commitment] simply contains a list of all the facts which affect marketable title to the Frankfort property and that no creativity was shown in the selection of these facts from the domain of facts that could have been included in the title commitment. We therefore conclude that the material copied from Mid America's title commitment lacks the requisite originality to merit copyright protection. . . .

Attorneys have done their bit to keep the copyright system presented with new issues. See, e.g., *Wheaton v. Peters*, 33 U.S. (8 Pet.) 591 (1834) (opining that the written opinions of the court are not copyrightable by the reporter of the Supreme Court decisions). Why do you think John West presented his reports in double columns? Made summaries of the opinions he printed, appearing after the case name with key numbers? Reported the counsels' names? Does LexisNexis have the right to insert the page numbers of West Reports in its computer copies of judicial decisions?

4. A product such as a database may be short on originality but long on commercial value. The news reported in the *International News Service* case may lack originality, but was none the less found to have a protectible value. *Feist* requires originality as a constitutional matter, regardless of value. How can *International News Service* and *Feist* be harmonized? See Steven Boyd, *Deriving Originality in Derivative Works: Considering the Quantum of Originality Needed to Obtain Copyright Protection in Derivative Works*, 40 Santa Clara L. Rev. 325, 344–349 (2000). However, if copyright protection for databases is limited by *Feist*,

the limitation has not stalled the development of the database industry, nor has it limited the industry's profitability. If you think otherwise, wait until you enter the practice of law and have to pay commercial rates for computerized legal research!

5.   The First Sale Doctrine. Originality is the *sine qua non* of a copyright, but no intellectual property, of any type, is worthy of the name "property" unless copies of the independently created and copyrighted work are alienable. Under the first sale doctrine, the transferee may resell the once alienated copy without infringing the copyright; that is, free alienation of copies is permitted when the copy is lawfully made or acquired. See 17 U.S.C. § 109. This doctrine has common sense behind it: if you buy a copy of a book, you should be able to resell it after reading it. This rationale has personal and market-wide consequences. The bookseller who buys a book at wholesale prices is free to retail the book at whatever price the seller chooses. See *Bobbs-Merrill Co. v. Straus*, 210 U.S. 339 (1908). This "free alienation" doctrine strikes a balance between an author's rights in the copyrighted work and the need for public access to it. Because the doctrine permits the creation of secondary markets in copyrighted works: you can rent a movie at a price less than a first run theater ticket would cost, or check out a library book at no cost. It provides many consumers with an opportunity to see, read, or use copyrighted works. If a work is worth a copyright, it's also worth allowing the public access to it. The doctrine comports with property law's long-held policy against restraints on alienation. See generally Donald Chisum & Michael Jacobs, Understanding Intellectual Property Law 4-119 (1992).

RANDOM HOUSE, INC. v. ROSETTA BOOKS LLC
283 F.3d 490 (2d Cir. 2002)

PER CURIAM.

Random House, Inc. appeals from the denial of a preliminary injunction that sought to enjoin appellee Rosetta Books LLC ("Rosetta") from continuing to sell as "ebooks" certain novels whose authors had granted Random House the exclusive right to publish, print, and sell their copyrighted works "in book form." The denial of a preliminary injunction is generally reviewed for abuse of discretion. See *Zervos v. Verizon New York, Inc.*, 252 F.3d 163, 172 (2d Cir. 2001).

A party seeking a preliminary injunction in this Circuit must show: (1) irreparable harm in the absence of the injunction and (2) either (a) a likelihood of success on the merits or (b) sufficiently serious questions going to the merits to make them a fair ground for litigation and a balance of hardships tipping decidedly in the movant's favor. *ABKCO Music, Inc. v. Stellar Records, Inc.*, 96 F.3d 60, 64 (2d Cir. 1996). Because, however, an exclusive licensee can, as here, sue for copyright infringement, see 17 U.S.C. § 501(b), and because a prima facie case of copyright infringement gives rise to a presumption of irreparable harm, the requirement of proof of irreparable harm can in such a case effectively be met by proof of a likelihood of success on the merits. *ABKCO Music, Inc.*, 96 F.3d at 64.

Here, however, the district court did not abuse its discretion in concluding that appellant had not established the likelihood of its success on the merits. To be sure, there is some appeal to appellant's argument that an "ebook" — a digital book that can be read on a computer screen or electronic device, see *Random House, Inc. v. Rosetta Books LLC*, 150 F. Supp. 2d 613, 614–15 (S.D. N.Y. 2001) — is simply a "form" of a book, and therefore within the coverage of appellant's licenses. But the law of New York, which determines the scope of Random House's contracts, has arguably adopted a restrictive view of the kinds of "new uses" to which an exclusive license may apply when the contracting parties do not expressly provide for coverage of such future forms. See *Tele-Pac, Inc. v. Grainger*, 570 N.Y.S.2d 521 (N.Y. App. Div. 1991). In any case, determining whether the licenses here in issue extend to ebooks depends on fact-finding regarding, inter alia, the "evolving" technical processes and uses of an ebook . . . and the reasonable expectations of the contracting parties "cognizant of the customs, practices, usages and terminology as generally understood in the . . . trade or business" at the time of contracting, *Random House*, 150 F. Supp. 2d at 618 (citing *Sayers v. Rochester Telephone Corp. Supplemental Management Pension Plan*, 7 F.3d 1091, 1095 (2d Cir. 1993)). Without the benefit of the full record to be developed over the course of the litigation, we cannot say the district court abused its discretion in the preliminary way it resolved these mixed questions of law and fact.

As to the alternative way of satisfying at least the second requirement for a preliminary injunction, i.e., showing sufficiently serious questions going to the merits to make them a fair ground for litigation and a balance of hardships tipping decidedly in the movant's favor, here the balance of hardships tips, if anything, in appellees' favor. For while Random House expresses fears about harm to its goodwill if Rosetta is allowed to proceed with its sale of ebooks, Rosetta, whose entire business is based on the sale of ebooks, raises a reasonable concern that the proposed preliminary injunction will put it out of business or at least eliminate its business as to all authors who have executed similar contracts. As the district court found, such legitimate concerns outweigh any potential hardships to Random House . . . which, if it ultimately prevails on the merits, can recover money damages for any lost sales. Thus, without expressing any view as to the ultimate merits of the case, the Court concludes that the district court did not abuse its discretion in denying Random House's motion for a preliminary injunction, and consequently the judgment is affirmed.

NOTES

1. Why didn't the book publisher just seek permission from its authors to create its own ebook business? Is this publisher's lawsuit anti-competitive? If the publisher was planning to enter the ebook market, would a preliminary injunction be granted?

2. Collective works present special problems. The collective work may be copyrighted as a whole, but so may the contributions of freelance writers and illustrators. A publisher is privileged to reproduce a separately copyrighted work — e.g., an article or illustration — in the original work to which contribution was made, or any revision of it, or any later work in the same series. 17 U.S.C. § 201(c). The creation of electronic databases from copyrighted material first released in hard copy has given rise to the issue of whether the database is a "revision" (or new version) of the original release or an infringement of copyright. See *New York Times Co. v. Tasini*, 533 U.S. 483 (2001). A user of the database might be able to generate a revision of a copyrighted article, but that user's initial perception of the database is not of a revision of the original collective work. The database itself stores and permits retrieval of the article in a new, not just a revised, context within all stored materials, effectively overriding its author's right to control reproduction or distribution of the original. *Id.* (so holding).

3.   An architectural design may be copyrighted. When copied without a license, a copyright infringement action may be barred by laches, even if suit is filed within the three year limitations period set by Congress, when the plaintiffs knew of the infringement and did not bring suit promptly. This is the rule in all but the Fourth Circuit Court of Appeals, where there is an outright prohibition on the use of the laches defense for actions brought within three years. See *Lyons Partnership, L.P. v. Morris Costumes, Inc.*, 243 F.3d 789, 797–798 (4th Cir. 2001) ("First, laches is a doctrine that applies only in equity to bar equitable actions, not at law to bar legal actions. Second, we note that, in any event, in connection with the copyright claims, separation of powers principles dictate that an equitable timeliness rule adopted by courts cannot bar claims that are brought within the legislatively prescribed statute of limitations." Thus, ruled the court, "when considering the timeliness of a cause of action brought pursuant to a statute for which Congress has provided a limitations period, a court should not apply laches to overrule the legislature's judgment as to the appropriate time limit to apply for actions brought under the statute."). The Fourth Circuit's prohibition on the use of laches in the face of the three year statute of limitations requires twin assumptions that three years is both the maximum and the minimum time for filing suit and that Congress has done all the balancing of incentives necessary and proper for achieving a just result. In your previous study of adverse possession rules for personal property, you saw that the doctrine of equitable tolling for a statute of limitations is available to plaintiffs, even in jurisdictions where the law of adverse possession is based on a statute.

The Sixth, Ninth, and Tenth Circuits have taken a more flexible view. See *Chirco v. Crosswinds Communities, Inc.*, 474 F.3d 227 (6th Cir. 2007), *cert. denied*, 551 U.S. 1131 (2007). *Chirco* held that: "Because the defendants have established . . . that the plaintiffs knew of the defendants' challenged construction plans and activities and yet failed to take readily-available actions to abate the alleged harm, and because the defendants and innocent third parties have been unduly prejudiced by that inaction, we AFFIRM the judgment of the district court insofar as it dismisses the plaintiffs' efforts to mandate the destruction of the [defendants'] project." See also *Jacobsen v. Deseret Book Co.*, 287 F.3d 936, 950 (10th Cir. 2002) (ruling "[r]ather than deciding cases on the issue of laches, courts should generally defer to the three-year statute of limitations" and recognizing a laches defense in some circumstances). Perhaps the circumstances in which laches and equity should be used was best put by Learned Hand in his opinion in *Haas v. Leo Feist*, 234 F. 105, 108 (S.D.N.Y. 1916): "It must be obvious to everyone familiar with equitable principles that it is inequitable for the owner of a copyright, with full notice of an intended infringement, to stand inactive while the proposed infringer spends large sums of money in its exploitation, and to intervene only when his speculation has proved a success. Delay under such circumstances allows the owner to speculate without risk with the other's money; he cannot possibly lose, and he may win." Accord, *Kling v. Hallmark Cards, Inc.*, 225 F.3d 1030, 1036–42 (9th Cir. 2000) (engaging in laches analysis in a copyright infringement action).

Laches is an unintentional and negligent failure to assert one's rights. It is an affirmative, equitable defense requiring a showing of (1) delay and a lack of diligence by the party against whom the defense is asserted, causing (2) hardship to the party asserting the defense. What if the hardship is on innocent third parties? Should those hardships be considered? If a home is built using copyrighted designs, should the hardship to the homeowner be considered? What other hardships might arise in this situation? If an injunction is barred by laches, should the plaintiff still obtain damages?

III. MORAL RIGHTS OF ARTISTS

Carter v. Helmsley-Spear, Inc., 71 F.3d 77, 81–83 (2d Cir. 1995):

The term "moral rights" has its origins in the civil law and is a translation of the French *le droit moral*, which is meant to capture those rights of a spiritual, non-economic and personal nature. The rights spring from a belief that an artist in the process of creation injects his spirit into the work and that the artist's personality, as well as the integrity of the work, should therefore be protected and preserved. See Ralph Lerner & Judith Bresler, Art Law 417 (1989) (Art Law). Because they are personal to the artist, moral rights exist independently of an artist's copyright in his or her work. See 2 Nimmer on Copyright 8D-4 & n.2 (1994) (Nimmer).

While the rubric of moral rights encompasses many varieties of rights, two are protected in nearly every jurisdiction recognizing their existence: attribution and integrity. See Art Law at 420. The right of attribution generally consists of the right of an artist to be recognized by name as the author of his work or to publish anonymously or pseudonymously, the right to prevent the author's work from being attributed to someone else, and to prevent the use of the author's name on works created by others, including distorted editions of the author's original work. The right of integrity allows the author to prevent any deforming or mutilating changes to his work, even after title in the work has been transferred.

In some jurisdictions the integrity right also protects artwork from destruction. Whether or not a work of art is protected from destruction represents a fundamentally different perception of the purpose of moral rights. If integrity is meant to stress the public interest in preserving a nation's culture, destruction is prohibited; if the right is meant to emphasize the author's personality, destruction is seen as less harmful than the continued display of deformed or mutilated work that misrepresents the artist and destruction may proceed. See Art Law at 421.

Although moral rights are well established in the civil law, they are of recent vintage in American jurisprudence. Federal and state courts typically recognized the existence of such rights in other nations, but rejected artists' attempts to inject them into U.S. law. Nonetheless,

American courts have in varying degrees acknowledged the idea of moral rights, cloaking the concept in the guise of other legal theories, such as copyright, unfair competition, invasion of privacy, defamation, and breach of contract. Nimmer at 8D-10.

In the landmark case of *Gilliam v. American Broad. Cos.*, 538 F.2d 14 (2d Cir. 1976), we relied on copyright law and unfair competition principles to safeguard the integrity rights of the "Monty Python" group, noting that although the law "seeks to vindicate the economic, rather than the personal rights of authors . . . the economic incentive for artistic . . . creation . . . cannot be reconciled with the inability of artists to obtain relief for mutilation or misrepresentation of their work to the public on which the artists are financially dependent." *Id.* at 24. Because decisions protecting artists rights are often "clothed in terms of proprietary right in one's creation," we continued, "they also properly vindicate the author's personal right to prevent the presentation of his work to the public in a distorted form." *Id.*

. . . California was the first to take up the task of protecting artists with the passage in 1979 of the California Art Preservation Act, Cal. Civ. Code § 987 et seq., followed in 1983 by New York's enactment of the Artist's Authorship Rights Act, N.Y. Arts & Cult. Aff. Law § 14.03. Nine other states have also passed moral rights statutes, generally following either the California or New York models.

. . . The issue of federal protection of moral rights was a prominent hurdle in the debate over whether the United States should join the Berne Convention, the international agreement protecting literary and artistic works. Article 6b of the Berne Convention protects attribution and integrity, stating in relevant part: "Independently of the author's economic rights, and even after the transfer of the said rights, the author shall have the right to claim authorship of the work and to object to any distortion, mutilation or other modification of, or other derogatory action in relation to, the said work, which would be prejudicial to his honor or reputation." Berne Convention for the Protection of Literary and Artistic Works, art. 6bis, S. Treaty Doc. No. 27, 99th Cong., 2d Sess. 41 (1986). * * * Congress passed the Berne Convention Implementation Act of 1988, 102 Stat. 2853 (1988), and side-stepped the difficult question of protecting moral rights. It declared that the Berne Convention is not self-executing [and that] existing law satisfied the United States' obligations in adhering to the Convention. . . .

Two years later Congress enacted the Visual Artists Rights Act of 1990 (VARA or Act), 104 Stat. 5089, 5128–33 (1990). Construing this Act constitutes the subject of the present appeal. The Act "protects both the reputations of certain visual artists and the works of art they create. It provides these artists with the rights of 'attribution' and 'integrity.' . . . These rights are analogous to those protected by Article 6bis of the Berne Convention, which are commonly known as 'moral rights.' The theory of moral rights is that they result in a climate of artistic worth and honor that encourages the author in the arduous act of creation." H.R. Rep. No. 514 at 5. . . .

Its principal provisions afford protection only to authors of works of visual art — a narrow class of art defined to include paintings, drawings, prints, sculptures, or photographs produced for exhibition purposes, existing in a single copy or limited edition of 200 copies or fewer. 17 U.S.C. § 101. With numerous exceptions, VARA grants three rights: the right of attribution, the right of integrity and, in the case of works of visual art of "recognized stature," the right to prevent destruction. 17 U.S.C. § 106A. For works created on or after June 1, 1991 — the effective date of the Act — the rights provided for endure for the life of the author or, in the case of a joint work, the life of the last surviving author. The rights cannot be transferred, but may be waived by a writing signed by the author. Copyright registration is not required to bring an action for infringement of the rights granted under VARA, or to secure statutory damages and attorney's fees. 17 U.S.C. §§ 411, 412. All remedies available under copyright law, other than criminal remedies, are available in an action for infringement of moral rights. 17 U.S.C. § 506.

MARTIN v. CITY OF INDIANAPOLIS
192 F.3d 608 (7th Cir. 1999)

WOOD, J.

We are not art critics, do not pretend to be and do not need to be to decide this case. A large outdoor stainless steel sculpture by plaintiff Jan Martin, an artist, was demolished by the defendant as part of an urban renewal project. Plaintiff brought a one-count suit against the City of Indianapolis under the Visual Artists Rights Act of 1990 ("VARA"), 17 U.S.C. § 101 et seq. The parties filed cross-motions for summary judgment. The district court granted plaintiff's motion and awarded plaintiff statutory damages in the maximum amount allowed for a non-willful statutory violation. Neither party is satisfied.

I. BACKGROUND

Plaintiff is an artist, but in this instance more with a welding torch than with a brush. He offered evidence to show, not all of it admitted, that his works have been displayed in museums, and other works created for private commissions, including a time capsule for the Indianapolis Museum of Art Centennial. He has also done sculptured jewelry for the Indiana Arts Commission. In 1979, at the Annual Hoosier Salem Art Show, plaintiff was awarded the prize for best of show in any medium. He holds various arts degrees from Purdue University, the Art Institute of Chicago and Bowling Green State University in Ohio. Plaintiff had been employed as production coordinator for Tarpenning-LaFollette Co. (the "Company"), a metal contracting firm in Indianapolis. It was in this position that he turned his artistic talents to metal sculpture fabrication.

In 1984, plaintiff received permission from the Indianapolis Metropolitan Development Commission to erect a twenty-by-forty-foot metal sculpture on land owned by John LaFollette, chairman of the Company. The Company also agreed to furnish the materials. The resulting Project Agreement between the City and the Company granted a zoning variance to permit the erection of plaintiff's proposed sculpture. An attachment to that agreement and the center of this controversy provided as follows: "Should a determination be made by the Department of Metropolitan Development that the subject sculpture is no longer compatible with the existing land use or that the acquisition of the property is necessary, the owner of the land and the owner of the sculpture will receive written notice signed by the Director of the Department of Metropolitan Development giving the owners of the land and sculpture ninety (90) days to remove said sculpture. Subject to weather and ground conditions."

Plaintiff went to work on the project and in a little over two years it was completed. He named it "Symphony #1," but as it turns out in view of this controversy, a more suitable musical name might have been "1812 Overture." Because of the possibility that the sculpture might someday have to be removed, as provided for in the Project Agreement, Symphony #1 was engineered and built by plaintiff so that it could be disassembled for removal and later reassembled. The sculpture did not go unnoticed by the press, public or art community. Favorable comments admitted into evidence and objected to by the City are now an issue on appeal and their admissibility will be considered hereinafter.

The trouble began in April 1992 when the City notified LaFollette that there would be public hearings on the City's proposed acquisition of various properties as part of an urban renewal plan. One of the properties to be acquired was home to Symphony #1. Kim Martin, president of the Company and plaintiff's brother, responded to the City. He reminded the City that the Company had paid for Symphony #1, and had signed the agreement with the Metropolitan Development Corporation pertaining to the eventuality of removal. Martin stated that if the sculpture was to be removed, the Company would be willing to donate it to the City provided the City would bear the costs of removal to a new site, but that plaintiff would like some input as to where his sculpture might be placed. Plaintiff also personally appeared before the Metropolitan Development Commission and made the same proposal. This was followed by a letter from plaintiff to the Mayor reiterating the removal proposal. The Mayor responded that he was referring plaintiff's proposal to his staff to see what could be done.

The City thereafter purchased the land. At the closing, plaintiff again repeated his proposal and agreed to assist so Symphony #1 could be saved and, if necessary, moved without damage. The City's response was that plaintiff would be contacted in the event the sculpture was to be removed. Shortly thereafter, the City awarded a contract to demolish the sculpture, and demolition followed, all without prior notice to plaintiff or the Company. This lawsuit resulted in which summary judgment was allowed for plaintiff. However, his victory was not entirely satisfactory to him, nor was the City satisfied. The City appealed, and plaintiff cross-appealed.

II. ANALYSIS

Although recognized under the Berne Convention, the legal protection of an artist's so-called "moral rights" was controversial in this country. The United States did not join the Berne Convention until 1988 when it did so in a very limited way. Then Congress followed up by enacting VARA in 1990, with this explanation found in the House Reports: "An artist's professional and personal identity is embodied in each work created by that artist. Each work is a part of his or her reputation. Each work is a form of personal expression (oftentimes painstakingly and earnestly recorded). It is a rebuke to the dignity of the visual artist that our copyright law allows distortion, modification and even outright permanent destruction of such efforts." H.R. Rep. No. 101-514, at 15 (1990).

VARA seems to be a stepchild of our copyright laws, but does not require copyright registration. * * * VARA provides: "The author of a work of visual art . . . shall have the right . . . to prevent any destruction of a work of recognized stature, and any intentional or grossly negligent destruction of that work is a violation of that right." 17 U.S.C. § 106A(a)(3)(B). The district court considered Symphony #1 to be of "recognized stature" under the evidence presented and thus concluded that the City had violated plaintiff's rights under VARA. That finding is contested by the City.

"Recognized stature" is a necessary finding under VARA in order to protect a work of visual art from destruction. In spite of its significance, that phrase is not defined in VARA, leaving its intended meaning and application open to argument and judicial resolution. The only case found undertaking to define and apply "recognized stature" is *Carter v. Helmsley-Spear, Inc.*, 861 F. Supp. 303 (S.D.N.Y. 1994), aff'd in part, vacated in part, rev'd in part, 71 F.3d 77 (2d Cir. 1995). Involved was an unusual work of art consisting of interrelated sculptural elements constructed from recycled materials, mostly metal, to decorate the lobby of a commercial building in a borough of New York City. *Carter II*, 71 F.3d 70, at 80. Part of the work was "a giant hand fashioned from an old school bus, [and] a face made of automobile parts. . . ." *Id.* Although the Second Circuit reversed the district court and held that the work was not a work of visual art protected by VARA, *id.* at 88, the district court presented an informative discussion in determining whether a work of visual art may qualify as one of "recognized stature." See *Carter I*, 861 F. Supp. at 324–26. That determination is based greatly on the testimony of experts on both sides of the issue, as would ordinarily be expected. The stature test formulated by the New York district court required: "(1) that the visual art in question has 'stature,' i.e. is viewed as meritorious, and (2) that this stature is 'recognized' by art experts, other members of the artistic community, or by some cross-section of society. In making this showing, plaintiffs generally, but not inevitably, will need to call expert witnesses to testify before the trier of fact." *Carter I*, 861 F. Supp. at 325.

Even though the district court in this present case found that test was satisfied by the plaintiff's evidence, plaintiff argues that the *Carter v. Helmsley-Spear* test may be more rigorous than Congress intended. That may be, but we see no need for the purposes of this case to endeavor to refine that rule. Plaintiff's evidence, however, is not as complete as in *Carter v. Helmsley-Spear*, possibly because

Symphony #1 was destroyed by the City without the opportunity for experts to appraise the sculpture in place.

The City objects to the "stature" testimony that was offered by plaintiff as inadmissible hearsay. If not admitted, it would result in plaintiff's failure to sustain his burden of proof. It is true that plaintiff offered no evidence of experts or others by deposition, affidavit or interrogatories. Plaintiff's evidence of "stature" consisted of certain newspaper and magazine articles, and various letters, including a letter from an art gallery director and a letter to the editor of The Indianapolis News, all in support of the sculpture, as well as a program from the show at which a model of the sculpture won "Best of Show." After reviewing the City's objection, the district court excluded plaintiff's "programs and awards" evidence as lacking adequate foundation, but nevertheless found Martin had met his "stature" burden of proof with his other evidence.

Included in the admitted evidence, for example, was a letter dated October 25, 1982 from the Director of the Herron School of Art, Indiana University, Indianapolis. It was written to the Company and says in part, "The proposed sculpture is, in my opinion, an interesting and aesthetically stimulating configuration of forms and structures." The Indianapolis Star, in a four-column article by its visual arts editor, discussed public sculpture in Indianapolis. This article included a photograph of Symphony #1. The article lamented that the City had "been graced by only five pieces of note," but that two more had been added that particular year, one being plaintiff's sculpture. It noted, among other things, that Symphony #1 had been erected without the aid of "federal grants" and without the help of any committee of concerned citizens. Other public sculptures came in for some criticism in the article. However, in discussing Symphony #1, the author wrote: "Gleaming clean and abstract, yet domestic in scale and reference, irregularly but securely cabled together, the sculpture shows the site what it might be. It unites the area, providing a nexus, a marker, a designation, an identity and, presumably, a point of pride."

The district judge commented on the City's hearsay objection to plaintiff's admitted evidence as follows: "The statements contained within the proffered newspaper and magazine articles and letters are offered by Martin to show that respected members of the art community and members of the public at large consider Martin's work to be socially valuable and to have artistic merit, and to show the newsworthiness of Symphony #1 and Martin's work. These statements are offered by Martin to show that the declarants said them, not that the statements are, in fact, true. . . . The statements contained within the exhibits show how art critics and the public viewed Martin's work, particularly Symphony #1, and show that the sculpture was a matter worth reporting to the public. Therefore, the statements contained within these challenged exhibits are not hearsay because they are not being offered for the truth of the matters asserted therein."

We agree with the assessment made by the district court. * * * In the present case, the author of the letter and the newspaper writer were not reporting as the truth what others reportedly said about the sculpture, but only expressing their own opinions. We find the article and the letter, as examples, admissible for this unique and limited purpose as the district court permitted.

Next the City claims that the Project Agreement entered into pre-VARA by plaintiff and the City encompassed many of plaintiff's rights under VARA. There-fore, the City argues, that whereas plaintiff failed to remove his work within the time allowed in the contract, plaintiff waived any cause of action he might have had under VARA. That failure was the City's, not plaintiff's, as under the Agreement the City was obligated to give the owners of the land and the sculpture ninety days to remove the sculpture. The City, after discussing with the Company and plaintiff possible other uses for the tract and the removal proposal, failed to give the required notice and went ahead and demolished the sculpture. Nothing had happened between the parties prior to that which could constitute a waiver of any rights by the Company or plaintiff. Plaintiff had no notice of the City letting a contract for Symphony #1's demolition and no notice when that demolition would actually occur. After the preliminary and ongoing discussions plaintiff and the Company had with the City, when there was no immediate threat of imminent demolition, plaintiff had the right to continue to rely on the specific notice provided in the Agreement, unless it had been waived, which it was not.

* * * Under 17 U.S.C. § 106A(e)(1), an artist may waive VARA rights "in a written instrument signed by the author," specifying to what the waiver applies. There is no written waiver instrument in this case which falls within the VARA requirements.

In spite of the City's conduct resulting in the intentional destruction of the sculpture, we do not believe under all the circumstances, particularly given the fact that the issue of VARA rights had not been raised until this suit, that the City's conduct was "willful," as used in VARA, 17 U.S.C. § 504(c)(2), so as to entitle the plaintiff to enhanced damages. This appears to be a case of bureaucratic failure within the City government, not a willful violation of plaintiff's VARA rights. As far as we can tell from the record, those VARA rights were unknown to the City. The parties proceeded under their pre-VARA agreement which the City breached. However, plaintiff retained his VARA rights. As unfortunate as the City's unan-nounced demolition of Symphony #1 was, it does not qualify plaintiff for damages under VARA. * * * Being fully satisfied with the district court's careful resolution of these unique issues and the resulting judgment, the district court's finding is affirmed in all respects.

MANION, J., concurring in part and dissenting in part.

* * * VARA was not designed to regulate urban renewal, but to protect great works of art from destruction and mutilation, among other things. 17 U.S.C. § 106A(a). In order to restrict VARA's reach, the Act was limited to preventing destruction of works of art that had attained a "recognized stature." 17 U.S.C. § 106A(a)(3)(B). The court correctly notes that a natural reading of this term indicates that it has two elements (which correspond to its two words): (1) merit or intrinsic worth; and (2) a public acknowledgment of that merit by society or the art community. As the district court in *Carter v. Helmsley-Spear, Inc.* stated: "the recognized stature requirement is best viewed as a gate-keeping mechanism — protection is afforded only to those works of art that art experts, the art community, or society in general views as possessing stature." 861 F. Supp. 303, 325 (S.D.N.Y. 1994), rev'd in part and aff'd in part, 71 F.3d 77 (2d Cir. 1995). So I concur with the court on this point.

I dissent, however, because summary judgment is not appropriate here. A plaintiff cannot satisfy his burden of demonstrating recognized stature through old newspaper articles and unverified letters, some of which do not even address the artwork in question. Rather, as the district court stated in *Carter*, in "making this showing [of recognized stature] plaintiffs generally, but not inevitably, will need to call expert witnesses to testify before the trier of fact." 861 F. Supp. at 325. Instances where expert testimony on this point is not necessary will be rare, and this is not one of those exceptional cases where something of unquestioned recognition and stature was destroyed. * * * While the very publication of newspaper articles on a work of art may have bearing on the "recognized" element, there has to be some evidence that the art had stature (i.e., that it met a certain high level of quality). The newspaper articles are hearsay and not admitted for the truth of the matter asserted in them. Construed in the light most favorable to the defendant, they cannot demonstrate by a preponderance of the evidence that the plaintiff's art was of a recognized stature, and that no reasonable jury could find otherwise. Experts need to weigh in here, and the trial court and perhaps this court need to come up with a clearer definition of when works of art achieve "recognized stature."

For now, however, those who are purchasers or donees of art had best beware. To avoid being the perpetual curator of a piece of visual art that has lost (or perhaps never had) its luster, the recipient must obtain at the outset a waiver of the artist's rights under VARA. Before awarding building permits for erection of sculptures, municipalities might be well advised to obtain a written waiver of the artist's rights too.

NOTES

1. VARA cases are reviewed in Christopher Robinson, *The "Recognized Stature" Standard on the Visual Artists Rights Act*, 68 Fordham L. Rev. 1935, 1948–1959 (2000). Some state moral rights statutes require, like VARA, that a work have a "recognized stature," but an equal number do not. *Id.* at 1942–1943. Do you think that a work installed without permission and removed without having been viewed by the public is entitled to VARA protection? See *Pollara v. Seymour*, 206 F. Supp. 2d 333 (N.D.N.Y. 2002). What about graffiti? A mural with an anti-smoking, anti-drug, or anti-drinking message? Painted by children? If a work is found to have the originality necessary for copyright, should it also have a "recognized stature"?

2. *Carter v. Helmsley-Spear, Inc.*, 71 F.3d 77 (2d Cir. 1995), cited and excerpted *supra*, held that a "walk-through sculpture" commissioned by a tenant for an office building lobby, was made for hire and therefore not protected by VARA. The court concluded that the artists had complete artistic freedom, controlling the manner and means of producing the sculpture, requiring great skill in its execution, and retaining the copyright on the work — all factors weighing against "work for hire" status; however, on the other side of the scale, the court concluded that the artists were employees, giving them a weekly salary, health and other insurance, paid vacations, unemployment insurance (which they used after the work was done), workers' compensation, and social security benefits. Nonetheless, the court was generous in its analysis of artists' rights, stating as follows, *id.* at 80, 85–86:

On this appeal we deal with an Act of Congress that protects the rights of artists to preserve their works. * * * American artists are to be encouraged by laws that protect their works. Although Congress in the statute before us did just that, it did not mandate the preservation of art at all costs and without due regard for the rights of others. . . .

Plaintiffs John Carter, John Swing and John Veronis (artists or plaintiffs) are professional sculptors who work together. . . . On December 16, 1991 SIG entered into a one-year agreement with the plaintiffs "engaging and hiring the Artists . . . to design, create and install sculpture and other permanent installations" in the building, primarily the lobby. Under the agreement plaintiffs had "full authority in design, color and style," and SIG retained authority to direct the location and installation of the artwork within the building. The artists were to retain copyrights to their work and SIG was to receive 50 percent of any proceeds from its exploitation. On January 20, 1993 SIG and the artists signed an agreement extending the duration of their commission for an additional year. . . .

The artwork that is the subject of this litigation is a very large "walk-through sculpture" occupying most, but not all, of the building's lobby. The artwork consists of a variety of sculptural elements constructed from recycled materials, much of it metal, affixed to the walls and ceiling, and a vast mosaic made from pieces of recycled glass embedded in the floor and walls. Elements of the work include a giant hand fashioned from an old school bus, a face made of automobile parts, and a number of interactive components. These assorted elements make up a theme relating to environmental concerns and the significance of recycling.

. . . The district court . . . established five factors which would be relevant in nearly all cases: the right to control the manner and means of production; requisite skill; provision of employee benefits; tax treatment of the hired party; whether the hired party may be assigned additional projects. * * * Our review . . . persuades us that the factors that weigh in favor of finding the artists were employees outweigh those factors supporting the artists' claim that they were independent contractors. One of the factors that did not persuade us was the appellants' simplistic contention that usage of the words "employ" or "employment" in the agreements . . . establishes that the plaintiffs were employees. The use of these terms does not transform them into "magic words" imbued with legally controlling significance. Again, we emphasize that despite the conclusion reached we do not intend to marginalize factors such as artistic freedom and skill, making them peripheral to the status inquiry. The fact that artists will always be retained for creative purposes cannot serve to minimalize this factor . . . even though it will usually favor VARA protection. Also, that the work was produced on the employer's premises is a necessary incident to all nonremovable art and therefore should not carry great weight. Similarly, we were not swayed by the boilerplate contract language or the accounting decision to deduct taxes. As discussed earlier, the moral rights of the artist whose artistic work comes under VARA's umbrella are to be protected, not ignored. . . .

Moreover, because the . . . test is fact-dependent, future cases involving the work for hire question will not always fit neatly into an employee or independent contractor category. We also recognize that by counting indicia such as health insurance and paid vacations against the artists' independent contractor status, it may appear that artists regrettably are being forced to choose between the personal benefits inuring in an employment relationship and VARA's protection of the artists' work afforded only to independent contractors. Of course, when an employer today denies an artist "basic attributes of employment" like vacation time or health benefits, such denial will be wholly inconsistent with a "work for hire" defense.

Consequently, while the existence of payroll formalities alone would not be controlling, in combination with other factors, it may lead to a conclusion that a given work is one made for hire. Such other factors include: plaintiffs under their contract could be and were in fact assigned projects in addition to the work in the lobby; they were paid a weekly salary for over two years for a contracted 40 hours of work per week; they were furnished many of the needed supplies necessary to create the work; and plaintiffs could not hire paid assistants without defendants' consent. These factors, properly considered and weighed with the employee benefits granted plaintiffs and the tax treatment accorded them, are more than sufficient to demonstrate that the artists were employees, and the sculpture is therefore a work made for hire as a matter of law.

MOAKLEY v. EASTWICK
666 N.E.2d 505 (Mass. 1996)

GREANEY, J.

We allowed the plaintiff's application for direct appellate review to resolve issues under the so-called Art Preservation Act, G. L. c. 231, § 85S (Act) . . . , effective April 7, 1985. By his complaint in the Superior Court, the plaintiff, John C. Moakley, an artist, brought a claim under the Act against the defendants, the Grace Bible Church Fellowship, Inc., Grace Bible Church, and Maurice T. Eastwick, the pastor of the church. . . . The plaintiff sought a declaration of his rights, injunctive relief, and the assessment of damages. The plaintiff appeals from a judgment entered in favor of the defendants. . . .

The dispute concerns a work of art, created by the plaintiff, which is located on the grounds of the former First Parish Unitarian Church in East Bridgewater, now owned by the church. The church argued that the Legislature did not intend that the Act's provisions were to be applied to works of fine art created before the law became effective. Stating that the content of the work was "problematic from a religious standpoint," the church also contended that, if the work was protected by the Act, and its provisions required the church to maintain the work on its property, then the Act, as applied, violated the church members' constitutional rights to freedom of religion and worship, as guaranteed by the First Amendment to the United States Constitution, as well as . . . art. 2 of the Declaration of Rights of the Massachusetts Constitution. The judge concluded that the plaintiff's work was protected by the Act, but that the "application of the statute to the defendants [would offend] [art.] 2." The plaintiff asks us to reverse the judgment for the defendants, to declare that his work is protected by the Act, to enjoin the church permanently from tampering with the work, and to assess damages for tortious infliction of emotional distress. We conclude that the Act does not apply to the plaintiff's work and that he is not entitled to damages on his tort claims.

The facts found by the judge are as follows. In 1971, the plaintiff, an established sculptor and potter, was commissioned by the pastor of the First Parish Unitarian Church in East Bridgewater to create and install a work of art on church property. The result of this commission consisted of a sixty-eight foot long concrete block wall to which the plaintiff affixed a mural composed of approximately 600 separate ceramic tiles, organized into ten panels (work). The work constituted an historical "time line," in relief, of events and social trends in East Bridgewater from its earliest days to the time of the commission. The final panel of the work contained references to social issues in the 1960's and 1970's, including drug use, environmental pollution, nuclear war, and civil unrest. The judge found that the plaintiff had invested substantial time and emotional resources in the work, and that it was "an expression of [the plaintiff's] personality." The judge also accepted the testimony of two experts that the wall with the affixed mural "was a work of fine art of recognized quality."[3] Because of the method of its construction, the work cannot be moved intact from its present site.

In October, 1989, the property on which the work is located was acquired by the Grace Bible Church Fellowship, Inc., for use as a house of worship for members of the church. The property was dilapidated when the church acquired it. On October 21, 1989, shortly after the purchase was complete, approximately sixty members of the church joined in a "clean-up day." The church intended to remove the work in its entirety, and, at some point during the clean-up day, a substantial portion of the east end of the wall, constituting about one-seventh of the entire work, was demolished. The judge accepted as credible testimony by the pastor of the church that the work was objectionable to the church on religious grounds, and that it was for this reason that the church had decided to remove it.

The plaintiff was informed of the partial destruction of his work by the chairwoman of the East Bridgewater Historical Commission. On the basis of the Act, he obtained a preliminary injunction prohibiting the church from causing or permitting any further physical defacement or alteration of the work.[4] On appeal, the plaintiff argues that the judge erred in concluding that the Act, as applied, would violate the defendants' rights under art. 2. We need not reach this

---

[3] General Laws c. 231, § 85S (1994 ed.), protects "works of fine art," which are defined, in subsection (b), as "any original work of visual or graphic art of any media which shall include, but not limited to [sic], any painting, print, drawing, sculpture, craft object, photograph, audio or video tape, film, hologram, or any combination thereof, of recognized quality." In determining whether a work is one of "fine art" within the meaning of the Act, a judge is directed to rely "on the opinions of artists, art dealers, collectors of fine art, curators of art museums, restorers and conservators of fine art and other persons involved with the creation or marketing of fine art." § 85S(f).

[4] Subsection (c) of the Act provides, in part, that "no person, except an artist who owns or possesses a work of fine art which the artist has created, shall intentionally commit, or authorize the intentional commission of any physical defacement, mutilation, alteration, or destruction of a work of fine art."

constitutional issue, because we agree with the defendants' contention that the Act was not intended to apply retrospectively to works created before its enactment and owned by someone other than the artist.

Because the plaintiff sought relief under the Act, which we have not previously had occasion to consider, we begin by discussing the Act's content and its relation to existing law. According to a commentator, the Act follows similar legislation in the States of California and New York "in attempting to graft onto a generally inhospitable common law tradition the civil law concept of droit moral, whereby a creative artist retains certain inalienable rights with respect to his or her creation before and after publication, display or sale." Koven, *Observations on the Massachusetts Art Preservation Act*, 71 Mass. L. Rev. 101, 101 (1986). The primary goal of the Act is to safeguard the professional reputations of Massachusetts's artists by protecting the work which forms the basis of the artists' reputations. See G. L. c. 231, § 85S(a). To this end, the Act protects what has been referred to as the "Right of Integrity," Koven, *supra* at 103, by prohibiting the physical defacement or alteration of a work of fine art for the lifetime of the artist and for fifty years thereafter. § 85S(g).[7] The Act also protects what has been referred to as the "Right of Paternity," see Koven, *supra*, that is, the right of the artist to claim authorship of his work, or "for just and valid reason, to disclaim authorship of his work of fine art." § 85S(d). The rights of integrity and paternity are enforceable by the artist, or his duly authorized representative, by an action in the Superior Court. § 85S(e). The Act deals separately with "fine art [that] cannot be removed from a building without substantial physical defacement, mutilation, alteration, or destruction of such work." § 85S(h). As to these works, the rights and duties created under the Act are forfeited, "unless expressly reserved by an instrument in writing signed by the owner of such building and properly recorded prior to the installation of such art." *Id.* The Act creates new rights for artists with respect to their work after it has left their hands, and it creates new duties for owners of fine art, who may not alter, destroy, or grossly neglect a work of fine art in their possession that is subject to the provisions of the Act. § 85S(c).

The defendants contend that, in the absence of a legislative directive mandating retrospective application, the Act, which alters the relationship and expectations of artists and owners of art, should not be applied retrospectively to an owner of a work of fine art that was created and permanently left the artist's possession before the effective date of the Act. We agree with the defendants that the text of the Act and its legislative history compel the conclusion that it does not apply to a piece of fine art, like the work, whose creation preceded the enactment of the protective legislation.

Whether a new law applies retrospectively is a question of legislative intent. "In the absence of an express legislative directive, this court has usually applied 'the general rule of interpretation . . . that all statutes are prospective in their

---

[7] Because its provisions only apply for fifty years after an artist's death, much of what the general public would consider "fine art" clearly is not protected by the Act. * * * As has been previously noted, the legislation serves primarily to safeguard artists' professional reputations by preserving the integrity of the creative work which forms the basis for those reputations. The Act's preservation function is subsidiary to this main purpose.

operation, unless an intention that they shall be retrospective appears by necessary implication from their words, context or objects when considered in the light of the subject matter, the pre-existing state of the law and the effect upon existent rights, remedies and obligations. * * * It is only statutes regulating practice, procedure and evidence, in short, those relating to remedies and not affecting substantive rights, that commonly are treated as operating retroactively. . . ." *Fontaine v. Ebtec Corp.*, 415 Mass. 309, 318, 613 N.E.2d 881 (1993).

As the judge noted, the Act does not expressly address whether its provisions should apply retrospectively to work created before its enactment. * * * Nonetheless, the text of the Act poses barriers to its application to works created prior to its enactment. The Act exempts from its protections fine art attached to a building, which cannot be removed without defacement or destruction, unless the rights and duties created by the Act are "expressly reserved by an instrument in writing signed by the owner of such building and properly recorded, prior to the installation of such art." G. L. c. 231, § 85S(h). This condition obviously could not be satisfied with respect to a work of art created as an integral part of a building prior to the Act's effective date. Thus, at best, the Act could only apply selectively to some works of fine art created prior to its enactment, and it could not apply to most works of immovable art, which may, in fact, face the greatest risk of defacement or destruction because an owner cannot otherwise dispose of such a work.

In addition to the forward-looking nature of the reservation provision in § 85S(h), there are other compelling reasons to conclude that the Legislature's failure to provide for retrospective application of the Act represents a deliberate choice that should be respected by this court. A comparison of the texts indicates that the Act was modeled on the so-called California Art Preservation Act, Cal. Civ. Code § 987, enacted in 1979 (1982) (California Act). In most respects, the Act follows quite precisely the language of the California Act.

There is, however, one omission from, and one addition to, the Act, both bearing directly on the question of retrospective application. Where the California Act (§ 987[j]) provides that it shall "apply to claims based on proscribed acts occurring on or after [the effective date of the Act] to works of fine art whenever created," the Act is silent on this point. In addition, the Act will not protect a work of fine art which is attached to a building and cannot be removed unless a preservation restriction . . . has been recorded prior to the work's creation. The California Act also requires the recordation of a preservation restriction applicable to the work be recorded prior to the work's creation, but does not require that the restriction be recorded before such work is created or installed.

The legislative history of the Act strongly suggests that the changes just described were deliberate and, consequently, supports the view that the Legislature did not intend the Act to apply retrospectively to works created before its enactment. Prior to its enactment, a different version of the Act had been proposed. That version included the language, found in the California Act, which would have made the Act applicable to "works of fine art whenever created." *Id.* at 4. * * *

Statutes in other jurisdictions, comparable to the Act in that they protect works of art from destruction, mutilation, or alteration, all address specifically whether their provisions apply to works of fine art created prior to enactment. See Visual

Artists Rights Act of 1990, 17 U.S.C. § 106A(d)(1) & (2) (1994); Cal. Civ. Code § 987(j); Conn. Gen. Stat. Ann. § 42-116t(g) (1995); Pa. Stat. Ann. tit. 73, § 2110(b) (1993). It is worth noting that the Legislatures responsible for these various laws have chosen differently on this point. The Federal Act applies to works created on or after the effective date of the statute and to works created prior to the statute's effective date "but title to which has not, as of such effective date, been transferred from the author." Connecticut's Act, enacted in 1988, applies only to works created on or after October 1, 1988. In contrast, as has been previously noted, the California Act applies to works of fine art whenever created, as does the Pennsylvania Act (although the Pennsylvania Act has the additional limitation that it applies only to works of fine art displayed in a place accessible to the public). We may infer from these diverging approaches that our Legislature is not alone in having concluded that the rights and duties created by legislation like the Act sufficiently alter the expectations and responsibilities of owners or possessors of fine art, that these duties should not be imposed on a person who acquired a work of fine art that was created before such duties were imposed by law. * * * We agree with the defendants that the Legislature did not intend the Act to apply to preexisting works of fine art. * * * The judgment is modified . . . and, as so modified, is affirmed.

NOTES

1. Artist's rights that can be disclaimed, waived, but often not transferred, may pose problems when changes are made in the ownership of a building in which the art is located. Does VARA or the state statutes just reviewed create problems of marketable title? When might such a right be the subject of a title insurance claim? See Stephen Snively, *Artists' Rights Meet Property Rights: An Invisible Restraint*, Prob. and Prop. (Nov./Dec. 1995), at 18.

2. The California Resale Royalties Act, Cal. Civ. Code § 986 (2003), states that if a work of fine art by a living artist either is resold in California or is resold by a California resident, its vendor shall pay the artist 5% of its sales price when the price is more than $1,000. *Morseberg v. Balyon*, 621 F.2d 972 (9th Cir. 1980). Would you recommend such a provision be included in a statute providing for artists' moral rights? Of the reach of the California Act, one court said that it:

> . . . was the first statute in the United States to recognize that an artist has personal rights in his or her work which are retained even after the work has been sold. This bundle of rights is known by the French term droit moral, translated into English as "moral rights." Among these moral rights, which are also known as the "right of the author's personality," is the right of integrity, which includes the right to object to the destruction of one's work and to prevent its mutilation, distortion, or alteration. Karlen, *Moral Rights in California* (1982) 19 San Diego L. Rev. 675, 684–85. The classic example of a violation of the right of integrity occurs when the owner of a work of art alters it and then continues to display it. Professor Karlen states, "[T]he artist must be entitled to certain rights in order to survive as a professional. For instance, the artist must be able to require credit for his work in order to establish a reputation. Conversely, he must be able to disassociate himself from work which is not his including his work which

has been so badly altered that it no longer expresses his creative efforts. Further, to mount exhibitions, especially retrospective ones, he should have access to works he has created earlier in his career. To do so, he must be able to locate the owners of the works and to prevent destruction of the works. To effectuate the right to restrain destruction, the artist should have the right to repair damaged works or to conserve decaying works so that careless abandonment does not put the work of art beyond redemption. . . ." Karlen, *supra* at 682.

Lubner v. City of Los Angeles, 53 Cal. Rptr. 2d 24, 26, 28 (Cal. Ct. App. 1996), stating the facts of the case and rejecting the plaintiff's claim as follows:

> In a factual scenario that seems to have been taken from a law school hypothetical, two artists lost much of their life work after a city trash truck parked at the top of a hill rolled down and crashed into their home, damaging the house, two cars and their artwork, which included paintings, drawings, prints and posters. We are asked to permit the artists, Martin and Lorraine Lubner, to recover damages based on either loss of reputation or emotional distress. Even though we sympathize with appellants, established law does not permit us to recognize the type of damages they seek. * * * Though Professor Karlen states that the artist must be able to prevent the destruction of his or her art, the context of the statement indicates that he is referring to intentional destruction. The ideas expressed by the commentators cited here and others we have read do not support the position that the theory of moral rights justifies finding in section 987 an implied remedy for destruction due to simple negligence. The Lubners offer no justification for so reading section 987. Furthermore, the plain language of the statute does not support the Lubners. . . .

IV. THE RIGHT TO PUBLICITY

A right to publicity permits famous persons to control and benefit from the commercial use and value of their identities, including their names, likenesses, images, and voices. It requires the appropriation and unauthorized use of the person's identity, to the defendant's advantage and the plaintiff's injury. See *Eastwood v. Superior Court*, 198 Cal. Rptr. 342 (Cal. Ct. App. 1983). Its development can be traced to the right of privacy-the right to be let alone. See Samuel Warren & Louis Brandeis, *The Right to Privacy*, 4 Harv. L. Rev. 193 (1890). The law of privacy worked well enough to protect private persons against the unauthorized use of their names and images. See *Pavesich v. New England Life Insur. Co.*, 50 S.E. 68, 81 (Ga. 1905) (citing the Warren and Brandeis article). For famous persons and celebrities, however, the protection it offered proved inadequate; they, after all, seek the public eye, so claiming emotional injury from publicity was paradoxical. And famous people often work hard to create sustainable identities. Once they have, control over the extent, manner and timing of their commercial exploitation goes to the core of what they do. After several decades of judicial hesitation, courts began to recognize that famous persons have a property right in their identities. The following case is the leading one recognizing this right was property.

HAELAN LABORATORIES, INC. v.
TOPPS CHEWING GUM, INC.
202 F.2d 866 (2d Cir. 1953)

FRANK, J.[*]

After a trial without a jury, the trial judge dismissed the complaint on the merits. The plaintiff maintains that defendant invaded plaintiff's exclusive right to use the photographs of leading baseball-players. Probably because the trial judge ruled against plaintiff's legal contentions, some of the facts were not too clearly found.

1. * * *

(a). The plaintiff, engaged in selling chewing-gum, made a contract with a ball-player providing that plaintiff for a stated term should have the exclusive right to use the ball-player's photograph in connection with the sales of plaintiff's gum; the ball-player agreed not to grant any other gum manufacturer a similar right during such term; the contract gave plaintiff an option to extend the term for a designated period.

(b). Defendant, a rival chewing-gum manufacturer, knowing of plaintiff's contract, deliberately induced the ball-player to authorize defendant, by a contract with defendant, to use the player's photograph in connection with the sales of defendant's gum either during the original or extended term of plaintiff's contract, and defendant did so use the photograph.

Defendant argues that, even if such facts are proved, they show no actionable wrong, for this reason: The contract with plaintiff was no more than a release by the ball-player to plaintiff of the liability which, absent the release, plaintiff would have incurred in using the ball-player's photograph, because such a use, without his consent, would be an invasion of his right of privacy under Section 50 and Section 51 of the New York Civil Rights Law; this statutory right of privacy is personal, not assignable; therefore, plaintiff's contract vested in plaintiff no 'property' right or other legal interest which defendant's conduct invaded.

Both parties agree, and so do we, that, on the facts here, New York law governs. And we shall assume, for the moment, that, under the New York decisions, defendant correctly asserts that any such contract between plaintiff and a ball-player, in so far as it merely authorized plaintiff to use the player's photograph, created nothing but a release of liability. On that basis, were there no more to the contract, plaintiff would have no actionable claim against defendant. But defendant's argument neglects the fact that, in the contract, the ball-player also promised not to give similar releases to others. If defendant, knowing of the contract, deliberately induced the ball-player to break that promise, defendant behaved tortiously. See, e.g., *Hornstein v. Podwitz*, 254 N.Y. 443, 173 N.E. 674.

Some of defendant's contracts were obtained by it through its agent, Players Enterprise, Inc; others were obtained by Russell Publishing Co., acting indepen-

---

[*] Judge Jerome Frank is best remembered today for his book, Law and the Modern Mind (1930) (arguing for the importance of a judge's psychology in law making).

dently, and were then assigned by Russell to defendant. Since Players acted as defendant's agent, defendant is liable for any breach of plaintiff's contracts thus induced by Players. However, as Russell did not act as defendant's agent when Russell, having knowledge of plaintiff's contract with a player, by subsequently contracting with that player, induced a breach of plaintiff's contract, defendant is not liable for any breach so induced; nor did there arise such a liability against defendant for such an induced breach when defendant became the assignee of one of those Russell contracts.

2. The foregoing covers the situations where defendant, by itself or through its agent, induced breaches. But in those instances where Russell induced the breach, we have a different problem; and that problem also confronts us in instances — alleged in one paragraph of the complaint and to which the trial judge in his opinion also . . . refers — where defendant, 'with knowledge of plaintiff's exclusive rights,' used a photograph of a ball-player without his consent during the term of his contract with plaintiff.

With regard to such situations, we must consider defendant's contention that none of plaintiff's contracts created more than a release of liability, because a man has no legal interest in the publication of his picture other than his right of privacy, i.e., a personal and non-assignable right not to have his feelings hurt by such a publication.

A majority of this court rejects this contention. We think that, in addition to and independent of that right of privacy (which in New York derives from statute), a man has a right in the publicity value of his photograph, i.e., the right to grant the exclusive privilege of publishing his picture, and that such a grant may validly be made 'in gross,' i.e., without an accompanying transfer of a business or of anything else. Whether it be labeled a 'property' right is immaterial; for here, as often elsewhere, the tag 'property' simply symbolizes the fact that courts enforce a claim which has pecuniary worth.

This right might be called a 'right of publicity.' For it is common knowledge that many prominent persons (especially actors and ball-players), far from having their feelings bruised through public exposure of their likenesses, would feel sorely deprived if they no longer received money for authorizing advertisements, popularizing their countenances, displayed in newspapers, magazines, busses, trains and subways. This right of publicity would usually yield them no money unless it could be made the subject of an exclusive grant which barred any other advertiser from using their pictures.

We think the New York decisions recognize such a right. See, e.g., *Wood v. Lucy, Lady Duff Gordon*, 222 N.Y. 88, 118 N.E. 214. We think *Pekas Co., Inc. v. Leslie*, 52 N.Y.L.J. 1864, decided in 1915 . . . , is not controlling since — apart from a doubt as to whether an opinion of that court must be taken by us as an authoritative exposition of New York law — the opinion shows that the judge had his attention directed by plaintiff exclusively to Sections 50 and 51 of the New York statute, and, accordingly, held that the right of privacy was 'purely personal and not assignable' because 'rights for outraged feelings are no more assignable than would be a claim arising from a libelous utterance.' * * *

We said above that defendant was not liable for a breach of any of plaintiff's contracts induced by Russell, and did not become thus liable (for an induced breach) when there was assigned to defendant a contract between Russell and a ball-player, although Russell, in making that contract, knowingly induced a breach of a contract with plaintiff. But plaintiff . . . has a valid claim against defendant if defendant used that player's photograph during the term of plaintiff's grant and with knowledge of it. It is no defense to such a claim that defendant is the assignee of a subsequent contract between that player and Russell, purporting to make a grant to Russell or its assignees. For the prior grant to plaintiff renders that subsequent grant invalid during the period of the grant (including an exercised option) to plaintiff, but not thereafter.

3. We must remand to the trial court for a determination (on the basis of the present record and of further evidence introduced by either party) of these facts: (1) the date and contents of each of plaintiff's contracts, and whether plaintiff exercised its option to renew; (2) defendant's or Players' conduct with respect to each such contract. Of course, if defendant made a contract with a ball-player which was not executed — or which did not authorize defendant to use the player's photograph — until the expiration of the original or extended term of plaintiff's contract with that player, or which did not induce a breach of the agreement to renew, then defendant did no legal wrong to plaintiff. The same is true of instances where neither defendant nor Players induced a breach of plaintiff's contract, and defendant did not use the player's photograph until after the expiration of such original or extended or option term.

If, upon further exploration of the facts, the trial court, in the light of our opinion, concludes that defendant is liable, it will, of course, ascertain damages and decide what equitable relief is justified. Reversed and remanded.

NOTES

1. Do you think that the right of publicity should be based on compensating a person for the labor put into creating an identity, or on the right to control it? If a movie star drives her car on a public street and the car's manufacturer films the star driving there, is the star's right to publicity violated when the manufacturer uses the film in an advertisement? See Alice Haemmerli, *Whose Who? The Case for a Kantian Right of Publicity*, 49 Duke L.J. 383 (1999). Just benefiting from a famous identity might be found to be unjust enrichment. See *Zacchini v. Scripps-Howard Broad. Co.*, 433 U.S. 562 (1977) (holding that taping and broadcasting the plaintiff's "human cannonball" act in its entirety violates the right of publicity, being not just the appropriation of the plaintiff's reputation, but the appropriation of the very activity by which he acquired his reputation, the court stating: "no social purpose is served by having the defendant get free some aspect of the plaintiff that would have market value and for which he would normally pay." *Id.* at 576.). The Supreme Court's right of publicity includes a right of performance. If assignability is the key to the *Haelan Laboratories* opinion, isn't the right not to assign or to withhold one's identity or performance protected as well?

2. For a discussion of *Haelan Laboratories*, see J. Gordon Hylton, *Baseball Cards and the Birth of the Right of Publicity: The Curious Case of* Haelan

Laboratories v. Topps Chewing Gum, 12 Marq. Sports L. Rev. 273 (2001). The right of publicity is today recognized in a about half the states, either by judicial opinion or in 16 states, by statute. Compare *Gregory Hetter, M.D. v. The Eighth Judicial District Court of the State of Nevada*, 874 P.2d 762 (Nev. 1994) (holding that the Nevada right of publicity statute was an exclusive remedy and involving a plastic surgeon publishing a before and after picture of the plaintiff and held liable for damages), with *Eastwood v. Superior Court*, 198 Cal. Rptr. 342 (Cal. Ct. App. 1983) (using plaintiff's photograph to sell newspapers violates both the common law and California statutory right, and holding that the California statute provides remedies in addition to those provided by the pre-existing common law).

The right is also sometimes grounded on the doctrine of misappropriation, deceptive trade practice statutes, or other distinctive statutory codifications. See, e.g., Restatement (Third) of Unfair Competition § 46, at 528. Moreover, its origins in the right to privacy have never entirely disappeared. The extent of the right is thus defined under state law and varies considerably from state to state. Thus imitating a singer's voice and song style for a voice-over in an advertisement gives rise to a cause of action to protect this right. See *Midler v. Ford Motor Co.*, 849 F.2d 460 (9th Cir. 1988). See also *White v. Samsung Elecs. Am., Inc.*, 971 F.2d 1395 (9th Cir. 1992) (giving the plaintiff Vanna White a cause of action against a firm creating a robot resembling her).

MARTIN LUTHER KING, JR. CENTER v. AMERICAN HERITAGE PRODUCTS
296 S.E.2d 697 (Ga. 1982)

These are certified questions regarding the "right of publicity." The certification comes from the United States Court of Appeals for the Eleventh Circuit. The facts upon which the questions arise are as follows: The plaintiffs are the Martin Luther King, Jr. Center for Social Change (the Center), Coretta Scott King, as administratrix of Dr. King's estate, and Motown Record Corporation, the assignee of the rights to several of Dr. King's copyrighted speeches. Defendant James F. Bolen is the sole proprietor of a business known as B & S Sales, which manufactures and sells various plastic products as funeral accessories. Defendant James E. Bolen, the son of James F. Bolen, developed the concept of marketing a plastic bust of Dr. Martin Luther King, Jr., and formed a company, B & S Enterprises, to sell the busts, which would be manufactured by B & S Sales. B & S Enterprises was later incorporated under the name of American Heritage Products, Inc.

Although Bolen sought the endorsement and participation of the Martin Luther King, Jr. Center for Social Change, Inc., in the marketing of the bust, the Center refused Bolen's offer. Bolen pursued the idea, nevertheless, hiring an artist to prepare a mold and an agent to handle the promotion of the product. Defendant took out two half-page advertisements in the November and December 1980 issues of Ebony magazine, which purported to offer the bust as "an exclusive memorial" and "an opportunity to support the Martin Luther King, Jr., Center for Social Change." The advertisement stated that "a contribution from your order goes to the King Center for Social Change." Out of the $29.95 purchase price, defendant Bolen testified he set aside 3% or $.90, as a contribution to the Center. The advertisement also offered "free" with the purchase of the bust a booklet about the life of Dr. King entitled "A Tribute to Dr. Martin Luther King, Jr."

In addition to the two advertisements in Ebony, defendant published a brochure or pamphlet which was inserted in 80,000 copies of newspapers across the country. The brochure reiterated what was stated in the magazine advertisements, and also contained photographs of Dr. King and excerpts from his copyrighted speeches. The brochure promised that each "memorial" (bust) is accompanied by a Certificate of Appreciation "testifying that a contribution has been made to the Martin Luther King, Jr., Center for Social Change."

Defendant James E. Bolen testified that he created a trust fund for that portion of the earnings which was to be contributed to the Center. The trust fund agreement, however, was never executed, and James E. Bolen testified that this was due to the plaintiffs' attorneys' request to cease and desist from all activities in issue. Testimony in the district court disclosed that money had been tendered to the Center, but was not accepted by its governing board. Also, the district court found that, as of the date of the preliminary injunction, the defendants had sold approximately 200 busts and had outstanding orders for 23 more.

On November 21, 1980, and December 19, 1980, the plaintiffs demanded that the Bolens cease and desist from further advertisements and sales of the bust, and on December 31, 1980, the plaintiffs filed a complaint in the United States District Court for the Northern District of Georgia. The district court held a hearing on the plaintiffs' motion for a preliminary injunction and the defendants' motion to dismiss the complaint. The motion to dismiss was denied and the motion for a preliminary injunction was granted in part and denied in part. The motion for an injunction sought (1) an end to the use of the Center's name in advertising and marketing the busts, (2) restraint of any further copyright infringement and (3) an end to the manufacture and sale of the plastic busts. The defendants agreed to discontinue the use of the Center's name in further promotion. Therefore, the court granted this part of the injunction. The district court found that the defendants had infringed the King copyrights and enjoined all further use of the copyrighted material.

In ruling on the third request for injunction, the court confronted the plaintiffs' claim that the manufacture and sale of the busts violated Dr. King's right of publicity which had passed to his heirs upon Dr. King's death. The defendants contended that no such right existed, and hence, an injunction should not issue. The district court concluded that it was not necessary to determine whether the "right of publicity" was devisable in Georgia because Dr. King did not commercially exploit this right during his lifetime. As found by the district court, the evidence of exploitation by Dr. King came from his sister's affidavit which stated that he had received "thousands of dollars in the form of honorariums from the use of his name, likeness, literary compositions, and speeches." The district court further found that "Dr. King apparently sold his copyrights in several speeches to Motown Records Corporation."

On plaintiffs' appeal of the partial denial of the preliminary injunction, the Eleventh Circuit Court of Appeals has certified the following questions: (1) Is the "right of publicity" recognized in Georgia as a right distinct from the right of privacy? (2) If the answer to question (1) is affirmative, does the "right to publicity" survive the death of its owner? Specifically, is the right inheritable and devisable? (3) If the answer to question (2) is also affirmative, must the owner have commercially exploited the right before it can survive his death? * * * As noted by the Eleventh Circuit, this case raises questions concerning the laws of Georgia as to which there are no controlling precedents directly on point. . . .

The right of publicity may be defined as a celebrity's right to the exclusive use of his or her name and likeness. *Price v. Hal Roach Studios*, 400 F.Supp. 836, 843 (S.D.N.Y. 1975); *Estate of Presley v. Russen*, 513 F.Supp. 1339, 1353 (D.N.J. 1981), and cases cited. The right is most often asserted by or on behalf of professional athletes, comedians, actors and actresses, and other entertainers. This case involves none of those occupations. As is known to all, from 1955 until he was assassinated on April 4, 1968, Dr. King, a Baptist minister by profession, was the foremost leader of the civil rights movement in the United States. He was awarded the Nobel Prize for Peace in 1964. Although not a public official, Dr. King was a public figure, and we deal in this opinion with public figures who are neither public officials nor entertainers. Within this framework, we turn to the questions posed.

1. Is the "right of publicity" recognized in Georgia as a right distinct from the right of privacy?

Georgia has long recognized the right of privacy. Following denial of the existence of the right of privacy in a controversial decision by the New York Court of Appeals in *Roberson v. Rochester Folding Box Co.*, 64 N.E. 442 (N.Y. 1902), the Georgia Supreme Court became the first such court to recognize the right of privacy in *Pavesich v. New England Life Ins. Co.*, 50 S.E. 68 (1905).

In *Pavesich v. New England Life Ins. Co.*, *supra*, the picture of an artist was used without his consent in a newspaper advertisement of the insurance company. Analyzing the right of privacy, this court held: "The publication of a picture of a person, without his consent, as a part of an advertisement, for the purpose of exploiting the publisher's business, is a violation of the right of privacy of the person whose picture is reproduced, and entitles him to recover without proof of special damage." 50 S.E. at 68. If the right to privacy had not been recognized, advertisers could use photographs of private citizens to promote sales and the professional modeling business would not be what it is today.

In the course of its opinion the *Pavesich* court said several things pertinent here. It noted that the commentators on ancient law recognized the right of personal liberty, including the right to exhibit oneself before the public at proper times and places and in a proper manner. As a corollary, the court recognized that the right of personal liberty included the right of a person not to be exhibited before the public, saying: "The right to withdraw from the public gaze at such times as a person may see fit, when his presence in public is not demanded by any rule of law is also embraced within the right of personal liberty. Publicity in one instance and privacy in the other is each guaranteed. If personal liberty embraces the right of publicity, it no less embraces the correlative right of privacy; and this is no new idea in Georgia law." 50 S.E. at 70. * * *

Observing in dicta that the right of privacy in general does not survive the death of the person whose privacy is invaded, the *Pavesich* court said: "While the right of privacy is personal, and may die with the person, we do not desire to be understood as assenting to the proposition that the relatives of the deceased can not, in a proper case, protect the memory of their kinsman, not only from defamation, but also from an invasion into the affairs of his private life after his death. This question is not now involved, but we do not wish anything said to be understood as committing us in any way to the doctrine that against the consent of relatives the private affairs of a deceased person may be published and his picture or statue exhibited." 50 S.E. at 76.

Finding that Pavesich, although an artist, was not recognized as a public figure, the court said: "It is not necessary in this case to hold, nor are we prepared to do so, that the mere fact that a man has become what is called a public character, either by aspiring to public office, or by holding public office, or by exercising a profession which places him before the public, or by engaging in a business which has necessarily a public nature, gives to everyone the right to print and circulate his picture." 50 S.E. at 79–80. Thus, although recognizing the right of privacy, the *Pavesich* court left open the question facing us involving the likeness of a public figure.

The "right of publicity" was first recognized in *Haelan Laboratories v. Topps Chewing Gum*, 202 F.2d 866 (2d Cir. 1953). * * *

In *Palmer v. Schonhorn Enterprises*, 232 A.2d 458 (N.J. Super. Ct. 1967), Arnold Palmer, Gary Player, Doug Sanders and Jack Nicklaus obtained summary judgment against the manufacturer of a golf game which used the golfers' names and short biographies without their consent. Although written as a right of privacy case, much of what was said is applicable to the right of publicity. In its opinion the court said (232 A.2d at 462):

> "It would therefore seem, from a review of the authorities, that although the publication of biographical data of a well-known figure does not per se constitute an invasion of privacy, the use of that same data for the purpose of capitalizing upon the name by using it in connection with a commercial project other than the dissemination of news or articles or biographies does.

> "The names of plaintiffs have become internationally famous, undoubtedly by reason of talent as well as hard work in perfecting it. This is probably true in the cases of most so-called celebrities, who have attained national or international recognition in a particular field of art, science, business or other extraordinary ability. They may not all desire to capitalize upon their names in the commercial field, beyond or apart from that in which they have reached their known excellence. However, because they presently do not should not be justification for others to do so because of the void. They may desire to do it later. It is unfair that one should be permitted to commercialize or exploit or capitalize upon another's name, reputation or accomplishments merely because the owner's accomplishments have been highly publicized."

In *Haelan Laboratories, supra,* the court was concerned with whether a celebrity has the right to the exclusive use of his or her name and likeness. In *Palmer, supra,* the court was concerned with whether a person using the celebrity's name for the user's commercial benefit has the right to do so without authorization. At this point it should be emphasized that we deal here with the unauthorized use of a person's name and likeness for the commercial benefit of the user, not with a city's use of a celebrity's name to denominate a street or school.

The right to publicity is not absolute. In *Hicks v. Casablanca Records,* 464 F.Supp. 426 (S.D.N.Y. 1978), the court held that a fictional novel and movie concerning an unexplained eleven-day disappearance by Agatha Christie, author of numerous mystery novels, were permissible under the first amendment. On the other hand, in *Zacchini v. Scripps-Howard Broadcasting Co.,* 433 U.S. 562 (1977), a television station broadcast on its news program plaintiff's 15-second "human cannonball" flight filmed at a local fair. The Supreme Court held that freedom of the press does not authorize the media to broadcast a performer's entire act without his consent, just as the media could not televise a stage play, prize fight or baseball game without consent. . . . [T]he Court said (433 U.S. at 576): "The rationale for [protecting the right of publicity] is the straight-forward one of preventing unjust enrichment by the theft of good will. No social purpose is served by having the defendant get free some aspect of the plaintiff that would have market value and for which he would normally pay."

The right of publicity was first recognized in Georgia by the Court of Appeals in *Cabaniss v. Hipsley,* 151 S.E.2d 496 (Ga. App. Ct. 1966). There the court held that the plaintiff, an exotic dancer, could recover from the owner of the Atlanta Playboy Club for the unauthorized use of the dancer's misnamed photograph in an entertainment magazine advertising the Playboy Club. Although plaintiff had had her picture taken to promote her performances, she was not performing at the Playboy Club. The court used Dean William Prosser's four-pronged analysis of the right of privacy, saying: "Dean Prosser has analyzed the many privacy cases in an article entitled *Privacy,* published in 48 Calif. L. Rev. 383 (1960), and in reviewing the cases he suggests that the invasion of privacy is in reality a complex of four loosely related torts; that there are four distinct kinds of invasion of four different interests of plaintiff; that there are four disparate torts under a common name. These four torts may be described briefly as: (1) intrusion upon the plaintiff's seclusion or solitude, or into his private affairs; (2) public disclosure of embarrassing private facts about the plaintiff; (3) publicity which places the plaintiff in a false light in the public eye; (4) appropriation, for the defendant's advantage, of the plaintiff's name or likeness." 151 S.E.2d at 499–500. Finding no violation of the first three rights of privacy, the court found a violation of the fourth, saying (*id.*): "Unlike intrusion, disclosure, or false light, appropriation does not require the invasion of something secret, secluded or private pertaining to plaintiff, nor does it involve falsity. It consists of the appropriation, for the defendant's benefit, use or advantage, of the plaintiff's name or likeness. . . . 'The interest protected (in the "appropriation" cases) is not so much a mental as a proprietary one, in the exclusive use of the plaintiff's name and likeness as an aspect of his identity.' Prosser, *supra,* at 406." Although Ms. Hipsley was an entertainer (i.e., a public figure), the court found she was entitled to recover from the Playboy Club (but not from the magazine which published the Club's ad) for the unauthorized use of her photograph.

However the court noted a difference in the damages recoverable in traditional right of privacy cases as opposed to right of publicity cases saying (*id.*): "Recognizing, as we do, the fundamental distinction between causes of action involving injury to feelings, sensibilities or reputation and those involving an appropriation of rights in the nature of property rights for commercial exploitation, it must necessarily follow that there is a fundamental distinction between the two classes of cases in the measure of damages to be applied. In the former class (which we take to include the intrusion, disclosure, and false light aspects of the privacy tort), general damages are recoverable without proof of special damages. *Pavesich v. New England Life Ins. Co., supra.* In the latter class, the measure of damages is the value of the use of the appropriated publicity."* * *

Thus, the courts in Georgia have recognized the rights of private citizens, *Pavesich, supra,* as well as entertainers, *Cabaniss . . . , supra,* not to have their names and photographs used for the financial gain of the user without their consent, where such use is not authorized as an exercise of freedom of the press. We know of no reason why a public figure prominent in religion and civil rights should be entitled to less protection than an exotic dancer or a movie actress. Therefore, we hold that the appropriation of another's name and likeness, whether such likeness be a photograph or sculpture, without consent and for the financial gain of the appropriator is a tort in Georgia, whether the person whose name and likeness is used is a private citizen, entertainer, or as here a public figure who is not a public official.

In *Pavesich, supra,* this right not to have another appropriate one's photograph was denominated the right of privacy; in *Cabaniss v. Hipsley, supra,* it was the right of publicity. Mr. Pavesich was not a public figure; Ms. Hipsley was. We conclude that while private citizens have the right of privacy, public figures have a similar right of publicity, and that the measure of damages to a public figure for violation of his or her right of publicity is the value of the appropriation to the user. *Cabaniss v. Hipsley, supra.* As thus understood the first certified question is answered in the affirmative.

2. Does the "right of publicity" survive the death of its owner (i.e., is the right inheritable and devisable)?

Although the *Pavesich* court expressly did not decide this question, the tenor of that opinion is that the right to privacy at least should be protectable after death. *Pavesich, supra,* 50 S.E. at 76.

The right of publicity is assignable during the life of the celebrity, for without this characteristic, full commercial exploitation of one's name and likeness is practically impossible. *Haelan Laboratories v. Topps Chewing Gum, supra,* 202 F.2d at 868. That is, without assignability the right of publicity could hardly be called a "right." Recognizing its assignability, most commentators have urged that the right of publicity must also be inheritable. Felcher and Rubin, *The Descendibility of the Right of Publicity: Is there Commercial Life After Death?,* 89 Yale L.J. 1125 (1980). . . . The courts that have considered the problem are not as unanimous. In *Price v. Hal Roach Studios, supra,* 400 F.Supp. 836, the court reasoned that since the right of publicity was assignable, it survived the deaths of Stanley Laurel and

Oliver Hardy. Other decisions from the Southern District of New York recognize the descendibility of the right of publicity, which has also been recognized by the Second Circuit Court of Appeals (*infra*).

In *Factors Etc., Inc. v. Pro Arts, Inc.*, 579 F.2d 215 (2d Cir. 1978), Elvis Presley had assigned his right of publicity to Boxcar Enterprises, which assigned that right to Factors after Presley's death. Defendant Pro Arts published a poster of Presley entitled "In Memory." In affirming the grant of injunction against Pro Arts, the Second Circuit Court of Appeals said (579 F.2d at 221): "The identification of this exclusive right belonging to Boxcar as a transferable property right compels the conclusion that the right survives Presley's death. The death of Presley, who was merely the beneficiary of an income interest in Boxcar's exclusive right, should not in itself extinguish Boxcar's property right. Instead, the income interest, continually produced from Boxcar's exclusive right of commercial exploitation, should inure to Presley's estate at death like any other intangible property right. To hold that the right did not survive Presley's death, would be to grant competitors of Factors, such as Pro Arts, a windfall in the form of profits from the use of Presley's name and likeness. At the same time, the exclusive right purchased by Factors and the financial benefits accruing to the celebrity's heirs would be rendered virtually worthless."

In *Lugosi v. Universal Pictures*, 603 P.2d 425 (Cal. 1979), the Supreme Court of California, in a 4 to 3 decision, declared that the right of publicity expires upon the death of the celebrity and is not descendible. . . . Bela Lugosi appeared as Dracula in Universal Picture's movie by that name. Universal had acquired the movie rights to the novel by Bram Stoker. * * * The majority of the court held that Lugosi's heirs could not prevent Universal's continued exploitation of Lugosi's portrayal of Count Dracula after his death. The court did not decide whether Universal could prevent unauthorized third parties from exploitation of Lugosi's appearance as Dracula after Lugosi's death.

In *Memphis Development Foundation v. Factors Etc., Inc.*, 616 F.2d 956 (6th Cir. 1980), Factors, which had won its case against Pro Arts in New York (see above), lost against the Memphis Development Foundation under the Court of Appeals for the Sixth Circuit's interpretation of Tennessee law. There, the Foundation, a non-profit corporation, planned to erect a statue of Elvis Presley in Memphis and solicited contributions to do so. Donors of $25 or more received a small replica of the proposed statue. The Sixth Circuit reversed the grant of an injunction favoring Factors, holding that a celebrity's right of publicity was not inheritable even where that right had been exploited during the celebrity's life. The court reasoned that although recognition of the right of publicity during life serves to encourage effort and inspire creative endeavors, making the right inheritable would not. The court also was concerned with unanswered legal questions which recognizing inheritability would create. We note, however, that the court was dealing with a non-profit foundation attempting to promote Presley's adopted home place, the City of Memphis. The court was not dealing, as we do here, with a profit making endeavor.

In *Estate of Presley v. Russen, supra*, 513 F.Supp. 1339, the court found in favor of descendibility, quoting from Chief Justice Bird's dissent in *Lugosi v. Universal Pictures, supra*, 603 P.2d at 434, and saying: "If the right is descendible, the individual is able to transfer the benefits of his labor to his immediate successors and is assured that control over the exercise of the right can be vested in a suitable beneficiary. 'There is no reason why, upon a celebrity's death, advertisers should receive a windfall in the form of freedom to use with impunity the name or likeness of the deceased celebrity who may have worked his or her entire life to attain celebrity status. The financial benefits of that labor should go to the celebrity's heirs. . . .' " 513 F.Supp. at 1355.

For the reasons which follow we hold that the right of publicity survives the death of its owner and is inheritable and devisable. Recognition of the right of publicity rewards and thereby encourages effort and creativity. If the right of publicity dies with the celebrity, the economic value of the right of publicity during life would be diminished because the celebrity's untimely death would seriously impair, if not destroy, the value of the right of continued commercial use. Conversely, those who would profit from the fame of a celebrity after his or her death for their own benefit and without authorization have failed to establish their claim that they should be the beneficiaries of the celebrity's death. Finally, the trend since the early common law has been to recognize survivability, notwithstanding the legal problems which may thereby arise. We therefore answer question 2 in the affirmative.

3. Must the owner of the right of publicity have commercially exploited that right before it can survive?

Exploitation is understood to mean commercial use by the celebrity other than the activity which made him or her famous, e.g., an inter vivos transfer of the right to the use of one's name and likeness.

The requirement that the right of publicity be exploited by the celebrity during his or her lifetime in order to render the right inheritable arises from the case involving Agatha Christie, *Hicks v. Casablanca Records, supra,* 464 F.Supp. at 429. The *Hicks* court cited [cases in which the requirement was dicta — Eds.]. Moreover, the *Hicks* court held that the fictional account of Agatha Christie's 11-day disappearance was protected by the first amendment. Thus, the finding that exploitation during life was necessary to inheritability was actually unnecessary to that decision. Nevertheless, the *Hicks* dicta has been relied upon. See *Groucho Marx Productions v. Day & Night Co.,* 523 F.Supp. 485, 490 (S.D.N.Y. 1981). However, in this case, involving the Marx brothers, it was found that, although Leo and Adolpho Marx ("Chico" and "Harpo") had not made inter vivos or specific testamentary dispositions of their rights, they had earned their livelihoods by exploiting the unique characters they created and thus had exploited their rights to publicity so as to make such rights descendible. Thus, even in the Southern District of New York where the requirement arose, exploitation beyond the "activity which made him or her famous" is not now required.

The cases which have considered this issue, see above, involved entertainers. The net result of following them would be to say that celebrities and public figures have the right of publicity during their lifetimes (as others have the right of privacy), but only those who contract for bubble gum cards, posters and tee shirts have a descendible right of publicity upon their deaths. That we should single out for protection after death those entertainers and athletes who exploit their personae during life, and deny protection after death to those who enjoy public acclamation but did not exploit themselves during life, puts a premium on exploitation. Having found that there are valid reasons for recognizing the right of publicity during life, we find no reason to protect after death only those who took commercial advantage of their fame.

Perhaps this case more than others brings the point into focus. A well known minister may avoid exploiting his prominence during life because to do otherwise would impair his ministry. Should his election not to take commercial advantage of his position during life ipso facto result in permitting others to exploit his name and likeness after his death? In our view, a person who avoids exploitation during life is entitled to have his image protected against exploitation after death just as much if not more than a person who exploited his image during life. Without doubt, Dr. King could have exploited his name and likeness during his lifetime. That this opportunity was not appealing to him does not mean that others have the right to use his name and likeness in ways he himself chose not to do. Nor does it strip his family and estate of the right to control, preserve and extend his status and memory and to prevent unauthorized exploitation thereof by others. Here, they seek to prevent the exploitation of his likeness in a manner they consider unflattering and unfitting. We cannot deny them this right merely because Dr. King chose not to exploit or commercialize himself during his lifetime. Question 3 is answered in the negative. . . .

NOTES

1. One of the elements of the right of publicity created in this opinion is that the defendant obtain some financial gain from the use of the likeness. In what situations without financial gain might the right still be worth protecting? See *Parks v. LaFace Records*, 329 F.3d 437 (6th Cir. 2003) (protecting civil rights activist Rosa Parks' right to publicity when her name was the title of a rap song); and see generally George Smith, *The Extent of Protection of the Individual's Personality against Commercial Use: Toward a New Property Right*, 54 S.C. L. Rev. 1 (2002).

2. The descendibility of the right of publicity was the issue that galvanized many state legislatures into action. For example, the Tennessee legislature codified the right in 1984. See David Bodette, *Use It (Every Two Years), or Lose It (Forever) — Tennessee's Personal Rights Protection Act and the Post-Mortem Right of Publicity*, 33 U. Mem. L. Rev. 83 (2002). Under its statute, the right is descendible for ten years after a celebrity's death, during which time it must be used or exploited in some way, and thereafter, once used or exploited, it extends perpetually unless it has not been used for two years. *Id.* at 84–85. The most usual statutory treatment of the right is to limit it to a term of years, ranging between 20 and 100 years after the person's death. *Id.* at 99, n. 103 (listing state statutes). California's statutory right lasts 70 years. Cal. Civ. Code § 3344.1(h). What is the effect of requiring that heirs use or exploit the right? What would have been its effect if it controlled the *Martin Luther King Jr. Center* case?

3. *Swidler & Berlin v. United States*, 524 U.S. 399 (1998), held that attorneys may not release communications with clients subject to the attorney-client privilege, even after the clients' deaths. Is this case (belatedly) relevant to the issue in the *King Center* case? And if an action for defamation is personal and dies with a plaintiff, shouldn't a publicity right die as well? See William Binder, *Publicity Rights and Defamation of the Deceased: Resurrection or R.I.P.?*, 12 J. Art & Ent. Law 297 (2002).

4. What is today descendible, may tomorrow be bankable. What problems would you foresee making a right of publicity the subject of an assignment, a mortgage or other security instrument, an asset in a bankrupt's estate, or marital property subject to a divorce proceeding? If a right can last a century, as under California's Civ. Code § 3344, op. cit., would a registry of such rights facilitate their use? At what cost? See generally Melissa Jacoby & Diane Zimmerman, *Foreclosing on Fame: Exploring the Uncharted Boundaries of the Right of Publicity*, 77 N.Y.U. L. Rev. 1322 (2002).

STEPHANO v. NEWS GROUP PUBLICATIONS, INC.
474 N.E.2d 580 (N.Y. 1984)

WACHTLER, J.

The plaintiff, a professional model, claims that the defendant used his picture for trade or advertising purposes without his consent, and thus violated his statutory right to privacy (Civil Rights Law, § 51) by publishing a picture of him modeling a "bomber jacket" in a magazine article containing information regarding the approximate price of the jacket, the name of the designer, and the names of three stores where the jacket might be purchased. Plaintiff also claims that the defendant's conduct violated a common-law right of publicity. The trial court granted summary judgment to the defendant concluding that the article reported a newsworthy event of fashion news, and was not published for trade or advertising purposes. A divided Appellate Division reversed and denied summary judgment finding that factual questions were presented as to whether the defendant had used the plaintiff's picture for trade purposes and whether the article constituted an advertisement in disguise. The defendant has appealed by leave of the Appellate Division which certified a question as to the correctness of its order.

In the summer of 1981 the plaintiff agreed to model for an article on men's fall fashions. The photographic session took place on August 11, 1981. The defendant used two of the photographs taken during that session to illustrate an article entitled "Classic Mixes", which appeared under the heading "Fall Fashions" in the September 7, 1981 issue of New York magazine. Another photograph taken during the session was used, a week earlier, in the August 31, 1981 issue of New York magazine, in a column entitled "Best Bets". That column, a regular feature in the magazine, contains information about new and unusual products and services available in the metropolitan area. One of the items included in the August 31 column was a bomber jacket modeled by the plaintiff. The text above the picture states: "Yes Giorgio — From Giorgio Armani. Based on his now classic turn on the bomber jacket, this cotton-twill version with 'fun fur' collar features the same cut at a far lower price — about $225. It'll be available in the stores next week. — Henry Post Bomber Jacket/Barney's, Bergdorf Goodman, Bloomingdale's."

It is the plaintiff's contention that he agreed to model for one article only-the September 7, 1981 article on Fall Fashions-and that the defendant violated his rights by publishing his photograph in the August 31 "Best Bets" column. The complaint alleges two causes of action. First the plaintiff claims that the defendant violated his civil rights by using his photograph for trade or advertising purposes without his consent. In his second cause of action the plaintiff claims that the defendant's conduct "invaded plaintiff's right of publicity". On each cause of action the plaintiff seeks $350,000 in compensatory damages and an equal amount in exemplary damages.

The defendant's answer asserts several affirmative defenses. The primary defense is that the photograph and article relating to it involve matters of legitimate public interest and concern and thus do not violate the plaintiff's rights under the Civil Rights Law (§§ 50, 51), or any common-law right of publicity. The defendant also urged that the second cause of action, for invasion of the plaintiff's right of publicity, does not set forth a claim "separate and distinct" from the first cause of action. * * * In the motion for summary judgment the defendant urged that the complaint should be dismissed because the plaintiff's photograph was not published for trade or advertising purposes. * * *

The trial court granted summary judgment to the defendant concluding, on the basis of the exhibits submitted, that the bomber jacket item was a "newsworthy observation" and was not published for advertising or trade purposes within the contemplation of the statute. The court also held that the inclusion of information concerning the availability of the jacket at certain stores, which currently advertised in the magazine, was not sufficient to sustain the claim that the item had been published for trade or advertising purposes "without a further showing of benefit to defendant".

The Appellate Division reversed and denied the defendant's motion for summary judgment. * * * Finding that the "form and presentation" of both articles were identical the majority held that a reasonable person could conclude that the August 31 article was also used for trade purposes. "The real question", the majority stated, "is whether the public interest aspect of the August 31, 1981 article is merely incidental to its commercial purpose". The majority held that it "is also possible that this article constituted an advertisement in disguise since many of the magazine's advertisers were mentioned in the copy." We now reverse.

Section 50 of the Civil Rights Law prohibits the use of "the name, portrait or picture of any living person" for advertising or trade purposes without the person's consent and declares a violation of the statute to be a misdemeanor. Section 51 of the statute provides civil remedies, including injunctive relief, compensatory damages and, if the defendant acted knowingly, exemplary damages.

The statutes have their origin in this court's 1902 decision in *Roberson v. Rochester Folding Box Co.* (171 NY 538). In that case it was held that a young woman whose picture had been used by the defendant on flour advertisements without her consent could not recover for a violation of her right to privacy because no such right was recognized at common law. The Legislature responded the following year by amending the Civil Rights Law to establish a statutory "right to privacy" (citation omitted). Since the adoption of the statutes, this court has repeatedly held that the right of privacy is governed entirely by statute in this State [*Arrington v. New York Times Co.*, 55 NY2d 433 (further citations omitted)].

Section 51 of the Civil Rights Law has been applied in cases, such as the *Roberson* case, where the picture of a person who has apparently never sought publicity has been used without his or her consent for trade or advertising purposes (see, e.g., . . . *Flores v. Mosler Safe Co.*, 7 NY2d 276). In such cases it has been noted that the statute serves "to protect the sentiments, thoughts and feelings of an individual" (*Flores v. Mosler Safe Co.*, *supra*, p 280).

This history has led some courts to conclude that the statutory right to privacy is limited to the type of case which originally prompted its enactment and thus would not preclude the recognition in this State of a common-law "right of publicity" in cases where the defendant has exploited, without consent, and usually without payment, the name, picture, or portrait of an individual who has consciously sought to establish a publicity value for his personality (see, e.g., *Haelan Labs. v. Topps Chewing Gum*, 202 F2d 866, 868; *Factors Etc. v. Pro Arts*, 579 F2d 215). The statute, however, is not limited to situations where the defendant's conduct has caused distress to a person who wishes to lead a private life free of all commercial publicity.

By its terms the statute applies to any use of a person's picture or portrait for advertising or trade purposes whenever the defendant has not obtained the person's written consent to do so. It would therefore apply, and recently has been held to apply, in cases where the plaintiff generally seeks publicity, or uses his name, portrait, or picture, for commercial purposes but has not given written consent for a particular use (*Welch v. Mr. Christmas*, 57 NY2d 143). Thus where the written consent to use the plaintiff's name or picture for advertising or trade purposes has expired or the defendant has otherwise exceeded the limitations of the consent, the plaintiff may seek damages or other relief under the statute, even though he might properly sue for breach of contract. The right which the statute permits the plaintiff to vindicate in such a case may, perhaps, more accurately be described as a right of publicity (citation omitted). In this respect the statute parallels the common-law right of privacy which generally provides remedies for any commercialization of the individual's personality without his consent [see Prosser, *Privacy*, 48 Cal L Rev 383, 403; (further citations omitted)]. Since the "right of publicity" is encompassed under the Civil Rights Law as an aspect of the right of privacy, which, as noted, is exclusively statutory in this State, the plaintiff cannot claim an independent common-law right of publicity.

The only question then is whether the defendant used the plaintiff's picture for trade or advertising purposes within the meaning of the statute when it published his picture in the "Best Bets" column without his consent.

The statute does not define trade or advertising purposes. However, the courts have consistently held, from the time of its enactment, that these terms should not be construed to apply to publications concerning newsworthy events or matters of public interest (*Binns v. Vitagraph Co.*, 210 NY 51, 52 . . . ; *Pagan v. New York Herald Tribune*, 32 AD2d 341, affd 26 NY2d 941). The exception reflects Federal and State constitutional concerns for free dissemination of news and other matters of interest to the public, but essentially requires an interpretation of the statute to give effect to the legislative intent (citations omitted). We have recently noted that this exception should be liberally applied (*Arrington v. New York Times Co.*, *supra*, p 440).

The newsworthiness exception applies not only to reports of political happenings and social trends, but also to news stories and articles of consumer interest including developments in the fashion world (*Pagan v. New York Herald Tribune*, *supra*). Nevertheless, the plaintiff contends that the photograph in this case did not depict a newsworthy event because it is a posed picture of a professional model taken at a photographic session staged by the defendant. However, the event or matter of public interest which the defendant seeks to convey is not the model's performance, but the availability of the clothing item displayed. A fashion display is, of necessity, posed and arranged. Obviously the picture of the jacket does not lose its newsworthiness simply because the defendant chose to employ a person to model it in a controlled or contrived setting.

The fact that the defendant may have included this item in its column solely or primarily to increase the circulation of its magazine and therefore its profits, as the Appellate Division suggested, does not mean that the defendant has used the plaintiff's picture for trade purposes within the meaning of the statute. Indeed, most publications seek to increase their circulation and also their profits. It is the content of the article and not the defendant's motive or primary motive to increase circulation which determines whether it is a newsworthy item, as opposed to a trade usage, under the Civil Rights Law (*Arrington v. New York Times Co.*, *supra*, p 440).
* * *

The plaintiff's primary contention is that his picture was used for advertising purposes within the meaning of the statute. Although the article was not presented to the public as an advertisement, and was published in a column generally devoted to newsworthy items, the plaintiff claims that it is in fact an advertisement in disguise. In addition, although the defendant has submitted affidavits that the article was published solely as a matter of public interest, without any consideration for advertising concerns, and that the magazine received no payment for including the item in its "Best Bets" column, the plaintiff nevertheless contends that he has presented sufficient facts to require a trial on the issue.

The facts on which the plaintiff relies are entirely circumstantial. He does not claim to have personal knowledge, or direct proof, that this particular article was actually published by the defendant for advertisement purposes. The circumstances on which he bases his claim are (1) the fact that the news column contains information normally included in an advertisement identifying the designer of the jacket, the approximate price, and three places where the jacket may be purchased, and (2) the fact that some or all of those stores mentioned in the article had previously advertised products in the magazine. Those circumstances are not enough to raise a jury question as to whether the article was published for advertising purposes.

The plaintiff does not dispute the fact that the information provided in the article is of legitimate reader interest. * * * In short, the plaintiff has not presented any facts which would set this particular article apart from the numerous other legitimate news items concerning new products. He offers only his speculative belief that in this case the information on the jacket was included in the defendant's column for advertising purposes or perhaps, more vaguely, to promote additional advertising. That, in our view, is insufficient to defeat the defendant's motion for summary judgment. The rule exempting articles of public interest from the operation of the Civil Rights Law would, as a practical matter, lose much of its force if publishers of articles which are at least prima facie newsworthy were required to incur the expense of a trial to meet such general and insubstantial accusations of disguised advertising. . . .

Finally, it should be emphasized that we do not mean to suggest that a publisher who has employed a professional model to pose for pictures to be used in an article may avoid the agreed fee, or otherwise ignore contractual arrangements, if the model's pictures are used to illustrate a newsworthy article or one involving matters of public interest. Although the complaint alludes to an agreement between the parties, the plaintiff has not sought to enforce a contract or recover damages for a breach. Since the plaintiff chose to frame his complaint entirely in terms of rights covered by the Civil Rights Law, which we have concluded is not applicable in this case, the complaint should be dismissed. Accordingly, the order of the Appellate Division should be reversed, the complaint dismissed and the certified question answered in the negative.

NOTES

1. Does this case square with *Haelan Laboratories*? Judge Frank's *Haelan Laboratories* opinion, and the right recognized therein, was overruled by another federal court 37 years later. See *Pirone v. MacMillan*, 894 F.2d 579 (2d Cir. 1990) (holding that N.Y. law did not contain an independent right of publicity permitting the daughter of Babe Ruth to enjoin a publisher from using her father's photograph without authority, and citing *Stephano*).

2. There is no doctrine of fair use in right of publicity law, as there is in copyright law. Should there be? Famous people are likely to have docudramas made about their lives and in the course of these, some scenes may be shaped to fit the drama as much as the facts. Or secondary characters may be presented as they appeared to shape the primary characters' life, not as they were. See Matthew Stohl, *False Light Invasion of Privacy in Docudramas: The Oxymoron Which Must be Solved*, 35 Akron L. Rev. 251 (2002).

3. A claim for infringement of the right may be pre-empted by federal copyright law when the likeness has been copyrighted-for example, as with an actor's performance in a copyrighted movie. See, e.g., *Fleet v. CBS, Inc.*, 58 Cal. Rptr. 2d 645 (Cal. Ct. App. 1996), and the following.

WENDT v. HOST INTERNATIONAL, INC.
197 F.3d 1284 (9th Cir. 1999)

ORDER.

The panel has voted to deny the petition for rehearing. * * * The petition for rehearing is denied and the petition for rehearing en banc is rejected.

KOZINSKI, J., . . . dissenting from the order rejecting a rehearing en banc.

Robots again. In *White v. Samsung Elecs. Am., Inc.*, 971 F.2d 1395, 1399 (9th Cir. 1992), we held that the right of publicity extends not just to the name, likeness, voice and signature of a famous person, but to anything at all that evokes that person's identity. The plaintiff there was Vanna White, Wheel of Fortune letter-turner extraordinaire; the offending robot stood next to a letter board, decked out in a blonde wig, Vanna-style gown and garish jewelry. Dissenting from our failure to take the case en banc, I argued that our broad application of the right of publicity put state law on a collision course with the federal rights of the copyright holder. See 989 F.2d 1512, 1517–18 (9th Cir. 1993). The conflict in *White* was hypothetical, since the defendant (Samsung) did not have a license from the Wheel of Fortune copyright holder. Here it is concrete: The panel holds that licensed animatronic figures based on the copyrighted Cheers characters Norm and Cliff infringe on the rights of the actors who portrayed them. As I predicted, *White*'s voracious logic swallows up rights conferred by Congress under the Copyright Act.

I.

Though a bit dated now, Cheers remains near and dear to the hearts of many TV viewers. Set in a friendly neighborhood bar in Boston, the show revolved around a familiar scene. Sam, the owner and bartender, entertained the boys with tales of his glory days pitching for the Red Sox. Coach piped in with sincere, obtuse advice. Diane and Frasier chattered self-importantly about Lord Byron. Carla terrorized patrons with acerbic comments. And there were Norm and Cliff, the two characters at issue here. Norm, a fat, endearing, oft-unemployed accountant, parked himself at the corner of the bar, where he was joined by Cliff, a dweebish mailman and something of a know-it-all windbag. After eleven years on the air, the gang at Cheers became like family to many fans, ensuring many more years in syndication.

Defendant Host International decided to tap into this keg of goodwill. After securing a license from Paramount, the copyright holder, Host opened a line of Cheers airport bars. To help get patrons into a Cheers mood, Host populated the bars with animatronic figures resembling Norm and Cliff: One is fat; the other is dressed as a mailman.

Plaintiffs George Wendt and John Ratzenberger, the only actors who ever portrayed Norm and Cliff, sued Host for unfair competition and violation of their right of publicity. Paramount intervened, claiming that its copyright preempted any claim Wendt and Ratzenberger might have under state law. The district court granted summary judgment for the defendants because it found that the robots didn't look like the plaintiffs: "There is [no] similarity at all . . . except that one of the robots, like one of the plaintiffs, is heavier than the other. . . . The facial features are totally different." Relying on *White*, the panel here reverses but offers little explanation beyond the curt assertion that "material facts exist that might cause a reasonable jury to find [the robots] sufficiently 'like' [Wendt and Ratzenberger] to violate" their right of publicity.

II.

This case, unlike *White*, pits actor against copyright holder. The parties are fighting over the same bundle of intellectual property rights — the right to make dramatic representations of the characters Norm and Cliff. Host and Paramount assert their right under the Copyright Act to present the Cheers characters in airport bars; Wendt and Ratzenberger assert their right under California law to control the exploitation of their likenesses. But to millions of viewers, Wendt and Ratzenberger are Norm and Cliff; it's impossible to exploit the latter without also evoking thoughts about the former.

So who wins? The Copyright Act makes it simple, at least insofar as the plaintiffs interfere with Paramount's right to exploit the Cheers characters. Section 301 of the Copyright Act preempts any state law "legal or equitable rights that are equivalent to any of the exclusive rights within the general scope of copyright[.]" 17 U.S.C. § 301(a). The copyright to Cheers carries with it the right to make derivative works based on its characters. See generally *Warner Bros., Inc. v. American Broadcasting Cos.*, 720 F.2d 231, 235 (2d Cir. 1983) (Superman copyright belongs to Warner Brothers). The presentation of the robots in the Cheers bars is a derivative work, just like a TV clip, promotion, photograph, poster, sequel or dramatic rendering of an episode. Thus, under federal law, Host has the unconditional right to present robots that resemble Norm and Cliff.

Instead, the panel allows the plaintiffs to pick up where Vanna left off: Copyright or no copyright, anyone who wants to use a figure, statue, robot, drawing or poster that reminds the public of Wendt and Ratzenberger must first obtain (and pay for) their consent. This cannot be squared with the right of the copyright holder to recreate Norm and Cliff however it sees fit. At the very least, Paramount must be able to reproduce the characteristics that bring Norm and Cliff to mind.

The problem lies with the sweeping standard we adopted in *White*. The right of publicity, as defined by the state courts, is limited to using a celebrity's name, voice, face or signature. See, e.g., *Stephano v. News Group Publications, Inc.*, 474 N.E.2d 580, 583–84 (N.Y. 1984) (finding right of publicity under New York law limited to statutory protection of "name, portrait or picture"); *Lugosi v. Universal Pictures*, 25 Cal. 3d 813, 828, 603 P.2d 425 (Cal. 1979) (Mosk, J., concurring). . . . A copyright holder can generally avoid using any of these tangible elements in exploiting its copyright. *White* exploded the right of publicity to include anything that brings the celebrity to mind. See *White*, 971 F.2d at 1399. It's inevitable that so broad and ill-defined a property right will trench on the rights of the copyright holder. According to the panel, Paramount and Host may not use Norm and Cliff in a way that reminds people of the actors who played them and whose identity is therefore fused in the public mind. This is a daunting burden. Can Warner Brothers exploit Rhett Butler without also reminding people of Clark Gable? Can Paramount cast Shelley Long in The Brady Bunch Movie without creating a triable issue of fact as to whether it is treading on Florence Henderson's right of publicity? How about Dracula and Bela Lugosi? Ripley and Sigourney Weaver? Kramer and Michael Richards?

When portraying a character who was portrayed by an actor, it is impossible to recreate the character without evoking the image of the actor in the minds of viewers. Suppose the Seinfeld minions create a spin-off called Kramer. One of the Seinfeld characters was Newman, a fat mailman. Suppose Wayne Knight — the actor who played Newman — won't do Kramer. So Kramer brings in someone else to play Newman, a corpulent actor who (when dressed as a mailman) reminds people of Wayne Knight. What happens when Knight sues? Under *White* and the panel decision here, Knight can go to trial on a claim that the new Newman evokes his (Knight's) identity, even though Castle Rock owns the rights to make derivative works based on Seinfeld. It would be no defense that everyone knows the new actor is not Wayne Knight; no one, after all, thinks the robots here or in *White* were, in fact, Wendt, Ratzenberger or White. So long as the casting director comes up with a new Newman who reminds the public of the old Newman (i.e. Knight), Knight has a right-of-publicity claim that will at least survive summary judgment. Under the unbounded right of publicity announced in *White*, copyright holders will seldom be able to avoid trial when sued for infringement of the right to publicity. Remember Vanna: Even though the robot looked nothing like her, a jury awarded her $400,000.

III.

The panel's refusal to recognize copyright preemption puts us in conflict with the Seventh Circuit in *Baltimore Orioles, Inc. v. Major League Baseball Players Ass'n*, 805 F.2d 663 (7th Cir. 1986). *Baltimore Orioles* held that the baseball clubs — not the players — own the rights to baseball telecasts under copyright law, and the players can't use their state law right of publicity to veto the telecast of their performance. This was so even though the telecast (obviously) used the players' identities and likenesses.

The Seventh Circuit acknowledged that the state law right of publicity gave the players a property interest in their actual performances, see *Zacchini v. Scripps-Howard Broadcasting Co.*, 433 U.S. 562 (1977), but held that this right could not trump the Clubs' right under the Copyright Act to control the telecast. See 805 F.2d at 678–79. * * * The plaintiffs' right to control the use of their likeness is preempted by Paramount's right to exploit the Norm and Cliff characters however it sees fit. If Wendt and Ratzenberger wanted to control how the Cheers characters were portrayed after they left the show, they should have negotiated for it beforehand.

IV.

Coming home to roost is yet another problem I warned about in *White* — that a broad reading of the state right of publicity runs afoul of the dormant Copyright Clause, which preempts state intellectual property laws to the extent they "prejudice the interests of other States." *Goldstein v. California*, 412 U.S. 546, 558 (1973). Just as a state law regulating the length of trucks is invalid under the dormant Commerce Clause if it poses an undue burden on interstate commerce . . . , so California's right of publicity law is invalid if it substantially interferes with federal copyright law, even absent preemptive legislation.

A copyright licensee must be able to exercise rights which are inherently federal in nature without worrying that 50 separate states will burden those rights. This is most obviously true when state law restricts the display of derivative works outside the borders of its state. Compare *Goldstein*, 412 U.S. at 558. Yet that is exactly what the panel approves here: Plaintiffs are using California law to stop Host from displaying a copyrighted work in Kansas City and Cleveland. Why California should set the national standard for what is a permissible use of a licensed derivative work is beyond me. Rather than construe the right of publicity narrowly to avoid this constitutional conundrum . . . , the panel compounds *White*'s errors by enforcing California's right of publicity way beyond California's borders. * * * As I noted in *White*, "No California statute, no California court has actually tried to reach this far. It is ironic that it is we who plant this kudzu in the fertile soil of our federal system." 989 F.2d at 1519. We pass up yet another opportunity to root out this weed. Instead, we feed it Miracle-Gro. I dissent.

NOTES

1. Is there a distinction between granting the actors who played Norm and Cliff a right of publicity in their fictional persona, and permitting a claim based on the commercial appropriation of their likeness? If artists have moral rights, then do Norm and Cliff have performance rights? See Michael Albano, *Nothing to "Cheer" About: A Call for Reform of the Right of Publicity in Audiovisual Characters*, 90 Geo. L.J. 253 (2001).

2. In the movie "Tootsie" Dustin Hoffman posed as a female. Using a picture of Hoffman's face as he appeared, dressed as a woman in the movie, a magazine publisher generated an unauthorized, computer digitalized picture of Hoffman with the body of a model wearing trademarked clothes he never wore in the movie. The picture was part of a feature called "Grand Illusions" and the caption under Hoffman's likeness was "Dustin Hoffman isn't a drag in a butter-colored silk gown by Richard Tyler and Ralph Lauren heels." Has Hoffman's right of publicity been violated? See *Hoffman v. Capital Cities/ABC, Inc.*, 33 F. Supp. 2d 867, reversed 255 F.3d 1180 (9th Cir. 2001), noted at 17 Berkeley Tech. L.J. 527 (2002).

V. TRADEMARKS

A trademark is a word or phrase that is used to distinguish a business, goods, or services in the marketplace. It may also be a symbol accomplishing the same end, but the distinction between a word, phrase or symbol is not critical to the law of trademarks. For example, the name of a corporation may be regarded as either a tradename or a trademark. The former is affixed to a business' operations or good will, the latter to its saleable goods. Both are protected by the law from use that is likely to cause confusion among consumers, even if the infringing use is non-competitive. Consumer confusion, not competition, is its core principal. From the consumer's perspective, a trademark saves the time and trouble it would take to study its holder's goods; it is thus a shortcut and a proxy for recognizing their quality. Trademark law thus has much to do with holders and consumers' interests in commerce; for that reason, it is, among the many types of intellectual property, the least property-oriented. See, e.g., *Mattel, Inc. v. MCA Records, Inc.*, 296 F.3d 894 (9th Cir. 2002) (holding that the song "Barbie Girl" by Abba, is not an infringement of Mattel's trademark in its doll and that for artistic works, infringement is found only where consumer confusion outweighs the interests of free expression, either by mockery or just to gain attention, so long as the public is not misled or told the holder produced the work). See also *Rogers v. Grimaldi*, 875 F.2d 994, 999 (2d Cir. 1989).

In order to sue an unauthorized user for infringement, the holder of the trademark must show: (1) its validity — that the public recognizes and uses it both to identify the plaintiff's business and to distinguish plaintiff from others; and (2) its infringement — that the defendant's action will likely cause confusion among consumers. Trademarks receive protection from state law. See *Alderman v. Alaska Guesttours, Inc.*, 32 P.3d 373 (Alaska 2001). As to trademarks used in interstate commerce, a stronger source of protection is federal law. See the Lanham Act, 15 U.S.C. §§ 1051–1129 (2003).

As to the first showing, of validity, an infringed mark can be shown either (a) to be inherently distinctive (that is, it can be arbitrary, fanciful, or suggestive, being altogether novel in some way) or (b) to have acquired a secondary meaning (that is, a mental association developed over time in consumers' minds between the mark and a single business, the plaintiff's). It is secondary just because its first meaning was the general understanding of the word, but out of this first meaning developed, over time, an association with the plaintiff's business as the unique source of goods. The actual name of a good or service is not protected, because it is not distinctive in either of the two ways just discussed. Personal names are considered inherently non-distinctive and gain protection only through their secondary meaning. See *L.E. Waterman v. Modern Pen Co.*, 235 U.S. 88, 94 (1914) (Holmes, J.).

As to the second showing, of infringement, the test is a "likelihood of confusion." Likely confusion is probable confusion. Confusion is a broad concept — pre-sale, post-sale, and point of sale confusion will all qualify. The test requires that an appreciable number, but not necessarily a majority or even a precise number, of consumers be confused. "Consumers" means both customers and potential customers.

Infringement claims have been made for "trade dress," the design and appearance of a product that make up its overall image presented to the consumer. Trade dress is a "device" or "symbol" for Lanham Act purposes. See *Best Cellars, Inc. v. Wine Made Simple, Inc.*, 2003 U.S. Dist. LEXIS 3958 (S.D.N.Y., Mar. 14, 2003) (concerning the interior design and product arrangement in a wine store and interpreting 15 U.S.C. § 1125(a), § 43(a) of the Lanham Act). Infringement actions are expensive. They typically require survey and marketing evidence. A trademark's use is encouraged because of the goodwill associated with it, but negative connotations can also be useful to consumers wishing to avoid some goods or services. Owners of trademarks having negative connotations will often seek to disassociate themselves with the mark, through bankruptcy or other proceedings. Should this be possible? See Note, *Badwill*, 116 Harv. L. Rev. 1845 (2003).

A federal trademark may also be the subject of an action for "dilution." See, e.g., 15 U.S.C. § 1525(c). Some state statutes have provided a similar action starting in the 1940s. Examples of trademark dilution would be Steinway aspirin, Buick shoes, or Kodak pianos. See Thomas McCarthy, *McCarthy on Trademarks and Unfair Competition* § 24.67 at 24-120; § 24.70 at 24-122 (2001). Dilution protects trademark owners from free riders on the substantial investment that they have made in their marks. See *I.P. Lund Trading ApS v. Kohler Co.*, 163 F.3d 27, 50 (1st Cir. 1998). In 1996 Congress amended the Lanham Act by protecting "the owner of a famous mark . . . against another person's commercial use in commerce of a mark or trade name, if such use begins after the mark has become famous and causes dilution of the distinctive quality of the mark." 15 U.S.C. § 125(c). See *Nabisco, Inc. v. PF Brands, Inc.*, 191 F.3d 208, 214–17 (2d Cir. 1999) (protecting the Pepperridge Farm Goldfish cracker against dilution); *Moseley v. V Secret Catalogue*, 537 U.S. 418 (2003) (holding that trademark owners were required to prove actual dilution, not merely a likelihood of dilution, that there was no such proof in this case sufficient to support the summary judgment issued below, and that difficulties in obtaining proof of actual dilution was not a reason for dispensing with this higher standard).

A trademark may not be infringed without being used first in time. If a trademark is distinctive, the first or senior user has priority of use, but for non-distinctive marks, priority is gained when the mark first achieves a secondary meaning. In an infringement action, this rule might require that a plaintiff show that it won the race to achieve that meaning. In practice, a plaintiff need only show the existence of the secondary meaning at the time and place that the defendant or junior user first began to use the mark. See *PaperCutter, Inc. v. Fay's Drug Co.*, 900 F.2d 558, 564 (2d Cir. 1990). To avoid priority issues from arising, a federal trademark may, but need not be, registered, unless it is immoral, deceptive, scandalous, or confusingly similar to a mark already in use. The registration is good for 10 years, and is renewable so long as the mark remains in use. See 15 U.S.C. § 1052(a)–(d).

15 U.S.C. § 1060(4) provides: "An assignment shall be void against any subsequent purchaser for valuable consideration without notice, unless [it] is recorded in the United State Patent and Trade Office within 3 months after the date of the assignment or prior to the subsequent purchase." What type of recording act is this? Would mortgagees of a trademark be protected as subsequent purchasers, or is this statute only meant to protect assigned users of the mark? Compare this statute with 35 U.S.C. § 261 para. 4 (the comparable section of the Patent Act), and see Comment, *Proposal for a Centralized and Integrated Registry for Security Interests in Intellectual Property*, 41 IDEA 297 (2002).

VI. PATENTS

The constitutional foundation of both copyrights and patents is the same. U.S. Const. art. I, § 8, cl. 8 uses both copyright and patent terms, referring, in the case of patents, to the promotion of progress in "science" and the "useful arts," "inventors," and their "discoveries." Either an original "manufacture" or a "composition of matter" is patentable. So is bacteria not found in nature that is useful in breaking down the components of crude oil. See *Diamond v. Chakrabarty*, 447 U.S. 303 (1980) (Berger, C.J.) (stating that Albert Einstein could not have received a patent for the equation $E = MC2$ any more than Issac Newton could have patented his laws of gravity).

Letter from Thomas Jefferson to Isacc McPherson (a Baltimore inventor), dated August 13, 1813, reprinted in part in Adrienne Koch & William Peden, The Life and

Selected Writings of Thomas Jefferson 629–30 (Modern Library ed. 1944):

> It has been pretended by some, (and in England especially,) that inventors have a natural and exclusive right to their inventions, and not merely for their own lives, but inheritable to their heirs. But while it is a moot question whether the origin of any kind of property is derived from nature at all, it would be singular to admit a natural and even an hereditary right to inventors. It is agreed by those who have seriously considered the subject, that no individual has, of natural right, a separate property in an acre of land, for instance. By an universal law, indeed, whatever, whether fixed or movable, belongs to all men equally and in common, is the property for the moment of him who occupies it, but when he relinquishes the occupation, the property goes with it. Stable ownership is the gift of social law, and is given late in the progress of society. It would be curious then, if an idea, the fugitive fermentation of an individual brain, could, of natural right, be claimed in exclusive and stable property. If nature has made any one thing less susceptible than all others of exclusive property, it is the action of the thinking power called an idea, which an individual may exclusively possess as long as he keeps it to himself; but the moment it is divulged, it forces itself into the possession of every one, and the receiver cannot dispossess himself of it. Its peculiar character, too, is that no one possesses the less, because every other possesses the whole of it. He who receives an idea from me, receives instruction himself without lessening mine; as he who lights his taper at mine, receives light without darkening me. That ideas should freely spread from one to another over the globe, for the moral and mutual instruction of man, and improvement of his condition, seems to have been peculiarly and benevolently designed by nature, when she made them, like fire, expansible over all space, without lessening their density in any point, and like the air in which we breath, move, and have our physical being, incapable of confinement or exclusive appropriation. Inventions then cannot, in nature, be subject of property. Society may give an exclusive right to the profits arising from them, as an encouragement to men to pursue ideas which may produce utility, but this may or may not be done, according to the will and convenience of the society, without claim or complaint from anybody.

Nice talk. However, the drafters of our federal Constitution, when using the phrase "useful arts," sought to expand the scope of our patent system in contrast to the English Statute of Monopolies, which restricts patents to "manufactures." "Useful arts" was thus intended to be more than "manual arts." Our patent statutes have reflected this broader scope. From the earliest, they included not just the equipment of the Industrial Revolution: methods and processes were referred to in the first statute and the present one. See John R. Thomas, *The Patenting of the Liberal Professions*, 40 B.C. L. Rev. 1139, 1144–1145 (1999).

Congress followed suit. The Patent Act declares that "patents shall have the attributes of personal property." See 35 U.S.C. § 261. Thus an inventor has the right both to use the patent and to assign it or the application for it to another.

A patent applicant must show three fundamental things in order to receive a patent. They are set out in 35 U.S.C. §§ 101 and 103: an invention must be new, useful, and not obvious at the time it was discovered. Its newness means its novelty compared to prior art exhibited in even earlier patent or product. If an invention is new but is just an easy-to-anticipate step, made by a person reasonably skilled in prior art (which may be a single patent), it is not obvious. Who is this ordinary, reasonably skilled person? Once made, many inventions seem obvious. The non-obviousness element serves to deny a patent that makes only minor improvements on an existing one, but has an element of hindsight in it. Events that occur after discovery (so called secondary considerations) are the only objective evidence for a patent claim. See *KSR Internat'l Co. v. Teleflex, Inc.*, 127 S. Ct. 1727 (2007) (an infringement action involving an automotive gas pedal that adjusted for the height of the driver and holding its patent invalid because of its obviousness). It is the claim in a patent, then, that confers a property right; this right involves only the right to exclude.

This right to exclude does not include the right to do anything more with a claim, as an owner of real property can do something with it. The right is also more difficult to enforce than it is with real property, which can be fenced and patrolled. It is further more expensive to enforce. The case of *eBay Inc. v. MercExchange, LLC*, 547 U.S. 388 (2006), below, highlights these differences. A patent is also limited in time; unlike the fee simple absolute, it is limited to 20 years from the filing of an application.

The patent system has come to include software programs, genetic fragments, and most recently, business methods. Thus, while the patent system has been dramatically expanded in recent years, the expansion has not been without administrative costs. As new subjects for patents are introduced, for example, new examiners must be hired and new types of patent searches devised. Until they are, the system will depend on private enforcement through infringement actions. An infringer need not have derived his product from the patentee, and patent law lacks a fair use exception known to copyright law. Disputes over the priority of a patent are frequent.

No mathematical formula, abstract idea, or algorithm — that is, a definite set of rules for making a mathematical calculation — for making a mathematical formula is patentable *per se*. Nor are the mental steps (the human thought or calculation) going into them. Business methods may, however, receive a patent as a "process" under § 101 of the Patent Act. One step in a process may involve the use of a programmed digital computer and be patent-eligible; patents involving computer programming for business methods have many times been issued. See *Diamond v. Diehr*, 450 U.S. 175 (1981), discussed in *State Street Bank & Trust Co. v. Signature Fin. Group, Inc.*, 149 F.3d 1368, 1370, 1374–75 (Fed. Cir. 1998) (describing a data processing system for implementing an investment structure developed for administering and accounting for mutual funds), cert. denied, 525 U.S. 1093 (1999). This debate revolves around the issue of whether a process consisting just of mental steps or ideas, when untied from technology, is patent-eligible. Algorithms, for example, may be very specific, describing operations performed by a computer, other machine, or human being. They do not exist in nature (they don't just describe radio waves or electricity), and do not describe ideas leading who knows where, but are instead prescriptive, human constructs. Tangible useful results must be claimed for a patent. For example, mathematical formulae to analyze electrocardiograph signals to detect particular heart activity are patentable because they change physical, electrical signals from one form into another — a number representing a signal related to the patient's heart activity; this is certainly not an abstract idea or natural phenomena. What about a hyperlink on a web site? If Amazon.com patents a one click (of a mouse button) method of making an internet purchase, does BarnesandNoble.com's Express Lane for purchasing a book infringe it? See *Amazon.com, Inc. v. BarnesandNoble.com, Inc.*, 239 F.3d 1343 (Fed. Cir. 2001). See John R. Thomas, *The Future of Patent Law: Liberty and Property in the Patent Law*, 39 Houston L. Rev. 569, 585 (2002). More will be heard on this matter. See *In re Bilski*, 545 F.3d 943 (Fed. Cir. 2008), *aff'd* 561 U.S. 593 (2010).

Although patent searches are inherently unreliable, the system is also increasingly dependent on good record keeping. In this regard, 35 U.S.C. § 261, para. 4, provides: "An assignment, grant, or conveyance [of a patent, patent application, or interest therein] shall be void as against any subsequent purchaser or mortgagee for a valuable consideration, without notice, unless it is recorded in the Patent and Trademark Office within three months from its date or prior to the date of such subsequent purchase or mortgage." This statute also provides that "patents shall have the attributes of personal property." *Id.* at para. 1. Clearly this statute permits a patent mortgage to be recorded. What type of mortgage? One that is a transfer of the title to the patent. Another type might have to be recorded under state law, under Art. 9 of the Uniform Commercial Code, unless that article is preempted by this federal statute. See U.C.C. § 9-302.

---

35 U.S.C. § 102(a) (2014)

A person shall be entitled to a patent unless — (1) the claimed invention was patented, described in a printed publication, or in public use, on sale, or otherwise available to the public before the effective filing date of the claimed invention; or (2) the claimed invention was described in a patent issued . . . , or in an application for patent published or deemed published . . . , in which the patent or application, as the case may be, names another inventor and was effectively filed before the effective filing date of the claimed invention.

NOTES

1. In January two years ago, A files to patent an invention, but delays further work on it. In January of this year, A begins reducing the invention to practice. A month later, in February of this year, B files and reduces the same invention to practice. Then A reduces the invention to practice. Under our system, who is the first inventor? See Donald Chisum & Michael Jacobs, Understanding Intellectual Property 2-190 (1992). "Actual reduction to practice requires a showing that the embodiment relied upon as evidence of priority actually worked for its intended purpose." *DSL Dynamic Sciences Limited v. Union Switch & Signal, Inc.*, 928 F.2d 1122, 1125 (Fed. Cir.1991). Under prior law, the performance of tests to determine

if an invention will work might be sufficient to establish a constructive reduction to practice as long as the testing conditions are sufficiently similar to those of the intended use of the invention: "There is certainly no requirement that an invention, when tested, be in a commercially satisfactory stage of development in order to reduce the invention to practice." 928 F.2d at 1126. If the last statement remains the law, then isn't filing the equivalent as a constructive reduction to practice?

2.   Section 102(a) describes what is called "prior art," which takes priority over a claimed invention. Prior art destroys the novelty of an invention. In 2012, § 102 was amended to change our "first to invent" patent system into a "first inventor to file" system more like a race recording act for real estate records. Would you expect different industries — for example, large pharmacology firms and intellectual technology companies — to have different reactions to this change? It is intended to harmonize our system with those of the European Union countries and Japan. One result of this change-over is more litigation over the derivation of a patent: was the idea for it misappropriated from another patent holder?

3.   A patent may be anticipated by a prior disclosure (made less than a year in advance of the application date for a patent). 35 U.S.C. § 102(a)(2). The disclosure must be available to the extent that persons interested and ordinarily skilled in the subject and exercising reasonable diligence, could locate it. There is no requirement that anyone actually locate it. Whether a reference is available is a question of law. Disclosures of more than one year may be prior art, taking priority over the claimed invention.

A college thesis is typically presented to a panel of faculty and defended in front of them. If approved, it may be certified as of publishable quality and sent to the college library, where it is catalogued and shelved. If a college student completes a thesis, has it sent to, catalogued in, and shelved in the college library, has it become a printed publication such that it is patent-eligible? What factors will be considered in deciding whether information is contained in a printed publication? See *In re Cronyn*, 890 F.2d 1158 (Fed. Cir. 1989); *In re Bayer*, 568 F.2d 1357, 1359 (CCPA 1978) (holding that a thesis was not a "printed publication" on receipt by a university library when the 3 member faculty committee approving it knew of its whereabouts in the library where it was available to them on request and that the thesis was not provided with wide public access when the department approving it indexed it in a "shoebox"); *In re Hall*, 781 F.2d 897, 898 (Fed. Cir. 1986) (holding that theses filed in the library of a German university where they were catalogued in a special theses catalogue was a "printed publication"). See also *E.I. Du Pont De Nemours & Co. v. Cetus Corp.*, 1990 U.S. Dist. LEXIS 18382 (N.D. Cal. Dec. 11, 1990). Could an accessible abstract take the place of an unrevealing title for an article? See *Mobil Oil Corp. v. Amoco Oil Corp.*, 779 F. Supp. 1429, 1489 (D. Del. 1991).

EBAY INC. v. MERCEXCHANGE LLC
547 U.S. 388 (2006)

JUSTICE THOMAS delivered the opinion of the Court.

Ordinarily, a federal court considering whether to award permanent injunctive relief to a prevailing plaintiff applies the four-factor test historically employed by courts of equity. Petitioners eBay Inc. and Half.com, Inc., argue that this traditional test applies to disputes arising under the Patent Act. We agree . . . .

* * *

According to well-established principles of equity, a plaintiff seeking a permanent injunction must satisfy a four-factor test before a court may grant such relief. A plaintiff must demonstrate: (1) that it has suffered an irreparable injury; (2) that remedies available at law, such as monetary damages, are inadequate to compensate for that injury; (3) that, considering the balance of hardships between the plaintiff and defendant, a remedy in equity is warranted; and (4) that the public interest would not be disserved by a permanent injunction. See, *e.g.*, *Weinberger v. Romero-Barcelo*, 456 U.S. 305, 311–313 (1982). . . . The decision to grant or deny permanent injunctive relief is an act of equitable discretion by the district court, reviewable on appeal for abuse of discretion. See, *e.g.*, *Romero-Barcelo*, 456 U.S., at 320.

These familiar principles apply with equal force to disputes arising under the Patent Act. * * * To be sure, the Patent Act also declares that "patents shall have the attributes of personal property," 35 U.S.C. § 261, including "the right to exclude others from making, using, offering for sale, or selling the invention," § 154(a)(1). According to the Court of Appeals, this statutory right to exclude alone justifies its general rule in favor of permanent injunctive relief. But the creation of a right is distinct from the provision of remedies for violations of that right. Indeed, the Patent Act itself indicates that patents shall have the attributes of personal property "[s]ubject to the provisions of this title," § 261, including, presumably, the provision that injunctive relief "may" issue only "in accordance with the principles of equity," § 283.

This approach is consistent with our treatment of injunctions under the Copyright Act. Like a patent owner, a copyright holder possesses "the right to exclude others from using his property." *Fox Film Corp. v. Doyal*, 286 U.S. 123, 127 (1932); see also *id.*, at 127–128 ("A copyright, like a patent, is at once the equivalent given by the public for benefits bestowed by the genius and meditations and skill of individuals and the incentive to further efforts for the same important objects" (internal quotation marks omitted)). Like the Patent Act, the Copyright Act provides that courts "may" grant injunctive relief "on such terms as it may deem reasonable to prevent or restrain infringement of a copyright." 17 U.S.C. § 502(a). And as in our decision today, this Court has consistently rejected invitations to replace traditional equitable considerations with a rule that an injunction automatically follows a determination that a copyright has been infringed. See, *e.g.*, *New York Times Co. v. Tasini*, 533 U.S. 483, 505 (2001). . . .

*   *   *

Because we conclude that neither court below correctly applied the traditional four-factor framework that governs the award of injunctive relief, we vacate the judgment of the Court of Appeals, so that the District Court may apply that framework in the first instance. In doing so, we take no position on whether permanent injunctive relief should or should not issue in this particular case, or indeed in any number of other disputes arising under the Patent Act. We hold only that the decision whether to grant or deny injunctive relief rests within the equitable discretion of the district courts, and that such discretion must be exercised consistent with traditional principles of equity, in patent disputes no less than in other cases governed by such standards. Accordingly, we vacate the judgment of the Court of Appeals and remand the case for further proceedings consistent with this opinion. It is so ordered.

CHIEF JUSTICE ROBERTS, concurring.

I agree with the Court's holding that "the decision whether to grant or deny injunctive relief rests within the equitable discretion of the district courts, and that such discretion must be exercised consistent with traditional principles of equity, in patent disputes no less than in other cases governed by such standards," and I join the opinion of the Court. That opinion rightly rests on the proposition that "a major departure from the long tradition of equity practice should not be lightly implied." *Weinberger v. Romero-Barcelo*, 456 U.S. 305, 320 (1982). . . . From at least the early 19th century, courts have granted injunctive relief upon a finding of infringement in the vast majority of patent cases. This "long tradition of equity practice" is not surprising, given the difficulty of protecting a right to *exclude* through monetary remedies that allow an infringer to *use* an invention against the patentee's wishes — a difficulty that often implicates the first two factors of the traditional four-factor test. This historical practice, as the Court holds, does not *entitle* a patentee to a permanent injunction or justify a *general rule* that such injunctions should issue. The Federal Circuit itself so recognized in *Roche Products, Inc. v. Bolar Pharmaceutical Co.*, 733 F.2d 858, 865–867 (1984). At the same time, there is a difference between exercising equitable discretion pursuant to the established four-factor test and writing on an entirely clean slate. "Discretion is not whim, and limiting discretion according to legal standards helps promote the basic principle of justice that like cases should be decided alike." *Martin v. Franklin Capital Corp.*, 546 U.S. 132, 139 (2005). When it comes to discerning and applying those standards, in this area as others, "a page of history is worth a volume of logic." *New York Trust Co. v. Eisner*, 256 U.S. 345, 349 (1921) (opinion for the Court by Holmes, J.).

JUSTICE KENNEDY, concurring.

* * * The traditional practice of issuing injunctions against patent infringers, however, does not seem to rest on "the difficulty of protecting a right to *exclude* through monetary remedies that allow an infringer to *use* an invention against the patentee's wishes." Both the terms of the Patent Act and the traditional view of injunctive relief accept that the existence of a right to exclude does not dictate the

remedy for a violation of that right. To the extent earlier cases establish a pattern of granting an injunction against patent infringers almost as a matter of course, this pattern simply illustrates the result of the four-factor test in the contexts then prevalent. The lesson of the historical practice, therefore, is most helpful and instructive when the circumstances of a case bear substantial parallels to litigation the courts have confronted before.

In cases now arising trial courts should bear in mind that in many instances the nature of the patent being enforced and the economic function of the patent holder present considerations quite unlike earlier cases. An industry has developed in which firms use patents not as a basis for producing and selling goods but, instead, primarily for obtaining licensing fees. (Citation omitted.) For these firms, an injunction, and the potentially serious sanctions arising from its violation, can be employed as a bargaining tool to charge exorbitant fees to companies that seek to buy licenses to practice the patent. When the patented invention is but a small component of the product the companies seek to produce and the threat of an injunction is employed simply for undue leverage in negotiations, legal damages may well be sufficient to compensate for the infringement and an injunction may not serve the public interest. In addition injunctive relief may have different consequences for the burgeoning number of patents over business methods, which were not of much economic and legal significance in earlier times. The potential vagueness and suspect validity of some of these patents may affect the calculus under the four-factor test. The equitable discretion over injunctions, granted by the Patent Act, is well suited to allow courts to adapt to the rapid technological and legal developments in the patent system. For these reasons it should be recognized that district courts must determine whether past practice fits the circumstances of the cases before them. With these observations, I join the opinion of the Court.

NOTES

1. When the patentee in an infringement case makes a showing of a likelihood of success on the merits, does a presumption of harm arise? If courts must articulate how they weighed the four factors for an injunction, may they give greater weight to one or another of them? Injunctions either preserve an exclusive right to an invention or deter others from using it. Might a finding of infringement still raise a presumption that a preliminary injunction is available? Might a presumption of unavailability more easily arise when (1) the defendant is not a direct competitor of the patent's owner, (2) the invention is but a small part of the defendant's product, or (3) the defendant did not copy from the owner? What if the defendant produced something covered by several patents? Would such factors make it more or less appropriate to decide patent infringement cases using real property law? See Peter S. Menell, *The Property Rights Movement's Embrace of Intellectual Property: True Love or Doomed Relationship?*, 34 Ecology L.Q. 713, 739–746 (2007). See also *Leading Cases*, 120 Harv. L. Rev. 332 (2006).

2. Are patents protected by the Takings Clause of the Fifth Amendment? If the government makes unauthorized use of a patent, the clause might protect the patent owner by providing compensation for its use. See *United States v. Burns*, 79 U.S. 246 (1871). Neither should a government employee be immunized from suit for

infringing it. But is the source of the compensation found in the Takings Clause? Patents might be analogized to personal property for this purpose, but if a patent is the grant of a limited monopoly to its holder, then further protection of a monopoly sits uneasily in the mind. And if patents are protected, then can copyrights be far behind? Will the patent holder seek the license fees that would have been earned if its use were authorized, or would he want compensation for his relinquishing it now and in the future? Is the compensation the result of an act of an abuse of its sovereign immunity, its power of eminent domain, or a compulsory license? See Adam Mosoff, *Patents as Constitutional Private Property: The Historical Protection of Patents under the Takings Clause*, B.U. L. Rev. 689 (2007). The Supreme Court has explored the use of the Takings Clause for real property, but its application to intellectual property remains unexplored. See *Zoltek Corp. v. United States*, 442 F.3d 1345, 1349 (Fed. Cir. 2006).

VII. IDEAS AS PROPERTY

GARRIDO v. BURGER KING CORP.
558 So. 2d 79 (Fla. App. 1990)

NESBITT, J.

George L. Garrido and his firm, The Garrido Group Advertising, Inc. [Garrido], appeal from a grant of summary final judgment in favor of the Burger King Corporation and Thomas Kupciunas [Burger King] entered on the ground of lack of subject matter jurisdiction. Garrido's complaint raised a number of legal theories based on Burger King's allegedly unauthorized and uncompensated use of ideas contained in a proposed advertising campaign. Based on the following rationale, we affirm the summary judgment inasmuch as it concerns the causes of action for conversion, theft and conspiracy. However, we reverse the summary judgment and remand for further proceedings on the claims for misappropriation, misrepresentation and implied contract.

Background Facts

In 1985, George Garrido, president of Garrido Group, an advertising company, telephoned defendant Thomas Kupciunas, Burger King's Vice President of Marketing, offering to make a presentation of a proposed advertising campaign. Burger King employees agreed to meet with Garrido representatives. At the subsequent meeting, which was the sole meeting between the parties, Garrido and two of his employee made their presentation to Kupciunas and two other Burger King employees. As part of the presentation, which focused on reaching the general fast food consumer market, and specifically, Hispanic consumers, the Garrido Group presented various written and visual materials, including a television storyboard, a series of slides, a demonstration tape of a musical jingle and a creative strategy statement. In the complaint, Garrido alleged that the proposed campaign was "to impress on the consumer's mind the specific notion that 'everywhere you go in America there is a Burger King town.'" As the presentation materials demonstrate and as the complaint alleges, the campaign themes were, "It's my Whopper, it's by Burger King" and "It's my town, it's my Burger King."

At the close of the presentation, Kupciunas told Garrido to contact him in seven weeks. Garrido called Kupciunas seven weeks later and several times after that, but was never able to speak with Kupciunas. Then, approximately nine months later, Burger King began an advertising campaign called "Burger King Town."

Garrido subsequently filed this suit, alleging the following causes of action against Burger King: (1) misrepresentation, (2) breach of implied contract, (3) misappropriation, (4) conversion, [and] (5) theft. . . . * * * Defendants ultimately moved for summary judgment on the ground that all the claims were preempted by the Copyright Act of 1976, 17 U.S.C. § 301. Summary judgment was granted and this appeal ensued. * * *

Copyright Preemption

The Copyright Act applies to causes of action based on "works of authorship that are fixed in a tangible medium of expression." 17 U.S.C. § 301(b)(1) (1976). A work falls into the subject matter covered by the Copyright Act even if the work "fails to achieve Federal statutory copyright because it is too minimal or lacking in originality to qualify, or because it has fallen into the public domain." H.R. Rep. No. 1476, 94th Cong., 2d Sess. at 131, reprinted in 1976 U.S. Code Cong. & Admin. News at 5747. The act does not preclude others from using ideas or information revealed in an author's copyrighted work; instead it protects only the author's original written form of expression of his ideas and information. See . . . 17 U.S.C. § 102(b). In other words, even though the ideas embodied in a copyrighted work are not themselves protected by copyright, they are preempted by the Copyright Act. U.S.C. 17 § 102(b). 17 U.S.C. § 102(b) states: "In no case does copyright for an original work of authorship extend to any idea, procedure, process, system, method of operation, concept, principle, or discovery regardless of the form in which it is described, explained, illustrated, or embodied in such work." It has been written that: "Section 102(b) is an embodiment of the idea-expression distinction in copyright law. The distinction between idea and expression, or the 'idea-expression dichotomy' as it is often called, is the term of art used in copyright law to indicate the elements in a copyrighted work which the grant of the copyright monopoly does not take from the public. It differentiates those elements in a copyrighted work which are protected from those which may be freely copied and plagiarized by the public. It is a limit of the protection extended by the statutory monopoly of copyright to subject matter included under [the act], not a definition of excluded subject matter." Abrams, *Copyright, Misappropriation, and Preemption: Constitutional and Statutory Limits of State Law Protection*, 1983 Sup. Ct. Rev. 509, 563.

In this case, the written and visual advertising materials plaintiffs presented to Burger King were copyrightable; thus, the ideas portrayed in those materials fell into the subject matter preempted by the Copyright Act. See *Flemming v. Ronson Corp.*, 258 A.2d 153, 157 (N.J. Super. Ct. 1969), aff'd, 275 A.2d 759 (N.J. 1971). Nevertheless, state law causes of action are not totally preempted by the federal act. Only those causes of action that involve rights equivalent to those protected by the act are preempted. 17 U.S.C. § 301(a) (1976). Section 106 of the act states that the rights within the general scope of copyright are those which prohibit reproduction, performance, distribution or display of a work. 17 U.S.C. § 106. Therefore, those state law causes of action which contain an element qualitatively different from a copyright infringement claim may be maintained.

As previously stated, the advertising materials which were the tangible expression of the plaintiff's ideas in the instant case fall within the subject matter of copyright. Consequently, protection of the ideas embodied in those materials is precluded according to the terms of the Copyright Act if plaintiff's causes of action are "equivalent to any of the exclusive rights within the general scope of copyright as specified by section 106." *Crow v. Wainwright*, 720 F.2d 1224, 1225–26 (11th Cir. 1983), cert. denied, 469 U.S. 819 (1984).

Application of the Copyright Act to Plaintiff's Claims

*   *   *

Misappropriation Claim

" 'Misappropriation' is not necessarily synonymous with copyright infringement and thus a cause of action labeled as 'misappropriation' is not preempted if it is in fact based neither on a right within the general scope of copyright . . . nor on a right equivalent thereto." House Judiciary Committee Report on the 1976 Amendments to the Copyright Act, No. 1476 at 132 reprinted at 17 **U.S.C.A. § 301.**

Plaintiff attempts to take its cause of action for misappropriation out of the realm of Copyright Act preemption by claiming that the ideas were disclosed in confidence to Burger King. In *Air Travel Assocs., Inc. v. Eastern Air Lines, Inc.*, 273 So.2d 3 (Fla. 3d DCA 1973), this court noted that a plaintiff must prove that the idea allegedly misappropriated was both secret and novel in order to recover. See *Official Airlines Schedule Information Serv., Inc. v. Eastern Air Lines, Inc.*, 333 F.2d 672 (5th Cir. 1964) [hereinafter *OASIS*] (essential elements of an idea misappropriation claim are that the idea was revealed in confidence and that the idea was novel). Based on the forgoing authorities, we hold that the allegations that Garrido's ideas were novel and confidentially conveyed to Burger King with the expectation of payment for their use and then misappropriated by the defendants state a cause of action which takes the claim outside Copyright Act preemption. * * *

Misrepresentation Claim

By the same token, the cause of action for misrepresentation is not preempted by the act since it raises the additional element of deceptive or fraudulent conduct in entering into a contract which is not an element covered by the act. See *Smith v. Weinstein*, 578 F. Supp. 1297 (S.D.N.Y.), aff'd, 738 F.2d 419 (2d Cir. 1984).

Novelty or Originality of Idea Requirement

Having held the misappropriation, misrepresentation, and breach of contract claims not to be excluded by the Copyright Act, we are next required to address the elements necessary to prove these causes of action when they involve the conveyance of an idea. While there is no Florida case addressing the exact factual situation before us here, the federal Fifth Circuit stated in *OASIS*, *supra* at 763–64: "[T]he idea must be novel; (2) the disclosure of the idea must be made in confidence, and (3) the idea must be adopted and made use of by the defendant." Courts adopting this rule have grounded it on the principle that an idea does not constitute property unless it is novel, and thus no recovery can be had for use of an "unnovel" idea. See, e.g., *Murray v. National Broadcasting Co., Inc.*, 671 F. Supp. 236 (S.D.N.Y. 1987), aff'd, 844 F.2d 988 (2d Cir.), cert. denied, 488 U.S. 955 (1988). "[W]hen one submits an idea to another, no promise to pay for its use may be implied, and no asserted agreement enforced, if the elements of novelty and originality are absent, since the property right in an idea is based upon these two elements." *Downey v. General Foods Corp.*, 286 N.E.2d 257 (N.Y. 1972).

An original or novel idea is not merely an innovative representation or adaptation of existing knowledge. It is not a variation on a theme. See *Murray*, 844 F.2d at 992–93. As stated in *Educational Sales Programs, Inc. v. Dreyfus Corp.*, 317 N.Y.S.2d 840, 843 (N.Y.Sup. 1970), "Not every good idea is a legally protectible idea." The court went on to state, "An agreement premised on the disclosure of a secret is a blind deal. When the purveyor of that secret exacts a promise of confidentiality, he knows what he is dealing with, but the recipient is in the dark. The enforcibility of such a threshold agreement — a promise in exchange for a revelation — turns on the value of the disclosure." 317 N.Y.S.2d at 844. If the idea revealed turns out to be one already within the public domain, then it cannot constitute a protectible property right which can be misappropriated or contracted for. Consequently, the novelty requirement prevents a person from being able "by contract [to] monopolize an idea that is common and general to the whole world." *Soule v. Bon Ami Co.*, 195 N.Y.S. 574, 575 (N.Y. App. Div. 1922), aff'd, 139 N.E. 754 (N.Y. 1923). For these reasons, we adopt the novelty requirement in cases involving state law causes of action based on the conveyance of an idea.

In the instant case, Burger King did not raise the novelty issue as grounds for summary judgment. Defendant moved for summary judgment exclusively on the ground that all of plaintiff's causes of action fell within the scope of the federal Copyright Act. . . . The trial court heard oral argument on the claim contained within this motion. The court did not determine the novelty issue nor make any factual findings on any other issue. *** However, in order to decide the novelty issue, factual inquiries leading to a determination of the merits of the case are required; the motion for summary judgment submitted by Burger King and granted by the trial judge required a purely legal decision on subject matter jurisdiction.

Burger King claims there is evidence in the record showing conclusively that Garrido's ideas were not novel and furthermore that its 1985 advertising campaign, which was allegedly based on Garrido's ideas, was simply a recycling of a prior campaign it aired nationwide in 1976 and 1977. However, appellants have not had an opportunity to rebut those claims, nor has the trial court ruled on these disputed factual issues. Accordingly, this court refrains from affirming summary judgment on the ground that Garrido's ideas were not novel. Instead, we are required to reverse and remand for further proceedings at which point the trial court may assess the evidence and proceed further. Affirmed in part [as to claims omitted here — Eds.], reversed in part and remanded.

NOTES

1.   Many cases concerning property rights in ideas focus on the idea's novelty or originality. Is that just a shorthand way of saying that the possession of an idea is protected only when others don't know of it? Their not knowing puts its possessor in control of it. If I conceive of a scientific idea, then I can personally use it and I might even sell it to others who don't know of it. But if at the time I conceive of it, it was unknown to me but generally known to scientists, I cannot prevent scientists from using it and disclosing it to others. See Andrew Beckerman-Rodau, *Are Ideas within the Traditional Definition of Property?: A Jurisprudential Analysis*, 47 Ark. L. Rev. 603, 619–621 (1994). Isn't finding an idea novel also a way of saying that it has been reduced to a useable, concrete form? This might be akin to saying that it is capable of possession. As with all intellectual property law, protecting ideas as property has to reconcile the public's interest in access to new ideas and the unfairness of permitting someone to exploit commercially the idea of another. Thus a middle ground between the monopolistic protection afforded by granting a copyright or patent, and no protection, is needed. See *Reeves v. Alyeska Pipeline Service Corp.*, 926 P.2d 1130 (Alaska 1996).

2.   Should the disclosure of an idea have to be in confidence, as *Garrido* requires, or is it enough that it is novel, the defendant exploits it, and benefits thereby? Compare *Alevizos v. The John D. and Catherine T. MacArthur Fdn.*, 764 So. 2d 8 (Fla. App. 1999) (requiring confidential disclosure as a necessary element of an action for misappropriating an idea, but refusing to protect an idea for a type of real estate development already developed), with *Blackmon v. Iverson*, 2003 U.S. Dist. LEXIS 6614 (E.D. Pa., April 8, 2003) (not requiring confidential disclosure). Finally, if the disclosure is followed by a compensation agreement, is the fact that the idea is not novel a defense to enforcing it? See *Johnson v. Benjamin Moore & Co.*, 788 A.2d 906 (N.J. Super. Ct. 2002).

3.   Another type of idea protected as property is a trade secret. See *Peabody v. Norfolk*, 98 Mass. 452 (1868). It is a formula, pattern, program, device, method, technique or process useable or in continuous use in a trade or business that is not generally known, is kept secret (or disclosed only on condition of restricted use), and is of value, conferring a competitive advantage on that business. See Uniform Trade Secrets Act (1985), 11 U.L.A. 438 (adopted in most states) and Restatement (First) of Torts, § 757 (1939). Based on this definition, how do you think the law of trade secrets would differ from that of protecting ideas as property? See *McKay Consulting, Inc. v. Rockingham Memorial Hospital*, 665 F. Supp. 2d 626 (W.D. Va. 2009).

TABLE OF CASES

[References are to pages.]

A

A. D. Juilliard & Co. v. American Woolen Co.. .365
A. H. Fetting Mfg. Jewelry Co. v. Waltz 399
Abbott v. Bob's U-Drive. 374
Abbott v. Forward Design Development, Inc. . .199
Abel v. Girard Trust Co.. . . . . 191, 192
ABKCO Music, Inc. v. Stellar Records, Inc.. . .857
Academy Spires, Inc. v. Brown 335
Aczas v. Stuart Heights, Inc.. 485
Adair v. Bogle. 307
Adams v. First State Bank 75
Adams v. New Jersey S. B. Co. 43
Adams; State v.. 705
Agins v. Tiburon.693; 698; 702, 703; 714; 717; 722; 726; 748
Agway, Inc.; Commonwealth v.. 16
Air Travel Assocs., Inc. v. Eastern Air Lines, Inc. 907
Akins v. Texas 797
Albright v. Fish. 640
Alcaraz v. Vece. 346
Alderman v. Iditarod Properties 896
Alevizos v. The John D. and Catherine T. MacArthur Found.. 909
Alexander v. Andrews 548
Alfano v. Donnelly 300; 594, 595
Alleghney Airlines, Inc. v. Cedarhurst 148
Allen v. Hyatt Regency-Nashville Hotel 50
Allen; United States v. 72
Alliance Against IFQS v. Brown 15
Allied Inv. Corp. v. Jasen. 41
Allinder v. Bessemer C.I. & L. Co. 492
Allison v. Powell. 243
Allred v. Allred. 445
Alumni Control Bd. v. Lincoln 773
AM Leasing, Ltd. v. Baker 87
Amazon.com, Inc. v. BarnesandNoble.com, Inc.. .900
American Leasing v. Morrison Co. 245
Anderson v. Anderson 474
Anderson v. Carlson 408
Anderson v. Cold Spring Tungsten, Inc. 108
Anderson v. Ferguson 328
Anderson v. Gouldberg 36
Anderson v. Kennedy 468
Anderson v. Rosebrook 419
Anderson v. Sawyer 779; 781

Andrews v. Andrews 9
Andrus v. Allard 699; 719; 722
Angell v. Ingram, Wash.. 586
Angier v. Worrell. 244
Angle v. Slayton 526
Annicelli v. South Kingstown 715
Anzalone v. Kragness 63
Appeal of (see name of party)
Appel v. Presley Co.. 656
Application of (see name of party)
Arbenz v. Exley, Watkins & Co.. 380
Arcadia Development Corp. v. City of Bloomington 708
Arden & Howe Assocs., In re 377
Ardmore Park Subdivision Ass'n, Inc. v. Simon . 656
Ariz. Dep't of Revenue v. Ariz. Outdoor Advertisers, Inc. 92
Arkansas Game and Fish Comm'n v. U.S. 711
Arlington Heights v. Metro. Hous. Dev. Corp.. . .791
Armory v. Delamirie 36; 39
Armstrong v. Francis Corp. 171
Armstrong v. United States. 739; 747
Arnold Realty Co. v. Wm. K. Toole Co. 404
Arrington v. New York Times Co. 889, 890
Artesian Water Co. v. New Castle Cty. 179
Association of Friends of Sagaponack v. Southampton Zoning Board of Appeals. 814
Assocs. of Philipsburg v. Hurwitz. 625
Atlantic C.L.R. Co.; United States v.. 47
Atlantic Discount Corp. v. Mangel's of North Carolina, Inc. 325; 328
Atlas Assurance Co. v. Gibbs. 87
Ault v. Holden 502, 503
Aust v. Beard. 437
Austin v. Cambridgeport Parish 358
Austin Hill Country Realty v. Palisades Plaza . . 383

B

B.A. Ballou and Co. v. Citytrust 64
Baililes v. Cities Service Co. 436
Baker v. Carr. 795
Baker v. Latham Sparrowbush Assoc.. 289
Baker; State v. 814
Ballard v. Wetzel 85
Ballstadt v. Pagel. 164

[References are to pages.]

Baltimore Orioles, Inc. v. Major League Baseball Players Ass'n 894

Bancorp Leasing & Fin. Corp. v. Stadeli Pump & Constr., Inc.. .83

Bank of America v. J.&S. Auto Repairs 87

Bank of America Nat'l Trust & Savings Ass'n v. Moore 362

Bank of California, N.A. v. First American Title Ins. Co.. 572

Bank of Dallas v. Republic Nat'l Bank 281

Bank of Hawaii v. Horwoth 445

Bank of Mississippi v. Hollingsworth 545

Bank of New Glarus v. Swartwood 549

Bank of Powhattan v. Rooney 196

Barash v. Pennsylvania Terminal Real Estate Corp.. . . . . .317, 318

Barber v. Somers 469

Barger v. Barringer 154; 156

Barker v. Barker 292

Barker v. Bates 23; 33

Barnacle, In re 535

Barnes v. Davitt 408

Barrington v. City of Sherman 769, 770

Bartholomew v. Staheli 616

Bartlett v. Budd 14

Bartlett v. Zoning Comm'n of Old Lyme 718

Barton v. Thaw. 287

Barton Enters. v. Tsern 337

Barwick v. Barwick 39

Baseball Publishing Co. v. Bruton 301; 594

Bass v. Boetel & Co.. 404

Bass v. Moore 260

Bateman v. Maddox 402

Battistone v. Banulski 252

Baumgartner v. Meek 427

Bayer, In re. 901

Bd. of County Comm'rs v. Lowery 681

Beall v. Wilson. 292

Beard v. S/E Joint Venture. 464

Beardslee v. New Berlin Light & Power Co.. . .592

Beardsley v. Knight 487

Beaver Township School District v. Burdick . . .191

Beck v. Town of Raymond. 804; 807

Becker v. IRM Corp.. 346

Beckham v. Ward County Irrigation Dist. No. 1 . 196

Beckman v. Marshall. 157

Bedian v. Cohn. 520

Beer Co. v. Massachusetts. 696

Bell v. Gray-Robinson Const. Co.. 140

Bellarmine Hills Association v. Residential Systems Co.. 818

Belle Terre v. Boraas. 810

Bellman v. San Francisco High School Dist.. . . 134

Belmar Drive-in Theatre Co. v. Illinois State Toll Highway Comm'n 135

Belnap v. Blain. 446

Bemis v. The RMS Lusitania 34

Benchmark Land Co. v. City of Battle Ground. .735

Bennett v. Langham 189

Bennett Veneer Factors, Inc. v. Brewer 650

Bennis v. Michigan. 238

Benson, In re Estate of. 264

Berger v. State 818

Berman v. Parker . . . 674, 675; 678, 679; 749; 810;
812; 820

Bernard v. City of Bedford 770

Bernstein v. Bramble. 210

Bernstein v. Seglin. 397

Berzito v. Gambino 339

Best Cellars, Inc. v. Wine Made Simple, Inc.. . .896

Bethlehem Township v. Emrick 598

Bettcher v. Knapp 238

Beutler v. Maynard. 609

Bigham v. Madison 468

Billy Williams Builders and Developers, Inc. v. Hillerich. 468

Bilski v. Kappos 900

Bilski, In re. 900

Biltmore Village v. Royal 193

Binns v. Vitagraph Co.. 889

Birkenhead v. Coombs. 339

Bither v. Packard. 518

Bizzell v. Booker. 7

Black Jack; United States v. 801

Blackett v. Olanoff. 313; 318

Blackhawk Prod. v. Chicago Title Ins. Co. 572

Blackman; United States v. 623

Blackmon v. Iverson. 909

Blake v. Hynes. 184

Blank v. Borden 424

Blevins v. Barry-Lawrence County Ass'n for Retarded Citizens 647

Block v. Hirsh 686; 695

Blocker v. Blocker. 265

Blumberg v. Weiss. 158

Board of Comm'rs of Trego Cty v. Hays. 196

[References are to pages.]

Board of County Comm'rs of Cecil County v. Gaster 782

Board of Trade v. Dow Jones & Co. 845

Bobbs-Merrill Co. v. Straus 843; 857

Bobeck, In the Matter of 72

Bocchini v. Gorn Management Co. 315

Bode v. Flobert Industries, Inc. 598

Bodkin v. Arnold 324

Boekelheide v. Snyder 458

Bond v. A.H. Belo Corp. 63

Bookout v. Bookout 221

Boomer v. Atlantic Cement Co. 135

Boraas v. Belle Terre 810

Borders v. Roseberry 341

Bormann v. Board of Supervisors 146

Borough of (see name of borough)

Borruso v. Morreale 609

Bowditch v. Boston 685

Bradley v. Zoning Bd. of Appeals 776

Brandreth, Matter of 70

Brawley v. Copelin 488

Brazell v. City of Seattle 743

Brenner v. New Richmond Regional Airport Comm'n 151

Britton v. Chester 802

Brizendine v. Conrad 329

Brokaw v. Fairchild 212

Brokaw, In re 214

Brokaw's Will, Matter of 214

Bronx Investment Co. v. National Bank of Commerce 587, 588

Brooks v. Bankson 443

Browder v. Williams 464

Brown v. Columbia Finance Co. 292

Brown v. Lober 485, 486

Brown v. Seattle 743

Brown v. Southall Realty Co. 309

Browndale International, Ltd. v. Board of Adjustment 818

Brownell v. Briggs 221

Browning v. Sacrison 261

Brtek v. Cihal 503

Brumley v. Dorner 169

Bruyere v. Jade Realty Corp. 455

Bryant v. Willison Real Estate Co. 439

Buchanan v. Warley 812

Buckey v. Indianhead Truck Line, Inc. 62

Buckles v. Kennedy C. Corp 597

Bugryn v. Bristol 680

Building D, Inc., In re 554

Building Monitoring Sys. v. Paxton 411

Bunn v. Markham 65

Bunn v. Offutt 596

Burch v. Ned Power Mount Storm, LLC 166

Burchell's Estate, In re 271

Burggraff v. Baum 469

Burke v. Smith 154; 156

Burke v. Stevens 241

Burkhardt v. Smith 111

Burkholder v. Twinsburg Township Bd. of Zoning Appeals 777

Burns; United States v. 904

Burpee's Estate, In re 192

Burris v. McDougald 527

Burrow-Giles Lithographic Co. v. Sarony 852

Buss v. Dyer 607

Buster v. Newkirk 6; 10

Butler v. Buick Motor Co. 86

Butler v. Frontier Telephone Co. 149

Butler v. Wilkinson 445

Byrd v. Allen 204

Byrne's Estate, In re 187

C

Cabaniss v. Hipsley 882, 883

Cain v. Finnie 211

Caldwell v. Fulton 633

Calhoun v. Hays 191

California and Or. Land Co.; United States v. . . 526

California Trout, Inc. v. State Water Resources Control Bd. 17

Calonico; State v. 11

Calvery v. Calvery 267

Cameco, Inc. v. Gedicke 40

Camp v. Camp 232

Campbell v. Seaman 139

Campbell v. Westdahl 370

Candler Holdings Ltd. I v. Watch Omega Holdings 116

Cannefax v. Clement 444

Capital Assets Financial Services v. Maxwell . . 449

Capitol Chevrolet Co. v. Earheart 86

Capitol Records, Inc. v. Spies 848

Caples v. Ward 257

Carma Developers, Inc. v. Marathon Dev., Inc. . 373

Carpenter v. N.Y., N.H. & H. R.R. Co. 44

Carr v. Hoosier Photo Supplies, Inc. 59

[References are to pages.]

Carter v. Helmsley-Spear, Inc. . . . 860; 864; 866, 867

Carter, State ex rel. v. Harper, Building Commissioner. 824

Caruthers v. Leonard. 252

Case v. Minot. 314, 315

Casey v. Zoning Hearing Bd. 806

Cash v. Maddox 436

Cason v. Florida Power Co. 157

Caswell v. Bisnett 609

Causby v. United States 149

Causby; United States v. . . . 138; 149; 162; 695; 748

Caywood v. Jones 292

CCC Info. Servs. v. MacLean Hunter Mkt. Reports 855

Centex Homes Corp. v. Boag 465

Chambers v. Chambers. 219

Chandler Flyers v. Stellar Dev. Corp. 601

Chapin v. Freeland. 94; 105

Chapman v. Silber 346

Charles v. Henry 245

Charles E. Burt, Inc. v. Seven Grand Corp. 314

Chase v. Burrell 641

Chase v. Silverstone 173

Cheatham v. Gregory. 547

Cheever v. Pearson. 595

Cheney v. Village 2 at New Hope, Inc. 785

Cheney Bros. v. Doris Silk Corp 845

Cherberg v. Peoples Nat'l Bank of Washington. .318

Chergosky v. Crosstown Bell, Inc. 548

Cherry v. McCutchen 63

Chesebro v. Moers. 646

Chesley v. King 173

Chevalier; People v. 737

Chicago & Southern Air Lines v. Waterman S.S. Corp. 149

Chicago B. & Q. Ry. Co. v. People of State of Illinois ex rel. Drainage Commissioners 824

Chicago, Mobile Dev. Co. v. G. C. Coggin Co. . 493

Chicago, Peoria & St. Louis R. R. Co. v. Vaughn 218

Chicago Title & Trust Co. v. Shellaberger 295

Chirco v. Crosswinds Communities, Inc. 859

Christmas v. Exxon Mobil Corp. 131

Citizens for Covenant Compliance v. Anderson . 657

Citizens to Preserve Overton Park v. Volpe. . . .798

City of (see name of city)

Civello, State ex rel. v. City of New Orleans . . .825

Claiborne v. Wilson 289

Clajon Prod. Corp. v. Petera. 734

Claridge v. New Hampshire Wetlands Board . . .718

Clark v. Carter 240, 241

Clark v. Maloney 23

Clark v. McNeal 549

Clark v. Walker. 419

Clark v. Wells 83, 84

Clark, In re Will of. 225

Clark, Matter of v. Board of Zoning Appeals. . .789

Clark Oil & Refining Corp. v. City of Evanston . 795

Clarke; United States v. 747

Class v. Strack 222

Clawson v. Primrose. 158

Clearview Coal Co.; Commonwealth v. 685

Cleburne, City of v. Cleburne Living Center . . .819

Cline v. American Aggregates Corp. 174, 175

Clucas v. State of Alaska 12

Coalition Advocating Legal Housing Options v. City of Santa Monica 809

Cohen v. Hayden. 313

Cohen v. Perrino. 155

Cohn, Matter of 70, 71

Coley v. Walker. 66

Collins v. Smithson. 188, 189

Collinson v. John L. Scott, Inc. 160

Collis v. City of Bloomington. 735

Colonial Village, Inc. v. Pelkey 410

Columbus, City of v. Barngrover 172

Columbus-America Discovery Group v. Atlantic Mut. Ins. Co. 19; 34

Columbus-America Discovery Group, Inc. v. Unidentified, Wrecked and Abandoned Sailing Vessel. .35

Comcast Cablevision of Sterling Heights, Inc. v. City of Sterling Heights. 94

Commerce Trust Co. v. White. 513

Commonwealth v. (see name of defendant)

Commonwealth Bldg. Corp. v. Hirschfield 404

Complaint of Steuart Transp. Co., In re 17

Compton v. Rixey's Ex'rs 260

Concord Bank v. Gregg 469

Concrete Pipe & Products of Cal., Inc. v. Construction Laborers Pension Trust for Southern Cal. 723

Conklin v. Davi 459

Connecticut National Bank v. Lorenzato 536

Consol. Turnpike Co. v. Norfolk & O. V. Ry. Co. 218

Continental Oil Company, State ex rel. v. Waddill, Mo. 826

Cook v. Stearns. 595

Cool v. Cool 260

Coombs v. Aborn. 548

[References are to pages.]

Coombs v. Anderson. 184
Cornell v. Heirs of Walik 243
Cornell College v. Crain 89
Cornett v. Nathan. 430
Corrigan v. City of Scottsdale. 751
Costley v. Caromin House, Inc.. 815
Couch v. Eastham 222
Counce v. Yount-Lee Oil Co. 107
County of (see name of county)
Cowen v. Pressprich. 54, 55
Cozens v. Stevenson. 306
Craft; United States v.. 231
Crane v. McCormick. 426
Crenshaw v. Williams 462
Crescent Harbor Water Co., Inc. v. Lyseng. . . .552
Crocker v. Cotting 503
Crocker Point Association v. Gouraud 460
Cronyn, In re. 901
Crow v. Kaupp. 366
Crow v. Wainwright 907
Crowley v. Knapp 819
Cumberland Farms, Inc. v. Dairy Mart, Inc. . . . 410
Curtman v. Piezuch 604
Cushman Corporation v. Barnes. 618
Cutter v. Wilkinson. 831
CWC Fisheries, Inc. v. Bunker 12

D

D'Ambrosio, Estate of v. Comm'r 72
Dado v. Jeeninga 24
Dailey v. City of Lawton 798
Danforth v. United States. 748, 749
Daniels v. Pond 20
Danpar Assocs. v. Somersville Mills Sales Room, Inc.. 396
Dapson v. Daly. 9
Darling v. Ennis 113
Dauberman v. Grant 134
Davidow v. Inwood North Professional Group. .338; 387
Davidson v. Davidson 204
Davis v. Nolte 770
Davis v. Vidal 355
Davis v. Williams 340
Deal; State v.. 602
DeAngelo v. Brazauskas 88
Deason v. Findley 486
Decatur Ventures LLC v. Daniel. 453
Deem v. Miller. 265

Deen v. Baltimore Gas & Electric Co. 779
Deetz; State v.. 164
Deimeke v. State Highway Com.. 824
Deiss v. Deiss 295
Del Monte Dunes v. City of Monterey 735
Delanoy v. Delanoy 240
Deleon Enterprises, Inc. v. Zaino 466
Demmitt v. McMillan 113
Den Norske Am. Actiesselskabet v. Sun Printing & Pub. Ass'n. 461
Devins v. Borough of Bogota 120
DeWeerth v. Baldinger. 99, 100
DeWitt v. Pierson 315
Dexter, Matter of v. Town Bd.. 763
Di Leo v. Pecksto Holding Corp 609
Diamond v. Chakrabarty. 897
Diamond v. Diehr 899
Dickhut v. Norton. 411, 412; 414
Dillman v. Hoffman 163
Dispeker v. New Southern Hotel Co.. 52
Dixon v. Salvation Army. 441
Dobbs v. Knoll. 115
Doctor v. Hughes. 270
Doherty v. Allman 218
Dolan v. City of Tigard. 724; 732
Dolitsky v. Dollar Sav. Bank 50
Donnelly v. Robinson 516
Donnelly Adver. Corp. v. Flaccomio 403
Donovan v. Donovan. 240
Doughty v. Sullivan. 10
Dow; United States v.. 747
Dowd v. Ahr. 620
Downey v. General Foods Corp. 908
Droney v. Droney 94
Drummond v. White Oak Fuel Co. 130
Druse v. Wheeler. 301
DSL Dynamic Sciences Limited v. Union Switch & Signal, Inc. 900
Du Bois v. Nye. 440
Dunbar, People ex rel. v. Bejarano 225
Dunlap v. Bullard. 357, 358
Dwyer v. Skyline Apartments, Inc. 346

E

E.I. Du Pont De Nemours & Co. v. Cetus Corp.. 901
Eads v. Brazelton 17; 35
Earle v. Arbogast. 320
Earle v. Fiske. 526
Eastwood v. Shedd. 547

[References are to pages.]

Eastwood v. Superior Court 874; 878
eBay, Inc. v. MercExchange, LLC. 899; 901
Echo Consulting Servs. v. North Conway Bank . 316
Eckart, In re Estate of 593
Economy Rentals, Inc. v. Garcia 373
Edmonds, City of v. Oxford House, Inc. 820
Educational Sales Programs, Inc. v. Dreyfus
    Corp.. 908
Edwards v. Habib. 411, 412; 415
Edwards v. Sims 148
Edwards & Deutsch Lithographing Co. v.
    Boorman. 852
Effinger v. Lewis. 209
Egbert v. Egbert 520
Eggen v. Wetterborg 328
Ehrlich v. City of Culver City. 735
Eisenstadt v. Baird. 811
El Di, Inc. v. Town of Bethany Beach 670
Ela v. Bankes. 208
Eldred v. Ashcroft 850
Eliason v. Wilborn 558
Ellicott v. Mayor of Baltimore. 782
Ellish v. Airport Parking Co. of America, Inc.. . . 46
Ellsworth Dobbs, Inc. v. Johnson 432
Elon College v. Elon B. & T. Co. 48
Elwes v. Brigg Gas Co.. 33
Emmons v. Scudder 208
Empire Properties, Inc. v. Equireal, Inc. 438
Employment Advisors, Inc. v. Sparks. 385
Entelman v. Hagood 409
Ephrata Area Sch. Dist. v. County of Lancaster . 620;
    626
Epstein v. Rose. 609
Epting v. Mayer 186
Erhard v. F.W. Woolworth Co.. 338
Erickson v. Sinykin 30
Ernst v. Conditt. 361
Erwin National Bank v. Riddle 188
Estate of (see name of party)
Euclid v. Ambler Realty Co.. . . .163; 726; 730; 752;
           787; 804; 809, 810
Eureka Springs Sales Co. v. Ward 74
Eusco, Inc. v. Huddleston. 86
Evans, In re. 571
Everitt v. Higgins 92, 93
Ex rel. (see name of relator)
Executors v. Houston. 208

F

Factors Etc., Inc. v. Pro Arts, Inc.. . . . . . .884; 889

Fallbrook Irrigation Dist. v. Bradley 675
Far West Savings & Loan Assn. v. McLaughlin . 549
Favorite v. Miller 31
Fay v. Fay 296
Federal National Mortgage Ass'n v. Levine-
    Rodriguez. 550
Federal Trade Commission v. Ticor Title Insurance
    Co.. 567
Fedorko Props., Inc. v. C.F. Zurn & Assocs . . . 623
Feider v. Feider. 648
Feist Publications, Inc. v. Rural Tel. Serv. Co.. .853;
           855, 856
Feister v. Bosack. 353
Feld v. Merriam 347
Ferguson v. Caspar. 573
Ferguson v. Village of Hamburg. 138, 139
Fernandez v. Wiener. 226
Ferris v. Frohman 843
Fields v. Conforti. 404
Fierro v. Hoel 73
Fifth Avenue Coach Lines, Inc., In re 739
Finch v. Moore. 207
Finley v. Finley. 266
First American Nat'l Bank v. Chicken System of
    America, Inc.. . . . . 363; 367
First American National Bank v. Chicken System of
    America, Inc.. 368
First Citizens Nat'l Bank v. Sherwood 550
First English Evangelical Lutheran Church v. County
    of Los Angeles. 745; 750; 777; 830
First Escrow, Inc., In re 590
First Trust & Sav. Bank v. Guthridge. 88
Fisher v. Comer Plantation, Inc.. 453
Fisher, Matter of Estate of. 219
Fitzgarrald v. City of Iowa City. 151
Flamingo Ranch Estates, Inc. v. Sunshine Ranches
    Homeowners, Inc.. 656
Flax v. Smith. 606
Fleet v. CBS, Inc. 891
Fleming v. Griswold. 106
Flemming v. Ronson Corp.. 906
Fletcher v. Peck 798
Floreau v. Thornhill 462
Flores v. Mosler Safe Co.. 889
The Florida Bar Re: Advisory Opinion etc.. . . .390
Flureau v. Thornhill 463
Fodor v. First Nat'l Supermarkets, Inc.. 410
Fontaine v. Ebtec Corp.. 872
Fontainebleau Hotel Corp. v. Forty-Five Twenty-Five,
    Inc.. 156

[References are to pages.]

Food Fair v. Blumberg. 371
Ford v. Venard. 89, 90
Fort Worth, City of v. Johnson 768
Fossum Orchards v. Pugsley. 609
Foster v. Joice 209
Foulkes v. Sengstacken 588
Foundation Dev. Corp. v. Loehmann's 410
44 Plaza, Inc. v. Gray-Pac Land Co.. . . . .155; 160
Fowler v. Coates. 249
Fowler v. Perry 72
Fox Film Corp. v. Doyal. 902
Frank v. Visockas 654
Franks v. Pritchett. 30
Franza v. Olin 115
Fraser v. Fred Parker Funeral Home 141
Frederick v. Burg. 126
Frederick Ward Assocs., Inc. v. Venture, Inc.. . .550
Freedman v. Oppenheim. 460
Frenz' Will, In re. 219
Friedman v. Le Noir 325; 376
Friedman v. Marshall. 205
Frobig v. Gordon. 346
Fry v. O'Leary. 743
Fuhst, Matter of v. Foley 764
Fulton v. McBurnie 518
Funk v. Haldeman 633

G

Gaertner v. Donnelly. 594
Gallagher v. Magner. 801
Gallenthin Realty Development, Inc. v. Borough of
    Paulsboro. 681
Gallo v. Brooklyn Savings Bank 461
Ganje v. Schuler. 119
Ganter v. Kapiloff. 31
Gaona v. Gonzales. 552
Gardner v. Dillard 267
Gardner v. Keteltas. 306
Gardner v. Padro. 456
Garner v. Gerrish. 209; 214
Garrett v. Coast & Southern Federal Sav. & Loan
    Ass'n. 427, 428
Garrido v. Burger King Corp.. 905
Geer v. Connecticut. 10; 12
General Motors Corp.; United States v.. . . 744; 748
Geo. M. McDonald & Co. v. Johns. 545
George Washington Univ. v. Weintraub. 340
Gerlach Live Stock Co.; United States v.. 744
Gerlock v. Gabel. 245

Gerruth Realty Co. v. Pire. 452
Gheen v. State ex rel. Dep't of Health 509
Ghen v. Rich. 13; 616
Giannini v. First National Bank of Des Plaines. .465
Gilchrist v. Van Dyke. 533, 534
Gillet v. Roberts. 99
Gilliam v. American Broad. Cos. 861
Gillies v. Orienta Beach Club. 614
Gilman v. Bell. 280
Gion v. Santa Cruz. 614
Goddard v. Winchell. 21
Godfrey v. Zoning Bd. of Adjustment. 805
Goff v. Graham. 450
Goldblatt v. Hempstead. 717; 719; 830
Golden v. Ramapo Planning Board 808
Golden Nugget, Inc. v. American Stock Exchange,
    Inc. 849
Goldstein v. California. 894, 895
Golub v. Colby. 316
Gomillion v. Lightfoot. 797
Goode v. Village of Woodgreen Homeowners
    Ass'n 647
Goodman v. Resident Servs.. 416
Goodwin v. Wertheimer. 99
Gordon v. Bauer. 465
Gordon v. Schneiker. 391
Gordon v. Tafe. 469
Gordon v. Whittle 196
Gorieb v. Fox. 699
Gosselin; Commonwealth v. 12
Gowl v. Atlantic Richfield Co.. 778
Grace v. Koch. 111; 113
Grand Trunk W. R.R. Co. v. Acme Belt Recoating,
    Inc.. 593
Grange v. Korff. 641; 666
Gray v. Fitzhugh. 115
Green v. General Petroleum Corporation 134
Green v. Leckington. 63
Green v. Superior Court. 334
Greenberg v. State 151
Greenberg v. Stewart Title Guaranty Co.. 571
Greenfarb v. R.S.K. Realty Corp 644
Greenpoint Mortg. Funding v. Schlossberg. 550
Gregory Hetter, M.D. v. The Eighth Judicial District
    Court of the State of Nevada. 878
Griffin v. Illinois 811
Griffin v. Northridge. 132
Grimes v. Rush. 204
Griswold v. Connecticut 811; 813

Groucho Marx Productions v. Day & Night Co. . 885
Gruen v. Gruen 67
Gruman v. Investors Diversified Serv., Inc. 383
Grytbak v. Grytbak. 210
Guarantee Title & Trust Co. v. Siedhoff. . .197, 198
Guaranty Trust Co. v. New York & Q. C. R.
    Co. 644
Guggenheim v. City of Goleta. 711
Guilliams v. Koonsman 257

H

Haas v. Feist 859
Hadacheck v. Sebastian. 689; 716; 719
Hadley v. Baxendale. 461
Haelan Laboratories, Inc. v. Topps Chewing Gum,
    Inc. 875; 881; 883; 889
Haer v. Christmas 512
Haggerty v. City of Oakland. 289
Haggren v. State of Alaska 12
Hailey, Village of v. Riley. 613
Hairston v. Danville & Western R. Co. . . . 676; 685
Haldeman v. Bruckhart. 179
Hale v. Ward County. 131
Hall v. Gulledge 656
Hall v. Hall 187; 211
Hall v. Schoenwetter 37
Hall v. Wood 170
Hall, In re. 901
Halvorson v. Birkland 468
Hamaker v. Blanchard. 30
Haman, State ex rel. v. Fox 610
Hamilton v. City of Jackson. 252
Hamlin v. Pandapas 598
Hammond v. McArthur 240
Hancock v. Butler 268
Hancock v. Henderson. 601
Hannan v. Dusch. 302
Harbison, Matter of v. City of Buffalo 762
Harmon v. City of Dallas 770
Harper v. Virginia State Board. 811
Harper & Row, Publishers, Inc. v. Nation
    Enters. 851; 854
Harris v. Axline 468
Harris v. Brooks 179
Harris v. City of Wichita. 734
Harris, Estate of 240
Harris Trust & Savings Bank v. Beach 295
Harrison v. Mayor and Board of Alderman of City of
    Batesville. 776
Harrison v. Montgomery Co. Bd. of Educ. 371

Hart v. Farmers & Mechanics Bank. 534
Hart v. Socony-Vacuum Oil Co. 362; 366
Harts v. Arnold Bros. 323; 329
Hash v. United States 196
Haslem v. Lockwood 19
Hatch v. Riggs Nat'l Bank. 272
Haughwout v. Murphy. 238
Hawaii Housing Authority v. Midkiff . 674, 675; 678;
                                        695; 749
Hayes v. Aquia Marina, Inc. 616
Haywood v. Fulmer 301
Hearne v. Bradshaw 476
Heart of America Lumber Co. v. Belove 328
Heath v. Dodson 445
Hebe Co. v. Shaw 757
Heflin v. Phillips. 491
Heide v. Glidden Buick Corp. 100
Heins Implement Co. v. State Highway Comm'n.172
Henderson v. Hunter. 191
Hendricks, Appeal of. 199
Hendrickson v. Minneapolis Federal Sav. & L.
    Ass'n 242
Hendrickson v. Wagners. 172
Henningsen v. Bloomfield Motors, Inc. 334
Herpolsheimer v. Christopher 305; 391
Hersh Properties, LLC v. McDonald's Corp. . . .558
Herter v. Mullen 404
Heston v. Ousler 161
Hewitt v. Meaney 602
Hicks v. Casablanca Records. 882; 885
Hicks v. Farrell. 547
Higbee v. Chicago, B. & Q. R. Co. 789
Higgins v. Whiting. 332
Highway 7 Embers, Inc. v. Northwestern Nat'l
    Bank. 160
Hildebrandt v. Hildebrandt. 538
Hilder v. St. Peter. 335; 337; 339
Hilton; Commonwealth v. 10
Hinman v. Pacific Air Transport. 149
Hinton v. Bowen. 188
Hisaw v. Bishop 153
Hobbs v. Cawley. 362
Hodel v. Irving. 722
Hodel v. Virginia Surface Mining & Reclamation
    Ass'n, Inc. 697
Hodgson v. Perkins. 597
Hoel v. Flour City F.&T. Co. 48
Hoene v. Milwaukee. 162
Hoffman v. Capital Cities/ABC, Inc. 895
Hogue v. Port of Seattle 682

[References are to pages.]

Hollars v. Church of God of Apostolic Faith, Inc. 603

Hollingsworth v. Seventy Doubloons and Three Small Pieces of Gold 19

Holmes v. Coghill 281

Holy Properties Ltd., L.P. v. Kenneth Cole Prods. 381; 390

Home Builders Ass'n v. City of Scottsdale 735

Home Builders Association of Dayton and the Miami Valley v. City of Beavercreek. 735; 769

Home Builders Association of Northern California v. City of Napa 809

Hornsby v. Smith. 154; 156

Hornstein v. Podwitz. 875

Houghton v. Rizzo. 652

Houle v. Quenneville. 416

House; State v. 12

Howard v. Kunto. 114

Hulbert v. California Portland Cement Co. 139

Hulett v. Swift. 43

Humble Oil & Refining Co. v. Doerr. 520

Humphries v. Huffman. 113

Hunt v. City of San Antonio. 768; 770

Huntington v. Huntington Branch, NAACP. . . .801

Huntington Branch, NAACP v. Town of Huntington 801

Hurd v. Cushing 209

Huston Co. v. Mooney. 431

Hyland v. Borras. 63

I

I.P. Lund Trading ApS v. Kohler Co. 897

Idaho Water Resource Board v. Kramer. 611

Imas Gruner & Assoc. Ltd. v. Stringer 453

In re Estate of (see name of party)

In re (see name of party)

In re Will of (see name of party)

In the Matter of (see name of party)

Inclusive Cmtys. Project, Inc. v. Tex. Dep't of Hous. & Cmty. Affairs 801

Industrial Indem. Co. v. Columbia Basin Steel & Iron, Inc. 615

Ingalls v. Hobbs 333

Intel Corp. v. Hamidi 41

International News Service v. Associated Press . 833; 844, 845; 847, 848

Isen v. Giant Food, Inc. 288

Island Creek Coal Co. v. Rodgers. 128

Ivons-Nispel, Inc. v. Lowe. 612

J

J.C. Penney Co. v. Giant Eagle, Inc. 538

J.C. Vereen & Sons, Inc. v. City of Miami 193

J.H. Bellows Co. v. Covell. 329

J.T. Hobby and Son, Inc. v. Family Homes of Wake County, Inc. 819

Jaber v. Miller 360

Jackson v. Robinson 210

Jacobs v. Klawans 369, 370

Jacobs v. United States. 747

Jacobsen v. Deseret Book Co. 859

James v. Valtierra. 794

Jamesson v. Downtown Dev. Authority. 744

Javins v. First Nat'l Realty Corp. 333, 334

Jefferies v. The Great Western Railway 37

Jeffery Towers, Inc., Application of. 520

Jeffrey Towers, Inc. v. Straus 520

Jelco, Inc. v. Third Judicial District Court 445

Jenkins v. McKeithen 795

Jennings v. State 543

Jernigan v. Ham. 85

Jewelers' Mercantile Agency v. Jewelers' Weekly Pub. Co. 844

Johnson v. Benjamin Moore & Co. 909

Johnson v. Johnson. 238

Johnson v. Whiton. 183

Johnston v. Cosby 294

Jones v. Levin 346

Jones v. New Orleans & S. R. C. & I. Assoc. . . 217

Jones v. Oklahoma City 248

Jost v. Dairyland Power Coop. 141

Judson v. Los Angeles Suburban Gas Co. 134

Juif v. Dillman 252

Julian v. Christopher 369

Just v. Marinette 163; 709

Justice v. Nesquehoning V. R. Co. 217

K

K & L Distribs. v. Kelly Elec. 93

Kaiser Aetna v. United States 697; 720; 726

Karesh v. City Council of Charleston. 682

Katz v. Duffy. 315

Kaufman v. Federal National Bank of Boston . . 595

Keble v. Hickringill. 7

Kellogg, City of v. Silver Mtn. Corp. 502

Kelly v. Fairmount Land Co. 544

Kelly v. Tri-Cities Broadcasting, Inc. 362

[References are to pages.]

Kelo v. City of New London 672
Kennedy v. Kidd. 329
Kennedy v. Moog Servocontrols. 139
Kennedy Park Homes Ass'n v. City of Lackawanna. 794; 798
Kent's Run P'ship, Ltd. v. Glosser 622
Kentucky-Ohio Gas Co. v. Bowling. 138
Kenyon v. Abel 73
Keron v. Cashman. 24
Kessler v. Tortoise Dev., Inc. 466
Kessler, In re Estate of. 224
Ketchum v. Whitfield County 502
Key v. Alexander. 464
Keyes v. School Dist. No. 1, Denver, Colo. . . . 797
Keystone Bituminous Coal Ass'n v. DeBenedictis. 691; 714; 719; 723
Kies v. Warrick. 466
Kimball Laundry Co. v. United States.696; 738, 739
Kimmell v. Skelly 427
King v. H.J. McNeel, Inc. 153
King v. Moorehead. 339
King v. Reynolds. 303
King's Estate, In re. 476
Kingsley v. Gouldsborough Land Imp. Co.. . . .599
Kirby Forest Industries, Inc. v. United States. . .747
Kirk v. Schultz. 613
Kiser v. Clinchfield Coal Corp. 526
Kisil v. City of Sandusky 777
Klebs v. Yim. 125
Klie v. Broock 324
Kline v. Burns 316; 319
Kline v. 1500 Massachusetts Avenue Apartment Corp.. .350
Kling v. Hallmark Cards, Inc. 860
Koch v. Ellwood. 460
Koger Properties, Inc. v. Allen 169
Koontz v. St. Johns River Water Management Dist.. .735
Kordecki v. Rizzo 541
Korn v. Campbell 646
Kovarik v. Vesely 456
Kremen v. Cohen 41
Kresser v. Peterson. 506
KSR Int'l Co. v. Teleflex, Inc.. 899
Kula v. Prososki 751
Kutzin v. Pirnie. 465

L

L.E. Waterman v. Modern Pen Co. 896

L. Smirlock Realty Corp. v. Title Guar. Co. . . . 570
Laba v. Carey. 462
Labbe v. Steffens. 131
Lacey v. Floyd 267
Lach v. Cahill 454
Lacy v. Flake & Kelley Mgmt. 352
Ladue, City of v. Gilleo 827
Lake v. Sullivan 301
Lamar Advertising of South Georgia, Inc. v. City of Albany. 766
Lambert v. Matthews. 131
Landshire Food Service, Inc. v. Coghill 76
Lane v. Kennedy. 113
Larkin v. State Dept. of Social Services 820
Larned v. Hudson 208
Las Vegas Downtown Redevelopment Agency, City of v. Pappas 141
Laspeyre v. McFarland 39
Last Chance Ditch Co. v. Sawyer. 612
Laughlin v. Elliott 291
Lawall v. Groman 460
Lawrence v. Chicago Title Ins. Co. 571
Lea v. Hernandez. 208
Leadbetter v. Pewtherer 375
Lechner v. Halling 582
Leckey v. Lower Southampton Twp. Zoning Hearing Bd.. 785
Leeds Bldg. Prods. v. Sears Mortg. Corp.. 538
Legg v. Castruccio. 315
Lehigh Valley R. Co. v. McFarlan. 612
Lehmann v. Keller. 93
Leigh v. Green. 608
Leighton v. Leonard 650
Leo Sheep Co. v. United States 601
Leonard v. Autocar Sales & Service Co. . . . 312, 313
Leonard v. Fallas. 426
LeRoux v. Edmundson. 817
Lesher v. Strid 469
Leslie Pontiac, Inc. v. Novak 329
Letts v. Kessler. 154
Levy Leasing Co. v. Siegel 686
Lewis v. Marker. 505
Lewis v. Poduska 72
Lewis v. Premium Investment Corp. 450
Lewis v. Prendergast. 468
Libman v. Levenson 438
Lieb v. Webster. 586
Liesner v. Wanie 6
Liggett & Myers v. United States 739

Lighthouse Community Church of God v. City of Southfield 831
Liles Bros. & Son v. Wright 85
Lindholm v. Brant 82
Lindsay v. James 637
Lindsey v. Clark 635
Lindsey v. DeGroot 146
Lindsey v. Normet 409; 794; 801
Lingle v. Chevron U.S.A. Inc. 702
Linkous v. Candler 259
Livingston v. New York, O. & W. R. Co. 217
Lloyd v. Murphy 310
Locke v. Bort 452
Logan v. Moulder 487
Loretto v. Teleprompter Manhattan CATV Corp. 695; 710; 719
Los Angeles Brick & Clay Products Co. v. City of Los Angeles 134
Louis W. Epstein Family P'ship v. Kmart Corp. . 625
Lovejoy v. School District 110
Lubner v. City of Los Angeles 874
Lucas v. South Carolina Coastal Council . . 712; 718
Ludlow, State ex rel. v. Guffey, Mo. 826
Luette v. Bank of Italy Nat'l Tr. & Savings Ass'n 448
Lugosi v. Universal Pictures 884; 893
Lund v. Idaho & W. N. R. R. 743
Luter v. Hutchinson 97
Lutheran Church in Amer. v. City of New York . 829, 830
Luttinger v. Rosen 453
Lux v. Milwaukee Mechanics' Ins. Co. 826
Lynch v. Hill 158
Lynn v. Hall 292
Lyons Partnership, L.P. v. Morris Costumes, Inc. .859

M

M.L. Sigmon Forest Prod., Inc. v. Scroggins . . .378
MacArtor v. Graylyn Crest III Swim Club, Inc. . 176
Mackintosh v. Stewart 492
Maddocks v. Giles 172, 173
Magevney v. Karsch 189
Magidson, State ex rel. v. Henze 823; 826
Malek v. Patten 72
Malloy v. Boettcher 593
Manchester Dairy System, Inc. v. Hayward 470
Mann v. Lower Makefield Twp. 784
Mannin v. Adkins 628
Manufactured Housing Communities of Washington v. Washington 682

Marcus Brown Holding Co. v. Feldman 686
Margaret H. Wayne Trust v. Lipsky 432
Markese v. Cooper 411; 414
Marrs v. City of Oxford 824
Marsh v. Gentry 15
Marshall v. Salt Lake City 789
MAR-SON, Inc. v. Terwaho Enterprises, Inc. . . .397
Martha's Vineyard Scuba HQ v. Unidentified Vessel 34
Martin v. Adams 517
Martin v. Allen 419
Martin v. City of Indianapolis 862
Martin v. City of Linden 179
Martin v. Franklin Capital Corp. 903
Martin v. Music 620; 626
Martin v. Prairie Rod & Gun Club 294
Martin Luther King, Jr., Center for Social Change, Inc. v. American Heritage Products, Inc. 878
Mattel, Inc. v. MCA Records, Inc. 895
Matter of Estate of (see name of party)
Matter of (see name of party)
Matthys v. Swedish Baptist Church 147
Mau v. E.P.H. Corp. 419
Mauala v. Milford Management Co. 302
Maudru v. Humphreys 440
Maxwell v. Redd 485
Maze v. Gordon 426
McAvoy v. Medina 29
McCabe v. City of Parkersburg 122
McCagg, Estate of 97
McCarthy v. City of Leawood 734
McCarthy v. Pieret 70
McCartney v. Robbins 198
McCrady v. Mahon 470
McCusker v. Goode 655
McGinnis, In re 554
McGlashan v. Spade Rockledge Terrace Condo. Dev. Corp. 170
McGlynn v. Parking Authority of City of Newark .51
McGregor v. Provident Trust Co. of Philadelphia 158
McKay Consulting, Inc. v. Rockingham Memorial Hospital 909
McKee v. Gratz 7
McKelvy v. Cooper 110
McKibben v. Pioneer Trust & Savings Bank . . .294, 295
McLean v. Caldwell 364
McPherson v. Barbour 587
McShane v. City of Faribault 151; 706; 708

McWhorter v. City of Winnsboro 770
Meadows v. Brich 506
Mease v. Fox 335, 336
Medico-Dental Bldg. Co. of Los Angeles v. Horton & Converse 309
Melenky v. Melen 220
Melms v. Pabst Brewing Co 214, 215
Melson v. Ormsby 669
Melton v. Melton 199
Memphis Development Foundation v. Factors Etc., Inc. 884
Menlo Park, City of v. Artino 737
Mercantile Library Co. v. Fidelity Trust Co. . . .625
Merrill v. Grinnell 44
Meservey v. Gulliford 613
Messersmith v. Smith 537
Methonen v. Stone 542
Metropolitan Housing Development Corp. v. Arlington Heights 792; 794; 799, 800
Metzger v. Hochrein 162, 163
Meyer v. Law 116
Meyer v. Nebraska 813
Meyers v. Langley 419
Miami Beach v. State 158
Miami Beach, City of v. State ex rel. Fontainebleau Hotel Corp. 158
Michels Pipeline Constr., Inc.; State v. 178
Mid America Title Co. v. Kirk 855
MidCountry Bank v. Krueger 551
Midler v. Ford Motor Co. 878
Midrash Sephardi, Inc. v. Town of Surfside . . .831
Midway Auto Sales, Inc. v. Clarkson 74
Midway Protective League v. City of Dallas . . .770
Miebach v. Safe Title Ins. Co. 569
Miller v. Clary 644
Miller v. Dyer 441
Miller v. Emans 249
Miller v. Hoeschler 160
Miller v. Lutheran Conference & Camp Ass'n. .620; 629
Miller v. Metropolitan Water Reclamation Dist. . 120
Miller v. Schoene 690; 717
Miller v. Whitworth 352
Mills v. Embrey 234, 235
Milwaukee & Sub. Transp. v. Milwaukee County 739
Minneapolis Post Office Rifle & Pistol Club v. United States 744
Mission Covenant Church v. Nelson 818

Mitchell v. Foran 343
Moakley v. Eastwick 869
Mobil Oil Corp. v. Amoco Oil Corp. 901
Mobile Home Owners Protective Assoc. v. Town of Chatham .762
Modjeska Sign Studios, Inc. v. Berle 762
Moelle v. Sherwood 526
Mohr v. Midas Realty Corp. 160, 161
Moline, State ex rel. v. Driscoll 743
Monongahela Nav. Co. v. United States 739
Montauk Corp. v. Seeds 310
Monterey, City of v. Del Monte Dunes at Monterey, Ltd. .735, 736
Monumental Properties, Inc.; Commonwealth v. .540
Monypeny v. Monypeny 221
Moon v. North Idaho Farmers Ass'n 146
Moonlight v. Boyce 417
Moore v. East Cleveland 730; 814
Moore v. The Regents of the University of California 40
Moores v. Walsh 601
Mooring v. Brown 445
Morford v. Lensey Corp. 415
Morgan, Board of County Commissioners of County of v. Kobobel 141
Morgan Lake Co. v. N.Y., N.H. & H. R.R. Co. . 643
Morgenstern v. Eastman Kodak Co. 62
Morning Call, Inc. v. Bell Atlantic-Pennsylvania, Inc. 622
Morrell v. Rice 600
Morris v. Morris 219
Morris v. Ulbright 203
Morris County Land Improvement Co. v. Parsippany-Troy Hills Township 715
Morrison v. Bucksport & B. R. Co. 174
Morseburg v. Balyon 873
Moseley v. V Secret Catalogue 897
Moseley v. Zieg 505; 507, 508
Mosher v. Van Buskirk 237
Moss v. O'Brien 109
Moss Point Lumber Co. v. Board of Sup'rs . . . 322
Motion Picture Patents Co. v. Universal Film Co. 843
Mott v. Oppenheimer 645
Mountain Queen Condominium Ass'n v. Haan . .419
Mountain Side Mobile Estates Partnership v. Secretary of Housing and Urban Development 801
Mountain States Tel. and Telegraph Co. v. Kelton 552

[References are to pages.]

Moyer v. Martin 634

Moyer v. Wrecked and Abandoned Vessel known as the Andrea Doria 34

Mt. Healthy City School Dist. Bd. of Education v. Doyle 799

Mt. Holly Gardens Citizens in Action v. Township of Mount Holly 801

Mueller v. Novelty Dye Works 445

Mugler v. Kansas 689; 695, 696; 716; 719

Municipality of Anchorage v. Locker 572

Murphy v. Bolger 146

Murphy v. California 689

Murphy v. New Milford Zoning Comm'n 831

Murphy v. Smallridge 415

Murray v. Miller 221

Murray v. National Broadcasting Co., Inc. 906

Musgrove v. Cordova Coal, Land & Improvement Co. 490, 491

Muwonge, Antwaun A. ex rel. v. Heritage Mutual Insurance Co. 346

Myers v. Koenig 406

Mygatt v. Coe 486

Myrick v. James 175

N

NAACP v. Alabama 811

NAACP v. Button 811; 813

Nabisco, Inc. v. PF Brands, Inc. 897

Naftzger v. American Numismatic Soc'y 96

Nahrstedt v. Lakeside Village Condominium Ass'n 648

Napier v. Napier 300

Napier v. Springfield 608

Nappi v. La Guardia 789

Narragansett Elec. Co. v. Carbone 41

National Shawmut Bank v. Cutter 470

Neiss v. Franze 452

Nelson v. Oren 309

Nemmers v. City of Dubuque 751

Neponsit Property Owners' Ass'n v. Emigrant Industrial Sav. Bank 642

New York City Housing Auth., Matter of v. Muller 139

New York, O. & W. R. Co. v. Livingston . . 214; 216

New York Times Co. v. Tasini 858; 902

New York Trust Co. v. Eisner 903

New York, W. S. & B. R. Co., In re 217

Newman v. Carson 64

Newton v. Magill 543

Nicholas v. Adams 67

Nichols v. Day 289

Nichols v. Luce 600

Nicoll v. New York & Erie R.R. Co 249

Nies, In re 537

99 Cents Only Stores v. Lancaster Redevelopment Agency 680

Nollan v. California Coastal Comm . . .717; 724; 726, 727; 729, 730; 732

Nomar v. Ballard 160

Noonan v. Pardee 130

Noone v. Price 121

Northeast Coating Techs. v. Vacuum Metallurgical Co 41

Northern Indiana Public Service Co. v. Vesey . . 138

Northridge Bank v. Lakeshore Commercial Finance Corp. 520

Northwest Airlines v. State of Minnesota 149

Norwood, City of v. Horney 681

O

O'Connor v. City of Moscow 764

O'Donnell v. Robson 248

O'Donnell v. Weintraub 362

O'Keeffe v. Snyder 100; 102

O'Neil v. Atwell 161

Oakland, City of v. Oakland Raiders 736; 741

Official Airlines Schedule Information Serv., Inc. v. Eastern Air Lines, Inc. 907

Ohio, State of v. Shaw 11

Oldfield v. Stoeco Homes, Inc. 193

Oliver v. Zoning Commission 817

Olmstead v. United States 813

Omega Corp. v. Malloy 647

Opinion of the Justices 807

Oregon City v. Hartke 825

Orito; United States v. 731

Ortega v. Flaim 346

Osborn v. Cardeza 137

Otto v. Steinhilber 776

Overholtzer v. Northern Counties Title Ins. Co. . 569, 570

Overton v. Lea 188

P

P.H. Inv. v. Oliver 410

Paccar v. Schwab 87

Pacifica Homeowners' Association v. Wesley Palms Retirement Community 160

Packard-Bamberger & Co. v. Maloof 366

[References are to pages.]

Packwood, Succession of 225

Pagan v. New York Herald Tribune 889, 890

Paine v. Meller. 438

Palazzolo v. Rhode Island 723

Palmer v. Schonhorn Enterprises. 881, 882

PaperCutter, Inc. v. Fay's Drug Co.. 897

Pappenheim v. Metropolitan El. Ry. Co. 138

Paradine v. Jane. 320, 321

Paris Adult Theatre I v. Slaton. 813

Parks v. LaFace Records. 886

Parsons; State v. 11

Pasadena, City of v. City of Alhambra 174

Pate v. Riverbend Mobile Home Village 346

Patterson v. Reigle. 114

Pavesich v. New England Life Insur. Co.. .874; 880; 883

Payton v. New York 680

Peabody v. Norfolk. 909

Pearson v. Nelley. 191, 192

Peet v. Roth Hotel Co. 46

Pekas Co., Inc. v. Leslie 876

Pelham Esplanade, Matter of v. Board of Trustees 762, 763

Pell, Matter of v. Board of Educ.. 829

Pencader Associates, Inc. v. Glasgow Trust. . . .599

Pendergrast v. Aiken. 169

Penelko, Inc. v. John Price Assocs.. 361

Penn Central Transportation Co. v. City of New York . . .152; 690; 693; 695; 698; 706; 714, 715; 717; 722; 729; 829, 830

Pennsylvania Coal Co. v. Mahon . . . 683; 691; 701; 714; 719; 726; 732, 733; 749

Pennsylvania Northwestern Distribs. v. Zoning Hearing Bd. 766

People v. (see name of defendant)

People ex rel. (see name of relator)

People's Counsel for Baltimore County v. Mangione 784

People's Savings Bank v. Bates 546, 547

Peoria Heights v. Keithley. 247

Performance Systems, Inc. v. First American National Bank. 368

Perkinpine v. Hogan 622

Perkins v. Gosewehr. 453

Perry v. J.L. Mott Iron Works Co.. 320

Peters v. East Penn Township School Dist.. . . . 190

Peterson v. Superior Court. 346

Peterson v. Vasak. 775, 776

Peterson v. Wirum 456

Petrain v. Kiernan 544

Petty Motor Co.; United States v.. 748

Pharr v. Tippitt. 767

Phelps v. McQuade 74

Philadelphia, R. & N. E. R. Co. v. Bowman . . .218

Philbin v. Carr 113

Phipps v. Leftwich. 233

Phoenix Title & Trust Co. v. Old Dominion Co.. .521

Pierce v. Casady. 147

Pierce v. Northeast Lake Washington Sewer and Water Dist.. 160

Pierce Oil Corp. v. Hope. 689; 757

Pierson v. Post 1; 15

Pikeville Nat'l Bank & Trust Co. v. Shirley 67

Pilus v. Milford. 271

Pingleton v. Shepherd. 75

Pinzon v. A & G Props. 337; 341

Pioneer Trust & Savings Bank v. Mount Prospect. 730

Pirone v. MacMillan, Inc.. 891

Plymouth Coal Co. v. Pennsylvania. 685; 719

Pocantico Water Works Co. v. Bird. 140

Poletown Neighborhood Council v. Detroit . 680; 682

Polka v. May. 245

Pollara v. Seymour. 867

Pollock v. Morelli 319

Pollock v. Speidel 204

Ponsler v. Union Traction Co.. 328

Poole v. French. 198

Popov v. Hayashi 22

Popp v. Bond. 264

Popp, Succession of 225

Porter v. United States. 739

Porter v. Wertz. 76; 80

Portland Savings Bank v. Landry 518

Post v. Pearsall. 614

Potwin State Bank v. J.B. Houston & Son 520

Powell v. Pennsylvania. 689

Poyck v. Bryant 337

Prah v. Maretti. 161

Pratt v. State, Dep't of Natural Resources 703

Prentiss v. Gloucester 607

Presley, Estate of v. Russen 880; 884

Prete v. Cray. 125, 126

Price v. Hal Roach Studios. 880; 883

Proffitt v. Isley. 487

Progress Development Corp. v. Mitchell 798

Proprietors of Church v. Grant 358

Provident Bank v. Tri-County Southside Asphalt, Inc.. 73

PruneYard Shopping Center v. Robins 731

Public Beach, In re. 647

[References are to pages.]

Publications Int'l, Ltd. v. Meredith Corp. 855
Pugh v. Holmes 350
Pulchny v. Pulchny. 476
Pulcifer v. Bishop 110
Pumpelly v. Green Bay Co. 690
Purefoy v. Rogers 278
Purity Extract Co. v. Lynch 758

Q

Quincy Cablesystems, Inc. v. Sully's Bar, Inc.. . .41
Quinn v. Holly. 606

R

Radice v. New York 757
Rael v. Taylor 554
Rahm v. Domayer. 89, 90
Ramot v. Scotenfels 550
Ramsey v. Lewis. 160
Randall v. Chase. 595
Randall v. Kreiger 222
Random House, Inc. v. Rosetta Books LLC.857, 858
Rankin v. FPL Energy, LLC. 166
Rasmuson; United States v. 555
Rassier v. Houim. 166
RCA Mfg. Co. v. Whiteman. 842
Real Estate Bar Association for Massachusetts, Inc. v.
    National Real Estate Information Services. . .590
Reaume v. Brennan 333
Reaver v. Martin Theatres. 157
Reed v. Piedimonte. 608
Reed v. Reed. 811
Reeves v. Alyeska Pipeline Service Corp.. 909
Region II Child & Family Services, Inc., State ex rel.
    v. District Court of the Eighth Judicial
    District. 818
Register.com v. Verio 41
Reid v. Architectural Board of Review of the City of
    Cleveland Heights. 825, 826
Reid v. Mutual of Omaha Ins. Co. 385
Reinman v. Little Rock. 689; 719
Reiss v. Reiss. 241
Reitman v. Mulkey. 794
Rentz, In re Estate of 266
Residences at Riverbend Condo. Ass'n v. City of
    Chicago. 165
Reste Realty Corp. v. Cooper. . .318, 319; 329; 338
Rexroth v. Coon. 7
Reynolds v. Bagwell. 97
Reynolds v. Gagen. 289

Reynolds v. McCullough. 373
Reynolds v. Van Beuren. 594
Reynolds v. Van Wagoner 445
Rhodes v. Pioneer Parking Lot, Inc. 52
Rhue v. Cheyenne Homes, Inc. 647
Rice v. Boston & Worcester R.R. 248
Rich v. Downs. 526
Richardson v. Holman. 250
Richart v. Jackson 545
Richmond, City of v. United States. 797
Riddle v. Harmon 239
Ridenour v. Woodward 48
Rideout v. Knox 684
Rieger v. Wessel 641
Riggs v. Bank of Camas Prairie 47
Riley v. Bear Creek Planning Committee. 661
Ringwood Assocs. v. Jack's of Route 23, Inc. . . 338
Ritz v. Selma United Methodist Church 22
RMS Titanic, Inc. v. The Wrecked and Abandoned
    Vessel. .35
Roath v. Driscoll. 178
Roberson v. Rochester Folding Box Co.. . .880; 888
Roberts v. Hale. 189
Roberts v. Lynn Ice Co. 594
Roberts v. Martin. 181
Robertson v. Bertha Mineral Co. 616
Robinson v. Diamond Housing Corp. 411; 414
Robinson v. Glenn. 267
Robison v. Stokes 353
Robrecht v. Marling 307
Robroy Land Co. v. Prather 649, 650
Rocamora v. Heaney. 502
Roche Products, Inc. v. Bolar Pharmaceutical
    Co.. 903
Rockford Map Publishers, Inc. v. Directory Service
    Co.. 850
Rockwell v. Sun Harbor Budget Suites 352
Rodgers v. Tarrytown. 786; 789
Rodier v. Twp. of Ridley. 625
Rogers v. Cardinal Realty Inc.. 455
Rogers v. Grimaldi. 896
Rogers v. Rogers. 186
Rogers v. Watson. 638
Rogers; United States v. 219
Rogis v. Barnatowich 548
Rohde v. Beztak of Arizona, Inc. 160
Roper v. Durham. 155
Rose v. Chaikin 166
Rose v. Freeway Aviation 327

Rose Lawn Cemetery Ass'n v. Scott 599
Rountree v. Thompson. 321
Royster Guano Co. v. Virginia. 811
Ruckelshaus v. Monsanto Co. 676; 695
Rudnick v. Rudnick 595
Russell v. Hill 38
Ruston v. Centennial Real Estate 393, 394
Ryan, In re 533; 536

S

S.D.G. v. Inventory Control Co.. 379
Saelzler v. Advanced Group 400 352
Safe Deposit & Trust Co. of Baltimore v. Bouse.258
Sagamore Corp. v. Willcutt 381
Sain v. Silvestre 659
Saltus & Saltus v. Everett. 99
Samples v. Geary 47
San Antonio School Dist. v. Rodriguez 794
San Diego Gas & Electric Co. v. San Diego. . .707;
            714, 715; 747, 748
San Francisco Credit Clearing House v. Wells. . .97
Sanborn v. McLean 641
Sanden v. Hanson 397
Sander v. Piggly Wiggly Stores, Inc. 366
Santa Margarita Area Residents Together v. San Luis
            Obispo County 773
Sapper v. Mathers 191
Saratoga State Waters Corp. v. Pratt. 593
Sargent v. Leonardi. 654
Saveland Park Holding Corp., State ex rel. v.
            Wieland 825, 826
Say v. Stoddard. 207
Sayers v. Rochester Telephone Corp. Supplemental
            Management Pension Plan 858
Saylor v. Brooks 326
Scarberry v. Carr. 503
Scaringe v. J.C.C. Enterprises, Inc. 660
Schenck v. Barnes 221
Scherer v. Hyland 67
Schlesinger v. Reservists to Stop the War. 796
Schley v. Couch 33
Schmidt v. Quinn. 608
Schneiker v. Gordon 385; 391
Schork v. Epperson. 155
Schroeder v. William Morrow & Co. 851
Schuknecht v. Schultz 294
Schultz v. Pritts. 778
Schuman v. Greenbelt Homes Inc. 131
Schweiger v. Superior Court. 411; 414
Scott v. Jordan 135

Scranton v. Wheeler 719
SCRAP; United States v.. 795
Scruggs v. Dennis. 52
Sea Hunters, LP v. The Unidentified, Wrecked &
            Abandoned Vessel 35
Seaman v. Harmon. 221
Seaman v. Seaman. 517
Searl v. School District No. 2 in Lake County . .216
Sebald v. Mulholland. 645
Sebastian v. Floyd 450
Seeton v. Pennsylvania Game Comm'n 13
Segelke v. Atkins. 109
Seibel v. Higham. 515
Seitz Packing & Mfg. Co. v. Quaker Oats Co.. . .605
Seligman v. First Nat'l Inv., Inc. 458
Seminole County v. Mertz. 169
Seneca Nation v. Appleby 249
Senez v. Collins 107
Seton v. Swann. 116
Shamrock Hilton Hotel v. Caranas 58
Shanahan v. Collins 393
Shapiro v. Thompson. 811
Shenandoah Valley Nat'l Bk. v. Taylor 288
Shepard v. Village of Skaneateles 787; 790
Sher v. Leiderman 165
Sheridan v. Lucey 244
Sherman v. Town of Chester. 736
Sherwin v. Cabana Club Apts.. 419
Shields v. Kearney. 776
Shindler v. Grove Hall Kosher Delicatessen & Lunch,
            Inc.. 314
Shump v. First Continental-Robinwood Assocs. . 346
Sickman v. United States. 9
Sierad v. Lilly 318
Sierra Club v. Morton 796
Signal Management Corp. v. Lamb 397
Simis v. McElroy. 460
Simmons v. Perkins 613
Simon v. Eastern Ky. Welfare Rights Org. . 795; 797
Simons Land Co. v. City of Dallas 770
Simpson v. North Platte 730
Sinclair Pipe Line Co. v. Richton Park 806
Sipriano v. Great Spring Waters of Am., Inc.. . . .175
Skally v. Shute. 314
Skeen v. Clinchfield Coal Corp.. 287
Skelly Oil Co. v. Ashmore. 438
Skelton v. Martin. 551
Skelton v. Spencer 611
Skendzel v. Marshall. 450
Skinner v. Reed 770

[References are to pages.]

Slater v. Ward 609

Slotoroff v. Nassau Assocs. 147

Slutsky v. City of New York. 166

Smith v. Boyd 436

Smith v. City of Centralia. 743

Smith v. Clews. 79

Smith v. County of Santa Barbara. 151

Smith v. Diplock. 518

Smith v. Marrable 333

Smith v. McEnany. 317

Smith v. Reeder 409

Smith v. Roberts. 311

Smith v. Russ 74

Smith v. Simons 301

Smith v. Smith ex rel. Clarke 297

Smith v. Smith. 209

Smith v. Thomas. 488

Smith v. Vernon 452

Smith v. Weinstein. 907

Smith, In re Estate of 67

Smith, State ex rel. v. Superior Court. 743

Sneed v. County of Riverside 151

Snell v. Ruppert 605

Snow v. Van Dam 654

Snyder v. Waukesha County Zoning Bd. of
  Adjustment 777

Soares v. Town of Atkinson 805

Society for Ethical Culture v. Spatt 828

Society of California Pioneers v. Baker 96

Solana Land Co. v. Murphey 602

Sollers v. Sollers. 12

Solomon v. City of Evanston 795

Solomon R. Guggenheim Foundation v. Lubell . .97;
                                              100

Somers v. Kane. 88

Sommer v. Kridel 389

Soule v. Bon Ami Co.. 908

South Dade Farms, Inc. v. B. & L. Farms Co. . .606

South Dakota, State of v. Rumpca. 9

South Norwalk Lodge, No. 709 v. Palco Hats,
  Inc.. 609

South Staffordshire Water Co. v. Sharman. 27

Southern Burlington Cty. N.A.A.C.P. v. Mt. Laurel
  Tp.. . . . . .806; 808

Southwest   Weather   Research,   Inc.   v.
  Rounsaville. 166

Sowers v. Forest Hills Subdivision 166

Spade v. Lynn & Boston Ry. Co. 686

Sparkman v. Hardy. 321

Sparrow v. Vermont Savings Bank 340

Spear T Ranch, Inc. v. Knaub. 175

Speed v. Speed. 437

Speedy Muffler King, Inc. v. Flanders 536

Speelman v. Pascal 69, 70

Speer v. Donald. 89

Spencer's Case. 660

Sporn v. MCA Records 99

Sprague v. Kimball. 654, 655

Spur Industries, Inc. v. Del E. Webb Development
  Co.. 144

St. Johnsville v. Smith. 217

St. Paul Title Ins. Corp. v. Owen 489

St.   Stephen's   Church   v.   Church   of
  Transfiguration 249

Stamper v. Griffin 208

Stanley v. Georgia 813

State v. (see name of defendant)

State by Stuart v. Dickinson Cheese Co. 9; 16

State ex rel. (see name of relator)

State of (see name of state)

State St. Bank & Trust Co. v. Signature Fin. Group,
  Inc. 899

State Street Bank & Trust Co. v. Signature Fin. Group,
  Inc. 899

Statler Manufacturing, Inc. v. Brown 552

Stedman v. Gassett. 207

Steele v. Latimer. 344

Stein v. Darby 606

Steinherz v. Wilson. 503

Stephano v. News Group Publications, Inc. . 887; 893

Stephenson v. Warner 334

Stevenson v. Wallace. 597

Stewart v. Childs Co. 331

Stewart v. Long Island R. Co.. 354

Stonehedge   Square   Ltd.   Partnership   v.   Movie
  Merchants, Inc.. 391

Stop the Beach Renourishment v. Florida Department
  of Environmental Protection 702

Storey v. Central Hide & Rendering Co. 145

Stortroen v. Beneficial Finance Co.. 423

Stoup v. Robinson 328

Stover; People v.. 825

Stoyanoff, State ex rel. v. Berkeley 821

Strasser v. Stabeck 468

Stratton v. Mt. Hermon Boys' Sch.. 181

Strickley v. Highland Boy Gold Mining Co. . . . 675

Stuart v. City of Easton 192

Sturgill v. Industrial Painting Corp.. 580

Sturgis v. Bridgeman, L.R.. 757

Succession of (see name of party)

[References are to pages.]

Sun Cal, Inc. v. United States 397
Sundowner, Inc. v. King 153; 163
Superior Court; State v. 238
Surman v. Blansett. 466
Sutfin v. State of California 739
Suttle v. Bailey. 656
Suydam v. Jackson. 321
Swanson v. Safeco Title Ins. Co. 567
Swarth v. Barney's Clothes, Inc. 54
Swetland v. Curtiss Airports Corp. 149
Swidler & Berlin v. United States. 886
Swift v. Gifford 14
Szabo, In re Estate of 69

T

T.W.I.W., Inc. v. Rhudy 380
T. W. Phillips Gas & Oil Co. v. Lingenfelter. . .191, 192
Taber v. Jenny. 14
Tahoe-Sierra Preservation Council, Inc. v. Tahoe
    Regional Planning Agency 723
Taliaferro v. Salyer. 159
Tapscott v. Cobbs 24
Taylor v. Leardi 131
Tazian v. Cline. 598
Teaff v. Hewitt. 89
Teague v. Abbott. 72
Teague v. Sowder 189
Tele-Pac, Inc. v. Grainger 858
Telluride v. Lot Thirty-Four Venture, L.L.C. . . . 809
Tempur-Pedic Int'l v. Waste to Charity. 73
Tenhet v. Boswell 239
Tenn v. 889 Assocs., Ltd. 165
Tenn-Tex Properties v. Brownell-Electro, Inc. . . 319
Teodori v. Werner 338
Tequesta, Village of v. Jupiter Inlet Corp.. 170
Terry v. Lock 30
Tex. Dep't of Hous. & Cmty. Affairs v. Inclusive
    Cmtys. Project, Inc.. 801
Thodos v. Shirk 668
Thomas v. Liberty Mut. Ins. Co. 569
Thomas v. Pullman Trust & Savings Bank 294
Thomas v. Stewart 320
Thomas v. Thomas. 209
Thompson v. Baxter 206
Thompson v. City of Palestine 768; 770, 771
Thompson v. Dildy. 488
Thompson v. Godfrey 196
Thompson v. Poirier 318

Thomson, Estate of v. Wade. 592
Thornton, In re Estate of. 225
Thornton, State ex rel. v. Hay 614, 615
Thos. Cusack Co. v. Myers 595
Thrifty-Tel, Inc. v. Bezenek. 40
Thyroff v. Nationwide Mutual Ins. Co.. 41
Tide Water Pipe Co. v. Bell 632, 633
Timm v. Brown. 362
Tinicum Fishing Co. v. Carter 632
Tipton v. Town of Tabor 4
Tobin v. Larkin. 467
Toftoy v. Rosenwinkel. 145
Toledo Tr. Co. v. Simmons 30
Tom Growney Equipment, Inc. v. Ansley 87
Town of (see name of town)
Township of (see name of township)
Travis v. Moore 141
Treasure Salvors, Inc. v. Unidentified Wrecked and
    Abandoned Sailing Vessel 35
Trenton Banking Co. v. Hawley. 260
Trimboli v. Kinkel. 459
Trobaugh v. Trobaugh 211
Trustees of Calvary Presbyterian Church v.
    Putnam 248
Trustees of Columbia College v. Lynch. 646
Turner v. Mallernee 510
Turner v. Scobey Moving & Storage Co.. 58
Turner v. Valentine. 116
Tuscarora Club v. Brown 592
Tuttle v. Steele. 293
Tyler v. Fidelity & Columbia Turst Co.. 292

U

U.S. Fidelity and Guaranty Co. v. Douglas'
    Trustee. .292
U.S. Trust Co. of N.Y. v. O'Brien. 460
Uhes v. Blake. 593
Ulrich v. N.Y.C. & H.R. R.R. Co. 44
Umphres v. J.R. Mayer Enterprises, Inc.. 620
Underwood v. Gillespie 517
United Bank v. Allyn. 568
United Methodist Church v. Dobbins 248
United States v. (see name of defendant)
United Virginia Bank/Citizens & Marine v. Union Oil
    Co.. 286
University Park, City of v. Benners 768, 769
Unsel v. Meier. 205
Upington v. Corrigan. 249
Urosevic v. Hayes 126

[References are to pages.]

V

Vade v. Sickler 109
Vail v. Long I. R. Co. 249
Valatie, Village of v. Smith 761
Valley Chevrolet Co. v. O.S. Stapley Co. 88
Van Bibber v. Hardy 488
Van Sant v. Rose 646
Vardeman v. Llewellyn 419
Varga v. Credit Suisse 100
Vaughn v. Carter 478
Venuto v. Owens-Corning Fiberglas Corp. 160
Vermont Electric Supply Co. v. Andrus 339
Via v. Beckett 502
Viall v. Carpenter 608
Vieyra v. Engineering Investment Co., Inc. . . .344
Village of (see name of village)
Violi, In re Estate of 593
Volusia County v. Aberdeen at Ormond Beach,
    L.P. .735
Voorheesville Rod & Gun Club v. Tompkins Co. .457

W

Wacker v. Price 503
Wade v. Jobe 333
Waldorff Insur. & Bonding Inc. v. Eglin Nat'l
    Bank .548
Walker v. State 741
Walker v. Strosnider 122; 124
Walker v. Walker 221
Walker v. Wilson 549
Walker Rogge, Inc. v. Chelsea Title & Guar. Co. .571
Wallace v. First National Bank of Paris 267
Wallander v. Barnes 24
Walls v. Oxford Management Co. 352
Walsh v. Young 317
Walton v. Capital Land, Inc. 620
Ward v. Inishmaan Assocs. 352
Warner v. Rasmussen 386
Warner v. Tanner 208
Warner Bros., Inc. v. American Broadcasting
    Cos. .893
Warren v. Albrecht 293
Warren v. Blake 600
Warren Publ., Inc. v. Microdos Data Corp. . . .855
Warth v. Seldin 795
Washington v. Davis 797, 798
Waters v. Beau Site Co. 54
Waterton v. Linden Motor Co. 45
Watkins v. Dodson 406

Watkins v. Watkins 115
Watner v. P & C Food Mkts., Inc. 328
Watriss v. First Nat'l Bank 324
Watson v. Muirhead 460
Watts v. Krebs 236
Waxahachie, City of v. Watkins 769, 770
Wayne, County of v. Hathcock 680, 681
Weaver v. American Oil Co. 61
Weaver v. Ham 768; 770
Webb's Fabulous Pharmacies, Inc. v. Beckwith. .721
Webber v. Webber 220
Weinberg's Estate, In re 404
Weinberger v. Romero-Barcelo 902, 903
Weir v. Rahon 245
Welborn v. Society for Propagation of Faith . . .338
Welch v. Mr. Christmas 889
Wellwood v. Havrah Mishna Anshi Sphard Cemetery
    Corp. .607
Wendt v. Host Int'l, Inc. 891
Werner v. Graham 660; 665
Wesson v. Leone Enterprises, Inc. 337
West v. Inter-Financial, Inc. 453
West v. Smith 611; 613
West Almeda Heights Homeowners Ass'n v. Board of
    County Comm'rs 670
West Kentucky Coal Co. v. Dilback 130
The West River Bridge Company v. Dix 738
West University Place, City of v. Ellis 769
Westchester Day School v. Village of
    Mamaroneck 831
Westchester Reform Temple, Matter of v. Brown. .830
Western Land Equities, Inc. v. City of Logan. . .772
Westland Housing Corp. v. Scott 314
Westland Nursing Home, Inc. v. Benson 616
Westland Skating Center, Inc. v. Gus Machado Buick,
    Inc. .167
Wetherbee v. First State Bank & Trust Co. . 259, 260
Whalen v. Union Bag & Paper Co. 137; 139
Whatley v. Mitchell 66
Wheaton v. Peters 856
Wheeler v. City of Pleasant Grove 750
Wheeler v. Reynolds 221
Whelan v. Tobener 513
White v. Bernhart 155
White v. Samsung Elecs. Am., Inc. . . 878; 892, 893
White v. Smyth 236
White v. Western Title Ins. Co. 572
White Plains, City of v. Ferraioli 817
Whitehead Oil Co. v. City of Lincoln 509; 751

[References are to pages.]

Whitinsville Plaza, Inc. v. Kotseas 652
Wichita Properties v. Lanterman. 397
Wiese v. Thien 604
Wiggins v. Brazil Coal & Clay Corp.. 174
Wiley v. Lininger. 449
Wilk v. Vencill. 240
Willard v. First Church of Christ Scientist 593
Willcox v. Penn. Mutual Life Ins. Co. 226
Williams v. Deriar 208
Williams v. Foster. 62
Williams v. Haddock. 221
Williams v. Stewart 245
Willow River Power Co.; United States v. 744
Willowbrook, Village of v. Olech 736
Willson, In re Estate of. 445; 447
Wilson Sporting Goods Co. v. Pedersen 550
Wilsonville v. SCA Services, Inc.. 135
Wing Ming Properties (U.S.A.) Limited v. Mott
    Operating Corp.. 152
Wisconsin v. Yoder. 831
Wisnieski v. Coufal 431
Witter v. Taggart. 549
Woelfel v. Tyng 601
Woerz v. Rademacher 459
Wolofsky v. Behrman 463
Wong v. Di Grazia. 289
Woo v. Smart 66
Wood v. Board of County Comm'rs. 195
Wood v. Boynton 47
Wood v. Lucy, Lady Duff Gordon. 876
Woodbury Place Partners v. City of Woodbury. .750
Woodland Realty, Inc. v. Winzenried 452
Wool v. Fleetwood. 198
Woolley v. Newcombe. 460
Worth, County of v. Jorgenson 517

Worthington v. Moreland Motor Truck Co.. . . .380
Wright v. Baumann. 386; 395; 397
Wright v. Brady 415
Wright v. Cypress Shores Dev. Co.. 656
Wright v. Douglass. 221
Wright v. Emory 419
Wright v. Jenks. 198
Wright v. Rockefeller 797
Wroblewski v. Grand Trunk Western Railway
    Co.. 328
Wylie, In re Estate of 284

Y

Yannopoulos v. Sophos 244
Yao v. Chapman. 42
Yarbrough v. Yarbrough 189
Yee v. Escondido. 711
Yick Wo v. Hopkins 797
York v. Jones 42
Young v. Hichens. 4; 10
Young v. Wrightson 377
Young v. Young. 69, 70; 72
Youngs v. Carter. 221
Yuzefovsky v. St. John's Wood Apartments. . . .352

Z

Zacchini v. Scripps-Howard Broad. Co. . . . 877; 882;
                                      894
Zendman v. Harry Winston, Inc. 79
Zervos v. Verizon New York, Inc.. 857
Zoltek Corp. v. United States 905
Zych v. Unidentified, Wrecked, & Abandoned Vessel
    Believed to be SB "Seabird" 35

INDEX

[References are to pages.]

A

ABANDONED PROPERTY
Acquiring . . . 1[II]

ACCESSION
Generally . . . 1[VIII]

ADVERSE POSSESSION
Elements of . . . 2[I][B]
Future of . . . 2[I][C]
Personalty, of . . . 1[X]
Statutory basis . . . 2[I][A]

AESTHETIC REGULATION
Generally . . . 7[II][E]

AIRSPACE
Generally . . . 2[IV][A]

APPURTENANT EASEMENTS
Generally . . . 6[I][F][1]

ASSIGNMENTS AND SUBLEASES
Generally . . . 4[VIII]
Assumption and novation . . . 4[VIII][A]
Real covenants, assignments and . . . 4[VIII][C]
Transfer restrictions . . . 4[VIII][B]

B

BAILMENTS
Generally . . . 1[V]

BONA FIDE PURCHASERS
Generally . . . 1[VII]; 5[VI][D]
Lack of notice . . . 5[VI][D][1]
Payment of consideration . . . 5[VI][D][2]

C

CATEGORICAL TAKINGS
Generally . . . 7[I][B][3]

CLOSINGS AND ESCROW
Generally . . . 5[IX]

COMMON LAW
Land conveyancing . . . 5[IV][A]
Marital estates . . . 3[IV][A]

COMMUNITY PROPERTY
Generally . . . 3[IV][C]

COMPENSATION, JUST
Generally . . . 7[I][D]

CONCURRENT ESTATES
Characteristics, basic . . . 3[V][A]
Concurrent tenancies, creation of . . . 3[V][B]
Joint tenancies, termination of . . . 3[V][D]
Relations among concurrent tenants . . . 3[V][C]

CONTRACTS OF SALE
Generally . . . 5[III]
Chain of title, breaks in . . . 5[III][H]
Contingencies, contract . . . 5[III][C]
Disclosures . . . 5[III][D]
Equitable conversion . . . 5[III][B]
Express title standards . . . 5[III][I]
Implied contract terms . . . 5[III][G]
Remedies, contract (See REMEDIES)
Statute of frauds . . . 5[III][A]
"Subject to financing" contract terms, express . . . 5[III][F]
Time for performance of contract . . . 5[III][E]

CONVEYANCING, LAND (See LAND CONVEYANCING)

COPYRIGHTS
Generally . . . 8[II]

COVENANTS
Assignments and real covenants . . . 4[VIII][C]
Deed covenants (See DEEDS, subhead: Covenants)
Habitability, implied covenant of . . . 4[VI]
Implied covenant of habitability . . . 4[VI]
Quiet enjoyment, of . . . 4[IV]
Real covenants . . . 6[II]
Repair, to . . . 4[V]
Termination of . . . 6[IV]

D

DAMAGES
Generally . . . 5[III][J][1]

DEEDS
Covenants
    Generally . . . 5[IV][D]
    Breach of covenants . . . 5[IV][D][1]
    Running with land . . . 5[IV][D][2]
Mortgages, deeds characterized as . . . 5[V]

E

EASEMENTS
Generally . . . 6[I]; 6[II][E]
Appurtenant . . . 6[I][F][1]
Creation of . . . 6[I][A]
Gross, easements in . . . 6[I][F][2]
Implication
    Necessity, by . . . 6[I][B]
    Past use, by . . . 6[I][C]
Prescriptive easements . . . 6[I][D]
Termination of . . . 6[I][G]
Transferability of
    Appurtenant easements . . . 6[I][F][1]
    Gross, easements in . . . 6[I][F][2]

EQUITABLE CONVERSION
Generally . . . 5[III][B]

[References are to pages.]

EQUITABLE SERVITUDES
Creation . . . 6[III][A]
Enforcement . . . 6[III][B]

ESCROW, CLOSINGS AND
Generally . . . 5[IX]

ESTATES IN LAND
Concurrent estates (See CONCURRENT ESTATES)
Fee simple . . . 3[I]
Fee tail . . . 3[II]
Life estate . . . 3[III]
Marital estates (See MARITAL ESTATES)
Powers of appointment (See POWERS OF AP-
   POINTMENT)
Remainders
   Creation and classification of . . . 3[VII][A]
   Rules regarding remainders . . . 3[VII][B]
Reversions, reverters, and rights of entry . . . 3[VI]
Reverters . . . 3[VI]
Rights of entry . . . 3[VI]
Rule against perpetuities (See RULE AGAINST
   PERPETUITIES)
Statute of uses and executory interests . . . 3[VIII]

EVICTION, RETALIATORY
Generally . . . 4[XII]

EXACTIONS AND IMPACT FEES
Generally . . . 7[I][B][4]

EXCLUSIONARY ZONING
Generally . . . 7[II][C]
Federal courts . . . 7[II][C][1]
State courts . . . 7[II][C][2]

F

FEE SIMPLE
Generally . . . 3[I]

FEE TAIL
Generally . . . 3[II]

FINDERS' RIGHTS
Generally . . . 1[III]

FIXTURES
Generally . . . 1[IX]

G

GIFTS
Generally . . . 1[VI]

GROUNDWATER
Generally . . . 2[V][B]

H

HOLDOVER TENANT
Generally . . . 4[IX][C]

HOMESTEAD RIGHTS
Marital estates . . . 3[IV][D]

I

IMPACT FEES
Generally . . . 7[I][B][4]

IMPLIED COVENANT OF HABITABILITY
Generally . . . 4[VI]

**INTANGIBLE AND INTELLECTUAL PROP-
   ERTY**
Artists, moral rights of . . . 8[III]
Copyrights . . . 8[II]
Ideas as property . . . 8[VII]
Misappropriation of information . . . 8[I]
Moral rights of artists . . . 8[III]
Patents . . . 8[VI]
Right to publicity . . . 8[IV]
Trademarks . . . 8[V]

INTELLECTUAL PROPERTY (See INTAN-
   GIBLE AND INTELLECTUAL PROPERTY)

J

JOINT TENANCIES
Termination of . . . 3[V][D]

JUST COMPENSATION
Generally . . . 7[I][D]

L

LAND CONVEYANCING
Generally . . . 5[I]
Closings and escrows . . . 5[IX]
Common law conveyancing, history of
   . . . 5[IV][A]
Conflicts and ambiguities in descriptions
   . . . 5[IV][E][4]
Contracts of sale (See CONTRACTS OF SALE)
Deed covenants (See DEEDS, subhead: Covenants)
Government survey system . . . 5[IV][E][1]
Intent, delivery, and acceptance . . . 5[IV][F]
Legal descriptions
   Generally . . . 5[IV][E]
   Conflicts and ambiguities in descriptions
      . . . 5[IV][E][4]
   Government survey system . . . 5[IV][E][1]
   Metes and bounds . . . 5[IV][E][2]
   Recorded subdivision plat . . . 5[IV][E][3]
Metes and bounds . . . 5[IV][E][2]
Modern conveyancing . . . 5[IV][B]
Real estate agents . . . 5[II]
Recorded subdivision plat . . . 5[IV][E][3]
Recording acts (See RECORDING ACTS)
Short form deeds, statutory . . . 5[IV][C]
Title insurance . . . 5[VIII]
Torrens registration . . . 5[VII]

LANDLORD AND TENANT
Assignments and subleases (See ASSIGNMENTS
   AND SUBLEASES)
Covenant (See COVENANTS)
Creation . . . 4[II]

[References are to pages.]

LANDLORD AND TENANT—Cont.
Frustration . . . 4[III][B]
Habitability, implied covenant of . . . 4[VI]
Illegality . . . 4[III][A]
Implied covenant of habitability . . . 4[VI]
Quiet enjoyment, covenant of . . . 4[IV]
Retaliatory eviction . . . 4[XII]
Security deposits . . . 4[XIII]
Self-help, landlord's . . . 4[X]
Subleases (See ASSIGNMENTS AND SUB-
   LEASES)
Summary procedure . . . 4[XI]
Tenancies, types of . . . 4[I]
Termination (See TERMINATION)
Tort liability, landlord's . . . 4[VII]

LAND USE CONTROLS
Aesthetic regulation . . . 7[II][E]
Exclusionary zoning (See EXCLUSIONARY ZON-
   ING)
Residency restrictions . . . 7[II][D]
Zoning actions (See ZONING)

LATERAL SUPPORT
Generally . . . 2[II][A]

LAW OF NEIGHBORS
Adverse possession (See ADVERSE POSSESSION)
Air and light
   Airspace . . . 2[IV][A]
   Rights in . . . 2[IV][B]
Airspace . . . 2[IV][A]
Duty of support by statute, modifying . . . 2[II][B]
Lateral support . . . 2[II][A]
Light, air and
   Airspace . . . 2[IV][A]
   Rights in . . . 2[IV][B]
Nuisance . . . 2[III]
Subjacent support . . . 2[II][C]
Water rights (See WATER RIGHTS)

LIFE ESTATE
Generally . . . 3[III]

M

MARITAL ESTATES
Common law . . . 3[IV][A]
Community property . . . 3[IV][C]
Homestead rights . . . 3[IV][D]
Statutory changes . . . 3[IV][B]

MORTGAGES
Deeds characterized as . . . 5[V]

N

NONCONFORMING USES
Generally . . . 7[II][A][2]

NOTICE
Bona fide purchasers; lack of notice
   . . . 5[VI][D][1]

NOTICE—Cont.
Termination, notice of (See TERMINATION, subhead: Notice of termination)

NUISANCE
Generally . . . 2[III]

P

PATENTS
Generally . . . 8[VI]

PERIODIC TENANCY
Generally . . . 4[IX][A][2]

PERSONAL PROPERTY
Abandoned property, acquiring . . . 1[II]
Accession . . . 1[VIII]
Adverse possession . . . 1[X]
Bailments . . . 1[V]
Finders' rights . . . 1[III]
Fixtures . . . 1[IX]
Gifts . . . 1[VI]
Sales and bona fide purchasers . . . 1[VII]
Wild animals . . . 1[I]
Wrongful taking of possession . . . 1[IV]

POWERS OF APPOINTMENT
Generally . . . 3[IX]
Nature of powers . . . 3[IX][A]
Varieties of powers . . . 3[IX][B]

PRESCRIPTIVE EASEMENTS
Generally . . . 6[I][D]

PRIVATE PROPERTY
Taking of . . . 7[I][C]

PUBLICITY, RIGHT TO
Generally . . . 8[IV]

PUBLIC USE
Takings . . . 7[I][A]

Q

QUIET ENJOYMENT
Covenant of . . . 4[IV]

R

REAL COVENANTS
Generally . . . 6[II]
Assignments and . . . 4[VIII][C]

REAL ESTATE AGENTS
Generally . . . 5[II]

RECORDING ACTS
Generally . . . 5[VI]
Bona fide purchasers (See BONA FIDE PURCHAS-
   ERS)
Exclusions from recording act . . . 5[VI][F]
Grantor-grantee index . . . 5[VI][C][1]
History . . . 5[VI][A]

RECORDING ACTS—Cont.
Indexes
    Generally . . . 5[VI][C]
    Grantor-grantee index . . . 5[VI][C][1]
    Tract index . . . 5[VI][C][2]
Operation of recording acts . . . 5[VI][B]
Recording and indexing . . . 5[VI][E]
Tract index . . . 5[VI][C][2]

REMAINDERS
Creation and classification of . . . 3[VII][A]
Rules regarding remainders . . . 3[VII][B]

REMEDIES
Generally . . . 5[III][J]
Damages . . . 5[III][J][1]
Other remedies . . . 5[III][J][4]
Rescission . . . 5[III][J][3]
Specific performance . . . 5[III][J][2]

RESCISSION
Generally . . . 5[III][J][3]

RESIDENCY RESTRICTIONS
Generally . . . 7[II][D]

RETALIATORY EVICTION
Generally . . . 4[XII]

REVERSIONS, REVERTERS, AND RIGHTS
OF ENTRY
Generally . . . 3[VI]

RIGHT TO PUBLICITY
Generally . . . 8[IV]

RIPARIAN AND LITTORAL RIGHTS
Generally . . . 2[V][C]

RULE AGAINST PERPETUITIES
Generally . . . 3[X]
Orthodox rule
    Generally . . . 3[X][A]
    Reform of . . . 3[X][B]

S

SALES
Generally . . . 1[VII]
Contracts of sale (See CONTRACTS OF SALE)

SECURITY DEPOSITS
Generally . . . 4[XIII]

SERVITUDES, EQUITABLE
Creation . . . 6[III][A]
Enforcement . . . 6[III][B]

SPECIFIC PERFORMANCE
Generally . . . 5[III][J][2]

STATUTE OF FRAUDS
Contracts of sale . . . 5[III][A]

SUBJACENT SUPPORT
Generally . . . 2[II][C]

SUBLEASES (See ASSIGNMENTS AND SUB-
LEASES)

SURFACE WATER
Generally . . . 2[V][A]

SURRENDER AND ABANDONMENT
Corollary rule . . . 4[IX][B][2]
Traditional rule . . . 4[IX][B][1]

T

TAKINGS
Generally . . . 7[I]; 7[I][B]
Categorical takings . . . 7[I][B][3]
Exactions and impact fees . . . 7[I][B][4]
Federal Constitution . . . 7[I][B][1]
Impact fees . . . 7[I][B][4]
Just compensation . . . 7[I][D]
Private property . . . 7[I][C]
Public use . . . 7[I][A]
State Constitution . . . 7[I][B][2]

TERMINATION
Holdover tenant . . . 4[IX][C]
Notice of termination
    Periodic tenancy . . . 4[IX][A][2]
    Sufferance, tenancy at . . . 4[IX][A][4]
    Tenancy
        Sufferance, at . . . 4[IX][A][4]
        Will, at . . . 4[IX][A][3]
    Term for years . . . 4[IX][A][1]
    Will, tenancy at . . . 4[IX][A][3]
Periodic tenancy . . . 4[IX][A][2]
Sufferance, tenancy at . . . 4[IX][A][4]
Surrender and abandonment
    Corollary rule . . . 4[IX][B][2]
    Traditional rule . . . 4[IX][B][1]
Tenancy
    Sufferance, at . . . 4[IX][A][4]
    Will, at . . . 4[IX][A][3]
Will, tenancy at . . . 4[IX][A][3]

TITLE INSURANCE
Generally . . . 5[VIII]

TORRENS REGISTRATION
Generally . . . 5[VII]

TORT LIABILITY
Landlord's . . . 4[VII]

TRADEMARKS
Generally . . . 8[V]

V

VARIANCE
Zoning . . . 7[II][A][4]

W

WATER RIGHTS
Diffuse surface water . . . 2[V][A]
Groundwater . . . 2[V][B]

[References are to pages.]

WATER RIGHTS—Cont.
Riparian and littoral rights . . . 2[V][C]
Surface water, diffused . . . 2[V][A]

WILD ANIMALS
Generally . . . 1[I]

WRONGFUL TAKING OF POSSESSION
Generally . . . 1[IV]

Z

ZONING
Generally . . . 7[II][A]; 7[II][A][1]

ZONING—Cont.
Amendment . . . 7[II][A][3]
Exclusionary zoning (See EXCLUSIONARY ZONING)
Modern zoning techniques . . . 7[II][B]
Nonconforming use . . . 7[II][A][2]
Special exception . . . 7[II][A][5]
Variance . . . 7[II][A][4]